GOD AND THE RATIONAL MIND

GOD AND THE RATIONAL MIND

THE GROUNDS FOR KNOWLEDGE

Joseph L. Cartland

Paley, Whately, and Greenleaf Press

Greenwood, Wisconsin

Paley, Whately, and Greenleaf Press
P.O. Box 57
Greenwood, WI 54437

Second impression, with revisions, 2022

Printed in the United States of America

Scripture citations in this work are taken from several sources, the abbreviated notations of which follow the references for the corresponding biblical passages that are quoted herein. These notations appear below, along with, where appropriate, the express copyright wording that the publisher of the version prescribes.

Amplified®
Scripture quotations taken from *The Amplified Bible*. Copyright © 1954, 1958, 1962, 1964, 1965, 1987 by The Lockman Foundation. All rights reserved. Used by permission. (www.Lockman.org)

ESV®
Scripture quotations marked (ESV) are from The Holy Bible, English Standard Version® (ESV®), copyright © 2001 by Crossway Bibles, a division of Good News Publishers. Used by permission. All rights reserved.

KJV
Scripture taken from the Holy Bible, King James version.

NIV®
Scriptures taken from the Holy Bible, *New International Version®*, *NIV®*. Copyright © 1973, 1978, 1984 by Biblica, Inc.™ Used by permission of Zondervan. All rights reserved worldwide. (Note that the NIV employs a small-capital font in translating the name of God as 'the LORD' in certain passages, depending on the Hebrew word. I preserve the font in quotations.)

NKJV
Scripture taken from the New King James Version. Copyright © 1982 by Thomas Nelson, Inc. Used by permission. All rights reserved.

TLB
Scripture taken from *The One Year Bible, The Living Bible*. Copyright © 1985 by Tyndale House Publishers, Inc., Wheaton, IL. All rights reserved.

Library of Congress Control Number: 2017918891

ISBN: 978-1-947844-08-7 (hard cover)
ISBN: 978-1-947844-07-0 (soft cover)

My people are destroyed for lack of knowledge.

—Hos. 4:6 ESV

CONTENTS

PROLOGUE

THE QUEST

"Come now, let us reason together,"
says the LORD.

—Isa. 1:18 NIV

Not long ago, I attended a lecture by a noted physicist who was claiming that the universe arose from nothing at all, promoting his new, appropriately titled book as part of the session. God is not needed to account for existence as humans know it, he asserted; science can show how everything began. Rather than limit the presentation to his cosmogonic thesis, the physicist proceeded to attack the Scriptures. He flashed a slide on the screen that read, "In the beginning," quoting from the opening verse of Genesis. What follows, he remarked, referring to the rest of the Bible, is a collection of fables. Several chuckles reverberated through the auditorium.

With its emphasis on the explanatory power of physical laws, the position that blind mechanism rules reality has become increasingly popular in recent years, though the concepts that underlie it are centuries old. The position's adherents maintain that its depiction of origins—of the cosmos, life, and rational mentality—stands alone in its feasibility. Knowing that an account is correct requires that attendant beliefs be true and that they be anchored properly, for such is the essence of knowledge. One thus must ask how well the model of naturalism, grounded in mechanistic tenets, fares under the meticulous scrutiny of logic, as logic is more forceful than science, and it is in an important respect more extended in its reach.

God and the Rational Mind explores the scope of reality and how knowledge of that scope is possible. The book is developed in the vein of apologetics, but the approach is atypical. Aside from a measure of inquiry into scientific disciplines, the text incorporates a fair amount of metaphysical analysis. Although many points in the writing undoubtedly will capture the interest of the academic community, the book is not a philosophical treatise, nor is it intended primarily for scholars. It is a work of discovery, penned as a guide for the journeyer who is seeking answers to the profound questions that humanity faces. Pondering these questions brings forth the most comprehensive beliefs that people possess; ultimately, the answers that they embrace define their worldviews.

The discourse begins with a review of the historical quest for understanding as it unfolds in the writings of the ancient Greek philosophers. Initiated as a search for the foundation of things, the quest expands rapidly to other areas of investigation. It is here that one finds the roots of a conceptual split concerning reality. Is it limited in its extent to the natural, physical world, or does it include incorporeal elements? Is strict mechanism the sole governor of its operations, or does it embody purpose? The resultant controversy continues to pulsate in contemporary thought, and it is no less spirited now than it was in ancient times. How well each camp can lay claim to knowledge is a matter to be probed. As the book proceeds, the pivotal character of this issue becomes apparent.

The text is divided into three parts. The first section frames the groundwork for the undertaking; the next one delves into pertinent issues in considerable detail; the final part turns to an examination of the span of reality, determining how a grasp of that breadth is achievable. The chapter-by-chapter summary that I provide below prepares one for the topics that I cover. Each chapter serves as an independent study, yet all align in a meaningful progression, leading to the thematic conclusion of the work, and an epilogue underscores its thrust.

CHAPTER 1. The introductory chapter opens with a brief discussion of belief. Both knowledge and action rest on what one accepts as true; and, with regard to major issues, at least, one's convictions must be right. The text turns to the matter of knowledge itself, introducing the discipline of philosophy and its primary divisions. The mission in Western civilization to uncover core principles began in the early sixth century B.C. as a metaphysical search for the basis of all that is. A few thinkers in the vicinity of the Aegean Sea set out to give an account of their world. Seeing nature in its great diversity, these Presocratic philosophers, as they are known, inferred that something, seated more deeply than what they observed around them, must underlie all things, giving rise to their being and linking them through a common factor. This search for the well-spring of existence spread as others engaged in the pursuit. Differing theories developed, and the philosophical enterprise was born.

One key problem to arise during this period is that of change. The philosopher Heraclitus argues that everything is in constant flux. Such continual shifting seems to undermine the persisting identity of objects. If something changes with the passage of time, then it cannot remain the same; if everything changes with the passage of time, then nothing can remain the same. Without a way to lock identity, knowledge is not possible, for the mind cannot grasp something that is not fixed any more than the senses can do so. Current physics reveals that Heraclitean theory is not far from the mark: Change is indeed ubiquitous. Then, the concern is to understand how one can know. It is not a trivial matter. If the intellect cannot take hold of the objects in the world, then there appears to be little hope of coming to grips with issues of even greater import, and comprehending the range of reality may be out of reach. This puzzle—the problem of knowledge—must be solved if there is to be the assurance of truth.

CHAPTER 2. The problem of knowledge is duplex, calling into question both the objects that are caught in unremitting fluctuation and the subjects that are prone to error in perceiving them. Chapter 2 examines attempts by three major philosophers to solve the problem, focusing on the former aspect of it. Plato constructs an elaborate model, the theory of forms, as a solution. In his theory, Plato draws a sharp distinction between the objects of sensory experience—what he refers to as particulars—and the properties of which they partake—forms. The forms are immutable; for this reason, they can be grasped with the mind. It is they that are the truly real; it is they that are the genuine objects of knowledge. Things in the world are caught in Heraclitean flux, but the forms afford a measure of stability, offering a derivative knowledge of things through the qualities that those things exhibit. Plato criticizes his own theory, and one of his arguments against it demonstrates the damaging character of the very separation that he introduces to resolve the difficulty.

Two millennia after Plato put forth his system, René Descartes confronts that difficulty from a different perspective. He starts with what is certain. If he can establish a ground for knowledge that is indubitable, so he believes, then he can build a superstructure on it that is just as sure. The foundation that he lays is himself, as he cannot doubt his own existence as a thinking thing. From this bedrock, Descartes proceeds to God, arguing for the existence of the Deity. Finally, he contends that, because God is no deceiver, knowledge of the world, arising through sensory experience, is possible. Descartes's contemporaries attack his theory, as do his successors. If he cannot advance beyond the boundaries of his theory's foundation, then knowledge is limited to the self, and Descartes drifts into the dead end of philosophy: solipsism.

A surprising approach to the problem of knowledge takes shape nearly a century later. There is no problem concerning knowledge of the material world, for, according to George Berkeley, there is no material world. Only ideas and the minds that perceive them exist. Objects in the world of sense are merely clusters of ideas in the mind. One can know them because one is in intimate contact with them. Berkeley's immaterialism introduces insurmountable hurdles, the most troubling of which pertains to the preservation of an objective reality. The shortcoming is serious, and Berkeley's system does not stand, nor do those of his two predecessors.

CHAPTER 3. The second part of the book begins at this point, undertaking an in-depth analysis of the objects of perception to see whether flux is as destructive as some philosophers have believed. If object-identity can be preserved through change, then perhaps knowledge can be saved. The actual threat to things, however, is time, not change. Identity from one moment to another requires that things persist; shifts in properties and composition are irrelevant. A contemporary view, known as four-dimensionalism, introduces temporal parts as a way to explain continuance, but it brings with it absurdities. A more radical stance is mereological nihilism, which avoids the continuance puzzle by denying that compound objects even exist. This position fails as well. One soon comes to see that persistence lies in unity. The chapter brings to mind the strivings of the Presocratic philosophers to explain how a plurality of objects could come from a unary base of reality, and how a plural base could produce a unary object. The central discovery of this chapter is the role that the rational mind plays in bringing about singularity, paving the way for the possibility of identity through time.

CHAPTER 4. The work of beliefs in contributing to both knowing and doing is the topic of investigation in chapter 4 as the book extends the discussion of the problem of knowledge to the subjects of perception. Beliefs are antecedents of knowledge. According to the classic definition, knowledge is justified true belief. What serves as justification, however, is worth considering. Cartesian certainty is sufficient to play that part, of course, but one must ask whether it is a requirement. It is always possible, it seems, that one is mistaken in perception, in which case one does not know, as the corresponding belief is false. If it follows that it is possible that one is always mistaken in perception, then knowledge of the world may be unobtainable. At first glance, certainty appears to be indispensable. That reasoning is fallacious, however, and one learns how the certainty-uncertainty dichotomy gives way to a continuum that provides justification through the vanishing probability of error.

Beliefs are also antecedents of action. What a person values and what that person believes serve, in a joint manner, to set the stage for what the person does. Some authors see the actions of an agent in a causal light. In an extreme form, actions are determined with finality, and there is no freedom of choice. In a softer version, the agent's reasons operate as the causal factors; still, an agent's freedom seems to be subject to law-like conduct. The text presents arguments against both views. It proposes, as the general structure of an action, the intentional undertaking of a behavioral performance by an agent based on an expected, desired end state and relevant beliefs.

The more important the questions in life are, the more important it is to know—one's beliefs must be true. Does God exist? Is the presence of humans on the earth explained best in terms of purpose? Such questions demand answers. The first part of the chapter demonstrates how knowledge of physical reality is possible. One wonders, though, how knowledge of nonphysical reality, if there is such, is possible. Surely, if immaterial things, in fact, do exist, then the mind is a prime candidate. Accordingly, the book considers it next.

CHAPTER 5. This chapter pursues the issue of rational mentality. Is the mind distinct from the body? To uncover the truth requires delving into the topic of personal identity, looking preliminarily at how organisms differ from persons. Following a critique of the serial theory of the self, a philosophical thesis for which the eighteenth-century skeptic David Hume is the recognized proponent, I explore three major attempts to define personhood in terms of materiality: analytic behaviorism, mind-brain identity theory, and logical primitiveness. It is soon evident that none of these recent formulations is acceptable; one cannot dismiss the incorporeal character of the mind easily and maintain a tenable account of persons. Materialism's final effort is to postulate a relationship in which the mental in humans is associated with the physical through supervenience. This conjecture too is unconvincing. Given that all these attempts fall short of the mark, it seems that it is possible to discover a plausible account of immaterial reality with an even broader scope. With this prospect in view, the work turns in the chapter that follows to the question of the existence of the supreme immaterial entity—namely, God.

CHAPTER 6. Chapter 6 opens with a glimpse of the vastness of the cosmos. It is conceivable that God is behind this immensity. There are five main categories of proofs of God's existence. After a brief examination of Pascal's wager, the book initiates an analysis of each of the five types. Four of these types are covered in moderate detail, but the fifth proof—the teleological argument—is the primary focus. One form of it is the argument from design, which posits intelligent agency as the cause of the natural order. The argument is important in its own right, but it is known chiefly because it is the special target of modern antitheistic writings. I anatomize the proof, diagramming the reasoning, which lays out the elements of the logic in a clear fashion. A leading opponent of the idea that nature exhibits design is David Hume, and the chapter assesses three of his principal objections. As before, I diagram each of the constructions. The result is that the flaws in Hume's criticisms are laid bare. The objections that he raises are of particular significance because the contemporary evolutionist Richard Dawkins uses a thinly veiled version of one of them to launch his own offensive against the existence of God.

The text proceeds to a review of the positions of Ernest Nagel and Clarence Darrow. Both dispute the theistic-design model, but their arguments lack force. A further consideration makes it obvious that, if agency is not a factor in cosmic theory, then it is difficult to account for the exactness of the rate at which the particle-space in the nascent universe had to have expanded for there to *be* a universe, granting a big bang as the opening event. The approach of several scientists who reject intelligent design in favor of a universe that arose out of nothing—physicists Victor J. Stenger and Lawrence M. Krauss are noted representatives—is a key topic as the book begins its assault on atheism. The ensuing discussion demonstrates that the notion of such a starting point, when probed, proves to be nonsensical. In the end, skeptics may not find the argument from design to be compelling, albeit the objections to it in favor of a different conclusion are certainly not persuasive; but there is just something that is unsettling about the portrayal of a near-septillion-star universe, cast with almost unimaginable precision, as simply the product of chance. The chapter closes where it began, with a glimpse of the colossal proportions of the cosmos—but with a difference. One is left with a sense of wonder, reflected in the words of an ancient king.

CHAPTER 7. As there are arguments for God's existence, there are arguments against it. This chapter examines two forms of attack on theism that seem to be foremost in the thoughts of a number of authors: the argument from evil and the argument from complexity. With respect to the former attack, it is not surprising that David Hume resurfaces as a spokesperson. The argument purports to show that there is an inconsistency holding between the claimed attributes of God and the presence of evil in the world. The inquiry that follows unmasks the inadequacy of the thinking, whether evil is classified as morally reprehensible deeds or as suffering. The latter association is particularly weak because it necessitates the absolute preclusion of suffering, attending to neither prevalence nor intensity, if the line of reasoning is to have any merit at all. Whether it can be shown that God is not real is reduced to contingencies that no one could accept.

The argument from complexity is the handiwork of Richard Dawkins. In effect, as stated above, it is simply a remake of one of Hume's criticisms of the argument from design but with a different property as the crucial hinge. The argument commits multiple logical errors, as the analysis reveals, and it fails categorically. The case for rational disbelief, presented by two avid defenders, is unsuccessful.

CHAPTER 8. In titling this chapter, I take liberties with a memorable remark by the astronaut Neil Armstrong. As the chapter unfolds, the significance of the wording becomes clear. The discourse here is a continuation of my evaluation of Richard Dawkins's writings, comprising an extended refutation of his account of the appearance of biological forms and the development of organismal complexity. To explain life on the earth, one must show how it came to exist on the planet in the first place and how it came to be at its present state of sophistication. Dawkins finds the answers, he believes, in the anthropic principle and evolution. The chapter begins its investigation by scrutinizing Dawkins's argument for the advent of life based on, to use his terminology, the magic of large numbers. His anthropic-centered argument is fraught with mistakes, which the logical review exposes in order. A deeper concern, though, is that applying the principle in a global way to explain whatever one finds, regardless of the unlikelihood of finding it at a particular time and in a particular place, removes its utility altogether. If it ostensibly can serve to explain everything that is against the odds in an express set of circumstances, then it actually can explain nothing. In the course of the review, I explore the theory of abiogenesis—the arising of life from lifelessness—and uncover serious impediments that stem from the chemistry on which the theory depends.

Dawkins seeks to explain the emergence of complexity, once life begins, in terms of a recurrent sequence of random mutation and natural selection. An undirected process of genetic honing, biological progression has three essential factors: It is gradual, discriminative, and cumulative. To arrive at complex features or complex organisms, evolution must trudge up the mountain of improbability—a metaphor that Dawkins employs in his narrative. It is an exercise of small steps, each of which has to provide an advantage in survival and procreation to ensure retention in the related genes. Aside from mirroring the coordinated-attack problem, which is a quandary that has no solution, the minuscule-change approach that Dawkins adopts is mathematically indefensible. A look at the structure of DNA and the randomness of genetic mutation clarifies why the development of advanced characteristics of organisms cannot proceed as Dawkins suggests. If pronounced biological enhancement is to occur, then it must do so as sweeping change, perhaps coming about through the activity of regulatory genes that control morphological elements of the phenotype. The trouble with that premise, however, is that nonincremental realization of fully functional intricacy is precluded by the mathematics as well—by Dawkins's own admission.

The chapter concludes with the notion that the most problematic gap in the evolutionary account is not one that calls for a leap from a prebiotic mass to conscious humans but a leap from strict mechanism to purpose. It is a rift that, as the opening pages of the work bring to light, is traceable to early Greek thought.

CHAPTER 9. This chapter introduces the final part of the book, returning to a discussion of the span of existence. Any theoretical system that is a candidate for acceptance must be internally consistent—it cannot be in conflict with itself—but, if it is submitted as a depiction of objective reality, then it also must correspond to what, in fact, exists. Otherwise, like a great novel, it may tell a believable story with no details at variance, but it is fictitious. Ultimately, it is the child of futility. Given two models that diverge on the question of immaterial substance, only one can be correct. The task is to determine which of the two prevails.

Physicists Stephen Hawking and Leonard Mlodinow put forward a theory that purports to avoid the uncertainty regarding what is real by emphasizing the practicality of observation and prediction over any relation to independent being. They refer to their conceptualization as model-dependent realism. According to the thinking, if each of a pair of competing systems adequately portrays the same perceived phenomena, and the projections of each align with future events, then what one system sets forth as real is no more right in its rendering of the truth than the other. The chapter shows how the theory generates a contradiction.

In the quest to define the scope of being—whether immaterial things do exist—both science and metaphysics respond to the challenge, but there are limitations. Science is adept at exploring the physical universe, but it cannot peer beyond that domain to see what may lie there. Metaphysics is equipped to conduct an effective search for the nonphysical, but it must rely on axioms and logic to ground its discoveries. Science therefore lacks the extended range of metaphysics, and metaphysics lacks the observational substantiation of science. Looking at evidential factors can be a way to ascertain the truth, and doing so in the present matter proves to be informative. I take issue with Dawkins again in the analysis. He claims to base his position on a study of evidence, yet he is willing to embrace a conjecture for which there is no supporting evidence at all—while denying the veracity of an opposing position that is supported by a wealth of it. Such an approach bespeaks an inherent incongruity.

CHAPTER 10. A consideration of wisdom characterizes the final chapter. Both the wise King Solomon and the philosopher Albert Camus hold that life without God is totally meaningless. Although it may appear that they are in agreement, they differ markedly in what they take to be real. These men personify the deep division that is prevalent in current times between two models of reality, paralleling the duality of the ancients. I present the core tenets that each model encompasses. Principal findings of the preceding chapters intersect at this point to reveal that the footings on which the system of naturalism rests, its operations adhering to the dictates of mechanistic doctrine, break apart under the weight of reason. The very rationality that atheism trusts to secure its stance is, in fact, its undoing. As the chapter concludes, the issue of personal identity resurfaces to accentuate the failure of materialism and to suggest an alternative picture of the human entity that explains much.

Every person wants to understand why the cosmos exists, why there are living entities, and why beings with intelligence populate the earth. One wonders whether an immense, mindless unfolding of material interactions constitutes the whole of reality, or incorporeal mentality of grand proportions accounts for everything. In the end, each individual wants to know the truth about his or her own existence. Is all that there is in the fleeting flicker of a lifetime all that there is? Knowledge is not found in passivity here. One must choose to pursue it and act on that choice, considering carefully the path that lies ahead. The implications of the decision to step forward are profound, and the outcome, I would argue, is eternal.

That no appreciably inclusive work can be the fruit solely of the author's insight borders on the self-evident. This writing is a case in point. Classroom instruction through the years, thought-provoking dialogue with family, and indeed revelation—all contributed to the final product.

PART I

OF PHILOSOPHICAL UNDERPINNINGS

CHAPTER 1

THE NEED TO KNOW

There is a way that seems right to a man,
but in the end it leads to death.

—Prov. 14:12 NIV

As I was crossing a busy intersection on foot one day, I noticed a blind man, cane in hand, approaching from the other side. Having misapprehended the correct path for pedestrians, he was moving increasingly off course, veering toward a vehicle that had stopped at the light. The danger was apparent to me but not to him. "This way," I warned; "Sir!" I called. Undoubtedly, he was attuned to environmental sounds; his hearing was a sense on which he must have relied considerably in his life. He was able to localize my voice quickly. The man adjusted his direction, advanced toward my position, and stood directly in front of me, more closely than one typically would stand unless perhaps intent on confrontation. Staring, as it were, at my face, he exclaimed in an angry tone of voice that displayed his indignation, "I know where I am; what are you hollering at me for!" It was hardly the response that I expected. Surprised by his resentment, I paused, then replied in a restrained manner, "Just trying to be helpful," and continued onward to my destination.

Behavior that is marked by action toward some end makes up an integral and fundamental part of human existence. Daily life is filled with examples: preparing a bowl of oatmeal in the morning, submitting a sales proposal to a potential client at lunch, cutting the grass after work, or reading a bedtime story to the children. Although such occurrences may frame the activities of the day, some things that people do unfold in a more extended way. One may build a home library by collecting rare books, play a game of chess by letter with an overseas opponent, or carry out a strategy to save for early retirement. Whether actions take minutes or years to complete, in each case, if one looks carefully, then it becomes apparent that they rest on the agent's beliefs. When a person acts toward an end, that person takes a particular path that he or she believes will bring about the objective in mind. Even though beliefs play a central role in setting direction, they cannot assure an agent of a wanted result: If those beliefs are false, then the acts that are based on them quite likely will end in failure.

Contrary to his claim, had the man in the aforementioned narrative known where he was and where he was going—had his beliefs about his location and bearing been right—he would not have taken the path that placed him in harm's way. He trusted his senses to guide him, but, lacking vision, he did not possess the means to detect his error in the way that was available to anyone with sight. He struck out across the street, believing that he was progressing according to his plan, the aim of which was to put him in the proper place on the other side. Given the circumstances, he could discover the problem with his route only after interpreting the facts in light of those things that were perceptually familiar to him, which, in this instance, were what he could hear—the sound of my voice—and what he could feel—impact with a car.

It is evident that the desire to move toward goals is inherent in humanity. An individual acts in a certain way at a certain time in keeping with what he or she deems to be of value, coupled with a set of beliefs. Although a man might have dreamed on many occasions of vacationing in Paris, if he believes that he cannot afford the trip or that Paris has been destroyed by a drifting asteroid that collided with the city or that he is incarcerated in Leavenworth, Kansas, then he will act accordingly. Both reason and experience demonstrate that accepting something as true is no guarantee that it is true. Rather, it is only if the contents of one's beliefs mirror what obtains in reality that those beliefs indeed can be true, and knowledge, by any reasonable standard, can be claimed.[1] Discerning the truth therefore becomes paramount in reaching one's goals. Knowledge of the facts is the essential determinant of success in an agent's course, taking the agent where he or she wishes to go, both in the literal sense and

---

[1] Philosophers have advanced various theories concerning what truth is, but it generally is accepted that a meaningful declarative statement is true if, and only if, what it purports is actually the case. The declaration—in this instance, a statement that is expressed in a belief about the world—must *correspond* to the facts.

in the metaphorical one. The question that arises is then plain: How can a person be sure that his or her beliefs are right—how can one know?

Humans are inquisitive creatures. They want to understand; they want to uncover the truth. One sees this desire in the wonderful curiosity of children as they pry open playfully concealing hands to find what treasures lie inside. One sees it in the wonder of adults as they peer into telescopes and microscopes to find the treasures of outer space and inner space. Human history resonates with a thirst for knowledge, and the search to find it dates from antiquity. In the West, this quest is apparent in writings that arose in the area around Greece. Extant documents, authored by early thinkers there, reveal systematic attempts to identify the fundamental makeup of the world. These theorists were looking for, and hypothesizing about, the ultimate reality, something at the base of existence that could explain all things. Philosophers of old, they are known as the Presocratics because they were active primarily before the time of Socrates, who lived from about 470 to 399 B.C.[2] Their initial attempts at discovery and description led to more intricate engagements as the ancients expanded their search for knowledge of an undergirding reality to knowledge of foundational axioms and then to knowledge of knowledge itself. Puzzling issues began to form, and an enduring problem eventually surfaced, one that plagued philosophers for the centuries that were to come. Its impact on Western thought has been profound. In an important sense, the problem that daunted the great thinkers of bygone years as they sought the framework for a tenable theory of knowledge is one with greater implications than what those who encountered it envisioned. To understand the problem and its consequences, one must understand the historical context in which this puzzle developed. It was the search for the essential nature of things, the basis of reality, that led to the perplexity concerning knowledge and challenged notions that probably, until that time, had been accepted by the populace. Consider first then the course that the search for knowledge took, and perhaps it will become clearer precisely where it took humanity.

---

[2] Some authors render the term 'Presocratics' differently, yielding 'PreSocratics' or 'Pre-Socratics'. Except in quotations and in titles of works, I will continue to use the form that I give here.

EARLY WESTERN THOUGHT

The English word 'philosopher' is traced to the Greek word *philosophos*, which means 'lover of wisdom'. Inherent in the word are two Greek expressions: *philos*, which may be translated as 'loving' or as 'beloved'; and *sophos*, which is translated as 'wise' or 'learned'. Thus, a philosopher, so the etymology of the corresponding term suggests, is one who possesses a passion for a certain depth of understanding. Appropriately, those who take up philosophical pursuits seek to gain insight by searching for, and uncovering, fundamental principles. Like other disciplines, philosophy is partitioned into various fields of inquiry, treated as distinct disciplines (or subdisciplines), according to the specific area under examination. My primary concern in this work is with three broad areas of analytic, or analytical, philosophy: an enterprise of predominantly Western thought that adheres to established rules of logic, clarity of expression, and critical, systematic investigation. In the current era, the analytic vein is prevalent in British and American papers as well as Canadian and Scandinavian ones. Philosophical writings that appear in Australia and New Zealand also fall into this category, as a rule. Nonanalytic philosophy, as one may surmise, does not adhere to the rigorous methodology of its counterpart. Such movements in the West are associated primarily with continental Europe, especially Germany and France. With roots in the past, they gained a measure of momentum in the twentieth century; foremost examples are existentialism, to a large extent, and phenomenology.

The philosophical analysis that unfolds in this book centers on metaphysics, an examination of doctrines of reality; epistemology, an investigation of knowledge and belief; and logic, the structuring discipline that cuts across the other branches and forms their foundation by setting forth the rules that govern proper inference. Additionally, it touches briefly on ethics, an inquiry concerning morality, right and wrong, and good and evil.[3] There are further

---

[3] Another area that is common to philosophical study in the analytic tradition is the history of philosophy. Rather than focusing on a particular subject of inquiry— such as reality, knowledge, or morality—it approaches the examination of ideas chronologically, undertaking a critical assessment of the thinkers, the movements that they influenced, and the movements that influenced them.

divisions. Metaphysics itself is partitioned into cosmology, which is the study of the universe in its totality, including its structure; and ontology, a specialty that delves into theories of existence, or being. Again, there are subfields of inquiry among these divisions. For instance, cosmogony, which is the study of the origin and early development of the universe, falls under cosmology; and mereology, which is concerned with composition and the relationship between parts and the wholes that they form, is a section of ontology.

There are a number of other, specialized fields of investigation that come within the bounds of the philosophical enterprise. Indeed, the reach of philosophy is limited only by the variety of topics that it explores. These fields include, to list a few, philosophy of law, philosophy of science, philosophy of language, philosophy of mathematics, social and political philosophy, philosophy of religion, and aesthetics—this last field, which sometimes is placed in a separate category, focuses on art and beauty. All of them, however, share a key factor. They are concerned with underlying principles, ones that are not found strictly within the topics under philosophical investigation. These principles themselves are not subject to the direct observation and testing that science employs in discovery, not because they are too small or too far away but because they are not the sort of things that can be perceived by the senses. They must be approached through reasoning. Although, for example, one can see a painting and appreciate its beauty, exactly what it is that makes the painting beautiful, and what constitutes beauty itself, are matters that are taken up in aesthetics.

From a chronological perspective, the history of Western philosophical thought is separated into six major periods. With some allowance for the development of ideas during the earliest period as well as another, the following table depicts these general divisions according to centuries:[4]

---

[4] Opinions regarding the classification of periods differ somewhat, but the broad representation here is acceptable.

Philosophical Period	Beginning of Period	Ending of Period
Ancient	600 B.C.	300 B.C.
Hellenistic	300 B.C.	A.D. 300
Medieval	A.D. 300	A.D. 1300
Renaissance	A.D. 1300	A.D. 1600
Modern	A.D. 1600	A.D. 1900
Contemporary	A.D. 1900	Present

Greek thought dominates the ancient period. It is the age in which the great minds of Plato and Aristotle are brought to bear on complex problems. The earliest philosophical writings in the West, however, predate them by a few centuries and are traced to Ionia, a Greek-settled region on the edge of Asia Minor that figures prominently in Western history. There, in the coastal city of Miletus, just across the Aegean Sea from Athens, musings about the nature of reality began to take root. Seeing the world around them in its great variety, these thinkers reasoned that something, existing at a deep level, must underlie that diversity, giving rise to things and grounding their being. Although the ancient philosophers developed different theories to explain the grounding factor, their theories were predicated on the shared belief that all things have a common foundation. This universal core, so they thought, is the base of all reality. It is the unifying element that ties everything together. If one can grasp what it is, they conjectured, then one can understand better the cosmos that the senses detect. They set out to find it.

The ideas of the Milesians eventually spread to outlying areas, including the cities of Athens and, in southern Italy, Elea, stimulating others to delve into these mysteries. Beliefs about the metaphysical underpinning varied. Opposing theories began to develop. Philosophy had arisen.

Regrettably, only fragments of the writings of a number of these earliest philosophers remain.[5] Though the original texts are

---

[5] In this work, unless noted otherwise, I quote the fragments of the Presocratic philosophers from Kathleen Freeman, trans., *Ancilla to the Pre-Socratic Philosophers* (1948; repr., Cambridge: Harvard University Press, 1996). Freeman's *Ancilla* is an English translation of the fragments that appear in the fifth edition of a Hermann Diels compilation, revised by Walther Kranz, titled *Die Fragmente der*

lost, something about the lives and ideas of these men has been preserved in the writings of succeeding authors, and scholars have been able to draw on their works in ferreting out the views of the Presocratics. Reconstructing the accounts of the ancients based on comments by these writers, contemporary philosophers are led to different conclusions about certain details, but the information is sufficient for most to agree on the major theses. There are a number of authors to whom scholars turn. Some important ones include, from the fifth century B.C., the historian Herodotus; from the fifth to the early third centuries B.C., the philosophers Plato, Aristotle, who was a student of Plato, and Theophrastus, a pupil of Aristotle; from the first through the third centuries A.D., Plutarch, a biographer and historian, Hippolytus, a Christian theologian, and the doxographer Diogenes Laërtius; and from the sixth century A.D.—principally, at least—Simplicius, another doxographer. It is in an Aristotelian work that one finds a significant statement about some of the thinking of these original theorists. Aristotle identifies their exploratory efforts as a mission to isolate some material substance that lies beneath all things.

> Most of those who first philosophized regarded the material kinds of principles as the principles of all things; for that of which things consist, and the first from which things come to be and into which they are finally resolved after destruction (this being the persisting *substance* of the thing, while the thing changes in its affections), this they say is the element and the principle of things; and because of this they think that nothing is generated and nothing perishes, since such a nature is always preserved. Just as in the case of Socrates when he becomes noble or musical, we do not say that he is generated in the full sense, nor that he perishes in the full sense if he loses these habits, because Socrates himself as an underlying subject still persists, so it is in other cases; for there must be some nature, either one or more

---

Vorsokratiker, which translates the Greek fragments into German. Kranz produced a sixth edition as well, which was published in 1951–1952, with various printings that followed the initial publication. One may consult the bibliography for a reference.

than one, which is preserved and from which the others are generated.[6]

In this quotation, two important concepts emerge. One is that of the base of reality that these earliest philosophers were seeking. Aristotle refers to it in the passage as the principle of things or, more descriptively, the first principle. The Greek term for it is *archē* (ἀρχή). *Archē* is (1) that of which objects are made, that from which they come into being, and that to which they ultimately return, and (2) what serves as the metaphysical ground on which the existence of objects rests—some permanent thing that underlies and preserves their being as they change in properties. *Archē* is thus both originator and conservator of things. One can separate the notion of the source of something from its enduring foundation, however, and it is not entirely obvious to what extent these two aspects of reality are distinguished in the rudimentary metaphysics of the earliest Presocratic philosophers. Although it is perhaps not a distinction that some were able to see very clearly, Aristotle, writing a few centuries later, brings into focus the difference in his discussion of their theories. The considerably greater sophistication of Aristotle and the general philosophical status of his time may reflect a level of maturity of thought that the most ancient philosophers had not reached. Aristotle is cautious in his assessments, however, and philosophers rely on his statements as authoritative nevertheless.[7]

A second foundational notion, bearing a close relationship to *archē*, is denoted by the Greek term *physis* (φύσις). It is translated as 'nature', a word that also appears in the aforementioned passage from Aristotle. The term is the root expression to which the modern English words 'physics' and 'physiology' are traced. *Physis* is the essential constitution of things—what they are at the heart of their

---

[6] Aristotle, *Metaphysics*, A, 3.983b6–18, *Aristotle's Metaphysics*, trans. Hippocrates G. Apostle (Bloomington: Indiana University Press, 1966), 16–17. The term 'affections' in the passage refers to nonessential properties. Note that, in this work, I employ the concepts of property, attribute, and quality without any firm differentiation: a common current practice. Linguistic forms signifying them vary; 'order', 'ordered', and 'being ordered', for instance—all may point to the property of order.

[7] For an informative discussion of *archē*, see W. K. C. Guthrie, *A History of Greek Philosophy*, vol. 1, *The Earlier Presocratics and the Pythagoreans* (1962; repr., Cambridge: Cambridge University Press, 1967), 57–58.

being. Although an object's nature includes its organization and its behavior, the principal reference here is to its intrinsic elementary fiber. Thus, there is a point at which *arche* in the sense of persistent substrate and *physis* as the essential nature, or defining constituent, of a thing appear to touch. One scholar argues that the proper classification of what the ancients were seeking is not *arche*; it is *physis*.

> [I]n the fifth century B.C., the name φύσις was given to the everlasting something of which the world was made. That is quite in accordance with the history of the word, so far as we can make it out. Its original meaning appears to be the "stuff" of which anything is made, a meaning which easily passes into that of its "make-up," its general character or constitution. Those early cosmologists who were seeking for an "undying and ageless" something, would naturally express the idea by saying there was "one φύσις" of all things.
>
> The term ἀρχή, which is often used in our authorities, is in this sense purely Aristotelian. . . . But Plato never uses the term in this connexion, and it does not occur once in the genuine fragments of the early philosophers, which would be very strange on the assumption that they employed it.[8]

In my discussion of these ancient philosophers, I will not probe this distinction at length. The identification of a fundamental reality in the writings of the Presocratics is the primary interest here—what one contemporary philosopher calls, as it pertains to the substrate, *Urstoff*, a German word that expresses the idea of a primitive element.[9] It is more the metaphysical concept of a reality base than the terminology that is employed to refer to it that is the central concern, for it reinforces the role that the views of the Presocratics played in the historical development of a key philosophical problem. The noteworthy exception to this approach is the peculiar stance of the Pythagoreans. For them, the essence of things is not the first

---

[8] John Burnet, *Early Greek Philosophy*, 4th ed. (1930; repr., London: Adam and Charles Black, 1971), 10–11.
[9] See Frederick Copleston, *A History of Philosophy*, vol. 1, *Greece and Rome* (London: Search Press, 1946), 20.

principle but rather something that is generated by it. The distinction is also important in understanding one philosopher who was active around the end of the sixth century B.C. because, for him, inherent in the nature of things—that is to say, *physis*—is order.

With this preliminary examination in mind, I turn my attention to the Presocratics' theories. Consistent with Aristotle's recapitulatory assessment in the previously quoted passage, the philosophers of the ancient period face two fundamental questions in endeavoring to develop an adequate account of reality. They are

1. What underlies the generation of things?
2. What underlies the conservation of things?

These questions presuppose, of course, that things are generated and that they are conserved, but this understanding is a reasonable starting point for a philosophical inquiry, and it is the point from which the early thinkers embark on the quest. Their attempts to answer these questions bring other matters to light, and the scope of the philosophical investigations expands accordingly.

The two queries may be set forth about individual objects, or they may be set forth about all things taken collectively. Both ways introduce interesting issues, but it is in the latter sense that a definitive picture of reality emerges. The genuine weight of the queries will become apparent later in this work, for they resurface as divisional in the quest for knowledge. One's responses to them mark out, in large part, one's worldview, and, as it was then, it is now: The answer to one question may be the answer to the other as well.

One meaningful way to group the Presocratic philosophers is according to whether they deem the base of reality to be a single element or many elements. Although doing so diverges slightly from a strict chronological path, it does underscore the primary difference between the two schools of thought: monism and pluralism. It is a difference that is given in number: In the monistic view, one thing undergirds all existence; in the pluralistic view, more than one thing does so. This bifurcation leaves room for positions in which the fundamental substance is thought to be essentially one or many but in which it shares characteristics with both singularity and multiplicity. It is appropriate at this point to look briefly at the differing positions that arose among some of the major philosophers of those times.

Fundamental Monism

To anyone who cared to observe the physical world during the ancient period, it was clear that things come into being, change with the passage of time, and finally decay. Those who gave thought to what they observed would have seen this principle at work in the plants that they cultivated, watching the seeds that were sown in the spring become mature plants in the summer, only to waste away to dried husks after the autumn harvest. They would have seen its operation in their livestock and the members of their own families. Even artifacts, arising when produced and eventually succumbing to ruin, would have demonstrated the principle's applicability. Pondering this ubiquitous sequence brought with it the belief that some basic substance must persist through the change. The ancient Greeks identified four primary components of the natural world: earth, air, fire, and water. Therefore, it is not surprising that some of these things, occupying the material realm, function as the basis of reality in the theories of several of the early philosophers.

THALES. The most ancient Western thinker meriting the designation 'philosopher' is Thales from the city of Miletus. Although other writers predate him, they are principally creators of poetry and various prose compositions, and it is Thales who initiates the philosophical focus on the unifying substrate. Estimates of Thales's birth range from about 640 to 620 B.C., and scholars place his death sometime after 546 B.C. What scholars know of his view is entirely dependent on accounts that are recorded by others, as no writings that are unquestionably attributable to him have survived.

Plato reports a rather amusing anecdote about this earliest philosopher.[10] According to the story, Thales was mocked by a witty

---

[10] For this account, see Plato, *Theaetetus*, 174a, trans. F. M. Cornford, in *The Collected Dialogues of Plato, Including the Letters*, trans. Lane Cooper et al., ed. Edith Hamilton and Huntington Cairns (1961; Princeton: Princeton University Press, 1971), 879. Diogenes Laërtius also reports the incident, with slight

maidservant: It seems that he was gazing up at the stars and tumbled down a well. She scoffed at him for being so eager to know what was happening in the sky that he could not see what lay at his own feet. It is not known whether the story is true, or even whether Plato accepts it as true, but it is interesting in light of Thales's belief that the fundamental substance of the universe is what Thales presumably found at the bottom of that well: water. He claims that all things come from water, and, on the assumption that Aristotle's interpretation of Thales's philosophy is correct, all things *are* water.[11] The earth itself is, in fact, a floating disk. In speaking of the Presocratic search for first principles, Aristotle notes Thales's identification of it.

> [T]hese thinkers do not all agree as to the number and kinds of such principles. Thales, the founder of such philosophy, says that this principle is *Water* (and on account of this he also declared that the earth rests on water), perhaps coming to this belief by observing that all food is moist and that heat itself is generated from the moist and is kept alive by it (and that from which things are generated is the principle of all); and he came to this belief both because of this fact and because the seeds of all things have a moist nature, and water is the principle of the nature of moist things.[12]

Mythical Egyptian and Babylonian accounts of earth-supporting and primeval waters respectively might have influenced Thales. Perhaps too his opinion came to be reinforced through observing that water can change in its characteristics, becoming hard when taking the form of ice and hardly substantial when appearing as

---

variations. Consult his *Lives of Eminent Philosophers*, trans. R. D. Hicks (London: William Heinemann, 1925), 1:35. The full title of Diogenes's original work is *Lives and Opinions of Eminent Philosophers in Ten Books*.

[11] Some who study ancient philosophy believe that Aristotle may be attributing more to Thales than what is justified. They maintain that the theory that this Milesian presents may be only about the source of things, not about a substrate as well. See G. S. Kirk, J. E. Raven, and M. Schofield, *The Presocratic Philosophers: A Critical History with a Selection of Texts*, 2nd ed. (1983; Cambridge: Cambridge University Press, 2011), 93–95.

[12] Aristotle, *Metaphysics*, A, 3.983b19–28, 17.

mist. Thales infers that, although many things exist, all of them owe their existence to one fundamental element, one material substance. It is likely that he sees this substance as something that persists through change and thus what accounts for, in addition to the existence of things, their subsistence. Thales's chief contribution to the history of thought is not that it is water that is the primordial element but the idea that *something* must be. He is the first Western philosopher, as far as it is known, to set forth the claim.

ANAXIMANDER. Born in 611 or 610 B.C. and another Milesian, Anaximander became a young associate of Thales. He lived until 547 or 546 B.C. Only five fragments of his writings remain. Unlike the elder theorist, Anaximander does not see the base of reality as one of the four elemental substances but as something apart from, and beyond, them. He believes that these basic elements are in opposition, and he alleges that there would be no reasonable way to account for their continued existence if one were primary. It would have encroached on the others—something that Anaximander considers to be an instance of injustice—resulting in their extinction, and it is obvious that such a state of affairs has not arisen. One may consider the notion in this way: Fire dries wet things, but water extinguishes fire; therefore, if water were the core reality, then, in due course, all would have become water. The base of reality therefore must be something other than one of the four primary elements. Moreover, if the underlying reality itself is subject to alteration, then it becomes incumbent on a supporting theorist to explain how it can provide the continuity of objects through time. Given that the essence of a thing is the one constant during the variation in the thing's state, it is difficult to see how that which changes can be the preserving factor in that which changes. Perhaps this problem occurs to Anaximander as he begins his search for an alternative.[13] Thales argues that the primordial substance is water. On cold days during the winter months, a pond freezes, and the water in it becomes firm—firm enough for a person to stand on it and walk to the other side. During the heat of summer, much of the water in the pond disappears as the sun bears down on it, drying the pond and leaving a muddy residue.

---

[13] Kathleen Freeman raises this consideration in *The Pre-Socratic Philosophers: A Companion to Diels, Fragmente der Vorsokratiker,* 2nd ed. (1949; repr., Oxford: Basil Blackwell, 1966), 57.

On cool autumn mornings after a rain, the fog that develops is wet, but it is more like air than water. Anaximander probably reasons that, if Thales were correct in declaring water to be the base of existence, then it would be impossible for water itself to undergo such changes.

Anaximander holds instead that the fundamental reality is the *Apeiron*, which is rendered as 'the Boundless', 'the Unlimited', 'the Indefinite', or a similar appellation. The Greek word *apeiron* (ἄπειρον) is formed from two expressions: One means 'absence' or 'without'; the other means 'boundary' or 'limit'. The Boundless is indefinite in its spatiality: It has enormous extent—undetermined, although perhaps not infinite. It is unbounded in its temporality: It is eternal, neither coming into being nor ceasing to be. The Boundless is the neutral and indefinite base out of which definite things arise. In his search for the core reality, Anaximander's move away from the four basic constituents of the natural realm that figure prominently in Grecian thought sets his metaphysics apart from the theories of other philosophers of his day. According to Anaximander,

> The Non-Limited is the original material of existing things; further, the source from which existing things derive their existence is also that to which they return at their destruction, according to necessity; for they give justice and make reparation to one another for their injustice, according to the arrangement of Time.[14]

As in the theory of his Milesian predecessor, Anaximander's underpinning for reality is purely material. Philosophical thought had not developed to the stage of distinguishing clearly between the corporeal and the incorporeal. There is a faint glimmer of what is to come, however, in Anaximander's belief that the *Apeiron* directs the course of things. That assertion does not appear in the fragments, but a reference to the view appears in Aristotle.

> Everything is either a source or derived from a source.
> But there cannot be a source of the infinite or limitless,
> for that would be a limit of it. Further, as it is a

---

[14] Anaximander, frag. 1, 19. Freeman's translation employs the term 'the Non-Limited' rather than 'the Boundless', but they are equivalent expressions.

beginning, it is both uncreatable and indestructible. For there must be a point at which what has come to be reaches completion, and also a termination of all passing away. That is why, as we say, there is no principle of *this*, but it is that which is held to be the principle of other things, and to encompass all and to steer all, as those assert who do not recognize, alongside the infinite, other causes, such as Mind or Friendship. Further they identify it with the Divine, for it is 'deathless and imperishable' as Anaximander says.[15]

The Boundless may have a rudimentary awareness in Anaximander's metaphysics, but its steering is little more than a physical impulse. The notion of a purposive, directing force in the form of rationality does not emerge in philosophical musings until nearly a century later. Further years elapse before a distinction between driving principles and the material that they propel surfaces in the Presocratics, and between active mind and passive matter. (Note that, in philosophy, the singular terms 'mind' and 'body' usually denote the respective categories when no article or adjective precedes them.)

The world in which people live is not the only world, according to the common reading of Anaximander's theory; many other worlds are spawned by the Boundless. He attempts to explain the process that brought about the cosmos that humans experience. Anaximander believes the Boundless to be in constant and eternal movement, although the pattern of this movement is not obvious from the writings. Some have suggested that the motion is a vortex, but there is no support for this view aside from a remark by Aristotle, and the remark is not conclusive.[16] In Anaximander's account of the generation of the universe, a foundational pair of opposites appeared, perhaps arising directly from the Boundless, though a more likely scenario is that the Boundless fragmented, and the principal pair came from a detached piece. In either case, these opposites are the hot and the cold. The hot separated from the cold and encircled it as bark encircles a tree, according to the ancient philosopher, becoming

---

[15] Aristotle, *Physics*, 3, 4.203b6–14, trans. R. P. Hardie and R. K. Gaye, in *The Basic Works of Aristotle*, trans. E. M. Edghill et al., ed. Richard McKeon (New York: Random House, 1941), 259.

[16] See Kirk, Raven, and Schofield, *Presocratic Philosophers*, 127–28.

a ring of fire. It is possible that Anaximander sees this particular movement—the one that produced the primary division—as a vortex or even many vortices. This whirlpool motion is common to thinkers of the day, representing a mechanism by means of which things are spread apart. In such movement, heavier objects remain near the center while lighter objects move outward.

Surrounded by the ring of fire, the other three elements were taking shape. The cold at this point consisted of misty air encasing wet earth that had condensed out of it. The fire ring dried the earth, leaving the wet in the depressions, and it became the seas. Thus, the four elements—fire, the first to be isolated, then air, earth, and water—came into being from the two opposites that arose, directly or indirectly, from the Boundless. The fire ring disintegrated, breaking into separate rings, which revolved around the world like the rims of wheels and continue to do so. Air encloses those rings in such a way that fire shows only through apertures in each band. In the outer ring, there is a single opening, like the one in the nozzle of a bellows, so Anaximander believes, through which the sun shines. The diameter of that ring is twenty-seven or twenty-eight times that of the earth, which is shaped like a short cylinder, having a diameter that is three times its height. Closer to the earth is the moon ring, also with a single opening. Its diameter is eighteen or nineteen times that of the earth. The star ring may be multiple rings in Anaximander's theory; philosophers are not certain regarding this point. In any case, of the heavenly lights, the stars lie closest to the earth, and the fire that human observers see as stars shines through many small openings in the ring or rings. The turning of all these bands causes the light from these celestial objects to appear to move across the sky. In a significant advancement over his forerunner, Anaximander postulates that the earth holds its position, not because it floats on some substance, such as water, but because it is in a state of equilibrium. It lies at the center of the rings and is thus equidistant from each of them.[17]

---

[17] The variations in the dimensions of the sun ring and moon ring are attributable to reports from different ancient sources. Some contemporary scholars believe that the star ring, assuming that it is a single structure, exhibits, in the ancient philosopher's thought, a diameter of nine times that of the earth, following a pattern of multiples of three. Ring values of twenty-seven, eighteen, and nine are

Regardless of how strange this story is, and how inaccurate, Anaximander gives a description of the process that generated the world. There is no record of such in Thales. Assuming that the absence is because Thales did not offer a corresponding narrative rather than because his philosophy has survived only minimally in the writings of his successors, there is in Anaximander's creative handiwork the beginnings of a cosmogonic account: an explanation of the development of the material universe from a primal phase.

Before I leave the discussion of Anaximander, it is worth mentioning that he is the first of the Presocratics, according to Simplicius, actually to apply the term *archē*, which again is translated as 'principle', to the ultimate reality. Simplicius states,

> Anaximander says that the opposites are in the substrate, which is a limitless body, and that they are extracted from it; he was the first to call the substrate a principle.[18]

ANAXIMENES. The third Milesian of note is Anaximenes. He was born around 585 B.C., and the date of his death is thought to be between 528 and 525 B.C. Anaximenes is known to be a student of Anaximander. Virtually nothing remains of his writings, but there are fragments that reveal his thinking. The following pair suggests that, according to Anaximenes's metaphysics, what lies at the base of reality is air:

> As our soul, being air, holds us together, so do breath and air surround the whole universe.[19]

> Air is near to the incorporeal; and since we come into being by an efflux from this (*air*), it is bound to be both non-limited and rich so that it never fails.[20]

---

then reasonable reconstructions—their being products, in all three instances, of three and a number that is evenly divisible by three—particularly given the ratio of three to one for the earth's cylindrical dimensions.

[18] Simplicius, *On Aristotle Physics*, 1.4 150, 22–24, trans. C. C. W. Taylor, *Simplicius: On Aristotle Physics 1.3–4*, trans. Pamela Huby and C. C. W. Taylor (London: Bristol Classical Press, 2011), 60.

[19] Anaximenes, frag. 2, 19.

[20] Ibid., frag. 3, 19.

The other elements are formed from air through condensation and rarefaction, he claims. Air becomes wind when it is condensed, or thickened, and further compacting yields clouds, then water, earth, and finally stones. When rarefied, or thinned, it becomes fire. Air therefore lies along a density continuum. As the amount of it changes through compression or decompression, the properties of that which it composes change.

Anaximenes demonstrates this alleged principle through the first scientific experiment in the West on record. Blowing on one's hand forcefully through pursed lips causes the condensed air to feel cool to the hand. Blowing on one's hand gently with the mouth open wide causes the rarefied air to feel warm. This account of the phenomenon is not correct, of course. What happens is that air that is taken into the lungs is warmed by body heat. When the lips are squeezed together, and the air is blown out with force, the drop in pressure as the air is released and exits the mouth reduces the temperature of the air in accordance with physical law. The result is that the air is perceived as being cool. When released slowly, how- ever, the temperature of the air remains greater than the temperature of the skin, under normal conditions; thus, it seems to be warm.

What is noteworthy in Anaximenes's account, however, is that, although he appears to take a step backward by returning to one of the four elements, deeming it to be fundamental, he attempts to ground his supposition that there is one substrate and that it is air on a hypothesis that is supported by experiment and observation. More important, as scholars of ancient philosophy recognize, it is the concept that the *qualities* of things are brought about by changes in *quantity* that distinguishes Anaximenes from his predecessors, and it forms an essential part of this philosopher's cosmogony. Whether this notion originated with Anaximenes is uncertain, but it is certain that Anaximenes believes that variations in physical things occur as a result of variations in the amount of the basic material substance. As Thales is thought to hold, Anaximenes too accepts the existence of a single substrate as that which provides continuity through change. Unlike Thales, however, Anaximenes puts forth an explanation, which he bases on a hypothetical physical principle, to convey how change occurs; in this respect, his theory demonstrates progress.

As for the formation of the cosmos, Anaximenes offers his own version. Some of the existing substrate, air, condensed into earth.[21] The sun, moon, and stars were formed as mist rose from the earth and became rarefied, yielding fire. Having noticed that wide, flat surfaces present considerable resistance to wind, he maintains that the world, which he believes to be flat, is buoyed by air, as are the heavenly bodies. The air is in constant, eternal motion and apparently possesses the capacity to move on its own without the application of an external force. Like Thales, Anaximenes sees the earth as a floating disk; however, it does not float on water but on air.

The Milesians differ in their accounts of what lies at the ground of reality, but all see it as one thing, and that thing is material. They believe that the cosmos is filled with many objects, but each of them exists and subsists because of a single substrate. The next philosopher whom I will examine is likewise fundamentally monistic in his views, but he introduces a pair of novel ideas. One unsettles the foundation of subsistence through change in the objects in the world; the other challenges the notion that the world is entirely mechanistic.

HERACLITUS. The most enigmatic of all the ancient Greek philosophers, and one who influenced future thought to a great degree, is Heraclitus. His writings, of which more than 125 original fragments are preserved, along with a few questionable ones, are often cryptic, lending themselves to different interpretations of his meaning. Those who study ancient writers place Heraclitus's birth between 540 and 521 B.C. and his death between 487 and 480 B.C., although, for his death, a date a bit later has surfaced. Born of nobility in the city of Ephesus in the region of Ionia, he is scornful of his fellow Ephesians and criticizes certain philosophers of the day, claiming, "Much learning does not teach one to have intelligence."[22]

Central to Heraclitus's philosophy is the tension of opposites. Opposition is evident in the cosmos: light versus darkness, rest versus motion, good versus bad, and right versus left.[23] For him, the

---

[21] Freeman notes that the condensation of air that resulted in earth, in the cosmogony of Anaximenes, appears to have been direct and therefore must have been intense. See Freeman, *Pre-Socratic Philosophers: A Companion to Diels*, 68.

[22] Heraclitus, frag. 40, 27.

[23] The Pythagoreans, the earliest of whom predate Heraclitus by several decades, developed a Table of Opposites, which lists the pairs that are mentioned, along

diversity of things in the world is bound inextricably to a war that arises out of disparity. Conflict, he asserts, is necessary for existence. Unlike Anaximander, who sees the war of the opposites as encroachment, as something unjust, Heraclitus believes that this very strife is essential to reality itself. Says Heraclitus, "That which is in opposition is in concert, and from things that differ comes the most beautiful harmony."[24] Nothing exists independently but only in the context of, and as part of, the whole. Reality is one, subsisting in the conflict of the many: unity out of diversity in contention. As the strings of a lyre yield the musicality of the instrument only when the device exerts tension on them—relax the strings, removing the tension, and the music subsides—so conflict brings about the existence and continuance of the cosmos. Things arise out of the contention; they exist as a consequence of it. Dependent on the actuality of strife, things have no being apart from it. Heraclitus declares, "One should know that war is general (*universal*) and jurisdiction is strife, and everything comes about by way of strife and necessity."[25] The constant battle of opposites holds them in check, producing a balance that is necessary for existence and is, in fact, the underlying cause of it.

Heraclitus believes fire to be the ultimate reality. A common interpretation of Heraclitean philosophy is that fire is the material substrate out of which the many things that compose the world arise and to which they ultimately return, their subsisting in the constant tension of conflagration. The following pair of fragments points to the essential role that fire plays in his philosophy:

> This ordered universe (*cosmos*), which is the same for all, was not created by any one of the gods or of mankind, but it was ever and is and shall be ever-living Fire, kindled in measure and quenched in measure.[26]

---

with others. The Pythagoreans' inclusion of Limit and (the) Unlimited in the Table of Opposites suggests the influence of Anaximander. In turn, Heraclitus ostensibly draws on this analysis in formulating his own view that opposition is essential to the existence of the cosmos.

[24] Heraclitus, frag. 8, 25.
[25] Ibid., frag. 80, 30.
[26] Ibid., frag. 30, 26.

> There is an exchange: all things for Fire and Fire for all
> things, like goods for gold and gold for goods.[27]

Among contemporary philosophers, however, there is some disagreement concerning whether Heraclitus, in fact, accepts the existence of an ultimate substrate. According to this contrary view, fire is the universal medium of exchange into which all things can be converted, not an element that supports their physical composition. Like gold, it is a standard that provides consistency and measurement, but it would be erroneous to conclude that everything is fire at the base of its being.[28] Even if Heraclitus does embrace the notion of a universal, material substrate, it is unlikely that it is in the less developed sense of the Milesians. Despite the differing perspectives on Heraclitean thought, no one disagrees that fire is central to it. In combustion, the blaze is in a state of continual change, and this characteristic state provides a clue to a deeper tenet in the philosopher's metaphysics.

Other ancient authors are an aid to understanding Heraclitus's cosmogony; the fragments of his writings that remain provide little information.[29] The fragments do show, however, that Heraclitus takes fire to be the element that is converted into the others: "The changes of fire: first, sea; and of sea, half is earth and half fiery

---

[27] Ibid., frag. 90, 31.

[28] A view that is contrary to the substratum position is found in Michael C. Stokes, *One and Many in Presocratic Philosophy* (Washington, DC: Center for Hellenic Studies, 1971), 102–8. Stokes argues that fire does not operate as a substrate; rather, it stands in a relationship of mutual succession to all other things: They become fire in a cycle of exchange, but fire does not underlie them. He believes that Fragment 90, quoted above, provides support for this position. Catherine Osborne holds a similar view. She notes that one may buy bread with copper coins; the money serves as a standard of trade, but the copper coins do not underlie the bread's physical being. Likewise, Heraclitus sees fire as the means by which things are translated, not a substrate. Refer to Osborne's "Heraclitus," in *Routledge History of Philosophy*, ed. G. H. R. Parkinson and S. G. Shanker, vol. 1, *From the Beginning to Plato*, ed. C. C. W. Taylor (London: Routledge, 1997), 88–127. Also see Harold Cherniss, *Aristotle's Criticism of Presocratic Philosophy* (1935; repr., New York: Octagon Books, 1964), 380 ff.

[29] That Heraclitus develops a cosmogony is denied by Stokes. See Stokes, *One and Many*, 107. This stance is in keeping with the author's rejection of the idea that there is a substrate, in the Heraclitean view, one from which the cosmos sprang.

water-spout . . . Earth is liquified into sea."[30] This process of conversion appears to be akin to Anaximenes's condensation and rarefaction. In what Heraclitus sees as the downward path, fire condenses into water, and further condensation produces earth. In the upward path, earth rarefies into water and, from there, into bright and dark exhalations. During cosmic generation, the bright exhalations form the sun, moon, and stars. The dark, moist exhalations surround the earth, probably like mist, reducing the light from the bodies close to the earth, which are the moon and stars, but not the sun, which, he thinks, is farther away. The process of the exchange of elements is cyclical and continual, with their undergoing unending transformation through compression and decompression, returning to fire as the sequence completes. An open question in Heraclitean philosophy is whether the cosmos as a whole returns to fire at some point in a cycle of exchange: a periodic, global destruction and regeneration of all things in unison. Such universal conflagration is known as ecpyrosis.[31]

This discussion leads to what is the most important, but controversial, concept of Heraclitean philosophy. It is the notion of change. More than any other aspect of his writings, and perhaps of those of the Presocratics as a whole, this notion sets the stage for metaphysical thought in the succeeding centuries. According to a widely accepted view, Heraclitus believes change to be universal and constant. It is not entirely obvious from the extant fragments that he embraces the idea that change permeates the world to this extreme extent, and again there is disagreement on the issue among those who research ancient philosophy.[32]

There are unequivocal indicators in the fragments, though, and certain doxographic material supports the view rather convincingly. The concept is revealed in the aphorism 'All things are in a state of flux'; from Simplicius, the rendition 'Everything flows' comes.

---

[30] Heraclitus, frag. 31, 27.

[31] Copleston offers several reasons against adopting this view. See Copleston, *Greece and Rome*, 44–45. Also see Guthrie, *Earlier Presocratics*, 455–59.

[32] For opposing views with accompanying discussion, refer to Jonathan Barnes, *The Presocratic Philosophers*, vol. 1, *Thales to Zeno* (London: Routledge and Kegan Paul, 1979), 65–69; and G. S. Kirk, *Heraclitus: The Cosmic Fragments* (1954; repr., Cambridge: Cambridge University Press, 2010), 367–80.

Whether these expressions are genuinely Heraclitean in authorship, they are certainly so in their representation of his theory—in some sense, at least—as the quotations that are given below demonstrate. They are also in keeping with the view that the underlying reality is fire, an ever-changing phenomenon in which flames continually rise and drop around and above the material that they consume, which itself changes as it is reduced to embers and ash. Consider these key fragments from his writings:

> Those who step into the same river have different waters flowing ever upon them.[33]

> In the same river, we both step and do not step, we are and we are not.[34]

> It is not possible to step twice into the same river. (*It is impossible to touch the same mortal substance twice, but through the rapidity of change*) they scatter and again combine (*or rather, not even 'again' or 'later', but the combination and separation are simultaneous*) and approach and separate.[35]

Plato ascribes to Heraclitus, as does Aristotle following him, the doctrine that change occurs in everything and at every moment. One finds in Plato's works the remark, "the opinion of Heraclitus, that all things flow and nothing stands"; again, in another passage, he mentions,

> Heraclitus is supposed to say that all things are in motion and nothing at rest; he compares them to the stream of a river, and says that you cannot go into the same water twice.[36]

---

[33] Heraclitus, frag. 12, 25.

[34] Ibid., frag. 49a, 28.

[35] Ibid., frag. 91, 31. Aristotle alludes to the river passages, exemplified by this one and the previous two, in his *Metaphysics*.

[36] Plato, *Cratylus*, 401d and 402a respectively, trans. Benjamin Jowett, in *Collected Dialogues of Plato*, 438–39. There are additional passages in Plato's dialogues that point to the perpetual flux that Heraclitus proposes. See *Theaetetus*, 160d and 179d–180d.

Aristotle notes in his own writings that Plato believes the doctrine of flux to be an accurate portrayal of the Presocratic's theory, as the following passage reveals:

> For, having in his [Plato's] youth first become familiar with Cratylus and with the Heraclitean doctrines (that all sensible things are ever in a state of flux and there is no knowledge about them), these views he held even in later years.[37]

There are other supporting passages. According to Aristotle, it is "the view of Heraclitus that all things are in motion."[38] Elsewhere, in referring to the Heraclitean principle, he writes, "[T]he view is actually held by some that not merely some things but all things in the world are in motion and always in motion."[39]

Evidence for the idea that Heraclitus sees change as ubiquitous is thus ample. The waters of a river flow ceaselessly, bringing a state of steady motion. There is a certain ambiguity in Heraclitus's writings regarding the phrase 'same river', but fragment 91 suggests, as does an alternative translation of fragment 12, that not only are the waters within the river fluctuating constantly, but the river is doing so as well. If this rendering is correct, and I will adopt that view, then the river is not the same from one instant to the next; but, in denying sameness, Heraclitus is denying more than constancy of properties—he is denying conservation. It is not simply a case of varying waters that make up one river through time; there are, in fact, diverse rivers. A waterway is in a perpetual state of becoming something different because of flux and never, for more than an instant, *is*. With every

---

[37] Aristotle, *Metaphysics*, A, 6.987a32–35, trans. W. D. Ross, in *Works of Aristotle*, 700. Cratylus, a follower of Heraclitus, takes the position of his predecessor on flux to the logically extreme end, claiming, according to Aristotle, that one cannot step even *once* into the same river. Before one's foot enters the water completely, the river will have changed. This account appears in Aristotle's *Metaphysics*, Γ, 5.1010a10–14, in the aforementioned work, pp. 745–46. I extract quotations from Aristotle's *Metaphysics* from both this translation and the one that I cited earlier, depending on the passage.

[38] Aristotle, *Topics*, 1, 11.104b21, trans. W. A. Pickard-Cambridge, in *Works of Aristotle*, 197.

[39] Aristotle, *Physics*, 8, 3.253b9–11, 361. Another passage in Aristotle that refers to Heraclitean perpetual flux appears in 1, 2.405a25–28 of his *On the Soul*.

tick of the clock, the object that was is not now, and the object that is now will not be. The Heraclitean river serves as an analogue; it is a picture of the cosmos: Physical things mirror, to a degree, the active waters. There is no persistence. Pervasive and unremitting, change prohibits the endurance and stability that one associates with sensory objects. Nothing is static, staying the same through time. Each thing varies, moment by moment (however brief a moment actually may be), for, when a thing's properties shift, there is a shift in essence.

Whatever Heraclitus has in mind in uttering the river statements, they raise a crucial question: Is it possible for an object at one instant and an object at another instant to be the same object if they do not have everything in common? If such is not possible, then, according to the view that change is happening everywhere, all the time, the world seems to fall apart, and human understanding with it. The problem is not just that the ability of some substrate to hold things together is overrun by the relentless flux; it is that change, despite the presence of a substrate—fire or otherwise—seems to undermine *identity*. What appears to be one and the same physical entity is not one and the same as the continual shift in characteristics takes its toll. The upshot is that reality is fragmented, so much so that nothing is sufficiently substantial to be a genuine object—one that endures beyond an instant, at least—and therefore nothing is an object of knowledge. It does not remain long enough to be grasped with the fingers or the mind. The relentless change makes every physical object unique at every slice of time and, in so doing, sweeps away one's understanding of the world. The problem is thus both metaphysical and epistemological.

Heraclitean philosophy does not deny identity altogether, as certain fragments, especially this one, make clear: "The way up and down are one and the same."[40] One must put this fragment in perspective, however. It is about the union of opposites, not about the preservation of object-identity through time. Heraclitus is emphasizing the notion that contraries are inherent in things, in keeping with his belief that existence is dependent on strife. Things are at odds with themselves by virtue of contrary aspects, but it must be this way, or they would not exist at all. In Heraclitean cosmology,

---

[40] Heraclitus, frag. 60, 29.

the downward and upward courses through which the elements are exchanged are parts of the same recurrent, cosmic cycle. It is likely too that the philosopher has in mind a path for travelers. At any one instant, the path extends in two different directions—indeed, opposite directions. At that instant, it exists, despite its incongruent features, or rather because of them. That fact says nothing at all about its being the same path at distinct instants, though. Change changes everything, as it were. With its obvious, ongoing motion, the river is a fitting paradigm for Heraclitus's philosophical position. At some moment, and again at another, *a* river may exist because of intrinsic conflict—but not *the* river, though, because of change.[41]

Some scholars are reluctant to accept universal change as an accurate representation of Heraclitus's beliefs; however, many do accept it, and I will take his theory to be one of ubiquitous flux. Doing so is important not primarily because of Heraclitus per se but because of the implications that the notion of streaming properties has for subsequent philosophy, challenging both theories of being and theories of knowing. Aristotle rejects the Heraclitean doctrine of flux and argues against it; but Plato embraces it, along with its inevitable consequence for knowledge, and he devotes much of his writing to the development of a theory that seeks to save human-kind's comprehension of things in the face of a turbulent world.

Though change may be occurring steadily, Heraclitus does not equate flux with chaos. On the contrary, he believes that everything that happens to everything is in accordance with what he calls *Logos*, the Rationale of the Cosmos, a principle of universal intelligibility that transcends the perpetual process of change and the world of which it is part.[42] It is the operation of *Logos* that brings individual

---

[41] According to W. K. C. Guthrie, Heraclitus thinks that what can change into another thing and, on some occasion, change back must have been the same all along. The ancient philosopher's belief in the cyclical nature of time allows, based on this reading, for a return to the original state. If Heraclitus holds that such is the case, however, then it seems that it would be possible to step twice into the same river if one waits long enough, and that rendering is contrary to what frag. 91 asserts. Any prohibition would be a consequence of the limited life span of the individual who steps, not the logical prohibition of the preservation of identity as change occurs. It is doubtful, I think, that Heraclitus has such a scenario in mind.

[42] The Greek term *logos* (λόγος) is translated predominantly as 'word' or 'reason'. It is the root expression from which the English word 'logic' is derived.

material things into existence through the war of the opposites. It is the operation of *Logos* that drives things—perhaps even the cosmos itself—toward ultimate dissolution into fire. Finally, it is the operation of *Logos* that impresses order on the endless shifting that pervades material reality. Stated concisely, *Logos* is "the purpose which steers all things through all things."[43] Far from the nascent steering of things that one finds in the *Apeiron* of Anaximander, the *Logos* of Heraclitus is infused with the ability to guide things toward ends. *Logos* directs the unfolding of the cosmic system in accordance with order and purpose; nevertheless, it lacks the ability to conserve the objects that populate that system as it unfolds. Heraclitus stops short with the notion of *Logos*; he is, however, on the right path with his postulation.

Here then are the roots of what becomes a watershed notion in Western philosophical thought—the concept that there is an essential connection between the workings of the *material* world and *reason*, between *physical process* and *purpose*. This seminal idea developed well beyond Heraclitean metaphysics. It came to represent a dividing line between two broad groups of philosophers: those who accept, and those who do not accept, that all that there is—all reality—is corporeal. Heraclitus's *Logos*, to be sure, is linked to the physicality of fire, albeit not tightly; the thesis proposing existence apart from the material does not appear until several decades later. *Logos* is not an intelligent agent as such; nevertheless, it is a controlling principle that reflects the order that is the hallmark of intelligence. More than merely serving as an indicator in this respect, however, *Logos* represents that which is common to the rational minds of human beings: thought. There is reason to believe that the philosopher is not far from the truth. To know the truth, though, humankind needs to know what, if anything, rational mentality contributes to the order that the conservation of objects within the universe requires, and what role, if any, it plays in the order that the universe exhibits as a whole. It is a matter of principal importance.

Thus, one finds in the enigmatic Heraclitus the rudiments of two conceptions from which spring ponderous philosophical issues in future systems, including a number of systems in current times.

---

[43] Heraclitus, frag. 41, 27.

These conceptions unfold with force as defining factors in the quest for understanding. They are the following pair:

1. the pervasiveness of change, with its corresponding implications for identity and knowledge;
2. a universe, the workings of which are in accordance with an order that points to rationality—intelligence and purpose.

QUASI-STRICT PLURALISM

Reacting to the basic monism of their Milesian predecessors, a group of thinkers took a major departure in their stance. Founded by Pythagoras, this philosophical school was ascetic in nature and cloaked in secrecy; and, given that Pythagoras himself evidently wrote nothing, it is difficult to distinguish between his ideas and those of his devoted disciples. That difficulty is compounded by the longevity of the ancient philosopher's following, as it continued for many years after his death. A further complication arises from the fact that the perspectives of his followers differ among themselves, apparently creating sects within the overall philosophical genre. For these reasons, it is often better to refer to the movement than to the man in setting forth the approach.

It is clear, however, that mathematics is a central part of the doctrinal theses of the Pythagoreans as a whole, as indicated by the well-known theorem in geometry that bears the name of the school's founder. Closely allied with their interest in mathematics is a focus on musical sounds, for numerical qualities are inherent in the notes of a scale. Investigations in these areas brought with them the belief that the nature of things is something that is altogether pluralistic.

PYTHAGORAS AND THE PYTHAGOREANS. Pythagoras was born on the island of Samos, probably around 578 B.C.; he lived to approximately 510 B.C., perhaps a bit later.[44] He is credited with

---

[44] Diogenes Laërtius gives slightly different dates: approximately 582–500 B.C. Some contemporary estimates vary even further.

discovering the harmonic relationships in music. An octave, for example, exhibits the ratio of 2:1. If all things are equal, then halving the length of a vibrating string on an instrument, such as a lyre, produces a note that is one octave higher than the original in its fundamental tone. The frequency at which the shorter string vibrates is twice that of the longer one. To demonstrate this principle using a modern instrument, strike any open string on a guitar, then press that string against the fingerboard of the guitar at a point precisely in the middle of the string, between the nut and the bridge, and strike it again. The octave tone will be created.

In current times, one measures pitch by the number of cycles per second at which the object that is producing a sound vibrates. For instance, playing A above middle C on a piano that is in standard tune causes the appropriate string to vibrate at a fundamental frequency of 440 cycles per second, expressed as 440 hertz, as a rule, after the German physicist Heinrich R. Hertz. Ascend the keyboard an octave, and the fundamental frequency of that shorter string is doubled to 880 hertz. Similarly, the ratio of 3:2 generates the perfect fifth in music, and the ratio of 4:3 generates the perfect fourth. These ratios hold consistently, regardless of the instrument or the material that is producing the sound.

It is the numerical ratio, according to the Pythagoreans, that is the authentic expression of an undergirding reality. The foundation of things is material, they believe, but not in the sense of the familiar four elements. It is mathematical; instead of water or air or a similar substrate, reality lies in number. Aristotle says of their philosophy,

> Again, the Pythagoreans, because they saw many attributes of numbers belonging to sensible bodies, supposed real things to be numbers—not separable numbers, however, but numbers of which real things consist. But why? Because the attributes of numbers are present in a musical scale and in the heavens and in many other things.[45]

For the Pythagoreans, it is not that things just align with numbers in some way. They *are* numbers.

---

[45] Aristotle, *Metaphysics*, N, 3.1090a20–24, in *Works of Aristotle*, 918.

To understand how the Pythagoreans arrive at this strange conception, one must consider their philosophical perspective concerning the way in which things come into being. At the beginning is a pair of first principles: Limit and the Unlimited. Related to these two principles are Odd and Even. There appears to be some divergence within Pythagorean thought here, or perhaps ambiguity, which Aristotle's writings capture. Limit and the Unlimited subsume Odd and Even, so one view suggests, as broad categories subsume narrower categories.[46] Alternatively, Limit and the Unlimited are identical to Odd and Even respectively. The Unlimited is reminiscent of Anaximander. Reminiscent of Anaximenes, it is probably air. The influence of the Milesians is thus visible in the cosmogony of the Pythagoreans—not only in the fact that the latter put forth a generational account of the cosmos, as some of their predecessors had done, but also in their declaration of the first principles.

Limit, exhibiting definiteness and form, began to breathe in what surrounded it: the Unlimited, exhibiting neither of those characteristics. At this stage, it appears that Pythagoreanism takes divergent paths once again. There are two cosmogonic versions, although both of them portray the Unit as a crucial component of the creative process. In one narrative, the Unit arose from the acting of Limit on the Unlimited; in the other, Limit *is* the Unit—they are the same. In either case, the Unit itself is not part of the numerical sequence but rather stands outside it, serving as the progenitor. It is both odd and even. Evidently, the thinking here is that increasing an even number by one makes it odd, whereas increasing an odd number by one makes it even.

At any rate, through the activity of the Unit, the Unlimited was marked out, or measured, perhaps as, in an analogous way, a person might pencil sections of a plank for multiple cuttings and then saw the board into pieces of different lengths to build a structure. The procedure produced a stretch of numbers by means of the generation of definite, calculable amounts of the Unlimited—that is to say, for

---

[46] As I indicated earlier, the Pythagoreans set forth a table of pairs of contrasting principles—ten in all. The duo Limit and (the) Unlimited heads the list, followed by Odd-Even, One-Plurality, and seven other sets. The arrangement is probably indicative of the importance of the first pair.

the Pythagoreans, collections of points. Corresponding to each given aggregate is an integer that equals the precise number of points in that aggregate.

The next step in the process follows this pattern, treating numbers as points. It is the generation of geometric solids from the numbers. It is not difficult to see how an ancient philosopher might believe that numerical values can produce geometric shapes. The number 1 corresponds to a point, 2 to a line, 3 to a plane, and 4 to a solid. In geometry, it is true, for instance, that three points, not all of which are on the same line, determine a plane; and four points, not all of which are in the same plane, determine a geometric solid. In the former case, if one joins the points with lines, then the resultant figure is a triangle. In the latter case, if one joins the points with lines and the lines with planes, then the resultant figure is a tetrahedron. The Pythagoreans take this concept a step further, claiming that the number is to be *identified* with the plane or the solid, in that the number is the fundamental nature of it. Summing the first four integers in the arithmetic progression (specifically, $1 + 2 + 3 + 4$) produces the number 10, which holds special meaning for the Pythagoreans as the Decad, or quality of tenness. They depict it as the tetractys, a collection of ten dots in the general form of an equilateral triangle: one at each point of the triangle, two along each side, and one at the center of the triangle. Their interest in music and mathematics may intersect here. Not only are the fundamental harmonic relationships of octave, fifth, and fourth expressed with the numerals 1 through 4, but the Decad reflects the combination of the mathematical values corresponding to all four geometric constructs as well: point, line, plane, and solid.

Once geometric solids are produced in the Pythagorean system, it is a natural move to fashion objects in the world from these three-dimensional shapes, which is the final step in the overall generation. Physical things—or, more precisely, types of physical things, such as man, horse, tree, and so forth—are differentiated by the amount of the Unlimited that they contain. That amount is determined by the demarcating activity of the Unit, resulting in a collection of points, and that collection composes the thing. Thus, corresponding to every object—and even to concepts—is a number, which is the essential nature of the object, according to Pythagorean thought.

The obvious first error in the Pythagorean system is the confusion of the unit of arithmetic with the point of geometry; the second one is the assumption that the point of geometry has dimensional magnitude, like a dot. Reason seems to dictate that an arithmetical quantity is an abstraction, not something material, as the Pythagoreans think. It cannot be a point in space, let alone a physical body in space. Likewise, points and lines and planes themselves are mathematical constructs. Physical objects do have shapes, of course, but the shape of any object is a property of the thing, not the substance of it. The Pythagoreans use numbers as building blocks to assemble figures, and figures to assemble objects, conflating the abstract and the concrete. To their undoing, they fail to see that number and matter fall into fundamentally distinct ontological classes.[47] "They transferred their mathematical conceptions to the order of material reality," says Frederick Copleston.[48] Tangible objects in physical reality cannot be constructed from intangible elements of thought. Indeed, Aristotle levels a criticism at the idea of

> composing the heaven of numbers, as some of the Pythagoreans do who make all nature out of numbers. For natural bodies are manifestly endowed with weight and lightness, but an assemblage of units can neither be composed to form a body nor possess weight.[49]

Besides turning to the numerical in their metaphysical quest, the Pythagoreans differ from the monistic, substrate theorists in another sense. Those theorists take that from which things come—the first principle, or *archē*—and their essential nature, their constitution—*physis*—to be the same thing. For the Pythagoreans, however, the first principle is the pair of elements, Limit and the Unlimited, but the actual nature of things is number. Even though the joint first principle is that of which, and from which, numbers are made, numbers are the elements that underlie the world of objects

---

[47] One will recall that ontology is the branch of philosophy that deals with theories of being.

[48] Copleston, *Greece and Rome*, 35.

[49] Aristotle, *On the Heavens*, 3, 1.300a16–19, trans. J. L. Stocks, in *Works of Aristotle*, 441.

and frame its being. They constitute the true essence of things. As points compose lines, lines compose planes, and planes compose solids, it is the mathematical entities themselves that do the ontological work of making up the world. From the standpoint of ultimate elements thus, the Pythagorean metaphysics appears to be dualistic. From the standpoint of essence, though, it is wildly pluralistic.

In summary, the Pythagoreans see the core nature of each thing as numerical—in a literal sense; and numbers, they believe, are derived ultimately from the dual first principles of Limit and the Unlimited. The Pythagoreans' fascination with the ratios that are found in musical sounds leads them to embrace a philosophy with untenable consequences. Whether the Pythagoreans continued to cling to this stringent view of numerical primacy in light of irrational numbers, such as the circumference of a circle divided by its diameter, which cannot be expressed in terms of simple integers, is a topic of debate among those who study the ancient Greek literature.[50]

STRICT MONISM

Two men of keen intellect from the city of Elea adopt a philosophical perspective that represents a radical departure from others of its day. They believe reality to be singular; indeed, they conceive of it as unary in every sense. The Pythagoreans are in error, as there can be no plurality; and furthermore, Heraclitus is in error, as there can be no change. These two men, Parmenides and Zeno, set out to prove their thesis logically.

---

[50] B. A. G. Fuller states that later Pythagoreans apparently modified their position after it was recognized that lines—and, a fortiori, planes and solids—could not be constructed from pure mathematical points. In their altered view, things were like numbers, as opposed to being numbers (aggregates of points). Refer to Fuller's *History of Greek Philosophy*, vol. 1, *Thales to Democritus* (1923; repr., New York: Greenwood Press, Publishers, 1968), 110. Contrast this thinking, however, with that of Stokes, who asserts that the Pythagoreans might have been unwilling or unable to draw a distinction between imitating numbers and being numbers, or else they did not deem it to be problematic to hold both doctrines simultaneously. See Stokes, *One and Many*, 25. An informative discussion of this topic is found in Guthrie, *Earlier Presocratics*, 229–38.

PARMENIDES AND ZENO. Parmenides was born near the end of the sixth century B.C., possibly as late as 504, although some cite a date that is slightly earlier. He died around 456 B.C. There is no Pythagorean multiplicity, he claims. Reality is one—indeed, the *One*—and it cannot be otherwise. It is whole and without parts, indivisible, unchanging, unmoved, and eternal. It exists everywhere and forever the same. In his metaphysics, Parmenides draws a distinction between what he calls the Way of Truth and the Way of Belief, or Seeming. He summarily dismisses the constant change of Heraclitean philosophy and the world of shifting sensory experience as illusory. There is no becoming, nor is an instance of it possible. That which one's senses reveal is mere appearance; it is not real, and it cannot provide truth. Reality lies in the realm of the mind, the realm in which thought and logic operate. Parmenides maintains that thought and reality are, in fact, identical: "For it is the same thing to think and to be."[51] He offers forceful support for his stance in the form of a dilemma: a type of logical argument. The influence of Parmenides on the theoretical developments of those who follow him is undeniable. The next chapter will show how the Parmenidean notion that thought and reality are the same resurfaces in a special way in a brilliant theory that one of the world's greatest philosophers sets forth.

Zeno lived from approximately 490 to 430 B.C. A student of Parmenides, he demonstrates genius in his defense of, and support for, his mentor. Against the Pythagoreans, Parmenides argues that all is one; Zeno argues that all is not many. Zeno poses a series of paradoxical arguments that are designed to substantiate his view by demonstrating that, on the assumption that reality is a plurality and is changing, absurd consequences concerning composition, space, and motion arise. Prior to the creation of these arguments, the Pythagoreans had ridiculed Parmenides because of his opinion that existence is one and that the sensory world cannot be real. The unleashing of Zeno's paradoxes mutes much of their derision. They are potent logical tools in the hands of this philosopher.

Some authors question whether Parmenides actually takes a hard stance on the speciousness of sensory experience. Parmenides

---

[51] Parmenides, frag. 3, 42.

does not deny the reality of the physical world, says Wallace Matson. On the contrary, Parmenides holds that the world of sensory experience, although amenable to change, is real nevertheless, just not in the strict sense in which the world of thought is real. The correct rendering of this Eleatic's philosophy, according to Matson, is that of a dual structure: "Reality is of two kinds. One is composed of the objects perceived through the senses. This kind of existence is subject to generation and change. . . . The other reality is known by thought alone."[52]

That the physical world is completely unreal and therefore illusory, however, is clearly the commonly accepted position on Parmenidean philosophy. Kathleen Freeman makes a case for it.

> [I]f Aristotle was right, and Parmenides made any concession whatsoever to the world of phenomena, why did his views seem so absurd to his contemporaries? Zeno's defence was against those who poked fun at Parmenides, and he undertook to show that an acceptance of the Many produced results just as laughable as those derived from Parmenides' principle of the One. This proves that down to the time of Plato, nobody gave Parmenides any credit for having in any way accommodated himself to the visible world; they would not have found his results absurd if he had kept them to the realm of logic and had not insisted that they must be accepted against all the evidence of the senses.[53]

I will adopt this latter perspective in working through some of the logic of these Eleatics, as I believe it to be the right one.

At this juncture, a brief examination of the structure of reasoning is in order. This foundational discussion will aid one not only in comprehending the arguments of the Eleatics but also in assessing the strength of various positions that will be detailed in subsequent chapters.

---

[52] Wallace Matson, *A History of Philosophy* (New York: American Book Co., 1968), 31.
[53] Freeman, *Pre-Socratic Philosophers: A Companion to Diels*, 145.

ARGUMENT—THE TOOL OF LOGIC

One scholar of ancient philosophy puts it succinctly in stating, "Logic is a Greek discovery."[54] To appreciate the impact of the cases against plurality and against becoming, or change, that the two men from Elea raise calls for understanding the tool that they use to build devices with which to attack their philosophical adversaries. How can one demonstrate that, although the world appears to be composed of many things, it is not actually so? Moreover, it seems that the world is filled with change. How can it be shown that change is unreal? Although philosophers may advance theories that are contrary to what appears to be factual with respect to the world, proving that those theories reflect the truth requires that one go beyond mere observation. Perception cannot lead there: One simply cannot go, look, and see. The path to proof lies in reasoning.

The development of modern systems of logic owes much to the foundations that Aristotle builds; yet, even before his time, forms of reasoning were beginning to take shape. The Milesian philosophy represents early steps in this direction. In disagreeing with Thales, Anaximander suggests that, because the elements are in opposition, if reality were one of the elements, then everything eventually would have become that element. It is the Eleatics, however, who take rational analysis to new heights, engineering formidable devices in their attempts to prove that they are right.

To grasp the approach of the Eleatics, one first must gain an understanding of the structure of reasoning as it is set forth in the discipline of logic and in the basic unit of the logical enterprise: the argument. What grammar is to language, logic is to philosophical argumentation; logic furnishes the framework—the set of rules—that determines how reasoning is to be conducted. A writer supplies the content for a particular literary work. The author selects the nouns, verbs, adjectives, adverbs, conjunctions, and other parts of speech, along with punctuation, to build appropriate sentences and then groups them into paragraphs, thereby formulating the message that is to be communicated. It is the author's sentences, coupled with the arrangement of them in paragraphs, that express his or her thoughts.

---

[54] Barnes, *Thales to Zeno*, 3.

It is, however, the rules of grammar that specify the ways in which those elements of language may be assembled, and it is by means of these rules that the scaffolding for a meaningful text is possible. Without them, the intended message, in the best of circumstances, is compromised; in the worst, it is rendered nonsensical. The structure of a sentential formation is correct or incorrect, depending on whether it is in compliance with the rules or at odds with them.

Analogously, a philosopher creates the content of what the philosopher wishes to advance in support of a particular view: the message that is to be delivered. It is logic, however, that determines whether the formation of that content is acceptable and whether the reasoning is cogent or flawed. Logic provides the laws of the discipline, and philosophers must operate in accordance with those laws as they assemble arguments to make their cases. Otherwise, like a careless writer's products, laid out in poorly constructed sentences and paragraphs, their works, in the best of circumstances, will be reduced to ones that are untenable; in the worst, they will be reduced to nonsense. It is a failure that their opponents will not miss.

It is important to explain some concepts that are employed in logic. An argument is a complex of statements, some of which, the premises, portrayed as true, purport to establish the truth of another, the conclusion. Consider the following set of statements; call it Set 1:

> Everyone who eats carrots at least twice per week is
>   intelligent (premise).
> Johnny eats carrots at least twice per week (premise).
> Therefore, Johnny is intelligent (conclusion).

This group of sentences constitutes an argument and attempts to establish that Johnny is intelligent on the basis that people who eat carrots are smart and that Johnny is a frequent consumer of the orange roots. This argument is an example of deductive reasoning. In such reasoning, the premises offer allegedly decisive support for the conclusion: The premises are in position to certify the conclusion, in that, aside from the rules of logic, no information beyond what the premises present is required to establish what the argument is put forward to prove. In deductive logic, if an argument is valid, then the premises guarantee the conclusion's truth by virtue of the form of the argument, such that, *if* the premises are true, then the conclusion must be true: The conclusion of a valid deductive argument cannot be false if all the premises are true. The meanings of the terms that are in play, of course, must remain constant. Set 1 forms a valid deductive argument. An invalid deductive argument cannot establish its conclusion based on the declarations that appear in the premises, as it lacks a proper construction. An invalid deductive argument may have a false conclusion, even if all the premises are true.

In inductive reasoning, the premises lend support to the conclusion, but that support is not decisive. The premises can purport to establish the conclusion only with varying levels of assuredness or probability. The traditional conception of induction is that of reasoning from particular cases to general rules. For example, after having observed numerous times and in various circumstances that pieces of ice float on (liquid) water of sufficient depth whenever the two are placed together, one can conclude inductively that all ice floats on (liquid) water. Induction has come to be used in a broader way, which I will adopt. It includes any nondemonstrative reasoning, or reasoning in which the premises purport to offer evidence that the conclusion is true but cannot guarantee it, thus distinguishing it from deduction.[55] Call the following group of statements, representing a form of nondemonstrative logical composition, Set 2:

> Recent scientific studies show that 96.5 percent of people who consume at least three carrots per week excel in mathematics (premise).
> Johnny loves carrots and eats them every day (premise).
> Therefore, Johnny is doing well in algebra class (conclusion).

In Set 2, there is some evidence that, if the premises that the argument submits in support of the claim that Johnny is performing well in algebra class are true, then Johnny may be receiving high marks. His good performance, however, cannot be established with certainty based on the proffered justification. Perhaps Johnny is among the

---

[55] For a general discussion of inductive reasoning, including brief descriptions of the various forms, see *Encyclopedia of Philosophy*, s.v., "Induction."

unfortunate 3.5 percent who eat carrots and still struggle with mathematics. It is also possible that Johnny decided to skip school and go fishing on the day of the first exam.

There are many respects in which arguments can go awry in their structure, in the contents of the assertions that they put forth, or in both. Examine this group of statements, Set 3:

> Carrots are a good source of vitamin A, which is needed for proper retinal development; and any child who eats them is acting to ensure his or her ocular health (premise).
> Even children want to see well (premise).
> Johnny eats carrots (premise).
> Therefore, Johnny avoids reading the encyclopedias, with their tiny print, in the school library (conclusion).

The conclusion must follow from the premises. If an appropriate link is absent, then the conclusion—and, according to some logicians, the argument itself in a wider sense—is a non sequitur (adopted from Latin, indicating that it does not follow). In Set 3, there is a problem of relevance: The conclusion is not related to the information that is given in support of it. There is no connection between the supposed facts that are submitted in the premises and Johnny's refraining from perusing encyclopedias. Although all four core sentences in Set 3 may express the truth, the premises not only fail to establish the conclusion but also fail to offer any grounds for it. Sometimes, irrelevance arises in an argument because it does not address the issue: Its conclusion is not germane to the matter at hand. Then, the fallacy is *ignoratio elenchi* (Latin, pointing to ignorance of the refutation[s]).

Even in a valid deductive argument, some premises, perhaps all, may be false, regardless of the truth of the conclusion. Look again at the statements in Set 1. It could be the case that people who are not intelligent routinely eat carrots too. Maybe Johnny eats peas but never eats carrots. A sound deductive argument is one that is valid and that contains true premises exclusively. Sound deductive arguments establish the truth of their conclusions with certainty.

Arguments are usually far more complex than those that appear above, as one would expect, and logicians reduce the language of reasoning to letters and symbols to provide an effective way of depicting arguments and analyzing their structures. The symbolism facilitates the determination of validity. This work is concerned only to a limited degree with the symbolic representations that philosophers employ in logic, as words alone suffice, as a rule, for the relevant purposes. I would like to consider briefly a few symbols and their application, however; they will prove to be useful later.

Various systems of logic have been developed, but the basic modern system is propositional logic, or the propositional calculus. As the name suggests, it deals with propositions or statements. Occasionally, this system is referred to as sentential logic, or the sentential calculus.

Note that there is no universal agreement among philosophers regarding what propositions are and how they relate to language. One approach is to maintain that *propositions*—and *statements* as well—are what *declarative sentences* affirm. An alternative approach is to maintain that all three are identical: The corresponding terms are synonymous; they refer to *assertions*. Independent clauses of declarative sentences also may count as assertions, typically qualified by expressed conditions. There will be a few places in this writing where it will be beneficial to contrast the concepts, but it generally will not be necessary to do so; and, to simplify the discussion, I rarely will draw a line between them. I will treat them as effectively interchangeable. A proposition, statement, or declarative sentence—or sometimes an independent clause in a more restricted sense—asserts that something is the case; it sets forth an ostensible fact. The alleged fact is what is conveyed. This broader use will not introduce any difficulties. For the most part, the focus of the analysis is on what the language communicates, not the language itself. Where the investigation touches on the syntactical construction that bears the affirmation, as opposed to the affirmation proper, I will make the distinction clear.

Within the system of propositional logic, letters represent simple declarative sentences. It is possible to form compound sentences by using rules that govern how simple ones may be expanded, incorporating certain truth-functional operators, which capture matching truth-functions. The following operators are standard: *not*; *and*; *or*; *if* . . . , *then*; and *if, and only if.* Analogous to the variables in mathematical equations, the letters in propositional logic may stand for any appropriate simple declarative sentences; but again, like the variables in any single equation, the letters in any single argument must be employed consistently, standing for the *same* respective sentences throughout that argument.[56] It is important to mention here that individual letters in this work may signify things other than sentences and also may serve as merely uninstantiated variables. The context clarifies how these elements are to be construed.

To illustrate the symbolism of the propositional calculus, suppose that *p* represents the proposition 'Johnny eats carrots', and *q* represents the proposition 'Johnny is intelligent'. One might assert the sentence 'Johnny eats carrots, and Johnny is intelligent'. Logical shorthand is in place not only for the propositions in the calculus but also for the operators. Different symbols signify the specific functions, depending on the particular logical version that a philosopher selects, although there are a few traditional ones. The compound statement that appears above, for example, which comprises two propositions conjoined by the *and* operator, may be given in a fully symbolized form: $p \cdot q$.[57]

Truth conditions are established for statements that use truth-functional operators, such that the truth or falsity of any compound sentence that is formed within the system is determined by the truth

---

[56] More advanced systems exist. Predicate logic allows the ascription of properties and relations to all entities or to some; I will touch on it later. Modal logic deals primarily with possibility and necessity; deontic logic is concerned with obligation.

[57] Philosophy distinguishes between the mention of an expression and the use of it. In mentioning a term, phrase, sentence, or other locution, one is referring to the expression itself; in using it, one is referring to what it signifies. To mention, for example, a proposition in this work, I place it in single quotation marks—a standard approach, although some authors prefer italics—unless it is separate from the running text or is symbolized in full; in such cases, quotation marks are not needed. Note that punctuation generally falls outside the closing quotation mark when an expression is mentioned. Foreign terms that are not common in English are italicized; by convention, the mentioning of them relies on context for distinction (already exemplified in this work). Where I employ letters to stand for given objects or to function as variables, I italicize them; unless referring to the letter-names themselves, quotation marks are omitted. *Uppercase* letters, as a rule, point to *nonsingular* things: types, sets, properties, and so forth. *Lowercase* ones designate *individual* things, though I capitalize them in captions if needed. Certain letters appearing in science and mathematics are normally nonitalicized capitals. I retain that format, and, if giving another author's term, I keep the author's format.

or falsity of the simple sentences that compose it. These simple sentences may be regarded as atomic propositions. They are minimal assertions of fact, the truth of which depends directly on the purported state of affairs. When atomic propositions are linked by a truth-functional operator, or by multiple operators, the newly created compound proposition may be regarded as molecular. With two simple sentences (*p* and *q*) and two truth-values (true and false), there are exactly four possible combinations of truth and falsity for those sentences, as the table that I present below depicts:

p	*q*
True	True
True	False
False	True
False	False

Compound sentences that are formed with the *and* operator are true just in the case where both the simple sentences that are connected by the operator are true; they are false in every other case. For the compound sentence 'Johnny eats carrots, and Johnny is intelligent' to be true, it is necessary that both the simple assertions about Johnny be true. The following table gives the truth conditions of statements employing the *and* truth-functional operator:

		Conjunction (and)
p	*q*	*p · q*
True	True	True
True	False	False
False	True	False
False	False	False

Showing the other primary truth-functional operators and the corresponding truth conditions, this table completes the picture:

		Negation (not)	Disjunction (or)[58]	Conditional (if . . . , then)	Biconditional (if, and only if)
p	q	$-p$	$p \vee q$	$p \supset q$	$p \equiv q$
True	True	False	True	True	True
True	False		True	False	False
False	True	True	True	True	False
False	False		False	True	True

One need not be concerned with remembering the circumstances in which each of these operators yields true sentences. I provide them for reference. It is important, however, to take note of one form of proposition: the conditional. Special concepts apply to conditionals. In a statement of the form $p \supset q$, p is the antecedent, and q is the consequent. Philosophers say that p is sufficient for, or is a sufficient condition of, q and that q is necessary for, or is a necessary condition of, p. One may think of it in this way: If the conditional is true, then (1) the truth of p is sufficient to warrant the truth of q, and (2) the truth of q is necessary, given the truth of p. The antecedent of a conditional proposition therefore implies the consequent. Deductive arguments themselves may be set forth as conditionals, where the conjunction of the premises implies the conclusion. Consider an argument of the following configuration, where p_1, p_2, and p_3 are premises, and q is the conclusion; the three-dot symbol means 'therefore':

p_1

p_2

p_3

———

$\therefore q$

---

[58] The conditions that are shown here are for the inclusive form of the disjunction, which is by far the most common in logic. In this form, the proposition 'p or q' is true if p is true, q is true, or both are true. There is also an exclusive form. Disjunctions in the exclusive sense are true if either p or q is true, but they are false if both are true. In this work, I use the disjunction in the inclusive sense of its meaning.

The argument can be formulated as a proposition: $(p_1 \cdot p_2 \cdot p_3) \supset q$. It is making the claim that the premises, if they are true, jointly guarantee that the conclusion is true.

Before continuing, I want to cover one additional point. An argument represents or expresses a case of reasoning through a linguistic structuring, which may be symbolized; it culminates in the inferring of a seeming truth. The argument progresses, whether regarded purely in a procedural sense or in a psychological one, to the drawing of a conclusion. The associated terms, although not synonymous, often are used in a general, undifferentiated way, with the understanding that they simply refer to distinct aspects of a given premises-to-conclusion procession. In a work of this sort, there is little value in distinguishing sharply between an argument and the particular inferential chain to which it corresponds—something that is perhaps already apparent—as their interdependence suggests that a broad perspective is in order. Accordingly, I keep the analysis at that level.

THE DILEMMA

With this explanation of basic propositional logic in mind, consider now two specific types of arguments. The first type is the dilemma, an argument that poses two paths, which are exhaustive (there can be no others), both of which lead to unfavorable consequences. The effect is to undermine an opposing stance. Dilemmas fall into four main categories, but all of them share the characteristic of presenting an undesirable or unacceptable conclusion based on a strict duality.

In the thoughts of the ancient Greek philosophers, the dilemma is the logical counterpart to a charging bull. The bull's two horns represent the alternatives that the dilemma poses, each of which ends in philosophical impalement. It is beneficial to look at the four basic categories of dilemmas prior to proceeding to the reasoning that Parmenides advances in support of his position. Let p, q, r, and s stand for any statements. Dilemmas take one of the following forms:

Category	Structure	Components
Simple Constructive	If p, then q; and, if r, then q. p or r. Therefore, q.	Major Premise Minor Premise Conclusion
Simple Destructive	If p, then q; and, if p, then r. Not q or not r. Therefore, not p.	Major Premise Minor Premise Conclusion
Complex Constructive	If p, then q; and, if r, then s. p or r. Therefore, q or s.	Major Premise Minor Premise Conclusion
Complex Destructive	If p, then q; and, if r, then s. Not q or not s. Therefore, not p or not r.	Major Premise Minor Premise Conclusion

To illustrate, imagine that Jane is waiting for her friend Janice at a busy shopping mall. They had planned to shop together and had made arrangements several weeks earlier to meet at 9:45 a.m. at Entrance VI to take advantage of the greatest promotional sale in the mall's history. All stores are scheduled to open promptly at 10:00 that morning with unprecedented price reductions. At Entrance VI alone, hundreds of people are in position, ready for action. The price of every item in every store will be slashed to mere pennies on the dollar, and Jane knows that she must act quickly, as she enters the mall, to purchase any of the popular articles. Both ladies have been excited about the shopping spree. Although they have been close friends for years, they seldom have had an opportunity in recent times to meet for shared activities.

Janice, who has demonstrated an occasional lack of punctuality in the past, assured Jane that she would meet her at 9:45 a.m. at the entrance that they had selected. Jane assured Janice that she would wait for her before going into the mall, so that they could shop together. Janice had invited Jane to come to dinner at her home after the event, where they could look at all the bargains that they had acquired that day and assemble outfits from the new clothes. Jane was so eager that she arrived thirty minutes early and stood in the parking lot, holding a place for herself and her friend near the door, but, by 9:55 a.m., Janice was yet to appear. Jane was not able to reach her friend by cell phone. At the appointed time, the doors open. Jane is faced with a dilemma. If she waits for her friend, then she will miss the prime bargains, but, if she enters the mall to shop, then she will miss her friend. Jane must choose. Either she must wait for her friend, or she must not wait and go shopping. She cannot do both. Therefore, either she will miss the best offerings of the day, or she will miss her friend.

This incident does not pose a logical challenge in the way in which philosophical ones do. In Jane's case, the alternatives that are presented are ones of commitment and action. The incident serves the purposes here nevertheless by illustrating the dichotomy that dilemmas introduce. Jane's difficulty is captured by the form of the complex constructive dilemma. Suppose that p stands for the proposition 'Jane waits for Janice'; q represents 'Jane misses the prime bargains'; r stands for 'Jane goes shopping'; and s represents 'Jane misses Janice'. Jane's dilemma assumes the form that is shown below:

If p, then q; and, if r, then s.
p or r.
Therefore, q or s.

THE PARMENIDEAN DILEMMA. With a clearer understanding now of logical arguments and the nature of dilemmas, it is time to return to the Eleatics. Parmenides expresses his metaphysics in poetic verse, thus taking a rather challenging subject and adding to its complexity. In this notably opaque passage of Parmenides's work, translated directly from the Greek poetry, a forceful argument takes shape:

> A single story of a route still
> Is left: that [*it*] *is*; on this [route] there are signs
> Very numerous: that what-is is ungenerated and
>   imperishable;
> Whole, single-limbed, steadfast, and complete;
> Nor was [it] once, nor will [it] be, since [it] is, now, all
>   together,
> One, continuous; for what coming-to-be of it will you
>   seek?
> In what way, whence, did [it] grow? Neither from what-
>   is-not shall I allow
> You to say or think; for it is not to be said or thought
> That [*it*] *is not*. And what need could have impelled it to
>   grow
> Later or sooner, if it began from nothing?
> Thus [it] must either be completely or not at all.
> Nor will the strength of trust ever allow anything to
>   come-to-be from what-is
> Besides it; therefore neither [its] coming-to-be
> Nor [its] perishing has Justice allowed, relaxing her
>   shackles,
> But she holds [it] fast; the decision about these matters
>   depends on this:
> *Is* [*it*] *or is* [*it*] *not*? but it has been decided, as is
>   necessary,
> To let go the one as unthinkable, unnameable (for it
>   is no true
> Route), but to allow the other, so that it is, and is true.
> And how could what-is be in the future; and how could
>   [it] come-to-be?
> For if [it] came-to-be, [it] is not, nor [is it] if at some
>   time [it] is going to be.
> Thus, coming to be is extinguished and perishing not to
>   be heard of.[59]

An alternate translation provides a measure of clarity, presenting the passage in prose.

---

[59] Parmenides, frag. 8, *Parmenides of Elea: Fragments*, trans. David Gallop (Toronto: University of Toronto Press, 1984), 65, 67. The bracketed insertions are those of the translator.

There is only one other description of the way remaining, (*namely*), that (*What Is*) Is. To this way there are very many sign-posts: that Being has no coming-into-being and no destruction, for it is whole of limb, without motion, and without end. And it never Was, nor Will Be, because it Is now, a Whole all together, One, continuous; for what creation of it will you look for? How, whence (*could it have*) sprung? Nor shall I allow you to speak or think of it as springing from Not-Being; for it is neither expressible nor thinkable that What-Is-Not Is. Also, what necessity impelled it, if it did spring from Nothing, to be produced later or earlier? Thus it must Be absolutely, or not at all. Nor will the force of credibility ever admit that anything should come into being, beside Being itself, out of Not-Being. So far as that is concerned, Justice has never released (*Being*) in its fetters and set it free either to come into being or to perish, but holds it fast. The decision on these matters depends on the following: IT IS, OR IT IS NOT. It is therefore decided – as is inevitable – (*that one must*) ignore the one way as unthinkable and inexpressible (for it is no true way) and take the other as the way of Being and Reality. How could Being perish? How could it come into being? If it came into being, it Is Not; and so too if it is about-to-be at some future time. Thus, Coming-Into-Being is quenched, and Destruction also into the unseen.[60]

Unraveling the passage, one can extract Parmenides's argument. The philosopher is attempting to show that nothing can come into existence, and nothing can pass from existence. That which is, is—timelessly. Moreover, what does exist is singular, indivisible, and static. I will focus on the coming-to-be component of the argument. It will suffice for the current purposes.[61] Parmenides's reasoning is that the coming into existence of something would require that it arise from something that exists, as it is clear that

---

[60] Parmenides, frag. 8, as it appears in Freeman's translation in *Ancilla*, 43–44.

[61] There are significant implications of this coming-to-be issue. It is one that disturbs the current scientific community in its pursuit of cosmic origins—a topic of investigation in a subsequent chapter.

nothing at all can come from the nonexistent: That from which something comes must exist to serve as the underlying wellspring of the generative event. If, however, something comes into existence from that which already exists, then it actually already exists as well, so there is no coming into being. The argument is in the form of a dilemma. Here then is a reasonable rendering of the Parmenidean dilemma, with some interpretative structuring, as it pertains to arising. Note that, in stating that something is, the argument is stating that it exists.[62]

> If a thing comes into being, then it must come from being
>   or from nonbeing.
> If it comes from being, then it already is, and there is thus
>   no becoming; and, if it comes from nonbeing, then
>   nonbeing is, which is absurd.
> Therefore, there is no becoming, and what is, is.

The format of this reasoning does not fall exactly into one of the four patterns of dilemmas. It is more complex than the basic configurations that are listed above in the table. Further analysis shows that it is composed of five arguments, each of which corresponds to a valid deductive form (if the premises are true, then the conclusion must be true as well). The five arguments follow, along with the names of their respective forms. One will observe that a complex constructive dilemma appears in the third step. The locution 'a thing' in the arguments is a general reference; hence, the thrust of the chain of logic is the denial of the coming to be in each case of a thing—anything—with the result that the denial applies to everything, and there is no coming to be at all.

---

[62] This portrayal of the dilemma aligns, in the main, with Aristotle's synoptic version in *Physics*, 1, 8.191a23–33. Nonbeing (Not-Being, in the translator's rendering), to which the argument refers, is the nonexistent.

1. *Hypothetical Syllogism*

If a thing comes into being from being, then it already is.
If a thing already is, then there is no becoming for it.
Therefore, if a thing comes into being from being, then
    there is no becoming for it.

2. *Universal Instantiation*[63]

If a thing comes into being from something, then that
    something is.
Therefore, if a thing comes into being from nonbeing,
    then nonbeing is.

3. *Complex Constructive Dilemma*

If a thing comes into being from being, then there is no
    becoming for it (from 1); and, if a thing comes into
    being from nonbeing, then nonbeing is (from 2).
A thing must come into being either from being or from
    nonbeing.
Therefore, either there is no becoming for a thing, or
    nonbeing is.

4. *Disjunctive Syllogism*

Either there is no becoming for a thing, or nonbeing is
    (from 3).
It is not the case that nonbeing is.
Therefore, there is no becoming for a thing.

5. *Modus Ponens*

If there is no becoming for a thing, then what is, is.
There is no becoming for a thing (from 4).
Therefore, what is, is.

---

[63] This argument form is expressed in predicate logic, which I will discuss later. Making use of quantifiers, it is universal, applying to any x from which a thing originates (taking liberties with the representation of existence). The entire series of arguments could be stated more forcefully in predicate logic, but, if viewing *a thing*, and *something*, as anything, this simpler composition is adequate here.

There are three traditional ways to escape a dilemma. The ancient Greeks continue the analogy of a bull in defending against the dilemma's destructive power. As a tactic, one can attack the major premise, denying its truth: taking the bull by the horns. One can deny the truth of the minor premise: escaping between the horns. Finally, one can pose a counterdilemma by changing the structure of the propositions to create a more favorable outcome. The method that one might attempt to employ, successfully or unsuccessfully, would depend on the nature of the argument. To illustrate the last approach using Jane's dilemma at the shopping mall as an example, one might pose the counterargument that is shown below:

> If p, then not s; and, if r, then not q.
> p or r.
> Therefore, not s or not q.

In this rendition of the dilemma, Jane's circumstances allow her either to meet her friend or to take advantage of the sale. Either way, something positive is in store for Jane, as the following structure demonstrates:

> If Jane waits for Janice, then Jane does not miss Janice; and, if Jane goes shopping, then Jane does not miss the prime bargains.
> Either Jane waits for Janice, or Jane goes shopping.
> Therefore, either Jane does not miss Janice, or Jane does not miss the prime bargains.

This approach is hardly valuable in the case of the Parmenidean dilemma, rendering a fairly obscure logical chain nearly unintelligible. Inherent in the Parmenidean dilemma, however, are several assumptions that bring serious questions to light, and one might ask whether either or both of the premises of the argument in its core form can be challenged. It seems that a thing comes into being in the building of a house, the manufacturing of an automobile or a piece of equipment, and the sketching of a portrait. Surely, each item did not exist prior to the building, the manufacturing, and the sketching respectively. It is evident that a thing cannot come from nonbeing (the nonexistent), but it is not clear what it means to say that nonbeing exists. Is change the same as coming into being—might a thing exist, and remain in existence, yet be altered in its characteristics; or might an existent thing be reformed and thereby give rise to something new? It appears that the notion that change is impossible—based on the logic of the Parmenidean dilemma, at least—leaves room for doubt.

THE PARADOX AND THE REDUCTIO

A paradox is an anomaly that is generated when two propositions conflict with each other, or even contradict each other, but they are derived from acceptable premises through apparently solid reasoning.[64] In a paradox, lines of thought intersect at a point of incongruence. A modern example will suffice to convey a sense of how these paradoxes operate.

Consider the surprise test paradox, an instance of what is known as the prediction paradox. Suppose that a college class meets every day, Monday through Friday, for an hour. One Friday, the professor announces that he will give a surprise test, or pop quiz, sometime during the following week. It is a surprise, in that the students will not know which day the professor selects for the exam until the professor distributes it. For the professor's claim to be true then, two conditions must be met: (1) there will be a test next week, and (2) the students will not know on which day the exam will occur. So far, there seems to be no problem.

If, however, the professor waits until Friday to administer the test, then the test will not be a surprise. Given the fact that there will be a test that week, by the end of the class on Thursday, the students will know that the test will take place on Friday. If therefore Friday were the day, then the professor's claim that there will be a surprise test during the week would not be true. Friday must be removed from

---

64 One conception of a paradox is that of a self-conflicting statement, but the representation that I give is more accurate in the philosophical sense and aligns with those that are found in appropriate texts.

consideration, thus leaving Monday through Thursday as the only possible days. If the professor waits until Thursday, however, then again the test cannot be a surprise. Friday has been eliminated as a possible day for a surprise test; so, by the end of Wednesday's class, the students will know that the test will take place on Thursday. Thursday therefore must be eliminated as well. This reasoning can be repeated, eliminating Wednesday, Tuesday, and finally Monday. The consequence is that it is impossible for the professor to give a surprise test at all. Certainly, though, the professor can do so, as one can attest from one's own experiences. There is something very strange at work in this paradox. Recent attempts to resolve it are not particularly persuasive.

Now, of even greater impact on Pythagorean pluralism than Parmenides's dilemma was the destructive power of Zeno's paradoxes. Zeno created more than forty arguments designed to show that the Pythagorean view of reality is illogical. Most of these arguments are direct attacks on the plurality of being; four of them are indirect, targeting motion. There is little in the extant fragments from which to restate or recreate Zeno's proofs that pluralism is inherently self-refuting, and not one of his cases against motion has survived intact in the original texts. Accounts of his reasoning, though, are preserved in the writings of others, mainly Aristotle and Simplicius (and, to a limited extent, Plato); philosophers have relied on them to establish the logic. His paradoxes take a particular form, the reductio ad absurdum (adopted from Latin, indicating reduction to absurdity), the second type of argument that is under review here.

In such an argument, one presumes that a given proposition—typically, one that represents an opponent's view—is true and then proceeds to show that it leads to illogical consequences. If the argument is valid, then the presumption must be false. By assuming a philosophical perspective that is contrary to that of Parmenides and then producing an absurd conclusion from that assumption, Zeno attempts to show that Parmenides is right.

To attack plurality, Zeno supposes, in accordance with Pythagorean metaphysics, that reality is not singular. He reveals how the thinking that is based on this supposition ends in a contradiction. It follows that the supposition cannot be true. Reality is therefore singular.

Likewise, in arguing against the stance that reality is not static and immobile, Zeno assumes that motion is possible. If it is possible, then motion must be either continuous or discontinuous; that is to say, movement must occur either in one flowing stream or in a succession of discrete steps. Zeno's proofs seem to show that both these paths lead to unacceptable outcomes. It follows that the premise that motion is possible cannot be true. Reality is therefore fixed.

It is interesting that, in contemporary times, two and one-half millennia after this Greek philosopher wielded his paradoxes, Zeno's arguments continue to be subjects of analysis in scholarly circles. I will consider two of the paradoxes.

ZENONIAN ARGUMENT AGAINST PLURALISM. Zeno demonstrates that the Pythagorean pluralistic view forces one to accept the irrational position that things both do not have any size at all and indeed have infinite size. One must reconstruct the logic, extracting lines from Simplicius, where portions of the logic appear; the rest of it can be assembled to form the argument as it probably was presented initially. The following representation is a reasonable, summary rendition of the original thinking.

If existence consists of the many, as the Pythagoreans hold, then the many must be discrete, numerable units; it should be possible to count them, given that each is one. It must be the case that either these units have magnitude—size and thickness—or they have no magnitude. If they are units, however, then they cannot have magnitude, for what has size and thickness has parts, and what has parts is not one. If something of no magnitude were added to a thing, however, then it would not make the thing any larger; and, if something of no magnitude were taken away from a thing, then it would not make the thing any smaller. If a thing cannot be increased or decreased in size through the addition or subtraction of something respectively, then what is added or removed is, in fact, nothing. Therefore, for the units to exist, they must have magnitude. If the units have magnitude—that is to say, they are something rather than nothing—then each of them must have a specific size and thickness. Consequently, one part of the unit must be at a distance from another part of it. The part in front also must have size. Hence, a part of that part will be some distance in front of another part of it, and so forth endlessly, as no part will be the endmost one. Each part, because it has some magnitude, will be divisible, and what is divisible, in turn, will have parts. It follows that, if existence is a plurality of units, then there must be an infinite number of them, and an infinite number of things having size must yield an infinite size. Therefore, if reality is many, as the Pythagorean theory maintains, then it is both so small that it has no size at all and so large that it is infinite.

ZENONIAN ARGUMENT AGAINST MOTION. Suppose that the swift Achilles runs a race with a tortoise, and suppose further that the tortoise is given a head start. To catch the tortoise, Achilles first must reach the point where the tortoise was at the beginning of the race, but, by then, the tortoise will have advanced to another point. To catch the tortoise now, Achilles must reach that second point, but the tortoise will have advanced yet again. If space comprises an infinity of points, then this process must continue ad infinitum, Achilles always reaching the point where the animal was but never reaching the point where the animal is, as he cannot get through the infinite number of points necessary to reach the creature and overtake it.

Zeno's argument against motion presents what is known as an infinite regress: a destructive sequence in which each element relies on another one in the chain—typically, the one that precedes it—but the sequence is without end. (Note that, in mathematics, the terms 'sequence' and 'series' are distinguished by definition; I use the terms interchangeably in this work in the usual, broad sense of a succession.) The regress is initiated when the first additional element surfaces as an unavoidable consequence of a position or theory. It, in turn, generates another, and so forth to infinity. Once the regression commences with the first additional element, it cannot be halted. The requisite base from which to proceed—the end of the series—never can be reached; but it must be reached if the position or theory is to be tenable, and thus it fails. An infinite regress is not to be confused with an infinite progression, which is benign. In such a sequence, the number of elements is unlimited, but the position or theory does not rely on reaching the end of the chain to account for, or to establish, what it is embracing or proposing.

The infinite regress is a regularly used philosophical tool, and it appears in attacks on a number of systems. Plato, in fact, raises an objection to his own theory in the form of a regress, and I will take up his argument in the next chapter. Of particular interest, one will see in later chapters how the regress is mishandled by a philosopher of the modern era and by a contemporary biologist, both of whom employ the tactic in controverting the existence of God.

Zeno's paradoxes raise some important questions about space, time, and infinity. They have proved to be challenging to unravel, and one contemporary philosopher begins his analysis of the above-stated argument against motion with this claim: "In offering a solution of this paradox, I expect to meet the fate of so many who have tried before, namely demonstrable failure."[65] A complete discussion of Zeno's paradoxes lies outside the scope of this writing, but a few comments are in order. I will begin by taking a closer look at the first of the two arguments, which is directly against pluralism.

It is evident that one can divide into smaller pieces—conceptually, at least—anything to which one can assign a length. Perhaps the best way to understand the idea is to think of a line. Given that numbers are infinite, something smaller than the original thing can be described mathematically without limit; one merely generates a smaller fraction. Mathematically, one can mark—using numeral designations here for fractional values—the $1/2$-point of a line, the $3/4$-point, the $1/100$-point, and so forth. Even the tiny quantity $1/1{,}000{,}000{,}000{,}000$ can be reduced by adding one to the denominator, and reduced again by adding one to that new denominator. Increasingly larger denominators are possible, yielding increasingly smaller fractions.[66] In principle, the process could continue indefinitely.

Georg Cantor (1845–1918), who developed set theory, takes the notion of infinity to new ground. Cantor proved that there is more than one level of infinity. In his theory, the term 'cardinal number' indicates—in effect—how many elements a certain set contains. The cardinal number of the set {1,8,27,64,125}, for example, is 5. The set

---

[65] Gilbert Ryle, *Dilemmas* (1954; repr., Cambridge: Cambridge University Press, 1975), 37. Ryle's analysis of the paradox appears on pp. 36–53 of his work.

[66] There are names that are applied to certain extremely large numbers. A googol is defined as 10^{100}. A googolplex, larger still, is defined as 10^{googol}. Scientists believe that the number of particles in the universe is well less than a googol and therefore less than a googolplex. In practical terms, dividing any linear stretch by physical means into parts numbering a googolplex, or even a googol, is undoubtedly not a feat that can be achieved, but one can represent such tiny-dimension parts mathematically. For the moment, this representation is sufficient.

of positive integers contains an infinite number of elements (in this case, numbers). For the cardinal number of such a set, to which he applies the term 'transfinite cardinal', Cantor uses the symbol '$\aleph_0$', read as 'aleph-null' or 'aleph-zero'. Indeed, the cardinal number, or simply the cardinal, of the set of all rational numbers, which includes all positive integers, is also $\aleph_0$. This infinite set is denumerable, which indicates that the elements can be numbered. It is possible to put the elements of the set into a one-to-one correspondence with the positive integers: 1, 2, 3, and so forth.

There are infinite sets with contents that cannot be numbered. The set of all real numbers, which includes such elements as π, $\sqrt{2}$, and others expressing interminable, nonrepeating decimal numerics, is nondenumerable: There are more elements of the set than can be counted. Cantor showed that the cardinal of the set of real numbers is greater than that of the set of rational numbers. In fact, it equals two raised to the power of $\aleph_0$; that is to say, the number of real numbers is equivalent to two raised to the power of the number of rational numbers. It is the cardinal of the set of all mathematical sites that lie on a continuum—a line. In the case of a line and the fractions of it that can be created, one is not limited to rational numbers; one can create fractions using irrational numbers as well: $1/\pi$, for example.

What is happening as one divides a line into progressively more pieces with a series of cuttings—say, into segments of equal length with each new division—is that, by the very description of the process, the size of the pieces that result from the partitioning continues to decrease. As the dividing action approaches infinity, the line components approach the infinitely small. As noted, numbers are infinite, and one can assign—in theory, if not in practice—a fraction to any length that one wishes, indicating the proportional value of that line's extension relative to the original line. Provided that one can assign mathematically a size to smaller lines that make up the original line, those component lines have a describable magnitude. The division operation can be repeated without termination because it has been set up precisely to do so; one cannot reach a line the extension of which is zero through this process. The number of the line segments that are generated grows larger with every new division, but their size grows ever smaller, moving closer and closer to zero but never reaching it. If a line, a foot in length, is divided into twelve equal pieces, then each piece is an inch long. Conjoining all these inch-long pieces yields a line that is the length of the original one—namely, a foot. If that foot-long line is divided into a trillion equal pieces, then each piece is one-trillionth foot in length. A trillion such lines, placed end to end, produce a line that is a foot long. Regardless of the number of segments into which a line is divided, placing those segments end to end yields a line that is the length of the undivided one. Generalizing the outcome appears to generate a rule: Dividing anything that is x units long (inches, feet, meters, or some other standard of linear measurement) into n equal parts, where x and n are finite numbers, will yield pieces that are x/n units in length; and, if one places all n of the x/n pieces in a row, practical considerations aside, then the length of the result will equal the length of the original thing: x units.

On the surface, a difficulty arises when n in the aforesaid rule is infinite. Consider that one could determine mathematically a place on a one-foot line at any point between the two end points. The length of the segment from that point to one end of the line thus could be any fraction of a foot. To capture every possible fractional length requires using real numbers because one cannot represent all possible fractions using only rational numbers. Given that the cardinal of the set of real numbers is $2^{\aleph_0}$, it seems that there are in principle $2^{\aleph_0}$ infinitesimal, same-length fragments into which one could break the one-foot line—and hence that $2^{\aleph_0} \times 1/2^{\aleph_0} = 1$. On the contrary, the result is undefined. Unlike multiplication and addition, division and subtraction are not operations that are permissible on transfinite cardinals, for they lead to contradictory consequences.[67]

This discovery should not deter one from seeing the problem with Zeno's argument. Zeno asserts that the units that make up a thing either have magnitude or do not have it. Assuming that the statement is meaningful—that the term 'unit' is used properly—he is

---

[67] Cantor uses the symbol '$\aleph_1$' to represent the cardinal that is next to $\aleph_0$ in magnitude. He endeavored unsuccessfully to show that it is the cardinal of the real-number continuum. Kurt Gödel contributed to the solution, but it was Paul Cohen who finally demonstrated in 1963 that Cantor's hypothesis is independent of his other assumptions and thus neither provable nor disprovable in that context. If the cardinal of the set of real numbers is indeed $\aleph_1$, however, then one would find a clearer example of the impermissible operation in the pseudoequation $\aleph_1 \times 1/\aleph_1 = 1$.

correct. This statement exemplifies a basic rule of logic: the law of excluded middle. In truth, if a thing's extension is mathematically specifiable by a positive number, regardless of how small that number may be, then it has some size—notionally, anyway. Starting with something having magnitude and then dividing it into two or more pieces invariably will produce things that have magnitude. The puzzle rests on the assumption that an infinity of units having magnitude must combine to yield a product that is infinite in size, but that assumption is false. An infinity of bits that are infinitely small will not join to generate something that is infinitely large. If a finite thing is separated into some quantity of parts of equal magnitude, then the number of parts that result from the process is inversely proportional to their size, such that their union, no matter how many there are, remains finite. Indeed, adding the infinite string of common fractions

$$\frac{1}{2}, \ \frac{1}{4}, \ \frac{1}{8}, \ \frac{1}{16}, \ \frac{1}{32}, \ \frac{1}{64}, \ \frac{1}{128}, \ \ldots$$

yields a finite result. It equals 1.

Consider next the argument against motion. Referred to as simply Achilles, it is perhaps the most famous of Zeno's puzzles. One approach to take in coming to grips with the argument is to review the analyses that two philosophers of the twentieth century provide. Gilbert Ryle (1900–1976) begins by drawing an analogy. Suppose, he says, that a mother passes a cake around a table, instructing her children to take a piece in succession until the cake is gone. Each child, however, must take only half of what is left and pass it to the next child. The cake never will disappear, as she instructed them always to remove only part of the remainder, never all of it. The whole cake, however, consists, at any point in the process, of the aggregate of the pieces that the children took *plus* the piece that is still on the plate. In the same way, the entire race between the mythical hero and the tortoise cannot be captured by adding the increments that the paradox identifies. Once the race ends, one might go back over the entire course of the race and plant flags at increments of one-eighth the total distance. The last flag will be planted where the race ended. Suppose instead that one chooses to stick a flag at the halfway mark of the whole race, then at the halfway point of the second half of the race, then at the halfway point of the second half of that half, and so forth. Ryle notes the trouble with this procedure.

> We shall never be able to plant a flag just at the place where the race ended, since our principle of flag-planting was that each flag was to be planted half-way between the last flag planted and the place where the race ended. . . . At no stage does the distance between Achilles' start-line and the last flag to be planted amount to the whole distance run by Achilles. But conversely, at each stage the total distance run by Achilles does consist of the sum of all the distances between the flags *plus the distance between the last flag planted and the point where the race ended.* Achilles' whole course is not the sum of all of its parts but one; it is the sum of all of those flagged parts plus the outstanding unflagged one.[68]

Gregory Vlastos (1907–1991) takes on the paradox in a somewhat different way.[69] His analysis is fairly elaborate, but I will condense it here. Vlastos distinguishes between two types of sprints. The first is the standard traversal of a set distance between two marks—say, the starting line and the finish line of a race—in which a runner dashes nonstop from the beginning mark to the end mark. The second type of run is the traversal of any portion of the first type: any interval that is less than the total of that nonstop dash. Inherent in the argument is the assumption that Achilles will catch the tortoise if, and only if, a run by Achilles and a run by the tortoise reach the same point at the same time. The paradox, however, says Vlastos, rests on the fact that the second type of run is disguised as the first type.

Vlastos asks one to suppose that Achilles starts at a point S, using Vlastos's terminology, and his plodding, four-legged opponent starts at another point A somewhere in front of Achilles. There exists a point Q ahead of both of them, such that the fleet warrior will cover SQ in the same amount of time that the beast will cover AQ, and this point is the one at which Achilles overtakes the tortoise. The

---

[68] Ryle, *Dilemmas*, 41.
[69] Refer to Gregory Vlastos, "Zeno's Race Course," in *Studies in Greek Philosophy: Gregory Vlastos*, ed. Daniel W. Graham, vol. 1, *The PreSocratics* (Princeton: Princeton University Press, 1995), 201–4.

following diagram depicts the layout of the race, where the slower contestant is given the advantage:

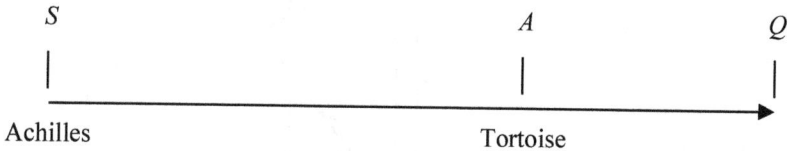

S   A   Q

| | |

Achilles   Tortoise

Time for Achilles to traverse SQ = time for tortoise to traverse AQ.

Figure 1.1

The paradox, by its construction, ensures that this event never will happen: It limits the runs to the second type and prohibits the occurrence of the SQ and AQ runs, for neither runner can make a run that ends *at Q*.

One can see from these analyses that the puzzle—because of the way that it is designed—restricts the race in such a way that the quick warrior cannot overtake the tortoise. The process of reaching a point where the tortoise *was* before the warrior can reach a point where the tortoise *is* constitutes an unending one because space comprises an infinity of points—mathematically, at least—and the tortoise is advancing continuously.

Perhaps an analogy from geometry will help to clarify the matter. Consider a particular geometric shape: the hyperbola. It is formed by the intersection of a plane with a right circular conical surface, such that the plane is parallel to the cone's axis, as shown in the diagram that follows:

Axis

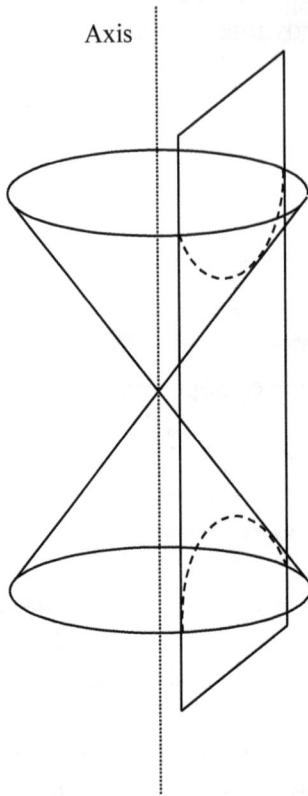

Figure 1.2

The curved lines that are created by this intersection can be graphed, with the center of the hyperbola positioned to coincide with the origin of the horizontal and vertical axes. A rectangle can be framed, the dimensions of which are set mathematically, such that the center of the rectangle lies at the origin of the axes, and each vertical side has a point in common with one of the two vertices of the dual-branch hyperbola. The diagonals of the rectangle can be extended to form the asymptotes, which are shown below:

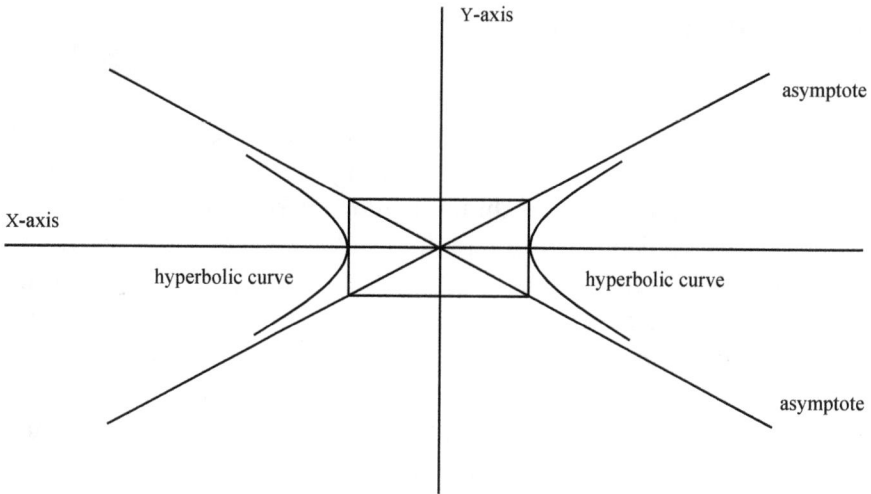

Figure 1.3

Each hyperbolic curve approaches, but never reaches, the diagonal lines of the asymptotes, regardless of how far the lines are extended in a finite space. The hyperbola is determined by formula not to intersect the asymptotes. Even if the lines are increased in length indefinitely, to any finite distance, the hyperbola's branches merely continue to approach the asymptotes, drawing ever closer to them but never meeting them. In an analogous way, the swift sprinter in the Achilles paradox is determined by design to approach ever closer to the tortoise but never to reach it. It is only in going beyond the puzzle's linguistic restrictions, only in breaking out of the box that Zeno creates, that the champion can overtake the beast.

Whether the Zenonian paradoxes are resolvable to the full satisfaction of the philosophical and mathematical communities, it is clear that they were powerful tools against the Pythagoreans. In this sense, they accomplished their purpose.

FUNDAMENTAL PLURALISM

A fourth Presocratic group consists of those who agree with the Milesians that materiality characterizes the cosmic foundation, but they maintain that conceiving of reality as a single element is misguided. The essence of things could not be reduced to such an extent; individual objects are built from a pool of basic corporeal components. These philosophers differ from the Pythagoreans, however, in their belief that something more substantive than numbers lies at the root of existence. In these later Presocratics, the influence of their predecessors is apparent, and there is an interweaving of both monistic and pluralistic principles to form a fabric of new ideas about the framework of nature.

EMPEDOCLES. Empedocles of Acragas in Sicily was born between 492 and 490 B.C. and died at the age of sixty.[70] From Parmenides, Empedocles inherited the belief that reality could not come into being, nor could it pass away. This view is expressed clearly in the intact fragments—of which there are about 160—of his original writings. The philosopher believes that reality is eternal; it is unchanging and indeed unchangeable. Taking a stand against those who hold that material things arise and cease, Empedocles remarks rather bluntly,

> Fools!—for they have no long-sighted thoughts, since they imagine that what previously did not exist comes into being, or that a thing dies and is utterly destroyed.[71]

Again, he declares,

> From what in no wise exists, it is impossible for anything to come into being; and for Being to perish completely is incapable of fulfilment and unthinkable; for it will always be there, wherever anyone may place it on any occasion.[72]

---

[70] Some estimates put the date of his birth a few years earlier; Diogenes Laërtius, however, places that event at 484 B.C.

[71] Empedocles, frag. 11, 52.

[72] Ibid., frag. 12, 52.

It is evident from this passage that Empedocles concurs with Parmenides in accepting the impotence of the nonexistent in any sort of generational role: That which does not exist cannot bring anything into existence. Reminiscent of the earlier, fundamentally monistic philosophers, Empedocles signals a return to the standard elements of matter as the bedrock of reality. Unlike the fundamental monists, however, Empedocles does not believe that one element can arise from another; the underlying core is unchanging. Water cannot become fire, as Thales would have one think, nor is it possible for air to become earth, as Anaximenes holds. Instead, all the world is constructed from a set of four essential components. Empedocles refers to these components in the extant fragments as "the four roots of things."[73] Not unexpectedly, they are earth, air, fire, and water. These roots exist eternally, giving rise to physical things out of the various combinations of them through mixing, although each retains its individual nature in the blend. The philosopher declares,

> And I shall tell you another thing: there is no creation of substance in any one of mortal existences, nor any end in execrable death, but only mixing and exchange of what has been mixed; and the name 'substance' (*Phusis*, *'nature'*) is applied to them by mankind.[74]

Material elements are not capable of bringing themselves together to form a mixture, he thinks. In this sense, they are passive. Thales argues that all comes from water, but he does not explain how it is that the substrate produces the physical objects that make up the world. To provide such an explanation, Empedocles postulates the existence of two prime forces: Affection and Strife. These cosmic drivers operate within a perpetual macrocycle; first one force dominates, then the other. As Affection prevails, the roots are forced together, blending them to create a sphere. It is the world of things as humans experience it. Strife then begins to work against the blend, separating the roots, bringing them back into their pure form. All the particles of a given root are held together in layers, with the earth at

---

[73] Ibid., frag. 6, 52.

[74] Ibid., frag. 8, 52. Freeman's translation of the upsilon in φύσις yields *phusis* rather than *physis*. It is an acceptable alternative.

the center. Affection begins its action of mixing again at this juncture, and the cycle restarts. Empedocles believes that the world is at the stage where Strife has begun to separate the mixture of the four elements. Note the Heraclitean influence here, both in the notion of a cyclical cosmic process and in the emphasis on Strife.

Although Empedocles reverts to the materialism that began with the Milesians, there is an important divergence from earlier philosophy. Here, the material elements are not self-moved but depend on basic forces to move them. Those forces are interlaced with the matter that they move rather than detached from it; however, they stand apart conceptually, in that the forces, unlike the elements themselves, are active. It is a departure that sets the stage for another Presocratic, Anaxagoras. In him, there is not only an actual separation of the passive from the active but a separation of the material from the immaterial as well; and the immaterial is, like the *Logos* of Heraclitus, rational.

Later philosophers, notably Aristotle, criticize Empedocles for making use of two additional forces in his metaphysics without explaining them. Finding the first two to be inadequate for his account, so goes the criticism, Empedocles adds Chance and Necessity. Although he does employ these notions, they are not cosmic drivers, positioned beyond the ones on which his philosophy relies.[75] Affection and Strife cause aggregation and segregation respectively, and those actions happen in accordance with possibilities, but possibilities do not compel them to happen. As a present-day illustration, consider a series of coin-tosses. The series may end with tails showing 50 percent of the time. The results are in line with the rules of probability, but the driver for the series of events and for the outcome is the propelling of the coin upward in combination with the force of gravity that reverses its course.

What is interesting in particular about Empedocles's use of chance is his explanation of the evolution of organisms in terms of the random shuffling of biological components, coupled with his elementary account of the survival of the best adjusted. Charles Darwin was not the first to articulate such ideas. Again, certain modern

---

[75] W. K. C. Guthrie notes this fact in *A History of Greek Philosophy*, vol. 2, *The Presocratic Tradition from Parmenides to Democritus* (1965; repr., Cambridge: Cambridge University Press, 1969), 159 ff.

conceptions reflect the theorizing of the Presocratics. (Note that both plants and animals are classified as organisms; however, in using the term 'organism' in this work, I am referring, as a rule, to animals.)

For Empedocles, the objects of the senses—what one sees, hears, touches, and so forth—are real, and they are subject to change. They are not, as Parmenides holds, merely illusory, nor is change itself illusory. Yet, in keeping with the Parmenidean view of reality, Empedocles believes that the roots of existence are unvarying and unending. It is the mixing by Affection that produces the material objects in the world and the separation by Strife that brings about their decay, but, through it all, the elements remain. It is clear that Empedocles attempts in his metaphysics to merge two views that had seemed to be irreconcilable.

ANAXAGORAS. Anaxagoras was born at Clazomenae near Smyrna in Asia Minor around 500 B.C. and lived until approximately 428 B.C. Like Parmenides, he holds that fundamental reality is unchangeable and neither comes into being nor passes away. Unlike that great thinker from Elea, though, he believes that physical things do undergo change; they are varying collections or mixtures of primary, unchanging elements. Anaxagoras refers in his writings to these elements as "the seeds of all Things . . . seeds infinite in number."[76] The combining, separating, and recombining of this vast multiplicity of seeds yields the great variety of physical things that are the objects of sensory experience. Reminiscent of Empedocles, Anaxagoras claims that individual things come into existence and cease to exist as respectively the seeds are mixed and separated.

> The Greeks have an incorrect belief on Coming into Being and Passing Away. No Thing comes into being or passes away, but it is mixed together or separated from existing Things. Thus they would be correct if they called coming into being 'mixing', and passing away 'separation-off'.[77]

Anaxagoras's philosophy thus draws on both Parmenides and Empedocles in allowing the permanence of a foundational universal

---

[76] Anaxagoras, frag. 4, 83.
[77] Ibid., frag. 17, 85.

core. Against Parmenides, however, he allows change in the form of alterations in physical things to which that core gives rise. Against Empedocles, he holds that the base of existence could not be just four things. Rather, the physical world in its diversity arose out of the amalgams of an infinity of elementary particles, each of which contains all characteristics within itself.[78] Everything is in everything, he declares. How can a thing, he queries, citing the parts of an organism, come from something that is completely different from itself: "How can hair come from not-hair, and flesh from not-flesh?"[79] The qualities of physical things exist eternally in the seeds, even before the things themselves arise from them, but it is through the predominance of one kind of seed that the particular characteristics of things appear. Says Aristotle of the Anaxagoreans,

> So they assert that everything has been mixed in everything, because they saw everything arising out of everything. But things, as they say, appear different from one another and receive different names according to the nature of the particles which are numerically predominant among the innumerable constituents of the mixture. For nothing, they say, is purely and entirely white or black or sweet, bone or flesh, but the nature of a thing is held to be that of which it contains the most.[80]

Anaxagoras postulates the existence of a cosmic driving force, but, in contrast to the cyclical duo of Affection and Strife in Empedocles's philosophy, this force is independent of the matter that it moves. It is the ultimate, initial cause of all movement in material things—the active, inducing the passive to respond to its controlling

---

[78] There is some disagreement among scholars concerning Anaxagoras's belief about the number of seeds. The common interpretation of his philosophy, according to one scholar, is based on the wording "seeds infinite in quantity" that appears in several of the fragments that remained of Anaxagoras's writings as late as the sixth century, when they were quoted by Simplicius. See Felix M. Cleve, *The Philosophy of Anaxagoras: An Attempt at Reconstruction* (New York: King's Crown Press, 1949). Cleve holds that it is questionable whether the quoted phrase refers to the number of *kinds* of seeds that exist or to the number of *particles* that make up the various kinds; consult p. 8 of his book.

[79] Anaxagoras, frag. 10, 84.

[80] Aristotle, *Physics*, 1, 4.187b1–6, 225.

influence. That influence is rational: Anaxagoras's term for it is *Nous*, which is translated as 'Mind'. An infinite and self-ruled power, *Nous* stands apart from the physical cosmos over which it exerts control. It is unique among the things that exist: Although there are things with *Nous*—that is to say, Mind—in them, such as man, *Nous* itself is not a mixture. It is pure; hence, it cannot lose its power through dilution. *Nous* does not create matter, which is composed of eternal particles, but it does set the particles in motion in Anaxagorean cosmogony. This movement is a vortex, a pattern that is common in Greek thought. Once the process begins, however, *Nous* backs away, leaving the formation of things to the mechanics of the cosmic whirlpool. As with the spinning of a toy top on the driveway after the child pulls the string and then stands aside to watch, physics alone takes over to maintain motion. The cosmogonic withdrawal disappoints both Plato and Aristotle, who were looking for a teleological account of the order that nature exhibits: an account that is marked by activity toward some end.

Nevertheless, Anaxagoras does take a bold step forward in separating passive elements from the active cause that moves them, and he identifies that cause with a reasoning entity. As opposed to a universe that is solely the product of natural forces, his is one in which an intelligence that is independent of the universe sets everything in place. This ancient writer brings to the forefront the notion that the physical is ruled by the mental, an express reflection of the philosophical emphasis on rationality that began with the *Logos* of Heraclitus. Albeit philosophers of this era may not have the tools at their disposal to expound on an immaterial existent (some scholars think that *Nous* is, in fact, material, yet others present solid evidence to the contrary), Anaxagoras pulls ahead of the pack. In any case, the split between the corporeal and the incorporeal is starting to mature.

LEUCIPPUS AND DEMOCRITUS. Virtually nothing remains of the writings of Leucippus except two fragments, and it is not clear whether he is the source of both. Two works are credited to him, although the authorship of neither is certain; his noted disciple might have penned at least one of them. It appears that Leucippus was active around 430 B.C. The exact dates of his birth and death are not documented, although it is likely that he was born before 460 B.C. in Miletus, Elea, or Abdera—a city on the north coast of the Aegean

Sea. Of the early Greek thinkers, Leucippus remains perhaps the most obscure.[81]

His disciple, Democritus, a native of Abdera, was born near 460 B.C., although some historians place the date of his birth later. Democritus lived to be quite old; he might have reached the century mark. A prolific writer, this philosopher created approximately sixty books in the course of his life, but not one has survived; only fragments remain. It is not entirely obvious where the ideas of the two men diverge, and, as a rule, they are joined in discussions of their philosophical perspective regarding being.

Building on the concepts of those who came before him, but departing in important ways, Leucippus is the first to put forth an atomic theory, an idea that is carried forward by his disciple; indeed, the two men have come to be known as the atomists. Leucippus and Democritus hold that atoms, together with the void of empty space in which they collide, constitute the whole of existence. These particles are "indivisible bodies, infinite both in number and in the varieties of their shapes."[82] By virtue of their minuscule size, they are invisible. Atoms move around continuously—and have done so eternally—in the emptiness of space, which is itself infinite, and they move apparently in a random way, coming into contact with each other in chance encounters. If compatible shapes collide, then they become entangled and form objects. When the atoms eventually separate because of impact with other atoms, where the collision is sufficient in force to disentangle them, the objects decay. Thus, change is accounted for on the basis of these conjoinings and disjoinings. Like miniature Parmenidean Ones, the elements themselves cannot change, but the arrangement and position of them can change, and do so, in a sort of cosmic dance of possibility.

With the hypothesis of the void therefore, Leucippus and Democritus offer a way to circumnavigate the dual Parmenidean problem of plurality and motion while paying homage to the great

---

[81] Some Greeks, including Epicurus, claim that Leucippus never existed. This view is difficult to accept, particularly in light of his being mentioned by both Aristotle and Aristotle's pupil Theophrastus; Theophrastus lived c. 371–c. 286 B.C. Other writers also mention Leucippus.

[82] Aristotle, *On Generation and Corruption*, 1, 1.314a22, trans. Harold H. Joachim, in *Works of Aristotle*, 470.

Eleatic. In summary, here is the problem as Aristotle presents it in one of his works:

> For some of the older philosophers thought that 'what is' must of necessity be 'one' and immovable. The void, they argue, is not; but unless there is a void with a separate being of its own, 'what is' cannot be moved— nor again can it be many, since there is nothing to keep things apart.[83]

The atomists' solution is to hold that, whereas empty space is not something, it is not nothing either. This paradoxical approach rests on their belief that only that which is corporeal is truly real, but corporeal reality need not be everywhere and continuous. If reality is composed of pieces, then it is not necessary that those pieces be juxtaposed and compacted, forming one undifferentiated, homogeneous chunk with no space anywhere in it. There can be areas where matter is lacking, and real things—pieces of matter—can move through these vacant places because those places, in fact, do exist. This scattered pattern is precisely the structure of the cosmos, they contend. Atoms are dispersed in the void, and the void is an empty, but *existent*, space.

> Leucippus and his associate Democritus declare that the *Full* and the *Void* are the elements, calling the one "being" and the other "nonbeing", that is, the *Full* or the *Solid* is being but the *Void* or *Rare* is nonbeing (hence they say that being exists no more than nonbeing, inasmuch as a body exists no more than void), and that these are the material causes of things.[84]

The atomists believe that they satisfy the Parmenidean requirement that reality must be a plenum—completely full—and still hold that it need not be a singularity, for the whole of being is contained in the atomic pieces that compose it. Contrary to the Parmenidean way of thinking, Leucippus and Democritus theorize that reality is pluralistic, that there is coming into being and ceasing to be, and that

---

[83] Ibid., 1, 8.325a4–6, 497.
[84] Aristotle, *Metaphysics*, A, 4.985b5–9, *Aristotle's Metaphysics*, 20.

motion is possible. Reality is many because the atoms are infinite in number. There is generation and decay because atoms combine and separate. There is motion because there is some place for atoms to go. Consider this passage in Aristotle on the atomistic solution:

> Leucippus, however, thought he had a theory which harmonized with sense-perception and would not abolish either coming-to-be and passing-away or motion and the multiplicity of things. . . . [H]e conceded to the Monists that there could be no motion without a void. The result is a theory which he states as follows: 'The void is a "not-being", and no part of "what is" is a "not-being"; for what "is" in the strict sense of the term is an absolute *plenum*. This *plenum*, however, is not "one": on the contrary, it is a "many" infinite in number and invisible owing to the minuteness of their bulk. The "many" move in the void (for there is a void): and by coming together they produce "coming-to-be", while by separating they produce "passing away". . . .'[85]

Although the atomists' theory, innovative for its time, offers a way out of the clutches of strict monism, it does so at the expense of declaring that what has no being and is therefore unreal—namely, empty space—exists. Indeed, materially empty space *does* exist, but the vacuum of space is as real as the particles in it, a rich scientific discovery with implications that extend well beyond the atomists' theory. There are things in the physical universe—setting aside the nonphysical for now—that are not matter, but they are surely part of physical reality. No one should expect these ancient thinkers to grasp the concept of energy as it is put forth in modern physics, of course. The atomists do believe that something other than matter exists, in the form of the void, yet they maintain that only material body can lay claim to reality. They fail to see that the existent and the real are one and the same. The inimitable Mr. Spock states the truth in declaring, "Nothing unreal exists."[86] The other part of the underlying

---

[85] Aristotle, *Generation and Corruption*, 1, 8.325a24–33, 498–99. The quotation marks are as they appear in the text.
[86] Mr. Spock, played by Leonard Nimoy, in the movie *Star Trek IV: The Voyage Home*, dir. Leonard Nimoy, 119 min. (Hollywood, CA: Paramount Pictures, 1986),

biconditional, which he does not state, is equally true: Nothing nonexistent is real.

In the Leucippean-Democritean model, countless universes arise out of the emptiness of space and the mass of atoms residing in it. Recalling the philosophy of Anaxagoras—and that of Anaximander before him—the vortex resurfaces in the metaphysics of the atomists as the motion that drives world generation. Smaller fire atoms are forced outward in the whirling motion, leaving the larger ones near the center to form earth as particles begin to attract others that are like themselves and coalesce. As is the case with Anaxagoras, the atomists declare that there is a propelling force that is inherent in the cosmos. Unlike Anaxagoras, though, they maintain that the impetus for cosmic process is mechanism, not intelligence.

The atomists put forth an idea—based on their position regarding the makeup of the universe—concerning the mechanics of sense perception: how atoms, which have no sensible qualities intrinsically, give rise to sensations. It is likely that the theory of perception is developed more fully in the writings of Democritus than in those of his mentor, and it is a theory that Aristotle criticizes, believing it to be one that reduces all sensations to touch. Consider the sense of sight. According to the rudimentary atomistic thought, an object in the environment constantly sheds material images of itself. These images are composed of atoms, as only atoms and the void exist. The images are impressed on the air; when shed by the object, they produce a likeness in the air, which serves as the means of propagation. These imprints of the original image bump into the soul through the eyes to generate the sensation of vision. One continues to see an object on which the gaze is trained because the shedding continues to occur. As the imprints travel to one's eyes, however, the air distorts them, so that they become increasingly indistinct with distance, ultimately fading altogether. The theory posits that one does not see things per se; one sees representations of those things, albeit material representations. By the very nature of sight, there is a separation between the perceived and the perceiver.

---

videocassette. Spock's statement was in response to a question that was posed by a computer: "What was Kiri-Kin-Tha's first law of metaphysics?" Following Spock's reply, the computer remarked, "Correct." With Spock and the computer in agreement, one's confidence in the truth of the statement ought to be high.

The atomic impact with a perceiver during a visual experience causes the sensation of color. Democritus attributes all the different hues that people experience to combinations of just four basic ones: white, black, red, and yellow. In keeping with his theory, each hue is associated with certain structural characteristics of the atoms that lie on the surface of the objects that people see. All other colors are created by the blending of the four basic ones as atomic particles of different configurations strike the eyes.

What of the other senses? Hearing is more direct. Atoms forming the imprint of the object, along with air that has been molded by the image into corpuscular chunks that are similar to the imprint, hit the ear, as opposed to merely the imprint itself—the active instrument in seeing. The sensations of taste, touch, and presumably smell, like vision, are caused by the varying sizes and shapes of atoms. Sweetness, for example, is the result of the tongue's contacting a set of atoms that are predominantly circular.

Thus, sensible qualities are not *in objects*, for objects are simply collections of atoms with no sensible qualities themselves: Atoms have no color and no sweetness. Perceived qualities are *in the perceiver*: They are subjective reactions by an observer to the impact of the atomic elements or their emanations. It is by custom or convention, Democritus claims, that humans ascribe sensible properties to things.

> Sweet exists by convention, bitter by convention, colour by convention; atoms and Void (*alone*) exist in reality . . . We know nothing accurately in reality, but (*only*) as it changes according to the bodily condition, and the constitution of those things that flow upon (*the body*) and impinge upon it.[87]

In a broad and basic sense, the premise of modern physical theory is evident in the philosophy of Leucippus and Democritus. For instance, the current scientific account of color resembles the Democritean model—in two ways. First, science reveals that the vast array of colors that humans experience actually can be traced to three primary ones and further that there are, in the majority of humans,

---

[87] Democritus, frag. 9, 93. The ellipsis as it appears here is part of the quotation.

three types of color receptors in the eyes. Each receptor is sensitive to a specific range of wavelengths in the spectrum of electromagnetic energy that corresponds to light.[88] Second, the concept of color is set forth in terms of the subjective interpretation of the wavelength of energy striking the retina. In this sense, color is, as Democritus thinks, in the perceiver. Although it is through contact with physical substance that sensory experience is possible in Democritean philosophy, one ultimately is removed from the true being of things in the process of perception. In a rather profound remark, Democritus asserts, "Man is severed from reality."[89] As one will see, the notion that people are not truly in touch with things—with reality, as it were—contributes to the perplexity of epistemological pursuits.

PHYSICS, METAPHYSICS, AND A RISING ENIGMA

Out of this mosaic of early Greek thought, three key problems emerge. Two of them, by now, may be apparent. The third is more veiled. To grasp the scope of the problems and why they persisted, one must understand first the difference between activities in the realm of science and those in the realm of philosophy. In science, the truth or falsity of declarations is determinable—in principle, at least—through perception. The senses are ultimately the faculties that allow one to ascertain the facts.

Technology, of course, might extend the capacity or the range of the senses through the use of various tools. Electron-scanning microscopes, radio telescopes, Geiger counters, oscilloscopes, sound-amplification devices, chemical-detection systems, video cameras aboard a Martian rover, sonar installations on submarines, and so forth—all allow people to enhance their capabilities to observe; but, in the end, it is through the senses that the potential for discovery arises. One still must listen to the sounds, detected and relayed by

---

[88] A small percentage of women carry a fourth receptor. Color receptors are known as cones.
[89] Democritus, frag. 6, 92.

audio sensors, perhaps also enhanced by them. One still must look at the images of the Martian landscape that appear on a video monitor.

The claims of science—because they pertain to phenomena that, under appropriate conditions, are subject to public examination—lend themselves to verification through observation, often by means of experimentation. One can determine the truth of a given claim by checking to see whether what it puts forward aligns with what perceptions reveal about the physical world. In some instances, it may take years to make such determinations. Declaring certain factors to be causal agents in disease generally follows a protracted period of research. Studies may be conducted throughout several decades to prove or disprove theories in pathogenesis.

Sometimes, assertions may be about the future or about the past. Years ago, my wife and I visited Gettysburg, Pennsylvania, the site of the well-known battle in 1863 that bears the name of the town. Aside from the museum, where a number of the artifacts had been preserved, the battleground area was open to visitors. They could see firsthand where the troops had been positioned for much of the encounter. Traveling the road opposite Cemetery Ridge, we drove along the Confederate artillery emplacements; an array of cannons formed an outline of the perimeter. I could envision the attack across that huge field on the final day of the battle. The terrain offered little protection from Union fire as Confederate soldiers charged toward the higher ground. It was sobering to reflect on the great loss of life, on both sides of the conflict, during those three days in July.

One particularly striking, but curious, reminder of the frenzy of the engagement was what lay in the museum. It was a piece of lead. More than a mere hunk of metal, though, it was the fusion of a pair of projectiles from discharged muskets. There had been so much arms fire during the encounter that two projectiles had collided in midair and merged to form a single mass. No one who is currently alive witnessed the Battle of Gettysburg, but there are written accounts of those who did witness it, and people trust their reports. Moreover, there are remnants of the event that serve as evidence of its occurrence as well as its intensity, and one can point—literally—to the items that are in the museum that is dedicated to its memory.

Consider, though, the claim by physicists that quarks exist. At one time, scientists deemed protons and neutrons to be fundamental, indivisible nuclear components. As is common knowledge now, each, on the contrary, is composed of minute units of matter called quarks. Until the construction of particle accelerators that were capable of demonstrating their existence, these subatomic entities, which were detected for the first time in 1968, were merely theoretical. Certainly, none ever had been demonstrated by experiment to be real. Quarks cannot be seen directly, given their size, but physicists note the diverse trails that follow collisions of atomic constituents in particle accelerators, indicating that quarks are part of the makeup of the universe. Postulating that they exist falls in the realm of science nevertheless because they are physical entities, things that are subject—in principle, at least—to sensory inspection. Indeed, scientists could have detected quarks, in the right circumstances, before they did detect them, a detail that is conditional: Had certain particle accelerators existed before they did exist (or had quarks been large, independent units), scientists could have proved, through observation, the existence of quarks before they did prove it. The important point is that it is not *actual* observation that is the hallmark of scientific activity, but it is rather the *potential* for it. To be science, assertions must be open to proof of truth through physical investigation; it must be possible *in principle* to determine their truth by using the senses. In science, observation is the route to discovery.

It is not so with metaphysics. This limitation is not a matter of degree; it is a matter of kind. Some types of assertions simply cannot be shown to be true or false based on information that the senses provide; it is not possible, even in principle. No amount of looking will tell one whether things are numbers or whether change is unreal. What surfaces in the thoughts and writings of the Presocratic philosophers as they set forth claims about reality is not physics; it is metaphysics. Taken literally, 'metaphysics' means 'after physics' or 'beyond physics'. Apparently applied originally to a set of writings of Aristotle that followed his work *Physics*, the term came to refer to an investigation of matters that transcend the natural, material realm. Metaphysical inquiries lie outside the ability of science to uncover the truth of assertions that are formed within the bounds of those inquiries. As they seek to uncover the foundation of the world, the ancient philosophers propose quite a variety of things as candidates for the ultimate reality, ranging from a sole substratum or element to a great many of them. The notion that some primary core exists is common to all these thinkers, but their views concerning what that base reality must be diverge markedly. The disagreement is so pronounced and so challenging to resolve because identifying *archē* or *physis* is not the kind of undertaking in which an individual can engage through the exercise of the senses. The exploration is not a scientific one, and observation will not work. It is not possible for the early philosophers to come upon what they are in search of by looking. In metaphysics, logic is the route to discovery.

Yet, science is on exactly the same quest: endeavoring to find a way to unify reality, tying all things to a single base. Recent advances in physics have led to the most encompassing scientific theory ever devised. The mission to pin down one master formula to explain everything in the universe—a theory of everything, or TOE—has gained considerable momentum in the last century and a half. As the science of matter and energy continued to make strides through the years, a rift emerged between the physics of the very large—namely, general relativity—and the physics of the very small—namely, quantum mechanics. The physics and mathematics that apply to celestial objects, such as planets and stars, are at odds with those dealing with the minuscule particles and forces of the subatomic world. They are just too different. Scientists have tried for quite some time to combine them, seeking a unique mathematical undercarriage for the whole of physical phenomena. A late development, superstring theory—typically referred to as simply string theory (the original version)—promises to be the master unifier of science. The theory holds that all matter and all forces in the universe are emanations from tiny, vibrating strings. Like different notes that oscillating violin strings produce, electrons and muons, gluons and photons, are the expressions of strings as they vibrate in different ways. These foundational strings (which some refer to as quantum strings) are almost unimaginably little, on the order of the Planck length, which is approximately 1.6163×10^{-33} centimeter. To put this remarkable size in perspective, suppose that a company, to promote its advanced capabilities, designed and manufactured a special metric ruler; one of the centimeters on the ruler was divided into Planck lengths. Suppose further that the company built a machine to count the tiny spans making up that centimeter, as the management team wanted to ensure the measuring tool's accuracy. If the machine could count those microspans at the rate of one per second, then it would take about twenty million billion billion years to complete the task.

Stranger still, traditional string theory requires the existence of six additional dimensions, which are curled tightly around every point in the four-dimensional space-time of common experience, bringing the total number of dimensions to ten. There are different versions of string theory, however—five in all. Depending on the particular model, the strings may be closed loops or open-ended structures. All these systems seem to describe reality, at least by virtue of the mathematics, but how can all these views of the universe be correct? In a comprehensive conjecture that is known as M-theory, there are actually seven extra dimensions. One great appeal of M-theory is that it brings together the various string theories—along with eleven-dimensional supergravity—in a common framework, showing that each variant of string theory is a single perspective on a broader reality.

To illustrate, picture oneself in a two-dimensional world, and imagine that it is possible to see things, such as lines, in this two-dimensional existence. Imagine further that there is a right triangle there, the sides of which are three, four, and five feet. Viewing the triangle from the plane in which it is situated and looking at each of the three sides dead-on, as it were, a viewer would see straight lines that are three, four, and five feet in length respectively. If the triangle were rotated in the plane, then the observer would see a single line, changing in length as the triangle turned. Exiting the world of two dimensions, however, and beholding the triangle from the top, one would realize that the three lines are, in truth, part of one and the same figure. Analogously, M-theory shows that the five string theories that describe the quantum world are merely different views of the same system, but M-theory introduces an extra dimension in doing so.

Many physicists believe today that these added dimensions are no less real than the ones of which people are aware. They have been overlooked because they lie beyond the human ability to detect them with existing equipment. As peculiar as it may seem to be, there is a certain elegance that issues from string theory and especially M-theory, the version that fuses the other theoretical renditions to form a cohesive whole. Ultimately, it may provide the answers to the most challenging mysteries of scientific inquiry. Not all scientists agree, however. Some think that string theory has been a disappointment. The search continues.

This question arises: Is string theory actually science? It is, after all, the physicists who are delving into these matters. One scientist claims that researchers eventually must be able to demonstrate the existence of strings through testing, not through mathematics alone. In a sense, experimental physics must underwrite theoretical physics. If trial cannot show that strings are real, he thinks, then string theory cannot be classified as science.

> String theory and string theorists do have a real problem. How do you actually test string theory? If you can't test it in the way that we test normal theories, it's not science; it's philosophy.[90]

Part of the problem with testing lies in the fantastically tiny size of the putative entities under investigation. The stage is set nevertheless for a number of creative experiments as scientists intensify the search for the diminutive, base-level filaments, and progress is occurring. Moreover, the intrinsic tension of the strings, which causes them to be so compressed, may be less than what was thought at first, leading to the idea that strings may be longer than the current theories hold and, if so, then potentially "subject to direct experimental observation by accelerators within a few decades."[91]

As noted earlier, though, the decisive factor in distinguishing science from philosophy, physics from metaphysics, is not whether observation is physically achievable but whether observation is conceptually achievable. Prior to the 1940s, humankind never had demonstrated that an explosion was possible through nuclear fission by initiating a chain reaction. In 1942, Enrico Fermi brought the first nuclear reactor into operation, thereby proving that fission could be

---

[90] Joseph Lykken of Fermilab, in *The Elegant Universe*, dir. Joseph McMaster and Julia Cort, disk 1, *Einstein's Dream*, dir. Joseph McMaster, 60 min. (Boston: WGBH Boston Video, 2003), DVD.
[91] Brian Greene, *The Elegant Universe* (New York: W. W. Norton and Co., 1999), 402.

sustained in a controlled environment. Its explosive potential, however, was yet to materialize. Theoretical physics had predicted a devastating discharge of energy, given the right conditions, but it was not until Julius Robert Oppenheimer and his team detonated a nuclear device on July 16, 1945, that experimental physics proved what theoretical physics had postulated. The resultant breaking of the strong atomic bonds in the radioactive plutonium-239 that fueled the bomb unleashed enormous power as a small part of the mass of the fissile material escaped in the form of energy in accordance with the famous equation of Albert Einstein, $E = mc^2$: Energy equals mass times a constant—the speed of light in a vacuum—squared.[92] In physics, and indeed in science in general, the theoretical should lead to verification through the experimental. The search for a fission weapon was always one of science; it was never one of philosophy. Technology extends humans' ability to see things, at least indirectly, but the objects of metaphysics are not the right sort of things to be seen at all. The infinitesimally small is unobservable by virtue of its size, not its nature, although the extra dimensions do add an element of complexity to the issue. It is reasonable to speculate that, with strings, increasing the ability to probe their small size could bring them in principle into the realm of the observable or, at any rate, provide indications in the four-dimensional experiential grid that they do exist. On the other hand, numbers cannot be seen—precisely because, according to a standard view, they are not physical entities

---

[92] Oppenheimer and his team also used uranium-235 for the fissile material in the construction of the initial set of nuclear bombs, but the plutonium implosion device was the first to be detonated. The scientists decided to employ implosion in this first weapon, as opposed to the simpler gun-barrel construction of the uranium bomb, because the presence of the isotope plutonium-240 in the radioactive material raised concerns about the possibility of a premature reaction if the other method were used. The uranium-based weapon was exploded over Hiroshima. A third bomb, utilizing plutonium, was dropped on Nagasaki. Einstein's original expression of the equivalency for which he is famous did not appear in the format that, as a rule, is articulated today. Einstein asserted that the mass of a body that is giving off energy L in the form of radiation diminishes by L divided by the square of the speed of light. His celebrated equation is a later rendering. Einstein set forth his groundbreaking formulation of the mass-energy relationship in a paper titled "Ist die Trägheit eines Körpers von seinem Energieinhalt abhängig?" ("Does the Inertia of a Body Depend upon Its Energy-Content?"), which he published in *Annalen der Physik* in 1905.

at all; they are abstract creations. Even if an infinitesimally small number were increased to a very large one, whatever that conditional statement might mean, a person still would not be able to see it. String theory lies in the realm of physics, not philosophy.

Someone may ask then why Thales's assertion that *archē* is water and Anaximenes's assertion that *archē* is air are not scientific claims. Water and air are clearly material substances, and inquiries concerning matter belong to the field of science. There is a marked difference, however, between stating that H_2O is water and stating that core reality is water. The first assertion is about the physical world; it is about the chemical constitution of a common material compound. The second assertion is not about the physical world. It is about the conjectured fundamental substratum that transcends the world, giving rise to it and upholding the things in it as they change.

Through findings in the area of chemistry, one can demonstrate that hydrogen and oxygen combine, under certain conditions, to produce water. An individual can set up an experiment in a laboratory to prove the truth of this notion, and prove it repeatedly. It is a well-established fact that is verifiable through experimentation and observation.

That water transcends the physical world and undergirds it, in contrast, is not a notion that can be verified through the senses. It is not the sort of thing that one ever could confirm by means of perception, no matter how elaborate the laboratory or any testing procedure might be. The fact that Anaximenes performed an experiment in support of his claim that *archē* is air does not alter the nature of the investigation. What the pseudotest purported to show in Anaximenes's system is that air changes in quality based on how dense it is. This idea was used to support the *philosophical* position that the whole of physical reality owes its being and persistence to air. Anaximenes's experiment and its accompanying concept are matters of science—or, more precisely perhaps, parascience—and observation is the path to discovery here. The ancient thinker's postulation, grounded in the experiment and the concept, is *not* science, however. It is not possible, even in principle, to observe that air is the transcendent underpinning that brings about the existence of all things, the substratum that provides the continuity of objects through change. Such a claim falls in the realm of metaphysics.

With the distinction drawn between the domain of physics and that of metaphysics, I want to return to the problematic issues that arise out of the philosophical musings of the early Greeks. These issues are interrelated. The first is *the problem of one and many*; the second is *the problem of change*.

In an effort to explain the observable, physical world, the philosophers of old turn to unobservable, metaphysical principles. The key assumption that they adopt in putting forth various systems is that the totality of what exists springs from something that is irreducibly primitive. In this belief, they are in agreement. Its nature, however, is a point of contention.

The theories of the Presocratics fall into four broad categories. Fundamental monism is the position that there are many things in the world, but they owe their reality to one elemental substance, and it is material. Diametrically opposed to this position is what I refer to as quasi-strict pluralism, the stance of the Pythagoreans. Theirs is the theory that there are many things in the world—although everything is traceable to two—but things are not constructed from some sole material element, which generates single entities, separate from each other. Rather, objects are *intrinsically* pluralistic, in that they are numbers; and not only are numbers many, but, with the exception of the mathematical unit—the number 1—they also carry plurality essentially. The third category is strict monism. In this view, there are not many things in any sense at all. Reality is singular in every respect. The final category is fundamental pluralism. Its adherents hold that there are many things in the world, and the reality base itself is many. This multitudinous base consists of material building blocks that combine, for one reason or another, to produce distinct objects. The table that I present below summarizes the views of the Presocratics whom I introduced in this chapter and identifies the underlying reality in their respective systems:

| | ── Base of Reality ── | |
Philosopher	Singular or Plural	Its Identity
Thales	Singular	Water
Anaximander	Singular	The Boundless
Anaximenes	Singular	Air
Heraclitus	Singular	Fire + *Logos*
Pythagoras	Plural	Numbers (traceable ultimately to Limit and the Unlimited)
Parmenides	Singular	One
Zeno	Singular	One (not many)
Empedocles	Plural	Roots (Earth, Air, Fire, Water) + Affection and Strife
Anaxagoras	Plural	Seeds + *Nous*
Leucippus / Democritus	Plural	Atoms in the Void

The difficulty here is that there appear to be many different things in the world, and those things themselves are made of many different parts. A tree has roots, heartwood, sapwood, bark, leaves, and seeds; and these parts are made of even simpler components. Cutting open one part—say, a seed—reveals additional parts. If reality is truly a multiplicity, then how it is that the many, varied parts cohere to form a single entity, unified in its being, poses a puzzle. What makes them all part of the same thing? The thinking can be expressed in another way: How can unity come from multiplicity and distinctness? Yet, if reality is singular, then how is it that uniquely different entities—trees, rivers, potatoes, and volcanoes—can exist, and how is it that the parts of a single entity, different in both qualities and operations, arise out of one base? How can multiplicity and distinctness come from unity? The following diagram captures the dual aspect of this problem:

THINGS

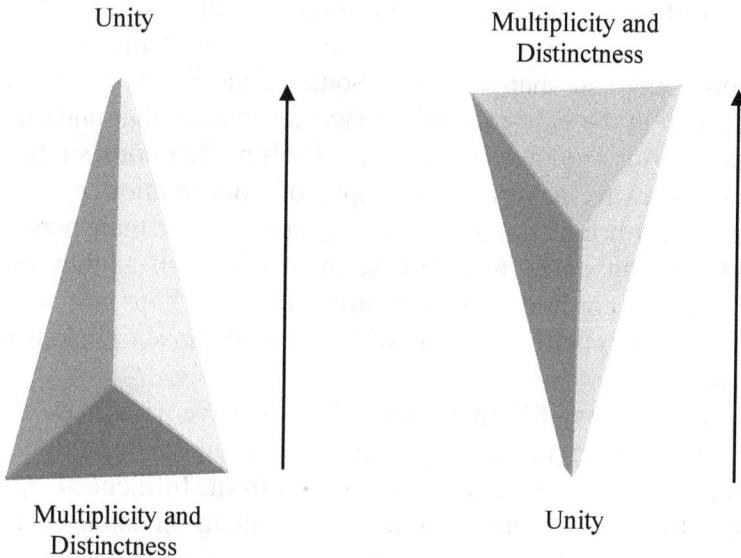

Figure 1.4

As discussed earlier, the proof of metaphysical claims rests not on verification by means of sensory experience but verification by means of inference. Unfortunately, little of the writings of the most ancient philosophers remains, although scholars have reconstructed their views from fragments, supplemented with reports from later philosophers. What is clear is that, although the earliest Presocratic philosophers do put forth metaphysical accounts in an attempt to explain the universe and its workings, these accounts are not grounded appreciably in logical arguments. It would take the Greeks several centuries after the rise of philosophy to formalize the discipline of logic in the writings of Aristotle. To be sure, there are elements of deduction inherent in even the systems of the Milesians as they reason that a common substrate is necessary to explain the cosmos. It is the Eleatics, however, who produce formidable arguments. Their influence on their Greek successors is indisputable.

The different accounts of the foundational core of things, and whether that core is one or many, point to a deeper, more ponderous question: How can change occur? Some of the Presocratics offer as an explanation the existence of a material substrate that underlies the physical world. The material substrate itself neither comes into being nor passes away, a sort of principle of conservation of ultimate matter. Yet, it brings things into being, provides for their persistence through shifting states, and absorbs them into itself as they eventually decay. According to this position then, perhaps not so much explicitly as implicitly, a thing's identity somehow is linked to the substrate.

The dilemma of Parmenides and the incisive paradoxes of Zeno force the problem of change—whether sameness through time is possible and, if so, then how—to the forefront. Influenced by these Eleatics, the Presocratics who come after them envision change as the combination of various nonchanging, elemental factors: roots, seeds, or atoms. Alterations in objects that one perceives are reducible to alterations in the location of immutable elements. As I will discuss in the next chapter, Plato claims that one must account for change in a different way. What is unchanging, in Plato's view, is not a collection of material particles that compose physical things but the qualities that those things exhibit. Objects change as they partake of different properties, but the properties themselves remain fixed. It is Plato's student Aristotle who takes the Milesian theory of the substrate to a higher level—denying, against his mentor, that ultimate reality lies in the attributes of things. It lies, he says, in the material as it exhibits those attributes. It is matter itself that endures through change, providing the substantive base of continuity that properties cannot provide. The process of variation in things is marked by matter's taking on a form that it did not have previously.

Consider an example of change and see where it leads. Suppose that a maple seed is planted in a field and a sapling appears. After a year, it is moved to another location in the same field, and to a third location two years later. In the course of time, it develops into a mature tree. Sometimes, its leaves are green; sometimes, its leaves are brilliant red; sometimes, it has no leaves. The branches increase in number as it grows, and decrease as it is pruned and weather takes its toll. It produces and releases seeds in season. Lightning strikes it during a storm, splitting the tree, and 20 percent of it lies on the ground; the remainder is pushed over 30° by the wind. Eventually, the tree is cut down, although the stump remains. The part that was felled is chopped into firewood, allowed to dry, and then burned, leaving only white ashes that are dumped back into the field where the seed was planted at the outset. Now, it is intuitive that, through all the years and all the changes, there was one tree. For a maple and, a fortiori, the *same* maple, to continue to exist through such dramatic alteration, the stance that something must be common to the tree at all points in time seems to be reasonable. One might represent the life of the tree—its duration—by the following diagram:

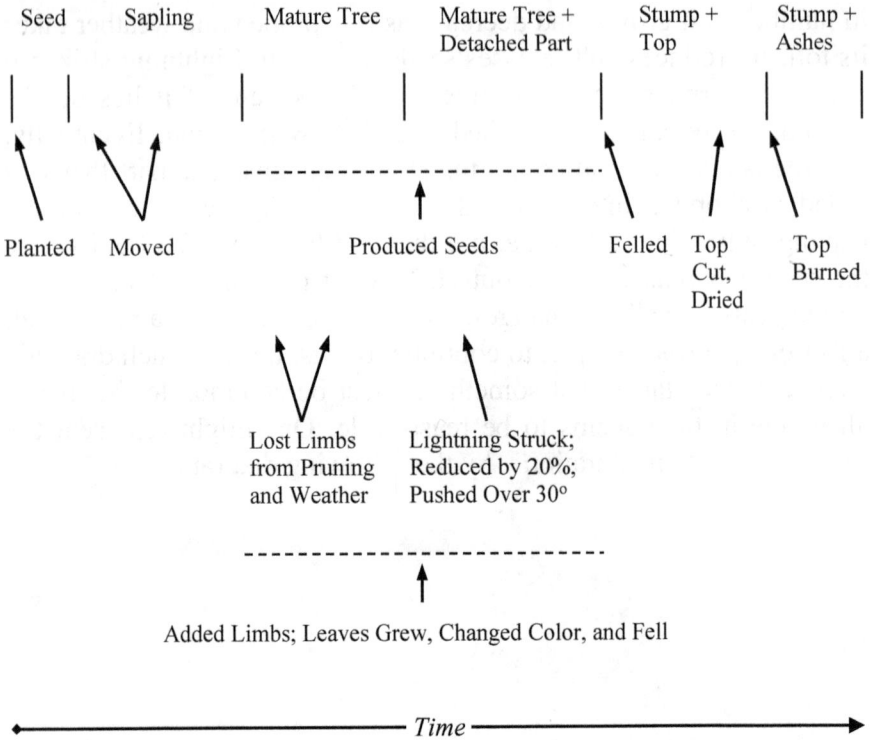

Seed	Sapling	Mature Tree	Mature Tree + Detached Part	Stump + Top	Stump + Ashes

Planted   Moved   Produced Seeds   Felled   Top   Top
                                                                        Cut,   Burned
                                                                        Dried

Lost Limbs   Lightning Struck;
from Pruning   Reduced by 20%;
and Weather   Pushed Over 30°

Added Limbs; Leaves Grew, Changed Color, and Fell

Time

Figure 1.5

In the thinking of a number of the Presocratics, the tree's continuity—perhaps its very identity—is linked to a foundational substratum that provides the necessary persistence through changing sets of characteristics. Thales, for example, asserts that water is the fundamental stuff supporting the alterations in properties. Anaximenes argues that air is the metaphysical glue and that things change as air is condensed or rarefied. Empedocles points to the four elemental roots that underlie all things, and he maintains that their mixing by Affection and separation by Strife yield change as people experience it. Anaxagoras explains that change is the result of the combining and disbanding of a great multiplicity of seeds, each in itself unchanging, each containing all characteristics. This blending and separation are the effects of motion that *Nous* initiates, bringing about manifested qualities of things as one type of seed becomes predominant in the mixture. Leucippus and Democritus believe that change occurs when compatible atoms cohere and occurs again when the collections break apart on impact with other atoms.

Whether it is water, air, roots, seeds, atoms, or some other substance, something allows an object, such as the maple, to change properties. In a metaphysical sense, the object holds together through its various states. The plant changes in many ways, but one can trace the adult tree to the seed from which it came and to the decaying stump and ashes that it eventually becomes. Its past and future seem to ride on the surface of something deep that is common to both and that makes the tree *this* tree. Although a satisfactory explanation of the relationship between the substratum and the qualities that it supports in a thing is lacking in these ancient accounts, each does attempt to show, at any rate, how it is that changes in properties take place.

There is, however, a more pressing difficulty here. Not all changes correspond to mere shifts in properties; some correspond to substitutions. In the case of the tree, one of its limbs may be severed and a limb from a different tree grafted in its place. Consider a more pronounced case of substitution: a lawnmower that, in the course of time, is exposed to extensive parts-replacement. After three months, the spark plug is exchanged for an aftermarket one. At the end of the first year, the broken handle and bolts securing it to the frame are replaced. The following mowing season, a new blade from a local repair shop is installed, the oil is changed, the air filter is replaced, and the tank, which was drained for winter, is filled. An unfortunate incident on the hillside cracks the frame; so, it has to be swapped for another frame. New all-purpose wheels and tires from the hardware store are purchased and mounted. When the engine fails and the crankshaft is bent following a battle with a root of a stubborn shrub, neither unit is found to be repairable. Another engine, complete with fresh carburetor, sits atop the machine now, along with a recently manufactured crankshaft. The end result of this continued process is that, after three years, *none* of the parts that were on the original device is still there. The thread that provides persistence for the tree—that it springs from a single source, a seed, and continues in some sense in the stump—does not apply here. There is no single point of origin for the three-year-old lawnmower. Even many of the parts that were installed came from different aftermarket manu-facturers and suppliers, and they were shipped from distribution centers in different states. This diagram depicts the changes:

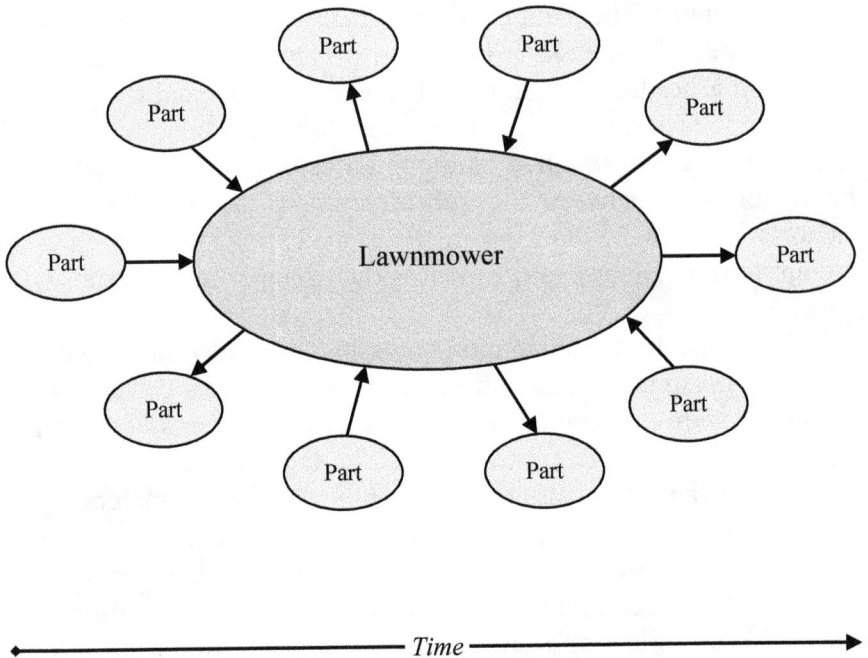

Figure 1.6

The lawnmower challenges one's sense of the identity of things. There is no common point of origin for the components that the machine comprises now, no anchor to secure the backward-traceable thread of its existence to some single beginning, as there is for the tree. There is no seed, as it were, from which the object that is presently at hand extends temporally. There is only a loosely conjoined set of parts, no one of which is an element of the set for the entire three-year duration of the machine.

The problem is, in this instance, a variant of the ancient Greek puzzle that is known as the ship of Theseus. In the puzzle, all the parts of a ship are replaced during a voyage, unsettling one's sense of sameness, as it is difficult to hold that the vessel that returns is the same ship as the one that departed. Later versions of the puzzle by philosophers introduce a new factor. Suppose that all the parts that were removed during the replacement process are used to construct a second ship. Now, which ship, if either, is the original one?

Here then is where many of the Presocratic positions concerning the rise of things from a common substrate begin to break down. Change in an object—one sort of change, at least—may lie not merely in the altering of properties but in the exchanging of parts as well; and all nonelemental physical things, by definition—including protons and neutrons—are composed of parts. So, even if a substratum might provide sameness through the former sort of change, it seems to be incapable of doing so through the latter sort. One could try to avoid the problem by saying that identity is maintained, despite the replacements, because all the parts issue from the same substrate, and it provides the continuity. If, however, one attributes the preservation of an object's identity, in the face of the exchange of parts, to the fact that the substrate that underlies the object and the parts is the same, then one would be forced to say that *everything* is the *same thing* because the one substrate underlies all physical reality. Lost completely is the individuation of objects, and, without individuation, there *are no* parts, which contradicts the initial supposition. None of the aforementioned accounts appears to be capable of explaining how identity is possible under such extreme conditions of alteration.[93] Two extraordinary, but conflicting, hypotheses are in place, ready to take on the problem: that of Heraclitus, who denies the reality of persistent identity; and that of his successor Parmenides, who denies the reality of change.

Reflect first on Parmenides, returning to the dilemma that he presents. Inherent in the dilemma is a principle in philosophy that lies at the bedrock of reason. Often given in its Latin form, the principle appears as the following statement:

---

[93] In fairness, I must note that present-day philosophy in general has fared little better with this problem.

Ex nihilo nihil fit.

What this key tenet asserts is that out of nothing, nothing comes—or, as it often is expressed, from nothing, nothing comes. It is important to understand the comprehensiveness of this tenet in the sense in which it is to be employed in any credible metaphysics. It is not the simple lack of some substantive existent that gives the rule its force but the consequence of such a lack. What the principle purports is tantamount to the assertion that there is no change from an absence of being. The nonexistent neither is nor does, and it cannot be the platform from which some difference develops—ever. The boundary between existence and nonexistence is a sharp one. It is the boundary between reality and nonreality because existence and reality are one and the same. Notwithstanding the atomists' perspective, that which exists, and indeed only that which exists, is real. In the nonexistent, there is no reality at all; a fortiori, there is no reality out of which something could come forth into existence, no opportunity for change to occur, no faculty to serve as the footing for an arising of any kind. There is only utter emptiness, a void in the strictest sense of the term, not in the sense in which the atomists employ it. Being is required for the begetting of being. Nonbeing cannot the basis for the begetting of anything. If the principle is correct, then not only is it true that nothing *does* come out of the nonexistent, but it is also true that nothing *can* do so, and it is this contention that constitutes the principle's quintessence.

The cosmos is an orderly system in which the things that populate it obey physical laws that govern their operations, laws that are so precise that mathematical equations can be applied to physical phenomena. By formula, the kinetic energy of a moving object equals half its mass times the square of its speed. In ballistics, one can calculate, using this formula, the kinetic energy of any projectile at any distance, provided that one knows the values of those two factors. No tenable system of physics or metaphysics describes a cosmos in which, barring the miraculous, a projectile appears spontaneously, out of nowhere, with no history, in the middle of a trajectory arc, complete with calculable kinetic energy. It is there because it has traversed the previous portion of its parabolic path, altered somewhat by air resistance, in accordance with the laws of motion. The cosmos as a whole is no less subject to orderliness than the things that lie in it and no less immune to the principle at hand; for, if the cosmos itself had a beginning, then it would be reasonable to hold that it too could have come to exist only if something already existed. It appears that Parmenides has this part right. Even Empedocles states the principle in his writings, declaring that generation from nonexistence is impossible.[94] Anaxagoras takes a comparable stance.[95] Finally, Aristotle emphasizes the truth of the maxim as well as its universal acceptance in saying,

> [E]verything that comes into being must arise either from what is or from what is not, and it is impossible for it to arise from what is not (on this point all the physicists agree).[96]

Despite the intuitively solid, logical force of the principle, some contemporary writers object to it on the grounds that, so they believe, things do pop into existence out of nothing. On what basis do they make such a claim, and what do they mean by the term 'nothing'? Do the cases that they present truly stand in violation of the principle? A full discussion of the thinking must await the appropriate time. Let it suffice for now to note that the question of the veracity of the tenet ex nihilo nihil fit is important. It will resurface as a pivotal issue, as the acceptance or rejection of the tenet comes with significant repercussions.

If one embraces this philosophical canon, then one is recognizing that existence is a precondition of coming to be; any such becoming requires that there be something already there. The Parmenidean dilemma, in contrast, takes the matter a step further. It contains this reasoning: There is no becoming; for anything that seems to come to be, *that* thing had to have existed prior to the apparent arising. It is not that some entity or entities must be in existence in advance; the entity itself must be in existence in advance. All change is purely an illusion. A much stronger stance, it is a troubling one. Parmenides moves from the position of his

---

[94] Refer to frag. 12 of Empedocles's writings; the quotation is above, p. 76.
[95] Refer to frag. 17 of Anaxagoras's writings; the quotation is above, p. 79.
[96] Aristotle, *Physics*, 1, 4.187a33–34, 224.

predecessors—namely, that something remains constant as things change—to the position that everything remains constant and that there is no change. In Parmenidean philosophy, change of any sort would be tantamount to penetrating the barrier between the real and the unreal. It is a barrier that logic declares to be, except in a special sense, impregnable.

Take the case of the lawnmower. As it is assembled at the factory, the parts are put together in a certain way, by design, to yield a functioning machine. The materials that make up those parts existed beforehand, but, until they were forged, molded, and stamped, they lacked the precision of structure that is required to build a working device. The lawnmower's raison d'être is the cutting of grass, which it cannot do until the pieces are joined in the proper configuration.

Parmenides would hold that there are no pieces. In fact, there is not even a lawnmower. The world of things is the world of mere appearance. The objects that people refer to in sensory perception are not real; they are illusions. Reality is indivisible, eternal, and immutable. It lies in the realm of thought.

Parmenides's philosophy leads to a predicament. Suppose that one stubs a toe on the aforesaid lawnmower while crossing the garage in search of a flashlight on a dark night when the power had failed. Parmenides, of course, would deny the reality not only of the machine but also of the foot that supposedly struck it. Few, however, with the occurrence of such an event, could accept that the lawnmower is illusory. Without seeing the contraption or thinking of it, one's mind is focused suddenly on the pain that stems from one's ostensible foot. If thought and reality are the same, as Parmenides claims, then surely thought itself includes all individual thoughts. So, the thought of the lawnmower that night—that particular thought—must be real. There is, however, no coming to be in his view. One wonders then where this thought has been if it did not arise that night in the garage. It was not in the mind of the one who kicked the machine, as it appeared abruptly along with the pain.

It seems to be far more acceptable to say that the thought did arise and that, by one of the fundamental principles that is inherent in Parmenides's own philosophy—out of nothing, nothing comes—it must have arisen out of something. Most persons would agree that, in fact, colliding with the machine lay in a succession of events that led to the thought.

My oversimplification hardly does justice to Parmenides's argument. He would hold that thought itself is whole and eternal, and speaking of individual thoughts of individual objects does not reflect the nature of the One. If, however, it is impossible to exit the mental world and still retain the mark of reality, then any explanation regarding the apparent, abrupt emergence of the idea of the lawnmower that night in the garage is bereft of substantive force. One needs the external world to explain the existence of human thinking—more accurately, some human thinking. Without it, one is left with an impoverished cosmos in which nothing *can* be explained, because there is nothing *to* explain. There is only the static One. Parmenides pays a high price to pose a solution to the problem of change and to bring order to existence.

The Eleatics deny even the reality of motion. This view cannot be reconciled either with the science of the celestial sphere or with that of the atomic sphere; neither astrophysics nor nuclear physics supports such a radical view. The Doppler shift in the light of distant stars proves that the great majority of galaxies are moving away from the Milky Way in a continuously expanding universe. Spiral galaxies themselves spin on their axes like cosmic pinwheels. Planets orbit stars that anchor them. Microcosms of planetary systems, atoms reveal a continuously moving particulate world where electrons buzz about nuclei, albeit not in the well-defined orbits that characterize celestial phenomena. String theory, as advanced by contemporary physicists, posits that particles of matter subsist in emanations from tiny strands. It is the very motion of those vibrating strands, borne out by the mathematics of the theory, that yields the quarks, electrons, and other bits that make up the world. Physics shows that not only is motion real, but, on the premise that string theory is right, motion is also essential to physical reality itself.

Parmenides has been criticized for introducing a fatal flaw in the concept of the immutable One. If being is static, and change is unreal, then it is necessary to give an explanation of how apparent change in the world has surfaced—to say from where this illusion has come. The philosopher can account for it only in terms of the finite human viewpoint. If there is a finite perspective, though, then it must coexist with the eternal One; thus, it is distinct from it. Reality is not unary, as Parmenides claims. This objection seems to present an insurmountable hurdle for him.

The more interesting view is that of Heraclitus. For him, change is ubiquitous and ongoing. Like his successor Parmenides, Heraclitus would declare that there is no lawnmower, persisting through time, but that declaration rests on completely different reasoning. It is Heraclitus's view that, because all is in constant flux, no object can continue, for nothing is the same thing at any two instants. The properties that one ascribes to a so-called thing are shifting moment by moment. The underlying assumption is that subsistence requires a thread of sameness. It is not difficult to see how this notion might be applied to the lawnmower example, where there is a recurring process of exchange of components, so that nothing of the original machine remains after a few years. It is not quite as straightforward in the case of the maple.

Still, even with the former example, there is ostensibly something that one calls a lawnmower, and its owner cuts grass with it. Can changing one part somehow undermine a thing's identity? If it could do so, then would Betty not have ceased to be herself when she had her first haircut and, whoever it was that she had become, the time thereafter? Saying just how much alteration, and just what sort of it, must happen before an object's identity dissipates is not so easy a puzzle to solve.

Change occurs at different rates. Some changes that one can observe directly appear to occur almost in an instant. A firecracker explodes; the lead in a mechanical pencil snaps when one writes with too much force; a camera flashes. Other changes occur more slowly. Organisms age, and glaciers move leisurely down mountains. Still others take decades, sometimes centuries, to see. The erosion of certain rock formations as they succumb to the effects of wind and water may not be observable in one lifetime. At whatever rate physical things change, however, it seems that change occurs and that it is inevitable. If Heraclitus is right, and flux is constant, then one reaches a state of bewilderment. Without something to hold things together metaphysically, there are no objects to be perceived, for, strictly speaking, there are no objects at all. There are only disjointed sets of instantaneous, property-laden slices.

The upshot of this discovery is both profound and disturbing. If no objects persist in the physical world, then there is nothing in the world about which one can have knowledge, for the mind cannot lay hold of things any more than the senses can do so. There is simply nothing for it to grasp. The question that I raised at the outset of this chapter resurfaces here: How can one know? A conundrum begins to form as a third problem emerges out of early Greek thought. It is a particularly disquieting one because, unlike its two predecessors, it is a puzzle that brings into doubt not only the objects in the world of the senses but also the subjects who sense them. It is *the problem of knowledge*.

Aristotle opens what is arguably his greatest work with this succinct statement: "All men by nature desire to know."[97] Atop the framework of the ancient philosophers' first principles sit the three pressing problems that I set forth in this section. There are, however, other matters that appear to lie deeper within. They are characterized by questions that bring division. Is all reality material, or is the immaterial just as real? Is the order of the cosmos the product of pure mechanism, or is it the handiwork of intentional activity? Perhaps addressing the immediate concerns will shed light on the others, for all seem to stem from common ground. Accordingly, I will delve next into the third problem in the trio, the problem of knowledge, and examine major attempts to solve it. Solving it is imperative, lest one have no understanding of the universe at all and, reminiscent of the blind man who drifted from his intended course at the intersection, no assuredness of direction—in this case, in the quest for truth. Unfortunately, efforts to gain freedom from its grip seem only to increase the perplexity.

---

[97] Aristotle, *Metaphysics*, A, 1.980a1, in *Works of Aristotle*, 689.

CHAPTER 2

EPISTEMOLOGICAL SYSTEMS

Though it cost all you have, get understanding.

—Prov. 4:7 NIV

One may be aware that the images that strike the human retina in vision are inverted and reversed; the pattern of light is altered as it passes through the cornea and lens in the front of the eye. The brain processes this visual information in such a way that the interpretation of the light energy that reaches the retina produces a perception that corresponds to the world. Things are upright, correlating with tactile and auditory sensations. What one seems to see, for example, in the upper right quadrant of the visual field is in harmony with what that person touches there and with the sounds coming from that location.

In the late nineteenth century, George M. Stratton, a professor at the University of California, conducted an interesting set of experiments on vision. Stratton wanted to learn whether inverted retinal images are necessary for people to see the world as upright. The professor developed an apparatus consisting of a pair of tubes containing biconvex (double-convex) lenses. The contrivance rotated the pattern of light passing through each tube 180° around its axis. As he looked through this device, it made things appear to be upside down and backward by causing the images that were presented to his retinae to be just the opposite: right side up and nonreversed. Stratton decided to limit the use of his invention to his right eye, keeping the tube for the other eye covered, as he found that it was too difficult to achieve convergence by allowing light to reach both eyes. As he gazed at his surroundings, the actual images that were striking his retina then were upright. The images were, in a manner of speaking, analogues of the real world. What he saw, however, was turned on its head. Things were misarranged. The scene on the street below him, the contents of his room, and even his own hands and feet—all looked upside down and reversed relative to their normal positions.

Stratton wore the contraption in the first experiment for more than twenty-one hours. In another trial, he wore it for eight days. Something strange happened in the course of the experiments. On occasion, Stratton reported that "everything was right side up."[1] What had looked upside down to him at first came to look normal at times. He concluded that the inversion of retinal images is not required for humans to see the world in the way in which they do see it.

In the century that followed Stratton's groundbreaking work, others performed similar experiments. Some thought that his findings were overstated.[2] An experiment with monkeys, however, which wore inverting prismatic glasses for months, produced results that suggested a large-scale reorganization of their visual cortices.[3]

Regardless of the degree to which the world appears to return to normal for one who wears inverting lenses for an extended period, what the experiment does is to underscore the point, which Democritus made twenty-three centuries earlier, that people are severed from reality.[4] What they see in the sense of the light that strikes their retinae, creating visual impressions, does not reflect the world as it is. The images are inverted; they do not correspond to reality as humans have come to believe it to be. One must ask then what has led people to form sets of beliefs about reality that are solid and enduring and that their experiences seem to support.

Clearly, any one belief about the world can be questioned. Often, one discovers one's own errors. For instance, as Jack drew

---

[1] George M. Stratton, "Vision without Inversion of the Retinal Image," *Psychological Review* 4, no. 5 (1897): 469.

[2] For an extensive analysis of the reversing-lenses experiment with a conclusion that is contrary to Stratton's, see Hubert Dolezal, *Living in a World Transformed: Perceptual and Performatory Adaptation to Visual Distortion* (New York: Academic Press, 1982).

[3] See Yoichi Sugita, "Global Plasticity in Adult Visual Cortex Following Reversal of Visual Input," *Nature* 380, no. 6574 (1996): 523–26.

[4] Immanuel Kant, a philosopher of the modern period, draws a distinction between things that people experience through sensory perception and things as they in themselves actually are. He claims that people cannot know things of the latter sort. Although they underlie appearances, they are removed from people; they are outside human contact. The influence of Democritus on philosophers that succeeded him is evident.

closer to the car, he realized that it was Amy, not April, who was behind the wheel. When Jill listened further, she found that she was mistaken: A cornet was playing the solo rather than a trumpet. If any given belief about the physical world can be wrong, though, then, so one would think, they all might be wrong. In perception, the following argument appears—initially, at least—to be applicable:

> It is always possible that one is wrong.
> Therefore, it is possible that one is always wrong.

People's intuitions tell them that, to know, they must be sure— absolutely sure. This need for certainty appears to lie at the very base of the concept of knowledge. If the abovestated reasoning is correct, however, then how can a person ever be sure? If one cannot be sure, then is knowledge even possible?

It seems that, if one is to know anything about the world, then there must be a firm link between the perceived and the perceiver, between the object of sense perception and the sentient subject. In the previous chapter, I demonstrated how Heraclitean flux, by generating uncertainties about the ontic integrity of things, brought a challenge to the notion that knowledge is obtainable: How is it that physical entities, which undergo constant change, hold together in such a way that there is a single thing to which one refers in language and that can be the object of knowledge? Philosophers came to realize that the world of corporeal objects—those things of which persons become aware through their senses—must be grounded in some fashion. If the properties of things are changing continually, then things ostensibly do not possess the solidity of being that is necessary for knowledge of them to be possible. Said differently, if the strong view of Heraclitus is right, then no substantive being is associated with any given sensory perception—there is no object of knowledge, for there is no genuine object at all.

As if Heraclitean flux were not disquieting enough, the possibility of error in perception brings a daunting challenge to knowledge from a markedly different angle. It raises concerns about the perceptual link itself and about the subjects who would come to know things by means of that link. If people are detached from physical reality, connected to it only through sensory impressions, then there seems to be no way for them to confirm the legitimacy of what their senses are telling them. People cannot step back and look around those impressions to see whether what appears is real or illusory, as every instance of looking is limited to what the senses themselves convey. Humans never can bypass their perceptions to observe things independently of those perceptions. Is it possible then for persons to be wrong—indeed, always wrong—about what they see, hear, and touch? If such is the case, then the consequence is that humans' ability to know the world around them slips from their grasp. By pointing to the dubious authenticity of the connection to the physical world in perceiving, emphasizing the accompanying lack of certainty for the perceivers, the argument presents a serious obstacle to knowing.

The problem of knowledge thus appears to cast doubts on both the things that would serve as the *objects* of knowing and the *subjects* who would know them or something about them. This two-faceted problem confronts anyone who would put forward an epistemological theory, and it is not one to be taken lightly. The following diagram illustrates the difficulty, in which each side of the perception event is called into question:

THE PROBLEM OF KNOWLEDGE

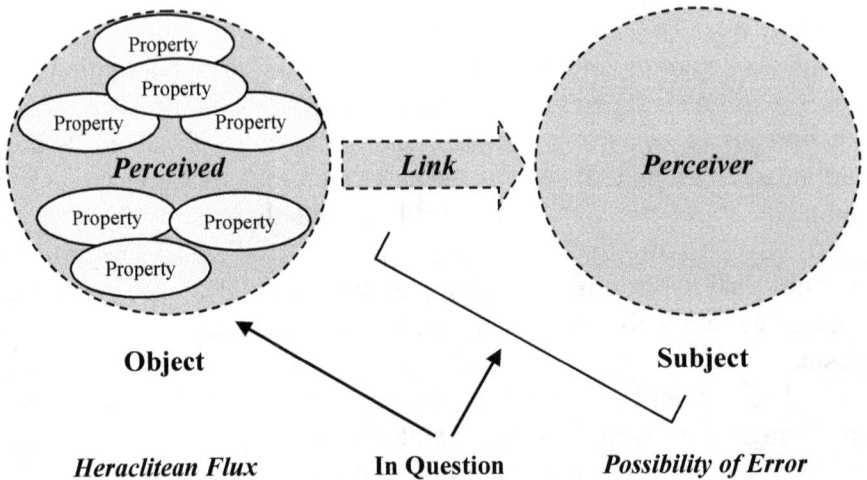

Figure 2.1

There have been numerous attempts by philosophers through the years to take hold of this perplexing matter. In this chapter, I will focus on three principal ones. Each represents an effort by a major historical figure to build a system whereby knowledge can be preserved. It is not practical to provide a comprehensive account of all aspects of these systems, or philosophical constructs, but I will try to bring forth the core notions with a measure of clarity. Albeit these constructs span many centuries, they grapple with a common foe.

PLATO

One of the world's most accomplished theorists, Plato was born in Athens or Aegina in 428 or 427 B.C., although estimates of the date of his birth vary slightly. His actual name, so it is thought, is

'Aristocles'; the term 'Plato' is a name or nickname that was given to him at some point in his life, and it means 'Broad' or 'Broady'.[5] Three possible reasons for the name are that he had a broad forehead, a broad upper body (chest and shoulders), or a broad perspective. His family was part of the Athenian aristocracy. The family lost influence, however, after supporting a political cause that failed. It is likely that Plato saw military service as a young man, fighting just before the end of the fifth century B.C. in the Peloponnesian War against the Spartan-led alliance. Plato witnessed the execution in 399 B.C. of Socrates, his friend and noted mentor, an alleged crime of whose was corrupting the youth of Athens with his philosophical discourse. Plato's account of the incident is heartrending. A learned scholar, Plato spent time in reflection, writing, teaching, and travel. He never married. Plato died in 348 or 347 B.C.

Plato founded the Academy in Athens, a school that was devoted to the study of mathematics, astronomy, physical science, and philosophy. The date of its establishment traditionally is set at 388 or 387 B.C., but evidence for these years is thin, and some scholars believe the founding of the school to be later. Students came to the Academy from Athens; however, the majority of the well-known individuals joined the school from other areas. The Academy existed for three hundred years before disbanding, but it was reinstituted later and persisted until its ultimate termination in the sixth century A.D. Plato's most renowned student, Aristotle—who is credited with, among other things, the development of formal logic—entered the Academy in 367 B.C. Following the completion of his studies, Aristotle continued his association with the institution for a period of time as a teacher. Aristotle lived from 384 to 322 B.C.

A prolific writer, Plato produced a considerable amount of intricate philosophical material, which, in the main, he presents in dialogue format. The authorship of a few of the dialogues has been challenged, but the standard position is that almost thirty of them are authentic, and additional ones may be attributable to Plato as well. In a number of these creations, Plato's thoughts are set forth as a discussion between his distinguished mentor, Socrates, and some

---

[5] The report about Plato's name comes from Diogenes Laërtius, although its truth is in question.

other figure. Often, Plato focuses on a question of the form 'What is Φ?' In the various discourses, Φ is something of which Plato wishes to uncover the essence. Included are such concepts as those of justice, temperance, beauty, courage, and virtue. Plato's ideas about knowledge proper emerge primarily in the *Theaetetus* and the *Republic*, although a discussion of the subject surfaces elsewhere in his writings.[6] The former dialogue is a treatise concerning what knowledge is not; it represents Plato's negative epistemological account. The latter work, which Plato composed before the *Theaetetus*, details his view regarding what knowledge is, representing his positive account. A key writing, the *Theaetetus* is a discussion between Socrates and a student of mathematics for whom the dialogue is named.[7] Depicted here in his youth, Theaetetus is a Greek mathematician, noted for his work with irrational numbers. In the dialogue, Theodorus, who is Theaetetus's teacher, introduces his student to the elder Socrates and instructs him to answer the philosopher's questions. In the typical Platonic fashion, Socrates begins by asking the young man what knowledge—the Φ in this dialogue—is. Again, in the typical fashion, the student responds by giving examples of the objects of knowledge. Socrates corrects the student, for the question is not what the objects of knowledge are, but what knowledge itself is. Here is a passage from the dialogue:

> SOCRATES: You hear what Theodorus says, Theaetetus. I do not think you will want to disobey him, and it would be wrong for you not to do what an older and wiser man bids you. So tell me, in a generous spirit, what you think knowledge is.
> THEAETETUS: Well, Socrates, I cannot refuse, since you and Theodorus ask me. Anyhow, if I do make a mistake, you will set me right.

---

[6] The dialogue *Meno*, for example, contains a discussion concerning knowledge, as does the *Sophist*. Other dialogues, including the *Cratylus* and *Timaeus*, also put forth applicable points.

[7] Scholars of ancient philosophy divide Plato's dialogues into three main categories based on the period of his life in which they were written: early, middle, and late. Disagreement about the timing of certain ones exists, but there is a general consensus with respect to the groups into which most of them fall. Plato penned the *Theaetetus* in the latter part of the middle period, or else the late period, of his life.

SOCRATES: By all means, if we can.

THEAETETUS: Then I think the things one can learn from Theodorus are knowledge—geometry and all the sciences you mentioned just now, and then there are the crafts of the cobbler and other workmen. Each and all of these are knowledge and nothing else.

SOCRATES: You are generous indeed, my dear Theaetetus—so openhanded that, when you are asked for one simple thing, you offer a whole variety.

THEAETETUS: What do you mean, Socrates?

SOCRATES: There may be nothing in it, but I will explain what my notion is. When you speak of cobbling, you mean by that word precisely a knowledge of shoemaking?

THEAETETUS: Precisely.

SOCRATES: And when you speak of carpentry, you mean just a knowledge of how to make wooden furniture?

THEAETETUS: Yes.

SOCRATES: In both cases, then, you are defining what the craft is a knowledge of.

THEAETETUS: Yes.

SOCRATES: But the question you were asked, Theaetetus, was not, what are the objects of knowledge, nor yet how many sorts of knowledge there are. We did not want to count them, but to find out what the thing itself—knowledge—is. Is there nothing in that?

THEAETETUS: No, you are quite right.[8]

Socrates is leading Theaetetus to define knowledge, to say what it is at the core. To understand the legitimacy or illegitimacy of the definitions that the young mathematician tenders as the dialogue progresses, one must understand what Plato sees as the standards that knowledge is required to meet. The concepts that Plato raises in the *Theaetetus* are central to his theory; it is appropriate to begin the investigation there.

---

[8] Plato, *Theaetetus*, 146b–e, trans. F. M. Cornford, in *The Collected Dialogues of Plato, Including the Letters*, trans. Lane Cooper et al., ed. Edith Hamilton and Huntington Cairns (1961; Princeton: Princeton University Press, 1971), 851.

THE CRITERIA AND THE DEFINITIONS

Plato believes that there are two essential principles to which any candidate for knowledge must adhere. Stated below, they are absolute maxims:

1. Knowledge is infallible.
2. Knowledge is of what is.

If one can be wrong about the putative object of knowledge, then one does not know, as knowledge requires certainty. Further, the object of knowledge must *be*; that is to say, it must be locked in ontic stasis. It cannot be undergoing change, for then one cannot know, as the would-be object is shifting even while one's belief about it is forming or while one is in the process of making some assertion about its properties.

In the dialogue, Plato's pursuits lead him to explore three possible characterizations. The standards that he sets forth—the aforestated principles—are especially applicable to the first of them.

PERCEPTION: THE PROTAGOREAN-HERACLITEAN SCHEMA

Theaetetus's initial attempt at a definition of knowledge, following his original confusion of knowledge with its objects—a mistake that Socrates corrects promptly—is to suppose that "knowledge is nothing but perception."[9] Through the character of Socrates, Plato proceeds to examine this proposed definition to see whether it satisfies the pair of criteria that he lays out in his philosophy. In doing so, he moves through a fairly elaborate discourse that covers a number of points. I will condense the discussion to the main components and order them for clarity.[10]

---

[9] Ibid., 151e, 856.

[10] In this section, I will draw on, with some elucidation, the analysis of the dialogue in Francis Macdonald Cornford, *Plato's Theory of Knowledge: The Theaetetus and the Sophist of Plato Translated with a Running Commentary* (1935; London: Routledge and Kegan Paul, 1949).

Two philosophical dicta converge in Theaetetus's definition of knowledge, thinks Socrates. The first is that of the philosopher Protagoras (c. 490–c. 421 B.C.). Protagoras, who is deceased by the time of the discourse, belongs to a group of thinkers who are known as sophists. These men traveled from place to place teaching rhetoric for a fee. Protagoras's most recognized statement is voiced in the *Theaetetus*, where Socrates quotes him as saying, " '[M]an is the measure of all things—alike of the being of things that are and of the not-being of things that are not.' "[11] In effect, Protagoras is claiming that whatever seems to a person to be the case is, in fact, the case. Examining the apparent relativism that is at the heart of the Protagorean doctrine, Socrates attempts at first to offer support for the late sophist's view in the interest of investigation. The same wind may feel cold to one person but not cold, or less cold, to another. The Protagorean stance is that it *is* cold to one and *not* cold to the other, for the wind *is* to a person just as it *appears* to that person to be. How can one explain this supposed state of affairs?

In terms of perception as it is discussed in the dialogue, there are two ways to view the phenomenon. The first way is to see the wind in itself as both cold and not cold; the property of coldness affects a given percipient, while the opposite property affects another. The second way is to see the wind in itself as neither cold nor not cold but instead taking on one property or the other when it is sensed: when the perceived object—the wind—meets the perceiving subject—the person or, more accurately, the sensory apparatus of the person. It is likely that the actual view of Protagoras is the former one.[12] Plato moves forward through the character Socrates, however,

---

[11] Plato, *Theaetetus*, 152a, 856.

[12] Cornford takes this position in *Plato's Theory of Knowledge*, 33–36. Logically, of course, it is not possible for the same thing both to exhibit and not to exhibit a given property simultaneously or, as expressed here, exhibit a property and its contrary. One might say that a car's trunk is cold, but its engine is warm and therefore not cold; or that the windshield is transparent, but the tires are opaque and therefore not transparent. It is clear that one is not referring to the same thing in each pair of assertions. Although the parts are parts of the same car, they are not the car itself, and the references in the statements concern the parts, not the whole. So, the car is not in an inconsistent state, exhibiting a property while failing to exhibit it in violation of logic. Further, if a property can apply meaningfully at all to a category of things, then either a thing of that kind has the property at a given

on the premise that the latter view reflects the Protagorean doctrine. Then, coldness is not a quality of the wind per se; it is not *in* the wind but rather how the wind appears to a person to be, and appearing-to and perceiving are the same thing, notes Socrates. Given that appearances are to each person just as the person senses them to be and that one cannot be mistaken, so it seems, about the appearances of things that one experiences, defining knowledge to be sense perception is on good footing at this juncture, satisfying the Platonic criterion of infallibility. The question, however, is whether appearances *are* at all.

Plato continues in the analysis to the second dictum that aligns with Theaetetus's definition—the Heraclitean doctrine that all things are in a state of flux. According to that view, there are no persistent, substantive things. A fortiori, there are no persistent substantive things to which one can refer. Instead, for the observer, there are constantly changing streams of appearances as things continually undergo alterations in properties. Consider this passage from the dialogue:

> SOCRATES: . . . All the things we are pleased to say 'are,' really are in process of becoming, as a result of movement and change and of blending one with another. We are wrong to speak of them as 'being,' for none of them ever is; they are always becoming.[13]

The objects in the world that the senses detect are transient; they are not fixed. These objects, however, are the very things that people perceive when they observe what lies around them. Thus, perception is not of what is, thinks Plato, but of what is in the process of becoming. Further, if Heraclitus is right, then not only are the objects of perception in flux, but the sensory organs of the perceiver are in flux as well. The consequence is that the Protagorean position that the appearances that a man experiences *are* for him is to be rendered

---

time, or it does not have it. The only way that both cold and warm (not cold) can apply to the same wind is with reference not to the thermal condition of a certain volume of air but to the subjective interpretation of the thermal condition by different individuals. In that case, though, the attribution is not applied to the wind itself.
[13] Plato, *Theaetetus*, 152d, 857.

as the appearances that a man experiences *become* for him, as those appearances vary with each passing moment.

Plato believes that perception is given in the interplay between the two elements that have a role in it: a constantly shifting object acting on a constantly shifting subject. The objects of sense, so goes the thinking, have no solid, enduring, independent qualities intrinsically. Apart from the percipient, they are neither cold nor not cold, white nor not white, loud nor not loud. Yet, without them, the subject has no sensations. The qualities that these objects possess, or seem to possess, are dependent on the interchange between the perceived and the perceiver. Plato proceeds to argue that this interdependence shows that, in perception, neither the object of sense nor the subject of sense can exist without its counterpart: "For there is no such thing as an agent until it meets with a patient, nor any patient until it meets with its agent."[14] The two sides of a perceptual incident—object and subject—are joined in an inextricable manner. Having put forth a theory of the mechanics of perception in the dialogue, Socrates elicits agreement from Theaetetus that this rendition aligns with the young student's notion of perception as it is employed in his definition of knowledge.

In the Platonic line of thought, flux guarantees that each perception is unique. An appearance arises for an observer, and only for that observer, at the instant of perception, and it vanishes at the next instant. Therefore, no person can have the very same sensory experience at two different times, nor can two persons have the same sensory experience at any one time. Whenever perception takes place, there must be something that is perceived and someone who perceives it, and the two are coupled only for the moment. This singularity adds weight to the idea, already in play, that perceptions cannot fail to be correct. One cannot contest how something appears to oneself to be in a perceptual event, and no one can contest another's perceptions. In sensory experience, what one seems to perceive, one does perceive.

Following the explication of the Protagorean and Heraclitean concepts that underlie the proposal that knowledge is perception, Plato launches his criticism. Directing his attention to the ancient

---

[14] Ibid., 157a, 862. The term 'agent' here refers to an active element, not a person.

sophist's man-is-the-measure axiom and the Theaetetean definition of knowledge that draws on it, he interleaves his comments about them. If knowing is perceiving, and every man is the best judge of his own perceptions, then no man is wiser than another. How is it then that Protagoras could justify teaching others and charging a substantial fee to do so, and wherein could one's comparative ignorance exist, such that it would make one sit at his feet to learn?

Further, if sensation and knowledge are equivalent, then there is a problem with past perceptions. The cessation of sensation eliminates knowledge that is given in memory; because of this fact, it eliminates perception as a candidate. No longer seeing something would be tantamount to no longer knowing it.

> SOCRATES: But suppose this man who sees and acquires knowledge of what he has seen, shuts his eyes; then he remembers the thing, but does not see it. Isn't that so?
>
> THEAETETUS: Yes.
>
> SOCRATES: But 'does not see it' means 'does not know it,' since 'sees' and 'knows' mean the same.
>
> THEAETETUS: True.
>
> SOCRATES: Then the conclusion is that a man who has come to know a thing and still remembers it does not know it, since he does not see it, and we said that would be a monstrous conclusion.
>
> THEAETETUS: Quite true.
>
> SOCRATES: Apparently, then, if you say that knowledge and perception are the same thing, it leads to an impossibility.
>
> THEAETETUS: So it seems.
>
> SOCRATES: Then we shall have to say they are different.[15]

To qualify as knowledge, perception must be expanded to cover images of previous sensations that are retained in the memory.

The most damaging problem that the Protagorean doctrine faces surfaces now. It is not perception but judgment that sounds the death toll. Plato argues that the Protagorean doctrine is self-refuting.

---

[15] Ibid., 164a–b, 869–70.

Extending it to beliefs in general—beyond just those arising from sense perception, where one cannot be mistaken about how things appear to be—results in an obvious contradiction: If Protagoras's axiom is true, then anyone who believes that Protagoras's axiom is false is right.

> SOCRATES: . . . Protagoras, for his part, admitting as he does that everybody's opinion is true, must acknowledge the truth of his opponents' belief about his own belief, where they think he is wrong.
> THEODORUS: Certainly.
> SOCRATES: That is to say, he would acknowledge his own belief to be false, if he admits that the belief of those who think him wrong is true?
> THEODORUS: Necessarily.[16]

As past perceptions present a challenge for Theaetetus's definition, judgments about future perceptions present a problem for Protagoras's doctrine. Plato argues through the character of Socrates in the dialogue that an expert can predict better than a layman what sensations will take place. Socrates gives a few examples to support the position. A doctor, he claims, may know that a person will not catch a fever and therefore will not have the accompanying sensation of heat, even though the layman demurs. Both cannot be right about the same future happening; the person either will have the given sensation or will not have it, and the doctor's judgment about another individual's coming sensory experience will prove to prevail in the face of the disagreement. Again, a vine-grower's judgment is more authoritative than a flute-player's with regard to the taste of the wine that will be produced from the grapes. A musician, Socrates continues, is in a better position than a gymnastic trainer to judge whether the trainer will perceive a piece of music, yet to be played, to be in tune. Once more, the chef's opinion about the sensations that will accompany a forthcoming meal, the philosopher argues, outweighs the belief of an attending guest who is inexperienced in cookery. On the premise that the Protagorean doctrine holds, they all are on equal ground. Contrary to the sophist's principle thus, not all opinions can

---

[16] Ibid., 171a–b, 876–77.

be true. Therefore, whereas the Protagorean maxim that man is the measure of all things may apply to all perceptions, it does not apply to all things, for it fails when extended to judgments.

It is interesting to note that a percipient need not be an expert to anticipate what sensations will occur. In fact, the percipient need not be even human. I recall a story that a relative told me about a dog that had encountered an electric fence, perhaps several times, in its past. Despite the discomfort of the shock that the fence administered, the dog, on a particular occasion, ran headlong toward the wire; apparently, the pasture on the other side was sufficiently appealing. As the creature approached the barrier, it began yelping. It seems that the dog was aware before it ever touched the wire of what sensations it was about to experience, and contact brought confirmation—a rather straightforward example of associated learning.

Plato focuses next on the Heraclitean doctrine of relentless flux. For there to be knowledge, there must be true statements, but the sureness of propositions about the things in the world is limited to an instant because those things are in a state of ongoing change. Moreover, if there is to be knowledge, then there must be stability in the meanings of words; otherwise, language is undermined. If the denotations of terms constantly shift, then the propositions that incorporate them do not put forth the same assertions from one moment to the next. Knowledge cannot be founded on such continual variability of meaning, for then even what the word 'knowledge' signifies would be fluctuating unpredictably and unendingly, along with statements that employ it. Therefore, whereas the maxim that all things are in a state of flux may apply to all sensory objects, it cannot apply to all things, for it fails when extended to language.

Finally, returning to Theaetetus's original claim, Plato proceeds to show that perception fails as a candidate for knowledge because what one knows lies beyond raw sensation. Judgments concerning concepts that apply across a range of things—existence and nonexistence, sameness and difference, unity and plurality, similarity and dissimilarity, odd and even, and so forth—come about only through thought. One may see a pair of objects in one's visual field, for example, but comprehending that they are similar in some respect and different in another requires a mind to compare and contrast them. The senses may provide the basic material of experience, but a person cannot gain an understanding involving any of the afore-mentioned notions through perception alone. One cannot obtain knowledge unless one can reach truth, and one cannot reach truth unless one can apprehend the existence of things. Doing so is a cognitive operation.

> SOCRATES: Is it possible, then, to reach truth when one cannot reach existence?
>
> THEAETETUS: It is impossible.
>
> SOCRATES: But if a man cannot reach the truth of a thing, can he possibly know that thing?
>
> THEAETETUS: No, Socrates. How could he?
>
> SOCRATES: If that is so, knowledge does not reside in the impressions, but in our reflection upon them. It is there, seemingly, and not in the impressions, that it is possible to grasp existence and truth.[17]

The limitations of perception disqualify it as a contender for knowledge.

So ends the refutation of Theaetetus's first definition. On the surface, perception as such seems to meet Plato's criterion of infallibility, but it fails to meet his criterion of being. It is the second point that is the crucial, underlying matter for Plato in the analysis, a matter that unfolds more explicitly elsewhere in his dialogues. The objects of sense are not the proper objects of knowledge at all, believes Plato, because knowledge must be of what is, and the objects of sense never are. They are caught in the Heraclitean stream of unremitting change and lack the necessary ontic stability. The Socratic denial of the accuracy of Theaetetus's definition in the dialogue dovetails with the Platonic theory about the authentic objects of knowledge, ones that *do* possess the requisite constancy.

---

[17] Ibid., 186c–d, 891.

PERCEPTION REVISITED: THE SENSE-DATUM SCHEMA

Reminiscent of Plato's *Theaetetus* and his principle of infallibility, a near-parallel philosophy of perception, known as the sense-datum theory, developed in the twentieth century.[18] The theory postulates the existence of sense-data associated with all appearances. In illusions, mirages, and reflections, the theorists note, one does not see objects as they are in reality. As a result of refraction, for example, a straight stick that is immersed in water looks as though it were bent. One does see something, however. What one sees therefore must be distinct from the physical object. Further, in normal cases of perception, where no illusion is involved, the appearances of objects vary with the circumstances. A dinner plate appears to be round if it is viewed from directly above its flat surface, but its appearance is elliptical when it is viewed from an oblique angle. The properties of material objects, though, are independent of the conditions under which they are observed.[19] Thus, what one perceives in gazing at the plate is, as before, something apart from the article in the environment.

In both types of cases, say the theorists, one is seeing sense-data; and, although a person can be wrong about a thing's properties when observing it, the person cannot be wrong about how a thing *looks* to him or her. A book, which appears to an observer to be blue, may not be that color in actuality. The fact that it looks blue to that observer, however, is not something about which the individual can be mistaken, according to the sense-datum theory. Appearances are incorrigible; they are susceptible neither to change nor to error. The

---

[18] A major proponent of sense-data is Alfred J. Ayer (1910–1989). For a discussion of the theory, consult his *The Foundations of Empirical Knowledge* (1940; repr., London: Macmillan and Co., 1958); and *The Problem of Knowledge* (London: Macmillan and Co., 1956). Other key supporters include Bertrand Russell, G. E. Moore, and C. D. Broad.

[19] This principle seems to apply to the world of macrophysical things well enough, where those things exhibit certain properties, regardless of any perceptual awareness on the part of sentient beings or the lack of such awareness. In the quantum realm, though, according to the standard view of contemporary physics, the act of observing a particle affects its state. Whether the state of a microphysical bit counts as a property of it, however, requires further investigation, which must await a suitable time.

important point from a philosophical perspective is that, by virtue of this putative certitude in perception, one may view sense-data as laying the foundation for knowledge, for the supposed incontrovertibility of sense-data seems to satisfy the Platonic dictate that, in knowing, one cannot be wrong.

The sense-datum theory has been attacked on a number of fronts by a number of philosophers. Gilbert Ryle argues that the theory leads to an infinite regress.[20] The proponents hold that having a visual sensation of something, say, a horse race, is explained in terms of having a glimpse of something else—namely, an appearance: a patchwork of colors associated with the horse race. This collage of colors, or each collage in a series of them, is a sense-datum. If, however, having a glimpse of a horse race requires having at least one sensation, then so too must having a glimpse of a patchwork of colors, generating yet another sense-datum to account for glimpsing the first one. Once this generation occurs, the process will continue ad infinitum, and the sense-datum theory is left powerless to explain perception because it never can get under way. Contrary to the theory, says Ryle, to say that a plate looks elliptical is not to draw on an extra object—namely, a look—that is actually elliptical. It is instead to compare tilted, round plates to nontilted, elliptical ones.[21]

Anther opponent is Roderick M. Chisholm (1916–1999). Chisholm points out that it is through faulty reasoning that the sense-datum theorists postulate the existence of appearances. One cannot conclude from the fact that something appears to be a certain way that something *is* that way. If a man catches sight of a boat, for instance, then one can infer that the boat looks a certain way to him, which, says Chisholm, is equivalent to saying that the boat presents him with an appearance. It is illogical to conclude from this fact, however, that the man sees an appearance. Chisholm believes that this sort of thinking constitutes what he refers to as the sense-datum fallacy. The problem does not end there. Once this fallacy is committed, the next step is to conclude that the man does not see a

---

[20] One will recall from chap. 1 that the infinite regress is raised by Zeno in his attack on the pluralists.

[21] See Ryle's arguments in *The Concept of Mind* (New York: Barnes and Noble Books, 1949), 210–22.

boat. The entire theory, alleges the author, rests on an improper inference.[22]

There are other problems with the theory. It violates the law, or principle, of parsimony, a practical scientific and philosophical tenet that dictates that entities should not be multiplied beyond necessity.[23] Given two theories, both of which explain some set of phenomena adequately, the simpler is to be preferred. The historically important discovery by Johannes Kepler (1571–1630) of the elliptical planetary orbits is a case in point. For centuries, it had been assumed that the heavenly bodies traveled perfectly circular paths, a notion stemming from the Aristotelian model (following Plato) of uniform circular motion. Like the operating of a cosmic clock, celestial objects moved across the sky affixed to giant, turning spheres—an early Greek thesis that Aristotle accepted. It was apparent, however, that the movements of the planets could not be explained easily based solely on bare, round orbits. Particularly problematic was their retrograde motion, seemingly reversing their courses at times. To account for the facts and to maintain a geocentric universe, Claudius Ptolemaeus, or Ptolemy (c. A.D. 85–c. 165), drew on the work of the astronomer Hipparchus to offer a solution that represented observational data with appreciable accuracy.[24] In addition to other special elements, the Ptolemaic system employed epicycles—circles on larger circles around which the planets traveled—adhering to Aristotelian thought concerning the circularity of motion but in few other ways. Nicolaus Copernicus (1473–1543) rightly put the sun at the center of the planetary grouping (an idea that actually arose in the third century B.C.), departing from the prevailing Ptolemaic geocentric structure. Kepler

---

[22] Chisholm's argument appears in *Perceiving: A Philosophical Study* (1957; Ithaca: Cornell University Press, 1969). See chaps. 8 and 10. The description of the sense-datum fallacy is on pp. 151–52 of Chisholm's book.

[23] This tenet frequently is referred to as Ockham's razor, after William of Ockham (c. 1285–c. 1349), who applied it in his writings, although the verbiage of this often-cited rendition of the principle, which I will treat as a law, is not found in the extant texts. The law can expand to include a range of elements on which a theory might draw: causes, events, distinct types of phenomena (in the broadest sense of the term 'phenomena'—it is the sense that I adopt in this work), number of assumptions, and so forth. The key notion, though, is that of simplicity, albeit what counts as simple is a study unto itself. 'Ockham' is spelled 'Occam' in some cases.

[24] Some hold that Ptolemy lived several years later.

was the one, though, who eliminated the circular paths in favor of a simpler system of elliptical orbits that accounted for the perceived astronomical movements.

The sense-datum theory holds that appearances exist and that there is one corresponding to each sensory phenomenon. Given that there are potentially many such appearances associated with an object, the theory generates numerous entities in an attempt to account for perception. A penny that is rotated on a transverse axis through the center of its rim presents an indeterminate, if not infinite, number of appearances to a viewer as an ellipse shrinks to a thin rectangle when the penny is viewed from the side, then enlarges to form a circle when it is viewed perpendicularly to the wide surface. Rather than seeing many distinct appearances that correspond to a single object, the law of parsimony would favor seeing a single object, the appearance of which differs under different conditions. This simpler account explains the facts but does not generate entities.

J. L. Austin (1911–1960) raises one of the most damaging arguments against the sense-datum theory. It is destructive not primarily because it shows that the theory fails but because it attacks the incorrigibility that lies at its base. It is this foundational characteristic that had held promise for the building of a system of empirical knowledge. Austin argues that descriptions of looks are not incorrigible; one may retract a claim about them.

> But certainly someone might say, 'It looks heliotrope', and then have doubts *either* as to whether 'heliotrope' is right for the colour this thing looks, *or* (taking another look) as to whether this thing really looks heliotrope. There is certainly nothing *in principle* final, conclusive, irrefutable about anyone's statement that so-and-so looks such-and-such. And even if I say, '. . . looks . . . *to me now*', I may, on being pressed, or after looking at the thing more attentively, wish to retract my statement or at least amend it. To rule out other people and other times is not to rule out uncertainty altogether, or *every* possibility of being challenged and perhaps proved wrong.[25]

[25] J. L. Austin, *Sense and Sensibilia* (1962; repr., London: Oxford University Press, 1970), 42–43.

Without incorrigibility, doubt enters. Where there is doubt, Plato's principle of certainty cannot apply and, so goes the thinking, there can be no knowledge. Austin's approach, however, is to deny that knowledge demands certainty. Plato's requirement, in this view, is too stringent; instead, Austin draws a parallel between knowing and promising.[26] A man may say that he knows something, and it may be discovered later that he was wrong—he actually did not know—just as a man may promise to do something and then fail to do it. The fact that it is possible for one to be wrong is no bar to saying, "I know," any more than the fact that it is possible that one will break one's pledge is a bar to saying, "I promise." One may be justified in saying that one knows or that one promises, asserts Austin, if that individual is in a position to do so, despite the fact that things may turn out contrariwise. Austin thinks that both expressions are performative in character: The individual uttering them is performing an act of guaranteeing.

If one clings to the position that people perceive appearances and not objects—a perspective that is discussed in the *Theaetetus* and reflected in the latter-day counterpart, the sense-datum theory—then an issue that is even more troublesome than those that Plato puts forward comes to the surface. It is the detachment from the physical world that such a position creates. To state that sensations are how they seem to be may provide the infallibility that Plato's epistemology dictates, setting aside Austin's point, but, whether such statements are true, they are, at best, trivial. To say that the book looks blue to a subject, on the premise that the sense-datum theorists are right, is to say nothing about the book but only something about the subject's current state of mind.[27] In line with the ideas of the atomists, one is left separated from the world, isolated from all but one's perceptions. How could knowledge of the universe be obtainable in such a system, closed in on itself and ultimately on oneself? Wherein could a person know anything about a world from which he

---

[26] This view is set forth in his work "Other Minds," in *Philosophical Papers*, ed. J. O. Urmson and G. J. Warnock, 3rd ed. (Oxford: Oxford University Press, 1979), 76–116.

[27] Austin claims that looks are not subjective, contrary to what the sense-datum proponents hold: "I am not disclosing a fact about *myself*, but about petrol, when I say that petrol looks like water." See Austin, *Sense and Sensibilia*, 43.

or she is removed in toto? Later in this chapter, I will show how one philosopher finds himself to be in a similar state and how he attempts to extricate himself from the system of knowledge that binds him.

True Judgment

Having eliminated perception as a candidate, Plato's dialogue proceeds with Theaetetus's supposing next, as a working definition, that knowledge is true judgment. It is a proposal that prompts Socrates to launch into an extended digression regarding false judgment to determine whether such a thing is even possible, and, if so, then what constitutes it. The excursion finally concludes with Socrates's admission that they were wrong to postpone the discussion of knowledge to pursue the concept of false judgment. That concept "cannot be understood," he says, before having "a satisfactory account of the nature of knowledge."[28]

Returning to Theaetetus's tendered definition following the diversion, Socrates dismisses the suggestion in short order. People may come to believe something that is, in fact, true, but on the basis of skillful persuasion rather than on the basis of any factual evidence in support of the belief. A legal trial provides an example.

> SOCRATES: And when a jury is rightly convinced of facts which can be known only by an eyewitness, then, judging by hearsay and accepting a true belief, they are

---

[28] Plato, *Theaetetus*, 200d, 907. In the digression, Plato introduces a pair of colorful comparisons to illustrate workings of the mind. He likens memory to a wax tablet in which impressions and conceptions are pushed into the soft material, where they are maintained; they are retrieved later in the process of remembering. Perhaps the more prominent illustration concerns the aviary, which he employs to draw a distinction between possessing knowledge and having it. As one may possess birds after capturing them and placing them in one's aviary, but not have a bird in the hand until entering the aviary and taking hold of it, one might have acquired knowledge and stored it in one's mind but not be attending to it. I will not pursue the analogies here. I will note, however, that a distinction in philosophy between dispositional beliefs and occurrent beliefs is somewhat reminiscent of the bifurcation that Plato sets forth in the latter illustration. It is a topic for later.

> judging without knowledge, although, if they find the
> right verdict, their conviction is correct?
>
> THEAETETUS: Certainly.
>
> SOCRATES: But if true belief and knowledge were
> the same thing, the best of jurymen could never have a
> correct belief without knowledge. It now appears that
> they must be different things.[29]

Believing something that happens by chance to be true is not knowing. It is easy to think of cases that support that fact. Obsessed with finding treasure and having heard on the news that a man in California found a collection of precious gems that were buried in his back yard, Clarence convinces himself that riches lay just beneath the surface of his own property in Maryland. He has no evidence to support the supposition but believes it nevertheless. Beatrice, who lives next door, never told anyone that she lost her grandmother's pair of rings. She dropped the rings at the cookout that Clarence held last year at his house, and, as it began to rain, they were pushed into the soft ground by the throng of guests. The diamond and ruby jewelry is covered now by a few inches of top soil and some leaves. Clarence believes correctly that gems of great value are in his yard, but he has no knowledge to that effect, as there is no justification for his belief, no appropriate reasoning lying behind it in the absence of observation.

TRUE JUDGMENT PLUS AN ACCOUNT

The final candidate for knowledge that Theaetetus presents in his discussion with Socrates is true judgment accompanied by an account. The first matter to which the dialogue turns here is the examination of a theory, the author of which is unidentified, that there are so-called first elements that compose everything. These elements are perceivable, but they are not knowable—a strange doctrine. It cannot be that the account that is necessary for knowledge is just the enumeration of these unknowable, composi-

---

[29] Ibid., 201b, 908.

tional elements, for then knowledge would consist of adding to a true belief a distillation into that which cannot be known. Such a position is unsupportable.

Plato, through Socrates, proceeds at this juncture to identify three possible meanings of 'giving an account'. If it merely were expressing a belief in words, then, because anyone who is capable of speech can express a belief, there would be nothing to distinguish between belief and knowledge. Verbalizing a belief that one possesses that is, in fact, true does not convert the unspoken belief into spoken knowledge by virtue of the utterance.

Socrates considers next whether giving an account is tantamount to analyzing something in terms of its fundamental parts. If so, then one who could list the parts of a wagon—wheels, axles, body, and so forth—would have knowledge of it, but providing a catalog of the components of a thing does not transform belief into knowledge. A wagon is not the mere collection of its constituents, and knowledge of it must include its technical nature or, stated differently, its operational utility.

Finally, Socrates examines whether the account that is assumed to be necessary for knowledge is equivalent to being able to name some uniquely distinguishing characteristic, something by which a thing differs from every other thing. This approach also fails, he believes. If a correct notion of Theaetetus does not include that which makes him unique, then there is no knowledge of him, as, in that case, he is not distinguished from other men. If it does include his unique differences, then the account adds nothing to the correct notion, as it already contains his distinguishing characteristics. An account cannot transform an accurate conception into knowledge by adding to the conception what is already in it. Plato, in the following passage, points to the stumbling block that this idea of an account introduces:

> SOCRATES: When we have a correct notion of the way in which certain things differ from other things, it tells us to add a correct notion of the way in which they differ from other things. On this showing, the most vicious of circles would be nothing to this injunction.[30]

---

[30] Ibid., 209d–e, 918.

This Platonic dialogue ends, like so many others, inconclusively. Plato has shown what knowledge is not, but not what knowledge is. It is through Plato's theory of forms, one of his greatest intellectual achievements, that one comes to understand his positive view regarding knowledge.

In present-day epistemology, a standard view of knowledge is that it is justified true belief, a depiction that is similar, in certain respects, to Plato's third version in the *Theaetetus*. Although this rendering commonly is accepted among philosophers as the correct one, a number of authors have challenged it. Indeed, Plato himself challenges a notion that is much the same. The ancient philosopher attempts to show that knowledge cannot be true judgment plus an account, but his use of the term 'account' is exceedingly narrow. Perhaps there is another, more appropriate way to represent the account that provides the necessary support for a belief. It is a matter to be explored.

The important point here is that saying precisely what knowledge is proves to be trying. All would agree that truth is necessary for knowledge, but, beyond that requirement, it is difficult to identify exactly what more is needed. Still, there is an unrelenting sense that knowledge must be anchored in some manner, whether it is through an account, justification, or another qualifying factor, lest one simply guess correctly and, in so doing, know. Plato looks beyond the physical world for that anchor and attempts to link what is known to what is ultimately real.

THEORY OF FORMS

Plato's thoughts about knowledge and his thoughts about reality converge in the theory of forms, where they are woven together to create a comprehensive philosophical tapestry. At its base, the theory is concerned with being; notions about believing and knowing are superimposed on this metaphysical framework and are inseparable from it. To understand Plato's epistemology then, one must understand his ontology. Several writers have produced books focusing on this major philosophical system that Plato advances, and one can turn to a variety of sources for further study.[31] I will cover its key points briefly.

For Plato, the things in the physical world rise and ebb in the constant current of Heraclitean flux. In themselves, they can be grasped firmly neither by the senses, as discussed above, nor by reason, for they are in a state of becoming and never are. The truly knowable is the genuinely real, Plato believes; and the genuinely real is not found in the individual, material objects in the physical world but in the immaterial entities that exist apart from the physical world and are apprehended by the intellect. Plato conceives of these entities as ideas, or forms.[32] He portrays them as unique, discrete essences; or as archetypes, or models. They are eternal, unchanging universals of which physical objects partake or in which they participate—to use Plato's concepts—as the objects manifest various qualities corresponding to these paradigms. For example, beautiful things, of which there are many, exhibit the associated quality because they partake of the one form Beauty, and this form imparts its character to the things that share in it: "[I]t is by [the form] beauty that beautiful things are beautiful."[33] Again, Plato asserts, "[W]hatever else is beautiful apart from [the form] absolute beauty is beautiful because it partakes of

---

[31] The bibliography lists several resources pertaining to Plato's philosophical concepts, and one may wish to scan it for suggested readings. The first part of Frederick Copleston's multivolume work on the history of philosophy provides a fine overview of relevant topics, as do vols. 4 and 5 of W. K. C. Guthrie's well-considered writings on Greek thought.

[32] Two Greek expressions that convey the notion of Plato's forms are *eidos* and *idea*, both of which are translated as the English word 'idea', but the translation is misleading. Plato is not referring to the idea that a person has in mind when, say, it occurs to that person how to repair the torn sail on a sloop or brace the sagging roof on the children's playhouse. The better choice is 'form'. Note that a number of authors capitalize the word 'form' when it denotes the Platonic construct, whereas others use the lowercase initial letter. The latter rendering is common in standard compilations of Plato's dialogues, and there is little to substantiate the capitalization other than convention and the prevention of confusion when the word is used in senses other than the Platonic one. I employ the lowercase format in this work, as a rule, capitalizing the term only where it refers to the unique form that bears the same name as the general class of them. In keeping with this approach, I capitalize all the names of Platonic entities—the individual forms, representing universals—in this text, unless quoting passages that use noncapitals.

[33] Plato, *Phaedo*, 100d, trans. Hugh Tredennick, in *Collected Dialogues of Plato*, 82.

that [form] absolute beauty, and for no other reason."[34] The form is thus the ideal, the exemplar, which accounts for things' exhibiting the properties that they exhibit at any given time. Beauty itself is immutable and permanent, in contrast to the fleeting presentation of this property in the beautiful things that populate the world. For Plato, stability lies in these incorporeal universals, not in corporeal objects.

The theory of forms runs like a thread through a number of Plato's dialogues, particularly during the middle period of his work and, to a lesser extent, the late period. Sometimes, it is expressed explicitly; sometimes, the expression is implicit. One author makes this statement about the theory's emergence in Plato's writings:

> If a graph were drawn of the appearance of the theory it would stay at zero for several of the earliest works, rise doubtfully in some of the so-called Socratic dialogues, leap up to maximum with the *Phaedo* and the *Symposium*, stay at that level in the central books of the *Republic*, the *Phaedrus* and the *Parmenides*, and then settle down to a level where the existence of some transcendental realities is definitely taken for granted but no full explanation of the extent of that belief is given, in spite of several outstanding questions clamouring for solution. In this last period the *Timaeus* is to some extent an exception.[35]

PLATO'S ALLEGORY—THE POSITIVE SIDE OF KNOWLEDGE

With this understanding, it is time to proceed to Plato's depiction of the structure of what amounts to a progression through various stages to the state of knowledge. To appreciate how Plato's theory of universals applies, a person must look at his dialogue *Republic*. The *Republic* provides an extended comparison that serves as a basis for coming to grips with the critical distinction in Plato's

---

[34] Ibid., 100c, 81.
[35] G. M. A. Grube, *Plato's Thought* (1935; repr., Boston: Beacon Press, 1968), 7.

philosophy between the world of physical objects and the world of reason. In the *Theaetetus*, as one saw, Plato presents primarily the negative view of knowledge. In the earlier-composed *Republic*, he presents the positive view. Plato believes that there are two fundamental categories or levels of apprehension. He sets forth this dichotomy by drawing an analogy with a line that is divided into two main sections, separating the *perceptible* from the *intelligible*: that which is apprehended by the *senses* from that which is apprehended by the *reason*. Perhaps the best way to examine the Platonic schema is to look first at the philosopher's famous allegory of the cave, which appears immediately after the simile of the divided line in the *Republic*.

Plato tells one to picture a subterranean cavern in which prisoners have been chained since childhood, their feet and necks bound in such a way that they face the interior wall of the cave with their backs to its opening. Prevented from moving their heads, the prisoners can see only the wall in front of them. A fire burns above and behind them, toward the entrance to the cave. Along a raised path between the prisoners and the fire, a low wall has been constructed. On the outer side of this wall, men pass carrying statues, which rise above the wall. These figures resemble different objects, including men and animals. The shadows of the sculptures appear on the rock surface of the cave in front of the prisoners. Sounds that those who are carrying the figures utter reflect from the rock face and thus seem to emanate from the shadows that appear there. The captives, who have no experiences to teach them otherwise, believe that the shadows correspond to what is real: "Then in every way such prisoners would deem reality to be nothing else than the shadows of the artificial objects."[36]

Suppose that one of the prisoners is released. He is compelled to turn and face the opening of the cave and walk around. Seeing his surroundings in the bright firelight is painful for him, and, if he were told that the statues that had cast the shadows on the wall of the cave were more real than the shadows of his lifelong experience, then he would not believe it. He encounters further pain when made to look

---

[36] Plato, *Republic*, VII, 515c, trans. Paul Shorey, in *Collected Dialogues of Plato*, 748.

at the fire itself. Eventually dragged by force out of the cavern, he stands in the light of the sun, blinded by the brilliance of daylight, unable to see the things in the environment. As his eyes adjust, he begins to see shadows of things, then reflections in water. Such images represent more directly the objects in the world, as there are no intermediaries in the form of look-alike statues that cast the shadows that he perceives now. Afterward, he comes to see physical objects themselves. Rather than sensing replicas of men and animals, he sees these things as they are. He looks next to the heavens: the stars and the moon. Finally, he gazes at the sun itself. If he returned to the cave at this point, then he would not be able to see because of the darkness; hence, he would appear to the prisoners who had remained there to be a laughable character. They would think that his eyes were ruined by the journey to the upper realm. If he tried to convince them of the truth and set them free, then, refusing to accept his report, they would resist to the point of taking his life if they could do so.

The story of the cave is intended to depict the levels of awareness and the ascent of the mind on its journey to true knowledge.[37] Using the analogy of a divided line, as mentioned above, Plato introduces the two principal, broad categories of mental apprehension: *doxa* (opinion) and *epistēmē* (knowledge). From the corresponding terms come respectively the English words 'doxastic' and 'epistemic'.[38] Each of these categories, in turn, comprises two levels. One can rise to the higher levels, with effort, through a sort of conversion at each step. Like the prisoners in the cave, humankind is chained in ignorance, unaware of its wretched state. It is through rationality, Plato believes, that people overcome the clutches of their dismal existence, reaching a state of true awareness. Consider then the path that the mind takes. It is a path from illusion or conjecture to belief to understanding and finally to reason. One who reaches the last stage reaches authentic knowledge.[39]

---

[37] I present an interpretation of the symbolism in the Platonic narrative that is in keeping with a traditional perspective, with my amplification. There are other perspectives, but the one that I adopt is substantiated by standard texts.

[38] The word 'doxastic' means 'pertaining to belief'; the word 'epistemic' means 'pertaining to knowledge'.

[39] See Plato, *Republic*, VI, 511d–e, 747.

Corresponding to each of the four levels of ascent from the cave is a state of mind, and corresponding to what the characters in the story see is an object of apprehension. I will summarize the symbolism after a brief explanation of each stage.

The prisoners who watch the shadows on the back surface of the cave represent those who are in the lower of the two stages of opinion. It is the bottommost position of all. What the men observe is misleading. Seeing the silhouettes and taking them to be the realities, they are deceived. Here, one senses images—imitations or copies rather than the originals that they mimic. The chained prisoners symbolize the mental state of illusion or mere rudimentary thinking; and the prisoners' seeing the shadows of the statues symbolizes humankind's perceiving the shadows and reflections of material objects.

The prisoner in the cave who is freed from his fetters sees, by the light of the fire, the statues that had cast the shadows on the rear wall of the cave. He represents one who is in the second phase of *doxa*; it is a higher form of opinion. The prisoner has progressed in his trek toward true knowledge, but he is yet to achieve it. The unchained prisoner in the cave symbolizes the mental state of belief, and his seeing the statues symbolizes humankind's perceiving physical objects in the world. These objects are the things of Heraclitean flux; changing constantly, they have no persistent being inherently.

On leaving the cave, standing in the light of day, the man in the allegorical account comes to see the shadows and reflections of the objects in the external realm as his eyes begin to adjust to the intense light. Like the prisoners who remain chained in the cave, this man too is seeing images, as opposed to originals, but they are formed directly by substantive things rather than by their proxies: the statues that merely resemble men and animals. They are the images of men and animals themselves. The man represents one who has reached the point of intellectualization. Apprehension has passed from the sensual to the conceptional, from grasping objects of perception to grasping objects of reason. Plato believes that the category of *epistēmē*, like that of *doxa*, is divided into two levels, and understanding falls in the first stage of *epistēmē*.

Herein lies the basic comprehension of elementary mathematical entities, which one may regard as intelligible individuals, as opposed to sensible individuals.[40] Although there are many objects that are in the shape of triangles, for instance, one can talk about a specific right triangle, the shortest sides of which measure three feet and four feet respectively. The Pythagorean theorem determines the hypotenuse of that triangle to be five feet in length. Yet, there is no actual figure in the world corresponding to this right triangle or to any triangle; such geometric constructs are two-sided figures. There are only rough approximations of the shapes of them. No physical entity in a given triangular shape is ever precise, and no two triangular entities are ever exactly alike in size. One simply cannot produce them in the realm of physical things. One can *conceive* of an authentic, particular *immaterial* right triangle, though, by *perceiving* a particular *material* right triangle of similar dimensions. The conceptualization that is based on the perception is what Plato has in mind for this phase of *epistēmē*. It is the grasping by the intellect of the actual, distinctive, geometric figure that the physical approximation represents; it is a shape the dimensions of which can be specified with all the precision that mathematics provides. The man who is outside the cave, yet to adjust to the sunlight, symbolizes the mental state of understanding. His seeing the shadows of physical objects in the area beyond the cave symbolizes humankind's taking hold of the intelligible individuals with which physical objects correlate.

The prisoner whose eyes have adapted to the brightness of the day, seeing the concrete objects around him clearly, represents one who has achieved the higher level of intellectuality. At this level lies the apprehension of the first principles, what the mind takes hold of through dialectic. It is the realm of pure cognition. It is the realm of the essences of things—universals, the forms themselves. One in this stage of ascension understands not just the immaterial triangle that a material structure mirrors but grasps as well the essential property

---

[40] See Plato's remarks in *Republic*, VI, 510b–511b (particularly, 510c–511a), 745–46. Frederick Copleston makes the point, which I believe to be correct, about abstract individuals. See Copleston, *A History of Philosophy*, vol. 1, *Greece and Rome* (London: Search Press, 1946), 157. For a discussion of this first level of true comprehension and the view that the objects of this level are mathematical entities, refer to pp. 156–59 of Copleston's work.

that all triangles share and that makes them what they are: Triangularity. Ultimately, the man gazes at the sun itself. This act points to the taking hold of the pinnacle of intellection: the supreme form—specifically, the Good. In the allegory, as noted earlier, those who remain in ignorance in the cave would reject the one who escaped from that state if he returned to the cave. They would kill the escapee, assuming that he tried to convince them of the truth, if they could lay their hands on him. There is no doubt that Plato's intent here is to portray the death of Socrates at the hands of the Athenian citizens. The man who sees the environment outside the cave with clarity symbolizes the mental state of knowledge; his seeing the objects in that environment symbolizes humankind's grasping the forms; finally, his seeing the sun symbolizes humankind's apprehension of the Good, which sits at the zenith of human comprehension.

The table that follows summarizes the psychological levels and the symbols that Plato employs to depict them. I present the information in a top-down fashion, underscoring the progression. The lowest state thus appears at the top of the chart. The names of the subdivisions of *doxa* and *epistēmē* are included for reference.

		Symbol in Allegory of the Cave	Mental Level	State of Mind	Significance of Mental Event
P R O G R E S S I O N	**Perceptible**	Chained prisoners—they see the shadows on the cave wall and take them for reality.	*Doxa*: level 1 (*eikasia*)	Illusion or thinking	Perception of images—seeing shadows and reflections of physical objects
		Released prisoner—he sees the statues that cast the shadows on the back wall of the cave in the firelight.	*Doxa*: level 2 (*pistis*)	Belief	Perception of physical objects
	Intelligible	Man who is forced to the surface—he sees the shadows and reflections of physical objects in the outside realm.	*Epistēmē*: level 1 (*dianoia*)	Understanding	Apprehension of elemental objects of reason: intelligible individuals
		Man on the surface whose eyes have adapted—he sees physical objects themselves in the light of the sun and finally the sun itself.	*Epistēmē*: level 2 (*noēsis*)	Knowledge	Apprehension of the forms, the highest of which is the Good

Figure 2.2

In Plato's ontology, the core of his philosophy, there are degrees of reality. Physical objects—the individual items of sensory perception, which Plato refers to as particulars—lack total being. Caught in flux, they are not entirely real, but they are not entirely unreal either. What reality they do possess is partial, incomplete.

Forms, in contrast, possess total being. They are fully real. Partaking of forms, particulars lie between absolute nonbeing and pure being.

As there are degrees of reality in Plato's philosophy, there are likewise degrees of awareness, as his story about the cavern reveals. One cannot know physical things, the things that never genuinely are. One does have a measure of realization with respect to them, however, by virtue of their participation in the forms. It is the forms that are the true objects of knowledge. It is through these universals that Plato's two epistemological dictates are satisfied: Knowledge must be infallible, and knowledge must be of what is. The mindfulness of particulars falls between total ignorance and pure knowledge; it is given in belief.

In his theory of forms, Plato seeks to bring together the corporeality of particulars and the incorporeal nature of properties. Here, the ever-changing world of perception intersects the stable world of reason. Authentic knowledge transcends the sphere of sense; one never can grasp sensory objects in the way in which one grasps the intelligible forms. An element of conceptualization is possible, however, because the mind can take hold of objects by taking hold of the forms that the attributes of those objects exemplify. Immune to the flux to which physical things succumb, forms lend a measure of weight to the world of appearances. Is it sufficient to anchor them against the raucous Heraclitean current? Perhaps it falls short in this regard, but it can dull the clamor—to a point. With his innovative theory, Plato provides a way to comprehend the world, albeit in an imperfect and derivative way. It is his solution to the problem of knowledge.

TROUBLE WITH THE THEORY

Setting forth a divergent theory, Plato's greatest student, Aristotle, becomes a staunch opponent of the philosophical system of his mentor, a system in which the realm of matter is separated from the realm of qualities that it exhibits. Plato himself spends much time considering his theory of forms and, in keeping with the Socratic tradition of open-minded inquiry, introduces a number of objections to his own creation. His dialogue *Parmenides* depicts a conversation between the elder Eleatic for whom the dialogue is named and a young Socrates, viewing his eminent predecessor with considerable wonder. In the dialogue, Plato attacks his own theory through the character of Parmenides, who is accompanied by his protégé, Zeno. I will take a look at some of the arguments that Plato presents in the text, but I want to begin with the criticism that Parmenides levels against the scope of the Platonic forms.

THE EXTENT OF THE INTELLIGIBLE

When queried, the character Socrates readily admits that there are forms for relations, such as likeness; for mathematical properties, such as unity and plurality; and finally for ethical and aesthetic qualities, including rightness, goodness, and beauty. Parmenides continues, however. Man, fire, and water—he wonders whether Socrates believes that there are forms of which these things partake. Socrates confesses that he is not sure. Parmenides presses further, asking whether there are forms for what he takes to be "undignified objects": hair, mud, and dirt. At this point, Socrates denies that the theory extends to such things, although it seems to him that this denial opens the door for an inconsistency.

> In these cases, the things are just the things we see; it would be absurd to suppose that they have a form. All the same, I have sometimes been troubled by a doubt whether what is true in one case may not be true in all. Then, when I have reached that point, I am driven to retreat, for fear of tumbling into a bottomless pit of nonsense.[41]

Parmenides attributes to Socrates's youth the hesitancy to propose forms for the mundane, as philosophy has no reluctance in embracing the consequences of its own devices.

---

[41] Plato, *Parmenides*, 130d, trans. F. M. Cornford, in *Collected Dialogues of Plato*, 924. The quoted phrase, preceding this passage, appears in 130c in this dialogue.

In the Platonic system, it is clearly the universals that bear the ontological weight. Where there are gaps in the framework of forms, the objects that copy them and depend on them are in danger of degenerating from partial reality to total collapse. With Parmenides's question about the extent of these immaterial entities, Plato faces a dilemma of his own making. Either there are forms for everything, including the commonplace, or comprehension of things, even in the derivative sense that his epistemology puts forward, slips from one's grip.

Plato did not develop his theory of forms as a result of an examination of language, and it is only after his writings had matured that he undertakes any in-depth grammatical analysis with respect to it. There is a point of intersection, however, between language and facts, between what a declarative sentence reports and a state of affairs that obtains in reality. Ascribing a property to an entity or affirming its involvement in a relation; attributing a condition to that entity, or an action by it or to it; and assigning that entity to a class—all are functions of sentential expression. In the dialogue *Sophist*, which succeeds the *Parmenides*, Plato explores the meaning of assertions and the mechanics of predication.

Before the discussion of the scope of forms continues, it is useful to see how Plato's theory can link that which is designated by the subject of a declarative sentence (not to be confused with the subject of perception or knowledge—a sentient being) to that which is designated by the sentence's predicative phrase. I will offer some brief, interpretative thoughts, focusing mainly on properties in my examples, but the analysis can be expanded to cover predication in general. A standard logical system, the predicate calculus, in fact, provides a structure whereby propositions are set forth in terms of properties and relations. Suppose that every true statement that refers to an entity, ascribing a property to it, mirrors a metaphysical relationship holding between an individual and a universal—in Platonic terms, between a particular and a form. A declarative sentence 'x is F', where the variable F represents a manifested quality to which the adjectival locution 'F' points, purports to link the thing that the variable x stands for—the individual that the word 'x' names—to the property—the universal F-ness—asserting that x exhibits that quality. The subject of the sentence and that which is expressed

145

about it in the predicate are linked linguistically through the copula—the verb, which, in this case, is the word 'is'. If the sentence is true, then the distinct thing that the subject of the sentence names and the property that the predicate adjective indicates are linked in reality as well. So, if the sentence 'Ken is kind' is true, then the person Ken partakes of, or participates in, the form Kindness, as the grammatical construction reveals. In giving an account of how things and properties bond, Plato's theory thus extends to language: What one says about things reflects the theory's inherent postulates. (Note that references to properties often appear in more than one linguistic format; cf. page 20, n. 6. Each member of a set of associated terms— 'solidity', 'solid', and 'being solid', for example—may serve to signify the same quality without introducing a firm distinction.)

Consider an illustration. There are many individual objects that are called trees. They are of different heights, different shapes and orientations, different colors, and different ages. Some shed their leaves in autumn; some do not shed them. Some bear edible fruit; some have cones; some produce winged seed pods. What makes them all trees is that they all share a certain core, distinguishing nature. If forms are sufficiently extensive in scope, then that nature is the form Tree, or Treeness—the essence of what it is to be a tree. Most living trees have brown trunks and, in the summer, green leaves; therefore, they share in other forms, such as Brownness and Greenness. Many green things that are not trees also share in these forms, including, for instance, a broken piece of multicolored pottery, which lies at the base of the oak in Johnny's yard, and his pet, lime-colored lizard, Snappy, which is on its trunk. Given the Platonic theory and its implications, if one says, "This thing is a green tree," or utters, "Snappy is green," then one is asserting that the objects that 'this thing' and 'Snappy' denote partake of, or participate in, certain forms: specific universals. A thing participates in the form Treeness for as long as it is a tree; in this sense, the thing's essential nature is grounded in that form, taking on the nature through impartation. The thing's participation in Greenness, however, changes with the seasons. Similarly, for part of its existence, the tree exhibits Tallness, which, in Plato's model, is a property. This shifting state of participatory affiliation is evident in the following diagram:

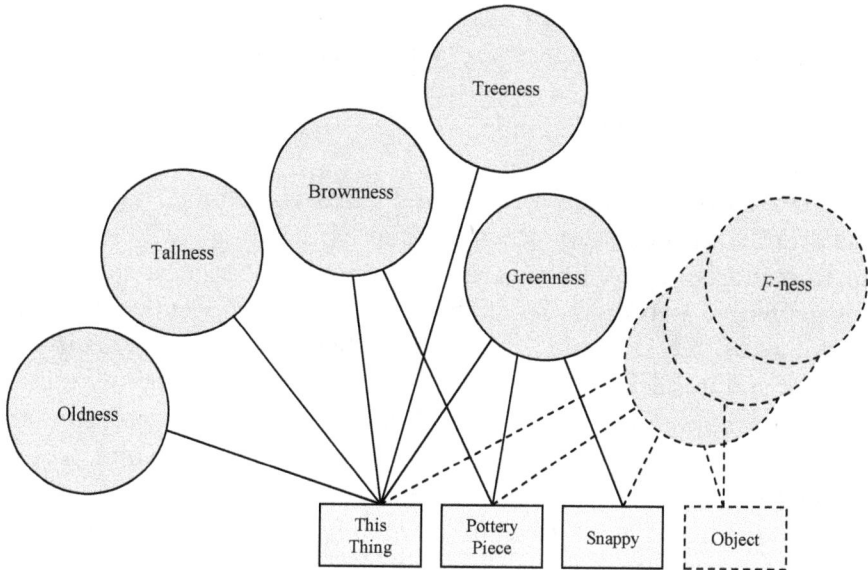

Figure 2.3

At least by the point in his career at which he writes the *Sophist*, Plato is ready to accept the broadening of his theory to encompass more than the noble concepts of justice, goodness, beauty, and the like. In keeping with his examination of language, Plato posits in that dialogue that all statements employ forms, and it is through predicative attribution that they do so. Plato claims that "any discourse we can have owes its existence to the weaving together of forms."[42] Some hold that Plato's assertion is problematic. It does not leave open the possibility of ascribing a single property to a particular. Combining things, including forms, requires there to be at least two entities for the joining to take place. In a statement with a syntactical formulation of 'x is F', if the variable x stands for a singular entity, such as Snappy, that the term 'x' names, and F stands for a displayed quality, such as (being) green, which the expression 'F' indicates, identifying the form—which is Greenness here—then

---

[42] Plato, *Sophist*, 259e, trans. F. M. Cornford, in *Collected Dialogues of Plato*, 1007.

only one form is in play. In this case, there is no weaving. Likewise, a proposition that is framed as '*x* is *Y*-ing'—where *x* represents a particular that the term '*x*' specifies, and *Y*-ing represents a state that the present participle '*Y*-ing' denotes—requires no blending of forms.

A reasonable interpretation of Plato's contention, however, is that forms are necessary for discourse as a whole—without them, there could be no predication, no ascription—not that all statements must involve two or more of them. Indeed, in the same dialogue, Plato gives an example in which an individual—Theaetetus—is named, and it is said of him that he is sitting or that he sits.

The important point is that Plato appears to be prepared to embrace the notion that there are forms for everything, which would include the things that one encounters regularly in the world—green trees and pottery pieces. Even in the *Republic*, which Plato composed earlier, he notes, "We are in the habit . . . of positing a single idea or form in the case of various multiplicities to which we give the same name."[43] In that dialogue, Plato moves straightway to propose forms for everyday objects—specifically, couches and tables. The ordinary no less than the exalted thus can lay claim to his ideal archetypes.

Although Parmenides's question about dirt and the like reveals, by Plato's own hand, an aspect of Plato's theory that he deems to be unpalatable, he has little choice but to accept it. Admitting the existence of forms for the commonplace and less-than-glamorous is hardly the problem that its counterpart is. If the forms are limited to a certain, noble group, then the theory loses its explanatory power. Moreover, the philosophical system that Plato has constructed is confronted either with the charge of arbitrariness in its ontological declarations or with the charge of inconsistency. No doubt, Plato is aware of the implication.

The theory of forms is an evolving doctrine in Plato's thought. He never rejects the sure ontological status of the forms, but his view regarding their range seems to shift. In the *Sophist*, Plato is willing to extend their scope beyond his commitment to it in the *Parmenides*, and he is willing even to extend the scope of reality itself. The forms-for-all-predicates approach, however, faces a significant challenge of

---

[43] Plato, *Republic*, X, 596a, 820.

its own, I believe. If forms are required for discourse, and every predicate that ascribes a property designates at least one of them, then forms are multiplied beyond all reasonableness because it is possible for the ascription to specify any numerical value. Johnny's pet lizard may be six inches long in June and seven inches long in September, growing during the summer. The statement 'Snappy is z inches long' singles out a different form for each value of z. Given that a mathematical infinity lies between six and seven, and each predicate that specifies Snappy's length designates a distinct form, there are an indeterminate, and perhaps infinite, number of forms to which Snappy's length corresponds as a result of growth—and maybe stretching to reach treats. It seems that Plato's theory violates the law of parsimony. Trouble is already afoot, but more is to come.

ARGUMENTS AGAINST THE FORMS

Following his critical remarks in the dialogue concerning the range of the forms, Parmenides launches a series of arguments directly against the Platonic theory, of which I will present three. The first two attack the relationship that holds between Plato's two sorts of entities, attempting to show that it leads to absurdities. The third denies that a relationship is even possible.

THE WHOLE-PART ARGUMENT. Parmenides notes that, if things partake of forms, then each thing's share must be either the whole of the form or part of it. Both alternatives are problematic. If it is the whole, then, because there are many things that exhibit a given property, the whole form will be in many things and consequently will be separate from itself. Socrates counters by saying that one and the same day is in many places at the same time; nonetheless, it is not separate from itself. Parmenides responds that Socrates ought to say, on that premise, that a sail, which is spread over a number of people, is in many places at the same time—a dubious analogy, but Socrates permits it. Only a part of the sail is over each person, not the whole sail. Therefore, the sail is divisible into parts. So it is with forms: Only a part of a form will be in a thing that partakes of it, not the whole form. Thus, the first concern—that the whole of the form

149

is in each thing that partakes of it—seems to be allayed for the moment, but the other takes its place: The form must be divisible into parts. According to Plato's theory, however, forms are indivisible, immutable wholes.

Furthermore, if it is only as part that the thing partakes of a form, then illogicalities result. Parmenides continues his criticism with these comments:

> Well, take smallness. Is one of us to have a portion of smallness, and is smallness to be larger than that portion, which is a part of it? On this supposition again smallness itself will be larger, and anything to which the portion taken is added will be smaller, and not larger, than it was before.
>
> That cannot be so.
>
> Well then, Socrates, how are the other things going to partake of your forms, if they can partake of them neither in part nor as wholes?[44]

There are only two ways, so the whole-part argument contends, that things could partake of forms, and neither way is logically acceptable. The theory of forms hence leads to the consequence that things cannot partake of forms at all.

It may be said in Plato's defense that Parmenides, in the dialogue, is assuming that forms, which are not material, can be sliced apart as though they were material. Even though the whole-part dichotomy may not apply to incorporeal entities—one cannot carve up a quality, say, justice or amicability or treachery, in the way that one would carve up a Thanksgiving turkey—there is still the problem of just how it is that things and forms come together. Plato employs the locutions 'partaking of' and 'participating in' to describe the relationship, but they lack true elucidatory strength.

THE THIRD-MAN ARGUMENT. The expression 'third man', as it pertains to the construction of the argument that is set forth in this objection to Plato's theory, originates with Aristotle.[45] That noted

---

[44] Plato, *Parmenides*, 131d–e, 925–26.
[45] The exact expression appears in a critique by Aristotle of Plato's theory of forms. See Aristotle, *Metaphysics*, A, 9.990b15 ff., trans. W. D. Ross, in *The Basic*

philosopher criticizes his teacher's theory of forms along the same lines as Plato's own criticism of it. Aristotle claims that a third man would be required to explain the commonality between an individual man and the form Man. The problem is that, by generating this additional entity, an unending chain is spawned.

In structure, the reasoning parallels Zeno's attack on motion that I discussed in chapter 1. The third-man argument attempts to demonstrate that the theory of forms introduces an infinite regress. In his dialogue *Parmenides*, Plato raises the thorny problem of self-predication: here, the self-ascription of properties. Things partake of forms and thereby exhibit qualities. Suppose that x_1, x_2, and x_3 are F. They all thus partake of the form F-ness$_1$. If, besides particulars, however, a property also exhibits the quality that corresponds to itself, then there must be yet another form to account for the fact that the individual things and the first form have that characteristic. Specifically, if x_1, x_2, x_3, and F-ness$_1$ are F, then there must be another form, F-ness$_2$, to account for the quality's being exhibited by the three things plus the first form itself. Parmenides questions the young Socrates in the following passage, drawing attention to the concern:

> How do you feel about this? I imagine your ground for believing in a single form in each case is this. When it seems to you that a number of things are large, there seems, I suppose, to be a certain single character which is the same when you look at them all; hence you think that largeness is a single thing.
>
> True, he replied.
>
> But now take largeness itself and the other things which are large. Suppose you look at all these in the same way in your mind's eye, will not yet another unity make its appearance—a largeness by virtue of which they all appear large?
>
> So it would seem.
>
> If so, a second form of largeness will present itself, over and above largeness itself and the things that share in it, and again, covering all these, yet another, which

Works of Aristotle, trans. E. M. Edghill et al., ed. Richard McKeon (New York: Random House, 1941), 707.

> will make all of them large. So each of your forms will
> no longer be one, but an indefinite number.[46]

It is difficult to see how largeness itself can be large. One is back to treating immaterial entities as though they were material. Self-ascription with respect to the forms, however, is a notion to which Plato subscribes. For him, the form Justice is just, and the form Beauty is beautiful. A form is the perfect instance of itself. Indeed, he claims, with respect to the qualities of heat and coldness, "[T]he name of the form is eternally applicable not only to the form itself, but also to something else, which is not the form but invariably possesses its distinguishing characteristic."[47] So, hot things, such as fire, are hot, and so is the universal Heat. The thinking seems to be that, if a form is to lend to things the quality that corresponds to it, then it must possess that quality; otherwise, it could not do so. It cannot give what it does not have.[48]

One might suppose that, if there are a great number of things that are large, then there is a sense in which Largeness is large because the set of things to which the property applies has considerable extension. 'Large' in this sense, however, does not mean 'of great physical size' any more than 'large number' means 'a number that occupies much space'. Parmenides invites Socrates to look at the form Largeness and large things in the same way, but one cannot look at them in the same way. Simply on the basis that a term is applied to two things, it does not follow that the term picks out the same property, especially so if those things are of distinct ontological classes. This issue will surface again in chapters 6 and 7 as I look at more recent arguments that, like this one, fail to distinguish between the different senses of a term as they apply to different categories. Parmenides's attack, as it stands, rests on an ambiguity. Had Plato

---

[46] Plato, *Parmenides*, 131e–132b, 926.

[47] Plato, *Phaedo*, 103e, 85.

[48] W. K. C. Guthrie makes the apt point that the Greeks' combining of the (definite) article with the adjective produces ambiguity; thus, 'the hot' may refer to hot things or to heat itself. In any case, notes Guthrie, the cause of particulars' being what they are is the forms' impartation of qualities. The forms themselves therefore must possess the qualities that they impart. Refer to Guthrie's *A History of Greek Philosophy*, vol. 5, *The Later Plato and the Academy* (Cambridge: Cambridge University Press, 1978), 43.

not accepted self-predication with respect to forms, the argument would hold no weight at all; however, he does accept it—in the dialogue, at least—even though it seems to produce nonsense. Treeness is not a tree. Greenness is not green. Largeness is not large.

The argument can appear to be more forceful if one draws on the appropriate property. Consider incorporeality. It is true, one may hold, that the number 3, the set of all even integers, the concept of rationality, and the property of incorporeality are incorporeal. If, as before, one maintains that the cause of something's having the property is an independent form, then a legitimate regress does appear to arise in this case. The difference, of course, is that all the items that are listed are immaterial; they belong to the same ontological class. The property can be applied without relying on an ambiguity. For the problem of self-predication to work in the third-man fashion, the property that is denoted in the predicate of the ascribing sentence must be applied in the argument in *exactly the same sense* to all the things to which it is ascribed. Otherwise, by switching the meanings, the argument that employs it is guilty of a logical error. Such errors are informal fallacies, or material fallacies, rather than formal ones, because they arise from content rather than structure.

When the material is mixed with the immaterial, different senses are inevitable. Plato is probably aware of the issue. In the *Republic*, he argues that a second form, which launches the regress, arises only if two forms, which are entities of the same order of being, share the property that matches their name. The fact that a physical couch partakes of the form Couchness does not cause a problem, he thinks. Only if Couchness is a couch will it surface, and the form itself is not a couch, for it is of an order of being that is distinct from the physical object.[49] Of course, one might argue that forms themselves are what they are because they too share a property, apart from the specific ones that correspond to the respective essences. Justice is a form, and so are Goodness and Beauty. They all are forms because they partake of the same universal: Form, or Formness. It is the form Form that imparts the

---

[49] See Plato, *Republic*, X, 597a–d, 821–22. Also see the discussion in Francis Macdonald Cornford, *Plato and Parmenides: Parmenides'* Way of Truth *and Plato's* Parmenides *Translated with an Introduction and a Running Commentary* (1939; London: Routledge and Kegan Paul, 1950), 87–90.

quality that defines their being. The regress thus seems to be inevitable.

THE TWO-WORLDS ARGUMENT. In his writings, Plato develops an account of being and knowing that incorporates elements of both Heraclitean and Parmenidean philosophy. Physical objects—the objects of sense perception—flow like a river, he thinks, in accordance with the ancient Ionian's doctrine of flux. They are neither entirely real nor truly knowable. Forms, on the other hand, are unchanging and permanent, and accessible only by the intellect. Each form is reminiscent of the One put forth by the great Eleatic philosopher. In attempting to bring together these two disparate kinds of things to formulate a comprehensive ontological-epistemological system, Plato must overcome the inevitable clash.

The two-worlds attack that Parmenides launches hits at the very heart of the theory of forms. Although widely regarded as fallacious, the argument points to a problem that may be damaging nevertheless. In the *Parmenides*, the Eleatic argues that the gulf between the perceptible and the intelligible cannot be bridged. The relationships in which each takes part are limited to entities of its own kind. When one speaks of an entity in the physical world, the reference is to that entity, not to immaterial, stand-alone properties that it may exhibit. If the reference is to Snappy's green color, for example, then the adjective may convey the name of a form, but the *lizard* is the object of the reference, not some *property* that the lizard exhibits. In this passage, Parmenides speaks with the young Socrates:

> Suppose, for instance, one of us is master or slave of another; he is not, of course, the slave of master itself, the essential master, nor, if he is a master, is he master of slave itself, the essential slave, but, being a man, is master or slave of another man, whereas mastership itself is what it is [mastership] of slavery itself, and slavery itself is slavery to mastership itself. The significance of things in our world is not with reference to things in that other world, nor have these their significance with reference to us, but, as I say, the things in that world are what they are with reference to one another and toward one another, and so likewise are the things in our world. You see what I mean?

Certainly I do.

And similarly knowledge itself, the essence of knowledge, will be knowledge of that reality itself, the essentially real.

Certainly.

And again, any given branch of knowledge in itself will be knowledge of some department of real things as it is in itself, will it not?

Yes.

Whereas the knowledge in our world will be knowledge of the reality in our world, and it will follow again that each branch of knowledge in our world must be knowledge of some department of things that exist in our world.

Necessarily.

But, as you admit, we do not possess the forms themselves, nor can they exist in our world.

No.

And presumably the forms, just as they are in themselves, are known by the form of knowledge itself?

Yes.

The form which we do not possess.

True.

Then, none of the forms is known by us, since we have no part in knowledge itself.

Apparently not.

So beauty itself or goodness itself and all the things we take as forms in themselves are unknowable to us.

I am afraid that is so.[50]

The argument purports to show that particulars relate strictly to particulars and that forms relate strictly to forms; no relation holds between the members of one class and those of the other. Humans can know only what lies in their own realm of being; they cannot have knowledge of forms. Given that forms are the only objects of knowledge, so Plato avers, it follows that people cannot have knowledge at all. Refer to Figure 2.4, which appears on the following page. Interpreting the argument in the *Parmenides*, one might say

---

[50] Plato, *Parmenides*, 133d–134c, 928–29. The brackets are in the translator's text.

that the relationships are horizontal, never vertical. The relationships RX_1 and RX_2 therefore never obtain; nothing can cross an ontological boundary.

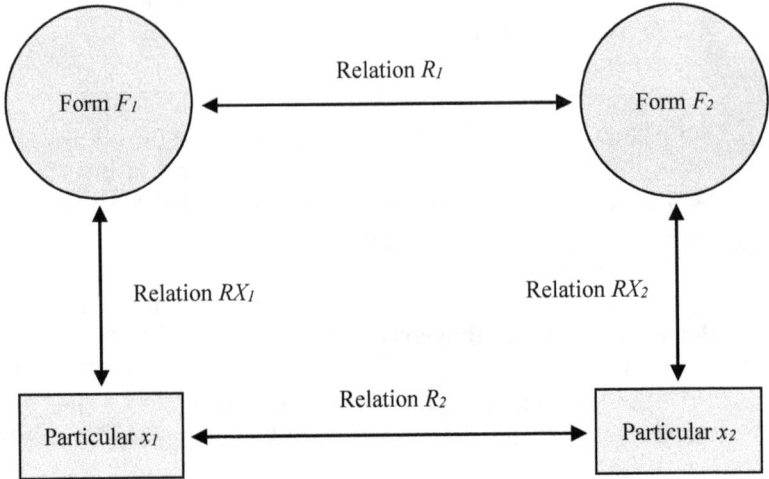

Figure 2.4

To reach its conclusion, the argument presumes that the master-slave relationship obtaining between two persons is the same relationship obtaining between the two applicable forms that those persons exemplify. Likewise, so the argument presumes, the known-know relationship holding between an object in the world and a sentient subject holds as well between any forms that the form Knowledge knows and the form Knowledge itself. In effect, the argument asserts that R_2 is reflected in R_1, such that the latter relation is the equivalent counterpart to the former one, but, of course, they are not equivalent. The forms Mastership and Slavery are associated, but they do not stand in the relationship that a master and slave stand to each other. The two forms are associated only by virtue of a connection that obtains between things that do stand in the given relationship. The father of the bride and the father of the groom are partnered through the marriage relationship in which the young couple stands, but the father of the bride is not married to the father of the groom. Further, it makes no sense to say that Knowledge bears the relationship of knowing to anything. Intelligent agents know, but it is meaningless to state that Knowledge knows. As one author notes, "Mastership is not *the master* of Slavery or of anything else. . . . The [f]orm [Knowledge] itself is not an activity existing in a mind and cannot know anything."[51] The argument mixes the relationships of distinct ontological orders. This issue will sound familiar, for a similar problem arises in the third-man argument. As one saw, though, Plato clings to the belief that forms are instances of themselves, manifesting their own essences. On this reading, Knowledge may be said to know, regardless of the ostensible senselessness of the claim, in which case Plato's theory cannot escape easily from the attack.

How exactly, to Plato's thinking, is the joining of material objects and immaterial forms possible, given that they are so different? Plato seems to be stretching for the relation when he stops short of a precise explanation.

> [T]he one thing that makes that object beautiful is the presence in it or association with it, in whatever way the relation comes about, of [the form] absolute beauty. I do not go so far as to insist upon the precise details.[52]

His stock description of the link, as I noted earlier, is that things partake of forms or that things participate in forms, but what it means to assert that such an affiliation obtains is unclear. If the way in which individuals and universals unite is reduced to metaphors, which is what Plato does in his analysis, then a genuine account of their interconnectedness is not put forth. The Eleatic philosopher takes that line of thought a step further in the dialogue by arguing that things, in fact, cannot unite with forms at all. They are entities of two completely different sorts, forever locked in their own isolated domains. Knowledge within the realm of human existence cannot reach beyond its boundaries to the essentially real. The forms are Plato's anchors for things. They provide the only measure of stability

---

[51] Cornford, *Plato and Parmenides*, 90.
[52] Plato, *Phaedo*, 100d, 82–83.

and continuity that the world of constant flux can experience. With his two-worlds attack through the character of Parmenides, Plato attempts to sever the ties to those anchors, and, if he is successful, then humankind is left adrift in uncharted epistemological waters. If knowledge must be infallible and of what is, as Plato thinks, then humans cannot know, for, unless they can reach the world of forms from their own world, all that they can take hold of are things that are becoming, not things that are. By separating the two sorts of entities completely, Plato's theory is in danger of total inefficacy. In the end, Parmenides acquiesces in the matter of separation, admitting that, despite the difficulties that the supposition of the existence of forms raises, forms are necessary for discourse to occur. If they do not exist, then there is nothing constant on which to fix one's thoughts in communication. Without that constancy, the meaning of the terms that people employ in language dissipates. Reminiscent of the *Theaetetus*, Parmenides's remark has a notably Platonic ring to it.

Perhaps, in the late dialogue *Timaeus*, Plato offers a way of escape from the Parmenidean argument. The soul, he says, lies in a third order of existence. Occupying a position between the two ends of the spectrum of reality, it has elements of each of the two opposed realms.

> Now God . . . made the soul in origin and excellence prior to and older than the body, to be the ruler and mistress, of whom the body was to be the subject. And he made her out of the following elements and on this wise. From the being which is indivisible and unchangeable, and from that kind of being which is distributed among bodies, he compounded a third and intermediate kind of being.[53]

As intermediaries, souls are in contact with both worlds. They perceive, and they conceive. They grasp corporeal objects, and they grasp incorporeal forms. Souls serve as the link between the sphere

---

[53] Plato, *Timaeus*, 34b–35a, trans. Benjamin Jowett, in *Collected Dialogues of Plato*, 1165. Note that the third order, for Plato, comprises both the World-Soul—that which permeates and moves the universe—and individual souls—the souls of persons.

of becoming and that of being. If, on the one hand, souls are purely immaterial, then they have to be able to connect to material things for perception to work. If, on the other hand, souls are purely material, then they have to be able to connect to the immaterial forms for intellection to work. Plato advances the thesis that they are both—a unique blend of the two. If such is the case, however, then the immaterial part of the soul must connect to the material part to produce the whole: a single entity that is capable of both sensation and reflection. Has Plato solved the two-worlds problem or merely pushed it back a step?

There is no reason, of course, to maintain that things of fundamentally different types are prohibited from interaction or from standing in a relationship to each other. The breaking of Timmy's arm when he fell from the tree house is related to his experience of pain, but it does not follow that the sensation itself is tangible, even though the arm is such. Again, imagine that an Athenian sculptor created a statue of Socrates and gave it to Plato, who set it by the entrance to the Academy. The statue is material, but its history during the prior year seems to be otherwise. The history of a thing may be viewed as a set of states of it, perchance in association with events in which it is either a cause or an effect of something, and it can be argued successfully that sets are incorporeal. Still, a thing stands in a relationship to its own past. The two are related uniquely.

The intrinsic separation in Plato's theory of forms does bring with it another, serious problem, however, and Plato's proposed third order of reality in the *Timaeus* only exacerbates this problem. Inherent in the Platonic system is a division between objects and forms. It is an ontological division between the partially real and the fully real. Reality, however, does not admit of degrees.[54] Part of a thing can exist, but nothing can exist partially. One thing can be heavier than another, greater in size, or less coarse; it can be more sour or less tuneful. Such is not the case with existence: Existence is not a predicable property—a widely accepted notion in philosophy. There can be no incomplete being. There can be no intermediate being. For anything at all that one may specify, either it exists, or it does not exist. Either it is absolutely real, or it is absolutely unreal. If

---

[54] This problem resurfaces in the philosophy of René Descartes—considered next.

the objects in the world of sense are fully real, then they are not becoming; instead, they *are*, in which case Plato's theory, with its postulation of the existence of forms, is superfluous. If the objects of sense are not real at all, however, then those objects do not exist. A total illusion, they are not even in a state of becoming. Plato's theory, in that case, is built on falsehood.

THE HARD LINE

Plato's ultimate solution to the problem of ontological separation is found perhaps in the *Sophist*. Plato's thoughts about reality evolve in the course of his writings, and this late dialogue reveals a view that reflects a softening of the hard line between the ontological categories of the perceptible and the intelligible—of particulars and forms. It marks a fundamental change in the definitive segregation on which his theory is built. One scholar of ancient philosophy offers these words: "I do not see how anyone can doubt that Plato [in the *Sophist*] is preparing the reader for a modification of his own metaphysics."[55] In that dialogue, Plato examines two opposing views of reality: materialism and idealism. Those in the former camp claim that the only thing that is real is tangible body: That which is palpable and offers resistance when it is touched is all that exists. Even the materialists would admit, however, that a soul can be just or unjust, wise or foolish. A soul comes to be that way, however, through the arising in it of justice or injustice, wisdom or foolishness, and whatever can arise in a thing must be real. Yet, justice and wisdom are neither visible nor tangible. So, even though they maintain that the soul consists of matter, albeit a special type, can the materialists say the same of justice and wisdom? Either they must deny the reality of these qualities, or they must deny that they are body.

Plato then posits that the distinguishing mark of reality is the power that real things have to act on other things and to be acted on

---

[55] Guthrie, *The Later Plato and the Academy*, 141. It should be noted that not all authors agree, but Plato's comments in the dialogue are clear.

by them. This approach is in keeping with the materialistic position, which holds that the sense of touch is affected by material objects through the capacity that they possess to bring about sensation. Physical objects are real; one can feel them. Matter affects things and is affected by things. Nevertheless, there are these other things—justice and wisdom—that also have the power to act, bringing about effects in people no less than concrete objects. One can discern the presence of justice in a person as much as one can discern the presence of the person's physical body. Justice and wisdom are real, but they are immaterial. Although Plato does not press forward to say that the forms that they exemplify—namely, Justice and Wisdom—are real, he has taken a firm step in that direction at this point in his analysis.

Having established the identifying mark of reality as this dual active-passive capacity, Plato turns his attention to the idealists, who deny the genuineness of material body and hold that the immaterial constitutes the truly real. Plato refers to these idealists as the friends of forms, proceeding to assess, in a not-too-subtle way, the veracity of his own theory. Plato's reasoning here is shaded, to a degree, but I will follow the path that he takes in the dialogue and attempt to expound it. The advocates of the forms assert that one interacts with the world of becoming through perception, but one interacts with the world of being through reflection. This interaction, however, appears to be a manifestation of precisely what has come to light, through his preceding analysis of materialism, as the twofold character of the real: It is the power to act on things and to be acted on by them.[56] The friends of forms claim, of course, that knowledge belongs to the realm of being; knowledge is of the changeless forms. An instance of knowing, though, is not a single-party occurrence, for it is a case of acting—in fact, of interacting—by means of the power to affect. What is affected in the act of knowing is both that which is known, or comes to be known, and that which knows, or comes to know. Therefore, the object of knowledge—reality as it is given in the forms—changes, not just the subject of knowledge—the soul—as a result of knowing. Both elements of the knowing relationship are

---

[56] Of note, the structure of this agent-patient relationship parallels what Plato advances in his interchange theory of perception as seen in the *Theaetetus*, which I discussed earlier.

influenced by the occurrence. The idealists assert, however, that reality is changeless. The obvious conclusion is that, if these two suppositions are correct, then one cannot know reality, and this result is hardly acceptable. Thus, either the active-passive interaction account of knowing, with its accompanying dual change-effects, is incorrect, or the objects of knowledge—that is to say, forms—change. Plato does not pursue further—directly, at least—the accuracy or inaccuracy of the agent-patient structure of knowledge, and he does not deny the immutability of forms. Plato proceeds instead to demonstrate that the condition that reality is completely unchanging is too strict, and it is too strict because the idealists' notion of reality is too restrictive.

Plato asserts that there can be no understanding without life, and both of them reside in the soul. In his philosophy, the soul is dynamic, not static. It moves, incessantly and perpetually; and it moves not incidentally but essentially.

> All soul is immortal, for that which is ever in motion is immortal. But that which while imparting motion is itself moved by something else can cease to be in motion, and therefore can cease to live; it is only that which moves itself that never intermits its motion, inasmuch as it cannot abandon its own nature; moreover this self-mover is the source and first principle of motion for all other things that are moved.[57]

To the ancient philosopher's way of thinking, motion is a type of change. If reality were without change, then, given that motion is the essential attribute of the soul, understanding would have no place anywhere in existence. It would not belong to the domain of becoming, for understanding has no footing where there is only constant flux. It would not belong to the domain of being, for, by the assumed principle, that domain is characterized by the immutable. Yet, these things—understanding, life, and soul—are surely real. Plato may be surmising here that, if there is knowledge at all, then the object of knowledge cannot lay claim to reality any more than the subject, despite the latter's nature. The contemplative soul cannot be

---

[57] Plato, *Phaedrus*, 245c, trans. R. Hackforth, in *Collected Dialogues of Plato*, 492.

relegated solely to the realm of becoming, and, if it is included in being, then so is its inherent movement.

On these premises then, one must make room within the real for that which changes. In what appears to be a rather remarkable shift in doctrine, Plato concludes that reality is to be found in the conjunction of the elements of the two categories on which he bases his philosophy. Says Plato, through a main character in the dialogue *Sophist*,

> STRANGER: On these grounds, then, it seems that only one course is open to the philosopher who values knowledge and the rest above all else. He must refuse to accept from the champions either of the one or of the many forms the doctrine that all reality is changeless, and he must turn a deaf ear to the other party who represent reality as everywhere changing. Like a child begging for 'both,' he must declare that reality or the sum of things is both at once—all that is unchangeable and all that is in change.[58]

In the end, it may be that Plato's ontology offers to things an anchor of their own, so that they no longer must rely totally on the weight of immutable universals to keep them from drifting into nonexistence. Plato never abandons forms, but the *Sophist* accommodates more than these universals in the global treasure chest of being. Even so, things continue to change, and change raises the troubling matter of identity. Without a way to lock things, how can they persist, moment to moment, as the same things? It seems that the problem of knowledge remains unresolved.

In the next section is another attempt to anchor things. Two millennia after Plato wrestled with the thorny problem of knowledge, a brilliant French philosopher with a unique approach tries his hand. That this philosophical puzzle persisted, crossing many centuries, points to the difficulty in solving it.

---

[58] Plato, *Sophist*, 249c–d, 994. The term 'forms' as it is used here refers to renditions of a doctrine, not to the Platonic forms.

RENÉ DESCARTES

Born on March 31, 1596, in Touraine, France, René Descartes was to become one of the greatest thinkers of the period. Along with Benedict de Spinoza (1632–1677) and Gottfried Wilhelm von Leibniz (1646–1716), Descartes belongs to a group of major philosophers who are referred to as the rationalists. Unlike the empiricists who, in the main, follow them, the rationalists accept the primacy of reason in knowledge, believing that knowledge is not fundamentally dependent on sensory experience.

Descartes lost his mother when he was only a year old. As a child of poor health, he was excused from morning exercises at school and given a private room. He spent much time lying in bed meditating, a habit that remained with him throughout his life and, no doubt, provided an opportunity for the development of what became his philosophical perspective. Though respectful of his teachers, he grew suspicious of the value of educational studies, finding only mathematics to be worthy of serious attention, providing a certainty and clarity that were lacking in the other disciplines. After taking a law degree, Descartes volunteered in 1618, at the age of twenty-two, for military service in Holland under the Dutch Prince Maurice of Orange. While there, Descartes conversed about physics, mathematics, and logic. After leaving the army, Descartes traveled in several countries in Europe, returning to Holland in 1628, where he spent the next twenty-one years. Having sold property in France, he became a man of means, which afforded him the opportunity to live in solitude and reflection. Although he was not without friends, Descartes never married. Continuing his life of thought, he corresponded with a few learned contemporaries—of note, the Franciscan friar Marin Mersenne—on a variety of topics. During this period, Descartes delved into the subject of geometry.[59] He experimented in optics and physiology, even grinding his own lenses and dissecting animals that he had acquired from the local butcher. An interest in

---

[59] The Cartesian coordinate system, which is basic to analytic geometry, is named for its founder, Descartes. Although the concept of the graph was introduced earlier, it was Descartes who developed the use of coordinate numbers and algebraic equations containing variables to express linear functions.

metaphysics and epistemology grew. He came to believe that, as he wrote later, all scientific inquiry, like a spreading tree, is linked to a common foundation. Ultimately, there is one science, he thought, and there is one method of scientific discovery that applies universally to all disciplines. Carrying his analogy further, Descartes supposed the roots of that tree of inquiry to be metaphysics. He supposed the trunk to be physics and the branches to be the other fields of scientific investigation. Thus, the whole of science is grounded in metaphysical principles. Reason provides knowledge. The role of science is verification: Through experimentation, science offers support for the truths that reasoning has revealed.

Late in his life, Descartes began to correspond with Queen Christina of Sweden, whom he came to know through the ambassador Pierre Chanut. Descartes presented to the queen a preliminary copy of his treatise *The Passions of the Soul*, which he published in 1649. Christina was so taken with Descartes's acumen that she pressed him to travel to Sweden and join her court, and she sent an admiral with a warship to escort him there. Reluctantly, he agreed, leaving Holland in that same year. The Swedish winters were difficult for Descartes. Perhaps worse still, the queen expected lessons in philosophy in her library at 5:00 a.m. For Descartes, who was accustomed to lying in bed meditating for long periods of time, the early risings, coupled with the cold, took their toll. Descartes died of pneumonia on February 11, 1650. Although Descartes created several scientific and philosophical works, his epistemological view unfolds primarily in *Discourse on the Method*, published in 1637; *Meditations on First Philosophy* with its *Objections and Replies*, released in 1641; and *Principles of Philosophy*, which appeared in 1644.

CARTESIAN DOUBT AND THE *COGITO*

Perhaps the one concept that is most applicable to Descartes's approach to knowledge is *doubt*. Cartesian doubt, however, is not the destructive disbelief of skepticism. It is instead a methodical and inclusive suspension of belief for constructive reasons, a doubt that is exaggerated, or, as Descartes describes it, "hyperbolical."[60] Its purpose is to discover truth. To this end, Descartes seeks first to lay the foundation by determining what it is possible to know with absolute certainty—what is, in fact, indubitable. Says the philosopher,

> Archimedes used to demand just one firm and immovable point in order to shift the entire earth; so I too can hope for great things if I manage to find just one thing, however slight, that is certain and unshakeable.[61]

Once again, certainty surfaces as a necessary condition of knowing. In this respect, Descartes's requirement is not unlike the first Platonic dictate, that knowledge must be infallible: Where it is possible to be wrong, there can be no basis for knowledge. For Descartes, the infallible is the indubitable. The central problem, as Descartes sees it, is that many beliefs have been tainted by misconceptions and preconceptions, calling into question the entire lot of them. One may hold, at a given time, particular propositions to be true, only to discover later that they are not true. How then can one be certain about any proposition? Descartes's quest for utter certainty leads him to lay aside the complete set of beliefs that he has come to embrace, doubting all that can be doubted in an effort to find that which cannot be doubted—some indubitable truth that would serve as the basis for his system of empirical knowledge. He notes,

> Some years ago I was struck by the large number of falsehoods that I had accepted as true in my childhood, and by the highly doubtful nature of the whole edifice that I had subsequently based on them. I realized that it was necessary, once in the course of my life, to demolish everything completely and start again right from the

---

[60] René Descartes, *Meditations on First Philosophy, Meditation VI*, in *The Philosophical Works of Descartes*, trans. Elizabeth S. Haldane and G. R. T. Ross (1911; repr., Cambridge: Cambridge University Press, 1967), 1:198.

[61] René Descartes, *Meditations on First Philosophy, Second Meditation*, in *The Philosophical Writings of Descartes*, trans. John Cottingham et al. (1984–1991; Cambridge: Cambridge University Press, 1997–2009), 2:16. I extract quotations in the section on Descartes from both this translation and the Haldane-Ross work, depending on the passage.

foundations if I wanted to establish anything at all in the sciences that was stable and likely to last.[62]

If this process of total expulsion seems to be extreme, consider an analogy that Descartes draws. Just as one rotten apple can spoil a whole basket of them, he notes, a single incorrect belief can corrupt one's whole collection of them. If one accepts as true a basic assumption that proves subsequently to be false, then all that is based on that assumption is suspect too. The only way to be sure that every apple is fresh or that every belief is true is to dump the bunch, then inspect each one carefully before accepting it. Descartes describes the method that a man would employ to accomplish the task at hand.

> Suppose he had a basket full of apples and, being worried that some of the apples were rotten, wanted to take out the rotten ones to prevent the rot spreading. How would he proceed? Would he not begin by tipping the whole lot out of the basket? And would not the next step be to cast his eye over each apple in turn, and pick up and put back in the basket only those he saw to be sound, leaving the others? In just the same way, those who have never philosophized correctly have various opinions in their minds which they have begun to store up since childhood, and which they therefore have reason to believe may in many cases be false. They then attempt to separate the false beliefs from the others, so as to prevent their contaminating the rest and making the whole lot uncertain. Now the best way they can accomplish this is to reject all their beliefs together in one go, as if they were all uncertain and false. They can then go over each belief in turn and re-adopt only those which they recognize to be true and indubitable. Thus, I was right to begin by rejecting all my beliefs.[63]

The French philosopher sets out at this point to do precisely what he sees as necessary for the building of a system of knowledge. The

---

[62] Descartes, *Meditations, First Meditation*, in *Writings of Descartes*, 2:12.
[63] René Descartes, *Objections and Replies, Seventh Set of Objections with the Author's Replies*, in *Writings of Descartes*, 2:324.

crucial question then becomes this one: What can be doubted? It is a question on which his entire epistemology turns.

Again, like Plato before him, Descartes examines sense perception to determine whether it can guide one to indubitable truth. The senses sometimes mislead, as when a person looks at an object in the distance, which appears to the person to be a certain way, but, upon closer inspection, the observer discovers that it is different from the way that it seemed to be at first. Even if the senses deceive an observer with respect to remote objects, Descartes continues, there must be times when they can be trusted.

> Yet although the senses occasionally deceive us with respect to objects which are very small or in the distance, there are many other beliefs about which doubt is quite impossible, even though they are derived from the senses—for example, that I am here, sitting by the fire, wearing a winter dressing-gown, holding this piece of paper in my hands, and so on. Again, how could it be denied that these hands or this whole body are mine?[64]

The philosopher's methodical doubt, however, leads him to reject as untrustworthy even such appearances as the ones that are noted above. Descartes is searching for the *indubitable*. His doubt is based not on practicality but on possibility; and it is possible to doubt that one is beside the hearth with one's notes. It is possible to doubt even that one has hands, or a body at all, for that matter, though the body clearly seems to be extended in front of the person. Consider, Descartes says, the beliefs of the insane. They maintain that they are dressed in purple when they are naked or that their heads are made of earthenware or that they are pumpkins. Even a rational person can be mistaken. Descartes asserts that, when it is evident to him that he is sitting by the fire with paper in hand, his experiences are the same as they would be if he were lying in bed, asleep, and dreaming of such an event. He would accept as real that which the dream conveys but later, when he awakes, would find that he has been deceived. There are no reliable criteria by means of which he can distinguish being awake from being asleep. The senses cannot be trusted *never* to

---

[64] Descartes, *Meditations, First Meditation*, 12–13.

mislead, and such trust is necessary if one seeks certainty. The senses, thinks Descartes, cannot produce indubitable truths.

One might wonder whether it is possible to be deceived when dreaming. Let s be a person and p be some proposition. To be deceived about p, the subject s must believe that p, where p is false. Philosophers generally identify two senses of belief: occurrent and dispositional. In the occurrent sense, a person holds that something is the case, and the notion that it is the case is presently before the person's conscious mind. One is thinking about it in believing it; that is to say, one is attending to the belief. For example, suppose that the teacher asks Johnny, "What is the capital of Spain?" He ponders the question and responds, "I believe that it is Madrid." Johnny's belief is occurrent. In the dispositional sense of belief, in contrast, a person accepts that something is the case, but the notion that it is the case is not presently before the person's conscious mind; the individual is not attending to it at the time. One is disposed nevertheless to affirm the truth of a given proposition and would do so if one were entertaining the notion. In the example that is mentioned above, Johnny might have been thinking about recess rather than what was going on around him in geography class. He still believes that Madrid is the capital of Spain, but his belief is dispositional, not occurrent, until the teacher prods him, and it will be dispositional again as his thoughts drift once more to the playground.[65]

With this division in mind, one might argue that a subject s cannot have occurrent beliefs while dreaming, because, by the very characteristic that distinguishes such beliefs, they are peculiar to a

---

[65] Rather than distinguish between two senses of belief, I think that it is more accurate, strictly speaking, to distinguish between two states of believing. If s believes that p, then s accepts p as true—as a statement of a fact—and, having done so occurrently, continues to do so even when s no longer is attending to p. At that point, the believing is dispositional. Subject s holds the belief—namely, that p—by virtue of having accepted it formerly; and s continues to hold it (until s no longer accepts it), even when s is not considering it in a conscious way, because the disposition continues. The belief that s possesses has not changed—it is still that p—but s's current awareness of it has changed. Thus, there is a shift in the state of believing but not in the belief itself. It may be useful to keep this difference in mind, but I will not make too much of it, and I will deem the broader and more common terminology to be adequate for conveying the core distinction between the occurrent and the dispositional.

conscious state. Any belief that *s* has while dreaming therefore must be dispositional. If *s*'s believing that *p* constitutes *s*'s having a dispositional belief, though, then *s*'s believing that *p* is tantamount to *s*'s believing that *p* occurrently, where *s* is awake and attending to the declaration that *p*. In this case, however, *s* no longer is dreaming. It follows that it is not possible to be deceived while asleep.

Whether such an argument is convincing, it does point to the fact that believing is complex. It includes not only a psychological state of cognizance and acceptance but a tendency, or disposition, to acknowledge the truth of certain propositions as well. I will note that, whereas one seems to perceive images in dreams that, of course, do not correspond to physical objects that lie in front of the dreamer, one's reasoning is not tricked so easily. Solving problems while asleep is a commonly reported experience. I can attest to the fact that it happens. Awakening one night with a solution to a challenge in my work that had beset me, I was sure that I had the answer. When I returned to the office the next day, I implemented the nighttime solution, and it was successful. On occasion, I have performed mathematical calculations in my sleep, amazed to learn as I awoke, following the first such incident, that it was possible to do so—and more amazed that my calculations were accurate. Descartes's general point, however, is not that it is possible to be right but rather that it is possible to be wrong.

It is certainty that he is seeking, and he looks at arithmetic and geometry to see whether they can provide the needed assuredness.

> For whether I am awake or asleep, two and three added together are five, and a square has no more than four sides. It seems impossible that such transparent truths should incur any suspicion of being false.[66]

Yet, believes Descartes, it is possible to doubt even the axioms of mathematics. He supposes that some evil genius, a being of great power and cunning, could pull out all the stops in an effort to deceive him. Descartes asserts that he cannot know that such is not the case, and, without that knowledge, he cannot be sure that what he takes to be elemental truths of arithmetic and geometry are, in fact, correct.

---

[66] Descartes, *Meditations*, *First Meditation*, 14.

Given that the existence of such a being is possible, thinks Descartes, mathematics cannot deliver indubitable truths.

With such extreme uncertainty facing him, Descartes endeavors to find whether there is anything at all that cannot be doubted, whether there is anything that can provide the requisite foundation for a system of knowledge. He determines that there is indeed something that is certain. No matter how extensive his doubt, he cannot be mistaken about his own existence: His very condition of being in doubt requires that a thing—namely, he himself—exist to experience the mental state of suspicion. Doubting—or, more generally, thinking—requires a subject, a thinker. Even an evil genius cannot deceive him here. For Descartes to doubt, he sees that his existence is necessary. In his most notable claim, the philosopher asserts,

I think, therefore I am.[67]

This assertion is known as the *Cogito*, for it typically is expressed in Latin: *Cogito, ergo sum*.[68] (Many commentators omit the comma.)

In the *Cogito*, Descartes finds, so he believes, the indubitable truth on which to base a system of knowledge. To develop such a system, though, requires that other truths be added, building on that foundation. From his initial discovery, Descartes proceeds in search of a criterion of truth that he can apply universally to derive other reliable propositions. The philosopher sees that, if he can identify such a criterion, then he will possess a tool with which to begin the construction. He examines the *Cogito* closely but discovers that there is nothing in it that can convince him that it is true other than the fact that its truth is conceived with a certain manifest clarity. He decides that propositions that are clear and distinct in their presentation of the

---

[67] This assertion, appearing here as it typically is rendered, is located in more than one place in the French philosopher's writings. For a pair of instances, see René Descartes, *Discourse on the Method, Part IV*, in *Works of Descartes*, 1:101; and *The Principles of Philosophy, First Part*, in *Works of Descartes*, 1:221. Note that the Haldane-Ross translation inserts the definite article in the title of the second of these writings; the translation by Cottingham et al. omits it. The full title of the first work, depending on the translator, is *Discourse on the Method of Rightly Conducting the Reason and Seeking for Truth in the Sciences*.

[68] Descartes writes in both Latin and French, although he prefers French here.

truth are ones on which he can depend. This clarity-and-distinction test becomes the method of identifying, in his epistemology, propositions that are acceptable. More than simply the foundation for knowledge thus, the *Cogito* also contains the means by which to increase knowledge, so Descartes believes, because it reveals the way in which truth can be determined.

For the two-part criterion to be useful, however, Descartes must say exactly what the words 'clear' and 'distinct' mean when applied to the conception of a proposition. He does offer a few remarks that he deems to be illuminating.

> I call a perception 'clear' when it is present and accessible to the attentive mind—just as we say that we see something clearly when it is present to the eye's gaze and stimulates it with a sufficient degree of strength and accessibility. I call a perception 'distinct' if, as well as being clear, it is so sharply separated from all other perceptions that it contains within itself only what is clear.[69]

There are problems. These definitions hardly make obvious what is intended by the terms. Indeed, given that clarity and distinction constitute the standard of truth against which all propositions are to be measured, one is left unclear about how to use it. Moreover, clarity is a property that is subject to gradation: There are degrees of it. Just how much clarity is required before a proposition is admissible, and how one can establish the extent of a proposition's clarity, are matters that must be settled before one can employ the test with any assurance of effectiveness. Descartes realizes that saying precisely what is conceived clearly and distinctly is not always easy.

> So I decided that I could take it as a general rule that the things we conceive very clearly and very distinctly are all true; only there is some difficulty in recognizing which are the things that we distinctly conceive.[70]

---

[69] Descartes, *Principles of Philosophy, Part One*, in *Writings of Descartes*, 1: 207–8.
[70] Descartes, *Discourse on the Method, Part Four*, in *Writings of Descartes*, 1:127.

A second difficulty is that, if even mathematical propositions are subject to doubt, then this measure of truth that Descartes has discovered surely ought to be so as well. The philosopher believes nevertheless that he can exploit his clear-and-distinct criterion as a working hypothesis. Eventually, though, its utility as a test of truth must be undergirded by something of considerable solidity if it is to have any genuine value. Descartes has in mind what would warrant the use of his standard of truth, but he must prove it.

Regrettably, however, his great discovery has placed him in quite a predicament. Having doubted everything that he can doubt— what his senses reveal, the existence of the physical world, that he has a body, and even mathematical truths—he is left only with himself or, more accurately, his mind. Descartes has landed in what is called solipsism. Like an abandoned boat that has drifted into the brackish backwaters of rational inquiry, caught in the eddies that entrap it forever, solipsism is the dead end of philosophy. This position in its epistemological sense holds that all that one can *know* is oneself; there is nothing else at all about which knowledge is possible. In its stronger, metaphysical sense, solipsism holds that all that *exists* is oneself or states thereof; there is nothing else in all reality. The solipsist has no reason to put forth a theory of knowledge, or any theory, because one in this position is presenting it only to oneself, and not by happenstance but by constraint. Solipsism prevents any other possibility. There is just nowhere to go.

FROM SELF TO THE WORLD

Descartes, though, sees a way out of the trap. Moreover, if he is successful, then not only will he have extricated himself from solipsism, but he will have established the veracity of his criterion of truth as well; finally, he will have accomplished his ultimate goal in setting forth a theory of knowledge. That goal is to provide an assurance of the corporeal world and, in turn, to warrant the pursuits of science. Like Plato, Descartes must anchor things in some manner, but, whereas ever-present flux threatens the existence of physical things for that ancient Greek philosopher, it is disbelief that challenges the Cartesian world, a doubt so pervasive that it calls into question all that the senses convey.

The first step in Descartes's solution is to prove the existence of God. If he can do so, then, because of God's perfect nature—He is liable to no defect and hence cannot deceive—God will ensure the legitimacy of the criterion of truth and will function as the guarantor of things. It is God who will provide assurance that, when one perceives things in the physical world, they actually exist. One may represent Descartes's approach in the following way:

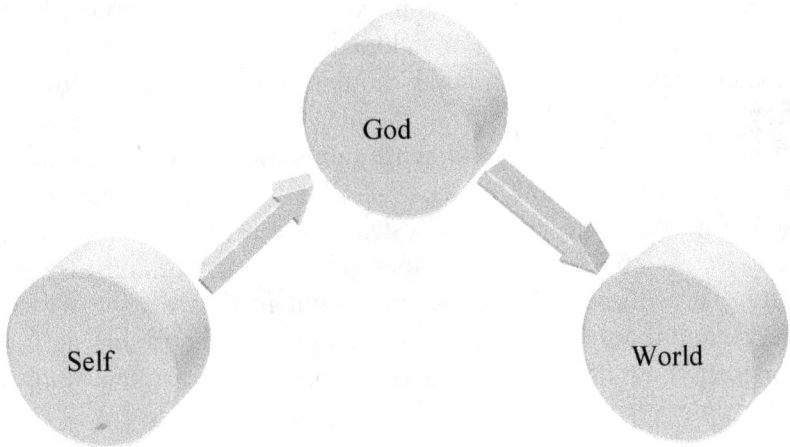

DESCARTES'S SYSTEM OF KNOWLEDGE

Figure 2.5

Descartes offers more than one demonstration in support of the existence of the Supreme Being, but the proof that appears below is the principal one, in keeping with his grounding of his epistemology in the self. At the current stage of the philosopher's development of a system of knowledge, he has shown only that he exists as a thing that thinks. Like a man, intending to cross a mountain stream by stepping on stones that protrude above the surface, Descartes, if he is to progress, must stand on the first stone and work his way across the philosophical waters; that is to say, he must move forward and outward from his own mind, which is precisely what he does.

To appreciate Descartes's argument requires understanding something about his theory of ideas and how ideas fit into his philosophy of being. For Descartes, what exists is substance. Strictly speaking, substance does not depend on anything else for its existence, and only God meets this criterion. Descartes believes, however, that he can continue with the terminology, recognizing that the concept of substance is one that includes, besides God (infinite substance), that which does not depend on anything other than God for its existence (finite substance). Substance may be either mental or physical, and, among the attributes of each type, there is an essential, defining one. The essential attribute of the mental is thinking; that of the physical is extension: occupying three-dimensional space. Descartes himself, as an incorporeal, thinking thing, is a substantive entity. Rocks and trees, as corporeal objects, are also substantive entities. Descartes, of course, must demonstrate that physical, extended entities exist, but he is heading in that direction.

In addition to substance proper, Descartes holds, there are modes: modifications that reflect the respective attributes of each type of substance. One may consider them to be the ways in which substance exists or is displayed. Thoughts are modes of mental substance, whereas shapes and motions are examples of modes of physical substance. A mode does not exist apart from the substance to which it corresponds; rather, it is dependent on it. There is no thought without a mind, although the thoughts of a mind—and certainly the thoughts among various minds—can differ. There is no shape without a physical object, although the shapes of a physical thing—and certainly the shapes among various physical things—can differ.

Descartes identifies three categories of ideas, each aligning with the source to which the occurrence of a given idea is traceable. The following chart describes these categories:

Idea Type	Distinguishing Factor	Example
Adventitious	Ideas that arise in the mind from sense perception	Idea of the maple in the front yard
Factitious	Ideas that are generated by the imagination	Astronomer's concept of the sun based on reasoning concerning its nature
Innate	Ideas that are inherent, in that one is born with the propensity for them to develop—clear and distinct ideas	Notion of God

Broadening the categorization, Descartes puts forth a distinction between formal reality and objective reality, and his proof of God's existence turns on this bifurcation. Formal reality is, for lack of a better description, actual being, the reality that a thing possesses inherently. If something exists, then it has formal reality; if an alleged thing does not exist, then it has no formal reality. As it pertains to ideas, formal reality subsists in what they are intrinsically: modes of thinking substance. In this respect, all ideas are on the same footing, as every one, regardless of type, has as much reality as every other one. Objectively, however, the reality differs markedly, as objective reality is linked to what the ideas signify. One must take care not to confuse the phrase 'objective reality' as it applies to Descartes's philosophy with the contemporary use of the phrase to refer to existence that is independent of an individual's subjective perceptions or thoughts. According to Descartes, objective reality is the reality of whatever it is that an idea symbolizes or represents. It pertains to the object of the idea, whether the object is something that actually exists, such as a horse, or something that does not exist, such as a unicorn.

For Descartes, reality, it seems, admits of degrees. Those ideas that represent substantive things, even if those things do not exist, have more objective reality than those ideas that represent the modes of things. One's idea of a tree is more real in this sense than one's idea of its rounded shape, as there is more to the physical body of a tree than there is to a property that it exhibits. Sam's factitious idea of a unicorn, arising from his imagination, has as much formal reality as Sally's adventitious idea of the tree, a maple, in her yard; and Sam's idea of the strange beast has objective reality as well because it signifies something substantive—a corporeal thing, occupying space—just as Sally's idea of the tree has objective reality. Unlike the tree, however, no unicorn exists; so, in this case, the thing itself, the beast—that which the idea signifies—has no formal reality. Whether there is something in existence to which an idea points determines whether that which the idea signifies possesses any formal reality, but its objective reality is linked to the sort of thing that it is, whether substance or mode, and, if substance, then whether infinite or finite. There are then three categories of being, marked by decreasing degrees of reality: infinite substance, finite substance, and mode.

One final distinction remains. Again, one must be careful not to be misled by the terminology. If a cause possesses the same degree of reality as its effect, then the reality of the effect is contained in the cause formally. If a cause possesses a greater degree of reality than the effect, then the reality of the effect is contained in the cause eminently. Effects can equal their causes, in terms of reality, or they can fall short of their causes, but they never can exceed them.

Incorporating Descartes's notions about substance, ideas, and causality, the key demonstration of the philosopher in support of the existence of God rests on a premise about himself. Descartes's reasoning is condensed here, to some extent, from the argument as it appears in its most detailed form in his writings. The argument contains other elements that are not presented, but they are tangential: more complementary in character and directed toward potential objections.[71] Consider now what Descartes offers as justification for his view. The premises and conclusion are numbered to facilitate readability.

---

[71] See Descartes's *Meditations, Third Meditation*, in *Writings of Descartes*, 2:24–36. There are various categories of proofs of God's existence. Descartes's primary demonstration is unusual, in that it includes elements of more than one category. For general information about the arguments that this philosopher advances for the existence of God, along with some of the pertinent concepts, one may refer to *Encyclopedia of Philosophy*, s.v., "Descartes, René."

1. There must be at least as much reality in the efficient and total cause of a thing as in the effect.[72]
2. Nothing can be without a cause; otherwise, something could proceed from nothing in violation of the afore-stated principle.
3. With respect to ideas, this principle applies not only to their formal reality (reality of ideas in themselves) but also to their objective reality (reality of what they signify), and the formal reality of the cause of an idea must be at least as great as the objective reality of the idea that it causes.
4. If the objective reality of an idea is sufficient to preclude its being in me either formally or eminently, then I am not the cause of the idea, and therefore some other thing exists and is its cause.
5. I have an idea of God, which, alone among my ideas, possesses objectively a supreme degree of reality because it signifies an infinite, perfect being.
6. The cause of this idea of God thus must possess formally a supreme degree of reality—the cause of my idea must possess within it a degree of reality that is at least as great as that which my idea signifies.
7. I cannot be the cause of this idea, as I am finite and imperfect, being in ignorance and doubt.
8. God, who alone possesses a supreme degree of objective reality and therefore a supreme degree of formal reality, caused this idea in me.
9. Therefore, God exists.

---

[72] The notion of efficient cause comes from Aristotle. It is the dynamic that one typically thinks of when referring to the cause of something—namely, that which brings about the effect. In essence, what Descartes is saying is that an effect cannot exceed that which brings about its occurrence. One will recall the philosophical principle *ex nihilo nihil fit*, a central piece of the Parmenidean dilemma. The axiom that Descartes employs here is related to that principle, in that it points to the impossibility of a thing's arising from a cause that is less substantive than it is, such that the product is greater than what produced it. If such could be the case, then one actually could get something from nothing, as it were. I will have more to say about this tenet in coming pages.

Essentially, Descartes is arguing that he has an idea of a perfect being. That idea must be caused by something that is perfect, as the effect (the idea of a perfect being) cannot be greater than the cause. Only the perfect God—infinite substance—could have produced that idea in him; no other source is perfect. Therefore, God exists.

From here, Descartes argues that, because God is perfect, He has no flaws and thus cannot deceive, as deception is wrong. So, the world that appears to be real is, in fact, real. Moreover, given that God cannot deceive, propositions that one apprehends clearly and distinctly are indeed true. Descartes believes that God's existence guarantees not only the corporeal world but the criterion of truth as well. Without God, the French philosopher's system of knowledge collapses.

For Descartes, knowledge arises from innate ideas, and one comes to know both physical and metaphysical principles by inference, deducing them from those implanted ideas. Sensory experience, or observation, serves to confirm the veracity of what one has discovered. Of course, by Descartes's own admission, people are sometimes wrong in their observations, in that what they believe that they perceive, they do not perceive, discovering their errors on closer inspection. Descartes must explain this phenomenon, lest his system of knowledge ultimately fail, unable to align the erroneous beliefs that people have about the physical universe, arising from perception, with the perfect nature of God. Descartes holds that beliefs are a matter of consent, that what one accepts as true is determined by the will. One is susceptible to the influence of sensory impressions that lead one astray. In such cases, according to the philosopher, a person's will outstrips the person's reason. Descartes maintains that humans are creatures with unlimited wills but limited intellects; he attempts to explicate the shortcoming in the following passage:

> So what then is the source of my mistakes? It must be simply this: the scope of the will is wider than that of the intellect; but instead of restricting it within the same limits, I extend its use to matters which I do not understand.[73]

---

[73] Descartes, *Meditations, Fourth Meditation,* in *Writings of Descartes,* 2:40.

People are occasionally wrong when they think that they perceive something clearly and distinctly, as they discover later. Consequently, it seems that a second criterion of truth is needed to ensure that what they believe that they perceive clearly and distinctly is, in fact, the case. If, because of failures of the human will, God cannot be the absolute guarantor in Descartes's system, then his system is in trouble.

ATTACKS ON CARTESIAN EPISTEMOLOGY

Descartes's philosophy is not without criticism. In general, the more ambitious and complex a philosophical system is, the more it invites opposing views, for the increased degree of construction brings increased opportunities for destruction. Before the publication of *Meditations on First Philosophy*, Descartes's friend Marin Mersenne forwarded the manuscript to a number of theologians and philosophers for comments. Descartes includes with his *Meditations* a set of their objections, along with his replies. Among his noted critics are three philosophers of the period: the Englishman Thomas Hobbes (1588–1679), and the Frenchmen Pierre Gassendi (1592–1655) and Antoine Arnauld (1612–1694). Aside from Descartes's contemporaries, later philosophers also challenge his view. I will look at two of the problems that the critics raise with regard to the Cartesian system of knowledge; these difficulties appear in the series of objections that accompany the *Meditations*.

Gassendi attacks the very basis of Descartes's philosophy, the *Cogito*. He contends that it is not the fundamental truth that Descartes believes it to be; rather, it is part of a syllogistic formation. It is, in effect, the tail end of an argument with an unstated major premise. An argument cannot be true or false; hence, it cannot play the role that Descartes's thesis requires. The Cartesian argument is shown here:

> If anything thinks, then it is.
> I think.
> Therefore, I am.

A truncated argument of this sort, in which part is missing, is an enthymeme.[74] One problem, as Gassendi sees, is that Descartes has not subjected the major premise to the methodical doubt. Thus, Descartes assumes it to be true in violation of his own method. Further, deductive arguments are valid or invalid, sound or unsound, as demonstrated in chapter 1, but they are not open to truth or falsity. So, if Gassendi is correct, then Descartes has not discovered in the *Cogito* a truth at all and, a fortiori, not one on which he can found an epistemological system.

Descartes holds that the *Cogito* does not present itself to the mind as inferential. He attempts to counter Gassendi's objection by arguing that not all knowledge is the product of deduction from universal propositions. Indeed, says Descartes, the opposite is the path to knowledge. One arrives at such propositions by finding out the truth concerning particular cases, and then, upon laying down the related universal assertions, one may deduce other cases from them.

> For it is certain that in order to discover the truth we should always start with particular notions, in order to arrive at general conceptions subsequently, though we may also in the reverse way, after having discovered the universals, deduce other particulars from them. Thus in teaching a child the elements of geometry we shall certainly not make him understand the general truth that *'when equals are taken from equals the remainders are equal,'* or that *'the whole is greater than its parts,'* unless by showing him examples in particular cases.[75]

What Descartes is advancing is akin to the traditional method by which scientists discover physical laws within associated fields of inquiry and employ those laws to predict future events. After using induction, basing it on the observing of specific instances, a scientist

---

[74] In classic syllogistic form, the argument is structured a little differently:
    All thinking things are.
    I am a thinking thing.
    Therefore, I am.
The two forms of the argument are essentially equivalent.

[75] René Descartes, "Letter from M. Descartes to M. Clerselier," in *Works of Descartes*, 2:127.

sets forth the statement of a relevant general principle. The examined instances may serve to confirm an original hypothesis or require it to be modified, possibly abandoned. Once the statement of the principle is established, the scientist extends its application using deduction. The simplified pattern that appears below illustrates the approach:

<u>Observation of particular cases</u>

At time t_1, subject s observed that an event of type A was followed by an event of type B.

At time t_2, subject s observed that an event of type A was followed by an event of type B.

At time t_3, subject s observed that an event of type A was followed by an event of type B.

. . .

At time t_n, subject s observed that an event of type A was followed by an event of type B.

<u>Inductive Step</u>

Therefore, events of type A invariably are followed by events of type B.

<u>Deductive Step</u>

Therefore, if an event of type A occurs in the future, then an event of type B will follow.

One may ask, though, how is it that Descartes can claim, as he does in his proof of God's existence, that there must be at least as much reality in the efficient and total cause of a thing as in the effect. This premise surely asserts a general principle, and it is a rather powerful assertion at that. Was the principle derived from observation of particular incidents? If it is so, then Descartes indeed has undermined his own philosophy by accepting as true particular propositions—namely, those instances of the general principle that led to his embracing it—without subjecting them to his methodical doubt. If it is not so, then Descartes's use of it in his proof of God's existence is at odds with his defense against Gassendi's attack.

Focusing on the proof and on Descartes's criterion of truth, both Gassendi and Antoine Arnauld charge Descartes with circular reasoning. Writes Arnauld,

> I have one further worry, namely how the author avoids reasoning in a circle when he says that we are sure that what we clearly and distinctly perceive is true only because God exists.
>
> But we can be sure that God exists only because we clearly and distinctly perceive this. Hence, before we can be sure that God exists, we ought to be able to be sure that whatever we perceive clearly and evidently is true.[76]

In his reply, Descartes invokes memory as his defense. He distinguishes between what one perceives clearly and distinctly at the moment and what one remembers to have perceived clearly and distinctly in the past. As one attends to the proof, it is the current clear and distinct perceptions that convince one of the validity of the argument for God's existence. Afterward, however, it is sufficient for one to remember perceiving something in a clear and distinct way to be certain of its truth. So, one takes note of the proof and accepts the conclusion, which asserts that God, who is perfect, exists; and, having proved that God exists and remembering the proof, one can use the clear-and-distinct criterion to discover other truths.

It is a bit surprising that Descartes employs the evil-genius hypothesis to call into question basic mathematical propositions, yet he trusts his own memory. Perhaps he just thinks that he proved God's existence but, in fact, never did so, deceived by the same hypothetical genius that brings doubt on arithmetic and geometry. One does not need even to invoke something other than memory itself and one's experiences using this faculty to call into question the authenticity of it—it is obvious that memory is not infallible, as any prosecuting attorney will attest. Given that it is not infallible, Descartes's employment of it contravenes his own epistemological principle. Moreover, the acceptance of Descartes's proof surely relies

---

[76] Descartes, *Objections and Replies, Fourth Set of Objections,* in *Writings of Descartes,* 2:150.

on memory even as the proof is unfolding for the individual who accepts it. One must keep in mind each premise in succession while working toward the conclusion, linking the premises together in a chain of reasoning.[77] By Descartes's own distinction, however, one cannot be sure that what one remembers perceiving clearly and distinctly earlier in the proof is true until one has completed the proof; thus, one never can establish the conclusion without falling into Arnauld's charge of vicious circularity.

In recent years, philosophers have raised other objections to Descartes's epistemology. For example, whereas it is true that the Cartesian self must exist if it thinks, the *Cogito* is charged expressly with begging the question: a fallacy in which an argument assumes in the premises, explicitly or implicitly, the exact issue at hand. Often in a circular mode, the conclusion is in the premises; here is a case:

> Although inclement weather and automotive failure are important factors, few people realize that the principal cause of accidents on American roads today is careless driving. Heedless motorists are practically ubiquitous. Our freeways are a prime example. Just look around. A cursory examination will reveal drivers darting back and forth as they change lanes, glancing at the scenery, talking on cell phones, texting, and even reading the newspaper. In fact, they spend as much time looking away from the road as they do watching the traffic formations that are developing ahead of them. Drivers are not paying attention. It is not difficult to see how this negligence can result in roadway incidents and accordingly that such a lack of care generates the bulk of collisions. We all pay the price for driver inattentiveness,

---

[77] Frederick Copleston states that, even if Descartes could avoid this problem by holding that memory is not employed in the proof—that is to say, rather than a chain of logical steps, one views it as an unfolding in oneself of the idea of perfection until the relation of self to God is realized—Descartes still faces the problem of the use of axiomatic, general principles in the proof. These axioms cannot be known to be right until it can be shown that God exists. Hence, the circularity remains. For a discussion of the extension of methodical doubt to memory and the problem of circularity in Descartes's proof, see Copleston's *A History of Philosophy*, vol. 4, *Descartes to Leibniz* (London: Search Press, 1958), 106–10.

and, provided that this pattern of motoring continues, it will retain its place of dishonor as the chief source of vehicle mishaps and the greatest threat to safety on the highways.

The argument sets forth—in this instance, with a shade of irony—the conclusion that the leading cause of traffic accidents in America is carelessness. It bases this assertion on the premise that carelessness causes the majority of traffic incidents, citing examples of careless driving. The conclusion effectively appears in the premises. In a similar way, so the criticism goes, Descartes's argument is flawed. By using the first-person pronoun in voicing the "I think" of the *Cogito*, Descartes assumes his existence before he has proved it and then asserts it in the conclusion: "I am." Descartes does not believe that the *Cogito* makes that assumption, but the point is a telling one.

The philosopher Bertrand Russell (1872–1970), one of the two founders of mathematical logic, suggests that what Descartes should utter is nonspecific: "'[T]here are thoughts.'"[78] Russell's point is that Descartes assumes that thoughts need a thinker, which has not been proved. Of course, Descartes assumes even more than that a thinker is required; he assumes that he is the thinker. Unfortunately, for Descartes, Russell's rendition would avoid question-begging at the cost of sacrificing the force of the Cartesian inference, as the conclusion, "I am," does not follow from the premise that there are thoughts. Even if thinking occurs, it need not be that of Descartes. The thoughts could be those of someone or something else. It cannot be shown that, because thoughts occur, Descartes—the "I" here—must be the thinker.[79]

Finally, one must note that the degrees-of-reality hypothesis that Descartes employs in the proof of God's existence is not supportable. Hobbes attacks Descartes on this very issue. As I indicated earlier, existence is not a predicable property of things and

---

[78] Bertrand Russell, *A History of Western Philosophy* (New York: Simon and Schuster, 1945), 567. Russell authored his groundbreaking work on mathematical logic in cooperation with Alfred North Whitehead. They published *Principia Mathematica* in three volumes from 1910 to 1913. Their *Principia* set the stage for logical systems of the contemporary period.

[79] Georges Dicker makes this point in *Descartes: An Analytical and Historical Introduction* (New York: Oxford University Press, 1993). See pp. 48–64 there.

is not amenable to gradation. Things can be more or less massive and more or less expansive. They can be more or less happy and more or less angry. Nothing can be more or less existent, however. Either a thing exists, or it does not exist. Either it is real, or it is not real. Like Plato, Descartes takes hold in his ontology of the erroneous notion of scalable existence.

Descartes's approach to building an epistemological system, founded on the certainty of the *Cogito*, reveals insight and ingenuity. As is the case with a number of others who set out on an ambitious course to undergird knowledge of the world, success for Descartes lies more in the unfolding of questions than in the proffering of answers. Although the problems that his critics raise present what appear to be genuine difficulties for him, the French theorist's self-outward philosophy underscores the quandary in which humans find themselves to be. A person may be sure of his or her own existence, but how does one bridge the gap between oneself and the physical universe? If certainty is required for there to be knowledge, then how can one know anything beyond oneself? If an individual cannot know, then the prospect of solipsism looms.

In the final section of this chapter, I will take a look at another approach to the problem of knowledge. It is not only imaginative but also unorthodox.

GEORGE BERKELEY

Born of English descent on March 12, 1685, at Kilcrene in the vicinity of Kilkenny, Ireland, George Berkeley is one of three main philosophers of the period composing a noted group: the empiricists. The other two in this group are John Locke (1632–1704) and David Hume (1711–1776). In contrast to the rationalists, whom Descartes exemplifies, the empiricists deny that any knowledge—of matters of fact, at any rate—is prior to experience; and, for them, sensory perception is the crucial element on which knowledge ultimately rests. Berkeley was to influence the views of those who followed him in the modern era through a radical departure from mainstream thought.

Berkeley entered Trinity College in Dublin at the age of fifteen and received his B.A. from there in 1704, becoming a fellow of the college in 1707. He published his first major work, *An Essay towards a New Theory of Vision*, in 1709; it advanced a novel view of the perception of distance. In the following year, he assumed duties as an ordained priest in the Protestant Church. One of Berkeley's early goals was to establish a college in Bermuda to provide a comprehensive education for entering students, both the sons of American colonists and Native American Indians, and to train them for Christian ministry. With the promise of financial assistance from certain supporters as well as the English government, he sailed for Rhode Island with his new bride in 1728, becoming the first major philosopher to travel to America. Settling in Newport, Berkeley planned, at first, to establish farms that would produce food for the college in Bermuda. In time, however, he questioned the prudence of his strategy and decided to build the college in Rhode Island instead of Bermuda. The money never came. After the death of their baby daughter, the Berkeleys returned to England in 1731. Berkeley was appointed bishop of Cloyne in Ireland three years later.

Berkeley continued his labors, writing a number of treatises and concerning himself with both the economic conditions around him and the health of people. His diocese was located in a poor area, undoubtedly contributing to his thinking. He proposed public works and education as a means to address poverty and published a manuscript in 1744 on the virtues of tar-water, which he had come to believe held medicinal value. A second edition of the work, which was published in the same year, expanded beyond the original subject to encompass an investigation of physical phenomena. It was Bishop Berkeley's final philosophical writing, although his last known work was a continuation of his thoughts about tar-water, published as part of his *Miscellany* in 1752. Berkeley died in Oxford on January 14, 1753. His primary contributions to epistemology are found in *A Treatise concerning the Principles of Human Knowledge* and *Three Dialogues between Hylas and Philonous*, published respectively in 1710 and 1713.[80]

---

[80] Berkeley's first edition of the *Principles* included a reference to *Part I* in the title. The second edition omitted it from the title page, indicating that Berkeley had

IMMATERIALISM AND PERCEPTION

The problem of knowledge persisted. The world of things remained at arm's length, leaving any philosopher who would know it to find a way to bridge the gap. The objects of understanding must be linked to the perceiver in some way, one that provides assurance of their veracity. To appreciate Berkeley's unique solution to the problem, one must look at his empiricist predecessor, John Locke, and the prevailing view of the times. That view is materialism, arising as a philosophical perspective out of work in the sixteenth through early eighteenth centuries by great scientists, such as Galileo Galilei, Robert Boyle, and Isaac Newton. The cosmos, from the standpoint of the physical science of the time, at least, was thought to reflect a machine-like nature: material bodies situated in space and time, the movements of which could be described with precision by mathematics. Accordingly, the fundamental properties of physical things were deemed to be the properties that the science of matter revealed them to be: movement, mass, shape, and so forth.

With the technical principles in place, the philosopher Locke draws a distinction between the primary qualities and the secondary qualities of things. Both are powers to produce ideas in a mind; however, the former qualities are absolutely inseparable from the material bodies that possess them, whereas the latter ones are merely the capabilities of material things to produce, by the actions of their primary qualities, ideas of sensation in perceivers. Locke also defines another category, that of tertiary qualities, which are the capabilities of bodies to produce changes in other bodies. The primary-secondary division, though, forms the main part of his philosophy. The table that appears below depicts Locke's trifurcation:

---

dropped his plans to publish a second part, although the designation appears in a heading of the text.

Quality	Distinguishing Factors	Identification
Primary	They are inseparable from bodies. One's ideas of these qualities resemble the qualities themselves. These qualities exist in bodies independently of any perceiver.	Solidity, extension (occupies space), figure, rest-motion, and number
Secondary	These qualities are the powers to produce sensations. One's ideas of these qualities do not resemble at all the qualities of bodies themselves. They are indicators of events that are occurring in real bodies.	Color, sound, odor, taste, and so forth
Tertiary	These qualities are the powers to produce changes in other bodies. They exist in bodies independently of any perceiver.	The ability of the sun to melt wax, for example

To demonstrate his point about the primary-secondary distinction, Locke notes that, if a person divides a grain of wheat into two parts, then each part retains solidity and extension. Those qualities must be in the object. Color, taste, and warmth, however, are not in objects *as such*. The red and white colors of porphyry vanish when in the dark. Pound an almond, he says, and both the color and the taste change. Impressions of hot and cold vary with the state of the perceiver and the conditions under which things are perceived. It is possible, the philosopher argues, for the same water, at the same time, to feel hot to one hand of an individual but cold to the other, though the same water cannot be both hot and cold. The corresponding qualities must not be in the water in the way in which primary ones are. (Cf. the illustration in the *Theaetetus* in this chapter, where Plato discusses how the same wind may feel cold to one person but, to another person, warm.)

Years ago, I conducted a pertinent Lockean-style experiment in an introductory philosophy course that I was teaching. I asked for a volunteer from the class and set before him a container of cold water and one of hot water. I instructed the student to immerse one hand in each container. The defect in an otherwise flawless experiment was that the hot water was extremely hot. The student wasted no time in letting me know. A moderate addition of cold water to that vessel brought it to a demonstration-perfect temperature. After he had soaked both hands for a bit, I asked the student to place his hands in a third container, which was filled with tepid water. The grouped looked on with anticipation as he announced that the water indeed felt warm to one hand and cool to its counterpart.

Locke's reasoning is problematic, however. As an almond that is pounded changes color, a grain of wheat that is divided changes figure and number—obvious to everyone, Locke included. The issue is that the wheat continues to possess primary qualities after the cutting event, just not the same ones; but similarly the almond continues to possess secondary qualities after the pounding event, just not the same ones. Moreover, whereas cutting a grain of some substance, say, salt or sand, alters its primary qualities of figure and number, its color may stay the same. One could make the case, based on this example, that it is color that is primary, for it is unaltered, and shape and number that are secondary. Again, if one covers the hands in addition to the eyes, then not only does the aforementioned porphyry produce no sensation of color in the dark, but it also produces no sensation of figure in the dark; and, if it is rotated in the light, then the appearance of the shape changes, whereas the red and white colors may remain.

One thus must question whether primary qualities are actually different from secondary qualities in essential respects. Although Locke's argument is not convincing, his distinction is an important one nevertheless. It points to a central concept of materialism, that things exist independently of sentient beings and possess, also independently of sentient beings, certain physical properties. Colors, odors, and the like, as perceived, however, depend on an observer; they are not—qua colors, odors, and so forth—inherent in physical things. It is a distinction that Berkeley challenges.

Against the backdrop of materialism and Locke's system, Berkeley presents his contrary position. Berkeley's early work on vision laid the foundation for his later thinking concerning what was to become a radical philosophy. In the book *An Essay towards a New Theory of Vision*, Berkeley argues that distance is not something that is perceived immediately through sight, but it is called to mind in the same way that a man's face conveys his feelings of anger. One cannot see distance, just as one cannot see a man's anger; what one sees, in the latter instance, is the man's face, and its expression suggests to the observer that he is angry. In his consideration of distance, Berkeley begins to ponder the issue of existence outside a perceiving mind, a view that matures as he turns his attention to Locke's analysis of qualities. Berkeley believes that Locke's division between primary qualities and secondary qualities is not tenable.

Berkeley contends that the qualities that Locke refers to as primary also change with changing conditions of observation. Distance, for example, can make the same object appear to be large or small. Reminiscent of Plato's writings, some of Berkeley's philosophical thought comes in the form of dialogues, where the character Philonous represents the proponent of Berkeley's theory. Notes Philonous, "[A]s we approach to or recede from an object, the visible extension varies, being at one distance ten or a hundred times greater than at another."[81] Such changes in size come about through the change in one's perspective. Further, says the philosopher, suppose that one views something through a microscope with one eye and views it directly with the other. The same object will look different to each eye. There is no more compelling reason to think that the qualities that are said to be bound inextricably to things—Locke's primary qualities—are intrinsic to those things than to think that heat is intrinsic to them. Turing Locke's example against him, Berkeley's protagonist in the dialogue makes the point in a discussion, with the character Hylas, which I cite below:

> *Phil.* . . . Was it not admitted as a good argument that neither heat nor cold was in the water because it seemed warm to one hand and cold to the other?
> *Hyl.* It was.

---

[81] George Berkeley, *Three Dialogues between Hylas and Philonous*, *The First Dialogue*, in *George Berkeley: Principles, Dialogues, and Philosophical Correspondence*, ed. Colin Murray Turbayne (Indianapolis: Bobbs-Merrill Co., 1965), 128.

> *Phil.* Is it not the very same reasoning to conclude
> there is no extension or figure in an object because to
> one eye it shall seem little, smooth, and round, when at
> the same time it appears to the other great, uneven, and
> angular?
>
> *Hyl.* The very same. But does this latter fact ever
> happen?
>
> *Phil.* You may at any time make the experiment by
> looking with one eye bare, and with the other through a
> microscope.[82]

To advance the philosophical view for which he is noted, Berkeley poses a succinct argument. First, however, he surveys the objects of human knowledge and sees that they all are ideas of one sort or another, specifically—as he orders them in this survey—ideas that are imprinted on the senses, ideas resulting from the passions and operations of the mind, and ideas that are formed by the memory and imagination. Berkeley then proceeds to make his case for immaterialism, arguing that to affirm the existence of matter without any perception of it is to embrace nonsense. Says the philosopher,

> That neither our thoughts, nor passions, nor ideas
> formed by the imagination exist without the mind is
> what everybody will allow. And it seems no less evident
> that the various sensations or ideas imprinted on the
> sense, however blended or combined together (that is,
> whatever objects they compose), cannot exist otherwise
> than in a mind perceiving them.—I think an intuitive
> knowledge may be obtained of this by anyone that shall
> attend to what is meant by the term "exist" when applied
> to sensible things. The table I write on I say exists, that
> is, I see and feel it; and if I were out of my study I
> should say it existed—meaning thereby that if I was in
> my study I might perceive it, or that some other spirit
> actually does perceive it. . . . This is all that I can
> understand by these and the like expressions. For as to
> what is said of the absolute existence of unthinking
> things without any relation to their being perceived, that
> seems perfectly unintelligible. Their *esse* is *percipi*, nor

---

[82] Ibid., 129.

is it possible they should have any existence out of the
minds or thinking things which perceive them.[83]

There is a class of things, Berkeley says, that cannot exist
unperceived. Thoughts, passions, and ideas that are formed by the
imagination—all require a mind, a perceiver. Yet, there is no reason
to distinguish in this respect between sensations and these other
mentally apprehended entities. Sensations, or what Berkeley calls
ideas of sense, cannot exist unperceived either. When a person
speaks of the existence of an object, such as a table, the person
means by the corresponding term the set of characteristics, perceived
through the senses, that the person ascribes to the object. If one
speaks of a table that one is not perceiving, then what he or she
means in doing so is the group of various properties, captured by the
sensory apparatus, that one would assign to it if it were in one's
presence, or else the group of properties that some other mind actually does assign to it at the time. No other meaning is intelligible.

Berkeley takes the line of thought one step further, holding that
the existence of objects *is* their being perceived. To declare that there
is some material container, as it were, devoid of all properties itself
yet holding properties that one ascribes to it, is to make a nonsensical
assertion. What people call physical things are, in actuality, no more
than collections of perceived qualities; they are concatenations of
sensations, ideas clustered together. An apple, for example, is "a
certain color, taste, smell, figure, and consistence having been
observed to go together" that perceivers count as "one distinct thing
signified by the name" that they give it.[84] There is no material object,
something that is independent of a mind's perceiving it. There is no
substratum. Matter does not exist. The whole of existence consists of
perceived ideas—sensations, thoughts, passions, memories, and
imaginations—and the active beings, which Berkeley calls minds or
spirits, that perceive them. Reality, claims Berkeley, is immaterial.

One may object that there is surely a difference between seeing
a table or an apple and imagining one. Berkeley agrees; sensations
differ from imaginings in several ways—namely, the following ones:

---

[83] George Berkeley, *A Treatise concerning the Principles of Human Knowledge,
Part I*, in *Principles, Dialogues, and Correspondence*, 23.
[84] Ibid., 22.

1. They are more lively, vivid, and distinct than ideas of
   imagination.
2. They have a steadfastness, order, and coherence that are
   lacking in imaginings, and they do not appear at
   random.
3. They are not subject to a person's will.

Berkeley's point is that one can distinguish between ideas of sensation and ideas of imagination but that ideas of neither category exist outside a perceiving mind. There is no material substrate out there, as it were, underlying the objects that one perceives. There are only ideas, whether of sensation or otherwise, and the minds in which they have their existence.

Berkeley maintains that the concept of a substratum, in fact, leads to an infinite regress. If the substratum is that which provides the support for the qualities of things—the substance that undergirds them—then it must be spread under those qualities. If it is spread under a thing's qualities, the set of which includes extension, then it is distinct from them. Nothing can be spread without extension, however; Berkeley reveals the upshot in these remarks:

> *Phil.* Consequently, every corporeal substance being the *substratum* of extension must have in itself another extension by which it is qualified to be a *substratum*, and so on to infinity? And I ask whether this be not absurd . . . ?[85]

Even if, Berkeley continues, the spreading is not literal, there still must be some sense in which the substance supports the qualities of an object. To do so, it must be extended; if one claims that it is not extended, then one cannot explain how it is that one thing, the substratum, can support something else, the qualities of objects. One is left with either the regress or an inexplicable relationship.

Paralleling Descartes's *Cogito*, a single aphorism captures the essence of Berkeley's philosophy: *Esse est percipi*, expressed in its Latin form. Berkeley alleges,

---

[85] Berkeley, *Three Dialogues*, *The First Dialogue*, 138.

To be is to be perceived.[86]

For the immaterialists, what people call things are bundles of sensations that have no existence apart from a mind's perceiving them.

If matter is unreal, and the existence of things is given in their being perceived, then what keeps the forks and knives from popping into, and out of, existence as one opens and shuts the kitchen drawer repeatedly? What happens to the tennis ball when both players blink as it crosses the net, propelled by a serve; how can it reappear in just the right place several feet farther along the same trajectory?[87] What could preserve the course of the ball if it ceases to exist—indeed, the net and the tennis court with it—for the momentary period that the opponents' eyes are closed? Berkeley is faced with a world that is annihilated instantly and recreated as quickly, time after time. In such a world, there can be no genuine persistence of things, no identity through time. There is no single tennis ball in the above-mentioned example but two or three or more.

Consider Roger, an avid numismatist. Thinking that he has acquired a rare coin, a fine specimen of which only four are extant, Roger clutches his prize to himself, only to find that there are hundreds of them, one for each instant that he gazes in his display case during the next decade. Like Descartes, Berkeley engineers a system that collapses without something to warrant the integrity of perceived objects, although the problem is not with the possibility of one's being deceived about them but with their continued existence during the times that they are not perceived by any person. Unlike Descartes then, who is trapped in solipsism without God to ensure the authenticity of perceptions, Berkeley must prove the existence of God to preserve the continuity of the world of things that humans

---

[86] The notion runs throughout Berkeley's writings. See, for example, his *Principles*, Part I, 65. The statement that captures Berkeley's ontology more completely is *Esse est aut percipi aut percipere*: To be is either to be perceived or to perceive. Berkeley believes that two categories of things exist: (1) ideas that are perceived by minds or spirits and (2) the minds or spirits that perceive them.

[87] A tennis professional can launch a ball at approximately 150 miles per hour in serving. Given a subsequent speed of, say, 130 miles per hour near the net, the ball would travel about nineteen feet during a blink, if the blink lasts 0.1 second.

experience. He attempts to do so. The bundles of sensation that people call things are conserved in the mind of God when people are not perceiving them. Here is his argument in a summarized format, which one may refer to as the passivity proof. The steps are numbered for convenience and subsequent reference.

1. Sensible things are ideas, there being no material substance.
2. All ideas are produced.
3. Unlike ideas of thought, passion, and imagination, ideas of sensation are not subject to my will.
4. Thus, I do not produce ideas of sensation.
5. Ideas do not produce themselves, as no idea can be the cause of another.
6. Some mind must produce them, as they are not produced from material substance and not produced from ideas.
7. Therefore, God produces them.
8. Therefore, God exists.

Berkeley's solution to the problem of knowledge is decidedly distinctive. One does not reach out to the world of things; instead, one pulls the world of things into oneself. Humans know objects because they are in intimate contact with them; objects are nothing other than collections of ideas—bundles of sensations. Berkeley avoids the severance-from-reality concerns, which Democritus introduces, at the expense of dispensing with matter altogether. What remains to be seen is whether the system that he builds is defensible against the predictable attacks.

PROBLEMS WITH BERKELEY'S SYSTEM

While in New England, Berkeley had met, and corresponded with, Samuel Johnson, the well-known English author and lexicographer. It is reported that, when asked about Berkeley's philosophy of immaterialism, Johnson kicked a huge stone with considerable force and said, "I refute it *thus*."

Few criticisms of Berkeley are as laconic as Johnson's quip, but the notion that matter does not exist is sure to raise concerns. Suppose that Sandra and Sally are viewing a daffodil. Given that, for Berkeley, things are no more than clusters of perceptions, existing in the mind, the question arises whether the ladies are viewing the same flower or different ones. If they are viewing the same flower, then Sandra and Sally must share a mind or, at least, share a mental part, as the identical bundle of sensations could not exist in two minds unless they were one and the same or, at least, conjoined. The problem might be depicted in the following way, where the configuration that is shown in either pattern *A* or pattern *B* must be the case:

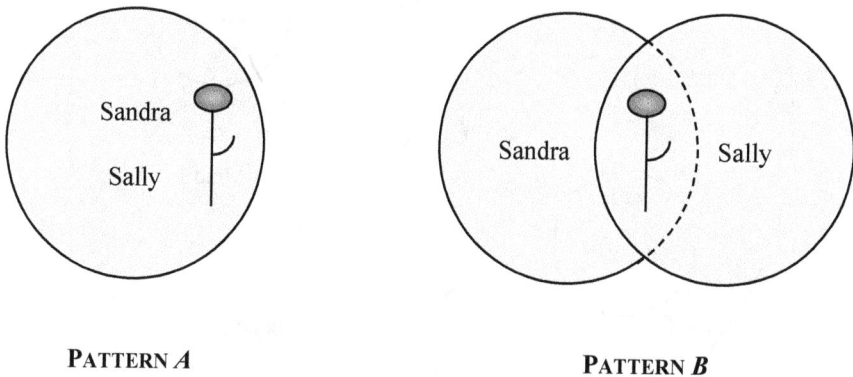

PATTERN *A*   PATTERN *B*

Figure 2.6

In fact, there must be a single mind for *all* people or, at minimum, one or more common parts where communal sensations occur.

On the other hand, if one denies that the ladies are seeing the same daffodil, then the world becomes a fragmented system in which there is no identity of objects. One returns to the problem of a multiplicity of entities that correspond to any perceivable thing that one cares to name, only here it is the consequence of the separation of sensations rather than the continualness of change. Although God, in Berkeley's view, preserves things, so that they do not blink into, and out of, existence, no two people ever can perceive the same object. Further, if objects are conserved in the mind of God, then where must perceivers be when they perceive them? It seems that, unless Berkeley can show otherwise, they all are in the mind of God:

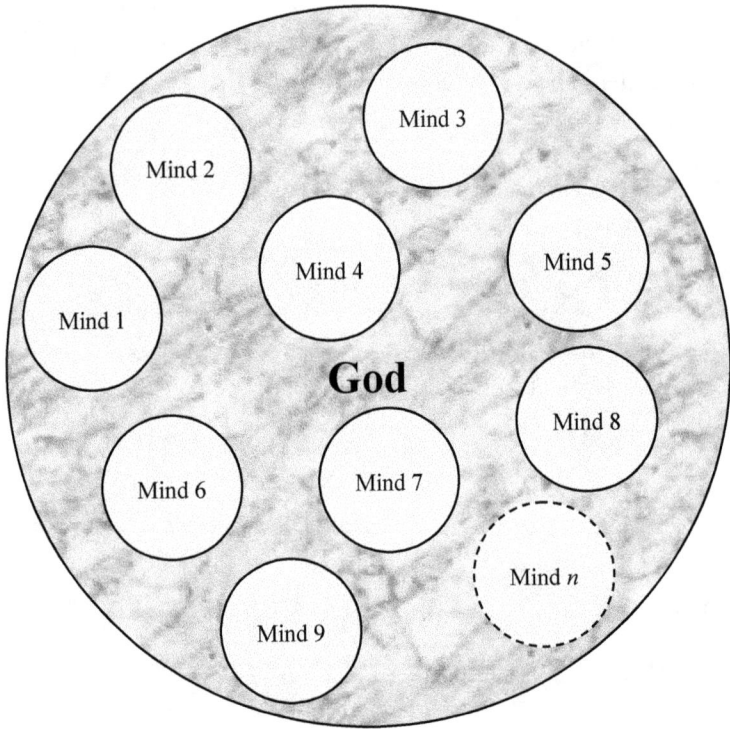

PATTERN *C*

Figure 2.7

Berkeley is willing to take a critical look at his own philosophy. Anticipating the inevitable objections, he attempts to address them in his published works. Berkeley is aware of the challenge of multiple persons' seeing the same thing, but his arguments in support of his view are hardly persuasive. In *Three Dialogues between Hylas and Philonous*, he tries to make a number of points in his defense. I will take a look at a pair of them.

One should note beforehand that there are two senses of sameness: *numerical identity* and *qualitative identity*. Consider this statement and the conditions under which it is true: 'John and Jim drive the same car'. Both men may take turns driving a single vehicle, or they individually may own automobiles that are of the same make, model, and year. In the former sense, the identity is numerical: There is just one car. In the latter sense, the identity is qualitative or, more accurately, quasi-qualitative: There are two cars with nearly the same properties. For objects to be truly qualitatively identical, they must have *all* properties in common. Aside from the same make, model, and year, for example, two automobiles that are identical in this sense must be the same shade of color, show the same mileage on their odometers, have dents in the passenger doors that are of equal dimensions and in corresponding places, reflect tread wear on their left rear tires that match exactly, have antennae that are bent at the same angle, display cuts in their passenger seats that measure thirty-two millimeters in length, and so forth. If one marks the properties with enough specificity, then it seems that there invariably will be *some* qualitative differences between two material objects that are distinct, although the differences may be minute.

The rationalist philosopher Leibniz, who predates Berkeley by about forty years, argues that there are no two discrete things that share all properties. It is not possible, he believes, for two things to differ numerically yet be exactly alike—that is to say, indiscernible. Expressed invariably in a negative formulation in his writings, Leibniz's assertion, in essence, is that, if two things are truly qualitatively identical, then they are also numerically identical. This principle—the identity of indiscernibles—typically is referred to as Leibniz's law. One interpretation of this law is that it holds as a matter of fact about the world, such that two things that appear to be similar in every respect will prove to differ upon close inspection. Leibniz's writings suggest, however, that he may have a stronger notion in mind, such that the indiscernibility of things is a logical guarantee of their identity. It is the stricter of the two readings, rendering identity independent of the empirical considerations that apply to the alternative view.[88]

The principle has been called into question in recent years, notably by the philosopher Max Black. Black makes a case for the possibility of a pair of separate objects, the properties of which are the same.

> Isn't it logically possible that the universe should have contained nothing but two exactly similar spheres? We might suppose that each was made of chemically pure iron, had a diameter of one mile, that they had the same temperature, colour, and so on, and that nothing else existed. Then every quality and relational characteristic of the one would also be a property of the other. Now if what I am describing is logically possible, it is not impossible for two things to have all their properties in common. This seems to me to *refute* the Principle.[89]

One wonders whether the two objects in Black's case can be exactly the same. If relational characteristics are allowed—Black allows them in his example—then it appears that a problem surfaces. The spheres will be in the space-time grid of the universe; and there are points asymmetrically locatable within that grid, such that, even though the spheres might stand in the same spatial relationship to each other, they would not stand in the same spatial relationship to a point that is not equidistant from the center of each of the spheres.

Further, for Black's objects to have all properties in common, it would be necessary for the respective compositions of those objects to be precisely the same. With the two iron spheres that Black

---

[88] For brief comments about the interpretations of the law and Leibniz's formulation, see *Encyclopedia of Philosophy*, s.v., "Identity." Note that some authors associate the law with a different principle (I will cover it soon). Note too that some see qualitative identity as spread along a continuum, where things can be more or less identical in this sense, depending on the extent to which they share properties. It is not the sense that Leibniz has in mind, and its application is stretched inappropriately, I think, for, unlike similarity, identity proper does not admit of degrees. I use the term 'quasi-qualitative' to denote sameness that is short of total resemblance.

[89] Max Black, "The Identity of Indiscernibles," *Mind* 61, no. 242 (1952): 156.

mentions, every microphysical particle in one sphere would have to be in a state paralleling that of a corresponding particle in the other sphere, where such correspondence would be determined by relative position. There would be a set of spatial relationships holding among the particles composing the first sphere, and a set of spatial relationships holding among the particles composing the second sphere, and the two sets—sets with many members because of the huge number of particles and their positions relative to others—would be equivalent. Owing to the geometric symmetry of a sphere, numerous sets of comparable relative positions within a given sphere would be possible—simply move the location point about the globe, maintaining its distance from the center—but not if one takes into account the space-time grid in which the globe is situated. Now, what is needed is a one-to-one correspondence between the particles making up the first sphere and those making up the second, a particle in each place within the second sphere matching one in the same relative place within the first sphere, where the particle in the second sphere is exactly like its counterpart in the first, sharing all its properties.

If the precise position of a microphysical particle is known, however, then the momentum of that particle cannot be ascertained with certainty, and conversely, according to quantum physics.[90] An inverse relation holds between an accurate determination of one of the paired elements and that of the other. One thus cannot know that any two particles for which one can establish the respective locations within each sphere share all properties if one counts momentum as a property. It follows, on that premise, that one cannot know that the spheres containing those particles are exactly alike in their attributes.

It is arguable nonetheless that the momentum of an object is not an attribute of the object at all. Consider everyday things. With a constant mass, momentum varies as a function of velocity, and how fast a thing is moving is extraneous; it has nothing to do with what that thing is in actuality. A dog, a car, and a rock may be traveling down a stretch of road at twenty miles per hour or at ten miles per hour, or all may be dead still on the pavement. Nothing about the rate of travel or a change in that rate either contributes to or alters the

---

[90] The Heisenberg uncertainty principle expresses this state of affairs in a formal manner.

characteristics of the objects, considered solely in themselves. The dog is still a golden retriever with a missing cuspid; the car is still a red Porsche with a loose fan belt; and the rock is still just a rock. Moreover, the failure to know the momentum of something may not be enough to topple Black's case, for he is concerned with the logical possibility of things' being numerically distinct yet qualitatively identical, not with whether one ever can know that they are so.

What is emerging here is that one need not enter Black's imaginary universe to see the merit of his objection; one can turn to the actual universe, to the subatomic particles of the quantum domain. For instance, the distinction between electrons, considered strictly in themselves—basic units that are components of matter—cannot be attributed to qualities that are intrinsic to them, because all electrons, as just electrons, are the same. They may vary in energy states, in quasi-spatial positions, and in association with the nuclei of atoms of different chemical elements, but one electron qua electron is exactly like any other. Outside the atomic world, it may seem that Leibniz's principle, even in its less-strict sense, applies, discounting Black's objection. If one determines the properties of macrophysical objects suitably, then, between any two objects that are distinct, it is likely that there will be *some* dissimilarity—discernible not just in principle but also in fact—although the variance may be slight. Such is not the case, however, when one descends into the area of the microphysical. Individual electrons are qualitatively identical—indiscernible not just in fact but also in principle—in that they have precisely the same defining properties, those *inherent* characteristics (setting aside the noninherent factors that the Pauli exclusion principle covers) that make them what they are essentially: elementary particles with the same mass, charge, and *absolute* spin value. If the sameness of things does not entail the sameness of their positions, given that location is contextual, then one is led to accept the thesis that different things can have identical sets of properties after all.

The more interesting issue, however, and one that is more central to this work, is whether *identical* things can have *different* properties. Crafting a tenable philosophy of identity through time turns on the ability to deal with this important question effectively. The principle of the indiscernibility of identicals, as it is known in philosophical circles, is, to be sure, even more suspect than its counterpart.[91] For now, note that, in day-to-day life, people typically call things the same that are alike in key properties but do not possess sets of properties that coincide exactly. It is the concept of the distinction between the two kinds of identity that is the principal concern in the analysis here.

Returning to Berkeley, I want to point out that he first seems to dismiss the problem of different observers' sensing the same object as a semantic issue and a matter of practicality. He believes that one may continue to say without confusion that people see the same thing, using the term 'same' in the qualitative sense, even if they do not see the same thing in the numerical sense; and no one is at a loss because of the usage. Yet, as is often the case in philosophy, practicality has little to do with building a defensible system.

Berkeley supposes a model-copy dichotomy next. Such a structure frequently is referred to as a division between types and tokens; for Berkeley, it is between archetypes and ectypes. Like duplicates of an original letter, printed on an office copier, ideas of sensation that arise in each person's mind are tokens of a type that is external to the individual mind; the type resides in the mind of God. The tokens are numerically distinct from each other but not qualitatively distinct. If Berkeley is successful in his approach, then perhaps he can address the problem that is shown in Figure 2.7 above. Assuming that God conserves the types, but persons experience the tokens, individual minds need not be inside the mind of God to experience sensations, but, of course, Berkeley must explain exactly how it is that the tokens are generated. According to the philosopher, God causes one's ideas of sensation in accordance with His will, but there is an obvious need for a more complete and compelling account of how God uses the types to produce the tokens and implant them in human minds.

Furthermore, if things are bundles of ideas of sensation—tokens grouped together—then one must ask what God's role is in the bundling activity that provides for the changing appearance of things. States Berkeley through the protagonist in his dialogues,

---

[91] Some writers equate Leibniz's law with *this* principle; others believe that the two mirror-image principles should be conjoined to provide a proper formulation of identity as Leibniz's law. The implications of each are significant—and significantly different—however, and I treat them as separate principles in this work.

"From all which I conclude, *there is a Mind which affects me every moment with all the sensible impressions I perceive.*"[92] As one watches objects in motion or things decay, one sees them go through many stages of change. Picture a basketball player, dashing past onlookers who are sitting in the stands. As the player drives toward the goal, his arms and legs are in constant motion, along with the ball. Each limb moves through its cycle, bringing alterations to the appearance of the athlete. A limb's motion is continuous, as is that of the player who is sprinting across the floor; so, an indefinite, maybe even infinite, number of positions correspond to his movement down the court. If each new appearance for an observer correlates with a different type in the mind of God, then one is challenged to understand what God is doing to produce the changing appearances. Moreover, given that the fans in the bleachers view the game from different angles, there must be a unique package of tokens for every observer. Is God bundling the types and then generating the tokens, all at great speed; or is He selecting the types quickly, generating the tokens, and then bunching the tokens together? Regardless of what God is doing, He is exceedingly busy. If, on the other hand, each new appearance of the player does not correlate with a different archetype, then Berkeley must explain how it is that the archetype itself changes to accommodate the changing, observed tokens. Such an account does not seem to be forthcoming.

In consideration of Berkeley's argument, it is important to note that the materialists, Berkeley contends, also hold that sensations are individual tokens of an external archetype, so that people do not see precisely the same thing. The archetype is in the material object. Tokens, the ideas of sensation, are unique to the perceiver. Yet, the materialists say that people, in looking at an object, see the same thing. So, claims Berkeley, materialism and immaterialism stand or fall together, as, in both accounts, everyone perceives something different in sense perception.

Berkeley's point about semantics, in the first part of his response to potential criticism, is superficial and does not address the real issue. In sensing, either all perceive the numerically same thing, or they do not perceive it. Berkeley appears to be embracing the

---

[92] Berkeley, *Three Dialogues, The Second Dialogue*, 157.

latter alternative. Thus, in a football stadium, packed with eighty thousand fans who are watching the game, not one of them sees the same event, or even the same football in play. There are tens of thousands of balls in that arena, each one a bundle of sensation tokens residing in a unique mind.

The second part of his response, drawing on a type-token structure, fares little better as Berkeley again skirts the issue. In question is the correctness of his own philosophy, and he cannot avoid its inevitable outcome: a fractured universe in which an indeterminate number of entities are generated. Neither of Berkeley's proffered defenses releases him from the problem of numerically distinct perceptions. Berkeley's philosophy constitutes a serious violation of the law of parsimony.

Moreover, Berkeley needs God to provide the continuity of things. Berkeley's critics find fault with his proof of God's existence, however. It does have problems. Consider more closely some of the argument's assertions, which I restate here, and the consequences for Berkeley.

Step 3   Unlike ideas of thought, passion, and imagination, ideas of sensation are not subject to my will.

Problem   The hallucinations that the delusional man seems to see are not subject to his will. Even a normal person has thoughts and passions that stand against his or her intent. Timmy did not want to daydream during the lecture, as he needed the information for the forthcoming exam, but he could not help doing so. Rachel tried in vain to overcome her anger at the cruel remark. In dreams, there are many ideas that one does not control by one's will.

Step 4   I do not produce ideas of sensation.

Problem   This step fails because of the problem with step 3. One has no assurance that one does not produce ideas of sensation, for one does produce them in dreams; and they are lively, vivid, and distinct, which, for Berkeley, are the defining marks of such ideas. Hallucinations, imaginings, and dreams—all are produced by the mind that perceives them.

Step 5   Ideas do not produce themselves, as no idea can be the cause of another.

Problem   Ideas do cause other ideas. Ann's seeing the bee caused her to imagine its stinging her. Arthur's fond thoughts of Emily caused him to remember her birthday and to think of the card that he wanted to purchase for her.

Step 7   God produces the ideas of sensation.

Problem   It cannot be shown with certainty that the mind that produces ideas of sensation is the mind of God. Even if it could be shown that a person is not the author of his or her own ideas of sense—and one has seen that there is no guarantee that he or she is not the author—it may be another finite mind (or even a set of them), although rather unlikely, that produces those ideas.

If Berkeley is not successful in proving God's existence, then his immaterialism reduces to a system with no cohesiveness whatsoever for objects, either spatially or temporally. Objects are discontiguous in space because they are no more than clusters of sensations, and each cluster is in a distinct mind of a perceiver. If that mind is located anywhere at all, then, unless every other mind is in that place too, the separation remains. Berkeley's view of sameness shows that Sandra's perception of a daffodil is numerically distinct from Sally's when both ladies are viewing the flower. Without God, there is no archetype, so there are no tokens of that type, only disjointed clusters that have no relationship to each other. One cannot talk to others about objects, for there is no common ground for discussion.

Worse still perhaps is the fact that objects are disconnected in time. There is a steady procession of unique objects as one blinks. Thus, not only are entities multiplied across minds; they are multiplied within a single mind as well. To adopt Berkeley's philosophy without the assurance of God is to embrace a universe that utterly disintegrates.

THREE ROADS TO THE WORLD

Part I of this work has laid the philosophical foundation for the inquiry that is to come. This inquiry must begin with the difficult problem of change. Introduced by the ancient Greeks, the problem is one that expands beyond its own immediate scope because it seems to be true that change undermines identity. The various substratum theories that arise out of early philosophical investigations make a case for explaining how alterations in properties might be possible. Where such theories flounder, however, is in giving an adequate account of the relationship between the substratum and the things that it supposedly supports, and in explaining how identity can be maintained through the substitution of component parts. The bundle theory that Berkeley puts forth, on the other hand, avoids the problem of the substrate-object relationship by denying that there is any substrate at all, but it fails to explain how identity through change—even a change in properties, let alone in parts—is possible. The crucial problem of knowledge, though, is the enemy of both approaches, in two ways. First, without an adequate account of continuance through different states and different components, objects fall apart and, with them, the ability to know. Second, if people are severed from reality, as Democritus declares, then, without a satisfactory means of bridging the gap, the things in the perceptible world remain out of reach, and knowledge of them slips from the grasp.

It is not surprising that the philosophical pursuit of a tenable system of knowledge has its roots in the ancient search for some underlying metaphysical principle on which to base the world of experience and account for change. The path to knowing somehow seems to rest on uncovering essential reality. One has seen how three exceptional philosophers tackle the issue in an effort to save the world that humans detect through their senses and to give an account of how knowledge of it is possible. Each philosopher attempts to forge the critical link between perceived objects and perceiving subjects. Of note, each one appeals to something eternal and changeless to do so. Their respective systems rely on something that is *outside* the realm of objects to provide the requisite ontic solidity for the things that are *inside* it.

For Plato, it is the forms. Plato sets forth two categories of entities: mutable things and immutable properties—particulars and forms. Without forms, there can be no knowledge in Plato's system, as things dissipate, receding into the roar of Heraclitean flux. Sensory objects are anchored by universals. It is through their participation in these universals that particulars gain a measure of reality, and people gain a measure of comprehension of them. Knowledge of corporeal objects is derivative and imperfect; it is possible only because forms provide a measure of fixity, allowing the mind to take hold of those objects in the limited way that it can do so.

Forms alone do not constitute order, however, and Plato turns to God to bring structure to existence and to explain how it is that the visible world came into being. In Plato's philosophy, God is the Craftsman, a role that Plato identifies in his dialogue *Timaeus*. Plato does not believe that God created the forms, but Plato does give an account of how God instituted order among them in establishing the cosmos. Man is the handiwork of this intelligent, celestial being, who made the immortal part of the soul of man—the rational constituent, Plato maintains—but trusted the completion of that mortal entity to lesser intermediaries. In recognizing divine perfection and the human striving to imitate it, Plato exhibits insight that gives one pause.

> God invented and gave us sight to the end that we might
> behold the courses of intelligence in the heaven, and
> apply them to the courses of our own intelligence which
> are akin to them, the unperturbed to the perturbed, and
> that we, learning them and partaking of the natural truth
> of reason, might imitate the absolutely unerring courses
> of God and regulate our own vagaries.[93]

In the Cartesian system, the eternal, changeless element is God Himself. Without God, Descartes's philosophy collapses into solipsism. The French philosopher begins his journey to find the key to knowledge of the world by establishing, first of all, something with certainty. He discovers the requisite assurance in the indubitable quality of the *Cogito*. If he can prove next that God exists, then he

---

[93] Plato, *Timaeus*, 47b–c, 1175.

can assert that the senses can be trusted because the perfect nature of God does not allow Him to be a deceiver. God is the guarantor of the veracity of perception, although, from time to time, one's boundless will leads one astray.

In the preceding pages, I analyzed Descartes's main argument for the existence of God. Ironically, Descartes's extreme doubt, the distinguishing mark of his approach to finding indubitable truth, undermines his own attempted proof. By casting doubt on even simple mathematical equations, Descartes takes away the legitimacy of using axioms in the proof that he advances. Descartes must make his case for God, however, for, unless he can show that God exists, all that he can know is himself.

Like Descartes, Berkeley finds the eternal element of his theory in God. Berkeley's approach, however, is radical. Unlike both Plato and Descartes, who reach out to the world, Berkeley brings the world to himself. He denies that material things exist, saying instead that the things that the senses reveal to perceivers are only clusters of perceptions, existing in the mind. The objects of knowledge are ideas, and one knows these objects because one is in intimate contact with them. Things themselves are real, says Berkeley, but they are not material. Berkeley's philosophy presents a world of order and coherence in which these incorporeal things are conserved in the mind of God. Objects are not annihilated and recreated every moment; God sustains their continued existence.

Remove God from Berkeley's system, and it flies apart like a fragile, crystal vase as it is splintered by a soprano. Knowledge of things loses meaning, for there are only fractured collections of ideas that are separated both by the boundaries of distinct minds and by periods of nonperception within the same mind. No two bundles can be numerically the same; therefore, there is no continuity for things, and all an object's history is erased with the blink of an eye. Without God, the orderly cosmos is no more.

For some philosophers then, God becomes the indispensable element of their systems—what makes them work, as it were. Not unexpectedly, the search for a way to prove the existence of God rises to a prominent place within the philosophical enterprise. Far more than simply a tenet in some theory of ontology or a necessary principle in an epistemological construct, the existence of the Creator of the unimaginably expansive universe is a matter of fundamental significance in its own right. The quest to find God through logical demonstration—or, more accurately, to demonstrate that He exists—is thus a principal part of any serious inquiry of sufficient breadth.

Before the text embarks on a journey to search the heavens, though, it is important to determine whether the thorny problem of knowledge derails attempts at discovery in the world of things. In this chapter, I examined three of the major epistemological systems that are found in the history of Western thought. The philosophies of Plato, Descartes, and Berkeley—each offers a way to provide an underpinning for the world of sense and to show how an understanding of it, whether limited or complete, is possible. All these systems are both ambitious and ingenious, yet, so one has seen, all of them fail. One is left with the unanswered question whether things are ever coherent enough, and beliefs ever sure enough, to say that one knows—whether, given both continual flux and sensory uncertainty, knowledge is obtainable at all.

PART II

BELIEVING AND KNOWING— LOOKING OUTWARD, INWARD, AND UPWARD

CHAPTER 3

THE OBJECT OF IDENTITY

He [Christ] is before all things,
and in him all things hold together.

—Col. 1:17 NIV

One of the more memorable toys of my childhood, although it was hardly a toy, was the microscope that I received as a gift from my parents. On second thought, I believe that it was Santa Claus who brought it to me. At any rate, it was a fascinating device for a school-age boy. With three levels of magnification, I could examine all manner of things to see how they are made. Nothing is immune to the curiosity of the young, and the microscope was a newfound means of discovery. Everything in the environment became a target. Tissue-thin layers of onion revealed a remarkable latticework of cells composing the bulb of the plant. Tiny insects displayed structures on their legs that could not be seen with the unaided eye. Even hair—human, or perhaps it was pet—looked completely different under magnification, where the highest power resolved the smallest surface details.

Unknown to me at the time, the philosopher John Locke, whose empiricist viewpoint I discussed briefly in the last chapter, had made similar discoveries three hundred years earlier.

> Thus Sand, or pounded Glass, which is opaque, and white to the naked Eye, is pellucid in a Microscope; and a Hair seen this way, loses its former Colour, and is in a great measure pellucid, with a mixture of some bright sparkling Colours, such as appear from the refraction of Diamonds, and other pellucid Bodies.[1]

---

[1] John Locke, *An Essay concerning Human Understanding*, ed. Peter H. Nidditch (1975; repr., Oxford: Oxford University Press, 1985), 301–2. The first edition of Locke's work appeared in 1689; it was dated 1690 on the title page.

Locke used his findings to support the assertion that qualities, such as color, are not in things in the way, for example, that the shapes of things are. Regardless of the accuracy of his claim, the microscope provided, for both the seventeenth-century philosopher and the latter-day lad who was to become one, a window on a foreign and exciting world awaiting exploration.

Aside from its utility as a scientific instrument, part of the appeal of the microscope—for a philosopher, at least—lies in the dramatic change that it brings to the appearances of everyday things. Under intense magnification, objects look radically different from the way that they look when observed with the naked eye. Despite these shifts in appearance, logical thinking seems to dictate that the objects themselves are the same; things are not undergoing the drastic changes that their appearances indicate as one views them first without the magnifying machine and then with it. They look so different from moment to moment because the conditions under which they are viewed are so different. It is the perceiving that changes, not the perceived or even the perceiver. Such changes are not surprising; one encounters them quite frequently. The drive to work reveals a myriad of diverse images as one sees cars, buildings, and trees from different angles and different distances. Reason combines appropriate groups of images, associating them with discrete objects. Notwithstanding the concerns of the sense-datum theorists, one understands that the sight of the rear of the truck now and the sight of the front a moment ago are merely two views of the same passing vehicle.

Often, though, it is not the conditions of the perceiving that are the variant factor. Something about the perceived object itself is not the same. A number of years ago, as an employee of a large corporation, I was transferred from my home in the South to an area of the Northeast where snow is common. The company required its managers who were positioned for reassignment to meet with both business leaders and client personnel in the new location for a period of assessment. During the onsite interview process, I inquired about snowfall in the winter months. My interviewers informed me that it was modest there; I should encounter no weather-related problems. Owning at the time, in addition to our family car, a compact SUV with four-wheel-drive capability and generous ground clearance, I decided to keep it, in spite of the reassuring comments by the staff. The vehicle was already several years old, so the potential for harsh environmental conditions was of little concern. Further, if it did snow more than anticipated, then I would be equipped to face the challenge of travel, or so I thought.

About a month passed as the company and I prepared for the move. I arrived for work near the end of April. In the interim, a single storm had dumped approximately three feet of snow on the township. The following winter set five records, including the coldest temperature ever recorded there and the most snow that the township had experienced in its history. The next winter broke that latter record by nearly a foot. The thermometer on my porch revealed a temperature of –27° Fahrenheit one morning. Whether it was during that year or another, I cannot say. I can say, though, that the winters there were very cold. The decision to keep that four-wheel-drive vehicle proved to be wise. I became lodged in the snow only once. A seasonal storm had left its mark that day. Traveling down a yet-to-be-plowed road, I found the snow on that remote stretch of asphalt to be as high as the bumper. Feeling invincible, I shifted into low, all four wheels locked and grabbing for traction. My confidence in the machine was misplaced. To my bewilderment, progress came to an abrupt halt. I tried to balance my perplexity with the obvious facts. How could this off-road engineering tour de force be *stuck*— what now? This situation cannot be the result of a lapse in judgment, I was sure; no, it must be a failure of four-wheel-drive technology. My house was miles away. It was a deservedly humbling experience.

Before my wife and I departed, so that I could begin my new assignment, it occurred to me that the old SUV needed a facelift. I drove it to a local detail shop to have it cleaned and waxed. This particular establishment had a reputation for quality workmanship, and the vehicle was going to look its best, I determined, as it set out on its journey northward. The interior was in excellent condition, but the exterior had faded severely. It was red; at least, it was that color originally. Red paint is notorious for losing its luster more quickly than other colors because of the particular pigment that is used, and the hot summer months in the South had taken their toll. I left the vehicle in the hands of the capable detail crew. I knew that it would be scrubbed well and polished when I returned; despite the faded paint, the makeover would prepare it for its forthcoming duty—a fitting send-off.

The cleaning job eventually was completed, and the firm let me know that my vehicle was ready. I went to the shop but did not see my SUV. I looked around the parking area. There were a few vehicles there awaiting the return of their owners, but mine was not to be found. I entered the work bays, but my SUV was not there. It was puzzling. What had they done with my vehicle? Had it been taken somewhere else for the final touches? I asked a person in the shop; he indicated that it was in the parking area. I checked again but did not locate it. I thought that he was mistaken, and I went back for further inquiry. He had to show it to me. I stared at it in suspended disbelief. That SUV is not *mine*, is it? It was mine. It had been transformed. Rubbing compound and machine buffing brought a rich, red finish that must have been similar to the hue of the paint when the vehicle was new. It was an *entirely* different color from what it was several hours earlier—so different that I did not recognize my own property. My key fit the ignition and started the engine. It was the same machine all right, but it had changed dramatically. It was the same machine, but it was also utterly different.

In the beginning chapters of this work, I noted how a problem concerning change emerges from the thinking of the ancient Greeks, bringing into question the stability of perceived objects. If a thing changes, then how can it be the same thing? Is there something about a physical object that allows it to persist through succeeding stages of alteration? In essence, how can identity through change be possible; and, if change is constant, as Heraclitus maintains, then how can there be any identity ever? From this puzzle about the lack of intransience comes a further issue: If things fall apart continually because of relentless flux, then there is nothing for one to lay hold of in perception; so, there seems to be nothing in the world around a person to know. Plato states the problem succinctly in one of his dialogues; it is a telling passage.

> SOCRATES: Nor can we reasonably say . . . that there
> is knowledge at all, if everything is in a state of
> transition and there is nothing abiding. . . . But if the

very nature of knowledge changes, at the time when the change occurs there will be no knowledge, and if the transition is always going on, there will always be no knowledge, and, according to this view, there will be no one to know and nothing to be known.[2]

As one will remember, this problem of knowledge presents itself as dualistic in character, bringing into question both the *objects* of perception and the *subjects* of perception. The former things are questionable because they are susceptible to change, the latter ones because not only are they susceptible to change, like their tangible counterparts, but they are prone to error as well. In this chapter, the focus is primarily on the object side of the problem and in particular the ravages of flux, setting aside, for the moment, the matter of the percipient subject. The concern here is to determine first of all *whether* things can cohere through change because, if they can do so, then knowledge of corporeal objects cannot be dismissed strictly on the basis of unremitting variation. Second, if it is indeed the case that identity through change is possible, then the charge is to discover *how* it is possible, to see whether there may be any approaches to the matter that hold promise.

A BRIEF GLIMPSE BACK

The problem of change is somewhat complex. It has been a subject of inquiry across a range of disciplines, and, in philosophy, a number of writers during the centuries since the controversy arose have explored the issue. Some have taken the path of Heraclitus in viewing change as constant and destructive to identity, whereas others have followed Parmenides in holding that change is unreal. Presocratic philosophy subsequent to the writings of the Eleatics is characterized by various theories that attempt to merge this pair of polarized perspectives. Empedocles, Anaxagoras, Leucippus, and

---

[2] Plato, *Cratylus*, 440a–b, in *The Dialogues of Plato*, trans. Benjamin Jowett (1892; repr., New York: Random House, 1937), 2:474.

Democritus—all hold that change occurs, but it lies in the mixing of certain elements, which themselves do not change.

In chapter 2 of this work, I discussed how Plato attempts to deal with the problem by drawing a distinction between two ontological categories. One is becoming; the other is being. The objects of sensory perception are always in a state of becoming, shifting constantly, caught in the eddies of Heraclitean flux. The things in the world never truly *are*. For Plato, physical things are not completely real.[3] Locked in a state of continual fluctuation, exhibiting first one group of properties and then another, they occupy a metaphysical place that is short of full existence. Plato postulates, on the other hand, that there are entities that are absolutely real and unchanging, the forms, which provide a measure of ontic stability for the variable physical things. For Plato, forms simply *are*. They are never in a state of becoming; they never undergo change. Although physical objects lack fixedness, they are protected from complete disintegration because of their participation in the changeless forms. It is the forms that provide the reality from which physical particulars draw the partial being that they have. The upshot of Plato's philosophy is that knowledge is possible because the objects of knowledge are abiding and immutable. Forms do not cease to exist, and they do not vary. The theory imposes a limitation on knowing, however: The authentic objects of knowledge are not found in the physical realm in which humans live. The grasp that people do have of the world is, at best, imperfect and derivative, and it is only because the perceptible partakes of the intelligible that it is possible at all.

Plato's student Aristotle takes issue with his teacher, albeit perhaps not at first. Aristotle inverts the structure of Plato's ontology, claiming that it is the individual, concrete, material objects that are primary, not the universal qualities that they exhibit. The properties of material things do not exist apart from the things in which those properties are manifested. Regarding change, Aristotle believes that there are three basic elements of it: the substrate, privation, and form. The substrate is matter. It is matter that persists through change,

---

[3] As noted in the previous chapter, Plato's stance regarding the reality of physical objects seems to shift toward the close of his philosophical career, but he never abandons the hard reality of the forms.

providing the requisite stability. Privation is the absence of a given form. Form corresponds roughly to an attribute or attributes that an object exhibits; it is the way in which the material that composes the object is displayed. It is important not to confuse this Aristotelian concept with the Platonic notion of an immaterial entity subsisting in a separate sphere. For Aristotle, a thing comes to have a certain form, which it did not have earlier, when matter assumes some new quality or qualities. The lump of material has the potential to exhibit characteristics that eventually will appear, but, until something causes them to appear, the pertinent form is not actualized in that particular corporeal mass. When it is actualized, change occurs.

It is through his introduction of the concept of privation and the thesis of potentiality that Aristotle seeks to address the Parmenidean dilemma with its denial of change. Being comes neither from being nor from nonbeing. What comes to be comes from the privation of a given form in a particular object. Material things have unactualized forms potentially, and it is out of this potentiality that new forms arise in them. Put succinctly, in change, the potential becomes actual. From privation comes exhibition. Underlying it all is the substrate, matter, which always exists and therefore exists through change, taking on a form that differs from the prior one. Given that it is persistent and eternal, the substrate is free of any nonbeing.

Aristotle's analysis of change points to four elements, or what he refers to as causes, and these elements form a key part of his system of physics and metaphysics.[4] One should think of these causes in a broad sense; collectively, they make things what they are. An illustration will clarify the idea. Suppose that a man molds a lump of clay into a bust of Socrates. The material cause of the bust is the clay: the tangible matter of which the object is made. The formal cause is the Socratic shape that the clay acquires through the action of the artist. The efficient cause is the driver for the change—in this case, the artist himself. The man initiates the change in the lump of clay, bringing about the actualization of the form of Socrates that the matter comes to exhibit. That form arises from the privation of it in the clay. Last, there is the final cause. This cause is the end toward

---

[4] For a brief overview of Aristotle's theory of change and associated concepts, see *Encyclopedia of Philosophy*, s.v., "Aristotle."

which the process moves. In the case of the artist, an intelligent being, it is the purpose for which he undertakes the molding of the clay. It is the objective with which the sculptor sets about his work. In Aristotelian philosophy, a final cause is not associated invariably with intelligent thought. It may be merely the terminal stage of a progressing course. For the man who is making a bust of Socrates, however, it is the artist's goal in performing the act.

Aristotle believes that knowing a thing properly requires comprehending it in light of these four central factors. He holds, not unlike Plato, that the genuine objects of scientific knowledge are universals. A scientist examines individual material trees, but it is the essence of trees, as plants, in general—treeness, as it were—that the scientist seeks to understand. Although the mind entertains that which is universal in this way, separating it from the things in which it is exhibited, Aristotle maintains, unlike Plato, that independent, incorporeal universals do not exist, as I noted above. They are not detached entities, subsisting apart from the concrete objects in which they are realized. The formal element makes an individual tree a tree, but it is the material element, matter, that makes it *this* tree. Form is only how the material is arranged. Without distinct, material trees, there is no treeness. Matter is the core element on which form is imposed, and physical reality consists of the union of the two.

Thus, Plato binds things to forms through participation, and Aristotle binds forms to things through the formal cause. The theory of neither provides an adequate account of conservation through change. Plato cannot explain how a thing has properties, and, a fortiori, how it comes to have different properties, without resorting to metaphorical language; and his view that sensory particulars bear a relationship to nonsensory forms is called into question in the *Parmenides* without satisfactory resolution. Aristotle relies on matter as the preserving constituent during a period of transition, yet science shows that it is not the ultimate substrate that Aristotle believes it to be. Quantum physics reveals that the distinction between particles and waves is not as clear as Aristotelian philosophy would require. Further, material particles can be annihilated through collisions with their antiparticles, and, depending on the circumstances, only energy emerges as the end product of such collisions. It seems that another way to look at the continuance of things is needed.

WAYS OF TRANSFORMATION

Change in the physical world is undoubtedly ubiquitous. Examples abound. On a galactic scale, an ongoing process of nuclear fusion, ultimately producing helium from hydrogen, fuels the thermonuclear furnaces of stars, such as the sun. Without such changes that affect the chemical elements that compose them, stars would be dormant masses, incapable of providing light and heat in an insipid universe. As these furnaces consume the available fuel and approach the burnout phase of their lives, red giants and white dwarfs form in the distant reaches of space. At the atomic level, physical things are in a state of constant change because such is the nature of particulate matter. It is dynamic. Electrons circle the nuclei of atoms in a lively cloud of continuous motion, and, if one drills down farther, then one enters a world that some physicists believe to be one that is pulsating with infinitesimal strings. It is the vibrations of these strings that give rise to the tiny units of matter and force that make up physical reality. The entire cosmos is abuzz with constant activity. At first glance, it seems not that there can be no objects *because* of change, as the traditional problem has been posed, but rather no objects *without* it. For the corporeal universe, change is both fundamental and essential. The view from the physical perspective is that there are never two consecutive moments in time at which all is precisely the same. Now, the question at hand is whether, given the state of the universe, objects can undergo alteration without losing their identity.

As one ponders this question, one can conceive of several ways in which change can occur. Given that change appears to be pervasive, it is valuable to look at each of these ways to see whether any may carry the seeds of destruction, as some have thought.

COMINGS AND GOINGS

The first thing to note is that change in which an object plays a part is not necessarily change in the object itself. For example, a shift occurs when a thing arises and another when it ceases to be—in spite of Parmenides's aversion to the idea. If a physical object comes into

221

being, then the state of the universe is altered because something is in it now that was not, strictly speaking, in it before. It makes no sense to say, however, that the object itself changes in such cases. If an object comes into existence at a certain time, then it did not exist prior to that time; so, whereas a change did take place in physical reality, the object did not change. The object did not exist previously; therefore, it was not there to undergo a process, *any* process, including a process of alteration. Only that which exists can change.

Likewise, if an object ceases to be, then a change does occur, but it is not a change in the object—*it* does not change to a different state, as *it* no longer is. Cessation marks the conclusion of a thing's being. There is a shift in the universe when a thing passes away, without doubt, but there is no variation in the object in question. To say that it changes to a state of nonexistence is to utter something that is nonsensical, for no object can exist in a state of nonexistence. Objects can change only if they exist on both sides of the process: at minimum, both at the onset of a given transformation and at the conclusion. For a thing itself to change, it itself must persist through the change.[5]

A brief investigation of this coming to be and ceasing to be is in order. How are they to be characterized? One way is to think of them as gradual processes. Some things may come on the scene or disappear rather quickly, as when a machine part is stamped from a metal plate or a bomb detonates. All arisings and passings are extended in the temporal dimension, however, requiring the passage of time to complete, no matter how brief; and a great number of them last hours, days, or even years. The Hoover Dam, as it is called today, was years in the making.[6] Substantial erosion of geological structures may require centuries to complete. Things come into existence through the duration of whatever process it is that results in

---

[5] Bertrand Russell makes a similar point with regard to locomotion: It requires that something be in one place and then in another place while remaining the same thing. If a particular thing is not here at one time and there at another, then it did not move. See Russell's *A History of Western Philosophy* (New York: Simon and Schuster, 1945), 151, n. 2.

[6] Originally, it was known as Boulder Dam because of its intended location. Its identity was changed to Hoover Dam and then back to Boulder before it was finalized under its current name in 1947.

their being, and their existence is not entire until that process is complete. Likewise, things cease to exist in the course of a process of gradual decay that results in their endings. This view can be depicted in the following way, where a thing originates or terminates gradually; the origination of a thing is shown:

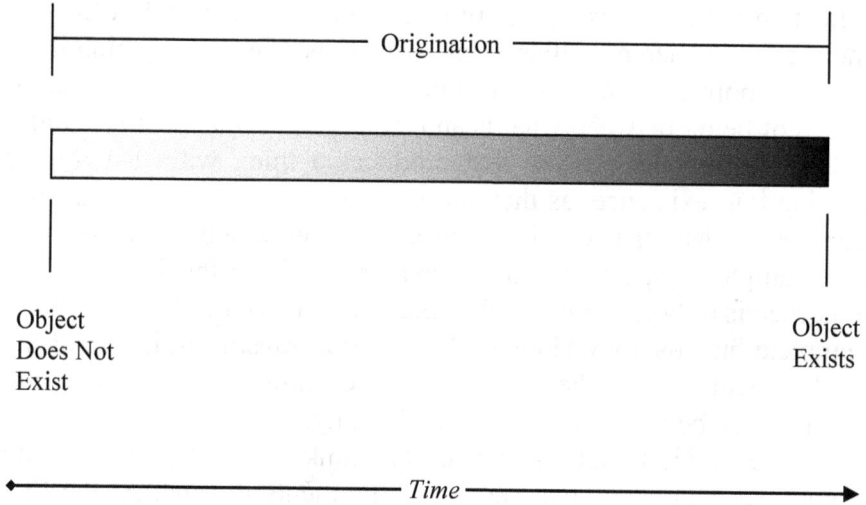

Figure 3.1

The problem with this approach is that it renders a coming to be and a ceasing to be as a progression and a regression respectively, in which, for the greater part of the process, a thing is only partially in existence. The construction of Hoover Dam took half a decade to complete; so, in what state was the structure after six months or a year or three years? Work on tunnels to divert water began in 1931; building of the upper cofferdam began in 1932; the first cubic yard of concrete in the dam proper was poured in 1933. The only response that can be given is that the dam was in a state of partial existence, and, by that statement, one would have to mean that it occupied a spot somewhere between the two ends of an existence scale, not unlike Plato's depiction of particulars, albeit for a different reason. Such a position is untenable. As was evident in the discussion of Plato, it is not possible for a thing to exist only somewhat. Either a thing is, or it is not. Existing is not like being big or heavy or thick; it is not like being flexible or resilient or absorptive. Existence is not a predicable property of things, and it does not admit of degrees. Things can be taller, more alkaline, or less reflective than other things. Things themselves can become taller, more alkaline, or less reflective with the passage of time. Nothing that exists, however, is more existent than any other thing that exists, nor can anything itself become more existent through time. There is no middle ground, no stages of being between what is and what is not. One must be careful not to confuse the process that produces a thing with that thing's coming into existence, as they are not the same. Certainly, part of a thing can exist—the foundation of a dam that is under construction, for example—but a thing cannot exist partially in the sense that its existence is only to a point. After three years of work, there was not a complete but shadowy Hoover Dam, as if a translucent image of the total structure could be seen when one squinted in the sunlight. Nothing can be in a state of fractional reality.

The obvious alternative is to think of origination as an occurrence that spans two successive moments in time. At the first instant, the thing that is about to arise does not yet exist; at the second, it does exist. One may think of cessation as a similar occurrence, spanning two successive moments in time. At the first moment, the thing that is about to terminate exists; at the second, it does not exist. A coming to be can be represented in this way:

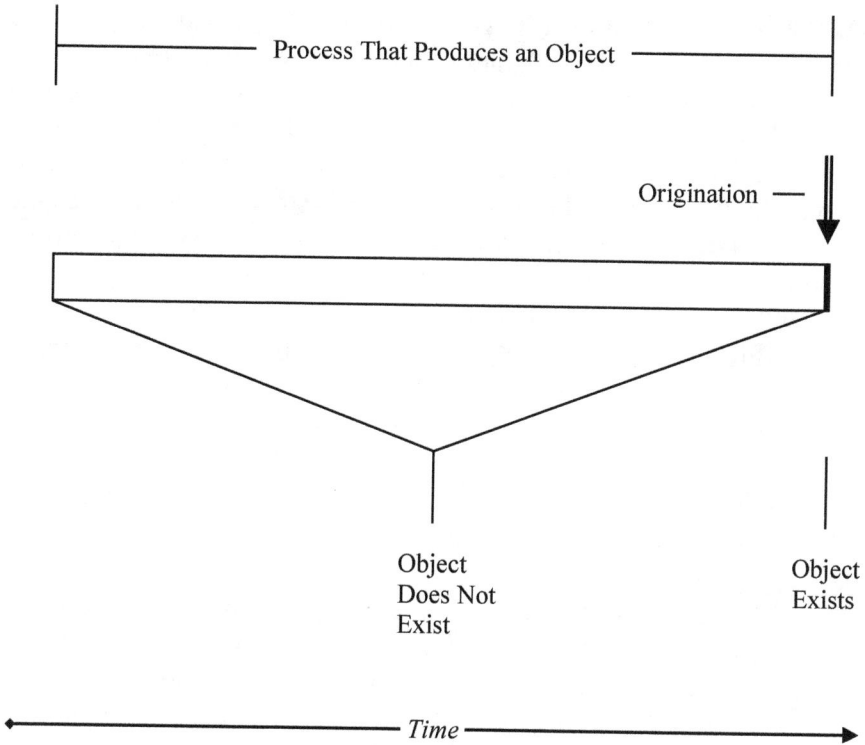

Figure 3.2

Whether time occurs in a continuous flow or discrete steps is a question for which the current state of physics cannot provide a definitive answer. It may be that what is known as the Planck time, after the physicist Max Planck (1858–1947), who formulated the quantum theory, sets the brevity limit. On the order of 5.3912×10^{-44} second, it represents the time that it takes a photon of light to cross the Planck length—again, approximately 1.6163×10^{-33} centimeter. I do not plan to explore the technicalities of time passage in detail, but I will say that, if time is continuous, and the number of moments that rest between any two points in time is indeterminate, then conceiving of the next moment in a series can be a bit challenging. In contrast, if time proceeds in quantifiable steps, then it is straightforward to speak of one moment's succeeding another immediately; it is the very next pace down the temporal progression. Either way, if a thing comes into existence, then it must jump into existence from nonexistence. There is no halfway site for the state of being where a thing can reside. It is all there, or it is not there at all. The following tenet expresses the proper concept of origination for objects in the universe, which lie within the boundaries of the stream of time; I use the lowercase Greek letter omega to represent an object and the symbol '<' to mean 'is earlier than':

> For any object ω that arises, its origination is such that there exists a moment t_2, such that ω exists at t_2, and, for any moment t_1, where $t_1 < t_2$, ω does not exist at t_1.

It is possible to state a condition that is slightly more descriptive if time is indeed incremental, where moments have well-defined edges:

> For any object ω that arises, its origination is such that there exists a moment t_2, and there exists a moment t_1, where $t_1 < t_2$, such that (1) ω exists at t_2, (2) ω does not exist at t_1, and (3) it is not the case that there exists a moment t_n, where $t_1 < t_n < t_2$.

Similar conditions can be put forth for cessation.

I want to note here that the points in this work do not depend on a particular representation of temporal structure. One may regard time as continuous or incremental with no impact on the arguments that I introduce. References to adjacent moments permit a clear discussion of the issues; so, in the analysis, I frequently portray time as passing in discrete blocks. The key matter is that certain times are prior to others; it is unlikely that anyone would contest that notion.

The process of erecting Hoover Dam lasted half a decade, but its origination—its coming into existence—occurred between one given instant and the next. At some point in time, the dam was not yet; at the next moment, it was. Thus, the origination was a temporally extended affair, in that it crossed more than a single instant—it crossed two—but that extension was minimal. Saying that a thing arises over a pair of moments avoids the illogicality of the alternative view, but it presents its own set of obstacles to surmount.

MOTION

All around, things appear to be in motion. One might ask if movement qualifies as a means of producing variation in a thing. An object, such as a child's toy top, may maintain its position, or place, on the sidewalk but spin on its axis; or, like a baseball, propelled by the pitcher toward the batter's box, an object may relocate in space from one place to another. A thing may tilt to one side, turn upside down, or tumble end over end down a hill. In the previous chapter, I discussed John Locke's distinction between primary qualities, which he believes to be inseparable from the things that exhibit them, and secondary qualities, which he classifies as simply capabilities to produce sensations in a perceiver. Locke holds that motion or, more accurately, rest-motion is of the former sort. It is true that rest and motion, as they apply to physical entities, cannot exist independently of things; there can be no rest and no motion unless there is something in existence that is resting or moving. Coming to be still as such, or coming to be in motion, does not entail modification of a thing itself, however. There need be no change in what one deems to be an object's inherent properties when the object moves. The flashlight in the glove box of my car is surely the same piece of equipment whether I am stopped at a traffic light, winding leisurely through a suburb, or traveling on the interstate at considerable speed. *Where* an object, as an entity, is at a given time, and where it is through time, are not central to its core being in the way that other dynamics are that may affect *what* it is. Where its parts are, relative to each other, however, may affect what it is—as I will show later.

Moreover, rest and motion can apply only with reference to some fixed standard. A rock in the Mojave Desert, lying in a depression, is undisturbed. It is therefore at rest. The earth, however, is rotating; hence, the rock is circling in space, and at hundreds of miles per hour at its latitude.[7] Further, the earth is revolving around the sun at nearly sixty-seven thousand miles per hour. There is more. The rock is being dragged through interstellar space at about half a million miles per hour as the solar system spins around the core of

---

[7] The speed of rotation of the earth is approximately 1,040 miles per hour at the equator, slowing as the poles are approached because of the spheroidal shape.

the Milky Way, which, in turn, is moving toward Andromeda; and both galaxies are hurling toward the Hydra-Centaurus supercluster at tremendous speed, all while the universe itself is expanding. Given these facts, the rock is clearly in motion. Without a system of reference, a contradiction arises. Movement of an object is relative; it is not a characteristic of an object apart from context. This relativity of movement applies as much to the atomic building blocks of things as it does to the objects that are constructed from them. The mere movement of an electron about the single-proton nucleus of a hydrogen atom does not alter what the electron is from moment to moment. Motion, along with its counterpart, spatial location, is a contextual property of things, not a property of things in themselves. Motion per se appears to pose little threat to the persistence of individual objects.

There are, of course, secondary changes that are brought about by motion or associated with it. Expansion, contraction, and similar shiftings of shape and size are changes that entail movement, but these changes seem to affect the object in some way, not merely its relative position in space. They are variations in its properties that are independent of where it is. Some things may bulge as they spin on their axes, and acceleration can compress objects that undergo it. Moving an object closer to the earth can affect its weight (which is distinct from its mass) because of gravity. As an object approaches the planet's surface from, say, the ionosphere, its weight increases, *ceteris paribus*. Indeed, an astronaut is virtually weightless in orbit but not upon returning to the earth; and a traveler will weigh more at the poles than at the equator partly because the poles are closer to the earth's dense core than the tropics, given the earth's enlarged center. Extreme gravity, such as that associated with the enormous masses of black holes, can elongate material that falls under its effect.

Consider the kinetic energy of a moving object, which changes with different speeds. A bullet that is fired from a rifle gains kinetic energy as it accelerates down the barrel, driven by enormous pressure from expanding gases, and then progressively loses it after emerging from the barrel as resistance from the atmosphere causes it to decelerate. The bullet's kinetic energy is dependent on both its mass and its speed, and mass is something that it possesses even at rest. Motion itself does not change *the bullet* through a change in kinetic energy. Rather, motion produces kinetic energy from the potential for it because of the bullet's mass.

In cases of this kind, changes in the qualities of a given thing are consequences of its overall spatial condition, including proximity to cosmic formations, or of its relocation in space. It is not directly by virtue of a thing's position within an area or its movement across that area that its continued identity can be brought into question, as such factors in themselves seem to be powerless to alter what the thing is in actuality. If a question does arise in these instances, then it is because of variations that *result* from position or motion.

PROPERTIES AND PARTS

There is a third way in which change conceivably can occur. It is through an alteration in the noncontextual properties that physical things exhibit or in the parts that compose them. Note that, when I speak of properties here, I am not introducing the Lockean division between primary qualities and secondary qualities; rather, I am treating properties in general as any attributes that a physical thing possesses independently of contextual factors. Context may provide an avenue for a property to be expressed, as when an object is fragile or top-heavy, but the *possession* of the property is not dependent on the circumstances in which the object is situated. In addition to rest-motion, Locke identifies other qualities of things that he believes are primary. These qualities include solidity, extension, figure, and number. Again, unlike secondary qualities—colors, sounds, odors, and so forth—the primary ones, according to Locke, are inseparable from objects themselves. Probing deep into the structural makeup of physical things, however, one finds that the notion of these qualities that Locke claims are in objects begins to break down. A piece of gold seems to be solid, yet extreme magnification would reveal that it is not truly solid. It is largely space. The gold appears to be solid because the atomic bonds that hold the components together do so with remarkable effectiveness. What does one say about extension? It is called into question by the fact that the greater part of matter, short of compacted cosmic objects, such as black holes, is empty. If to be extended is to occupy space, then, unless space itself occupies space, much of the lump of gold is not extended, for it is devoid of particulate matter. Looking further into the structure of things, an observer sees that even figure and number are not fixed. The shape of the gold is reduced to the shape of its moving subatomic parts, and the one chunk is, in reality, a myriad of minuscule pieces, all aflutter.

At any rate, regarding properties and parts, a person may argue that exhibiting certain characteristics is reducible to having certain material components. The element hydrogen, for example, exhibits the chemical properties that are peculiar to it because each atom of the standard element consists of a single electron whirling about a single proton. Such an argument would assume, of course, that everything is material, and this assumption is unwarranted. A concern still exists, though, even if the applicability of the possible reduction of properties to parts is limited to the realm of the physical. Besides strictly the makeup of things, the specific configurations of the components must be taken into consideration, as their presence alone cannot account invariably for the qualities that things exhibit.

Consider a pair of cases. The expression on Mr. Potato Head's face changes if a child turns the mouth upside down to form a frown where a smile existed before, although the set of parts remains constant.[8] The chemical compound octane consists of eight atoms of carbon and eighteen atoms of hydrogen, represented by the formula C_8H_{18}. These atoms can join structurally in different ways—eighteen ways in all—to form molecules that differ slightly from each other in the chemical properties that the molecules exhibit. The parts are exactly the same, but the properties vary as a function of the arrangements of the atoms. Such compounds, having the same atomic composition but distinct structures—and, as a consequence, distinct properties—are isomers.

One may argue as well that the converse is true, that being composed of particular material parts can be reduced to possessing certain properties. Having parts p_x, p_y, and p_z, so goes the thinking, is expressible in terms of having an X-part as a constituent, a Y-part as a constituent, and a Z-part as a constituent, where the variables in this latter group correspond to types. Defining the properties with enough

---

[8] 'Mr. Potato Head' is a registered trademark of Hasbro, Inc.

specificity, though, reveals that it is not the possession of an X-part, a Y-part, and a Z-part that matters but the possession of *this* X-part, *this* Y-part, and *this* Z-part—explicitly, parts p_x, p_y, and p_z respectively. Once a particular part is removed, even though a duplicate may be substituted, there will be a change in properties. The fact that the first item is not attached any longer to the object is sufficient to ensure a difference, regardless of how closely the two parts may match.

Whether it is true either that exhibiting properties or that having components can be expressed in terms of its counterpart, it is clear that changing a component entails a change in properties, even in the instance where a copy is substituted for the original one. The principal underlying reason is that any change requires time to complete. Change in an object is change *from* one state *to* another, different state. Logically, if there is but a single state, then there can be no change. Substituting a part in an object requires the removal of the first piece and the installation of the replacement. Thus, there will be at least some time during this exchange in which the properties of the object and its composition differ as the part is extracted and another put in its stead. This point is important because it will come into play in the next section, where I will argue for the possibility of persistence through time, in spite of a change in properties. Here, though, the primary concern is with distinguishing factors that apply to things qua things from those that do not so apply.

This third sort of change is not some modification of the state of the world as entities originate and terminate, nor is it merely and strictly a variation in position because of motion, either of the whole object relative to its environment or of its subatomic parts relative to each other. Instead, this category appears to involve a more fundamental alteration: a change in something about a thing itself, one that seems to be intrinsic. As a working principle then, I submit that, for a physical object, an *intrinsic change* is one in which there is a change in the object's noncontextual properties, whether properties of the whole or of a part (or parts); or a change in its composition through diminution, replacement, or augmentation. If such changes do occur, then it is they that most likely pose a threat to the identity of things because it is they that seem to affect what things, considered in themselves, are. They are alterations in the states of objects, without regard to background factors, even if those factors are causal agents of the changes.[9] Henceforth, in the main, I will use the term 'property' to refer to those qualities that things exhibit independently of context. Although there may be times when the sharpness of this distinction is less than ideal, it will suffice, as a rule; where the circumstances call for a precise line, I will draw one.

If change is constant in the universe, then, regardless of what sorts of events may be taking place, it is important to determine whether things themselves are caught in the frenzy. If they are susceptible to it, either through shifting attributes or through shifting constituents, then understanding the impact of such on their ontic integrity is imperative. In effect, the question that must be answered is not whether things can survive change but whether things can survive intrinsic change, as it is this sort of variation that threatens their identity.

PERSISTENCE AND INTRINSIC CHANGE

Every physical object exhibits a set of properties at a given time. Every physical object—save those foundational, presumably

---

[9] Some contextual factors, such as environmental lighting, may bring about apparent changes in an object, but they are not changes that affect anything that is inherent in the object. If a sheet of white paper is viewed in violet light and afterward in red light, then it will look different to an observer as the wavelength of the electromagnetic energy—the sort of energy that light is—that falls on it changes. The white paper reflects light in a broad range across the visible spectrum and does so when such broad-spectrum light is present. If, however, light with a wavelength of 400 nanometers, or 4,000 Å (violet), is present, and no other wavelength is present, then, *ceteris paribus*, the energy that the paper reflects is limited to that wavelength, making the sheet look violet. If light with a wavelength solely of 700 nanometers, or 7,000 Å (red), is present, then energy only with this longer wavelength is reflected, causing the paper to have a red appearance. The paper has not changed, just the wavelength of the electromagnetic energy that is striking it. Contrast this situation with one in which a person punches a hole in the piece of paper. The paper exhibits a torn spot, regardless of the environmental lighting. The focus of the analysis in this chapter is on changes in things themselves, removed from the physical context in which the things are positioned, even if contextual factors bring about whatever changes may take place.

indivisible entities that quantum physics recognizes—is also a composite and, by virtue of its being so, is made of certain material parts. Suppose that P_1 is the set of properties that an object ω_1 possesses at time t_1 and that C_1 is the set of component parts that ω_1 possesses at t_1. Again, suppose that there is an object ω_2 at time t_2 having sets of properties and parts P_2 and C_2 respectively. For a change of the sort under consideration to occur, it must be that the related set of properties or set of parts at time t_1 is not the same as it is at t_2, yet the object itself remains, which is to say that ω_1 is the same object as ω_2.[10] I want to formalize this notion by putting forth the *principle of intrinsic change*, or *principle IC*. With respect to time in the following construction, the symbol '$<$' means, as before, 'is earlier than'. It is sufficient to state simply that the two times that are given in the formulation are not identical, but specifying which is earlier helps to clarify the concept. Here then is the working principle, which gives the conditions under which intrinsic change occurs:

> PRINCIPLE IC. An intrinsic change in a corporeal object occurs if, and only if, there are two moments t_1 and t_2, where $t_1 < t_2$, and object ω_1 exists at t_1, and object ω_2 exists at t_2; and, given the set P_1 of properties of ω_1 at t_1 and the nonnull set C_1 of component parts of ω_1 at t_1, and the set P_2 of properties of ω_2 at t_2 and the nonnull set C_2 of component parts of ω_2 at t_2, it is the case that $P_1 \neq P_2$, or $C_1 \neq C_2$, but $\omega_1 = \omega_2$.

In essence, if change is to occur in an object, then not only must that object exist for more than a single moment in time—which is to say that its origination and its cessation cannot have an instant in common—but there also must be two points in time in the course of the object's existence, such that something about it is different at one of those times relative to the other.[11] Change in an object cannot

---

[10] I am using the term 'or' in the inclusive sense: One set, the other set, or both sets differ. Refer to the truth conditions of disjunctions in chap. 1.

[11] By employing an additional provision, the principle could be restricted to change that happened in the past. For example, it might contain a requirement whereby t_2, which, as specified, is an instant that follows t_1 and that falls within the period of existence of ω_2, is prior to the current instant. For the purposes here, though, it is

occur unless, stating the obvious, something changes; and what changes are the properties of the thing or its parts.

Note that there must be at least one part in each object, ω_1 and ω_2, a point that is of special relevance where the change is by virtue of an object's parts, and the *number* of parts changes. Everything is part of itself, in that a thing is included in its own being, just as a mathematical set is a subset of itself, albeit not what is referred to as a proper subset: one with fewer elements than the set of which it is a subset. A part therefore need not be less than the whole, although it is generally less. If the object has only one part, then it is an undivided unit—its one part is itself; that one part is the whole. If the object's set of parts is null, however, then the object does not exist, for, without any parts at all, there is no whole. There is simply nothing there. Thus, when an object undergoes change, neither the prechange state of the object nor the postchange state can be one in which there are no parts. If the former instance were to obtain, then it would constitute a case of the arising of that object. If the latter instance were to obtain, then it would constitute a case of the cessation of that object. I demonstrated previously that originations and terminations, although they are changes, are not changes in objects themselves. The set of parts of a thing that changes therefore cannot be empty.

A thing, at a particular time, could acquire a set of properties or parts different from the set that it had at an earlier time and then, sometime later, revert to the original state. Change still will have occurred—with regard to parts, the abovementioned parallel case of substitution provides a reason—even though there are two times at which a thing arguably may have the same qualities and general components. Principle IC does not say that there can be no change in an object unless, for *any* two distinct moments, the properties or parts are different, only that, for *some* two distinct moments, the properties or parts are different. What is required for change is that there must be at least one instant in time, during the span of a thing's existence, when not all its properties or not all its parts are the same as they are at some other instant. Principle IC captures this concept.

---

sufficient to look at an object across its span of existence, even if its existence may lie not only in the past but also in the future.

The distinction per se of different attributes or components at different times, however, is not sufficient. For example, one rock may be dark brown, weigh slightly more than a pound, and be shaped like a turnip at noon. Another rock may be light grey, weigh two pounds, and be as flat as a pancake at 1:00 in the afternoon. There are two different sets of exhibited characteristics and two different sets of parts at two different times, but there are two different rocks. For a change in a physical object to take place, such that the object is the *same* thing through that change, it seems that *something* pertaining to the object must remain. The notion is that, for an object to persist through a process of alteration, it cannot be the case that *everything about* the object at the latter time is different from what it was at the former time. There must be some thread of constancy, something that is not affected by the transformation process. In change therefore, the object that changes is different in some way and the same in some way—not unlike my SUV that was reconditioned by the detail shop. Although principle IC states that, in change, there are different properties or different parts that are associated with one and the same object at different times, it does not explain why the object remains. Suppose that all the properties or all the parts changed. How could a given object still exist in those circumstances? Principle IC hence appears to be incomplete. It describes what constitutes intrinsic change but not what constitutes continuance, nor does it specify what underlies that continuance. Ostensibly, a further principle is required, one that pertains to identity through time and that expresses formally what it is to be conserved. Having set forth at that point the conditions of identity in this additional principle, on the assumption that success in determining them is achieved, the analysis must proceed to the next step, which is to pin down the critical, stable element that bridges the gap between the prechange and postchange states of an object.

I will break down principle IC into its two constituents: changes in the qualities that things possess and changes in their makeup. It is important to examine each one in more detail to see whether a stabilizing factor can be discovered within either group.

FRAGMENTATION

Imagine that Donny is asked to slice a loaf of freshly baked bread for the Thanksgiving meal and that he accepts the dinner-table duty. If, in keeping with the theory of flux, things cannot survive a change in properties, then the warm, brown loaf that emerges from the oven is not the same object as the cool, pale one that entered it half an hour earlier. More obstacles arise as Donny undertakes the slicing. The loaf that has a cut in it that is 3.5 millimeters deep is not the same as the one that, a fraction of a second later, has a cut that is 4.5 millimeters deep—or the one afterward having a cut that is 4.55 millimeters deep or the one with a cut that is 4.555 millimeters deep, or 4.5555. A multitude of loaves, perhaps an infinity of them, arises and vanishes in succession.

The problem does not end with the bread; there is a problem with Donny too. In his carelessness, he cuts his finger as he slices the loaf. The person who has the injured finger cannot be the same one who set out to slice the bread, in the Heraclitean view, as each possesses a different set of characteristics. More problematic yet for this position is that the generation of two persons is just the beginning. Indefinitely many arise; in fact, it seems that there may be an infinity of them as the knife deals its blow. The person who has a cut in his finger that is 3.5 millimeters deep is not the same as the one who, a fraction of a second later, has a cut that is 4.5 millimeters deep—or the one afterward having a cut that is 4.55 millimeters deep or the one with a cut that is 4.555 millimeters deep, or 4.5555. If one says that Donny is the same person and that it is only his body that differs from moment to moment, then an even more troublesome difficulty arises. How is it that Donny is linked to an indefinitely large number, perhaps an infinite number, of unique bodies in a matter of milliseconds? Moreover, Donny is now in pain, whereas, just a bit earlier, he was not in pain. Regardless of the changes that affect his body thus, it has to be true that he himself changes, for this reason alone, on the premise that all shifts in properties bring shifts in the things that possess those properties.

If therefore there is no loaf of bread that persists through the slicing event, given the assumption that things cannot continue as themselves when their properties change, and, if there is no persistent

Donny, for the same reason, but instead merely a series of independent Donny-things, each corresponding to a different state, then the consequence is something that no one could accept. An inconceivably large number of objects and people arose momentarily and then ceased to be where what appeared to be Donny stood that night over what appeared to be the loaf of bread at the dinner table, each of these existents coming into being and then vanishing into oblivion, all in the blink of an eye. Whenever any change in a thing occurs, where one set of properties is exchanged for another set, one thing must be annihilated and another thing formed. Such multiplication of entities affects both the object of perception and the subject of perception. For any seemingly one thing that a person perceives, there is not one thing but a great many of them; and even the person who is perceiving is not one thing but a great many of them. There is no reasonable way to account for how the collections of independent slices of perceived and perceiver could hold together long enough to complete a perception as the objects that populate the universe are splintered—as is indeed the universe itself—into something that is incomprehensible.

Besides an extreme violation of the law of parsimony, a central problem here is that the momentary elements that form the human perceptions of one continued thing through time must come from somewhere, a truth that follows from the principle ex nihilo nihil fit.[12] Then, the matter to uncover is how this stream of elements, indeterminable in number, arises on the position at hand. One must explain how the subsequent things in a series—the second loaf and the second Donny, and every loaf and every Donny thereafter—come into existence.

DIMENSIONALITY

There is a view in contemporary philosophy that is known as four-dimensionalism, and it appears to fit well, in certain respects,

---

[12] One will recall the introduction of this principle in the discussion of Parmenides in chap. 1.

with Heraclitean metaphysics. Its name can be misleading, but it refers to the critical inclusion, in a certain way, of the temporal factor in setting forth an ontology of objects. In this view, things have instantaneous temporal parts. It seems to be obvious that houses, trees, and people have physical parts, and these parts are spread out in the three spatial dimensions: Different pieces of them occupy different locations in space. These same things, the theory of four-dimensionalism maintains, have temporal pieces as well, all of them occupying different moments in time. Where a road crosses a territory, every part of the road lies in a unique location within the region, but the parts are connected, in that, aside from their being spatially contiguous, they all are parts of the same road. Analogously, an object exists at multiple points in time, and a temporal part exists at each one of those instants, but the parts are connected, in that, aside from arising in the course of successive moments, they all are parts of the same object. A four-dimensionalist believes that ascribing momentary components to things is a way to account for change. Each part is unique and occupies a distinct place in the sequence of time; therefore, one part can possess properties that are different from another part, but identity is maintained because the parts belong to a single entity.

In referring to the existence of things through time, a typical four-dimensionalist says that they perdure. For this reason, four-dimensionalism is the theory of perdurantism, although a few philosophers reserve the name of the concept for one version of the temporal-parts model. The distinction will become clear shortly. I will use the expression 'four-dimensionalism' to refer to the general position that there are momentary temporal elements corresponding to every object.

The opposing view, three-dimensionalism, holds that things are present in their entirety at every moment of their existence. They are not split into individual pieces that lie across time, separated from other pieces at other times, though joined in a temporal series. Rather, things sweep through time as coherent objects, there in toto for the duration of their being. According to this position, things do not perdure but endure; thus, the theory is that of endurantism.

An illustration may underscore the difference. Imagine that one unrolls a big rug across the hardwood floor of a living room to cover it, as opposed to leaving the tightly curled rug bound with cord and rolling the intact bundle to the opposite end of the room. The former process distributes the rug across the floor of the room as each part of the rug rests on a section of the floor. The latter process relocates it by moving it as a unit through the room, so that, when the rug rests on a section of the floor, the whole rug—assuming that one makes allowances for the size of the bundle—rests on it. In both cases, the rug contacts the entire area of the room's base surface but in different ways. To complete the analogy, think of the expanse of the floor as time.

In summary then, what sets four-dimensionalism apart from its rival, three-dimensionalism, is its insistence on the existence of a plethora of fleeting pieces corresponding to every object in the world, and these pieces are not mere conceptualizations but actual things in physical reality. As Theodore Sider, a contemporary philosopher and one of the theory's leading proponents, declares, "Four-dimensionalism may then be formulated as the claim that, necessarily, each spatiotemporal object has a temporal part at every moment at which it exists."[13]

The principal employment of the perdurance-endurance phraseology, as it appears in the metaphysics of identity through time, is traceable to David Lewis (1941–2001), although the corresponding terms themselves did come to light earlier.[14] Lewis provides the following definitions; the expression 'iff' is philosophical shorthand for 'if, and only if':

> Let us say that something *persists* iff, somehow or other, it exists at various times; this is the neutral word. Something *perdures* iff it persists by having different temporal parts, or stages, at different times, though no

---

[13] Theodore Sider, *Four-Dimensionalism: An Ontology of Persistence and Time* (2001; Oxford: Clarendon Press, 2003), 59. Four-dimensionalism allows in principle the instantaneous temporal parts to compose temporal parts of longer duration, but the key notion for the theory is that there is a temporal part corresponding to every fleeting instant, no matter how brief.

[14] The distinction appears in Mark Johnston, "Particulars and Persistence" (Ph.D. diss., Princeton University, 1984). See his comments in the subsequent paper, "Is There a Problem about Persistence?" *Proceedings of the Aristotelian Society Supplementary Volumes* 61, no. 1 (1987): 107–35.

> one part of it is wholly present at more than one time;
> whereas it *endures* iff it persists by being wholly present
> at more than one time.[15]

Lewis's definition of persistence, as it stands, is inadequate, and his subsequent definitions that incorporate it are thereby inadequate. Without including another condition, what he defines in his first assertion is not persistence but multiple-moment existence, which logically is satisfied as easily by recurrence as by continuance. Nothing can cease to be and then reappear as the same entity, for nothing can exist in a state of nonexistence, only to come to exist again. Such resurfacing of the same entity is not possible. When a thing ceases, *it* ceases; *whatever* appears afterward is not *it*. A thing that comes afterward may look like the former thing. It even may be the same sort of thing. It cannot be the entity that ceased, however. Lewis's definition fails to take this point into account. Persistence is uninterrupted existence—whether time is represented as continuous, or it is quantized—not recurrent existence. A proper concept of persistence therefore requires the addition of this restriction: If a thing persists during a period of time, then there is no moment from the beginning of that period through the end of that period at which it does not exist. Formally capturing the notion is in order. I define it by means of the following biconditional—the *statement of persistence*; as before, the symbol '<' indicates 'is earlier than':

> STATEMENT OF PERSISTENCE (df.). For any object ω and any two moments t_1 and t_2, where $t_1 < t_2$, ω persists from t_1 to t_2 inclusive if, and only if, ω exists at t_1, and ω exists at t_2, and, for any moment t_n, where $t_1 < t_n < t_2$, ω exists at t_n.

In essence, a thing that persists from one moment to another moment exists at those two moments and continuously—in a *broad sense*—between them; that is to say, its existence is without interruption throughout the entire period that is marked by the two instants.

There is another problem with Lewis's definitions. The locution 'wholly present' is unclear. Philosophers' misunderstanding concerning the possible meanings of this phrase has resulted in

---

[15] David Lewis, *On the Plurality of Worlds* (Oxford: Basil Blackwell, 1986), 202.

attacks on three-dimensionalism that are sorely ill-founded. In speaking of perdurance, Lewis uses the phrase 'wholly present' to deny, in accordance with this view of persistence, that an object is complete at a given time—in the sense that there are other *temporal* parts of the object that exist at other times but not at the given time. In speaking of endurance as its alleged contrary, however, authors have taken Lewis's phrase to affirm, in accordance with that opposing view of persistence, that an object is complete at a given time—in the sense that, with respect to that time, it is true not only that there are no temporal parts lying elsewhere but also that there are *no parts at all* lying elsewhere. For now, bear in mind that unbroken existence is necessary for persistence, regardless of how persistence occurs. Lewis's distinction between perdurance and endurance provides a starting place, as the central question is whether things continue by virtue of having temporal parts, or they continue, albeit not by virtue of having them.

Given that (1) nothing can cease to be and then arise again as the same thing, as noted above; (2) a thing that exists at any two different moments thus must exist at every moment between those two moments, reflected in the statement of persistence; and (3) all things exist at the first moment that they arrive in being and at the last moment before they depart from it, in accordance with the previous analysis, I can extend the statement of persistence to propose another principle. I will refer to it as the *principle of continuous duration*, or *principle CD*.

> PRINCIPLE CD. For any object ω, if ω's origination corresponds to the pair of sequential moments t_{o1} and t_{o2}, and ω's termination corresponds to the pair of sequential moments t_{t1} and t_{t2}, where $t_{o2} < t_{t1}$, then ω persists strictly from t_{o2} to t_{t1} inclusive.

A persistent thing exists incessantly from the moment that its origination completes through the moment that immediately precedes the completion of its termination. For any thing that exists in passing—a thing that has a beginning and an end—what comes into being continues to exist, without interruption to its being, until it is no more.

Within four-dimensionalism, there are two primary versions, which are distinguished by their respective notions concerning how things are thought to persist. The dissimilarity is more than a nuance, but it is not quite a hard divergence. The first position is the so-called worm theory. This position has it that objects exist as spatiotemporal worms, as it were. Extending through the dimension of time, an object *is precisely* the sum of its transient parts: the current one in combination with all those that preceded it. Each of these parts is distinct from the others, and each exists only for a moment in a time-ordered series that forms the worm—a notional compilation that continues to grow with every passing instant until it ends. Of the two versions of four-dimensionalism, it is the worm theory that occasionally is identified as perdurantism.

The second position—the one to which Sider subscribes—is the stage theory. According to this view, objects are momentary phases. At any instant in time, an object *is precisely* the temporal part at that time. To highlight the difference between the two versions, suppose that an object ω persists from moment t_1 to moment t_3, existing at t_1, t_2, and t_3, where those moments lie in a temporal sequence from earliest to latest. Let ω at t_1 be o_1; let ω at t_2 be o_2; and let ω at t_3 be o_3. Imagine that the time is now t_3. A worm theorist says that ω is $o_1 + o_2 + o_3$ at this moment. A stage theorist says that ω is o_3 at this moment, but it *was* o_2 at a previous instant, and it *was* o_1 at yet another previous instant. Of whichever persuasion, a four-dimensionalist believes that an object subsumes temporal pieces, whether through the object's being identical to the whole collection of them, or through its being identical to each of them individually, one after the other. In actuality then, to refer to an object, crossing points in time, is to refer to individual, ontically substantive object slices, existing serially, linked together in some way or other in the course of the object's existence. With the exception of a problem that I will introduce in a moment, I will not make much of the distinction between the two flavors of four-dimensionalism. My interest is in the core premise of the theory, namely, that things *have* temporal parts—instantaneous, independent, and real.

Before continuing, consider a key argument that Lewis presents against a three-dimensionalist's depiction of reality. To understand exactly how the argument works requires recognizing the distinction between properties and relations. A property is an attribute of an entity and pertains to it directly; it is not necessary to introduce yet another entity when ascribing a property. A relation, on the other hand, pertains to an entity only in light of its connection to something, whether that connection is to one entity or to more than one.[16] Properties are *of* things—by themselves; relations are *between* things or *among* things—not by themselves. Being ambidextrous is exhibiting a particular property. Being taller than something else is standing in a certain relation.[17] Being between this object and that object is also to stand in a given relation.

The best way to represent the difference is by means of the logical system that is known as predicate logic, or the predicate calculus. This system is an extension of the propositional calculus that I covered in chapter 1. I will mention briefly some of its principal concepts, which are important for the discussion here but which will be even more so in a coming chapter. Having this foundation will prove to be central to a grasp of the issues.

In the predicate calculus, one can express declarations about properties and relations through symbolized sentential constructions. Different logical systems employ various elements to generate a properly assembled assertion in the system, what logicians refer to as a well-formed formula, represented by the shorthand term 'wff'. The generally accepted format is to let capital letters represent predicates, which link properties or relations to individual things, and to let lowercase letters stand for the things to which the properties or relations are assigned through predication.[18] Where the possession of

---

[16] Note that the things that are related may be the same thing; the relation of identity, for example, holds between anything and itself. What distinguishes a relation from a property is the number of entities or putative entities to which the function applies in a particular instance, regardless of whether the entities are actually distinct.

[17] One will recall from chap. 2 that Plato treats large, or largeness, as a form: a universal, or property. Strictly speaking, being large is a relation. A thing, considered in itself, is not large; it is large only in comparison with something. African elephants are huge, but not per se. To assert that they are huge is to claim that they are larger than many other things—other kinds of animals in particular. They are small, however, relative to blue whales, mountains, and planets.

[18] As indicated in the discussion in chap. 1, n. 57, I use a similar pattern for type-token distinctions, where capital letters represent types and lowercase ones

a property is expressed, a single lowercase letter follows the letter that represents the predicated property. Where the obtaining of a relation is expressed, two or more lowercase letters follow the letter that represents the predicated relation. Suppose that *A* stands for exhibiting the quality ambidextrousness, and *m* stands for the individual Mary. The assertion 'Mary is ambidextrous' is rendered as

Am

Similarly, one can convey the fact that John is taller than Mary, using the letter *T* for the obtaining of the taller-than relation and adding *j* for the person John. The corresponding statement is rendered as

Tjm

Suppose that Mary, John, and Karen are in the line at the grocery store preparing to pay at the register. Karen is in front of Mary, and Mary is in front of John. One can affirm the fact that Mary is between the other two persons. This spatial arrangement involves three entities. If *B* represents the obtaining of the in-between relation, and one adds *k* for the individual Karen, then the declaration may be formulated in the following manner:

Bmkj

The predicate calculus introduces quantification, affording a way to state, for example, that something has a certain property or that all things stand in some relation. The backward-E symbol, '∃', followed by a variable, is the symbol that systems of predicate logic typically employ to represent the English quantifier 'some' or '(there exists) a/an'. The inverted-A symbol, '∀', followed by a variable, or simply enclosing the variable in parentheses, is used in general to represent the English quantifier 'any', 'all', or 'every' in these systems. Again, depending on the particular logical framework that is in use, the symbolization varies, but the figures that I give here are

---

represent individual tokens. I take the same approach to classes and their members respectively, and to sets and the elements of those sets.

accepted standards. The predicate calculus is a powerful tool because it provides a way to communicate assertions that cannot be put across in the propositional calculus. This logical system allows one to say that someone is ambidextrous by stating that there exists a thing that is both a person and ambidextrous, incorporating the symbol for conjunction that chapter 1 identified. The form of this declaration is

$$(\exists x)(Px \cdot Ax)$$

In such affirmations, the quantifier is said to bind the variable. One could limit the application of the variable strictly to persons, if desired; then, it would not be necessary to employ the Px component in setting forth the symbolized assertion but merely the Ax component. The scope of the things to which the variable can apply is the universe of discourse, or the domain.

Note that the formatted statements that I present above are expressed in the first-order predicate calculus, where the variables that quantifiers bind are restricted to those that signify individual entities. In the second-order and further higher-order predicate calculi, quantifiers can bind lower-order predicate variables, signifying things other than distinct entities, such as properties that entities may exhibit, relations in which they may stand, and other intangible things.[19] One can use these more advanced systems to put forward declarations that are not possible in first-order predicate logic.

Continuing with quantification, one can say, for example, that it is not the case that there exists something that is taller than everything. One will recall the symbol for negation from the discussion of the propositional calculus earlier. Consider then this formulation of the claim:

$$- (\exists x)(\forall y)(Txy)$$

---

[19] Some higher-order systems employ quantifiers to handle predicates, which, in turn, incorporate properties or relations. Quantification can extend to groups of individuals, classes, or other entity-assemblages. The key difference between first-order systems and these more inclusive ones lies in whether the variables that the quantifiers can bind signify only discrete elements—typically, concrete items—as opposed to universals, or properties; sets; or other nonsingular things.

The statement, interpreted literally, is 'It is not the case that there exists an x, such that, for any y, x is taller than y'. Is the claim true?

With this introductory understanding in mind, I return to Lewis's argument, where he presents what he sees as the primary reason for rejecting endurantism.

> The principal and decisive objection against endurance, as an account of the persistence of ordinary things such as people or puddles, is the problem of temporary intrinsics. Persisting things change their intrinsic properties. For instance shape: when I sit, I have a bent shape; when I stand, I have a straightened shape. Both shapes are temporary intrinsic properties; I have them only some of the time. How is such change possible?[20]

Lewis says that one must take into account the intrinsic character of properties: They are possessed by objects in themselves. An object's shape, for instance, is a property that it exhibits independently of anything else. It is just bent or just straight. Lewis argues that, if endurantism—three-dimensionalism—were factual, then, because objects undergo changes in properties, there would be no possession of properties *simpliciter*. Things would possess properties only *at a time*. A man who is seated in a chair and then rises changes his shape from bent to straight. On the premise that three-dimensionalism is right, he is neither bent intrinsically nor straight intrinsically, but bent at a time and straight at another time. It follows that the presumed properties of things, which things have per se, are, in fact, relations. Therefore, the assertion 'John is straight' cannot be given as

$$Sj$$

but always must be set forth in relation to a time, where t stands for a specific time:

$$Sjt$$

---

[20] Lewis, *Plurality of Worlds*, 203–4.

because John's shape changes. Three-dimensionalism, according to the thinking, precludes one's declaring that something is simply straight. To account for the possession of properties *simpliciter*, one must hold to a view of objects that incorporates temporal parts. Lewis believes that therein lies the answer to his question about change. Temporally limited parts allow both the possession of intrinsic properties and the occurrence of variation in those properties.

This argument is not only rather strange; it also fails to be compelling. If a thing exists at all in the physical realm, then it exists at a time *and* in a place. How is it that having a property *now* is different—in a relational respect—from having a property *here*? For a four-dimensionalist, the fact that a temporal part exists only for a single instant guarantees that it will have the properties that it has for its entire existence, as long as that individual part is in view. It has them *simpliciter*. Now, if there are intrinsic properties, then the texture, or surface condition, of a thing qualifies as intrinsic with no less assurance than does its shape. A well-paved road, say, State Route 430, may be very smooth. As a result of the passage of time and heavy traffic, it may become uneven and full of potholes across its entire length. At first glance, it seems to be possible to eschew a reference to time and avoid involving a relation by adopting the theory of four-dimensionalism. One temporal part of the road is smooth *simpliciter*; a later temporal part is rough *simpliciter*. The change is explainable, according to four-dimensionalism, in terms of unique time slices of the road, some slices of which exhibit properties that differ from those of other slices.

Suppose, though, that the stretch of road from mile 168 through mile 201 is smooth; the remainder of the road is bumpy and full of ruts. It has been this way from the time that it was constructed because its foundation was laid improperly. Even if a temporal part of the *stretch of road* from mile 168 through mile 201 is intrinsically smooth, the temporal part of the *road* at that time is not intrinsically smooth. A reference to location is required. Thus, being smooth is transformed from a property ascription, as appears in the symbolized statement

Sr

where S stands for exhibiting the property smoothness, and r stands for State Route 430, to a relation ascription, such that the road is smooth in a place, symbolized by

Srp

where p represents the portion of the road from mile 168 to mile 201 inclusive. One could assume just as easily that this section of the road, and only this section, expands from two lanes to four, thereby changing its shape—the quality that Lewis selects in an attempt to make his case. Lewis surrenders the very intrinsic-property factor to which he points in support of a philosophy of four-dimensionalism. He cannot maintain it without undermining the holistic integrity of objects.

Those who subscribe to the existence of temporal parts of persisting things would be the last to deny the existence of spatial parts of composite objects, and accordingly Lewis's example of a bent man fails. John is not just a bent entity—the section of his body from his left ankle to his left knee is, in fact, as straight as a graphite arrow—even though he is sitting. A man is bent if some parts occupy certain spatial positions in relation to other parts. It is the geometric attitude of the parts to one another that defines the bend. Shape is not an intrinsic property of a man as a whole in the sense that Lewis has in mind, contrary to his contention.

Claiming that noncomposite things—namely, fundamental, physical particles—have intrinsic properties, even if composite ones do not have them, would not help a temporal-parts theorist here. An electron has a certain mass, charge, and spin for its entire existence, but such properties do not require a succession of momentary pieces. Physical laws determine that these properties are unchanging and indeed unchangeable. It is not necessary to refer to a time frame to enumerate the electron's inherent characteristics. Such properties therefore fit quite well with a three-dimensionalist's view of reality.

What is more, Lewis's argument turns back on itself. On the premise that there are temporal parts, those parts must be parts of something, and that something is said to be a persistent object. Identity through time is not possible, except on the condition that the instantaneous parts are linked to that object and, for each of those parts individually, linked at the one instant that the given part exists. Unless a four-dimensionalist is willing to forgo the identity of the ordinary things in the world, he or she must hold that objects stand in a relationship to their own temporal parts, and those parts shift with every tick of a four-dimensionalist's clock. When one refers to an object, one is referring to the object at that moment, for what the object *is* for a four-dimensionalist—whether worm theorist or stage theorist—changes from moment to moment. One cannot say that this object is ω *simpliciter*: There *is no* ω *simpliciter*; there *is no* just ω. Instead, this object is what it is just *at time t*. Four-dimensionalism thus expands the proposition that there exists something that is object ω, which the following formulation, albeit unorthodox, conveys:

$$(\exists x)(Ox)$$

to the proposition that there exists something, and there exists a time, such that this something is object ω at that time, as shown below:

$$(\exists x)(\exists t)(Oxt)$$

Three-dimensionalism has no such requirement. One who adopts the three-dimensional perspective can assert that this object is John without having to add a temporal reference. John's properties may change as time passes, but John himself—John's identity—is constant. For a four-dimensionalist, however, John himself is never constant; he is never simply John. Four-dimensionalism attempts to cling to *properties simpliciter* only to forfeit *identity simpliciter*. It is not an improvement; it is a loss.

Regardless of the version, four-dimensionalism faces a quandary that undermines it right out of the gate. Temporal parts are distinct entities: No two are identical. Suppose that object ω exists from t_1 to t_3, having, as outlined earlier, temporal parts o_1 to o_3 respectively. According to the worm view, at t_3, object ω is identical to $o_1 + o_2 + o_3$; at the next moment, t_4, assuming that ω continues to exist, ω is identical to $o_1 + o_2 + o_3 + o_4$. It is axiomatic that two things that are identical to the same thing are identical to each other. It follows that the two sums-of-parts are identical because ω is identical to ω, but, no matter how one thinks of the collection, the fact is that $o_1 + o_2 + o_3$ is not identical to $o_1 + o_2 + o_3 + o_4$.[21] Moreover, if a thing *is exactly* the sequence of its temporal parts, as a worm theorist holds, then the thing does not exist until all the temporal parts that compose it exist, for fractional existence is illogical. For there to be a complete complement of temporal parts, however, all of them prior to the final one must have come on the scene and vanished before the present moment, and the final one itself is on the brink of disappearing. The upshot is that there is, in truth, no object—and thus no object-identity—until the supposed object is passing away. Something is plainly wrongheaded about the reasoning underlying such a position.

The stage view has it that ω is identical to o_3 at the present moment, t_3, but, at the previous moment, t_2, ω was identical to o_2. Again, two things that are identical to the same thing are identical to each other. It follows that the two temporal parts are identical because—as before, axiomatically—ω is identical to ω. Yet, according to the theory, they are not identical; o_3 and o_2 are different parts. Sider claims that four-dimensionalism does not imply that identity through time is reducible to temporal parts, but, unless there is some atypical sense of identity on which four-dimensionalism rests, the theory, in either form, leads to a glaring contradiction. Three-dimensionalism faces no such problem: For any time that an object ω exists, it is identical to ω at any other time that ω exists, although the time factor does introduce additional philosophical considerations.

One cannot assume that persistence is the same thing as strict equivalence in a mathematical sense. Nevertheless, four-dimensionalism appears to be a nonstarter. It is worth investigating whether another notion of the identity relation may be afoot in the theory of temporal parts that can help to salvage it.[22]

---

[21] Though not with regard to temporal parts, Peter Simons makes a similar point in claiming that, if an object has different parts at different times, then it cannot be identical to the sum of its parts at any time, as, in that case, it would be different from itself. See his work *Parts: A Study in Ontology* (Oxford: Clarendon Press, 1987), 1.

[22] Presently, it will be clear that identity through time does not fall under the same rules as identity at a time, but, even so, the four-dimensionalists face the charge of contradiction. At any given time, a thing is necessarily identical to itself at that time. Whatever things are identical to ω therefore, regardless of when they are

RELATION AND GENERATION

The crucial question that arises for the four-dimensionalists is then twofold: *What* precisely is the relationship of one part to another, and of the parts to the whole; and from *where* do all the temporal parts of a thing come? Do the parts in this "crazy metaphysic" just pop into existence out of nothing in a continual procession, as one critic objects?[23] Does this scenario portray what is taking place in the four-dimensionalists' ontology, contrary to logic? If such not be the case, then it seems that the only candidate for a part's source, aside from perhaps the first one, is the previous member of the sequence. The warm, brown loaf on the table ultimately must be traceable in some way to the cool, pale one that entered the oven earlier; and the loaf that is sliced to a depth of 4.5555 millimeters somehow must have come from the loaf that has a cut in it that is slightly less deep. It could not have come from something in the immediate surroundings: a chair at the table; the dog under the table, waiting for a fallen crumb; or the set of knives in the kitchen drawer. There is no natural happening that suddenly would transform the seat, salivating dog, or set of silverware into the savory loaf. Each instantaneous part must arise from a predecessor—an ongoing process of generation in a cause-effect chain. Nothing else could account for such a speedy string of one-moment fragments.

This picture appears to be the accepted one. According to Sider, "The sensible four-dimensionalist will claim that current temporal parts are caused to exist by previous temporal parts."[24] Note that Sider is not alone in his belief that causality drives the process. Another four-dimensionalist agrees.

> The objects that I am defending do not just pop into existence. It is not as if there is empty space and then, poof, the space is filled. It is the causal mechanisms together with the material configuration of matter at any

---

identical to ω, must be identical to each other. It is a requirement that four-dimensionalism fails to meet.

[23] Judith Jarvis Thomson, "Parthood and Identity across Time," *Journal of Philosophy* 80, no. 4 (1983): 213.

[24] Sider, *Four-Dimensionalism*, 217.

given time that affect which parts will exist at the next moment.[25]

On the position of the four-dimensionalists, a thing subsists in a state of generating its own parts from its own parts, one at a time. If it is not a crazy metaphysic, then it is surely, at best, a bizarre one.

Both four-dimensionalism and Heracliteanism hold that reality consists of instantaneous slivers. There is a key difference, however. In the former view, things survive change, and, although they are, at base, transient parts, this division into parts is not because of change, which may, or may not, be occurring. In the latter view, things do not survive change, for nothing can be the same if it changes, and things are fragmented into transient parts because change is constant. Four-dimensionalism professes to connect the pieces, so that the entities to which they correspond perdure through time, regardless of whether a shift in properties occurs. In contrast, Heracliteanism lets them fly apart, driven by the machinery of flux. Change destroys any integrity that objects might possess, according to this latter philosophical stance, with the consequence that reality consists of an ongoing, innumerable stream of unconnected bits, each aligning with an instant in time, coming into being and then ceasing to exist immediately. Like the four-dimensionalists, Heraclitus must explain the origin of the slivers; he must offer a way to account for their existence. The river that is in front of a person now may not be the same body of water as the one that lay in front of the person a minute ago, but there must be something there at each moment, and that something is a river sliver in a stream of river slivers, each a slice of a different watercourse. If the slivers in this succession do not arise from some existent thing, then Heraclitean philosophy self-destructs because it violates the principle ex nihilo nihil fit—not as a one-time occurrence but with every change in properties; and change, according to the thinking, is continual. Without some way to explain the generation of the plenitude, Heraclitean metaphysics fails. In the philosophy of four-dimensionalism, on the contrary, object slivers are bound to each other in a relationship of cause and effect, and that causal link is explicit. It is perhaps the only choice open to

---

[25] Mark Heller, *The Ontology of Physical Objects: Four-Dimensional Hunks of Matter* (Cambridge: Cambridge University Press, 1990), 18.

Heraclitus, but he does not take it, and further speculation along these lines would be unsupported. Heraclitus does believe in a world that is ordered by *Logos*—the cosmic principle of rationality—where "all things come into being in accordance with this Law."[26] Absent an account of the mechanics of the generative process, the object slivers, regardless of whether they arise in an orderly fashion, form a disjointed universe. In light of this fact, I want to turn to Sider's causal-link theory to see whether it can unite, in any effective way, the pieces that make up the objects in the world. If it cannot do so, then it too is reduced to incoherency.[27]

Is it even possible for each new member of a series of temporal bits, ignoring the first one at present, to be brought into existence from a predecessor? Consider the sequence that Figure 3.3 represents. I will refer to the members of the sequence as elements.

---

[26] Heraclitus, frag. 1, in *Ancilla to the Pre-Socratic Philosophers*, trans. Kathleen Freeman (1948; repr., Cambridge: Harvard University Press, 1996), 24.

[27] The focus is on Sider in this analysis to determine whether the causal theory is adequate to account for the identity of objects. Heller agrees with him that the relationship of causality obtains among the temporal parts but takes a different view of identity. I will say more about Heller's position later.

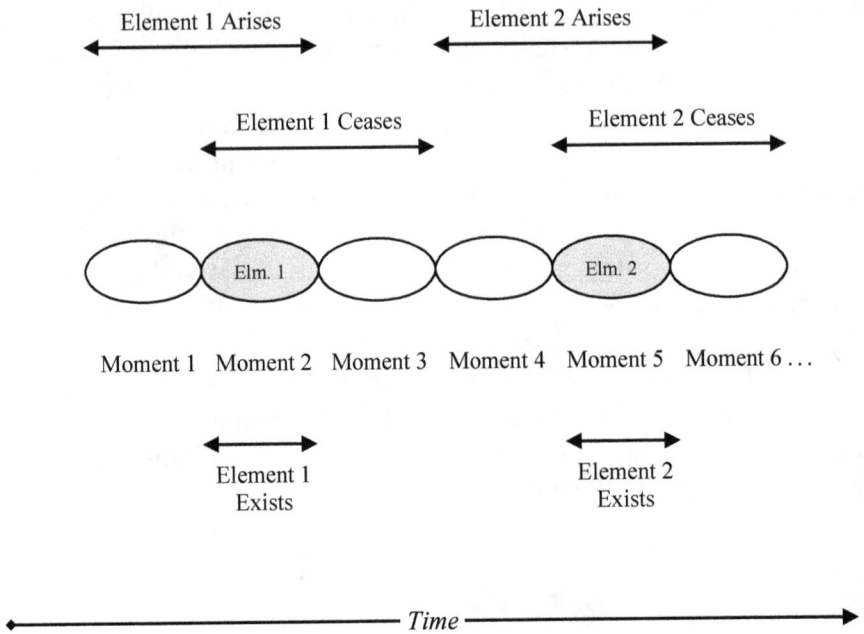

Element 1 Arises   Element 2 Arises

Element 1 Ceases   Element 2 Ceases

Elm. 1   Elm. 2

Moment 1   Moment 2   Moment 3   Moment 4   Moment 5   Moment 6 ...

Element 1   Element 2
Exists   Exists

Time

Figure 3.3

As one can see, an element of this series ceases to be before the next one comes into existence. The former element cannot give rise to the latter one—or to any other element of the series—as that which does not exist cannot do anything at all and, a fortiori, cannot generate anything. This scenario precludes any member of the series from being the progenitor of another member of that series.

Suppose, however, that there is an overlapping of arisings and ceasings. Elements still exist only for a single moment, but, as one element degenerates into nothingness, the next element of the sequence is coming into existence. The following diagram depicts this pattern:

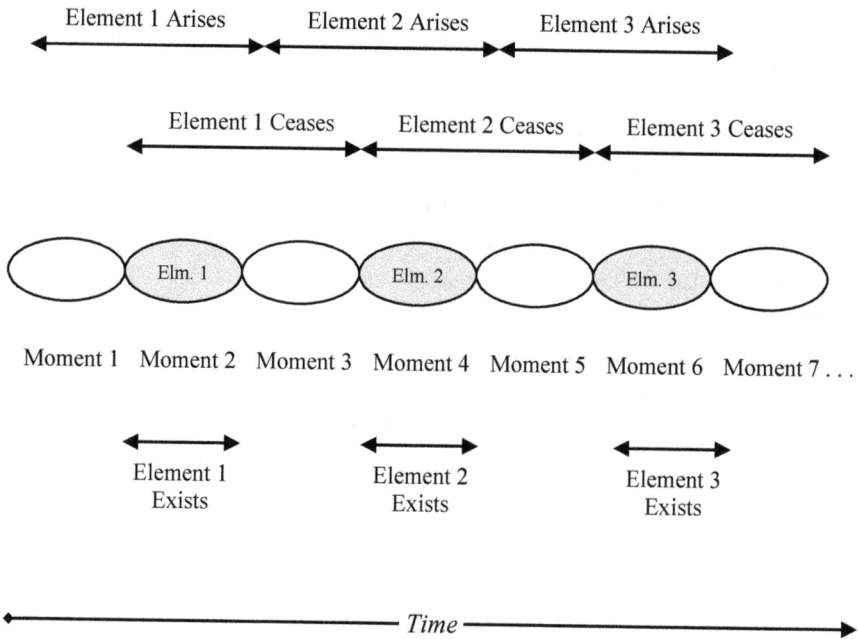

Figure 3.4

The problem is the same. The scenario in Figure 3.4 is not like that of a relay race, where the first runner's speed fades as the athlete hands the baton to the second runner, who is gaining speed. At the point in time that is marked by moment 3, element 1 does not exist. It is not that element 1 is fading; it is *gone*. A thing can serve as a cause only while it exists, for, as noted above, that which does not exist cannot do anything at all. It will not work to claim that element 1 initiates a causal chain that eventually results in the existence of element 2 but then ceases to be before its successor comes to exist.

Contrast such a case with that of a man at the Houston control center who, upon pressing a button and thereby sending a radio command to a spacecraft that is orbiting Neptune, dies—long before the spacecraft receives the message and responds to the instruction. The man is gone, but the orbiter will react four hours later. Here, there is a causal chain that links the sending of the message to the receiving of it as the radio signal traverses the distance between the two planets. The initiating of the signal by the man's pressing the button serves as a distal cause; it is a cause in a chain of causes that produces some effect, but not the cause that directly precedes the effect. Such an immediate cause is the proximal cause. It takes time for the signal to reach its destination, but the electromagnetic wave that carries the instruction does not cease to exist in the interim, nor does the causal chain cease to exist, for the signal is part of that chain. In Figure 3.4, there is no causal chain between element 1 and element 2. If element 1 were to generate element 2, then it would have to be the proximal cause, but, because it has ceased to exist by moment 3, it cannot be the proximal cause.

There is a third way. The series could be collapsed even further, such that the first element exists at the instant that is immediately prior to the existence of the second element. At moment 2, element 1 is, and element 2 is about to be; at moment 3, element 2 is, and element 1 has ceased to be. Figure 3.5 illustrates this scenario.

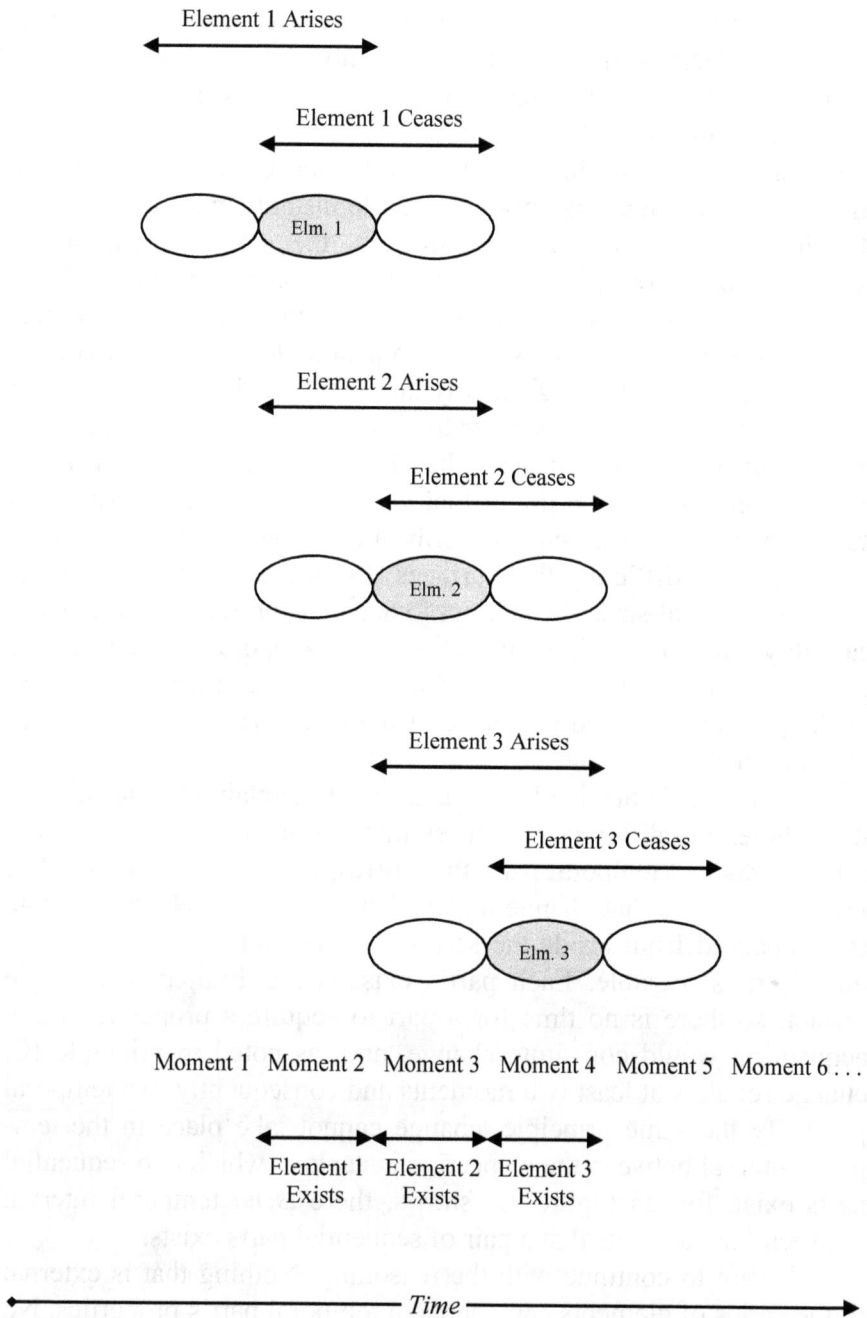

Element 1 Arises

Element 1 Ceases

Elm. 1

Element 2 Arises

Element 2 Ceases

Elm. 2

Element 3 Arises

Element 3 Ceases

Elm. 3

Moment 1   Moment 2   Moment 3   Moment 4   Moment 5   Moment 6 . . .

Element 1   Element 2   Element 3
Exists   Exists   Exists

Time

Figure 3.5

As one has seen, a coming to be must occur across two successive instants in time. At the first moment, the thing does not yet exist; at the second moment, it does exist. Likewise, a ceasing to be occurs in the course of two successive moments: A thing exists at the first moment of the pair but no longer exists at the second moment. If a thing exists only for a single instant, and it gives rise at that instant to something else—namely, the next element of the series—then it would have to come into existence in the mode of generating its own successor. It is not as though the first object comes into being simply with the potential to generate a second object; it comes into being actually doing so, for there is no time for it to acquire any properties other than what it already possesses. If it exists only for a single instant, then it has to be, and do, all that it ever is going to be, and do, at that very moment that it exists. Can such a metaphysical structure describe a plausible reality?

The core difficulty that surfaces here for Sider and other stage four-dimensionalists is the attempt to account for identity in terms of causality. In Sider's view, an entity *is* its temporal element at any given time, and each element amid the sequence of them is the effect of the previous one and the cause of the next one. This model faces several hurdles.

First, the theory is offered as a way to explain change because it attributes the different properties that entities possess at different times to distinct temporal parts that correspond to those entities. The fact, however, is that change undermines the theory. Neither change that is caused from inside the series nor change that is caused from outside it is possible. Each part's existence is limited to a single instant, so there is no time for a part to acquire a property, as any acquisition would constitute change, and, as noted in principle IC, change requires at least two moments and consequently two temporal parts. By the same principle, change cannot take place in the temporal interval between the respective instants at which two sequential parts exist, for, as Figure 3.5 shows, there *is no* temporal interval between the moments that a pair of sequential parts exists.

I want to continue with the reasoning. Nothing that is external to the series of elements can change a temporal part's properties. No external body can act on a part until the part exists, as the part is not there to be the object of the action. When a part does arise, its single-moment existence precludes the possibility of its changing because, as just stated, change requires at least two instants. It must be that some external cause starts the chain of elements, and some external cause stops it, but no external cause can act on any of its members to alter the member. It follows that a part must come into being with all the properties that it ever is going to possess. It can gain none, nor can it lose any. The problematic issue that results from this approach is that an entity that changes with the passage of time is nothing more than a string of things that do not change. How then is it possible for change to occur?

If change is to take place at all, then it must do so in the generation process: A temporal part that lacks property P generates a successor that has it. Where there is a cause-effect relationship in operation within a physical system, however, the effect cannot exceed the cause, in its totality, that generates it. One might deny that all events are caused, pointing to certain phenomena in the quantum realm, but such a stance is indefensible. I will take up the topic in a subsequent chapter, where I will show that the notion of uncaused events rests on a misconception. One might remark that not all causes are generative—that is to say, not all of them are ones that bring something into being. Four-dimensionalists, such as Sider, however, maintain that (1) every temporal part of an entity *is* caused and, setting aside the first one, is caused *by its predecessor* in the chain. Further, (2) the cause of every temporal part is that which *does bring* it into existence. With respect therefore to the metaphysics of four-dimensionalism's temporal-part identity-persistence thesis, causality is employed in the generative sense: In the context of the theory as a whole, it is the process of bringing into being.

To accept the philosophical tenet ex nihilo nihil fit is to accept its counterpart. Not only is it true that a thing cannot arise out of an absolute void, as in the invented case of *e* in Figure 3.6,

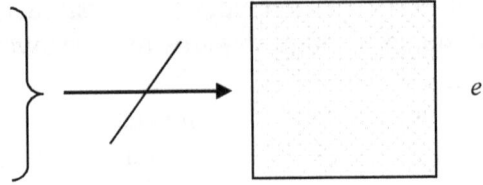

Figure 3.6

but it is also true that a thing that is caused to arise—to come into existence—cannot be made to do so from that which is insufficient to produce it. Consider for a moment a case in physics. If a hundred newtons of force are required to accomplish a certain task, for example, to cause an object of mass m to accelerate at v meters per second squared, and only ninety newtons of force are brought to bear on the task, then it is not possible, in the circumstances at hand, assuming that no other factors are involved, for the task to be accomplished.[28] Such an effect exceeds what is available to produce it. To assert that the occurrence is possible is to assert that an insufficiency is not an insufficiency, for it is tantamount to claiming that the effect-event can be produced, in part, out of an absence. In the illustration that I provide below, if c is insufficient to produce e, but e is produced, and there are no other dynamics at work, then something—namely, e—must come, in part, from nothing, clothed in the guise of deficiency:

---

[28] Acceleration is measured in distance per unit of time, per unit of time. An object, near the earth's surface, that is falling because of gravity, for instance, travels at approximately thirty-two feet per second at the end of the first second of its travel and sixty-four feet per second at the end of the next second, ignoring air resistance.

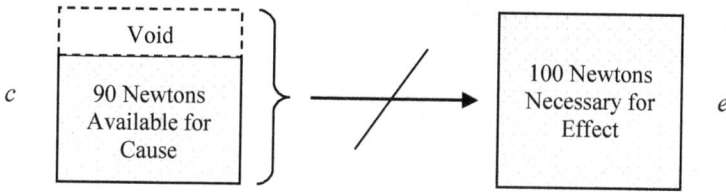

Figure 3.7

This state of affairs is illogical. That which does not exist—in this case, the void that is represented by the space above *c*—cannot produce anything. To think that nothing is actually something and that one can ascribe qualities or capabilities to it is irrational.

Proceeding with the analysis, I want to point out that certain changes that reflect increase likewise introduce a difficulty. Given that all the properties of a temporal part of an entity come entirely from the previous member of the chain, and nothing external to the chain ever can act as a cause—except perhaps to initiate the string of temporal-part-successor generation—Sider's four-dimensionalism is unable to explain how organisms grow. An adult cannot be greater in extension or weight or capabilities than the correlated infant. The theory cannot explain why the snowball at the foot of the mountain slope is larger than the one that was at the top a minute ago, though they are alleged to be the same snowball. Each temporal part is greater in size and mass than the preceding one as the chunk of material rolls downhill, yet nothing other than the previous temporal part can contribute to the obvious enlargement. In such incidents, things in the form of temporal components of objects are coming into existence out of an insufficiency. Sider's four-dimensionalism does not work as an account of the things that populate the world. The causal bond between parts that the theory proposes cannot explain change.

It is worth noting that, if one were to try to employ causality as a way to escape the spontaneous creation that seems to be inherent in Heraclitean theory, then the same problem that four-dimensionalism faces would exist there as well. There is no time for single-moment objects to acquire properties. Further, the acquisition alone, given that it constitutes change, would not be even possible in Heraclitean philosophy for another reason: Once an object changes, it is no longer the same object; thus, as before, each object must come to exist with all the properties that it ever is going to have.

On the causal approach, every object comes forth from its predecessor in a stream of slivers, owing all its attributes to the one before it. Although Heraclitean metaphysics is not concerned with maintaining the identity of things—and, in fact, finds none in the shifting objects in the world—it still would be charged with explaining how an effect can exceed the previous sliver-cause that produced it, if it were indeed so caused. The swollen waterway that is about to overflow its banks today may not be the same object as the placid river of yesterday, in Heraclitean thought, but one wonders how to account for the expansion in width, depth, and volume. Picture a river that is straight along a one-mile stretch, descending to the bottom at the same angle from each side, triangular fashion. Let PS_1 equal the following set of properties of the river:

$P_{1a} \rightarrow$ is 169 feet in width;

$P_{1b} \rightarrow$ is 101 feet in depth at the deepest point, which is in the middle, between the two banks;

$P_{1c} \rightarrow$ contains 45,062,160 cubic feet of water in a linear mile.

Let PS_2 equal this set (invented dimensions simplify the example):

$P_{2a} \rightarrow$ is 170 feet in width;

$P_{2b} \rightarrow$ is 102 feet in depth at the deepest point, which is in the middle, between the two banks;

$P_{2c} \rightarrow$ contains 45,777,600 cubic feet of water in a linear mile.

For illustration purposes, let element 1, a river slice, possess property-set PS_1 and element 2, the successor slice, possess property-set PS_2. Given the philosophy at hand, if one denies that a causal link is in place between elements, then they are popping into being out of thin air, as it were, and disappearing into thin air in defiance of a logical explanation. If one affirms that a causal link is in place, then, in the case here, element 1 must be the source of element 2; no other cause of element 2 is plausible. Further, in a metaphysics of objects that last only single instants, if element 1 generates element 2, then, apart from the properties that element 1 possesses, no cause of the properties that element 2 possesses is possible, as demonstrated above. Although, unlike for Sider, the postflood river for Heraclitus is not the same body of water as its preflood counterpart, the problem of increase remains nevertheless. One cannot get 715,440 cubic feet of water—the difference between a mile stretch of the rivers—out of the absence of anything there that is sufficient to produce it. The matter of property expansion is as destructive for Heracliteanism, with its momentary, one-off fragments, as it is for four-dimensionalism.

There are other hurdles that Sider must surmount in basing identity on a generative cause-effect relationship. The second challenge concerns the failure of causality to be either a necessary or a sufficient condition of identity. If a causal relationship between temporal parts is a necessary condition of the identity of an object, then, where there is no part-to-part causal connection, there is no identity. Things can, and do, cease to exist; thus, it is possible for one of the serial elements that make up a persistent thing to come into existence without generating a successor, so that the series can be stopped—say, by some external force that is potent enough to block the continued production and sever the causal link. If the last element can fail to generate a successor, then any one of them, it seems, can do so. If any one of them can fail to generate another, then so can the first one. It would be possible, in a four-dimensionalist's account of the world, for an entity to be composed of a single temporal part. The part does not cause another part in a string of them, nor certainly does it cause itself, as otherwise it would exist as a cause before it exists as an effect. It has no causal ties to anything else that makes up the entity, for nothing else does make up the entity, temporally speaking. It follows that, if a temporal-part causal relation is a necessary condition of object-identity, then identity is barred for such short-term existents—where there is no succession. That consequence, however, would be unacceptable for a four-dimensionalist, whether a worm theorist or a stage theorist, as both versions of the theory would have it that, where there is only one temporal part, a thing *is* its single temporal part at the single moment that the part exists. Thus, on a four-dimensional stance, identity does not require causality to be in operation, linking temporal constituents of a thing.

Alternatively, if a causal relationship between temporal parts is a sufficient condition of the identity of an object, then it must be that whatever a temporal part causes is part of that object. On what basis could one claim that a particular temporal part is not a member of the sequence that makes up the entity, where that part is the effect of one of the members of the sequence? With four-dimensional metaphysics and the role that temporal pieces play, could an element not be the cause of numerous effects? There is nothing to limit the chain of generation to one effect of a cause, as long as the properties of the effects do not exceed the capability of the cause to produce them. A typical four-dimensionalist would have to agree that multiple effects can arise from a single cause and further that multiple causes can produce a single effect. The theory is said to account for coincidence, where the time-components of things intersect or collocate, either by sharing their individual temporal parts for a period, in the worm view, or by forming mereologically composite temporal parts, in the stage view. As two roads may merge to create one highway, keeping their unique route numbers, then diverge miles from that point and finally remerge, so clay blocks may be joined and then diverge to form both a mass and a coextended statue of Mozart, before being smashed again into a lump. The clay mass and the sculpture occupy the same space-time segment, either as chunk plus statue or as chunk-statue. The temporal parts of the objects are traced causally to prior temporal parts of the united material, and the after-smashing lump's temporal parts are traced causally to those of the mass and statue. In coincidence, effects do not outstrip their causes, but there is a deviation from a one-to-one causal correspondence between, or among, temporal parts. Four-dimensionalists are wont to accept coincidence; so, for them, the single-to-multiple, and multiple-to-single, tree structures remain viable.[29] Consider this progression:

---

[29] It is one thing to hold that a single chunk of material can compose two objects simultaneously in the sense that there are two names for, or descriptions of, that one chunk, as in the example of convergent roads. It is quite another to hold that there are discrete objects occupying the same space simultaneously in the sense of strict collocation of matter. The former conception is unproblematic, but not even the theory of temporal parts can override the impossibility, barring a miracle, of the

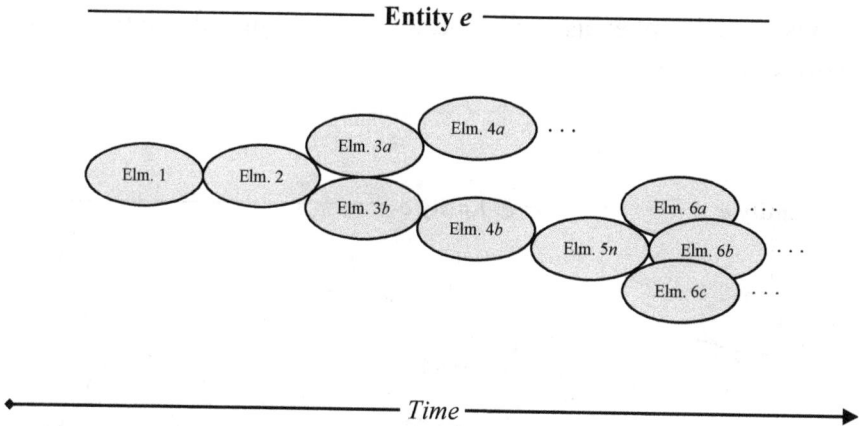

Figure 3.8

In Figure 3.8, one can see that element 2 produces two effects—there are two temporal parts that it generates, perhaps the early phase of a pair of small chunk-statues that arise from a single large lump, such that the collocated mass of the two does not exceed the mass of the one. Element $5n$ produces three. If causality is a sufficient condition of identity, then the result is a tree structure, such that, within the confines of physical law, anything and everything that is caused by a temporal part becomes part of the makeup of the entity—such is the concept of sufficiency. Identity cannot survive such total dissipation. It leads to illogical consequences. The ham on the table in the kitchen is a causal factor in Sidney's salivating; therefore, the dog's secretions, brought about by the slab of pork, somehow become part of the slab, even though Sidney never touched it, as temporal parts of the meat generate temporal parts of the drivel.

Furthermore, if causality is sufficient for identity, then whatever causes the supposed first element of the series to exist is itself part of the series, and whatever causes the cause of that first element

---

rightness of the latter, for physical laws prohibit it. The four-dimensionalist Mark Heller rejects coincidence for this reason. Beyond the causality problems that four-dimensional metaphysics faces, describing a single mass of matter in multiple ways does not succeed in showing that temporal parts are somehow at work.

to exist is a member as well, and so forth. Figure 3.9 represents a possible scenario.

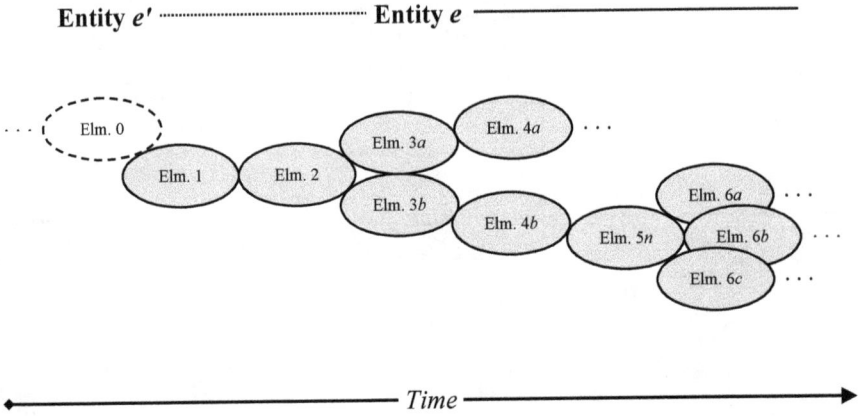

Figure 3.9

On the causal principle of four-dimensionalism, each temporal part has a cause of its coming into existence. In Figure 3.9, element 0, which is some temporal part of entity e', generates element 1, which is the first temporal part of entity e. If the cause-effect relationship sets forth identity through sufficiency, then element 0 must be a temporal part of entity e. Paralleling the query concerning the other end of the chain, as discussed above, is another question: On what basis could one claim that a particular temporal part is not a member of the sequence that makes up the entity, where that part is the cause of one of the members of the sequence? Ultimately, it appears that everything that is a progenitor of element 0 must be a temporal part of entity e. Therefore, e' and e are the same entity, even though, by hypothesis, entity e did not come into existence in the flow of time until after entity e' existed, which is impossible.

The end result of the sufficiency-of-cause approach is that whatever is caused by, or causes, any temporal part of an entity is itself part of that entity, which is an untenable consequence. It blends the distinct things that populate the world into an amorphous whole that is extended indefinitely in time—in both directions. In view of this fact, causality does not capture identity; through assimilation, it destroys it.

Attempting to modify the causal-sufficiency model to retain the critical link but eliminate extraneous causes and effects leads to another problem. Refer to Figure 3.9. Are there any grounds for saying, in an effort to rescue four-dimensionalism, that the early and late units, element 0 and, for instance, element 6c, are not temporal parts of entity e, thereby avoiding the problem of predecessor and successor causation? One cannot hold that only those temporal parts that are parts of e are parts of e without employing a useless criterion. The only other plausible option is to incorporate spatiality. If there are incorporeal things, then such an approach fails, of course, but I will set aside the issue of the nonphysical and see whether the criterion can be applied successfully to physical things. What the investigation will show is that adding the spatial factor to the causal relationship will not work.

Suppose that the claim is that element 1 and element 2 are temporal parts of entity e if, and only if, element 1 causes element 2 to come into existence, and element 2 occupies the same space as element 1. The consequence is that nothing ever could move without losing its identity.

If same spatial extension, rather than same spatial location, were the crucial component, then the result again would be unacceptable. One and the same balloon could not be inflated, nor could it be deflated, as there would be a different balloon at each instant: Every balloon temporal part would occupy more space or less space than the previous part occupied because of inflation or deflation respectively. Neither the inflating balloon nor the deflating balloon would be identical to the one in the original state. Moreover, given that sameness would not be preserved from moment to moment, if Henry inflated a balloon and released the air subsequently, then the object at the end of this two-step process could not be the same object as that with which he started, even though the two items may be indistinguishable.

One might wish to add spatial contiguity. Element 1 and element 2 are temporal parts of entity e, one could say, just in case element 1 causes element 2 to come into existence, and element 2 occupies either the same space as element 1 or a space that is contiguous with that of element 1. There is a hint of this approach in Mark Heller's remark about the configuration of matter; see the quotation on pages 251–52. Sider too alludes to the contribution of spatio-temporal unbrokenness in his account of persistence.[30] It may be assumed that such an additional factor allows not only movement but also growth, thus countering a difficulty that surfaced earlier. Coupling spatial contiguity with causality, however, does not rescue the theory. It raises what I will call the problem of eternal object-existence. If each element of a series pushes the next one into being as it itself comes into being, and whatever the element produces is part of the series, provided that the product is temporally continuous with its predecessor and occupies either the same space as, or a space that is contiguous with, its predecessor, then it is not clear how the chain ever could be stopped.

Once what one refers to as a loaf of bread comes into existence, it becomes eternal. To say that the loaf never ceases to exist leads to absurdities. The loaf is composed of material particles. It is eaten by four people and digested. Some of its material particles are assimilated through metabolic processes. They provide energy for the bodies of those people and rebuild their tissues. Thus, a portion of the particles of the loaf are retained in the tissues, while a portion of them are eliminated from the body. Even the dog under the table gets a bite. When the dog dies, is buried, and decays, the loaf goes on forever because its composite bits follow the path of conditions that define identity: Each temporal part of each material particle causes its temporal successor to come into being, and each successor temporal part occupies a space that is the same as, or contiguous with, the space that its predecessor temporal part occupied. Before long, the loaf is spread across three continents, appearing in both soil and water, and incorporated into the organs of different animals and the fibers of a few plants.

One could attempt to evade the problem by claiming that the loaf must remain intact, its physical bits conjoined, as a condition of

---

[30] Unfortunately, for him, there is an argument that demonstrates the inability of unbrokenness, under certain conditions, to distinguish between an object that is in motion and one that is at rest. I will discuss the objection in a moment.

identity. The loaf ceased to exist when a physical part of it was removed. The consequence of such a stand is even more dire. The loaf did not come to an end with the first slice; it ended when a tiny crumb fell from the crust while Judy carried it to the table. This approach leads one to say that nothing can persist if there is a loss of a single particle. Therefore, Judy herself ceased to exist during her trip across the kitchen, for she lost an eyelash on the way.[31] Surely, though, one should not be so quick to get rid of Judy.

Additional trouble arises for one who seeks to circumvent the problem of eternal elements by disallowing the disassembly of a thing into spatial parts, saying that the particles of the loaf, for instance, must remain juxtaposed. In that case, there can be no identity of anything the parts of which are not in intimate contact. There is no solar system, no Milky Way, no Orion Nebula. There is no set of desk accessories in the gift box, given that the stapler is not touching the letter opener, and the paperweight is on the other side of the molded container. No one owns a doll collection unless the dolls are dumped on top of each other in a trunk. No jigsaw puzzle exists until the pieces, scattered widely on the table, are inserted in place. Sally asks her husband, "Is that the same puzzle that you were planning to work on yesterday?" The question is meaningless because the locution 'same puzzle' is referentially vacuous. There are not even any atoms. It is impossible within the bounds of physical law for the electrons that encircle the nuclei of atoms to rest atop those nuclei because of the base energy that is inherent in any physical system.[32] In this universe, the electrons must remain apart from the nuclei for as long as the universe exists. If there are no atoms, however, then there are no objects that are made of them, including loaves of bread, and physical reality disintegrates.

Reliance on a causal connection to support a four-dimensional ontology seems to be misguided. A causal link cannot be necessary for identity, or else it would undermine object-identity altogether. As a sufficient condition, causality alone is too inclusive; causality combined with same spatial location or extension produces illogicalities; causality combined with spatial contiguity leads to unlimited

---

[31] The position that nothing can survive a loss of parts—any change that affects the parts, in fact—is mereological essentialism. The parts are as they are essentially.
[32] This energy is known as zero-point energy.

continuance, avoiding the irrationality of it only at the expense of being too restrictive. If causality is neither a necessary nor a sufficient condition of identity, then it cannot be set forth in the theory as a way to account for it. It is not an essential part of the concept; it is, at best, incidental.

Sider's four-dimensionalism faces a third hurdle in its reliance on causality, and it is a particularly serious one. Once the series of elements is initiated, so that new elements are coming into being with each successive instant, there seems to be nothing to block their prolongation. Until the entity itself ceases to exist—the sequential progression comes to a halt—the temporal parts are spawned like soap bubbles, blown from a child's toy. Why would the parts not remain in existence following their arising? They are, after all, independently existing things. What annihilates them? The cessation of the entity, of which the elements are temporal parts, may be explainable in the theory by the cessation of the generation of new temporal parts corresponding to the entity—blocked presumably by some cause that is outside the chain. The theory, however, is unable to offer an adequate account of the cessation of the temporal parts themselves. Without something to terminate them, they continue. Moreover, if they continue, then they too must have temporal parts, as the theory has it that every persistent thing has temporal parts, and those parts must have parts, and so forth. To claim that individual rudimentary temporal parts do not last beyond a sole moment on the stage of existence, by definition, is to impose an arbitrary, a priori limit. Causality is an empirical relation, not a logical one; it is a matter of fact that the relation holds where it does hold, not a matter of definition. Temporal parts are initiated by a cause, the theory asserts; unless there is a cause to terminate them, they will remain.

One could stop the progression of a chain of falling dominoes, placed on end in close proximity, by putting a foot down in the path, but stopping the progression does not cause the dominoes to cease to exist. Analogously, stopping the continuance of an object that is composed of temporal parts—terminating the further generation of them—is not the same as stopping the continuance of the temporal parts themselves, and there is no reason to think that the former event causes the latter one. It is not even whether the temporal parts *do* persist that undercuts four-dimensionalism but the fact that they *could* persist. According to the theory, there is one, and only one, temporal part of a given entity that corresponds exactly to each instant in time in the course of the entity's existence. What the possibility of continuance introduces, however, is an increase in the number of temporal parts that exist simultaneously at each moment in the progression of time. Instead of a string of parts, as shown in Figure 3.10,

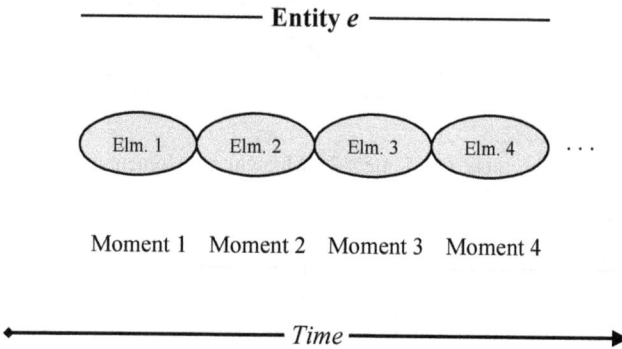

Entity *e*

Elm. 1   Elm. 2   Elm. 3   Elm. 4   . . .

Moment 1   Moment 2   Moment 3   Moment 4

Time

Figure 3.10

the result is the stacked wedge of Figure 3.11.

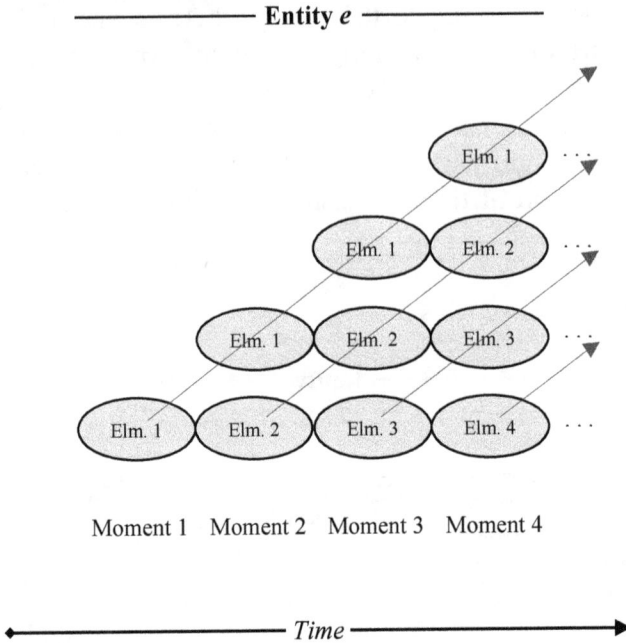

Figure 3.11

One may think that such continuance could benefit the theory, in that it might offer a way to address a problem, that of augmentation—apparent in the swelling-river case—by lumping together retained elements. If temporal parts are retained, then the requirement that a thing exist for two or more moments if it is to change is met. The thought will be short-lived, however, for such continuance leads to absurdities. First, according to the view of four-dimensionalism, an entity is identified with its temporal parts, either as the sum of all of them to date, for a worm theorist, or as the one at the present instant, every instant, for a stage theorist. If element 1 is Donny at moment 1, then, in a matter of nanoseconds, there will be a legion of Donny-things. Which one is the real Donny-sequence? If all of them are authentic, then one man has turned into an army of discrete beings, all of whom are identical to him, yet all of whom are distinct from him, which is logically impossible. If only one of them is authentic, then who are the others?

Second, an inconsistency arises from the possession of contrary attributes: Elements may possess different—and incompatible—sets of properties at the same moment in time. An entity may change from sitting to standing, brunette to bald, deflated to inflated, or blue to nonblue in the course of its existence. According to the theory, an entity is identical to its temporal parts. If therefore the parts, after springing into being, can continue, then the entity to which the parts belong may have properties that it cannot have simultaneously. It is impossible for anything to retain earlier characteristics of itself and still be the same entity, where those characteristics are mutually exclusive and exhibited at the same moment. By the rules of logic, no single thing can be both P and not P at once, where P stands for some property. With the causal generation that is inherent in four-dimensionalism, entity e may be both P and not P at a given instant, moment 4 in Figure 3.11, and this state of affairs cannot obtain—ever. It is one thing to take note of the different times that an entity exists. It is quite another to think, as the four-dimensionalists do think, that there are independent elements existing at those times, linked by an indispensable causal chain that constitutes the entity. The theory of temporal parts appears to be toppled by its own efforts to explain change.

There is one final possibility. Figure 3.12 represents it.

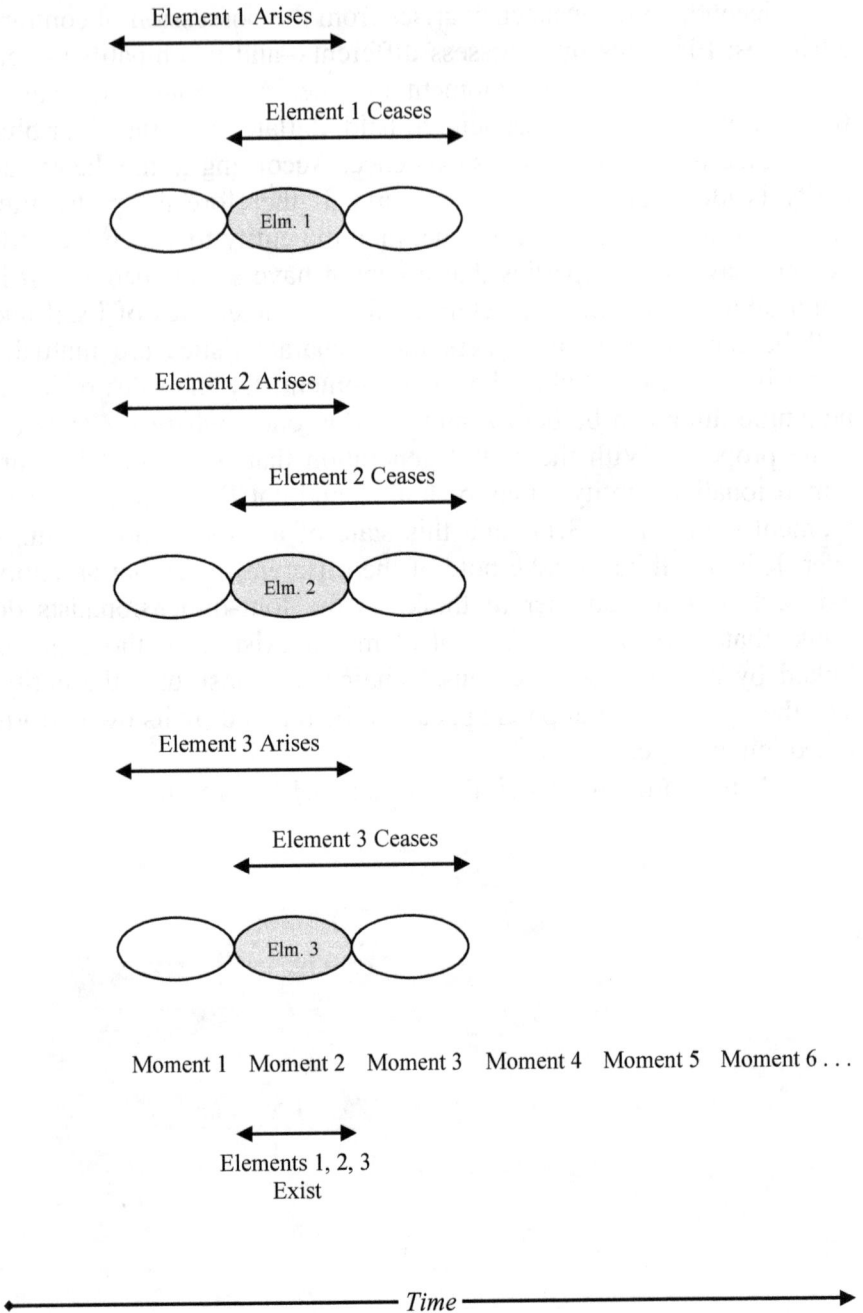

Figure 3.12

The problem here is that the elements exist all at once. There is only one element at one moment in time. Elements 1, 2, and 3 are the same element. There is no sequence of causally linked object slivers. There is no sequence, because there is no temporal succession; there is no causality, because no sliver can be the cause of itself. Even on the supposition that elements 1, 2, and 3 are distinct elements, coexisting at moment 2, there is still no sequence of causally linked object slivers. There is no sequence, because, as before, the objects exist simultaneously; there is no cause-effect relationship, because each element exists only for a single moment—the same moment— and it cannot bring into being anything until it exists. It follows that the first moment of existence for whatever that element produces, if it produces anything at all, must follow the moment at which the element itself exists. To condense the notion, think of it in this way: Nothing that exists only for one instant in time can spawn something that coexists with itself. The scenario that is represented above therefore cannot serve to support the claim that what one perceives as a single thing through time is actually a series of transitory elements, where each element of that series causes a temporal successor. A fortiori, the scenario cannot serve to support the claim that what one perceives as a single thing with variations in properties through time is actually a series of transitory elements, where each element of that series causes a temporal successor with properties that may differ from those that it possesses. The state of affairs that Figure 3.12 details is not a depiction of the structure of four-dimensionalism nor, for that matter, of Heracliteanism.

It is clear that none of the four scenarios will work. They are fraught with problems. No other portrayals are forthcoming. It is difficult to see how the universe of everyday objects, in reality, could be a universe of object slivers, each lasting no more than an instant, extinguished without adequate explanation. The existence of no member of the series can be explained by claiming that there is a previous one, serving as its progenitor. Causal generation cannot describe persistence. Without it, however, perdurance fails, and one is left with a plenum of disjointed temporal elements popping into, and out of, existence in violation of logic.

The consequence of this line of thought is that there is nothing to perceive and no person to perceive it. Both the reputed objects of perception and the reputed subjects are merely streams of fleeting, dissociated pieces, each of which disappears before perception can take place. A perception requires time to complete. The signaling information generally must traverse the space between the article in the world and the perceiver—true, as a rule, for visual, auditory, and olfactory data. It must stimulate the receptors of the perceiver's appropriate sensory faculty. It must travel the proper neural pathways to the perceiver's central nervous system. It must be interpreted by the perceiver. All the momentary elements that are needed for the process perish long before their respective functions can execute, and, without a way to link the pieces, there can be no perception of objects. Further, knowledge of the world, like perception, is not possible: The would-be objects of knowledge fall apart before they can be apprehended by the mind, and the would-be apprehender who is to know them falls apart before any apprehending can occur. Indeed, carried to its ultimate conclusion, if one views the universe as the totality of physical things, then there can be no universe at all.[33] There is merely a temporally stretched assemblage, possibly infinite, of universe slivers, no one of which has a connection to any other one, each appearing and then disappearing in a moment, with no accounting for how any of them came to be. Reality is reduced to a senseless morass from which a path of escape is not in the offing. Four-dimensionalism—let alone Heracliteanism—does not seem to be right.

The four-dimensionalists believe that they have set forth an ontology of objects that accounts for change. All the temporal pieces of a thing are stand-alone existents, independent of each other but forming a whole. Given that they all are distinct things, they can have different properties. The relationship between successive parts is simply cause and effect, but with a twist. Each of *a particular* entity's temporal parts, save the last, generates a successor that is

---

[33] From the standpoint of logic, it cannot be assumed that a whole has the same characteristics as its parts, even if all those parts have a quality in common. In this case, however, if the universe *is precisely* its parts, perhaps arranged in a certain way, then it is reasonable to think that the collection of physical entities is as susceptible to fragmentation as any of the physical entities that compose the collection. The consequence is that the coherence of the universe as a global system is undermined.

also a part of *that particular* entity. Sider calls the essential association the *temporal counterpart* relation—or the *genidentity* relation. Says Sider,

> For the temporal parts theorist, the world is a four-dimensional manifold of stages. The career of any persisting object is a sequence of instantaneous objects in this manifold—a path through spacetime. But it is only a small minority of paths through spacetime that correspond to careers of persisting objects. . . . The worm theorist will say that only a small minority of all the mereological sums of instantaneous stages count as continuants (objects of our ordinary ontology)—namely, those sums whose temporal parts stand in some 'unity' or 'genidentity' relation. The stage theorist will say that of all the paths through spacetime intersecting a given continuant (stage), only some of these paths include all and only that continuant's counterparts, where the relevant counterpart relation is just the worm theorist's genidentity relation.
>
> Thus an integral part of any four-dimensionalist view is the genidentity relation.[34]

What picks out, according to Sider, the *right* path through space-time—the path that includes all those, and only those, temporal parts that belong to the persisting entity—is genidentity. Parts are related by cause and effect, so the thinking has it, yet there is this vague, belonging-to-the-same-entity relational component. I already have shown that causality is neither a necessary nor a sufficient condition of identity and that coupling a spatial factor to causality is of no benefit. Contiguity, the most optimistic choice among such factors, raises the issue of eternal object-existence. In fact, given that various four-dimensionalists accept coincidence—material objects, in some way, can occupy the same spot simultaneously—the spatial aspect cannot play a part in delineating the careers of persisting objects.[35]

---

[34] Sider, *Four-Dimensionalism*, 224–25. The term 'mereological sum' refers to a composite—an assemblage of parts. One will recall from chap. 1 that mereology is the study of parts and wholes, and of the relationship between them.

[35] See my discussion of coincidence, pp. 264–67.

A further difficulty arises for spatial contiguity in a temporal-parts theory of persistence. One objector states that spatiotemporal uninterruptedness is insufficient to distinguish between two disks that are exactly alike and completely uniform, except that one disk is spinning and the other is stationary. In such a case, every temporal part of a disk will be like every other temporal part of it—true for both disks—and contiguity is valueless as an aid to differentiation. Sider attempts to rescue his theory by linking genidentity to the laws of nature—the laws of motion in particular—and introducing the global context in which those laws are in force, thereby helping to determine the facts in instances of this sort.[36] Sider admits, however, that the objection is formidable; he realizes that endurance theories are superior to his own in capturing common notions about motion in homogenous objects. If genidentity is to succeed as the mark of persistence for objects, then it seems that something more is needed.

What then could be the additional factor that makes genidentity work if it is not the very persistence that the theory is attempting to explain? Sider proffers a response to a core objection to the stage version of four-dimensionalism—the version that he adopts. His remarks are below:

> The first and most obvious objection is that it denies persistence over time. How could continuants be stages? Stages don't *continue*. If persons are instantaneous stages, then no person lasts more than an instant. However, as I will develop it, the stage view includes a counterpart theory of *de re* temporal predication, according to which instantaneous stages may nevertheless have temporal properties such as *being* F *in ten minutes*.
>
> According to my temporal counterpart theory, the truth condition of an utterance of 'Ted was once a boy' is this: there exists some person stage x prior to the time of utterance, such that x is a boy, and x bears the temporal counterpart relation to Ted. Since there is such a stage, the claim is true. Despite being a stage, Ted *was*

---

[36] Saul Kripke raises this objection against the theory of temporal parts. For a discussion of Kripke's argument and Sider's response to it, see Sider, *Four-Dimensionalism*, 224–36.

a boy; he has the historical property of *once being a boy*.[37]

Two problems immediately surface with this position. The first is the misconstrual of the expression 'being *F* in ten minutes'. It does not denote a property that is possessed by anything. To say that the pancakes will be too burned to eat in ten minutes is to say that the pancakes *will possess a property in the future*, not that they *possess right now a future property*. What could possessing a future property even mean? The future, instantaneous stage in which the property materializes is not identical to the present stage, by the theorist's own account, and the present stage will be long out of existence before the property is exhibited, by that same account. No one would say of a cat a decade before it is conceived that it has the property, right now, of being a three-legged animal in a little more than ten years. The term 'the cat' here could not apply to anything. It is referentially vacuous: There is nothing in existence that it denotes. It may be the case that Lucy will give birth far in the future, and it may be the case that a kitten that she bears at that time will have only three legs. If Lucy, in fact, does bring forth such an offspring, then the kitten to which she gives birth at that time will possess the property of having less than a full complement of appendages. A yet-to-exist kitten, however, cannot possess *now* any properties at all, for, by definition, there is no such beast in existence to possess them. A fortiori, a yet-to-exist kitten cannot possess *now* a property of having only three legs at some point in the future. Ascribing properties to an object that does not exist is misguided, even if, in the future, an object may come to exist and possess those properties when it does so. Sider is confusing the exhibiting of future characteristics of existents with the exhibiting of characteristics of future existents—things that will come to exist.

---

[37] Ibid., 193. Sider proceeds to claim that the relation may be analyzed, for persons, in terms of memory or bodily continuity, or it may be primitive—that is to say, not further analyzable. He does not pursue this matter. The use of memory as a criterion of personal identity is traceable to John Locke. Employing the criterion would not allow four-dimensionalism to escape the core trouble from which it suffers, however—trouble that has been brewing and is about to appear. Further, even if memory could serve as a way to determine the sameness of persons, it obviously could not serve as one for inanimate objects.

The second problem is that Sider has leveled Lewis's criticism of three-dimensionalism against himself. Being *F* in ten minutes is, if anything, standing in a relation, not displaying a property. The same is true of once being a boy. If Sider wishes to ascribe so-called future and past properties to his instantaneous stages, then he can do so only with reference to times.

There is, however, a more serious problem. Again, Sider states,

> 'Ted was once a boy' attributes a certain temporal property, the property of *once being a boy*, to me, not to anyone else. Of course, the stage view does analyze my having this property as involving the boyhood of another object, but *I* am the one with the temporal property, which is the important thing. The stage view is consistent with stages having temporal properties; it's just that temporal properties are given a counterpart-theoretic analysis.[38]

How does the philosopher know that *he* is the one with the temporal property? Trace the reasoning that one might expect to encounter in a friendly dialogue between a stage-view four-dimensionalist and an inquisitive interlocutor concerning identity.

FOUR-DIMENSIONALIST: This temporal part, existing right . . . *now* is Ted, who is living in Tennessee.

INTERLOCUTOR: Then, what is—or, I suppose, was—this other temporal part?

FOUR-DIMENSIONALIST: It was Ted too, but he was much younger at the time and living in Texas.

INTERLOCUTOR: Oh, I see. Well, what assurance does one have that the long-ago Texas-Ted part was really this Tennessee-Ted, as you say?

FOUR-DIMENSIONALIST: It is because the parts of both belong to the same temporal counterpart sequence—the same genidentity-related sequence—that they are both Ted.

INTERLOCUTOR: Oh, okay, but how can one be sure that they belong to the same temporal counterpart sequence?

---

[38] Ibid., 195.

FOUR-DIMENSIONALIST: It is because they are both parts of the same person, Ted, that they belong to the same temporal counterpart sequence.

As an account of how things can continue through time, the theory of temporal parts is circular. One cannot point to a specific causal sequence of parts to account for the persistence of a particular entity while, at the same time, pointing to *that very entity* to pick out the specific causal sequence of parts that are the parts of *it*. In the final analysis, if the only guarantor of the veracity of the sequence is the sequence itself, then four-dimensionalism fails as an account of object-continuance. If temporal parts exist, then, without a way to lock the right ones into place—an obstacle that began to come to light in the discussion of causality—the theory leaves open the door for what I will call *identity drift*; and the four-dimensionalists' embracement of coincidence serves indisputably only to exacerbate the problem. In Figure 3.13, one sees the conjectured temporal parts of two objects cross, and the result is ontological ruin.

Object 1

Temp. Parts: 1*a*　　　1*b*　　　1*c*　　　1*d*　　　1*e*

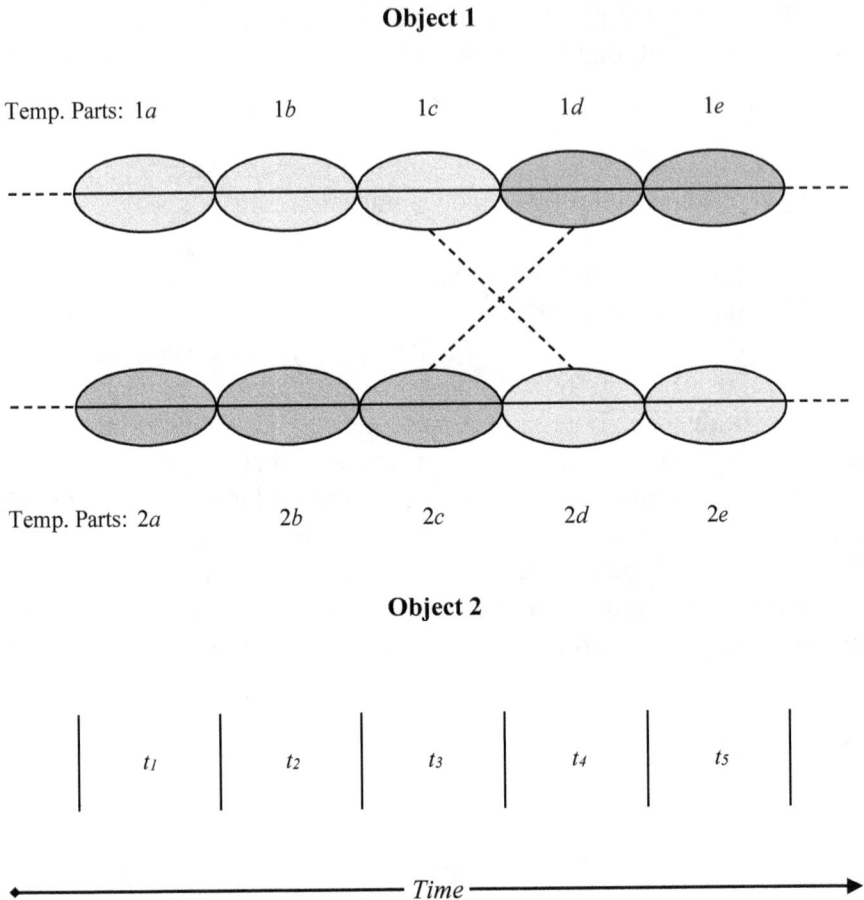

Temp. Parts: 2*a*　　　2*b*　　　2*c*　　　2*d*　　　2*e*

Object 2

t_1　　　t_2　　　t_3　　　t_4　　　t_5

━━━━━━ *Time* ━━━━━━▶

Figure 3.13

The four-dimensionalists attempt to put forth a position that breaks things into discrete temporal components. Being distinct, each component can have a set of properties that differs from the others, yet persistence is possible, so goes the thinking, through a relation of genidentity. Splintering an object into pieces is the easy task. Reassembling the pieces properly is not accomplished so readily— there is just no good way to put them in place again. All the king's horses and all the king's men could not piece poor Humpty together after his dreadful fall. The problem for the four-dimensionalists is more than just change; it is also, and of notably greater import, identity.

Surely, if persistence is possible, then a better explanation of it can be found. What is needed is an account that eschews the constant generation and annihilation of objects, and which does not depend on a plethora of causally linked, time-dependent pieces. If a plausible account is to be put forth, then it must do so in terms of something other than perdurance. Three-dimensionalism appears to be the logical alternative. Things must continue through time as wholes, not spread across time as series of individual parts. What, however, is it to be a whole?

SENSES OF IDENTITY

One might ask how such confusion about identity arose in the first place, how philosophy reached this peculiar frame of mind. In taking a look at the properties of things, one sees that there are seemingly two fundamental facts, which, when one fails to take them into account, give rise to the misunderstanding about identity through change. Here is the first: The concept of sameness is marked by divergence; there are two distinct senses of it, and the difference between them has been blurred. If the term 'same' means 'nothing different', then, by definition, a thing is not the same if it changes. To assume that this sort of sameness must hold for the identity of a given object through time, though, is to adopt an extreme position—one that, so I think, is indefensible. The requirement is simply too stringent. Suppose that an acorn falls from a tree and bounces off the roof of Tony's house on its way to the ground, leaving a small mark on a shingle. The consequence is that Tony's house—the dwelling that stood there a moment earlier—is no more. Striking a flower pot on his patio while en route to its destination, the acorn annihilates the container too by virtue of chipping the rim. Even the acorn is gone because of the slight depression on each side, resulting from the respective impacts. Underlying the identity-change perplexity is a piece of fallacious reasoning, which takes the form of the following argument, with numbered assertions:

1. If an object does not possess, at a given point in time, the same properties that another object possesses, at that point in time, then the two objects cannot be the same object.
2. Therefore, if an object does not possess, at a given point in time, the same properties that another object possesses, at a different point in time, then the two objects cannot be the same object.

The thrust of this argument becomes more clear when it is represented diagrammatically. Imagine that, at a certain moment, call it t_1, two different sets of physical properties are exhibited in the world.[39] The set of properties that some object exhibits at time t_1 is P_1, and another set of properties that some object exhibits at time t_1 is P_2, where $P_1 \neq P_2$. This state of affairs represents the premise of the argument. Refer to Figure 3.14.

---

[39] Time may be continuous and without discrete increments, or discontinuous and incremental—a detail that surfaced earlier. Nothing here hinges on the distinction, although the incremental portrayal provides a clearer picture of the main philosophical points. In either case, if Zeno's paradox is to arise, then it will show no favoritism. My intent is to give an account of alteration in things. Whatever duration a moment is, it is obvious that there are some times that are later than other times, and it is this temporal crossing, or moving through time, that is central to understanding the notion of change. As before, I will represent a minimal block of time, whatever that block may be, as t, followed by a subscript, and show it as a segment on a timeline.

Premise of Argument: Object 1 Cannot Be Object 2.

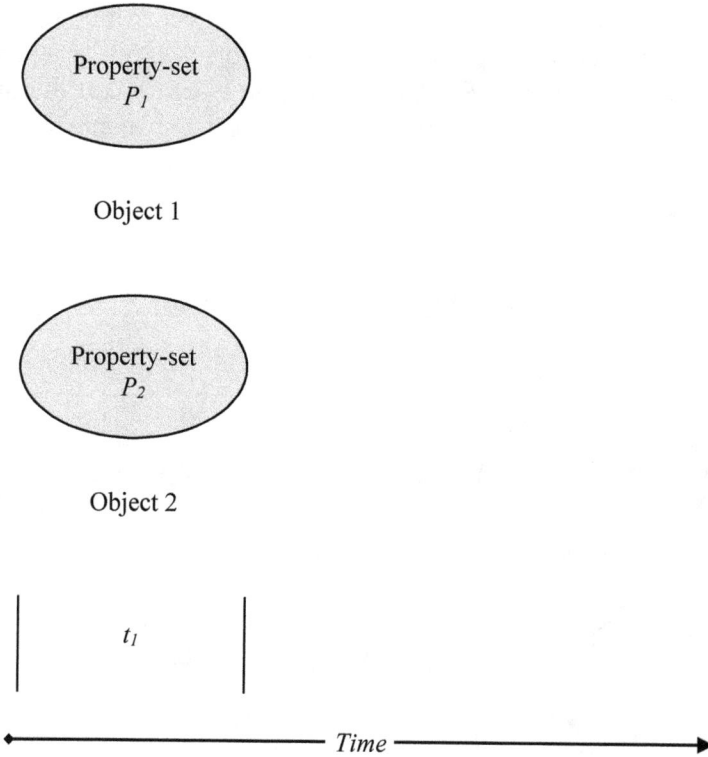

Figure 3.14

The premise is true. It is not possible for the two objects that are represented above to be identical: Their characteristics are *simultaneously* dissimilar. One will recall the discussion in the previous chapter regarding the principle of the indiscernibility of identicals. The counterpart to Leibniz's law, it states that, if two things are identical, then they must possess all properties in common. The principle is indisputable, but only if its application is limited to a single instant.

From the argument's true premise, the reasoning proceeds to claim, in effect, that time is not a factor in identity; only sameness of properties is a factor. The argument stretches the principle of the indiscernibility of identicals beyond its applicability. At two *different* times, t_1 and t_2, two distinct sets of physical properties are manifested in the world. The set of properties that some object exhibits at time t_1 is P_1, and the set of properties that some object exhibits at another time t_2 is P_2, where $P_1 \neq P_2$. The conclusion is again that the objects cannot be identical—they cannot be one and the same thing. See Figure 3.15.

Conclusion of Argument: Object 1 Cannot Be Object 2.

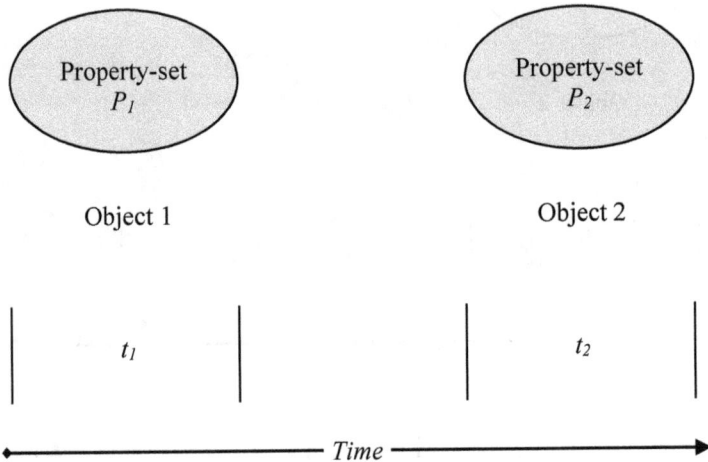

Figure 3.15

It is this fallacious reasoning that forms the foundation for the view that the constancy of Heraclitean flux destroys identity. Even some contemporary authors hold that changes in properties or states can have that ability. Flux need not destroy identity. The underlying argument is flawed because, albeit the premise is true, the conclusion is a non sequitur. One cannot infer that object-identity through time is subject to the same property-equivalence restriction that marks object-identity at a given point in time. A photograph is not a movie; a snapshot in time, whether physical or metaphysical, does not depict a continuance through time. Michael might have been quite pale when his college graduation picture was taken; therefore, if the person in the photograph has a suntan, so goes the reasoning, then it cannot be Michael. In the video segments of a weeklong adventure to the beach, however, one watches as a man works on his tan, suffering an unfortunate sunburn on the first day and eventually exhibiting a dark color. Regardless of whether the man in the video is pale, blister-red, or brown, surely it is the same man, Michael, and the same skin, Michael's skin, throughout the video. It is possible for a thing to have different properties at different times. If such were not the case, then there would be countless Michaels on the summer trek to the shore, all with the same, unique fingerprints. Such a consequence is indefensible.

In essence, the problem is that the argument conflates two fundamentally different types of identity with disastrous results. One saw in chapter 2 how a distinction is drawn between numerical identity and qualitative identity. I will provide a brief review here. Things are numerically identical by virtue of uniqueness. Things are qualitatively identical by virtue of the properties that they possess. Jeremy and Jason may own the same rare coin—say, a 1943 copper U.S. Lincoln cent, of which only a few were minted.[40] In the numerical sense of sameness, there is joint ownership of a single coin. There exists a 1943 copper penny occupying a specific location in space-time, and each man is part-owner of that one coin. In the qualitative sense of sameness, Jeremy has sole ownership of a penny, which he keeps in a safe deposit box, and Jason is the sole owner of a separate penny, which he hides under his mattress. Either may sell his coin, and, between the two of them, another remains. Of course, to be truly qualitatively identical, two things must possess even the minutest of details in common. The underlying argument against identity through change that is represented above is fallacious because it presumes that the requirements of numerical identity and

---

[40] The Lincoln series to which this particular coin belongs consists of 0.950 copper (plus tin and zinc). A critical shortage of that metal during War World II forced the U.S. Treasury Department to issue pennies in 1943 that were made of zinc-coated steel. A few coins were struck in error on the copper-based planchets, however.

those of qualitative identity track together without regard to the temporal factor, and that presumption is false.[41]

In summary, if one supposes that objects are *not* capable of intrinsic change—they cannot survive a shift in properties without an accompanying dissolution of identity—then, because different sets of properties, which persons associate with objects, are exhibited in the world at different times, there must be a different object corresponding to every individual set of characteristics. More succinctly, if things cannot change, but properties in the world do change, then each new set of properties that is associated with a thing signals the presence of a new entity. Any shifting in the qualities of things is accompanied invariably by the ceasing to exist of one object and the coming into existence of another. The upshot of this approach is that, if change is occurring continually in the universe, then so is this process of object-swapping, and all things collapse into streams of single-instant fragments. It is this view that depicts the Heraclitean canon that, because change is unremitting, no one can step a second time into the same river. That canon is underscored by Heraclitus's disciple, Cratylus, who denies, for the very reason that Heraclitus gives, that one could step even *once* into the same river.[42]

If one supposes, on the other hand, that things *are* capable of intrinsic change by virtue of a change in properties, then they must be able to persist through the change to undergo the progression from a given state to a different one. Nothing can change unless it survives the process, and, if *it* survives, then *it* remains. To maintain that change in a physical object destroys the object's ontic integrity is to subscribe to a view that is self-defeating. If corporeal things are

---

[41] Given that location, rest-motion, and positional attitude are not independent of context, according to my contention, they should be excluded from an authentic list of properties that determine qualitative identity. If one does not exclude them, then, in normal circumstances, true qualitative identity would entail numerical identity. Otherwise, it would be possible for two separate masses of matter that compose two separate physical objects and that have *all* properties in common to occupy the same place simultaneously, doing so not merely under different names or descriptions but in a strict physical sense in violation of the laws of nature. The determination of qualitative identity has to be limited to noncontextual properties as they are described in this chapter. Compare these remarks with the comments in the previous chapter on the identity of indiscernibles.

[42] See chap. 1, n. 37.

amenable to change through a shift in attributes, then, instead of being a threat to identity, Heraclitean flux, on the contrary, guarantees it. Refer to Figure 3.15. It is evident in this depiction that the only way that object 1 can *change to* object 2 is if object 1 *is* object 2. It is necessary that a thing continue through time, through a change, for it to be true that it changed, for nothing can be conserved through a period of nonexistence. If therefore things do change, then things do persist; and, if they persist, then, as is clear from the preceding analysis, they do so without temporal parts. In light of that fact, what role do properties play in persistence? If changes in properties—at least some of them—do not bring about, of necessity, the termination of things, then is it true that the preservation of properties—at least some of them—may effect the continuance of things?

ATTRIBUTING IT TO THE ATTRIBUTES

It is George Berkeley who takes the role of properties to the limit, claiming that things are the properties that minds perceive.[43] Following Berkeley, the bundle theorists probably would affirm that there is a fixed factor that anchors things when a shift in properties occurs. At first glance, at least, it appears to be so: They would say that it is the perceiver who provides the element of sameness through change, so that the stable element is the mind. If, however, an object undergoes a change, then it seems that the mind that is perceiving the object would change as well, given that the object is literally in the mind. The challenge for the bundle theorists, in actuality, is not any temporal-identity principle that may be discovered but rather the principle of intrinsic change: principle IC. If an object is nothing other than ideas of sense that are grouped together, then the object is identical to some set of perceived characteristics. Even an object's parts, those that are sensed, are perceived characteristics; and, if they are not sensed, then, according to Berkeley, they do not exist. Using the structure of Figure 3.15 as a backdrop, refer to principle IC.

---

[43] I covered Berkeley's theory in chap. 2.

Given Berkeley's view, object ω_1 in the principle *is precisely* the set P_1 at time t_1, and object ω_2 *is precisely* the set P_2 at time t_2. By the diagram's specified conditions, however, $P_1 \neq P_2$. The consequence for this theory is that no object remains the same object if anything about it changes. Altering one characteristic alters the group of characteristics, and, if the group changes, then *that* object ceases to exist. Things cannot be preserved through change in Berkeley's theory.

Appealing to Berkeley's type-token distinction in an attempt to provide a way for identity to be maintained through change does not help. If, like object tokens in the minds of humans, the perceived object types in the mind of God change, then the same problem surfaces to undermine persistence: Any change at all in perception destroys the object. If, on the other hand, there is no change among the object types, then God's mind is frozen. It is a static snapshot of perceived objects, limiting God in such a way that He never can perceive anything to be anything other than exactly what He perceives it to be at the present moment. An infinite God could not be confined to such a state without violating His essential nature. Even if He wanted to perceive something different about an object, He could not do so. The approach removes God's omnipotence. It also removes His ability to bring something new into being through creation, unless He cannot see what He is doing, in which case His omniscience vanishes.

Suppose that one responds by claiming that all objects, in the form of types, lie before God, in His omniscience, so that His perceptions are indeed static, as they are eternally complete. The tokens that people see do undergo change, however, exemplifying first one type and then another as God carries out His bundling work. It is *because* God does see all things that the types lie before him in a fixed state.

One still cannot escape the difficulty, however. This position is ultimately self-defeating. The only way to prevent change in the perceptions in the mind of God is to disallow His perceptions of the changing object tokens that human minds perceive. Practically Platonic, the position restricts God's world to the exemplified; the individual copies are beyond His experience. He has no way to see the things that humans see, even though, so Berkeley claims, He causes them. God therefore cannot be omniscient if one takes this stance. Moreover, as I noted earlier, it makes little sense to say, just to explain people's varied sense impressions, that God is engaged in a bundling activity at great speed. Think of the stream of different visual sensations that correspond to a dozen beach balls rolling down a hill. There are different patches of color appearing at an indeterminate number of different angles, all against a constantly varying background. To keep the balls from dissolving into a patchwork of myriad sensory fragments and losing the cohesion that is necessary for their identity, God must hold the object perceptions together, and do so by throwing a multitude of tokens at people, each assembled from a different set of types. Yet, God cannot behold what He is producing, which conflicts with His infinite nature. The type-token model is of no benefit to Berkeley in this matter. The consequence for him is the same: There can be no identity of objects through change—there is just no plausible way in his philosophy to connect the dots. Heraclitean flux wreaks havoc on Berkeley's theory.

As a digression, it is important to note that the material substratum theorists face an equally disturbing, albeit different, problem with identity. If objects can be the same by virtue of the substratum's preserving their individuality through change, then, because the same metaphysical foundation underlies them all—as in the case of Thales's water, for example—it seems that everything is the same thing, a point that chapter 1 introduced. Stated differently, if all things owe their identity to a substrate, and there is only one substrate for all things, then there is only one thing in existence. The theorists merely have exchanged the total absence of object-identity for the total absence of object-distinction. It is not an improvement.

An alternative might be to hold that the single substrate exists as separate instances—a piece of it here, a piece there—so that this chunk of it is distinguished from that chunk of it. Perhaps then, as long as the chunk itself remains invariable, the properties can come and go without affecting identity. One would be compelled, in that case, to set forth a criterion of individuation for the underlying core. Would it be the constancy of a given, separate chunk-amount of the substrate that counts? If so, then the loss or gain of any portion of it, whatever the substrate may be, would undermine identity. If it were water, as Thales holds, then Walter would cease to be the same individual when he perspires at the gym or drinks a glass of water.

When a mare eats a bale of damp hay, both the horse and the hay lose their identities through a merger, forming a new object, distinct from both the animal and the grass that it consumed. This approach cannot be right.

Berkeley aside, I have been making the case that a shift in properties qualifies as an intrinsic change in a physical thing. Perhaps what is required to anchor an object's identity is the constancy of certain properties; that is to say, some properties of the object must remain in place, as others change, to keep the object intact. It is therefore logical to ask whether particular ones are essential. The properties of things in the world vary widely, however, so it is unlikely that a general principle of identity that is based on certain, predetermined characteristics for all objects can be found. For such a principle to be grounded in this way would require that there be some set of properties that is common to all things as part of their essential being.[44] If some properties must remain with a thing through change, then the better question to ask concerns how many are required. Could it be that, if just a single attribute is maintained, in spite of a pervasive shift, then it is possible for an object to be sustained? The requisite additional principle that the present analysis is pursuing thus would hold that, as each change occurs in an object across a span of time, at least one property of that object has to remain fixed. Liken it to the constraint that applies to a man as he walks with deliberation across unknown terrain: He always must leave one foot firmly planted while he steps forward with the other to test the ground. This new condition would assert that it is the overlapping of properties that provides the crucial anchor for object-identity, so that the preservation of it is possible. With each successive alteration, at least one property from the previous phase appears in the new set of properties. Figure 3.16 depicts this pattern.

---

[44] Even mass and extension do not work. Mass falls short because photons are massless (at rest). A collection of gravitons may not be extended—in the space-time of the universe that humans experience, at least—if those particles are able to escape the common dimensional framework, as some physicists have suggested.

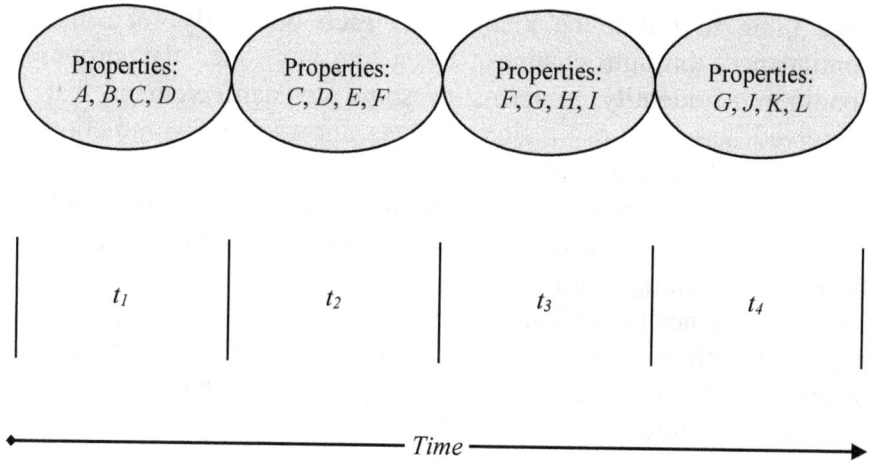

Figure 3.16

Basing identity on this overlapping of qualities, however, raises a serious problem. It allows the following circumstances to arise:

> The object at t_1 is the same object as the object at t_2.
> The object at t_2 is the same object as the object at t_3.
> The object at t_3 is the same object as the object at t_4.
> The object at t_1 is *not* the same object as the object at t_4.

Such a state of affairs will not do; it is contradictory. Pairs of successive stages cannot be daisy-chained together by means of common elements to ensure that identity through time is not destroyed. If something about an object must persist through a change for that object to continue, then it must be the *same* something that persists through *every* change in that object, or else it would lose its identity with a former version of itself by way of a subsequent variation. It is clear that what is required for an object's sustention is not identity through a given change but identity throughout the object's existence, from origination to cessation, *in the face of* any changes that the object may undergo. Otherwise, there is the potential for the object, with the passage of time, to violate logical rules by permitting two things that are identical to a third thing to fail to be identical to each other. By focusing on continuance through changes, taken one by one, the proposed condition of identity in terms of some constant element that is preserved across pairs of altered states allows the contradiction to arise and is therefore insufficient.

Part of the problem here is that, somewhat reminiscent of Berkeley, the approach seeks to bind a thing using its own attributes. Is it really a thing's attributes, though, that make it what it is? If identity does not lie with the qualities that a thing possesses, then a pervasive shift in them, even if that shift occurs all at once, need not destroy an object's identity. Such a pattern of abrupt change is reflected in Figure 3.17. Contrast Figure 3.17 with Figure 3.16.

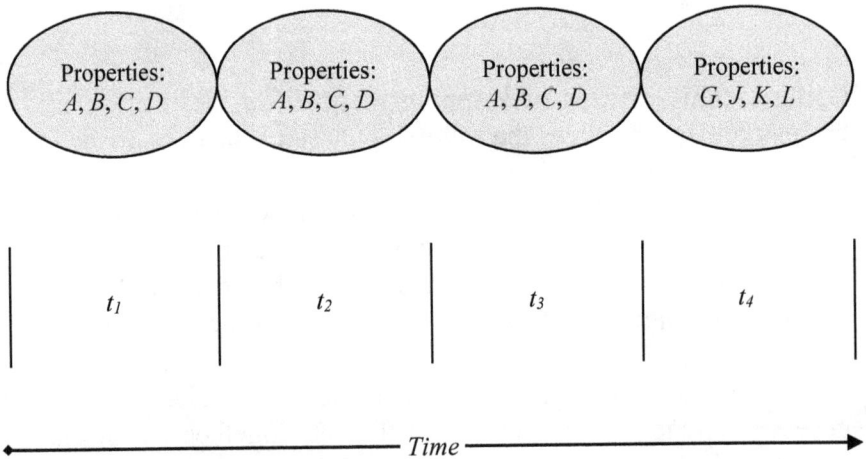

Figure 3.17

Despite the fact that there is a single occurrence of change involving *all* the thing's properties, the supposition is that it is still *possible* for the object at t_4 to be identical to the object at t_1.

To be persuaded that this supposition is true, consider an informative case. Imagine that Timmy and his father finished constructing, just hours ago, their first radio-controlled model airplane, a brilliant-silver-painted replica of the P-47N Thunderbolt that was put into production during World War II. They head for a nearby field to send the model on its maiden flight. Timmy's father starts the engine and, after a few final instructions, hands the controls to Timmy. The craft taxies down a dirt road that they chose for the airstrip and soars upward to two hundred feet. Timmy's inexperience is revealed almost immediately after takeoff as he tries to bank the Thunderbolt to the left. He loses control, and the aircraft plunges to the ground at full speed, bursting into flames. They rush to the crash site and extinguish the fire by throwing a blanket over it. What lies under the blanket does not resemble at all what Timmy flew minutes earlier.

Consider Lockean primary qualities. The object's extension and figure, or shape, are now different: It crumpled on impact, compressed, diminished through burning and releasing smoke, and melted into a form that is totally unlike that of an aircraft. Its solidity and texture—surface shape—are not the same: Once hard and smooth, it crumbles easily in the hand now and has a rough, uneven exterior. The number has changed: The airplane's tail broke when it crashed and separated from the fuselage, as did other parts; the object of a moment ago is no longer one thing but many. Its rest-motion has been altered. Moving at fifty miles per hour over the area before the accident, it lies still in the field now. Even Lockean secondary qualities have changed. The craft is charcoal-black and dull instead of pristine-silver and shiny. It smells of burned plastic and singed wood rather than paint and glue. The article's overall temperature has increased markedly. Other properties are also different: What is left is immobile; none of what were its controls operates; its chemical composition is unlike the previous one; it even has lost its aesthetic appeal. It is logically possible for the list to be exhaustive, such that none of the original properties of the object remains. For all this enveloping change in attributes, that which lies there in the scattered mass is surely Timmy's model airplane nevertheless. What else could it be? If it were not Timmy's P-47N, then why would these chunks of charred and mangled material be there? No other accounting for the substance that is on the ground in that place is realistic. Properties alone cannot be behind coherence; it seems that one must look elsewhere for what serves to anchor identity. Perhaps then the endurance of things can be ascribed to their sets of parts.

ATTRIBUTING IT TO THE AGGREGATE

The substratum theorists would agree that the persistence of things is factual, but, to explain it, they would point to some supporting base that is outside the arrays of characteristics that things possess. For them, the substratum is the stable element that underlies change. It is this core, infrastructural component of physical objects that provides the continuity that is needed to secure identity through shifts in properties. Part of the challenge for their position is to give a clear account of the essential connection between the substratum and a particular object's attributes, and such an account is scarcely forthcoming. What exactly is the relationship that joins ultimate reality to individual things; just how does the supposed underlying container hold things and their attributes together? There is no adequate description of the link.

Further, one may ask why there must be a metaphysical factor in the constituency of things. Perchance they can cohere without the substratum glue. Stated in another way, it might be that physical objects carry within themselves, within the bounds of the corporeality that frames them, their own determinants of identity. Maybe it is the actual *matter* that composes physical objects, in whatever form that the matter takes, that provides the requisite coherence. Aristotle might have been correct in holding that matter is the key to continuance through variation. Given that change involving a thing's material parts is intrinsic, as I defined such change, when an object's physical constitution differs with the passage of time, that object differs too. If one abandons the ancient philosophical idea that a primitive element, the *Urstoff*, somehow fastens the pieces of a thing in place, forgoing the metaphysical in favor of something that is solely physical, then how can anything persist if its material makeup shifts? When a physical part is removed from a thing, even if another part is substituted for the detached one, how can the thing—*that* thing—remain? Turning to materiality as the indispensable conservator seems to force one to discard the intuition that identity can be preserved through a change in composition, so that a thing's makeup must be totally static.

It appears that John Locke adopts a no-change-in-parts stance for inanimate masses. According to Locke's reasoning, collections of simple, material particles, where those particles are not organized to form a living entity, cannot maintain identity if the parts change. Says the philosopher,

> Let us suppose an Atom, *i.e.* a continued body under one immutable Superficies, existing in a determined time and place: 'tis evident, that, considered in any instant of its Existence, it is, in that instant, the same with itself. For being, at that instant, what it is, and nothing else, it is the same, and so must continue, as long as its Existence is continued: for so long it will be the same, and no other. In like manner, if two or more Atoms be joined together into the same Mass, every one of those Atoms will be the same, by the foregoing Rule: And whilst they exist united together, the Mass, consisting of the same Atoms, must be the same Mass, or the same Body, let the parts be never so differently jumbled: But if one of these Atoms be taken away, or one new one added, it is no longer the same Mass, or the same Body.[45]

Locke ties the sameness of a chunk of matter to the sameness of its components. Removing one particle undermines the identity of the cluster.

If Locke uses the terms 'Mass' and 'Body' to refer simply to the individual parts taken collectively, as one set, then the claim is a tautology—it is always true—and uninformative. It would be tantamount to saying that all the parts cannot be the same unless all the parts are the same. The collection is just the parts that compose it. Think of a set of paperweights. To assert that there are a hundred paperweights in this set of a hundred paperweights, but only if not a single one is removed or another one added, is to utter a true statement. It is a statement, however, that lacks informational value.

If, on the other hand, Locke uses the terms 'Mass' and 'Body' to indicate some one thing aside from the simple aggregate of parts that compose the mass, or body, then the terms must refer to an *object* that is formed by the group of atoms, in which case his argument does not succeed. Consider the logical fallacy that results from

---

[45] Locke, *Essay*, 330.

concluding that, because all the individuals that make up a group have a given property, the group itself has that property. This error is the fallacy of composition. The group *may* have the property, but one cannot determine that it does have it on the basis of the attributes of the components.

For example, each bolt in a case of five thousand may weigh one-quarter ounce, but the case of bolts does not weigh one-quarter ounce; it weighs more than seventy-eight pounds. Locke holds that atoms maintain their identity because they do not change; likewise, a mass of atoms, as a singular thing, maintains its identity, as long as its atomic constituency does not change. In putting forth the sameness of unchanging parts as the basis for the sameness of an unchanging whole—specifically, a whole the particulate count of which stays constant—Locke is inferring, so the current reading suggests, that the rule of immutability that applies to the components of a thing when determining identity applies as well to the thing of which they are components. Echoing the reasoning that is behind the fallacy of composition, such thinking is not correct; the flaw arises from the extension of the application of a principle, however, rather than from the extension of the ascription of a property. If Locke is not making this inference, then he is putting forth the assertion regarding the identity of a mass, or body—in the sense of a singular object—without a basis. It is then an arbitrary assumption.

If an atom of hydrogen is pulled into intergalactic space by some massive celestial entity passing within a few light-years of the Milky Way, then is the galaxy destroyed by the event? Even Locke believes that, when the parts are organized in such a way that they take the form of a living organism, the resultant collection is exempt from his same-atom restriction, and the parts can change without thereby abolishing a thing's identity. In instances of this sort, he avers, identity is not tied to material makeup. Locke claims, "In the state of living Creatures, their Identity depends not on a Mass of the same Particles; but on something else."[46] If Locke is right in what he says here—and he is right on this point—then why is it so, and why would nonliving things not be exempt as well? One must question whether the sameness of an inanimate thing, where that thing is taken

---

[46] Ibid.

to be a singularity—that is to say, not mere piled up particles but an object—depends on the sameness of its particulate mass.

Even among contemporary philosophers, there are those who contend that composite things cannot undergo any change in parts whatsoever without a loss of their identity. No matter how small and insignificant changes may be, they will result in the demise of the affected objects. As mentioned briefly earlier, this position is mereological essentialism: Compound things, so goes the thinking, have their parts essentially. One cannot take a ride down the Mississippi River in this view. There is no such river. Instead, there is a swarm of rivers, arising as the waters flow, losing material through evaporation and the emptying into the delta after gaining material from other water sources and from the erosion of the banks. Each passing moment ends the waterway that was and brings into existence the one that is. Even the paddlewheel boat on which a passenger travels during the voyage is a host of momentary vessels as the waters wear away, in an ongoing stream, the atomic particles of the wooden boards that compose the boat. Heraclitean in its underlying premise, this philosophical stance flies in the face of the law of parsimony.

There is yet a more extreme position regarding composites. Mereological nihilism contends that, because it is possible for the material constitution of what people think of as individual, compound objects to change, there can be no compound objects at all, not even people. It is a position that leads to its own set of absurdities. In a subsequent section, I will take a detailed look at the paradox that inspires this bizarre thinking. I want to proceed now, however, as though common sense prevails until proven to be wrong.

A narrative may shed some light on the issue. Beverly is riding her bicycle after school on a sunny afternoon in the spring. As she pedals home, a tiny particle of synthetic rubber falls from the front tire of her bicycle. When she applies her brakes and slows to watch a butterfly searching for nectar, another particle falls from the tire, and yet another as she reaches her destination and takes a turn into the garage. To hold that Beverly rode several bicycles home that day as a consequence, not one, would be a stretch of reason. She never left the seat, never stopped, and never relaxed her firm grip on the handlebars during the outing. Albeit a change in matter—and thus mass—occurred each time that a small piece of rubber compound fell from the machine's tire, surely what Beverly was riding on the trip was her only bicycle: the one that she received as a gift on her tenth birthday, the one with the bend in the front fender. It is more sensible to say that she has no other bicycle to ride than to say that she has owned four different bicycles within the last hour, only one of which exists now. If a change in composition through the loss of a few particles of matter undercuts identity, then counterintuitive cases, such as this one, surface.

More concerns await. Suppose that Beverly's father removed the wheel from her bicycle to inspect the tread before she began her journey that day. At that point in time, it was no longer part of Beverly's bicycle; therefore, if things cannot survive a compositional change, then her original bicycle ceased to be, and something else stood in its place. Curiously, according to the mereological essentialists, the wheel was the same wheel because it did not lose any of its parts. After Beverly's father reinstalled it on the frame, however, the resultant bicycle could not have been the same bicycle; the original one terminated, and, as I argued formerly, what ends cannot reappear. Imagine that, in his clumsiness, the man knocked the chain off the sprockets several times during the reassembly, threading it back carefully following each mishap. A different machine must have sprung into existence with each incident. Such a position is hardly believable.

One may argue that the continued existence of a bicycle wheel guarantees the continued existence of the bicycle to which it belongs, even when the wheel is not attached to the frame. The same is true of the chain. A thing's parts need not be together; if the parts persist, then the whole persists. The consequence of this stance, however, is that, if Beverly's father were to grind his daughter's bicycle to dust and scatter it over the county, then the machine would continue to exist, even though there is nothing that Beverly could ride to the park after school. Ultimately, nothing ever would cease to be, as long as the matter that composes it persists in physical reality. The problem of eternal object-existence surfaces again here—but from a different angle. This entire approach is simply not tenable.

One could say that the removal of matter is destructive only if the amount of it is significant relative to the whole. Imagine that each particle that was dislodged from the tire on the child's bicycle on the three occasions was equivalent to, expressed as a common fraction, $^1/_{100,000}$ of the mass of the machine that morning. The mass of the bicycle at the end of the afternoon jaunt is thus equal to 99.997 percent of the original mass. If one deems the loss of tire material to be too small to count, then suppose that the loss each time measured $^2/_{100,000}$ of the pretrip mass, so that the mass of the bicycle at the end of Beverly's ride is 99.994 percent of the original. Are the machines still the same? What if the loss measured $^1/_{22,351}$ or $^5/_{1,067}$ or $^8/_{413}$? Discarding a sameness-of-matter principle in favor of some near-equivalence-of-matter does not provide any better basis for identity.

So, the simple reduction of material seems to pose little threat to identity, and there is no indication that either the substitution of material or the addition of it is any more threatening. Robert's knee replacement today removes a portion of bone in the joint and inserts a synthetic substance. Certainly, Robert is still the same person as he was before the surgery, even though he does not know where he is because of the effects of the anaesthesia; and his body is certainly the same body as before, even though an engineered apparatus takes the place of a portion of the tissue in his knee. He responds to the name 'Robert' and remembers the injury that resulted in the surgery. He has the same retinal profile, which is unmistakable evidence of individuality, given that he is not an identical twin. Dental X-rays would reveal that it is indeed Robert's physical being that is in the hospital bed. As for addition, Robert weighs thirty pounds more now than he weighed when he was a teenager, but to hold that the presently hospitalized body is not the same one as that of the adolescent Robert would be unfounded. There is the C-shaped scar on his arm, a consequence of the accident when he was nine. He recalls his father's taking his picture at the reunion when he was twelve and again during the sports event when he was twenty; the scar is visible in both pictures. If it is not Robert's body now, or was not at the prior time, then whose is it, or was it, and how did Robert come to have it?

If identity is to be grounded in materiality, then one may think that the continuance of an object requires the constancy of some portion of matter; and thus either (1) for any variation in components that a thing undergoes, from one state to the next, there is some set of material parts, perhaps with a single member, that remains the same through that specific variation, or (2) for all variations in components that a thing undergoes, there is one set, remaining the same throughout, from inception to demise. Figure 3.18 depicts the first condition.

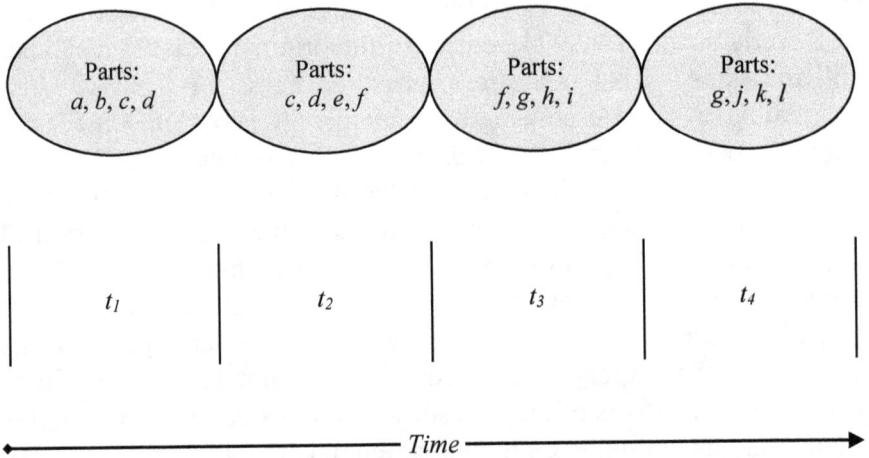

Figure 3.18

This pattern is exactly that of Figure 3.16, and it will lead to the same contradiction. Whether the focus is on properties or parts, holding onto a set of common elements between pairs of successive alterations never will work.

If the alternative condition is in force, then a single core portion of matter must stay intact through all changes in a thing for the entire span of its existence. Is this long-term preservation of a central material piece what is required? Picture a tree that took root where it was planted fifty years ago and continued to live. Through the years, it incorporated a large amount of matter, increasing in height from twelve inches to forty-five feet. One can track the tree's growth from seedling to maturity, and one can cut it in half and look at the rings that mark the years of its existence. It is weathered and listing, and a few limbs are sagging, but on what basis could one hold that the tree is not the same plant as the seedling, even though its composition has changed dramatically since its early days, and none of the atomic particles that were in the sapling remains in the old tree? Tracing the life of the plant through the years speaks more about its identity than the physical bits that form its roots and trunk, its limbs and leaves. The matter that makes up the tree is not the factor that distinguishes it. This principle would apply to other things as well, it seems; no suitable grounds for denying it are apparent.

With this analysis in mind, one can set forth an illuminating declaration concerning materiality and identity. It is one that appears to be defensible.

> COMPOSITION HYPOTHESIS 1. Physical things can be the same, even if their material composition is different.

It is important to give some thought now to a different sort of case. Suppose that a set of sterling silver tableware is melted and formed into a bust of Socrates, so that the matter that makes up the bust is the same as the matter that made up the silverware. The material stays fixed in this example, but such an account of change does not address the problem of continuity. One would not say that the bust *is* the set of knives, forks, and spoons, in spite of the fact that the metal in each instance is the same. The bust came into being when, for example, a renowned sculptor produced it. It was not formed until the artist's assistant melted the silverware, which was manufactured by machines in a factory that closed last year. The statue originated long after the utensils came to be. Of course, the silverware and the likeness of Socrates have different purposes; yet, imagine that the set of silverware is melted, only to form another set of silverware that looks exactly like the first set. It would be counterintuitive to assert that the sets are numerically identical, even though they serve the same ends, are qualitatively indistinguishable, and are made of the same mass of metal. The second set did not come to exist until after the first set was heated in the crucible; they have different points of origin. If things do not have a common origin, then they cannot be numerically identical. Any alleged entity that originates more than once would have to cease to exist and then come into existence again. Such a sequence is not possible; whatever ceases to be does so permanently. John Locke takes note of the point on origins in his writings, asserting,

> [O]ne thing cannot have two beginnings of Existence,
> nor two things one beginning. . . . That therefore that had
> one beginning is the same thing, and that which had a
> different beginning in time and place from that, is not
> the same but divers [sic].[47]

For a more convincing illustration, suppose that there is an interim step: A serving tray is made from the first set of silverware and melted later to form the second set. It is even more challenging now to maintain that the two sets of silverware are identical. They may have the same material composition, but one is compelled to say that they are distinct.

A decisive case is Billy's dog. Brute is a St. Bernard. The atomic particles that Brute's body contains at two minutes past four o'clock on Wednesday afternoon may be exactly the same as those that made up two gaggles of geese, strolling along the shores of separate lakes on a given morning 3,428 years ago.[48] Certainly, no one would hold that the dog *is* the collection of birds; neither would one hold that the canine's body *is* the set of avian bodies. The dog is one organism and never could fly; the geese are many organisms and never could bark. Surely, these facts provide a clue to the nonidentity of the things in question, but the more telling issue is continuance: The geese ceased to be centuries ago, and, as I affirmed before, nothing that ceases to be can remain in a state of nonbeing, only to reemerge. Any existent that ceases, ceases; *it* never will be again, and whatever arises afterward is not *it*, necessarily so, although the material particles that compose it may be precisely the same. Relying on the constancy of matter to drive identity generates consequences that are unacceptable. Comprising the same physical substance does not appear to be the factor that preserves individuality, and one can advance a second tenet concerning materiality and identity, which is given here:

---

[47] Ibid., 328.

[48] A similar case is raised in the philosophical literature, where the molecules that make up one thing eventually become the components of another thing of a different sort. The identity of two objects requires something other than identical sets of component molecules. Moreover, as electrons can jump from atom to atom, one must determine first of all what 'same molecule' means.

COMPOSITION HYPOTHESIS 2. Physical things can be different, even if their material composition is the same.

If one accepts Composition Hypotheses 1 and 2, then one is led by the conjunction of the pair to conclude that a thing's physical makeup cannot provide the basis for either a necessary or a sufficient condition of its uniqueness: A difference of materiality does not preclude identity, nor does the sameness of materiality guarantee it. Matter is not a deciding factor in establishing whether one thing is identical to another.

In the final analysis, it seems that something in this quest—as I have portrayed it—to understand what lies behind preservation through change is misguided. Attempts to anchor a thing by taking hold of its properties or its parts fail to provide a suitable foundation for identity. A sign of what actually is needed already has surfaced. One must extract identity from a thing by focusing on duration, not the absence of change. For sameness to be possible, there must be a thread of continuance from a thing's origination to its termination. Change, whether to properties or to parts, causes one to question identity, but it is, in truth, time that sets the stage for the entire quandary. Object-identity boils down to identity through time, regardless of whether a thing has dissimilar properties or parts from one moment to another. Without continuity throughout the span of its existence, there can be no sameness of an object. Change is merely a catalyst that brings to the forefront philosophical concerns over differences, but whether a thing changes or does not change is, in the end, irrelevant. Whatever accounts for identity through variation must account for identity through none; whatever holds a thing in ontic stasis must be insensitive to the extent of variation. Essentially then, and here is the important point, *change is incidental* to the actual problem of temporal identity.

At this point, having defined persistence in a prior segment, I wish to propose the *principle of temporal identity*, or *principle TI*, as the statement of conditions under which the numerical identity of objects at diverse times obtains. In the declaration that appears below, and the one that follows it, the symbol '$<$' means, as noted previously, 'is earlier than'; the symbol '$\in$' stands for 'is an element of':

PRINCIPLE TI. For any two objects ω_1 and ω_2 and any two moments t_1 and t_2, where $t_1 < t_2$, and where ω_1 exists at t_1 and ω_2 exists at t_2, ω_1 is numerically identical to ω_2 if, and only if, the set S_1 of all propositions that are true of ω_1 at t_1 are true of ω_2 at t_1, and the set S_2 of all propositions that are true of ω_2 at t_2 are true of ω_1 at t_2, even though it is not the case that, for any proposition p, $p \in S_1$ if, and only if, $p \in S_2$.

Two things at different times can be the same thing, even if intrinsic change occurs. For any pair of numerically identical objects, every proposition that is true of one at any given moment is true of the other at that moment; but a proposition that is true of an object at one moment may not be true of the same object at another moment—because of change. Such propositions, of course, include assertions about the properties and parts that objects possess. Principle TI captures the state of affairs in accordance with which two temporally distinct things are one.

From the abovestated principle, one can deduce that numerically identical objects that exist at different times also exist at the same times because assertions that are true of one at a particular time are true of the other at that time. An associated formulation—the *persistence corollary of principle TI*—furthers this thought, drawing on the definition of persistence. These concepts are linked through close affiliation and a measure of interdependence. Here, the triangle formally completes by conjoining the notion of numerical identity and that of persistence in the following biconditional:

PERSISTENCE COROLLARY OF PRINCIPLE TI. For any object ω_1 and any two moments t_1 and t_2, where $t_1 < t_2$ and where ω_1 exists at t_1, there exists an object ω_2 at t_2, such that ω_1 is numerically identical to ω_2 if, and only if, ω_1 persists from t_1 to t_2 inclusive.

The numerical identity of two objects, at two different respective times, is a condition that is logically equivalent to that of a specific continuance of the earlier-existing object: An identical counterpart to that object exists later if, and only if, the object persists between the two times inclusive. It is a simple assertion, but there is an important consequence: A persistent object has a history—the set of all occurrences in which the object has been a participant—and its historical record as of any particular moment is contained in its chronicle as of any later moment. A thing's history is changing constantly, building on the past with the passage of time. The worm theorists take this developing history to be single-instant elements strung together and identify the string with the object itself, but this conception is misguided. The fact that an object can exist at more than one moment does not imply that its existence is tied to independent, temporal pieces, each of which appears and disappears instantaneously. Given different points in time, if objects that exist at those points are actually the same object, then the history of any one of them is encompassed by the history of any succeeding ones, but there is no implication of a string of object slices. One might represent this finding in the following way:

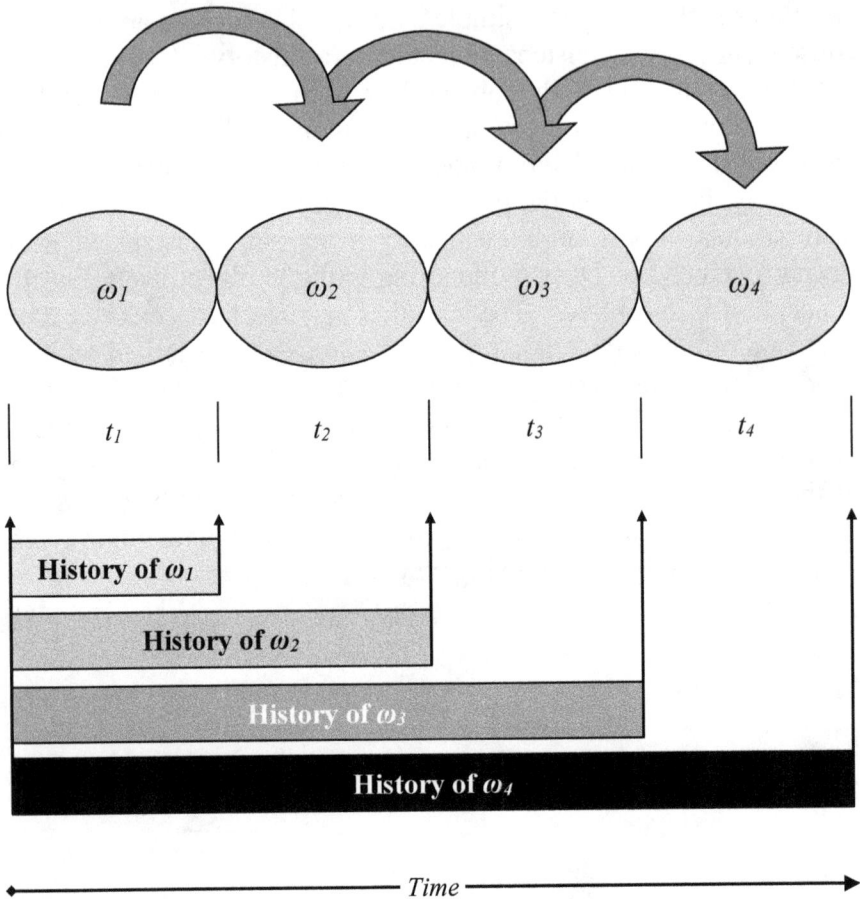

Figure 3.19

The history of object ω_2 includes the entire history of object ω_1. The history of object ω_3 encompasses all that of ω_2 as well as that of ω_1; and the history of object ω_4 includes the total histories of ω_3, ω_2, and ω_1. The past of each successive object in the series includes the past of the predecessor object in the series and, a fortiori, includes the predecessor's origin, a fact that Locke recognizes as definitive in the matter of identity. The series is unique. At any point in time, nothing else encompasses the past in this way; only that of the object itself. Objects ω_1, ω_2, ω_3, and ω_4 are one and the same, even though change might have taken place. It is the *history* of an object that is increasing with the passage of time—not, as the worm theorists have it, the *object itself* owing to the sequential accumulation of temporal pieces.

Principle TI and the corresponding notions offer an explanation of what continuance is, but they do not explain why it happens. Even with an acceptance of three-dimensionalism as the right theory of preservation through time, rejecting the temporal-parts approach, only the mechanics of persistence are illuminated. The foundation for it remains shrouded. Therefore, principle TI, as it stands, although clear in its rendering of truth, lacks the full explanatory weight of a substantial metaphysical finding.

ORIGINATION, TERMINATION, AND UNITY

Return for a moment to the case of Timmy's first flight to look at a different, but related, quandary. Examining the incident further, one may want to maintain that the boy's airplane, after the crash, ceased to be identical to the earlier counterpart because its raison d'être is flight, and it lost the capacity to be airborne. Regardless of changes that may affect other properties, when a thing that is created to perform some primary function cannot perform it, its continued identity is lost. The latter thing cannot be the same as the former one.

This stance would be unfounded, for the consequence would be that any machine that failed to operate, even if all its parts were intact, would cease to be the same as the one before the failure. It would not be reasonable to hold that, when Timmy's model airplane stops running because of a clogged fuel line or a fouled glow plug, that particular toy thereby ceases to exist. Is it not still Timmy's airplane, even though he cannot start the engine? A dehumidifier that no longer removes moisture from the environment because of a faulty compressor or iced-over coils does not come to an abrupt end; it merely is not working at the moment. After the ice melts on David's dehumidifier, and it begins operating properly, would one hold that the unit that is in a thawed state now is, in reality, a new device? Indeed, it might have been running all the while because the blower motor continued to force air over the coils, but the machine as a whole did not perform its intended duty. Suppose, to press the issue, that a tree fell on a power line, and David lost electrical service to his house as a result. The dehumidifier is not capable of running, given the circumstances. If one were to rely strictly on functionality, then a new dehumidifier would spring into being when the restoration of the service causes a moisture-reducing appliance to begin operating again in his basement. The primary function of a machine is set forth by design—a key concept in defining the *sort of thing* that it is and consequently in establishing whether a particular thing is an instance of that sort. Design in itself, however, is not what determines when an *individual of that sort* is no longer the same individual. Being a member of a certain kind is not the same as being numerically identical to a member of that kind.

Suppose that one takes the different position that Timmy's airplane ceased because there was just too much change for it to continue to be. What lies before him is an amalgam of melted plastic, splintered wood, and twisted metal. Perhaps it is the wreckage of what was once Timmy's model, but it is not the model itself. A person thus could avoid having to say that things can endure such a dramatic and sudden alteration in properties as that which befell the ill-fated P-47N. When events of this type occur, things simply end.

In taking that stance, one, it seems, would trade the problem of identity for another problem—that of termination: determining just how much change an object can tolerate before it ceases to be. The challenge then would not be that of saying that two objects, which differ markedly in properties, are identical, or perhaps that two object slivers, which differ markedly in properties, are slivers of the same thing. It would be that of saying exactly when a thing ends. Is this exchange equitable, or is the resultant problem greater than the difficulty that one had hoped to surmount? Identity and termination are not independent of each other. The connection is a topic for exploration.

The question of termination is not limited to property changes. One saw earlier how a total exchange of parts can test one's sense of identity, but it does not destroy identity, for sameness is not dependent on the material parts of a thing. A lawnmower—Bobby's *only* lawnmower—can survive, even when all the parts are replaced, so common sense has it. Suppose that, in removing its parts, though, one does not replace them. The spark plug may be unscrewed and used on an outboard motor at the lake. The handle may be loosened, removed from the frame, and given to a neighbor. A wheel may be taken off the machine and installed on the son's soapbox racer. One of the engine mounting bolts may be removed and stored in a spare parts bin or even inadvertently discarded. If one continues down this path, then, at some point in time, nothing will be left. Surely, when that state is reached, the lawnmower will have ceased to be, but is there still a machine if one has only a cotter pin in hand? Alternatively, if one sets out to build a lawnmower and picks up a cotter pin, then does the lawnmower exist at that juncture; or, if Timmy carves an aileron from a sheet of balsa wood, then has a model of the P-47N sprung into being? Did Hoover Dam arise when the first cubic yard of concrete was poured? The problem of termination and the problem of origination are two sides of the same coin; they are mirror images of each other, lying at the extreme ends of the temporal spectrum of a thing's existence. See Figure 3.20 below. What makes the ends of this stretch of being, with respect to an object, comprehensible seems to be a rather puzzling matter.

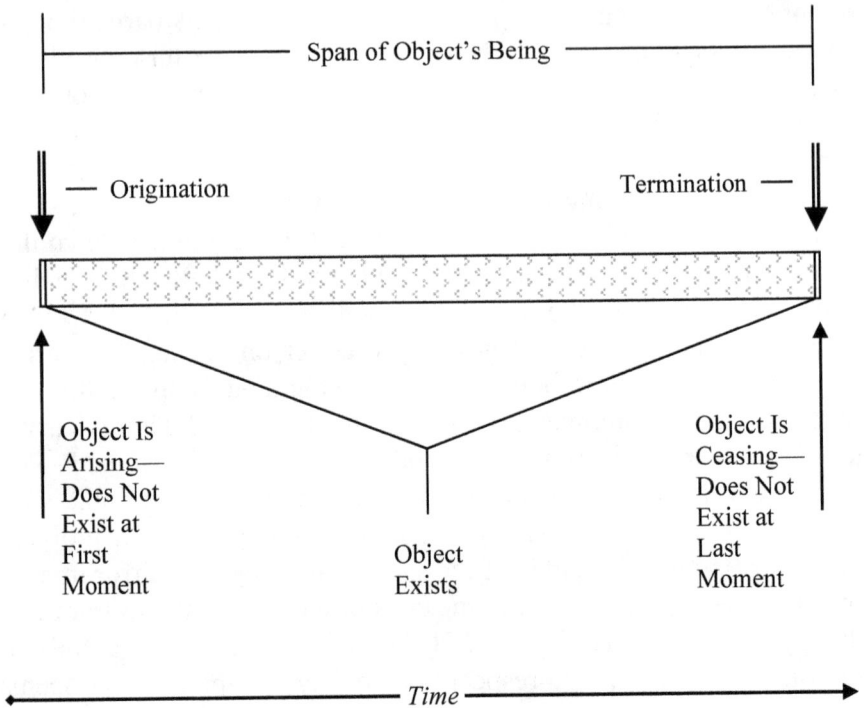

Figure 3.20

In an important sense, inanimate hunks of material, whether lawnmowers or model aircraft, are simply hunks of material. The fact that the hunks may have a purpose, in that they have been designed to perform some operation, helps one to conceive of them as unified. One still does so, however, even without a purpose. A lump of dirt sitting atop a rock is distinguishable from its environment by a person who is perceiving it. Yet, there is nothing special about the lump itself that provides a metaphysical basis for singularity. It is just that the particles of soil are set apart from their surroundings by dirt-to-atmosphere and dirt-to-rock boundaries, which appear to become increasingly imprecise as one views the lump under greater and greater magnification. Given the proximity and coherence of the soil particles and their separation from dissimilar environmental elements, a percipient sees the material as a distinct object, so the percipient refers to the collection of matter as one thing. The perceived individuation remains, even if the collection of material lies on something that is composed of the same substance: a lump of dirt that is sitting on a dirt road, for example. Under conditions of change, however, the cohesion that seemed to be there begins to break down. Place the piece of dirt in a bucket of tepid water, and it fragments in the course of several hours. Initially, the borders are altered; the periphery begins to disintegrate. The size of the lump reduces gradually until, at last, there is only a bucket of muddy water. The material is still there in the bucket, but there is no lump. At what point did that lump cease to be that lump, or even *a* lump? The bounds—both spatial and temporal—of physical objects, particularly where there is a loss of material, seem to suffer from a lack of clarity, and the events that mark their terminations can be remarkably fuzzy.

OBJECTIONS TO OBJECTS

That fuzziness is captured by two positions that threaten to undermine the objects of day-to-day experience, but for different reasons. Outside the world of subatomic physics, the entities that people encounter have parts, so common sense would reveal. If physical objects are something other than mere particulate collections, however, then questions concerning their quiddity arise. Two ways of thinking about composite objects remove the vagueness that is associated with their composition in a radical way: They remove the objects altogether.

MEREOLOGICAL NIHILISM

There is a position in philosophy that holds that macrophysical objects, as composites of physical parts, do not exist. According to this position, the atomic particles that make up such would-be things as bricks, boats, and baseballs exist, arranged correspondingly in a brick-like, boat-like, and baseball-like manner, but the collectives themselves, as objects, are not real. There are no bricks, no boats, and no baseballs. Such a view is known as mereological nihilism. A mereological nihilist denies that things have parts: There are no aggregate objects; reality is composed only of simple things. Though these simple things may be grouped together, they do not form singular entities. This position is a version of eliminativism, albeit an eliminativistic philosophy may target things other than aggregate entities for dismissal, such as the mind: a common focus. A variant of the position has it that certain things—living organisms, for example—are real, despite the fact that they are composites, but no other composite objects are real. This view may be classified as mereologically quasi-nihilistic.

A contemporary proponent of a mode of this philosophical approach is Trenton Merricks.[49] He argues that baseballs do not exist, on the grounds that they cause nothing that the atoms that compose those supposed objects do not cause. If what people refer to as a baseball crashes through what they refer to as a window, then the breaking of the glass is not overdetermined; that is to say, the breaking is not caused both by the atoms that make up the alleged sports object and by that alleged object itself, and it is the atoms, taken jointly, that do the work. Claims Merricks, "The shattering of the window is caused by those [constituent] atoms, acting in concert."[50] A so-called baseball is simply a group of microphysical bits that are arranged in a certain fashion—namely, baseballwise. It is by virtue of these bits that the window breaks; the collection causes nothing beyond what the particles bring about. In contrast, persons, because of consciousness, *do* cause things that their physical parts do not cause. They are therefore objects. He sets out the distinction:

> Sometimes my *deciding* to do such and such is
> what causes the atoms of my arm to move as they do.

---

[49] Peter van Inwagen also argues against the existence of common material objects on the basis of composition but admits the existence of organisms, although his reasoning differs from that of Merricks. I will focus on the latter philosopher, whose account is more recent, but see van Inwagen's *Material Beings* (Ithaca: Cornell University Press), 1990.

[50] Trenton Merricks, *Objects and Persons* (Oxford: Clarendon Press, 2001), 56.

Presumably my so deciding won't ever be the *only* cause of their moving. There will also be a cause in terms of microphysics or microbiology, in terms of nerve impulses and the like. But at some point in tracing back the causal origin of my arm's moving (if it is intended), we will reach a cause that is *not* microphysical, that just is the agent's *deciding* to do something.

. . . [E]verything a *baseball* would cause—if it would cause anything at all—would be caused by its atoms. Moreover, . . . the baseball is causally irrelevant to what those atoms cause.[51]

Merricks thus uses the criterion of causality to eliminate the inanimate objects of everyday experience but preserve persons, as opposed to another philosopher, whom I will discuss next, who discards both. With regard to the question whether nonhuman organisms exist as composites, Merricks does not offer a definitive answer.

Merricks is correct, in that persons are fundamentally different from nonliving things, but dismissing ordinary aggregates as objects so quickly, purely on the basis of causality, raises problematic issues. It is doubtful that an effect that a collection causes is never anything other than the effect that the sum of the components of that collection causes. Consider a molecule of water. There is a difference between a collection of atoms that is configured as a bundle and a collection of them that is bound together as a molecule, for a molecule is generally a compound, and it exhibits causal properties that the composite atoms, even if they are acting in concert, do not exhibit. (Technically, atoms of elements are regarded as molecules as well; the atoms of certain elements are affixed to like ones in nature, albeit no compound results.) The formula for water is H_2O: two atoms of hydrogen joined to one atom of oxygen. Hydrogen and oxygen are gaseous at $-20°$ Celsius and standard pressure; water is solid. At $-20°$, water can cause things that the atoms that make up the compound cannot cause, such as sinking a ship in motion by ripping a hole in its hull.

Could one say that it is the arrangement of the hydrogen and oxygen atoms forming the molecules of water that imparts their properties and hence what they can cause, just as the atoms of the

---

[51] Ibid., 110.

baseball must be held together to break the window? Mere bundled atoms do not fuse to yield molecules; the causal capacities of molecules are distinct from those of the atoms that compose them. Is it the configuring of the parts moleculewise that makes the difference? In theory, if not in practice, one could disassemble a baseball into its atomic bits and reunite all the parts, but in a different way—creating, say, a slightly different shape, with some of the stitching on the inside—and it would retain its chemical properties and cause what a thing with those properties causes. If a molecule is disassembled into its constituent atoms and reassembled in a different way, however, then the molecule's chemical properties can change; consequently, what the set of atoms can cause changes. Both a molecule of fructose and a molecule of glucose have the chemical formula $C_6H_{12}O_6$. These compounds are structural isomers: distinct substances with different physical arrangements and different qualities but with the same number of atoms of the same elements. Accordingly, fructose and glucose exhibit different causal capabilities. Fructose produces a much greater sensation of sweetness when in contact with the tongue than does glucose, and both substances produce a sensation of sweetness that is lacking in the taste of their component elements: carbon, hydrogen, and oxygen. It seems, on the basis of Merricks's causality criterion, that some innate aggregates are indeed units.

One need not stop at the molecular level. Atoms are composites too, the properties of which are determined by their compositions. Remove a proton from an atom of the element mercury, and gold results. Add a proton to mercury, and thallium results. Not only do these substances differ in chemical properties, but they differ in causal properties as well. Gold is not toxic; it does not cause death through ingestion of moderate amounts of it.[52] Thallium is highly toxic, and ingestion of small amounts of it causes death in animals. The varied causal properties are attributable to the number of protons that a given material has, as it is this atomic number that is unique for each element.[53] In fact, even protons themselves are composites,

---

[52] At one time, a special restaurant customarily spread gold on its bowls of soup. Although gold is nontoxic, consumption of it in large quantities could lead to other problems and should be considered to be imprudent.

[53] Removing or adding an electron too, in conjunction with the corresponding change in the number of protons, would maintain a neutral charge, but it is the

consisting of simpler particles. A proton contains two up quarks and one down quark. Does one say that the only things that exist are the basic building blocks that are identified in the standard model of particle physics?

Merricks makes it clear, though—and it is important to note this fact to capture his view accurately—that it is not the physical bits per se that matter. Instead of atoms, one could scale down to the elementary particles that make up atoms, or scale up to collections of them in the form of molecules. What matters for him—what determines whether a putative object exists—is the absence of causal overdetermination. He declares, "Then, for material objects, *to be is to have non-redundant causal powers.*"[54] The world of everyday experience is filled with what one thinks of as objects, but they are no more than particulate groupings with no causal efficacy beyond that of their constituent parts. Aggregates are individuals if, and only if, they cause things by themselves, he thinks. It is this point that distinguishes Merricks's eliminativistic ontology.

It may seem that Merricks's position provides a tidy solution to the problem of object-identity. There are no aggregate, inanimate objects, in his view, so there are no objects to retain identity through time. The problem disappears because the objects disappear. Given this approach, however, the common sense of daily life is turned into something truly bizarre. For example, one never can acquire an item of personal property, such as an automobile. Vehicles do not exist; a person can purchase only sets of atoms. "Here is a nice bunch of atomic bits," touts the salesman at the dealership. "Take them for a spin, and you need not worry about their falling apart, as the strong nuclear force will keep the bundled nucleons in check," he states reassuringly. The main problem, though, is that, because no macrophysical objects exist, and the alleged objects to which people refer are really nothing but clusters of atoms, any changes in respective atom-sets with the passage of time preclude relevant continuance. Two sets that do not have all members in common cannot be the same sets. In mathematics, the set

---

number of protons that determines the element. Note that the three elements that are mentioned have markedly different physical properties. Of the three, for example, only mercury is a liquid at room temperature.

[54] Merricks, *Objects and Persons*, 115.

$$\{1,2,3,4,5,6,7,8,9\}$$

is not equivalent to the set

$$\{1,2,3,4,5,6,7,8\}$$

This notion will have a familiar ring. A Heraclitean-like problem of identity simply resurfaces in a different form.

Suppose that a man wishes to make a chest in his woodworking shop. He begins sanding what one calls a board to build what one calls a drawer. The would-be plank's thickness is reduced nonstop in the course of a minute and, with the diminution, a steady loss of atoms. As each atom flies off the surface, a unique particle-set is brought into being. The atoms that are shed in this ongoing process are not part of a board, Merricks must say, because boards do not exist in his view. There are only assemblages of particles: an original board-collection and subsequent, different board-collections that surface as the matter that composed the original one decreases with each micromovement of the would-be sander. Indeed, in place of a board, there are trillions of board-collections as unique sets arise and vanish, lasting only nanoseconds, for the duration of the sanding.

Further, each atomic set will have different causal properties because the mass of any given collection will be slightly different from all the others. Merricks's ontology gives up objects in favor of generating a plethora of independent particle-groups—hardly a fair trade. It is unclear how the particle-groups are associated. Perhaps it is through the relationship of a proper subset to a set, such that each thinner plank-set is a proper subset of the one that preceded it in the sanding process. If one employs the subset relationship, then what one thinks of as a board extends far beyond the woodworking facility, for everything constitutes a proper subset of a set that contains it and at least one other member. The supposed entity that one refers to as a board encompasses the air around it, the building in which it is located, the planet earth, the Milky Way, and even distant galaxies. It would be more sensible to say that the board exists and is pared down in size by the sanding—a straightforward assertion.

If one attempts to avoid the problem of overinclusion by limiting the particle-set, from which the subsets are taken, to the material composing the original board, then there is still a problem. Microscopic wood chips are flying everywhere, and minute bits of sawdust are suspended in the air, embedded in the equipment, and wedged in the woodworker's hair. Particle-sets that one calls planks are spread all over, which scarcely fits the notion of them. Merricks cannot claim that these collections are not planks, but the big chunk that is left on the sanding table is a plank, for then he would be arguing against his own theory: Planks do not exist, he says. He cannot claim that collections with their pieces spread across space are not plank-like, but the big chunk is plank-like, because the only truly relevant differences between them, in the theory at hand, are the location of the pieces and the amount of material. If the woodworker breaks a board neatly into thirty pieces and then places the pieces carefully in the same order on the shop floor, then the atoms are juxtaposed, as before, and in the shape of a plank. All the material is still there, but it would be untenable to hold that it is now plank-like. As it is, it never could serve to make a drawer.

The key problem for Merricks, though, is that, if the sanding continues, then eventually all that is left of the board is a mass of tiny wood fibers and sawdust flecks. If one drops that material in its entirety on the woodworker's foot at once, then the craftsman would take little notice. If one drops the same material on his foot before the sanding, then it would break two of his toes. The presanded plank has causal powers that are beyond that of a mere collection of atoms acting in concert. The presanded plank thus, using Merricks's own criterion, exists, despite his argument that such objects do not exist.

It will not help to say that the atoms of the presanded plank are organized plankwise, whereas those of the postsanded plank—the same atoms—are not organized in that way, claiming that it is the atoms' arrangement, not the group of atoms per se, that serves as the key differentiating factor. It is not necessary even to sand the board to generate the problem. Walking at three miles per hour, the woodworker accidentally strikes the metal door of the shop with the corner of the plank. A dent in the door results. He does so again at the same speed, but, this time, he hits the door with the plank turned in such a way that its broad surface touches the door. No damage results. Not a quick learner, he repeats the series several times, with like outcomes. Therefore, the same collection of particles, arranged in the same plankwise manner, both does cause, and does not cause, a dent. The plank-turned-corner-to-the-front has causal properties that the plank-turned-face-to-the-front lacks, even though the collection of atoms and their arrangement do not vary with orientation. For Merricks, there is no object above and beyond the atomic particle-set, arranged in the form of the alleged object. Let p_c represent the plank with its corner turned to the front and p_f represent the plank with its face turned to the front. Let S equal the set of atomic particles arranged plankwise and E stand for a door-dinging type of event. The following construction, numbered for readability, captures the issue:

1. p_c causes events of type E.
2. p_f does not cause events of type E.
3. Therefore, p_c has causal powers that p_f lacks.
4. $p_f = S$.
5. Therefore, p_c has causal powers that S lacks.
6. S = the collection of particles that compose p_c.
7. Therefore, p_c has causal powers that the collection of particles that compose p_c lacks.
8. To be an object is to have nonredundant causal powers.
9. Therefore, p_c is an object.

One as easily could have produced a contradiction, showing, for example, that $p_c = S$ and $p_c \neq S$.

It will not do to claim that one must include, in addition to the particles that make up the board and their arrangement plankwise, the angle of the particle-set relative to the door, in determining whether an object exists. If the man had been moving at an appreciably different pace, then the outcome of the p_c incident and that of the p_f one would have been the same. At one-third mile per hour instead of three miles per hour, neither plank-set would have caused a dent. If the man had been moving at ten miles per hour instead of three miles per hour, then both plank-sets would have dented the door. The causal criterion is simply inadequate to distinguish between objects and nonobjects.

What does Merricks have in mind in saying that the window-breaking event is not *overdetermined*? He thinks that the whole as a single object does not exist, on the sole basis that the parts do all the causal work; the whole is doing nothing more than the parts are doing. It follows that, where the parts do not do the causal work, they must not exist either. Certain atoms are almost inevitably superfluous in any occurrence. Tommy is using a biconvex lens to focus the sun's rays to ignite a piece of paper. Suppose that the lens is formed rather poorly, so that the portion of the glass near the edge of the lens fails to concentrate the light energy, dispersing it instead. The atom-set at the center of the lens is doing the causal work; the atom-set on the periphery is causally irrelevant to the ignition. One cannot conclude that those atoms making up the outer area do not exist. It might be objected that they can cause other things, even if they are not involved in the burning of the paper. What counts is the fact that they can cause *something*. If such is the case, then it seems that one first of all must detail the defining event before determining causal relevancy; and, if that relevancy is the critical factor in existence, then an atom-set sometimes exists and sometimes does not exist, depending on the circumstances and what is taking place. This consequence is hardly acceptable.

Again, one must ask what Merricks means in saying that the atoms of a thing act *in concert*, as when, for example, a baseball breaks the window. Is the idea simply that the atoms are lumped together, so that they form one close-proximity bundle, serving as the joint cause of some effect? If so, then anything that is touching a putative object must be included in the set and thus part of the cause. Suppose that John is holding a baseball when it breaks the window: He pushes it through the glass. Given the fact that they are in contact, John and the baseball that he is holding constitute a set. John himself, though, is an object, according to Merricks, because he possesses consciousness and thereby exhibits causal properties that are independent of those that the atoms of his material body exhibit. That which is holding the baseball—call him baseball-man—is therefore an object, for baseball-man, by virtue of John's being a conscious person, causes things beyond the set of atoms that make up baseball-man. According to Merricks, though, what one calls the baseball, taken independently, is not an object. The result is that a set of atoms that is not an object becomes part of an object merely through the contact of some members of that set with what is an object. His theory turns a nonobject into an object—or part of one, at least—

through incorporation. This whole approach simply lacks a measure of reasonableness.

Additional problems stem from incorporation. Suppose that Monte's father gives what one refers to as a baseball to Monte as a present for his birthday. It is old and fairly dirty, and has some writing on it: obviously used. Seeing the condition, Monte is highly disappointed, as he wanted a new ball. On closer inspection, he notices that the writing on the baseball, to his amazement, is an autograph of Lou Gehrig. He knows that it is authentic because his father, who is an avid aficionado of sports memorabilia, never would have given him an imitation. He is now ecstatic. The atoms, however, have not changed. It is not the atoms of the ink arranged as they are on the atoms of the ball that make the difference here. If the writing had been exactly the same, but no one bearing the name 'Lou Gehrig' had been a famous player for the New York Yankees—a fan with that name caught the ball in the stadium and signed it—then there would be no excitement on the part of Monte. If the writing had not been exactly the same but had been placed there by the famous Lou Gehrig nevertheless—signatures by the same individual do vary somewhat—then the excitement would remain. The physical configuration of the ink in itself is irrelevant. It is the *source* of the writing in the signing event—its being put there by one of the most notable figures in sports—that carries the causal weight. The writing on the baseball derives its precipitating power from its history rather than from the particles of the ink that compose it, even though the writing, considered as a physical collection of atoms, *is* the ink. The autographed baseball hence causes something that the atoms that compose it do not cause; neither the number of atoms nor their configuration is a causal factor. It follows that the autographed baseball, given Merricks's theory, is an object over and above the atoms that make up that ink-laden relic, which contradicts his postulation. There is nothing about the old, scribbled-on ball's collection of atoms, taken as a collection of atoms, that causes Monte's excitement. His excitement arises instead from something about the artifact—namely, its extreme scarcity and worth, coupled with Monte's valuing it highly and believing that it is authentic. The object of that value and belief, however, is not a bunch of atoms but a rare, Gehrig-autographed baseball from the late 1920s.

Consider a different problem that incorporation introduces. Imagine that Monte and Milton decide to play catch with Monte's treasured possession. Imagine further that, in the course of the boys' tossing the baseball, an atomic bit somehow breaks loose from the leather hide of the ball and sticks to Milton's leather glove, and a like atomic bit separates from Milton's glove and sticks to the hide of Monte's ball. Given that an atom from the original ball-collective is now part of the glove-collective that belongs to Milton, is Milton part owner of a Gehrig-autographed baseball; and, given that an atom of the glove-collective is now part of the baseball-collective, is Monte part owner of the leather mitt? If one answers this question in the affirmative, then ownership of any would-be object that one may possess can be undermined by any change in the atom-set of that object. Billy's driving an ATV across Phil's farm will result in joint ownership of both the vehicle and the land. Such a consequence is unsupportable. If, on the other hand, one answers the question in the negative, then ownership is not dependent on the atoms that make up the things that people supposedly own. The upshot is that, where possession continues through atomic loss or gain, as is the case with Beverly's bicycle, things exist apart from the mere sets of atoms that compose them. What else could these things that people possess be but the objects that they believe them to be? Merricks maintains that causal overdetermination makes objects as wholes irrelevant while preserving their parts. It seems, however, that the right of possession makes the parts irrelevant while preserving the objects as wholes. It is a point that, in the end, will prove to be pivotal.

Thus, one concern with Merricks's account is that he couches his ontology solely in terms of causality pertaining to the dynamic world of microbits: the atoms of baseballs and the displacing of the atoms of windows that they shatter. In relying on causality as the mark of distinction, Merricks's account is focused too narrowly on the physics to capture the breadth of relevant factors. There is more at hand in an assessment of object-existence than raw physics. Not everything is reducible to the laws that govern particle interactions; there are other distinguishing relationships. The abovementioned instances point to what may be the crucial, underlying element.

If composite, inanimate things do exist, then the reason that they exist is not to be found in Merricksian causal nonredundancy.

Eliminating aggregate objects on the basis that they are irrelevant in bringing about effects falls short of a satisfying story. It is important—and fair—to note that some compound things, even according to Merricks's criterion, are not causally redundant: a molecule of water, for example. If one accepts his quasi-nihilistic thesis, then aggregates do exist as individual objects. One's sense, however, is that far larger aggregates exist too—those things, such as bricks, boats, and baseballs, that people encounter in their daily lives.

OUT OF BOUNDS—NIHILISM OVER THE EDGE

The problem of imprecise boundaries is one that was familiar to the early Greek thinkers. At one end of a spectrum, a given term clearly seems to apply. At the other end, it clearly seems not to apply. Where to draw the line is the challenge. Logic would dictate that it must be drawn somewhere, as the term ceases to be applicable at some point between the two ends of the spectrum. Eubulides from Miletus—the home of the earliest Presocratic philosophers—is credited with putting forth a classic puzzle that is based on this sort of apparent imprecision. It is the problem of the heap, known as the sorites paradox. The paradox derives its name ultimately from the Greek root term for heap, *sōros* (σωρός). Here is a typical rendering:

> If a huge number of grains of wheat are piled together, then they form a heap.
> If one grain of wheat is removed from a heap, then a heap remains.
> Therefore, the removal of each grain of wheat in succession will continue to leave a heap, even when only a single grain is left.

Some philosophers have taken the sorites paradox seriously, enough so to believe that it is sufficient to undercut the existence of ordinary objects. If there were such things as tables and stones and yo-yos, thinks Peter Unger, then they would be just the material of which they are made. One can remove that material piece by piece, atom by atom. The removal of a single atom from what lies there, however, never can scribe the difference between the presence of a table or a stone or a yo-yo and the absence of one. Human notions of certain molecules may carry with them the requisite precision, where such molecules are determined by an exact number of component atoms, but notions of ordinary objects are notably imprecise. It is not reasonable to hold that the removal of one atom leaves a table in existence, while the removal of another atom eliminates its existence entirely, Unger maintains. The reasonable position to take, he says, is to hold that the table never did exist.

Unger does not stop there, however. In the same way, he believes, one can demonstrate that not even people exist. Like tables, they can be deconstructed one piece at a time—in this case, by the unit of the cell. He asks one to imagine a process in which Unger himself is under such disassembly. At some point, life-support systems will be employed. Nourishing fluids will be pumped into him, and the requisite electrical stimulation will be provided. As the process continues, one can see, so he argues, the illogicality of an ontology that includes such composite objects: There is no reasonable place to draw the line.

> Cell after cell is pulled away. The remaining ones are kept alive, and kept functioning. . . . Sticking to what might here most plausibly be considered myself, then, at a certain point we are down to a brain in a vat and, then, half a brain. So far, so good; but then we get down to a third of a brain, then a sixteenth. Still later, there are only fifty-three neurons in living combination. Where at the end, there is but one living nerve cell, and then it too is gone. Where will I disappear from the scene? Realistically, now, will the removal of a single cell ever . . . mean my disappearance from reality? While that may be a 'logical possibility', it does not compel belief. The conclusion of our argument, in contrast, is quite compelling: I do not disappear at any time, because I was never around in the first place.[55]

---

[55] Peter Unger, "I Do Not Exist," in *Perception and Identity: Essays Presented to A. J. Ayer, with His Replies*, ed. G. F. Macdonald (Ithaca: Cornell University Press, 1979), 244–45.

For Unger, composite things, both inanimate and animate, are unreal. If they were real, then they would be subject to the illogicality of sudden disappearance through decomposition. He admits that he is not sure even about the existence of atoms, but whether there are any is a sidebar to his core position.[56] His stance is part metaphysical, part linguistic-conceptual: There are no compound entities existing in physical reality that correspond to the general terms that people use to denote those putative entities. Without a major restructuring of human concepts and language—a reformation that is not likely to be forthcoming—nothing is singled out by composite-object names, and one is forced by reason into "an acceptance of nihilism."[57] Unger is aware of the ludicrousness of adopting a philosophy of extreme denial. He forges ahead to embrace it nevertheless, as he believes that there is no way around it, given the state of human modes of thought and expression. Accordingly, it appears that, says Unger, "[A]n adequate philosophy of nihilism . . . is the only adequate philosophy there can be."[58] In the final analysis, Unger concludes,

> I do not exist and neither do you. . . . There are, then, no tables or chairs, nor rocks or stones or ordinary stars. Neither are there any plants or animals. No finite persons or conscious beings exist, including myself Peter Unger: I do not exist.[59]

Who said so? It is the first question to ask in response to Unger's remarks. If no one exists, then there is no one—no thing, in fact—to generate the utterance. If no one exists, then, in Unger's

---

[56] Theodore Sider believes that Unger's position is closer to mereological essentialism than to nihilism, more explicitly, to mereological nihilism. Unger walks a fine line perhaps between the two, but it seems that he leans toward nihilism in holding that it is more logical to deny the existence of composite objects than it is to admit their existence and accept the consequences—namely, that they could cease to exist by the removal of a single part. For a further discussion of Unger's use of the sorites paradox to argue against the existence of persons, see his "Why There Are No People," *Midwest Studies in Philosophy* 4, no. 1 (1979): 177–222.

[57] Unger, "I Do Not Exist," 248.

[58] Ibid., 251.

[59] Ibid., 236.

pronouncement, "I do not exist," there is nothing to which the subject of the sentence could refer: The word 'I' is a nonreferring term. The sentence itself is therefore meaningless. There is not even anyone to develop the concept that no one exists; a fortiori, there is no Peter Unger to develop the concept that Peter Unger advocates— namely, that neither Peter Unger nor anyone else exists.

Such a position could not be anything but completely self-defeating. One can utter with meaning a proposition that denies the existence of a putative class of objects. A statement that asserts that there are no living passenger pigeons, for example, is not only meaningful but also true, as the species became extinct years ago. What one cannot utter with meaning is a statement that purports to deny the existence of the very one who utters it. In his zeal to underscore the problem of composition, Unger has landed in a sinkhole. There is value in reviewing his reasoning here, however, because the senselessness of Unger's claim of a nonexistent self only adds weight to the position that what makes things unique—what makes them individuals, or particulars—is not the material of which they are composed. One must look elsewhere for it.

Eventually, Unger comes to dismiss this extreme view of objects, but he does so in favor of one that is even more bizarre. In a later work, he returns to the sorites paradox to argue, not for his nonexistence altogether but instead for his gradated existence. "Although perhaps not as notably so as clouds, or even bricks, we are *gradual* beings," avers Unger.[60] Subjects are not absolute entities; they are not all-or-nothing things. As his cells are peeled away one by one, Unger claims, "I will . . . fade out of existence."[61]

Unger has fallen into the trap of confusing the existence of part of a thing with the partial existence of a thing. The bumper of his car may lie in the driveway after Bobby backed into the garage door that morning while he hurried to work. It is true that the car in the parking lot at the office an hour later is not all there if one means that it is missing a part. It is senseless, however, to say that the car is not all there if one means that it has moved partway into nonexistence. Existence is not an attribute; it does not lie on a continuum; it does

---

[60] Peter Unger, *Identity, Consciousness, and Value* (New York: Oxford University Press, 1990), 64.
[61] Ibid., 197.

not admit of degrees. Existence and nonexistence are absolutes. The fading Cheshire Cat in Wonderland is just a fantasy. Reducing the material presence of a person or the person's abilities by extracting cells from the body does not diminish the person's being in some way. Just as a statement of the form 'I do not exist' is meaningless, so are its counterparts: 'I do not exist fully' and 'I am not completely here'. If a thing x exists, then *that* thing, x, exists. It is not possible for x to be both in existence and not in existence. Nothing can have a foot in both camps. The propositions 'I, Peter Unger, do not exist fully' and 'I, Peter Unger, am not completely here' are tantamount to asserting that the entity to which the pronoun 'I' refers both is, and is not, an existent thing. Although odd, the assertion can be expressed in the following manner, where T represents the holding of the identical-to relation, and u stands for the individual Peter Unger:

$$(\exists x)(Txu) \cdot - (\exists x)(Txu)$$

That declaration is a contradiction.

If removal of bits from Unger's body through time were to bring about the gradual cessation of Unger himself, then there would be no Peter Unger, for there would be no identity. How could two things be the same if one of them is completely there in reality and the other is not quite all there, not in the sense of missing parts but in the sense of diminished being? What sense could one make of the supposed notion of decremental reality? Aside from diminished bodily mass, Unger may possess, at some point in his life, only 79 percent of the physical and mental abilities that he possessed at an earlier age, as measured by some set of tests, but to conclude that Unger at the later time is 79 percent existent and 21 percent nonexistent is to adopt the absurd. If claims of partial reality were meaningful, then it seems that the truth of statements about the existence of things would fall across an entire spectrum, with the consequence that the statement 'I exist' may be only 79 percent true. A rule of logic, the law of bivalence, which is related to the law of excluded middle, precludes values for propositions other than true and false. Under the gradual-being hypothesis, the rule must be rejected in favor of recognizing an indeterminate number of truth-values, and that toll is an exorbitant one to exact. What Unger's argument shows, if anything, is that persons are not their physical bodies, and their existence is not tied to their extension in space, nor is it tied to the capabilities of that extended form. The *existence* of a person is not something that one can scrape away with pumice.

BOUND TO BE

Metaphysical positions that attempt to eliminate objects altogether, whether because of presumed causal redundancy or because of apparent imprecise boundaries, leave one unsatisfied. People are wont to say that aggregates do exist as individual objects; further, their intuitions tell them that those objects, in fact, do cause things to happen and do have boundaries. Of the two proposed cases against aggregates that I raised, the problem of boundaries may appear to be the more troubling one as the sorites paradox takes hold. Despite the difficulty in finding the limits of things, however, one should not be deterred from claiming that things have them.

Any composite, physical object that one can name is subject to degradation and, with such, there comes a time when it ceases to exist. It is a contingent thing, and contingent things exist in passing.[62] At some stage of their being, things that exist in passing are no more. If one accepts that cessation occurs over two adjacent moments in time, as I argued earlier, then there must be a time at which lumps of dirt and heaps of grain cease to be. The issue that surfaces is how to discover those end points. As it is, the better question to ask is whether the points that mark such endings can be *discovered* at all.

Part of the counterintuitiveness that emerges in such cases is a reflection of another, deeper problem that the ancient Greeks raised,

---

[62] One may take the position that a notable exception is the universe as a whole: a composite that does not exist only in passing. Whether even the universe is future-unrestricted in the temporal sense, however, is called into question—from different standpoints. For the astrophysicists, it may collapse into a singularity at some juncture, although, according to current scientific thinking, the evidence suggests that it will not do so, given its observed state. For the theologians, the present heavens and earth will pass away, and God will bring into being a new heaven and a new earth. Either way, cosmic continuance, in the present form, is not assured.

one that I discussed in the first chapter. It is the problem of one and many. If all is not one, then the universe is a universe of many things, and some of these things seem to be aggregates that are built from simpler components. Any shifting in the components causes the question of sameness to arise, particularly if those components are not replaced. It is becoming evident that what makes identity possible, and what makes it comprehensible, is *unity*. There must be some way to lock things, as it were, into singularities. Both Heraclitus and Parmenides take this locking to the extreme: The first denies continuance; the second denies change. Heraclitean philosophy holds that there is no locking and therefore no persistent object, for all the things in the physical world are in a state of constant fluctuation. Parmenides applies the locking to everything as a whole. For him, all that exists is the indivisible and immutable One. Reality for Parmenides has no parts, nor does it ever change in any way. Such a view avoids the total dissolution of objects that Heraclitus would have, and the accompanying preclusion of identity through time, but it pays too high a price to do so.

On reflection, it is evident that the requisite unity, as it pertains to objects, is twofold. What must be unified are both (1) the physical parts that compose a thing at a given time and (2) the different time segments in which such a thing exists. Thus, the following two requirements hold for an object if it is to be a unit:

Unity

Spatial   At any one moment, any spatially spread parts of an object must achieve unity through conjunction.

Temporal Across an interval of multiple moments, the units that are conjoined spatially must achieve unity through persistence.

Now, with respect to the composition issue, one must ask what it is to be singular. Consider the two structures that I give below. The first figure represents a physical object that is not a composite; the second figure represents one that is a composite.

Structure 1: Noncomposite, Unary Object

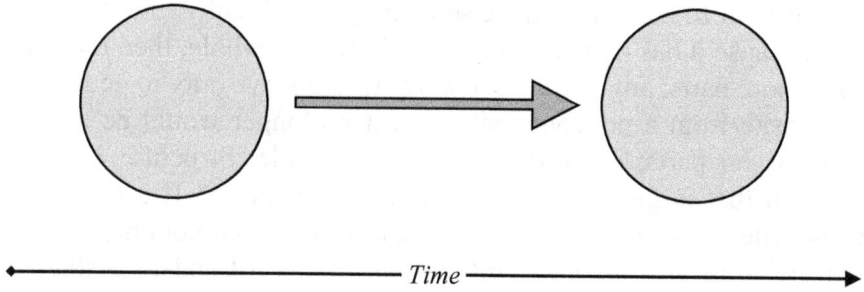

Time

Structure 2: Composite Object

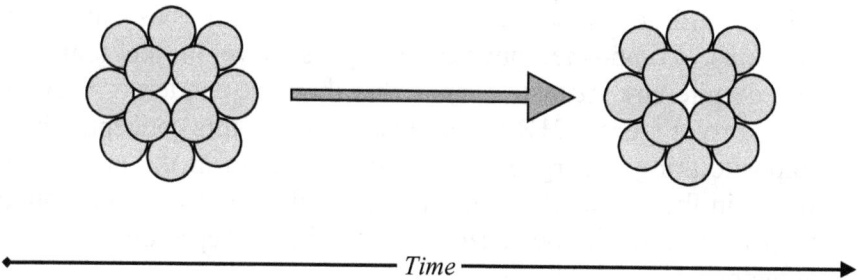

Time

Figure 3.21A

One understands that, if an entity is singular, in that it is a fundamental, undivided—even indivisible—thing, then affirming its oneness in space and its continuance through time without a disruption to its uniqueness, until it ceases to be, is not particularly problematic. When a thing is a unit because it has no parts other than itself as a whole, it is not subject to degradation of identity through the *loss of parts*, as the loss of any material would be the loss of the whole.[63] Further, without parts, other than itself as a whole, there can

---

[63] One will recall that anything is considered to be a part of itself. In accordance with a mathematical principle, a set is a subset of itself, just not a proper subset.

be no *substitution of parts* in the thing, for any substitution at all would remove, and replace, the whole and, in so doing, remove what was there at first and introduce something else. Finally, if a thing is a unit because it has no parts other than itself as a whole, then it cannot have more parts; any *addition of parts* would serve only to generate a composite from a noncomposite, and it no longer would be a thing that has no parts, other than itself as a whole. Structure 1 in the diagram that is given above illustrates these facts.[64] If a thing is a composite, as depicted in Structure 2, however, then not only is there a question of *how far it extends in space* before it ends, but there is also a question of *how far it extends in time* before it ends, for it is subject to the parts-shifting concern.

The principal matter is to determine what underlies persistence. What one sees is that a thing continues through time—staying the same thing—for as long as its unity remains uncompromised. It is a straightforward, even self-evident, concept, but it has important implications. Composite, physical things survive in the temporal stream, despite any intrinsic change that they may undergo, because of singularity. Figure 3.21B is a representation of this concept, where a composite thing undergoes a shift in parts, both in the number of them and in their properties, but maintains its identity, being bound together as a unit. The outer ring in the diagram represents the unifying factor.

---

[64] In the physical universe, only the fundamental particles of quantum physics (and presumably the correlated theoretical strings) qualify as unary by virtue of having no parts. Even then, their unity may be unclear, as particles can behave like waves.

Structure 3: Composite, Unary Object

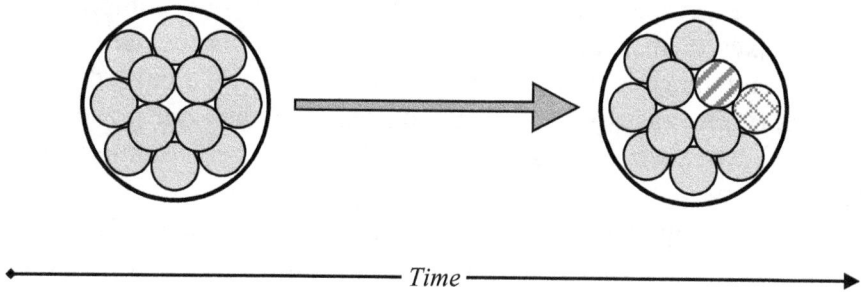

Time

Figure 3.21B

If this analysis is correct, then it is the monadic status of things that makes their persistence possible. How can any compound object satisfy this condition? By definition, a compound object is not monadic. Its structure is such that it contains parts other than itself as a whole. The solution to the quandary is that the unary character of a composite object cannot be attributed to its material configuration. That character must lie elsewhere. As I set forth previously in a pair of hypotheses, a thing's composition is neither a necessary nor a sufficient condition of its individuality. Object ω is not ω by virtue of its makeup. Objects are not simply collections of physical pieces.

It is incumbent on one who would pursue this matter to determine how fusion is achieved in objects. If a thing can possess parts and yet be unary, then what compresses the component pieces with such metaphysical might? As Figure 3.21B illustrates, it is not so much ontological fusion as ontological encapsulation. It is not the joining of parts per se that forms a unit but the existence of a unifying factor that encases them in some way. The key to under-standing the unity of objects is to uncover precisely what dynamic possesses the capability to turn many into one through encasement, as the things in the day-to-day world—those things that people perceive through their various senses—are composed of numerous parts; and these things, insofar as they persist, are collections of material parts traversing collections of sequential moments. Quite likely, herein lies the solution to the problem of knowledge regarding objects. If one comprehends what locks the physical things of common experience into singular entities, then one comprehends what makes them persist—I will say endure at this juncture—for a thing's endurance is its continuance intact: a whole, a unified being. In turn, if one grasps what makes things endure, then one grasps how knowledge of them is possible in a world of flux because the objects of that knowledge are constant.

In keeping with my earlier promise, I want to touch on the vagueness of David Lewis's use of the phrase 'wholly present'. Besides Lewis's objection to an endurance-based ontology, an objection that fails, there is another attack, which employs Albert Einstein's theory of special relativity. I will cover it briefly. The argument, which Stephen D. Hales and Timothy A. Johnson submit, begins with a premise about what it is to endure.

> We can formulate this as a necessary condition for endurantism: something is an enduring object only if it is wholly present at each time in which it exists. An object is wholly present at a time if all of its parts co-exist at that time. Put contrapositively, the principle states that if an object is not wholly present at each time at which it exists (if all its parts do not co-exist at each time at which it exists) then it is not an enduring object.[65]

From this premise, the argument proceeds to deny that endurantism can be right. The reason, it purports, is that the parts of an object can exist at different times in different reference frames because of relative motion with respect to the object, in accordance with the theory of relativity. The authors give an example: Events at both ends of a train—explosions that destroy parts of it—that is traveling at a substantial fraction of light-speed may happen at the same time from the point of view of a commuter at the center of the train. The traveler's frame may be regarded as the rest frame for the object. These same events, however, would happen at other times for an observer who is standing on a platform near the tracks as the train speeds past, where

---

[65] Stephen D. Hales and Timothy A. Johnson, "Endurantism, Perdurantism, and Special Relativity," *Philosophical Quarterly* 53, no. 213 (2003): 532.

the observer on the platform is exactly opposite the passenger on the train when the events take place with respect to the passenger. The explosion at the front of the train would occur for the spectator on the platform after it occurs for the traveler, and the parallel event at the rear of the train would occur for the one by the tracks before it occurs for the one on the train. The train therefore has proper parts at separate times. The cosmos is dynamic. For all physical things, there are frames that are in motion in relation to the things' respective rest frames; so, "[E]very object has proper parts at different times," Hales and Johnson assert, concluding, "[N]o object wholly exists at each moment of its existence, and endurantism as defined . . . is false."[66]

The authors take an object's being wholly present at every moment of its existence to mean that, for any moment that the object exists, all the proper parts of the object exist at that moment: the hallmark of endurantism, so they stress. Can such a severe restriction ever be applied in a reasonable way? It is not necessary to turn to special relativity to see that the notion—taken literally, at least—cannot be an acceptable depiction of endurance.

Timmy lost his appendix when he was eight years old. After removing it, the surgeon sent it to the lab, where it was examined and destroyed. Timmy's tonsils were extracted when he was nine. Using a container of formaldehyde, the lab preserved the extracted material. Abnormally, a tonsil on one side of the boy's throat grew back when he was ten, along with an extra piece of tissue there. Some of Timmy's parts are gone; some remain untouched; some remain but are unattached; some are present now that did not exist previously.

For an object to endure is not for it to have all its spatially extended components present, intact, and joined to it at each moment at which it exists. That view is mereological essentialism. A thing endures if it sweeps through time as a *unit*, as *one thing*. The point of three-dimensionalism—endurantism—is that temporal parts are a fiction. It is not the unrelated idea that a persisting object never can suffer a change in makeup, or else it would not be wholly present, on the basis that the existence of its parts would not coincide.

The Hales-Johnson contention rests on the supposition that an object's physical parts are displaced temporally because of relative

---

[66] Ibid., 535.

motion. The heart of the issue for them, it seems, is that, because of this displacement, all a thing's parts fail to be present at a time, not in the sense that some of them that were there last year are not there now but in the sense that they both are, and are not, parts of it at that time, depending on whether the rest frame of the object or an inertial reference frame, moving with respect to the object, is considered.

On that reading, one ought to say that the aforesaid train has incompatible property-sets. Imagine that it has been covered totally with phosphorescent paint, emitting light after exposure. Albeit uniform in color, the train, in a fundamental way, takes on different hues as a unit because of relative motion. From the passenger's viewpoint, the train, prior to its reaching the platform, is green; but, from the perspective of the observer, standing by the tracks, the color of the approaching train shifts toward violet because of the Doppler effect. After it passes, the train is still green for the traveler, but, for the one on the platform, the color shifts toward red as the train recedes into the distance. If this situation presents a concern for endurance, then it presents a more serious one for perdurance: The transitory temporal parts of *the train*—the object as a whole—are both green and not green during entire sequences of time that those temporal parts exist.

An entity may have different properties or parts at discrete instants yet retain its unity, in keeping with endurantism. If an incident-moment for an entity relative to its rest frame corresponds to an earlier or later moment relative to another frame, owing to motion, then, with respect to a single frame, the given entity's rest frame, those moments are, in fact, discrete. Neither the commuter nor the bystander is perceiving a train that is exhibiting conflicting properties, being both green and not green simultaneously; logic has it that no one thing is capable of that feat. The apparent inconsistency arises only in a cross-frame context, where one frame is set against another. It is the same for the parts. To extend through time as a unit, an object at instant t_1 need not have everything in common with that object at a different instant t_2. In the example of the train, t_1 is distinct from t_2 as a consequence of the relative motion of two frames. In the case of Timmy, t_1 is distinct from t_2 as a consequence of the history within one frame. In both instances, there is a spread in time, but to postulate that it produces a disjointed entity, whether in the former instance or the latter one, leads to a disputable conclusion.

Special relativity appears to be no more challenging for endurantism than the simple passage of time as the parts of a thing come and go during the normal course of its existence. It shows only that time references are not fixed to the point of unalterability.

THE GREAT UNIFIER

I would like to take another look at the sorites paradox to see whether there is a way to resolve its puzzlement. Contemporary philosophers have proposed a number of solutions to the paradox. One response, which is based on concepts that are employed in multivalued logic systems—systems in which truth-values other than true and false apply to sentences that are formulated in the given language—is to identify interim stages of heaps. Here, one finds partial heaps, varying in levels of entirety between the two ends of a spectrum. I believe that this approach introduces a significant problem. The phrase 'partial heap' must mean either 'part of a heap that exists' or 'a heap that exists partially'. The second way presents an impossibility. As noted on several occasions, nothing can be in a state of fractional existence. Either a thing is, or it is not. There is no middle ground where shades of being can lie. Opting for the first alternative, however, saying that a partial heap is in existence, does not provide an escape from the difficulty; one still must cope with setting the conditions that determine what counts as a heap. Until establishing those conditions, either explicitly or implicitly, one cannot make sense of the claim that a partial heap rests before the eyes. One cannot understand the meaning of a locution that consists of a noun and an adjective that modifies the noun unless one understands what the noun itself means, even when the adjective is in common usage. Suppose that one makes the following assertion:

A partial x, but not a whole x, is on the table.

Part of something can exist, but a statement that makes a declaration about part of something can be true only in the case where the referring term has meaning. The sentence that is shown above can have a truth-value and, in fact, can be true, only if (1) the term 'x'—following the instantiation of the variable—denotes something, as do the other terms in the sentence, and (2) some portion of an x, which is less than all of one, is there on the table. If the term is referentially impotent, not in the sense that it ostensibly points to something that does not exist but in the sense that it does not point at all, then, although the sentence has the appearance of making a claim that may, or may not, be factual, as determined by conditions that obtain in the world, the sentence is instead nonsensical. Where the expression 'x', replacing the variable with a word, has no meaning, a sentence cannot assert that an x is not there in toto, nor can it assert that something less than an x is there in toto. To see the issue more clearly, substitute the fabricated word 'zaptonogyte' for the variable in the term 'x' in the sentence. The resultant proposition is neither true nor false, and it is not partially true. It is meaningless.

WITH METRICS IN MIND

The notion of established metrics may help to shed some light on a way to settle the matter. In marking distance, quantity, time, and other such facets of the physical universe, humans have instituted various units of measurement and normalized them as a means of structuring the world. They have defined what an inch, a foot, and a meter are. They have set forth what a gallon is, and a liter. They have divided time into various units, including years, days, hours, minutes, and seconds, breaking seconds into smaller parts—a picosecond, for example.[67] A foot could have been the height of an average horse; a gallon could have been defined as equal to five quarts; an hour could have been a hundred minutes. The volume of a quart could have been

---

[67] Timing errors in digital equipment, such as disk players, constitute jitter, and jitter is measured in picoseconds. A picosecond is 0.000000000001 second, a remarkably brief duration. There are as many picoseconds in a second as there are seconds in almost thirty-two thousand years. Far shorter still is an attosecond: 0.000000000000000001 second. A later chapter will employ attoseconds in setting forth a critical illustration.

greater than it is, and minutes could have stretched far longer than they do stretch, so that there were only ten in a day. These things are what they are by convention. Once they are established, however, propositions that employ them are like all other propositions that assert facts about the world. They are either true or false by virtue of circumstances; they fall under the same principles of truth that govern all assertions about states of affairs that obtain in reality. Thus, it is through proclamation that the sequence of letters *f-o-o-t* denotes the distance in space that it does denote, but it is through application of that proclamation that one can assert that Johnny's pet lizard, Snappy, is a foot long after three years on a diet of insects and leftover pizza.

Consider now this pair of assertions.

1. Carl has a metal rod embedded in his left foot.
2. Carl is standing with the front of his left foot two yards from the wall.

Given that all the terms in these sentences are meaningful, the truth-value of each assertion hinges on physical reality. If a doctor implanted a titanium shaft in one of the tarsals in Carl's left foot during the reconstruction that followed his accident, then statement 1 is true. If there is only tissue in that foot, then it is false. If the tip of Carl's great toe on his left foot is, in fact, six feet from the wall—on the premise that a yard equals precisely three feet—then statement 2 is true. If he is only three feet away from the wall, then it is false. One cannot eliminate the metallic composition of Carl's foot without changing the truth of the sentence about it. Likewise, one cannot change the distance that Carl stands from the wall without changing the truth of the proposition about his position relative to it. There is an important difference, however, and it is that the truth of the first of the propositions that appear above depends on the physical state of affairs obtaining in the world, whereas the truth of the second depends both on the state of affairs in the world and on an established standard of measurement. If humankind had determined a yard to be any length other than what it is—a little longer or a little shorter—then, although Carl stands in exactly the same place, what sentence 2 expresses would be false. The physical circumstances would not have changed, only the relevant conventional measure of distance.[68]

Consider again the concept of termination. In day-to-day life, this problem of the endings of things simply does not surface. A lady at a picnic asks her son whether the half-eaten drumstick on his plate is the same piece of chicken that he took from the basket an hour ago. Perhaps he is not hungry, she thinks, but she is worried that the quality of her cooking is declining. In another instance, a man asks his wife whether the roll of paper towels on the holder is the same roll that she placed there last week, as he is surprised by its girth. He is hoping that the family finally is taking his request for conservation seriously. No one is perplexed by such cases. Only when philosophy takes hold of a straightforward and simple issue does obscurity reign.

There are times, however, when it may be important for some reason, philosophical or otherwise, to determine when things of a given sort end. Suppose that someone, attempting to understand the game of checkers, asks when a given bout is over. The answer is that it is over when one of the two players captures all the other player's pieces, an opponent concedes the match, or a stalemate is reached and declared by mutual consent. Of course, one competitor could become angry, flip over the board, and walk away, or both of them could become tired and dump the checkers back into the box. Such conclusions are merely the cessation of activities. They are not endings at all in the proper sense of the term but aberrations: There are no official rules that govern the events as described. These aberrant games conclude by virtue of an unwillingness on the part of a player or both players to continue, not by virtue of the standards that are set forth in the handbook. In general, once the opponents start a game upon the movement of the first piece, the game continues, and it continues as *one* game of checkers—the *same* game—until, by the

---

[68] One could say that, just as the term 'yard' denotes a certain distance by virtue of decree, the other words in propositions 1 and 2 depend on declaration for the assignment of meaning. The words 'metal', 'rod', 'left', 'standing', and so forth could have signified things other than what they do signify in current usage. It is not necessary or helpful to delve into the matter for the discussion here. Meaning is a topic that is explored in the philosophy of language; an analysis of it would take the discussion far afield. The examples that I provide in this section are of things that are established on the basis of standards—measurements and rules—and are sufficient for the purposes at hand.

rules, it terminates through a win, a concession, or a stalemate. It does not matter whether it takes seconds, minutes, or hours for a player to make a move when it is the player's turn; it is one game until it ends.

The rules could have been different from what they are. A game could have ended when the first king was crowned, or when a player lost all his or her pieces except one. The rules that determine when the game is over are established by custom. There is nothing more at work here, no metaphysical constraint that forces the game to stop at a certain point in its progress. Some endings come about not through *discovery* but through *declaration* or *definition*.

Persistence, termination, and identity are linked in an inextricable way. A thing that has come into being persists—that is to say, it continues to exist without a break in its existence—until it terminates, at which point, it no longer persists. Underlying this truth are the statement of persistence and principle CD. Nothing can continue to exist beyond the boundary of its own termination: A thing cannot come to be, cease to be, and then come to be again. Thus, the conditions under which a thing persists and the conditions under which it ends are codetermined—in an inverse manner: Whatever sets one also sets the other by preclusion.

The determination of the continuance and cessation of things as it applies here is not to be viewed in the causal sense, as when, say, a dilapidated shed in a man's field continues to stand or is blown to bits with a stick of dynamite, but in the sense of fixing the conditions under which things of a given sort persist and under which they end. Whatever persists must continue as the same thing, maintaining numerical identity through time, until it no longer exists, a fact that is given in the conjunction of principle CD and the persistence corollary of principle TI. Thus, the conditions under which a thing persists and the conditions of its identity through time are codetermined as well—but not inversely: Whatever sets one also sets the other by correspondence. If the end of something is fixed by instituted rules, then correspondingly so is its identity. If rules are enacted to establish when any given game of checkers begins and when it ends, then those rules make it true that it is one and the same game between those two events because, if the game has started but not yet ended, then *it* is continuing.

Is it not the same with composite, inanimate, physical things? A lump of clay is made of many parts, but one sees it as a single thing. One understands its spatial limits, as an aggregate, because one can see where the dirt ends, more or less, and the environment begins, more or less. Consider temporal limits. When the lump disintegrates in a bucket of water, it ceases to be something that is perceived to be unified. The particles that made up the clod still exist, of course, but they are not together now in the manner in which they were together previously. The clod is no more. Again, one sees a stone as a single object, distinguished rather easily from its surroundings, but it erodes under the forces of wind and water until there is nothing left that one is disposed to call a stone. It will take longer for the stone to wear away than for the clod to fall apart, but the issue of dissipation is the same.

Look at another case. The way to Grandmother Gertrude's house is overlaid with stones for the first nine miles, becoming dirt-surfaced for the next five, turning afterward into two parallel, dirt tracks for another three miles, fading into a rough, indistinct path for a mile through the woods, and finally becoming nothing more than an area where it appears as though a vehicle might have depressed the foot-high grass across a narrow, 880-yard-long pasture. *Where* does the road end? Weather and wear take their toll on the way in time, degrading it substantially across its entire length of eighteen and one-half miles, so much so that most of it is no longer even recognizable as a means of travel. *When* does the road end? Both the spatial and the temporal aspects of things point to a need for specific boundaries, but it is the latter aspect that is the more pressing concern, for the overarching question is about the impact of change through time on the knowledge of objects.

As this analysis continues, I wish to focus on the macro-physical—the things that are outside the atomic realm. It is these things that make up the world of perceptual experience, and it is the possibility of knowing these objects, where such knowledge arises through perception, that is of interest in this chapter. As an aside, however, it is worth noting that, even when one delves into the microphysical, oneness and sameness are called into question. A molecule of a compound substance, say, sodium chloride—common table salt—is deemed to be a unit because it is the smallest chunk of material that exhibits certain properties, and those properties are not exhibited by the constituents in themselves. Why would those properties make a collective a singular entity? Two atoms of helium do not bond to form a joint molecule under normal conditions—helium is an inert gas—yet that collective too is the smallest chunk of material that exhibits certain properties that are not exhibited by its atomic constituents in themselves. The relative atomic mass of the chunk is 7.94 times that of an atom of ordinary hydrogen, for example, a property that neither of the atomic components of the collective exhibits individually.[69] Moreover, a molecule can be split into its constituent atoms, and those atoms can be separated further into protons, neutrons, and electrons. The protons and neutrons are composites as well and can be split into quarks and gluons. The nuclei of atoms of elements can shed associated electrons to create charged structures, or ions, and those nuclei may gain other electrons subsequently to form complete, electrically neutral atoms once again. In these cases, are the atoms the same ones as before, provided that their nuclei remain intact, or did the original atoms terminate? There was a change in material pieces, not unlike the installation of new wheels on a lawnmower, but, so one has seen, matter is not the key to identity. The sameness or difference of atoms, if it is to make sense in any way, seems to depend on people to declare, as the question of the continuance of atomic building blocks does not appear to be meaningful without a benchmark to establish what counts as unity and what counts as cessation.

In fact, without benchmarks, there can be no grounds for holding that the world is characterized by the individuation of composite, physical objects at all. There is no dividing of things into distinct entities because, at the quantum level, there is only a soup of subatomic particles: a place here or there more densely packed with matter than another place; an area here or there where like atoms or molecules are clustered, a group of particles held in close proximity by natural forces. Without individuation, though, there *is no* object, except perhaps the universe as a whole; therefore, there is no object

---

[69] The calculation is based on values that are given in J. S. Coursey et al., "Atomic Weights and Isotopic Compositions," Physical Measurement Laboratory, National Institute of Standards and Technology, accessed October 20, 2014, nist.gov/pml/data/comp.cfm. These values are also available elsewhere.

to cease to be, except perhaps the universe as a whole. If objects are to be formed within the physical universe, then they must be carved out of this particulate soup by that which possesses the ability to do the work.

There is another reply to the sorites paradox that holds more promise. It rests on the setting of a limit below which no heap exists. The idea is that a heap must have at least some predetermined number of grains. That requirement can expand to include other restrictions; for example, each grain must be in contact with at least one other grain, and a certain ratio of height to width is necessary. Some philosophers raise an objection here, however. Suppose that the predetermined number of grains is n. Then, where n grains are stacked together, a heap exists, but, where $n-1$ grains are stacked together, no heap exists. This distinction, according to the objectors, is totally arbitrary and should be dismissed.

The trouble with the objection is probably obvious: It assumes that one must search for some principle of meaningful demarcation *within* a collection of material itself, and there *is none*. To object that setting a limit is arbitrary and valueless is to miss the point entirely, and the point is that there is no basis for what constitutes a heap awaiting discovery. What marks the ends of composite, inanimate, material things is not strictly physical, and it is not metaphysical. It is a matter of mandates and metrics applied to physical circumstances. As Carl's distance from the wall, expressed in yards, depends on both his location in the room and on established measurements, so too a heap must be defined before statements about one can be grounded. An independent marking of the terminal points of composite objects as they dwindle with the passage of time, founded on some philosophically rich, fundamental, and discoverable principle, is not something that is forthcoming. In day-to-day life, the problem of heaps seldom surfaces. A truckload of dirt, dumped on a construction site, is a heap; a pinch of salt, set aside to be added to the gravy at the right time, is not one. Whether one speaks of lumps and rocks, or heaps and piles, if it is important to be clear and precise, then a standard must be instituted. One may say, for instance, that stuck-together clay forms a lump when its circumference at the greatest line exceeds three inches; or its volume at a certain temperature and atmospheric pressure is at least twenty cubic centimeters; or its mass exceeds a hundred grams or seventy grams or twenty and one-third grams. The lump ceases to exist when it falls below the specified measurement. One may set forth similar conditions to determine what counts as a rock, saying that it is no longer a rock but a pebble when erosion reduces its maximum diameter to less than an inch or three-quarters inch or eighteen millimeters; or its mass becomes less than twenty-four grams or fourteen grams. In turn, one may say that the pebble comes to an end when it erodes to one-third the value of a particular foregoing dimension or one-fourth the value of a particular foregoing mass. In defining the terms that are used to refer to objects of a specific sort, humans are setting forth the conditions under which things qualify for inclusion in the set of objects that are picked out by the sortal terms. When change in the course of time alters those things to the point where they no longer satisfy the specified conditions, they cease to be elements of the given set. People do not *detect* such things strictly by looking a little more closely with no explicit criterion; they *define* what counts as one of them.

A material aggregate—a lump of clay or a stone—exists as an individual only where the conditions that underwrite the identifying of the aggregate as a single item of a specific sort are supplied through the creation of a standard. Such standards are put in place solely by thought. It is therefore the rational mind that brings unity to the aggregate, yielding one lump or one stone. It is the same with heaps. A collection of grains of wheat or some other substance does not form a singular object—a heap or a mound or a pile—unless the understanding provides unity; and it is the understanding that must determine the rules that govern the formation and elimination of such objects, whether those rules are based on volume, mass, number of grains atop each other, the ratio of the height of the collection to its width, or some other criterion or set of criteria. There *is no* unary heap in physical reality subsisting independently of rational mentality, only particles occupying certain positions in space-time that are relatively close to other particles like themselves. As the collection diminishes piece by piece during an extended period of time in the sorites fashion, no answer to the question of the heap's cessation, in a world without appropriate standards, emerges, for there is no way to decide definitively that a heap exists. Unless there is some method of determining unity for things of a given sort, the quandary over the termination of those things will continue. If there is to be a rule, however, then it is up to rational agents to do the work of setting it. Where it is important enough to have conclusive answers, standards must be established. Such standards are arbitrary, of course, insofar as they are subjective; they could not be otherwise. They are based on decree, not discovery; but they are no more arbitrary than the ones that allow a person to say, truly or falsely, that a man is standing two yards from the wall or that the line at the end of this sentence is an inch long: _____.

At this juncture, I want to revisit the matter of multivalued logic systems. One perhaps would be inclined to say that no one ever can produce a line that is exactly an inch long. Humans can do no better than to approximate it, and those approximations are reflected in their assertions. Thus, drawing on the concepts that are inherent in multivalued logic systems, one may hold that sentences about the numerical values of the lengths of lines are neither true nor false *simpliciter*. Instead, they are nearly true or highly false; they are just barely true or not quite true or essentially false. With this pattern in mind, one may think that it is reasonable to hold that such variability applies to heaps and piles. A sentence declaring, for example, that there is a heap of dirt in the back yard or a pile of snow in the driveway may be somewhat true or completely false, according to the view.

There are two different senses of measurement at work here, one pertaining to the presence or absence of metrics and one pertaining to degrees of accuracy. The force of the sorites paradox hinges on there being no standard at all. One can count the number of grains in a collection with great care, assuming that grains can be identified as being such.[70] Yet, doing so will not deliver an answer to the question whether there are sufficient grains in the collection to equal or exceed the lower limit of a heap. A physical state of affairs without an associated benchmark with which it can be compared tells one nothing. In front of an observer may be a billion grains. Is this grouping a heap? If one cuts it in half, then is it still one? In the

---

[70] Grains themselves are made of particles and, in turn, are subject to the same paradox of gradual disintegration. The concept on which the presently unfolding solution to the paradox of the heap is based will apply equally well to the disassembly of a grain.

absence of a criterion, no matter how carefully a person measures, the boundary of a heap never can be found, even in principle. On the other hand, there is a conventional length for an inch. It may be beyond one's ability to measure it accurately to within an increment of extremely small magnitude, say, the radius of a proton, but this inability is imposed by a material world and practicality, not, in contradistinction to the alternative, by the absence of any criterion whatsoever. One can discover whether something is an inch long, and with acceptable precision, by testing its length against a standard. No such test can tell a person whether a heap lies before the eyes, as there is no standard at all for one. Herein is the difference.

If the assessment that I am offering is correct, then the borders of compound, inanimate, corporeal entities are determined by rational thought. Amalgamations do not exist as single objects in themselves; only the various bits that constitute them at any particular moment in time exist independently of the mind. Humans observe a material world—an objective, physical reality—but they provide the structure that binds the contents of that world into singularities. The mind imposes on matter the lines that demarcate units, as unified collectives, of a given sort. By the setting of rules, the understanding glues aggregates together, tracing the edges of things as objects to determine how far they extend in space and in time. It thereby fixes their ends, not in the sense that it annihilates matter but in the sense that it determines the conditions under which articles corresponding to a given sortal term cease to be. It is rationality that yields the unity that object-identity requires. The truth of statements about the identity of material things therefore depends not only on the conditions that obtain in reality but also on accepted conventions. One provides the raw material; the other provides the framework. Composite, nonliving, physical things *as singularities* have no being, no identity, apart from the mind. In saying so, I do not mean that one certain mind or another is necessary for object-identity but that such identity as a whole depends on the existence of rational thought. It is not that one is creating an entire set of corporeal entities out of thin air by thinking of it.[71] One is detecting an objective, real,

---

[71] Rational minds do play a part in the reality that humans experience, albeit in a different way. Beliefs are part of the mental landscape, and beliefs, coupled with words, can have tremendous efficacy.

physical cosmos by means of perception, but dividing it by means of intellection. In stark contrast to a strange theory that will come to light later, one is not generating reality, only deciding how to slice it.

Imagine a universe in which no mind exists. In such a universe, there are bits of material with different chemical compositions, and some of these granules lie next to others like themselves. Matter exists with or without humans. Pieces of a substance may remain in close proximity because of physical forces, and like components may stick together because of chemical cohesion. The forces of nature explain why basic parts coalesce to form collectives, but they can explain neither how those collectives yield discrete, monadic entities at a given moment in time nor how those monadic entities achieve persistence across many moments. Things as clustered particles are held together by the properties of matter and the physics of particle interactions. Things as objects are held together by reason, for this kind of coalescence is beyond the capabilities of pure material substance and physical forces. The oneness of objects is there not because of nature but because of rationality. Even though objects are formed out of matter, they are not physical things. They are *conceptual* things.

The upshot is important. A pair of factors must come into play for there to be intrinsic change in the world of things: (1) a shift in the properties or parts that make up a certain material collective and (2) the mind to give that collective unity. Without the former element, there is *no change in an object*; without the latter element, there is *no object to change*. I noted earlier that there are two fundamental facts, a lack of understanding of which contributes to the mistaken belief that intrinsic change is not possible. Where change involves properties, the ambiguity of the concept of sameness surfaces to obscure the truth by blurring the distinction between the two senses of it. Where change involves parts, the reliance on materiality as the guarantor of object-sameness leads to the same mistaken belief. The reason that it is mistaken is now clear. Here then is the second fundamental fact: The bonding that is required for material aggregates to be objects does not lie within those aggregates. To look inside them in a search for an understanding of identity is to look in the wrong place, for the unity of composite, inanimate things does not come from *within* but from *without*.

Enduring objects are wholly present, not because all their physical parts are stuck together, as those who have been misled by Lewis's remarks think. Enduring objects are wholly present because they are singularities. Changes by themselves therefore lack the efficacy to destroy an object because the limits of a physical thing's endurance as a single entity are fixed apart from the substance that composes it.

Merricks is right to recognize that persons cause things that their collections of atoms do not cause, but he seeks to eliminate other aggregate objects based on the belief that the atoms of those things do all the causal work. Unger questions, with some insight, the vagueness of terms that refer to objects that have parts, for those parts can be removed one at a time, but he gives up too quickly and rejects the existence of common objects altogether. Both positions are deficient. Perhaps, in an unexpected way, Berkeley is nearly on the mark in his theory: Without the mind, objects do not exist—just not in the way or for the reason that he thinks. Berkeley holds that things are not material; they have no being aside from a mind that senses them, as their essence lies in their being perceived. The truth is that objects are material and that matter does exist independently of its being perceived, at least by human minds. The materiality of things is governed by physical laws apart from personal perceptions. The oneness of nonsentient, macrophysical objects, though, because they are collectives, is governed by thought. Their individuality as persistent entities lies in their being conceived as singularities. The critical factor in an ontology of objects is not *perception* but *conception*. In the end, it is mind that generates one out of many.

AGAINST CONVENTION

Before the discussion concludes, it is worth considering two views that are at odds with a convention-based delineation of enduring objects, contrary to the position that I have championed in this chapter. In his attempt to uphold four-dimensionalism, Mark Heller argues that the putative objects of everyday life, such as tables and chairs, are not truly objects, strictly considered, for the supposed conditions of their persistence—as well as their alleged essential properties—rest on convention; and, where convention is the basis for boundaries, there is no genuine entity. Heller equates objects instead with hunks of material. He states,

> This text is devoted to developing an ontology of four-dimensional hunks of matter. I argue that every filled region of spacetime is exactly filled by one such object.[72]

Indeed, whatever matter lies in such a region *is* that object: "A four-dimensional object is the material content of a filled region of spacetime."[73] Rather than embrace the setting of object boundaries by means of standards, Heller looks for them in physical substance itself. He believes that matter offers the needed precision: The margins that mark intervals of time mark ipso facto the limits of existence for objects along the temporal dimension. Claims Heller,

> The temporal boundaries of *four*-dimensional hunks are not selected by us. Every pair of times forms the temporal boundaries of whatever hunks of matter exactly fill that temporal interval. A given four-dimensional object goes out of existence at the time that it does because the object's boundaries are its defining characteristics. The material content of either a temporally larger or temporally smaller region of spacetime is, by definition, a different four-dimensional hunk of matter.[74]

Each different lump of material in space-time is a different object, and each part of an object is one as well: "A spatiotemporal part, as long as it has greater than zero extent along every dimension, is itself a four-dimensional object."[75]

On the surface, Heller's approach may seem to offer an appealing solution to the problem of beginnings and endings, despite the other problems that four-dimensionalism faces, which I have detailed in the foregoing pages. Its drawbacks are revealed, though,

---

[72] Heller, *Ontology of Physical Objects*, ix.
[73] Ibid., 10.
[74] Ibid., 53.
[75] Ibid., 11.

with regard to the spatial aspect. One must ask what Heller has in mind in saying that objects are hunks that fill space. The only things that fill space in a literal sense, as he recognizes, are subatomic bits. Even atoms consist of extensive, empty expanses, speaking in relative terms. There are great gaps between their nuclei and the electrons surrounding those nuclei in orbital clouds, and between the electrons in one shell and those in others. Heller thinks, so it appears, that one can view atoms as disjointed objects because an empty area

> does not contain an object nor any part of an object. So, for instance, if there really is empty space between the parts of an atom, then atoms are really scattered objects, since the region of space that an atom exactly fills at any given time is not connected. Similarly, those everyday objects around us that are composed of atoms are also, on the present hypothesis, scattered objects.[76]

Given his hunk ontology, the criterion of individuation for spatiotemporal things rests on the presence of matter. It is difficult to see what justification Heller could have for allowing bits of disconnected matter to be objects, whether atoms or things that are made of them. At any rate, on the supposition that dispersal does not preclude the presence of objects, the universe, scattered across the vastness of space, surely must be counted as one. For Heller, parts of objects are also objects. It follows that there are as many objects in existence, at any given time, as there are elementary particles in the universe. Further, because any set of two or more particles, separated by a space, also must be an object—if for no other reason than that the grouped bits form part of the cosmos, scattered as it is—every one of those sets is an object that must be included in the list. Contemporary estimates place the number of atoms in observable physical reality at approximately 10^{80}, within a few orders of magnitude; the quantity of particles is thus greater. The number of sets that can be formed as combinations of any detached two particles, any detached three, any detached four, and so forth is almost incomprehensible.

It does not end there. One must multiply the result by the number of temporal segments in history—every different pair of

---

[76] Ibid., 7.

times marks the temporal boundaries of a material object, thinks Heller—plus all the incremental supersets of those segments. The consequence is something that no one could embrace. It constitutes a radical violation of the law of parsimony, and the fact that matter is in constant motion seems to exacerbate the problem.

The upshot of Heller's ontology is therefore unacceptable. There are so many objects that the term 'object' loses all meaning. If one endeavors to remedy this unpalatable outcome by saying that matter must be compacted to a specific extent in a particular region of space for there to be a scattered object in that place—x particles per cubic meter—then one would be compelled to *declare* what density is adequate for object-existence: to pronounce the value of x. In this case, however, objects are conventional after all, which is what I have argued in this chapter.

A more interesting line of reasoning against conventional objects is put forth by another author. Tobias Hansson Wahlberg claims that, although persistence as a matter of convention is not problematic in the sense of assigning meanings to relevant terms, persistence never can be a matter of convention in the sense of determining physical reality to be a certain way by virtue of applying those terms. No theory of the temporal continuity of objects, whether a theory of three-dimensionalism or of four-dimensionalism, is exempt from this restriction, so he claims. Consider briefly a series of arguments that Wahlberg raises in opposition to convention-based continuance. There are six objections.[77] To set the stage for his objections, Wahlberg supposes that an object a exists *at one time* and that an object b exists *at another*—assume that it is later—and he uses the equal sign to signify their numerical identity.

His first pair of objections raises questions about the capabilities that are associated with declaratory occurrences. If persistence could be established by convention in the more substantial sense, then one would be imputing to humankind some strange power to alter reality by legislating, at a distance, that $a = b$. Furthermore, this power would involve reverse causality. Where the declaration that $a = b$ is issued after the time of the appearance of the latter of the two

---

[77] See Tobias Hansson Wahlberg, "Can Persistence Be a Matter of Convention?" *Axiomathes* 21, no. 4 (2011): 507–29.

objects, the effect of the declaration that brings about the identity would predate its announcement. Reverse causality, however, is a highly doubtful phenomenon.

A third objection claims that, given the two objects a and b, if it is by convention that $a = b$, then the predicate 'is conventionally identical to a' is applied truly to b. By Leibniz's law, on the premise that $a = b$, what is true of b is true of a. It follows that the predicate 'is conventionally identical to a' is applied truly to a. It cannot be the case that $a = a$ by convention, however, for a thing is identical to itself independently of any declaration.

Another objection asserts that, if persistence is a matter of convention in the stronger sense of determining reality, then things could stand in a contradictory state simply by a decision to issue a pronouncement. One decision would force the identity of a and b; another would force their nonidentity.

The last pair of objections focuses on the unconditional character of the identity relation. In his first argument of the pair, Wahlberg contends that identity is a relation that holds necessarily, such that, if $a = b$, then a statement asserting that $a = b$ is a necessary truth, which is to say that it is not logically possible for it to be false. This necessity of identity is based on the assumption that the terms that denote a and b are rigid designators—expressions that name the same thing in all possible worlds. The concept of rigid designation is traced to Saul Kripke.[78] The term 'possible world' in a philosophical context refers to a comprehensive set of envisaged circumstances, especially as the set is described by various propositions that purport to express facts about it. There is a possible world in which, say, George Washington was the third president of the United States, not the first, and attained a military rank of colonel but never general. In using a name, thinks Kripke, one is referring to a particular entity, and *that entity* is the same individual object—the same person in the example here—regardless of what the circumstances may be, even if one learns that George Washington's real name was 'Chad Jackson'. On the premise that identity is conventional, argues Wahlberg, whether $a = b$ is something that is determined by decision because,

---

[78] For the primary explanation of a rigid designator, see Saul Kripke, *Naming and Necessity* (Cambridge: Harvard University Press, 1980), 48.

by hypothesis, it is a matter of proclamation. Suppose that it is so decided in the case of a and b. It follows from the necessity of identity that it could not have been decided that $a \neq b$, but this limitation contradicts the notion that identity is a matter of choice.

The final argument asserts that, if identity is determined by convention, then it is determined by something that is outside the things that are identical; specifically, it is determined by those who set the conventions. External relations are contingent, however, not necessary; that is to say, it is logically possible for them not to hold where they, as a matter of fact, do hold. The identity relation, on the other hand, is necessary: The relation follows from the things that are related by it irrespective of outside factors. It is therefore an internal relation, not an external one. Whether $a = b$ therefore cannot be a matter of convention.

None of these objections is effective against the theory that I have advanced. In matters where one is required to be precise, standards must be established before statements about persistence are amenable to the affixing of truth-values. Wahlberg's first two objections assert that conventions in the stronger sense must hold power over nature, given a notion that persistence is determined by persons. This reasoning is incorrect. Persons set standards by means of declaration, but those standards are merely tools by which persons measure nature. A pressed-together collection of dirt that is put into a bucket of water or a mass of pushed-together sand that is being blown away a grain at a time by the wind will be a clod or a heap respectively, and each will persist as a singular object, only if people define the corresponding limit. Measuring a rug with a ruler does not *make* the rug nine feet long, but it is true that it *is* nine feet long because the people of a society *decide* how long a foot is. When an inanimate object qua object terminates is likewise up to them because that of which they are declaring termination is not the material substance but the collective as a unary thing, and that unary thing is identical to itself until it terminates. The material lies in nature independently of any convention; the object that it forms, however, if it forms one at all, does not so lie.

The third objection conflates identity *through time* and identity *at a time*. As I have argued at length, the numerical identity of objects that exist at distinct moments is not based on the possession of identical sets of properties and parts, nor are propositions that are true of the later member of an identical pair of entities always true of the earlier member, and conversely. To support what he contends, Wahlberg turns to Leibniz's law. One will recall that this law—the identity of indiscernibles—holds that, if two things have all qualities in common, then they cannot be different things; they are identical. This principle is not relevant to his argument, however, as his objection relies on the alternative notion that, if two things are identical, then they must share all qualities. What is true of one must be true of the other. It is the flip-side of Leibniz's law, as the law typically is stated, that is related to his case: the indiscernibility of identicals. To be fair, I want to note that he apparently intends to refer to the latter principle; certain authors think that the law concerns it rather than its counterpart, or covers both tenets in an inclusive formulation (cf. page 203, n. 91). Ambiguity seems to be at work here. In any event, the argument fails. If identity through time were constrained by the same requirement that pertains to identity at a time, then nothing would retain its identity from one moment to another if it changed at all. Tom is six feet tall today, but he was an inch shorter a year ago, as he is still a developing teen. Using Wahlberg's terminology, let a stand for Tom a year ago and b stand for Tom now. The predicate 'is taller than a' is applied truly to b, but it cannot be applied truly to a, even though a is numerically identical to b. Tom has persisted, and something is true of him now that was not true last year. A predicate need not apply in the same way to a persistent thing at distinct times.

Numerical identity at a time, however, *is* based on possessing identical sets of properties and parts, and propositions that are true of one member of an identical pair of objects, at a given moment, are always true of the other member at the same moment. If it were not so, then, contrary to the indiscernibility of identicals, it would be possible for an object to be identical to itself yet exist in a contradictory state, both having, and not having, a certain property at a particular instant, which is illogical. The relevance of both Leibniz's law and its complement is limited to things at the same moment. By the very conditions that Wahlberg sets forth in his series of arguments, the objects in question exist at separate times. Persistent identity does not require indiscernibility. The boulder that is perched on the cliff now is the same one that was there last year, even though erosion has decreased its diameter by two millimeters. Identity at an instant, on the other hand, does require indiscernibility.

Here is the heart of the matter. As Wahlberg sees, everything is identical to itself. On this basis, he argues that it is incorrect to hold that $a = a$ by virtue of convention, as self-identity is independent of societal declarations. Composite, inanimate objects qua objects exist, however, only if conventions establish the criteria for their inclusion in a set of things to which a sortal term is applied. In the absence of rules, the seeming identifiers 'a' and 'b' are nonreferring terms: They give the appearance of pointing to things in reality, but they do not point to anything at all. In this case, neither '$a = b$' nor '$a = a$' is true; rather, both expressions are meaningless. Thus, a is indeed conventionally identical to b, *and* to a, not in the sense that edicts hold sway over the logic of the identity relation but in the sense that there is no identity of either a or b without the rules (cf. page 434, n. 30).

The fourth objection misses the mark altogether. If there is no agreement, then there is no convention. It is not as though half the observers declare that a foot is the length of the Brooklyn Bridge and half declare that it is the diameter of a vinyl album. Without the standard, there almost assuredly will be disagreement, but it is illogical to think that such disagreement creates an inconsistent state of existence. The discrepancy is in the defining of the term, not in the employing of it, and, once the metric is fixed by convention, there is no discrepancy at all; and such is the case with persistence.

The last two objections seek to eliminate conventional identity just by assumption. In presupposing that the names of a and b—that is to say, 'a' and 'b'—are Kripkean rigid designators, Wahlberg's first argument of the pair falls short in its portrayal; Kripke claims,

> If 'a' and 'b' are rigid designators, it follows that '$a = b$', if true, is a necessary truth. If 'a' and 'b' are *not* rigid designators, no such conclusion follows about the *statement* '$a = b$' (though the *objects* designated by 'a' and 'b' will be necessarily identical).[79]

Identity may be maintained under varying designations, but it is certainly not the case that it is maintained invariably and with

---

[79] Ibid., 3. Wahlberg refers to nonrigid designators later but assumes rigidity here.

necessity under those designations, for the circumstances could have been otherwise than they are. Roger is the tallest individual ever to be born in Wales, according to records. Many there refer to him by the nickname 'Mr. Max-Height of Wales', strictly because of his stature. In using the tag, people mean to characterize him as the tallest native of the country. Had he not been so, he would not have been given this nickname. Roger is also the only person ever to be born with three thumbs on his left hand, as reported in public documents. Some refer to him warmly by the identifier 'Mr. Most-Thumbs', strictly because of his deformity. In using the label, people mean to characterize him as the human being possessing the greatest number of thumbs in history. Again, had he not been so endowed, he would not have been given this nickname. It is not necessary that the tallest native of Wales is the only person to be born with three thumbs on his left hand, and it is not necessary that either of these persons is Roger, even though they are, in fact, he. It is a contingent matter that these unique, descriptive nicknames apply to the same man. Someone else *could have* been born in Wales who is taller than Roger, and yet another person, instead of Roger, *could have* been born who has more thumbs than he. In that case, the appellations that are applied to Roger would have been applied to another person or to other people. Considered in light of their floating applicability, the tags are not rigid, although the person to whom they apply as a matter of fact—namely, Roger—is identical to himself. That two things are identical under the same context-appropriate appellation or description is, *ceteris paribus*, both necessary and independent of external factors. That two things are identical under different appellations or different descriptions may be both contingent and dependent on factors that are external to the objects.

Consider now a heap. Given conditional identity, there is no heap in existence unless there is a firm standard. Let the standard of a heap be some set S of criteria, say, at least 1,400,600,000 grains of a substance—wheat or some other material—in an area, such that each grain is in contact with at least one other grain of the same sort of substance. Once the standard is set, a heap is before an observer where those definitive conditions are met. Suppose that a heap actually lay there yesterday, which was Friday, and suppose further that one also lies there today. Like all objects, a heap persists until it

357

terminates. Let yesterday's heap be heap$_{fri}$ and today's heap be heap$_{sat}$. Heap$_{fri}$ contained 1,400,600,220 grains of wheat; heap$_{sat}$ contains 220 fewer grains because a mouse feasted on the wheat at the base overnight. Nothing else about the heap changed. One can assert truthfully the proposition that heap$_{fri}$ is numerically identical to heap$_{sat}$ because the two objects, which are designated by the corresponding heap-terms are, in fact, numerically identical objects at different times. The proposition is not a necessary truth, however; the identity on which the proposition rests is assured only on the condition that S is established and that the criteria that it sets forth are met. The names 'heap$_{fri}$' and 'heap$_{sat}$' are not rigid designators, for S *could have* been different. For 'heap$_{fri}$' and 'heap$_{sat}$' to be meaningful terms, they must pick out specific objects in the world, but objects *as* objects—singular entities—require conditions of existence *as* objects, and the identity of those things therefore depends on those conditions. By assuming that the names of a and b are rigid designators, Wahlberg's fifth objection begs the question. A designation can be rigid only if external factors play no crucial referential role—no part in determining objects as such and accordingly when they are the same—and this issue is the very one in contention. If specified conditions fix the identity of inanimate, material aggregates as unary things, then they do not do so with necessity, and they are not unalterable. They are outside the things to which they apply.

Wahlberg's final case relies on the putative necessity of the identity relation, as presented in his previous argument, to support the premise that the relation is internal—a notion that is again traceable to Kripke.[80] What is missed, however, is that time itself is a relational factor that is *external* to the objects that are said to be identical, and time is a critical element of Wahlberg's declaration that $a = b$. Wahlberg's case is precisely that of objects that exist at different times. Persistence is not the same as strict equivalence; identity *through time* does not fall under the same rules as identity *at a time*, a concept that this chapter has supported in detail. By definition, persistence introduces the temporal aspect.

An analogy in which different places rather than different times are in view may serve to clarify the matter. When one says that

---

[80] Ibid., 3–4.

County Road 225 = State Route 14 along this stretch, one is not saying that the identity relation holding between the two roads is necessary and internal: The two roads diverge a few miles from this location. One heads north toward Maple City; the other bears west toward Heartsong Village. County Road 225 = State Route 14 only in a certain place. The material in the world that the names of the two roads denote is exactly the same in every respect, but only here, along this section of asphalt. The identity relation holds with restrictions in this case. It holds just where the roads come together on the segment *here*, and the modifier 'here' introduces an external factor.[81] Wahlberg's employment of properties of the identity relation in his concluding two arguments against a convention-based portrayal of persistence closely aligns them, and the two arguments appear to go down together.

Kripke's analysis provides the basis for Wahlberg's rigid-designator objection, but it also provides the basis for its undoing. As for Kripke himself, he goes on to claim, as the earlier quotation reflects, that, where terms designate objects that are identical, those objects themselves are necessarily identical, even if the terms that designate them are not rigid. Is he right? Care must be exercised in speaking of the term that is used to denote an object. The being of a person, or even a living, nonhuman organism, does not depend on circumstances, regardless of what the circumstances are. The Roman statesman Cicero is the individual Tully. The corresponding names are rigid designators, and the persons whom the names designate are necessarily the same person in reality, regardless of what else was happening in the world during the second and first centuries B.C., where the man was day by day, what he was doing daily, and what

---

[81] One will recall the example that I used earlier in defending endurantism against Lewis's argument from temporary intrinsics. Lewis claims that things have properties *simpliciter* but that endurantism precludes their doing so. A reference to time must be included in assigning properties to things under endurance theory, he thinks. Perdurantism, however, is open to the other side of the coin. A reference to location must be included in assigning properties to things under perdurance theory. A man who is bent is not bent *simpliciter* but only with reference to a place on his body. Similarly, in the discussion of the identity relation as it is represented in Wahlberg's objection, it is clear that an external factor must be incorporated to portray persistence, even apart from convention, because persistence entails a temporal element. Persistent identity is not identity in absolute isolation.

day of the week it was. The intrinsic personhood—the inherent identity—of an individual in the world is not affected by conditions that are external to the person. Although they might have had an effect on his mood, his health, or his weight, conditions could not have altered who Cicero was during his lifetime. Kripke's claim is true for persons.[82] Person-identity, however, is not object-identity, and person-identity through time is not object-identity through time; so, one must ask whether Kripke's principle is universal. Suppose that the standard of a heap were set at 1,400,600,100 grains rather than 1,400,600,000. The expression 'heap$_{sat}$', in that case, would be a nonreferring term because the collection falls below the adjusted grain-count requirement for a heap. It follows that the proposition 'heap$_{fri}$ = heap$_{sat}$' would be neither true nor false; it would be meaningless. The truth of the statement of equivalence depends on the terms' being designators, whether rigid or otherwise, for specific objects; their designating depends, in turn, on the existence of objects to which they refer; and there being objects *as* objects depends ultimately on established standards that determine the conditions of existence for entities of a given sort—not as mere assemblages of material particles but as units.

Composite, inanimate things that exist at different times and that are identical are not identical of necessity, for objects qua objects are not simply the raw assemblages of physical particles that compose them. If they were just those sets, then the identity would be logically necessary, and Kripke would be right; but alas persistence through a change in parts would evaporate. As it is, suitable rules must be established for their existence and accordingly their persistence. The material that makes up compound objects is there, with or without minds, but not the objects. If the conventional rules

---

[82] It is important not to assume that personhood is tied to materiality, such that the body of Cicero the person must have been exactly the same material body as the one that existed and to which his contemporaries referred in using his name. If who Cicero is as a person is independent of his physical being, then he could have existed as the same individual but existed with a different physical realization. This complication is not germane to the points here about rigidity of designators. Once Cicero came to be, it was that body that was tied to him, and this condition remained constant throughout his lifetime. I mention the matter because the notion will be a critical part of a discussion later in this work regarding what does constitute the identity of persons.

are missing, then the objects are missing as well; the consequence is that there are no objects to which the identity relation can be ascribed with meaning, let alone with truth. Those rules could have been different from what they are. Thus, Kripke's claim, if it is correct for objects, is correct only in a limited sense: The purported necessity of the identity of identical items follows from the fixing of the conditions under which aggregate, inanimate items of a given sort *exist*—and accordingly *persist*—although the conditions themselves are not a matter of necessity.

It is not unusual for roads to overlap in places. So, does one say that County Road 225 is State Route 14 and that County Road 225 is not State Route 14? Everything is identical to itself, regardless of what one calls it, but the necessity of equivalence is subject to restrictions. If it is the physical pavement to which a person refers by the names of the two roads, then there is a contradiction, unless the strips of pavement are distinguished with a reference to location; in that case, however, an external factor is involved, so the relation is not strictly internal. If it is not the physical pavement to which a person refers, then there is still a contradiction without a reference to location. Aside from this fact, though, if the names do not designate the material substance of which the roads are made, then what else could they designate except conceptual constructs that employ external factors by virtue of conventions? I will leave the matter for one to ponder further.

CONCLUSION

The problem of identity through change is a specious puzzle. Change is not the threat to objects that some philosophical systems have proposed, for it is incidental to the continuance of an object along the course of its existence. The right question to pose concerns what makes the object the same through *time* rather than what makes it the same through *change*. When alteration affects the properties that anything possesses, confusion arises because of the failure to distinguish between numerical and qualitative identity. In saying that the model airplane that lies crumpled in the field is the same one that Timmy and his father built last month in their garage, what one means is that the shattered device that is in front of Timmy and the one that he and his father constructed several weeks ago have a common history. The fact that the machine's properties have changed markedly during the last hour as it took flight on its maiden voyage is no threat to its uniqueness. Numerical identity at a time entails qualitative identity at that time, but numerical identity through time certainly does not entail qualitative identity through time.

The more difficult problem arises over the reputed degeneration of objects through a modification of their material makeup. I have shown that matter is not what holds the objects in the world together and, paralleling the point, not what determines their identity. If it were so, then neither a loss of it nor a gain would be possible without undermining their integrity. Such is not the case. Two things can be the same, even if their material composition is different, and two things can be different, even if their material composition is the same. For this reason, changing the constituents of an object, even all at once, is not, apart from other dynamics, adequate to destroy it, for an object is not just a collection of parts.

The aim of the analysis in this chapter has been to demonstrate that knowledge of the items that populate the world is not prohibited by the fluidity that characterizes them. Change presents no insurmountable hurdle to knowing, as the locking that allows humans to know things is not accomplished through quiescence but through ontological encapsulation—more literally, unification. Although properties and parts do vary, things persist because of unity. I have maintained that persistence is in accordance with a three-dimensional account of continuance, not a four-dimensional one. The principal matter, in actuality, however, is not *how* things persist but the fact that they *do* persist because, if things continue through time, then knowledge cannot be dismissed on the basis of a fragmented reality. The problem of knowledge no longer can stand on the assumed metaphysical fracturing of objects as a result of change to make its case. Fluctuation per se of neither properties nor parts is sufficient to undermine identity.

When it is important enough, people establish benchmarks to provide common ground in determining the presence or absence of various sorts of objects; and accordingly the persistence of those objects depends on the conditions that those benchmarks set forth. Whatever continues must do so as the *same* thing from its inception to its demise. This concept is precisely that of temporally extended numerical identity. Comprehending the continuance of nonliving, physical things that make up the world and that people can see, hear, and touch comes through an understanding that, viewed in an inclusive way, what an object is, is what it was; or, more accurately, what it is, is what it has been being all along. To know a thing in the sense of grasping its identity across a temporal span is to understand at least some part of its history—to know what is true of it at times other than the present moment. It is just that the rational mind fixes the limits of its existence as *that* object—one thing, individual and unary—even as the constitution of the aggregate of material particles that form its physical being shifts. The mind brings together, into a single entity, the spatially spread, physical pieces that compose the object and the temporally spread moments that reflect its unique history.

The duration of an object and its susceptibility to change are represented by Figure 3.22. Its existence begins at t_1; its origination corresponds to the sequential pair of moments t_0 and t_1. At each successive moment after it comes into being and before it ceases to be, either it exhibits a change, vis-à-vis the previous moment, or it does not exhibit one. The moment t_n marks the last instant of its existence, and it terminates from t_n to t_{n+1}.

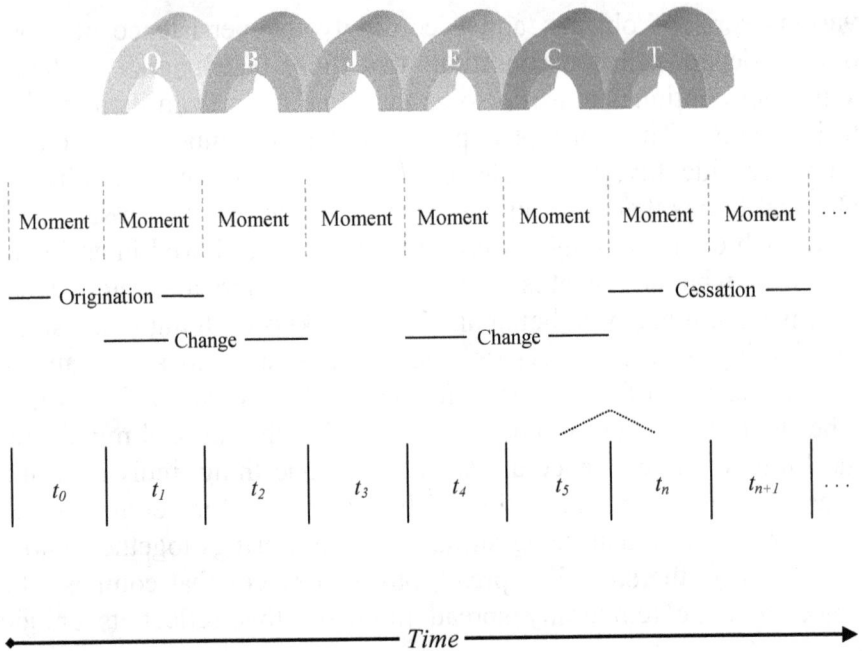

Figure 3.22

In this chapter, the challenge has been to direct the gaze outward to the universe of things to see whether one may be able to comprehend those things in the face of unremitting flux and, if so, then to determine what accounts for the persistence that makes grasping them possible. This study has brought to light some interesting aspects of identity and the role that rationality plays in marking the bounds of physical objects. Still, it is unsettling to think that the very existence of some things as units depends on the mind. It seems that there is more to the matter when one looks at the world of creatures and in particular humans. Living beings exhibit a certain autonomy that is absent in the collections of particles that constitute nonliving objects. Barring the anomalous, the end of life of an organism, in contrast to the end of a clod or a stone, is not set by convention; it is observed—if it is known by people at all.

Consider the common freshwater creature *Amoeba proteus*. It is a self-contained, single-cell entity that is composed of interdependent parts that operate together in such a way that the parts support the functioning of the entity as a whole, sustaining it and continuing its kind. It moves through its environment, takes in food, protects itself from harm, and reproduces. Until the discovery of unicellular organisms by Anton van Leeuwenhoek in the seventeenth century, no one had knowledge of such things. Their being is not contingent on the presence of humans at all, and neither are the moments that mark their beginnings and their endings as living entities. These microscopic creatures continue entirely independently of anyone's cognizance of them. Even if there were no human mind to conceive of its being, the life span of any given amoeba would be the same. In a remote wetland, it comes to be, lives, changes, and divides or dies, all unknown to any person. That lack of awareness has no bearing on the period of its existence. One wants to understand how it is that things that are alive hold together where no person knows of them. Unicellular organisms have no minds, even more assuredly no intelligent minds, and plants are certainly without rational thought. Yet, trees, for example, take in materials, create food for themselves through photosynthesis, grow, seal wounds, extend their roots toward water, and even reproduce. Living organisms clearly seem to have an identity apart from human awareness. They are active systems rather than passive masses—Locke is following the right intuition here. If the oneness that characterizes life does not come from persons, though, then what is its source? How is one to account for it? Why are the criteria of identity different for biological entities?

I will take up these questions at the appropriate time. There is much work to do first. In sensory events, it is not only the perceived *objects* that play a part but the perceiving *subjects* as well, and the problem of knowledge is not only about how *things* can be known but also about how *persons* can know them. What remains to be shown is that the imperfect character of the subjects is not a barrier to their knowing.

I would like to begin to look inward now at those subjects to see whether it is possible to learn anything about what it is for them to know. Surely, any proper analysis of the matter must include an examination of beliefs, for it is they that serve as the crucial link between the perception of things and the knowledge of them. If the analysis is successful, then chapter 5 can proceed on a firmer footing, focusing on the essential characteristics of the existents that are perceiving and knowing—namely, persons. Perhaps the investigation will lead to even more important discoveries.

CHAPTER 4

A CERTAIN FRAME OF MIND

Every prudent man acts out of knowledge.

—Prov. 13:16 NIV

There was no doubt that it was going to be a fascinating vacation. Our family packed the car with all the necessities and headed for the Great Smoky Mountains National Park. What awaited us did not disappoint us. There were winding two-lane roads through the highlands and the unmatched scenery of America in the middle of the last century. Cold cherry cider at a roadside establishment accompanied a welcomed pause in the travel, while local articles piqued the curiosity. A swinging footbridge in the area spanned a rushing creek some distance below, where the stones were worn so round and smooth that they looked more like artifacts than objects belonging to the natural world. That bridge lived up to its name. Holding onto the ropes for dear life, we crossed its considerable length with a considerable amount of uneasiness.

My father bought a leather bullwhip for me at some point during the excursion, and I fancied myself to be some sort of woodsman as I learned to make the characteristic cracking sound. The firsthand discovery of its ability to inflict pain was inevitable, I suppose. My most aggressive, overhead maneuver—performing it without the requisite care on one occasion—put a mark on my neck that persisted for a number of weeks. The fond recollections of the time far outweighed this disturbing one, however. It was the best that Appalachia had to offer to a boy of my age. My love of the mountains never left me, and trips to the Blue Ridge Parkway in the years that followed carried with them that same element of wonder.

The most memorable incident for me on that trip, however, came at a remote country store along the way. After stopping for refreshments, we spotted a black bear on the wooded hillside across the road, eighty yards or so in the distance. The bear was far enough from us to pose little threat, so we left the car and went into the store. My father informed the proprietor that we had noticed the animal, and, to our surprise, the man was not surprised at all. The bear is especially fond of chocolate sodas, he told my father. Buy one and remove the cap, get in the car, lower the window, and let him see the soft drink, the man suggested; he will come and take it. Caution was not a factor to be considered, from my perspective; I just *had* to see such a thing. I do not recall how much persuasion it took to convince my father of the value of this extraordinary opportunity, but he always had been somewhat adventurous anyway, so only a little prompting probably was needed. He bought the soda.

As I returned to the car with great expectations, my level of excitement was off the scale. My father did as he was instructed; he lowered the window and, holding the treat securely, extended his arm toward the bear. As soon as the animal saw that bottle of cold, sweet, chocolate soda, he headed straight for the car—no doubt, with great expectations too. When he reached us, he grabbed the drink with both paws. Palms gripping it tightly, he plopped on his rear end with such force that the jolt caused his fat body to ripple like an oversized serving of gelatin. Placing the mouth of the bottle in his own mouth and tilting the bottle skyward, the bear gulped that soda in a record-setting, nonstop feat, and it all was over in a matter of seconds. Then, he looked at my father, and I knew what he wanted—he wanted another one. All this action was just too thrilling to let it end. Oh, we must do it again, my excitement told me, and I pleaded with my father to get him a second soda. Understandably, with the bear just outside the vehicle, paternal prudence prevailed, despite my father's adventurous streak, and we left. I suspect that the owner of that store made a decent living by selling those chocolate drinks. The bear undoubtedly did not fare too poorly either.

Years later, during a summer of my high-school days, our family took another vacation to the mountains; this time, though, it was to the Rockies. My sister had completed a session in Colorado as part of an academic program, and my parents and I journeyed to the state to meet her and to bring her home for a few weeks. Having been enamored of the highlands of Appalachia since childhood, I was destined to find my first trip to the towering Rockies to be unforgettable. The terrain was indeed riveting, with a certain allure about it that captured my thoughts. It was an exciting time. It was also August and hot. The cooler air at higher elevation, however, was about to take the edge off the heat. Touring the territory near Colorado Springs, we could see Pikes Peak in the distance. It was our outing, so we decided to divert our course and ascend that mountain. As we went up, the temperature went down. At the outset of that diversion, the day was sweltering, but, when we arrived at the destination and stopped the car, the temperature had plummeted to the freezing zone. Standing there in my casual shorts, I stared at the snow around me. I was aware of the relationship between altitude and temperature, but such a dramatic change in mere minutes left an impression on me that lasted well past the inexperience of my youth.

Something even more fascinating than Pikes Peak lay ahead of us. During the trip, we visited several states in the region, enjoying the varied scenery. One day, as we traveled along a remote highway in Utah, our vehicle seemed to develop a problem. My father noticed that its forward movement was inhibited, as though the brakes were engaged, despite the perceptibly downhill route. We were far from any place to have the car inspected, so the only practical option was to press onward. Mile after mile, the car dragged. Finally, we spotted a service station and stopped for assistance.

My father explained the problem, hoping that it could be corrected. After all, home was quite a distance from there. Curiously, the gentleman at the station asked from which direction we had come. My father responded, noting our course. It was astounding, even bizarre, to learn that we had been traveling *uphill* for miles, not *downhill*, as had seemed to be beyond question. I suspect that my father received the news with a bit of disbelief, but the attendant convinced him when he said that people regularly stop at the station to express the same concern. It was the perspective. The topography of the land, the horizon, and the highway—together they imparted a sense that the road led downward. What that perspective conveyed was convincing, but it was wrong. It skewed the frame of reference, distorting the perceptions and resultant beliefs.

Earlier in this work, one saw how the problem of knowledge presented itself as a twofold challenge. The previous chapter examined the object side of the puzzle. In this chapter, I will focus on the subject side; in particular, I will examine beliefs. The main purpose is to understand the principal role that they play in knowledge and ultimately in people's lives, and to see why that role is so important. It is by means of the senses that people commonly come to hold beliefs about the world; so, if one is to have knowledge, then one's perceptions must give rise to beliefs that are true and are grounded satisfactorily. If those perceptions lead one astray, as in the family trek through Utah, then one cannot know. Must beliefs be certain, however, for there to be knowledge; must they be infallible? If so, then what makes them immune to error?

Besides their link to knowledge, beliefs are associated with actions, and in a special way. Coupled with values, they position one for decisions and, in accordance with those decisions, the purposeful deeds that result. They help to form the frame of reference out of which one acts. In the abovementioned narrative regarding our excursion, my father's stopping the car was based on his belief that the brakes were malfunctioning, which, in turn, was linked to his belief that the vehicle was traveling downhill. He valued our safety, so he did what any responsible husband and parent would do: He pulled aside when the appropriate opportunity presented itself. Given his concern for his family's welfare and what he believed at the time, one hardly could imagine that he would have done otherwise.

It is evident that both knowing and acting depend in some sense on believing. Understanding what beliefs are therefore seems to be a reasonable place to start the analysis. The character of their crucial dual role may emerge from the study with some clarity.

THE DISTINGUISHING MARK OF BELIEFS

One prominent theorist of the contemporary period is Gilbert Ryle, whom I introduced in chapter 1. Ryle's analysis of the mind and mental phenomena proved to be a turning point. (Note that, in philosophy, the concept of phenomena often includes psychological factors of experience, not just the sensory apprehensible.) I will look at Ryle's ideas in detail later. Here, Ryle presents his view of belief, which he treats as a tendency to carry out particular activities:

> Belief might be said to be like knowledge . . . in
> that it is 'propositional'; but this, though not far wrong,
> is too narrow. Certainly to believe that the ice is
> dangerously thin is to be unhesitant in telling oneself and
> others that it is thin, in acquiescing in other people's
> assertions to that effect, in objecting to statements to the
> contrary, in drawing consequences from the original
> proposition, and so forth. But it is also to be prone to
> skate warily, to shudder, to dwell in imagination on
> possible disasters and to warn other skaters. It is a
> *propensity* not only to make certain theoretical moves
> but also to make certain executive and imaginative
> moves, as well as to have certain feelings. But these
> things hang together on a common propositional hook.[1]

To believe something, according to Ryle, is to be inclined to behave in a certain way, to be prone to make particular moves under certain conditions. He construes beliefs in terms of hypothetical statements: what a person *would* do in specific circumstances. There is nothing else to them, no mental happenings, hidden beneath the surface, serving as causes of overt behavior. Beliefs are to be *identified* with propensities, which are manifested in physical conduct when the occasion is right.

It is true that what a person believes is linked to what the person does, or tends to do, but the relationship of being linked is not that of identity. There is more to believing than acting, or being disposed to act—and there is more to acting than believing. To say that a belief *is* the tendency to behave in a specific manner, that they are identical, is to omit an important part of what it means to believe; and phrasing it in terms of what an agent would do, or how a person would act under certain conditions, leads to strange consequences, to say the least.

Suppose that a man, who has lived at 1412 Main Street for the past twenty years, is injured in a serious automobile accident while returning home from work one evening. The paramedics arrive just

---

[1] Gilbert Ryle, *The Concept of Mind* (New York: Barnes and Noble Books, 1949), 134–35. The emphasis is mine. One should take care not to confuse the concept of dispositional beliefs with Ryle's depiction of beliefs overall as mere dispositions to act. His goal is to replace all subjective, mental goings-on with objective behavior.

in time to prevent his demise. He lies in an intensive care unit on life support, totally paralyzed because of the site of the severance of the spinal cord. The man is conscious but unable to move or to speak. He is incapable even of opening his eyes. His doctors say that his condition is permanent.

Does the man believe that his home address is 1412 Main Street? Yes, a behavioral theorist must say, because, if he *were* back to normal and *could* move, then he would provide the location of his residence when asked; he would go there, settle into his recliner, pet the dog, and turn to channel three to watch reruns of old Westerns. Regrettably, the man succumbs to his injuries a few hours later and expires in the hospital. Does the man still believe that his home address is 1412 Main Street? On the premise that beliefs are simply inclinations to act, it seems that he does so. What is to prevent one from saying now that, if he *were* back to normal and *could* move, then he would provide the location of his house when asked; he would go there, settle into his recliner, pet the dog, and turn to channel three to watch reruns of old Westerns?

If beliefs are certain propensities, and those propensities are given in hypothetical statements, then one must apply those statements uniformly to ferret out beliefs. There is no justifiable way to account for the difference between the two aforementioned states of affairs. One always can describe a set of conditions under which a person's behavior would exhibit a certain pattern. It will not work to argue that the deceased lack the tendencies that are to be called beliefs, to say that these tendencies cease when the person dies. The man on life support lacks the same tendencies. He no longer has the capacity to move his limbs, to utter words, or to blink. Yet, one has no hesitancy in saying that he believes that his house is on Main Street. Indeed, he knows where he lives and, no doubt, wishes that he could go there.

Dispositions are useful, of course, in helping one to assess what an individual does believe, for the actions mirror the person. By watching someone, particularly across an extended period of time, an observer generally can gain a sense of that person's take on things, seeing evidence of the values that form the person's character and the beliefs that the individual holds. One comes to understand what a person is on the inside, as it were, through observing the person on the outside: noting the individual's conduct. Consider the following words of Jesus Christ:

> For every tree is known by its own fruit. For *men* do not gather figs from thorns, nor do they gather grapes from a bramble bush. A good man out of the good treasure of his heart brings forth good; and an evil man out of the evil treasure of his heart brings forth evil. For out of the abundance of the heart his mouth speaks.[2]

Behavioral performances are the key indicators of the beliefs that a person has, and one's behavior aligns with corresponding propensities to act. One does not have to be acting currently, or even disposed to act currently, in accordance with a given propensity, however, for it to be true nevertheless that the person possesses a given belief, just as one need not be thinking about a proposition at the moment for it to be true that the person believes it. Beliefs can be occurrent, in that they are presently before the mind, but they need not be present for one to hold them. When asked in what year the American Civil War began, Johnny is thinking about the date at that very instant, but he still may believe that it began in 1861 while he is playing softball after school. The subject of history is far from his mind on the playground, though the conviction remains. It is dispositional at that juncture, not occurrent, but Johnny's holding the belief in that mode entails the continuation of his acceptance of the date as correct, not some behavioral proclivity.

In summary, although beliefs underlie propensities to perform in certain ways, it would be a mistake to conclude that beliefs are nothing apart from those propensities to perform, that they are identical to them or, in the case of occurrent beliefs, identical to those propensities presently carried out through behavior. One's actions echo one's beliefs, to be sure, but the acting itself is not the believing; rather, it issues from it. A man may lack the capacity or the tendency to act on what he believes because of, say, paralysis, yet it is clear that he may possess the corresponding belief, in spite of his limitation. If, in an effort to save the behavior-based theory, one says that the man does have the tendency because he would execute

---

[2] Luke 6:44–45 NKJV.

certain deeds, were he not paralyzed, then it seems that one would be compelled to conclude that the deceased also believe. Doing so, however, introduces an incorporeal part of the human entity, and Ryle's whole point in proposing his theory is to account for the mental activity of humans in strictly physical terms, eliminating the existence of immaterial minds, to say nothing of immaterial spirits. In the end, Ryle's approach to beliefs leaves one not only unfulfilled but unconvinced as well. Another way to account for them is necessary.

Stating exactly what beliefs are may not be as important as pinning down their role and determining why that role is crucial, but taking a look at some of their defining characteristics can be illuminating. To believe something, one must accept it as true, as I noted previously; and accepting it as true is tantamount to putting one's trust in its veracity. A belief entails a commitment, either explicitly or implicitly, and either occurrently or dispositionally—in the traditional sense of that notion—to a proposition that asserts an ostensible fact. It is holding that something is the case. Beliefs are *about* things. The proposition that one accepts in believing ascribes something to the object of the belief—what it is about. Thus, to say that a belief is true is to say that the propositional ascription is true.

I want to put forward a working principle to capture the concepts: To believe any atomic proposition p is to accept that what p purports corresponds to a state of affairs that obtains in the system of reference, where the obtaining of that state of affairs is time-linked to the ascription as set forth in p; and the belief is true if, and only if, p is true. That statement requires unraveling a bit.

First, consider the term 'time-linked'. The idea that I wish to convey by this term is that the time frame in which the state of affairs obtains is denoted by the tense and aspect of the verb in the syntactical construction of p. It may be that p refers to the present, the past, or the future, and p may express something that is temporally bound, continuous, or recurrent. For example, these three sentences express different temporal periods with respect to a belief:

> Jeff believes that the car is in the garage.
> Jeff believes that the car was in the garage.
> Jeff believes that the car will be in the garage.

Consider now three more sentences with clauses that also bear distinct temporal indicators. Other verbal configurations are possible in the language.

> Jeff believes that the car has been in the garage all day.
> Jeff believes that the car had been in the garage all day by
>   the time that Jennifer arrived.
> Jeff believes that the car will have been in the garage all day
>   by the time that Jennifer arrives.

All these sentences could be represented by this structure:

> Jeff believes that *p*.

In each of these formations, *p* stands for the assertion in the clause following the word 'that'. The car is the object of the belief that Jeff possesses: His belief is about the car; he thinks that something concerning it is factual. The state of affairs that obtains—namely, the car's being in the garage—is the essential component, ascribed to the vehicle, but it may be that the state of affairs did obtain, will obtain, has been obtaining, and so forth. One's belief is true only in the case where there is a period of time, corresponding to what *p* expresses, in which the state of affairs that is identified by *p* obtains. Of course, other restrictions, as specified in *p*, also apply.

The other key locution is 'system of reference', which parallels 'universe of discourse' in logic. Sometimes a belief may pertain to events in a play or individuals in a novel. Having read *Moby-Dick* recently, Jeff believes that Captain Ahab is consumed with revenge as he seeks the white whale. Jeff does not think that Captain Ahab exists or that he ever did exist. Within the scope of the novel, statements about the characters can be true or false, but those statements are limited to the sphere in which they apply—namely, the fictional account as Herman Melville created it. The one who holds the belief understands this limitation, and the relevant system of reference is identified, explicitly or implicitly, by the clause *p*, as shown below:

> Jeff believes that Captain Ahab is consumed with revenge
>   [in the novel *Moby-Dick*].

In this declarative sentence, whether the prepositional phrase that is enclosed in brackets is stated or implied, the system of reference is Melville's novel. Such a declaration does not apply to reality. Jeff's beliefs are correct or incorrect—true or false—with regard to a fictional account. They are correct if they agree with that account, incorrect if they do not agree. Of course, if Jeff thinks that *Moby-Dick* records historical events and that Ahab is a real person who is full of vengefulness, then his beliefs are false, even though they may be accurate in terms of the fictional narrative. He is in error because he thinks that something exists that does not exist. His beliefs do not align with objective being, which the system of reference, in this case, encompasses now. It is sometimes important to specify the critical scope to add clarity to the claim about a belief.

Generally speaking, however, the system of reference that is identified in a belief is reality: that which actually exists. Naturally, many of one's beliefs pertain to the physical world, such as Jeff's judging the car to be in the garage, but beliefs need not be concerned only with material entities. One may think, for instance, that, in addition to sensible bodies, Platonic forms exist. Here, the thinker considers objects to be real but considers some of them—namely, forms—to be incorporeal. The system of reference is still reality. The person holds, correctly or incorrectly, that forms are part of the sum of all that is, although it is through a metaphysical account that the individual comes to acknowledge their existence.

Contrast this acceptance of Platonic forms with other beliefs about immaterial things. Jeff believes that the measure of the circumference of a circle is always its diameter times π and that the sum of the interior angles of a triangle invariably equals two right angles, or 180°. Circles and triangles are two-dimensional figures, which cannot be observed in corporeal existence. The system of reference is reality nevertheless: Jeff holds that the postulates of geometry are abstract and that they apply to the figures in the world—those that one draws on tablets, blackboards, and sidewalks—to the extent that those figures approximate the perfect two-dimensional constructs, as defined by mathematics. Jeff believes that this particular, well-drawn circle on the sidewalk is such that its measured circumference is very close to its measured diameter times π. If it were possible to draw it perfectly and in two dimensions, then its circumference indeed would be precisely the product of its diameter and π. Jeff is not assigning independent, incorporeal existence to abstractions but merely using them as paradigms that aid in making calculations in the corporeal realm.

One's beliefs, although true in relation to a given system of mathematics, are not universally true, however, because that mathematical system may be one of several competing models. Jeff's beliefs about two-dimensional circles and triangles in planar structures are true in the Euclidean system, but they are, in fact, false in other systems. In Lobachevskian geometry, the ratio of the circumference of a circle to its diameter is greater than π:1, and the sum of the interior angles of a triangle is less than two right angles. In Riemannian geometry, the ratio of the circumference of a circle to its diameter is less than π:1, and the sum of the interior angles of a triangle is greater than two right angles. Here then are three coherent systems that, with strict interpretation, are in conflict with each other, and no more than one of them can apply to a given geometric space.

If the space is flat, as typified by the surface of a glass top on a table, then the sum of the interior angles of a triangle in that space equals two right angles. A triangle that lies across the curvature of a saddle—a hyperbolic shape—has interior angles that sum to a value that is less than two right angles. A triangle on the surface of a (smooth) basketball—a spherical shape—is such that its interior angles sum to a value that is greater than two right angles. The following diagram illustrates this state of affairs. The single-line arrows represent incompatibilities; the large, double-line arrow aligns with the one system that depicts space corresponding to the surface of the spherical object in physical reality.

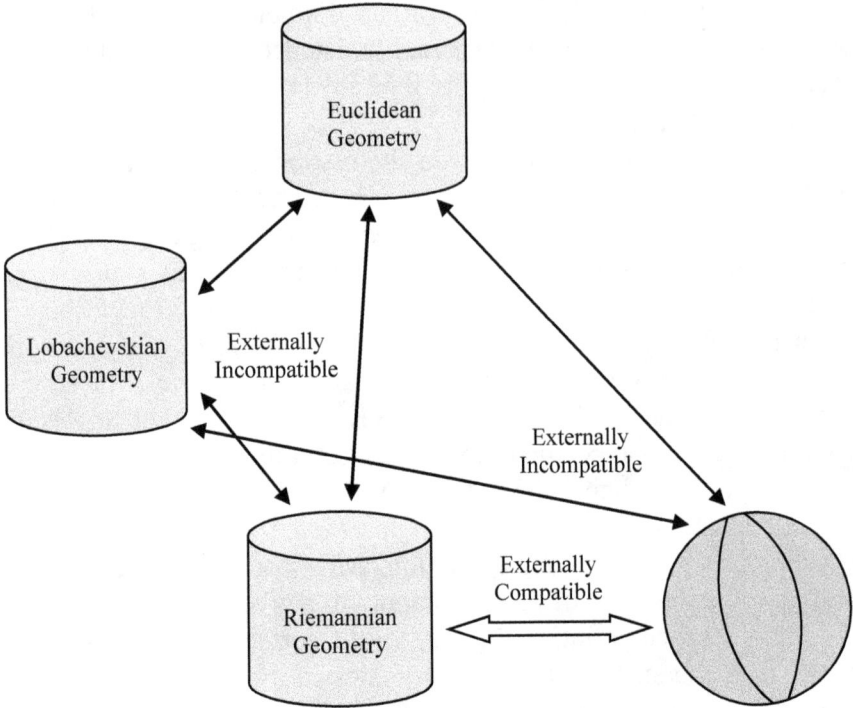

Figure 4.1

When one extends these plane-geometry concepts to solids, to the cosmic spatial structure, the issue to explore is what system depicts the space of the universe as a whole. In accordance with Albert Einstein's theoretical predictions, light rays bend around massive objects, such as stars. The standard rendering of this finding is that space—more accurately, space-time—warps in the vicinity of these masses, reflecting Riemannian geometry. Taken globally, though, is the universe flat or curved; and, if curved, then is it bent negatively, in an open, hyperbolic fashion, or positively, closing in on itself? The amount of substance that the universe contains is the key factor. Scientists have pursued an answer to the question, and the most recent data indicate that the universe is flat to within a very small margin of error in measurement. Consider then this diagram:

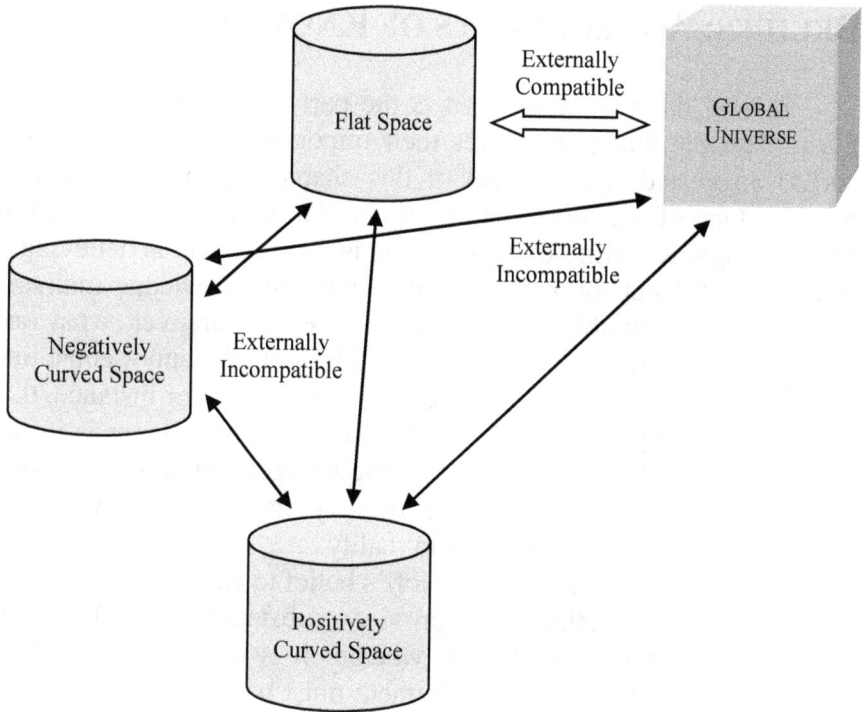

Figure 4.2

The truth of beliefs about circles and triangles is established by a set of mathematical axioms, postulates, and deductions serving as the system of reference. As with Jeff's notion of Captain Ahab, the beliefs may be true within the confines of a particular system but false outside it. If the system of reference does not correspond to what actually exists, or the postulations that it puts forward are in conflict with objective facts, then the beliefs will fail when they are extended to reality. A given belief may be true merely by chance, but there would be no underlying support for it. The context in which its truth-value was formulated no longer would apply when it is moved beyond the boundary of the original framework. It is not grounded. Such ungrounded beliefs about reality never can qualify as candidates for knowledge.

BELIEFS: ANTECEDENTS OF KNOWLEDGE

If, as I have maintained, it is the part that beliefs play in the lives of people that underscores their importance, then what is that part? I suggested at the outset of this chapter that it is essentially twofold. One of the functions of beliefs is to serve as *preconditions of knowledge*. Knowing that something is the case entails believing it to be true. All but the most extreme views of knowledge maintain that, to know something, one must believe it. Moreover, what one believes must correspond to the facts; false beliefs cannot constitute knowledge. Thus, it is not possible for Jeff to know, for instance, that the car is in the garage unless (1) Jeff believes that the car is in the garage, and (2) the car is, in fact, in the garage, which is to say that the state of affairs that is identified by the proposition that is expressed in Jeff's belief obtains in reality.

More is needed, though, for Jeff's belief to count as knowledge. There must be something that provides substance to his belief. It must be supportable. Otherwise, whether it is true or false, it is a guess. Accordingly, a third requirement must be met if there is to be knowledge: (3) Jeff's belief about the car has to be grounded suitably—something has to give it weight. Whether with explicit affirmation or through implication, contemporary philosophy prior to the middle of the twentieth century generally had come to regard knowledge as *justified true belief*. As a rule, the conception is presented in terms of a specific set of conditions, as identified below. The variable s represents a subject—some sentient being—and p stands for a proposition.

> It is the case that subject s knows that p if, and only if, the following conditions hold:
>
> 1. Subject s believes that p.
> 2. It is true that p.
> 3. Subject s is justified in believing that p.

It is the combining of these three conditions that establishes what it is to know. Each of the conditions is necessary for knowledge, and jointly they are sufficient: A subject can have no knowledge that p

unless all of them obtain, and, if all do obtain, then the subject indeed does have knowledge that p.[3]

This stance exhibits certain similarities to the one that Plato suggests in his *Theaetetus*, where he considers whether knowledge might be true belief plus an account. It is a view that Plato rejects. Here is his reasoning: Either one's notion of a thing does not include its uniquely identifying characteristic or characteristics, in which case it is not distinguished from other things, so there can be no knowledge of it; or one's notion of a thing does include its unique characteristic or characteristics, in which case the account adds nothing to the idea of the thing, as the account merely restates something that already is contained in the concept. Thus, knowledge is not true belief plus an account.

There is a problem with Plato's representation of knowledge in the *Theaetetus*, and the problem has two parts. Depicting the knowing of a thing solely as the identification of some unique quality that it possesses, a quality that separates it from other entities of its sort, is to misconstrue in general what it is to know. Much of knowledge concerns facts about things where uniqueness does not play a central role. As indicated above, because beliefs are represented by propositions—believing *that p*, where *p* signifies some assertion—if knowledge is anchored true belief, then knowing that something is the case must incorporate the proposition that is expressed in the belief. To know then in this sense means to know *that p*.

What then is the critical account in such instances? Tim knows that this tulip is red because he and others have observed it closely. This tulip is not alone in being red; there are many other red tulips, and there are white and yellow ones too. Tim's true belief that this one is red is justified by the verification that observation yields, not by any unique quality that this particular flower exhibits. The account here is the explanation of how it is that he came to accept

---

[3] In definitions of knowledge, the crucial justification component takes different forms, depending on the author. Roderick M. Chisholm selects "has adequate evidence for" as a qualifier. See his *Perceiving: A Philosophical Study* (1957; Ithaca: Cornell University Press, 1969), 16. Alfred J. Ayer says that a person who knows should "have the right to be sure." See Ayer's *The Problem of Knowledge* (London: Macmillan and Co., 1956), 34.

that this tulip is red, not a characteristic, or an exhaustive set of characteristics, that this tulip alone possesses.

Accounts even may include elements of reasoning. Brad knows that a member of the Martin family could not have committed the crime. He saw all of them at the concert when the heinous act was carried out across town. Brad realizes that a person cannot be in two places simultaneously, so he deduces that none of them could be the guilty party. It is not anything unique about the family members themselves that leads to the knowledge of their innocence. There were other people at the performance and, of course, other people who were not there. Brad knows that the Martins are innocent because his observation, coupled with his deduction, provides an acceptable account of his coming to know. There is a solid explanation that grounds his belief. When he so testifies in court, his testimony will exonerate Mr. and Mrs. Martin, and their two sons.

The second part of the problem for Plato is his use of the term 'knowledge'. Knowing Theaetetus, to follow Plato's example, in the sense of being familiar with his individuality is not knowing in the sense of understanding that something is true. Knowing people is having a relationship with them, being acquainted with them in more than a casual way. It is knowing who they are by means of interfacing. Such knowledge is not *propositional*; it is *experiential*— through interaction, not simple perception. It plays a very important role, which will come to light later, in the overall understanding that humans possess, but it is not grasping facts about persons, although one also may know, of course, that particular assertions about them are true. What it would entail to give an account, in the meaning at hand, of that familiarity is not even clear. As they pertain to knowledge, accounts are offered in support of beliefs, not relationships.

I have noted that believing that something is the case is rendered propositionally. One could explain how one came to be acquainted with a person or object (or, as some would say, a place, such as a city—although a city may be viewed as a collection of various objects in a certain arrangement within specific geographic coordinates), but this coming to know falls outside the scope of Plato's use of the term. That use is limited to having a notion of the entity's uniqueness, something peculiar to it in itself. To the extent therefore that familiarity qua familiarity with someone or something is to count as knowledge, in alignment with Plato's discussion, an account fails to be applicable, let alone a requirement. To the extent that knowledge of someone or something encompasses beliefs in facts concerning that person or object, however, an account is both applicable and required. That sense, however, is not the sense in which Plato employs the concept in his analysis of the relevant tendered definition in the *Theaetetus*. One cannot dismiss—based on Plato's considerations in the dialogue, at least—the justificatory, grounding element of knowledge.

It is apparent that knowing is a dual-aspect phenomenon. Propositional knowledge concerns facts: declarations that specific conditions obtain with respect to certain things. Experiential knowledge concerns familiarities: being acquainted directly with certain individuals or things. Jeff's knowing that the car is in the garage is an instance of the first sort; Jeff's knowing Jennifer is an instance of the second.[4] In both cases, the *object* of knowledge is a particular entity, not the universal attributes in the Platonic sense that it may exhibit, although, when the knowing is propositional, what is known *about* the entity is given in what the proposition ascribes to it; and such ascriptions frequently point to attributes.

More recently, though, the true-belief-plus-account rendition of knowledge has been challenged on the basis of other considerations. In a well-circulated paper, Edmund Gettier poses a pair of cases to show that the standard definition is inadequate.[5] I provide here a somewhat condensed version of one; the other is similar. Assume

---

[4] Some philosophical writings include what would constitute a third sort: *knowing how*, separating it from *knowing that*. The former sort of knowledge pertains to skills or to abilities to do particular things, in contrast to propositional knowledge, which pertains to facts. Accordingly, it has received little attention in the field of epistemology in the last few decades. These uses of the term 'know' are quite different, and the shared terminology, so I hold, is more a result of phraseology than of any metaphysical commonality. It is knowledge of truths—as they are expressed in statements—that is central to the quest for understanding. There is, though, the other form of nonpropositional knowledge: experiential. Distinguishing it from its fact-based counterpart is important, but further discussion must await the appropriate time. The primary charge here is to uncover how beliefs that correspond to assertions can yield knowledge.

[5] Edmund L. Gettier, "Is Justified True Belief Knowledge?" *Analysis* 23, no. 6 (1963): 121–23.

that Mr. Smith has compelling support for the truth of the proposition 'Jones owns a Ford' because Mr. Jones, in Smith's recollection, at any rate, invariably has owned a Ford and just offered Smith a ride in one. Smith does not know the whereabouts of Mr. Brown but, on the basis of the aforesaid proposition, accepts the following one: 'Either Jones owns a Ford, or Brown is in Barcelona'. Recall the discussion of propositional logic, presented in chapter 1. A compound proposition of this sort is a disjunction: two or more statements that are joined by the *or* operator (here, as usual, in the inclusive sense). The proposition is true where at least one of the disjuncts—one of the statements that make up the disjunction—is true. So, the assertion 'Either Jones owns a Ford, or Brown is in Barcelona' is true if Jones owns a Ford; it is true if Brown is in Barcelona; and it is true if Jones owns a Ford, and Brown is in Barcelona. It is false only when Jones does not own a Ford, and Brown is not in Barcelona. Suppose that Brown is, in fact, in Barcelona. Gettier argues that Smith is justified in believing the truth of 'Either Jones owns a Ford, or Brown is in Barcelona', even though he does not know where Brown is, because he believes that Jones owns a Ford. (Note that a disjunction is implied by any of its disjuncts.[6] Therefore, if any disjunct of a disjunctive proposition is true, then the disjunctive proposition itself is true.) Says Gettier, given that the proposition 'Either Jones owns a Ford, or Brown is in Barcelona' is true, Smith believes it to be true, and Smith is justified in believing it to be true, it follows that Smith knows it—according to the commonly accepted definition of knowledge—although Jones does not own a Ford and merely was driving a rental car when he offered Smith a ride. If Gettier's counterexample is cogent, then the standard view of knowledge is incorrect.

Reactions to the Gettier problem spawned a series of responses, and the discussion has continued. Some philosophers take exception to Gettier's claim that Smith is justified in his belief—in the requisite sense, at least—for the belief, despite its being true, rests on false reasons. The "possession of such grounds could not constitute possession of knowledge," contends one author; indeed, he states, "I

---

[6] Generally, disjunctions are represented as propositions that are composed of two disjuncts, but they may have more than two. The same truth conditions, however, apply to all disjunctive statements. The statement 'p or q or r' is true in every case except where all three disjuncts are false.

should have thought it obvious that they are too weak to serve as suitable grounds."[7]

Other philosophers attempt to block the counterexample by adding a fourth requirement to the traditional set. Further counter-examples surface, however, purporting to show that the amended set of conditions is still inadequate. Some philosophers choose to hold that the quandary that Gettier raises is inescapable; knowledge never can be equated with justified true belief or some version of it. One such author claims that underlying the trifold set of conditions that constitute the standard definition of knowledge is what is referred to as the coordinated-attack problem. That problem as it is portrayed has no solution. This conundrum arises when two or more independent factors must align to produce some result jointly, where each factor relies on coordination or communication, literal or metaphorical, with the other or others. An example from the literature will help to illustrate.

> A group of gangsters are about to pull off a big job. The plan of action is prepared down to the last detail. Some of the men are holed up in a warehouse across town, awaiting precise instructions. It is absolutely essential that the two groups act with complete reliance on each other in executing the plan.
>
> Of course, they will never get around to putting the plan into action, because the following sequence of events is bound to take place.
> 1. A messenger is dispatched across town with instructions from the boss.
> 2. The messenger reaches his destination. At this point both parties know the plan of action. But the boss doesn't know that his message got through (muggings are a common occurrence). So the messenger is sent back, to confirm the message.
> 3. The messenger reaches the boss safely. Now, everybody knows the message got through. Of course, the men in the warehouse are not aware that step 3 [the messenger reaches the boss safely] occurred, and must

---

[7] D. M. Armstrong, *Belief, Truth, and Knowledge* (Cambridge: Cambridge University Press, 1973), 152–53.

be reassured. Off goes the messenger.

4. Now the men in the warehouse too know that step 3 was successful, but unless they communicate their awareness . . .

. . . .

. . . .

Note that the needs of both parties are quite reasonable. They simply want to reach a state where

(1) The original message (i.e., the plan of action) is successfully delivered, and

(2) Both parties know that they are in mutual agreement that (1) occurred.

The sequence cannot terminate successfully.[8]

To ensure the necessary coordination, validation of the receipt of each communication is required prior to acting. Without that validation, the agents cannot act in full assurance that they share the requisite information. The independent informational factors must converge at a common point in time. Given their independence, however, communication between them is necessary for information sharing, and the communication is invariably subject, at minimum, to a delay in delivery and, at maximum, to a corruption of the information or a failure in delivery. This messaging structure prevents the essential convergence, where all agents possess the same information at the same time. If therefore, before two or more agents can perform any synchronized, joint action, each must wait for confirmation from the other or others of the delivery of a message, where the confirmation itself is a message that requires delivery and confirmation, then an infinite regress launches as the circularity turns vicious.

L. Floridi argues that this situation is the very one that the prevailing account of knowledge faces. The problem that the Gettier counterexamples introduce and the coordinated-attack problem are logically equivalent, according to Floridi. In the standard definition of knowledge, the trio of conditions represents a sufficiency: If those conditions are met, then knowledge is guaranteed. The difficulty

---

[8] E. A. Akkoyunlu, K. Ekanadham, and R. V. Huber, "Some Constraints and Tradeoffs in the Design of Network Communications," *Association for Computing Machinery SIGOPS Operating System Review Newsletter* 9, no. 5 (1975): 73–74.

arises over the meeting of those conditions with infallible assurance. With respect to knowledge of some proposition p, the author claims,

> Since the tripartite account [of knowledge] aims at establishing necessary and sufficient conditions for propositional knowledge, the question whether GP [the Gettier problem] is solvable in principle is equivalent to the question whether there can be a time t at which the n (for $n \geq 2$) agents involved are successfully coordinated with respect to p. In the case of a message-passing system, the latter question is modelled as the question whether there is a communication protocol that can guarantee coordination between the n agents at a certain time in the future with respect to p. No protocol satisfies these requirements. . . . As long as there is a possibility that the message may be lost or corrupted—and this possibility is guaranteed by the empirical and hence fallible nature of the interaction between the agents— common information is unattainable, even if the message is in fact delivered.[9]

Coordination of independent factors in a distributed arrangement—in the case here, truth and justification—never can be achieved with absolute certainty. Floridi contends that the standard definition of knowledge requires this level of coordination in just such an arrangement; therefore, he argues, the definition is not acceptable.

> [I]t would be a mistake to interpret the coordination problem as a mere message-passing issue. For the latter is not the difficulty itself but an elegant way of modelling the dynamic interactions between $n \geq 2$ agents (resources, processes, conditions, etc.) to prove that the goal of ensuring successful coordination in a distributed system, such as the tripartite account [of knowledge], is insurmountable. The real difficulty is that, if T [truth] and J [justification] are independent (as they should be, given the fact that we are speaking of empirical, fallible knowledge), the logical possibility of a lack of

---

[9] L. Floridi, "On the Logical Unsolvability of the Gettier Problem," *Synthese* 142, no. 1 (2004): 68.

coordination is inevitable and there is no way of making sure that they will deliver knowledge in a Gettier-proof way.[10]

It is not easy to see how the truth of a proposition and the justificatory support for it can be analogous to the components of a coordinated attack that is, by its structure, dependent on the certainty and integrity of the synchronized interaction of the factors or agents that play a role in it. What exactly is this coordination between truth and justification that Floridi believes to be crucial—how is it to be characterized? It does not seem to matter. Floridi states,

> Regarding . . . the unspecified nature of the relation of coordination between *T* [truth] and *J* [justification] . . . it is *useful* to keep the relation unspecified precisely because this makes the result applicable to any interpretation of it. . . . And it is *not necessary* to specify the nature of the coordination relation. This is so because the failure to deliver propositional knowledge does not depend on a particular interpretation of it.[11]

The principal thrust of Floridi's reasoning is that multiple, independent conditions never can combine, in any circumstances, to warrant a specific consequence that relies on the set of them. It is logically possible that, despite the joining of the conditions, they will not be in lockstep, which is a requirement for the outcome to appear with certainty. Given the standard definition of knowledge, the conjunction of the three stated conditions is a guarantee that one knows because their joint sufficiency renders the result certain. According to Floridi's analysis, however, the potential for the failure of truth and justification to unite to ensure that a subject's belief counts as knowledge demonstrates the inadequacy of the trifold account of knowing. As long as the *possibility* of a lack of coordination exists, there can be no guarantee; and that possibility is not eliminable.

---

[10] Ibid., 74.
[11] Ibid., 73.

Perhaps one should not be so hasty in dismissing the standard definition. Floridi's alleged coordination requirement cannot be set forth as a general principle. Simply by virtue of the fact that multiple independent conditions are individually necessary for some state of affairs to obtain at a particular time, the assurance of their combined sufficiency to produce a certain outcome is not precluded. There is a genuine sense in which a theoretical account can be undercut by an interdependence that generates a vicious circularity, as one sees in the coordinated attack, and I will bring to light one later in this work that falls to an unusual instance of it, but one must question whether such is the case where knowing is concerned. In the standard definition, knowledge is realized *if* the trifold set of conditions is met. A problem arises only if one condition cannot hold unless, or until, another holds, and the other cannot hold unless, or until, the one holds. To generate the destructive infinite regress, each condition must depend on the other in either a logical binding or a temporal one. That configuration is not universal, and it is not applicable here.

Indeed, if one were to adopt Floridi's requirement in a broad way, then one would be compelled to question definitions that are not dubious and even to eliminate physical laws where two or more factors serve jointly as a precipitating cause. A commonly accepted depiction of causality is in terms of sufficiency: The cause, whether a single driving element or a group of coupled elements, is sufficient for the effect. If the conditions that constitute the cause of some phenomenon in particular circumstances occur, then the phenomenon—the effect—is the consequence. Causal laws thus may be expressed in the form of conditional statements, which conform to the simple structure that is shown below, assuming the absence of an opposing situation.[12] (Note that some cause-effect links are nonphysical, so one will see later, but the same structure applies.) Letters represent types of events or states, which cover specific instances—tokens.

---

[12] In the case of miraculous events, physical laws may be set aside, but incidents of this sort do not count against there being physical laws, nor do they count against the representation of them as conditional statements expressing causal relations. If a supernatural event takes place, then, by definition, it falls outside the laws of nature. Note that I distinguish between physical laws themselves, which obtain in nature apart from human mentality (unlike, for example, laws of a society), and the statements that convey those laws, which humans publish after discovering them.

$$C \supset E$$

where

C = cause
E = effect

Given that causes can be compound, requiring more than one factor to bring about the effect, the antecedent of the conditional statement may be a conjunction. The following proposition expresses a causal connection where the cause has multiple factors:

$$(C_1 \cdot (C_2 \cdot \ldots \cdot C_n)) \supset E$$

Mix finely ground potassium nitrate, powdered charcoal, and elemental sulfur in appropriate proportions, and, by definition, gunpowder results. The three chemicals are independent of each other, but they assuredly make gunpowder when they are united, even if each ingredient is added in sequence. When a quantity of the dry mixture is placed in a contained space that offers satisfactory resistance and is ignited, an explosion assuredly occurs. Where the conditions are met, the detonation is guaranteed by virtue of physical, causal laws. The fact that a person, in attempting to make a batch of the substance, may mistake sodium chloride (salt) for potassium nitrate (both are white and crystalline in appearance) is not relevant. The point of the definitional sufficiency is that, *if* (1) finely ground potassium nitrate, (2) powdered charcoal, and (3) elemental sulfur are intermixed in the correct ratios, then the resultant material is gunpowder. Again, the fact that a person may succeed in making gunpowder but, in attempting to create an explosion, may fail to seal it is irrelevant. The point of the causal law sufficiency is that, *if* (1) a quantity of dry gunpowder is (2) packed in a sealed container, offering proper resistance, and (3) ignited, then an explosion occurs.

Even introducing independent agents who must communicate and coordinate their efforts to produce a detonation does not show that the sufficiency fails. Suppose that, after obtaining permission from local authorities, John, Jack, and Jim prepare to demolish a stump in John's field using standard gunpowder. They estimate the quantity that is needed based on information that they find at the library. To produce an explosion, they must combine the right ingredients.[13] Their plan is to pack the gunpowder inside a large hole in the side of the stump, cover it tightly, and insert a fuse for ignition. The ingredients, though, are not available in a single location, so they decide to distribute their efforts. John heads for a chemical supply business for the potassium nitrate. Jack sets out to purchase charcoal briskets at a home goods establishment and then to proceed to his house, where he will pound them into fine powder. Jim thinks that he can purchase elemental sulfur at a pharmacy downtown and leaves to go there. Once the first man delivers his compound, he notifies the others by means of a text message. At that point, there is nothing more that he must do. Another will deliver his ingredient and inform the others. His task is complete. Whoever is last will combine his substance with the other chemicals, pack them well, seal the site, insert the fuse, and light it, igniting the mixture. It is true that each man must act, and, if any one of them fails to do so, then a detonation will not occur; however, there is no circular messaging here, undermining the efficacy of their efforts. John could have lied about completing his part, and the white substance in the hole is the result of a sugar spill from an outdoor-cooking class. He could have been mistaken, delivering the wrong chemical compound or the wrong amount of it. Jack could have gone inadvertently to the stump in a neighbor's field, and the black substance in the hole in the stump on John's property is finely sifted top soil from a nearby garden. The point is that the outcome—namely, the explosion—is assured as a consequence of the physical laws of nature, provided that the conditions are met. The logical possibility that any one of the conditions might not have been met—that any of the three men might have failed in his assignment—is entirely immaterial. *If* the necessary chemicals are conjoined properly to make gunpowder, *if* they are sealed, and finally, *if* they are lit, then the detonation is sure to occur. Conjunction does not require that each chemical ingredient of the three-member set wait for another ingredient to appear before it can be deposited, forming some endless loop of crippling delay. Here is where the dependency lies: The *outcome*—the occurrence of the explosion event—is dependent. It is dependent on the existence

---

[13] There are certain substitutes that could achieve the desired result, but gunpowder proper consists of the substances that are mentioned. In the example then, the three ingredients are necessary to produce a gunpowder explosion.

of a complete ingredient-set that is sealed and set on fire. There is no dependence of the set's components on each other as such and no dependence of the delivery of any component on the delivery of another. Sulfur is just sulfur; its presence in the demolition area is in no way contingent on the presence of an additional component, nor is Jim's act of bringing it contingent on the act of another on the team.

Is it not the same with the definition of knowledge? The conditions of knowing include both truth and justification. If a proposition is true, then it is just true, regardless of whether there is overwhelming support for its truth or no support at all. Its being true is contingent neither on one's belief about it nor on any justification. A proposition that is not true, however, cannot be justified, nor can it be known; and seeming facts that are not true cannot provide justificatory support for a proposition, nor can they contribute to knowing it. As knowledge must be based on truth, the justification for knowledge, in turn, must be based on truth, and it must be germane and substantial. Erroneous, irrelevant, or inconsequential information cannot ground any belief whatsoever.

The point of the standard definition is that justification is required. If the supposed backing for a belief falls short, for whatever reason, then it cannot serve as justification. It is possible that a believed proposition is false, and it is also possible that the seeming grounds for it are wrong, but neither of those possibilities counts against the definition. It is enough for the belief to be true and the justification to be right for there to be knowledge; they need not be utterly infallible as well. There is a dependence inherent in the standard rendering of knowledge, but Floridi misconstrues it. Knowledge depends on the satisfaction of its three conditions. From the logical perspective, knowledge is assured, by virtue of definition, whenever its conditions are met. The challenge comes in saying when the conditions are met—and in particular when the justifying evidence carries enough weight—not whether there is a logical possibility that those conditions may fail to be satisfied. That possibility is always present, but it has no bearing on the definition, for the definition is couched in terms of the conditional: *If* the set of conditions holds, then one knows. A proposition is anchored by a set of facts, expressed in the form of true statements, where that set lends strong support to the truth of the proposition. The proposition and the justificatory support for its truth converge on the end result—knowledge—not on each other in some unending loop, even though the justification aims at the truth of the proposition. Underlying the relation between them is induction, not deduction. Unlike the relation of logical implication that obtains between the trifold set of antecedent conditions (belief, truth, and justification) and the consequent (knowledge), the relation that obtains between a true empirical proposition and its grounding facts is based on *probability, not logical necessity*.

Actually, I do not think that the cases that Gettier presents run counter to the standard definition of knowledge at all. The whole problem with the Gettier proposal centers on this concept of justification. It is more complex than Gettier assumes. His argument begins to break down when making the transition from the logical to the psychological. As stated above, a disjunction is true if at least one of its disjuncts is true. Serving as the consequent of a conditional proposition, a disjunction is warranted, through logical implication, by any of its disjuncts: $p \supset (p \vee q)$. The implication thereby justifies the disjunctive proposition because the rules of logic demand the truth of the disjunction based on the truth of one of its atomic components. The case that Gettier presents, however, supposes that the *belief* in one of the disjuncts justifies the *belief* in the disjunction, even when that disjunct itself is false—a conspicuously different matter. Thus, one must question what the essential support for believing the disjunctive proposition is; one must ask how it is that the justification for embracing it arises.

Support for the disjunction must rest on one of the two statements that are given below:

1. If it is true that p, then it is true that p or q.
2. Given that it is true that p, it is true that p or q.

Statement 1 is not equivalent to statement 2, and believing statement 1 to be true is not the same thing as believing statement 2 to be true. Inherent in statement 2 is a declaration regarding the truth of p, a declaration that is lacking in the first statement. Statement 2 can be recast as a valid argument with statement 1 as its major premise, which the following construction demonstrates:

If it is true that p, then it is true that p or q.
It is true that p.
Therefore, it is true that p or q.[14]

The counterintuitiveness of Gettier's scenario seems to rest on a blurred concept of justification, as revealed in the assertions that are set forth in statements 1 and 2. In that scenario, Smith believes in the truth of the disjunction because there is a chain of reasoning that leads him to accept it. Statement 1 asserts that a disjunction is implied by one of its disjuncts. Implication is sufficient justification for one's accepting the disjunction but only on the supposition that the disjunct that implies it is true. If the disjunct is false, then one cannot be sure whether the disjunction is true until the truth of the other disjunct is determined. At least one of them *must* be true for the disjunction to be true. If Smith's reasoning is simply that which is reflected in statement 1, then Gettier cannot make his case, for the belief is too weak to support it. Smith's belief would be conditional. He would hold merely that, *if* Jones owns a Ford, then the disjunction 'Either Jones owns a Ford, or Brown is in Barcelona' is true, and no knowledge about Jones or Brown is forthcoming from such a conjecture. Under the standard definition of knowledge then, Smith does not know. If, on the other hand, Smith's reasoning is that of statement 2, which is presumed by the Gettier example, then Smith is *not justified* in his belief. Deduction that rests on falsity can justify nothing; it cannot lead to knowledge, as the false never can provide the logical underpinning for the true.

As explained in chapter 1, a deductive argument may be valid and have a true conclusion yet fail to be sound because at least one of its premises is false. In the same way, a chain of reasoning—an argument—that undergirds a true belief can justify the claim that one knows to be factual what that belief conveys only if the argument that reflects that reasoning is sound. In any sense of the term, what is known can be only what is true, and each step in the deductive process, in turn, must stand on the truth, or there is no justification for belief in the truth of the conclusion. There is no knowledge

---

[14] The argument takes the form of *modus ponens*. One will recall that *modus ponens* appears as one of the five logical constructions constituting the Parmenidean dilemma.

without that justification; there is only a guess. The sole reason for Smith's believing in the truth of the proposition 'Either Jones owns a Ford, or Brown is in Barcelona' is his mistaken belief about Jones. Where reasoning is involved in the acquisition of knowledge, individual beliefs cannot be justified apart from the logical process that leads to them. One cannot carve out a belief from the context in which one comes to hold it. Smith is not justified in believing the disjunction to be true, even though it happens to be true, because the reasoning that underlies the truth of the disjunction is *deductive*, and the deduction is flawed. Gettier does not succeed in destroying the standard definition of knowledge.

Now, consider the false disjunct, 'Jones owns a Ford'. Gettier holds that Smith is justified in believing the statement to be true because of strong supporting evidence. What is happening is that Smith comes to believe the statement based on an implicit *inductive* argument. I can represent Smith's reasoning in the following way:

> As far as I can remember, Jones has owned a Ford.
> Jones offered to me just now a ride in a Ford.
> Therefore, Jones owns a Ford.

There are therefore two kinds of argumentation at work in the Gettier example. The reasoning that leads to Smith's belief in the true disjunction is deductive. The reasoning that leads to Smith's belief in the false disjunct on which his belief in the disjunction is based is inductive. In the first chapter, I indicated that an inductive argument establishes its conclusion only with varying levels of strength or probability. The premises of the argument that is shown above suggest that the conclusion is correct, but, of course, they do not guarantee it. There is no constraining, logical implication in induction. Explaining why one has come to hold a belief is not the same thing as justifying it. A false belief can be explained, but it never can be justified.

Consider an illustration. A man is condemned to die on strong evidence of murder. The jury is convinced unanimously, beyond all reasonable doubt, that the defendant is guilty of the crime. The prisoner is executed. Through records, brought forth later, it is discovered that his genetic material matched that of a patient in a foreign hospital, where he spent six weeks in traction as a result of a serious accident. He could not have committed the murder, as he was out of the country at the time, but his attorney was not able to obtain the hospital records until two years later when the laws of that country changed to permit it. Although each member of the jury could explain why he or she condemned the man with a judgment of guilty, not one of them would say that justice was served, for the wrong man was executed, and the murderer is still at large. Their collective action was explainable, and it was understandable, but it was not justified. Admittedly, the issue here is moral rightness, not logical rightness, but the case illustrates a principle that is common to both: Justification requires truth.

The Gettier case can be strengthened, however. Suppose that the night before Jones offers a ride to Smith, Jones buys an antique Ford to restore. The car is not operational, and Jones tows it to his garage, planning to start the restoration next month. In this case, Jones actually *does* own a Ford. One can eliminate the disjunction and replace it with the true, atomic proposition: 'Jones owns a Ford'. It seems nevertheless that Smith does not know that Jones owns one. Smith is basing his belief on historical information—namely, Jones's record of owning and operating Fords as a primary means of transportation—and on what he sees—namely, the rental car that Jones is driving. Smith is completely unaware that Jones purchased the antique automobile only hours earlier. The problem with justification therefore remains. Given that Smith has no idea that Jones just parked an old Ford in his garage, the fact that Jones owns such a vehicle can play no part in Smith's holding his belief and thus cannot serve as justificatory support for it.[15]

Infallibility is another matter altogether. Indeed, if one is to view the logical possibility of a coordinative misstep as an impediment to knowledge, as Floridi does, then one ought not to stop there. The logical possibility of error exists with perception alone; there need not be multiple factors involved for that potential to manifest itself. Look at the earlier case again. When Jeff sees the car in the

---

[15] Richard G. Meyers and Kenneth Stern make a similar point in "Knowledge Without Paradox," *Journal of Philosophy* 70, no. 6 (1973): 147–60. The fact that one is not cognizant of evidence that would validate the belief precludes its playing a justificatory role.

garage, is this sensory input sufficient for his belief to yield knowledge? Does perception have the wherewithal to ground beliefs? Can Jeff know based on what he perceives; and, if so, then what does it take to say truthfully that he does know?

So many of persons' beliefs about physical reality arise through the senses. In their role as preconditions of knowledge, beliefs serve as the important link between sensing and knowing. It is uncertainty, as expressed through the possibility of error in perception, that has been taken to be the sentinel that closes the door to knowledge. In the second chapter, I presented an argument that works against the prospect of ever knowing anything about the world because of this ubiquitous potential for error in perception. I would like to revisit the argument now. In perception, so goes the thinking, the following reasoning applies:

> It is always possible that one is wrong.
> Therefore, it is possible that one is always wrong.

In essence, the argument postulates that one can be deceived, on any single occasion, about what one thinks that one sees, hears, touches, and so forth. If a person can be wrong on any occasion, though, then the chance for error to occur must surface each time that a person perceives something: In *every* individual instance of perception, beliefs about what one's senses tell him or her *can* be wrong. The upshot is that it is possible for the entire set of one's beliefs, arising through perception—all of them—to be false. If such can be the case for one person, however, then it can be the case for all persons. I can restate the reasoning in a more pertinent way, assigning an apt title:

The Argument from the Possibility of Error

> It is possible for any given belief arising out of perception to be false.
> Therefore, it is possible for all beliefs arising out of perception to be false.

As it stands, the argument is not forceful. The conclusion does not follow from the premise. Imagine that a bag of twenty lemons is dumped on the kitchen counter. It is possible for any given lemon to lie to the left of the others, but it is not possible, of course, for all the lemons to lie to the left of the others.

Consider a different case. Let the set K consist of the statements that are shown below; each is identified by a unique letter:

$$K = \begin{cases} \text{Statement } p: \text{There is a maple in my yard.} \\ \text{Statement } q: \text{There is a maple in the yard of} \\ \quad \text{my neighbor George.} \\ \text{Statement } r: \text{There is an oak in my yard.} \\ \text{Statement } s: \text{There is no maple in my yard.} \\ \text{Statement } t: \text{ Statement } r \text{ is false.} \end{cases}$$

It is possible for any given statement in K to be false, but it is not possible for all of them to be false. If p is false, then s cannot be false. If r is false, then t cannot be false. It is the interrelatedness of certain sentences in the set, their mutual dependence, that brings about this state of affairs because of the inconsistencies among them.[16]

The fact that not all statements in K can be false, however, does not mean that different conditions could not obtain in some other set. Suppose that there is a grouping of five statements, composing the set K', as appears here:

$$K' = \begin{cases} \text{Statement } p: \text{There is a maple in my yard.} \\ \text{Statement } q: \text{There is a maple in the yard of} \\ \quad \text{my neighbor George.} \\ \text{Statement } r: \text{There is an oak in my yard.} \\ \text{Statement } s: \text{There is no spruce in my yard.} \\ \text{Statement } t: \text{ Statement } r \text{ is true.} \end{cases}$$

---

[16] For the sake of clarity, note that such interrelatedness is not that of circularity, as may be introduced by a coordinated attack involving multiple agents. It is a logical relation holding between propositions based on the propositions' meanings and on specified conditions of truth. The set of sentences could be reengineered to produce a problematic circularity, to be sure, but it does not produce it as it stands, and there is nothing to be gained by pursuing the topic. It is the interrelatedness of perceptions and their giving rise to beliefs that constitute the point to be illustrated at present.

In this group, all the statements could be false. There is an interrelatedness here too, but it is inherently supportive. Statement *t* refers to statement *r*, but it is the job of *t* now to uphold *r*, not to refute it. A relation of affirmation holds in this set rather than denial as appears in *K*. There are no inconsistencies in this second collection of propositions.

In attempting to make its case, the argument from the possibility of error disregards the interrelatedness and mutual support that characterizes perceptions, but one cannot ignore perceptual reciprocity any more than one can ignore the propositional relations of *K'*. Even if the argument is invalid and cannot establish its conclusion, though, this finding may be of little comfort. That lack of cogency does not mean that the conclusion is unquestionably false; as I demonstrated in the first chapter, an invalid argument may have a true conclusion. Although it is an illegitimate step to infer that all perception-derived beliefs might be wrong on the basis that any one of them might be wrong, there still may be no logical assurance that any of those beliefs is right. All that one can say is that the argument itself is faulty. Furthermore, regardless of whether all beliefs gained through perception are wrong, it clearly seems to be the case that some of them are wrong, as one discovers. How then can one determine categorically *which* beliefs? Where uncertainty prevails, how can there be knowledge? In short, if people *can* be wrong, then how is it possible to know?

Besides the argument from the possibility of error itself, there is a correlated piece of reasoning underlying the whole issue: The fact that beliefs that are gained through perception are *susceptible* to error constitutes adequate grounds for dismissing the possibility of knowing anything about the world. It is not necessary to show that all beliefs may be wrong, for the logical uncertainty of beliefs in general is sufficient to block knowledge: If *any* belief at all *can* be wrong, then certainty can be ascribed to *none* of them, for they all are exposed to error; and, without certainty, there can be no knowledge. This correlated argument can be set forth as the construction that I present below, where the premise of the argument from the possibility of error resurfaces, essentially intact, in a conditional proposition. Numbered steps facilitate reading.

The Argument for the Indispensability of Certainty

Part I

1. If it is possible for any belief arising out of perception to be false, then it is not possible for certainty to arise out of perception.
2. It is possible for any belief arising out of perception to be false.
3. Therefore, it is not possible for certainty to arise out of perception.

Part II

4. It is not possible for certainty to arise out of perception (from Part I, step 3).
5. Where certainty is not possible, knowledge is not possible.
6. Therefore, it is not possible for knowledge to arise out of perception.

It is this very concern about certitude that lies at the core of René Descartes's methodical doubt. In his quest for knowledge, he is searching for something with respect to which it is impossible for him to be wrong, some bedrock truth that can become the foundation on which he can build his epistemology. Descartes sets out to find certainty, but he does not find it in perception; he does not find it even in mathematics. It is the *Cogito* that halts Descartes's search. He believes that it has to be the case that he thinks because he is in doubt, and it is impossible for him to doubt without thinking, as doubting is a form of thought; hence, his existence as a thinker is assured.

The truth-value of some propositions is fixed, such that it cannot be other than what it is. What determines the truth-value of such propositions and their fixedness, however, is not always the same. Consider a pair of statements: Set 1 below. It is not possible for either proposition to be true. The reasons for the respective impossibilities in the two cases differ, however. The order of the set reflects the forcefulness of the individual principles that impose the corresponding restrictions: The proposition that rests on the greater principle appears first. The analysis in the remainder of this section will follow this order; the logical generally will precede the physical.

Set 1: Cannot Be True

> *a*. The boy Jimmy is five feet tall, and he is not five feet tall, at time *t*.
> *b*. The boy Jimmy is five thousand feet tall at time *t*.

In sentence *a*, the impossibility is because of logical preclusion. Whatever the height or other characteristic that a sentence of this structure ascribes to Jimmy is irrelevant. It is by virtue of the form of the statement—asserting that both *p* and not *p*—that the statement cannot be true. The impossibility arises because logical rules prevent Jimmy's being *anything* while simultaneously not being it. One is incapable even of imagining a world in which he could be what the sentence claims that he is. In sentence *b* in Set 1, however, there is a violation of physical laws, not logical ones. Here, the ascribed property or relation *does* matter. It is a fact that Jimmy is not thousands of feet high, but this extreme height is not possible: In the natural world, the physiology of humans prevents it. The statement cannot be true, barring the setting aside of the laws of nature, but its falsity is not because of its form; rather, it is because it asserts that something is the case that is never the case, and further cannot be the case, in physical reality. Although one can imagine a universe in which humans grow to be so tall, that universe is not the one that humans know. It is logically possible for Jimmy to be five thousand feet tall, but it is plainly not physically possible.[17] This latter sort of possibility is referred to as nomological because it is determined by

---

[17] The division between the logical and the physical is somewhat reminiscent of the distinction, put forth by the philosopher David Hume, whom I introduced earlier, between propositions concerning relations of ideas and those concerning matters of fact. Hume holds that any proposition that purports to impart truth but that does not fall into one of these two categories is to be rejected, and he uses the division, albeit erroneously, as a basis for a sweeping dismissal of both theology and metaphysics. The notion is referred to as Hume's fork. His remarks appear in *An Enquiry concerning Human Understanding*, published originally in 1748 under the title *Philosophical Essays concerning Human Understanding*.

the physical laws of the universe.[18] A near-mile-high child is a *nomological* impossibility.

Consider another pair of statements. Here, not only are both propositions true, but it is also impossible for them to be false. As before, underlying the first proposition in the set is the principle that carries the greater weight.

Set 2: Cannot Be False

a. It is not the case both that the boy Jimmy is five feet tall at time *t* and that he is not five feet tall at time *t*.

b. It is not the case that the boy Jimmy is five thousand feet tall at time *t*.

In Set 2, sentence *a* cannot be false, for logical rules enforce its truth, such that its denial is a contradiction. The thrust of the affirmation can be represented this way: not both *p* and not *p*. No matter what one substitutes for the variable *p*, where *p* is a sensical assertion, the instantiation renders sentence *a* incontrovertible. The sentence has to be true because its form guarantees it, regardless of circumstances. One cannot imagine a universe in which it would be possible for it to be false. Sentence *b* in this set is also assuredly true, but its veracity is not linked to its form but to the fact that human physiology makes it so. It is true without exception by virtue of the laws of nature.

It may be valuable here to touch on a pair of logical elements that have surfaced in this work—necessary conditions and necessary truths—to emphasize the distinction between them. One will recall the discussion in chapter 1 regarding conditional propositions. In a statement of this form, the consequent is a necessary condition of the antecedent, such that, if the statement is true, then, provided that the antecedent is true, the consequent has to be true. A conditional statement that is true, however, need not be so—often, it is not so— by virtue of logical rules: There is no contradiction in denying it.

---

[18] Laws other than physical ones could come into play. For example, it is not possible under American law for the speaker of the house *as such* to be the commander-in-chief of the armed forces. That role belongs solely to the president of the United States. Generally, however, in philosophical contexts involving the truth-value of propositions, 'nomological' refers to the laws of nature. Statements reporting such laws are simply true; what they proclaim aligns with experience.

As I noted earlier, a causal law may be expressed as a conditional statement, asserting that the cause is a sufficient condition of the effect, and the effect is thus a necessary condition of the cause. That the causal-law conditional statement holds, however, is not a matter of reason; it is a matter of fact. Material reality could have been otherwise than it is; apples that break loose from trees could have moved toward the sky rather than the ground. Physical, causal laws are not logical warrantors but nomological ones; they do not reflect the hard constraints of logic but the systematic operations of the cosmos. Sentences that express them are not necessary truths.

In summary, there are different determinants of the truth-value of propositions for which that truth-value is preset. Almost universally, when philosophers speak of the modality of necessity, it is with reference to propositions that are underwritten by logical rules rather than physical regularities. Accordingly, necessary truths are, in the language of the discipline, true in all possible worlds, not just the actual world. One must exercise care in investigating philosophical writings nevertheless to ascertain the author's intent in a specific context. Each proposition in Set 2 above asserts what must be the case, but only the first one is logically necessary. The second, though undeniably true, is contingently so. Its sureness is not absolute; it holds only in the limited, nomological sense. It is not a necessary truth in the strict sense.

In the latter half of the twentieth century, Saul Kripke put forth a case for yet another sort of necessity. A statement asserting, for example, that water is H_2O is necessarily true, thinks Kripke, but its unconditional truth is not because of either logical restrictions or nomological ones; the limitations are metaphysical. Appropriately, philosophers apply the locution 'metaphysical necessity' to facts of this sort. Science reveals that the substance that people refer to by the term 'water' is such that its essential properties could not be different from what they are without the failure of the substance to be what it is. Water is a chemical compound that is formed from two atoms of hydrogen and one atom of oxygen. The term 'water' is more akin to a proper name, thinks Kripke, than is assumed. When one uses that term, whatever it picks out in reality is the very same thing as what the term 'H_2O' picks out in reality, science's having discovered the molecular structure of the compound. The relation between the two things holds unconditionally. The copula 'is' in such propositions is the link of identity, not predicative ascription.[19] Water and H_2O are *exactly* one and the same, and their being so is the case everywhere and in all circumstances—all possible worlds.

Although Kripke's thesis has gained wide acceptance in philosophical circles, it raises some concerns—for me, at least. That the terms 'water' and 'H_2O' denote the same thing—they have identical referential extension, which is to say that whatever one term singles out, the other does so as well—appears to be a requirement for statements that employ them, given that those statements are to carry the weight of necessity in Kripke's view. It is the supposed invariableness of the chemical composition of water that makes the statement 'Water is H_2O' true without exception. A proposition that reports the atomic number of an element falls under the same principle because, says Kripke, "[S]tatements representing scientific discoveries about what this stuff *is* are not contingent truths but *necessary truths in the strictest possible sense.*"[20]

I think that isomers, which I mentioned in the previous chapter, introduce a complication. Both the statements 'Fructose is $C_6H_{12}O_6$' and 'Glucose is $C_6H_{12}O_6$' are true. If Kripke's analysis were right, then these statements, it seems, would be metaphysically necessary, where the terms 'fructose' and 'glucose' operate, as they allegedly do in the case of water, as quasi-proper names. Two things that are equal to a third thing are equal to each other, however. The result is that fructose is glucose—necessarily so—but, of course, fructose is *not* glucose. They exhibit significantly different qualities.

One could object that it is not the mere chemical elements of a compound that make it what it is but the arrangement of the atoms that compose the molecules of that compound. Although molecules of fructose and glucose are made of the same number of atoms of the same elements, they differ in their physical arrangements. Once structure is introduced as a required component, however, statements that link the names of substances to their chemical constitution either fail to be statements of strict identity—and therefore obviously fail to be metaphysically necessary—or change from statements of strict

---

[19] See Saul Kripke, *Naming and Necessity* (Cambridge: Harvard University Press, 1980), 106 ff.

[20] Ibid., 125. The second emphasis is mine.

identity to statements asserting that the substances are tokens of types. Kripke sees such type-based assertions as metaphysically necessary too; a proposition declaring that a tiger is an animal is an example.

On this reading, perhaps the two sugars can be viewed as instances of a chemical type: $C_6H_{12}O_6$. What about water? On the planet earth, natural water contains not only simple hydrogen in its makeup but also deuterium. Deuterium is an isotope of hydrogen with a neutron in the nucleus of the atom. A tiny amount of tritium is present as well. Tritium is a radioactive isotope of hydrogen with two neutrons in the nucleus. (Isotopes of oxygen also may be present.) I will focus on deuterium, as it is sufficient to make the point. A molecule of water that is made of deuterium is a molecule of heavy water and is represented by the formula ^2H_2O, or sometimes by D_2O. Thus, when one is referring to water—the common material of which a lake consists—there are two possibilities. (1) One is referring to a substance that contains both H_2O and ^2H_2O, in which case it is not true that water is identical to H_2O. Instead, water is $H_2O + {}^2H_2O$. That which is not true, though, cannot be necessarily true, metaphysically or otherwise. (2) Alternatively, following the structure of the statement 'Fructose is $C_6H_{12}O_6$', one may be referring to water as a token of the type H_2O. It is also a token of the type ^2H_2O, however. Now, $H_2O \neq {}^2H_2O$, and no instance of the first type can be an instance of the second type; they are different substances and are mutually exclusive things. One is a compound that is formed from simple hydrogen, having only a proton for a nucleus, and the other is a compound that is formed from deuterium, having a proton and a neutron for a nucleus. The nucleus is either neutron-laden or not neutron-laden; there is no middle ground. So, the statement 'Water is H_2O' cannot be metaphysically necessary, for the statement 'Water is ^2H_2O' has no less claim to the truth than its counterpart, and water cannot be identical to two things that exhibit conflicting formations.

If one attempts to remove deuterium from consideration by *defining* water as H_2O, distinguishing it from water in general and from heavy water in particular, then metaphysical necessity vanishes, replaced with logical necessity. Kripke's point, though, is that statements that are metaphysically necessary are *not* necessary by virtue of logical laws. Such laws obviate any need to base necessity on discovery—a key component of the concept of metaphysical necessity. Statements that are true by definition are true a priori, *not* a posteriori, as would be required by Kripke's position on such necessity.

Kripke could reverse the order of the terms in his assertion, yielding 'H_2O is water' instead, expressing, one supposes, that the chemical compound is a token of the type water. In that case, one also would have to uphold '^2H_2O is water', and Kripke would have to abandon the metaphysical necessity of his original statement about water. One is left with water's being a mixture. What follows is that, if there is to be metaphysical necessity here, then both 'H_2O is water' and '^2H_2O is water' are necessary statements. Given their necessity, however, the latter statement indicates that it is an impossibility for water to exist without taking an isotopic form because the Kripkean necessity is not set forth definitionally but empirically. Such a state of affairs is simply unbelievable, particularly if one introduces a third token: tritium. Kripke's claim seems to be slipping between the fingers. I will leave the topic for others to pursue.

I want to return to the arguments that present the supposed difficulties. Consider first the argument from the possibility of error. From the standpoint of logic, any belief about what is perceived can be wrong, but it also can be right. Indeed, there is no logical prohibition against one's *always* being *right* in one's perceptions. Again, from the standpoint of logic, the proposition that it is possible for one always to be right is no less plausible than the proposition that it is possible for one always to be wrong. Thus, one could reformulate the argument from the possibility of error to produce an opposing argument that is on equal footing, as shown below:

The Argument from the Possibility of Correctness

It is possible for any given belief arising out of perception to be true.
Therefore, it is possible for all beliefs arising out of perception to be true.

Without question, error precludes knowledge; it is clear that one cannot know what is not true. The acquiring of knowledge that is based on beliefs that are gained through the senses, however, does not require that it is *impossible* for one to be wrong, only that one is *not* wrong. It is not a matter of *logical compulsion* or *nomological compliance* but *empirical truth*. Charlie may be in the living room or in the den. Either location is possible. Statements reporting his whereabouts are true or false, depending on the actual circumstances that obtain. One may know where he is by looking. The possibility that he could have been elsewhere in no way bars that knowledge, for he is, in fact, in the den. In perception, being correct is not the result of the constraints of reason or the limitations that are imposed by physical law but the ascertaining of the facts by means of the senses. In the world, human beings live under the rules of probability. Human beings are not wrong all the time, nor are they right all the time. Neither is logically impossible or even physically impossible, but neither is feasible. Both lie at the extreme end of the spectrum of what can happen in material reality. The mathematics of probability ensures that propositions reporting conditions that bear a radical level of unlikelihood are, as a *matter of fact*, excepting supernatural intervention, not true. What they purport is precluded from the realm of actuality by a pronounced lack of potentiality. Such statements are nonstarters. They express *probabilistic implausibilities*, as I will call them, for they are surely false, not because of logic or physical law but because of the rules of chance; and the greater the odds are against their being true, the closer they come to expressing *practical impossibilities*.

There are then propositions that owe their truth-value to the principles of logic. Their truth-value is invariable. There are propositions that owe their truth-value to their correspondence to the facts or their lack of correspondence. Their truth-value depends on the conditions that obtain in reality. In some cases, these propositions may be invariably true or false, like their logic-based counterparts. That invariability may be traceable to nomological restrictions, but alternatively it may be traceable to probabilities that apply to the real world. Statements of that sort, if true, are just never false, regardless of circumstances, and, if false, are just never true.

The upshot is that either the conclusion of the argument from the possibility of error—that all beliefs that are gained through perception might be wrong—is trivially true, or it is undeniably false.

In the logical sense of possibility, it is trivially true, as there is no contradiction involved, provided that no two beliefs are inconsistent. One can conceive of a world in which such a thing happens, albeit with some difficulty, but it is of no consequence. One also can conceive of a world in which all one's beliefs are true. In the sense of what can happen in material reality as a matter of fact, however, the argument's conclusion is false. A world in which people could exist in an ongoing state of pervasive and total error regarding their perceptions could not be the world of humankind. For the conclusion to be true, it would have to be possible in the physical universe for every perception of every person, day after day, year after year, to be wrong. Under such conditions, the reality that humankind experiences would cease to be. The very notion borders on the senseless. *Everything* that people ostensibly see or hear or touch as they travel along the interstate one morning during rush hour, going to work or to the airport to catch a flight, would be deceptive. Other cars, the highway, the road signs, the exit ramps, the steering wheel, the dashboard gauges, the brakes; and, for the pilot, the airplane wings, the runway, the cockpit instruments, the navigator, the messages from the tower, and the landing strip at London—all would be illusory. No one would survive in such a universe. Not only is the argument from the possibility of error invalid, as I showed earlier, but the conclusion itself fails as well. If all beliefs about what is perceived were wrong, then existence for each person would be fleeting, to say the least, and, in the end, there would be no humans to experience perceptions.

I wish to examine now the argument for the indispensability of certainty. Consider Part I. The problem here is again that, although it is logically possible in every case for a belief about the world, arising from perception, to be false, it is also logically possible in every case for it to be true. The only beliefs for which error is *logically impossible* are those that are represented by propositions the truth-value of which is determined not through correspondence to some actual state of affairs in the world but rather by virtue of form. The statement 'Tonya's tricycle has a bent frame, or her tricycle does not have a bent frame' must be true—it is logically impossible for it to be false—but such propositions are not really about the world at all. If Part I of the argument is concerned with logical possibility and logical certainty, then it is trivial. Under the guise of an argument pertaining to beliefs arising from perception, the argument turns on a notion that actually has nothing to do with perception, for perception pertains to the physical world. If, on the other hand, the argument is not concerned with logical possibility, then it is the feasibility of circumstances in the world with which it is concerned. In that case, both its premises are misguided. Certainty arises through perception when there is no reasonable chance of error, when the perceptions are so grounded in careful, even corroborating, observation that the truth is assured.

As Jennifer lays the king of hearts on the table, to the surprise of the other players, and takes the trick in the final round of the championship, her team's opponents see the card and sigh, while her partner, Jackie, laughs aloud and says to herself, "I didn't think that she had it!" Those watching the match applaud. Is it logically possible that the card is not really the king of hearts, although everyone present thinks that it is the king? It is logically possible, as it could have been the queen that she played; but the chance for something to have been other than it is does not make it different. Aside from logical possibility, can the card be a card other than the king, as the four players believe it to be? No, the card is what it is. Its being something else is a probabilistic implausibility. The observations of scores of people converge at a point of empirical certainty; the card *is* the king, and all can see that it is so. Part I of the argument avoids triviality at the expense of failing to establish its conclusion.

As for Part II of the argument, the first premise, which is the conclusion of Part I, is not established, given that Part I failed. Furthermore, the second premise is not true. In knowledge, it is not whether a proposition about perceived things *can* be false that counts but whether it *is* false. Knowing that p does not require that not p is *impossible*, only that not p is *not the case*. Jackie sees that Jennifer played the king of hearts, even though she could have played the queen; it was in her hand. As four attentive players and numerous onlookers gaze at the table, there is no question about the card that Jennifer played. What it could have been is irrelevant. That it is the king is unmistakable.

Descartes argues, as I discussed in chapter 2, that, just as one rotten apple can spoil an entire basket of them, so one tainted belief can undermine the rest. To a point, Descartes is correct, in that the interleaving of an individual's beliefs creates a general perspective that influences how the person perceives things. In spite of the Cartesian-revealed exposure to corruption of the entire set of beliefs through their interconnectedness, there is a positive aspect of this nexus. Ironically, it serves to guard against the very corruption to which the set is exposed. Analogous to the affirmation that is inherent in the aforementioned set K', the interdependence of beliefs can uphold them. Like corroborating evidence at a trial, beliefs fit together in a system of mutual support that underlies one's judgments about what one perceives through the senses.

When Jeff sees a car in the garage, other senses often come into play to confirm the visual impression. He can start the engine, and hear the belts whirring and the valves clicking; he can take hold of the steering wheel and the dashboard; he can smell the exhaust. Jeff can open the hood and lift the battery, feeling its considerable weight. He can ask his wife what she sees in the garage and listen to her response. He can watch his children jump into the back seat. He can drive to the neighbor's house and take him to the auto parts store to buy a new water pump, which they install in the vehicle. As the evidence mounts, the possibility of error becomes infinitesimally small. The complex of beliefs that forms a frame of reference for Jeff offers protection against misjudgment in perception.

In keeping with Descartes's tenet, it is true that one wrong belief may taint others, although it is hardly likely to taint them all, but that principle is a two-sided blade. The opposite edge is that many true beliefs, arising from a diversity of perceptions, form an interlocking web that is not penetrated easily by candidates for deception. There is a pragmatic operational efficacy at work here, which is why one looks for the strings when one sees a puppet moving around on the stage. Logical reasoning balances perceptions, each against the others and against a preestablished frame of reference, while convergence helps to anchor them. Acting on the data that the senses provide, reason assesses their correspondence to what is real. The truth is that beliefs about what one detects in perception *are* right much of the time, and those times that they are right position one to know. Sometimes, a single perceptual event is sufficient. Alex sees that his class ring is still on his finger after his somersaulting water-skiing fall; Allison hears that the radio is still on in the kitchen as she prepares to retire for the evening. Where perceptions converge, however, assuredness is taken to another level. Knowledge about the world can be conclusive because corroboration of facts is available both to an individual person and to other people through observation, carrying with it a pledge of truth. The inter-relatedness of perceptions in day-to-day existence ensures that it is implausible to the point of a practical impossibility for all of them to be wrong.

As shown, no belief about the physical world is *logically* unassailable, for one always can conceive of its being erroneous. Beliefs can be *empirically* definitive, however, in that their being erroneous would stand in contradistinction to such an overwhelming body of other perceptions and accepted facts that it is unreasonable to reject them. Some philosophers, because of the assumed require-ment for logical certainty, have become skeptical, wondering how one can come to know at all. Descartes thinks that he has to ground knowledge of the world in the indubitable character of the *Cogito*, and the sense-datum theorists think that they have to ground knowledge in the seemingly incorrigible patches of color that they see whenever they open their eyes. Underlying this thinking is a dichotomy that the traditional view puts in place, wherein a belief is either logically certain or not logically certain, and wherein only beliefs of the former sort are candidates for a foundation on which to build a system of knowledge. Unlike enlightenment in logic or pure mathematics, in which new information comes through deduction from axiomatic propositions, understanding of the physical world arises through discoveries that are based on observation. Knowledge of corporeal reality is not grounded in logical necessity but in empirical surety, in facts that reason renders unfailing by the veri-fiability that perception brings. People are to count as knowledge those true beliefs about the world that fall at the high end of a continuum of probability that is undergirded by experience, and everyone serves as a juror in the court of understanding. Just how low the chance of error must be is a determination that is up to them collectively, but, at some point, the truth of a given belief about the perceived world is assured.

It is time to dismiss this insidious dichotomy that has led some philosophers astray through the years in their efforts to understand what characterizes knowledge of the physical world. The following diagram represents that division:

THE TRADITIONAL DICHOTOMY

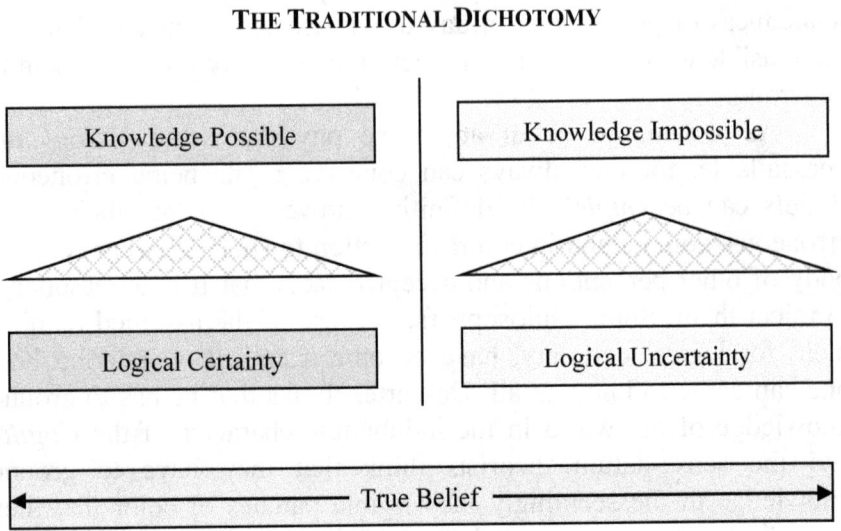

Figure 4.3

In its stead should be the continuum that underlies empirical knowledge. Figure 4.4 illustrates this concept.

THE EMPIRICAL CONTINUUM

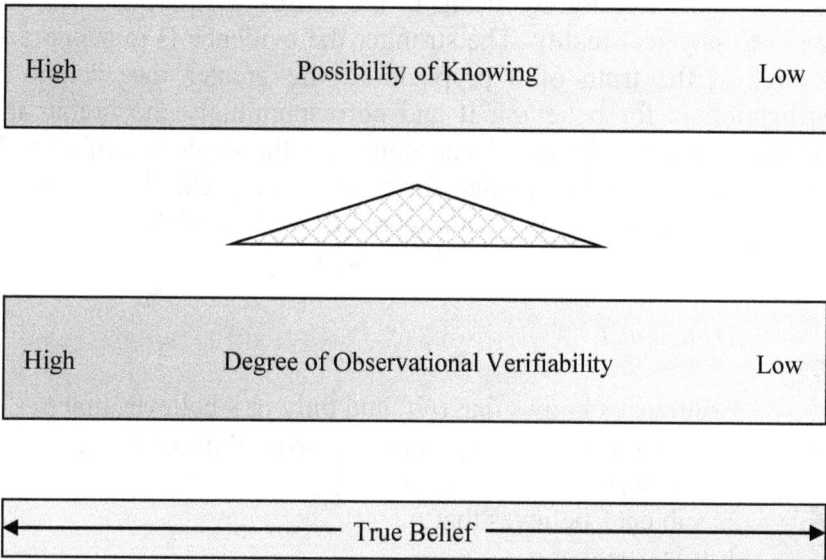

Figure 4.4

To rise to the level of knowledge, true beliefs about physical reality must be justified; they must be grounded sufficiently: There has to be something that provides adequate substance to them. The classic position about knowing has this part right. Being grounded in a suitable way, however, is not being logically incontestable; it is not being infallible. It is being right—substantially empirically verifiable. Observation is not only the fundamental method by which humans come to hold beliefs about the physical universe; it is also the means by which those beliefs come to be anchored. It is on the foundation of perception that discovery of the world rests. The reciprocity of perceptions underwrites their veracity as they join to offer common support for a given truth. In the world of sense, convergence is the warrantor of knowledge.

In the final analysis, what it means to know is represented by a pair of arguments, where the conclusion of one argument lends credence to a premise of the other. Wherever there is justified true belief, there is knowledge because justified true belief *is* knowledge. Justification itself, however, is external to this trio of conditions. It is based on substantiation by means of the senses, for propositions that pertain to physical reality. The stronger the evidence is in support of a belief in the truth of a proposition, the greater the weight of justification is for believing it and correspondingly the higher the likelihood that one knows. I can complete the depiction of knowledge by adding to the earlier formulation to yield the following structure. Again, the steps are numbered to aid in readability.

Argument 1

1. Subject *s* knows that *p* if, and only if, *s* believes that *p*, and it is true that *p*, and *s* is justified in believing that *p*.
2. Subject *s* believes that *p*.
3. It is true that *p*.
4. Subject *s* is justified in believing that *p* (see Argument 2 below).
5. Therefore, subject *s* knows that *p*.

Argument 2

1. One is justified in believing that *p* to the extent that one has evidence for the fact that *p*.
2. Subject *s* observes states of affairs or events $x_1 \ldots x_n$.
3. States of affairs or events $x_1 \ldots x_n$, reported in statements of fact $e_1 \ldots e_n$, constitute strong evidence for the fact that *p*.
4. Therefore, subject *s* has strong evidence for the fact that *p*.
5. Therefore, subject *s* is justified in believing that *p* (corresponds to premise 4 in Argument 1 above).

What it is to know is rendered with rigidity because it is given in definition. The variability comes in justification. If true beliefs fall in the high range of the empirical continuum—and only if they do so—then they qualify as knowledge about physical reality. People can know because it is often exactly where they do fall.

It is clear that the attack on knowledge from the possibility of error in perception is misguided. It emerges from a misunderstanding regarding the concept of certainty and its role in knowing. One will remember that the problem of knowledge rises to challenge both the objects and the subjects in perceptual events. In the previous chapter, I demonstrated that change in itself is no threat to the continued integrity of objects and therefore does not preclude one's knowing. In the current chapter, I have investigated the subject side of the matter to see whether one can know, despite the potential for mis-judgment. With the analysis completed, it seems that this two-sided problem has been rendered innocuous.

BELIEFS: ANTECEDENTS OF ACTION

This chapter began with an account of a family trip to the West. Returning to that account, one can see how my father's actions were tied to his beliefs. He stopped the car when he sensed what seemed to be a mechanical malfunction. Believing our course to be downward, he held the related belief that there was a problem with the brakes; thus, he pulled aside to have them inspected and, once the problem with them was identified, repaired. His beliefs positioned him to act just as he, in fact, acted. In the context in which the events took place, was my father's action unavoidable? Given similar circum-stances on a different occasion, he would have done exactly the same as he did on this occasion. Any rational, caring spouse and parent would have acted in an identical manner.

Such uniformity sets the stage for a philosophical stance that holds that beliefs have no bearing whatsoever on what one does; things must happen exactly as they do happen. According to the reasoning, whether an event will occur is preset; it is determined before it unfolds. Humans live in a universe that is governed by causality, and, in such a universe, every occurrence follows a fixed course, dictated by preceding causes. It does not matter whether the occurrence is some unobserved happening on a distant planet or the seemingly purposeful behavior of a human being on the planet earth; everything is necessitated beforehand. If a stone is dropped, then it falls. Barring something to prevent it, the consequence is inescapable. Humans are no different, so goes the thinking. Their acts are only events in a causal chain. Whatever one does, one could not have done otherwise, for it is impossible for things to take place in any way different from the way in which they, in fact, do take place. All events, including human actions, are compelled. The notion that one acts out of a set of beliefs is rendered hollow in this view, as one has no option but to do what is inevitable. This position is a mode of what is known as determinism, a theory that I will cover briefly.

DETERMINISM

There are different versions of determinism, but all share the thread of inevitability. Every event that occurs is such that no other event could have taken place under the conditions of its occurrence. Given that actions are events, merely a special type involving rational agents, determinism threatens to remove choice, and thereby accountability, from agency. The idea is that one cannot refrain from doing what one does, as all actions are predetermined; therefore, one cannot be liable for one's acts. Outlined below are several versions of the theory. There are others, but these renditions constitute the core of the position. In each case, there is some factor from which an alleged compulsion emerges.

LOGICAL DETERMINISM

If a certain event happens on a particular day—say, the attack on Pearl Harbor on December 7, 1941—then it seems that it was true years before that time that it *will* happen on that day. Thus, it cannot be prevented, and there is nothing to be gained in trying to do so.

416

Herein lies the view of logical determinism, referred to, in some contexts, as fatalism. Logical determinism maintains that every statement is either true or false; therefore, if it is true that a subject s will do an action a tomorrow, then it is not within s's power to alter that fact. The agent s does not have the ability to change the course of events, even those events that are s's own actions. In its extreme form, such a deterministic stance denies that humans have free will.

The position can be formulated in terms of a logical dilemma. Let the variable s be a subject and a be a performance by the subject, constituting an action. The variable p will equal this proposition:

Subject s will do action a tomorrow.

The dilemma surfaces in the manner that is shown below:

If p is true, then it is not within s's power not to do a; and, if p is false, then it is not within s's power to do a.
Either p is true, or p is false.
Therefore, either it is not within s's power not to do a, or it is not within s's power to do a.

Aristotle suggests that propositions concerning future events—ones involving human decision, at least—are neither true nor false when given. Other philosophers take a similar, or even more rigid, view. A proposition of this sort becomes true or false after the event that it reports either has occurred or has failed to occur. So, if the thinking is correct, then the minor premise of the abovestated dilemma is groundless. In this way, the problem might be avoided. The compulsion is absent because sentences that are about the future have an undetermined truth-value or have no truth-value at all.[21]

---

[21] In logic, intuitively enough, whether a sentence is true or false determines its truth-value. Thus, logical systems are nearly universally two-valued systems; the values are *true* and *false*. Basic assumptions in logic are that (1) every meaningful declarative sentence must be either true or false and that (2) no sentence asserting a proposition and its negation can be true. These postulates correspond respectively to the law of bivalence—which is related to the law of excluded middle—and the law of noncontradiction. There are systems that put forth other values, such as *undetermined* or *neither true nor false*. The type of objection that Aristotle and later philosophers raise is consistent with systems in which more than two values

The problem here, I believe, is that the solution is misguided. Perhaps this fact will become more clear when opposing the fatalistic line of reasoning with a counterdilemma.

> If p is true, then it is within s's power to do a; and, if p is
>   false, then it is within s's power not to do a.
> Either p is true, or p is false.
> Therefore, either it is within s's power to do a, or it is within
> s's power not to do a.

The pressing issue is why the compulsory quality of the theory seems to vanish so quickly when the dilemma is reformulated. Is there a metaphysical force at work in the dilemma or merely a linguistic one?

To answer this question, consider a statement of the following form. Call it q; let t represent some date in the future.

> Event e will happen on t.

For example, suppose that event e stands for the bombing of Pearl Harbor, and t signifies December 7, 1941. Suppose further that t has come and gone, so that the present date is now two years after t. It makes no sense to assert q at this juncture. The future tense of the verb (will happen) is not consistent with the past period of time that t specifies. Statement q cannot become true or false once the event e either happens at t or does not happen at t. If anything, it *ceases* to be true or false because it becomes meaningless. To say that the bombing will occur on a particular day two years ago is to utter something that is nonsensical. It is not that q is suddenly open to truth when t does arrive but rather that one *knows* at that point whether it *was* true, whereas one did not know previously. Knowing that a statement is true, however, is not the same thing as a statement's being true. The following proposition was obviously correct even when no one knew it:

---

are inherent. The previous chapter touched on such multivalued logic systems. A full discussion of them lies outside the scope of this work; suffice it to say that they have not found wide acceptance. Although some writers believe that they may have uses in quantum mechanics, I hold that truth is not subject to such variance.

The world is spheroidal in shape.

It is just that people eventually discovered the truth of what it reports. One cannot say of a proposition, simply because the truth of it is not known, that it has no truth-value. If such were the case, then even propositions using the past tense would be neither true nor false if no one knew. So, taking the view to the extreme, the following statement presents a problem:

The giant redwood Big Ed fell yesterday, toppled by the severe storm.

It is neither true nor false, on the premise at hand, given that no one has been in the forest to look. Such a position is indefensible. Imagine that two rangers take a trip into the woods to discover the facts. Both see a large tree, a redwood, on the forest floor. Ranger Tolberson thinks that it is Big Ed. Ranger Jackson disagrees, convinced that it is Fat Willie instead. Does the statement about Big Ed remain neither true nor false until there is some consensus or concession? Must Ranger Carter come to the scene of the fallen giant to put an end to the deadlock?

One cannot reduce truth about physical reality to psychological states or to affirmations by the majority. Humans may not know, now or ever, the truth of certain propositions, such as those about the particulars of microevents in the far reaches of intergalactic space. Yet, this lack of knowledge has no bearing on the states of affairs that obtain in those distant places—the singularity of compound objects, as discussed earlier in this work, is a different matter, of course. Assertions that people may make about those places are still amenable to the test of truth. People know what is required for those assertions to be true or false, even if no one can travel there to take an up-close look.

It is not the case that statements about events that have not yet come to pass have no truth-value, and it is not the case that their truth-value compels people to act, such that persons are without the freedom to choose. The lack of knowledge of the truth or falsity of a statement in no way makes it neither true nor false, whether it is a statement about the future, the present, or the past; and the fact that *s* will do *a* in the future is no more compulsory than the fact that *s* is doing *a* now or that *s* did *a* yesterday. The truth of a proposition about *s*'s doing *a* is determined by the occurrence of the action; *s*'s action is not determined by the truth of the proposition about it. There is an asymmetry at work here, but determinism misconstrues it. The theory reverses the order.

It is as if one takes a photograph of a mountain across a valley. The photograph and the mountain have a distinct similarity: The picture is a miniature, virtually two-dimensional representation of the scene; it reflects what one sees when one gazes beyond the camera's lens. The picture, however, is dependent on the mountain, and the expanse between it and the observer, not conversely. What the camera captures on film or other medium appears as it does because of the existence of the natural, geological structure that looms in the distance; the geological structure does not appear as it does because of the picture. Analogously, determinism treats sentences about the future that are true as ontologically prior, constraining reality to conform to what they purport. Just as a snapshot reflects things that lie in reality as the image of them is presented to the camera, however, sentences about the actions of agents, whether about the future or otherwise, only reflect reality; they do not establish it. To hold that events must be as they are solely because a sentence says so is to build into linguistic expressions an efficacy that they in themselves do not possess.[22] As I will argue below, this notion of asymmetry arose in a similar way centuries ago.

THEOLOGICAL DETERMINISM

Here, the supposed compelling force is the omniscience of God, coupled with the notion that truth is not limited by time. If a statement about some occurrence is true, then God knows it, even in the case where the event has not yet happened, for He knows what

---

[22] Declaratory authority is not to be confused with determinism. Indeed, people do have the ability to effect change by virtue of what they say, though not because of some intrinsic semantic dynamism but because of the authority that is granted to the agent who is making the declaration. Refer to, for example, Mark 11:22–23.

will happen. If God knows that a future event will occur, however, then it must come to pass. The principle holds, regardless of whether those events are human acts. If God knows that *s* will do *a* tomorrow, then there is no way that *s* cannot do *a* tomorrow. The agent must do so because God's knowledge is infallible. Therefore, *s* is not free to act otherwise than in accordance with God's knowledge.

Again, this argument for determinism rests on a mistaken notion. Although God could force things to turn out to be a certain way, given His omnipotence, one cannot assume that His omniscience so forces them. As the medieval theologian St. Augustine (354–430) claims, God foresees events because they are going to occur; they do not occur because He foresees them. In terms of agency, it is not that *s* will do *a* because God knows it but rather that God knows it because *s* will do it. St. Augustine remarks further that God exists independently of time, so that all history is before Him as the present is before people. A man might know that something is true in the present—for example, that his friend Roger is standing on the terrace—but that knowledge in no way forces Roger to be there. Knowing does not compel events to occur. Roger is on the terrace because he chose to be there. If Roger will be on the porch tomorrow, then God knows it because He knows the future as surely as He knows the present and the past, but God's knowledge does not constrain Roger, so that he can go nowhere but the porch.

PHYSICAL AND PSYCHOLOGICAL DETERMINISM

Philosophical views of the modern period often focus on causation. Thomas Hobbes believes only in materiality, thereby denying the existence of both immaterial mind and immaterial spirit. Human behavior is the goings-on of matter and as such is necessitated by, and in accordance with, physical laws. Deliberation, he claims, is the vacillating between conflicting impulses of nearly equal force; eventually, one of them prevails, and the agent acts. Hobbes believes that human actions are caused and thus determined, but they are caused by the will and hence to be regarded as free. Liberty is the freedom to act in accordance with the will, not the lack of causation. One is free to act if nothing stands in the way of what one wills to do.

Although there are a number of significant problems with Hobbes's materialism, one pertinent issue surfaces regarding his treatment of the will. Portrayed as mechanistic in nature, a person chooses based on the stronger of two impulses. Hobbes's view cannot account for instances in which the alternatives are of equal force, yet the agent chooses nevertheless. The classic example is Buridan's ass, most likely put forward in criticism of the moral philosophy of Jean Buridan of France (c. 1295–c. 1356). The illustration, however, arose in a slightly different form in the writings of Aristotle and later in those of the Arabic philosopher Ghazali (1058–1111).[23] Here is the case: Suppose that a hungry donkey is suspended between two bales of hay that appeal to the animal equally. If Hobbes were right, then the beast merely would respond to the stronger of two impulses. Given that the impulses are of equal force, the donkey inevitably would starve to death, a consequence that no one could believe actually would happen. The theory is just false.

Imagine that the dealer in a bridge game decides to entertain the other players by showing them a card trick. He spreads the deck, fan-style, face down on the table and says, "Pick a card, any card." From the back, the cards look identical. The stimuli are the same. Are three people frozen in indecision for hours until the host asks them, at last, to leave? No, they all make a choice.

The philosopher David Hume, who is known for his marked skepticism, takes a divergent view of causation, which forms the basis for his theory of action. Causation is constant conjunction, he says, whereby events of one type precede those of another type repeatedly. Causes only come before effects; they do not compel them: There is no deep-seated metaphysical constraint at work. The relation is one of simple temporal succession. Human actions are such that certain motives result consistently in certain behavior; hence, thinks Hume, actions are caused, and determinism is correct.

---

[23] The common view is that the case of Buridan's ass arose as an attack on Buridan's theory of the will. According to Buridan, one always wills the greater good. If one cannot judge which of two possibilities holds the greater good, however, then the person's choice is delayed until the person can make that determination through a further examination of the values that are inherent in each.

Free actions arise from the motives of the agent. Like Hobbes, Hume believes that freedom is the ability to act in accordance with one's will; actions are not free if they are caused by something other than one's will. So, he maintains, determinism and free will are not inconsistent.

The general criticism of the views of these philosophers is that the concept of freedom that they employ is incorrect. As it applies to determinism, freedom is not the liberty that people have to act as they will. Certainly, there is a type of liberty in a society that permits citizens to follow their pursuits unimpeded, as long as they stay within the rule of law; and, as individuals, they are at liberty to act in accordance with their desires. Determinism, however, is not about impediment; it is about avoidance. It is not that one can act in accordance with one's will that represents freedom of choice; it is instead that whatever one does, one could have done otherwise if one had so chosen. Determinism holds that events, including actions, must occur as they do; therefore, one is not free to act in any way other than the way in which one does act. Thus, determinism undermines free will. If free will is abolished, then, continuing in this vein, so is accountability, as one cannot be responsible for what one cannot avoid doing.

Determinism falls short of the mark. In physics, one can calculate the trajectory of a projectile under standard geological and atmospheric conditions if one knows its initial velocity, the angle at which it is propelled, and its ballistic coefficient. In a sense then, one can say that the shell, fired from the artillery piece on the hill, will strike the village at the town square, even before it hits. The mathematical calculations show that it is so. Yet, there is no compulsion here. The round simply follows a path that is prescribed by physical laws. The shell's striking the village is not certain, as it may explode prematurely, or it may collide with a flock of birds en route and be diverted from its course. That diversion, though, is also in accordance with physical laws. If the diversion occurs, then determinism claims that it was the diversion that was inevitable all along, not the destruction of the community's town square. The problem here is that *whatever* happens, whether probable or improbable, expected or unexpected, in line with similar occurrences in the past or out of line with them, determinism claims that it was to be. Scientific claims are valuable precisely because they have the potential to be falsified. Science advances hypotheses about material reality, and those hypotheses are subject to refinement or refutation if relevant incidents prove them not to be true. The demonstration of their truth or falsity comes through experimentation and observation. Determinism makes no such claims, however. It merely asserts that whatever will happen, will happen. Hence, whatever does happen, determinism has it that it could not have been otherwise. Claims of this sort are uninformative and point to a philosophical view without merit. One might not know beforehand what will occur, but, after some event *e* does occur, the statement that *e* was inevitable lacks the potential falsifiability that is required of proper assertions of science. To declare that *e* was to happen because it did happen imparts no knowledge to the hearer. Contrast the claims, which are specified below, of two artillerymen upon the firing of a howitzer—one who embraces the science of ballistics, the other who adopts the concepts of determinism:

Ballistician	We have aligned the howitzer. The shell will strike the village at the town square.
Determinist	The shell will strike where it will strike. If it strikes the village at the town square, then it could not have landed any other place.

Viewed in this way, determinism is, at best, trivial. At worst, it is indefensible.

The more pressing concern, though, is that determinism simply fails to explain the richness and complexity of human behavior. Humans live in a world of agency. People are fundamentally different, in important ways, from inanimate objects. They do not track prescribed paths like mere artillery shells. They deliberate, choose, and act in accordance with those choices. They plan and carry out those plans. They are moved by compassion and by anger. They are motivated by things that they value. They hoard and give away, follow habitual patterns and envision change, and cogitate and imagine.

I am reminded of an account concerning the actions of an abusive spouse. The man beat his wife on more than one occasion, venting his rage. The man claimed that he became so angry that he could not refrain from hitting her. In a session with a counselor, the counselor asked the man why he did not go ahead and just kill her. The man was taken aback by the question. He did not want to kill her; he never let it go that far. The counselor pointed out to the man, rightly so, that, if he could keep himself from killing her, then he could keep himself from striking her. The man's anger influenced his actions, without doubt, but there was no coercion—he could have done otherwise than he did. He could have resisted the impulse. He had a choice. The man was presented with an opportunity to act against his anger, but he did not do so. There is no compelling inevitability inherent in human action, only an impetus that is related to the deed.

One can follow the inclination or stand opposed to it. The notion that all that people do is unavoidable is just inconsistent with reasonable views of humanity. If all events are determined, then everything that one does was to be. Accordingly, no one is to be praised or blamed, recognized for achievements or chided for failures. Determinism reduces the actions of agents to the reactions of physics. The upshot of the position is that one should do nothing at all, for, no matter what one does, one cannot make a difference. It is an idea that has not found much favor in philosophical writings, although certain scientists seem to have embraced it, to their detriment. Determinism provides an impoverished and truncated view of people and of their ability to effect change in the world in which they live.

I want to look further into the workings of human actions. Discovering how beliefs are linked to behavior may help to illuminate why it is that people do what they do and what consequences may be in store for them.

MIND IN ACTION

Much of day-to-day life consists of simple acts. Straight-forward and transparent in their execution, there seems to be little question about what is happening in such instances and why. Some things that people do are undertaken just for the fun of doing them. There is no substantive goal in mind, only carefree enjoyment. Children throw rocks into a stream or skip down the street or kick dandelions as they walk across a meadow. Other acts are goal-directed performances, in that people execute them to accomplish specific ends. One takes shirts to the cleaners on the way to work or prepares a candlelight dinner for a special anniversary or vacuums the house before the guests arrive for a party. Still others appear to exhibit characteristics of both kinds: One plays checkers for the fun of the game but also to win. Many human actions are recognizable for what they are because one sees the agent's physical activity—his or her bodily movements—and understands what is occurring. In the cases where those actions correspond to intended ends, the purpose that the agent has in mind in performing them is often something that one can surmise with a reasonable measure of assurance. Indeed, the philosopher Donald Davidson (1917–2003) maintains that actions *are* the movements that people make in carrying out deeds. He states,

> We must conclude . . . that mere movements of the body—these are all the actions there are. We never do more than move our bodies: the rest is up to nature.[24]

I believe that this position is incorrect. Albeit the physical body is a fundamental part of human action, some behavioral perform-ances by persons are not expressed through movements, but they surely count as acts nonetheless. It is not difficult to think of examples. With eyes closed, a young girl is making a concentrated effort not to move as the radiologist X-rays her injured leg. She is trying to do what the doctor asks, even though it is painful. A sunbathing college student lies motionless to maximize the amount

---

[24] Donald Davidson, "Agency," in *Agent, Action, and Reason*, ed. Robert Binkley, Richard Bronaugh, and Ausonio Marras (Toronto: University of Toronto Press, 1971), 23.

of exposure on a certain area of her back. She believes that she can accomplish her objective by remaining fixed in a particular position. The appearance of the girls is the same as it would be if they were unconscious, yet each is aware and engaged in an act. There are other examples. An experienced hunter is immobile, holding his breath as his wary prey looks in his direction. Certain models simulate manne- quins as they stay still for long periods of time, displaying the latest fashions. In all these cases, the absence of physical movement is no bar to comprehending what the persons mindfully are doing. There is an explanation for the motionlessness in each instance because there is an identifiable purpose for it. Aside from his view that all actions are simply movements by the agent, there are other problems with Davidson's theory; I will cover them in the next segment.

On the other hand, of course, not all bodily movements are associated with acts. Certain behavior is involuntary. Rather than actions, these events are reactions. They are not things that are performed in the capacity of agent. Kerry's leg extends a few degrees when the physician taps his knee just below the patella. He sneezes in the presence of pepper, cats, and freshly cut grass. He ducks when a sudden, loud noise startles him. Kerry's movements are the result of reflexes. Though physical behavior takes place, the behavior does not correspond to any act on his part. The movements are involuntary and not the outward expression of deeds that he undertakes as an agent.

Instances of agency hence may, or may not, involve the moving of a person's body, and the moving may, or may not, signal instances of agency. It follows that the link between the two is not sufficiently strong for it to be a qualifying factor. Acts are not definable strictly in terms of the varying positions of the human frame.

Some conduct even appears to blur the distinction between what one may think of as an action and what one may classify as a reaction. A man jerks the steering wheel to the left to avoid hitting a dog that dashes in front of his car. One may suppose that the subject is fond of animals and does what he can to protect them. There is thus a general principle to which the man adheres and that may be associated with what he did in this case, but there is also a situational shift that brings about a reflex-like movement, a response that was acquired perhaps through years of driving. It is hardly a matter of resolve, it seems, but rather a matter of conditioning. One may argue that it is accurate to describe the man's turning of the wheel as both—partly action and partly reaction, containing elements of each. It would be challenging to defend such a view, however. If it is possible to ascertain what it is that makes an event an act, then it is likely that one can say which of the two it is, for it is evident that actions have an intrinsic quality that distinguishes them from reflexes and related reactions.

Whether there are such compound cases, a great part of human activity—a broad spectrum of behavioral incidents—obviously consists of things that people do in the role of agent. Given that actions are not mere changes in positions of the body, as Davidson maintains, what then is the structure of these occurrences, and why do they happen? If physicality is not the key, then do actions rest on a mental foundation; and, if so, then how does this mental under-pinning come into play? What is the identifying mark of agency?

THE VALUE-BELIEF PAIRING

Actions are events of a particular type; they are performances that people undertake with intent. If one *intends* to do something, determined to see it through, circumstances permitting, regardless of whether there is a goal in doing it and whether it is accompanied by bodily movement, then agency is at work. Indeed, if intention lies in one's mind, then how the event unfolds in the world—even *whether* it unfolds—is not essential to its being a case of agency. Andy meant to catch a monarch butterfly as he swung his net over the unsuspect-ing creature, but he caught a viceroy butterfly instead, occasioned by mistaken classification: The two insects have very similar appear-ances. In capturing the viceroy, he did not do what he intended to do—in the fullest expression of his intent. It was not what he had in mind to do, but his doing was intentional nevertheless. His sweeping the flowers with the net was something that he did on purpose. It was an act. Sissy meant to check the fourth box on the fifth question of the multiple-choice test. She knew the correct answer, but, in her haste, she marked the third box. Her marking was intentional, despite the fact that her marking the third box as such was not intentional. Sissy acted when she made her selection and put pencil to paper.

Among the events that may be categorized as actions, one can narrow the scope of the discussion a bit by focusing on those cases in which the agent does something for the purpose of effecting some state of affairs. Instances of this sort, in fact, seem to constitute the majority of deeds—perhaps, one may argue, nearly all of them. Human beings act in such a way that their individual actions, so they believe, will bring about, or may bring about, the accomplishment of a certain goal, whether immediate or otherwise. People ponder and choose; they consider and elect; and they deliberate and decide—all with an objective in mind. Their performances are willful, purposeful behaviors that are intended to realize some end.

In his work *Nicomachean Ethics*, Aristotle claims that deliberation concerns means, not ends. One might paraphrase Aristotle's claim roughly in this way: People do not decide what they want, only how to get it. Says the philosopher,

> We deliberate not about ends, but about what promotes ends. A doctor, for instance, does not deliberate about whether he will cure, or an orator about whether he will persuade, or a politician about whether he will produce good order, or any other [expert] about the end [that his science aims at] [sic]. Rather, we lay down the end, and then examine the ways and means to achieve it.[25]

One may object that people sometimes do deliberate about ends. Both the cherry pie and the apple cobbler look appetizing; Betty must decide which one she wants for dessert. She ponders the options and selects the cobbler, and consuming it is the end that she has in mind. In reality, though, the satisfaction of her sweet tooth is the objective here. How better to satisfy her craving in the particular circumstances is what she undertakes the deliberation process to achieve. Taking a high-level view of actions makes it manifest that

---

[25] Aristotle, *Nicomachean Ethics*, 3, 3.1112b, *Aristotle: Nicomachean Ethics*, trans. Terence Irwin, 2nd ed. (Indianapolis: Hackett Publishing Co., 1999), 35. The first two bracketed insertions are those of the translator.

ends are set according to what people *value*—in an encompassing sense—and that the paths to getting what they value in various cases are linked to decisions that are based on what they *believe* to be true: People believe that the means that they choose will lead to the attainment of the respective goals. Ends themselves, of course, can be means to more extensive goals, a matter that I will discuss later.

It would be beneficial to look closely at an example of action to see whether one can drive out a structure that may apply in a general fashion. Begin by considering the following statement:

> Jimmy ate the peas that were on his plate.

This sentence reports an act—it is evident that the eating was not a mere reflex motion; it was intentional. The report of that act, though, is limited to the physical behavior. Independent of context, one does not know why Jimmy ate the peas. Did he think that they were jelly beans? Was he hungry? To provide a fuller description of an act, as reflected in the observed conduct—to tell what is going on, so to speak, when a person acts—the sentence relating the event must include a clear reference to something more: It must indicate what prompted the incident. Consider a few additional statements:

> Jimmy ate the peas that were on his plate because he did not wish to appear to be impolite.
> Jimmy ate the peas that were on his plate because his friends dared him to do it.
> Jimmy ate the peas that were on his plate because his mother threatened to spank him if he refused.

In these instances, the outward behavior that the statements identify is the same, but different reasons are apparent. The sentences report the physical aspect of the performance—the boy's eating the peas—and his eating was plainly deliberate; but each sentence also offers a partial account of why he did it: The word 'because' in the sentence conveys the motive that was behind his behavior. In each case, two things were at work, expressed either explicitly or implicitly in the description of his act: (1) something that was important to the boy and (2) a set of beliefs that the boy possessed. Jimmy had in mind what he willed to do, and he believed that eating what lay in front of him was sufficient to bring about the actualization of it. He may, or may not, have thought that the things that were on his plate were peas, but he did think that consuming them would accomplish a desired result, whether it was avoidance of impropriety, the gaining of peer respect, or freedom from punishment through obedience.

As a rule, actions that are directed toward an end that the agent intends to realize, the sort with which I am concerned here, share this form. They arise out of something that the agent sees as valuable in the circumstances, expressed in the form of what the agent wills, coupled with beliefs that the agent possesses at the time. What the agent wills is typically what the agent desires or wants, or something that he or she deems to be of worth or importance. Occasionally, of course, one may will to do what he or she does not want to do: going to the dentist for a root canal, for example, or following orders from a superior to undertake a laborious task. It is the broader goal that is in mind. It is appropriate to view acts in terms of an inclusive perspective on the agent's values, for one wills what one sees as worthy for one reason or another, even if it may be unpleasant. It is the *will* that one expresses in acting—and acts begin when the will is fixed.

At any rate, outward behavior—bodily movement—is not the mark of agency, although the behavior is usually in concert with it. Instead, agency is characterized by mentality, and mentality is inseparable from it. Doing with intent—exercising one's resolve to do—is what qualifies the event as an action. For the most part, this carrying out of the will is in accordance with one or more values and a set of beliefs, throwing rocks and kicking dandelions perhaps put aside. The relationship is not simply one of concomitance. Valuing and believing are bound to doing with a cord of rationality. Jointly, they serve in such cases as the foundation for the intention that is central to acting. They explain *why* a person is acting, though not necessarily *the act* itself: *what* the person actually is doing in acting, as Andy and Sissy show. I will refer to such goal-oriented actions as *end-state actions* (or *acts*), for performances of this sort signal the presence of an objective that an agent means to achieve in executing a deed. I will call *value-factors* those things that a person regards as valuable at the time of the performance of an end-state act and that operate as motives behind the person's intentional behavior. So, end-state actions are events in which an agent purposively undertakes, through the exercise of the will, a behavioral performance, whether that performance involves movement or no movement, to effect a specific state or condition because of the agent's value-factors and beliefs.

It is not an uncommon view in philosophy that acting for a reason includes in some sense the two features that I identified above: valuing, of one sort or another, and believing. Returning to Donald Davidson, one finds that he makes the following claim:

> What is the relation between a reason and an action when the reason explains the action by giving the agent's reason for doing what he did? . . .
> . . . Whenever someone does something for a reason, . . . he can be characterized as (*a*) having some sort of pro attitude toward actions of a certain kind, and (*b*) believing (or knowing, perceiving, noticing, remembering) that his action is of that kind. Under (*a*) are to be included desires, wantings, urges, promptings, and a great variety of moral views, aesthetic principles, economic prejudices, social conventions, and public and private goals and values in so far as these can be interpreted as attitudes of an agent directed toward actions of a certain kind.[26]

Then, Davidson asserts,

> Giving the reason why an agent did something is often a matter of naming the pro attitude (*a*) or the related belief (*b*) or both; let me call this pair the *primary reason* why the agent performed the action. . . .
> The primary reason for an action is its cause.[27]

It is quite a list that Davidson offers as extensions of the expression 'pro attitude'. The locution is probably broad enough to cover them, given that Davidson, following this passage, allows attitudes to include both long-term character traits and single-incident fancies,

---

[26] Donald Davidson, "Actions, Reasons, and Causes," *Journal of Philosophy* 60, no. 23 (1963): 685–86.
[27] Ibid., 686.

but there is a problem with his depiction of the structure of actions. Davidson says that they are *caused* and that it is the attitudes and beliefs that do the causing. By use of the term 'cause', Davidson is referring to the efficient cause; that is to say, that which brings about the effect. It is in this sense that the term is used in ordinary language. If one strikes a nail with a hammer, then the hammer's slamming into the nail with a certain velocity is the efficient cause of the nail's sinking into the board.[28]

Suppose that a man lights a fire in the fireplace on a cool night. According to Davidson's analysis, the desire to start a fire and the belief that what he is doing is lighting one as he holds the burning match beneath the kindling constitute together the cause of the man's act of igniting the wood splinters. This interpretation of what is happening cannot be right. The man's act causes a fire to start at the hearth, and his valuing warmth and his belief that he is setting the kindling ablaze are key elements of the event, but the desire and the belief, even if they could serve as a cause, could not serve as the cause of his *action*. End-state acts are those that are marked by the aim to accomplish some objective. As noted above, acts are distinguished from mere physical activity by virtue of, and only by virtue of, the mentality of the agent. The difference between Sarah's foot's tapping because of a series of muscle twitches and Sarah's tapping her foot to aid her in keeping time with the music as she plays the flute does not lie in the observable physical behavior. It lies in Sarah's intent; and the intent points to the reason that is behind her activity—behind what her corporal being is about at the moment. The behavior may be exactly the same, whether it is involuntary or deliberate. In foot tapping, without intending in mind, there is no act; without some objective in mind, there is no end-state act. The motivation for acting is given in Davidson's pro attitude, whether it is characterized as a desire, a wanting, or some other psychological factor in his list. United with the matching belief, it constitutes the primary reason for the doing, Davidson maintains. If the primary reason is part of the action, however, which it must be to advance a foot-tapping affair from a clonic spasm to an end-state action, then it *cannot* be the efficient cause, even in part, of the action. Otherwise, it

---

[28] Refer to Aristotle's four causes, which are described in chap. 3.

would be the efficient cause of itself, and it is not possible for anything to be such a cause.

There are two problems with Davidson's notion. First, a thing must *be* before it can *do*, a principle that the last chapter covered in some detail. If a thing could be the efficient cause of itself, then it would have to exist, to serve as the cause, before it exists, to serve as the effect of that cause, which is absurd. Second, a cause must be logically distinct from its effect, as the cause-effect relation is contingent, not necessary—a universal tenet in philosophy.[29] If a thing could cause itself in the sense at hand, even in part, then that cause would stand in the relation of identity to its effect, for it is itself, or part of itself, and identity is a logical relation, not a contingent one.[30]

This problem of logical separation has not escaped the notice of others. A. I. Melden contends that Davidson's theory violates the separation rule, and he declares,

> [T]he interior event which we call 'the act of volition'. . . must be logically distinct from the alleged effect—this surely is one lesson we can derive from a reading of Hume's discussion of causation. Yet nothing can be an act of volition that is not logically connected with that which is willed—the act of willing is intelligible only as the act of willing whatever it is that is willed.[31]

---

[29] David Hume argues against any necessary link between cause and effect. As I mentioned above, according to Hume, there is merely constant conjunction, which gives rise to one's making the connection between the two. One observes that occurrences, which one refers to as causes, precede other occurrences, which one refers to as effects. The regularity with which instances of the first type come before instances of the second type leads to the ascription of a causal connection, but there is no logical compulsion at work. In philosophy, as pointed out earlier, a generally accepted way of expressing the cause-effect relationship is as a conditional proposition.

[30] In chap. 3, I covered how declarations of identity for objects rest on standards that the individuals of a society establish. There is no logical necessity in the establishment of one particular standard, as opposed to another, for objects corresponding to a given sortal term. Once the standard is set, so that the identity of objects of a given sort is determinable, however, those objects stand in a relation of identity to themselves and thus stand in a necessary relation because everything is necessarily identical to itself. Such necessity hence, resting on a prior declaration of conditions, applies in a restricted sense.

[31] A. I. Melden, *Free Action* (1961; London: Routledge and Kegan Paul, 1967), 53.

Davidson attempts to defend his theory against such notions with the following explication:

> Someone might be tempted into the mistake of thinking that my flipping of the switch caused my turning on of the light (in fact, it caused the light to go on). But it does not follow that it is a mistake to take 'My reason for flipping the switch was that I wanted to turn on the light' as entailing, in part, 'I flipped the switch, and this action is further describable as having been caused by my wanting to turn on the light'. To describe an event in terms of its cause is not to identify the event with its cause, nor does explanation by redescription exclude causal explanation.[32]

It is true that to describe an action in terms of its primary reason—a pro attitude plus a belief—which, according to Davidson, is its cause, is not to identify the *action*, taken in its entirety, with the action's cause, but it *is* to identify a *component of the action* with the action's cause. In putting forth his view of act structure, Davidson is embracing this identity, an approach that cannot be correct. The flipping of the switch in his example is not an (end-state) act without the wanting that underlies the intent. The part of a behavioral event that makes it more than an inadvertent lurch, a pathological twitch, or a common reflex is mental. It is the defining factor. Davidson says that the act of flipping is caused by the wanting; but, if the wanting is part of the act, then it *cannot* be its cause: The whole includes the part.

Furthermore, a causal structure produces counterintuitive cases. To set the stage for one such case, consider a scenario (expanding the previous example) that Davidson presents. If a man (Davidson, in his scenario) flips the light switch, turns on the light, illuminates the room, and unknowingly alerts a prowler to the fact that he is home, then he does only one thing, avers Davidson, not four, although there are four descriptions. There is a single bodily movement—the flipping—but it is described in terms of increasingly encompassing circumstances. A man's wanting to turn on the light explains his flipping the switch, but it does not explain his alerting the prowler.

---

[32] Davidson, "Actions, Reasons, and Causes," 695.

Suppose that the light switch is next to the switch for the ceiling fan; it sits just to the right of it. John wants to turn on the light, but, in his clumsiness, he turns on the fan instead. If Davidson were right in saying that acts are redescribable in terms of their causes, and those causes are pro attitudes plus beliefs, then would one not be inclined to say that John's wanting to turn on the light and his belief that he was doing so caused him to activate the fan switch? This consequence is hardy acceptable. More problematic, though, would one not be inclined to say that John's wanting to turn on the light and his corresponding belief that he was turning on the light caused him *not* to hit the light switch? What sense does this act description make? John's failure to accomplish what he wanted was not caused by a desire to accomplish it and a belief that he was doing so. Moreover, he had neither a pro attitude toward not turning on the light nor a belief that he was not turning on the light; yet, not turning it on is precisely what he did. It would be more reasonable simply to deny that his unsuccessful act was the effect of an efficient cause, contrary to Davidson's stance. If a particular act is not so caused, though, then others surely may follow suit. In any event, Davidson's theory seems to falter.

Davidson goes on to say that reasons explain what one does when the act is described in one way but not necessarily in another way. To avoid a problem here, Davidson puts forth a condition of primary reasons.

> R is a primary reason why an agent performed the action A under the description d only if R consists of a pro attitude of the agent toward actions with a certain property, and a belief of the agent that A, under the description d, has that property.[33]

Perhaps employing Davidson's condition can avoid the consequence that I noted above by limiting the applicability of the reason to an appropriate description of the action, but, in the end, it does not rescue him. Suppose that John's wife, Martha, noticed one day, while John was at the office, that the ceiling fan was not working. Martha called an electrician, who discovered a faulty wall switch and

---

[33] Ibid., 687.

replaced the mechanism. Unfortunately, the electrician crossed the wires during the repair, so that the switch on the left operates the light now, and the one on the right controls the fan. That evening, John decides to turn on the light to thumb through a chapter of a book that he has been reading. By accident, he flips the left switch, and the bulb illuminates.

Consider the consequences of Davidson's theory; I will use his terminology in my analysis. Let *A* under description *d* be John's flipping the light switch. *R* consists of John's wanting to turn on the light—that is to say, his pro attitude toward actions that have the property of lighting the bulb in the socket—and his belief that what he is doing is turning on the light—that is to say, his belief that his action of flipping the light switch has the property of lighting the bulb in the socket. Davidson claims that the primary reason for an act both explains the act and serves as its cause. Then, what one has, given Davidson's analysis, is this representation:

Case 1.

Act *A* under description *d*:

John's flipping the light switch

Primary reason *R*:

John's wanting to turn on the light and John's believing that he is turning on the light

R explains *A* under *d*:

John's wanting to turn on the light and John's believing that he is turning on the light explain John's flipping the light switch.

R causes *A* under *d*:

John's wanting to turn on the light and John's believing that he is turning on the light cause John's flipping the light switch.

The rendition of this event, however, based on Davidson's criterion, neither explains it nor provides the cause of what happened. As for the explanation, John's desire to turn on the light and his belief that he was doing so do not yield an adequate account of his act of flipping the light switch. Although he intended to turn on the light, in keeping with his wanting, he intended to do it by activating the right-hand switch, which had been the light switch ever since he purchased the house—until today. He hit the wrong one by mistake; it is just that his doing so had a favorable outcome. Something is missing in the explanation if one relies simply on Davidson's primary reason to explain the event. As for the cause, the Davidsonian thesis fails to provide a link between what John meant to do and what he, in fact, did. To offer a causal account of any sort necessitates adding another element to the mix, something along the lines of crossed wires, plus poor coordination, lack of attention, or careless execution. There is a gap between the wanting-plus-belief and the act that cannot be bridged, in a Davidsonian view of action, because the belief about the switch could have played no causal role at all in the switch activity and the light's being turned on by John. His physical performance was not in accordance with that belief, even though he did what he wanted to do under the label 'turning on the light'.

The problem becomes more apparent if I describe John's reason for acting in more detail, including an additional condition in its portrayal.

Case 2.

Act *A* under description *d*:
John's flipping the light switch

Primary reason *R*:
John's wanting to turn on the light by flipping the right-hand switch and John's believing that he is turning on the light by flipping that switch

R explains *A* under *d*:
John's wanting to turn on the light by flipping the right-hand switch and John's believing that he is turning on the light by flipping that switch explain John's flipping the light switch.

R causes *A* under *d*:
John's wanting to turn on the light by flipping the right-hand switch and John's believing that he is turning on the light by flipping that switch cause John's flipping the light switch.

Davidson's declared condition is that, if R is the primary reason for an action under a given description, then R equals a pro attitude toward actions having a certain property, coupled with the belief that what one is doing is an instance of performing an action, under the description, with that property. In Case 2, Davidson's condition is satisfied. John did hit the light switch and turn on the light, as a matter of fact. John wanted to turn on the light and wanted to do it by hitting the right-hand switch. He thought that he was doing so when he acted. Indeed, he still may think so, unaware that he hit the left-hand switch. It is clear in Case 2, however, that R, which includes the references to the switch, does not explain John's act under the stated description d. What John wanted to do in the depiction of R and believed that he was doing in the depiction of R is not what he actually did, nor is it what he would have done had he acted in accordance with that desire and belief. If he had carried out his intent successfully, then he never would have performed A—he would not have flipped the light switch and turned on the light—because the right-hand switch controls the fan. R therefore cannot *explain* A. More important, even if reasons could be causes, R could not have *caused* A. There can be no causal link between John's desire and belief, and his switch flipping; the left-hand switch lights the room.

One must be careful in viewing purposeful behavior as effects in a causal chain. Actions must include the psychological factors that make them what they are. Singled out by mentality, they are operations of the will. If one holds that actions are caused, then would one hold that the mental elements that are part of them—essentially, in fact—are caused too? If so, then one is close to viewing persons as automata, compelled to dance to the beat of determinism. Mental phenomena can, and do, serve as causes; certainly, they can bring about other mental phenomena.[34] One's remembering the loss of a loved one may bring feelings of grief and depression; and one's realization of what just happened following the collision on the highway may bring a sense of regret and despair. To think, however,

---

[34] Apart from the hypothesis that mental phenomena cause actions, some philosophers hold that they cause bodily movements. Others, such as Gilbert Ryle, seek to disprove that there exist hidden, mental happenings serving as antecedent causes at all, let alone antecedent causes of physical behavior. Both of these views lead to problems, as the next chapter will demonstrate.

that the whole lot of mental happenings is merely a set of passive effects unfolding in a precipitating sequence is to mischaracterize the mind. Persons do not act in the manner in which billiard balls roll across the felt on impact, rebounding and colliding with others that lie in their paths. Consider the following illustration:

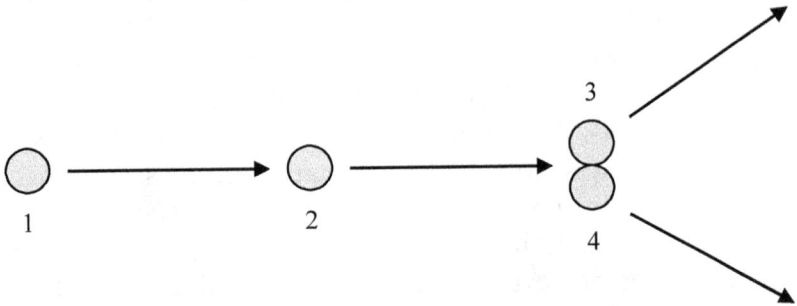

Figure 4.5

When a player strikes ball 1 with the cue, it moves, and the speed and direction of its movement are in accordance with the force and angle of the striking. The ball hits another—namely, 2—causing it to slam into 3 and 4, which also move. Human actions do not resemble the movement of ball 2; they are not occurrences that occupy passive middle positions in some series of events. They are not episodes in which agents do no more than react blindly to whatever forces are applied to them, taking paths that are prescribed by the rules of physics.

Such a concept of action is all wrong from the start. Suppose that a man stretches his left arm across the dinner table in an effort to retrieve the salt, which is just out of range of his fully extended hand. As his arm goes out, so do his watch and wedding ring. He does not move his arm and then move his watch and ring, nor does he move his arm *to* move them. They go with the reaching. As long as he is wearing them, the movements are inseparable. His intention is to take hold of the salt shaker; he is not even presently cognizant of the fact that he has on the jewelry. His movements might be just the same, however, if he decided to show a guest his new watch, stretching over the table to display the prized possession. When a person acts, the behavior is the physical manifestation of the agent's intent. It is the volitional expression through the materiality of his or her being. If the event is an end-state action, then what is expressed reflects both a value-factor and a belief, perhaps more than one of each, as the agent sets out to effect some state of affairs in the world. The body is the means by which one brings about a desired state in physical reality, but the bodily movement is not the deed. The deed at the dinner table is the *man*'s reaching, not his body's reaching. The movement of his arm is the spatiotemporal actualization of what he is doing. The jewelry goes out when the man extends his append-age. The appendage goes out when he reaches for the salt—it is a part of his action of reaching. In both cases, there is an accom-paniment, but only in the former case does it stand in relation to the principal event as merely a concomitant element.

In summary, a Davidsonian-style theory does not offer a proper picture of human action. An action is not the behavior with which it is associated, even behavior that is described in a certain way. To think so is to miss the whole point of agency, mistakenly picking out the bodily goings-on as the essential factor. Further, it is not some-thing that is caused by a wanting, or similar attitude, and a belief, for those elements form an integral part of the act itself. They therefore cannot serve as its cause without leading to the absurdity that a thing is its own efficient cause. Finally, an action is not an inert link in some blind sequence that is ordered by the various laws of nature, as physical determinism would have it. To take this position is to reduce the will to a cog in the cosmic machinery, moved by the mindless dynamics of nature, with no chance to do something other than what has been decreed by the strict canons of physics.

Rather, agency lies *outside* the chain of events that lead to action. Far from their being carried along by causal sequences, agents *start* them—agents are *initiators*. Billiard balls have no choice, as it were, but to respond to forces that are applied to them. Agents do have a choice in responding to forces that are applied to them. There are impulses that influence a person's behavior, and they put the person in a *position* to choose a course, but the precursor causal chain stops with the individual. One is impelled, but not compelled; stirred, but not bound; prompted, but not coerced. The interleaving of value-factors and beliefs is a necessary condition of end-state agency, not a sufficient one. It forms the scaffolding from which human action issues, but it does not form its constraint. It scribes the why of intent, not the why of physics.

There are, of course, consequences to what people do in a physical world, and those consequences are events that people themselves launch, some of which may end at points of decision for other people. Those others must choose as well. Where the will operates, regardless of the occurrences that may lead to it, one finds an interruption in the mechanistic movement of things. Life presents circumstances to individuals every day, but those circumstances provide merely the backdrop for the choices that they make. It is the *agent* who determines what he or she does, not the events that lead to that determination. Situations arise; persons deliberate and decide on a particular course; they interact with their material surroundings through their behavior—it is this progression that defines how end-state doings unfold. One may picture it in the following way:

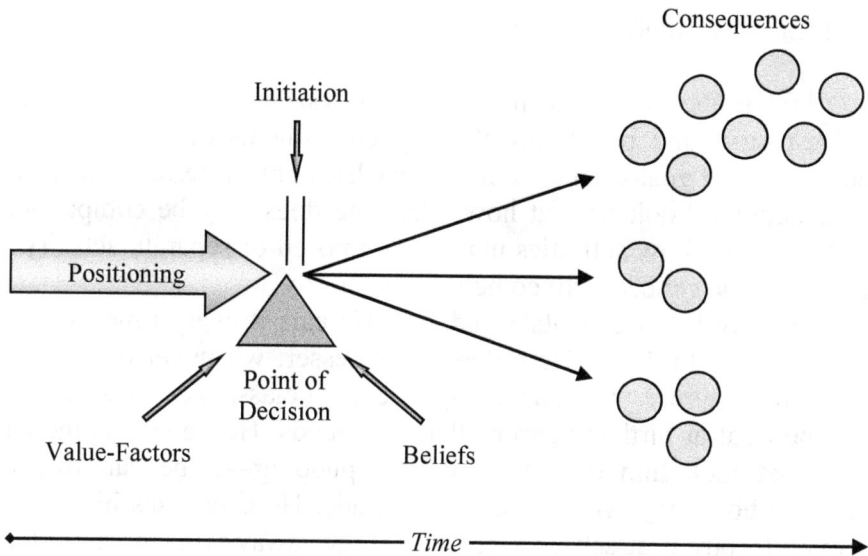

Figure 4.6

In acting, ones causes things to happen by the exercise of the will, but the exercise of the will in acting is not, in turn, the product of causality. It is the beginning of it.

A driver cuts off a man abruptly on the freeway. Rocks on the shoulder fly up and nick the paint on his brand-new car—barely a week old and three hundred miles on the odometer. A cup of coffee in the holder on the console spills into the gear-shift housing and down onto the carpet. Papers for the conference, lying in the front seat, scatter about the vehicle. Anger flares. Retribution is foremost in his thoughts. What happens next is up to him. Humans are beings who are free to choose. The ability to decide is an essential part of their rational nature. In agency, the capacity for initiation is inherent.

BELIEFS AS PROGENITORS

What one can establish from the analysis at this juncture is that value-factors and beliefs are the key components of any adequate description of goal-oriented doings, or what I have referred to as end-state actions. Look now at how what one does may be compound; that is to say, how activities may be composed of separate acts. The import of the concept will come to light shortly.

Jimmy loves chocolate pudding. He eats it every time that he has a chance to do so. He orders it for dessert whenever the family goes out to dinner. When asked by parents of classmates, he selects it for the treat at birthday parties that he attends. He trades his model cars that took him days to build for pudding—if he can find a neighborhood boy who agrees to the trade. He even uses his lunch money to buy it at school when he can get away with the act. One afternoon, Jimmy discovers a freshly made half gallon of it in the refrigerator at home. It is irresistible. He scurries to the tree house with his prize and begins consuming it with the zeal of a bear that is emerging from its long, winter slumber. Toward the end of the spree, however, that enthusiasm wanes. Jimmy becomes satiated and eventually overly full of pudding. He begins to loathe the sight of the next bite of it, yet he presses onward, for he is a determined young man, always stubbornly striving to complete whatever he starts.

When one gives an account of an end-state act, one must point to something that is important enough to the agent to provide an impetus for the agent's conduct, and it is reflected in the agent's purpose for doing what he or she does. Along with a corresponding belief, it is why the agent acts, executing a deliberate deed, although, contrary to Davidson, it does not function as a cause. At the outset of the afternoon affair, Jimmy's wanting the pudding and his thinking that he was eating it could explain his activity, but not toward the end of the event. After twenty minutes of gorging, he becomes nauseated at the thought of another spoonful. The original value-factor, in conjunction with the belief, no longer can account for the incident.

One may be inclined to argue that what lay behind the boy's taking the snack to the tree house in the first place was really the desire to complete tasks and that he believed that he could satisfy this general desire by eating the pudding—the container of it was just the means to accomplish his objective. Although it was overshadowed by the extreme fondness for pudding, that attitude came into play when the fondness gave way to repulsion. This explanation hardly seems to be credible, however. Surely, if Jimmy had dropped the giant bowl after three bites, and it had crashed into the ground, then it would not have been the desire to finish a task that he had started that brought disappoint and tears but the sudden, unexpected loss of the pudding itself. His heart was set on *it*—the object of his gastronomic yearning—not on the admirability of tenacity. He would scramble to the ground to retrieve what he could retrieve, knowing that he would not be able to complete the task of eating the bowl of pudding, as some of it, soaking into the dirt, would not be recoverable. He would be glad that a portion, at least, remained edible, and he would gulp what he could get.

A more accurate depiction of the happening, I think, is that Jimmy's wanting the pudding was the initial motivation for devouring it, but sheer determination replaced that motivation at some point during his time in the tree house. Albeit he continued to eat, there was a change in the reason that he did so in the course of the activity. For the first fifteen bites, he was carried along by his craving for the delicacy; for the final fifteen, doggedness—a strong desire not to let the treat beat him kept him going. All the while, his belief that it was pudding that he was eating remained unchanged. On the thirty-fifth bite, halfway through the gorging incident, maybe both motives were at work.[35] If an outlook shift occurred, though, then there must have

---

[35] If one takes this approach, then one must be careful, lest one allow the individual acts of eating a spoonful to be broken down into further components. The result would be that, to explain what Jimmy is doing, one would need to give the reason for his moving the spoon the first four inches toward his mouth, then the first two inches, then the first inch, and so forth. This account begins to parallel a Zenonian paradox in which one never can reach the end of an infinite series of acts and thus never can explain why Jimmy ate the pudding at all. There is an entire field of philosophy devoted to the individuation of actions, a topic that I will not pursue here. Suffice it to say that the philosopher Alvin Goldman maintains that the right way to divide actions is according to a type-token distinction. Actions are different events if they are instances of different types. Albeit Goldman's analysis is appreciably more involved than this distinction, I believe that it leads to an infinity of actions for every deed that one carries out because of tokens of numerically quantifiable act types, as just noted. Such a stance is untenable. Goldman's view is

been a change in action. Explanations of end-state actions rest on the agent's value-factors and beliefs, and one must individuate actions in view of these basic elements when the performance takes place. It is the thing that the agent values at the time of the act and on which the behavior turns that, when coupled with what the agent accepts as true, explains what is happening. One can refer to Jimmy's consuming the whole bowl of chocolate pudding, but Jimmy's doing so is an event that is composed temporally of three actions, each with similar bodily movements but with different desires. It is a *composite action*, one might say, an action that has other ones as components, such that, in doing them, a person has done it. Eating all the dessert is something that Jimmy did, but no single motive spanned the entire activity. His consuming the pudding extended through a period during which three value-factors came into play, along with one shared belief. The value-factors differentiate the behavioral episodes:

> Jimmy's eating the chocolate pudding out of a desire for it, in accordance with his fondness for it;
> Jimmy's eating the chocolate pudding out of a desire for it, in accordance with his fondness for it, and the determination to finish what he started;
> Jimmy's eating the chocolate pudding out of the determination to finish what he started.

It is evident that, aside from a change in value-factors with the passage of time, composite actions can arise in a different way. A man may play a game of chess to be victorious in a match, for example. The playing of the game consists of a series of individual acts as the man moves his pieces about the board in response to the changing placement of his opponent's pieces. Here, the compounding is not owing to a shifting motivation for the suite of moves—his overall purpose was, and is still, to win the game—but to tactical acts that are performed to accomplish a strategic objective. Each move may carry with it a unique desire in light of the configuration of the pieces on the board, but the overarching goal remains fixed. Once he

---

detailed in his work *A Theory of Human Action* (Englewood Cliffs, NJ: Prentice-Hall, 1970).

defeats the challenger, his act of winning the game can be divided into a sequence of compositional acts: his moving his knight to there, his rook to here, and his queen to the king's bishop three.

Often, such composite acts are extended doings. They are associated with long-term goals that are based on substantive values, and they may take years to complete. The structure of such actions, however, remains the same as that of their shorter-duration siblings. Consider Kim. She intends to obtain a college degree. It is very important to her, and she has been planning for college since the tenth grade. Kim has shown great promise in biology and plans to major in that discipline. Having completed the requirements for admission to the three schools of her liking—achieving a satisfactory score on the SAT, requesting a copy of her high-school transcript, submitting official application materials, arranging for financial aid, and so forth—she sets the stage for reaching her goal. College is a four-year journey, and Kim realizes that she must pass certain required courses along the way to obtain a bachelor's degree. She must follow the prearranged path. After being accepted by her first choice among the schools to which she applied, Kim is excited about her future. She receives a catalog from the college and reviews the requirements for a degree in her selected field. She must enroll in courses in cell biology, organic chemistry and its lab that runs through the summer, marine ecosystems, and human physiology, to list a few. Analogous to her performing actions that were necessary for her to be accepted to the program, Kim's completing these required courses constitutes a group of actions that are necessary for her to achieve the final result. Although she may wish to understand organic chemistry because of an interest in it, and learning more about it becomes in this sense an end in itself for her, in the context of her overall education, completing the course is an interim act, in that it is required for her B.S. in biology. Kim believes that she must pass specific courses to obtain what she regards as valuable: a diploma. Therefore, she sets out to do so. She takes a series of steps that are designed to move her increasingly toward the desired end. In the strategic sense, what Kim is doing is obtaining her college degree. The account of her action will contain a reference to the conjunction of what she values and what she believes. One might represent Kim's action in this way:

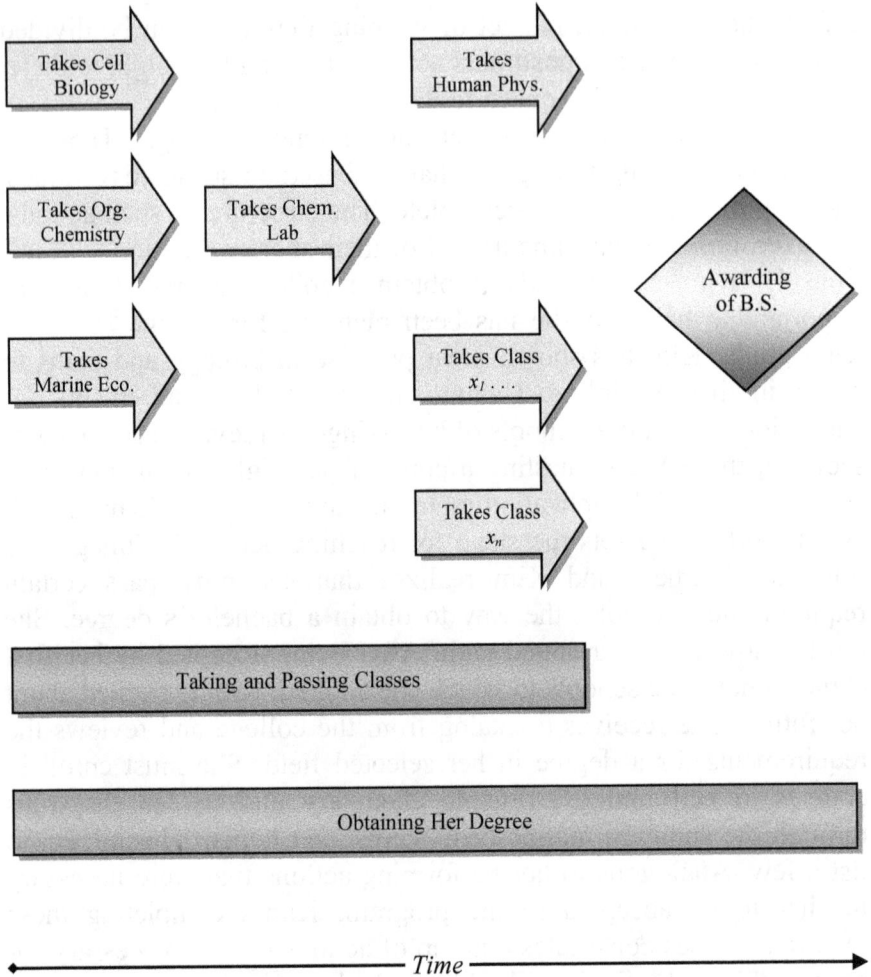

Figure 4.7

Beliefs prepare a person to do what he or she does, not in the sense that they *force* the person to perform but in the sense that they *position* the person to perform. One can trace actions—in principle, at least—to an underlying set of those beliefs. They explain, in part, why agents do what they do because, as noted earlier, actions align with what agents see as valuable and what they take to be true. Kim can drop out of school, if she wishes. Given that she desires to complete the science curriculum, however, if she does continue along her path, then what she is engaged in doing is traceable to her conviction that it will lead to graduation. Beliefs thus function as progenitors. Like a grid, they interlock to form the structure in which an agent ponders, decides, and sets out on a given course. Coupled with their value-factor counterparts, beliefs form the ordered system out of which one acts; these two elements unite to serve as the core of deliberate human behavior.

In practical terms, the achievement of goals that an agent establishes for himself or herself, because the agent sees them as valuable, is founded on what the agent accepts as factual. Whether composed of correct beliefs or incorrect ones, a person's perspective sets the stage for the person to do whatever deeds the person does. It is in the capacity of the second of their primary functions, which I am identifying now, that beliefs have such a significant bearing on people's lives. Beliefs are *precursors of action*. If a person accepts the truth of a proposition p—believes that p—then the person, in normal circumstances, and in light of what the person values, will act accordingly.

In the course of a life, what a person comes to hold as true forms for that person a frame of reference, a dynamic standard in accordance with which he or she makes judgments. As in the family trek that I reported at the beginning of this chapter, this framework plays a significant role in building and shaping new beliefs, which, in turn, mold the set itself. It can be compared to a collection of rules that govern an individual's patterns of thought. One interprets objects of perception—material things and events in which they take part— and objects of reflection—concepts, conjectures, hypotheses, and so forth—in terms of this preexisting network that was stitched together by reason. Arising from sights and insights, newly adopted beliefs are formulated against the background of accepted ones, and what one considers to be true is dovetailed into the structure that was laid down in the past. In this ongoing process, logic balances the recently encountered against the firmly established to form a coherent picture, adjusting some beliefs, supplementing others, and abandoning a few altogether.

Then, what if one's beliefs are wrong? What if a person is convinced that he or she knows, as my father was convinced about the incline of the road in Utah, but the person does not know? In a move of unprecedented boldness, Descartes tries to solve the problem by throwing out all his beliefs and starting over, accepting nothing as true unless he finds it to be indubitable. An extreme approach, it is scarcely a method that realistically one could, or should, embrace. It is certainly not a method that one could employ in any practical way. The question of correctness that Descartes raises is a genuine concern, however. If one's beliefs are false, then what one does is misguided. The person acts not out of knowledge but out of ignorance. What the person sets out to achieve quite likely will not be achieved. All rational people want, at minimum, what is best for those who are dear to them and for themselves. In view of that fact, one must be careful to ensure that the lattice that is formed by the interleaving of one's beliefs is of proper construction. Beliefs must be true and must be grounded appropriately. Where they go astray, there can be no knowledge; and, where there is no knowledge, the outcome is clearly at risk. One might get by, as it were, acting on a true-by-happenstance opinion on occasion, but such acts never can be consistently successful. It is not a pattern on which anyone can depend. On the contrary, knowing is required. It is here, in the realization of goals, of what one regards as desirable, that the two functions of beliefs—as preconditions of knowledge and as precursors of action—converge. If one is to succeed, and this point is key, then both these states of affairs must obtain:

1. One's beliefs must be true and must be grounded adequately—one must know.
2. One must act in accordance with that knowledge.

To fail in either case is to fail entirely.

Suppose that a critical belief in an agent's grid of beliefs is false. It is critical because, if the agent acts on it in a given context, then the goal will be forfeited. In this end-state action, the agent will have missed the mark. A simple diagram may help to illustrate the problem. The dashed lines indicate false beliefs.

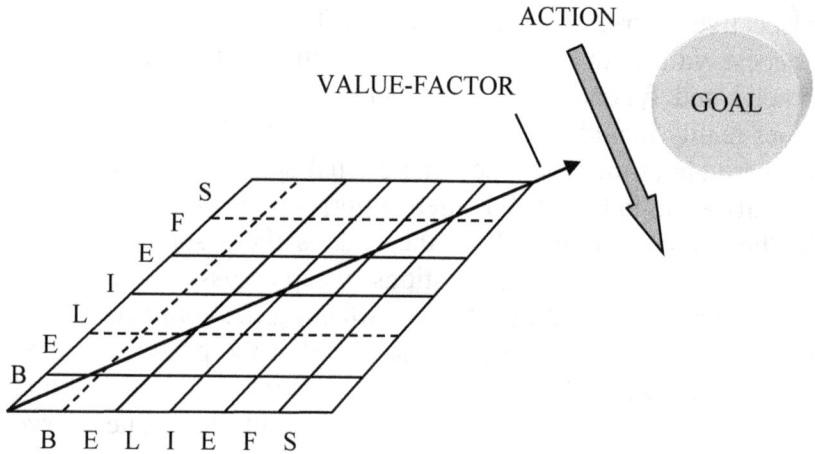

Figure 4.8

Kim's pursuit of a degree, for example, must be based on the truth, lest she fail to fulfill her dream. If she does not know that she must take a course in organic chemistry to receive a diploma and believes instead that calculus and quantum mechanics are requisites, then she will not graduate with her class. Even if she knows that organic chemistry is required, but she does not act on that knowledge and register for the course, she will not graduate with her class. What she values will be delayed and, in the extreme case, lost altogether.

The consequences of falling short, either in knowing or in acting on that knowledge, may present even more serious problems. The demolition expert on the police team may be right nearly all the time in his opinions about the wires and timing mechanisms that he sees connected to various detonation devices, but a single wrong belief—or a single failure to act on a right one—can be fatal. It is not how often one is right that counts but whether one is right about the things that truly matter. The import of this principle is compounded by the fact that many beliefs do not rest on observation, for the objects of those beliefs are not amenable to the senses.

At the terminus of the spectrum of actions lie certain things that people do that are based on goals of the most inclusive and enduring kind. They are global ends that pull people toward them during the respective courses of their lifetimes. These actions are tied to the deepest values that humans possess and to beliefs that are both crucial and fundamental. Such beliefs frame personal worldviews. Does reality include the incorporeal? Does God exist, and, if so, does He care about me? Do I have an eternal spirit? What constitutes my identity as an individual? Is there a purpose for me—for each of us—in the scheme of things? In the end, is there something more? A person's answers to these questions sweep across the mental grid in a comprehensive and decisive way, affecting the entire set of what the person accepts as true and ultimately what the person does. No one can afford to be wrong here. If one is wrong, then that which one values most of all—that which one seeks with the greatest fervor and commitment—never will come to pass.

Consider the Apostle Paul, who, after his conversion on the road to Damascus, spent the remainder of his life suffering and persecuted for the cause of Jesus Christ, about whom he preached without reservation. He came to serve with great passion the one whom he so passionately had denied. Paul's belief in Jesus as the Son of God was unwavering; his steadfastness was undiminished by his trials.

> I have worked much harder, been in prison more frequently, been flogged more severely, and been exposed to death again and again. Five times I received from the Jews the forty lashes minus one. Three times I was beaten with rods, once I was stoned, three times I was shipwrecked, I spent a night and a day in the open sea, I have been constantly on the move. I have been in danger from rivers, in danger from bandits, in danger from my own countrymen, in danger from Gentiles; in danger in the city, in danger in the country, in danger at sea; and in danger from false brothers. I have labored and toiled and have often gone without sleep; I have known hunger and thirst and have often gone without food; I have been cold and naked. Besides everything else, I face daily the pressure of my concern for all the churches. Who is weak, and I do not feel weak? Who is led into sin, and I do not inwardly burn?[36]

---

[36] 2 Cor. 11:23–29 NIV.

If there were nothing beyond the ephemeral, then Paul's great sufferings because of his beliefs and his preaching would be pointless. Says this spiritual warrior, "If only for this life we have hope in Christ, we are to be pitied more than all men."[37]

NEXT STEPS

This work began with a problem, one that is put forth best in the form of a question: How is knowledge of the world possible, given that the objects of perception are changing constantly, and the subjects of perception are prone to error? Chapter 3 demonstrated that the metaphysical instability of a Heraclitean universe cannot destroy the objects that lie in it and thus cannot preclude knowledge of those objects; the mind provides a unity that holds sway over the roar of flux. The current chapter has shown that the possibility of error on the part of subjects is no bar to knowing, for knowledge is not given in logical certainty. Where the senses are the means by which one acquires truth, a single glance in the right circumstances may be enough, but sensory corroboration is definitive in warranting the veracity of perceptions. Objects of sense become objects of belief as a subject's thoughts about them take shape; ultimately, they may become objects of knowledge.

An individual therefore can move forward with the assurance that he or she can know. The investigation here has focused the attention inward in the search for understanding, revealing the essential characteristics of beliefs and the role that they play in persons' lives. One has come to see the conditions under which beliefs yield knowledge and how they position persons to act. Some beliefs are far-reaching in their implications and all-embracing in their scope; they form the cornerstones of the most closely held, global views. Thoughts concerning God, eternity, self, and purpose pass through the mind as the thinker stands on the thin line of time that is called the present, remembering the past and envisioning the future. The

---

[37] 1 Cor. 15:19 NIV.

need to discern the truth about God is indisputable. The other three matters hinge on that discernment. Knowledge requires that beliefs be both true and justified, but what justifies belief in God is something to be explored. One wonders whether reason can provide sufficient grounds to accept that God exists. Furthermore, if coming to know is only part of the answer because one also must *act* on what one knows, then, even if a person finds God, the question of what to do next remains.

I will take up these matters soon enough, but, before looking upward to the heavens to see what thoughts may arise in the search, I want to continue to look inward for a bit longer, for there is yet a fundamental issue that one must consider. It has become clear at this point just how important the mental facet of humankind is. The mind brings unification to material collectives and identity to the objects that result; it forms beliefs and holds knowledge; it makes actions out of behavior. What exactly, though, is the mind? It is surely a crucial part of humanity. Do people then have a foot in both the corporeal and the incorporeal? Wherein lies the identity of persons as individuals? Who—or what—*are* they?

CHAPTER 5

MENTAL MATTER

What is man, that thou art mindful of him?

—Ps. 8:4 KJV

Pets and children go hand in hand. It is an association that is beneficial to families. Growing up with animals taught my sister and me valuable lessons about caring for living things and about the behavior of different creatures. Cats and canines, goldfish and a black fish, turtles and tadpoles, hamsters and a horse—all were present. There was a parakeet with an amazing vocabulary. By imitating what he heard, that bird learned to say the name of my dog Toby. On one occasion, the bird was on the porch and began to call Toby in a loud voice. The parakeet's cry had just the right intonation, and the dog came running, expecting to be fed. What awaited him was a noisy bird in a cage. He appeared to be perplexed by the whole affair; we were amused by it.

Toby was an unusual dog. Fairly aggressive, even for a male, he demonstrated a leaning toward hostility at an early age. He was merely four weeks old when we brought him to our house, so young that his eyes had not yet opened. As we introduced him to the other two dogs, the adult male suddenly growled, and Toby began to bark—without hesitation and with considerable passion for a puppy. Although he could see nothing at all, he was ready for a fight. In later years, there were fights, and we were forced more than once to separate Toby from some other combatant.

Toby had a gentle side too, though, and he was especially fond of cats. Having been raised with them, he seemed to regard them as relatives. The extent to which he accepted this other species became apparent as he grew older. I still can picture him with one cat underneath him—partially, at least—and another on top as he lay in his bed: perhaps a pillow-and-cover arrangement for comfortable sleeping on that day. It was fitting that, when one of his slumber partners bore kittens, eventually taking little notice of them, Toby stepped in to become the surrogate mother. He sometimes sat by the basket in which we had placed the kittens and watched them. If one of them climbed out of its home, then Toby was there to look after the wanderer. Given his tendency to be aggressive, Toby's softer side seemed to reflect an inborn incongruity. Had Toby perceived that the little ones were being threatened, I suspect that, like any proper would-be mother, he would have intervened in a decisive way.

The dual nature of Toby was never more evident than it was one night when I approached him outdoors. At first, he did not recognize me. He responded to my presence with a posture of uncertainty, but it was obvious that he was prepared to attack: ears up and forward, sharply focused stare, and teeth set. It was surprising, even disturbing; my own dog was ready to turn on me. I called his name, and he changed in an instant. His ears went down; his tail began to wag. He acted friendly; his behavior indicated that he was excited to see me. Toby was prepared to lick at that point rather than bite. The dog came to view me as someone whom he trusted, as a member of his family. He was able to link the person in front of him that night to a person whom he had known since he was a puppy—the same person as his owner. In short, Toby identified me. What *was* it, however, that the dog identified?

THE IDENTITY OF SELF

"Who are *you*?" said the Caterpillar.

This was not an encouraging opening for a conversation. Alice replied, rather shyly, "I—I hardly know, Sir, just at present—at least I know who I *was* when I got up this morning, but I think I must have changed several times since then."

"What do you mean by that?" said the Caterpillar, sternly. "Explain yourself!"

"I ca'n't explain *myself*, I'm afraid, Sir," said Alice, "because I'm not myself, you see."

"I don't see," said the Caterpillar.

"I'm afraid I ca'n't put it more clearly," Alice replied, very politely, "for I ca'n't understand it myself, to begin with; and being so many different sizes in a day is very confusing."

"It isn't," said the Caterpillar.

"Well, perhaps you haven't found it so yet," said Alice; "but when you have to turn into a chrysalis—you will some day, you know—and then after that into a butterfly, I should think you'll feel it a little queer, wo'n't you?"

"Not a bit," said the Caterpillar.

"Well, perhaps *your* feelings may be different," said Alice: "all I know is, it would feel very queer to *me*."

"You!" said the Caterpillar contemptuously. "Who are *you*?"[1]

In Lewis Carroll's familiar work about a little girl's adventures in a strange land, one of the many peculiar characters in that playful story opens a dialogue with Alice by asking a question. The caterpillar endeavors to learn the little girl's identity. On the surface, his inquiry is straightforward enough, but it contains an element of stark profundity. It seems that Alice can say who she is only if there is such a thing as a self to whom she can refer—and not just any self but one particular self: herself. If one is to make sense of personhood at all, then there must be a way of linking subjects who exist at different times and in different states—a way to say, for instance, that the little girl who is speaking to the caterpillar at the moment is the same person who earlier today was as large as a house but is now quite small. Such claims appear to require that there be a single being who exists through time and through change and with respect to whom it is possible to make various ascriptions.

A central part of the overall quest of this work is to understand how knowledge is to be characterized and how one comes to possess it. Where knowledge concerns the world that humans perceive

---

[1] Lewis Carroll, *Alice's Adventures in Wonderland* in *The Complete Works of Lewis Carroll* (New York: Vintage Books, 1976), 53–54. *Alice's Adventures in Wonderland* was published initially in London in 1865. Writing under his pen name, Charles Lutwidge Dodgson (1832–1898) created the narrative.

through their senses, both the perceived and perceiver have a part to play. One saw earlier how the identity of the objects of perception can be maintained through time. It is important to determine how the identity of the subjects of perception can be maintained through time as well. If there is a self, a subject that somehow is bound together to form an essential part of what it is to be a person, then ascertaining precisely what that self is becomes paramount. One may believe that it is simply the mind, the same unifier that holds compound, inanimate, physical things together. One must ask, though, from where this sense of *I* that humans possess comes. Does it point to a real, persistent substance, perhaps apart from the body and even the mind; and what role does it play in connecting one's present state to previous states? In effect, the question to be posed is this one: How is personal identity possible? It is a question that demands an answer.

As one would expect, various philosophical theories have been advanced to give an account of the self and of what gives rise to its identity. Perhaps the most notable treatment is found in John Locke, who turns to consciousness as the hallmark of a person and to memory as the crucial factor that both distinguishes one person from another and explains the continuance of the individual. Consider briefly the thinking that underlies this notion.

The last chapter revealed that Locke ties the identity of an inanimate mass to its material components. It is not the same, however, with living entities, he says, and, on this point, he gets it right. I will pick up his words again, beginning with a sentence from a previous quotation, where the philosopher declares that what achieves continuance in animate things is not matter.

> In the state of living Creatures, their Identity depends not on a Mass of the same Particles; but on something else. For in them the variation of great parcels of Matter alters not the Identity: An Oak, growing from a Plant to a great Tree, and then lopp'd, is still the same Oak: And a Colt grown up to a Horse, sometimes fat, sometimes lean, is all the while the same Horse: though, in both these Cases, there may be a manifest change of the parts.[2]

---

[2] John Locke, *An Essay concerning Human Understanding*, ed. Peter H. Nidditch (1975; repr., Oxford: Oxford University Press, 1985), 330.

Next, Locke describes the dissimilarity between man and person. Man, he claims, is a living organism, an animal, the identity of which is tied to its physical form.

> An Animal is a living organized Body; and consequently, the same Animal . . . is the same continued Life communicated to different Particles of Matter, as they happen successively to be united to that organiz'd living Body. And whatever is talked of other definitions, ingenuous observation puts it past doubt, that the *Idea* in our Minds, of which the Sound *Man* in our Mouths is the Sign, is nothing else but of an Animal of such a certain Form.[3]

A person, on the other hand, is

> a thinking intelligent Being, that has reason and reflection, and can consider it self as it self, the same thinking thing in different times and places; which it does only by that consciousness, which is inseparable from thinking, and as it seems to me essential to it: It being impossible for anyone to perceive, without perceiving, that he does perceive.[4]

Locke then puts forth the claim that consciousness is the key to personal identity.

> For since consciousness always accompanies thinking, and 'tis that, that makes every one to be, what he calls *self*; and thereby distinguishes himself from all other thinking things, in this alone consists *personal Identity*, *i.e.* the sameness of a rational Being: And as far as this consciousness can be extended backwards to any past Action or Thought, so far reaches the Identity of that

---

[3] Ibid., 332–33.

[4] Ibid., 335. The distinction between human qua organism and human qua person is important, but I will not follow Locke's terminology quite as rigidly as he, who provides, as the abovementioned quotations show, separate definitions of man and person. Where it is necessary to mark the difference, however—and it will be so in later sections—I will be clear in my use of terms.

> *Person*; it is the same *self* now it was then; and 'tis by
> the same *self* with this present one that now reflects on
> it, that that Action was done.[5]

In essence, whereas sameness of man lies in the continuance of life that is communicated, to use Locke's terminology, to material particles that are organized into a certain form, sameness of person lies in consciousness as far as it extends into the past—that is to say, consciousness as it is exhibited in memory. The philosopher believes that memory is the sole necessary and sufficient condition of personal identity through time. Person s_1 is the same individual as person s_2 if, and only if, s_1 remembers doing or thinking something that s_2 did or thought.

Before I look at criticisms of Locke's theory of personal identity, I want to turn my attention for a moment to the concept of animal that he raises. Although his definition is somewhat vague, and, as a consequence, the criterion of identity that he bases on it is likewise vague, the notion is worth exploring.

OF ORGANISMS

From the investigation in a previous chapter, one has learned that the end points of existence—origination and termination—are bound to identity in an inextricable way, such that the conditions that define the end of an inanimate object define its identity as well. Could the same be true of living things? Such an assertion would not mean, of course, that the car that ran over Carla's cat, Buddy, is responsible for the animal's individuality but rather that the logical scaffolding that allows one to say truthfully that something has ceased to be is also the scaffolding within which true statements about identity are molded. It is just that one does not rely on conventional standards, in the case of cats, to determine when the animal is no more—when the unique creature that all Carla's friends know, or knew, as Buddy is gone. As long as Buddy is alive, there is

---

[5] Ibid.

no trouble in identifying him. He is Carla's only pet; he is the third animal to arrive in Bonnie's first litter; he is the cat that ate Timmy's goldfish. One need consult no rules of convention to understand what it means to be the same cat.

Not unexpectedly, one also has a grasp of what it is for Buddy's life to cease to be. When an animal succumbs to the grip of death, its life terminates by definition, as the death of the organism is the cessation of life. Although one may not know exactly what pair of successive moments corresponds to its demise—remember that both originations and cessations require two instants to take place—it assuredly passes away. Anyone who has witnessed the death of an air-breathing creature, in fact, has seen what it is for a living being no longer to have the breath of life in it. Such an event is unmistakable, and no philosophical analysis is needed to comprehend what has happened.

There will be times, however, when tracing a life to the point of cessation seems to introduce an element of uncertainty, and plainly the originations of organisms can be a point of contention among advocates of specific views. On closer inspection, however, these cases are not as problematic as they appear to be at first glance.[6] People have made puzzles where none existed. For example, in the reproductive cycle of the common freshwater organism *Amoeba proteus*, the cell undergoes mitosis, a serial process in which the nucleus of the cell divides following the duplication of DNA: the genetic material. Accompanied by proteins, DNA makes up the animal's filamentous chromosomes.[7] As mitosis draws to a close, the process of cytokinesis ensues, whereby the cytoplasm separates. The cell membrane first becomes pinched in the middle, then pulls apart at the junction, enclosing the two sets of interior cellular components, and division concludes as membrane continuity is established individually for each new cell. With that continuity comes autonomy

---

[6] Certain living things present borderline cases: grass, for instance. It does have recognizable parts (roots, blades, and so forth), however, working as a whole to keep the plant alive and growing; and, if a patch of it dies, then that patch stands out from the living sod that is around it.

[7] 'DNA' is the common acronym for deoxyribonucleic acid, the fundamental compound that contains the instruction-sets for living things. Its sister compound is ribonucleic acid; 'RNA' is the common acronym for it.

and, with autonomy, two organisms. The offspring come into being as the original amoeba ceases to be.

Whereas both new cells arise from a single original cell, they are distinct from it and from each other: Each of the two new amoebae is a complete, living entity, with the proper chromosomal count, capable of metabolism and reproduction on its own. Although the two daughter cells can be linked to a common source, each one has an identity apart from the parent cell from which it came and apart from the other, sister cell. Their lives take different paths. One may stay in the pond; its counterpart may be scooped into a jar and taken to a laboratory. The original cell that begat them is a single organism, but, once they come into being, and at every point thereafter, the two offspring creatures do not have the same histories. As demonstrated earlier, unless two things have the same histories, they cannot be identical.

Amoebae reproduce asexually. Consider the principles that are at work in sexual reproduction, as in viviparous life forms: those that bear live young—most mammals fall into this category.[8] Albeit they are living cells, sperm and ova are not bionts, but they are parts that combine to make them, each of these cells, or gametes, supplying half the chromosomes that are needed to yield a complete, paired array.[9] A zygote, the product of the gamete union, comes to be as the haploid predecessor cells join and cease to be. So, whereas neither of these generational elements is an organism, a zygote *is* an organism, one at the earliest point in an unfolding history. It is undeveloped at this juncture; yet, it is a living entity, embedded with the full number of chromosomes, right for its species. It operates as a unit to sustain vitality, grow, and progress to a more mature stage. The only puzzle of origination here involves saying precisely when fertilization completes with the emergence of a diploid nucleus, not how much mass must have developed in vivo before the organism arises or whether

---

[8] A platypus is an unusual mammal, in that it is oviparous. It produces eggs; after a period of partial incubation within the parent's body, the animal lays the eggs, and they hatch outside the parent. A spiny anteater is an oviparous mammal as well.

[9] Biologists apply the term 'diploid' to cells (or to their nuclei) that possess these paired sets, distinguishing them from the single-set gametes, where the term 'haploid' applies. Gametes are the mature, end products of processes, different for sperm and ova, that reduce the quantity of chromosomes to half the full number.

the product of procreation actually has left the womb. As I have discussed at length, a macrophysical thing's material does not make it what it is, nor does a thing suddenly become an organism in the postpartum state—to hold otherwise leads to an untenable position. Suppose that the gestation period of a particular mammalian species is n months. Then, any offspring that are brought forth at month $n–1$ would be organisms if the criterion were simply separation from the parent, whereas in vivo offspring at month $n–1$ would not be organisms. The individuals of both groups, however, have the same operational parts, kick in the same way, and even look alike. They are just in different places. A prior chapter revealed that *where* a thing is, disregarding other factors, does not affect *what* it is. Imagine that there are identical twins; one is removed from the mother through surgery, while the other is left in the uterus. Attributing the applicability of the term 'organism' to one and not to the other is a contrived distinction. Mammalian life begins with the zygote. It is this first DNA-complete cell—housing an entire complement of the genetic substance—from which an adult develops, directly or indirectly, that marks the starting point of an organismal life stream, not some step between conception and delivery, or the delivery itself.[10]

It is important to note that there are phases through which individuals pass on their way to maturity, and one may ask when specific phases begin and end. One may want to know the conditions under which Tyler's little tadpole became a frog, or Carla's kitten became a cat. Both the tadpole and the kitten changed into the adult creatures of the respective species, but how can one identify those points of change on the continua of their existence? This problem is simply another case of the sorites paradox. It is just this sort of matter that has created the confusion over the beginning of being for an organism, with the resultant social and moral debate. When a

---

[10] In some respects, the case of identical twins is similar to that of an amoeba, in which an original amoebic cell terminates with the arrival of its successors. The bodies of identical twins have a common source but not a common history. If, soon after the zygote arises, the tiny cellular mass that exists, call it a, splits into two separate units—let them be b and c—then the resultant entities follow different paths and develop into distinct adults. If one of the new units—say, b—subsequently splits to generate d and e, then identical triplets emerge. Entities c, d, and e exist at this juncture; a and b have ceased to be. So, c arose before d and e, but the DNA is uniform, though slight mutational divergence typically occurs eventually.

sexually reproducing animal *qua example of the species* arises is clearly recognizable: It arises with the expression of life through the zygote—the fundamental cell to which its existence is uniquely traceable.[11] When an animal *qua phase of its development* arises, on the other hand, is not as clear. To determine in any consistent way at what point, for instance, the tadpole stage of a frog ends requires that there be some standard, and rational thinking must set it. Like other measurements that humans have established, such a standard would not rest on metaphysical grounds but on convention. There is no undergirding reality-principle in operation, for it is not metaphysics that marks the terminal points of the phases of living things but decree. One may say that an animal is no longer a tadpole when the ratio of the length of its tail to the length of the rest of its body is 1:12, or its mass is 67 percent of the average mass of those animals in its species that have reached a certain age and that were evaluated in a recent scientific study. Perhaps a tadpole ceases to be when its front legs are a specific length, or, where one employs a functional criterion, the creature no longer relies on larval gills for respiration. Rational minds—persons—must decide.[12] There is an obvious parallel between the endings of composite, inanimate, material objects and the endings of developmental phases of organisms.

To allow, however, this lack of phasic clarity in the absence of established rules to cause one to think that origins of animals qua examples of the species are really origins of animals qua stages of development is to commit a very serious error in reasoning. The two are not the same. One cannot assume that the beginning of an organism is equivalent to the beginning of a developmental phase that leads to maturity—a phase in particular that appears late in the maturation process of the creature. The sorites paradox serves to

---

[11] Again, identical twins come from a single DNA-complete (diploid) cell, but the initial, defining element of each twin proper is a biological unit that is produced from the division of the early, developing life form into discrete existents. Strictly speaking, it is not the zygote itself; so, this case varies from the norm. Such twins thus originate with the two cellular entities that arrive with the separation, though their source is the zygote, and it is from one or the other of this pair of entities that the respective courses of growth proceed uniquely. Note that one could substitute the term 'kind' for 'species' in the italicized phrase, if desired, to include hybrids.

[12] The rational mind that brings singularity to material collectives need not be human; it may be divine.

obfuscate the matter, but it never can provide a way of moral escape by reducing the issue to one of perspective. The identity of an individual is affixed permanently to the identity of a unique initial stage through an exclusive, uninterrupted series of progressive steps that reflect its subsistence. See Figure 5.1; the pattern will look familiar.

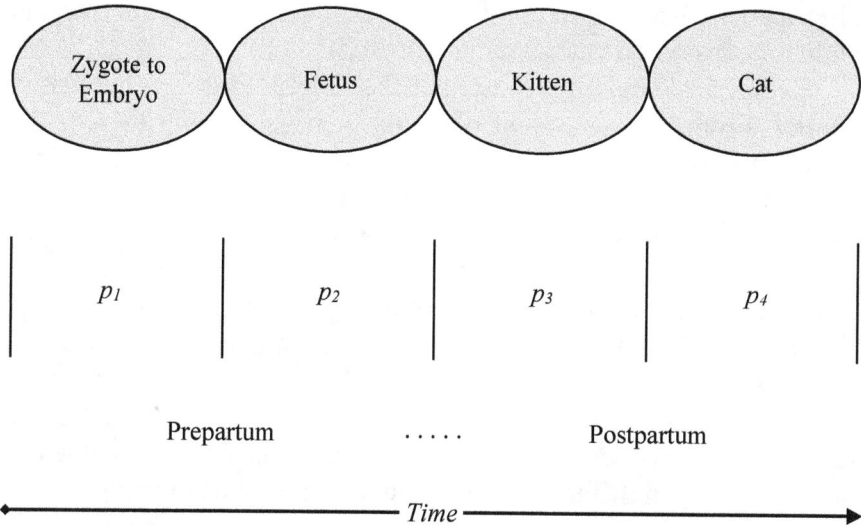

Figure 5.1

Here is the thinking:

The object that exists in period p_3 is an organism.
The object that exists in period p_2 is not an organism.
Moral obligations apply only to organisms.[13]
Therefore, whatever moral obligations apply to the object
   that exists in period p_3 do not apply to the object that
   exists in period p_2.

---

[13] This line of thought is addressing the duty to observe rights that pertain to beings, not obligations to conserve energy, protect natural resources, preserve geological structures, or other such directives as one may consider to be ethical.

There is a logical flaw in this argument. It echoes the flaw that led to the conclusion that Heraclitean flux destroys identity. Things do not cease to exist, and other things suddenly spring into existence in their place, simply because of a change in properties. Refer to Figures 3.16 and 3.17 on pages 293 and 294 respectively. There, the elements represent successive moments; here, they represent periods, or groups of successive moments, but the concept is the same. Two things at different times may be identical, even if they do not share all properties, because time may bring changes in the properties that a thing possesses, yet the thing itself persists.

Numerical identity must not be confused with qualitative identity. From the standpoint of logic, there is nothing to preclude the identity of the objects in periods p_1, p_2, p_3, and p_4 in Figure 5.1. In fact, the point is that they *are* identical: A viviparous mammalian life form, regardless of its current stage and its species, had its beginning in the zygote, the first step in ontogenetic progression, leading to the embryonic segment. It did not begin to exist at the outset of p_3 or of p_4. Certainly, the kitten here is not the cat in one sense: It is not yet mature. The kitten is indeed the cat, though, in this sense: It is an earlier phasic instance of the same animal. There is historical continuity. The objects occupying the various periods are merely one and the same entity in different temporal stages during its development to adulthood. The second premise of the argument is not supportable.

Returning to Locke and his claim that an animal is a living, organized body, one finds in his theory that the identity of the animal is determined by the life that makes that body a viably functioning entity. Sameness of an animal is tied to sameness of life; therefore, it seems that, where the life ends, so must the animal. The consequence is that the end of an individual creature's life is the end of the individual creature, although the body itself may remain. This consequence rings true.

Buddy has ceased to be, but there is a physical aggregate that is left, and this collection of matter falls under the same rules of convention that apply to the termination of other composite, material things. While Buddy was alive, the question of the identity of his body did not surface, even though time brought major changes as he grew from a kitten into a cat. His death, however, highlights the principle that the mind is the unifier of the matter of inanimate things, even of nonhuman things that were once animate, because now one must *decide* how much corporal loss can take place before the cat's body no longer exists. Is 40 percent of the predeath mass of the animal sufficient to maintain the identity of the body? Is 25 percent enough to ensure persistence? Will 9.33 percent suffice? What if the torso and cranium are intact, but much of the natural material of the extremities is no longer present? If all tissues except the skeleton and teeth have decomposed, then is it still Buddy's body underneath that pile of rocks on the hill? Suppose that only a rib is left, or a splinter of a rib, because of unusual soil contaminants. Without standards, one falls into the sorites-engendered absurdities into which Peter Unger falls, as noted in the preceding chapter. It appears that the truth of propositions about the end of *Buddy* is independent of the truth of propositions about the end of Buddy's *body*. Statements of the former sort are grounded in circumstances, whereas statements of the latter sort also depend on some set of accepted standards to establish their truth.[14]

One may be inclined to say that the termination of the body aligns with the termination of the organism if it undergoes sudden disintegration, as, for example, in the case of an explosion where it is blown to bits. Under normal conditions, however, such is not the case. Thus, one is constrained to think that a creature as an individual is distinct from its physical being and that what makes an organism a unique, singular entity is something other than the pure physicality of the corpus. I can construct an argument that purports to establish this distinction; it appears below. I number the steps for comparative purposes.

---

[14] One can imagine cases in which a mandate may be involved in saying that a life has ceased to be, as when a court must decide whether Alistair Charrington, a wealthy businessman, is still alive following the dreadful crash. On limited life support, the accident victim breathes with assistance from a machine, but there is no evidence of skeletal muscle movement and no indication of forebrain activity. His family, anxious to receive the considerable inheritance, seeks a declaration from the legal system that would terminate their injured relative officially, regardless of whether his heart beats on its own. Such cases do not count against the notion that, by and large, the end of life is something that people witness, not something that people decree; whereas, for the body itself, decree is an essential part of marking the end.

1. An organism terminates upon death.
2. An organism's material body does not terminate upon death (except perhaps in atypical cases).
3. Two things the cessations of which do not coincide cannot be the same thing.
4. Therefore, an organism is not identical to its material body.

It could be alleged that a cat, whether dead or alive, is still an existing organism; there is merely a change in properties when it passes away. Until Buddy's body is gone, Buddy remains. As with Timmy's airplane when it strikes the ground (an incident that is covered on page 295), Carla's pet continues, even after a catastrophic event brings a dramatic and encompassing change in properties. Hence, one might deny the truth of the first premise of the argument. An organism's life terminates upon death—but not the organism.

On the face of it, this stance seems to be reasonable. Certainly, *something* remains when a cat is crushed beneath a car wheel. To say that it is the cat that remains, however, because the cat *is* its physical body—to assert that it is identical to the thing that is lying under the car—leads to a problem. Chapter 3 established that aggregates of matter cannot achieve object-identity on their own. If matter were responsible for sameness, whether for inanimate things or animate ones, then illogicalities would be the result. An automobile would cease to be the same vehicle if a hubcap broke loose from a rim on a trip to the mountains, or the driver added air to a tire, although the VIN never changed. Likewise, Buddy's losing a claw in a fight last week with a tabby in the vicinity would undermine his being, as would his gaining two pounds after Carla overfed him during the holidays. It looks as if one can explain identity only by drawing on something else, something that is not matter. For the nonliving things in the world, it is the mental that provides unity, and I think that one has to hold that the mind too unifies the corpus of a cat that is no longer alive. Even so, if it is life that holds an animal together through time to achieve identity before its death, then how is one to characterize it? This life to which Locke refers and to the continuance of which he attributes sameness is not the collection of material particles that make up the body. So, is it something immaterial?

One may argue that the biological entity itself generates its own unity, that there is no need for an immaterial thread of life to bind it into a singular thing. Albeit there are many physical parts, they work together for one overarching end. That end is life: the continuance of the individual—and furthermore the species. Action toward an end in this way, however, is not like the universe's moving toward a terminal state of maximum entropy. Both occurrences may point to Aristotle's final cause, which I discussed earlier, but only the former one suggests that the workings are directed toward accomplishing an end rather than merely drifting toward it in alignment with the laws of physics. Instances of the former sort appear to bear the mark of rationality. When things without understanding, whether pansies or paramecia, behave as though they possess it, doing things that can be described with plausibility as activity in accordance with reason, one introduces rational mentality beyond the human kind. Conceivably, such rationality is traceable to God. If one objects to the existence of the immaterial, claiming that reality is purely physical, then it seems that one has opened the door to a larger problem.

Perhaps one will say that the concept of behaving in accordance with reason is too strong, and it presumes the presence of a mind where there is none. That an organism continues to live, with or without human mentality, is simply a biological fact, and its being alive through time is sufficient to yield its identity. There is a group of ongoing processes that collectively one can consider to be life; and, provided that those processes continue, the identity of the organism is assured. One need not bring in the immaterial to hold living beings together. The reputed thread of life is merely an unbroken chain of biochemical workings, and it is through this enduring chain that unity is accomplished.

To avoid admitting the existence of immaterial things, suppose that one defines an organism as simply a biological complex of heterogeneous, interdependent, physical parts that, through metabolic activity, operate jointly in such a way that they sustain the operation of the complex as a whole, something that the parts could not do individually. On this basis, maybe one could say that the life to which Locke refers is nothing other than a group of metabolic processes. So, perchance one still can cling to the notion that the cat is material in its essence; it is just that there are certain biochemical happenings that the matter making up the cat's body undergoes. Where those happenings cease, life ceases, and, where life ceases, so does the creature, even though a corpse is left. One therefore may not dispute the premises and the conclusion of the argument that appears above but hold that the cat is corporeal nevertheless. Such a position would reformulate the argument to read:

1. Life is nothing other than specific metabolic processes that certain concatenations of material particles undergo, where such concatenations of material particles constitute the body of an organism.
2. The metabolic processes that are the life of an organism terminate upon death because death is simply the cessation of those processes.
3. An organism's material body does not terminate upon death (except perhaps in atypical cases).
4. Two things the cessations of which do not coincide cannot be the same thing.
5. Therefore, the metabolic processes that are the life of an organism are not identical to the material body of the organism, although it is the material of that body that undergoes those processes.

Implicit in this argument is the notion that it is not necessary to draw on something other than the corporeal to account for organism-identity, that the sameness of an organism is linked to a group of ongoing physical happenings that are precisely what it is for that entity to be alive. There is no unseen, dynamic, intrinsic life-strand that explains the oneness of things—no core, immaterial element that provides the reason for it. There is only a steady sequence of chemical events. Thus, it may seem that one can avoid the problems that arise from linking organism-identity to matter, while still subscribing to a materialistic view of things, by focusing on this continuing metabolic chain. Buddy persists as the same animal for as long as metabolism persists in a particular bundle of material particles. Terminate the metabolic processes, however, and Buddy terminates, regardless of whether the matter that made up his body remains for some time in its bundled state.

If one accepts this argument and its account of identity, then counterintuitive cases surface. When virtually all liquid water is removed from the tissues of organisms, metabolism halts completely. What is surprising is that metabolism can be reinitiated in certain species if sufficient water becomes present for rehydration. The desiccated state that is associated with the disruption of biochemical activity in these species is anhydrobiosis. It is not possible for metabolism to occur in this state. James S. Clegg, a researcher in the field, makes the point.

> [O]ne is compelled to conclude that the removal of all but, say, 0.1 g H_2O / g dry weight (easily achieved by anhydrobionts), will inevitably result in the cessation of metabolism. For example, one can calculate that this amount of water is insufficient to hydrate intracellular proteins, without which a metabolism is obviously not possible.[15]

Examples of animals that experience anhydrobiosis include rotifers and nematodes.[16]

Now, if an organism is nothing other than a group of ongoing metabolic processes (life) that are taking place in a particular collection of matter (body), and the identity of the organism lies in the continuance of those processes, then it has to be true that the organism terminates when it is dehydrated to the point that metabolism is halted. When these processes end, the organism must end as well. Nothing can exist in a state of nonexistence, only to come to exist again, a point that I made clear in several previous passages. The animals that emerge from anhydrobiosis therefore cannot be the same ones that entered that strange state. How then did they spring into existence fully developed? The consequence of

---

[15] James S. Clegg, "Cryptobiosis—A Peculiar State of Biological Organization," *Comparative Biology and Physiology – Part B: Biochemistry & Molecular Biology* 128, no. 4 (2001): 615. I am indebted to Clegg for his direction on this issue through correspondence.

[16] The absence of liquid water also can occur through low temperatures. Where metabolic cessation takes place as a result of freezing, the static state is cryobiosis. Examples of animals that experience this condition include some frogs and species of insects.

attempting to avoid immateriality in portraying life seems to be unacceptable, even for those who embrace the view that there is no life apart from matter and its interactions.

Suppose that one claims that the metabolism has not terminated in this peculiar state; rather, it merely has been suspended. Metabolism is to be viewed in a more long-term fashion, so that the biochemical events that constitute metabolic processes are subsumed under a broader process that includes both active and inactive states. In the building of a house, for example, construction continues for many months, although there are recurrent periods of inactivity as the workers leave the job site to go home at the end of each day of labor. Until the house is completed, and the workers leave for the last time, it appears to be the same operation of building. The notion can be depicted in the following manner, where a segment, exemplifying this progression, is shown:

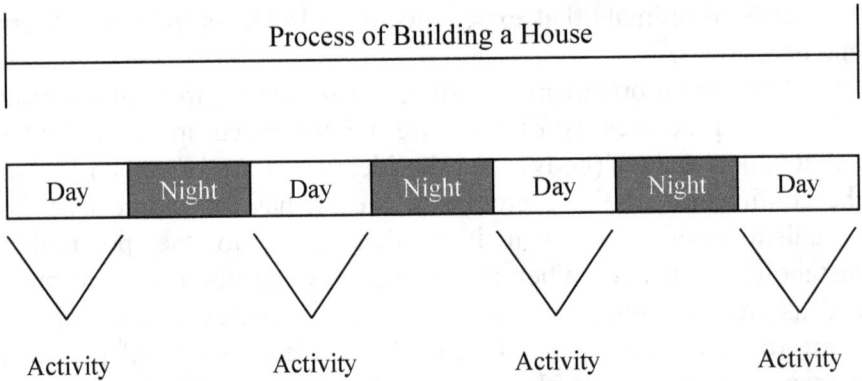

Figure 5.2

It could be argued, in a similar fashion, that an organism can maintain identity through recurrent periods of total biochemical inactivity because the process of metabolism is sustained, provided that one takes a sufficiently temporally extended view of things. Although conditions at the cellular level are completely static, life as metabolic activity continues, and, by virtue of that continuance, the organism does so as well.

The analogy does not work, however. The periods of activity that Figure 5.2 depicts are distinct groups of occurrences that somehow must be joined for there to be an enduring process that encompasses them, uniting them to generate a singular, long-term performance. Pouring concrete, framing, wiring, installing plumbing, laying brick, painting, and so forth—the various activities are related because there is a common goal. The workers are engaged in constructing a house by assembling materials in accordance with the architect's plan. Sawing, hammering, and painting in themselves do not constitute making something. One could be doing these things to try one's hand at honing a new skill, to demonstrate a technique, or to test a set of tools. One even could be doing them just for fun. It is only if the actions are aimed at a common end—in this case, building a house—that they become linked, being part of a broader whole. It is not necessary that the individuals act with full knowledge of the crafts of the others. The carpenter may not understand why the pipes that are behind the wall that he is building must be of a certain configuration for the plumbing to work properly. He does understand, however, why the wall must be constructed in a certain way; and, regardless of the comprehensiveness of the understanding of the workers, what they are doing is building a house, as the architect and the contractor can attest. If they depart from the plans, then both the architect and the contractor undoubtedly will intervene. The *process* that is the *building of a house* is meaningful only in the context of the intended product; that is to say, the course of action is meaningful only if it is set against a backdrop of the end toward which the work is directed.

Therefore, for there to be a *single* process that is composed of periods of doing, interrupted by periods of quiescence—in house building, at least—there must be an outcome toward which the tasks that the workers are performing converge. Otherwise, there is activity, but there is no course of assembling a complete product during a period of time. It is the *end* that defines the process that leads to it. This notion is correct, even if the goal is intended but is not accomplished. The contractor may run out of funds or discover a major problem with the design; a fire may destroy the half-finished structure; the land may be sold, the would-be house razed, and an archery range erected in its place. Despite these possibilities, it is true nonetheless that what the tradespersons were doing before the work stopped was constructing a dwelling.

Where all actions are of the same sort, as in felling a large tree with an axe in the course of three days or plowing a large field with a tractor in the course of three weeks, there is still a global goal to which each day's work points. It is this goal that binds the discrete events to yield the single operation of which the events are components. Without that end, there is nothing to unite the intermittent activity. If the actions are not undertaken to accomplish some common end, then they are simply independent happenings, unlinked by anything except perhaps resemblance; and so there is no process, one extending beyond the first occurrence of the cessation of activity. The end that gives rise to such a process, however, is not the process itself but that toward which it moves. It lies outside the series. The analogy of intermittent goings-on is put forth, however, to save the notion that life *is* metabolism, that they are the same thing: Nothing that is external to the series of metabolic events figures in the concept of it. The analogy therefore fails.

Furthermore, the common end toward which activity progresses in building, felling, and clearing bespeaks purpose; the respective operations occur because of intention. Thus, not only is an extraserial factor—the goal—required for there to be an extended process in such instances, but rational mentality is required as well because purpose entails intelligence. Attempting to cling to the analogy yet still contend that metabolism, considered comprehensively, extends through periods of dormancy, as with house building, compels one to account for the end that defines the affair. To do so requires turning to rationality, which is something that lies outside the metabolic operations of rotifers and nematodes. Moreover, it is beyond their capabilities.[17]

---

[17] It is not even necessary that human beings undertake the construction work in building a house. Robots with no understanding but with sophisticated electronics employing the appropriate sets of instructions can perform the tasks. Ultimately, rationality must lie at the base of the activity, however, as the design, construction, and programming of the robotic machines, and the positioning of them on the site to perform the tasks, require understanding.

Pursuing the line of objection further, one may argue that a process does not require a purpose. Consider the famous geyser Old Faithful. The geyser's eruptions occur at fairly regular intervals, but they do not take place nonstop. Yet, there is no purpose here, it may be said, no intelligence that has some objective in mind for these things. There are only physical occurrences that are caused by other physical occurrences. It could be the same with metabolism: There are only biochemical events and nothing more. Even though metabolism is suspended from time to time, there is a process—the same process—in continued operation. Consequently, identity can be maintained through static periods, despite the absence of a goal.

Logically, there are only two options with regard to the geyser activity: Old Faithful's eruptions are part of a process, or they are not part of one. Either way, there is a problem for the objector. If the former option is the case, then one must include all the elements that make up the phenomenon: the heating of the water underneath the ground, the building of pressure as steam forms, the sudden release of that pressure as water blasts upward, the seeping of water back underground, and so forth. This cycle is ongoing; only the actual eruptions are occasional. The comparison to anhydrobionts thus does not hold, for the geyser activity is not intermittent after all. The activity is *not* suspended. As with the bobbing of a cork on a line when a fish has taken the bait—the cork sporadically rises above the surface and then falls beneath it—there is no break in motion, although what one sees comes in discrete packets of movement.

On the other hand, if one looks only at the temporally disrupted events that are referred to as eruptions, then there is nothing that combines them into some cohesive singularity. There is no overarching process. Each eruption is a distinct happening. They may be similar; they may be tokens of a type; but the temporally unjoined episodes in the sequence alone no more form a singular process than three spatially unjoined lines in a plane form a triangle. Just as a man may saw boards on different occasions, his doing so is not part of building a house unless he is working toward that end. He merely is sawing, and his activity on Wednesday is separate from his activity on Monday. The events of each day are unconnected occurrences, related by similarity of movement but not by the way in which two things that are constituents of one and the same whole are related.

In summary, metabolism is precisely the goings-on of chemical interactions within the cells, tissues, and organs that compose the body of a beast. They are one and the same. Where there are no goings-on, there is no metabolism; and, where there is no metabolism, there are no goings-on. The halting of all biochemical activity of an organism is the conclusion of metabolism, not its suspension. The reformulated argument, however, has it that life *is just* metabolism. If therefore metabolism concludes, then life concludes and, with it, the beast and its persistent identity. Taking a view of organismal life as a coalescent process that extends beyond the cessation of active, biochemical events, so that one may account for the continuance of anhydrobionts through static states, is to see life as comprising something other than those events—specifically, the end that is required to unite them—which contradicts the proposed position. Further, to posit the right kind of end as a way to stretch life across periods of metabolic dormancy introduces purpose. The point of the reformulated argument, however, is to define life purely in terms of mechanism. Again, the result is an inconsistency.

Finally, one may argue that it is structure, as opposed to biochemical processes—whether those processes are occurring in actuality in an active state or occurring in potentiality in an inactive one—that accounts for life in organisms. In light of the existence of anhydrobionts, this approach may have some appeal in certain circles. Accordingly, if the identity of an organism lies in the life of it, then a living thing presumably would be the same entity through time because of the configuration of its body parts. Even if metabolism ceases for a period, the animal's body continues in the same arrangement of cells or tissues, awaiting metabolic resumption.

This objection rests on the same misconception that has surfaced before. Matter never can be the determinant of the identity of composites as objects—singular entities—and the arrangement of matter as a distinguishing mark gains nothing over the mere collection of it. Neither sameness of structure nor difference of it has any bearing on numerical identity. Organisms of the same species have the same, or nearly the same, general arrangement—identical twins, barring major alteration events, are prime cases—but they are distinct beings. The cat Buddy is not his sole brother, Butch, an identical twin. Alternatively, if an organism loses a body part, then its structure changes; yet, if it lives, then does it not persist as the same thing? Persistence is carried in life, but life is not carried in configuration. An adult frog is the numerically same entity as the newly hatched tadpole from which it developed, but there are differences in form. One has legs and no tail; the other has no legs but a tail. A swallowtail egg, larva, pupa, and winged butterfly exhibit different structures. They are one and the same creature nevertheless: Destroy the egg, and there will be no larva; destroy the larva, and there will be no pupa; destroy the pupa, and no butterfly will emerge from the cocoon. Remove an ear, a forelimb, a tail, or a spleen from a mammal, and the identity is not altered. Take away the cilia that protrude from the anterior end of the anhydrobiotic rotifer, and it still will be the same creature, although its physical organization will have changed dramatically. Scientists have come to rely on the physical arrangement of tissues in organisms to help in classifying them, but there is unquestionably no necessary link between structure and organism-identity, for qualitatively identical structure cannot yield numerical identity, nor can qualitatively distinct structure prevent it.

It will not do to counter with the claim that it is not overall structure that accounts for life and identity but rather a certain core arrangement of material components. The loss of a limb, one might say, may not end the life of a being; however, alter the core organization of that matter—remove a key part—and life ceases, just as a car can operate without a back seat but not without an engine. Life thus can be defined in terms of essential structure rather than structure *simpliciter*. Consider, however, that planaria, or flatworms, can be sliced transversely into numerous parts from head to tail, and each part will develop into a complete organism. One must question then what counts as the essential structure of the creature. Maybe it is the head; possibly, it is the tail or one of the pieces in the middle. Each sliced section of the flatworm differs significantly from the others, yet each section must be alive, as otherwise no fully mature creature could grow from it. Once regeneration occurs, the structure of each organism is, for all practical purposes, qualitatively the same as the others—all are anatomically indistinguishable—but there are multiple, distinct, living entities at this point. Life is necessary both for organisms and, in accordance with Locke's thinking, for their identity as individuals. It is not so with essential structure, however; it is necessary for neither.[18]

Where does all this analysis about organisms lead? It is correct to say that an organism is a type of physical system, something to which I alluded earlier, and, in the case of the organismal system, it is characterized by *synergism*. A system in this sense is a complex of interdependent parts that are typically heterogeneous performing operations that are typically diverse in a joint, ordered manner, such that the complex as a whole performs a central, defining operation that the individual parts cannot carry out on their own.[19] Synergistic systems are commonplace among things that are the products of design. Grandfather clocks, lawnmowers, automobiles, belt sanders, and dehumidifiers—ordinary machines exemplify such systems. Disassemble a clock, and it will not keep time. No component of a dehumidifier, apart from the rest of the contraption, will keep the basement dry. The parts of a machine are joined specifically for the purpose of performing a particular, central task through their collaborative workings. The separate performances of the parts *converge* on the performance of the whole; what they do, they do in support of what it does. That global performance, however, is not the mere conjunction of the workings of the constituents but something else. Marking time is more than the mechanical rotation of wheels and the moving of metal hands as the weight that drives the gears on the grandfather clock descends to the floor. Lowering the humidity in

---

[18] A question that arises with regard to such an incident is whether all the planaria that come from the original creature are new planaria—analogous to the case of amoebic reproduction, where the parent cell begets two daughter cells—or one of them is the same as the original creature. Without specifics of the cutting operation, and a discussion of the microbiology and morphology of the animal, a clear answer is not forthcoming. What is clear, though, is that, at most, one of the new creatures is identical to the initial creature because the identity of organisms is the identity of individuals. Given that numerically identical things must share the same origin, as already noted in this work, the reasonable position to take is that each regenerated worm is distinct from the initial one, and the initial one ceased to be with the completion of the first severing event. I will not pursue the matter further here, however; it would divert the discussion from its central course.

[19] It is possible for there to be more than one defining operation of a synergistic system, although multiple operations probably point to a set of activities that are performed in support of, or in conjunction with, a principal one. In my inquiry, I will focus on the primary work of the complex, considered in its entirety.

an environment is more than the compressing of a coolant and the turning of a fan. The operation of a machine as a whole is its *function* in the strong sense that it explains the workings of each of its individual constituents—why each one does what it does—but the workings of no individual constituent explain the operation of the whole. It is in light of the function of the device, taken in its entirety, and only in that light, that the doing of each part achieves work that can be portrayed in a meaningful way, somewhat as the building of a house is what accounts for the various activities of the individual laborers. The operational convergence in complexes of the synergistic sort is forward-looking. It is teleological. A synergistic system's function is the end toward which the activities of the individual parts converge.

Note that it does not follow from the fact that something is performing a function, of course, that it exhibits a multifarious configuration. A boomerang is designed to execute a function, but it is a monolithic device. Even a rock can perform a function on a temporary basis—say, propping up a lawn chair with a broken leg. Regardless of the object and whether it is complex or simple, functionality in the sense at hand is end-oriented. Synergistic systems are special cases, however, because they are complexes of parts, the individual operations of each of which are oriented toward the *same* end.

Further, it does not follow from the fact that something is classified as a system that it is synergistic and thereby performing a function. A simple collection of material things that are arranged in a certain way, perhaps engaged in one or more activities, can be a system. A volcanic mountain range of twenty peaks, extending along the western perimeter of an area, for example, could constitute a geological system simply by virtue of contiguity, configuration, and similarity of eruptive events. It lacks, however, the important characteristic of the cooperative operation of the parts through which they enable an operation of the whole that depends on them but is separate from the sum of them.

Where the organismal system is concerned, the characteristics include both complexity and collaboration. The immediate parts that make up the whole are, in many cases, in the form of subsystems—lymphatic, nervous, immune, circulatory, and so forth—each with its own parts, in turn, working together to support a particular operation. Those subsystems then work collaboratively in support of the over-arching function of the whole, and that function is the life of the creature. Life is something that cannot be captured adequately simply by enumerating metabolic activities. It stands apart from the bare collection of them. Life is the object of the organismal system; it is that toward which the parts of the system converge in their respective movements.

There is a difference between the careening of a group of meteors toward the earth, caught in the planet's gravitational field, and the pressing forward of leucocytes in a cheetah's bloodstream, driving in a headlong rush toward the infected cut on its paw. The movement of the disease-fighting cells is explainable, and arguably defined best, in terms of purpose and its accompaniment—namely, reason—factors that indeed may be external to the system that expresses them rather than internal, which is evident in the case here. Although some organismal systems plainly exhibit a measure of inherent mentality, as many pet owners can attest—and I will cover a few telling examples later in the chapter—they and, a fortiori, their parts do not exhibit the understanding that accompanies inherent rationality. They behave, but not in the capacity of reasoning agents; they perform, but not in the role of sapient beings. Humans are not just smarter animals; they have fundamentally different psyches, contrary to a widespread opinion among biologists that all living things—and even nonliving things—lie on a continuum. Organismal systems as such do not possess the ability to weigh the downstream consequences of their behavior, bearing in mind specific purposes for doing what they do, intending to achieve certain envisioned goals as part of a long-term strategy. A horse eats a bale of hay because of hunger. It does not eat to live. It does not study climate patterns and consider whether it should save some of the food for another day in anticipation of a coming famine, rationing a limited supply to maximize the life-sustaining effect of the sustenance. It does not question whether, in an altruistic gesture, it should toss a portion to the mule in the stall next to it to keep its companion in good health. A dog performs procreative activity because of a biological drive. It does not do so to have a family, nor does it take into account the extended responsibilities of raising young ones, preparing them for futures in a harsh environment. The psychological aspect of behavior that animals display is grounded in the natural characteristics of the organism proper: instinct, imprinting, conditioning, habit, and so forth. Organisms qua organisms do not possess the grasp that characterizes intellection: reflection, abstraction, empathy, judgment, imagination, supposition, and purpose. Much less then do their parts do so. The functioning, whether of the whole or of the parts, in accordance with rationality therefore suggests that the end-directed activities of organisms and their components are attributable to something that lies outside them.

I have argued that identity is given in unity. Aggregate, inanimate objects, including those that are synergistic systems—machines—require standards to determine their persistence as individuals. The central function of a machine may play a role in the setting of those standards, and it certainly plays a role in defining the sortal term that is applied to the device, be it vehicle or vacuum cleaner; but it in itself is not what makes the machine one thing or makes it the same thing through time. An automobile is still the same vehicle if it loses the capacity to operate for a period of time because of a faulty fuel pump. The VIN verifies this fact. Even if a standard of persistence of aggregates that are machines were to be based on function, whether actual or potential, it would serve only to highlight the fact that rationality is a necessary condition of object-identity. Not only is it the case that there must be rationality to establish the convention, but it is also the case that the core function of a designed contrivance is a vacuous conception outside the context of purpose, and purpose requires a mind.

Organisms, however, are notably unlike other synergistic systems in a key respect: The identity of an organism *is* found in the end-facing function of the whole. Life as it is sustained binds the parts and their operations into a cohesive unit through convergence. It is life that accounts for the being's autonomy and its persistent identity. Regardless of whether an organism is highly active or completely inactive, if it is not dead, then it is alive, and, if it is alive, then its identity is maintained by virtue of that life. When an organism as such ceases to be living, passing into the fixed state of death, that organism, that animal, barring the clearly anomalous, ceases to be. What is left is not a nonfunctioning organism; it is a carcass.

The precise notion of life, however, is difficult to capture, in spite of varied attempts in recent years to state what it is. It extends beyond simple metabolic events and organizational arrangement. Indeed, it appears to be apart from the physicality that is essential to the very expression of it. There is something about the identity of living things—and, so one may argue, about life, considered in its entirety—that eludes the limitations of a monistic view of reality in which only the tangible exists. One cannot count on matter itself or on material process or on material structure to explain how living organisms continue through time as distinct individuals. Despite the trend to the contrary in philosophical circles today, one may not be able to rule out incorporeality without great difficulty in presenting an adequate account of the identity of animate entities.

No case would be more decisive than that of humans, for they exist not only as organisms but also as agents; they are rational beings who are capable of deliberation and the intentional acts that follow it. Unique among creatures on the planet, humans are persons. Ultimately, it is this concept of personhood that one must come to understand. Locke holds that personal identity is not grounded in materiality. He believes that the essential element is consciousness—what one thinks of as the mental part of humans—as it is bound together through time by memory. What this mental facet is, though, has puzzled philosophers. Conceivably, it is something other than a person's physical being, something that is truly incorporeal. In a moment, I will take a look at three related arguments that purport to establish that it is so. As the examination in the coming pages of this chapter unfolds, the discussion will alternate in order and in primary focus, with some regularity, between the physical and the mental, and between the physical and the nonphysical, depending on the topic. In the end, insights into the character of the rational mind and its place in personhood are in view.

OF PERSONS AND AGENTS

Locke's criterion of personal identity brought with it a number of concerns, which his critics were not hesitant to introduce. How does one know that a memory is correct? Simply on the basis that someone seems to remember witnessing an event, one cannot be certain that he or she actually saw it. Memories can be faulty. To be sure that a memory is genuine, one would have to know that the person who seems to recall the event does recall the event, but to know that the person does recall the event requires that one know that he or she is the same person who witnessed it. The memory criterion thus fails because it presupposes what it is meant to determine. In essence, it is circular.[20]

There were other criticisms. Thomas Reid (1710–1796), for example, argues that the memory test leads to unacceptable consequences. Suppose that a man has made a career of the military. As a general, he remembers a brave deed that he performed as a young officer years ago. The officer who performed that deed remembered a flogging that he received as a boy for stealing fruit from an orchard. The general, however, does not remember the flogging. The general is therefore the officer, and the officer is the boy, but the general is not the boy.[21]

Certain philosophers attempted to rescue Locke from this counterexample with more elaborate renditions of recollection. Some of these attempts were more successful than others. Suffice it to say that both sameness of the body and memory continued to be foremost in the thinking of subsequent writers who focused on the problem of the self. For one such philosopher, memory, so I plan to show, becomes a two-edged sword—David Hume's theory of the self is surely one of the most radical of all.

To understand Hume's theory, it is important to take a cursory look at his concept of perceptions. Hume includes in perceptions all mental elements, everything that is found in consciousness, and divides them into two groups: impressions and ideas. Impressions are emotions, passions, and sensations. In general, they strike the mind

---

[20] Joseph Butler recognizes this problem with Locke's account. See Butler's discussion of personal identity in *The Analogy of Religion, to the Constitution and Course of Nature. To Which Are Added Two Brief Dissertations: I. On Personal Identity.—II. On the Nature of Virtue*, 23rd ed. (Philadelphia: J. B. Lippincott and Co., 1902), 318. Butler's work was published originally in 1736.

[21] This argument appears in Thomas Reid, *Essays on the Intellectual Powers of Man* (1785; repr., Cambridge: MIT Press, 1969), 357–58.

with a level of force and vividness that ideas, which are faint copies of impressions—copies that appear in thinking and reasoning—lack. Seeing a ripe persimmon is an example of an impression. Closing one's eyes and remembering the orange fruit that one saw, and imagining it on a shelf in the pantry, are examples of ideas. An individual's impression of a persimmon must precede his or her idea of one; a person can have no memory of seeing a persimmon until the person actually has seen one. Certain ideas may precede certain impressions, however, as when one's memory of a painful incident brings about a strong emotion, such as fear; but ultimately the impression of the original, painful incident sits at the base of the chain.[22]

According to Hume, seeing a thing, though, should not lead one to accept the existence of an object in some external world of corporeal things that gives rise to perceptions, let alone to accept its continued existence when unobserved. Humans do embrace both as a matter of course, but it cannot be reason that leads them there. Maintaining his skepticism, Hume holds that all that one ever has access to is what lies in one's own consciousness. To hold that there is a physical world of things to which perceptions correspond is to move beyond the bounds of human reach. People believe that such a world exists because of the regularity with which they experience impressions. Impressions of sense—seeing the kitchen table day after day, for instance—arrive with a certain recurrent similarity. There is a constancy to them, and, even in the face of change in the impressions, there is still coherence. The collection of impressions that a person experiences now, which the person associates with the table, resembles the set that surfaced a minute ago, the day before, and

---

[22] Hume separates ideas further into the simple and the complex. Simple ideas—the thought of an orange patch of color, for example—cannot be broken down into parts. All simple ideas are copies of impressions, as are memories, even though the latter are complex. Imaginations, though, may, or may not, correspond to direct impressions of what is imagined in its entirety. Imagining, for example, a unicorn cannot be a copy of an impression of one, for no one ever has seen such a thing, but this complex idea may be reduced to simpler components, in the Humean view (beast, white, horn, and so forth), and these components correspond to impressions. It would be a serious mistake, however, to claim that ideas can be assembled from other ideas, as one would assemble a birdhouse. I will take up this issue later. For now, note that memories, for Hume, cannot precede their matching impressions.

even last year. It is the imagination that fills in the gaps, tying together the string of discrete, interrupted impressions in a unified way: "The smooth passage of the imagination along the ideas of the resembling perceptions makes us ascribe to them a perfect identity."[23] It is memory, however, working in concert with imagination, that is key in bringing about the acceptance of a persistent external reality. Memory's role is underscored by the fact that the sensory impressions of a given object, such as a table, may be sporadic and infrequent. Acting on sensations and on recollections of previous, similar sensations, the mind produces a tendency to believe that there is an actual, physical table, which corresponds to one's perceptions and which continues to exist during those times when one is not experiencing table impressions. For Hume, imagination and memory thus account for one's practical belief in an enduring material universe.

As belief in temporally continuous things in a corporeal world is unwarranted, so too, Hume thinks, is belief in a temporally continuous self or mind. Hume argues that there is no persistent *I* underlying perceptions—no constant entity, existing through time, to which the perceptions are attached. Indeed, there is no self at all in the sense that one normally thinks of it. There are only perceptions. The appearance of a self arises from an uninterrupted string of them.

> It must be some one impression, that gives rise to every real idea. But self or person is not any one impression, but that to which our several impressions and ideas are suppos'd to have a reference. If any impression gives rise to the idea of self, that impression must continue invariably the same, thro' the whole course of our lives; since self is suppos'd to exist after that manner. But there is no impression constant and invariable. Pain and pleasure, grief and joy, passions and sensations succeed

[23] David Hume, *A Treatise of Human Nature*, in *David Hume: The Philosophical Works*, ed. Thomas Hill Green and Thomas Hodge Grose (1882, 1886; repr., Frankfurt am Main, Germany: Scientia Verlag Aalen, 1964), 1:494. Hume's work typically is referred to by its abbreviated title; the full title of the writing is *A Treatise of Human Nature, Being an Attempt to Introduce the Experimental Method of Reasoning into Moral Subjects*. Hume's *Treatise* was published originally from 1739 to 1740.

> each other, and never all exist at the same time. It
> cannot, therefore, be from any of these impressions, or
> from any other, that the idea of self is deriv'd; and
> consequently there is no such idea.[24]

As one looks closely at the mind in Hume's theory, it is clear that it is just a collection of related perceptions, nothing more. Referred to as the serial theory, or the bundle theory, of the self, the thesis identifies the mind with a string of impressions and ideas, elements that form its associated content. The mind has no continued existence that is independent of its own perception events, nor do those perception events have an existence that is independent of the mind to which their respective occurrences are linked. Herein, I believe, lies a problem for Hume.

Ideas are copies of impressions; therefore, ideas are dependent on the prior impressions that they resemble. Now, if there is no continuous self, only a bundle of impressions and ideas at any given moment in time, constituting a mind, then all that can keep ideas of memory from blinking out of existence is the set of impressions to which they are traced and on which they ultimately depend. Suppose that Jim visits Yellowstone National Park. In Humean terms, perhaps one should say that Jim experiences a series of impressions that he correlates with the famous national park. For the sake of the example, however, I will use more familiar terms. Suppose further that, on Friday, the last day of his visit, Jim sees the geyser Old Faithful erupt. In his excitement, he decides to step over a rope that is blocking access to a temporarily restricted area; his intent is to get a better look. For the remainder of the day, it may be that he can remember the magnificent sight of the water's blasting skyward as the pressure built beneath it to the point of forcing its escape—and remember his improper act as well. After retiring for the evening, though, he reaches a state of dreamless sleep sometime during the night, and, in this state, there are no perceptions.[25] Until he begins to dream again, or he awakens, there are no impressions and no ideas, no seeing things and no thinking of them. On Saturday morning,

---

[24] Ibid., 533.
[25] If dreamless sleep is not convincing in this example, then substitute a coma or a state of anaesthetization.

however, Jim remembers the awesome eruption scene at the park. From where did that idea come? According to Hume, it must have come from an impression—but what impression? It can be only the one that the idea resembles. Yet, Jim has no forceful and vivid perception of the geyser on Saturday; that is to say, he has no impression of it, as he is not sensing it at the time. He is on an airplane heading back to his home in Virginia. One of the following four conditions therefore must be true:

1. Jim remembers Old Faithful because the memory persisted outside any mind and returned later to Jim's mind from wherever it had persisted.
2. Jim remembers Old Faithful because the memory persisted in another conscious mind, or other conscious minds, and returned later to Jim's mind.
3. Jim remembers Old Faithful because, although the memory ceased to exist, it reappeared in Jim's mind.
4. Jim remembers Old Faithful because Jim's mind persisted through a period of unconsciousness, and his memory was preserved.

The first option will not work. Memory events are elements of consciousness and as such cannot exist outside it. It is not as though one can remove them from the mental realm, store them on a shelf, and return them when desired. Mental phenomena are not self-sufficient. Despite the criticism of Bertrand Russell, René Descartes has this point right: Thoughts require a thinker.[26] It is nonsensical to suggest that a memory could exist unattached to any mind; indeed, if such were possible, then it also would be possible for a memory to exist in the absence of any mind at all in existence. Memories are derivative: They depend on previous experiences. The authentic recollection of the nonillusory sight of a red sports car can take place only if a genuine experience of seeing a red sports car did take place, but that event could not have happened without a perceiving mind to receive and attend to the visual image. A sensory occurrence is a two-part operation. It requires both an object that is perceived and a

---

[26] I mentioned Russell's criticism in chap. 2.

sentient subject that perceives it. If no mind exists, then no sensory phenomena exist either; and, if no mind exists, then it is possible that no mind ever existed, in which case no sensory phenomena ever existed either. Without such phenomena, however, no memories that are derived from them are possible.

The second option may evoke thoughts of George Berkeley and his theory that things are conserved in the mind of God when they are not perceived by human minds. Berkeley's theory regarding conservation, however, which has its own set of difficulties, is an attempt to account for objects of sense when no human mind is perceiving them. Berkeley would not say that two human minds can share the same memories.

If one presses the issue, then it seems that again an absurdity is reached. Suppose that the second conscious mind, where Jim's memory is stored—lay aside the problem of how it could be trans-ferred between minds—also lapses into a dreamless sleep state. There then must be a third mind to hold Jim's memory and to explain its existence on Saturday morning. The third mind, however, may fall into the same state, and so forth. Potentially, the end result is that there may need to be a group of other minds to account for any individual's memories, and ultimately amnesia is found to be a social failure rather than a neurological or psychological one. Such a conclusion does not fit the constraints of reason. Even more prob-lematic, the memories, barring a problem with one's faculty of recollection, are not distinguishable from each other, their being copies of the same perception. Hume writes,

> [W]e shall here content ourselves with establishing one general proposition, *That all our simple ideas in their first appearance are deriv'd from simple impressions, which are correspondent to them, and which they exactly represent.*[27]

Continuing, he asserts,

> 'Tis evident, that the memory preserves the original form, in which its objects were presented, and

---

[27] Hume, *Treatise*, 314. Memories, though not simple, he thinks, are still copies.

> that where-ever [*sic*] we depart from it in recollecting any thing, it proceeds from some defect or imperfection in that faculty.[28]

The consequence is that it would be impossible to know who had the original impression. Jim remembers seeing Old Faithful, but he may be remembering an event that he never witnessed, which again defies logic.

The third option is a logical impossibility. As I argued in chapter 3, nothing can exist in a state of nonexistence, only to reappear at a later time. One can forget something and remember it subsequently, but such a sequence is not that of the existential termination and regeneration of a given memory. If a thing ceases to be, then, whatever it is that follows, it cannot be the thing that once was and then was not. The memory cannot come to exist after it ceases, nor can a copy of it come to exist and resurface in Jim's mind, for, by hypothesis, the memory ceased to exist; there is therefore nothing in existence to copy. Even if the copy were produced in Jim's mind prior to his falling asleep, it would have disappeared along with the original when Jim reached the unconscious state.

The greater problem here, though, is that, for Hume, there is no persistent self underlying perceptions. The mind subsists only in its perceiving. The mind *is* the collection of impressions and ideas; where they cease, with the loss of consciousness, the mind cannot continue. Jim's mind therefore ceases to exist in the dreamless-sleep state. Not only then does the memory vanish, but, because the series of perceptions is the mind, and this serial mind is the only self in any sense whatever, Jim vanishes as well. Not even Jim can survive a period of nonexistence. Hume admits, "When my perceptions are remov'd for any time, as by sound sleep; so long am I insensible of *myself*, and may truly be said not to exist."[29] Although memory plays a significant role in Hume's theory of perceptions, it is his undoing. There is no way to account for ideas of memory where there are gaps in awareness. Hume cannot explain adequately how Jim could have a recollection of what he experienced at the grand park on the previous

---

[28] Ibid., 318.
[29] Ibid., 534.

day nor, because Jim ceases to exist that night, explain why anyone at all could have the recollection that one would attribute to him. Hume has discarded the self only to undermine his own theory.[30]

Although Hume would reject the fourth option, it stands apart from the others in sensibility. If Jim's mind did persist through a period of unconsciousness, then it seems that Jim also must have persisted. Otherwise, it is difficult to see how the persistent mind, which must be *someone*'s mind—and must be so *at whatever time* that it exists—could be *his* mind. Some may hold that memories are preserved in the brain, which endures through a state of unawareness, and that the mind continues because the brain continues, for the mind *is* the brain: They are the same thing. Soon, I will examine the theory that the mind and the brain are one and the same. Certainly, they are closely connected, but whether they can be identical is another issue. In any case, a mind is bound in an intricate way to personhood. To assert that a particular person's mind continues unaware entails that there is a particular person to whom the mind belongs or, at least, with whom it is associated in a special way, and that the one to whom it belongs, or with whom it is associated, continues with it. If every human mind must be someone's, however, then Jim's mind surely must be his; thus, if it persists through a state of dreamless sleep, then so must he. According to this reading then, it appears that Jim's personal identity is preserved, in contrast to Hume's nightly destruction of it. Saying exactly what the person—or the element of personhood—that persists is, though, becomes the challenge.

The concept that seems to be emerging here is that underlying the question of *who* a person is, is the foundational question of *what* a person is. To answer the former question, one first must answer the latter one. Ascertaining precisely how this entity is put together may make it possible to gain some insight into what yields personal identity. The place to start such a metaphysical investigation is the mind. What is it; how is it to be classified? Are there in people distinctly different components with different natures—are persons

---

[30] In the end, Hume admits that his account of the self is "very defective" in showing how distinct perceptions can be joined to form personal identity. See his comments in the appendix to the *Treatise*, 559. Also see Frederick Copleston's discussion in *A History of Philosophy*, vol. 5, *Hobbes to Hume* (London: Search Press, 1959), 304–5.

strictly material beings, or are there immaterial parts or sides? I want to turn to some philosophical theories about the constitution of the human entity and the essential character of its mentality.

THE MECHANICS OF THE MENTAL

In their quest to determine what sets humans apart from other living things, philosophers through the years have settled on various qualities that, so they believe, produce the exclusivity. Plato focuses on the physical aspect, defining man as a featherless, biped animal, after which the cynic Diogenes of Sinope (c. 404–c. 323 B.C.) plucked a bird and brought it into the lecture hall, declaring, "Here is Plato's man."[31] His gesture resulted in an expansion of Plato's definition to include broad nails, which birds do not have. One can imagine other cases, though, in which further refinement along such lines would be required because of atypical characteristics, either of what one takes to be clearly human or of what one takes to be clearly fowl. Delineation by means of the corpus is a problematic course to follow.

Abandoning the effort to draw on the physical aspect to isolate human beings, other theorists turn instead to the mental. Aristotle holds that rationality is the differentiating factor.[32] A qualifying mark that succeeding scholars mention is risibility: the capacity to grasp the point of a joke—to laugh. Both faculties are peculiar to people, to be sure. Beasts do what they do based on inbred traits, conditioned responses, and other behavioral dynamics; people reason, and they express amusement. The rational mind seems to be indispensable as a delimiting feature. As Locke sees centuries later, it is an essential

---

[31] Diogenes of Sinope, as reported in Diogenes Laërtius, *Lives of Eminent Philosophers*, trans. R. D. Hicks (London: William Heinemann, 1925), 2:43. Some estimates of the birth of Diogenes of Sinope place it several years earlier.

[32] Diogenes Laërtius reports that Pythagoras, who lived two centuries before Aristotle, also sets man apart on the basis of rationality, claiming, "Intelligence and passion are possessed by other animals as well, but reason by man alone." See ibid., 347. Note that Aristotle says too that only man discerns good and evil.

part of what it is to be a person, and he relies on it to distinguish the organismal aspect of human beings from their personal aspect.

Indeed, people possess a range of psychological attributes—aesthetic, affective, and cognitive—that separate them from other creatures. The ability to appreciate beauty in its various forms, even to create it, is noteworthy. A hiker is struck by the kaleidoscope of colors on a fall morning as the sun penetrates the leaves overhead. A listener is drawn into the airy, recurrent cycles of a concerto by Johann Sebastian Bach, or the soulful tone of a solo cello playing in a minor key. People possess as well the ability to feel, whether compassion, grief, envy, indignation, happiness, admiration, anger, chagrin, or other emotions. Of importance, people are beings that are capable of reflection. They can ponder their awareness of themselves, their beginning, and their mortality. They can wonder whether there is a plan for their lives in the thoughts of God and what the future holds for them. They can stare into space and speculate about what may lie beyond the observable universe, or gaze into a microscope and contemplate what drives cells to undergo mitosis. They can imagine what it would be like to fly without the aid of machines, soaring above the clouds. They can solve problems in calculus—sometimes. Human beings are cogitative and ratiocinative. Whether they have the answers or only the questions, they can inquire, deduce, conjecture, consider, plan, envision, and analyze—in short, they can think. One of the salient, uniquely identifying attributes of humanity is surely intelligent, rational thought. To understand themselves then, human beings need to understand what the mind is, as it must be this element, in whatever way that it may be characterized, that accounts for intelligence. The mind, however, is not something that can be clutched with the hands as one would take hold of a soccer ball. One cannot place it under a microscope to examine it. Instead, it seems to be something incorporeal—not made of matter in the least. The mind is, after all, the seat of thought.

As philosophers began to take up the study of mentality in earnest, they attempted to delve into the concepts that appeared to be essential to it, such as those of volition, choice, motive, intention, emotion, desire, belief, and action. The philosophy of mind—and in particular contemporary action theory—started to flourish as an area of inquiry in the middle decades of the twentieth century. The aforementioned concepts proved to be difficult to capture, however, and even more difficult to define with any clarity. Questions arose concerning the general nature of mental happenings. What precisely are motives? How is one to describe the difference between my hand's moving and my moving my hand? Do mental events induce physical behavior and, if so, then how? What does the term 'intelligence' mean? How should intention be depicted? It became evident from the ensuing analyses that attempting to pin down the various things of the mind, and indeed the mind itself, brought forth some interesting, but perplexing, issues to address. Predictably, opposing systems developed.

One sees in the early Greeks the beginnings of philosophical views that assign a key role to rationality or mentality in explaining the universe. The *Logos* of Heraclitus and the *Nous* of Anaxagoras are ordering forces in the ideas of those philosophers, playing active roles of a sort in the workings of the cosmos. The primary hypothesizing that carves out the mental in humankind, however, can be traced to Plato. He argues that the minds of people exist prior to the physical bodies in which those minds are housed, and they continue to exist after those bodies have expired, a position on which he draws to explain the apparent presence of innate knowledge in people.[33] In his dialogues, Plato portrays Socrates as an intellectual midwife who assists the youth of Athens in giving birth to ideas that they themselves possess, ideas that allegedly were acquired in some previous existence. Through his incisive questions, Socrates elicits responses from his hearers that lead them to understanding as they follow a chain of proper reasoning. In the Platonic composition *Meno*, for example, Socrates brings forth geometric truths from a boy, ones to which the lad had not been exposed. In reality, the boy deduces mathematical facts under Socrates's guidance and probing, but Plato supposes that the soul, being immortal, comes to hold pertinent true beliefs that were acquired in a prior lifetime, then recalled.

It is René Descartes, however, who sets forth a thesis about the nature of two unlike elements of the human entity, and he attempts to explain how they are related. Descartes is the principal founder of the modern theory of mind-body dualism, in which minds are considered

---

[33] Plato's theory is that of recollection. A related notion is in Presocratic thought.

to be incorporeal substances with essential attributes that differ in distinctive ways from those of the sensible bodies that serve as the counterparts. There are philosophers, however, who do not accept that such entities as independent, immaterial minds exist. This metaphysical view is, in fact, the prevailing one today. Surely, though, some things that people do must count as intelligent behavior, whether it is playing hide-and-seek in a park, playing chess in a tournament, or playing Macbeth in a high-school drama class. If there are no incorporeal minds as people have come to think of them, then the challenge becomes to find a logical way to explain intelligent actions. If they can be explained without employing the notion of incorporeality, then the question that arises next is whether such explanations are ever adequate.

MIND AND BODY—DUALISM AND MONISM

Descartes holds that minds and bodies are not only distinct things but distinct kinds of things as well, not sharing the same nature. One finds this pair of arguments in the *Sixth Meditation*; I condense his reasoning a bit:

> The mind is thinking and unextended (does not occupy space).
> The body is extended (occupies space) and unthinking.
> Therefore, the mind and the body are distinct.[34]

> The mind is indivisible.
> The body is divisible.
> Therefore, the mind and the body are distinct.

---

[34] In their translation of the *Meditations*, John Cottingham et al. note that 'body' as it appears in this section of the original Cartesian work is ambiguous. One could take the term to refer to corporeality in general, without the definite article, or Descartes's body in particular, employing the definite article. See René Descartes, *Meditations on First Philosophy, Sixth Meditation*, in *The Philosophical Writings of Descartes*, trans. John Cottingham et al. (1984–1991; Cambridge: Cambridge University Press, 1997–2009), 2:54, n. 2. I proceed using the article.

In keeping with his methodical doubt, Descartes puts forth other reasoning in an effort to show that the mind cannot be the body. As a thing that thinks, the mind must exist wherever doubting exists because doubting is a form of thinking. To say that one doubts but does not think is contradictory. The body, however, need not exist, and doubting its existence poses no contradiction. In his *Discourse, Part IV*, Descartes argues,

> It is absurd for me to doubt that I am thinking.
> It is not absurd for me to doubt that my body exists.
> Therefore, the mind and the body are distinct.

After Descartes, the course of philosophy reflected a deep division between those who accepted the existence of immaterial minds and those who rejected it. The split surfaced, and persists today, in part, because one can point to physical things, either in actuality or in principle, but such is not the case with incorporeal things. "Look, there is Deborah's car!" says Jason, pointing to the antique Aston Martin under the tree, surprised to find it after the theft. Everyone present can gaze at the vehicle and understand that it is the object about which Jason is speaking. They can examine it: touch the dashboard, open the glove box, lift the hood, and check the trunk. They can attach a chain and tow it away. Day-to-day life is filled with observation of material objects, and demonstrative expression—pointing to a thing—is a basic means of identifying that to which an individual intends to refer in communicating with others. Defining an object by pointing is ostension, as when one answers the question, "What is a duck?" by extending one's index finger toward the thing in the pond. It is not a flawless means of expression, as the questioner may take the pointing to indicate floating or feathered or far away; in general, though, cases of ostension, particularly when supported by additional cases of it in other circumstances, make the point—no pun intended. In matters pertaining to the physical world, communication rests, at base, on the ability to train the attention of others on a physical thing by means of a physical act. These material things to which people can point include their own bodies. They are publically observable things.

When one speaks of minds, however, where one means some immaterial part or side of individuals, there is no pointing. One cannot say, "Look, there is Deborah's mind!" Even if the hearer stares attentively, Deborah's mind cannot be seen. One can gaze into her eyes and into her ears. One can perform a CAT scan and an MRI. Still, her mind cannot be found. Neither radiologist nor neurologist can show it to others. In contrast to what is true of bodies, observation does not work as a way of locating minds if they are indeed immaterial things; and pointing does not work as a way of showing them—directly, at least—to others.

Given such unobservability, the position that immaterial minds exist has been challenging to defend. Compounding the problem is the fact that identifying exactly how an incorporeal, thinking part of a person and a corporeal, unthinking body are joined is not an easy philosophical task to undertake. Descartes struggles to explain the relationship, but it is clear to him that the mind and the body, though distinct substances, are linked in an intricate way nevertheless.

> Nature also teaches me by these sensations of pain, hunger, thirst, etc., that I am not only lodged in my body as a pilot in a vessel, but that I am very closely united to it, and so to speak so intermingled with it that I seem to compose with it one whole. For if that were not the case, when my body is hurt, I, who am merely a thinking thing, should not feel pain, for I should perceive this wound by the understanding only, just as the sailor perceives by sight when something is damaged in his vessel.[35]

One way of addressing the difficulty that dualism raises is to assert that it is a spurious problem. As I noted, many philosophers resort to denying the existence of immaterial minds altogether, not to mention immaterial spirits. All that exists is physical, they say; reality consists only of the things in the corporeal universe. Although

---

[35] René Descartes, *Meditations on First Philosophy, Meditation VI,* in *The Philosophical Works of Descartes,* trans. Elizabeth S. Haldane and G. R. T. Ross (1911; repr., Cambridge: Cambridge University Press, 1967), 1:192. Descartes holds that it is the pineal gland in the brain that serves as the point of conjunction between the mind and the body.

dissention does persist, materialism has become the battle cry of contemporary metaphysics as one author after another seeks to do away with the mind as something that is fundamentally dissimilar to the body. Again, one finds the roots of this materialistic position in the Presocratic philosophers. Milesian writers, such as Thales, look to physical things as the ultimate substance while they seek to explain the workings of the world. The thinking probably reaches its most prominent form of the period in the ideas of Leucippus and Democritus, who portray reality as consisting of corporeal atoms and their mechanical movements in a void. Mirroring these views during the modern period, around the time of Descartes, Thomas Hobbes declares that the whole of existence is corporeal; there is no part of the universe that is not body. According to Hobbes, given that substance is solely body, the locution 'incorporeal substance' is self-conflicting. Consistent with the mechanistic approach of the ancient atomists, Hobbes puts forth the view that all mental states are simply matter in motion. Ruling out immaterial substance on the basis of definition or fiat, however, does not eliminate it.

The philosophy of materialism generally comes in two forms. In the stronger sense of it, only matter and energy in space-time exist. It is this form that the position takes, as a rule. In contemporary times, some philosophers prefer the term 'physicalism' for this stance. All reality is physical, so they hold, but there may be things that, although part of the universe, as defined by physics, are not, strictly speaking, material. Forces and space itself may be cases in point. In the weaker version of materialism, the theory holds that everything that exists is completely dependent on matter for its being. This view admits the existence, for instance, of nonphysical properties, along with the physical things that exhibit them, but denies that properties themselves have any reality apart from those physical things. There is a certain variance in the terminology here; some philosophers refer to this latter view as materialism and separate it from physicalism. In the following quotation, one author offers a succinct explanation of what he takes to be the principal difference:

> [P]hysicalism is the view that everything is physical,
> including all the properties; materialism is the view that

> all things are physical, but not necessarily the prop-
> erties.[36]

According to the weaker view of materialism, one can speak of mental phenomena, as distinguished from the physical body of an individual—mental properties are not *reducible* to physical prop-erties—but, in the final analysis, what exists is matter.

The key concept for these doctrines is that the physical is either all that there is or, at minimum, what is ontologically primary. In any event, so goes the thinking, there are no incorporeal substances: no independently existing minds and no spirits. In light of this point, I do not make a hard distinction in this work between the terms 'materialism' and 'physicalism'.

It is not possible to demonstrate, from the standpoint of logical necessity, that sentience is a physical thing, for there is no outright contradiction in asserting that a thinking being with no material body exists. If there is to be a connection between mind and matter, then it must be a contingent one—it must be a fact about the world—and accounts of the mind-body link in terms of pure materiality must proceed accordingly. In language, one can ascribe a variety of properties and states to humans, and some of them are mental. Although it may be said of a man that he weighs two hundred pounds or that he is blue eyed and bald, it also may be said of him that he is stubborn or smart or in pain or feeling sad or planning his next move in the chess game. Both sorts of ascriptions are applicable. If, as the advocates of materialism hold, there is no incorporeal substance that makes up people, then it becomes incumbent on the adherents to explain how it is that one can talk about human behavior as though there were incorporeal minds. In short, materialism must account for consciousness, and it must explain intelligence. Can it do so?

I turn initially to the theories of three philosophers of the contemporary period as they seek to provide a picture of humankind that does not resort to the Cartesian model. In time, two of these theories fell largely from favor as opposing proposals stepped in to replace them. Of note, however, one of the two has seen a resurgence in recent years. The other continued to be considered but lost ground

---

[36] Anthony Dardis, *Mental Causation: The Mind-Body Problem* (New York: Columbia University Press, 2008), 133.

to a depiction of the mind that gained popularity in the closing decades of the last century. Aside from their historical significance, there is value in critiquing these systemic constructs to determine from a fresh perspective whether materialism in any form is right.

ANALYTIC BEHAVIORISM

Hobbes's materialism and its reduction of mind to matter in motion served as a backdrop for the development of a contemporary restatement of this position in the form of behaviorism. The approach regards behavior as the defining mark of an organism; it replaces immaterial mental states with physical conduct. The operations of all organisms—and humans are not to be excluded—can be explained in purely physical terms, so the reasoning has it. Thus, the putative private workings of an individual's mind are to be identified with overt, bodily movements. Beginning with the ideas of J. B. Watson (1878–1958), an American psychologist, and continuing with those of B. F. Skinner (1904–1990) and others, behaviorism captured the attention of philosophers. By merging the mental into the material, as it were, it brought with it an attractive way to give an account of consciousness without resorting to the existence of incorporeal things. Objective and public, bodily activity is something that can be observed by many, unlike the subjective and private happenings of Cartesian mentality, which lie outside the realm of the perceptible.

In its most crude form, however, behaviorism is especially unsavory. If having a pain is equivalent to behaving in a certain way, then a man is not in pain if he is not wincing, moaning, and uttering, "Ouch," or a similar interjection. Surely, he could be controlling himself, so that he remains quiet, even though he aches. If he does writhe, grimace, and say, "I am hurting," then he could be faking it. Behaviorists focus on the body; so, suppose that Tom's hand moves. Different possibilities surface, including—starting with a base-level event—his hand's moving as a result of its being pushed by a falling tree limb, his hand's moving as a result of a neurological ailment that produces uncontrollable twitches, and his hand's moving because he wants to remove a quarter from his pocket. The first movement is not something that Tom does at all. The second is something that one could say only in a limited sense that he does: the sense of doing that applies to nonsentient entities. It is not intentional, not out of agency. One might say more accurately that his body does it but that he, the person, does not do it. Such a stance would lead one to conclude that Tom's physical being is not Tom, which raises a problem in itself for a materialistic behaviorist. Again, Tom sneezes when suffering from allergies, but the sneezing is a reaction to a stimulus, not an action of an agent. It is something that Tom's body is doing; it even may take place against his will. The moving that occurs in the third instance diverges from the others. It is something that Tom does, and he does it on purpose. It is a willful, deliberate deed, and he has an objective in mind in doing it. Behaviorism blurs the distinction in these cases.

In an attempt to bolster the theory, one may narrow the scope of what is classified as behavior to include only those movements that are not the result of events that are outside the control of the organism. Thus, when a falling tree limb bumps into Tom's body and generates movement, that movement is not behavior. The problem is that the concept of stimulus-response is part of the very essence of the modern behavioral theory. Stimuli are things that bring about responses in organisms; and not only is it true that the responses are typically movements of one or more parts of the body, but it is also true that the stimuli are typically outside the control of the individual. If Tom swats at an elusive bee that is buzzing around his ear, then he is responding to a stimulus. His hand motions are linked to a physical going-on that is beyond his ability to restrain—namely, the bee's activity near his head. If therefore responses to factors that are outside one's control do not count as behavior, then the swatting incident is no more a case of behavior than the tree-limb incident, and that consequence is simply false.

To address this issue, a behaviorist needs to distinguish clearly between two sorts of events: (1) those in which the movement is not initiated by the person and (2) those in which the movement is initiated by the person in response to a stimulus. What does it mean, though, to say that a person initiates the movement? Would initiating it not be something that the person purposely *does*, as opposed to something that *happens to* him or her? The distinction between happening-to events of sort (1) and doing events of sort (2) appears to underlie the difference that one identifies intuitively between the moving of Tom's hand because he has an uncontrollable twitch— triggered here by something that is internal to his body rather than external—and the moving of his hand because he wants to get a coin. The modification itself is problematic, however. By introducing the concept of doing through the exercise of the will, performing in accordance with the manifestation of intention, it begins to point to something other than pure behavior as the mark of mental phenomena. It seems that refinements are needed for behaviorism to work.

Some philosophers put forth innovative concepts in an effort to make it work and to explain mental states in terms of physicality, developing entire systems to confront the dualistic approach. It is not surprising that Gilbert Ryle is one such writer. Perhaps more than any other philosopher, Ryle sets out to destroy the notion of the mental as a realm of existence separate from that of the material. In objecting to Cartesian dualism, Ryle charges the French philosopher with what he calls "a category-mistake."[37] Whereas one can describe acts in mental terms, one is not talking about anything that is apart from the overt, physical expressions of them. To illustrate, Ryle says,

> A foreigner visiting Oxford or Cambridge for the first time is shown a number of colleges, libraries, playing fields, museums, scientific departments and administrative offices. He then asks 'But where is the University? . . .' It has then to be explained to him that the University is not another collateral institution. . . . The University is just the way in which all that he has already seen is organized.[38]

The visitor has taken the scholastic institution to be a thing other than the collection of structures that compose it. The institution, however, is not another member of the set of things that the visitor has seen; in seeing them, he has seen it. Similarly, contends Ryle, there are not mental events that are distinct from the physical acts to which one ascribes a correlation. Describing things in mental terms is simply a

---

[37] Gilbert Ryle, *The Concept of Mind* (New York: Barnes and Noble Books, 1949), 16.
[38] Ibid.

different way of characterizing human actions. Against those who accept the existence of an immaterial, reasoning part of humans, Ryle argues,

> They postulate an internal shadow-performance to be the real carrier of the intelligence ordinarily ascribed to the overt act, and think that in this way they explain what makes the overt act a manifestation of intelligence. They have described the overt act as an effect of a mental happening.
>
> In opposition to this entire dogma, I am arguing that in describing the workings of a person's mind we are not describing a second set of shadowy operations. We are describing certain phases of his one career; namely we are describing the ways in which parts of his conduct are managed.[39]

Ryle conjectures that all psychological notions can be interpreted in terms of behavior; however, much of the time, that behavior is potential. Rather than depicting mental factors, such as intelligence, as incorporeal personal elements, they are to be portrayed dispositionally. Intelligence is the ability to do particular kinds of things, and it is characterized by being *disposed* to act in a certain way when certain circumstances obtain. Dispositions are represented by hypothetical statements, what Ryle portrays as law-like propositions, which, paralleling standard causal statements, take an alternative conditional form: 'Whenever an instance of X occurs, an instance of Y occurs'. Consider two of Ryle's illustrations. A glass has the property of being brittle. Brittleness is just a tendency to shatter whenever struck with force. A glass is disposed to fly into fragments if an object ever hits it, even though it is possible that such an occurrence never happens. A sugar cube is soluble in water. To say that a sugar cube is soluble is to say that a dry sugar cube, if placed in water, would dissolve. It is disposed to dissolve under specific conditions—namely, upon becoming wet.

Likewise, if placed in the appropriate circumstances, then an intelligent being would act in such-and-such a manner. For example,

---

[39] Ibid., 50. For Ryle's application of his theory to belief, see chap. 4.

if Bobby sits down to a game of chess, then he would move his pieces in accordance with the rules, although, at present, he may be building a birdhouse. Bobby knows the rules; he knows how to play the game. More important, he knows how to play competently and does so whenever he faces an opponent. Not only can he recite the rules, but he can employ them as well and execute successful strategies in doing so. He possesses the capability, and, when the time is right, from that capability emerges certain overt behavior. It is the manifestation, in a given instance, of particular capacities and inclinations, specific abilities and tendencies, that singles out rationality. An intelligent act is not the end product of some causal chain stemming from an immaterial mind, thinks Ryle; it is simply the proclivity to do things in a special way as that proclivity is expressed corporally when appropriate circumstances support it. If one looks for mental causes in explaining actions, then he or she is looking askew. The individual should look instead for the propensities that underlie conduct. Ryle replaces the thinking substance of Descartes with occurrences of physical behavior, executed in accordance with law-like assertions.

As one turns to the motives of actions, the differences between Descartes's dualistic theory of humankind and Ryle's monistic theory step forward to stand in stark contrast. In the Cartesian view, the statement 'He boasted from vanity' is a causal statement, where the antecedent cause is a mental impulse, and the effect is the overt, physical, boasting behavior. According to Ryle, however,

> [I]t is to be construed as saying 'he boasted on meeting the stranger and his doing so satisfies the law-like proposition that whenever he finds a chance of securing the admiration and envy of others, he does *whatever he thinks* will produce this admiration and envy'.[40]

It is interesting that Ryle leans on behavior to account for thinking and other mental workings, but, in the case here, he relies on thinking to explain how mental workings are really just behavior. He seems to be going in circles. At any rate, in asking why a glass broke, says Ryle, one may be asking for the cause—a rock struck it;

---

[40] Ibid., 89. The emphasis is mine.

or one may be asking for the reason—it possesses the property of being brittle. Analogously, in inquiring why someone boasted, one may be asking what sparked this episode or asking why the person does this sort of thing. If asking the latter question, then what one is seeking is an explanation of the action. The following diagram sets forth a general depiction of the difference between the two theories:

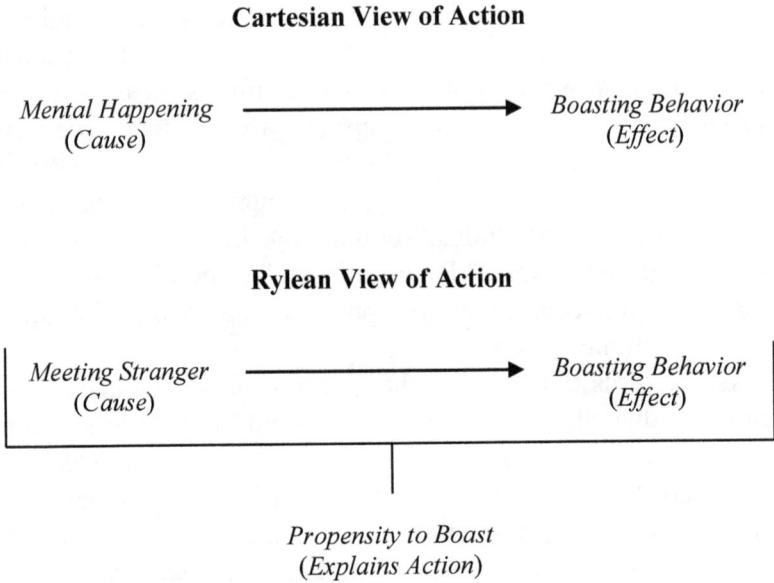

Cartesian View of Action

Mental Happening   ⟶   *Boasting Behavior*
(Cause)   *(Effect)*

Rylean View of Action

Meeting Stranger   ⟶   *Boasting Behavior*
(Cause)   *(Effect)*

Propensity to Boast
(Explains Action)

Figure 5.3

Ryle's primary concern in developing his philosophy of mind is twofold: (1) to show that there is no immaterial, thinking part of people from which the causes of behavior originate and (2) to show that phenomena that are classified as mental are nothing more than modes of conduct. Ryle challenges the demonstrability of an existent mental substance separate from the physical—a place where such things as volitions, motives, intelligence, intentions, emotions, and beliefs are housed. Doing something intelligently, intentionally, or cautiously is one event, not two. It is the manner in which physical performances unfold, represented by instantiated hypothetical statements. For Ryle, a mind is merely a body in action, or potential action, described in a particular way. Following Ryle's critical work, authors, no doubt, became more wary of using words and phrases that even *seemed* to point to putative mental occurrences.

Some philosophers dared to delve more deeply into the matter, however, and not all of them agreed with Ryle. Charges along these lines surfaced: Ryle defines mental states in terms of the disposition to behave in certain ways, but the behavior that is associated with a given mental state can be specified only by referring to the mental state itself. To be in mental state *m* is to be disposed to conduct oneself in a manner that is consistent with being in mental state *m*.

Anthony Kenny takes issue with Ryle on other grounds, accusing him of failing to see that his own theory is, in fact, a causal one. Drawing on an expression of a cause-effect link, Kenny offers the following case:

> It is ironic that Ryle, having attacked the 'impulse' theory of motives for wrongly regarding explanation by motives as a type of causal explanation, should himself offer a theory which is, on his own view of causation, no less causal. For if to offer X as a causal explanation of Y is roughly to say that whenever X then Y, then Ryle's explication of "he boasted from vanity" as "whenever an opportunity for boasting arrives, he takes it" construes "he boasted from vanity" as a causal statement. His theory differs from the one he rejects only in that it offers public circumstances, instead of private impulses, as the cause of the boasting.[41]

In accordance with the ideas of G. E. M. Anscombe, another philosopher of the contemporary period, Kenny goes further, finding fault with Ryle's analysis of motives. One may do things from a given motive yet not behave in accordance with some law-like proposition. Kenny states, "[I]t seems possible to act out of vanity

---

[41] Anthony Kenny, *Action, Emotion, and Will* (1963; Atlantic Highlands, NJ: Humanities Press, 1976), 79.

once in a while, out of impatience without being an impatient man, and out of remorse without being chronically remorseful."[42]

This view is correct. In fact, if one pursues the issue of motives, then one will see that Ryle's dispositional theory faces a difficult challenge on another front. Suppose that Tom and his best friend, Frank, served together in combat. One dreadful day, a soldier in the platoon spotted an enemy tossing a grenade toward the unit. The soldier shouted, "Grenade!" as the destructive device sailed directly toward Frank. Tom was near him at the time. He saw the grenade as it was on its downward arc and hurled himself in that direction, coming between it and his friend. Tom took the brunt of the blast, saving his friend's life at the expense of his own. He was awarded a medal posthumously for bravery in the line of duty, and he became a local hero. His hometown erected a monument in his memory, and many went there to honor one of their own who had fallen. Now, all the following statements cannot be true:

> s_1. Tom sacrificed himself intentionally to save the life of his best friend.
> s_2. Tom attempted to use his friend to shield himself from the grenade but stumbled into its path.
> s_3. Tom committed suicide to escape the horrors of war, unaware that Frank was nearby.

Until the incident, those people who knew Tom pictured him as just an ordinary man. He never had displayed bravery before or displayed cowardice. He never had experienced bouts of depression and, despite the war, had enjoyed the camaraderie of his fellow soldiers. Why did Tom do what he did; what was his frame of mind as he moved his body? People believe that he acted out of laudable bravery in an effort to protect his friend, even though it could have cost him, and did cost him, his life. Perhaps, though, he acted out of fear, and his own clumsiness resulted in his death. Again, he could have acted out of disillusionment and despair; seeing an opportunity to end his life without suspicion, he decided to do so, not knowing that Frank

---

[42] Ibid., 77. Also see G. E. M. Anscombe, *Intention*, 2nd ed. (1963; repr., Ithaca: Cornell University Press, 1974), 21.

was in the path of the grenade. What makes one of the three sentences that is shown above true and the other two false is not something about Tom's body hurling through the air but about Tom. In its raw form, behaviorism cannot capture the distinction, as the behavior—namely, jumping in front of the grenade—would be the same in each case, regardless of the motive that was behind this once-in-a-lifetime event.

Ryle defines motives in terms of propensities, and he claims that one *explains* what people do by referring to those propensities. The throwing of the grenade triggers Tom's behavior. For Ryle, however, the motive for the act was a specific instance of a general behavioral rule.

> The imputation of a motive for a particular action is not a causal inference to an unwitnessed event but the subsumption of an episode proposition under a law-like proposition.[43]

The problem for Ryle is that there *is no* applicable law-like proposition in the grenade case; therefore, there is nothing under which to subsume a proposition about the episode. Tom never had exhibited—and, of course, does not exhibit now—a tendency to be brave or cowardly or suicidal. This incident thus cannot be included under *any* such general tendency. If there is no tendency, however, then there is no motive, given Ryle's analysis, and that predicament is destructive for Ryle. Diagrammatically, Ryle's account of the happening reduces to the structure that appears in I below:

I. Tom Acts.

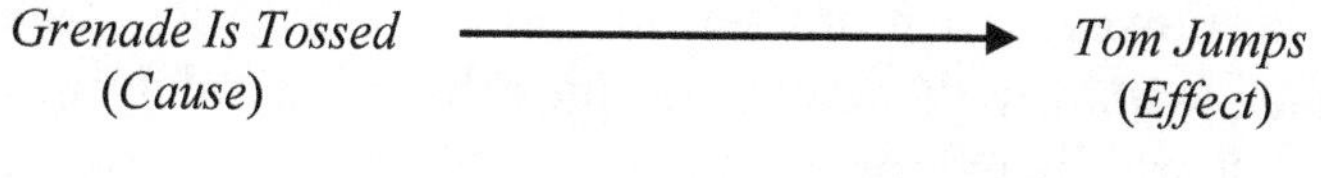

Grenade Is Tossed   ———————▶   *Tom Jumps*
    (Cause)   *(Effect)*

Figure 5.4

---

[43] Ryle, *Concept of Mind*, 90.

This motiveless event looks like another one, which is depicted in structure II in the following diagram. In reality, it is not far from mirroring the base-level event that is shown in III.

II. Tom Moves.

Tom's Muscles Twitch   ⟶   *Tom's Hand Moves*
   Uncontrollably   *(Effect)*
      (Cause)

III. Tom Moves.

Tree Limb Falls   ⟶   *Tom's Hand Moves*
  and Hits Tom   *(Effect)*
    (Cause)

Figure 5.5

Ryle's theory cannot handle the grenade incident. It degrades Tom's performance to nothing more than physics. None of the three sentences—s_1, s_2, or s_3—is false, given Ryle's theory of motives; neither is any one of them true. As explanations for what happened, they all are meaningless. Tom *did* act, though, and he did act *for a reason*. There *was* a motive behind his behavior, along with a matching belief; there *is* an explanation for why he did what he did. In attempting to dismiss the Cartesian model of man, Ryle has thrown out the baby with the bathwater.

There is, however, a more serious problem with Ryle's entire thesis—in fact, with any thesis that defines the mind solely in terms of behavior. Clearly, behavior can be an indicator of the existence of a particular mental state or event when certain circumstances obtain. The yelling of an obviously injured person and the yelping of an animal in the same condition is solid evidence that the individual creatures are experiencing pain. One can see the damaged tissue on the hand or the paw, and the person or animal is doing what an alert organism typically does when hurt. Ryle, however, takes such correspondence too far. He *equates* mental phenomena with physical conduct, actual or potential. In denying the existence of the immaterial and aligning intelligence with a disposition to act in specific ways, a theorist is destined to discover that it becomes difficult to stop the application. If intelligence is merely behaving in a manner that is consistent with what one categorizes as intelligent, then things to which no one would wish to ascribe intelligent behavior look suspiciously like thinking beings.

Plants turn toward the sun consistently, maximizing the light that falls on their leaves. I have one in my home that I must rotate periodically to keep it relatively straight, as it tends to lean toward the light entering a glass door, exemplifying the phenomenon of phototropism. Plants of some species even track the sun during the day as it moves across the sky, taking full advantage of the light; and they do so day after day. This movement is particularly valuable in northern regions, where it contributes to their warmth. What does one say, that they want more sunlight and have found a way to get it, that they have reasoned out a solution? The plant Venus's flytrap exhibits predatory behavior. It remains virtually motionless with the clustered leaves open to passing insects. When an unsuspecting fly ventures into the opening, the spiked blades close upon the prey in a fraction of a second—considerable rapidity for a plant—after which the flytrap digests the animal at its leisure. Is the plant planning its moves, employing an effective strategy to secure nourishment, and completing an objective as part of a suite of survival tactics; or is it instead annoyed by flies, buzzing around it relentlessly, and determined to put an end to the nuisance? Echoing the pattern in Figure 5.3, does the following illustration not fit the leaning-plant circumstances? Indeed, it seems to fit quite well.

Rylean View

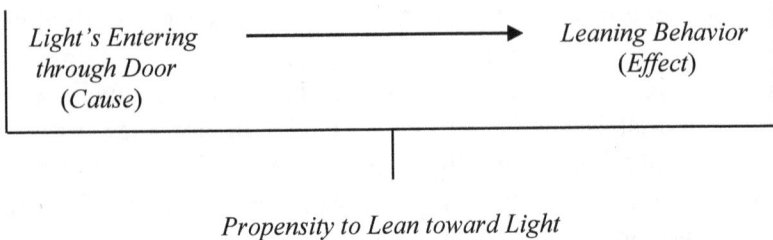

Propensity to Lean toward Light

Figure 5.6

Ryle attempts to distinguish behavior that corresponds to intelligent capacities from behavior that does not correspond to them. Examples of this latter sort are doing things by habit or luck. Ryle claims that intelligence is not represented by what he calls the single-track dispositions that nonintelligent behavior exemplifies. Saying something by rote, for instance, as the result of being drilled, does not reflect the higher-level activities that correspond to judgment. Manifold dispositions are associated with rational capacities, he declares, and these are revealed when the circumstances promote it. Acting out of intelligence involves more than behaving in accordance with one tendency. It is multifarious. It is to be able to do something repeatedly and to do it in various circumstances, accompanied by various related behaviors. It is to possess a complex of associated abilities of which the given performance is an actualization. Ryle avers,

> In judging that someone's performance is or is not intelligent, we have, as has been said, in a certain manner to look beyond the performance itself. . . . We are considering his abilities and propensities of which this performance was an actualisation. Our inquiry is not into causes (and *a fortiori* not into occult causes), but into capacities, skills, habits, liabilities and bents. We observe, for example, a soldier scoring a bull's eye. Was it luck or was it skill? If he has the skill, then he can get on or near the bull's eye again, even if the wind

strengthens, the range alters and the target moves. . . . He generally checks his breathing before pulling the trigger, as he did on this occasion; he is ready to advise his neighbor what allowances to make for refraction, wind, etc. Marksmanship is a complex of skills, and the question whether he hit the bull's eye by luck or from good marksmanship is the question whether or not he has the skills, and, if he has, whether he used them by making his shot with care, self-control, attention to the conditions and thought of his instructions.[44]

This distinction is a questionable one because habits may be complex, involving several behaviors grouped together, not just one. Aside from that fact, consider the case of the light-maximizing plants, which I set forth above. One might suggest, along Rylean lines, that their behavior of leaning toward the sun indicates a single-track disposition (the tendency to lean toward light) and is therefore not to be classified as astute. One still cannot deny, however, based on Ryle's criterion—namely, that intelligence is picked out by multifaceted behavior manifesting diverse dispositions—that plants are intelligent entities. The inclinations that one sees in them are not single-track proclivities but are varied and compound. Plants do more than turn toward the sun; their roots grow toward water as well. They protect themselves from harm through the use of chemicals and defensive parts, and they offer insects something of interest that facilitates the dissemination of pollen. Some close their leaves in response to adverse conditions. Like a marksman who adjusts for the varying factors of wind, range, and movement of the target, plants alter their behavior in response to environmental changes. If I move the houseplant that is by my glass door to a different location near that door, then it adjusts the angle at which it leans. Put it in front of a window across the room, and it would appear to ignore the door altogether, preferring to grow toward the new, better source of light. Owners of septic systems have little doubt that trees will find supplies of water, which is why the roots can damage the field lines of those systems. Common mimosas contract their branches almost

---

[44] Ibid., 45. The phrase 'occult causes' here refers to hidden, mental causes, the existence of which Ryle denies.

instantaneously when touched or exposed to excessive heat. Morning glory blooms fade when the temperature rises after sunrise, and rhododendrons draw their leaves into a tight configuration when the temperature falls. In fact, while living in the Northeast, I became fairly adept at determining the temperature during the winter months just by looking at the rhododendron plants in the hedge in front of our living room window. When their leaves curled tightly about themselves and hung straight down in the morning like icicles, I did not need to look at the thermometer; I knew that it was going to be a very cold day. Given Ryle's theory, and the consistently repeated behavior of flora across a range of diverse activities in an ostensible attempt to survive, saying that a particular person possesses intelligence but that a particular plant lacks it seems to be self-conflicting.

Even if one dismisses the case of plants, other things present a challenge for a behavior-based theory, as a tendency to perform in certain ways in accordance with an apparent purpose is not limited to living organisms. The context-sensitive operations of machines can be multidimensional, varied, and complex in response to changing conditions. Years ago, I applied for a position in a large corporation and was invited to visit one of the primary offices for testing as part of the application procedure. Seated in a waiting area after arriving at the facility, I watched with interest as a robot began delivering mail to employees. Navigating the work areas with remarkable adroitness, it was making the rounds. The device appeared to be quite clever, going precisely where it needed to go to find the recipients. I am sure that some of the employees—intelligent beings, no doubt—would have done a poorer job of finding their fellow workers in such a huge building than that machine. Technology has progressed since then, and, as the progress continues, the capabilities and tendencies of future contrivances may be surprising. Advances in cybernetics and artificial intelligence show that machines can be equipped with the capacity to adapt to contextual changes and not to do things merely by rote. Automata can be endowed with the ability to mimic human behavior in subtle and crafty ways. Military drones can roam the countryside looking for targets of opportunity, and they very likely will form a formidable future force. Their performances can be extraordinarily intricate and multifaceted—far from the actualization of any single-track disposition. Focusing on tendencies as a way to explain intelligence and to characterize rational behavior may allow a theorist to avoid admitting of immaterial minds, but it does so at the great expense of obscuring a fundamental mark of humanity.

To object that plants and machines are not intelligent beings, and therefore the principle of dispositional activity cannot be applied to them, would be to commit an error in reasoning in a blatant way. One cannot assume that certain things are intelligent and that certain things are not intelligent, so that one can exclude those that one wishes before applying the criterion of intelligence that is supposed to separate them. It is the work of the proposed distinguishing factor to accomplish that task. Behavior may point to intelligence, but intelligence is not simply to be identified with activity, regardless of the intricacy of the movements; and, if it does so point in the case of plants and machines, then it points to mentality that is external to the physical systems that exhibit the behavior. That fact alone stands against the theory. Ryle's analytic behaviorism is not persuasive.

MIND-BRAIN IDENTITY THEORY

Regardless of the seeming impoverishment that it brought, contemporary philosophy embraced the notion that the human being is purely a corporeal entity. Writers continued to seek to explain mental phenomena without invoking happenings in an incorporeal substance as materialism took on a familiar tone in philosophical works. Nothing other than the physical is to be found in people or, for that matter, anywhere, so the supporters claimed. Immaterial entities have no part in the realm of reality. Philosophy is fickle, however, and analytic behaviorism eventually lost ground to other physicalistic theories. By the middle of the twentieth century, the notion that mental phenomena are merely states of, or operations of, the brain had taken root in the writings of some. The mind *is* the brain, so they assert; the two are actually one. The author J. J. C. Smart (1920–2012), for example, argues that there is reason to view organisms as just physiochemical mechanisms. Smart alleges that philosophical analysis does not support a Cartesian view of humans:

> [T]here are no philosophical arguments which compel us
> to be dualists.
>   The above is largely a confession of faith. . . . A
> man is a vast arrangement of physical particles, but there
> are not, over and above this, sensations or states of
> consciousness. There are just behavioral facts about this
> vast mechanism.[45]

From the standpoint of ontology, Smart accepts the view that reality
is entirely material. It is interesting that he does so principally on the
basis of what he refers to as faith. At any rate, in his theory, sensations are *numerically identical* to brain processes.[46] They are *exactly*
the same thing.

> When I say that a sensation is a brain process . . . ,
> I am using "is" in the sense of strict identity. (Just as in
> the—in this case necessary—proposition "7 is identical
> with the smallest prime number greater than 5.") . . . I do
> not mean just that the sensation is somehow spatially or
> temporally continuous with the brain process. . . . I wish
> to make it clear that the brain-process doctrine asserts
> identity in the *strict* sense.[47]

Smart's theory is that of type-materialism: It identifies types of
mental events with types of physical events, and every instance of a
specific mental type is an instance of a specific physical type.

     Hilary Putnam raises one early objection to the identification of
the mind with the brain, basing his argument on what is known as
multiple realizability. Putnam argues that mental phenomena, such as
being in pain, can be realized in various kinds of organisms having
physiologies that differ markedly from that of humans. It is a mistake
to hold that a given type of mental state corresponds to only one type
of physical state.

---

[45] J. J. C. Smart, "Sensations and Brain Processes," *Philosophical Review* 68, no. 2
(1959): 143. Other theorists of the period are U. T. Place and Herbert Feigl.
[46] Refer to the distinction between numerical identity and qualitative identity, as
discussed in the section on George Berkeley in chap. 2 and the section on senses of
identity in chap. 3.
[47] Smart, "Sensations and Brain Processes," 144.

Consider what the brain-state theorist has to do to make good his claims. He has to specify a physical-chemical state such that *any* organism (not just a mammal) is in pain if and only if (a) it possesses a brain of a suitable physical-chemical structure; and (b) its brain is in that physical-chemical state. This means that the physical-chemical state in question must be a possible state of a mammalian brain, a reptilian brain, a mollusc's brain (octopuses are mollusca, and certainly feel pain), etc. At the same time, it must *not* be a possible (physically possible) state of the brain of any physically possible creature that cannot feel pain. Even if such a state can be found, it must be nomologically certain that it will also be a state of the brain of any extraterrestrial life that may be found that will be capable of feeling pain before we can even entertain the supposition that it may *be* pain.[48]

Putnam's objection constitutes a serious blow to the identity theory of mind. In its place, Putnam introduces his own view of mentality: functionalism, the notion that the mental is defined not by the contents of consciousness but by the causal role that it plays in the biological system. That theory too is not without problems; I will have a bit more to say about it in a moment.

One of the noted opponents of mind-brain identity theory is Saul Kripke. Kripke inquires whether certain brain tissue that is associated with pain—namely, C-fibers—can be stimulated without the occurrence, out of logical necessity, of the corresponding sensation. If so, according to the philosopher, then the theory is false. He remarks,

> In the appropriate sentient beings is it . . . possible that a stimulation of C-fibers should have existed without being felt as pain? If this is possible, then the stimulation of C-fibers can itself exist without pain, since for it to

---

[48] Hilary Putnam, "The Nature of Mental States," in *Philosophical Papers*, vol. 2, *Mind, Language, and Reality* (Cambridge: Cambridge University Press, 1975), 436. The paper was published originally under the title "Psychological Predicates," in *Art, Mind, and Religion: Proceedings of the 1965 Oberlin Colloquium in Philosophy*, ed. W. H. Capitan and D. D. Merrill (Pittsburgh: University of Pittsburgh Press, 1967), 37–48.

> exist without being *felt as pain* is for it to exist without
> there *being any* pain. Such a situation would be in flat
> out contradiction with the supposed necessary identity of
> pain and the corresponding physical state, and the . . .
> [same] holds for any physical state which might be
> identified with a corresponding mental state.[49]

Returning to Kripke's concept of rigid designators, as I discussed in chapter 3, one sees that, so Kripke argues, if the identity theory of mind were correct, then 'C-fiber stimulation' and 'pain' would be rigidly designating terms. The link between them therefore would be necessary, and it would not be possible for C-fibers to be activated without there being a sensation of pain. Plainly, it is not impossible, thinks Kripke. God could have constructed humans in such a way that the firing of these particular fibers led to some other sensation or to no sensation at all. Just creating the tissue does not guarantee ipso facto that pain will be felt, rather than a tickle, when the fibers are stimulated. "[T]he stimulation could exist without the pain," Kripke maintains, so the relation between the two cannot be identity.[50]

I noted in chapter 3 that there is good reason to take the stance that identical composite objects are not—in an important respect— identical of necessity. Objects qua objects are not simply the sets of physical particles that compose them. Rules must be established for the existence of inanimate, material collections as units and likewise their persistence as units. In the case here, however, Kripke is right, assuming that one expands the reference to C-fibers to include, as a set, any neuronal tissue the stimulation of which is accompanied by pain (current science identifies additional pain-bearing tissue in the nervous system). Mind-brain identity theory holds that, in sensation, there is just a physical event that is taking place, and the two names that are applied to it refer in all circumstances to exactly it, and it is not possible for it to be otherwise. The theory's assertion, as Kripke shows, is just false.

Aside from the criticisms of Putnam and Kripke, I believe that Smart's approach leaves him open to a few problems for other

---

[49] Saul Kripke, *Naming and Necessity* (Cambridge: Harvard University Press, 1980), 151.
[50] Ibid., 154.

reasons. One must be clear with regard to the meaning of the term 'sensation'. Is activity of neural tissue in response to a stimulus to be part of the corresponding concept? Given mind-brain identity theory, it seems that it must be so; but, if it is so, then, contrary to Smart, sensations need not involve the brain and hence cannot be identical to encephalic processes. Certain environmental circumstances evoke movement of the body through reflexes. In such cases, peripheral nerves that are triggered transmit impulses to the spinal cord, which initiates behavior long before the brain can receive the information, process it, and direct the appropriate muscles to contract. This movement is particularly important under extreme conditions, where it plays a protective role. If one leans on a stove's burner, unaware that it had been turned to the high setting ten minutes earlier, then one will jerk the affected hand away virtually instantaneously because of the intense heat. In this withdrawal behavior, the reflex arc, which is the path that the nerve impulses travel in the episode, does not include the brain. The neural transmission goes to, and returns from, the spinal cord, which prompts the physical response. The shortened path minimizes damage to the hand. Only after the limb's withdrawal will the accompanying signals reach the brain. Smart could not deny that such incidents involve genuine sensations. Experiencing what the senses communicate constitutes the very essence of sensory impressions. If there were no sensation in the aforementioned case—no successful sensory input—then the hand would not move, as there would be nothing to indicate a problem.

For obvious reasons, it would not do for Smart to declare that only those certain sensations that are actually brain processes are, in fact, brain processes, as such a declaration would be trivially true and uninformative. Moreover, it would be of no value to his case, as the point that Smart is attempting to establish is that sensations—taken inclusively—as a type of phenomena are identical to events in the brain. He cannot assume that all sensations are brain events without begging the question. If Smart argues instead that sensations, as neural events, can rise to the level of conscious awareness, and only if they do so are they to be classified as brain processes, then his position would lead to unsupportable consequences. No sense could be made of the claim that one was not aware of any pain during the past hour, but it was definitely there nonetheless. If there is no sensation of pain of which one is mindful, then there is no pain at all. To be hurting, one must experience it, and experiencing it, in this instance, means having the sensation in a conscious way.

Suppose that Lindsey injures her foot. Suppose further, given the envisioned conscious-awareness modification of Smart's theory, that she alternates numerous times during the day between being aware of the pain in her foot and then not being aware of it. It is nonsensical to assert that there are two kinds of pain at work—one that is felt, one that is not felt. The concept of unfelt pain is illogical. One does not have a toothache unless one feels it. The existence of pain is given in the experiencing of it; Kripke's remarks indicate as much. The conscious sensation *is* the feeling. There is no meaningful way to distinguish Lindsey's sensation of pain from some alleged cloaked counterpart. One could attempt to differentiate them only on the basis of a thesis that presumes that both must be there in a subject and that they must be unlike. It would be a contrived distinction. One would be constraining the conditions that obtain in reality to reflect the conditions of a theory, not building a theory to reflect the conditions that obtain in reality. The cart would be pulling the horse. If Lindsey is conscious, then either she is *experiencing pain*, or there is *no pain at all*—it just does not hurt.

A renewed interest in the idea that the mind and the brain are identical surfaced in recent years, with a proffered defense of it against Putnam's telling multiple-realization objection. Thomas W. Polger contends that the evidence for Putnam's assertion is weak.

> First we need evidence that mammals, reptiles, and mollusks experience pain, and indeed that they experience the same kind of pain sensations as humans and thus as one another. If they cannot all have at least some sensations of exactly the same kinds, then there is no question of them multiply realizing any one kind of sensation. . . . Second, we need evidence that the brain processes that realize pain in each kind of creature are of neurobiologically distinct kinds. What reason do we have to support this contention?[51]

---

[51] Thomas W. Polger, "Are Sensations Still Brain Processes?" *Philosophical Psychology* 24, no. 1 (2011): 10. For another account that argues for a return to

According to Polger, even the significant differences in the physical structures of various kinds of organisms is insufficient to warrant one's concluding that there are neurological differences among them.

One does not need to introduce organisms of different species, however, to counter Smart's theory. One does not need even to bring in different organisms of the same species. The essence of Smart's view is that mental things, at least states of consciousness, such as sensations, are purely physical goings-on in the brain. It is not that the two are merely temporally coexistent. They are absolutely and strictly identical in the way that the names 'Cicero' and 'Tully' pick out the same, unique individual: There is only one Roman statesman by either name. Such strict identity, despite Polger's skepticism, leads to a demonstrable contradiction. Consider how this trouble for Smart and any supporter of his position arises.

Electromagnetic energy in the universe exists across a broad spectrum. The energy is classified according to ranges in which its wavelength falls. Gamma rays, X-rays, ultraviolet light, visible light, infrared radiation, microwave radiation, and radio waves—all are electromagnetic energy in different parts of the continuum, listed here in order of increasing wavelength. The wavelength becomes more extended, *ceteris paribus*, as the frequency decreases. An analogous phenomenon exists in sound energy, where short wavelengths correspond to high frequencies and long wavelengths correspond to low frequencies. The descending notes that one hears on a guitar are sound waves of increasing fundamental wavelength and correspondingly declining frequency, produced by strings vibrating in a medium through which the sound waves can propagate: in this case, air. Unlike sound, however, electromagnetic energy needs no medium through which to propagate; it crosses even intergalactic space.

The portion of electromagnetic energy that is classified as visible light corresponds to wavelengths ranging from approximately 380 nanometers to 740 nanometers. The human eye contains two types of photoreceptors: rods and cones. Cones respond to certain wavelength-segments of the visible spectrum, giving rise to the sensation of colors through the interpretation of the cones' signals. In

mind-brain identity theory, see Christopher S. Hill, *Sensations: A Defense of Type Materialism* (Cambridge: Cambridge University Press, 1991).

the norm, there are three types of cones.[52] The ranges of their responses to stimuli overlap, but they generally are distinguished by the three wavelength spans to which they are most sensitive: short, medium, and long. Humans see visible light at the shortest wavelengths as violet. The longest wavelengths, humans see as red. These two hues are among the spectral colors. They can be produced by splitting a beam of white light into component wavelengths—what happens when, for example, sunlight passes through a prism. It is a phenomenon that Isaac Newton discovered. Human eyes detect hues according to where the energy falls on the continuum from 380 to 740 nanometers. The other spectral colors—indigo, blue, green, yellow, and orange—correspond to increasing wavelengths that fall between the two spectral extremes of violet and red.[53] It is the activity of the cones and the interpretation by the brain of the sensory information that the cones provide that allow people to experience color.

Interesting things happen when light of different wavelengths is combined. Aside from splitting a beam of light, by which Newton produced the spectral colors, the scientist found that, if he passed the resultant multicolored beam through a second prism, recombining the colors, then white light was regenerated. The fact is that, if all wavelengths between 380 and 740 nanometers are merged, then what one sees is the color white. One need not blend all wavelengths to produce white light, however. One can generate it by combining the three primary colors: blue, green, and red. In fact, mixing just two shades—blue, or bluish violet, and yellow, for instance—produces white light. Additional hues result from joining two of the three primary colors of light. These secondary tints are cyan, magenta, and yellow. The human eye-brain system can detect at least ten million different colors.[54] This fascinatingly large palette is a consequence of the blending of light energy at various wavelengths and intensities, creating an array of perceived, nonspectral variations.

Impulses from the photosensitive cells of the retinae of humans progress along a particular path in the cranium, traveling to the optic

---

[52] As mentioned earlier, a small percentage of women have a fourth type of cone.

[53] Not everyone includes indigo in the list.

[54] See Deane B. Judd and Gunter Wyszecki, *Color in Business, Science, and Industry*, 3rd ed. (New York: John Wiley and Sons, 1975), 245.

chiasma, or optic chiasm, then onward to the thalamus-housed lateral geniculate nuclei, finally extending to the primary visual cortex. (Nerve signals that control the size of the pupil in response to light intensity take a somewhat different course.) The neural pathways converge at the optic chiasma, such that impulses originating from the nasal side of each eye cross before going to the appropriate lateral geniculate nucleus. This structure is a factor in binocular fusion—the perception of a single composite visual image from two eyes. I present a simplified diagram below to illustrate the crossover:

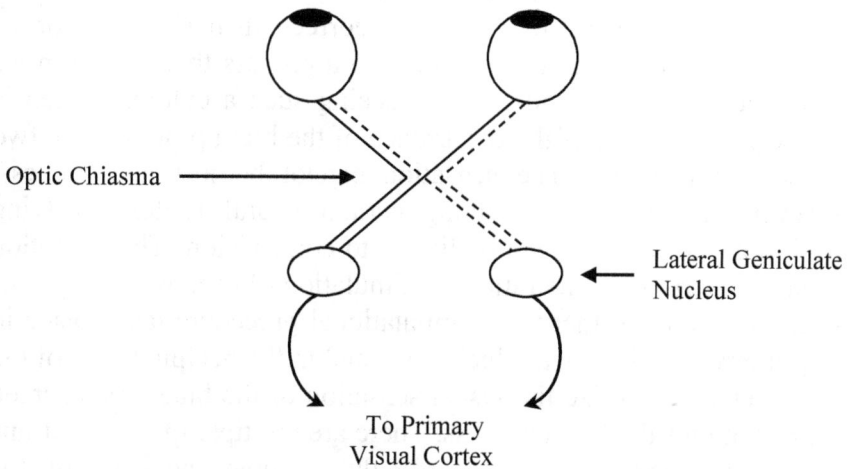

Optic Chiasma

Lateral Geniculate Nucleus

To Primary Visual Cortex

Figure 5.7

Now, suppose that a normal subject with uniform, perfect sight in each eye—call the subject *s*—who is participating in an experiment is wearing glasses that block much of his lateral peripheral vision. Each lens of the glasses is colored a distinct blue-green shade, similar to cyan. Seated in a chair in a windowless, featureless room, *s* stares at a white, back-lit, translucent screen through the lenses, so that the screen looks bluish green to him. Nothing other than the screen is visible to him. He repeats this exercise several times, shutting his eyes for a period of time between incidents as part of the experiment. While his eyes are closed, an assistant removes s's glasses and reinstalls them on s's head, after which s opens his eyes again to stare at the screen. On the tenth such occurrence, the assistant extracts the blue-green lenses, replacing one with a blue lens of a particular shade and the other with a green lens, also of a certain shade. When s opens his eyes, the screen will appear to him to be bluish green. If the colors and tinting of the lenses are sufficiently precise, then s will not be able to distinguish between the color sensation that is brought about by the matching lenses and the sensation that is brought about by the different lenses. The partial crossing of the neural pathways and the brain's interpretation of the data join to yield duplicate experiences.[55]

If mind-brain identity theory is correct, then s's sensation of seeing a colored screen is equivalent to a process that occurs in s's brain. Moreover, every instance of seeing such a colored screen is precisely an instance of the occurrence of the brain process: The two are strictly identical. The sensation cannot be just any process, however, as only activity along certain neural routes involving specific groups of cells can be linked to color vision. The operation includes determining the ratios of stimulation of each of the types of cones. It is thought that this computational procedure takes place in the primary visual cortex, which is located in the occipital lobe of the brain. Let V symbolize the visual sensation of the blue-green screen and P stand for the brain process. There are multiple incidents of this sensory phenomenon and accordingly multiple incidents of the process, even within s alone; so, V and P represent types of which each sensory instance and each brain process is a token respectively.

---

[55] One need not conduct such an elaborate experiment to demonstrate to oneself the apparent blending effect. Stand in bright sunlight with one eye covered or tightly closed for about a minute. Next, stare at a piece of white paper with the open eye, then shut that eye and glance with the other one for a moment. The paper will look dark to the first (open) eye and bright to the second—a clear difference. Gaze at the paper now with both eyes, and its degree of brightness will appear to be between the two levels. People's eyes adjust rather quickly to the intensity of light, so this effect will be short-lived. It does illustrate, however, the in-between phenomenon that is caused by different sensory signals from each eye. There will be other differences, of course, between seeing with each eye individually and seeing with both eyes together, such as the impression of depth in the latter case, but it is the degree of brightness of the binary visual image that is the point here.

For the sake of simplicity, I will limit the example here to one subject, s, rather than numerous subjects. Thus, s's in-general sensing of the blue-green screen, whenever such a thing may happen, is the visual sensation V, and each instance in which s actually does sense such a thing is a token of that type; refer to such tokens in this way: $v_1, v_2, v_3, \ldots, v_n$. Likewise, the in-general firing of certain neurons in a certain sequence in s's brain, whenever such a thing may happen, is the process P, and each case in which those specific neurons do fire in the given order on some given occasion is a token of that type; call these tokens $p_1, p_2, p_3, \ldots, p_n$. At 10:30:01 on Monday morning, when the subject s sees the screen while wearing the blue-green lenses and experiences the corresponding sensation of color, a particular instance of a sensory event, say, v_1, which is a token of type V, occurs. Likewise, a particular instance of a physical process, say, p_1, which is a token of type P, occurs. To assert that sensations are strictly identical to brain processes is to assert that $v_1 = p_1$, and it is to assert further that every instance of V is in the *strict* sense of identity an instance of P.

On the tenth trial of s's experiment, however, a shift in circumstances takes place. Whatever series of brain events that is under way now cannot be the same as the one that was under way prior to the change. There is a difference in the wavelength components of the energy that is entering s's eyes and thus in the matching signals from the cones. In the first nine instances, a single wavelength entered both eyes. In the current trial, there are two different wavelengths, each one entering a single eye. With this variation in the conditions, the brain's determination of color that results from its assessment of the cone-provided data also must vary. Some brain process other than P has to occur as the brain takes into account the disparity of the signals arriving from the eyes and produces a unified, common sensation from dissimilar wavelengths. The impression of seeing a blue-green screen is alleged to be exactly equal to the former sequential firing of neurons. What there is now, however, is the impression of seeing a blue-green screen that looks the same as the earlier screen, but it results from blue light's entering one eye, coupled with green light's entering the other eye simultaneously. The subject s can discern no difference in the appearances of the screen under the two distinct conditions. Refer to the altered process as *PX* and any tokens of this type as px_1, px_2, and so forth. So, when *s* sees the screen after the exchange of the lenses, the sensation is of type *V*, but the brain process is of type *PX*, where $PX \neq P$. It follows that, although $v_1 = p_1$, in the theory under review, $v_{10} = px_1$; and *no* instance of type *PX* is qualitatively identical to *any* instance of type *P*, for they are different physical happenings. Qualitatively, v_1 is indistinguishable from v_{10} because the sensations seem to *s* to be precisely the same. The problem for the proposed identity of the mind and the brain arises in this way: It is not possible for two things at two respective points in time to be qualitatively identical and be numerically identical to two corresponding things, at those same respective points in time, that are qualitatively distinct. The conjectured mind-brain equivalence of Smart and others allows indistinguishable instances of visually experiencing a blue-green color on different occasions to be numerically identical to unlike physical occurrences on those same occasions, and such a state of affairs cannot obtain—ever. The problem becomes more clear when I represent it diagrammatically, as shown here (taking liberties with the temporal depiction), revealing the relations that emerge from the postulates of the theory:

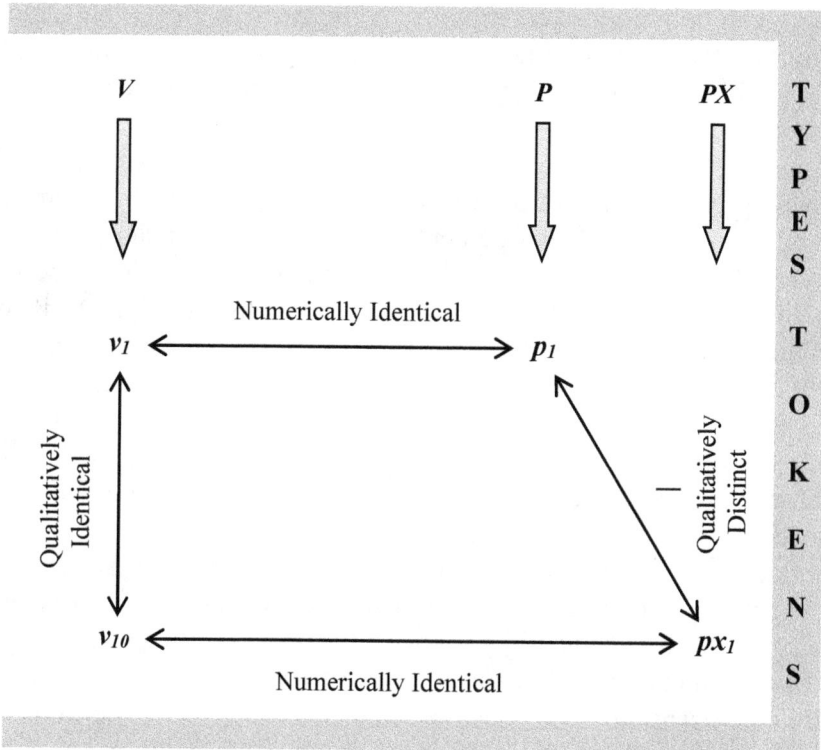

Figure 5.8

It does not matter whether the experiment that I outlined ever, in fact, results in no detectable dissimilarity. It is sufficient to undermine mind-brain identity theory simply to demonstrate that it is *possible* for the subject to discern no difference while wearing the altered glasses. It is unquestionably possible—nomologically, not to mention logically; binocular color fusion has been proved in various trials by researchers. Generating a definite sensation of yellow from red and green light, where one color is presented to each eye, has been achieved.[56] One author remarks, "There is no color-sensation,

---

[56] See the report by W. C. H. Prentice, "New Observations of 'Binocular Yellow,'" *Journal of Experimental Psychology* 38, no. 3 (1948): 284–88. One also may wish to see R. W. Pickford, "Binocular Colour Combinations," *Nature* 159, no. 4034 (1947): 268–69.

which can be produced by mixing two lights in one eye, that cannot be duplicated by supplying the two lights, independently, one to each eye."[57] If an attentive perceiver cannot distinguish between two visual perceptions, then, because those perceptions exist only as part of the sensory experience of that perceiver, no qualitative difference can be present. It is not a case here of two physical objects in the world; it is a case of two perceptions in the mind of the perceiver. Given that appearances *are just* the totality of their perceived qualities (blue-green shade, square shape, and so forth), if no difference between, or among, appearances can be discerned, then they are qualitatively identical. This scenario demonstrates that the theory leads to a contradiction.

A supporter of the theory might attempt to amend it, saying that, even if two sensations are qualitatively identical, the counterpart processes need not be qualitatively identical, only sufficiently similar—alike in certain key respects. Strict identity is the very core of the theory, however, and it could not be maintained under such a change. The theory would collapse. It cannot permit even a single alteration in the firing of a single neuron to occur without varying the equivalent sensation. Besides, the change would have no ground on which to stand. What would 'sufficiently similar' really mean? What would count as the key respects? If one defines a sufficiently similar brain process to be a brain process that is identical to the particular sensation, then one's associated argument would beg the question. If one means that qualitatively identical sensations are to be equated with certain processes involving neurons in the same areas of the brain respectively, then, because *s*'s seeing a lady in a green dress and his seeing a horse in a brown harness involve areas of the brain that are the same as those that *s*'s seeing a man in a blue suit involve, the sensation of seeing the lady and that of seeing the horse would be qualitatively indistinguishable from the sensation of seeing the man, which is false. Humans' brains play an essential role in their perceiving the world, but to claim that sensations *are exactly* brain processes to avoid accepting the existence of immaterial things brings one to an untenable position. It does not account for the perception, let alone

---

[57] Gordon Lynn Walls, *The Vertebrate Eye and Its Adaptive Radiation* (Bloomfield Hills, MI: Cranbrook Institute of Science, 1942), 90.

the perceiver. It is not difficult to generate other counterexamples to the thesis of mind-brain identity, and, despite the renewed support for it in recent times, Smart's conjecture is demonstrably false.[58]

LOGICAL PRIMITIVENESS THEORY

Consider next the position of the philosopher P. F. Strawson (1919–2006). Strawson rejects both (1) the austere view that there is no subject to which conscious experiences can be assigned—a view that aligns with Hume's denial of a persistent self and one, Strawson believes, that Ludwig Wittgenstein (1889–1951) held at one point— and notably (2) the stance that there is an independent, incorporeal substance that is the subject of experiences: the thinking self of Descartes's dualistic system. Here, he condenses Descartes's theory:

> When we speak of a person, we are really referring to one or both of two distinct substances, two substances of different types, each of which has its own appropriate types of states and properties; and none of the properties or states of either can be a property or state of the other. States of consciousness belong to one of these substances and not to the other.[59]

---

[58] Although I will not pursue the matter, another example that proves the identity theory of mind to be false is that of attention. Experiments demonstrate the ability of an individual to focus on something in particular in perception while ignoring extraneous sensory data. Not seeing or not hearing something, which is present but ignored by an observer as a result of attention, can be indistinguishable from not sensing it because it is absent, where otherwise like conditions obtain. The brain employs sensory gating to remove the irrelevant information. Perception involving the active exclusion of specific data is linked to a brain process that differs from the process that sustains perception in which those elements are just missing, even though, to the perceiver, the respective sensory events may seem to be the same. The pulvinar of the thalamus plays a key role in selective attention, serving an early gating function, while the parietal lobe provides subsequent fine-grained selection. Refer, for instance, to Marie T. Banich, *Cognitive Neuroscience and Neuropsychology*, 2nd ed. (Boston: Houghton Mifflin Co., 2004), 258.

[59] P. F. Strawson, *Individuals: An Essay in Descriptive Metaphysics* (1959; repr., London: University Paperbacks, 1974), 94.

Strawson claims that the concept of a person is, in his terminology, logically primitive. It is misguided to see a person as an amalgam of two completely different kinds of things. Rather, one should see a person as a member of a class of entities that are metaphysically fundamental and with respect to which one can make dissimilar ascriptions. A person is not two things—a mind and a body—stuck together, but a single thing to which it is possible to attribute disparate sorts of conditions and qualities. One might say, to use some of Strawson's examples, that an entity of this type is in pain or is playing ball, reflecting states of awareness, and one also might say that it weighs ten stone or is in the drawing room, pointing to physical features or circumstances. The appropriateness of applying, to the *very same thing*, predicates that pertain to the mental and those that pertain to the physical is the defining mark of personhood.

> [T]he concept of a person is to be understood as the concept of a type of entity such that *both* predicates ascribing states of consciousness *and* predicates ascribing corporeal characteristics, a physical situation &c. are equally applicable to an individual entity of that type.[60]

Strawson's view of a person is rather like that of a book on a shelf in the den. It may be said to be the seminal work that changed Jack's way of thinking about the American Civil War. It also may be said to be the nine-pound object that fell on Jack's toe and broke it. One can refer to different aspects of the object and ascribe different kinds of properties to it. It is controversial, and it is massive. It is written in an elegant style, and it is four inches thick. There is only one object, however, and that object is a physical thing occupying a place in space. Identity requires materiality, according to Strawson, and that requirement extends to persons too. Individuals, whether they are inanimate objects or persons, are grounded in the corporeal.

What this parallel shows, though, is that the mere ascription of different sorts of properties is insufficient to distinguish persons from other things. Objects, such as books, can be subject to predication in which the properties that one ascribes to them differ in basic ways. It is when those ascriptions credit states of awareness to entities,

---

[60] Ibid., 104.

however, if Strawson's theory holds, that one singles out persons. The reason that the Cartesian independent self fails as that to which one could attribute mental states that are not one's own states, so Strawson contends, is that it is impossible to identify that alleged self as a stand-alone entity. A Cartesian ego could not be recognized by the would-be attributer. One cannot discern others if one can discern them only as subjects of experience. In his analysis, Strawson calls predicates that point to states of consciousness P-predicates. Predicates pertaining to material bodies he calls M-predicates. What his theory turns on is this point: Being able to apply both P-predicates and M-predicates to a thing is what classifies it as a person.

One can use those same predicates, however, with reference to dogs. Consider first the M-predicates. Their applicability is obvious: The animal is black, weighs sixty pounds, has four legs, and is equipped with a tail. Strawson's P-predicates also apply. Anyone who has owned a dog can confirm the fact that 'is in pain' and 'is playing ball' are plainly relevant expressions. I remember accidentally stepping on my puppy's foot when I was a boy. Whitey— fittingly named, given his totally white coat—yelped uncontrollably. Such yelping was a clear indication of a measure of misery. I was sure that the rest of his life would be marked by blame—blaming me for hurting him. My mother convinced me that he knew that I did not intend to injure him. A caring and compassionate parent, she was concerned as much for my feelings of regret as for the dog's feelings of discomfort. Still, it grieved me, but, after a while, I came to let go of the incident as much as Whitey already had let go. We remained buddies. I suppose that children and puppies are equally resilient.

Aside from the aforementioned P-predicates, there are others that apply as much to animals as they do to humans. Although she chased balls that I tossed for her, a favored Labrador retriever that I recall was so taken with catching a Frisbee in flight that, when opportunities for play arose, her behavior sometimes suggested a certain intransigence.[61] In one particular instance, I was busy at work, sawing a large piece of wood for some home project, but Liza was not to be ignored. With my Frisbee in her mouth and her tail wagging, she stood in front of me, first on one side of the board and

---

[61] 'Frisbee' is a registered trademark of Wham-O, Inc.

then on the other, indicating that it was time to play. I continued my work, paying her no attention. Liza was not deterred. She repeated the series—but to no avail. Finally, Liza dropped the toy on the board almost under the saw, bringing the work to a halt. In a rather humorous way, Liza's conduct demanded that I take notice of her. Her persistent manner made it clear that it was time for a game of catch; and how could anyone resist responding positively to such a relentless performance by such an adorable creature?

Then, there was the cat Cookie. As mothers go, she was unique. It must have been a difficult day for her, and tempers can be short at those times. The challenges of rearing offspring can weigh on any cat, I suppose, but she resembled a strict authoritarian more than a gentle nurturer. I do not know what her kitten had done, but, whatever it was, it was not received well. Cookie snatched the youngster by the back of its neck, plopped on her side in the yard with the kitten in tow, and proceeded to smack the little creature repeatedly in the rump with her hindfeet. Cries of distress from the stricken were in vain. Over and over, Cookie kicked her baby until, at last, she released it, and it ran away from her with all the speed that its legs could deliver. A cat-administered spanking—it was not something that I ever expected to see, and I never have seen it again. It would be a mistake to view the event as an attempt to correct the kitten, issuing from some vague parental hope of altering its future behavior through proper discipline. It was instead a reaction to the youngster's behavior at the time. There is no question, however, that a Strawsonian P-predicate applies to Cookie here. She displayed a state of awareness by her conduct, and the negative reinforcement that resulted probably taught that kitten a lesson, so to speak, thwarting, through association, any such future shenanigans.

Strawson has it that the applicability of both psychological and physical predicates to things separates persons from other sorts of entities. Although dogs and cats lack the distinctive characteristics of rationality and never can qualify as agents, they plainly do exhibit states of consciousness; therefore, given his theory, it would seem that dogs and cats are persons. By adopting the phrase 'type of entity' in defining a person as the sort of thing to which both P-predicates and M-predicates pertain, Strawson must mean that whatever entity falls into the collection of things to which one can refer in using those predicates is a person. He cannot carve out what one thinks of as human beings to define the type. To object that dogs and cats do not count, as they are not persons, would constitute fallacious reasoning. One cannot assume that certain things are persons and that certain things are not persons, so that one can exclude the latter group in order to employ the criterion that supposedly differentiates them. How is it possible to know, though, that Whitey's wailing, Liza's prancing, and Cookie's kicking actually indicate states of awareness, that one was in pain, another was ready to play, and the third was unyielding in the strict treatment of its offspring? Strawson holds that one applies many, but not all, P-predicates to oneself on the basis of experiencing what the predicates denote, but the justification for applying P-predicates to something else is behavior.

> What I have said is that one ascribes P-predicates to others on the strength of observation of their behaviour; and that the behaviour-criteria one goes on are not just signs of the presence of what is meant by the P-predicate, but are criteria of a logically adequate kind for the ascription of the P-predicate.[62]

Strawson's method of discernment does not work. If the term 'others' means 'other persons besides oneself', then one would be required to know that something is a person before ascribing a state of consciousness and therefore before applying the concept of personhood and any corresponding P-predicate. That approach is obviously unsatisfactory. If, in contrast, 'others' means 'other things besides oneself', then Strawson's approach forces one to identify numerous things as persons, including those that no one ever would think of as being such. On the supposition that the behavior criterion is sufficient to warrant the attribution of a state of consciousness, many animals have states of consciousness because their behavior shows that it is the case. Both Whitey and I cry out and limp when an injury to a foot occurs. There is nothing sufficiently substantive to distinguish between the behavior of Liza and that of a mute human who wants to play with a Frisbee. Both grip the device, say nothing, and indicate by their anxious bodily movements that—from their

---

[62] Strawson, *Individuals*, 106.

respective viewpoints, at least—it is playtime. A spanking is a punitive smacking on the rump, regardless of the species of the sufferer.

The problem does not end there. In philosophy, a general objection has been raised against the notion that behavior is a way to determine whether conscious minds other than one's own exist. If observed activity is the discriminating factor, so goes the dissenting position, then this factor must be extended to behavior overall. I might surmise, for example, that a can that is rolling down a hilly street does so because it wants to get to the next block. The consequence for Strawson is that cans may be persons too.

Ryle makes use of the concept of single-track dispositions in an attempt to isolate habit and chance behavior from intelligent performances; for him, intelligence is characterized by a complex of appropriate tendencies. One may think that something similar could save Strawson from the cans-are-persons result. After all, the rolling incident is only one uninterrupted occurrence, with no multifarious characteristics exhibited. It is not difficult to envision episodes, however, in which the can appears to rest for a while against the curb to compose itself and then push off again to move farther down the street. It may cross over to the other side where there is more shade to continue its journey on a hot day. One may imagine that it does so just as the traffic subsides, thereby avoiding being crushed. It stops close to another can in an ostensible act of friendship, finally rolling to touch it—more than friendship, it is evidently romance, which could explain the can's coming down the hill in the first place. A romantic relationship is undoubtedly very important to a can. Albeit such apparently intelligent activity may not be recurrent, it may recur frequently, depending on wind speed, surface conditions, number of cans, and other elements of the surroundings. In any case, it points to the problem of using behavior as a guarantor of sentience. Turning to conduct to anchor the applicability of awareness-expressions seems to undermine Strawson's theory concerning what it is to be a person. In fairness, I must note that reliance on behavior also figures in some systems that accept the immaterial; George Berkeley's system is one.

Given that the suitable use of P-predicates scarcely can be limited to what one thinks of as members of the human kind, crediting to such use the ability to separate persons from nonpersons is an unsupportable approach. Strawson's portrayal of personhood loses value as the terminology loses meaning, and the theory, like other theories that are founded on the behavioral criterion, drifts toward a world in which even plants and inanimate objects are persons. It is noteworthy that Strawson's position that the concept of a person is logically primitive leans slightly toward the Cartesian view that he rejects, for Descartes himself declares that he, the mental entity, is so intermingled with his physical body that he seems to be a unified whole consisting of both substances. Strawson differs from Descartes, in that Strawson claims that there are not two discrete things that are linked in some special configuration but rather a single thing, and it is grounded in materiality. Strawson attempts to address the disparate-substance problem by denying that mental attributions apply to a mind that exists in the form of some distinct, incorporeal entity. Although he does admit that one can imagine his or her continued existence after death, all such notions of an immaterial self so conceived, he alleges, are derivative and logically secondary to the notion of a person: "[I]n order to retain his idea of himself as an individual, he must always think of himself as *dis*embodied, as a *former* person."[63] One's very identity, thinks Strawson, is tied to the whole, but a person is not put together from parts to form a whole. It *is* the whole. Fracturing it, while conceivable, leaves something that is meaningful only in terms of that off which it was broken. The primary concept of a person, says Strawson, is that it is a type of being that "necessarily has corporeal attributes as well as other kinds of attributes."[64] After a person has been identified, one can talk about his or her individual consciousness, but Strawson maintains that the order cannot be reversed.

> [O]nce we have identified a particular *person*, there is nothing to stop us, and nothing does stop us, from making identifying references to a particular of a different type, namely the consciousness of that person. It is in this way that the concept of a particular consciousness can exist, as the concept of a non-basic, non-primary type of particular. And only in this way.[65]

---

[63] Ibid., 116.
[64] Ibid., 133.
[65] Ibid.

In the final analysis, Strawson declares that the proper understanding of humankind rests on the conception of personhood as logically elementary—singular in nature—not fused in the Cartesian sense. Persons are not made of distinct components, let alone made of distinct components, one of which is immaterial. Persons are basic and of one substance, and that substance is matter.

One has seen the inadequacy of Strawson's theory. His dual-predicate distinction does not succeed, and he has produced an explanation of mentality that is no more persuasive than Ryle's. The critical failure of his view, however, lies in the acceptance of the metaphysical irreducibility of personhood in accounting for the identity of an individual. His theory leads to the stance that, without a material body, there can be no meaningful idea of the self. This view is just wrong. One *can* conceive of one's identity—and that of other persons—apart from a mass of protoplasm, or even a former mass of it, and, as I hope to show in due time, one *must* do so. For now, ponder the following portion of a dialogue, as recorded in the Scriptures, between Jesus and some unbelieving Jews of His day. It is a profound exchange—not simply because Jesus's declaration reveals that the essence of His being is independent of the material body that those around Him see but for another reason as well: The declaration attests to Jesus's actual identity in a way that the Jews, familiar with the Pentateuch, could not have missed.

> Jesus replied, ". . . Your father Abraham rejoiced at the thought of seeing my day; he saw it and was glad."
> "You are not yet fifty years old," the Jews said to him, "and you have seen Abraham!"
> "I tell you the truth," Jesus answered, "before Abraham was born, I am!"[66]

Persons are indeed unique among living entities. In the end, however, what accounts for their being that way is not captured by the Strawsonian structure.

---

[66] John 8:54–58 NIV.

SUPERVENIENCE THEORY

Three major materialistic portrayals of humankind fail to be convincing. Is there something left that will preserve the attributes that are unique to people while adhering to the constraints of a reality that is thought to be purely physical? I turn now to a metaphysical position that attempts to steer a precarious course between the mind and the body. Some philosophers see it—or, at least, one of its inherent tenets—as the long-awaited, concluding chapter on building a material model of humans.

Near the end of the twentieth century, the philosopher Donald Davidson advanced a representation of the mental unlike those of his predecessors. Davidson's view is known as anomalous monism. It is anomalistic because it denies that there are strict laws under which mental phenomena fall. In rejecting such laws, Davidson's account diverges from a type-materialism theory of mind, thereby circumventing some of the criticisms that are leveled against the thesis of identity that Smart and others adopt. Mental events are typeless tokens, according to the theoretical view. They are single instances that are not governed by any rules of nature that link them to material reality, or even to each other, although they are, in the end, nothing different from material reality, which is governed by those rules. For Davidson, the mental is not conceptually or nomologically reducible to the physical, but it is ontologically reducible to it because mental things *are* physical things; those things are, in actuality, the same. Each mental token is a physical phenomenon, only not a token of any specific type of physical phenomenon, as the mind-brain identity adherents would have it. Davidson's theory is therefore monistic because it declares that only one kind of thing is found in reality: physical. It is his conjecture that mental phenomena *supervene* on physical phenomena.

Various authors characterize supervenience—or alternatively supervention—somewhat differently, and a number of versions of it appear in the literature. Indeed, the amount of ink that writers have spilled over analyses of the notion since Davidson's employment of it is a bit surprising, even for philosophy. Broadly speaking, though, the concept is that of a relation of *covariant dependence*. For a thing x to supervene on a thing y is for y—the subvenient element—to determine with finality x—the supervenient element—such that, for any change in x, there must be a change in y underlying it, although a change in y need not force a change in x. In essence, x is wholly dependent on y, and y completely determines x.

An analogy may help to clarify the covariant-dependency relation. Suppose that one looks at the image of an apple in a mirror. The mirror-apple is totally dependent on the real apple in front of it, as it is nothing but a reflection. Take away the piece of fruit in the room, and the image disappears. Assuming constant conditions of lighting, angle of observation, and so forth, any change in the mirror-apple comes about only through a change in the real apple, although a change in the real apple may not produce a change in its facsimile: A bite out of the side away from the mirror, for example, would not be visible in the reflection. In one sense, the image is different from its authentic counterpart. It does not have the same qualities. The mirror-apple is not a material object in three-dimensional space. It does not have a circumference of nine and one-half inches. One cannot hold it in one's hand and feel its weight or detect its delicate scent. One cannot roll it across the counter. The image has no independent existence. Whether one is viewing the apple by means of the mirror's reflected light or looking directly at it, there is only the single piece of fruit among the things that are real. In this sense, the mirror-apple may be deemed to be just the apple in the room—despite the fact that it is not conceptually reducible to it—for, in looking at the reflection, one ultimately is looking at the apple. It is not a perfect comparison, but it illustrates the critical relation.

The stance of anomalous monism is that there are no laws linking the psychological to the physical. Causal connections, which *do* correspond to physical laws, are attributable to the material base on which the psychological supervenes. The mental can play a causal role in a material world because of, and by means of, this physical, subvenient undercarriage. The mind qua mind cannot be boiled down further, in that it cannot be captured by descriptions or principles that apply to the material world, for psychology is not biochemistry. Phenomena that are the elements of consciousness are characterized in a way that is fundamentally different from the way in which their underlying material base is characterized. In the final analysis, however, the material world is all that there is. Mental events therefore cannot exist apart from the physical events on which they supervene. The mind is entirely dependent on, and controlled by, the body because, quintessentially in humans, there is nothing else there. In the following passage, Davidson sets forth his view:

> Anomalous monism resembles materialism in its claim that all events are physical, but rejects the thesis, usually considered essential to materialism, that mental phenomena can be given purely physical explanations.
>
> Although the position I describe denies there are psychophysical laws, it is consistent with the view that mental characteristics are in some sense dependent, or supervenient, on physical characteristics. Such supervenience might be taken to mean that there cannot be two events alike in all physical respects but differing in some mental respect, or that an object cannot alter in some mental respect without altering in some physical respect. Dependence or supervenience of this kind does not entail reducibility through law or definition.[67]

Although the concept of supervenience was not new to philosophy at the time of Davidson's employment of it, the concept was new to the philosophy of mind, and writers latched onto Davidson's theory with a passion, whether in opposition to it or agreement with it.[68] Davidson's critics did not hesitate to respond with charges of epiphenomenalism: The mental is merely incidental to physical phenomena; it is not part of any relevant process, exerting no influence on anything that happens in the world. The theory, according to the opponents, makes the mental completely causally inert: If the physical is doing all the causal work, then the mental

---

[67] Donald Davidson, "Mental Events," in *Essays on Actions and Events* (Oxford: Clarendon Press, 1980), 214. The article appeared first in *Experience and Theory*, ed. Lawrence Foster and J. W. Swanson (Amherst: University of Massachusetts Press, 1970).

[68] One philosopher who has written much on the topic of supervenience believes that the first occurrence of it in a philosophical context is in a work by Gottfried Wilhelm von Leibniz. See Jaegwon Kim, "Supervenience as a Philosophical Concept," *Metaphilosophy* 21, nos. 1–2 (1990): 5. Two philosophers of recent history, R. M. Hare and G. E. Moore, adopt the approach in an effort to explain morality.

plays no role at all. The charge raised some serious concerns for the Davidsonian perspective.[69]

There were also supporters of this new theory—some aspects of it, at least. Many turned to supervenience with a focus on properties, seeing it as a way to permit some things about humans to be expressed in terms that refer to states of mind, while preserving the stance that nothing other than the physical exists. Supervenience, so goes the thinking, brings mental events close enough to physical events to be them in actuality, but not so close that these mental events cannot have distinct properties—specifically, those properties that characterize them uniquely as phenomena of consciousness. For the supporters, this nonreductive physicalism seemed to offer the best of both worlds—monistic materialism with a dualistic flair, etching the fine line that they wished to walk. At base, a human being is simply a mass of protoplasm; but, because of supervenience, one can speak of this being, in light of its consciousness, as though it were something other than a collection of chemicals arranged in a certain way.

A form of nonstrict materialism, supervenience is thought to allow for property-dualism, in which there are both nonphysical and physical properties, without embracing the division of Cartesian substance dualism. Herein lies its attraction for some. If an ontological system can make room for dissimilar qualities while, at the same time, avoiding the rift that a two-category structure occasions, then perhaps it is possible to uphold a philosophy of monism that does not discount the psychological. Favoring the idea, one author asserts,

> All mental things are physical things (as they must be, if, as materialism says, everything is physical). And two things that are physically just alike will be mentally just alike as well. While we cannot pretend that we know this for certain, we have an enormous amount of evidence to believe that it is true. In short: mental properties supervene on physical properties.[70]

---

[69] See, for example, Ted Honderich, "The Argument for Anomalous Monism," *Analysis* 42, no. 1 (1982): 59–64; and Jaegwon Kim, "The Myth of Nonreductive Materialism," *Proceedings and Addresses of the American Philosophical Association* 63, no. 3 (1989): 31–47.

[70] Dardis, *Mental Causation*, 172.

In the end, this philosopher accepts that humans have a "dual nature," but concludes nevertheless that "the world is, and . . . we are, physical through and through."[71]

The Indispensable Mental Element

One problem facing any theorist who holds that the mind is ultimately matter is the issue of awareness. Everything that exists is strictly physical, according to this view. The mind is therefore physical. How is it possible then to account for phenomena of human consciousness, given that they as such are strikingly different from physical states? Seeing wispy clouds against the blue sky and hearing the tone of a bassoon, and appreciating the beauty of each; feeling embarrassed and feeling forsaken; or thinking about a friend's troubled past and thinking about an algebra problem—none of these phenomena as experiences is remotely like a physical event. How does one get from the biochemical nervous system to the perceptive-aesthetic, affective, and cognitive conditions of human mentality? It is a gap that is difficult to bridge.

A contemporary author, who supports the physicalistic position, acknowledges the problem of consciousness; his solution is that the correct picture of mentality is near enough to physicalism to overlook this impediment to embracing it.[72] I believe that this stance is a distortion. Either the mind is matter, or it is not matter. Either there are no immaterial things, or there are immaterial things. Substantive existence is the very issue at hand. In this respect, being close has no place in an ontological theory.

The concern in my analysis is whether it can be shown with an adequate measure of assuredness that materialism is right and that the mind is altogether corporeal—albeit, with supervenience in view, perhaps something with properties that cannot be ascribed to a subvenient, physical body on which it depends. The other theories that I have examined in this chapter fall short of eliminating incorporeal

---

[71] Ibid., 174.

[72] Jaegwon Kim takes this stance. See his *Physicalism, or Something Near Enough* (Princeton: Princeton University Press, 2005).

substance; one might wonder whether Davidson's version gains anything in an effort to do so. Is supervenience a genuine answer to the centuries-old question about the contrasting facets of humans, or is it rather just a bit of metaphysical trickery?

To begin to answer that question, consider again the case of the autographed baseball that I introduced in chapter 3. Monte was excited to learn that the ball bore the signature of Lou Gehrig, the famous player for the New York Yankees. It is important to understand exactly what that autograph is. Look first of all at the obvious physicality of it. There is a clear sense in which it is ink in a particular configuration on the surface of the baseball; it is a material thing. The ink alone, however, does not constitute an autograph; much less does it constitute Lou Gehrig's autograph, even if it spells his name. To qualify as an authentic signature, the ink must have been placed there by Gehrig himself with the intention of inscribing his name on the ball. It follows that the autograph, although it is the ink scribbling, is not the ink scribbling *simpliciter*. The inscription has to be an instance of deliberate writing, deposited by the hand of the person whose signature it is. What makes the *ink* an autograph is the *act* of Gehrig's writing his name for the purpose of marking the occasion through his signing the ball. If Gehrig had gone through the motions with no pen or other writing instrument in hand, then there would have been no autograph, for there would have been no ink. If the writing had been placed on the ball by a machine that was programmed to generate an unusual pattern of scribbling, then there would have been no autograph, nor would there have been one if someone had placed a pen in Gehrig's hand while he slept and moved his hand just so: In neither instance would there have been an act of Gehrig's signing his name. It takes both the *ink* and the *act* to create the authentic inscription. They both are constituents of one and the same thing. Each is necessary, and neither by itself is sufficient. Consider the diagram that I provide below. It shows an autograph to be the fusion of two things.

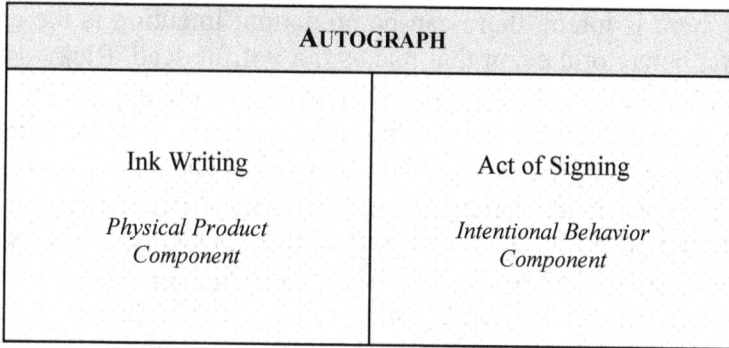

AUTOGRAPH	
Ink Writing *Physical Product Component*	Act of Signing *Intentional Behavior Component*

Figure 5.9

Given the concept of supervenience, is it correct to say that the autograph supervenes on the ink and that the mind supervenes on the body in a similar way? It might seem to be true. The autograph is inherently dualistic, incorporating a material piece and a rational, mental piece; nonetheless, in the end, the writing itself is what lies in physical reality. The problem with this approach, however, is that supervenience requires that the physical base fix absolutely that which supervenes on it. If that requirement is to hold here, then there can be no difference in the autograph without a difference in the ink. Such is not the case, however. The ink lines on the baseball could be exactly the same, yet Gehrig never signed it. Someone else, or some apparatus, wrote his name on the ball. The simple fact that a thing, which is not classified as physical in one respect, may issue forth through physical expression is inadequate to guarantee that supervenience is at work and that, ontologically speaking, the thing that is in question is strictly physical through and through.

As I noted, the ink lines constitute one element of the autograph: the physical piece. The act of signing constitutes the other. Acts, in turn, are composites; there are both physical components and rational, mental components. One has seen that the physical is not sufficient to warrant the presence of an action. A jerk, caused by some external force; a spasm; and a common reflex—all lack the mentality that is essential to the existence of a case of agency. The conduct of an individual may be the same in various instances, but, unless there is intent, there can be no action; intention is the critical part of a behavioral event that makes it a willful deed. Ricky's foot's tapping because his trouser leg is caught in a spinning pulley at the factory as the radio blares may be just like Ricky's tapping his foot to keep time with the music while he works. The first occurrence is something that is happening to him; the second occurrence is something that he is doing with a purpose in mind. Only the latter one is a case of agency. As the autograph is a combination of the material, ink inscription and the act of putting it there, so too the act of signing the baseball is a combination of depositing the ink on the ball, by moving the pen in hand, and the crucial intention, which points to the reason that is behind the moving. This figure shows the structure:

AUTOGRAPH		
Ink Writing	ACT OF SIGNING	
	Moving Hand with Pen *Physical (Bodily) Component of Act*	Intention *Rational (Mental) Component of Act*

Figure 5.10

If supervenience theory were right, then, for every mental difference, there *would have to* be a physical difference. It would be a mistake thus to assert that an act supervenes on the physical behavior that corresponds to the act, for markedly different mental states can correspond to identical behavioral incidents—so different that one incident may be the result of an accident or a series of quivers, whereas the other is a deliberate doing. The Ricky scenarios demonstrate how disparate states of mind can be associated with the same physical movement. Davidson declares, as quoted in chapter 4,

"[M]ere movements of the body—these are all the actions there are."[73] If the body, insofar as it moves, is to be the anchor for human actions, then supervenience cannot work as an account of mentality. It fails to capture the mental dynamic that separates acts from mere events—and one act from another with equal motion but a different purpose. How then can the mind be wholly dependent on the body?

The proponent of mind-body supervenience may claim that it is not an individual's bodily motions, taken in isolation, that one must consider but the individual's entire physical state, which includes the individual's brain. There is something special about Ricky's head when his foot-tapping behavior is intentional; a neurological factor is what accounts for the dissimilarity. It cannot be just any neurological factor, however, lest the thumping of Ricky's foot, traced to brain damage from the affliction Sydenham's chorea, which causes uncontrollable tremors, be counted as intentional, even if the unfortunate incident at the factory is not classified likewise. Does this approach succeed as a way to skirt the movement problem?

PROBLEMATIC PHYSICALITY

The difficulty that is raised by the cases involving Ricky reveals a second and more serious challenge for a materialistic theory of mind: providing an acceptable account of human action. A materialist must align the core dogma of the position with the presence of free will, unless he or she wishes to adopt the stance that there is none, and it is not easy to defend that stance. The theory lacks a satisfactory means to explain purposed deeds, which are based on freedom of choice, in a physical universe that is governed by the fixed laws of nature. If all events are the workings of physics, determined by those laws, then there is no room for the intentional doings of agents, and the deliberation and the decisions that precede them. Without intention—without the will—there is no agency at all, regardless of whether supervenience is part of the package.

---

[73] Donald Davidson, "Agency," in *Agent, Action, and Reason*, ed. Robert Binkley, Richard Bronaugh, and Ausonio Marras (Toronto: University of Toronto Press, 1971), 23.

Suppose that Susie is in a dentist's office awaiting her appointment. Her mother told her that she might have a cavity. Susie is nervous. She knows what cavities entail: the dreaded lidocaine shot, the piercing sound of the drill, and the potential for pain as the lidocaine fails to deaden the nerve effectively. She decides to distract herself by thinking of something that is pleasing to her. She brings to mind her birthday party last month, with the presents, the cake, and the hilarious skit by the clown. It works. Susie's memory of the delightful occasion absorbs her. Now, if the supervenient element is determined by the subvenient element, then one must ask what determines the intention to think pleasant thoughts—on what base it supervenes. By reflecting intentionally, Susie performs an act; she does something on purpose, and her doing so brings about a particular mental state. Her act is, in fact, an end-state act because she is attempting to effect a state of affairs that she values at the time (a pleasant frame of mind), resting on her belief that what she is doing (turning to memories of an enjoyable occasion) will produce that state. If supervenience is in operation, then her act brings about a physical state on which the mental state supervenes. By forcing herself to think certain thoughts, what is Susie doing? Is she putting herself into a particular state of mind or a particular state of brain?

Presumably, a supervenience theorist would answer this question by saying that Susie is putting herself into a particular state of mind—comforting thoughts—by bringing about a particular state of brain on which that particular state of mind supervenes. The act of putting herself into a particular state of mind, however, like all acts, requires a mental element itself—*intention*. If the mental element of intending supervenes on a physical undercarriage, then it really must be the brain that is putting itself into a different state. How is one to explain such an occurrence? If, as the monistic materialists hold, all is physical, ontologically speaking, then all events are physical and have purely physical causes. The brain's change to another state thus must be the effect of some physical cause. That cause, though, must be the effect of some physical cause—another event in the brain, it would seem—and that cause the effect of some other physical cause, and that cause, in turn, the effect of yet another, and so forth. It is just one long causal sequence in a closed box that cannot be opened with a metaphysical crowbar. What happened to Susie—the agent who is responsible for the change in mental state—in all this bustle; is she just along for the ride? Why does one even need her at all? Surely, one would not attempt to avoid the problem by saying that Susie *is* her brain. Doing so would introduce the absurdity of Peter Unger's position, which I discussed in chapter 3. Existence is not decremental; *Susie herself* cannot disappear like Carroll's fanciful Cheshire Cat with the loss of an encephalic neuron or two.

Physical things are reactive; they are passive. Like billiard balls colliding on a table, they respond blindly to the forces that are applied to them in accordance with the laws of nature, a point that I put forth previously. Physical things are incapable of independent initiation; they can do no more than what nature determines that they do. They are marionettes, swaying to the tug on the strings by the causality puppeteer. Brain tissue can change only in response to something that causes it to change. Without intention, there is no plausible way to account for the initiation of changes that lie apart from the mechanistic sequence of cause and effect. Only agents can initiate such changes and reset the course of events, driving them toward a calculated end. It is *Susie* who is pulling calming thoughts from her memory. Her brain surely plays a part in the event, but it cannot be that which originates it. Her brain is a physical organ that merely responds to impinging causal forces that drive its molecules like miniature billiard balls, the neurons undergoing an exchange of sodium and potassium ions, thereby inducing the propagation of impulses—nerves transmit signals through an electrical differential that is generated by the influx and efflux of these elements. As Lou Gehrig's signature on the baseball is the result of intention, Susie's change in mental state is the result of intention, although it is through physical means that the outcome in each case is realized—without overt movement, for Susie. Focused on eliminating the bathwater, supervenience theory dumps the baby, and all that is left is an empty tub. It is a recurring theme among materialistic theories of mind.

In channeling her thoughts, Susie has a goal in mind. She is doing something for the purpose of accomplishing—that is to say, *to* accomplish—an objective; it is an end-state act. Her act is based on a mental pairing: a value-factor (a desire to be in a pleasant emotional state) and a belief (that turning to memories of an enjoyable occasion will produce a pleasant emotional condition). As phenomena of the psyche, those two elements must supervene on the physical as well if supervenience theory is to be characterized as consistent. Ontologically speaking therefore, the brain must be drawing on itself *for the purpose of* producing a state of itself.

It is simply implausible to hold that a purely physical thing alone can perform in this fashion, where it not merely brings about a particular state but further *to* bring about a particular state—and, what is more, one that it envisioned. A mechanistic process in itself never can occur with purpose, nor can it ever account for it. The physical brain's transmission of neural signals per se bears only the inherent mark of mechanism; anything further is external to the chemicals that compose the brain and to the ionic transfers that brain tissue undergoes. The rational mind's expression of intention, in contrast, bears an inherent mark of teleology. This rift is one that physicalism is ill-equipped to handle. Equating the passive happenings that involve the bodies of persons with the active doings of those same persons removes the very essence of actions: intention.

When Tommy knocks Johnny down on the playground at school, the first matter to determine in investigating the incident, after assessing injuries, is why it occurred. If Freddie tripped while they all were running toward the ball and fell headlong into Tommy, then no blame whatsoever can be placed on the boy in the middle. His body merely reacted to the accidental blow from Freddie and followed the path that physics specified, resulting in the collision with Johnny. On the other hand, if Tommy shoved Johnny because he wanted to hurt him for winning the race yesterday—a race in which Tommy took second place—then there is not only blame but appropriate punishment as well. In the mechanistic view of things, there is neither *freedom of choice* before a deed nor *accountability* after it, for the body simply responds to the physical forces that move it. The human experience loses the humanity that distinguishes it from the nonsentient workings of the cosmos.

Besides, it is difficult to accept that mental states cannot differ at all unless physical states differ. This thesis is the essence of supervenience, but I believe that there are grounds for dismissing it. No logical prohibition against such unilateral variance exists: There is no contradiction in asserting that covariant dependence is a false notion. If therefore mind-body supervenience is to hold, then it must hold as a matter of fact, not a matter of reason. Susie possesses a vague memory of the polka-dot outfit that the clown wore at her party, but she does not remember clearly how many dots the costume contained. An art teacher asks Susie to draw the clown as accurately as possible on a large piece of poster board. She does so, putting forty-nine red dots on his white costume, depicting the clown from a face-on perspective. She remarks truthfully that she thinks that the picture looks like the clown. Later that day, the teacher requests that Susie redraw the clown on a second piece of poster board. The picture this time contains fifty-one dots. When asked whether she believes that the drawing looks like the clown that she saw, she responds truthfully in the affirmative. Susie's pictures express in a genuine way what she recalls. The variability of her handiwork stems from the quality of the memory. Had the clown had only one large red dot at the center of the chest of the costume, Susie's respective depictions of that particular outfit, barring unusual circumstances, would have been the same. If the theory of supervenience were tenable, then there would be variation in the brain state that underlies the variation in the remembrances.

Recent experiments with mice show that the neurons that are activated in an original incident in which the mice experience fear are the same ones that are activated when the subjects recall the incident.[74] Whether the findings apply to humans is undetermined; nevertheless, the extension is possible, perhaps likely. With the current level of knowledge of neuroscience, it would be speculative to maintain that the memory of the perceptive element of an event, like the emotive element—fear, in the case of the mice—is linked to an invariant set of neurons, but it also would be speculative to hold the contrary. There seems to be insufficient support for a universal

---

[74] Leon G. Reijmers et al., "Localization of a Stable Neural Correlate of Associative Memory," *Science* 317, no. 5842 (2007): 1230–33. Subsequent recollections, one would think, would involve—or, at least, could involve—the same neurons as well. From the earlier discussion, it is clear that a cell, like the organism of which it is a part, retains its identity for as long as it continues to function—for as long as it continues to live. Thus, further analysis regarding what 'same neuron' means would be superfluous, and I will set it aside. It is possible for a given set of neurons to fire on more than one occasion because it is possible for them to persist. Coupled with the experimental findings, this possibility presents a challenge to the supposition that brain states fix mental states, given the variance in memories.

thesis that one's memory—a mental part of an individual—can vary in *no* respect unless one's brain—a physical part of the individual—varies. If it cannot be proved that mental change accompanied by physical invariance is an utter nomological impossibility, regardless of circumstances, then supervenience is not only unconfirmed but also far too reliant on conjecture to serve as the basis for a theory of mind. As it stands, there is no justification, whether philosophical or evidential, for forcing its adoption. It is therefore the notion of a supervenient relation that is speculative; and, if Susie's second recollection of seeing the clown from the front does involve the same neurons, then, of course, supervenience theory is shown to be false.

Even if the covariant dependence of the mind on the body did describe the state of affairs in the world, exactly what it would establish is open to question. Susie's mother cannot remove her wedding ring. With lubricant and much tugging, it simply will not slip over her knuckle, which enlarged over the years since the ceremony. Whenever she extends her hand, the ring goes with it. Whenever she retracts her hand, the ring follows suit. The ring's movements are covariant with, and dependent on, the lady's movements, but the ring is not the lady or any part of her. They are separate entities; they are individuals. Distinct conditions mark their uniqueness, and different times correspond to their originations and eventual terminations as physical things. A relation of covariant dependency in itself does not necessitate the identity of things that stand in that relation.

A supporter of mind-body supervenience may respond that the movement analogy is informative but insufficient to down the concept. It is not movements that are to be taken into account in covariant dependency but properties, and property-covariance is not contingent but necessary. Covariance, as it pertains to supervenience, is a relation among sets of properties, so that necessarily, for any property P_1 in the supervenient property-set that a thing possesses, there is a property P_2 in the subvenient property-set, such that the thing possesses P_2; moreover, whatever possesses the latter property possesses the former one.[75] Further, says the advocate, any change in

---

[75] This rendering is essentially equivalent to Jaegwon Kim's weak covariance II, the position that he ascribes to Donald Davidson. Kim offers a stronger version of covariance, adding necessity to the last clause in the statement, making it *necessary* that whatever possesses the subvenient property, P_2, possesses the

the supervenient property-set must be accompanied by a change in the subvenient property-set, although the converse is not true. If this condition holds, then, according to supervenience theory—in the present context, at least—the things that exhibit those properties are, in reality, the same thing, although their properties are not identical.

As a principle, the thinking is clearly incorrect. Consider a case in mathematics. Necessarily, every positive number is a square of some number. The square is determined strictly by the number, the root, of which it is the square, such that, if the square changes, then the root also must change, although the root can be different without a difference in the square. For example, it is necessarily true that

$$4 = 2^2, \text{ and } 4 = -2^2$$

but also true, as is obvious, that

$$4 \neq 2, \text{ and } 4 \neq -2$$

There is a relation of covariant dependency here, but it is insufficient to demonstrate that the relata are one and the same thing. Indeed, they are *not* one and the same in the example that is given.

The example can be extended to parallel the property-dualism of the supervenience theorists. The square, the integer 4, possesses properties that its roots do not possess. It equals the number of lines in a rectangle, the number of sides in a tetrahedron, and the number of players in a bridge game; it is half the cube of 2; it is the number

---

supervenient one, P_1. See Jaegwon Kim, "Supervenience as a Philosophical Concept," 9 ff. Note that the stronger version, by including the qualifier, increases the likelihood of failure. It is a standard principle in philosophy that raising the level of aggressiveness of a claim requires raising the level of defense that is needed to support it against counterexamples. The assertion 'Some x are Φ' is true if there exists a single x that is Φ. Contrast this statement with 'All x are Φ'. For this proposition to be true, it must be the case that no x is not Φ, and finding a single existing instance of an x that fails to be Φ is sufficient to disprove the assertion. Finally, consider this statement: 'Necessarily, all x are Φ'. It declares that it is *impossible* for an x not to be Φ. There cannot be any circumstances—at any time, in any place—where there is an x that is not Φ; there is no possible world where one can exist. The point of this sidebar is that, if weak covariance fails to hold, then, a fortiori, the stronger version will fail.

of 440-yard footraces in a mile; and so forth. Conversely, the roots, 2 and –2, possess properties that the square does not possess. One of them is equal to the number of protons in an atom of helium; the other is the negation of the only even prime number; and so forth. Even if mental properties were to supervene on physical properties that are distinct from them, standing in a relation of covariant dependence, that relation would not show that the mind is, in reality, just the body—and this point is the crucial one.

Not only does the theory that Davidson launched fail to do justice to the essential concepts of agency, but it also follows a problematic path in relying on a supervenience relation as the way to an ontological merger. Like other attempts to turn mind into matter, supervenience theory produces a system that lacks adequate explicatory power. It is appropriate to close this discussion with a quotation from a philosopher who has written much on the topic:

> Supervenience is not a metaphysically deep, explanatory relation; it is merely a phenomenological relation about patterns of property covariation. Mind-body supervenience, therefore, *states* the mind-body problem—it is not a solution to it.[76]

MAKING SENSE OF THE MIND

Even though there is disagreement among philosophers concerning what the mind is, all philosophers, regardless of their respective positions, agree that humans are capable of engaging in mental activities, however those activities may be portrayed. The existence of the events of consciousness is undeniable. Now, the mind is strictly a corporeal thing, or it is not strictly a corporeal thing; it is purely a substance belonging to the physical world, or it is something of a very different character. The view of materialism, of course, is that the mind *is* material or, at least, that it is traceable to

---

[76] Jaegwon Kim, "The Mind-Body Problem after Fifty Years," in *Current Issues in Philosophy of Mind*, ed. Anthony O'Hear (Cambridge: Cambridge University Press, 1998), 10.

the varying arrangements and movements of matter. The mind, so goes the opinion, is *not* different in its quintessence from the things that a person sees and touches in the world. All that is, is physical. There is no Cartesian mental substance existing alongside the corporeal. At base, nothing other than matter and energy in space-time exists or ever did exist. I believe that this stance, exemplified by the four theories that I have reviewed in this chapter, leads to the intractable quandaries that have become apparent.

One may argue, along a different line, that the mind is not to be equated *exactly* with physical being, and, as a consequence, certain difficulties may be averted. Perhaps it is best, one may say, to view the mind as something that is emergent: either a set of novel properties that surfaces from material configurations—much as the properties of chemical compounds differ from the properties of their constituent elements—or alternatively a function of the ordered physical parts and their interactions. There is only matter and the results of its arrangement; thought is simply something that comes forth from particular concatenations of materials. If one fits the pieces together in just the right way, then conscious awareness appears. Make brain tissue out of various compounds and provide life support, and thinking emerges as a result of the collective activity of the physical parts as chemicals drive the mechanism. One might liken the case to that of an internal-combustion engine, where the machine's operation arises from the proper conjoining of the mechanical components, but the device does not operate until the apparatus is assembled. Once it is bolted together, if one provides fuel and the necessary impulse to start it, then the engine runs.

Emergentism—a theory that novel characteristics, such as mentality, arise when biochemical interactions reach a certain stage of complexity—appeared in the philosophical literature in the early decades of the 1900s. It lost support in the years that followed, although it has resurfaced, to a certain extent, in recent times. The theory that mental properties supervene on physical properties resembles that of emergentism quite closely—in the writings of some emergentists, at least—with its core premise of dependence on physicality.[77] Restructured in a more modern form, albeit perhaps

---

[77] Kim makes this point in "Supervenience as a Philosophical Concept," 4 ff.

unintentionally, supervenience theory seems to have had more success in garnering supporters than its counterpart. I do not plan to take up a discussion of emergence in detail, having touched earlier on the trouble that the property-supervenience conjecture faces, but the concept of it is worth exploring briefly as it pertains to function rather than properties.

It is important to draw a distinction between the concept of function as something that emerges from the interactions of the physical components of a thing, and the theory of mind that is known as functionalism. This theory is the view that the mind is just a causal-functional role that a given biological organization assumes. The mind is not something that comes forth from matter per se; it is a process that is carried out within the organism. As with a computer, certain inputs produce certain outputs in living beings: Stimuli bring about responses. For this reason, mentality can be realized in various organisms with significantly different neurobiological formations—a point that Putnam advances in his criticism of mind-brain identity theory.

Authors have attacked functionalism on several grounds. For one, the input-output operation fails to provide an adequate account of consciousness. A man in a room with nothing more than a set of books, paper, and a pencil could produce proper answers to questions that are passed to him, written in a language that he does not know. By consulting the instructional guides, he could respond in an appropriate manner, although he has no knowledge whatever of the language, or even of the symbols that are used in the language, and understands neither the questions that are passed to him nor the answers that he writes on the paper and returns to the inquirer. Functioning properly in an input-output fashion is not a satisfactory depiction of mentality.[78]

A second objection to functionalism concerns its inability to handle the very thing that it is put forth to explain. Mental states are object-oriented; they are *about* things. Functionalism cannot capture this aspect. Says one philosopher,

---

[78] John Searle proposes this counterexample to functionalism. See John Searle, "Minds, Brains, and Programs," *Behavioral and Brain Sciences* 3, no. 3 (1980): 417–24.

An even more fundamental problem . . . is encountered in the "aboutness" which is the very essence of an intentional state. There just is such a thing as thinking about something, worrying or hoping that something may happen, believing that so-and-so is the case, deciding on a certain course of action—and in such cases one ordinarily has a distinct, conscious awareness of the intentional object of one's mental state. . . . [T]he claim that a person is in such an intentional state is clearly *not equivalent*, logically or conceptually, to any causal-functional description of the person. The causal-functional properties of the state identified by functionalism can be *completely described and explained* in terms of the physical structure and behavior of the state in question and its relations to other physical states. There simply is no place in such a description for the "aboutness" which is essential to intentional states as such. . . . If . . . [causal-functional states] do not involve "aboutness," then they just are not intentional states. . . . If they do, then a crucial, and logically essential, aspect of these states has been left unexplained; we still have no idea how the "aboutness" is to be incorporated into a materialistic worldview.[79]

Returning to the concept of emergence, I believe that viewing function in light of such a concept in an attempt to explain mentality leads to a dilemma. If the functionality that arises out of the conjoining of the physical parts is not anything that is ontically over and above the collection of those parts as they stand in certain relational positions, even where those positions may be shifting dynamically, then there is no actual emergence; there is only redescription. This perspective is essentially no different from that of Ryle. As erosion is a function of the actions of wind, water, and ice, in which particles of geological structures are moved from one place to another, the function of the aforementioned internal-combustion engine is really nothing but a certain way of describing the movement of its pieces. The machine has the capacity to operate and is disposed to do so

---

[79] William Hasker, *The Emergent Self* (Ithaca: Cornell University Press, 1999), 31–32.

when the right circumstances appear. In seeing the parts interact and the crankshaft turn, one has seen the function. So it is with the mind: The matter that makes up a person is disposed to do certain things that one calls mental. When the material behaves in a special way, one has seen the rational mind. What results from this approach, however, as is the case with Ryle's account, is that one is forced to ascribe intelligent thought to entities to which one's ascribing it is illogical. Asserting that thoughtful behavior characterizes a man's turning the crank on an appliance for making homemade ice cream, while denying that thoughtful behavior characterizes a motor's doing the same thing, constitutes a contrived distinction.

On the other hand, if function is something that is ontically over and above the physical parts and their physical interactions, not merely a redescription, then what is it? By the law of excluded middle in logic, the emergent thing is material, or it is not material. There is no other possibility; a sentence declaring that one state of affairs or the other obtains must be true. If it is material, then it is generated in violation of the physical law governing conservation in the universe: Its mass-energy arises in addition to what already exists in the totality of the physical realm and indeed arises ex nihilo. It follows that it has to be immaterial and ontically so. That consequence, for a materialist, however, simply will not do.

A further problem surfaces. Imagine a universe that is devoid of all thought. In this universe, there is a planet on which a basic engine, complete with fuel, was assembled by chance. Imagine now that the engine is running. One need not be concerned about the improbability of such an occurrence for this exercise, only that the machine exists and that no minds ever have existed. The spark plug ignites the fuel; the piston moves up and down; the valves open and close at the appropriate times; the crankshaft rotates. The motion of the parts, however, is nothing more than the ongoing relocation of material in space. As with rocks, blown from a volcano, tumbling down the mountainside in this imaginary, mindless world, there is only the raw physics of the process. To say that the machine is performing a function, where the term 'function' refers to something other than the simple movement of matter, is to utter a nonsensical pseudoproposition. Indeed, even to say that there is a machine here is nonsensical.

If therefore 'function' is not merely an equivalent form of the expression 'dynamic configuration of matter', then the logical alternative appears to be a term that is without import apart from a backdrop of rationality.[80] The claim that something is performing a function in this sense is meaningful only in the context of purpose because function in this sense connotes end-oriented activity. It is the same, strong meaning of the term that came to light earlier in the discussion of the life of organisms. Purpose, of course, requires a rational mind. Further, where there is no purpose, no proceedings that are grounded in reason, there can be physical goings-on in accordance with the laws of nature, but there can be no function that concerns doings to realize a goal.

On a breezy day at the park, a large stick is sitting atop several leaves on a picnic table; the leaves are fluttering a bit in the wind. Why is the stick there? Consider a pair of explanations. (1) It is there because the windy conditions caused the stick to break off the tree over the table, and it landed on some leaves that the wind had blown there. (2) It is there because Mary placed it there to keep the leaves that she had gathered from blowing away, as she plans to use them in her nature project for school. The outcome in each case is the same: The stick prevents the leaves from blowing away, but only in the second case is it there *to* prevent the leaves from blowing away. In the first case, the stick is just there. In the second, it is there for a reason; it is there to perform a function in the sense of accomplishing an objective.

The existence of such goal-orientation depends on the existence of understanding, which is a mark of rational mentality. So, if a mind is a function in the sense at hand, then ultimately a mind depends on a mind for its existence, either another one or itself. The first option leads either to an infinite regress—for any mind that exists, a second mind must be there to account for the existence of the first, and a

---

[80] One might contend that 'function' can mean 'covariant dependence', as one thing varies as a function of another, but this notion as it pertains to mentality is nothing other than that of supervenience, which I already have argued is an unsatisfactory account of the mind. Moreover, if such function were emergent, then it would not differ from the first concept that I outlined above, as it would not represent an ontic addition to matter and its interactions. No other clear use of the term is forthcoming.

third mind for the second, and so forth—or to a mind, at the base of the series, that depends on itself for its existence, which is the second option.

The notion of a self-dependent mind, however, proves to be problematic for the materialists. The premise under review is that mentality is not *exactly* physicality; a conscious mind is not *equated* with a collection of matter but rather comes about from the way in which the material aggregate is arrayed. Its existence is traced to chemicals and their patterns of interaction. Remove the chemicals, and one removes the mind. It follows that the mind is dependent on configured material for its existence. If a mind depends on itself for its existence, however, then either its existence is independent of other things altogether, including the chemicals, or its existence is partially dependent on itself and partially dependent on something else. With regard to the first condition, to declare that the existence of a mind is not dependent on other things at all, yet it is dependent on other things—specifically, configured material—is to put forth an outright contradiction. With regard to the second condition, which is partially self-dependent existence, the concept is incoherent. Even if it were intelligible, though, matter and its interactions alone would be insufficient to account for the existence of a mind, for they could not generate it on their own, given that, by hypothesis, the mind depends, in part, on itself for its existence, and it is not identified with a set of materials. As a final point, if the mind were identical to the matter-based emergence instead of being a product of it, then, because the alleged emergence itself is not matter but is totally dependent on matter and its arrangement, there would be no self-dependence, whether in whole or in part. The idea that mentality is an emergent function cannot be right.

There is something more weighty in the wings. If the existence of anything is *ever* self-dependent, then it is logical to maintain that it is *always* self-dependent, for its existence depends on nothing other than itself. In that case, it is eternal because, if its existence depends on itself alone, then its existence is independent of all other things, and therefore nothing that is outside it can bring about its nonexistence. No obstacle would have the wherewithal to block its continuance. The implications are profound. One author puts forward the notion in this way:

> That which even for a single instant is the sufficient reason of its own existence is self-existent. But a nature which is capable of self-existence needs not to wait for the action of an efficient cause in order to exist; it must have existed from all eternity. Probably most people imagine that, once constituted, the substance can somehow conserve itself unless brought into contact with hostile agencies which are too powerful for it. Yet to say that a thing conserves itself is to say that its persistence through each successive moment is to be attributed to its own existing nature.[81]

If there is any rational mind that depends solely on itself, then it is not human, for humans are contingent beings with contingent minds. They come into existence. Although the analysis took an unexpected course to reach this juncture, the notion that rational thought is eternal is an important one. Does rationality, the very principle of order that some ancient Greek philosophers put forth as the key to existence, lie in the eternal mind of God? Are Heraclitus's notion of *Logos* and Anaxagoras's concept of *Nous* closer to the mark than what may appear at first glance to be the case? Did order issue forth from God in cosmic design? Reflect on the opening passage in the Gospel of John concerning Jesus Christ:

> In the beginning was the Word [*Logos*], and the Word was with God, and the Word was God. He was with God in the beginning.
> Through him all things were made; without him, nothing was made that has been made. In him was life, and that life was the light of men.[82]

The next chapter will pursue the exact questions that have come to the forefront here.

---

[81] George Hayward Joyce, *Principles of Natural Theology*, 2nd ed. (London: Longmans, Green and Co., 1924), 62.
[82] John 1:1–4 NIV.

PUTTING THE PARTS TOGETHER

Materialists see one kind of thing in people. Substance-dualists see two, and those two are very different. I have discussed the shortcomings of materialistic theories at length. If persons are more than material, though, comprising the immaterial as well in their makeup, then one must ask how things that are so unlike can relate to each other. This interface problem is the first for those who hold that the mind is nonphysical. Contemporary supervenience theorists face exactly the same problem, however. Philosophers who subscribe to the property-dualism that underlies the theory—some versions of it, at least—must explain how a physical body can serve as the basis for mental properties, which these philosophers classify as nonphysical.

One may be reminded of the two-worlds attack on the theory of forms that Plato raises in the dialogue *Parmenides*, as I covered in chapter 2. In this criticism, Plato surmises that entities of different ontological sorts cannot be joined, thereby undermining his own attempt to merge particulars and forms, although he does present a mitigating account in the *Timaeus*. If one distinguishes between a physical world of matter and a nonphysical world of mind, then this problem seems to resurface. It is the problem of describing how things that are fundamentally dissimilar can interact.

Plato's theory of forms falls short, in part, because it attempts to account for the union by relying on metaphorical language. There is no solid philosophical doctrine that prohibits the interrelatedness— even the conjunction—of entities belonging to categories that differ in significant ways.

An analogy that employs mathematics may help to elucidate the concept. There are various views regarding the ontological status of numbers. Whether one holds numbers to be nonabstract entities— a general view that is referred to as nominalism—or assigns numbers to a class of metaphysically substantive, immaterial, abstract entities that exist independently of human thinking—a view that is referred to as Platonism—one can ascribe differing properties and relations to them.[83] Clearly, whatever stance an individual takes, numbers and

---

[83] One version of the former position sees numbers as strictly marks on a piece of paper or other medium. An alternative version, which is known as psychologism,

sets are not only distinct mathematical entities but also, one could argue convincingly, distinct sorts of mathematical entities, not sharing the properties that make them what they are. A number can be an integer that is ≥ 107 and < 108, but a set cannot be such. A set can be empty, or null, but a number, even 0, cannot be null. There are prime numbers, but there are no prime sets. One can calculate the cube root of a finite negative number, but not the cube root of a finite negative set. Numbers can be members of sets, but not conversely. These disparate entities can be coupled nevertheless through a mathematical relationship. For example, the set of rational numbers includes the integers 1, 2, and 3 as elements; and a set may contain both numbers and other sets as elements. One even can define numbers in terms of sets. The definition of the number 2 can be stated in the following manner:

> df.
> 2 = the set of all sets K, such that, for any x and any y, x is an element of K, and y is an element of K, and x does not equal y; and, for any z, if z is an element of K, then z equals x, or z equals y.

This statement defines the number 2 as the set of all sets that contain two, and only two, members.

A set is not a corporeal thing, but the elements of the set can be corporeal or incorporeal. There can be a pair of shoes on the doorstep, just as there are two square roots of the number 4. There can be a pair of neutrons in the nucleus of an atom and two theories on the origin of the cosmos. A set of two things, in fact, can contain an element from each category: one leather glove and one idea of historical importance. It is, as it were, twoness—two of anything—that constitutes the essence of a pair.

As a further example of the concept, consider the predictability that the laws of nature provide. Science formulates these laws as abstract assertions that capture the regularity of the workings of the

---

postulates that numbers are ideas in the mind. What both forms of nominalism have in common is the representation of numbers as nonabstract things. As for the latter position, it is so named because it aligns with the view of Plato regarding the independent existence of incorporeal forms.

physical cosmos. Gravity ensures that objects that are in close proximity accelerate toward each other at a certain rate in a vacuum, given their respective masses and the distance between them. The law of gravity allows one to predict the outcome of an event in which two bodies of known masses are separated by a specified distance. Some laws pertain explicitly to causal links between types of physical phenomena. Water, which is densest just under 4° Celsius, expands, *ceteris paribus*, if the temperature descends from there, dropping below that point of greatest density. If the temperature reaches the freezing mark at 0° Celsius, then ice forms. It is the expansion of water as it freezes that accounts for the rupture of unprotected pipes in one's home on a cold night. Again, igniting gunpowder in a confined space results in an explosion, where the increase in pressure is sufficient to burst the container. The following proposition is an apt way of representing causally linked events, a general notion that came to light previously:

If an event of type X occurs in the circumstances-set C, then an event of type Y occurs.

Events of type X are physical occurrences—they are incidents in which physical things take part—and they cause physical occurrences of another type—namely, Y. Suppose that an X-event does occur. If the statement of the law is an accurate depiction of reality, then one can affirm that a Y-event happens as well and furthermore can explain why it happens. Without the law, there is no predictability. Without the causal event of type X, there is no satisfaction of the precondition that corresponds to the law, although obviously an event of type Y may happen because of some other precipitating incident.

Yet, the law-statement is an abstraction. It is not physical, nor is the law that it conveys. They are not material things. The law links types of events. Types are not material. The law allows predictions with nomological sureness. Predictions are not material. Specific occurrences of the types that are covered by the law are part of the goings-on of a material cosmos nevertheless. One knows that, if a particular event x_1 takes place in the right circumstances, then, with the law in force, the particular event y_1 occurs as an effect. It is the joining of the physical event and the nonphysical law that determines that another physical event also happens. Material and immaterial ride together on the same train of conclusiveness.

Such conjunctions as those that are set forth above suggest how existents belonging to distinct ontological categories can relate. Then, one might propose, without introducing an illogicality, that a physical body and a nonphysical mind could be linked in some way. In view of this fact, an answer to the puzzle about the ontological character of the mind begins to take shape when one turns one's attention to a key aspect of humanity: agency.

As discussed in this chapter, synergistic systems are characterized by the presence of interrelated parts that work together in support of a central operation that the parts cannot perform on their own. The operation of the whole is possible only if the parts carry out their respective roles. In the case of organisms, this core operation is the life of the complex. It is its function; it is the end toward which the parts undertake their individual activities and by virtue of which those activities are explicable. Ordinarily, not all parts are necessary, of course, but certain ones must be performing their duties, so to speak, for the complex itself, under normal conditions, to achieve its principal, defining work—such parts are essential to the function.

A meaningful parallel develops as one recognizes that a human agent is also a system. It is a complex that is composed of both an organism, *Homo sapiens*, and a rational mind, the two parts working synergistically to enable the complex to undertake actions—nearly universally, end-state ones—in a physical cosmos. Both a body and a mind are needed for human agency to be possible in the world in which humans live, and both are needed to account for it. From the standpoint of logic, an intelligent agent can exist without a body, for there is no logical necessity that agency be physical or be linked to an organism, but an intelligent agent cannot be a *human agent* in the absence of the organismal constituent.[84] Without the organism, there

---

[84] Human agents are ones that exist in a world of physical things, and physicality is not only an essential attribute of their being but also a necessary condition of their actions as humans. There is nothing to preclude, on the basis of logic, the existence of nonphysical intelligent agents, however. The organismal component of humans is therefore necessary for human agency but not for agency altogether.

is no physical presence in the form of a human body to bring about changes within material reality. Likewise, from a logical perspective, a human organism can exist if rationality—the ability to reason—is lost, but the *human agent* cannot exist apart from that rationality. If there are no mental sensibilities, then there is no intention and so none to accomplish an objective, no cognizance of purpose, no deliberation and weighing of options, and no considered choice— there is no willful setting of a course, traced to value-factors and beliefs, to realize an aim. The goal-oriented activity of intelligent entities is forward-looking; it is doing to attain what is envisioned. It is not pushed from the rear but pulled from the front. It is not mechanistic but teleological. The rational thought that accounts for this teleological activity in the case of agents is part of the system itself. Agents are endowed with reason.

If it is possible for a whole to comprise fundamentally dis-similar parts, and I believe that one can see that it is possible, then there is no logical prohibition against the inclusion of such parts in the structure of a system, where the operations of the parts converge on the operation of the whole. The structure of human agents thus recalls the structure of actions: There are both physical and mental constituents. The relation holding between the body and the mind in human beings is therefore, I submit, that of part to part. An agent is not primitive in the Strawsonian sense but a composite that forms an ordered whole, a system, the function of which is the faculty of the expression of the will in acts—and I will stress end-state acts here— through realized behavior, typically, but not invariably, involving movement. Such expression issues forth in intentional, purposed performances in a material universe. The existence of the body is a necessary condition of the manifestation of physical behavior; likewise, the existence of the mind is a necessary condition of the manifestation of reason. It would be a mistake to hold that the capacity to throw a rock *is* the body, and it would be equally erroneous to hold that the capacity to express the will *is* the mind. Such misstep would come very close to the error that Ryle commits in his analysis, taking the disposition to behave in certain ways to be the intelligent mind itself. The ability that something possesses and that which possesses it are distinct things. It is the potential to exercise, by corporal means, volition, taken as a global attribute of the human agential system, that joins the physical and the mental systemically, resulting in a unified whole. Acts come in discrete blocks of doing, but agency itself is an enduring part of the rational human entity. It lies within the system's inherent structure. The table that I present below summarizes the thesis. In keeping with the general pattern of the discussion to this point in this section (and in some other places in this chapter), the corporeal, base element appears first:

	ORGANISM	**HUMAN AGENT**
Entity type	Synergistic system	Synergistic system
Parts / subsystems	Cells, tissues, organs composing broader subsystems: lymphatic, nervous, immune, circulatory, and so forth	Organism, rational mind
Ontological category of parts	Physical	Physical, nonphysical
Central operation that parts cannot perform in isolation	Life: its continuance	Agency: faculty of the expression of the will in end-state acts through behavior in a physical world
Category of central operation	Teleological; it is function in end-oriented sense	Teleological; it is function in end-oriented sense
Rationality associated with central operation	External	Internal

Figure 5.11

Even if one accepts this analysis as accurate, however, there is an apparent problem for substance-dualism. A prevalent view of the universe is that it is a closed structure in which every caused event within it has a physical cause that is also within it. One never needs to exit the physical realm to find what precipitated any physical event: The universe is a single matter-energy net, vast in scope, in which lie all causes and effects. Stated succinctly, this idea of causal closure reads, "If a physical event has a cause at *t*, then it has a physical cause at *t*."[85]

---

[85] Kim, *Physicalism*, 15.

In itself, the closure hypothesis may seem to be innocuous. The materialists, however, set forth a further hypothesis, which asserts, in essence, that the total physical cause of a physical event is sufficient for the effect. Nothing but physics is needed to account for anything that ever happens in the cosmos, to the extent, at least, that what happens involves physical things and is the effect of some cause.[86] Causes can consist of multiple factors, of course. The car moves because of the activity of the pistons, the valves, the camshaft, the transmission, the wheels, and so forth. All are necessary, given the structure of the machine, and, although no one of them alone is sufficient to make the car travel on level ground, their proper operations, when taken collectively, can produce the effect. Analogously, in the portrayal of agency that I am presenting, both a living organism and a rational mind—and it is the latter one that bears the will—are necessary for the agent of which they are parts to perform an act, and it relies on the agent's body. Neither alone is sufficient; it takes the pair: one physical, one nonphysical. If, however, the hypothesis of the causal sufficiency of the physical is correct, then, unless one is prepared to accept overdetermination—tossing in a mental cause, even though it is not needed to provide a full report of the occurrence—an immaterial mind is superfluous. Actions can be explained completely in terms of physical causes; introducing anything further is ill-conceived.

Not everyone accepts the closure and sufficiency of the physical. One philosopher rejects it outright, stating that closure cannot explain rational inference—the means by which one comes to hold beliefs. If mental goings-on have no impact on events, and instead physics is the driver for everything that happens, then no one ever comes to believe a proposition because of good reasons; rational support for the proposition is irrelevant to one's taking it to be true. Such a notion is obviously false.[87]

---

[86] Generally, the principles are couched in provisional terms to allow for the possibility of uncaused events. Some physicists hold that there are such events in the quantum world. I believe that their conceptualization is based on a misunderstanding of causality, and, in the next chapter, I will point to the source of that confusion. At least, though, in the macrophysical realm, causation among physical phenomena is accepted by most as the norm.

[87] See Hasker, *Emergent Self*, 64 ff.

Another author takes exception to the concepts underlying the hypotheses, claiming that they reduce causality to the mere activities and properties of subatomic particles: "[W]hat happens at the micro-level determines everything else that happens."[88] For any event that takes place, one must drill down into the structure of physical reality until one reaches the quantum foam to identify the true, root cause. There is no room for higher-level causes. One cannot say even that the acidity of a liquid caused the litmus paper that contacted it to change color; the precipitating phenomenon is situated much more deeply: "The actual causal transaction . . . took place at the micro-physical level."[89] If the position disallows causal claims pertaining to ordinary chemical reactions, then it surely subverts causal notions that are found in law and morality, the author believes. She con-cludes that the approach ultimately undermines most of science and, as for common sense, nearly all of it.

In asking why an individual did what he or she did, one finds that there are two sorts of responses to the inquiry. Consider this passage from John Locke's writings concerning a man who is in a room with the door secured. Although Locke is addressing the issue of liberty, his example is apropos because it shows how both mech-anistic and teleological explanations can account for physical states.

> [S]uppose a Man be carried, whilst fast asleep, into a Room, where is a Person he longs to see and speak with; and be there locked fast in, beyond his Power to get out: he awakes, and is glad to find himself in so desirable Company, which he stays willingly in, *i.e.* prefers his stay to going away. I ask, Is not this stay voluntary? I think, no Body will doubt it: and yet being locked fast in, 'tis evident he is not at liberty not to stay, he has not freedom to be gone. So that *Liberty is not an* Idea *belonging to Volition,* or preferring; but to the Person having the Power of doing, or forbearing to do, accord-ing as the Mind shall chuse [*sic*] or direct. Our Idea of Liberty reaches as far as that Power, and no farther.[90]

---

[88] Lynne Rudder Baker, "Metaphysics and Mental Causation," in *Mental Causa-tion,* ed. John Heil and Alfred Mele (Oxford: Clarendon Press, 1993), 87.
[89] Ibid., 90.
[90] Locke, *Essay,* 238.

There is a purely physical cause of the man's being in the room, in that the door is locked. He could not exit, even if he tried. By focusing strictly on this physical cause, however, one neglects the fact that, had the door been unlocked, he still would be there. In this case, the otherwise-in-play physical condition of the door would not be sufficient to account for the man's state: He is in the room, and the door is not preventing his leaving. It is his intent to remain where he is, and intent is forward-looking. He chooses to remain, and that choice explains his being there no less than the status of the door.

I recall traveling on a four-lane highway one Saturday morning. I had proceeded only a few miles toward my destination when I saw that traffic on both sides of the median had come to a halt. Even an ambulance was at a standstill. It did not take long to see why. A truck with no driver was circling across the road repeatedly at a respectable speed. Apparently, the truck had slipped into gear, with the engine running, after the owner had exited the vehicle. With the steering wheel turned toward one side, it continued its threatening maneuver, slamming into a mailbox near the road as it made its rounds. Finally, a man tracked alongside the truck and opened the door on the driver's side. He was able to jump into the vehicle, gain control of it, and bring it to a stop.

Without someone to direct it, a truck can proceed on its own, but it cannot drive itself to the next city by depending on its mechanical parts. There is a marked difference between the cause of the motion of the vehicle—pistons, valves, camshaft, transmission, wheels, and so forth—and the cause of the motion of the vehicle that results in a hundred-mile journey along a winding highway, through towns and countryside, detouring on occasion to stop at a scenic overlook, with no mailboxes demolished in the process. The purely mechanized operations of the physical components of the truck can propel it, but they alone are not sufficient to account for its staying the course. For that event, there must be not only the workings of the machine but also the actions of an intelligent being—namely, the driver (or an apparatus that is programmed by an intelligent being to simulate one). It is the combining of the physical causes with the mental activity that produces the physical effect: keeping the vehicle traveling in the lanes, making the correct turns, and stopping when traffic signals so require, until it arrives at the destination. Even if the causal closure hypothesis were to hold, the sufficiency hypothesis would be unconvincing. To assert that physics is adequate to account for every event that happens in the cosmos is exceedingly ambitious. One may turn there to find the cause of the movement of photons in a laser but not the cause of a chess player's losing a match when his opponent moved a rook and trapped the player's king. That causal explanation does not require descriptions in physics but rules of convention, and those rules are nonphysical.[91] The concept may apply with no problem to the exposure of hidden geological structures through the erosion of surface features but not to Kyle's engagement to Karen when he surprised her with a ring that he had hidden in her dinner napkin. Karen's acceptance of his proposal, placing the ring on her finger, caused her to be engaged, yet the engagement is not traceable to laws of nature but to protocol, commitment, and societal norms—all nonphysical things. Reducing cause-effect occurrences to the interchange of material particles in space-time leaves out the very heart of events that marks them as human actions; it not only fails to explain the incidents but bankrupts the character of them as well.

Sensations and emotions are classified as mental phenomena, even by those philosophers who deny the existence of incorporeal things, and nothing precludes the interaction of the physical body with these phenomena. Cutting one's finger with a saw results in the sensation of pain and the emotion of anger, maybe even thoughts of some catastrophic end to the tool's existence. Excitement or rage results in heightened blood pressure, and severe anxiety increases perspiration. These interactions, whether one is a monist or dualist, are undeniable. The causal problem is not about such cases, though. It is about agency. It is not about how an *organismal system*, as I defined it, reacts to stimuli but about how the intentions of an *agential system* can correlate with corporal conduct. A finger-cutting causes one to hurt, but neither the cutting nor the hurting causes one to hurl the saw across the yard. The act is the expressing of the will. Materialists cannot offer a satisfactory account of action—how it is

---

[91] Although with regard to a different point, Baker advances similar scenarios involving causation where it is clear that the causal relationship is not one of mere particle interactions. A man's failing his French course, for example, may cause him to be ineligible to play NCAA Division I basketball. See Baker, "Metaphysics and Mental Causation," 91–92.

possible in a purely material being—because physical things lack the ability to initiate events independently of the blind forces of nature that propel them. If all that exists is physical—a universe of physical things in which every physical event has a physical cause that is governed by deterministic laws—then all that a would-be agent ever does is react; he or she never acts. As a consequence, there are no human actions at all.[92] The behavior of people is simply one more cog in the cosmic machinery. It is a very high price to pay to eliminate the incorporeal. Supervenience offers, prima facie, a way of escape, but, in the final analysis, it is impotent. Here is why: The subvenient, physical base is locked in the deterministic, causal order, but it is the base itself that determines the mental element that supervenes on it; therefore, *in supervenience theory, the mind is determined no less than the body.* There is no place here for the fundamental constituent of personal freedom: choice.

Now, turning to the efficacy of mentality, consider that, among philosophers today, there seems to be a standard rendering, perhaps a near-universal one, of causality as it pertains to the human entity. It portrays the mind, however it is characterized, as standing in a cause-effect relationship to the body, inducing its movements when they are intentional. A mental event precedes a bodily event, and, contrary to the Rylean view, the first produces the second. Says one theorist,

> Let us first review some of the reasons for wanting to save mental causation—why it is important to us that mental causation is real. . . . In voluntary actions our beliefs and desires, or intentions and decisions, must somehow cause our limbs to move in appropriate ways, thereby causing the objects around us to be rearranged.[93]

---

[92] One author argues that asserting that all occurrences can be explained in mechanistic terms is self-defeating because the act of asserting the claim is inconsistent with what it asserts. Putting forth the claim is an act; it is explainable only with reference to intent. If all is mechanistic, however, then the complete explanation lies in the neurological happenings in the brain, and such explanations proscribe purposive behavior. The consequence is that people do not do things for reasons, and actions therefore fall by the wayside. This position is given in Norman Malcolm, "The Conceivability of Mechanism," *Philosophical Review* 77, no. 1 (1968): 45–72.

[93] Kim, *Physicalism*, 9.

Against this entire picture, I am arguing that, when a person acts, the mind and the body do not stand in a relation of cause to effect. Mental phenomena do not cause actions—I showed in the previous chapter how such a notion results in an absurdity—but mental phenomena do not cause the bodily movements that are associated with actions either. Both an agent's mental activity and the agent's physical activity are parts of the workings of a broader entity. They are components of a synergistic system. It is the *system* that acts; it is the *agent* who moves his or her limbs, thereby bringing a change in the state of the physical world. What a person qua agential system does is a function of the elements that make up a whole. Indeed, the doing of an agent, taken globally, *is* its function actualized. Instead of the common view, diagrammed in structure I below, I believe that the correct depiction is structure II:

I. Mind-Body Causality

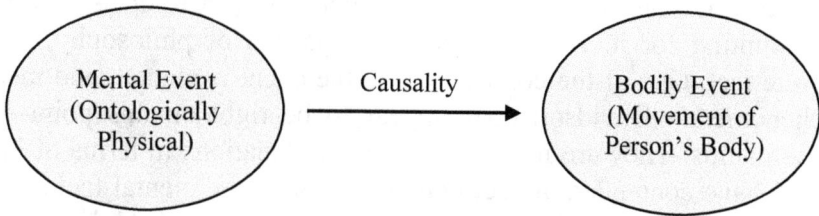

II. Mind-Body Synergism

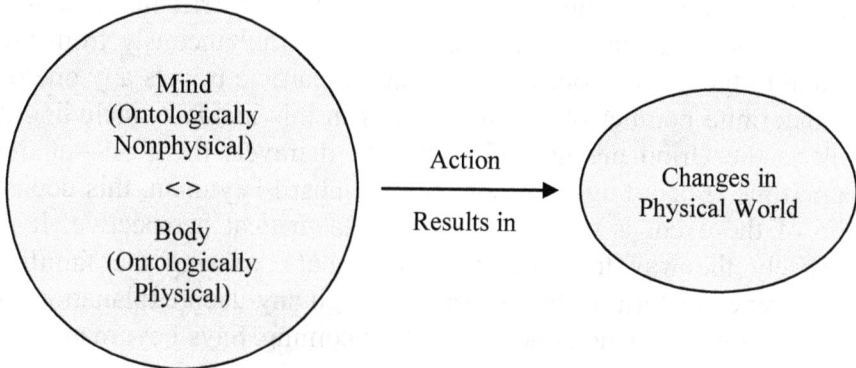

Figure 5.12

Explaining at a neurochemical level precisely what is taking place within a person when he or she performs an intentional deed is a challenge that shows no favoritism. It is, for different reasons, as unsympathetic to monist as it is to dualist. If one looks at the interplay of the immaterial and the material, then perhaps one sees that the crucial question for the dualist is not how it happens—how the nonphysical element of an agent works synergistically with the physical element in the execution of purposed deeds—but whether it, in

571

reality, does happen. Indeed, it may not be meaningful to ask for a further description: There may be no strict law under which an instance of interplay falls and to which one can refer as a way of accounting for it. Maybe it is, in the jargon of philosophy, just a brute fact. One of the contributors to the event is mental, and mental phenomena—Davidson does appear to be right on this point—are anomalous: They are not amenable to explanations in terms of laws. As I have contended, an act *must* incorporate the mental factor to be an act at all, regardless of what a person's body is doing in performing it. Therefore, given that some things that an individual does are deliberate, if the mind is truly immaterial, then the interaction of the nonphysical and the physical—their conjunction—is certain.

Unquestionably, some events that are relegated to the realm of the physical are no less obscure. It is difficult to see how an electron that is fired toward a detection screen through a barrier that contains a pair of slits can take every possible path simultaneously from the source to the destination. It is not that the particle travels any one of an indefinite number of possible routes in this incident, including a trek to the Orion nebula and back, but it travels them all—at the same time. According to the physicist Richard Feynman, this depiction of the event is correct, from a mathematical perspective. It is precisely the way to represent what occurs, causing the familiar interference pattern on the screen, although any deep explanation of the bewildering phenomenon is not forthcoming. Says Feynman,

> [T]he more you see how strangely Nature behaves, the harder it is to make a model that explains how even the simplest phenomena actually work. So theoretical physics has given up on that.[94]

Certain things that happen in the microphysical arena must be accepted at face value. Whereas one may put forth a theory that describes observed phenomena with meticulousness, understanding them is a different matter. Feynman recognizes this fact, and one finds in his writings the following statement:

---

[94] Richard P. Feynman, *QED: The Strange Theory of Light and Matter* (Princeton: Princeton University Press, 1985), 82. Feynman was awarded the Nobel Prize in physics in 1965. Recent double-slit trials have produced further bizarre results.

> I think I can safely say that nobody understands quantum mechanics. . . . Do not keep saying to yourself, . . . 'But how can it be like that?'. . . Nobody knows how it can be like that.[95]

In the consideration of the human entity as it is brought to light especially by actions, what one can show is that joining dissimilar things is feasible, even if the joined elements are of ontologically distinct categories. The demonstration in itself is important. The supervenience theorists who embrace immaterial properties in an attempt to explain mental phenomena in a purely physical world are forced to agree. Thus, a person is left with a choice between two competing accounts, one, and only one, of which is inconsistent with a plausible depiction of humanity. The choice alone is a case in point.

AN OPEN DOOR

In one of his dialogues, Plato writes,

> [T]hey lay hold upon every stock and stone and strenuously affirm that real existence belongs only to that which can be handled and offers resistance to the touch. They define reality as the same thing as body.[96]

He is referring, of course, to those who deny the existence of the incorporeal, which is grasped not by the hands but by the mind. In the present age, this camp would be that of the strict materialists or physicalists as they set forth their ontological theses. Regardless of whether one accepts the existence of immaterial things, theories that

---

[95] Richard P. Feynman, *The Character of Physical Law* (Cambridge: MIT Press, 1965), 129.

[96] Plato, *Sophist*, 246a–b, trans. F. M. Cornford, in *The Collected Dialogues of Plato, Including the Letters*, trans. Lane Cooper et al., ed. Edith Hamilton and Huntington Cairns (1961; Princeton: Princeton University Press, 1971), 990.

limit one to a view of the world and of humanity where immateriality is excluded entirely are theories that fail to convince the cautious that they are right. Given the difficulties with portraying rationality—and in particular purpose—in materialistic terms, it appears to be more reasonable to hold that the correct view of reality includes the immaterial than to rush headlong to embrace materialism.

In chapter 5, one has come to see certain limitations of the attempts to equate reality with physicality, grounding mind in matter in their wake. Those efforts do not offer a solid underpinning for the identity of living things, and they provide an adequate account of neither mental experiences nor human action. The natural senses of a human may bring no direct perception of the incorporeal, except, one might say, in the case of properties; however, an examination of incorporeality is perhaps not to be dismissed so readily as the mere illusory ramblings of the woefully uninformed. If the door to an immaterial reality is open, then should one not enter through it in the quest for truth? Truth is, after all, the object of all genuine inquiry.

I wish to turn next to the arguments for the existence of the supremely immaterial being, God, in whose image, the Scriptures say, man is created. A coming chapter will revisit the matter of persons, taking a further look at how these unique entities are structured, for the answers to the questions about personal identity that the current chapter raised at the outset are yet to materialize in their entirety. It is evident from the analysis thus far that human agents are more comprehensive than the organismal systems that they comprise. Are persons likewise more inclusive than agential systems, or are the two parts that join to form those systems exhaustive? A thorough examination of personhood is critical. What results from the investigation of the matter is a grasping of the foundation on which personal identity rests, for a person's makeup truly does underlie who the person is.

CHAPTER 6

SEARCHING FOR GOD
ON A COSMIC SCALE

Anyone who wants to come to God
must believe that there is a God and that
he rewards those who sincerely look for him.

—Heb. 11:6 TLB

Years after the trip, my father enjoyed telling the story of our first family outing to the coast. I was very young at the time and have only a vague recollection of what is undoubtedly the great appeal of the beach for all children: a huge supply of sand in which to dig. My father's subsequent account of the event is more clear in my memory. Long before we left home, he began to impress on my sister, who is nearly two years my senior, just how large the ocean is. As far as the eyes can see, all the way to the horizon, there is nothing but water. The ocean is immense, extending from the shore for miles and miles.

The time that he invested in convincing my sister of the vastness of the deep yielded an unexpected return. As she listened attentively to his words, her imagination began to form a picture of what the ocean must be like. In her youthful mind, it was big—very big. After arriving at our destination, we headed for the beach in due course, making our way onto the sand at the water's edge. My sister stood there affixed, staring out to sea. Nothing but water lay before her, stretching to the horizon far in the distance. My father asked what she thought of the ocean, curious to learn what sense of magnitude her first sighting of the Atlantic evoked. Her surprising reply was that it was not as big as she had thought. It could not have been any bigger. From where she stood on the shoreline, it must have looked infinite. Somehow, though, in her imagination, it had been bigger still.

One's sense of scale, even in the imagination, is challenged by astral discoveries of recent years. As late as the first part of the twentieth century, it was a common belief that the galaxy in which humans live was the entire universe. Nearly two centuries earlier, the philosopher Immanuel Kant (1724–1804) had proposed that the numerous dim, elliptical structures that one could see with a telescope were not solitary stars but "systems of many stars," similar to "the stellar system in which we find ourselves. . . . [T]hese elliptical figures are just universes and, so to speak, Milky Ways."[1] Contrary to Kant's conjecture, however, the hazy, cloud-like patches of light were regarded by most observers as nebulae: gaseous phenomena in intragalactic space. Using the most powerful and sophisticated astronomical device of its day, the hundred-inch Hooker telescope at the Mount Wilson Observatory in California, Edwin Hubble trained his gaze in the 1920s on a few of these formations—one near the constellation Pegasus in particular. An amazing discovery awaited him. Hubble was studying supergiant variable stars, or Cepheids, that were embedded in the alleged nebulae, but these stars, which are very bright during a portion of their respective luminosity cycles, were extremely faint when Hubble beheld them. Indeed, they were too faint to be part of the Milky Way. The cloudy object that Hubble saw near Pegasus thus did not lie within the galaxy but far outside it. Hubble realized that the object was not a gaseous nebula at all; it was, in fact, a galaxy—one of many. Focusing on what astronomers refer to now as the spiral galaxy Andromeda, or M31, Hubble concluded that its distance from the earth was nearly a million light-years.[2] Kant had been right.

Following Hubble's finding, the cosmos that scientists thought that they knew, as immense as it was believed to be, was replaced with something that one scarcely could comprehend. Two trillion or more galaxies populate the vastness of space, according to current

---

[1] Immanuel Kant, *Universal Natural History and Theory of the Heavens*, trans. W. Hastie (Ann Arbor: University of Michigan Press, 1969), 63. Kant published his work in German in 1755.

[2] Later refinements to the cosmic analysis using the telescope at Mount Palomar Observatory, with its mirror of two hundred inches—twice the diameter of the Hooker's mirror—revealed the actual distance to be about two and one-half million light-years.

astronomical assessments, and the stars number in the hundreds of sextillions to as many as a septillion. The Milky Way alone contains at least two hundred billion stars. The cosmos is stupefying in its enormity.[3]

The search of the heavens continued. For several years, Vesto Slipher at the Lowell Observatory in Arizona had been measuring and cataloguing the radial velocities at which the mysterious nebulous objects—which proved to be galaxies—were moving, relative to the earth, basing his measurements on the shifts in the spectra of light that they emitted. It appeared, in fact, that these remote, immense aggregates of stars were receding, on the whole, and at great speed, as the Doppler effect showed. Georges Lemaître, a Belgian physicist and astronomer, realized that the rapid dispersion of galaxies had significant implications. In 1927, he published a paper in which he proposed that the universe itself was expanding. It was not a notion that Hubble was inclined to accept, even years later, despite his acknowledgment of red shifts and their association with galactic recession. Hubble proceeded with his work, and, just before the turn of the decade, he determined that the velocity of the retreat of a galaxy was proportional to its distance—the farther that one of these colossal stellar assemblages was from the earth, the faster it was moving away. Collaboration with Milton Humason, another researcher who was conducting studies of outlying objects using the Mount Wilson facility, brought confirmation of this linear velocity-distance relation.[4] Hubble remained skeptical of the notion that recession was linked to cosmic expansion, but the evidence that space was spreading out in all directions was mounting.

The concept of a distending universe, in conjunction with the observational data, led Lemaître in the early 1930s to champion the view that the cosmos had a highly compact beginning—what Lemaître referred to as a primeval atom. This densely compressed mass disintegrated, blasting outward, in a manner of speaking,

---

[3] The estimated number of galaxies—previously placed at a hundred billion—is based on the perceptible universe; the actual value could be greater. Some scientists think that the stars in the Milky Way number about four hundred billion.

[4] The relation is given in a formula, which sets forth Hubble's law. It had been suggested initially by Lemaître. Atypically, the distance between Andromeda and the Milky Way is decreasing rather than increasing.

sending material into space as the universe extended into the void. The big bang theory, as it came to be called later, although in a disparaging manner, stood in stark contrast to the competing view of the universe as a steady state system, characterized by the continual generation of matter with no initial, violent event.[5] The big bang view aligned with Albert Einstein's theory of relativity, but the great physicist was reluctant to accept it at first. Eventually, however, Einstein became convinced of this rendering of the cosmic beginning. It is reported that, following a talk by Lemaître at a conference, Einstein stood, applauded, and declared that Lemaître's account was the most beautiful and satisfactory explanation of creation to which he ever had listened.

As the years passed, the theory of a turbulent birth gained wide acceptance among astrophysicists as the correct celestial model, owing, in part, to the work of Stephen Hawking. Hawking attempted to show, by reversing time conceptually, that the universe contracts as it shifts to earlier states, similar to a great star's collapsing under the force of gravity to form a black hole. If this process is carried to the limit, then the universe shrinks to the point of maximum compression—a notion that originated with Lemaître. On reaching this condition of ultimate density, it becomes what is referred to as a singularity. From that point, if one runs the tape forward again, as it were, there is a discharge of cosmic proportions, forcing all that makes up the physical universe outward in every direction at extreme velocity. What one sees in present times, a ballooning universe containing countless stars, is the result of that tumultuous occurrence.

The energy that is inherent in the theoretical big bang and subsequent cosmic unfolding is virtually incomprehensible. The magnitude of the happening is compounded because, so cosmologists believe, visible material makes up only a small percentage of what exists in the universe. The remaining material substance is in the form of dark matter, and the quest to understand it better is afoot. Without postulating its existence, however, it is difficult to explain the speed at which the underpopulated, outer fringes of galactic formations move. They should rotate about the centers of the

---

[5] The initial event of the theoretical big bang is depicted popularly as an explosion, although that depiction is technically incorrect. Like an explosion, however, it resulted in extremely rapid dispersion, according to the supposition.

respective galaxies more slowly than the clusters of stars that make up the bulk of the observable structures, but they do not do so. Dark matter—and a universe filled with it—is a way to account for certain astronomical observations, such as this one.

Then, there is the enigmatic cosmic constituent: dark energy. Current findings in astrophysics suggest that most of the universe is composed of this still-conjectural building block. It exerts negative pressure, acting contrary to gravity, causing the repelling of matter rather than the attracting of it. Scientists postulate that dark energy accounts for the increasing rate at which galaxies overall are receding from each other at present in the expanding celestial sphere. It is driving the cosmos apart. The latest data show that the composition of the universe is 4.6 percent ordinary matter, 24.0 percent dark matter, and 71.4 percent dark energy.[6] It is a fascinating system.

The uncovering in recent years of the Higgs boson, with its accompanying field, casts considerable doubt on the authenticity of a cosmogonic big bang. The discovery indicates that the universe, in fact, never would have formed, given the standard scenario. It would have collapsed within microseconds of the supposed original event.[7] Nevertheless, such a beginning remains the prevailing model among contemporary cosmologists. If the big bang did occur, then is it to be taken as the moment of creation? Did God step out of eternity to bring into existence all that humans have come to view as physical reality? Beliefs about the existence of God and His attributes are fundamental to one's beliefs about one's own being. They define who one is, or who one thinks that he or she is, and how one interacts with others and the world. They scribe the path that a person follows in day-to-day life. Whether God is real is a matter of profound importance to an individual personally as he or she executes current actions and plans future ones. Of all the issues that one encounters in

---

[6] These values are supplied by WMAP Science Team, "WMAP Produces New Results," reported as of April 8, 2013, National Aeronautics and Space Administration, accessed May 20, 2013, map.gsfc.nasa.gov/news. Other sources may vary.

[7] See Malcolm Fairbairn and Robert Hogan, "Electroweak Vacuum Stability in Light of BICEP2," *American Physical Society Physical Review Letters* 112, no. 20 (2014): 201801-1–201801-5, accessed July 20, 2015, journals.aps.org/prl/pdf/10.1103/PhysRevLett.112.201801. The authors propose a pair of paths that might save the big bang, but they recognize that there is currently no known physics that can support either of those alternatives.

life, of all the things that one seeks to know, surely the question of God's existence is a question that must be answered.

Besides the spiritual impact, the matter holds interest for many on intellectual grounds. As noted in chapter 2, certain metaphysical-epistemological constructs implode or explode without God to secure them. So, it is not unforeseen that theologians and philosophers would take hold of the problem, offering proofs to support their positions. Blaise Pascal (1623–1662) puts forth what is perhaps the most unusual argument for accepting the existence of God. Unlike proofs that attempt to demonstrate, on metaphysical bases, *that* God exists, Pascal's line of reasoning is set up to reveal why one *should believe* that God exists. Known as Pascal's wager, the argument examines the four possible states of affairs pertaining to the matter.[8] I can represent the possibilities with the following matrix:

	God exists.	God does not exist.
Person believes in God.	o_1	o_3
Person does not believe in God.	o_2	o_4

According to Pascal's analysis, if God exists, and one believes in Him, then the outcome o_1 is infinitely positive for that person. If God exists, and one does not believe in Him, then the end result o_2 is overwhelmingly negative for that person. If God does not exist, though, then it does not make much difference, in the end, what one believes; nothing awaits him or her after the present life either way—outcomes o_3 and o_4. The theists would realize the greater benefit nevertheless, Pascal maintains, because the positive qualities that are associated with a life of faith outweigh the luxuries that the world offers to one who turns aside. Thus, the rational stance is to adopt the

---

[8] The argument appears in Blaise Pascal's *Pensées de M. Pascal sur la religion, et sur quelques autres sujets*, published posthumously in French in 1670. For a recent rendition of this work by Pascal, see *Pensées*, trans. W. F. Trotter; *The Provincial Letters*, trans. Thomas M'Crie (New York: Modern Library, 1941), 79–85.

belief: "If you gain, you gain all; if you lose, you lose nothing."[9] There is value in knowing the truth, of course, but the import of Pascal's possibility assessment lies in the proposal that accepting the existence of God leads to a desirable future.[10]

Although this approach is innovative and fascinating, it is difficult to see how anyone could come to believe in God based on a consideration of risk and reward; no doubt, Pascal was aware of the limitations of his proposal. A person even might accept that, *if* God exists, then believers would be in a better position for eternity, yet that person still may not think *that* God exists. It is probable that Pascal devised his wager to show those individuals who had not made up their minds about spiritual matters that believing is the more advantageous path.[11] He intended it to bring about a disposition to accept the existence of the Deity. Further, as a mathematician, Pascal quite likely hoped that his schema would appeal to those for whom the element of chance in gaming activities was of interest. By focusing on polarized consequences, his matrix of possibilities does bring to mind the importance of one's beliefs about God, but it lacks the efficacy to convince one that He exists. The way to that knowledge must lie elsewhere.

ARGUMENTS FOR THE EXISTENCE OF GOD

There are a number of arguments that are put forward to prove the existence of the Supreme Being. In a previous chapter, I covered in detail attempts by René Descartes and George Berkeley, cast

---

[9] Ibid., 81.

[10] Pascal's wager has its critics. Alan Hajék claims that Pascal's reasoning is not cogent. See "Waging War on Pascal's Wager," *Philosophical Review* 112, no. 1 (2003): 27–56.

[11] For the Christian, of course, it is belief in Jesus Christ and the acceptance of His sacrificial atonement for human sin that is the key to the future, believing not only in God but also in the Son of God. As the Scriptures state succinctly, "He who has the Son has life; he who does not have the Son of God does not have life" (1 John, 5:12 NIV).

within the concepts of their respective philosophical systems, to show that God is real. In general, the cases for God's existence may be placed together according to the basic tenets that the reasoning expresses. With regard to the major arguments that have been advanced in the course of philosophical history, five patterns emerge as primary; they are listed below:

> The cosmological argument
> The henological argument
> The ontological argument
> The anthropological argument
> The teleological argument

This chapter will look at proofs corresponding to each line of reasoning, devoting the greatest part of the analysis to the last of them. It serves, in one structuring, as the key argument in the ongoing debate over intelligent design and thus bears critical ties to theories of origins. Some of the issues in the arguments touch on the scientific, but the demonstrations operate mainly in the realm of the philosophical; and, one will remember, logic is the route to discovery in this enterprise. If any of the proofs can stand against the objections of those who critique them, then perhaps genuine progress is possible in building a framework for a set of true beliefs. The next chapter will analyze two chief arguments against the existence of God to see how they fare in comparison with their positive counterparts.

Before I attend to the first proof, a comment about the concept of God is appropriate. Philosophers raise the point that it is important to state one's meaning in saying that God exists. There are many and varied theories about who, or what, God is. For example, pantheism maintains, on the whole—albeit one finds different versions of the doctrine—that all the universe is God, and God is all the universe. God is identical to the system itself. Deism holds that there is a cosmic originator, but, after establishing the universe with immutable physical laws and setting it working, this initiator refrained from any intervention; there is no divine immanence. The concept of God that Plato presents in the *Timaeus* appears to be that of deism. Having generated the universe, utilizing the forms, the celestial Craftsman withdrew and left the system to continue without further involvement on his part. In the proofs that I will examine in the sections that follow—and, as a rule, in this entire work—I will intend the word 'God' to refer to the Creator, the God of Judaism and Christianity, who is perfect, transcendent, immanent, infinite, eternal, unchanging, incorporeal, omnipresent, omnipotent, benevolent, and omniscient.

Tracing Back—The Cosmological Argument

As its name suggests, the cosmological argument attempts to prove that God exists based on assertions about the cosmos. The English word 'cosmos' comes from a Greek term meaning 'order'. The cosmological argument is understood best as a group of arguments that are related by the shared notion that the world of experience points to a beginning, and agency is behind it. Some authors limit the use of the label to a particular form of the general argument—namely, one that is based on causality—but, in keeping with the established approach, I will not make that distinction here. The reasoning has its roots in ancient philosophy. Plato holds that living entities originate motion; inanimate things cannot move unless they are set in motion by something else. All motion (in the current world order, at least) is therefore attributable to the actions of that which can move itself—specifically, soul: "[T]he soul is the first origin and moving power of all that is, or has become, or will be. . . . [S]he has been clearly shown to be the source of change and motion."[12] Aristotle makes a case for an unmoved mover by arguing that only that which is actual can bring that which is potential to action. If each object in motion requires an actual moving cause to move it, then the cosmos must have a prime mover—for Aristotle, a final cause—that was the impetus for the present motion of things.

Others through the centuries employed the argument in their works, but it takes on its full form in the writings of the medieval theologian and philosopher Thomas Aquinas (c. 1224–1274). In his work *Summa theologiæ*, St. Thomas, as he commonly is known, puts

---

[12] Plato, *Laws*, 10, 896a–b, in *The Dialogues of Plato*, trans. Benjamin Jowett (1892; repr., New York: Random House, 1937), 2:638.

forth five arguments for God's existence, three of which can be classified as cosmological.[13] They are summarized below.

ARGUMENT FROM MOTION.[14] It is evident that things in the world are in motion. Motion is nothing other than the reduction of a thing from potentiality to actuality. Nothing can be reduced from a state of potentiality to one of actuality except by that which is already in a state of actuality. Therefore, whatever is in motion is brought to that state by something else that is already in motion; that thing, in turn, by yet another that is in motion. This chain of events, however, cannot continue to infinity, as there would not be an original mover and thus no subsequent motion at all. This first mover must exist, and everyone understands that the first mover is God.

ARGUMENT FROM EFFICIENT CAUSE.[15] There are causes and effects in the material world, and there is an order of causes within the causal chain: initial, one or more intermediate, and final. It is not possible for a thing in the world to be the cause of itself, as then it would have to exist before itself, which cannot happen. To remove the cause, however, is to remove the effect. If the causal chain were infinite, then there would be no first cause, and, as a consequence, there would be no effect. Obviously, there are effects in the world. A first cause therefore must exist, and this first cause is understood by everyone to be God.

ARGUMENT FROM POSSIBILITY AND NECESSITY. It is possible for things that one finds in nature either to exist or not to exist, for it is clear that they are generated, and they decay. Their existence is not necessary. If it is possible for a thing not to exist, then there was a time when it did not exist. If this principle holds true for everything,

---

[13] The five arguments appear in Latin and English in Thomas Aquinas, *Summa theologiæ*, 1a.2.3, trans. Timothy McDermott, vol. 2, *Existence and Nature of God* (Cambridge: Blackfriars, 1964), 12–17. Dominican clergymen renamed the work *Summa theologica*. Some philosophers do not place the third argument, which relies on the concepts of possibility and necessity, in the cosmological grouping, although it commonly is classified as a member of that set.

[14] Some renditions of the Latin in the Thomistic work translate *motus* as 'change' rather than 'motion', but the ideas that are inherent in the readings are parallel.

[15] As a reminder, the concept of efficient cause stems from Aristotle's four senses of causality, as identified in chap. 3. It plays a part in Descartes's argument for God's existence; refer to chap. 2. An efficient cause is something that brings about the effect: for instance, the hammering that drives a nail into a board.

however, then "once upon a time there was nothing."[16] In that case, given that a thing can come into being only by something that already exists, there would be nothing at the present time, which contradicts observation. It therefore cannot be true that the existence of all things is merely possible, such that they need not exist; there must be something the existence of which is necessary. Now, an entity that is necessary owes its necessity to another entity, or it does not owe it to another entity. It is not possible to go back to infinity in necessary things the necessity of which is owed to something else—the argument from efficient cause demonstrates that such regressive sequences eventually must terminate. It follows that there must exist a necessary being the necessity of which is owing to itself and is the foundational cause of necessity.

These arguments begin with an observation of the cosmos, where it is evident that things are in motion or that things have causes or that things can come into existence and pass away. Each puts forth the existence of a sequence that yields the current state and explains its arising. The arguments then move backward in the sequence to examine how it is that the current state logically could have come to be. All the arguments embrace the same principle: The sequence cannot be infinite. There must be a primary instance—the beginning of the procession—whether it is the first mover, the first efficient cause, or the foundational being whose existence is necessary. The primary instance in the series is God.

Given that a prominent feature of the cosmological argument is its disallowing an infinity of prior elements, it is not surprising that one criticism of the argument turns to the supposed inadmissibility of an infinite series and rejects it. Such an array can be described mathematically. One may hold that the integers constitute an infinite progression, where one can create the next member of the chain by adding the number 1 to the present integer repeatedly. Likewise, one can produce an infinite string by an ongoing operation of subtracting the number 1 from the present integer. There are insufficient grounds in the argument itself, one might say, for denying an infinite past.

The philosopher William Lane Craig points out that there is an important difference between an infinite set and an infinite serial

---

[16] Aquinas, *Summa theologiæ*, 1a.2.3, 15.

array. A set is given all at once; a series is generated by a continuing or recurring process. The set of natural numbers is infinite, but one never can generate it by repetitive addition. Regardless of how many times one performs the procedure and how much time is allowed, one cannot complete the process to reach infinity. There forever will be another possible iteration. The same is true of the negative integers. One cannot start with the number −1 and reach the end of a decreasing run through recurring subtraction. No infinite set will result from either approach; and no infinite series is possible in physical reality: One cannot reach the present time by initiating a temporal progression in an infinite past, adding moments one after another. The objection is relegated solely to the realm of thought.

A core problem with the common criticism of the cosmological argument is that it misses St. Thomas's point. He is not suggesting the impossibility of an infinite series. Rather, St. Thomas is claiming that there must be some primary instance on which the whole sequence of movements or causes depends, the existence of which is required to account for the sequence itself. The things in the material universe are not self-initiated; they cannot be the cause of themselves, nor can they be the cause of their own continuance. Instead, they must rely on something else. It makes no sense to think of things' moving or reacting to causes unless one envisions something that is ultimately responsible for the whole group of presently observed occurrences. If one takes away the first instance in the sequence, then the entire chain disappears, leaving one with no motion and no effects in the current world. It is not the notion of an infinity of links in the chain that St. Thomas rejects but the different notion of having a chain at all if there is no explanation for its initiation.

There is another aspect of the argument that comes into play. Picture a large rock tumbler, a device that is used to polish stones by agitating them inside a container that is filled with a slightly abrasive agent. Suppose that a number of stones are inside the compartment and that the unit is operating. Tossed against each other, the stones cause other stones to move in an ongoing state of successive impact. Two sorts of causality are at work in this illustration. (1) Something must account for the series of incidents in which pebbles are pushing other pebbles off their respective courses. Stone *a* moves stone *b*, *b* moves *c*, and so forth, but why are the stones bumping into each other in the first place? What is responsible for all this activity—what launched it? (2) Something must account for the conservation of the series. Why is the motion continuing—why is it that the activity is happening at this point rather than having ceased before now? In both cases, the answer is that an entity apart from the series is responsible. It is the motor-tumbler assembly that started the movement of the rocks; it caused the rock-bumping events to take place. It is also the motor-tumbler assembly that maintains the constant motion of the rocks. Even if one imagines that the unit has been running forever, one still cannot explain the activity adequately without making reference to the machine that is responsible for it. There is something that is independent of the stone-jostling series that not only *starts* it but also *sustains* it.

Apply the concept now not to movement but to being. As for the things that exist in the cosmos—the things that can be detected by means of perception—there must be something that brings them into being and something that conserves their being, sustaining them in existence. Both are causal factors, and both produce effects, but the factors are dissimilar in their operations. Philosophy regards the first sort of cause (the more familiar sense) as a cause *in fieri*, the second one as a cause *in esse*. If things are dependent on something other than themselves for their coming into existence, then they are dependent on something other than themselves for their continuance. Recall a passage from a work by the philosopher George Hayward Joyce, presented in chapter 5 with reference to a related point:

> That which even for a single instant is the sufficient reason of its own existence is self-existent. But a nature which is capable of self-existence needs not to wait for the action of an efficient cause in order to exist; it must have existed from all eternity. . . . [T]o say that a thing conserves itself is to say that its persistence through each successive moment is to be attributed to its own existing nature.[17]

---

[17] George Hayward Joyce, *Principles of Natural Theology*, 2nd ed. (London: Longmans, Green and Co., 1924), 62. See chap. 3 of Joyce's work for a full discussion of his argument.

Joyce is correct. The things of perceptual experience come and go. They do not bring themselves—indeed, cannot bring themselves—into existence. They are not self-existent. Whatever entity is not self-existent, however, must depend on something else for its being, and not only for its generation but for its conservation too: What lacks independent existence has the ability to effect neither its origination nor its sustention. Its being requires both a cause *in fieri* and a cause *in esse* that are outside it. The upshot of this line of reasoning seems to be that the self-existent, and therefore the eternal, must account for the things in the world. The proponent will claim that such a designation applies to, and only to, God, having presumed that the self-existent is singular. Aside from this issue, one might wonder whether there is a way around the freighted conclusion.

It appears that each of the Thomistic proofs assumes that the sequence in discussion is an open-ended linear progression, albeit one that must be grounded in something that is ontically solid, something that undergirds the series of contingent members and explains its existence. That undergirding unit is the initiator of the series, which extends forward in time from that point. Suppose, however, that a series of things is linked to itself. Instead of a straight line, in which each link in the chain is dependent on the former one until the beginning is reached, as shown in Figure 6.1,

Series Elements

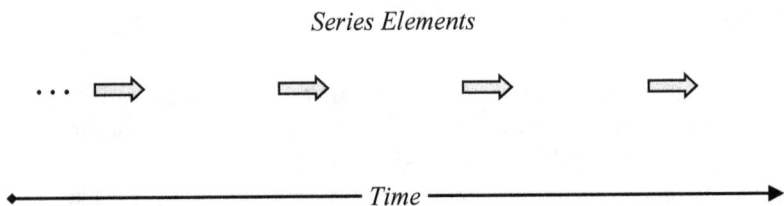

Figure 6.1

there could be a loop, as the following diagram illustrates:

Series Elements

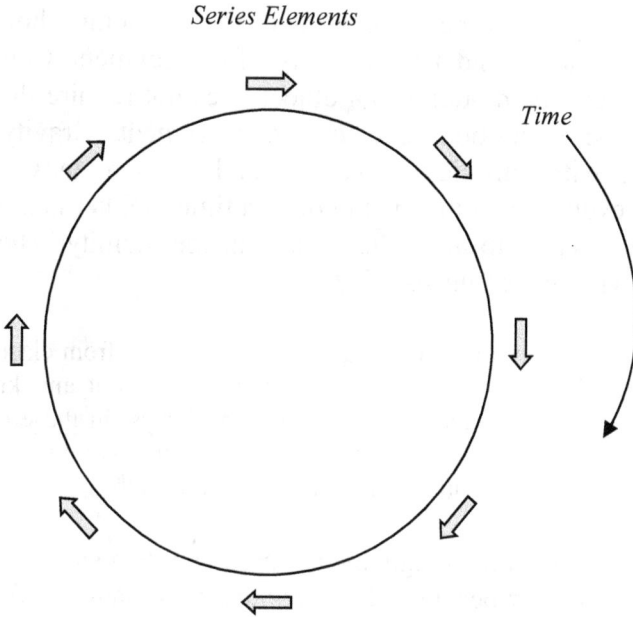

Figure 6.2

In this case, the sequence itself is finite (although it need not be), but it could recur an infinite number of times. Hence, there conceivably could be a causal chain that is not infinite in length and is such that the current state depends on a previous one; yet, there is no first link. It seems, however, that, where contingent beings are under consideration, the loop configuration loses applicability. In a finite circular progression, a thing ultimately becomes the cause of itself, initiating a chain of causes that causes it, and this scenario represents an illogicality. Nothing can cause itself to come into existence, for then it would exist, before it exists, to serve as the cause that brings it into being—a point that appears in St. Thomas's second abovestated argument. Further, and more important, if every member of the set is dependent for its being on another member of the same set, then accounting for the existence of the set itself becomes a problem. One is faced with explaining how the set arose, the issue at the very heart of the Thomistic arguments.

There is another concern with the reasoning, though, that may be apparent. Consider St. Thomas's first argument. Contrary to what is claimed, the motion of an object does not require that some other object be in motion to cause its movement. Gravity causes two objects with sufficient proximity and mass to move toward each other, even if, at some given point in time, neither is moving relative to the other or to any other object in the vicinity. The philosopher David Hume recognizes this fact.

> Motion, in many instances, from gravity, from elasticity, from electricity, begins in matter, without any known voluntary agent; and to suppose always, in these cases, an unknown voluntary agent, is mere hypothesis; and hypothesis attended with no advantages.[18]

Add to Hume's list magnetism, which causes a stationary iron object to move simply because of its nearness to a magnetic field. The body is not set in motion by some other body in motion but by a force. There are other examples. Electromagnetic energy in the form of infrared light or microwaves, for instance, can boil water in a container, thereby creating movement, where there was none, by converting the liquid water to steam, which rises and creates surface turbulence. One might say that the energy is in motion, given its wave nature, but it is not moving in the sense that the argument employs. St. Thomas's way of thinking reduces the observed motion of objects to kinetic, material causes, but there are other phenomena that produce movement at a macrophysical level, and their doing so is independent of any body that is already in motion.

Immanuel Kant criticizes the cosmological argument from a different perspective, contending that it violates an important tenet. He declares,

> The principle of causality has no meaning and no criterion for its application save only in the sensible

---

[18] David Hume, *Dialogues concerning Natural Religion*, in *David Hume: The Philosophical Works*, ed. Thomas Hill Green and Thomas Hodge Grose (1882, 1886; repr., Frankfurt am Main, Germany: Scientia Verlag Aalen, 1964), 2:426. Hume's work *Dialogues* was published posthumously in 1779.

world. But in the cosmological proof it is precisely in order to enable us to advance beyond the sensible world that it is employed.[19]

Kant continues, noting the problem of inferring a first cause from the impossibility of an infinite series.

The principles of the employment of reason do not justify this conclusion even within the world of experience, still less beyond this world in a realm into which this series can never be extended.[20]

Kant's central point is that the cosmological argument rests on the notion of cause-effect, but this notion is applicable only in the context in which people understand it and give it significance. That context is the universe of the empirical. The cosmological argument employs the notion in an attempt to prove a transcendent cause—that is to say, one that lies outside the perceptible world in which the human idea of causality is framed. One cannot exit the system in which a concept is meaningful to use that concept elsewhere, Kant posits, because its utility is confined to the system whereby the denotation of the corresponding term is imparted.

The philosopher is not banning discovery. Kant is not asserting that it is impossible to go to places, so to speak, where one has no experience; he is asserting that one cannot leave the realm of experience itself and continue to make use of its structuring elements. Kant's claim is in keeping with his bifurcated system of knowledge. In the world of appearance, the senses are at work, furnishing the basic data on which the mind acts to bring order to perceptions. It is in this realm of phenomena, Kant holds, that human understanding operates. One cannot move beyond an appearance to something as it really is—*das Ding an sich*: the thing-in-itself. Direct contact with it is not possible, in Kant's view, a point that I noted briefly earlier in

---

[19] Immanuel Kant, *Immanuel Kant's Critique of Pure Reason,* trans. Norman Kemp Smith (1929; repr., New York: St. Martin's Press, 1965), 511. Smith takes his translation from the second edition of *Critique of Pure Reason,* which Kant published in German in 1787. Kant does not reject the existence of God, but he does reject the traditional arguments that are set forth to prove it.

[20] Ibid.

this work.[21] In a somewhat similar way, if God is not part of the causal chain of the empirical universe, acting as a member of it—indeed, the initiating member—but is instead external to it, then He is out of the range of human experience, Kant argues. To extend the idea of causation to God is thus to violate its appropriate use.

To be sure, there are many concepts and associated terms that cannot be carried across an ontological threshold without a change in meaning, even a loss of it—a matter that I will cover in detail later—but the principle is not universal. A person understands the statement 'God is benevolent', for instance, and the person would have gained a grasp of the indicated attribute by observing individuals and their deeds. In the case of certain concepts and terms, their applicability can be barred from the extension because, but only because, one limits the applicability to the sensible world by *presupposition*. Further, there are some areas along the periphery of the thinking here, within the physical domain, that seem to challenge Kant's purported rule, and theoretical physics stands at the extreme outer edge. It might be argued that one must begin where one is to go anywhere at all. How else would one get there? It is the nature of discovery to stand on what is known and to postulate, to infer, and to envision what must be, and people sometimes do venture outside the system. They can take with them on the journey only what they have. When physicists talk of the six-dimensional Calabi-Yau spaces in which particles operate, they are going beyond the experiential realm of the universe to form theories about how *physical* reality must be. Figure 6.3 shows a rendition of a Calabi-Yau manifold.[22]

---

[21] See chap. 2, n. 4.

[22] I wish to thank Andrew J. Hanson of Indiana University, who produced this particular Calabi-Yau image for this work, kindly granting permission to include it. Hanson used the Mathematica software from Wolfram Research, Inc., to create it.

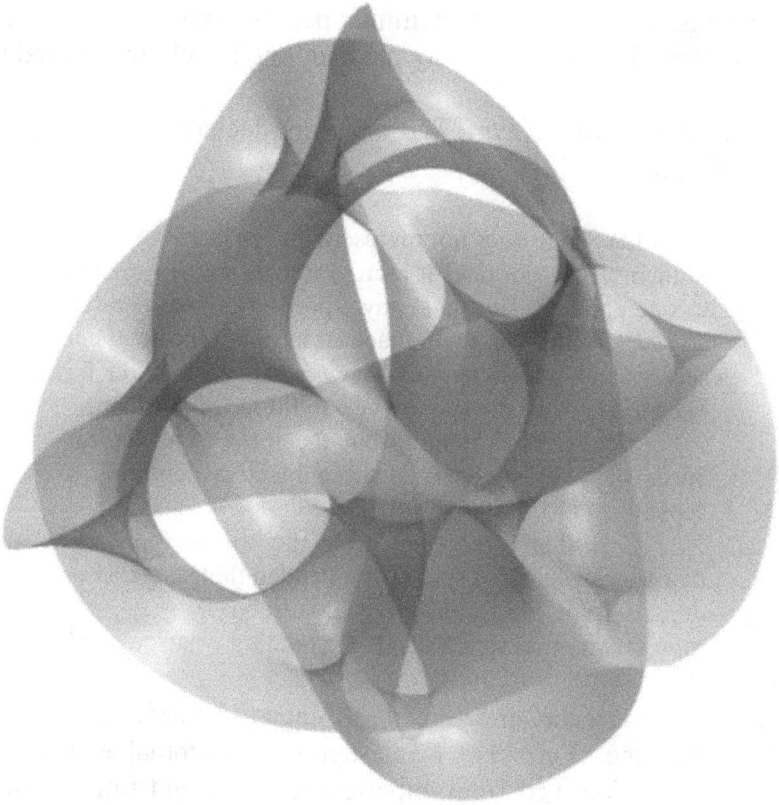

Figure 6.3

These tiny, hyperdimensional pieces of territory wrap around each point in the space-time grid of the universe like intricate, twisted bubbles in which particles can escape from the four dimensions of common experience. Postulations about these other dimensions are grounded nevertheless in concepts that are derived from scientific observation within the known dimensions. One comprehends what it means to say that a particle moves in another dimension and to say that a particle acts as a cause in that dimension, even if one is not sure how to get there. It is the process of adding the theoretical to the established that is a major part of what it is to learn. Science, however, deals with the physical cosmos, regardless of the number of dimensions, and, with this in mind, perhaps one has not left the system after all. With feet firmly planted, one merely has leaned over the balcony.

In his *Critique of Pure Reason*, Kant declares that space is not part of objective reality.

> (*a*) Space does not represent any property of things in themselves, nor does it represent them in their relation to one another. That is to say, space does not represent any determination that attaches to the objects themselves, and which remains even when abstraction has been made of all the subjective conditions of intuition.
>
> (*b*) Space is nothing but the form of all appearances of outer sense. It is the subjective condition of sensibility.
>
> It is, therefore, solely from the human standpoint that we can speak of space, of extended things, etc. If we depart from the subjective condition . . . , the representation of space stands for nothing whatsoever.[23]

In sensory experience, one perceives things to be ordered in space as well as in time. Yet, says Kant, neither perceptual element is a concept that is derived from experience. Space and time are mind-imposed forms, and all appearances of things take these forms. According to him, space is not out there, as it were, and its representation has no meaning apart from the subjective human component. One cannot detect objects in additional dimensions; therefore, where the spatial dimensions exceed three, as in the case of the Calabi-Yau manifolds, perception is precluded. Presumably, Kant would say that Calabi-Yau spaces are not only unreal but are bereft of significance too.

It is true that one interprets objects in a spatial way; one determines them to be closer or farther away, for example. Binary vision provides perceptional cues from two different points in space. The human brain utilizes the associated parallax, which helps to

---

[23] Kant, *Critique*, 71. Kant opposes both Isaac Newton's view of space as absolute and objective, and Gottfried Wilhelm von Leibniz's view as a relation among material bodies. Kant believes instead that space is something that humans contribute to their own perceptions of things as dimensionally extended.

impart a sense of depth. As a rule, a person with sight in only one eye has trouble locating an object in the depth plane because of the loss of simultaneous signals from two distinct angles, although other clues, such as the known size of an object in the visual field, can help. Even hearing is binary. An individual uses the information that two ears provide to localize sounds. Minute temporal differences in the arrival of a given sound, where one ear receives the noise slightly before the other, coupled with variations in amplitude and phase, allow a person to pinpoint the source—for a broad portion of the frequency range to which humans are sensitive, at least. Where the sound originates in a plane that dissects one's head vertically, front to back, such that the sound energy arrives at each ear simultaneously and in phase, one generally cannot tell from which direction the noise comes. That one *interprets* sensations in such a way that the locating of things spatially is achievable, however, does not mean that space has no existence apart from human observers.

The problem for Kant is that his view is at odds with contemporary physics. Relativity demonstrates that he is in error. The space-time grid exists independently of the humans who perceive the clusters of matter that are embedded within it. It encases every collection of material, curving all the more tightly, according to the standard view, around the more massive chunks. What one refers to as the moon Titan is forced to orbit what one refers to as the planet Saturn, and Saturn is forced to orbit what one calls the sun, precisely because the moon and the planet follow the warps in space-time that are created by the large relative masses of the material aggregates around which they revolve. The bending of space-time is independent of the experience of human beings; indeed, the warping of dimensions predates their arrival. Kant's writings, of course, appeared more than a century before Einstein's groundbreaking work; Kant did not have access to the information that is available today in the field of physics.

Another objection that some raise against the third version of the cosmological argument concerns St. Thomas's reasoning about contingency. He states that, because it is possible for a thing in the world not to exist, at some point in time, it did not exist. Such things are contingent beings: Their existence is not logically necessary. Given that this fact applies to all the objects in the world because they all are contingent entities, at some point in time, nothing would have existed, without there being some entity the existence of which is necessary—that is to say, an entity the nonexistence of which is impossible.

The problem with the argument is that one cannot conclude that nothing existed at a time in the past—nor, for that matter, will exist at a time in the future—on the basis that things can exist or not exist. The reasoning takes the form that is shown below:

> For any object x, there is a time t, such that t predates the arising of x.
> Therefore, there is a time t, such that, for any object x, t predates the arising of x.

The argument is invalid. What may be true of every individual object at one time or another need not be true of every individual object at the same time. The argument exchanges the order of the quantifiers to produce the error—a problem resembling one that surfaced earlier. For every person, there is a time at which that person was conceived, but it is not true that there is one particular time at which every person was conceived.

This line of thinking may highlight the flaw more clearly; let the individuals to whom the sentences refer be adults:

> For any human member h of a population, there is a human navel n in that population, such that h does not possess n.
> Therefore, there is a human navel n in a population, such that, for any human member h of that population, h does not possess n.

The conclusion does not follow from the premise, and it is false. There are human navels that do not belong to Nelson, to be sure—Nancy's, for example—but it is not the case that there exists a human navel that belongs to no one. There can be a human navel only if there is a human, or was a human, in which it is, or was, embedded. A navel cannot exist on its own.

There could be a series of contingent things, each of which comes into existence—and thus did not exist at some point in time—

and which exists long enough to generate something else, without there having to be one time when nothing existed. I might represent the series in the way that appears below. Each depicted thing is a contingent being, and the bar underneath it, terminated by vertical lines, represents the thing's span of existence in time. The generation regresses to an undetermined past.

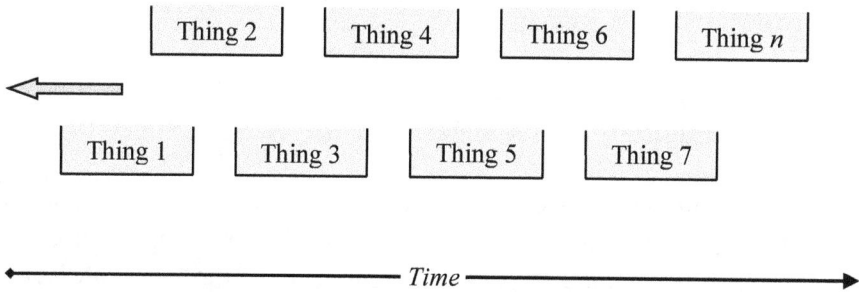

Figure 6.4

Of course, the principal issue that arises over contingency is the same one that arises over movement and causation. Contingent beings lack the power to initiate their own existence. Although any given one may depend on another, and that one on another, and so forth, it is an explanation for the series itself that is needed. Without something that is outside the sequence of contingent entities to account for the existence of the sequence, the entire chain collapses.

Aside from this issue, there is one premise of the Thomistic argument that I find to be of particular interest. St. Thomas claims that, if it is possible for a thing not to exist, then, at some time, its nonexistence is actual. The matter of nonexistence pertains to both ends of the duration of an object, both its origination and its cessation, but the greater matter for St. Thomas in the argument is the former event. He is attempting to show that there is something that existed in the past, the existence of which is necessary. One may see his premise as an instance of a more general principle: Whatever is possible is, at some time, actual.[24] Where one speaks of events, the principle may be stated in this way: Given enough time, all possible events occur. There is a somewhat narrower form of this restatement that is commonplace: If anything can go wrong, then it will go wrong. As is evident, this assertion expresses what is referred to as Murphy's law.[25] Is it true that, simply because an event is possible, it must occur at some juncture?

To answer that question, one must distinguish between two distinct statements, as identified in the following pair, where *p* stands for any declarative sentence:

> It is logically possible that *p*.
> It is logically impossible that not *p*.

If the first statement is true, then *p* may, or may not, be the case. If the second statement is true, then *p* *must* be the case. Logic demands it. One can deny that *p* and yet hold to the truth of the first statement. Without introducing a contradiction, one cannot deny that *p* and yet claim that the second statement is true.

Now, let *p* stand for the statement that event *e* occurs. Substituting for *p* in the abovesaid pair of statements yields this set:

> It is logically possible that *e* occurs.
> It is logically impossible that *e* does not occur.

---

[24] Some theorize that everything that is possible is actual, albeit not necessarily in the universe of common human experience but in one or more parallel universes. Time is not so much a critical factor as divergence into alternate realities. The position introduces illogicalities, which I will look at briefly later. In the discussion of the proposed principle here, it is the universe that humans know that is in view.

[25] For a discussion of the history of Murphy's law, see Fred R. Shapiro, ed., *The Yale Book of Quotations* (New Haven: Yale University Press, 2006), 529. According to Shapiro, the earliest documented wording of the essence of the so-called law appeared in a different form in 1941 in George Orwell's "War-time Diary." A variant of the law-statement allegedly surfaced in 1949 at Edwards Air Force Base in California when project manager George E. Nichols heard Edward A. Murphy Jr. speak of an improperly prepared experiment. Nichols averred, in an interview in 2003, to have said at the time of the incident, "If it can happen, it will happen." The first documented instance of the law, presented in its current form, is traced to John Sack; it was given in an epigraph in *The Butcher: The Ascent of Yerupaja* in 1952. Shapiro provides other references as well.

The distinction here is the same as the one in the previous pair of statements. It is only in the latter sense that the occurrence of *e* is logically necessary. Events in the physical world may happen, or they may fail to happen: It is possible for any of them not to occur, for they are not compelled by the laws of logic.[26]

St. Thomas claims that things may, or may not, exist; yet, one may think, based on his premise about their actual nonexistence at a point in time, that their coming into existence is compelled after all. Here is why: If all possible events become actual, given enough time, then all things that have come to exist *had* to come to exist—their emergence is inescapable—albeit the timings of the arrivals could have varied. The very existence of those things demonstrates that it is possible for them to have come to be, and, under the principle at hand, what is possible must be actual at some juncture. The case is misleading, however. It is not true by the rules of logic that an infinity of time drives all potential events to actual events.

Picture Tommy, who is running barefoot back and forth across a large field near his house. He continues his activity for much of the day, chasing his new dog, which appears to enjoy evading him. Hour after hour he runs. It becomes his routine. He does it again the next day, and the next. Sixty-four feet from the western side of the field and ninety-nine feet from the northern edge, a small ant bed lies hidden in the grass. Tommy seldom goes over that way, but he may

---

[26] Consider that events the occurrences of which are told in advance by God, as reported in the Scriptures, must happen, but they must do so for a reason other than logical necessity. Given the essential attributes of God—including omnipotence, omniscience, and truthfulness—if God exists, then what the future reveals cannot be other than what He so declares. God is in control of all events and invariably knows what is forthcoming. Events that are mentioned in prophecy are secured by the characteristics of the Deity rather than the rules of logic. Of course, one could build a valid deductive argument to demonstrate that such incidents must take place, employing premises about God's nature. Supported by logical principles, the conclusion would follow from premises that are supported by theological principles; thus, both disciplines would play a part in the chain of reasoning. One must be cautious not to confuse prophecy with theological determinism. The omnipotent, omniscient God allows free agents to choose, but the unfolding of events in accordance with those choices will align with God-inspired prophetic utterances. The decision of the Jewish religious leaders to have Jesus crucified by the Romans conformed to prophecy; nevertheless, it was still their decision. They chose the path that they took, and God knew that they would do so.

do so eventually. Will Tommy step on the ant bed? Perhaps he will land there. Time serves to increase the probability that a state of affairs will obtain, but it does not force it to do so. Time cannot make a contingency logically necessary. If the boy's activity stretches across months, then the likelihood that ants will bite him assuredly rises, but that event never can attain logical certainty. The probability of its occurrence cannot be 1.0. For all useful purposes, however, the actualization of contingent events can be so close to certainty that it is not reasonable to deny that they will come to pass. Tossing a fair coin fifty times will produce an outcome that includes tails on some occasions because probability calculations virtually guarantee it. The endorsement is practical, not logical.[27] The failure of heads to appear even once in so many trials is a probabilistic implausibility, a notion that I presented in chapter 4. Such is the character of the universe.

The thrust of the story is that an event's being possible does not make it necessary. Said in another way, if it is possible for it not to happen, then it just may not happen; and, if it does happen, then its occurrence is a matter of fact, not a matter of reason. An event that is not constrained by logic—denying its occurrence does not introduce a contradiction—stands at the crossroads of alternative paths. If the probability of its taking place is high enough, then it is a sure thing, but the surety is because of the mathematics of chance, not because of the rules of logic.

Returning to Murphy's law, one finds the limitations of it to be obvious now. Whether the supposed law applies to given instances in physical reality or does not apply to them is determined by circumstances, not by strict deduction. Even if everything that can go wrong, in fact, does go wrong, it did not have to be that way. If something can go wrong but has not done so to date, then one may have to wait to see what the future holds in store.

There is a final form of the cosmological argument to take into account. With roots that predate St. Thomas by centuries, it is a contemporary defense that is put forth by William Lane Craig. Craig begins with a straightforward representation of the reasoning, as shown below:

---

[27] The odds are greater than a quadrillion to one against the appearing of heads every time in fifty tosses.

1. Everything that begins to exist has a cause of its existence.
2. The universe began to exist.
3. Therefore the universe has a cause of its existence.[28]

The argument is valid by virtue of its form. One will ask, though, whether it is sound.

Consider the first premise. The skeptic David Hume proclaims, " 'Tis a general maxim in philosophy, that *whatever begins to exist, must have a cause of its existence.*"[29] The maxim, he maintains, is "not intuitively certain."[30] It appears that he means that there is no logical contradiction in asserting that a coming-to-be event that has no cause can take place. One can imagine its happening, so there is no absurdity. One may think that, if Hume is right, then Craig's argument is a nonstarter.

It is true that, from the fact that one can imagine something, one can infer that it is not logically impossible, but it still may be nomologically impossible. Refer to the discussion in chapter 4 of the distinction between the two sorts of impossibility. The philosopher G. E. M. Anscombe rightly dismisses Hume's contention, finding it to be impotent.

> For if I say I can imagine a rabbit coming into being without a parent rabbit, well and good: I imagine a rabbit coming into being, and our observing that there is no parent rabbit about. But what am I to imagine if I imagine a rabbit coming into being without a cause? Well, I just imagine a rabbit coming into being. That this *is* the imagination of a rabbit coming into being without a cause is nothing but, as it were, the *title* of the picture. Indeed I can form an image and give my picture that title. But from my being able to do *that*, nothing whatever follows about what is possible to suppose

---

[28] William Lane Craig, *The Kalām Cosmological Argument* (London: Macmillan Press, 1979), 63. The essence of the argument can be traced to the Christian theologian and philosopher John Philoponus, who composed his works during the sixth century. The term *kalām* is Arabic for 'speech'; it came to represent a movement within Arabic thought, notes Craig.

[29] David Hume, *A Treatise of Human Nature*, in *Philosophical Works*, 1:380.

[30] Ibid., 381.

'without contradiction or absurdity' as holding in reality.[31]

Craig offers support, empirical as well as logical, for the coming to be of the universe—the second premise of his deductive argument. With regard to the former support, Craig raises two points. The expansion of the universe suggests an absolute beginning, which is consistent with the prevailing theory among scientists that a big bang event launched the cosmos several billion years ago. Furthermore, says Craig, if the universe had existed infinitely in the past, then, as a closed system, it would have reached a state of thermal equilibrium by now, in accordance with the second law of thermodynamics. The universe, however, is in disequilibrium; it has not reached a state of maximum entropy, where no further thermal activity occurs and where all is completely uniform in temperature. It follows that there could not be an infinite history, but, without it, the universe must have come into being. By the first premise, this event requires a cause. Craig believes that this cause of the arising of the universe is explained best by supposing a personal being who created it—namely, God.

As proponents of a big bang cosmogony, atheists who oppose Craig's line of reasoning generally do not object to his premise that the universe began to exist. Some do object, however, to his premise that everything that begins to exist, and therefore the universe, has a cause of its coming to be, turning to reputed incidents in quantum physics to support their position. I will examine their objections in conjunction with the discussion of the teleological argument.

As for the logical support that Craig offers for his premise, consider one of his arguments. Noting that Georg Cantor's work on transfinite numbers provides the tools to understand infinity, Craig, paralleling Anscombe, points out that one cannot move from the thought of numerical infinity to reality. It is absurd to hold that a library actually could contain an infinite quantity of books. Suppose that each book is either red or black and that the colors of the books alternate on the shelves. The number of red books equals the number of black books because, in an infinite set of alternating items, there

---

[31] G. E. M. Anscombe, " 'Whatever Has a Beginning of Existence Must Have a Cause': Hume's Argument Exposed," *Analysis* 34, no. 5 (1974): 150.

are as many of one as of the other. The infinite set of positive integers, for example, is such that there are just as many odd numbers as there are even numbers. The absurdity surfaces when one realizes that the number of red books equals the number of red books plus the number of black books, just as the cardinal of the set of odd positive integers equals the cardinal of the set of all positive integers, both odd and even.[32] The mathematics of infinity is limited to the realm of thought—for objects, at least. There is no comparable way, in Craig's view, that it can be applied to the realm of material reality.

In the end, though, even if the cosmological argument can establish that there is a cause that gave rise to the cosmos—a transcendent cause—it does not follow that this cause is the Judaeo-Christian God. In the last chapter, however, I described how agency lies outside the causal chains of events that unfold in the physical universe. Agents can initiate such chains, but their actions do not fall under the strict physical laws that govern nature. Agents are not constrained in their actions by a deterministic world. If there is a cause that started it all, then there is good reason to think, following Plato, that it is indeed characterized by agency.

Continua—The Henological Argument

Referred to on occasion as the degrees-of-perfection argument, the henological proof attempts to demonstrate the existence of God based on the gradation of things. The proof is so designated because it purports to show that a number of qualities point to one God: The first part of the name of the proof is traced to a Greek term meaning 'one'. It is again Thomas Aquinas who presents the argument in its most well-known version. The demonstration, which appears in his *Summa theologiæ*, is summarized here.

Properties admit of degrees. Some things are more good, more true, more noble, and so forth than other things. The comparative expressions 'more' and 'less' apply according to whether a thing approximates the superlative. Something is hotter than something

---

[32] See Craig, *Kalām Cosmological Argument*, 82 ff.

else, for example, if it more nearly resembles that which is the hottest of all, which is fire. There is therefore something that is best and truest and most noble. As Aristotle notes, the things that are greatest in truth are the things that possess being most fully. When various things possess a property in common, the one that possesses the property most fully is the cause of it in all the others, just as fire is the cause of all things' being hot. Hence, there must be something that, for all things, is the cause of their being, their goodness, and whatever other perfections they possess. This cause is God.

The point of the argument is that, because qualities can be present in things to varying degrees, there is a scale for qualities. There must be a maximum for the genus. This maximum is also the cause of things' having those qualities. St. Thomas believes that a thing is perfect to the extent to which it is actual, and it is imperfect to the extent to which it is potential. Think of it in this way: A person who is actually benevolent is more complete in benevolence, more perfect in his or her exhibiting the quality, than one who is potentially benevolent but has not reached the stage of actually being that way. According to St. Thomas, that which possesses the super-lative degree of a thing is that in which the property is actualized to the full extent. With respect to that particular quality, when it is maximized, there is no potential. Things in which the property is actualized must have the actualization of the property caused in them by something else with at least as much of that property actualized because only the actual can bring the potential to actual. That which possesses a positive quality to the extreme thus must be the cause of it everywhere—one cause, generating the manifestation of the property across a multiplicity of things. The superlative degree of perfections—and here St. Thomas is speaking of sublime qualities, such as truth, unity, goodness, and nobility—must rest with the being in whom those perfections are actualized completely. That being is God. Therefore, God exists. The Aristotelian overtones in Thomistic thought are evident.

There are obvious problems with this argument. One objection that philosophers raise is based on the notion that comparatives need not require a superlative to be employed or understood. For instance, something can be longer than something else, but one cannot infer from this fact that there is a longest thing. A fishing pole that is ten feet in length is longer than another that measures only nine feet. One is comparing the poles with each other, or with a standard unit of measure, not with some object of greatest length. There is a scale; there is just no maximum. St. Thomas is not justified in claiming that, because the characteristic of nobility varies among people, there must be a perfectly noble being.

Another difficulty that St. Thomas faces, I believe, arises from his claim that the entity that possesses a property to the greatest extent is the cause of that property in everything else that possesses it. This claim is twofold: There is a single cause of a given property, and the maximum is that cause. He uses the example of fire. Occupying the uppermost position on the scale of heat, so he maintains, it is responsible for the heat in the things that exhibit hotness. One can heat things through friction, however, as when an Eagle Scout builds a fire by rubbing sticks together, or a truck's brakes reach a point of burning as the driver attempts to slow the vehicle's descent down a mountain road. Here, the heat causes the fire, not the other way around. Radiation also can heat things, as the pavement on a sunny day in summer demonstrates when one steps on it in bare feet, or a bowl of oatmeal from the microwave oven proves when it burns one's tongue. The energy of the moving molecules of a particular substance corresponds to its thermal level, and increased molecular energy need not be the result of fire.

How does one identify the superlative here? Consider the scale of temperature. On the low end, it is absolute zero, the coldest possible temperature, where no thermal energy can be extracted from a material body. This temperature is 0 K, which is equal to –459.67° Fahrenheit. Whether there is a highest temperature is questionable, but it generally is thought to be the Planck temperature—the initial temperature of the universe, according to physicists who subscribe to the big bang theory—which is approximately 1.4168×10^{32} K, or about two hundred fifty-five nonillion degrees if expressed on the Fahrenheit scale. A nonillion is written with thirty zeros after the initial digit. The higher on the scale a thing measures, the hotter it is. Yet, the Planck temperature does not cause a thing to be hot.

St. Thomas's argument, however, is concerned with the maximization of the property in a thing, not the gauge that determines its level. One might say that it is the maximum of what the scale measures that corresponds to the superlative, not the maximum spot on the scale itself. In this case, it is thermal energy; and, continuing this thought, one might say that it is the thermal energy of the big bang that is the ultimate cause of all heat today. Yet, thermal energy is not literally the cause of heat. It *is* heat—more accurately, its transfer is heat. This energy causes *things* to become hot, but, even so, it is not correct to state that it in itself is the sole and ultimate source of all heat in the world. The abovementioned examples show that kinetic energy can be converted to thermal energy and that electromagnetic energy also can be converted to it. For St. Thomas's argument to work, there must be one cause at the top. Without that singular, supreme cause, his argument stumbles, as the varying degrees of perfection in the world need not point to one entity as the source. To succeed, the argument requires convergence.

Other properties come to mind: fragility, viscosity, flexibility, hardness, buoyancy, and acidity, to list a few. It is not true that whatever possesses one of these properties to the greatest degree is the cause of it in other things. The most acidic of all substances, as far as it can be determined, is fluoroantimonic acid, but it in itself does not impart acidity to aspirin (acetylsalicylic acid) or lemon juice (contains citric acid). That characteristic is attributable to the donation of hydrogen ions (or, as generally stated, protons) by substances. The thing in which a given property is maximized need not be the cause of that property in other things—and, as a rule, it is not the cause—any more than the strongest person in the world has to be the cause of strength in everyone else. Individual things possess properties to varying degrees, but those things are typically only the conduits through which the properties are manifested, seldom their sources.

OF NECESSITY—THE ONTOLOGICAL ARGUMENT

This succinct argument is perhaps the most philosophically interesting of the proofs of God's existence. The argument is classified as ontological because it proceeds from the standpoint of being; the first part of the term for the argument is derived from a Greek expression meaning 'being'. St. Anselm (c. 1033–1109), abbot of Bec and subsequently archbishop of Canterbury, sets forth the original version in his work *Proslogion.* It predates St. Thomas's series of arguments by nearly two centuries. Here is a generalized formulation of the proof:

> That than which nothing greater can be conceived is God.
> That which exists in the understanding and also in reality is greater than that which exists in the understanding alone.
> If that than which nothing greater can be conceived were to exist only in the understanding, then something greater would be conceivable because it would be possible to conceive that it also exists in reality.
> Therefore, that than which nothing greater can be conceived must exist in reality.
> Therefore, God exists in reality.

A fascinating argument, it seeks to prove the existence of God based on the conception of God. One can envisage a being that is the greatest of all. Actual existence surpasses mere conceptional existence. By His nature, God lacks no perfection; God is the greatest of all beings. If He were to exist only in one's mind, then one would be able to think of a being who is greater still. That than which none greater can be conceived therefore must exist in reality. Hence, God is real.

Gaunilo, a Benedictine monk of Marmoutier and contemporary of Anselm, attacked Anselm's argument not long after it appeared. Gaunilo holds that no concept itself can imply that there is something in existence to which it corresponds. He draws a parallel: One might visualize a perfect island, an island that outclasses all others, but it does not follow that, because one can think of it, it must exist. As for an island, he is correct, but Anselm counters the objection by stating that his argument cannot be applied to islands or anything else the nonexistence of which is conceivable. An entity than which nothing greater at all can be conceived must exist because, if the entity did not exist, then something greater could be envisioned. Such an entity cannot be thought of as nonexistent. In short, the argument does not apply to *contingent* beings; it applies only to a *necessary* being. It is not possible to consider a necessary being apart from its existing.

Other philosophers since Anselm have employed this argument. René Descartes, for one, presents a version in his writings, supplementing his principal argument, which is based on the cause of his idea of perfection.[33] Descartes maintains that the notion of a triangle includes certain attributes that define what it is to be that three-sided figure. A triangle contains three interior angles, the sum of which always equals two right angles. That uniformity is bound inextricably to triangularity, being part of the essence of it, and is thus inseparable from the corresponding idea. In a similar way, the attribute of existence is bound inextricably to God. He is a necessary being: His essence includes existence, ensuring that He is real. He cannot be otherwise, nor can one imagine otherwise. Says Descartes,

> From the fact that I cannot think of a mountain without a valley, it does not follow that a mountain and a valley exist anywhere, but simply that a mountain and a valley, whether they exist or not, are mutually inseparable. But from the fact that I cannot think of God except as existing, it follows that existence is inseparable from God, and hence that he really exists. It is not that my thought makes it so, or imposes any necessity on any thing; on the contrary, it is the necessity of the thing itself, namely the existence of God, which determines my thinking in this respect. For I am not free to think of God without existence (that is, a supremely perfect being without a supreme perfection).[34]

---

[33] Descartes's idea-of-perfection argument (detailed in chap. 2), which incorporates premises about Descartes's own reflection, may be classified as an ontological proof, although it comprises elements of other lines of reasoning. These elements include causality, which is a factor in the cosmological argument, and the human state—here, of Descartes—which is an aspect of the next proof to be covered: the anthropological argument. In this respect, it varies from a strict ontological demonstration. Brief commentary on the blended character of Descartes's principal argument is available in Augustus Hopkins Strong, *Systematic Theology* (1907; Valley Forge, PA: Judson Press, 1972), 1:86.

[34] René Descartes, *Meditations on First Philosophy, Fifth Meditation*, in *The Philosophical Writings of Descartes*, trans. John Cottingham et al. (1984–1991; Cambridge: Cambridge University Press, 1997–2009), 2:46. Note that Descartes's point about triangles, which he applies analogously to the necessary existence of God, is true in Euclidean geometry, but, of course, in the later Lobachevskian and Riemannian geometries, the defining attributes diverge.

A criticism of the ontological argument appears in the writings of Immanuel Kant—and later, Bertrand Russell. It turns on the impermissible treatment of existence as an attribute. One can ascribe various properties to an entity and thereby extend the concept of it, but appending existence to the list yields no extension; it is not a property in the inventory. One merely posits that there is something that corresponds to the described thing. " '*Being*' is obviously not a real predicate; that is, it is not a concept of something which could be added to the concept of a thing," declares Kant.[35] The existence of a thing is a matter of fact, not definition; it can be affirmed or denied.

Is the objection central to Anselm's argument? The existence *span* of a thing is an attribute of it (a common, adult mayfly lives a day; God, who is sui generis, is eternal), but existence *simpliciter* is a state, a condition, expressible in terms of sets. From the fact that a thing exists, even if timelessly and necessarily, it does not follow that existence is a property of it; and, from the fact that existence is not a property, it does not follow that it is not assignable. Here is the issue: If it is possible that a being, the nonexistence of which is impossible (a necessary being) exists, then is it necessary that this being exist?

Use of the ontological argument has waned in recent times, but it continues to have advocates. It is worthy of further study.[36]

HUMANITY—THE ANTHROPOLOGICAL ARGUMENT

The next major proof of God's existence derives its name from a Greek word that means 'man'. The primary representative of the general inferential form is the moral argument, and I will focus on it in the discussion. This proof differs notably from the others, in that it does not attempt to demonstrate God's existence through reasoning about the cosmos or the graded properties of things that are within it, nor does it draw on the nature of a necessary being. The proof points to moral law instead and argues for its source. A rendition is below:

---

[35] Kant, *Critique*, 504.

[36] One contemporary philosopher offers a revised version of the argument, which employs modalities, that he believes to be sound. See Alvin Plantinga, *God, Freedom, and Evil* (1974; London: George Allen and Unwin, 1975), 104–12.

609

> Law implies a lawgiver. We cannot have a command without a superior who issues the command. . . . There can be no obligation where there are not two persons concerned—a superior having authority and a subject who owes obedience to his commands. No man can impose a law upon himself. For law binds the will: and so long as no superior authority commands us, we remain at liberty to choose either alternative. I cannot owe a debt to myself. If the moral law binds us, as we know that it does, this can only be because it comes to us from one who can claim the duty of obedience from us. An essential note of morality is lacking unless we recognize that the command is imposed by an external authority, and yield obedience to it as such.
>
> This is not to say that the moral law is arbitrary. We have seen that it is not so: that it is revealed to us by reason as the rule of life involved in our rational nature. It is *natural* law. But only if there be an authority who commands me to observe the natural order, does it acquire the character of *law*.
>
> If, then, we ask who it is who thus commands, there can be but one answer. The moral law, as we have seen, has the note of necessity. The authority who imposes it must then be final. Only when a command issues from the supreme and ultimate authority is it in the strict sense necessary. The lawgiver who commands me is, then, the source and fountain of morality, the supreme arbiter of right and wrong. But He who possesses these attributes is God.[37]

One criticism of the argument is that, whereas it is true that a command requires that there be a commander, there is nothing inherent in commands themselves that imply morality. A command may be issued in a nonmoral context. For example, the order from the drum major to break to the right during the halftime performance by the school band at the homecoming game has no ethical or moral implications. Failing to obey the order might create havoc on the field, but it in itself is not ethically wrong. It could be said that disobeying marching rules, as with moral ones, carries punishment:

---

[37] Joyce, *Natural Theology*, 156–58.

additional after-hours practice sessions, being barred from playing during the next three games, expulsion from the band, and so forth. Nevertheless, there is no moral deliberation and no accompanying decision to do what is right or what is wrong in a failure to comply *simpliciter*.

The moral argument, however, is concerned with commands that do carry moral weight. The point of the proof is that there is a lawgiver for the mandates that people recognize as morally obligatory. It may be objected subsequently that doing the right thing might not owe its rightness to a command. One may commit oneself to a set of principles or policies that are not given under the authority of a commander. If such can be the case, though, then one must question how it can be determined that the policies are actually moral ones; one must ask in what way they came to be. If Vivian is following a set of guidelines that she herself created, then no moral obligation is associated with the action. When she fails to adhere to her diet on Tuesday because of a friend's birthday party—the cake was too tempting to resist—her failure disappoints her and causes her to gain a pound, but, unless it constituted gluttony or broke a promise or violated a specific divine directive, it was not morally wrong. As Joyce notes in the preceding passage, one cannot owe a debt to oneself. To object that one is obligated to oneself to refrain from intentional self-injury, for example, or to avoid committing suicide, is to mischaracterize that to which the debt is owed. These acts are wrong by virtue of a moral law that prohibits them—a law that sits outside the individual who executes any deed of this sort and that issues from authority—not by virtue of a decision of the agent who chooses, whether capriciously or otherwise, to behave in such a manner. That one ought to avoid harming oneself is not an obligation to oneself but a duty under external governance. Contrast this matter with another one. Jackie thinks that she looks better in blue than in brown and believes that she always ought to look her best. Here, it is the 'ought' of means to a desired end—feeling good about herself—that is at work, not the 'ought' of obligation. The same sense of the term is in force when one says, "Charlie ought to leave now if he wants to avoid the rush-hour traffic." What Charlie ought to do has nothing to do with morality. It is the same with Jackie. She selects the brown dress for the class reunion. Her act is neither moral nor immoral.

Consider the drum major example again. The command to break to the right does not convey a moral obligation, but the reason for the disobedience may have much to do with morality. If the noncompliance with the order is the result of inattentiveness or ignorance, then one can be displeased with the band member for not staying alert during the performance or not practicing sufficiently. If, on the other hand, sabotage is intended, then one finds it to be an ethically disturbing event. Strictly speaking, depravity does not lie in executing wrong behavior, or failing to execute right behavior, in the appropriate context; it lies in the corresponding intention, resting on the motive. A man who hands hungry children apples because he thinks that they are bombs has done a good thing for the young ones, but his action is despicable. He wants to hurt others. It is not enough for one just to act in the right manner; the intent with which an agent undertakes an act must be examined. The morality of deliberate conduct cannot be judged apart from the motives that are behind it.

How then does the awareness of doing right or wrong arise in people; from where does it come? An advocate of the moral argument would hold that it is the recognition of obligatory compliance, expressed in the commandments of God, that imparts the sense of rightness and its contrary. If one claims instead that people gain this sense from the laws of the land, then one must ask on what the laws of the land are founded. If they emerge from common, accepted practices of a society, from the thoughts of the men and women who constitute the social order, then the challenge is to account for universality and consistency. Those laws are subject to alteration in many ways. The persons who set forth law-bearing proclamations— whether dictators, assemblies of governing representatives, or adjudicators who issue pronouncements—may effect formal change in an existing law by means of fiat, constitutional process, or interpretation respectively. A law may change informally through the lack of enforcement because its applicability has diminished; it remains a part of the record but is ignored within the society. Finally, the society itself may tumble. Given the inevitable ethical relativism that results from these states of affairs, an explanation of how it is that rules carry the mark of morality is in order. There has to be something to make obligations moral rather than legal, practical, or efficient. Without divinity, without holiness, one is left wanting deeper principles to secure them. When one removes God from consideration, one removes the moral anchor.

Systems of human-based morality have arisen in an effort to address this issue and define some maxim by which one can decide with consistency whether something is right or wrong. I will take a brief look at one of these systems: utilitarianism. This system of ethics originated with the English philosopher Jeremy Bentham (1748–1832). Other utilitarians of note include the theorists John Stuart Mill (1806–1873), Henry Sidgwick (1838–1900), and G. E. Moore (1873–1958). The view holds that the rightness or wrongness of an action is determined by its consequences. The act that brings about the greatest good is the right act; any other, given the circumstances, is wrong. For the theory's founder, the greatest good is to be defined in terms of the overall pleasure or happiness for the greatest number of people, although subsequent utilitarians have included less hedonistic factors. There are two versions of utilitarianism: act and rule. According to the former position, each individual act itself must be assessed in light of its consequences. With regard to the latter position, it is the type of action that must be considered when looking at results.[38]

Such a theory is ripe for attack, and the critics do not miss the opportunity. It is not difficult to conceive of cases that align with utilitarian guidelines but stand squarely against one's sense of moral rightness. Consider act-utilitarianism. Suppose that a man brings kettles of steaming soup to the downtown mission on some winter day, mistakenly believing it to be poisoned. His action maximizes happiness. The recipients enjoy a hot meal, and the man, leaving the scene hurriedly, believes that they soon will be dead, which brings him great delight. All who are involved in the incident are made more content by the man's behavior, although one would be hard-pressed to characterize it as anything but deplorable. Utilitarian doctrine misses the point. Morality is more about *reasons* than it is about *consequences*.

Basing the rightness of actions on their outcome to the exclusion of overarching, independent principles of morality surely

---

[38] Additional information about utilitarianism and the distinction between the two versions is available in *Encyclopedia of Philosophy*, s.v., "Utilitarianism."

produces a logically twisted system of ethics. On June 25, 2010, the Associated Press released a news story stating that British health experts had determined that a human fetus could not experience pain before the age of twenty-four weeks, as the neural pathways had not developed sufficiently to allow for it.[39] So, they concluded, no change in the law, which permitted abortions up to that point in fetal development, was needed. The underlying premise is that it is not ethically wrong to destroy the fetus, given that, in theory, the fetus cannot suffer.

The atheist Richard Dawkins agrees: "The most important moral question in [the] abortion debate is 'Can it feel pain?'"[40] Thus, the determinant of whether a particular action is ethically permissible—the moral watershed—is the suffering of the object of the action. The outcome is what marks the act as one that is morally acceptable or depraved. Although Dawkins is addressing the issue as it pertains to entities in vivo, he cannot disallow the extension of his criterion to individuals in general without putting forth a contrived distinction. The argument may be stated broadly in this way:

> It is not wrong to do something to subject *s* if *s* does not suffer as a result.
> Doing (act) *a* to *s* in the set of circumstances *C* does not cause *s* to suffer.
> Therefore, it is not wrong to do *a* to *s* in *C*.

Such thinking leads to failure by any rational standards. To fill in the picture, suppose that a medical patient seeks help from her physician, only to become a casualty of the practitioner's irregular activity. Seeing an avenue for research, the physician elects to take advantage of it; unfortunately, that election proves to be disastrous. Consider the following argument; I number the steps to facilitate readability:

[39] Assoc. Press, "Fetus Can't Feel Pain before 24 Weeks, Study Says," reported by NBC News, June 25, 2010, accessed November 19, 2013, www.nbcnews.com/id/37920310/ns/health-health_care/t/fetus-cant-feel-pain-weeks-study-says.
[40] Stoyan Zaimov, "Richard Dawkins Claims Unborn Children Are 'Less Human' Than Pigs; Stirs Firestorm," *Christian Post*, March 14, 2013, accessed April 29, 2013, www.christianpost.com/news/richard-dawkins-claims-unborn-children-are-less-human-than-pigs-stirs-firestorm-91911/#.

1. Betsy, an adult with no living relatives, checked into a hospital to have a benign tumor in her brain removed.
2. While she was anaesthetized, her doctor decided to carry out experiments on her, without her foreknowledge, to increase his understanding of neural pathways.
3. Betsy died as a direct result of the experimentation.
4. Betsy did not suffer from the experimentation, for she was anaesthetized during the procedure.
5. Therefore, the doctor's action was not morally wrong.

Perhaps a more telling case is in order. Fred, who has neither family nor friends, is the victim of an intrusion. The following argument, its steps numbered, unfolds:

1. A thief broke into Fred's house at 3:00 a.m.
2. Fred was asleep at the time and not dreaming.
3. Concerned that the homeowner might awaken, the thief shot him twice in the head.
4. Fred never regained consciousness.
5. Fred did not suffer, for he was unconscious when the shooting occurred and remained so until his death.
6. Therefore, the action of the thief was not morally wrong.

The moral character of an act is attributable to its intent—ultimately, to the motive, serving as a value-factor, underlying the intent—not to its outcome. Utilitarianism opens the door for very troubling cases.

It may be objected that, in evaluating rightness, one must consider what reasonable, benevolent people generally would do, not the single acts of the sadistic, reckless, or criminal. It is these general rules that determine right acts. Rule-utilitarianism theory fails too, however. The classic illustration of this fact is the execution of the innocent. To prevent the perishing of many in an uprising, the sheriff of a small, Western town agrees to lynch a prisoner, forgoing the trial, even though he knows that the man is not guilty of a crime. One person dies rather than scores in a fierce gun battle. According to utilitarianism, it was the right thing to do, and it can be adopted as a rule of practice because, in similar circumstances, the right course of action for reasonable people will be to put a rope around the incarcerated man's neck: Sacrificing one person to save many is a proper principle—one that all people should adopt. No, hanging the innocent, regardless of consequences, cannot be universally good.

There are additional difficulties for utilitarianism. One criticism that is leveled against it is that an agent does not know ahead of time, in all likelihood, whether an act will maximize happiness. There is then no way to ascertain whether what one is doing is ethical. There is no moral guide, and one acts blindly. Some have suggested that the right act is the one with the highest *probability* of maximizing happiness. Given this stance, one would not have to know how things turn out in the end, as it were, only know which of the possible courses of action carries with it the best chance of generating the most happiness. This approach strikes me as incredible. Aside from the insurmountable task of generating a workable formula, the tactic reduces morality to mathematics, and, if all people were to try their best to do the right thing, then the most ethical person among the lot would be the one who excels at calculating probabilities.

Further, imagine that, of several possible acts in a set of circumstances, the probability of each one's producing an ideal result is exactly the same. Does one say that such acts are neither right nor wrong, that they are devoid of moral ascription or are morally neutral? If morality does not apply to such acts, then why would it apply to acts that are just like them in other circumstances, where the probabilities shift slightly? How is it that performing a deed today would be wrong, according to the theory, but performing it tomorrow would be neither right nor wrong: One of the persons who would have been saddened by the act passed away during the night? More problematic still, if a second such person had died, then the act suddenly would become right: The happy would outnumber the sad.

Finally, I believe that degrees of happiness must be taken into account. Through a corporate downsizing four months ago, Kerry is out of work and seeking employment. At this juncture, he has interviewed for three positions and sits by the phone daily hoping for a call. Alecayson Industries is a possible employer. Kerry likes the corporate culture but has some concerns about the amount of travel. The compensation plan, however, is attractive. Zaltred Corporation, a firm with a substantial market share, holds promise. Founded by a family friend, the company offers stability, Kerry believes—which interests him considerably following his recent layoff experience—as well as opportunities for promotion. Relocation to the corporate office would be required, though, which disappoints him a bit. At the third company, Perikronon Enterprises, Kerry seems to have found his dream job. The eighty-year-old firm is established, reputable, progressive, and innovative in its solutions for its customer base. The compensation plan is the best of the three, and Kerry would be able to remain in his current location. The program that he would enter as a management candidate at Perikronon all but assures him of rapid advancement. If Kerry is asked to work for any of the three companies, then he will be happy. If Perikronon extends an offer, then he will be ecstatic. Certainly, the level of happiness can vary.

In assessing the outcome of an action to determine whether it happened to be right or wrong, a utilitarian either (1) has to allow only two values to count in the tally—happy, unhappy—as the theorist measures the potential good of the result or (2) has to allow a range of values, perhaps an indeterminate number of them—degrees of happy and unhappy. If the utilitarian takes the former path, then a hundred people who are barely above indifferent in their happiness as a result of an action outweigh ninety-nine who are absolutely miserable as a result. According to the utilitarian, the deed was the right thing to do because more persons were pleased by it than displeased. This verdict is not only counterintuitive but untenable as well. If, on the other hand, the theorist takes the latter path, then, to determine the rightness or wrongness of an act, the theorist must be able to measure the extent to which each affected person is glad or sad as a consequence and then presumably compute the arithmetic mean. Doing so requires a scale. If ecstatic is ten, and miserable is zero, then is fairly happy six and two-fifths, seven and one-third, or eight and seven-ninths? Utilitarianism cannot provide a clear means of distinguishing between levels of pleasure, compounding the trouble in assigning a happiness value to the outcome of actions. Aside from this practical difficulty, the core problem with this approach—and, to a lesser extent, even with the other one—is that happiness is subjective. People change. Jack may be happy on Tuesday as a result of some deed that was performed on Monday and a bit perturbed by it on Wednesday after he thinks more about it.

Jack is not alone. Hundreds of people may be happy on Tuesday and perturbed a day later, some of whom revert on the following day to their original feelings. The very same act then would be both right *and* wrong, or else its ethical character would shift wildly between the two extremes. This verdict too is counterintuitive and untenable.

The moral argument has not found favor with everyone. Still, there remains common to humankind a sense of morality, of right and wrong; and those who do not accept that moral obligations align with the commandments of God are compelled to look for an alternative way to account for rightness and the origin of people's sense of it.[41] Utilitarianism is of no value here. Something is just out of place—not merely in principle but in practice too—if one has to check the consequences of actions to see whether they were right. Morality becomes largely a matter of chance, governed not by adherence to directives that are established by God, or even by societal law, but by the mathematics of probability. Indeed, utilitarianism may not be able even to pronounce the status of an already-performed action as its consequences continue to develop, and all the aftereffects are not yet in view. A putative system of ethics that is not capable of stating whether an act is right or wrong is not a system of ethics at all. In their efforts to explain moral concepts and set forth a structure of right behavior apart from God-instituted principles, philosophers have produced a theory that is sorely deficient in merit.

UNIVERSE BY DESIGN—THE TELEOLOGICAL ARGUMENT

This last proof, and the one on which I will spend much of the remainder of the chapter, is so named because it attempts to demonstrate the existence of God from the notion of purpose. The

---

[41] Some have attempted to explain the human sense of morality in evolutionary terms, tying the development of it, despite its seemingly altruistic character, to some advantage in the battle for survival. I will have enough to say about the theory of evolution later without taking up a criticism of this incredible notion. The discipline of ethics, although not a major philosophical focus in this work, is not to be excluded. Ideas concerning morality, because they are central to an argument that purports to prove that God exists, are pertinent to this section's discussion.

term for the argument is based on a Greek word meaning 'end'. In a sense, it is the mirror image of the cosmological argument. Rather than argue that things are as they are because they are pushed from the rear by some force, the teleological argument holds that things are as they are because they are pulled from the front by some end toward which they move or in accordance with some purpose that shapes their course. In the cosmological argument, one is reminded of the Aristotelian concept of efficient cause, whereas, in the argument here, the Aristotelian notion of final cause comes into play.

A common form of the teleological argument is the argument from design. It purports to show that the universe of human experience points to rational agency that fashioned it and its components intentionally. It is the teleological argument that serves, in large part, as the basis for the controversy in recent times concerning intelligent design. Theorists on each side of the issue put forth some version of the reasoning in support of their decidedly polarized positions. In the current chapter, I will explain how the argument is constructed and note several key objections to it. In chapter 7, I will take up the negative mode of the argument as it is wielded by the atheist Richard Dawkins to see whether his inversion of it carries any weight.

St. Thomas poses a teleological argument in his work *Summa theologiæ*. Considering the guidedness of nature, St. Thomas notes that things that lack awareness—unthinking, material bodies—act toward ends, rather than by accident, in obeying the laws of the natural order. Whatever lacks awareness cannot move toward a goal unless it is directed by something with awareness and intelligence, as an arrow that is moving toward its mark does so only because it was directed by the archer who shot it. It follows that there must be some intelligent being who is directing all natural things to their end. This being is God.

It is the theologian and philosopher William Paley (1743–1805) who provides the more familiar, modern rendition of the teleological argument in his book on natural theology. Paley imagines crossing a heath and, in doing so, strikes a stone with his foot. Asked how the stone came to be there, he perhaps would surmise that it had lain there for eons; it would be hard to prove otherwise. Suppose, though, he says, that he finds a watch. Asked the same question about its history, he would be compelled to believe that the instrument was designed and built for a purpose because its assembly reveals that it is, and indeed has to be, the product of intention.

> [W]hen we come to inspect the watch, we perceive (what we could not discover in the stone) that its several parts are framed and put together for a purpose, e.g. that they are so formed and adjusted as to produce motion, and that motion so regulated as to point out the hour of the day.[42]

Something that is designed must have a designer. One can conclude with surety that there was an intelligence that was responsible for the existence of the watch, for, declares Paley, "[T]he watch must have had a maker."[43]

Paley states that none of the factors that are listed below counts against the fact that the existence of the watchmaker is the only plausible explanation for the existence of the watch:

1. One never has seen a watch made, never has known a watchmaker, and does not know how to build a watch.
2. Sometimes, the watch is inaccurate in its timekeeping.
3. One does not know the function of some of the parts.

Furthermore, asserting any of the following statements would in no way persuade a person that the watch had no designer:

4. The watch is one of the possible combinations of materials.
5. There is a principle of order which had disposed the parts of the watch in their present form.
6. The mechanism of the watch is no proof of contrivance.
7. The watch is simply the result of the laws of nature pertaining to metals.
8. One knows nothing at all about the matter of the watch.

---

[42] William Paley, *Natural Theology: or, Evidences of the Existence and Attributes of the Deity, Collected from the Appearances of Nature* (1802; repr., Boston: Lincoln and Edmands, 1829), 5.
[43] Ibid., 6.

The human eye, in all its intricacy, continues Paley, must owe its existence to a designing agent, just as the watch owes its existence to one. Like a telescope that focuses light rays by means of lenses, the eye is an instrument that focuses light on the membrane within it (the retina) to create visual images. Paley goes on to describe the skull structures that support and protect the eye, the brow that prevents perspiration from invading it, and the eyelid and tear secretions that clean it and keep it moist, all of which point to intelligent design by the Creator. One can conclude on this basis that God exists.

The proof unfolds as an argument from analogy. Such arguments take a particular approach. Two things are similar, in that they have some property or properties in common. One of those things has a further property or stands in a certain relationship to something else. Therefore, it is probable that the other one also has that further property or stands in that same sort of relationship to another thing. This argumentation method surfaces in philosophical writings at times in an attempt to prove the existence of minds other than one's own, offering perhaps a way to escape the clutches of solipsism—in its milder rendering. I know that my body behaves in a certain way because, so a person reasons, I am a being with a mind. I notice that other bodies, which resemble my own body, behave in a fashion similar to the way in which I behave. Hence, those other bodies must be behaving as they do because they belong to beings with minds.

In Paley's use of the argument, he claims that a manufactured device, the timepiece, is like a human eye in the display of functional intricacies. Both exhibit a certain order of operation. The contrivance reflects purpose; it is the way that it is by design. The eye also must be the product of design because, like its time-keeping counterpart, it reflects purpose in its arrangement and function. Often, the argument from design is expanded to include the world or the universe, where the argument points to the ordered character of nature as a whole. Such order, according to the proponents, can be only the product of intelligent agency.

One might represent the argument from analogy in the way that is shown below if one is drawing it based on the exhibition of some set of properties: one or more. In this diagram, and in the similar ones that follow, solid lines indicate observed similarities or known relationships. Lines showing a pattern of dashes indicate inferences.

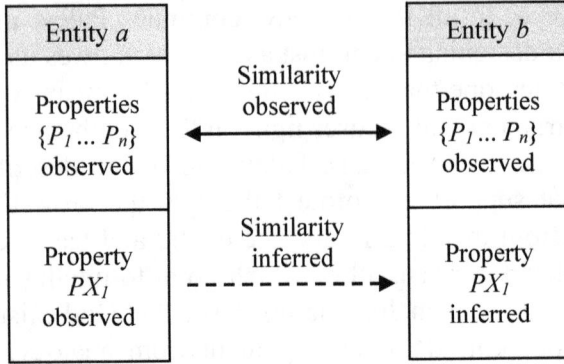

Figure 6.5

Where the analogy is based on a relationship, one may represent it in this way:

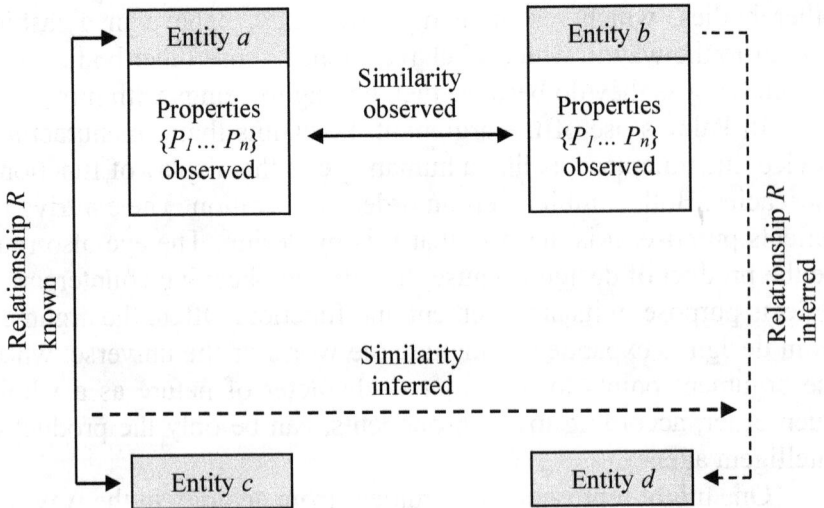

Figure 6.6

When the argument from design is used to support the view that there is a God who caused the universe to be, and to be as it is—namely, possessing functional order, a condition that is indicative of purpose—the argument is represented more appropriately by combining the two diagrams that appear above to yield this pattern:

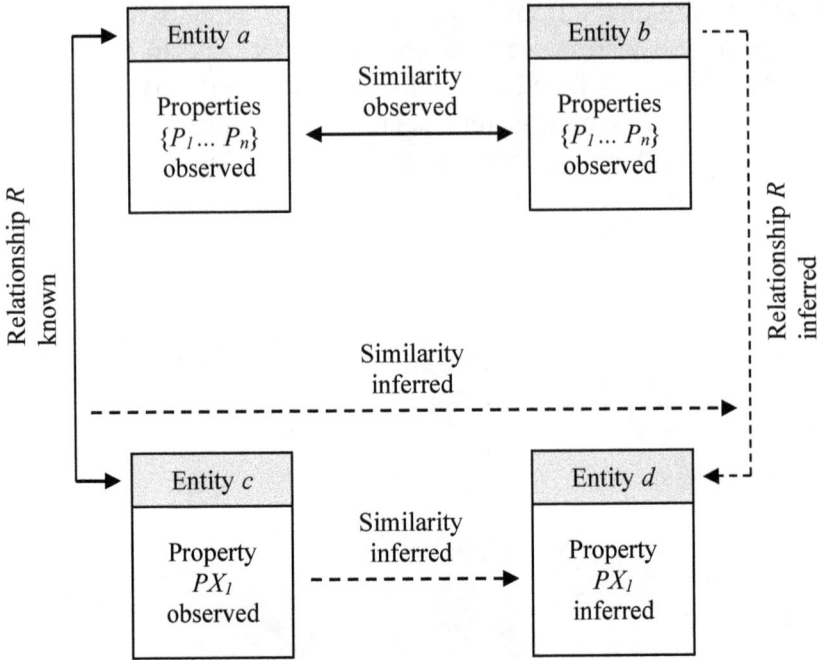

where

    a = machine
    b = nature—either a thing that exhibits functional order,
        such as an eye, or the functionally ordered universe
        as a whole
    c = human
    d = God
    P_1 = functional order
    PX_1 = intelligence
    R = the relationship of effect to cause—specifically,
        designed-produced to designer-producer

Figure 6.7

With regard to a machine, it is clear that it was designed and constructed purposely because it exhibits an order that bespeaks intentional function, its parts operating toward a particular end. Likewise, biological features, and indeed the cosmos as a whole, exhibit functional order. It follows that they too, one must think, were designed and constructed purposely. In the case of the machine, the designer, manifesting intelligence, is human—and is observed to be such. In the case of eyes and the cosmos, it is God.

DAVID HUME'S OBJECTIONS IN THE DIALOGUES

In his *Dialogues concerning Natural Religion*, David Hume advances a series of criticisms of the argument from design. His philosophy in the work is developed as a discussion among three individuals: Cleanthes, who represents the theistic position that nature exhibits design, which proves that God exists; Philo, his skeptical opponent; and Demea, who plays the role of catalyst, more or less—believing in God but rejecting design as an acceptable basis for such a belief, turning instead to a form of the cosmological argument. The text is created in the style of a letter in which another character, Pamphilus, writing to Hermippus, recounts the conversation. Hume's writings precede Paley's work on natural theology by a number of years, but the reasoning that Paley advances represents well the position against which Hume takes a stand.

It is likely that Philo voices most closely the stance of Hume, but the philosopher masterfully weaves the discussion in his *Dialogues* into a general challenge to theism, using each of the characters to convey his ideas. Early in the work, Hume sets forth the notion that one is not justified in drawing conclusions about the origin of the whole based on the operations of the parts. One thus cannot infer that the universe is the handiwork of an intelligent agent by using the thinking human as a model. The declaration misses the point, as Hume surely sees. Although it is illogical to argue from the possession of a property by a thing's parts to the possession of it by the whole (cf. the description of the fallacy of composition—given in chapter 3), the argument from design does not proceed in this way. If active design is necessary for the operation of even a single part, then a designer must exist. The character Cleanthes, in fact, presents the example of the eye; it is a part of a whole, but its structure and workings point to an intelligent source. If the eye is actually the product of design, then there has to be a designer who conceived the plan. Such reasoning does not prove that the source is God, although it lends weight to that position, but the origin-of-the-whole tactic in itself is largely ineffective against the case for a teleological account.

The most important of Hume's objections attempts to extend the analogy on which the argument from design rests, seeking to undermine the argument's conclusion by drawing additional similarities. I will concentrate on this line of reasoning in my analysis. A subsequent objection follows a like pattern but with a different focus, and a third attacks the reputed resemblance between the noted effects. An examination of these two counterarguments is beneficial, and I will review them as well. Although Hume raises other points, these three cases constitute a principal facet of his thinking. His primary goal is not to show directly that God is nonexistent but to discredit the design argument. To grasp the full import of the obstacles that Hume introduces, one must place them in the context of his broader philosophy—his view of the serial character of the mind in particular. It is critical that one take care not to overlook this detail.

FIRST CONSIDERED OBJECTION

Laying the foundation for his overall attack on the argument from design, Hume presents what he sees as a core concept of it.

> Throw several pieces of steel together, without shape or form; they will never arrange themselves so as to compose a watch: Stone, and mortar, and wood, without an architect, never erect a house. But the ideas in a human mind . . . arrange themselves so as to form the plan of a watch or house. Experience, therefore, proves, that there is an original *principle of order* in mind, not in matter.[44]

The central question to ask here at the outset, with respect to the first objection that I will examine, is this one: What exactly does Hume

---

[44] Hume, *Dialogues*, 395. The emphasis is mine.

mean by 'order'? That this question is pivotal will become apparent as the analysis proceeds.

Hume turns to the alleged similarity between the mind of a human and the mind of God. According to the argument from design, both possess the property of intelligence. Hume subtly posits that, if one accepts that similarity, then one must look at other properties that are common to the two. He directs his attention first to the human mind. In keeping with his theory of the self in the *Treatise*, as discussed in chapter 5, Hume believes that the mind consists of distinct elements that are ever-changing, appearing in succession. In fact, the mind *is* the elements that compose it, nothing more. Its order is given in the arrangement of those elements, and that arrangement is transient concatenation. Hume reaffirms this concept of the mind—what he refers to in the passage that I provide below as the soul of man—through the character Demea.

> Our thought is fluctuating, uncertain, fleeting, successive, and compounded; and were we to remove these circumstances, we absolutely annihilate its essence. . . .
>
> . . . [C]onsider what it is you assert, when you represent the Deity as similar to a human mind and understanding. What is the soul of man? A composition of various faculties, passions, sentiments, ideas; united, indeed, into one self or person, but still distinct from each other. When it reasons, the ideas, which are the parts of its discourse, arrange themselves in a certain form or *order; which is not preserved entire for a moment, but immediately gives place to another arrangement.*[45]

Hume widens his contention, stating that, if one is going to claim that the mind of God—the intelligent Designer of the world—is similar to that of the human—the intelligent designer of artifacts—then one must accept too that God's mind resembles the human mind in being characterized by discrete mental elements that surge and ebb in an ongoing, perceptual string. The philosopher maintains that God's

---

[45] Ibid., 405–6. The emphasis is mine.

mind indeed could not be fixed in a single state of perfect uniformity and immutability. The declaration to that effect, in this case, comes through the character Cleanthes.

> For though it be allowed, that the Deity possesses attributes, of which we have no comprehension; yet ought we never to ascribe to him any attributes, which are absolutely incompatible with that intelligent nature, essential to him. A mind, whose acts and sentiments and ideas are not *distinct and successive*; one, that is wholly simple, and totally immutable; is a mind, which has no thought, no reason, no will, no sentiment, no love, no hatred; or in a word, is no mind at all.[46]

For Hume, the conscious human mind is characterized by elements that appear in a serial fashion. The mind of God therefore must be ordered—in the same way. Is succession then the essence of mental order? At this point in Hume's overall contestation, at least, it seems to be the case, but his application of the concept already is showing signs of vagueness.

Hume moves now from, with reference to Figure 6.7, a horizontal property resemblance (mental to mental, material to material) to a vertical one, applying order to both the mental and the material. It is a critical shift in the reasoning. Hume asserts that causality cannot characterize the former realm any less than the latter one; moreover, if the two are alike, in that they are ordered in a similar manner, then that likeness must result from like causes.

> [A] mental world, or universe of ideas, requires a cause as much, as does a material world, or universe of objects; and *if similar in its arrangement must require a similar cause*. For what is there in this subject, which should occasion a different conclusion or inference? In an abstract view, *they are entirely alike*; and no difficulty attends the one supposition, which is not common to both of them.
>
> Again, . . . neither can . . . [experience] perceive *any material difference in this particular, between these*

---

[46] Ibid., 407. The emphasis is mine.

two kinds of worlds, but finds them to be governed by similar principles.[47]

Essentially, what Hume is arguing is that the psychological and the physical are under the rule of parallel principles; and, given that both are caused, if they are similar in order—and presumably thereby similar in being ordered—then their causes must be similar.

Turning to causes of ordered entities, Hume poses what is, in effect, a dilemma. He claims that, with respect to arrangement, one has no reason to treat the mind of God differently from the way in which one treats the world. Any ordered thing is produced by either (1) something that is outside it or (2) itself. If one accepts the first condition, then, in the case of the world, it may be said that the cause of it is God, on the assumption that God indeed designed it; yet, what caused the ordered mind of God? It is necessary to trace God's mind to another intelligence, for there must be a cause that is outside God—a further designing mind—that brings about the ordered mind of God. Such a requirement is no less definite, thinks Hume, than that God, as an external cause, is needed to bring about an ordered world. A designing agent is necessary to generate the second mind for the same reason, however, and that mind likewise requires a designing agent, and so forth. The result is an infinite regress, which is unacceptable. On the other hand, if one accepts the second condition and says that the cause of the ordered mind of God lies within God's mind itself, then why not make the same claim for the world?

> How therefore shall we satisfy ourselves concerning the cause of that Being, whom you suppose the Author of Nature, . . . the ideal [i.e., mental] world, into which you trace the material? Have we not the same reason to trace that ideal world into another ideal world, or new intelligent principle? But if we stop, and go no farther; why go so far? Why not stop at the material world? How can we satisfy ourselves without going on *in infinitum*? And after all, what satisfaction is there in that infinite progression? . . . If the material world rests

---

[47] Ibid., 407–8. The emphases are mine.

upon a similar ideal world, this ideal world must rest upon some other; and so on, without end. It were better, therefore, never to look beyond the present material world. By supposing it to contain the principle of its order within itself, we really assert it to be God.

To say, that the different ideas, which compose the reason of the Supreme Being, fall into order, of themselves, and by their own nature, is really to talk without any precise meaning. If it has a meaning, I would fain know, why it is not as good sense to say, that the parts of the material world fall into order, of themselves, and by their own nature.[48]

Concluding that a self-arranging system of ideas is not any more reasonable than a self-arranging system of matter, Hume summarizes his thoughts in the following passage:

An ideal [i.e., mental] system, arranged of itself, without a precedent design, is not a whit more explicable than a material one, which attains its order in a like manner; nor is there any more difficulty in the latter supposition than in the former.[49]

Hume asserts that, if one puts forth a proof of the existence of God, basing it on design, then one should be prepared to accept the notion that the cause of the mind of the Deity is like the cause of nature on the premise that both God's mind and nature reflect order. I can capture the thinking by modifying the general structure that I provided in Figure 6.7; see page 624. The bold, dotted lines that are shown in Figure 6.8 represent Hume's extension; four of those lines depict relations of similarity that Hume is advancing. Entities and properties remain solid-line boxes. Expanded entity details in this diagram, and in the two that come afterward, help to clarify relevant concepts. Refer to Figure 6.7 for the legend and labels, which are not repeated here.

---

[48] Ibid., 408–9.
[49] Ibid., 411.

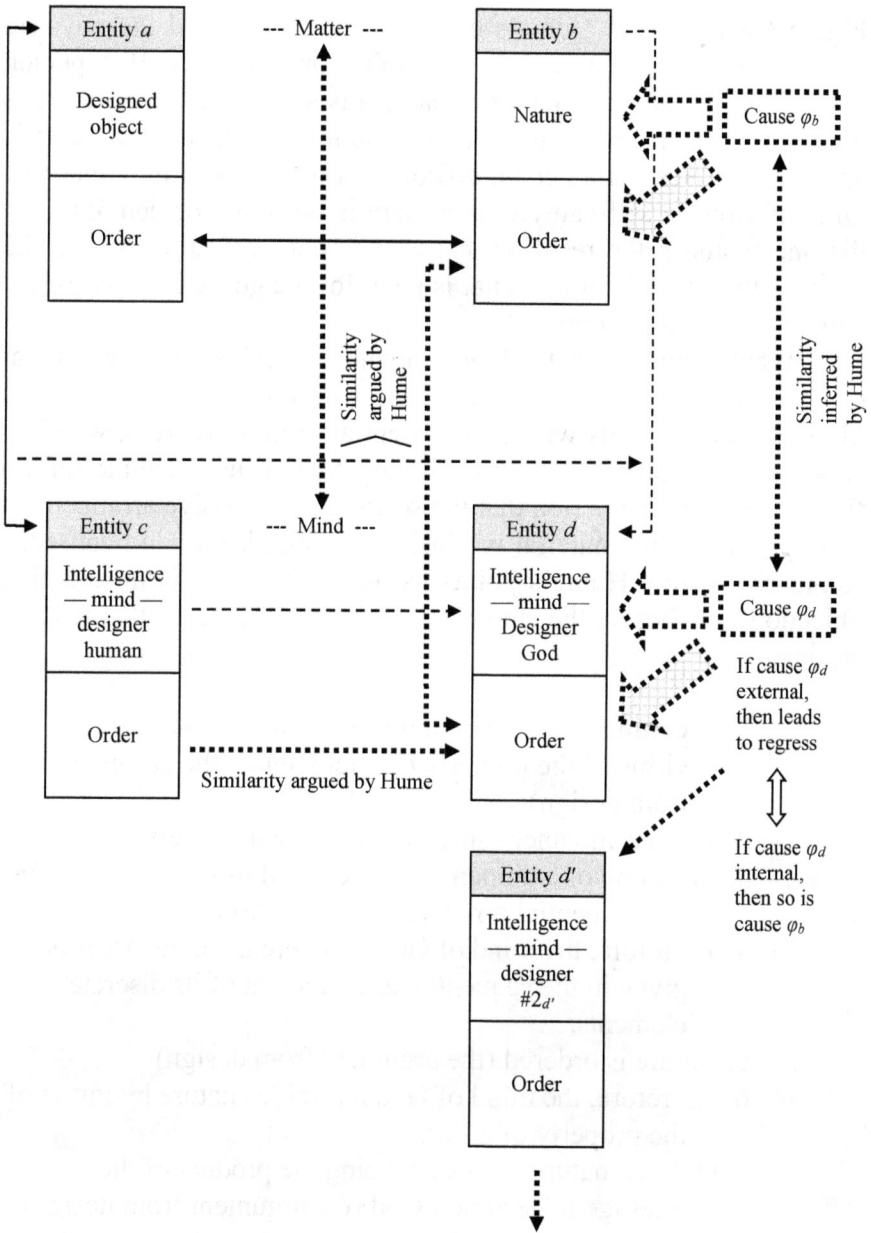

Figure 6.8

Figure 6.8 illustrates Hume's case that the mental and the physical must track together in whichever option one chooses. If a person denies that the order of the one (nature) is self-caused, then there is no basis for affirming it in the other (the mind of God); the result is an infinite regress. If a person affirms that the order of the other (the mind of God) is self-caused, then there is no basis for denying it in the one (nature); the result is that God is not needed to explain the order of the natural world. What is good for the goose is good for the gander, or so Hume thinks.

What Hume hopes to show ultimately with his argument is that one cannot use the ordered state of the world to prove the existence of God. Unless one is willing to accept an infinite regress, which is an indefensible position in which to land, there is no reason to refrain from embracing the notion that the seemingly purposive arrangement that appears in the material world is self-caused, not God-caused. I summarize below Hume's points as they unfold in his meandering objection; numbering the steps facilitates the reading of this lengthy argument:

1. The mind of God resembles the mind of a human by virtue of the property of intelligence (the argument from design).
2. The resemblance must extend to other properties.
3. The mind of a human is ordered, and its order is given in the sequential arrangement of its discrete elements.
4. Therefore, the mind of God is ordered, and its order is given in the sequential arrangement of its discrete elements.
5. Nature is ordered (the argument from design).
6. Therefore, the mind of God resembles nature by virtue of the property of order.
7. Ordered nature is caused, being the product of the intelligent Designer, God (the argument from design).
8. The mental requires a cause no less than the physical.
9. Therefore, the ordered mind of God is caused.
10. The cause of a thing is either external to it or not external to it.

11. If the cause of the ordered mind of God is external to God's mind, then the cause lies in another mind; but, like the cause of God's mind, there must be a cause of that (ordered) mind that is also external to it, and so forth, which leads to an infinite regress.
12. An infinite regress is not defensible.
13. Therefore, the cause of the ordered mind of God is not external to itself.
14. The mental and the physical are similar by virtue of their being ordered and so must have similar causes, their being governed by similar principles.
15. Therefore, the cause of the ordered mind of God must resemble the cause of ordered nature.
16. Therefore, the cause of ordered nature is not external to itself.
17. Therefore, God is not needed to explain ordered nature, as nature is self-ordered.
18. Therefore, the argument from design fails, and the existence of God is not proved.

There are significant problems with Hume's argument. First of all, if Hume relies on the application of the term 'order' to the mind by pointing to the succession of thoughts as they arise, in accordance with his theory of the self, then his vertical property-resemblance relation fails because of irrelevance. Nature does exhibit a temporal arrangement, like Hume's depiction of the mind, but a temporal arrangement is not what is needed. There is a glaring distinction between the order that a sequence of things exhibits and a thing's being ordered in the functional sense. Consider a watch. Take the parts of the device prior to assembly, throw them in a paper bag, shake it several times, and dump the collection on the table. Clearly, there is a chronological order here: The first to fall from the bag is the winding knob; then the primary gear rolls out of the bag; the spring comes next, followed by the crystal and the hour hand; and so forth. Furthermore, there is a spatial order: After the dumping, the winding knob lies just to the left of the primary gear; the spring is three inches directly to the right of the crystal; the hour hand is a foot below it; and so forth. Regardless of the sequence in which the pieces exit the bag and where they land on the table, there will be an order: a particular temporal and spatial organization. There is no watch, however, no operational machine, because such order alone is not sufficient. What matters is the shape of the parts, their placement relative to each other, and their being in their proper positions at the proper time. It is *this* sort of order that yields a functioning system, and it is *this* sort of order to which the argument from design refers in pointing to machines and nature, *not* sequential occurrence. The order that a functioning system exhibits is beyond that of a simple temporal chain, even though whatever processes it performs must occur in some sequence. It is the cooperative workings of the parts in achieving a common end that distinguishes a pattern that is associated with design from a mere serial happening.

A further difficulty arises for Hume over his vertical twisting of resemblance. Hume posits that the wellsprings of mental things and physical things ought to rise and fall together. If Hume is going to argue—focusing on God and nature—that the cause of an ordered mind must be like the cause of ordered matter, then he must embrace the consequences of his own reasoning. Given his goose-gander principle, one must hold either that (1) neither the human mind nor the watch is self-ordered or that (2) both of them are self-ordered. On Hume's premise that the ideas of the human mind arrange themselves, it seems that the human mind is self-ordered—a concept that dovetails with his corresponding conjecture about matter. Therefore, by Hume's own principle, the various parts of the watch must have assembled themselves to generate a functioning device, which is ludicrous.

If Hume intends the concept of a self-ordered system to single out one in which the whole orders the things within it, as opposed to one in which the parts of the whole order themselves—that is to say, the human mind orders the ideas in it; the ideas do not order themselves—then he is in no better position. By such an application of the principle at hand, the watch assembled its own parts to construct itself, which is as ludicrous as its counterpart. For the watch to have assembled its parts to build itself, it would have had to have existed before it existed, which is an illogical stance.

Plainly, it cannot be that the mindless forces of the material universe assembled the watch. Such assembly would be tantamount to the instrument's arising—alloy gears, steel spring, polished face, jeweled case, and all—by the chance construction of its components and the subsequent chance joining of those components to form the operating piece of equipment, which is an untenable view by anyone's standards.

Whether the wheels and levers of the watch connected themselves, thereby forming a functioning, time-keeping apparatus; or the already-existing watch brought itself into existence by assembling its own parts; or the universe as a whole did it, the consequence is the same. Hume draws a parallel between the cause of God's mind and the cause of nature in an attempt to show that it is no more reasonable to assert that God's mind is self-caused than it is to assert that the world is self-caused. Hume's doing so, however, compels him to draw the same parallel between the cause of the human mind and the cause of artifacts, and the result is absurdity.

In continuing his assault on the argument from design, Hume takes an interesting turn, denying that order is an essential property of either mind or matter. He does so in an effort to underscore his premise that the psychological and the physical must track together.

> We have also experience of particular systems of thought and of matter, which have no order; of the first, in madness; of the second, in corruption. Why then should we think, that order is more essential to one than the other?[50]

Surely, though, even a mind that is mad has thoughts, if it is conscious, at least, and those thoughts come in a series, appearing in the form of a continual progression. If therefore it is possible for a mind to have no order, as Hume declares, then 'order' cannot mean 'sequence' after all. So, what is its distinguishing mark? What is it for a mind to be ordered? Can this shift to a different sense of the term rescue the philosopher?

Hume asserts that, when the mind *reasons*, the ideas array themselves in a certain *order*—see the pertinent quotation, earlier in this section. Given that, in the end, order, as Hume employs the concept of it with respect to the mental, is at odds with a simple

---

[50] Ibid., 409.

consecutive pattern, one must ask if it is, in his view, the rational thinking of the sound minded. Is it the coherent pondering of the lucid, presumably "consisting of distinct ideas, differently arranged; in the same manner as an architect forms in his head the plan of a house"—drawing on a passage in Hume's text?[51] Maybe it is so, but, if an ordered mind is the same as a rational mind, then Hume's objection, based on vertical property resemblance, still fails: It is not possible for the material world to be ordered in a comparable way— only minds can reason; only minds can be rational. It is nonsensical to ascribe rationality to the physical objects in the cosmos, whether sticks or stars. Hume cannot erect his intended cross-category bridge, and his madness-corruption division only highlights the problem.

It is evident that one never could base the premise that mind and matter must be alike, and the respective causes themselves of that alikeness must be alike, on some overarching principle of dual ascription of attributes. More to the point, merely because one can ascribe properties, which are identified by the same term, to both mental and physical entities, it does not follow that the properties, which are denoted by that term, are the same properties. In many cases, attempting to set forth such a duality creates nonsense, for the similarity must be more than linguistic; it must be real.

Consider first, in keeping with the general flow of Hume's approach, the ascription of a mental attribute.

> Jonathan is happy today because he learned that his
> measured intelligence is high—his IQ is 152.

The statement may be true, but applying the same attribute to a physical object is illogical. The sentence appearing below is neither true nor false; it is meaningless:

> This metal rod is happy today because it learned that its
> measured intelligence is high—its IQ is 152.

Consider now physical qualities. Assume that Rusty is holding a solid rod of pure nickel; the following proposition is true:

---

[51] Ibid., 407.

The specific gravity of the rod that Rusty is holding is 8.9.[52]

This assertion also may be true:

The bowling ball in Jerry's hand weighs sixteen pounds.

If one attributes a quality of physical things to a nonphysical thing, however, then one says something that is neither true nor false. Instead, it is entirely devoid of meaning. The following sentence exemplifies the senselessness:

The specific gravity of the set of natural numbers is 8.9.

Again, attributing a quality of physical things to a mental element as such, as in this sentence, is irrational:

Jerry's memory weighs sixteen pounds.

In both cases, one has produced nonsense.

It is thus clearly illogical to accept as meaningful the attribution of properties universally across the mental-physical split, where one speaks of mental things qua mental and physical things qua physical. Is it possible to accept, though, that at least some properties apply to both the mind and the body; and, if so, then can order, or being in an ordered condition, be among them? Is it true that an ordered mind is like an ordered world—or an ordered component thereof?

On the surface, it seems that there may be a few qualities, or perhaps even relations, that could find expression in both categories. Robert's mind is brilliant, as is the sun. William's temper is short; so is the right sleeve on his coat. Both Justin's perspective and his driveway are broad. Martha's mind is open, and the door to her porch is open too. The adjectival terms that appear in these sentences apply grammatically to both mental objects and physical ones, but it is

---

[52] Specific gravity is a measure of density, reflecting the ratio of the mass of a given volume of a substance to the mass of an equal volume of a standard material. In the case of liquids and solids, the standard material is usually water at its densest point: 3.98° Celsius. As a rule, 4° is used for measuring. By ascribing a determinate specific gravity to a material, one utters a statement that is either true or false.

obvious that the meanings of the respective terms vary, depending on that to which they refer. Although there is a single linguistic modifier in each instance, it points to decidedly different characteristics. A brilliant mind possesses extraordinary capacities for learning, understanding, reasoning, and insight. A material thing is brilliant in the case where it emits electromagnetic radiation within a certain frequency range with a certain intensity; and such a measure applied to a mind is illogical. A short temper is one that surfaces with little provocation. A short sleeve is one that does not extend to the wrist; and a temper cannot be short in this way. A broad perspective is a viewpoint that is characterized by its encompassing many factors. A broad driveway is one that spans a greater-than-typical distance across the dimension that is perpendicular to the intended path of travel; and applying this description to someone's outlook generates nonsense. An open mind is one that is receptive to new ideas or to the suggestions of others. An open door is one that permits passage or is ajar; and ascribing such a state to a mind is irrational. When one fails to distinguish between two senses of a term, or among more than two, and employs those senses in an argument that relies on them, the fallacy of equivocation results. This flaw is a specific form of the fallacy of ambiguity. Equivocation occurs in any argument where the meaning of a term changes, either between two premises or between one or more premises and the conclusion. It also can surface within a proposition, be it premise or conclusion, if the term appears more than once in that proposition with a deviation in meaning. To see at a basic level how equivocation creates a logical error, consider the trivial construction that follows:

> Katie missed her father when he left for work.
> To miss something is to shoot at it but fail to hit it.
> Therefore, Katie shot at her father when he left for work but failed to hit him.

The term 'miss' is used in two different senses, of course. The first one is that of a feeling of longing for something that is familiar to a person; in this case, it is the fellowship of a parent. The second is that of poor marksmanship. The argument plainly does not establish its conclusion, for the variation in denotation undermines the reasoning.

As I noted earlier, such missteps constitute informal, or material, fallacies: Their erroneousness does not stem from an argument's structure.

Albeit with a trace of subtlety, Hume commits this same error. How can the terms 'order' and 'ordered' be applied to a mind in any way that is even remotely like the way in which the argument from design applies them to physical things? Nevertheless, this illicit parallel is precisely what Hume draws in his objection, and it topples his argument as a consequence. A physical system of the sort that is under consideration—a watch or an eye, for instance—is ordered by virtue of synergism. It is ordered because the various material parts that compose it interact collaboratively and thereby perform an identifiable operation as a unified whole, which the parts, taken individually, cannot perform, although the parts, at least certain ones, are necessary for the whole to execute the operation. The parts carry out specific activities that are explicable only if they are viewed in terms of a holistic collective—a concept that I introduced earlier in this work. What is required for an operational material system to be ordered in this sense is a given spatiotemporal arrangement of particular constituents. It is this organized array that underlies the methodical action of the compound, where the action of the compound bespeaks purpose or, at minimum, mindful utility. For the whole to achieve an end that the components cannot achieve on their own, those pieces must be configured in a precisely defined manner: Their arrangement is by design.

If a mind is ordered at all, then it cannot be ordered as a constructed device or a system of nature is ordered. Gears and levers in themselves do not mark time, only when they are engineered with a given intention, assembled according to an exact pattern, and supplied with stored energy in the form of a wound spring, battery, or other power source. Likewise, photosensitive cells cannot produce vision in humans unless they are arrayed across retinal tissue in the eye, held in place within the structure, and connected to appropriate neural pathways. No one could assign any meaning to a proposition that asserts that a mind, like a thing of matter, is ordered by virtue of heterogeneous, juxtaposed, tangible parts, working in an integrated fashion, performing something that is possible only in a cooperative context. Minds as such are not material; they as such are not

extended in space. Hume's parts thereof, the elements of consciousness (in themselves, legitimate phenomena), are no more material
than the minds qua mental entities to which they correspond, and
analyzing them in terms of functional arrangement, as if they made
up physical devices or the parts of them, creates nonsense. Neither
minds nor mental items are mosaics, built by arranging collections of
constituents just so. An architect's plan for a house is not a group of
idea-pieces, sweeping across some screen of consciousness in the
"most rapid succession imaginable" yet captured somehow and put
together to form a well-ordered whole idea.[53] The notion is senseless.

When Frieda is looking for her car in the airport parking lot,
her thoughts are of the car, but she is not assembling the concept of
the vehicle in her mind by thinking of the pistons, the fuel pump, the
camshaft, the rocker arms, the timing belt, the transmission, the
wheels, the brake pads, the bearings, the constant-velocity joints, and
a host of other parts. She is thinking of her automobile as a whole
and wondering where she parked. The car requires a fuel pump to
run, but Frieda's idea of a car does not require her to have an idea of
a fuel pump; she does not know that her car even has such a thing.

In the physical world, there are physical objects. If a composite
object in the world is ordered in the functional sense, whether it is a
machine or a natural system, then it has that property because its
components stand in a certain spatiotemporal relation to each other—
and those components typically have components that do the same: a
car engine, for example. Then, carrying out their particular activities, the parts converge on a common end. If one agrees with Hume
that the mind has component, mental elements, then, to be ordered,
were the term 'ordered' to have the same meaning in the two cases,
one would expect the idea itself of a thing to be a composite, the
parts of which cooperate to yield the whole idea. To say that the
things of the psyche are amalgams of spliced-together mental bits is
to express something that has no meaning. A fortiori, to say that the
juxtaposed parts of ideas, à la the juxtaposed parts of machines, work
together, producing complete ideas, is to utter nonsense. A mechanic
can disassemble Frieda's automobile and lay the parts about the shop
floor. Those parts, at least most of them, are necessary for the car to

---

[53] The quoted phrase appears in Hume, *Dialogues*, 406.

be a car, and it will not operate in that role until the mechanic puts the parts together again in a specific way. No one can disassemble Frieda's idea of an automobile, however, and lay the parts anywhere at all. Frieda's notion of a car does not depend on there being ideas of the parts of the car, much less there being parts of the idea of the car. Her notion is not a compiled complex of pieces, whether immaterial or material. Both Frieda's mind and her thoughts are quite unlike her vehicle. If a mental thing as such is ordered, then it *cannot* be ordered in the same way that a physical thing is ordered, in the mode that the argument from design sets forth.

An illustration from mathematics may be helpful. I will use as an example the set S of integers between 1 and 50 inclusive, where each integer appears uniquely in the set. Let R stand for the binary relation less-than.[54] First, a relation has the property of irreflexivity where, for any element x of a set, it is not the case that the relation holds between x and x. The relation R is irreflexive because no number in the set S is less than itself. Second, a relation exhibits asymmetry where, for any two elements x and y of a set, if the relation holds between x and y, then it does not hold between y and x. R is asymmetric: With respect to the set S, if one number in S is less than another, then the converse is not true. Third, a relation has the property of transitivity where, for any elements x, y, and z of a set, if the relationship holds between x and y, and it holds between y and z, then it holds between x and z. The relation R is transitive because, if one number in S is less than a second number, and the second number is less than a third, then the first is less than the third. Given these three properties of the relation R, R is a strict order on S. This order is not attributable to the collaborative workings of various material parts. Its comes about through the properties of a relation on a set, and it bears no resemblance to the order of a corporeal thing.[55]

In summary, the argument from design points to specific arrangements of physical things, aligning with systemic functions. The argument contends that those functions, in turn, point to a particular mental property that accounts for them: intelligence. Hume's

---

[54] A binary relation is one that holds between two things.

[55] For information on strict order, one may refer to Alex Sakharov, "Strict Order," MathWorld—a Wolfram web resource, created by Eric W. Weisstein, accessed April 24, 2013, www.mathworld.wolfram.com/StrictOrder.html.

objection to the argument fails predominantly because it attempts erroneously to attribute a given property to entities in disparate categories by applying a single expression to both groups. Whenever a certain term is used to describe two things, it does not follow that what the term denotes in the respective cases is identical, especially if the objects of attribution belong to different realms. Whereas there is nothing to prohibit the application of a predicative locution to an entity comprising ontologically distinct parts—the human agential system, for example—using the locution with regard to the ontologically distinct parts themselves, or to other such things, in the same sense by adopting Hume's pattern is illogical. Whatever the adjectival expression 'ordered' might mean as it pertains to mind—if it means anything at all—the meaning cannot be the one that applies to matter, whether machines or the things of nature. The only way in which it could so apply is in the sense of temporal progression, but that meaning is not the one that the argument from design employs, nor ultimately is it one to which even Hume himself holds fast. The properties to which Hume refers in using the expression unquestionably stand apart. His argument is guilty of equivocation.

If, in all instances, terms could extend across categories, which differ at a fundamental level, and still retain their meanings, then Plato's third-man argument in the *Parmenides* could launch the regress that he introduces in an effort to confront his own theory. In that argument, the philosopher attributes largeness to an immaterial form just as he attributes it to material things; surely, though, they cannot be large in the same sense, if Plato's form can be large in any sense whatsoever.[56] Like the ancient Greek philosopher's argument, Hume's regress never gets off the ground, and for the very reason that Plato's regress stumbles, albeit the two vary in constructional respects. This point is important because the evolutionist and atheist Richard Dawkins makes this exact mistake, in a more blatant way, in his attack on theism. Unlike Hume, who attempts to show that the argument from design cannot make its case for the existence of God, Dawkins takes the assault a step further, endeavoring to show that God almost certainly does not exist. I will examine the fallacy more closely when I take up Dawkins's argument in the next chapter.

---

[56] See the discussion of the third-man argument in chap. 2.

SECOND CONSIDERED OBJECTION

The next objection in the *Dialogues* that I will consider also relies on an expansion of the argument from design. Hume begins by taking note of a portion of the underlying reasoning, which is that a similarity between effects points to a similarity between their causes.

> [T]ake a new survey of your principles. *Like effects prove like causes.* . . . Now it is certain, that the liker the effects are, which are seen, and the liker the causes, which are inferred, the stronger the argument. Every departure on either side diminishes the probability.[57]

From this position of effect-effect likeness and cause-cause likeness, Hume proceeds, as before, to turn the resemblance of properties to the vertical plane. He asserts, "[T]he cause ought only to be proportioned to the effect."[58] This assertion, however, does not follow from the concepts that are expressed in the argument that Hume is criticizing. It is Hume's conjecture. Drawing on this conjecture, Hume contends that it is unreasonable to ascribe the attributes of infinity and perfection to the cause of the world, given what is observed in nature.[59] The universe, as far as one can tell, insists Hume, is neither infinite nor perfect. Refer to Figure 6.9. See Figure 6.7 for relevant tags; variance from that basic structure reflects the shift in Hume's line of attack here, which includes his conjectured, general cause-effect relational principle. The bold, dotted lines show Hume's application of the principle to specific properties.

---

[57] Hume, *Dialogues*, 411.

[58] Ibid., 412.

[59] Hume also argues that ascribing unity to the cause of the world, using observation to support the ascription, is unfounded. Even if intelligent agency is the cause, Hume says, there is no reason to believe that the world is the result of a single agent's work rather than that of a group. The argument is similar to the one under examination, in that it attempts to cast doubt on an aspect of the cause, but differs in two ways. First, the objection is not based on the observation that the effect lacks the attribute of unity but is based instead on a sister premise that there is nothing in the effect to give a reason to believe that the cause has that attribute. Second, any casting of doubt does not rest on Hume's postulate concerning proportionate causes. In my analysis in this section, I will focus on the argument that incorporates this postulate, but both arguments face a similar problem.

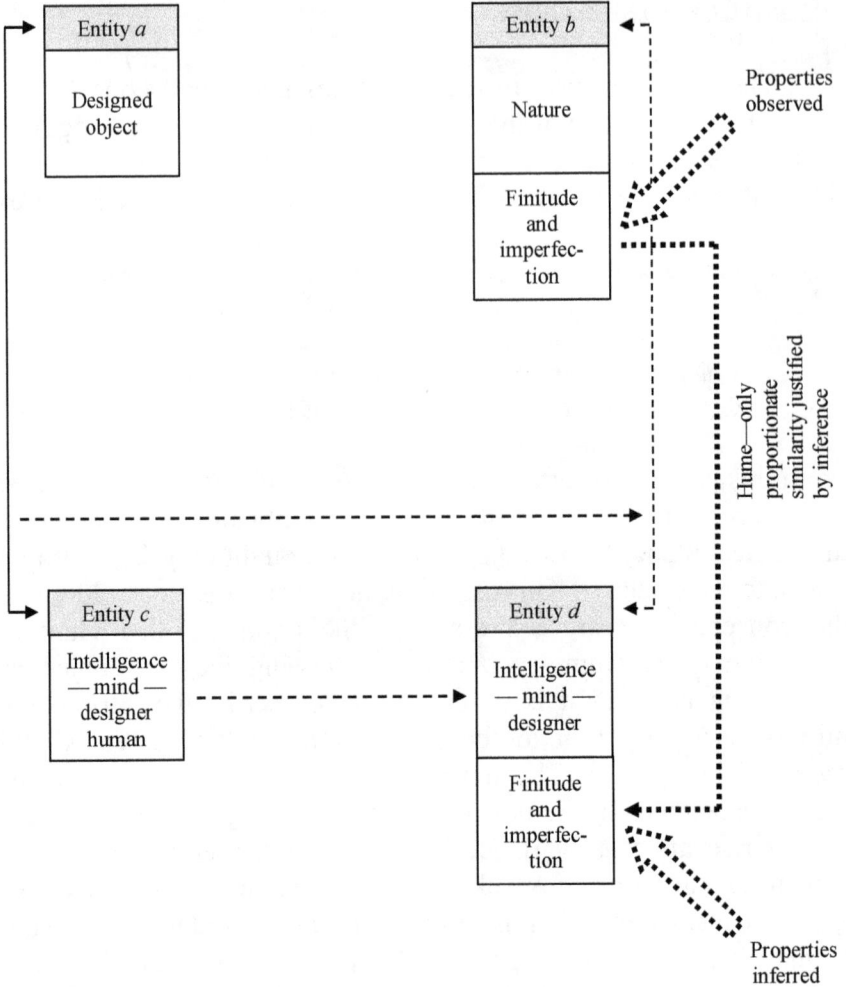

Figure 6.9

The essence of Hume's postulate concerning proportionate causes is that one cannot go beyond what one sees to infer something greater in the cause of it; at best, one is justified only in inferring properties to the same degree. Therefore, so he holds, one is not warranted in ascribing certain attributes to that which designed nature—supposing it to be designed—because those attributes are not perceived in nature itself. If God engineered it, then His attributes are in doubt.

It may be that a cause is far greater than what it produces, in that the potential—the capability or capacity—to yield greater effects exists in the cause, even if the potential is not actualized in the observed effect. One cannot know, however, based solely on what one perceives in the result, whether it is so. A stick-man picture of a family on a picnic at the park could be the product of a first-grader, or it could be the product of a renowned artist who merely was passing time by showing a first-grader how to sketch. Strictly from observing the drawing, one cannot infer that it is the handiwork of an accomplished portraitist, although one can conclude that it is the product of design, despite the fact that the designer may be unknown. Though a world-class portrait could have been produced only by some person or persons with advanced skills, a stick-man picture could have been produced by a child or a gifted adult—a fact that is perhaps suggestive of the formal-eminent distinction that Descartes employs in his reasoning.

Viewed in this way, Hume's conjecture seems to be right, but it proves to be problematic. Aside from the vertical ascription of property similarities, as it were, one key difference between Hume's objection and the argument to which he is objecting lies in how properties are attributed to their causes. In building the analogy, employing the premise that what one observes is the fruit of agency, the argument from design credits to the inferred cause a property— namely, intelligence—that is *necessary* for the cause to yield the observed effect—specifically, purposeful arrangement—as purpose is a facet of intelligent thought. It is the minimum that is needed for the explanation, not the maximum or some proportionate degree. That quality is *not* one that either of the effects in the argument can possess at all: It is senseless to ascribe intelligence to a manufactured device or to nature. Following the argument's inferential step to intelligent agency, Hume attempts to impose limitations on one's knowledge of the *inferred* causal agent's properties using properties that the corresponding effect allegedly *does* possess. He does not address the core point of the argument from design.

It is important to note that a cause may have many characteristics that cannot be determined by looking at what it causes. Consider first this sentence and its adjectival signifier; it is integral to the argument from design, and it is true:

> If nature is the product of design, then the cause of nature
> *must* be intelligent.

Contrast that statement with two others, appearing next, which are integral to Hume's objection and which, one may think, are also true:

> If nature is finite, then the cause of nature *may* be finite.
> If nature is imperfect, then the cause of nature *may* be
> imperfect.

There is no necessity here, only possibility. Ignorance of some properties of a cause has nothing to do with knowledge of others. One could say just as well,

> If nature is mostly brown, then the cause of nature *may* be
> mostly brown.

This statement is of no value, regardless of a person's position on the existence of God. Indeed, a cause may not be even *like* its effect—in virtually *any* respect. By examining Stephanie's cedar chest, what does one know about the cause of it, other than that the cause is intelligent because the chest is obviously a designed and put-together product? Is the cause made of wood, as is the effect? Does it have four round feet—one at each bottom corner—and a lid that opens on top? Does it contain a pair of blue quilts? Are the majority of its parts less than an inch thick and sealed with a high-quality, satin lacquer? The chest is very different from that which created it.

If causes need not possess the properties that their effects possess, then they need not be limited to possessing them to some proportionate degree. To assume that they must do so brings false conclusions. Hume's gradation postulate, were it true, would lead one to think that the properties of causes vary with the matching properties of the effects—an increase in the extent of a property in the effect would correlate with an increase in the extent of that property in the cause; a decrease in the extent of it in the effect would correlate with a decrease in the extent of it in the cause. There are two pocket watches on a table. The one on the left is 10 percent larger in its greatest dimension and 15 percent heavier than the other.

It is logical to infer that each is the product of intelligent design. It is not logical to infer that the cause of the watch on the left is 10 percent larger in its greatest dimension and 15 percent heavier than the cause of the watch on the right. Ben, who designed and built the more substantial device, is six inches shorter and sixty pounds lighter than Bob, who built the other one. Moreover, there might have been only one watchmaker—say, Ben—who designed both watches and assembled them during the same general period of time. It would be inconsistent to assert that Ben is larger in his greatest dimension and heavier than Ben himself at that time. Hume's conjecture, if taken as a general principle of attribute ascription, is false. In summary then, herein lies the first problem with Hume's objection.

Inherent in the argument from design is a dual-step logical construction. It concludes (1) that the world is the product of intelligent agency and (2) that this agency is to be identified with God. Hume's objection concerning the properties of the cause of the world bears essentially no relevance to the first step. The fact that one cannot know strictly by looking at nature whether the cause of it is infinite and perfect says effectively nothing about the argument's affirmation that nature was designed and hence the fruit of rationality. With respect to this element of the reasoning, his protestation has no force. Hume, in fact, concedes the point, in a rather noncommittal manner, as Philo addresses Cleanthes in the following passage:

> [A] man, who follows your hypothesis, is able, perhaps, to assert, or conjecture, that the universe, sometime, arose from something like design: but beyond that position he cannot ascertain one single circumstance.[60]

The relevance of Hume's objection is limited to the second step. It is true that the argument from design does not prove that God exists, only that, if the analogy that it sets forth is accepted, then holding that nature is the result of intelligent thought is justifiable. One cannot conclude that God is the agent who is behind it.

On the other hand, the options are quite narrow, which points to the second problem with Hume's objection. His proportionate-cause tenet works against him. One may be unwarranted in inferring from

---

[60] Hume, *Dialogues*, 414.

what one perceives of the cosmos that the cause of it is infinite, but, whether the cosmos is finite or infinite, Hume's postulate serves only to underscore the fact that the cause of it is surely grand. Although one may not know whether an unobserved cause is greater than its observed effect, in that it may possess capabilities that are beyond those that are manifested, one *can* know nevertheless that, where a relationship between the two phenomena does obtain, the observed effect does *not* exceed the capabilities of the unobserved cause to produce it. In any such relationship, whatever gives rise to a thing, whether that thing is an object, an event, or a state, must be sufficient for it to appear, given appropriate circumstances.[61] If a dozen sticks of dynamite are necessary to bring down the old building, and the demolition crew uses only eight, then one can be sure that the edifice will not be razed. In light of the enormity of the universe and the mass-energy that is inherent in the system, if it is the product of design and accompanying formation, then that which conceived it and brought it into being undoubtedly must possess awesome ability.

This analysis leads to further trouble for the philosopher. As before, Hume is attempting to treat attributes of the mental as though they were attributes of the material because one can ascribe properties to each using a common name. Consider the property of being infinite; turn first to the material. To say that the universe is not infinite must mean something akin to claiming that the number of particles in the universe is limited or that the totality of energy is not boundless or that space-time does not extend indefinitely—perhaps a combination of these things. Different conditions could be advanced, but the important issue is that, as a physical structure, the limitations of the universe are physical limitations. On an elementary level, and just for illustrative purposes, one might posit a simple criterion of finitude, based on this notion, for the universe as a physical system. Restricting the criterion to particulate count yields this statement:

---

[61] As I remarked earlier, some atheists deny that everything has a cause, pointing to reputed cases in the quantum realm; thus, if they are correct, then seeming effects can exceed causes in the sense that these presumed effects may not be the products of anything at all. That position is ill-conceived, as will become apparent soon enough, but the point here is that, if phenomena of type X cause phenomena of type Y, then, if an instance of X occurs, then, *ceteris paribus*, an instance of Y occurs, and the latter instance cannot outstrip the former one.

> A physical system ψ is finite if the set E of elementary particles that compose ψ is such that the cardinal of E is less than $\aleph_0$; and it is infinite otherwise.[62]

This criterion of finitude, employing the elementary particle count, could not apply to a mind. A finite, rational mind in the cognitive sense is one that possesses limited knowledge: It does not know everything. No human knows the exact number of molecules, at a given moment yesterday, that composed the outer crust, to a depth of twenty miles from the surface at each point of it, of the outermost planet orbiting the most massive star with a planetary complement in the Andromeda galaxy. Then, one might say that a criterion of the finitude of the mind rests on the extent of understanding, as represented in the following way:

> The mind of subject s is finite if there is an atomic proposition p, such that p expresses a supposed fact, exclusive of a chained reference, and s does not know the truth-value of p; and it is infinite otherwise.[63]

By including a modal operator, the criterion could be stated more broadly, asserting that the mind of a subject is finite if it is *possible* for there to be an atomic proposition, purporting to express a fact, the truth-value of which the subject does not know, and infinite otherwise. The given rendition will serve the purposes here nonetheless.

It is possible—indeed, likely—that the set of all atomic propositions that purport to express facts is finite; that is to say, the

---

[62] For an explanation of the symbol '$\aleph_0$', see the discussion of Zeno's paradoxes in chap. 1. Recall that Craig argues against an actual infinity of things; see pp. 602–3.

[63] Atomic propositions are defined in the discussion of truth-functional operators in the section on arguments in chap. 1. The criterion excludes chained references to eliminate propositions that refer strictly to other propositions. One can generate a trivial, infinite set of atomic propositions merely by allowing propositions to point to other ones: For example, p_1 = 'Sirius is the brightest star, other than the sun, when viewed from the earth'; p_2 = 'p_1 is true'; p_3 = 'p_2 is true'; and so forth. Of course, one might use sets to handle the chaining en masse, where the truth-value of every member of the set would be determined by the statement at the base of the references, and capture the set as a whole, but I think that this approach presents a complication that is excessive for the current exercise.

cardinal of the set of knowable propositions about reality may be less, and is probably less, than $\aleph_0$. Hence, it is possible for a mind to be infinite, possessing unlimited knowledge, even though the number of elements that determine infinitude or, at least, potential infinitude is finite. The same is not true of a physical system; it is not possible for the system to be infinite unless the quantity or reach of a constituent that determines infinitude is unlimited. Given the criteria that I suggest above, the infinity of a mind cannot be like that of a physical system. It is not the criteria themselves that are important but the fact that the term 'infinity' cannot be applied in the same sense to occupants of disparate realms. Hume again crosses boundaries illegally.

Take a look at the property of perfection and what it means to say that nature is not perfect. One might hold that perfection in the cosmic system is the exhibiting of, and complying with, physical laws that can be described with the precision of mathematics. If one adopts this sense, however, then, contrary to Hume, one could say that nature *is* perfect because events in physical reality occur in accordance with universal laws that are expressed in mathematical formulations. As far as one can observe in reality, the pressure of a given mass of a gas (an ideal gas is assumed) that is maintained at a constant temperature in a confined area is inversely proportional to its volume—a statement of Boyle's law. One has come to understand the relationships among phenomena in the world because the laws are in force with an exactness that allows predictability without variance within the scope of their macrophysical applications.

The only exception to this rule is the suspension of the laws of nature by the supernatural intervention of God. These suspensions are miracles. Thus, if one accepts that miracles occur, then there is solid evidence that supernatural intelligence exists, which works against Hume in his assault on the argument from design. If one rejects the occurrence of miracles, then the invariance that characterizes physical laws, reflecting perfection, would point, if one were to allow Hume's postulate about equivalent-degree causality to stand, to perfection in the source of nature: the Supreme Being who authored the universe, according to the argument from design.

Regardless of how one defines perfection, however, Hume still faces finding a meaning for the corresponding term that is common to minds and matter. If one disputes the physical-law basis, then does one say that a perfect universe is a symmetric universe? Is it a universe in which all planetary orbits are circular? Whatever perfection in the material realm is, it cannot be the perfection that distinguishes God, revealed in the completeness of the essential attributes of His divine nature. None of those attributes applies to physical things as such, nor is it possible for any of them to apply in that way. One cannot employ terms loosely in an attempt to draw a property similarity between observed effects and inferred causes, whether within domains or, without doubt, across them.

Skeptics may agree with Hume, holding that one does not know, based on what one sees of the cosmos, that the cause of the world is infinite, and perhaps does not know that it is perfect, but Hume's path to that point is strewn with logical impediments. In the end, if Hume is going to embrace a commensurate-cause thesis, then he must embrace its consequence as well. It seems to be true then that one can know more about the cause of nature than Hume is willing to admit. This verse from the Scriptures is telling:

> For since the creation of the world God's invisible qualities—his eternal power and divine nature—have been clearly seen, being understood from what has been made, so that men are without excuse.[64]

It is a point to ponder.

THIRD CONSIDERED OBJECTION

Hume continues his discussion of the argument from design by forming an attack from another angle. The world, he states, resembles an animal or a vegetable more than it does a contrivance. He concludes,

> [T]here are other parts of the universe (besides the machines of human invention) which bear still a greater resemblance to the fabric of the world, and which

---

[64] Rom. 1:20 NIV.

therefore afford a better conjecture concerning the universal origin of this system. These parts are animals and vegetables. The world plainly resembles more an animal or a vegetable, than it does a watch or a knitting-loom. Its cause, therefore, it is more probable, resembles the cause of the former. The cause of the former is generation or vegetation. The cause, therefore, of the world, we may infer to be something similar or analogous to generation or vegetation.[65]

In Figure 6.10, I show the directional change in Hume's approach. He targets the horizontal link here, questioning the supposed resemblance between the world and machinery. Nature is more akin to living things than to nonliving ones, Hume contends, and, on this basis, he hypothesizes that the generative cause of nature is more likely to resemble objects in the former group than those in the latter group. As before, bold, dotted lines in the diagram reflect Hume's reasoning; one may refer to Figure 6.7 for relevant supporting information.

---

[65] Hume, *Dialogues*, 421.

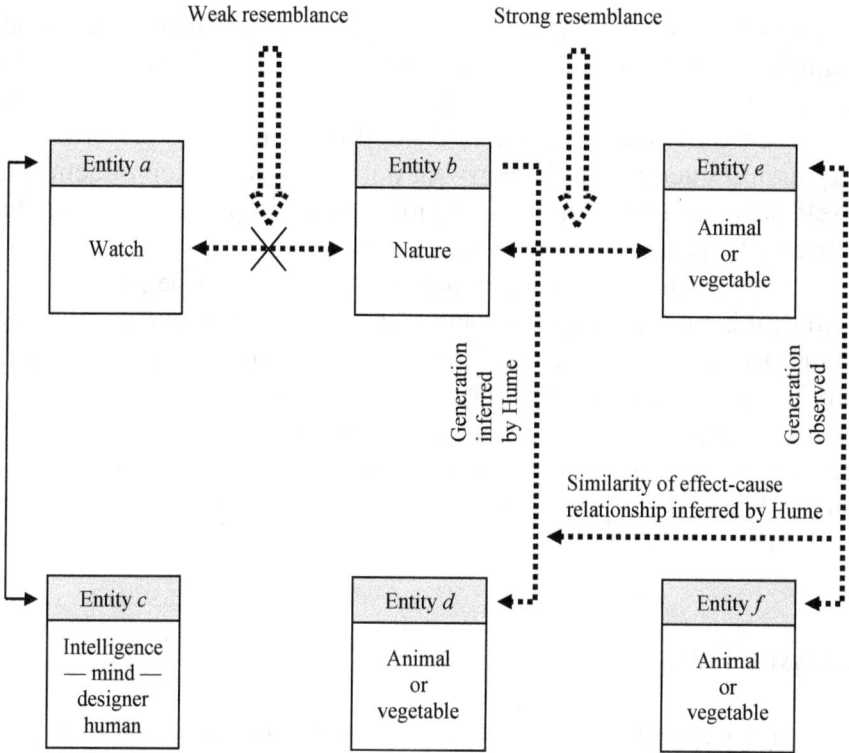

Figure 6.10

Those in philosophical circles have pointed out that Hume's objection leads to an infinite regress. It is ironic that he poses an objection to the argument from design that raises the very difficulty that he intended to inflict on the argument's supporters. Procreation produces offspring that resemble the parents. If the world is the descendant of other worlds through a process of reproduction, then its forerunners likewise must be worlds, which must have arisen in the same way. One is forced, in that case, to postulate the existence of another pair of worlds for each member of that pair, given a dual lineage, and so forth ad infinitum. One cannot explain the present world without explaining the opening incident in an endless series.

Hume's defense may be found in his claim that resting one's cosmogony on reproductive propagation is no more problematic than resting one's cosmogony on rational agency; prior causes elude both camps. What Hume misses is the fact that an intelligent being who can create ex nihilo is a plausible precipitating dynamic because, as discussed previously, agency is the ability to initiate a performance, expressing intention in the carrying out of the deed. Reproduction in itself never can explain the start, for it turns in perpetuity to predecessors. Thus, it never can capture initiation.

One might look for an explanation concerning beginnings in a primeval bang for the cosmos and a chance chemical event, followed by protracted evolution, for life. An understanding of the present world surely demands an account of its roots. Regardless of the status of any pertinent narrative, though, Humean dependence on generation remains hollow. As I will explore in due course, the atheist Richard Dawkins believes that he has the answer.

COSMIC ORDER

Two authors, writing in the twentieth century, offer another pair of criticisms of the teleological argument, centering again on the concept of order. First, consider the objection of Ernest Nagel. Physicists have noted that the laws of nature are describable in mathematical terms, and, from this truth, some of them have concluded that nature is the product of a divine agent who employed mathematics in framing it. The fact that one perceives an orderliness when beholding the universe, though, is not in itself sufficient proof of intelligent design, says Nagel. One cannot assume that the tools of physics would be useful only if the universe displayed some special kind of order, for, from a mathematical perspective, any order—even chaos—can be described.[66] Further, according to the second author, who is Clarence Darrow, to say that something is orderly is to say that it is fashioned after some norm or pattern, but the underlying

---

[66] Nagel presents this argument in an essay titled "A Defense of Atheism." The essay appeared first in *Basic Beliefs*, ed. J. E. Fairchild (New York: Sheridan House, 1959). A revised version, from which I take the objection here, is printed in *A Modern Introduction to Philosophy*, ed. Paul Edwards and Arthur Pap, rev. ed. (New York: Free Press, 1965), 460–72.

pattern for the human idea of order, as is the case with other ideas, is just the universe itself. To declare that the universe exhibits order is to declare no more than that the universe is like itself.[67]

I find these objections to be unconvincing. That the laws of nature reflect numerical precision is interesting—and the extreme degree of that precision has surfaced only in recent years—although, as Nagel indicates, one cannot deduce from the fact that the laws of physics can be represented by various formulae that an intelligence produced the universe, which stands in accordance with them. His objection, however, is based on the claim that any order at all can be portrayed in mathematical terms.

In attacking the teleological argument as he represents it in this criticism, Nagel's objection has nothing to do with the concept of order that appears in the standard argument from design. Recall the example that I mentioned earlier in which the parts of a watch, prior to assembly, are placed in a bag, shaken, and dumped onto a table. Regardless of the sequence in which the parts fall onto the table's surface and where they land, there will be some order or other—temporal and spatial. Some parts drop onto the table at the outset of the dumping, others at its conclusion, most in the interim period. Some parts lie close to others, even touching; some lie farther apart and to the left; some are beneath. This concept of order, however, is irrelevant. The notion of order on which the central argument from design relies is one that points to the cooperative interaction of the parts of a thing, explicable only with reference to the functional performance of the whole, and, so goes the reasoning, such systemic operation requires intelligent design.

Imagine that there are two groups of pebbles, several yards apart, on a moderately rocky beach; each group is composed of thirty-four stones. Figure 6.11 depicts the patterns.

---

[67] Clarence Darrow expresses this objection in *The Story of My Life* (New York: Charles Scribner's Sons, 1932), 414.

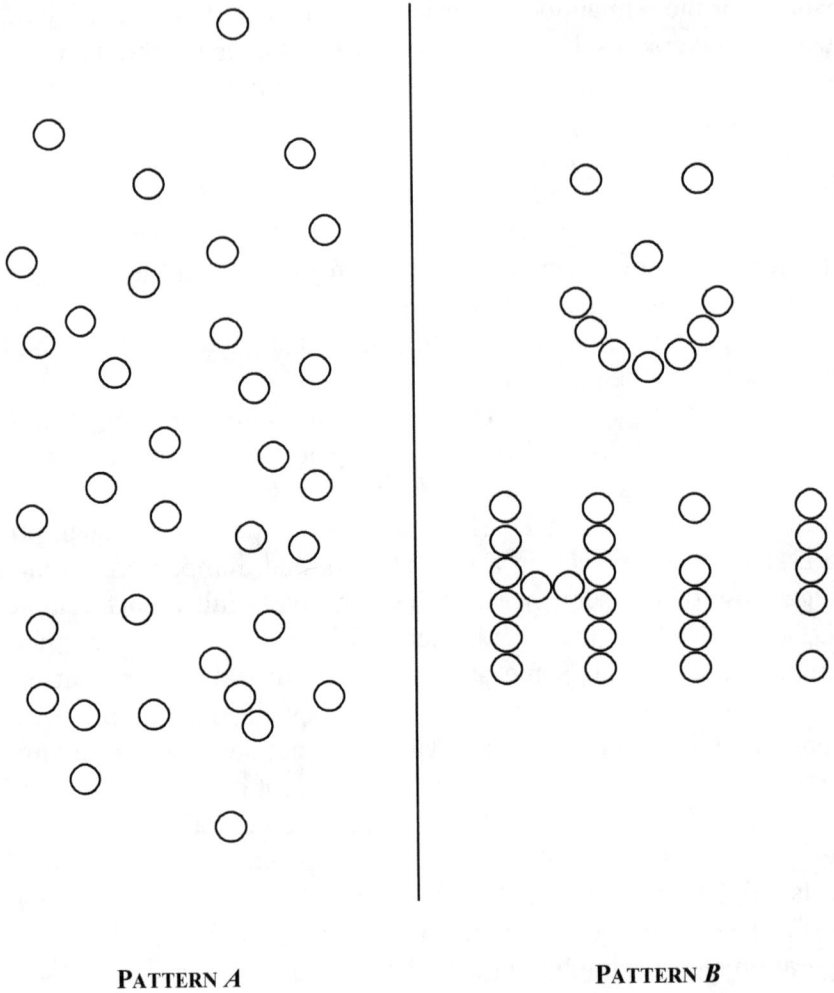

PATTERN *A*   PATTERN *B*

Figure 6.11

Both these arrangements can be identified in mathematical terms; both exhibit *an* order. There is something special about pattern *B* nevertheless. Order as it has been wrought by intelligence is not like order as it has been wrought by mere natural forces; it is not simply one more random pattern among all possible arrangements, each of which is equal to the others. On the contrary, it carries with it a mark of distinction, and that mark is a reflection of intention, of action. Nagel's objection is ineffectual.

In his case against the teleological argument, Clarence Darrow says that, because the human understanding of order is derived from what humans perceive in physical reality, they could not see the universe as anything but orderly. Why does he think that the concept of order depends on observation of the universe, and why does he think that people cannot conceive of order apart from what they see? There are numerous concepts that are not the strict products of observation: those of truth, incorporeality, justice, abstraction, contradiction, and infinity, to list a few. It is easy to envision a cosmos that is infinite in spatial dimensions—as opposed to, say, planetary count, as Craig would argue—but no one has observed such a thing. What people see is surely expansive, and, though space may extend infinitely, people do not see that it does so. How then did they come to have an idea of infinite space if the concept of it depends purely on what they see?

Moreover, many things that people observe in the universe are not orderly. Mt. St. Helens erupts at irregular intervals. When it does erupt, there is a chaotic expulsion of molten lava, rocks, and ash. To hold that humans could not see the universe as anything but chaotic on the basis that their notion of chaos is derived from observation is to adopt an untenable position. Neither the timing of the eruption events nor the occurrence of the events themselves convinces one that the universe is characterized by chaos any more than the tumultuous ride on the interstate, resulting from the sudden blowout of a nail-pierced front tire, convinces the driver that the car is not the product of well-ordered engineering and construction.

It is important to note that, if one embraces science's prevailing cosmogonic theory of a big bang launch—a contemporary atheist has few, if any, options—then one is faced with explaining the extraordinary precision with which the cosmos was spun. In astronomy, the concept of critical density is foundational. It is the density of a flat universe; and it is needed to halt the expansion of the universe without pulling it back to a compact state. The capital Greek letter omega symbolizes the cosmic density numeric. If $\Omega < 1.0$, then the combined mass of all that is in the cosmos is too slight for the associated gravity to overcome the extension, and the dispersion will continue indefinitely. If $\Omega > 1.0$, then that mass is sufficient in principle for the gravity of the system to reverse the extension and return the universe to a compressed formation, mirroring its early state. If $\Omega = 1.0$ (the density is critical), then the mass is just the right amount to halt the distension without reversion, *ceteris paribus*, albeit the long-term expansion-accelerating effect of dark energy is still an open question.

Now, the density that the universe exhibited at the outset, asserts the scholar Robert Dicke, determined its very subsistence. If the density had not been on the mark, then there would be no universe. Extreme precision was needed to yield the critical value:

> [A]ny significant deviation [of omega] from 1 in the earliest universe would have led, effectively and almost immediately, to the end of the universe: either an exponential expansion toward infinity or a collapse. Calculating backward, the closer and closer you got to the Big Bang, the closer and closer omega must have been to 1. At three minutes after the Big Bang, omega would have been within a hundred-trillionth of 1. At one second after the Big Bang, omega would have been within a quadrillionth of 1—that is, between 0.999999999999999 and 1.000000000000001. The earlier in the universe you calculated, the more decimal places you added. At some point in the calculations you simply conceded: Omega as good as equaled 1.[68]

Although the density must have been just right for the universe that humans observe to have arisen, if the universe is larger than what one can see, then, according to the physicist Alan Guth, omega could have varied without ensuring annihilation. Guth recognizes nevertheless the stunning exactitude that was required of the nascent cosmos for it to have come to exist as it does at present. He postulates that the rate at which the primal universe was expanding had to have been precisely the rate that was necessary to maintain the system. If the speed of the particle-space distension had been any greater, then the material in the universe never would have collected to form the cosmic structures that are currently in place. The matter would have

---

[68] These comments by Robert Dicke are reported in Richard Panek, *The 4 Percent Universe: Dark Matter, Dark Energy, and the Race to Discover the Rest of Reality* (Boston: Houghton Mifflin Harcourt, 2011), 128.

scattered too quickly to coalesce. If the speed had been any less, then the material would have collapsed upon itself following the initial event because of the force of gravity. Likewise, no cosmic structures would have formed. Guth notes that an accuracy of measurement to fifteen decimal places was required at a second after the big bang, but Guth applies it to speed rather than density.

> What was always needed, and nobody had really pointed this out, was that you had to assume that the expansion rate of the early universe was tuned almost exactly right—that is, almost exactly the right expansion rate, so that the universe would be just on the verge of eternal expansion versus eventual collapse. If one talks about the universe at a time of about one second after the big bang, this tuning, this precise fixing of the expansion rate, had to be done to an accuracy of about fifteen decimal places. If the universe just expanded one part in the fifteenth decimal place faster than we thought it had, it would fly apart without galaxies ever having a chance to form. If the universe at one second after the big bang were expanding with one number less in the fifteenth decimal place than what we thought, then the universe would collapse before galaxies had ever had a chance to form. To make the universe work, the universe had to be perched just on this borderline.[69]

Accuracy of this order, as is apparent, is equivalent to one part in a quadrillion.

To put this degree of accuracy in perspective, imagine that a car is traveling on the interstate at sixty miles per hour. Imagine further that the car continues on the journey, day and night, nonstop, for ten thousand years. Upon concluding this ten-millennia journey, the car will have traveled more than five billion miles: 5,259,487,519 miles, to be precise, taking into account the standard tropical year of 365.242188792 days. If, at the end of that ten-thousand-year trek, the car had rolled just *one-third inch* more or *one-third inch* less, then its

---

[69] Alan Guth, in *Stephen Hawking's Universe*, Educational Broadcasting Corp., vol. 6, *An Answer to Everything*, 60 min. (Boston: PBS Video, 1997), videocassette.

actual speed would have been sufficiently off the mark to undermine the crucial exactitude. The cosmic scales that underlie the existence of things in the universe must be balanced with astounding rightness. Although it may be that any pattern can be described mathematically, as Nagel declares, the more fascinating point is that there is a pattern at all, one the mathematics of which reveals the amazing precision of the existing order.

If the cosmos is merely the product of blind mechanism, then one is left with the question of why it formed—regardless of what initiated the process—because the probability of formation appears to be exceedingly remote. It is a matter that one must address in any account of the existence of the universe. Some hold that the precision is in a sense self-explanatory. If the cosmogonic facts had been different, then there would be no cosmos today and thus no humans to observe it. Given that humans do exist and behold the precision, the cosmos could not have been otherwise. Does such a standpoint actually account for the astonishing exactness? The answer must await the appropriate time. I wish to turn now to the most bizarre of all cosmogonic ideas. It is the notion, which some authors have advanced in recent years, that the generation of everything is traced to nothing.

NOTHING, NOTHING AT ALL

As noted in chapter 1, there are scientists who take exception to the principle that out of nothing, nothing comes, holding that certain phenomena violate it. For example, they claim that, in the quantum world, the sudden generation of photons in excited atoms—atoms that are in a state of heightened energy—is uncaused. When atoms absorb energy, electron energy values increase, then rapidly fall, giving rise to photons. These quanta of energy are discharged from the atoms in spontaneous emissions following the atoms' momentary change of state. Another instance is found in virtual particles, which, they say, pop into existence with no cause to produce them. Virtual particles are matter-antimatter pairs that appear abruptly, then disappear almost immediately as the opposite-charge units come together and annihilate each other. They exist for such a short period of time that they cannot be detected directly.[70]

It is important to distinguish between the concept of causality and that of coming to exist, and to distinguish as well between the concept of arising uncaused and that of arising out of nothing. Not everyone is careful to do so. Some comments by the physicist and atheist Victor J. Stenger are in order; he asserts,

> In fact, physical events at the atomic and subatomic level are observed to have no evident cause. For example, when an atom in an excited energy level drops to a lower level and emits a photon, a particle of light, *we find no cause of that event.* . . .
> . . . The photons emitted in atomic transitions *come into existence spontaneously.*[71]

Stenger believes that not all events are caused and, of greater consequence, that not all coming-into-existence events are caused. In arguing against the concept that whatever begins to exist must be caused, he makes the following, problematic claim:

> While . . . [the statement that whatever begins has a cause] can be challenged on a number of fronts, let me just mention one rebuttal that has been made from physics. Quantum electrodynamics is a fifty-year-old theory of the interactions of electrons and photons that has made successful predictions to accuracies as great as twelve significant figures. Fundamental to that theory is the *spontaneous appearance* of electron-positron (anti-electron) pairs for brief periods of time, *literally out of "nothing."* Thus we have a counter example to [the] statement . . . [that whatever begins has a cause, namely,] something that begins without cause.

---

[70] Scientists sometimes point to a third instance as a reputed case of uncaused events: the Casimir effect, in which a small force changes the position of closely aligned metal plates in a vacuum. The reasoning is the same, however, and I will focus on the other two examples in the analysis in this section. They are sufficient for the purposes of the discussion.

[71] Victor J. Stenger, *God: The Failed Hypothesis—How Science Shows That God Does Not Exist* (Buffalo: Prometheus Books, 2007), 124. The emphases are mine.

The momentary pairs of subatomic bits to which Stenger refers in this passage are virtual particles.[72]

There are two interrelated problems with Stenger's assertion. First, he is confusing the notion of an uncaused event with that of coming out of nothing. Even if there are uncaused events, it does not follow that there are uncaused generative events, and, even if there are uncaused generative events, it does not follow that what is generated comes out of nothing. Second, his concept of the locution 'out of nothing' is distorted because his concept of that which is denoted by the term 'nothing' is distorted. It is not the denotation that appears in the canon ex nihilo nihil fit. Admittedly, something's coming into being ought to be subject to explanation—why it happened—and it is often the case that proper explanations of events are formulated in terms of cause and effect. When one speaks of a generative cause—that which brings a thing into being—one means an efficient cause in the Aristotelian sense. It is the driver for the origination event that results in the existence of the generated thing. It makes it happen. Lacking a generative cause, however, is not equivalent to arising from a void, and claiming that one sort of event is possible is not the same as claiming that the other sort is possible.

As a simple conceptual exercise to illustrate the point, imagine that a lump of clay in the form of a sphere is sitting atop a table. In the course of thirty seconds, the sphere becomes two cubes. All the material that was in the sphere, and only that material, is present now in the pair of cubical blocks. One can confirm this fact by inspection and accurate measurement. The gradual transformation preserves the spatiotemporal stability of the material as it separates and reforms. Imagine now that the table is empty—for the sake of the example, assume that no material substance is on it or in the vicinity above it. Suddenly, two lumps of clay in the shape of cubes appear on the table's surface. One has no way of explaining either this event or the aforementioned one. No cause of the change in either instance is identifiable.

There is a clear difference between the two cases, however. In the first imaginary episode, the cubes of clay that are currently on the

---

[72] This extract regarding virtual particles is from Victor J. Stenger, "The Other Side of Time," Secular Web, accessed October 21, 2014, infidels.org/library/modern/vic_stenger/otherside.html. The emphases are mine.

table came from the sphere of clay that was there earlier, even though any account of how it happened is not forthcoming. In the second imaginary episode, the cubes did not come from it or from any substance. There is preservation of matter in the first case; there is none in the second. Claiming that either of these events could be an actual phenomenon in nature without supernatural intervention would be unfounded; it is obvious that one can imagine things that are not nomologically possible.

The point is that something's arising uncaused is not identical to something's arising out of nothing. They are distinct concepts, and I plan to show that both of them are, in fact, false. Even on the supposition that the first cube-event is possible in the world, it would not follow that the second event, which contravenes the physical law governing conservation in the universe, also would be possible. Whether uncaused events occur or do not occur is irrelevant to the truth of the metaphysical canon at hand. According to that principle, the *coming* into existence of a thing requires the *being* in existence of something already. Reality sits on both sides of any pair of moments that constitutes an origination; refer to the structure of such events, as detailed in chapter 3. The canon ex nihilo nihil fit is not about causality per se but about the preconditions that permit arisings to take place. Stenger is not alone in the conflation of these concepts.

Extend the exercise to the quantum realm. In the phenomenon of spontaneous emission, photons, which are quanta of electromagnetic energy, do not spring into existence out of utter nothingness. When atoms absorb energy, they become excited for a short period of time, raising the probability of finding associated electrons farther from the nucleus, corresponding to increased energy values. This state is not maintained, and the affected electrons in those excited atoms collapse in position, releasing photonic energy in accordance with the law of conservation. The heightened-energy state is usually very brief, on the order of 10^{-8} second, although longer durations are possible.[73] Such incidents are not examples of emergence ex nihilo: There would be no spontaneous emissions if the atoms that absorbed energy and then released it did not exist; or they did not exist in an

---

[73] This value is cited in Raymond A. Serway and John W. Jewett Jr., *Physics for Scientists and Engineers*, 7th ed., vol. 2 (Belmont, CA: Thomson Brooks/Cole, 2008), 1244.

excited state; or the energy that they absorbed and emitted afterward did not exist. Stenger's conceptualization is incorrect.

A more interesting case is that of virtual particles. A foundational tenet in quantum physics is the Heisenberg uncertainty principle. It holds that it is not possible to determine absolutely both the position of a particle and its momentum. The more tightly determined that one of the two conjoined elements is, the less so is the other one. There is an uncertainty that extends to time and energy as well. It provides for momentary ripples in the energy of a system without violating the law of conservation. As physicists note, if a particle and its antiparticle, such as an electron and a positron, appear and then disappear quickly enough, colliding as a result of their opposite-charge attraction, then the uncertainty of the mass of the particles can exceed the mass. In that case, one cannot be sure whether the particles had mass, and a pair of such entities with no mass does not increase the energy of the system. The overall energy level stays constant, within the limits of uncertainty, provided that the shifting is exceedingly short-lived. For virtual electrons and positrons, that brevity is on the order of 10^{-21} second.

There is a problem with Stenger's use of the transitory pairs to support his stance. Specifically, even if it were true that virtual particles could come into being uncaused, they would not come into being literally out of nothing, contrary to what he alleges. Inherent in any quantum physical system, there is zero-point energy, the residual that remains in the system at its lowest-energy state, or ground state. Indeed, a totally vacant space, completely devoid of all that can be removed from it, retains energy. It is the vacuum energy of space, a phenomenon that science clearly recognizes. In a recent work, two physicists report, "[T]here is no such thing as empty space. . . . [S]pace is never empty."[74] Another scientist writes, "The quantum vacuum . . . is by no means a simple empty space where nothing ever happens or a pure abstract concept of quantum field theory."[75] Others agree; this assertion appears in the literature: "[T]he vacuum is

---

[74] Stephen Hawking and Leonard Mlodinow, *The Grand Design* (New York: Bantam Books, 2010), 113.

[75] Astrid Lambrecht, "Observing Mechanical Dissipation in the Quantum Vacuum: An Experimental Challenge," in *Laser Physics at the Limit*, ed. Hartmut Figger, Dieter Meschede, and Claus Zimmermann (Berlin: Springer-Verlag, 2002), 197.

actually something complex, structured, multivalued and full of information."[76]

Consider these synoptic remarks by yet another physicist:

> Zero-point energy . . . means that there is always some energy present in any system, no matter how hard you try to extract all the energy. Even empty space has zero-point energy, which leads to . . . spontaneous emission of photons from atoms and tiny forces (called "Casimir forces") between metal plates in a vacuum. The zero-point energy of empty space can even produce short-lived pairs of "virtual" particles.[77]

Subsequently, he states,

> In quantum physics, even a perfect vacuum is a constant storm of activity, with "virtual particles" popping into existence for a fleeting moment, thanks to zero-point energy, then disappearing again.[78]

Finally, Stenger avers,

> Normally we think of the vacuum as being empty of matter and energy. However, according to general relativity, gravitational energy can be stored in the curvature of empty space. Furthermore, quantum mechanics implies that a vacuum could contain a minimum *zero-point energy*.[79]

When regarded from a macroscopic perspective, empty space appears to be an area with nothing in it. When one drills down into the microscopic, subatomic world, however, one finds a boiling sea of energy. The pseudovoid of space is not an absolute blank. It is not nothing. It is something. It exists. It is out of this dynamic backdrop

---

[76] J. Rafelski and B. Müller, *The Structured Vacuum: Thinking about Nothing* (Frankfurt am Main, Germany: Verlag Harri Deutsch, 1985), 8.

[77] Chad Orzel, *How to Teach Physics to Your Dog* (New York: Scribner, 2009), 53.

[78] Ibid., 191. Here, the author broadens the quoted term to include 'particles'.

[79] Stenger, *Failed Hypothesis*, 151.

of energy that virtual particles arise and vanish as quantum fluctuations occur. Virtual particles do not arise from nothing; they arise from what is already there. As for the prior case of spontaneous emissions, this same backdrop of energy can bring about excited states of atoms and spur the release of photons. Stenger's claim that something is coming out of nothing, in both situations, runs contrary to the facts.

Aside from the foregoing concern, why does Stenger think that certain events are uncaused? One of the identifying characteristics of causal relationships is sufficiency, a concept that I introduced previously. If a particular set of conditions—an event or a state (possibly multiple events or states)—is the cause of another particular set of conditions—a further event or state—then the former set is *sufficient* for the latter set; this relation is expressed in a conditional proposition, which captures the causal law. If the former conditions, in fact, obtain, then, *ceteris paribus*, so do the latter conditions; and, if the latter conditions, in fact, do not obtain, then, *ceteris paribus*, neither do the former conditions.[80] If one puts a sugar cube into hot water in

---

[80] Effects may be brought about by various causes, of course. A hurling rock or a shrieking shrill soprano may shatter a glass. Either of these causes is therefore sufficient, in a specified set of circumstances, for the effect, and the effect is thereby necessary for the cause: It must occur if the cause occurs, given the circumstances, assuming that the statement regarding the cause-effect relationship is true. In propositional logic, a conditional statement—which expresses sufficiency—is true by pronouncement, however, if the antecedent is false. See the discussion of the truth conditions of atomic propositions in chap. 1. A conditional statement with a false antecedent is a counterfactual. One must take care, in putting forward assertions that affirm the obtaining of cause-effect relationships, to prevent error owing to the truth of counterfactuals. For example, consider the following sentence: 'Eating ten pounds of lead every day for a year causes an adolescent consumer to live to be more than a hundred years old'. Representing this causal statement as the appropriate conditional proposition yields this sentence: 'If an adolescent eats ten pounds of lead every day for a year, then that person thereby will live to be more than a hundred years old'. No one ever has eaten ten pounds of lead in a day, let alone each day for a year, so, by the truth conditions that are established in propositional logic, the statement is true because the antecedent is false. No doubt, if a few people tried the lead diet, then one would learn rather quickly that the supposed cause-effect relationship does not hold. Nevertheless, it is sufficiency, which is inherent in conditional statements, that is a central mark of causality. It is just that it must be coupled with empirically substantiated facts—reflecting actual occurrences—lest a counterfactual compel one to embrace an

normal circumstances, then it dissolves; the circumstances, of course, include certain relevant factors, such as the absence of heat-resistant and moisture-resistant material on the exterior of the cube, and so forth. In light of the facts, if the sugar cube remains intact, then, *ceteris paribus*, it has been kept out of the water. One can prevent its dissolving by leaving it on the counter. Again, if one shoots the potent, seventy-caliber express rifle into a piece of ordinary plywood at ten feet, then a hole in the board results. If the board is left unscathed, then, *ceteris paribus*, the rifle has not fired a round into the board. One can prevent the bullet-inflicted puncturing by leaving the rifle in the rack. These activities can be repeated with the same outcomes. Each time that one drops a sugar cube into hot water, it dissolves. Each time that one fires the oversized rifle into a plywood board at close range, a hole results, although, considering the recoil of this firearm, one is not likely to repeat the affair too often. The regularity of recurring episodes of the preconditions followed by the postconditions is what leads the scientific community to formulate statements of laws of nature, such laws reflecting cause-effect relationships. Refer to the inductive-deductive approach to the development and use of law-statements—see chapter 2.[81] The regularity that underlies the laws forms the very foundation of science, which relies on the predictability that the laws provide within their joint purview.

A central problem with Stenger's view is that the cases that he mentions fit—quite well—the pattern of causation as it is given in

---

affirmation of a causal relationship that obtains nowhere in reality. As an aside, counterfactuals have become a special topic of study in philosophy with an accompanying expansion of the analysis of their truth conditions.

[81] Sometimes, one bases a conclusion about a cause-effect relationship on a single instance. The destruction of the space shuttle *Challenger* was caused by a failure of the O-rings on the solid-fuel booster rockets. Given sufficient evidence, a unique occurrence may be all that is needed to understand what caused an effect, as is true of the breakup of the shuttle. One could envision a similar occurrence in similar circumstances, although it is extremely unlikely that comparable preconditions and postconditions will resurface. In such single-instance events, one is not interested in formulating a statement of a law of nature but in providing an account of something that happened, although the laws of nature do lie behind what happened, and it is by virtue of them that the given effect-event ensued. As a rule, propositions that express physical laws are set forth based on the observation of recurring sequences, prompting one to infer that correlated physical links are in place and so to declare it. The laws, once discovered, allow predictions of future incidents.

sufficiency. When atoms are excited by an influx of energy, the atoms absorb the energy and release it subsequently as photonic emissions. The absence of emissions entails the absence of excited atoms. Again, when zero-point energy is present in a system—and it is present in any physical system—virtual particles appear in a vacuum. Such coupled phenomena are consistent and predictable. If no virtual particles were to appear in a vacuum, then zero-point energy would be absent. The presence of particles is thus necessary, given the presence of the base energy: The failure of the successor to be there guarantees that the predecessor is not there. By logical rules, it follows that the preconditions are sufficient for the postconditions.

Where then is the supposed lack of a causal link? The so-called spontaneity of certain occurrences in the quantum realm—photonic emissions and virtual-pair generations—seems to lead Stenger to hold that these happenings are uncaused; if so, then his thinking fails to capture the essence of causality. Predicting *when* an event will take place is not the same as predicting *that* it will take place. Causality is defined by the invariable accompanying of preconditions by postconditions, in specified circumstances, such that the exclusion of the latter set warrants the exclusion of the former set, and this structure is *exactly* what one sees in the phenomena that he puts forward as counterexamples.

Stenger probably is viewing causes as strictly triggering events, not states. Hence, he is looking for occurrences that precipitate the aforementioned happenings. Such a view is incorrect, for assuredly states can serve as causes. There are many examples. The truck was parked on the old bridge, causing the structure to collapse suddenly sometime during the night because of the substantial weight of the vehicle and the weakened condition of the bridge's supports. If one points to the event that preceded the state of the truck's resting atop the bridge—namely, someone's driving the truck onto it—then one must point equally, for example, to the influx-of-energy event that brought about the excited state of the atoms that released the photons as an efflux of energy in an emission event. Either way, it is clear that a cause-effect relationship holds.

The assertion about uncaused arisings of particles is echoed nevertheless by the physicist and cosmologist Lawrence M. Krauss. I want to take a brief look at comments by him regarding the question of something's coming from nothing as it allegedly applies to virtual particles.

> [M]erely defining "nothingness" as "nonbeing" is not sufficient to suggest that physics, and more generally science, is not adequate to address the question. Let me give an additional, more specific argument here. Consider an electron-positron pair that spontaneously pops out of empty space near the nucleus of an atom and affects the property of that atom for the short time the pair exists. In what sense did the electron or positron exist before? Surely by any sensible definition they didn't.[82]

It is not obvious what Krauss has in mind in this passage. He seems to be making the following argument:

> The electron-positron pair did not exist before it came into existence.
> Therefore, the electron-positron pair came into existence out of nothing.

The first statement is certainly true—but trivially so. Things, whether particles or otherwise, plainly do not predate their own existence; it is logically impossible for them to do so. It assuredly does not follow from this truth, however, that they must have come out of nothing. The second statement thus constitutes a non sequitur. Refer again to the structure of originations that I gave in chapter 3. The car in Pete's garage did not exist before it was manufactured. The swimming pool in Cory's back yard did not exist before the excavation was finished and the concrete poured. The painting *Mona Lisa* did not exist before Leonardo da Vinci put brush to canvas; indeed, the painter himself did not exist before he came into being. The issue here is that it is illogical to hold that, if a thing, such as a pair of virtual particles, comes to be, even comes to be suddenly, then it must come out of the void of nothingness. In view of the possible choices in Krauss's

---

[82] Lawrence M. Krauss, *A Universe from Nothing: Why There Is Something Rather Than Nothing* (New York: Free Press, 2012), 146.

example, it seems that the scientist is facing a dilemma. Either empty space is something (that is to say, not nothing), or it is nothing. If it is something, then what pops out of empty space, to use Krauss's phrase, as given in the preceding quotation, does not pop out of nothing. Therefore, it is not true that virtual particles come out of nothing. If, on the other hand, empty space is nothing, then how can it be curved, bending around massive objects—or flat, for that matter? How can it even have a shape at all, as the physicists, including Stenger and Krauss, declare? How can it expand—indeed, faster than the speed of light—in the inflationary model of the universe? Consider these remarks by Krauss:

> Special relativity says nothing can travel *through space* faster than the speed of light. But *space itself* can do whatever the heck it wants, at least in general relativity. And as space expands, it can carry distant objects, which are at rest in the space where they are sitting, apart from one another at superluminal speeds.[83]

The nonexistent has no properties and, a fortiori, no shape. It cannot expand; it cannot do anything. Krauss's example rests on a mistaken concept.

Perhaps Krauss is thinking that the electron-positron pair comes from nothing because, unlike Pete's car, it does not come immediately from other material. One can trace the metal in the pistons, gears, fenders, and wheels to various ores, but one cannot trace the virtual particles to other material bits in some uninterrupted chain of predecessor material. Matter and energy are two sides of the same coin in the physical universe, however. It is because of this fact that nature moves from one form to the other with regularity, and the mass of matter is linked to an equivalent amount of energy through Einstein's celebrated equation. People can bring about the exchange themselves. In a nuclear-fission bomb, for example, a portion of the mass of the fissile material is released in the form of energy when the devastating device is detonated; and, in engineered circumstances, collisions of photons can produce material particles. The appearance of those microbits is not an instance of matter's arising from nothing

---

[83] Ibid., 96–97.

any more than the appearance of virtual particles is one. These phenomena are not leaks; they are not void-seepages. Virtual particles are spawned by the zero-point energy that is inherent in a system. They do not come into existence from sheer nonbeing, nor do they disappear into it. A straightforward case of exchange, the energy that was there to give rise to the particles is returned upon their collapse.

To believe that virtual particles constitute a counterexample to the principle ex nihilo nihil fit is to misunderstand the principle altogether or, at least, to misunderstand the meaning of the term 'nothing' in the principle's employment of it. 'Nothing' means *'nothing'*—literally, strictly, exhaustively, and absolutely. It does not mean 'something other than'. Krauss seems to admit that identifying empty space with nothing is inadequate, as his following comments about cosmic inflation indicate:

> [T]he observation that the universe is flat and that the local Newtonian gravitational energy is essentially zero today is strongly suggestive that our universe arose through a process like that of inflation, a process whereby the energy of empty space (nothing) gets converted into the energy of something.
>
> . . . [I]t would be disingenuous to suggest that empty space endowed with energy, which drives inflation, is really *nothing*.[84]

Krauss offers an alternative depiction of nothing, which does not draw on the vacuum of space. I will take it up in a moment.

REAL AND UNREAL—THE VALUE OF THE VOID

The occurrences of spontaneous emissions and virtual-particle generations are local phenomena, but the genuine weight of the principle ex nihilo nihil fit becomes evident when it is taken globally: On the condition that nothing was, nothing is; and, on the

---

[84] Ibid., 152.

condition that nothing is, nothing will be. It is *this* contention that unsettles those who seek to explain the existence of the universe without introducing agency. Behind the quarrel that Stenger and Krauss have with the principle as it may pertain to quantum phenomena is a more ponderous issue. It is stated best in the form of a question: If something can come from nothing, then why not everything, where 'everything' is taken to mean 'the sum of physical reality'—that is to say, the universe? Of course, if all can spring forth from naught, then one can account for the existence of the cosmos without reliance on God. The quantum-sphere examples that these scientists raise merely serve as the springboard to a declaration of their atheistic stance. The tacit reasoning appears in the following argument; the steps are numbered for reference:

Part I

1. If something arises uncaused, then it comes from nothing.
2. There are things that arise uncaused.
3. Therefore, there are things that come from nothing.

Part II

4. If something comes from nothing, then it is possible that everything comes from nothing.
5. There are things that come from nothing (from Part I, step 3).
6. Therefore, it is possible that everything comes from nothing.

The first premise of Part I is false. It rests on a mistaken notion. To lack a cause of an arising, even if such were possible, would not be to arise out of a sheer void, as I demonstrated. The second premise is based on a theoretical view that some physicists have adopted, and I endeavored to show that it too is false. It embodies an incorrect view of causality; the phenomena that Stenger and Krauss put forward as representatives of uncaused events are submitted unsuccessfully. Thus, Part I of the argument is not sound and consequently does not establish its conclusion. Its conclusion is, in fact, false.

Likewise, Part II is not sound. Note the first premise, step 4. From the fact that an assertion may be true of one thing, it does not follow that it can be true of everything. There is something in the cosmos that comes from hydrogen and oxygen—water, for example. It does not follow that everything, all physical reality, can come from those two elements—salt comes from sodium and chlorine. Again, let the universe of discourse be persons. Someone in the world may be taller than everyone else in the world. One cannot conclude from this fact that it is possible that everyone in the world is taller than everyone else in the world. Such a state of affairs is barred by logic. The conditional statement that is presented in this step is not defensible as it stands. Step 5 is the false conclusion of Part I. Therefore, the conclusion of Part II is not established, and, as I hope to show in the next section, it is also false.

NOTHING AND EVERYTHING

A brief article by Edward P. Tryon offers a cosmogonic hypothesis that draws on the popular view that the universe is traceable to a primeval event, but he postulates further that the event issued from a vacuum, which, as I noted, is endowed with energy. States the scientist in the paper, which appeared in the 1970s,

> Here I propose a specific big bang model which I believe to be the simplest and most appealing imaginable—namely, that our universe is a fluctuation of the vacuum, where 'vacuum fluctuation' is to be understood in the sense of quantum field theory.[85]

The notion caught on, and, in the decades that followed, other scientists took up the charge. Though hardly touting an original concept by that point, they expounded on Tryon's hypothesis to underscore the assumed mechanistic cosmic beginning, attempting to obviate the need for God to explain the origin of things. According to

---

[85] Edward P. Tryon, "Is the Universe a Vacuum Fluctuation?" *Nature* 246, no. 5433 (1973): 396.

the thinking, as long as the net energy in the universe remains zero, where the positive energy of matter is balanced by the negative gravitational energy, the universe can develop into its current state from a meager wavering in the vacuum without violating the law of conservation.

A recent work by physicists Stephen Hawking and Leonard Mlodinow contains the following claim:

> Because gravity shapes space and time, it allows space-time to be locally stable but globally unstable. On the scale of the entire universe, the positive energy of the matter *can* be balanced by the negative gravitational energy, and so there is no restriction on the creation of whole universes. Because there is a law like gravity, the universe can and will create itself from nothing. . . . Spontaneous creation is the reason there is something rather than nothing, why the universe exists, why we exist. It is not necessary to invoke God to light the blue touch paper and set the universe going.[86]

This assertion is somewhat muddled. As a minor point, it is not entirely clear whether the authors are saying that the force of gravity accounts for the universe's arising, or the law of gravity does so. Presumably, they mean gravity in the former sense; the law merely ties the force to its effects by universalizing the application to things with mass and by supporting predictions, which are based on the universalization, about occurrences.

There are other difficulties with the passage, and they are more serious. The first problem is that the claim by Hawking and Mlodinow that the universe can, and will, create itself is, taken literally, logically absurd. If any existent thing could have created itself, then it would have had to have existed before it existed, which is a logical impossibility. Only that which exists can act as a cause, a point that I have expressed on several occasions. That which does not exist cannot do anything at all and hence cannot cause anything. A fortiori, it cannot cause anything to come into existence, and therefore it cannot cause itself to come into existence. Contrary to the

---

[86] Hawking and Mlodinow, *Grand Design*, 180.

authors' claim, the universe cannot create itself. The position that they espouse is self-refuting.

The second problem concerns the authors' remark that, because of gravitational law, the universe arose from nothing. What do they mean by the term 'nothing'? If one takes their assertion in what I will call the strong sense of the term, then one arrives at a contradiction. They would hold that, prior to the coming into existence of the universe, nothing existed, but something existed—namely, gravity— which Hawking and Mlodinow draw on to explain the arising of the universe from nothing. Gravity cannot predate the arising of the universe if the universe is predated entirely by nothing. On the other hand, if gravity arose along with the universe that it supposedly explains, then gravity, in fact, could not serve as an explanation for the arising, as it could have had no part in it.

Elsewhere, Hawking makes a related declaration; consider this remark:

> As the universe expands, it borrows energy from the gravitational field to create more matter. The positive matter energy is exactly balanced by the negative gravitational energy, so the total energy is zero.[87]

To maintain conservation in accordance with the physical law that governs it, the amount of energy in a closed system must be fixed. If there were no energy, then that no-energy state would be permanent. Any arising of energy in the universe must be in compliance with the rule of physics. Certainly, there is no energy in nothingness, for there is no existent thing there. Then, the problem, if one is to argue that the universe arose out of nothing, is to preserve the state of no energy while allowing the production of what exists in the cosmos. What Hawking and Mlodinow theorize to dodge the problem, following Tryon's postulation, is a process whereby a balance between the positive energy of matter and the negative gravitational energy is maintained, such that the sum remains zero. In this scenario then, the universe pulls itself up by its own bootstraps, taking care, as it were, to comply with the law of conservation of energy. This case of no

---

[87] Stephen Hawking, *The Universe in a Nutshell* (New York: Bantam Books, 2001), 91.

energy is *not* that of *nonexistent energy*. Far from it, it is that of zero *net* energy—a critical distinction.

Picture two seesaws at a schoolyard. The beams of both are parallel to the ground. No one is sitting on the first one, but Billy and Bobby, two boys of equal weight, are seated on the second. One might suppose that they climbed aboard near the middle, the same distance from the fulcrum, and slid backward at the same rate, maintaining equilibrium. When a teacher finds them on the playground, they are occupying the positions that are shown in the seesaw on the right in Figure 6.12.

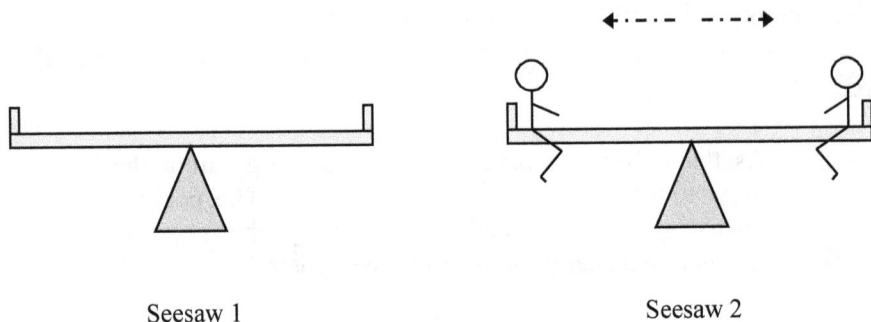

Seesaw 1   Seesaw 2

Figure 6.12

Even though both seesaws are in perfect balance, leaning neither to the left nor to the right, there is an obvious difference. Only the first one is empty; no one is riding it.

A crude illustration perhaps, it represents nevertheless, in a somewhat comparable way, the physicists' suggestion that the universe can come forth from nothing, as long as the energy of matter is offset by gravitational energy, thereby avoiding a conflict with conservation. The Hawking-Mlodinow account, however, is not that of arising out of nothing. In holding that things can spring into being out of a void, they are using the term 'nothing' to mean 'something other than'. Although gravity can *arrange* matter, it cannot account for why the energy, from which matter—virtual or otherwise—is supposed to have come, is there in the first place. If the energy were not there, then the universe would not be able to borrow it, as Hawking imagines. Nothing, not even the universe, can borrow from what does not exist. Contrary to their assertion about spontaneous creation, Hawking and Mlodinow do not explain why there is something rather than nothing. Billy and Bobby are existent entities, but, like most active boys, they moved; in this case, they slid backward on the board. Self-organization is not self-genesis.

Others take a position that is similar to that of Hawking and Mlodinow, as evidenced by this affirmation by a pair of astronomers:

> The idea of a zero-energy Universe, together with inflation, suggests that all one needs is just a tiny bit of energy to get the whole thing started (that is, a tiny volume of energy in which inflation can begin). The Universe then goes through inflationary expansion, but without creating net energy.[88]

From where does the energy to launch the process come? It is not surprising that these astronomers turn to the frenzy of virtual particles, correlated with quantum fluctuations, as a source and, also not surprising, think that the source can be nothing. They assert,

> According to quantum theory, there is a natural way that the energy may have come out of nothing. . . . [I]t turns out that "virtual" pairs of particles and anti-particles can spontaneously form and quickly disappear without measurably violating the law of conservation of energy. . . . These spontaneous births and deaths are called "quantum fluctuations."[89]

What follows is a summary of the general sequence that many of the scientists who are under discussion in this section put forward as an account of the beginning of the universe. Quantum fluctuations occur. These fluctuations correspond to the generation, and nearly

---

[88] Jay M. Pasachoff and Alex Filippenko, *The Cosmos: Astronomy in the New Millennium* (Fort Worth: Harcourt College Publishers, 2001), 375.
[89] Ibid.

instantaneous annihilation, of virtual particles in tiny vacuum spaces. As long as the existence of the particles is brief enough to be within the constraints that time-energy uncertainty imposes, the phenomenon does not violate conservation. The rapidity with which the matter-antimatter pairs collapse following production smoothes the overall energy level, absorbing the slight variances within the bounds of uncertainty, so that it remains at an average of zero. In one particular fluctuation, however, a difference occurs as a consequence perchance of different initial conditions. The tiny space-cum-virtual-particles undergoes a sudden, dramatic, and very brief inflation as space moves away from the initial energy incident far faster than the speed of light, dragging whatever is in that space with it. The inflation period ends, but expansion continues at a less brisk pace. The creation of matter is fueled by gravity, balancing the positive energy with the negative. Once the initial seed of energy exists, given the right circumstances, inflation can be off and running as the seed takes root, and the universe is born.

It is quite a story. Even those who believe that it is feasible call it an "admittedly speculative hypothesis."[90] One wonders exactly how everything gets under way, given that, if truly nothing exists, then there is nothing to fluctuate. Is this account simply a global version of nothing's equaling something? A universe that comes from energy oscillations is *not* a universe that comes from nothing; so, is the thinking that nothing itself is fluctuating, or is it rather that something that came from nothing is fluctuating? The stance that appears to be the trend is traceable to a twentieth-century article by a physicist who claimed, "The answer to the ancient question 'Why is there something rather than nothing?' would then be that 'nothing' is unstable."[91] Stenger seems to concur, accepting the alleged instability of nothing as a way that one might account for the universe's arising from it.

> Does this imply that we have explained how the Universe came from nothing (assuming that it did)? The meaning of the word *nothing* is a source of endless

---

[90] Ibid., 376.
[91] Frank Wilczek, "The Cosmic Asymmetry between Matter and Antimatter," *Scientific American* 243, no. 6 (1980): 90.

debate. How do you define nothing? What are the characteristics of nothing needed to define it? If it has any characteristics, any properties, then would it not be something?

I have defined the void as what you get when you remove all the matter and energy. No physical quantities are measurable in the void. The void does not kick back when you kick it. If this void is not "nothing," then I do not know what is. But if the void is unstable, then we have "something" existing as another phase or state of nothing, the way ice and steam are different phases of water.[92]

This passage is fraught with problems. Nothing is not something that is left over after one extracts all the matter and whatever energy can be removed, leaving only the vacuum energy of the system. As noted earlier, the vacuum is not nothing; "[I]t is a mistake to think of any physical vacuum as some absolutely empty 'void'."[93] A more pressing concern is that the confusion in the passage results in an inconsistency that ushers in a meaningless claim. Stenger correctly implies in the first paragraph that nothing—pure emptiness—lacks any properties; otherwise, nothing would be something. Immediately afterward, he states that nothing is the void, and suggests that the void is unstable. Instability, however, is a property. The passage is in conflict with itself. Only existents can exhibit properties or stand in relations to existents. Nothing is not something that exists. One cannot ascribe properties to it. To assert that it is unstable is to put forward a statement that is without any meaning. Stenger's misstep extends to his implication that nothing must have properties for it to be defined; however, it is the *absence* of properties, not the *presence* of them, that captures the concept.

Krauss fares no better. He abandons, at least, the idea that the term 'nothing' could apply properly to empty space and the energy within it, but, in shifting to a new concept of nothing, he makes the same mistake as his predecessors.

---

[92] Victor J. Stenger, *The Comprehensible Cosmos: Where Do the Laws of Physics Come From?* (Buffalo: Prometheus Books, 2006), 171–72.

[93] Christopher Ray, *Time, Space, and Philosophy* (London: Routledge, 1991), 205.

> [Q]uantum gravity not only appears to allow universes to
> be created from nothing—meaning, in this case, I
> emphasize, the absence of space and time—it may
> require them. "Nothing"—in this case no space, no time,
> no anything!—*is* unstable.[94]

Krauss's claim that nothing—no anything—is unstable is totally
nonsensical. Nothing is nonbeing. It *is exactly* nonbeing. It *is strictly*
equivalent to nonbeing, to nonreality. It is the complete absence of
any existent whatsoever. The unreal cannot possess attributes—*any*
attributes. To ascribe either stability or instability to nothing results
in a declaration that is utterly meaningless.

One can capture the notion of nothingness by a statement in
logic using quantification to cover both properties and individuals—
possible in the second-order predicate calculus. Refer to chapter 3 for
a general discussion of predicate logic. A straightforward way to
express the notion is to assert that there is no property, and there is
no entity, such that the entity exhibits the property.[95] One may
represent the statement in this way, where the variable Φ ranges over
properties and x ranges over individual entities; other, equivalent
renderings are possible:

$$- (\exists \Phi) - (\exists x)(\Phi x)$$

Conceivably, one could take the philosophical position that it is
possible for properties to exist—Platonic forms, for example—even
if there are no things that exhibit them. Further, one may hold that it
is possible for a thing—some conjectural primitive substance, for
example—to exist without any properties. It would follow that the
affirmation that is given above may open the door for there to be
something other than a void. It would be quite difficult to defend that
stance.

One can put forth an alternative nevertheless that avoids the
concern by using the terms of set theory, also making use of the
concept of reality. The approach would be to equate nothing with the

---

[94] Krauss, *Universe from Nothing*, 170.
[95] One can extend the notion to cover relations, but the extension is not needed:
The absence of properties ensures the absence of relations, except maybe identity.

set R, such that all things that are constituents of reality are elements of R, and R equals the null set.

When one focuses too closely on the physical framework, one will fail to see the point. Something cannot be another phase or state of nothing as Stenger says. Nothing cannot be, or be in, *any* phase or state. It has no properties. It does not exist.[96] Nothing is not a matter of physics but of metaphysics. Physics cannot show one nonbeing.

I am reminded of the existentialist Jean-Paul Sartre, who argues that, if he looks in a cafe, expecting to see Pierre, but he does not see him, then what he discovers is Pierre's absence; the absence is actually something—he discovers it. The view is senseless. Sartre should conclude only that Pierre is not in the cafe when he looks, not that the nonappearance of the man somehow bears ontic solidity.[97]

Instead of Sartre, perhaps it is Lewis Carroll of whom I should be reminded. He depicts the mistaken thinking in an amusing, but more pointed, way, as this passage reveals:

> "I see nobody on the road," said Alice.
> "I only wish *I* had such eyes," the King remarked in a fretful tone. "To be able to see Nobody! And at that distance too! Why, it's as much as *I* can do to see real people, by this light!"[98]

If it takes instability to push nothing into something, then, if there is ever truly nothing at all, then there never will be a universe—any universe—because it is nonsensical to hold that something can come from an unstable absence of anything in existence. Only the existent can be stable or unstable. Absence can be neither of them. Absence cannot be anything at all. The preclusion is not a scientific one; it is a logical one.

---

[96] Without doubt, nonexistence is not a property—recall the discussion of the ontological argument and the fact that existence is not a predicable attribute—and attempting to ascribe nonexistence as an attribute results in sheer nonsense.

[97] See Jean-Paul Sartre, *Being and Nothingness*, trans. Hazel E. Barnes (New York: Philosophical Library, 1956), 9–29. Sartre's work was published originally in French in 1943.

[98] Lewis Carroll, *Through the Looking Glass*, in *The Complete Works of Lewis Carroll* (New York: Vintage Books, 1976), 223. Carroll's work was published initially in London in 1872, several years after *Alice's Adventures in Wonderland*.

There is a different way to account for the universe, one that does not suppose that everything sprang from nothing. It is the description of the cosmic arising that theists believe to be right, set forth succinctly in the book of Isaiah: " 'Has not my hand made all these things, and so they came into being?' declares the LORD."[99] Whether one accepts it as the correct portrayal of the origination of physical reality, the portrayal of that origination is, at least, meaningful: The declaration makes sense. In this respect, it stands in stark contrast to its primary contender.

On the surface, it may seem that the principle ex nihilo nihil fit faces a challenge on another front. Predictably perhaps, it pertains to the theistic account of origination—namely, creation—where a generative force brings things into existence. In Judaeo-Christian thought, this force is God. Even though, in the creation of the universe, a physical reality appears where none was beforehand, the generation does not proceed out of the total lack of anything in existence; by hypothesis, the essential, creative factor—specifically, God—must exist for there to be an act of creation. The generation proceeds rather out of the lack of any physical thing in existence. It is the beginning of the being of nature, but it is not the beginning of being. Creation, of course, is not limited to the corporeal—to assume otherwise is to make an unwarranted supposition. I will focus on the physical cosmos in the discussion here, however.

In creation, physical things have a beginning, in that the substantiveness of their being is an entirely new thing, just now present in the realm of reality. That beginning is traceable nevertheless to that which preexists. In this case, the preexistent is also a precipitating cause. Things are brought forth by that which is prior to them and is external to the realm of physicality in which they emerge. What is prior to them and apart from the initial physical emptiness is the Creator. If the external, creative force is omitted, leaving only the pure emptiness, then nothing can come of it— literally. In creation, one might say, the physical is brought into being in the absence of anything that is physical—no initial matter or energy or even space-time—but it is not brought into being in the absence of anything at all, for it is the effect of existent agency that

---

[99] Isa. 66:2 NIV. For the NIV use of the special font, here and elsewhere, see p. iv.

has the ability to generate. The locution 'creation ex nihilo' is applied to such an act, but it is important to understand that the 'ex nihilo' (or 'out of nothing') component of the locution does not apply to that which is doing the creating. There can be no creation, ex nihilo or otherwise, if there is nothing in existence to perform the creative deed. Of logical necessity, creation entails something that creates. In Judaeo-Christian thinking, that dynamic is God. Whether one accepts the reality of this Supreme Being, postulating His existence does not stand in contradistinction to the principle.

Krauss, though, presents an argument against the compatibility of the tenet ex nihilo nihil fit and the existence of the Creator.

> [T]hose who argue that out of nothing nothing comes seem perfectly content with the quixotic notion that somehow God can get around this. But once again, if one requires that the notion of true nothingness requires not even the *potential* for existence, then surely God cannot work his wonders, because if he does cause existence from nonexistence, there must have been the potential for existence.[100]

Krauss is correct, in that there can be no actual existence without the potential for it. Only the potentially real ever can be genuinely real. The problem with the argument is that Krauss's use of the concepts of both potentiality and nothingness is skewed, and he fails to take hold of the tenet because of it. To say that there is a potential for some event to occur is to say that its occurrence can take place. Events are context-dependent, however. The potential for their occurrence is not free of the circumstances in which they are embedded. Davey has the potential to knock the ball out of the baseball park during a game before the season ends, although there are only two competitions left. His father has been coaching him on his stance, his swing, and his timing. Davey placed a fly ball over the fence in practice three weeks ago. His last one in a game sailed over third base, barely inside the line, and landed just two feet short of the fence. The boy's heart is set on reaching the milestone; it will be the first of his career in this middle-school league. It is possible that he

---

[100] Krauss, *Universe from Nothing*, 174.

will accomplish his objective; it is within his capabilities to bring it to pass. Yet, that potential occurrence is contingent, not absolute. If Davey falls sliding into home and breaks both his arms, then he will not be able to swing at all until well after the season ends. The potential for him to realize his dream suddenly disappears. The occurrence of a home run is not unqualified. It is not unconditional. It is dependent on the unfolding of events in the relevant context. There is no iron-clad assurance at work here.

The fundamental import of the philosophical principle at hand may be expressed in this way: What comes to exist can do so only if something exists. As I mentioned previously, philosophers use the locution 'possible world' in building a specific, comprehensive set of circumstances. The term does not refer to an actual structure but to the totality of a given set of states of affairs, especially as those states of affairs are captured by propositions that purport to present facts about them. For instance, there is a possible world in which the sun is a double star two hundred million miles from the earth, sugar tastes sour, and Davey made a perfect score on his first geometry test—not the world that humans know—among other circumstances. An inclusive description of pertinent conditions defines the possible world. If a statement is true in all possible worlds, then it is logically necessary; its denial is a contradiction. To say that no number is greater than itself is to put forth a statement that is true in all possible worlds. To say that Davey has the potential to lob a ball over the fence is not to assert that it can happen in all possible worlds; it can happen only in a world in which he does not break his arms or suffer some other catastrophe—or any number of other conditions prevail.

Krauss removes the core contingency that makes creation ex nihilo possible. It is not that there is a potential, regardless of the circumstances, for the universe to arise where no physicality exists. The potential is there only if something exists before the universe arises, and what exists, in the case at hand, has the ability to create ex nihilo. It is *because God exists* that the conditions that are necessary for a physical universe to come into existence in the absence of all physicality obtain. Krauss misses the point. True nothingness, to use his phrase, indeed does preclude the potential for existence, but, if something exists—specifically, God—then it is *not the case* that there is true nothingness. Change the circumstances, though, remove *everything*, including God, and the potential for existence vanishes like Davey's dream of glory. If there is genuinely nothing, then there *is no* potential for there to be something, and herein lies the essence of the canon. Krauss builds his case around a mishandling of the key concepts. In the end, his argument actually offers support for the philosophical principle under review instead of opposition to it.

Ultimately, to avoid absurdities, it seems that the various scientists whom I covered in this section could use 'nothing' only in a weak sense of the term. In this sense, 'nothing' does not mean 'absence of being' but rather 'something other than'. Their claims then would be merely that the universe sprang into being by virtue of something that was already there. The theists would agree, but they would say that it is not energy but agency that lies at the base. Who is right?

THE NEED TO KNOW—REVISITED

Although his wager about eternity was elementary and incomplete, Pascal did underscore, at least, the awesome weight that the question of God's existence thrusts on humankind. The simple desire to know on intellectual grounds is prevalent among people, but one's belief in the Supreme Being is tied to far more than one's curiosity. It is central to a perspective about life and its value. It shapes the ideas regarding right and wrong. It molds the thinking about whether there is a specific purpose for each individual and whether, at the end of the day, there is continued existence in an eternity. If humans are merely beings of happenstance in a great cosmos of chance, honed perhaps across eons by natural selection, then anything that is beyond the ephemeral slips from hope's grasp. All that one is, is all that one is today; so, " 'Let us eat and drink, for tomorrow we die.' "[101] Standards of right conduct become self-based or, at best, society-based, and hedonism begins to sink its roots in the soft ground of relativism. Subject to the whims of the times, morality

---

[101] 1 Cor. 15:32 NIV; cf. Isa. 22:13.

is up-anchored and humanity is set adrift. Whether God exists is a matter that extends beyond the mere inquisitive nature of persons. It defines them. It is not surprising that history reflects a focus on the question. To be sure, people want to know, but, more important, they need to know.

The arguments for the existence of God that I have discussed in this chapter may not convince one to abandon a contrary, nontheistic position, but the objections to those arguments surely convince no one to retain it. The wonder of the universe somehow seems to transcend all that logic. On a cold, clear night in the heart of winter when everyone else in the house is asleep, one might want to dress warmly, go outside, and gaze up at the heavens in the silence, taking a few moments to ponder what an amazing thing lies before the eyes. Two trillion galaxies are out there, hundreds of sextillions of stars— an enormous expanse. The amount of material that is sailing through the vastness of space is staggering. Given that mass and energy are interconvertible, the exchange itself is staggering. Einstein's well-known equation reveals the sheer magnitude of such a thing. If just half a teaspoon of common sugar were transformed into the energy that corresponds to its tiny mass, then the resultant release would be equivalent to three times the energy that was discharged in the nuclear blast that destroyed the city of Hiroshima in 1945.

Somewhere in the distance a dog may bark, bringing back for a bit an awareness of the world in which the daily demands of life unfold: completing the report tomorrow for the audit committee, replacing the broken sprocket wheel on the daughter's bicycle, finding that special gift for the close friend's wedding on Saturday, or maybe cutting down the leaning tree that threatens the roof. Then, all is quiet again. The thoughts return. One can imagine what it would be like if the mass of all the matter in the cosmos were changed into equivalent energy. Perhaps more impactful, one can imagine the stupendous amount of energy that it would have taken to produce all that cosmic matter—what an awesome realization it is. Even if the lot of it might sum to zero, it is surely far from nothing, and, if . . . no, concentrating so intensely on the physics leads one to overlook the wonder of it all. David, king of Israel, understood; he penned these words:

The heavens declare the glory of God;
    the skies proclaim the work of his hands.
Day after day they pour forth speech;
    night after night they display knowledge.
There is no speech or language
    where their voice is not heard.
Their voice goes out into all the earth,
    their words to the ends of the world.[102]

Is anyone listening?

---

[102] Ps. 19:1–4 NIV.

CHAPTER 7

IN DENIAL

In his pride the wicked does not seek him;
in all his thoughts there is no room for God.

—Ps. 10:4 NIV

The college years hold special memories for me. It was a time of discovery, with many frontiers to explore—academic, psychological, social, and political, to list a few—and many avenues for exploring them. At the university that I attended as an undergraduate, entering students were required to live in a dormitory for the initial semester, after which they could move to off-campus locations, if desired. In retrospect, I believe that the administrators were wise to make such a requirement. Hardly a model of maturity at seventeen, I found my first weeks in this environment of freedom to be filled with opportunities for adventure. During the months that were to come, my friends and I launched into numerous escapades, far from the rigidity of the classroom, some of which risked life and limb. A favorite of ours was a trek to the trestle near the dormitory that offered, among other things, a device that was ready-made for vertical hiking. I recall waiting anxiously on one occasion for the next train to come our way, then climbing down from the tracks to just below the railroad bed on the aging structure, its wooden beams crisscrossing beneath us as if to provide strategically placed stepping points. With tons of machinery and freight above us and a dizzy drop to the underlying terrain, it was simply great fun to hang onto the old trestle while the train roared past. For us, caution was of little value in the quest for excitement, but we all survived. It is good to be alive.

Dormitory life brought its own set of challenges. My roommate was a person whom I had met during my high-school days, so we had a head start on adjusting to the circumstances. Mike and I were committed enemies in the twelfth grade, though—something about a girl whom I liked—but, by the time that we enrolled in our college courses, we had come to be close friends. That friendship would last a lifetime. The girl, however, faded from my life as we grew apart. Mike and I did honor her with a song that I had written in memory of the romance, our guitars harmonizing better than our voices on my soulful masterpiece. She never had the opportunity to hear it, which, no doubt, spared my feelings in more than one way. I think that I still can recall the chords. All right, how did it go? Yes, I remember— Dmaj7, then G6: *San-dy* . . . *San-dy* . . . .

Mike talked in his sleep. Had I known, it might have prepared me for what was going to happen. It was the middle of the night, sometime during that initial semester. All was quiet. I was sleeping soundly, dreaming of Sandy perhaps. Suddenly, Mike sat straight up in his bed and exclaimed in an alarming, frantic way what I am certain was, "Quick! Somebody's pouring water on the radio!" Such news at 2:00 in the morning, or whatever time it was, can be rather startling. I sat straight up in my bed: horizontal to vertical in an instant, dreams to reality in a fraction of a second. My mind was reeling, trying to process this new piece of information—only a few seconds to formulate a plan of action. What do we do? Where is the intruder? Why would anyone do such a thing? Do we even have a radio? Critical moments passed. My mind began to focus. Rationality was beginning to return. Wait a minute—what sense does what he said make; what is going on here? There must have been sufficient light from the window to see Mike's face. I looked at him. His eyes were glazed, his countenance blank. Like a tabula rasa, that iconic prior-to-experience mind in John Locke's philosophy, no functioning psyche existed behind that stare—not one, in any event, that had made the leap to consciousness. "Go back to sleep, Mike," I told him. He lay back in his bed, and I in mine, but I am not sure that sleep in the dormitory ever was the same for me after that incident.

The following semester was an improvement—in some ways, at any rate. Mike and I left the campus and joined three other friends in renting a house. It was an ideal place to live. More adventures awaited, not the least of which was an experiment that went wrong, frightfully so. I was confident that it was going to be awesome, a great work in the distinguished field of chemistry. I had made concoctions before; occasionally, I varied the components, but this one was a standard assembly, with one exception: It was big. What followed never should have happened: The thing ignited in the kitchen. The waste of a prized ingredient was disappointing. Trying to extinguish the blaze once the reaction started was futile. I attempted to halt its progress, though, and reached for the closest available tool: a broom—just not the best piece of equipment to use for flame-control. It burned too. The fire that was associated with the chemical reaction was too hot for normal measures to be effective. It continued until the process came to an end through the depletion of the compounds. General visibility in the house was only a few feet, approaching no feet at ground zero. An impressive result maybe, but the location of the burn event was not in the plan. Good science cannot be rushed, I suppose. With the windows open, we sat outside on the porch, waiting for the smoke to clear; it took about an hour. A neighbor had called the fire department. I suspect that the municipal employees in a college town are accustomed to such things. The episode did not stop us from conducting other experiments, one involving . . . but it may be wise to remain silent on some matters.

Despite the risk of collateral damage from our activities, college life persisted. Mike and another of our group entered the army. The rest of us pursued our studies. After graduation, I worked in the private sector for a period of time, then returned to the university to enroll in graduate school. The dormitory where I had lived had been reestablished as a residence hall for mentally challenged individuals. The basketball courts were intact, probably the original ones, still there from my early college days, so I decided on a particular occasion to spend some time tossing the ball at the hoop.

A strange feeling accompanied my being on the premises again as reminiscence took me to a bygone season of camaraderie. Much had changed since my semester in the dormitory—admittedly, more in me than in the grounds. No students lived there at that point, only persons with special needs. A young inhabitant from the facility stood nearby; I passed the ball to him to take a shot. It arced into the hoop as though guided by lasers. He had another chance to miss when I passed the ball to him a second time, but it was a repeat performance. We moved around on the court. I took shots and grabbed the rebounds. Time after time, I threw the ball to him. Shot after shot, his execution was perfect. We continued to play. Some of my attempts to hit the net were successful; some of them missed the mark. The young man never spoke a word. I do not believe that he was capable of speaking, but he understood what he was to do: put the ball through the hoop.

His consistency in accomplishing the objective was astounding. Regardless of where he stood, regardless of the angle or distance to the goal, he sailed that ball into the net with the precision of a neurosurgeon. It was not a typical afternoon workout on the courts. Assuming that memory serves me well, and I am confident that it does so, I can aver that he never missed—never, not even once. My skill in the sport stood in stark contrast to his ability. It was fascinating to watch this young man in action. Although his intellectual faculties were seriously deficient, he possessed a remarkable capacity to visualize trajectories in varying circumstances and to hit the target with unfailing accuracy.

There are times, however, when hitting the mark is not hitting the mark at all, so to speak. It is not the accuracy of the aim that is in question but the legitimacy of the target. During World War II, both the Allies and the Germans deployed fake tanks. The devices served a dual purpose: They gave the appearance of a formidable force, and they helped to protect the real tanks by diverting the focus of the enemy. A direct strike on one of these posturing decoys would demolish it, but it had no impact on the ability of the actual armored division to engage in combat.

There is a parallel to this case in philosophical circles. One who takes a stand against a position must identify correctly what lies in the sights before launching an attack. If the target is a counterfeit, then, even if the aim is sure, nothing is gained. From such faulty identity stems the logical fallacy of straw man. In committing this fallacy, one confronts a misrepresentation of the opposing position (or perhaps a weakened version of it) in setting forth an argument rather than confronting an accurate portrayal of the opponent's view. The assailing philosopher fires at a mock tank, as it were, and the imitation is usually one that the philosopher has created. The real war machine, the one that threatens to dismantle the assailant's own chain of reasoning, is left unscathed. Such arguments are doomed to failure. I will show in this chapter how that fallacy operates in two major attacks on the existence of God.

ARGUMENTS TO THE CONTRARY

In the previous chapter, I examined five patterns of proofs of God's existence—concentrating on the ostensible purposiveness of nature. Not unexpectedly, philosophers have criticized each of them, but the criticisms themselves are subject to criticism. In the philosophical enterprise, such is the way of things. Of course, an argument that is not compelling may have a true conclusion nonetheless. If the proofs that I covered are not universally persuasive, then that fact says nothing about whether God exists, only that one cannot get there through the metaphysics in view. Still, the notion that there is a principle of rationality underlying the workings of the world and the life within it—a principle that several ancient Greek philosophers recognized—does give one pause. Is intelligent design behind the cosmos, or is this design merely apparent? One author, whom I will discuss in a moment, endeavors to prove that it is illusory.

As one would anticipate then, just as there are arguments for God's existence, there are arguments against it. I turn my attention now to two main lines of thought that writers have advanced in support of atheism. The first seeks to draw an inconsistency between the divine attributes of God and the conditions that people experience in the world. It is an old argument, dating back centuries, although it continues to surface. The second is a more interesting construction and, in the form that it is presented, more recent. It is an inversion of the argument from design that, echoing the tactic of David Hume, attempts to produce an infinite regress based on property ascriptions. One will see that these arguments fail to be credible, but the analysis of them is worthwhile nevertheless, as it serves to underscore the limitations of metaphysics in the pursuit of existent divinity.

ARGUMENT FROM EVIL

Introduced by the Greek philosopher Epicurus (341–270 B.C.), this classic argument for atheism centers on the characteristics of a divine being and the appearance of evil in the world. According to the reasoning in its more modern form, if God is perfectly powerful, then He can prevent evil; if He is perfectly good, then He is opposed to it. Given that evil exists, it must be that God does not exist. The skeptic Hume puts forth perhaps the most succinct representation of the argument; he says,

> Is he [God] willing to prevent evil, but not able? then is he impotent. Is he able, but not willing? then is he malevolent. Is he both able and willing? whence then is evil?[1]

There is more than one category of what philosophers deem to be evil. I will focus on the two primary forms. In one mode of the argument that is based on the concept of it, evil is associated with morally reprehensible deeds that are performed willfully by agents. In another, it is associated with afflictions and suffering, which may be caused by disease, lack, or traumatic occurrences, such as natural disasters. Albeit the things in this latter category may be undesirable, they, considered in themselves, cannot be evil. Evil is a quality that is ascribable only to moral agents and what is linked to their agency. It entails core iniquity or malicious intent, and intent, whether it is directed toward good or harm, requires a mind. A car door that shuts on Joan's finger is not intrinsically evil, even though the pain that the incident brings may be great. The closing might have been an act of cruelty by her cousin, an act of carelessness by her aunt, or no act at all, simply an accident that was caused by the car's rolling when the emergency brake failed. Only the first event carries with it malice aforethought. Unless sickness, trauma, and the like are brought about by an intelligent agent for the strict purpose of causing harm, they are neither evil things nor the products of evil. The question of why suffering exists if God exists remains, however. Despite the fact that suffering cannot be classified as a form of wickedness, it still may seem to be in conflict with God's goodness—on the surface, at least.

A number of attacks have been directed at the argument from evil, but some of these supposed defenses are devoid of merit. One such defense posits that God may exist, but He is finite, not infinite,

---

[1] David Hume, *Dialogues concerning Natural Religion*, in *David Hume: The Philosophical Works*, ed. Thomas Hill Green and Thomas Hodge Grose (1882, 1886; repr., Frankfurt am Main, Germany: Scientia Verlag Aalen, 1964), 2:440.

lacking either supreme power or supreme goodness. This objection is self-defeating. The very concept of God, as identified in the previous chapter, is that of an infinite being.[2] The arguments that are put forth for His existence employ the notion that God is both powerful and good without limit. To deny that God has these characteristics is to deny, through redefinition, that God exists. It is as though one applies the term 'rokorestrian' to any geological structure on the earth, the summit of which is no less than 31,510 feet above sea level, and then asserts that rokorestrians exist but that the highest ones are never greater than 29,029 feet in height.[3] To make that claim is tantamount to altering the meaning of the term to allow for the existence of the structures, or else maintain a contradiction. The proffered defense that is based on finitude actually supports the argument against which it is raised. One cannot uphold the existence of the infinite God by arguing that He is not infinite.

A second objection is that what one sees as evil in the world is an illusion that is attributable to limited understanding. An alternative take on this objection is that what one calls evil is real, but it is evil only when it is viewed in isolation. Something is judged to be evil because of one's narrow perspective.

To say that evil is an illusion is misguided. There is no justification for such a view. One could argue just as easily that good is an illusion, that it is because one's understanding is limited that one thinks otherwise. Both positions are distortions of reality. I remember watching a documentary years ago on the My Lai incident that took place during the Vietnam War. A woman had lost her children in the mayhem that befell that hamlet, and she was in the pits of despair, weeping for her dead family. An interpreter translated her lamentation as she groaned the words from the depth of her grief. Struggling to understand, she asked why life was so hard. Her question was striking in its profundity. Life *is* hard. Says Jesus, "In this world you will have trouble."[4] There is surely evil in the world;

---

[2] John Hick makes this point, claiming that solving the problem by ascribing finitude to God is abandoning the fundamental premise of the Hebrew-Christian belief that God is a sovereign, infinite being. See Hick's *Philosophy of Religion* (Englewood Cliffs, NJ: Prentice-Hall, 1963), 40.

[3] The latter height is the elevation of Mt. Everest, as recent calculations confirmed.

[4] John 16:33 NIV.

open any newspaper, or listen to the evening report on the radio. Anyone who hears about the kidnapping and murder of a child would be hard-pressed to hold that evil is an illusion. Those who take this path may have admirable intentions, but to deny that evil is real is to disregard the words of the God the existence of whom they are trying to defend: "I will punish the world for its evil, the wicked for their sins."[5]

The alternative stance with respect to the objection—that evil is real, though only when it is viewed in isolation—is misguided as well. It sometimes may take an encompassing outlook to apprehend a quality of something, but to hold that what one sees as evil is merely the product of an inadequate perspective, a fact that one will recognize when the big picture emerges, is to cling to an aberration. Things happen in the lives of people, not necessarily ones that they bring on themselves by their own actions. They may be brought on them by the actions of others; and many of these happenings, whether desirable or undesirable, can be viewed as components of something more global, something that is genuinely good. Being a component of something that is good, however, does not make the component itself good. It still can be evil. One cannot assume that the properties of a whole are properties of each of its parts. It does not follow from the fact that a softball team is the best in the state's middle-school league that each member of the team is the best. The famed Green Valley Warriors may be undefeated, but the group's pitcher has a mediocre record, easily outclassed by a number of other pitchers in the same club. The Warriors win or lose as a team, though, and they are going to the playoffs. To conclude that the pitcher must be the best because the team is the best is to commit the logical fallacy of division. Likewise, there can be evil, even if it is part of an overall good.

---

[5] Isa. 13:11 NIV.

EVIL AND AGENCY

I want to look more closely now at the argument as it pertains to agency, returning to the question of suffering in due course. There is a view that humans are beings with free will and that they sometimes do commit evil acts; but a world in which there is no evil at the hands of humans, because there is no free will, is a world without humankind. To prevent their doing evil is to take away their humanity and turn them into automata. This challenge to the argument from evil takes a step toward the unfolding of what I believe is its major problem. A subtle fallacy is at work in the argument, as Hume presents the reasoning in the aforementioned passage: It contains two implied declarations about God, without which it cannot establish its conclusion. One of those declarations, however, is false. When one completes the logical form, it appears as it does below. The steps are numbered for reference.

The Argument from Evil—Standard, Completed Form

1. If God is omnipotent, then He can prevent evil.
2. If God is benevolent, then He desires to prevent evil.
3. If God is omniscient, then He knows when evil will occur unless He acts to prevent it.
4. Therefore, if God exists, then He invariably will act in a way that prevents the occurrence of evil.
5. Evil exists.
6. Therefore, God does not exist.

The first add-on proposition appears in premise 3: God is omniscient. (Hume does include a like premise elsewhere.) If God is going to act against potential wrongdoings, then it is not enough that God be both powerful and good. He also must be aware of the impending evil: Being capable of preventing evil and desiring to prevent it would not result in its preclusion unless God knew about it beforehand. Atheists would not object to incorporating the proposition into the argument, as it would serve only to strengthen their stand, it seems; and, given that omniscience is an attribute that God possesses, according to the Judaeo-Christian view, theists would accept its truth.

The second appended proposition appears in step 4 of the argument. It is a specific instance of a broader principle on which it relies for support. One may put forth the principle in the following way:

> For any set of circumstances C and any evil deed d that could happen in C, a being who (1) possesses the capability to prevent the occurrence of d in C, (2) has good intentions, and (3) has an adequate understanding of the relevant facts will act to prevent d in C before it occurs.

As for God, His power, goodness, and knowledge are infinite. If therefore the principle is true, then these attributes must combine to prohibit evil in *every* possible case, *never* allowing it to happen, even if God might take action, punitive or otherwise, subsequently. God always must crush evil in advance. This supposed state of affairs is reflected in the conditional statement that is expressed in step 4.

This step does not follow from the first three premises, however. Furthermore, neither it nor the general principle of which it is an instance is true. The principle is a fabricated requirement. It is founded on what someone *thinks* that a good being—and therefore God—should do about evil, stemming from an incorrect notion of goodness. To argue against the existence of the Judaeo-Christian God based on the premise that He is good, one must attack the existence of Him in accordance with the right concept of His being, as revealed in the Scriptures, and the right concept of what it is to be a good agent.

Actions can encompass more than the immediate and often do so, and they may entail events, including other actions, that lead to an intended end. Refer to Figure 4.7 and the associated discussion in chapter 4. Global goals take precedence over local events. A long-term objective may be good, corresponding to a good purpose, but people have free will, and one cannot hold that all the acts that others perform in conjunction with a good plan will be good too. The characteristics of the parts may differ from those of the whole. Just as one cannot assume that the performance of the pitcher from Green Valley is excellent based on the fact that the performance of the school's team overall is excellent, the path to something beneficial may not be invariably beneficial in its entirety.[6] A benevolent God grants the freedom to choose, but those choices may lead to undesirable consequences because of the choices of others. Willing the best for someone does not entail blocking the person from the experiences of life. If it were so, then the only good parent would be the one who locks his or her child in the house until the child reaches adulthood. It is inevitable that schoolmates and playmates will act unkindly to the youngster at some point in the course of his or her maturation. A parent is not malevolent in allowing the child to develop socially, even though the parent (1) could prevent the occurrence of incidents that cause hurt feelings, (2) does not want such incidents to occur, and (3) knows that they indeed will take place unless the parent acts to avert them through isolation.

Moreover, the intention itself to do evil is evil. In fact, it is the intention with which an act is performed that imparts its moral character. Did Molly slap Millie because she was trying to smash the mosquito on her playmate's neck before it drew blood or because she wanted to hurt Millie for walking home with her boyfriend, Mickey, not knowing that the mosquito was preparing to strike? The unfolding of the physical event in the two cases is identical; the motive is the key, defining factor. Unless something happens to block it—say, physical prohibition, a changed mind, loss of memory, or pangs of conscience—a malevolent act will follow an agent's will to execute it, and the underpinning for the intention to execute it is a malevolent motive, joined by a related belief. If God is to prevent all evil, then He must prevent not only the acts but the intentions as well. He must not allow anyone to entertain certain thoughts or to possess certain attitudes. He must control people to the point that they cannot do, utter, or think anything that is wrong. He must remove their ability to make moral choices—to choose the good or the wicked, the virtuous

---

[6] One must not confuse this statement with the notion that the ends justify the means. The goodness of an act issues from the principles on which the agent undertakes the performance. Where other agents are involved in one's planned course of action, those agents may commit evil deeds, although both the intent of the planner and the outcome are good. A benevolent agent's global action cannot be construed to excuse the wicked deeds of others that the global action may comprise, but the agent acts, *despite* these interim, evil deeds, and regularly acts knowing what will happen.

or the iniquitous. In short, He must reduce humans to something akin to androids.

What god is *this* one? It is certainly not the God of the Bible, who permits free agents to act in accordance with their volitions but punishes the unrepentant for their deeds. God does not move to prevent evil in every set of circumstances, but He assuredly does move to balance the scales. No demonstrable notion of the Judaeo-Christian God includes this preventative constraint. To attempt to establish the conclusion, the argument from evil must ascribe to God unlimited power, goodness, and knowledge. Given, however, that the argument posits that the being the existence of whom it wishes to deny is God, it must allow the entire set of unbounded qualities that are attributed to Him.

God is righteous and fair without limit. He is also eternal. Even a cursory examination of the biblical account of the character of God reveals that unqualified justice is a facet of His being. God is absolutely just in executing judgment against all iniquity—at some point. Holding that His time frame for acting against evil is always prior to the occurrence of evil, however, is not supportable. Preemption is not a necessary condition of the existence of an omnipotent, benevolent, and omniscient being. One might ask well of Hume, if God always prevents evil, so that it never occurs, then *whence justice*? A judge whom one respects for acts of integrity is one who condemns the guilty and acquits the innocent, not one who sentences a person before a crime is conceived and ultimately accomplished. A price must be paid for the commission of evil deeds by agents with free will, but justice is rearward-looking, not forward-looking. An eternal God can ensure that the demands of justice *and* goodness are satisfied in accordance with His long-term plan.

> Jesus told them another parable: "The kingdom of heaven is like a man who sowed good seed in his field. But while everyone was sleeping, his enemy came and sowed weeds among the wheat, and went away. When the wheat sprouted and formed heads, then the weeds also appeared.
>
> "The owner's servants came to him and said, 'Sir, didn't you sow good seed in your field? Where then did the weeds come from?'

> "'An enemy did this,' he replied.
>
> "The servants asked him, 'Do you want us to go and pull them up?'
>
> "'No,' he answered, 'because while you are pulling the weeds, you may root up the wheat with them. Let both grow together until the harvest. At that time I will tell the harvesters: First collect the weeds and tie them in bundles to be burned; then gather the wheat and bring it into my barn.'"[7]

In this parable, righteousness prevails, but at the harvest, which represents the end of the age. The burning of the weeds symbolizes the judgment of God against the unrighteous lost among humankind. Action against evil is not overlooked, even though it is delayed. It is because of the *justice* of God that it is not overlooked; it is because of the *goodness* of God that it is delayed.

> The Lord is not slow in keeping his promise, as some understand slowness. He is patient with you, not wanting anyone to perish, but everyone to come to repentance.[8]

The conflicting state that the argument from evil purports to establish fails to materialize. An inconsistency can arise only if one assumes that God acts, necessarily and universally, in a manner that precludes the occurrence of every trace of evil because absolute goodness cannot allow any of it—at any time, in any place—to surface. Such a concept of goodness rests on a manufactured restriction. It stems from the belief that God *ought* to be a certain way in the expression of His character, but it is at odds with the way that God *is* in the expression of His character, as revealed in the biblical account. God may permit wickedness to obtain, despite the fact that He is opposed to it, because it suits His broader purposes, and those purposes are good. The argument from evil relies on the assumed, erroneous notion that beneficence entails preemptive exclusion. By employing this false idea, the argument attacks a caricature of God, an invented being who differs from the one the nonexistence of

---

[7] Matt. 13:24–30 NIV.
[8] 2 Pet. 3:9 NIV.

whom it is attempting to demonstrate. Such misrepresentation results in the fallacy of straw man, and the argument does not succeed.

There is another side of this form of the argument from evil, and it is the problem of its origin. The concern is that of accounting for the arising of evil in a good creation that was brought about by a good God. If everything that exists at some point in time is good, then how could some things—namely, Satan and the horde of fallen angels, and then humankind—become evil at a later point in time? As one author puts it,

> The simple presence of free will is not enough to explain the origin of evil, in as much as we still must ask how a good being would be inclined freely to choose evil. The inclination for the will to act in an immoral manner is already a signal of sin.[9]

The problem of the origin of evil is one that has educed various perspectives. I will not spend much time on it here, but it is worth noting its major points. Some philosophers have concerns about the emergence of evil from a created being who is perfectly good, though finite, as such an appearing would contradict a logical tenet: Evil would come from nothing, violating the basic principle ex nihilo nihil fit. If, on the other hand, evil arises from the potentiality for it in the being, then how can the being be perfectly good before the downfall?

The answer, it is clear, is that one cannot ascribe a property to an entity that possesses the potential for the actualization of that property unless the property is actualized. Jill is a brunette. She can dye her hair red at any time to change her appearance, if she wishes, but she never has red hair, for she never dyes it. A being may be good by virtue of creation because of the goodness that flows from the nature of the Creator, but the being may become evil by virtue of a will that loses its steadfastness as the agent chooses the path of wickedness. The potential itself of an agent to do evil is not evil any more than the potential of a student to fail algebra is a failure of algebra. Robbie *could have* gone fishing on the day of the final

---

[9] R. C. Sproul, "The Mystery of Iniquity: Right Now Counts Forever," *Tabletalk* 32, no. 12 (2008): 6.

exam, but he resisted the urging of the other boys in the area and went to school; he passed algebra. Following his neighbor's inflammatory remarks, Raymond *could have* opted to get even with his neighbor when the opportunity arose—he had the ability—but this fact does not demand a moral categorization of the possibility, especially a negative one. To say that a character failure arises from nothing in violation of ex nihilo nihil fit is illogical. Evil is not an entity; it is an attribute, a quality. Evil arises when the agent chooses wrongly from among potential courses of action. It is *actual* failure, not *potential* failure, that mars the agent's record. Indeed, it is *because* Raymond practiced restraint and did his neighbor no harm, whether in deed or word or thought, that one lauds his self-control.

I noted in chapter 4 that initiation lies at the heart of agency. Intentional doings begin with the agent's resolve, and evil begins in the same place. It does not come from nothing; it comes from the determination to do, and that determination is possible only if the potential for it exists. Nothing can occur in actuality unless it can occur in potentiality; that is to say, that which *does* happen must be only that which *can* happen. The potential for something to happen, however, is not the happening itself. Moral failure is inapplicable—it is bereft of all applicability of ascription—until the determination to proceed is complete; and that determination to proceed is in accordance with the free will of the agent as the agent decides on a course of action. Just as the possibility of winning the raffle is not the actuality of winning the raffle, it is not the temptation to do evil that is wrong but the yielding to that temptation that is wrong. Temptation underscores *choice*, not *occurrence*.

> For we do not have a high priest [Jesus] who is unable to sympathize with our weaknesses, but we have one who has been tempted in every way, just as we are—yet was without sin.[10]

A lack of sin is not the result of the lack of potential for it. In fact, it is the potential to act either justly or unjustly, rightly or wrongly, that defines the freedom of will that people possess. People decide. People make the election. They bring forth actual good or evil in

---

[10] Heb. 4:15 NIV.

accordance with the potential to do; and, when they do, that doing may be virtuous or blameworthy.

Cheating is wrong. Few would disagree. If no one ever cheated, then it still would be wrong, but there would be no concrete instance of its occurring. A student who is tempted to cheat on an exam does not cheat until succumbing to the temptation to take the easy path. Knowing that it is unethical, the student decides to proceed and glances at a classmate's paper. Whether an individual does evil or does not do it, it is *the individual* who makes it so. Without the possibility of choice, all humanity drifts toward the distortion of determinism. The problem of the origin of evil is not really very different from the problem of its presence. In either case, if one denies the existence of God, then it cannot be because of the argument from evil, as the argument does not carry the logical force that is needed to establish its conclusion.

EVIL AND SUFFERING

A second form of the argument from evil attempts to make the case that suffering is incompatible with God's existence. I noted earlier that suffering in itself is not evil, but there are those who attempt to include it as a form of evil when arguing against God. As before, the thinking is that an omnipotent God could prevent suffering and that, if He is truly good and cares for people, then He would prevent it. Given that people do suffer in this life, there can be no God.

St. Augustine, who spent much of his life delving into the problem of evil, concluded that evil can subsist in one of two modes: (1) deviation from good by free agents; (2) the punitive natural suffering, as ordained by God, that results from such deviation. Put succinctly, there is sin, and there is the pain of punishment for having committed it. Some suffering is surely attributable to the penalty for wrongdoing, as young Eddie's painful spanking for an act of deliberate disobedience demonstrates. His distress does not prove that his mother is not good or that she does not love him. Eddie took the path of noncompliance and bore the consequences of his act.

The argument based on suffering, however, is not about punishment for wrongdoings, which is not evil in the sense that the argument adopts. The point is that dreadful things happen to decent people. It is suffering when one has not committed a related, morally wrong act that is the concern. God would not let it happen, one may be inclined to say, if He is both powerful and good. In reply, one might note the fact that humans live in a world that is replete with sin, and one should expect to see the suffering of many because of it. Indeed, in the biblical account, the ground itself is cursed because of the moral failure of man.[11] The consequences of humankind's fall are profound and far-reaching; yet, just as all are subject to suffering in a troubled and fallen world, so all are subject to blessing: "He [God] causes his sun to rise on the evil and the good, and sends rain on the righteous and the unrighteous."[12] The atheists will reject the explanation, of course, and object to its employment in response to a line of reasoning that attempts to raise an inconsistency in the very foundation on which the explanation is set forth. That rejection is irrelevant, however, as it is not whether the account is factual that is at issue but whether the existence of God is incompatible with the reality of affliction. It is not an empirical question but a logical one.

To work, the argument must show that God and suffering are mutually exclusive. From the standpoint of logic, however, there is no irreconcilable situation to be uncovered. Suffering is commonly undesirable, to be sure, but something's being undesirable in no way makes it morally evil, nor does it make it morally good. Bobby does not care for strawberries in the least; he dislikes the taste of them. Even desserts—normally, his favorite—are shunned if he detects strawberries on the first bite. His finding them to be unappealing has no moral component, nor does his eating them, if he so chooses, in spite of their unwelcome taste. Such things are neither ethical nor unethical, good nor bad; neither are the strawberries themselves, even though they cause an unpleasant sensation for Bobby when he puts them in his mouth. Morality does not apply. Suffering is unwanted, but it is morally indifferent, although persons' responses to it clearly may be otherwise. In fact, in stark contrast to the

---

[11] See Gen. 3.
[12] Matt. 5:45 NIV.

atheists' perspective, the biblical account declares that the very God the existence of whom the atheists wish to deny is a being who Himself suffers.

> The LORD saw how great man's wickedness on the earth had become, and that every inclination of the thoughts of his heart was only evil all the time. The LORD was grieved that he had made man on the earth, and his heart was filled with pain.[13]

It is a poignant passage. God's pain is caused by humanity's evil. Far from its being incompatible with suffering, God's inherent goodness is the express reason for His brokenheartedness. It is an arresting thought. If an atheist wishes to counter the existence of the God of the Bible based on suffering, then the atheist must confront the target as it is, not as he or she wants it to be. Once again, the claim by one who takes the stance that God and suffering cannot coexist is based on how the person thinks that the God of the Bible *ought* to be, not on how He *is*.

Rather than focusing on suffering in the world, an atheist could allege instead that benevolence and suffering cannot coexist in the same being—they cannot be in the same entity contemporaneously. Given this conceptualization then, the portrayal of God in the above-mentioned passage would reveal that He does not exist: His continuous benevolence is inconsistent with any instance of His being in pain. This approach, after all, would be the more direct route. Here is the form of the argument, with numbered steps:

1. For any entity x and any time t, it is not possible both that x is benevolent at t and that x suffers at t.
2. Assume that God exists.
3. God is always benevolent.
4. There is a time t_a, such that God suffers at t_a.
5. Therefore, there is a time t_a, such that God is benevolent at t_a and also suffers at t_a.
6. Therefore, God does not exist.

---

[13] Gen. 6:5–6 NIV.

Such an argument would not work, of course. The first premise of the argument is false. With a different instantiation of the variable *x* that appears in that premise and slight modifications elsewhere, one could build a parallel argument to prove that virtually no human being exists. The compassionate acts of people in behalf of others who are suffering are not inconsistent with people's being grieved by the suffering that they see. In truth, it is because of their benevolence that they suffer too. One surely experiences emotional trauma in seeing a critically injured child at the scene of an accident or a crime, and it is accompanied by a strong desire to help. It is absurd to conclude that such caring entities cannot exist. Similarly, it is because of God's inherent goodness that He is grieved by human wickedness, but it does not follow from that fact that His existence is disproved. Indeed, the Scriptures report that God sent His own Son to suffer and die because justice demands payment for wrongdoing—human wrongdoing. The sinless suffered for the sinful. There is no logical contradiction to be unearthed here. A beneficent God not only can allow suffering, but He also can direct it for good—human good.

Suffering for having done no wrong is puzzling, though. It seems to go against one's sense of rightness. It seems to be unfair. It may be unfair, but again, considered in a global sense, something more encompassing could be afoot. The biblical account of the Apostle Paul's view of suffering provides a fitting backdrop.

> For our light and momentary troubles are achieving for
> us an eternal glory that far outweighs them all. So we fix
> our eyes not on what is seen, but on what is unseen. For
> what is seen is temporary, but what is unseen is eternal.[14]

In this passage, Paul weighs the temporary against the permanent. He was mistreated intensely for his belief and his testimony, yet he sees his suffering as minor and fleeting in light of a far different future. Regardless of whether one introduces the biblical account and the perspective to which Paul adheres, the notion that goodness and pain cannot coexist is indefensible; and to argue that there is no God on the grounds that people sometimes hurt is simply frivolous. One could argue just as well that Timmy has no mother, because he fell

---

[14] 2 Cor. 4:17–18 NIV.

and skinned his knee. Of course, he has a mother; she is an important part of the causal chain that brought Timmy—and his knee—into the world. His mother could have prevented his injury by forbidding him to run, overriding his will; however, as noted earlier, learning comes through experience, and experience sometimes is accompanied by hurtful things. Acting in goodness does not entail acting to avert all pain. Would a benevolent mother, although she did not want her child to fall, have stopped his playing tag with the other children in the neighborhood, sacrificing his continued physical, psychological, and social development just to avoid the injury, even if she knew that he eventually would require a bandage and perhaps sutures? Would that action be one of virtue and wisdom? The long-term plan out-weighs the inevitable tumble to the ground. Timmy cried when he fell and hurt his knee—so did the person who could have forestalled it: his mother.

The point of this story is not that one should disregard encounters with pain but that arguing against the existence of God on the basis of them lacks any credibility. It is remarkable that there are those who seem to rest their denial that God is real on the fact that life is not one long walk in the park. It is not sensible to think that the raison d'être of human existence on the planet is the evasion of discomfort at all costs, that in avoidance of it somehow lies the highest good—a very strange doctrine. For the atheistic stance even to be worth considering, a *contradiction* must stem from asserting that the goodness of the infinite God and the actuality of suffering can exist together, but the concept of benevolence no more includes prevention of pain than it includes prevention of abject turpitude.[15]

---

[15] Indeed, one may argue effectively that suffering plays a critical part in the growth of an individual and, in the long run, serves to further the individual's development in a way that could not occur in its absence. I will not pursue the issue here, other than to note that the Scriptures, which the atheists reject, hold that suffering is fundamental to one's progress toward maturity: "[W]e also rejoice in our sufferings, because we know that suffering produces perseverance; persever-ance, character; and character, hope" (Rom. 5:3–4 NIV). Can a person mature in character without enduring things that try the person? Unless one's corners have been rounded by the challenges of life, one is seldom in a position to counsel or lead others from a seasoned perspective. A husband and father who has not experienced brokenheartedness over family matters lacks the empathetic viewpoint that he needs to guide couples who are contemplating marriage, divorce, or raising

One cannot misconstrue pertinent concepts and thereby define God out of existence with the argument from evil as suffering. It will not work.

What truly underscores the problem with this form of the argument from evil, however, is its inherent reliance on two related notions. The first notion is that, if suffering is inherently evil, then any suffering, regardless of the *number of instances* of it, entails the presence of evil. A single case of suffering by a single sufferer is sufficient. Suppose that four people receive moderate burns in a hotel fire. One is normal, and three have congenital analgesia, a disorder in which an individual is born without the ability to feel physical pain.[16] If one points to the lone victim of the fire who endured pain and claims that God must be nonexistent because that person suffered, then one could point to the three who did not encounter pain, and did not give the burns even a second thought, and argue instead that God must exist because they did not suffer in the unfortunate affair. If the argument from evil is to establish its conclusion, then it cannot permit *any* suffering at all in this incident and, by extension of the principle, *any* suffering among the members of the population at large. Otherwise, the proffered proof against the existence of God depends on the individuals or instances that one selects to make the case, which results in, at best, an exceptionally weak argument from which the conclusion cannot be derived and, at worst, an absurdity.

The single-instance sufficiency leads to the second notion. If suffering is inherently evil, then all suffering, regardless of the *degree* of it, must be evil. It cannot be that only some of it is evil.

---

children. The military officer who never has been in combat is ill-prepared to take command as the battalion faces an entrenched and formidable enemy. The manager who never has assumed the responsibility for a team and dealt with the many personnel issues that come about from such a role will struggle to bring unity to a disparate group and instill in them a common vision as they take on a crucial project. An objector may claim that such cases bear no weight, as development could have taken place in the absence of suffering because there is no logical requirement that suffering accompany growth. Perhaps it is so, but there is surely no logical prohibition either. Whether pain and development are linked as a matter of fact, it is evident that the coexistence of good and suffering does not introduce an inconsistency.

[16] Alternatively, this condition is known as congenital insensitivity to pain, or CITP.

One would not expect otherwise, for then, besides the obvious element of subjectivity, the proof against God's existence would rest on factors that are both variable and arbitrary. One would be forced to decide how much discomfort is required for there to be no God, and one would be compelled to classify uncomfortable experiences using a common scale, even if they cannot be compared with each other with any reasonable assurance.

Does the suffering that accompanies a broken arm exceed that of a spurned lover's broken heart? What about the discomfort of walking into the bright sunlight after leaving a darkened room or the sadness of seeing a friend make poor choices or the disappointment of getting something other than what one wanted for a birthday gift? Are any of these greater than stepping on a rock in one's bare feet or experiencing acid reflux or being frustrated over losing a game of chess to an unskilled opponent? How does the pain of depression over the loss of one's job or life savings or self-respect compare with the pain of losing one's finger, one's mobility, or one's spouse? It seems that a theorist would need to build a scale of suffering and say that whether it can be demonstrated that God does not exist depends on the level of pain. In the event that a person claims to have experienced a discomfort incident at a rating of at least y on a scale of x–z, God cannot be real. The charge then would be to determine how to quantify so subjective a thing as discomfort.

The further charge would be to determine whether the anguish of one person—suffering that is near the high end of the x–z scale— is of more weight than the mild discomfort of many and, if so, then how many. If a person has a higher tolerance for pain than another or is numbed with medication or is filled with adrenalin following the onset of a threatening situation, then that variability too must be taken into account, as if such would be possible. Clearly, it just will not do to say that the nonexistence of God can be shown only if suffering reaches a certain level of intensity. Whether God exists is a matter of what occupies reality, and, if one is to demonstrate that it is not *possible* that He exists, then one will need something more than a survey on how people feel—and how they feel on a given day.

If suffering is evil, intrinsically evil, and, if it is thereby incompatible with the goodness of God, then the magnitude of it, whether in *prevalence* or *intensity*, is irrelevant. God must prevent *all* of it: all instances and all degrees. If there is any suffering what-soever, then God cannot exist, for, so goes the thinking, the perfect power, benevolence, and knowledge of the Supreme Being would not allow evil of any amount or to any degree or of any kind to surface. If one is going to hold that suffering is evil, then *none* of it can be tolerated, no matter how few the occurrences or how slight the pain; and, because suffering is subjective, the claim, "I am hurting," perhaps accompanied by some appropriate supporting evidence, is adequate validation. Take a look now at the argument from evil as it is revealed to be with regard to suffering; the steps are numbered, as before:

The Argument from Evil—Suffering as Supposed Evil

1. All suffering is evil.
2. Discomfort is a form of suffering.
3. Disappointment is uncomfortable.
4. If God exists, and, if He is omnipotent, benevolent, and omniscient, then He invariably will act in a way that prevents the occurrence of evil.
5. Therefore, if God exists, then He will not allow suffering.
6. Jenny is having a bad-hair day.
7. She is experiencing disappointment.
8. Therefore, God does not exist.

Any atheist who hangs a hat on a bad-hair day is not one to be taken seriously. One should not see this rendering of the argument as an attempt to trivialize the human experience. Suffering is a solemn thing. Anyone who has lived long enough to be reading this work will have been bruised by the painful incidents of life, and the pain is not always tied to the physical. Some of the anguish that humans undergo can be pronounced, even excruciating, pushing them to the point of desperation. Regardless of the state of misery in the world and the extent of it in any individual's life, however, the argument from evil that is based on it must embrace the reasoning that appears above, ludicrous as it is.

Before leaving the topic, I want to take a moment to look at a variant of the argument from evil as suffering that attempts to disprove God's existence from a different perspective. Rather than aim at a logical inconsistency holding between God's attributes and the presence of suffering in the world, this variant seeks to show that the existence of God is improbable because there is a considerable amount of distress on the earth. The rate of occurrence is too high to maintain that it is likely that God exists. He would disallow such widespread misery on the premise that He is real. A close sister argument alleges that a large percentage of the suffering on the planet is severe and unjustifiable, a state of affairs suggesting that a good God, who would not permit it to happen, is probably unreal.

With regard to the extent of suffering as the evil-rendering vehicle in the logic, the argument is self-defeating. I already have shown how reliance on the number of instances undermines the proposed case against God's existence. Either suffering is evil, or it is not evil. If it is evil, then how is it that the omnipotent, wholly benevolent, and omniscient God can tolerate some of it but cannot tolerate very much of it? If it is not evil, then, no matter how much of it there is, the sum of it cannot point to the nonexistence of the wholly benevolent God.

In an effort to escape the dilemma, one could not take the path of declaring that the probability of God's existing is inversely proportional to the rate of occurrence of suffering. That tactic would not uphold the hypothesis of nonexistence. Whatever probability that one would assign to the permanent existence of an infinite being would change with every tick of the clock and every sampling of the population—a frail bit of reckoning. Furthermore, if one were to base the probability of God's existence simply on the rate of suffering, then, just as one declares that His existence is improbable when the rate of occurrence is high, it appears that one would be compelled to declare that His existence is probable when the rate is low. The upshot is that, because there are living organisms on the earth currently, creatures that are experiencing suffering, the eternal God, in all likelihood, does not exist; but, before sentient beings were present, the existence of the eternal God was actually a certainty, or nearly so. At minimum, one would have to say that the argument is too irregular to establish its conclusion: Sometimes, the argument could demonstrate that the existence of God is quite improbable; sometimes, the argument could demonstrate that it is quite probable.

This approach is unusually muddled and implausible. It reflects a particularly poor piece of reasoning.

Another path that may seem to be open is to hold that suffering is not evil at all until it reaches a certain level of prevalence—whatever such a thing might be—and it becomes evil at that time. This position is also untenable, however. It would be as if one declares that murder is not evil, unless it happens too often, in which case it becomes immoral. Imagine an attorney who freely admits that the defendant murdered the victim but argues for his client's release on the grounds that murder rates are low in general and that there has not been another instance of such an act in the town for more than thirty years, let alone a homicide using the type of weapon that the defendant employed. Thus, murder is not a vice, and his client did nothing wrong. No person—no judge and no juror—would accept the argument. The frequency of the occurrence of homicide is not related, even remotely, to its standing in violation of a moral code. Whether no one commits the deed or everyone commits the deed, murder is a transgression. How much of it takes place is not the factor that defines its ethical or legal character. In an analogous way, if suffering is evil, then the frequency of the occurrence of it is not relevant to its being so; hence, the amount of it that is found in the world can have no bearing on the matter of God's existence.

If, on the other hand, suffering is inherently not evil, then multiple instances of it, regardless of how many there are, cannot sum to something that is evil. Piling up individual cases of suffering that are not evil will not produce a collection of them that is evil by crossing a threshold. The benign cases cannot contribute wickedness to the pool, and nothing else could contribute it to the pool. It is all or nothing with suffering: Either it is evil, irrespective of the amount of it, or it is not evil, irrespective of the amount of it. The argument from the extent of misery purports to rest its opposition to the existence of God on the fact that anguish abounds, but it actually turns on the very premise on which its more stringent counterpart turns, and it fails for the same reason.[17]

---

[17] It is important to distinguish the purported evil of much suffering from the evil of the impiety of excess, such as gluttony. Eating is not wrong, but gluttony is wrong. One cannot draw a parallel here to make the case that suffering is wicked only when it is excessive. The evil of gluttony is not tied inherently to the sum of

Consider the sister argument. One may object that it is only pointless suffering that matters: suffering that is unjustifiable or senseless, such as the trauma that is linked to sweeping epidemics. Suffering is not evil per se; it is evil when it is not reasonable.

What could such a claim mean? It could not be meaningful without a distinction between two types of affliction: the justified and the unjustified. What criterion, though, could one use to differentiate them? If justifiable suffering is any that is explainable, then no suffering for which one knows the cause is evil. The argument cannot succeed on this basis. There is little suffering for which the cause is unknown. The proponents of the argument intend to show that the misery that results from epidemics, such as the bubonic plague that decimated Europe centuries ago, is senseless. The cause of the disease is known, however, along with the neurological discomfort that is associated with it. This line of assault is ineffectual because, given the rendition of the argument here, the premise that such suffering is senseless fails.

If instead justifiable suffering is to be identified with suffering that is tied to a purpose, then it is evident that Sam's pain from the surgery that removed his inflamed appendix is justifiable, but so is the pain resulting from the torture of innocent children at the hands of a sadist, as it too is done with a purpose in mind. This approach obviously will not work. Perhaps one responds by saying that suffering that is brought about by good intentions, rather than evil ones, is suffering that is justifiable. The pain that is inflicted by Sam's surgeon is therefore morally distinguishable from the pain that is inflicted by the sadist. The logic, however, is flawed. One cannot use ascriptions of good and evil to distinguish between good and evil. Moreover, suppose that, although Sam's surgeon wanted to help Sam to overcome his medical problem, the doctor took pleasure in bringing about his patient's pain and intended to cause Sam to suffer. Given the reasoning at hand, the patient's suffering is both justifiable and unjustifiable. Clearly, this approach will not work either.

It appears that nothing is left for the proponents of the argument from evil as senseless suffering except to conclude that it is the

---

multiple bites of food but to the self-indulgence that it expresses, the disregard for the deleterious effects that it has on the body, and the lack of self-control from which it issues.

outcome that separates the reasonable from the unreasonable. Reminiscent of utilitarianism and the failures that accompany it, one would need to know how much good must result from suffering for it to be acceptable and how long one must wait to know whether it is so.[18] What may seem to be unreasonable to one person, however, may not seem to be that way to another, and what may seem to be unreasonable today may not seem to be that way tomorrow. Timmy thought that the suffering that his tetanus shot brought about was unreasonable. Neither the pediatrician nor Timmy's mother thought so; a few years later, Timmy did not think so either.

One might say in reply that what the majority of rational adults think is the factor that determines reasonableness; the views of the immature and inexperienced are to be discounted. This attempt to salvage the argument fails as well. The collective mindset of the rational people of a society cannot be the element that renders suffering justifiable or unjustifiable, reasonable or unreasonable, innocuous or harmful. The fact that societies in the past embraced the burning of their children in sacrificial rituals to a pagan god, such as the Ammonites did in worshipping Molech, in no way justifies this act or the suffering that accompanied it. Ancient societies' deeming it to be acceptable and modern, civilized ones' deeming it to be deplorable are together enough to show that surveying the population cannot mark the distinction between sensible suffering and its opposite. The argument never can escape the grip of subjectivism, and that characteristic brings about its downfall.

Ironically, even an atheistic naturalist must see value in suffering. One experiences the discomfort of thirst when deprived of water and of hunger when deprived of food. Those discomforts lead to drinking and eating, without which one will not last beyond a few days or a few weeks respectively. Further, pain can etch the memory, so that the precipitating circumstances will be avoided in the future. For an evolutionist, suffering cannot be categorically bad if survival is worthwhile—and, of course, survival lies at the very heart of evolutionary theory. Some suffering thus must be a good thing, given that view, because it aids the sufferer in the continuance of life. Hence, an evolutionist who seeks to disprove the existence of God on

---

[18] See the discussion of utilitarianism in the previous chapter.

the presumption that suffering is evil would land at a point of self-induced contention.

EVIL AND ITS PRONOUNCEMENT

There is a final problem with the argument from evil against God's existence. All forms of the argument hinge on the premise that evil exists in the world. One must ask on what basis the claim can be put forward. The issue is the identification of the conditions that determine the truth or falsity of the premise. For it to be true that evil exists, there must be something that establishes the fact. Suffering does not work as a criterion, as already shown, so the task of serving as the guarantor falls to iniquity: What counts as evil must be substantiated by some set of principles of rightness, code of ethics, or moral law. The argument purports to demonstrate that God does not exist; therefore, it plainly cannot draw on absolute moral standards, as dictated by God, in an effort to prove the presence of evil. One cannot have one's cake and eat it too, tacitly using God to show that God does not exist. The truth or falsity of the proposition that evil exists must be set in another way. It is not the content of the standards that may be employed in demonstrating the presence of evil that matters. Whether those standards align perfectly, partially, or not at all with the principles that the Bible sets forth is not relevant to the issue. What matters is the unconditional applicability of the standards—an unwavering set of them that can lock down the truth with finality.

Such strict universality points to the question of source. God cannot be posited as the source, or else the argument would trip itself right out of the gate. Aside from God, what other source is there? It must fall to humans, individually or collectively, to declare what is good and what is evil. Without universally accepted moral laws, however, there are no absolute rules, and inclusive and unreserved acceptance is not forthcoming. Views at any given time vary both among individuals of a society and among societies themselves, and views at different times vary for a particular individual and for a particular society. What if one could find, without relying on God, just a single act that everyone would agree is malicious—would this finding be sufficient to declare that there is evil? In this country, slaying infants is murder and prohibited by law. One may say that such an act is evil by virtue of its violating the laws of the state. It is difficult to believe that anyone actually could think that tormenting and killing the young of a civilization is good. As I indicated above, however, an accepted practice in some early cultures was to sacrifice children by burning them. Kings Ahaz and Manasseh of ancient times even sacrificed their own sons in the fire. If the God of the Scriptures, who condemned such acts as evil, does not exist, then moral absolutes are not simply elusive; they are absent, as the variability of the views of individuals and societies ensures that precepts are not fixed.[19] Tossing innocent babies into the flames to torture and destroy them then would not be evil, for there are exceptions to its denunciation. With no moral absolutes, how could one pronounce with assurance that the evil on which the argument against God's existence rests is anything more than an ascription based not on objective fact but on subjective opinion, which varies with the time and place? If one cannot so pronounce, then the argument fails. It seems that one needs for God to exist to capture absolute standards, and one needs absolute standards for the argument against God's existence to get off the ground; hence, the logic is self-refuting.

It is not even necessary to point to such extreme cases to show variance. A vegetarian may contend that eating meat is morally wrong, while others enjoy a tasty steak; and, if evil is equated with violation of societal law, then it may be good today to travel a certain stretch of County Road 23 at fifty miles per hour but evil tomorrow when the speed limit is reduced. Even if all agreed at some point in time on what counts as wrong, another day surely may bring dissent.

Ironically, even some who seek morality in human dictates agree that the concepts of right and wrong are senseless without moral absolutes. The ethicist Richard Taylor claims, "The basis for morality is conventional, which means the rules of morality were fabricated by human beings over many generations. . . . These rules

---

[19] See 2 Kings 16:1–4, 17:16–17, 21:1–17; 2 Chron. 28:1–4, 33:1–9; Ps. 106:37–38; Jer. 7:30–31, 19:4–5, 32:35; and Ezek. 16:20–21, 36, 20:31, 23:37. Note the contrary, corrective action of King Josiah in 2 Kings 23:10.

were not the invention of God."[20] Yet, he holds that "the concept of moral obligation [is] unintelligible apart from the idea of God. The words remain, but their meaning is gone."[21] As the philosophical community withdrew from the idea of an existent utmost authority from which morality derives its force, reasons Taylor, it held onto the religious underpinning for the concept: the directives of the Deity. The result, he says, is that the notion of ethical conduct as that which aligns with the commandments of an ultimate lawgiver lingers, but it is left ungrounded, having abandoned the foundation that imparted its significance. Modern philosophical attempts to maintain "discourse on moral right and wrong, in the absence of any reference to divine law, became entirely empty and meaningless" because they "*cast aside* the context that gave it [the distinction between moral right and wrong] meaning, namely God's will."[22] Taylor believes that the answer to this seemingly self-conflicting situation lies in recognizing that ethics is not about duty in the first place but about aspiration. The proper concern of ethics is not obligation to authority but the achievement of personal excellence, an idea that he derives from ancient Greek concepts of virtue.

Among other troubling matters, one core problem with his approach, I submit, is that it does nothing to establish or reestablish the applicability of moral ascriptions. Taylor correctly sees that the removal of absolutes undermines the meanings of statements that incorporate moral terms, but he fails to see that an ethics of aspiration surely does likewise: It renders all propositions that purport to ascribe moral properties devoid of truth-value, guaranteed to be the case by the inherent variability of human opinion. To relativize the essence of what is good and what is not good is to sound the swan song of any system of ethics and the attributions that issue from it. The context to which Taylor refers in the quoted passage is not a mere vestige of some bygone perspective. It is instead the very

---

[20] Richard Taylor, "Is the Basis of Morality Natural or Supernatural?" a debate between Richard Taylor and William Lane Craig at Union College, Schenectady, New York, October 8, 1993, accessed November 4, 2015, www.leaderu.com/offices/billcraig/docs/craig-taylor1.html.

[21] Richard Taylor, *Ethics, Faith, and Reason* (Englewood Cliffs, NJ: Prentice-Hall, 1985), 84.

[22] Ibid., 90.

structure that defines the moral character of actions. It is what determines the truth or falsity of moral ascriptions. Without it, there can be no ethics; there is only a pseudoethical house of cards that will collapse as societal currents change.

The fundamental stumbling block for the argument from evil against the existence of God is that there is a serious problem with this proposition:

Evil exists.

The proposition appears as a premise—step 5—of the standard, completed form of the argument. One must accept (1) that the truth of the proposition cannot be established; (2) that it is false because there can be no evil, given that no standards can be instituted across all times for all individuals and cultures; or (3) that the statement is true at some times and with respect to some sets of standards, false at other times and with respect to other sets of standards. The first option undermines the argument completely because the truth of one of its premises is indeterminable. The second option also undermines the argument completely because one of its premises is indeed false. The third option produces an argument with an intrinsically variable and context-dependent premise, the supposed truth of which shifts unpredictably. A premise of this sort is incapable of supporting the argument's conclusion. It is relativistic, erratic, and contingent. Whether it can be shown, in this case, that God is a nonexistent being depends not in any way on objective reality but on a philosophical soup du jour. Such reasoning is impotent.

One will recognize that statements both about the existence of evil and about the existence of unary, composite objects, as discussed in chapter 3, must rest on standards. A heap today may not be a heap tomorrow if there is a change in the specifications, even though the particles that compose the material collection are exactly the same. All that rides on it, however, is the existence of the heap itself, as the unary character of the collection is determined through conception. The existence of the particles, on the other hand, is determined by physical reality. The insurmountable hurdle for the argument from evil is that it attempts to prove the nonexistence of something based on the existence of something else, but the existence of the latter thing is based on rules that cannot be established with constancy unless the former thing exists, which is precisely what the argument is attempting to deny. One cannot use alterable standards to put forth ontological assertions beyond that to which the standards apply—and especially so when the assertions rest on standards that are both unalterable and contrary to the standards that one uses.

To avoid going too far afield on this topic, I want to leave the alleged inconsistency that arises from accepting both the existence of God and the presence of evil. As one has seen, there is no inconsistency. I will move to the other attack on the theistic view. It is advanced by an atheist who believes that reliance on God to account for the world leads to a logical problem of a different sort.

ARGUMENT FROM COMPLEXITY

One of the most vocal advocates of atheism in contemporary times is Richard Dawkins. He states his position clearly in a recent work.

> I am not attacking any particular version of God or gods. I am attacking God, all gods, anything and everything supernatural, wherever and whenever they have been or will be invented.[23]

A central challenge to theorists is to explain how it is that things came to be the way that they are—how the grand array of life on the earth came to be there. One way to provide an account of the present state of the planet is to track the course to the past in search of exactly what happened to bring life to where it is. William Paley finds what he believes is the answer in intelligent design: the handiwork of God. Dawkins finds his answer in probability and process: a fortuitous beginning followed by a cycle of random change and targeted retention. Dawkins is an evolutionary biologist and ethologist—important to know because his belief in Darwinism

---

[23] Richard Dawkins, *The God Delusion* (Boston: Houghton Mifflin Co., 2006), 36.

plays a significant role in his stance. A comprehensive discussion of the theory of evolution is tangential to the core theme of this writing, but I must delve into the theory to a fair extent to present an adequate depiction of Dawkins's program.

With a rather harsh treatment of the principal position that is opposed to his own, Dawkins sets out to prove two things: (1) It is not logical to postulate that God exists; (2) it is not necessary to postulate that God exists, for one can account for life on the earth, in all its great variety, without resorting to God. Chapter 6 showed how the argument from design attempts to establish God's existence on the basis of the functional intricacy that nature exhibits. Dawkins maintains that complex organisms and the intricate parts thereof are not the products of intelligent agency but rather the products of something entirely different. Far from its supporting the existence of the creative Designer, complexity, in his view, works against it.

It is this notion of complexity, together with the improbability that is associated with its arising by chance, that lies at the center of Dawkins's argument. Indeed, it runs like a thread through his entire account. In this chapter, I will take a look at Dawkins's idea that the nonexistence of God is almost certain. In the next chapter, I will analyze his thesis concerning life, both how it arose in a Godless universe and how it came to be at its present, highly developed state through evolution. If the thread begins to unravel, then the analysis will have proved to be on the mark.

No Chance

To support his atheistic view, Dawkins attempts to turn the argument from design on its head. The very complexity on which the argument relies to prove the existence of God demonstrates, so Dawkins contends, just the opposite. Theists assert that complex organisms and their elaborate parts cannot arise suddenly out of a random assemblage of material. Chance never can account for such statistically improbable occurrences. The complex things that make up the world therefore must be the work of an intelligent, designing agent—namely, God. Design, however, says Dawkins, is illusory.

The natural temptation is to attribute the appearance of design to actual design itself. In the case of a man-made artefact such as a watch, the designer really was an intelligent engineer. It is tempting to apply the same logic to an eye or a wing, a spider or a person.

. . . The temptation is a false one.[24]

The problem, he says, is that an actual complex thing—a product of design—forces one to explain the appearing of the complex designer.

[T]he designer hypothesis immediately raises the larger problem of who designed the designer. The whole problem we started out with was the problem of explaining statistical improbability. It is obviously no solution to postulate something even more improbable.[25]

According to Dawkins, that which designed the complex thing must be a complex thing itself; therefore, the coming into existence of this designing entity is no less statistically improbable than the coming into existence of what it designed. To assert that complex things could not have arisen by chance and thus were conceived and created by God is to assert further that the designing God could not have arisen by chance. He also must be complex and hence must be designed. By the same logic, that second designing entity must be the product of an intelligent act, leading to yet another step. The result is an infinite regress. Dawkins claims that the reasoning that he proffers based on the improbability of complexity constitutes a

powerful argument . . . I have alluded to it several times already. The whole argument turns on the familiar question 'Who made God?', which most thinking people discover for themselves. A designer God cannot be used to explain organized complexity because any God capable of designing anything would have to be complex enough to demand the same kind of explanation in his own right. God presents an infinite regress from which

---

[24] Ibid., 157–58.
[25] Ibid., 158.

> he cannot help us to escape. This argument . . . demon-
> strates that God, though not technically disprovable, is
> very very improbable indeed.[26]

A powerful argument, is it? I will offer my own assessment of the logic.

In summary, it is manifest that complex entities cannot arise by happenstance. Some hold that the complexity in nature is owing to the work of the intelligent Creator: God designed the natural world and brought it into being. Dawkins claims that, if one says that things in the biological realm, because of their complexity, must have been engineered, then one is forced to say the same of God, or else one would fail to apply the requirement consistently. What is good for the goose is good for the gander, so to speak: What applies to one complex thing applies to another. The goose-gander principle leads straight back to Hume, as one might have suspected. Underlying Dawkins's reasoning is a form of Hume's attack.[27]

The gist of Dawkins's argument—that one needs to account for God's complexity and accordingly His coming to be—is not one that originates in Dawkins's writings; similar thinking appears in earlier works. Even apart from Hume's *Dialogues*, a clear example is found in a book by the philosopher John Stuart Mill, who asks the very question that Dawkins asks, with the same implication of regression. Mill attributes the musing to his father, who led him to believe

> that the question, "Who made me?" cannot be answered,
> because we have no experience or authentic information
> from which to answer it; and that any answer only
> throws the difficulty a step further back, since the
> question immediately presents itself, Who made God?[28]

Dawkins refers to the case for intelligent design as "the creationist's wearisomely recycled argument."[29] Yet, one finds that

---

[26] Ibid., 109.

[27] One may wish to review the discussion of Hume's goose-gander approach in the section on the teleological argument in the previous chapter.

[28] John Stuart Mill, *Autobiography of John Stuart Mill* (New York: Columbia University Press, 1924), 30.

[29] Dawkins, *God Delusion*, 121.

Dawkins repeats his own argument in his writings. It seems that he rests his atheistic position directly on it.

Perhaps the best place to start an analysis is with a diagram of Dawkins's reasoning, as I did with Hume's, because Dawkins's argument is a thinly veiled remake of the eighteenth-century philosopher's foremost objection to the argument from design. Refer to Figure 6.8 in the last chapter, where I depicted Hume's attempt to introduce an infinite regress based on the notion that designed and designer have a property in common: order. The designed-designer commonality that Dawkins puts forth is merely a different, but related, property: complexity. Below, I show Dawkins's attempt to establish a Humean-style regress. As before, solid lines and dashed lines depict features (those that are applicable here) of the standard format of the argument from design as I have represented it; see Figure 6.7 in the previous chapter. The bold, dotted lines in Figure 7.1 illustrate key elements of Dawkins's extension. All boxes are shown with solid borders; expanded entity boxes provide relevant detail.

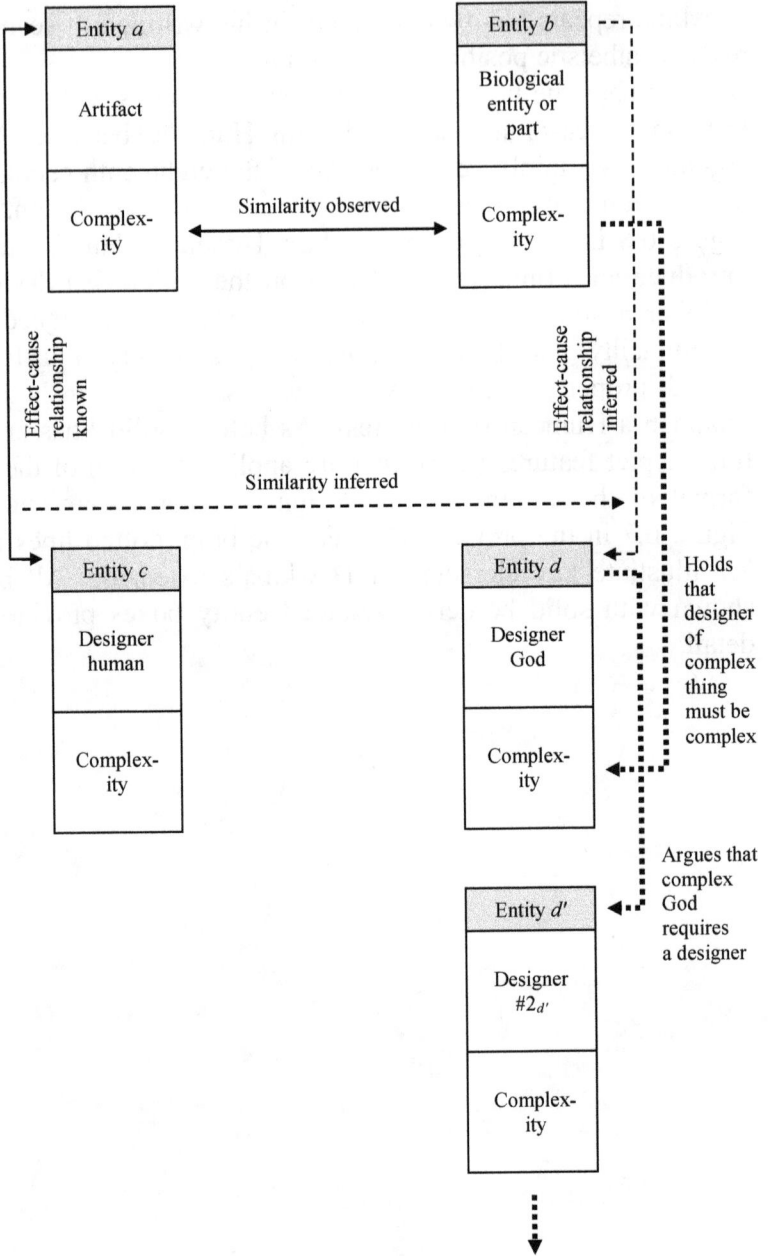

Figure 7.1

Why would one assume that the property of a thing that is designed must be found in its designer too? Certainly, it could not be a general principle to which one could subscribe. Gerald, an accomplished jeweler, designs and builds pocket watches in the small shop that is behind his house. Currently, he uses the same pattern for all of them. Each watch, placed vertically in his display rack, is three inches tall, weighs two and one-half ounces, keeps time accurately, and is made of metal on one side and glass on the other. Gerald exhibits none of these properties. He is six feet tall, weighs two hundred pounds, cannot keep time accurately, and is made of neither metal nor glass on either side. How then would one justify the claim that God must be complex on the grounds that what He designs is complex? Given that the principle cannot be general, it must be specific to a property—in this case, complexity: Intelligent designers of complex things must be complex as well. That qualification alone would be insufficient to establish an infinite regress; it results only in ascribing a particular property, in the present context, to God. To generate the regress, one must add that, if a complex thing is the product of intelligent design, then the intelligent designer of that complex thing, being complex itself, also must be the product of intelligent design—an even more ambitious notion. Without that notion, though, there is no regress.

The problem for Dawkins here is that he is trapped by the very regress that he hoped to use against the theists. If one can account for an intelligent designer only in terms of another intelligent designer, then look at the diagram of Dawkins's reasoning as it appears now:

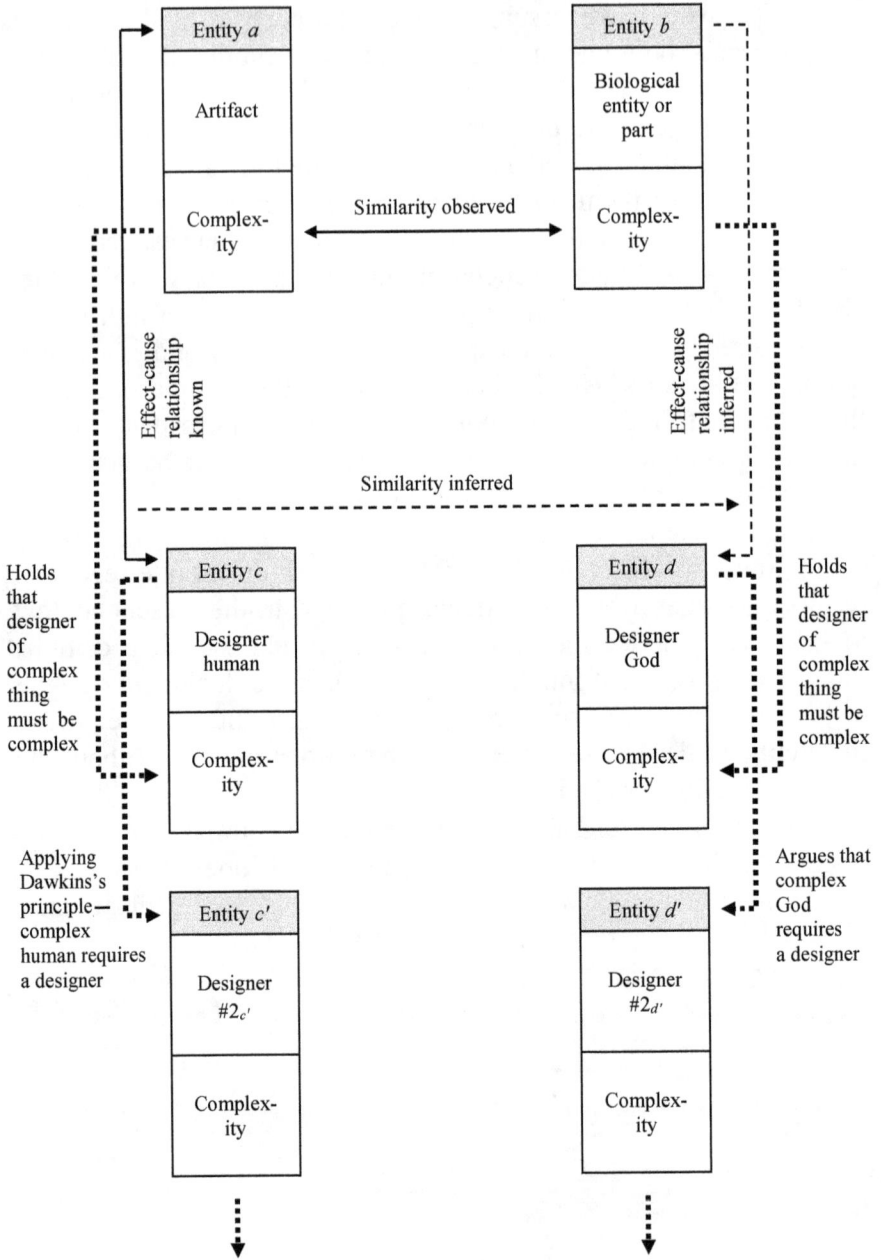

Figure 7.2

Dawkins's argument lands him squarely in a dilemma of his own making. Although he charges the theists with failing to apply the design principle consistently, Dawkins himself is exposed to the charge. One must ask whether he is as eager to embrace an infinity of designers for humankind as he is for God. Dawkins asserts that complex artifacts are the result of intelligent design, but the intelligent designers themselves—that is to say, the humans who fabricated them—are not the result of intelligent design. If therefore he relies on a principle that intelligent designers themselves must be designed, then his position is blatantly self-refuting. If he does not rely on such a principle, then there is no requirement that an intelligent designer be designed by some other intelligent designer; thus, he cannot launch the regress against the theists.

Dawkins would deny that the principle applies in all cases. What is good for the goose may not be good for the gander after all. On what basis then might one draw a distinction between a designer who is human and the Supreme Designer, who is God? The distinction in Dawkins's case can be based on his supposition that there is a third possibility for humans: There is a way to account for their coming to be that avoids both the statistical improbability of their arising by chance and the alleged unacceptability of their arising by design. That way is natural selection; humanity is the product of an evolutionary course. Complexity is a ground-up thing, believes Dawkins, coming about from the simple by a process of gradual change. Contrary to what is true of human beings, so goes the thinking, no such third possibility exists for the complex God of theism: Either He sprang into existence by accident against all odds, which is statistically unpalatable, or He Himself is the product of design, coming into existence as the result of another designing agent's work, which generates a regressive sequence. One cannot explain His existence, as one can do for humankind, without taking one of these two troublesome paths.

A clue to one problem here already may be evident. Dawkins can avoid the dilemma only if he supposes that there is another option for giving an account of the existence of people—one that relies neither on chance nor on design. Why then would he assume that there is not another option for giving an account of the existence of God—one that relies neither on chance nor on design? Dawkins limits the ways of explaining God's existence to two, but the limitation is spurious. In fact, not only is it the case that another way is genuine, but it is also the case that, of the alternatives that Dawkins does submit, neither is even possible for reasons that are manifest. In attempting to lock the theists into a pair of destructive choices to explain God's being, Dawkins introduces the fallacy of false dilemma—the first error to note in his argument. It is a matter to investigate.

The task at hand is to understand two things. Each represents a core element of confusion in Dawkins's writings, and that confusion is ruinous. This key set is shown below:

> 1. what it means to explain something and in particular to explain a thing's coming into existence;
> 2. what it is to be complex.

Dawkins forms a special parallel between the two, holding that, just as explanations regarding how complex things work are given in statements about the operations of their simpler parts, explanations regarding how complex things came to be are given in terms of their emergence from simpler predecessors. He says,

> We concluded that the behavior of a complicated thing should be explained in terms of interactions between its component parts. . . . But another kind of question is how the complicated thing came into existence in the first place. . . . I shall just mention that the same general principle applies as for understanding mechanism. . . . We shall explain its coming into existence as a consequence of gradual, cumulative, step-by-step trans-formations from simpler things, from primordial objects sufficiently simple to have come into being by chance.[30]

Is his explanation acceptable?

---

[30] Richard Dawkins, *The Blind Watchmaker: Why the Evidence of Evolution Reveals a Universe without Design* (1986; repr., New York: W. W. Norton and Co., 2006), 22.

ON EXPLANATION AND ETERNITY

Exploring the concept of explanation is important at this juncture. In science and in philosophy, explanations commonly adhere to the covering-law method, where that which is to be explained—the explanandum—is derived from the statement of a law (or sometimes laws) under which the explanandum is subsumed, and a reported set of applicable circumstances.[31] The law is expressed in the form of a conditional statement—referred to as simply a conditional in the language of logic. As a reminder, a conditional has the following structure: 'If p, then q', where the variables p and q represent propositions. One will recall that, in a statement of this form, p is the antecedent, and q is the consequent. If the conditional is true, then the truth of the antecedent guarantees the truth of the consequent—without variance. Taken together, the covering-law conditional, and the description of the circumstances in the antecedent, constitute the explanans.

On the whole, explanations of physical phenomena are based on laws that reflect cause-effect relationships. Law-expressions are generally the end products of induction following observed recurrent instances. Not all explanations are of this sort, however, as when one offers accounts of the acts of agents. Actions are not reducible to the causal principles that govern the universe, a point that I argued previously. On occasion too, the covering laws may be probabilistic rules. One explains why Stewart had an accident by pointing to the likelihood of collisions when people drive under the influence of alcohol, as statistical records indicate, and to Stewart's inebriated state. A cause-effect relationship often underlies probabilistic explanations along these lines, though, but it is not so much explicit as implicit. Accordingly, in the case of Stewart, his intoxication is an effect of his consumption of ethanol, as the molecules of the substance interfere with the transmission of nerve impulses in the brain. That impairment decreases one's ability to control a vehicle and thereby increases the risk of a crash. Unless the probabilities on

---

[31] The model is detailed by Karl G. Hempel and Paul Oppenheim in "Studies in the Logic of Explanation," *Philosophy of Science* 15, no. 2 (1948): 135–75. An overview of the model is available in *Encyclopedia of Philosophy*, s.v., "Explanation in Science."

which explanations draw are extreme, citing physical, causal laws usually affords stronger support in explaining things than citing their probabilistic counterparts: Those laws are unvarying within the confines of a closed, deterministic, macrophysical system, provided that other factors do not intervene; and, when stated with adequate specificity, carry a fair amount of weight in giving an account.[32] At a basic level, the explanation concerning why event y happened, or why y appeared, follows the structure of a deductive argument (the first premise is to be viewed as tenseless) that includes a reference to a type-token relationship. I show the form here, with numbered steps:

1. If phenomena of type $X_1 \ldots X_n$ occur (or are present), then phenomena of type $Y_1 \ldots Y_n$ occur (or are present).
2. Phenomena $x_1 \ldots x_n$ occurred (or are present).
3. Therefore, phenomena $y_1 \ldots y_n$ occurred (or are present).

For example, to explain the sudden formation of a particular precipitate in a test tube, one points to (1) a deterministic, causal law, stated in the form of a conditional that declares that, if two certain chemical substances are combined, then the precipitate forms, and (2) the adding of one of these chemical substances to the other. Again, to explain why sulfur dioxide is in a room, one points to (1) a conditional that states that, if elemental sulfur is heated to a certain temperature in an oxygen-rich environment (so that it burns), then sulfur dioxide is present as a result, (2a) the availability of elemental sulfur, and (2b) the heating of it to a certain temperature in an atmosphere with a high oxygen content. Substituting for the variables in the structure that is outlined above may yield, with respect to the latter example, an explanation in this manner, with numbered steps:

1. If sulfur is burned, then sulfur dioxide is present there.
2. Someone placed a three-ounce pile of sulfur in a bowl on the kitchen counter and then lit it.
3. Therefore, sulfur dioxide is present in the kitchen.

---

[32] See the discussion in chap. 2 on the inductive-deductive approach to discovering physical laws in science and expressing them, extending the laws to future instances of specific types of events.

One could expand this minimal explanation by incorporating other law-statements to provide additional information, such as the linking of sulfur dioxide to a pungent odor.[33] The configuration that appears below is a suitable representation of an expansion; the additional numbered steps show how the argument is completed:

Part I

1. If sulfur is burned, then sulfur dioxide is present there.
2. Someone placed a three-ounce pile of sulfur in a bowl on the kitchen counter and then lit it.
3. Therefore, sulfur dioxide is present in the kitchen.

Part II

4. If sulfur dioxide is present in a place, then one can detect a pungent odor there.
5. Sulfur dioxide is present in the kitchen.
6. Therefore, one can detect a pungent odor in the kitchen.

Of course, the amount of the substance must be sufficient for one to discern it, although, in the case of this particular gas, not much is required. The explanation could be extended further by, say, tying the odor to a threshold of parts per million of sulfur dioxide.

The conditional under which the explanandum is subsumed also may be formulated in terms of the properties of things, and those properties may not be merely incidental but essential. Suppose, for example, that someone wants to know why particular objects are so heavy for their small size. One would respond by saying that they are made entirely of lead—or gold, platinum, iridium, osmium, or some other metal with a similar mass-to-volume ratio. A person then might ask why things that are made of lead are that way. In effect, what the person actually is asking is why lead is that way. There are a number of paths that one might take in preparing a reply, but ultimately they end in the same place. One could note that lead has a high specific gravity or talk about its atomic structure. One could remark that lead

---

[33] Having burned sulfur in our kitchen as an adolescent, I can attest to the odor of the suffocating gas as well as the fitting reprimand that I received as a consequence of my experiment.

is dense; its being dense—that is to say, its having a highly concentrated mass—in a solid state, characterizes this chemical element
essentially.[34] The respondent is explaining why lead things are
heavy, even if fairly small, by pointing to the fact that they are made
of a substance that has particular chemical and physical properties by
its nature. As before, one is offering an explanation in terms of a
conditional and a reported instance that the corresponding law
covers. The explanation might assume the form that follows, its steps
numbered. Although simplistic, it serves the purpose of illustration.

1. If an object is made of lead, then it is dense—and
   accordingly rather heavy for its size.
2. These objects are made of lead.
3. Therefore, these objects are dense—and accordingly
   rather heavy for their size.

Suppose, though, that one asks not why these objects are dense,
or even why lead is dense, but why lead came to be that way—how it
happened that lead acquired the property of being dense. What would
this question mean? A chemist can talk about the generation of the
heavier elements in stars or the degeneration of uranium as it turns
into an isotope of lead in time. What the chemist cannot do is explain
lead's coming to be dense because it did not *come* to be dense. It *is*
dense—always. Whenever the element is formed, its chemical and
physical properties come with it. Lead as such can no more acquire
the quality of being dense—which lithium lacks—than it can acquire
its atomic number. Lead has been dense for as long as there has been
lead, just as it has been metallic and malleable, with an atomic
number of 82. All that one can do in response to the inquiry is to
point to the essential properties of the material. The substance—
timelessly—is what it is and the way that it is in the universe. To be

---

[34] Density can be quantified, if one desires, providing a benchmark for determining
whether a substance is dense based on the ratio of the mass of a given volume of it
to the mass of an equal volume of a standard substance at a set temperature and
pressure. Being dense then can be treated as a relationship of being more dense
than the reference, of having a greater mass, for a given volume, than, for example,
water. For the purposes here, and with respect to elements, it is sufficient to treat
being dense, or mass-concentrated, as simply the displaying of a property.

lead is to be a chemical element with specific characteristics. It is nonsensical either to affirm or to deny that an essential attribute of a thing is acquired by it, as if the potential for the thing to come to possess the attribute exists; so, it is illogical to seek an explanation of how the attribute arose in it. No rational narrative of such is possible.

Having provided this general understanding of explanations, and what sort of conditions are open to them, I return to Dawkins and the complexity of God. The first of the two central confusions in Dawkins's account that I mentioned earlier arises here. He glosses over the distinction between a pair of related concepts, which these phrases denote:

1. the coming into existence of an entity;
2. the existing of an entity.

What each of these expressions refers to respectively is not the same. The first describes an event; the second describes a state of affairs. There is another dissimilarity. If one assumes the backdrop of a temporal nexus, then one might say, with regard to a given entity, that the first presupposes the following condition. As before, the symbol '<' indicates the earlier-than relation.

> There is a time t_1, and there is a time t_2, where $t_1 < t_2$, such that entity e exists at time t_2, and it is not the case that entity e exists at time t_1.

No matching presupposition is associated with the second.

As it pertains to the Supreme Being, the concepts that are to be differentiated emerge in this pair of phrases:

1. the coming into existence of the complex God;
2. the existing of the complex God.

Is either the purported event that expression 1 describes or the state of affairs that expression 2 describes explainable?

One must distinguish between asking for an explanation of how it is that the complex God could have *come* into existence and asking how the complex God could *be* in existence. A person who poses the former question seeks a reply that offsets the statistical improbability of a chance occurrence, but no meaningful reply is forthcoming. Here is why: The Judaeo-Christian God, as I identified Him early in the previous chapter, is unlike the things in the world, in that His coming into existence is not a possibility. In this respect, God is sui generis. An entity that comes into being, whatever it is, cannot be God. It is not that the entity's arising constitutes some statistical anomaly or empirical unlikelihood. It is precluded on the basis of logic. By definition, God is an eternal being. He has no beginning and no end. If He exists, then He always does so. It is part of what it is to be infinite in attributes. One might deny the existence of the Judaeo-Christian God, claiming that the characterization of God does not pick out anything in all reality, but one cannot deny that, if God does exist, then He is unconstrained by temporal limits.

As an illustration of the point, consider that it is possible that there are no bachelors who are forty-two and one-half years of age in Iceland, but, if there are any, then one can be sure that they are not married. Marriage is precluded for forty-two-and-one-half-year-old Icelandic bachelors not by occurrence but by the meanings of the pertinent terms. The Judaeo-Christian God did not arise—indeed, *could not* arise—because eternity is an indispensable part of the being of God. It is illogical to think that an eternal entity's coming into being can be an actual happening, let alone that it is explainable. The supposed event that expression 1 depicts is not subject to explanation, as any such account would be nonsensical.

On the other hand, if one assumes the second sense of existence in asking for an explanation, then what is it that one is seeking? The covering-law model does not work. There is no applicable conditional rule and thus no antecedent to which one can make reference. To insist on an explanation under a covering law and in precipitating circumstances is to misapply the explanatory power of the method by attempting to employ it where it cannot be employed. Statements about the existence of an eternal entity are not reducible by further demands for explanations in terms of efficient causes. One can account for the *existence qua existence* of something that is eternal only in terms of its being unlimited.

In dismissing limits, one thinks of those limits as temporal: If a thing is eternal, then there is no point in time at which it does not exist. It is not necessary to refer to time in capturing the essence of the concept, though. In fact, it may be important not to do so: On the premise that time had a beginning—a view that both the Bible and accepted science uphold—the concept cannot be put forth effectively using temporal language. One can define eternal existents by making reference to conditions, however. The key issue is that there cannot be any circumstances in all reality, physical or otherwise, in which an eternal entity is absent—that is to say, fails to be among what is in the state of existence. I can represent the notion in this way:

> For any entity x, x is eternal if, and only if, for any exhaustive nonnull set R of real elements, x is an element of R.

No complete set of real things, if there are any real things at all, excludes an eternal existent. Whatever objects there are in reality under whatever conditions obtain, an eternal thing is present—it exists. Given that this representation by means of set-inclusion can account for the substantive being of things apart from temporality, it depicts the unlimited existence of an entity independently of either a beginning of time or the lack thereof. Whether one believes that it is possible for things to exist without such limits, the idea is not difficult to grasp, and even some physicalists embrace it. Regardless of the scope of reality—whether it is restricted to the physical or includes the nonphysical—eternity is an established concept. If there are eternal things, then they simply exist.

Dawkins's argument based on complexity presupposes that the first of the two aforementioned senses of existence—God's coming to be—applies. To initiate a regress, he *must* assume that God is impermanent. Without that assumption, the regress is a nonstarter. What god, however, is *this* one? The question is one that already has surfaced in this chapter. For Dawkins to propose atheism as the right picture of reality by arguing against the existence of the Judaeo-Christian God, he must set his sights on that particular entity, and that particular entity is "eternal, immortal, invisible, the only God."[35] Any other perspective is a distortion, and an argument against a distortion commits a fallacy: straw man—the second error to note in

---

[35] 1 Tim. 1:17 NIV. On the start of time, see 1 Cor. 2:7; 2 Tim. 1:9; and Titus 1:2.

Dawkins's chain of reasoning. Dawkins has twisted the concept of God into something that fits better with his view, but, in so doing, he has gone considerably wide of the mark. If God did not have a beginning, then one can give no account of His emergence, for there is none to be had. One cannot explain the coming to be of something that did not come to be. Dawkins's conjectures about God are incorrect; his notion of the frame of existence is too narrow.

As I underscored earlier, before Dawkins could pose an infinite regress utilizing his idea of complexity, he would have to show that an intelligent designer must be designed, which works against his own argument and places him in a dilemma. Aside from that fact, and more to the point here, he must offer a convincing proof that God could not have existed from eternity and promote the upshot that the Judaeo-Christian depiction of God is not an appropriate representation. Dawkins has to demonstrate that, if God exists, then He would have to be locked into the causal, contingent, physical universe like the things of common experience and, like them, must have arisen. Dawkins offers no such proof, only a passing, unwarranted guess that it is true and a disappointing dismissal to the effect that holding God to be eternal is a "lazy way out."[36] The charge is faulty. Dawkins fails to take hold of the point. It is not *lazy* to refer to God's eternal nature; it is *necessary* to do so. Dawkins mistakes inapplicability for laziness, as one might do who demands that a chemist explain how density arose in lead or how lead came to be a metal, not understanding that those characteristics are defining marks of the substance. Lead did not come to be that way; it is just that way. Again, the prohibition is not physical but logical. That which is not dense in a solid state or is not metallic, whatever it is, cannot be lead. That which is not eternal, whatever it is, cannot be the Judaeo-Christian God. The eternity of God is a matter with which Dawkins must deal if he is to submit a case against God's existence. No support for the necessity of redefinition appears in Dawkins's conjecturing, no argument against the nature of God, no proof of His supposed coming to be. Dawkins simply avoids the issue.

Needless to say, there is, contrary to Dawkins's stance, another option; and it is exactly the one that theism puts forth: God did not

---

[36] Dawkins, *Blind Watchmaker*, 200.

arise by chance or by design, for God did not arise at all. He has existed eternally. The affirmation is straightforward. As Dawkins points to humankind without drawing on theistic design, so theism points to God without drawing on a Dawkinsian coming-into-being event. Dawkins could attempt to disallow eternal things altogether and thus the Judaeo-Christian God with them, but he cannot do it on the basis of statistical improbability, as it is irrelevant. With its ill-founded assumption, Dawkins's argument is doomed from the start. Atheism needs far more than what Dawkins provides. Even so, more trouble looms ahead.

What about eternal things—is it possible for something always to have been? I want to return to the fundamental philosophical tenet ex nihilo nihil fit that I introduced in chapter 1. According to the axiom, for all things that come into being, there must be something to which their being is traceable, at least in principle. As revealed in the previous chapter, which covered the axiom in more detail, it is important to recognize the not-so-subtle distinction between arising uncaused and arising from nothing. It is a difference that has escaped the attention of a number of writers who argue against the tenet and even those who argue for it. An absolute void—pure nothingness—cannot be the backdrop against which anything at all comes to be. If nothing at all exists, then nothing at all ever will exist or can exist. Think of it in this way: If there were no creative God, no universe, no ordinary or dark matter, no quantum fluctuations or virtual particles, no vibrating strings, no energy in any sense, no space-time, no force, no mind, no spirit, no properties, no thing of any sort whatsoever in the realm of reality, then there always would be absolutely nothing.

Consider the place where Dawkins arrives as he brushes over the eternity of God. In accordance with the law of physics governing conservation, in a closed system, barring an act of creation ex nihilo, energy cannot be generated, and it cannot be destroyed. Within the limits of the principle of uncertainty in quantum theory, what there is of energy, there is—no more, no less. Whatever happens, whatever physical processes occur, the total amount of energy in a closed system remains constant. This state of fixed energy is that of the universe, according to the general view of science. One is faced then with explaining the fact that energy exists. It could not have generated itself, for then it would have had to have been in existence to have been the generative instrument that brought it to be, with the consequence that it would have had to have existed before it existed, which is illogical. There are therefore three possibilities regarding energy: (1) It did not arise; (2) it arose from something—that is to say, from something that existed; or (3) it arose from nothing—that is to say, not from anything that existed. Recall from the discussion in chapter 1 that existence and reality are one and the same.

I would like to look at each of these three possibilities. (1) If energy did not arise, then its past is eternal—and, given that its destruction is nomologically impossible, its future is endless as well. One therefore could not deny the feasibility of an eternal existent. (2) If energy arose from something, then either that thing's being regresses to eternity, and thus there is an eternal existent (the view of theism), or that thing, in turn, arose either from something or from nothing. Assume that it arose from something. If this second thing is eternal, then again one could not deny the feasibility of eternity. If the second thing arose from something, then the same three options would surface. This chain must end in something that is eternal or not end at all or end with nothing as the starting point. If the chain ends in something that is eternal, then, once more, one cannot dismiss eternity as infeasible. If it does not end—there is no first generative event—then the chain itself must be without beginning; it is eternal. One hence could not deny the feasibility of eternity. If it ends in nothing, then, whether it is at this point or from the initial step, one arrives at the final possibility, which is (3) energy arose from nothing. It is clear from the last chapter that the concept of something's arising from nothing is not tenable. Physicists Victor J. Stenger and Lawrence M. Krauss try to explain how the entire universe could have arisen from nothing, but their accounts in terms of instability are self-refuting, and their use of the word 'nothing' is faulty. Yet, even if Stenger were right, and nothing and something were merely alternate phases of each other, the nothing-something pseudocontinuum itself would be interminable. Here is why: By the law of excluded middle, it is the case that either there is nothing, or there is not nothing, and not nothing is the same as something. Therefore, if the pseudocontinuum of nothing-something were to describe reality, then it would have to be ceaseless. There is no other path to take; one of the two states must obtain. Eternity thus cannot be avoided, regardless of the position that one adopts on generation, even the mistaken view of the abovementioned scientists.

Whether energy itself is eternal, or it arises, either immediately or mediately, one must accept the fact that the idea of eternity is not only reasonable but also indispensable. This discussion brings to mind St. Thomas Aquinas, who rightly declares, "[S]omething that does not exist can only be brought into being by something already existing."[37] The core underlying principle concerning preexistence in generation is manifest, and it is correct. There are no credible grounds for Dawkins's dismissal of the eternity of God. If a state of eternity is logically possible, then Dawkins's cavalier remark about laziness is shortsighted, and it undermines any support for his view. More than just a logical possibility, however, a state of eternity, so I am arguing, is inescapable.

ON INTRICACY AND IMPROBABILITY

I wish to focus now on the second confusion that surfaces in Dawkins's account: what it is to be complicated or complex. As a way of countering Dawkins's attack on intelligent design, some have suggested, in line with traditional thought, that God is not complex, and Dawkins objects to this idea. God may be complex—in some sense—but the problem is that Dawkins misconstrues the concept, and, in doing so, he introduces yet another flaw in his logic. What does it mean to ascribe complexity to God, and does the term 'complex' signify something different from what it signifies in other ascriptions? Dawkins believes that complexity is to be understood in terms of probability. He puts forth the following claim:

> A complicated thing is one whose existence we do not feel inclined to take for granted, because it is too 'improbable'. It could not have come into existence in a single act of chance.[38]

---

[37] Thomas Aquinas, *Summa theologiæ*, 1a.2.3, trans. Timothy McDermott, vol. 2, *Existence and Nature of God* (Cambridge: Blackfriars, 1964), 15.
[38] Dawkins, *Blind Watchmaker*, 22.

It is doubtful that Dawkins posits this statement as a definition, but, if he does so, then it is not acceptable. Complexity must be independent of how people feel. In evolutionary theory, to which Dawkins subscribes, complicated creatures and their intricately functioning parts arose long before humans. For an evolutionary biologist, such as Dawkins, the statement that appears above could not be a definition without introducing an inconsistency. Probability is independent of people's take on it. The chance of rolling double sixes on a given throw of the dice in a game of craps is $^1/_{36}$, expressed as a common fraction. Even though Jack may feel lucky tonight and feel sure that he is going to be a winner, the probability remains unchanged. If complexity is linked not to improbability itself but to how one is inclined to interpret that improbability—whether one's sense is that the unlikelihood is too great for something to have happened just by chance—then complexity and improbability have to be discrete concepts.

In a subsequent writing, Dawkins makes a stronger claim, leaving out the affective element and asserting simply that the two concepts are one: "And complicated is just another word for improbable."[39] In a more recent work, he reaffirms this definition, stating,

> The opposite of simple is statistically improbable. Statistically improbable things don't spontaneously spring into existence: that is what statistically improbable *means*. The beginning had to be simple.[40]

The definition fails, of course. It is not what one *means* by 'statistically improbable'. John's winning the lottery is certainly statistically improbable, yet what could be simpler? He drove down to the filling station in his area, bought a ticket, and waited for his number to be selected at random. No doubt, what Dawkins intends is to portray complex things as those for which the arising of them in view of the properties that they possess is highly improbable, so

---

[39] Richard Dawkins, *Climbing Mount Improbable* (1996; repr., New York: W. W. Norton and Co., 1997), 77.

[40] Richard Dawkins, *The Greatest Show on Earth: The Evidence for Evolution* (New York: Free Press, 2009), 416–17.

much so that the existence of things with those properties could not have come about directly by chance. Even this extension, however, does not work. Walking along a seldom-used trail in the woodlands, Larry finds a rock that is a chartreuse color on one side and a purple color on the other. It is statistically improbable that it just happened to come to be that way and further that it just happened to be there. The object's unusual coloring is, in fact, the accidental outcome of a child's art project. While making her poster for school, Missy spilled chartreuse paint in her back yard. Some paint, as chance would have it, landed on a rock near the table where she was working and covered the rock's top surface. That night, a raccoon overturned the rock in search of food and pushed it several inches away. Continuing with her handiwork on the following day, Missy spilled paint again—this time purple—and, as chance would have it, it landed on the same rock. Several weeks later, a tornado swept through the family's neighborhood, lifting the rock and depositing it in the woods. Through a series of chance events, the rock came to have its quite unusual color properties and came to be where it is. What lies in Larry's path nevertheless is not a complex thing. It is just a rock.

A deeper problem emerges with his definition, though, for there is a further inconsistency afoot in Dawkins's writings. Dawkins believes that complexity can come about only by means of development from the simple. It cannot arise spontaneously, and there is no other path, he thinks, to get there. The beginning of life therefore had to be simple, as only the simple can come to exist by chance. Dawkins asks one to assume that the prospect of the occurrence of such an event is one in a billion.

> [A] billion billion is a conservative estimate of the number of available planets in the universe. Now, suppose the origin of life, the spontaneous arising of something equivalent to DNA, really was a quite staggeringly improbable event. Suppose it was so improbable as to *occur on only one in a billion planets*. . . . [W]e are talking about odds of one in a billion. . . . [E]ven with such absurdly long odds, life will still have arisen on a billion planets.[41]

---

[41] Dawkins, *God Delusion*, 137–38. The emphasis is mine.

Dawkins's inference is flawed because his computation is incorrect, vitiating the logic. I will come back to this point later in the work. For now, note that one chance in a billion, applying Dawkins's own standards, constitutes an extreme improbability. That long-shot value is precisely what he postulates nonetheless for the coming into existence of what he sees as the simplest of all forms of life: the initial DNA-like replicator from which all biological entities, and all biological complexity—on the earth, at least—supposedly sprang. By his own definition, however, that first life form cannot be simple, for its arising is extraordinarily improbable in his view, and simple and improbable, he declares, are opposites. Dawkins's fusing of nonsimplicity and statistical improbability is self-defeating.

Dawkins attempts to improve the odds of the appearance of life by pointing to the large number of planets in the universe, increasing the opportunity for life to spring into being somewhere. I plan to take a look at his reasoning in detail in the next chapter, but, for the moment, consider that what he apparently wishes to hold is that the probability of a DNA-surfacing event is low in the case of one planet and high in the case of many planets. The approach does not help him in forming his definitional rendering: *Equating* complexity with improbability forces the same thing to have conflicting properties. He must choose a domain for the probability: either a single planet or all planets. Given the reciprocity that he assigns to the corresponding terms, he cannot hold that the occurrence is improbable here or there but probable somewhere; for to do so is to maintain that the arising of life here or there is complex, but the arising of life in the cosmos is simple, even though the arising here or there is an instance of the arising in the cosmos. In effect, it is tantamount to contending that no single thing of sort Y in any given place has the property Φ, but a single thing of sort Y in some place has that property. As in mathematical formulae, where various equal values can be substituted for variables without altering the correctness of those formulae, terms in objective propositions normally may be replaced with definitionally equivalent ones without altering the truth of those propositions. With the equivalence that Dawkins submits, however, substitution in his own assertions leads to a contradiction. It is true that a complex thing is not likely to be the product of a chance event, but complexity and statistical improbability are not interchangeable. By attempting to unite two concepts that are distinct—that of a property and that of the prospect of an incident—Dawkins introduces inevitable absurdities.

It is Dawkins's framework of materialism that sets the stage for the problem. He believes that reality is composed solely of physical things and that biological individuals thus fall into this category: Living systems—that is to say, organisms—and their operational components, such as eyes and wings, are complex in light of the configuration of their constituents. Dawkins continues his notion that complexity and improbability are the same, and here one sees that he ties these conditions to the arrangement of parts, where the parts so configured perform something useful. He remarks,

> To say that an object like an eye or a protein molecule is improbable means something rather precise. The object is made of a large number of parts arranged in a very special way. The number of possible ways in which those parts could have been arranged is exceedingly large.
>
> . . . Of all the trillions of possible arrangements of the parts of an eye, only a tiny minority would see. . . . There is something very special about the particular arrangement that exists. All particular arrangements are as improbable as each other. But of all particular arrangements, those that aren't useful hugely outnumber those that are. Useful devices are improbable and need a special explanation.[42]

As before, Dawkins is blending a property itself with the unlikelihood of the random arising of something that has it.

Perhaps I can extract his key concepts and offer some clarity:

1. Complex things are made of numerous parts that are arranged in special ways, such that the arrangements of those things are useful.
2. Complex things arise from simpler things.
3. The arisings of complex things are events that carry a low probability of occurrence.

---

[42] Dawkins, *Mount Improbable*, 77–78.

With these points laid bare, how could Dawkins argue against God on the basis of complexity? Regarding the second and third points, I already have dismissed their applicability to an argument against the existence of God because God did not arise. Turn to the first point. Given his approach to explaining things by making reference to their component parts, perhaps Dawkins is looking for an account of the assumed-to-be-complex, existent God by alluding to the assumed-to-be-present parts that compose Him, as though He were an entity so composed. To expect an explanation in terms of parts, however, is to take for granted that the object to be explained *has* parts and—for a materialist, at least—in the way that a machine or a biological entity has them. Such is not the case with God. He is not a material being. *If* God is complex, then it is by virtue of the attributes that characterize His essential nature and the unlimited capabilities that are inherent in Him. His complexity, *if* He is complex, *could not* stem from a large number of components that are arranged in some useful way, much as a horse's parts—heart, liver, lungs, and other vital organs—are arranged. Horses are physical entities that come into being and are subject to death and decay when some of those critical parts no longer perform. Horses are ephemeral. They are contingent. The complexity of a physical entity is very different from any complexity that a nonphysical entity may exhibit. Again, if one is to argue against the existence of the Judaeo-Christian God, then one must argue against the existence of a being who is not corporeal, for the position of the theists is given clearly in the Scriptures: "God is spirit."[43] A spiritual being is incorporeal. So is a mathematical set. So is a law of nature, and, whereas the law governs physical phenomena, it itself is immaterial. Dawkins never draws the crucial distinction between the two senses of complexity, even merging them in his consideration of the concept of a multiverse: the notion that there are numerous other universes existing in parallel with the one of which humans are aware. What he claims in this respect follows:

> The key difference between the genuinely extravagant God hypothesis and the apparently extravagant multiverse hypothesis is one of statistical improbability. The

---

[43] John 4:24 NIV.

multiverse, for all that it is extravagant, is simple. God, or any intelligent, decision-taking, calculating agent, would have to be highly improbable *in the very same statistical sense* as the entities he is supposed to explain. The multiverse may seem extravagant in sheer *number* of universes. But if each one of those universes *is simple in its fundamental laws*, we are still not postulating anything highly improbable. The very opposite has to be said of any kind of intelligence.[44]

The contrasting notions of simplicity and complexity and of probability and improbability, as they apply to the distinct categories of matter and mind, body and intelligence, are themselves distinct; and, where the corresponding terms are employed, they plainly are employed in disparate senses, not, as Dawkins holds, in the very same sense. If God is, in fact, complex, then He is decidedly not complex in the way in which biological things are complex, nor is He amenable to the statistical principles that one might apply to corporeal reality. Dawkins shuffles complexity and improbability together, and he fails to scribe a line between the applicability of complexity to material things and its applicability to things that are not material. If complexity were the same thing as improbability, then it would be possible for Boyle's law pertaining to gases, for instance, to be complex only if it were highly unlikely. Unlikely to what, one must ask—to obtain in the cosmos, to cover physical phenomena, to exist, to come to exist? Such thinking is not sensible. What does Dawkins maintain that it is for something to be simple in its laws—does he mean that the things that are governed by the laws are simple or that the laws themselves are simple? Consider first that he intends to convey the former sense. Dawkins asserts that, unlike mere collections of physical particles, living organisms—the higher forms of life, at least—are complex. Even the bodies of living beings, however, are subject to physical laws, and Dawkins admits as much, as the following passage demonstrates:

---

[44] Dawkins, *God Delusion*, 146–47. The first and third emphases in the quotation are mine. Note that the postulation of a multiverse out of which arose the known universe still does not avoid the issue of eternity. Either there is an eternal series, or there is an eternal generative existent. The multiverse postulation merely pushes the issue to another step.

745

> Is this to deny that living things obey the laws of physics? Certainly not. There is no reason to think that the laws of physics are violated in living matter.[45]

If the simplicity of physical laws indicates, in his view, that the things that are governed by those laws are simple, then advanced biological entities and their parts, which are governed by physical laws, are simple after all; therefore, their direct arising is not improbable, which contradicts his core position. If he abandons the idea that the simplicity of physical laws determines the simplicity of what is governed by them, then his multiverse line of reasoning is a nonstarter. Whichever path he chooses, he falters. The first sense of law-simplicity thus cannot work.

If Dawkins means instead that the laws themselves are, or can be, simple, then the problem that he faces topples his own argument against God. Physical laws are not material and, of course, have no material parts. They associate sets of physical phenomena, reflecting the way in which material reality operates. These laws, which are expressed in abstract propositions, link types of phenomena in a particular way, so that the tokens of those types fall under the governing principles that are inherent in the laws. To think that simplicity and complexity as they pertain to the immaterial are tied to the relative dearth or plenitude of physical parts, arranged in a just-right way, is to misunderstand the notions altogether. If simplicity and complexity are properties that can be ascribed meaningfully to immaterial things, then those properties are surely distinct from ones by the same names that apply to machines and organisms.

Some examples from mathematics may help to elucidate the matter. A complex number is one that has a specific structure; it generally is rendered in accordance with a strict, standardized formulation, which I provide here:

$a + bi$

where

the letters a and b represent real numbers
the letter i represents the imaginary number $\sqrt{-1}$

---

[45] Dawkins, *Blind Watchmaker*, 17.

That which the mathematical construct symbolizes is said to be complex because of the imaginary number, but such complexity is by definition. 'Statistically improbable'—the meaning that Dawkins gives to the term 'complex'—has no meaning when applied to a number. One can ascribe odds to rolling double sixes on a pair of dice on a given throw. One cannot ascribe odds to the integer 6 itself, let alone two of that integer. Such an attempted ascription results in sheer nonsense.

What about sets? Is a set that contains sets of ordered pairs of numbers as members more complex than one that contains only individual numbers? If so, then the set of all sets that contain as a single member an ordered pair of even integers that are greater than 1 and less than 5,

$$\{\{<2,2>\},\{<2,4>\},\{<4,2>\},\{<4,4>\}\}$$

is in this sense more complex than the set of all integers between 1 and 9 inclusive,

$$\{1,2,3,4,5,6,7,8,9\}$$

because of the properties that this former set exhibits, despite the fact that it has fewer members. Even in a derivative sense, the complexity of sets of sets of ordered pairs is attributable neither to their development in the course of time by a Dawkinsian process of "gradual, cumulative, step-by-step transformations from simpler things" nor to their being "[s]tatistically improbable things."[46] As for the former idea, one could assert with no greater inanity that the number 3 is built through a period of time by means of a steady progression from a trio of units—the number 1—or that it develops from a quartet or sextet of fractions: $3/4$ or $1/2$ respectively, expressed numerally. Such declarations would be nonsensical. As for the latter matter, a set is simply what it is. To say that sets that contain sets of ordered pairs as members are more improbable than sets that contain only individuals is to say something that is utterly meaningless. Even a Platonist, who

---

[46] See the corresponding passages from Dawkins's works *Blind Watchmaker* and *Greatest Show on Earth*, quoted on pp. 728 and 740 respectively.

believes that numbers are real in the strong, ontological sense, would not hold that statements about their probability make any sense at all. One is attempting to cross categories illegally in attributing improbability to mathematical objects themselves.

In his reasoning against God, Dawkins fails to distinguish between the application of the term 'complex' to corporeal objects and to what he refers to as "any kind of intelligence."[47] This failure generates the fallacy of equivocation—the third error to note in Dawkins's argument. It is the same error that Hume commits. One will recall that equivocation arises from a change in the meaning of a term in an argument. The shift may take place between two premises or between one or more premises and the conclusion; on occasion, it may occur within a single proposition, whether premise or conclusion. Consider a simple illustration. Suppose that a man sets out to help a sick neighbor by cutting his neighbor's grass. One may see the following reasoning; its components are numbered for readability:

1. Tommy saw his father drive the lawn tractor across Gary's yard on Saturday morning.
2. A yard is three feet.
3. Therefore, Tommy saw his father drive the lawn tractor across Gary's three feet on Saturday morning.
4. Driving a lawn tractor across feet causes injury to the creature or creatures whose feet they are.
5. Therefore, Tommy saw his father cause injury to Gary on Saturday morning.

Both 'yard' and 'feet' are used with different meanings in this construction, of course, with comical results. The argument is guilty of the fallacy of equivocation. This logical mistake is analogous to the mathematical error of inconsistent instantiation of variables in an equation. In each case, there is a defective outcome: one of reasoning, the other of computation. In the abovestated inferential chain, the problem is obvious, but the fallacy of equivocation is usually far more subtle. Ponder the closing argument by a defense attorney as

---

[47] See the corresponding passage from Dawkins's work *God Delusion*, quoted on p. 745.

the lawyer addresses the jurors in an imaginary trial. It may proceed along these lines:

> We all have heard the facts. I ask you to consider carefully, though, how you interpret those facts. The prosecution has presented its case in an attempt to persuade you that my client is guilty, that he acted with malice aforethought. Mr. Brown's reasoning, however, was that a wrong that had been done to him ought to be corrected. Certainly, all of us have the right to seek justice. Perhaps his action did reflect poor judgment. Perhaps he should have taken the time to think about the consequences of what he was about to do. How many of you never have acted in anger or been driven to see a wrong reversed? Mr. Brown did exactly what each of you would have done in the same circumstances. Mr. Brown is not evil; he is not a malevolent being, lying in wait for some unfortunate victim. All who know him know what sort of kind and giving man that he is. He could not have acted out of malice, for it is not his nature: He is just not a malicious person. He acted out of a sense of rectification. Yes, he is to be blamed, and blamed for a regrettable failure, but that failure is one of reasoning, of judgment. It is a breakdown of thought, not will. My client is not guilty of the crime with which he is charged so recklessly.

There are a number of problems with this argument. Equivocation is one of them. The word 'malice' in the legal locution 'malice afore-thought' denotes an intent to do harm. The defense attorney attempts to recast the word, so that it points to something that issues from or that characterizes a trait of the individual, as opposed to designating the intention with which a specific act of the individual was per-formed. The attorney then argues that his client should be released on the basis that he could not have acted out of malice, for such a thing is at odds with the traits that the man possesses. The shift in meaning generates the logical fallacy. Aside from that fact, though, it is clear that the concept is false. A gentle person can become very aggressive in certain circumstances; a careful individual can throw caution to the wind on occasion; and one who is quite impatient can endure a prolonged wait sometimes with remarkable composure.

Now, regarding Dawkins's complexity argument, there are two possible readings, both of which result in breakdowns in reasoning. Viewed in the first way, it contains two meaningless premises; viewed in the second way, it is guilty of the fallacy of equivocation. I set forth the argument here, condensed, with numbered steps:

1. There are complex (sense-1) biological things in the world.
2. Theists agree that complex (sense-1) things, including complex (sense-1) biological things, could not have arisen by chance.
3. Theists claim that complex (sense-1) biological things are the product of intelligent design—namely, the work of God.
4. An intelligent entity that designs things, including complex (sense-1) biological things, must be complex (sense-1 / sense-2).
5. Therefore, God, the intelligent Designer, must be complex (sense-1 / sense-2).
6. Therefore, God could not have arisen by chance.
7. Therefore, God, like complex (sense-1) biological things, must be the product of intelligent design.
8. Therefore, there must be another intelligent designer who designed God, and that designer must have been designed, generating an infinite regress.

The truth of step 4 is disputable, for, as I discussed, the properties of an effect need not be possessed by the cause of that effect. I will proceed nevertheless. If, on the one hand, the second occurrence of 'complex' in step 4 is used in sense-1 (pertaining to the corporeal), then the assertion in that step is misapplied: If it is meaningful to ascribe complexity to an intelligent agent, in the capacity of intelligent agent, then that complexity *cannot* be given in the same way that the complexity of a physical thing, whether a manufactured object or an organism, is given. That sense is carried to step 5. It is obvious that, if one can ascribe complexity to an entity, without uttering nonsense, by virtue of its being a rational designer, then any complexity that one ascribes to that entity by virtue of that entity's role as reasoning engineer is assuredly not the complexity that one ascribes to a living beast by virtue of its various organs, working together to maintain viability. *Whatever* it may be for intelligent agency *qua intelligent agency* to be complex, if the property of complexity is applicable at all, then that complexity manifestly is *not* there because of a collection of material parts, performing in concert to provide the continued operation of an organized, physical system.

A materialist may claim at this point that intelligence is a property that emerges from the functioning of the brain, which is a corporeal thing. I covered some problems with the concept of emergent mentality in chapter 5, but, even if the claim were true, it would not count as a counterexample. Intelligent agency, considered in itself, is not the physical neuron-parts of the cerebral cortex, with their ionic transfers, and cannot be in any sense complex in the way in which the brain is complex. This truth becomes more clear when one looks at step 5 of the argument. The complexity of God—if God is indeed complex—is surely not identical to, nor does it emerge from, a physical brain or other physical organ belonging to God.

Despite this fact, one may wish to assert that mental properties supervene on physical properties—a common position for a materialist. I argued at length against this position in chapter 5, but, even so, note that the error of a change in meaning remains; in fact, it is underscored. Mental properties and states are distinct from physical ones. They are not coascribable: One cannot attribute to a human agent's mind *as such* what one attributes to the agent's physical being, nor is the converse permissible. Mildred is sad because she has gained weight. It is nonsensical to say that that which is sad qua sentient being has gained weight, and it is nonsensical to say that that which has gained weight qua physical body is sad. If one tries to merge the mental and the physical by using a single term for both types of attributions, as Dawkins attempts to do in his argument, then the error results. Complexity is not something that can be ascribed in the same sense to both an intelligence and a physical entity any more than being unyielding, immature, quick, or any of a number of other characteristics can be applied to both in the same sense. Of course, given that the intelligent agent in the argument is God, supervenience of the mental on the physical is not even applicable, for God is incorporeal.

On the other hand, if 'complex' is used in sense-2 in step 4—some sense different from that of sense-1, *regardless* of what this other sense may be—then the argument rests on equivocation to reach its conclusion. It is therefore fallacious. Step 5 is equally problematic. Like Hume, and even Plato before him, Dawkins ascribes properties that bear a common name across sets of entities that are not simply different; they are different in fundamental ways. It is a ruinous mistake.

Underlying steps 6 and 7 is a cloaked false dilemma atop which Dawkins erects his straw man: the first two fallacies that I discussed in relation to Dawkins's argument. The Judaeo-Christian God, if He exists, is not the product of anything. He did not arise by chance or by design; He did not arise at all. Dawkins is jousting with a metaphysical opponent whom—or rather that—he himself invented.

In setting forth his grounds for atheism, Dawkins spins a dilemma against his own position, although he does not articulate it. Refer to Figure 7.2 in this chapter. The dilemma becomes evident when one makes the following term-substitutions in the argument as I detailed it above: 'artifacts' for 'biological things', 'atheists' for 'theists', and 'humans' for 'God', making 'Designer' a lowercase, plural word in step 5 to ensure proper grammar. With those changes, look now at steps 6 and 7 of the argument. Dawkins would find the statement in step 7 to be particularly unpalatable, one would think, as it contradicts the evolutionary theory to which he subscribes. The problem, though, is that, to avoid the infinite regress that is identified in the last step, Dawkins must posit a third option, but there is no more reason to do so in the version that substitutes the three terms that I propose than there is in the original. The argument from the improbability of complexity weaves a troubled tapestry of errors. It is not surprising that it fails.

In the end, it seems that Dawkins's chain of reasoning is the lazy path. It assumes, without even an attempt to ground the assumption, that God is neither eternal nor—as far as His complexity is concerned, at least—immaterial. Ironically, what Dawkins's analysis based on complexity leads one to see, if one sees anything, is that an existent God who designed the personal human entity did not come into being and is not a physical life form like the biological creatures that populate the planet—a result that Dawkins undoubtedly did not want.

To be sure, given that Dawkins attempts to make use of a Humean-style criticism of the argument from design, he invites its contrary aspect. As noted in the previous chapter, Hume postulates that causes ought only to be proportioned to their effects, and he employs this tenet to argue against the infinitude of the Supreme Designer based on the apparent finitude of nature. A corollary, however, which I presented as well, is that great effects require great causes. It is a more forceful principle, and Dawkins is obliged to agree with it. He contends that an entity that designs complex things must be complex too, and indeed more so than what it produces: Dawkins maintains that the intelligent agent is even more improbable, to use his particular phraseology, than the complex things that the agent supposedly designs. There are two trillion or more galaxies in the known universe, hundreds of sextillions of stars, perhaps as many as a septillion. Dark matter and dark energy fill the cosmos, according to the current thinking in science. If there is a God who brought about a law-adherent system of such magnitude that operates with great precision, then, whether He is infinite or finite, He is surely awesome.

At this point, it should be apparent that Dawkins's upturned version of the argument from design is not a logically compelling construction. Even though Dawkins cannot demonstrate the nonexistence of God with his reasoning based on complexity, he offers nevertheless an account of life that does not employ the activity of a creative being. I will continue with Dawkins in the next chapter as I consider his explanation of how sophisticated biological entities came to be on the earth. It is a two-part program: (1) a beginning that is founded on a chance event and (2) a progression that is founded on more chance events, coupled with nature's selection of the fittest—those, in a given population, that produce the most offspring. Both parts raise troubling questions.

REDEFINING THE SEARCH

Some have made up their minds that there is no God. Turning to certain metaphysical arguments with confidence, they seek to prove that nothing in all reality corresponds to the notion of the Creator. I remember conversing years ago with a professor who served as the chair of the Department of Philosophy and Religion at a regional university. With a terminal degree in philosophy from a respected institution, his educational background, coupled with his teaching experience, qualified him well for the position. The professor told me about his students' exposure to the argument from evil as he laid out the logic in one of his courses and about their coming to realize that there is, as he put it, "no way out." He believed—I took it that he did so, at least—that he was fulfilling his role as educator, opening their impressionable minds to see the alleged truth of atheism. No way out, he says? It is just not true. One needs only to look with a bit more care.

The evolutionist Richard Dawkins thinks that he has boxed God into a corner of nonexistence in his remake of Hume's objection to design as a basis for a theistic view. Referring to a philosopher-friend, Dawkins appears to be confident that his complexity-based argument is solid as he quotes supporting remarks by his associate; and Dawkins declares,

> Dan Dennett rightly describes it as an 'unrebuttable refutation, as devastating today as when Philo used it to trounce Cleanthes in Hume's *Dialogues* two centuries earlier. . . .'[48]

An unrebuttable refutation, he says? It is just not true. One needs only to look with a bit more care.

God is not amenable to discovery in the way in which one may come upon a heretofore-unknown comet or a never-before-seen species of deep-water fish. It is not by means of observation—of scientific inquiry—that the spiritual is uncovered, for, even if one searched the entire universe with a radio telescope and did not find

---

[48] Dawkins, *God Delusion*, 157.

God, it would not follow that He does not exist. Science does present discoveries that evidence the existence of the Creator, but science cannot point directly to Him, just as it cannot point directly to a mind, a feeling, a concept, or the set of rational numbers. Science is a discipline that is concerned strictly with the physical. Ostension has no application outside the realm of corporeality. Science cannot peer past the edge of mass-energy in space-time to catch sight of what may lie there.

In the quest to find answers about origins, to see beyond the world of perceptual experience to a reality that undergirds it, human-kind has set foot on the trails of philosophical reasoning. It has journeyed into the metaphysical to determine whether one can locate God with the tools of the trade. In this quest, however, metaphysics does not yield universal acceptance. Arguments for God's existence meet criticism from the philosophical community, but the cases that are put forth against it surely fare less well. Although many have sought to establish a position on the matter, the naysayers—whether opposed to the reality of divinity or opposed to the rejection of it—are waiting in the wings.

If science cannot show one whether God is real, and meta-physics is not definitive here, then how can one answer the question about His existence; and, if one does learn that there is a God, then how can one know anything about Him? If knowledge is to be gained in this pursuit, and that knowledge is to be the basis for actions in life, then there has to be another way to ascertain the truth. One must redefine the search. In a later chapter, I will do so, but there is more work to do before then. Dawkins, in an attempt to explain biological complexity, advances a model of life that eschews design. It is important to examine it next.

CHAPTER 8

ONE GIANT LEAP TO MAN'S KIND

[B]etween us and you a great chasm has been fixed.

—Luke 16:26 ESV

I love ice cream. I suppose that I always have loved ice cream, and the homemade kind is definitely the crème de la crème. I still can recall those summer days of my youth when the old ice-cream freezer became the center of attention. It was more than the final result of the process that made the experience memorable, but the end product was surely at the top of the list. Pour the ingredients, mixed by my mother's accomplished hand, into the canister, drop in the dasher, secure the top, and the assembly was ready to be loaded into the wooden bucket, weathered from its years of service. Next, the layering came: ice, then rock salt, more ice, then more rock salt, all the way to the top. As good as it was, the ice cream came at a price: Turn the handle until the handle will turn no more. Even now, I can see the silver cylinder whirling just beneath the uppermost chunks of ice, spinning my thoughts to other things and other days, breaking the monotony of the toil. The cranking continued—rotation after rotation; it seemed as though it never would end. My father relieved me from time to time, but I knew my job. Turning became harder and harder as the mixture became harder and harder. It was boy versus machine, and I was determined not to let the machine beat me. I pressed onward until, at last, physics triumphed as freezing brought all motion to a halt. It was over, and the reward for the labor was just around the corner. Remove the crank, pack the top, cover, and then wait, which was harder to do than turning that handle another round. Invariably, it was worth it.

Years later, someone gave an electric ice-cream maker to me. A plastic tub with a motor on top, it was much less toil-intensive than the manual kind. Mix a batch; throw in some ice and salt; plug the contraption into an AC outlet; get a chair and relax. Ice cream is wonderful, no matter how it is made, but alas something seemed to be lost in the transition to modern technology. The woody, salty smell of that aging bucket, worn from years of action; the gear mechanism with its familiar, grinding sound; and the loosely fitting handle that made it happen—all were vestiges of another era, and all were lost or misplaced as time took its toll. What that assemblage brought forth, however, was the pinnacle of frozen treats. Maybe, in the final analysis, it was the effort that preceded the reward that made it such a treasured commodity.

Ice-cream parlors offering a range of flavors became popular through the years. One establishment touted thirty-one different ice creams and sherbets to try. From peppermint stick to pineapple sherbet, there was something for everyone at Baskin-Robbins.[1] A patron could order a triple serving. It was a great way to taste multiple kinds at a single sitting. Of course, unless one exercised great care, the individual scoops tended to merge. How well does banana nut fudge go with butterscotch ribbon? Do cherry macaroon and chocolate mint taste good together? With so many choices, one must try them all to be sure, but I doubt that anyone would complain about the assignment. A purist could order three scoops of the same flavor. Broaden the standards a bit, and one could keep two scoops the same, varying the third, then switch. The daring could mix three different ones. Given thirty-one flavors, if a person could consume one triple-scoop portion every fifteen minutes—not a problem for a professional—then, eating eight hours per day, six days per week, it would take about six and one-half months to sample every such configuration of scoops. As the number of flavors increases, the time that is needed to eat all the configurations rises disproportionately. Triple the flavors for this triple-scoop endeavor, and it would take

---

[1] Famous for its thirty-one flavors, the Baskin-Robbins enterprise had its beginning in a pair of ventures by two brothers-in-law: Burton Baskin and Irvine Robbins. Robbins opened the first store, Snowbird Ice Cream, in 1945 in Glendale, California. Baskin followed in 1946 with Burton's Ice Cream Shop in Pasadena. The operation acquired its current identity in 1953 and continued to expand, both in stores and in flavors. For a history of the company, see Baskin-Robbins, "Our History," accessed July 24, 2013, www.baskinrobbins.com. A list of the original thirty-one flavors is available at the following posting: Sporcle, "Baskin-Robbins 31 Flavors," accessed July 31, 2013, www.sporcle.com/games/g/baskinrobbins. 'Baskin-Robbins' is a registered trademark.

one almost fourteen years to make it through the mound of desserts. Triple twice more, and one would have had to have started nearly ten thousand years ago, close to the dawn of the earth's Holocene epoch, as the geologists define it, to have any chance of finishing in the foreseeable future.[2] Such is the force of combinatorial mathematics. I love ice cream, though; I am up to the challenge. What time does this place close?

Evolution is predicated on the belief that geological time is sufficient to allow random changes and subsequent selection to overcome extraordinary odds. Those odds, in turn, are predicated on a vast array of possibilities. As this chapter will reveal, the numbers that underlie the unfolding of life, as reflected in its biomolecular machinery, give one pause. With applicable mathematics in mind, I turn to the evolutionary narrative as presented by Richard Dawkins.

THE PROGRAM

To account for the existence of living entities on the earth, one must explain two things: how life itself arose on the planet and how the particular organisms, or kinds of organisms, came to be. To explain the first matter, Richard Dawkins, whose argument against the existence of God I reviewed in the last chapter, relies on what has come to be called the anthropic principle. The name of the principle suggests that it is man-centric, and there is indeed an element of such on which it is based. Although there are variations on a theme, so to speak, the anthropic principle, on the whole, recognizes that there are a number of fundamental constants of the universe and corresponding physical laws, such that, if those factors had been slightly different, then the existence of humankind—in fact, that of carbon-based life in general—would not have been possible in the cosmos. For example, changing the value of the strong nuclear force would

---

[2] According to its website, the giant of frozen treats has introduced more than a thousand different flavors since its inception in 1945. That many choices would add several more millennia to this taste experiment.

result either in no chemical elements besides hydrogen or in no hydrogen at all and thus no water. Neither possibility is compatible with life as humans know it to be. Dawkins gives the name 'Goldilocks' to these values, for the numbers must be, as the childhood story goes, just right. Notes Dawkins,

> The anthropic answer, in its most general form, is that we could only be discussing the question in the kind of universe that was capable of producing us. Our existence therefore determines that the fundamental constants of physics had to be in their respective Goldilocks zones.[3]

A universe that was capable of *producing us*, he says—inherent in his phraseology is an assumption that the universe itself is that which brought about living things; that is to say, its efficient cause, its source. That very notion, however, is what he is attempting to show. There is a difference between humans' arising in such a universe and their being produced by it. A subtle problem is already at work.

Dawkins applies this cosmic principle to the earth in an effort to show how life emerged in the world. It is the initial thrust in working toward an account of the existence of the numerous and intricate biological forms that populate the planet. His proposal is below. Part of the passage appeared in the previous chapter.

> Again, as with Goldilocks, the anthropic alternative to the design hypothesis is statistical. Scientists invoke the magic of large numbers. It has been estimated that there are between 1 billion and 30 billion planets in our galaxy, and about 100 billion galaxies in the universe. Knocking a few noughts off for reasons of ordinary prudence, a billion billion is a conservative estimate of the number of available planets in the universe. Now, suppose the origin of life, the spontaneous arising of something equivalent to DNA, really was a quite staggeringly improbable event. Suppose it was so improbable as to occur on only one in a billion planets. A grant-giving body would laugh at any chemist who admitted that the chance of his

---

[3] Richard Dawkins, *The God Delusion* (Boston: Houghton Mifflin Co., 2006), 144.

> proposed research succeeding was only one in a
> hundred. But here we are talking about odds of one in a
> billion. And yet . . . even with such absurdly long odds,
> life will still have arisen on a billion planets—of which
> Earth, of course, is one.[4]

Once life begins, according to Dawkins, a developmental mechanism takes hold to support its continuance. Evolution comprises several factors that can introduce dissimilarities within a biological population, but, to account for the great diversity and complexity of life, evolutionary theory turns to a principal, driving instrument of change. It is a two-part affair. Stating it succinctly, genetic mutations occur at random; these chance events constitute the first step in the process. Most mutations create no advantage for the mutant offspring in survival and reproduction; many actually have disadvantageous effects. Occasionally, however, some do yield a benefit, and nature targets, as it were, the organisms that bear these favorable alterations, positioning them to pass their characteristics to the next generation through heredity. This faux targeting of properties marks the second step in the process: natural selection. Evolution is ongoing and cumulative, inching toward complexity across extended periods of time. Ultimately, the world arrives at its current state. The course of nature is not one of steered progression but mindless meandering as nature blindly shapes its own future.

Dawkins draws an analogy in his writings between the progression of life toward increased biological sophistication and the ascension of an imaginary geological structure to which he gives the name 'Mount Improbable'. At the crest of the metaphorical mountain lies a complex organism or a complex part of one. The steep cliffs on one side of the structure represent the improbability that such intricate things could come to exist in a single random change, bounding directly to the highest point. On the other side of the mountain, there is a gentle slope leading to the summit. This gradual rise in elevation represents the path that living things supposedly take as natural selection hones them through incremental variations. Here, nature is not facing the stunning leap of improbability to the peak but a less threatening, serial course of small steps upward—improvements

---

[4] Ibid., 137–38. The galaxy-count has increased, but it offers no help to Dawkins.

through which increasing complexity is realized. Each step is improbable, but only somewhat so, and the collection of them eventually leads to the greatest heights. It is the factor of accumulation through heredity that makes up the footholds that allow nature to push its way slowly up the mountain, capturing beneficial changes from past generations and building on them. Dawkins refers to his symbolic mountain rather frequently in his writings, even including a reference to it in the title of one of his books.

Such is Dawkins's explanation of how the world of diverse, biological entities came to exist. I will start by examining the first step in his account of life: the simple arising. The analysis will move next to the second: the progression from that modest start to the present stage of highly developed organisms. Volumes have been written on the theory of evolution. Much material argues for it on scientific grounds. Other material points to inadequacies on the same grounds. Sometimes, dissenting facts force a reassessment of a prominent theoretical model. As a case in point, recent discoveries of soft tissue in the remains of dinosaurs—examples include skeletons of *Tyrannosaurus* and a horn of *Triceratops*—have disquieted the scientific community. Tissue of this sort perishes rather quickly on the geological time scale, lasting a few thousand years, at most; but it has surfaced in animals that, according to evolutionists, became extinct many millions of years ago—about sixty-six million for the two examples that I give here. The findings present an inconsistency for evolutionary theory's purported unfolding of biological existence, yet corroborating evidence continues to appear.[5] Support for such

---

[5] Some examples from the scientific literature regarding discoveries of soft tissue include the following ones: Sergio Bertazzo et al., "Fibres and Cellular Structures Preserved in 75-Million-Year-Old Dinosaur Specimens," *Nature Communications* 6, article no. 7352 (2015): 1–8, accessed July 17, 2015, www.nature.com/ncomms/ 2015/150609/ncomms8352/full/ncomms8352.html; Małgorzata Moczydłowska, Frances Westall, and Frédéric Foucher, "Microstructure and Biogeochemistry of the Organically Preserved Ediacaran Metazoan *Sabellidites*," *Journal of Paleontology* 88, no. 2 (2014): 224–39; Mark Hollis Armitage and Kevin Lee Anderson, "Soft Sheets of Fibrillar Bone from a Fossil of the Supraorbital Horn of the Dinosaur *Triceratops horridus*," *Acta Histochemica* 115, no. 6 (2013): 603–8, accessed November 2, 2016, www.sciencedirect.com/science/article/pii/ S0065128113000020; Robert R. Reisz et al., "Embryology of Early Jurassic Dinosaur from China with Evidence of Preserved Organic Remains," *Nature* 496,

findings comes from another source as well: carbon-14 dating. This radioactive isotope has a half-life of about 5,730 years. After nine or ten iterations, it effectively vanishes; each atom leaves a nitrogen nucleus and emitted particles. Thus, any sample that tests positive for the isotope cannot be much older than fifty thousand years. Some examinations of dinosaur remains using this dating method have revealed ages that are in the thousands of years. The specimens could not be even a million years old, let alone tens of millions.[6] Attempts to explain these incongruities are under way, focusing, in the former case, on how the tissue could be preserved. Another possibility, of course, is that paleontologists are wrong about the ages of the beasts, which is what the abovesaid evidence plainly indicates, raising difficulties having wide-ranging consequences. The controversy persists.

In a work of the sort that I am undertaking here, narrowing the scope of the analysis is important, lest the discussion drift too far afield in paleontological and related matters. Therefore, I will focus on the two key elements of Dawkins's program of life, his attempt to describe certain biological phenomena as he sees them. The two are

---

no. 7444 (2013): 210–14; Mary Higby Schweitzer et al., "Molecular Analyses of Dinosaur Osteocytes Support the Presence of Endogenous Molecules," *Bone* 52, no. 1 (2013): 414–23; Johan Lindgren et al., "Microspectroscopic Evidence of Cretaceous Bone Proteins," *PLOS ONE* 6, no. 4 (2011): e1–e11, accessed November 2, 2016, journals.plos.org/plosone/article?id=10.1371/journal.pone.0019445; Mary H. Schweitzer et al., "Biomolecular Characterization and Protein Sequences of the Campanian Hadrosaur *B. canadensis*," *Science* 324, no. 5927 (2009): 626–31; John M. Asara et al., "Protein Sequences from Mastodon and *Tyrannosaurus* [*r*]*ex* Revealed by Mass Spectrometry," *Science* 316, no. 5822 (2007): 280–85; Mary Higby Schweitzer, Jennifer L. Wittmeyer, and John R. Horner, "Soft Tissue and Cellular Preservation in Vertebrate Skeletal Elements from the Cretaceous to the Present," *Proceedings of the Royal Society B* 274, no. 1607 (2007): 183–97, cor. 274, no. 1629 (2007): 3183; Mary Higby Schweitzer et al., "Analyses of Soft Tissue from *Tyrannosaurus rex* Suggest the Presence of Protein," *Science* 316, no. 5822 (2007): 277–80; and Roman Pawlicki and Maria Nowogrodzka-Zagórska, "Blood Vessels and Red Blood Cells Preserved in Dinosaur Bones," *Annals of Anatomy* 180, no. 1 (1998): 73–77.

[6] A pair of articles pertaining to carbon-14 dating of fossils appears here: John Michael Fischer, "Carbon-14-Dated Dinosaur Bones Are Less Than 40,000 Years Old," accessed November 5, 2016, www.newgeology.us/presentation48.html; and Josef Holzschuh, Jean de Pontcharra, and Hugh Miller, "Recent C-14 Dating of Fossils Including Dinosaur Bone Collagen," accessed November 5, 2016, www.sciencevsevolution.org/Holzschuh.htm.

1. the *beginning*—in terms of probability;
2. the wandering toward *complexity*—in terms of gradual change.

The concept beneath Dawkins's program is that, by providing explanations that do not go beyond the natural world, one does not need

1. *creation* to account for the beginning;
2. *intelligent design* to account for complexity.

Dawkins is not proposing merely an alternative to creation and intelligent design as an account of how things came to be the way that they are on the earth. He is arguing ardently in favor of that alternative on both counts: the origin of life and the materialization of advanced biological development. Indeed, he states, "In any of its forms the God Hypothesis is unnecessary."[7] Further, he declares, "Evolution is a fact."[8] As the prior chapter clearly revealed, what Dawkins is putting forward in his writings is a model of existence that excludes the supernatural altogether. There is no room for God in Dawkins's theory. I will proceed with that understanding.

An appreciation of the biology that gives rise to Dawkins's overall position is beneficial, particularly as it applies to the building of organismal complexity, and it is important to cover it to a fair extent. For the most part, however, the forthcoming investigation will center on how well the philosophical implications and the mathematics of the Dawkinsian conceptional framework align with reality. Beyond such central matters, a sobering question lies just beneath the surface of evolutionary theory. It is one that the theory is ill-equipped to answer, for science can offer only what it has. In the end, whether Dawkins's program carries enough logical force to convince one of its truth is the issue of the day.

---

[7] Dawkins, *God Delusion*, 46.
[8] Richard Dawkins, *The Greatest Show on Earth: The Evidence for Evolution* (New York: Free Press, 2009), 8. The assertion that evolution is a fact is found as well in Dawkins, *God Delusion*, 300.

SPONTANEITY OF OLD

Before I continue, a slight diversion is in order; it is one that is relevant nevertheless. Years ago, it was a common belief that living things could come into existence from nonliving material: frogs out of mud, snakes out of horsehair lying in a puddle of rain water, and maggots out of decaying flesh, to list a few. This theory is known as spontaneous generation. In 1668, the Italian scientist Francesco Redi conducted an experiment to see whether rotting meat could bring forth life. He placed animal tissue in flasks, using cloth and paper as coverings for some, while another was left open. Only in the open flask did maggots appear, as it was the one flask into which flies, which were attracted by the odor, could enter. Had the meat been the source of the larvae, the larvae would have appeared in all the flasks, so reason would dictate. The theory of spontaneous generation was disproved conclusively in the nineteenth century by the French chemist Louis Pasteur. In a noted experiment, Pasteur filled a long-neck flask with a nutrient-rich solution. He heated the neck and bent it into an S-shape. Next, he boiled the solution, which killed all microorganisms that were present and also caused water vapor to condense in the curve of the neck, forming an airtight seal. No airborne organism could enter the flask through the seal and thereby taint the solution. A year and a half later, the liquid was still free of contamination.

It is ironic that evolutionary biologists have traveled full circle concerning the concept of life's arising from lifelessness. The modern adaptation is more sophisticated, attributing the life-giving substance to a soup of prebiotic chemicals, or maybe a buildup of inorganic crystals, in which some extraordinary, precipitating event or group of events occurred, resulting in a self-replicating molecule or molecular apparatus. The underlying concept of life's arising from nonlife is the same nonetheless. One thing that makes the modern version more palatable perhaps is the assumption that it was highly unusual. Says Dawkins, "[T]he origin of life was (or could have been) a unique event which had to happen only once."[9] It took place when no one was looking, given that no human existed at the time.

---

[9] Dawkins, *God Delusion*, 139.

Experiments, such as those of Redi and Pasteur, can be performed repeatedly today, however, and one can demonstrate satisfactorily that spontaneous generation of biological entities does not occur. One is not hesitant to eat canned goods if they are processed properly, sealing them well and heating the contents to a high temperature for a certain period of time. No one expects to find life in there: No informed person believes that it can be generated from the contents, even if the key chemical elements that are necessary for DNA are present. When an occasional spoiled product does appear, the problem is attributed to improper sealing or faulty heating. There are many opportunities for life to arise from lifelessness, but such an event never is observed; and one eliminates spontaneous generation as a possibility. Still, many scientists believe, as does Dawkins, that some unique, or near-unique, lifelessness-to-life incident, or series of incidents, to which humans can trace their own history must have taken place, for they are alive to consider it. What was it about that peculiar life-starting event that made it possible when one does not see it happen at all currently? Was it simply an accident, bound by the rules of probability to happen somewhere—so, why not here?

One might say that the aforementioned comparison is unfair. It is not appropriate to characterize the event that brought life to the lifeless earth as old-fashioned spontaneous generation. It was not the sudden appearance of an organism itself, be it maggot or microbe. It was a much different affair, just the right combination of materials—hydrogen, oxygen, nitrogen, carbon, and phosphorous—in just the right environment, yielding a DNA or RNA molecule that was embedded in a structure from which all organisms sprang. The incident is presumed to have been rare, possibly singular. It is presumed further that, setting aside the work of Redi and Pasteur, the failure to observe even one occurrence is no bar to its having happened. An aberrant event, it took place in a special environment—quite unlike that of the earth now—and one should not expect to see it occur again. The launch-of-life episode need not be subjected, and perhaps cannot be subjected, to trials that may show that such a thing is not factual, even though proper scientific standards require hypotheses to be potentially falsifiable. The lack of experimental evidence, an advocate may say, ought not to dissuade one from accepting the conjecture, as the failure to observe snakes emerge from horsehair may count against the theory of spontaneous generation. Snakes do not lie at the very base of biochemical life; DNA, or a molecule that is similar to it in certain respects, occupies that place. Whereas the probability of a sudden, undirected assemblage of the parts that are necessary to produce a functioning multicellular organism is too remote ever to have occurred, the probability of a sudden, undirected piecing together of a self-replicating structure, albeit surely low, is not, Dawkins thinks, unreasonably low. It is the anthropic principle that improves the odds, he says—what he refers to as large-number magic. I will leave this digression on spontaneous generation here and turn to Dawkins's argument that leans on the anthropic principle.

GETTING STARTED: AN ANTHROPIC ARISING

Dawkins asks one to assume with him that the chance of the spontaneous arising of something akin to DNA is one in a billion. Some scientists estimate the number of planets in the universe to be at least a billion times a billion, and Dawkins maintains, on that basis, that there must be a billion planets where the lifelessness-to-life event would occur—not *could* occur but, given his assumption of the probability, *would* occur. More than arguing only that life originated somewhere among the planets in the universe from one or more random events, though, Dawkins proceeds to conclude that, because there are intelligent beings on the earth who are looking for life elsewhere, this planet must be among the distinctive group. In essence, his principal assertion, resting as it does on his assumed probability, is that life sprang into existence by a chance occurrence, without design, not just someplace but *here*: This one-in-a-billion, long-shot incident is part of the earth's history.

I will take up his reasoning beginning with a partial restatement of a previous quotation.

> [S]uppose the origin of life, the spontaneous arising of
> something equivalent to DNA . . . was so improbable as
> to occur on only one in a billion planets. . . . [E]ven with

such absurdly long odds, *life will still have arisen* on a billion planets—of which Earth, of course, is one.

This conclusion is so surprising, I'll say it again. If the odds of *life originating spontaneously on a planet* were a billion to one against, nevertheless that stupefyingly improbable event *would still happen* on a billion planets. The chance of finding any one of those billion life-bearing planets recalls the proverbial needle in a haystack. But we don't have to go out of our way to find a needle because (back to the anthropic principle) any beings capable of looking *must necessarily* be sitting on one of those prodigiously rare needles before they even start the search.[10]

Next, Dawkins claims that his logic destroys the intelligent design theory.

Even accepting the most pessimistic estimate of the probability that life might spontaneously originate, this statistical argument completely demolishes any suggestion that we should postulate design to fill the gap.[11]

Finally, he says,

The anthropic principle states that, since we are alive, eucaryotic and conscious, our planet *has to be* one of the intensely rare planets that *has bridged all three gaps.*[12]

---

[10] Dawkins, *God Delusion*, 137–38. The emphases are mine. Technically, if the chance of the occurrence of some event is one in a billion—a probability of 10^{-9}— then the odds are 999,999,999 to one, not a billion to one, as Dawkins states. Dawkins does not distinguish in his postulations between probability and odds. Given the magnitude of the numerical values that he mentions, however, it makes little difference, and I will not quibble over the distinction in my analysis. Except where it affects the accuracy of a calculation, I will take his expressions of probability and odds to be more or less interchangeable.

[11] Ibid., 139.

[12] Ibid., 140–41. The emphases are mine. The term 'eucaryotic' refers to the type of cells that make up the bodies of more advanced organisms. These cells, in contrast to bacteria, have nuclei, mitochondria, and other special components. The typical spelling of the term 'eucaryotic' in American works is 'eukaryotic'.

A strange argument, it all seems to be a little fast. A closer look at its structure is in order. It takes the form that is shown below; I number the steps for reference:

Dawkins's Anthropic Argument

Part I

1. [Assume that] the chance of x's happening on a given planet is one in 10^9.
2. [Assume that] the number of planets where x could happen is 10^{18}.
3. It follows that the number of planets where x would happen is (at least) 10^9.

Part II

4. If a planet is populated by y, then x happened on that planet.
5. The planet earth is populated by y.
6. Therefore, x happened on the planet earth.

where

x = an instance of a random lifelessness-to-life episode
y = complex, intelligent life (living organisms)

This argument contains both logical and mathematical errors. I will start with Part I. From where did Dawkins's assumption of the chance that appears in the first premise come? Undoubtedly, he employs the one-in-a-billion figure because it represents a very low likelihood, but he grabs it strictly out of thin air, so to speak. There is categorically *nothing* to support that number: no science, no metaphysics—nothing. To assume a numerical value by picking it to suit one's purposes can aid in demonstrating a point, as long as it is clear that the consequence of any argument that is based on that assumption is contingent on the accuracy of the number. Humans are imaginative beings, and such assumptions are often useful in helping them to envision things in search of the truth. In the case of Dawkins, though, his narrative concerning life on the earth comes to rest on a supposition—if one is indeed to put any trust in his purported probability. Unless Dawkins can find a way to account for the existence of biological entities without introducing the activity of an intelligent agent, his entire naturalistic theory collapses around him with a thud. Such a detail is thus a crucial element of his thesis.

Even if one could speculate about the probability of the emergence of chemical self-replication on a planet, however, any assigned mathematical value would not be meaningful apart from relevant contextual factors. What common fraction represents the likelihood of one's rolling two sixes, or boxcars, on a pair of dice: $^1/_{36}$, $^1/_{20}$, $^1/_6$, or some other value? The question cannot be answered; it is incomplete. There is no probability *simpliciter* here. The probability is contingent on the number of rolls of the dice, which, in turn, may be governed by the rate of generating throws and the allotted time. If one can toss the dice about every three seconds during a nine-second trial, managing three attempts to hit double sixes in that span, then the probability is 0.0810399520—a little less than $^1/_{12}$, in common-fraction form—that at least one roll will result in boxcars. Time is hence a key factor in determining the chance that a particular event will occur in the unfolding of phenomena. Dawkins realizes that the time for progression of life is capped, but he does not address—with respect explicitly to time—the fact that his one-in-a-billion chance of the occurrence of the random opening event on a given planet varies inversely with the level of development on that planet. I will explain.

Dawkins does not specify the period of time to which the probability that he submits applies. In light of his remarks, however, one would think that he intends the probability of the emergence of the initial replicator-molecule on a particular world to pertain to the full span of that world's existence. For the earth, that period, in the view of contemporary science, is about four and one-half billion years (four billion six hundred million is the usual number). Then, the position is that a patriarchal molecule has one chance in a billion of surfacing on the earth during the planetary period of four and one-half billion years. Dawkins is therefore off to a rather rocky start. According to evolutionary theory, there are subsequent developmental events, occurring much later, that are dependent on that emergence. For example, *Homo sapiens*, so goes the theory, is a relative latecomer. To allow sufficient time for humans to develop from the initial DNA or RNA replicator, the arising of that extraordinary molecule must be pushed back to the first billion years or so. In effect, this reduction in time also reduces the chance of its occurrence, *ceteris paribus*, just as limiting the dice-throwing scenario to three seconds, instead of nine, decreases the probability of hitting boxcars from 0.0810399520 to the lesser number of 0.0277777778 if one manages but a single throw. It follows that Dawkins's proposed one-in-a-billion chance is actually appreciably less, at least on the planet earth—the likelihood on each of the other planets in his many-planet grouping presumably will vary notably. One cannot consider merely the probability of life's appearing on the earth. If one wishes to propose a fortuitous arrival, then one must consider its happening in a condensed time frame. Dawkins is aware that the biological development that he proposes is a protracted process, of course, but he neglects to describe adequately the impact of the time that is associated with it on the probability that he states.

Continuing the analysis reveals that there is more to Dawkins's number grabbing than meets the eye. In an interesting twist, he picks for the probability of the spontaneous arising of life a mathematical value that puts the likelihood in a Goldilocks zone of his own. If it were substantially less, then his anthropic-basis reasoning would be pointless in an attempt to account for this initiating event, as the odds would be prohibitive. If it were substantially greater, then, based strictly on the numbers, it would be difficult to defend the position that such an event is an atypical occurrence in planetary circles. The numerical value that Dawkins uses in his assumption must fall within a critical, just-right range, giving one the distinct impression that the supposed chance is more the product of need than a hypothesis to probe. Even on the supposition that the spontaneous emergence of life without intervention is a physical possibility, the notable lack of grounds for Dawkins's estimate of its probability leads one to question whether the chance of an occurrence of this sort might not be far from one in a billion. Maybe it is one in a nonillion or one in a tredecillion.[13] Maybe it is one in a thousand or one in five.

At one chance in a tredecillion, the outcome is much more bleak than the one that Dawkins advances, despite his assumption of

---

[13] A nonillion equals 10^{30}, as indicated earlier. A tredecillion equals 10^{42}.

a billion billion available planets. The probability of life's arising, in this instance, is so extraordinarily minute that to maintain that it will happen or that it has happened—on *any* planet in *any* galaxy *anywhere* in the universe—would be irrational. On the other hand, if the chance is one in five, then it assuredly will be happening and has been happening virtually *everywhere*, and prudence would dictate that one check each can of chicken soup carefully before serving it to the family. Strange things may be going on in there after all, especially given the antioxidizing properties of certain additives.

The point is that merely picking a number on which to base a fundamental tenet that is central to one's case—in the present matter, the dawn of biological existence—is to proffer an account that lacks any substantive explanatory merit. The numerical value that Dawkins gives in the first premise is thus unwarranted, as its authenticity cannot be established either by empirical methods or by logical ones. Dawkins's claim that applying statistics, employing his imaginary odds, demolishes any reason to postulate intelligent design is surprising. His confidence in his made-up number is misplaced.

A further difficulty with Dawkins's argument occurs in the first premise of Part I. It is subtle, but it is logically destructive. To assign a probability at all—any probability other than zero—to the occurrence of a mindless lifelessness-to-life event is to say implicitly that it is a possibility: a physical possibility here. The issue on the table is whether life did come—indeed, *can* come—from lifelessness without the introduction of agency. Again, one must be careful to distinguish between, on the one hand, life's arising from a mass of chemicals by a chance occurrence in a purposeless world and, on the other hand, its arising from a mass of chemicals by the action of an intelligent being who is capable of generating it. The fact that life exists, and exists on the planet where humans dwell, demonstrates that its existence is physically possible in the universe. One cannot deduce from the fact that life exists, however, that its arising from an inert mass without willful intervention is physically possible as well. To assume that it is so is to put forth the exact notion that is in question. Only that which is possible is actual. By supposing that abiogenesis is possible, the argument, in a somewhat cloaked manner, commits the fallacy of begging the question. This fallacy is underscored by the reasoning in Part II, where the error is overt.

The second premise of Dawkins's anthropic argument is also speculative, albeit plainly not as recklessly so as the first premise. One can perceive stars with the unaided eye; with other means, one can perceive them even in the far reaches of space. Until recent years, planets could not be detected beyond the solar system with surety. Astronomical viewing has continued to improve, though, and, following the launch in 2009 of NASA's spacecraft *Kepler*, scientists have discovered other planetary systems. Astronomers know now through observation that outlying worlds exist, but they still cannot know whether there are many of them, let alone billions. A few of the aforesaid systems are of interest because they contain planets that are orbiting their respective stars at distances that place them in zones of presumably moderate temperatures. The composition of the atmospheric gases of none is discernible, however, as of this writing, and whether any of them can sustain life, of course, is unknown. The best that scientists can do is to hypothesize that gaseous environments elsewhere in the universe resemble local conditions, arriving at that hypothesis by means of an argument from analogy. As I have noted, although such arguments are useful, they cannot establish their conclusions with certainty, a fact that Dawkins himself embraces in attempting to counter the argument from design.

With regard to the billion billion planets to which Dawkins refers, it appears that he is concerned in this respect only with the number of planets in the cosmos, not with the number of ones with life-enabling capabilities. It may be that he intends his stated chance of life's arising to perform an extra duty, functioning as a limiter that narrows the pool of planets to all those that can initiate life and maintain it, theorizing, if so—amazingly—that a living thing arose on every world that is capable of sustaining it.

This numbered logical sequence is behind the second premise:

1. Humans observe that there are planets circling a local
    star: the sun.
2. They observe that many other stars populate the universe.
3. They observe that there are planets circling at least some
    of those stars.
4. Therefore, there are many other planets circling other
    stars in the universe.

Although there is scientific support for the view that undetected planets fill distant regions of the universe, the support is derived through an inference that is based on generalization from a few known cases. A further, speculative move is required to reach the conclusion that there are many planets—a billion billion—that may provide a platform for life's emergence. At the far end of this speculative exercise is Dawkins's proposed probability by which he lands on an alleged group of worlds that can sustain life.

Turn now to statement 3 of Dawkins's anthropic argument: the conclusion of Part I (page 768). A fallacy that surfaces here is the result of a mathematical error. Dawkins uses numbers in an effort to reach the conclusion of this part, but his computation is incorrect. The proper value cannot be obtained simply by performing this calculation: $10^{-9} \times 10^{18} = 10^9$. If the chance of the occurrence of x (an instance, a token of a type) on a planet is one in a billion, and there are a billion billion planets where it could happen, then it does not follow that x will occur on a billion or more planets. What follows is that there is a probability of 0.5000063084 of a billion or more incidents of x—almost an even split.[14] The idea in step 3 must incorporate a reference to probability. The mistake creates a non sequitur.

Further, in arriving at the conclusion, Dawkins is endeavoring to prove one of two things. If his inference is to show that something is possible or probable based on the assumption of other possibilities or probabilities, then nothing is gained. Said in another way, if one assumes a chance of $1/n$ for an independent instance of some type of event to happen, and one assumes that there are n^2 opportunities for an instance of that type to happen, then one can assign a *probability* for n occurrences. The argument would be trivial, impotent—reduced to a mere computation. One could say just as well that, if the chance that a white hippopotamus will dart in front of a speeding train at a railroad crossing in a particular American state is one in a hundred, and, representing opportunities, there are ten thousand crossings in that state where it could happen, then the probability is a little greater than 50 percent that an albino hippo will be knocked into the weeds

---

[14] The Department of Mathematics and Statistics at Auburn University provided assistance in determining this figure, for which I am grateful. A normal distribution was used for the calculation. Probability applies to future events, but, to capture Dawkins's argument properly, it is necessary to represent his case in broad terms.

at least a hundred times. One could add a time frame to the story, but, with or without it, the thinking, in spite of the accuracy of the calculation, is obviously unfounded; the claimed chance of an incident, by any standards, ludicrous.

It is more likely that Dawkins is attempting to show instead that, if one accepts his one-in-a-billion assumption and accepts his supposition concerning the number of available planets, then one must accept the conclusion as reporting conditions in reality. The trouble thus, apart from the mathematical problem, is that, if this second interpretation of Part I of Dawkins's argument is correct, then he is trying to use the numbers in steps 1 and 2 to prove that life actually *did* arise spontaneously on many planets. To reach this point, he is taking one of two paths. The first path is to assert that the two premises do not present assumptions but facts. This approach is indefensible. As I have indicated, the likelihood of life's arising cannot be given a definitive numeric, and it is only through baseless speculation that Dawkins assigns a mathematical value to it at all. There is no reason whatever to believe that he is right about his conjectured odds or, more important, that odds even apply. Premise 1 cannot be put forward as a declarative proposition with the introductory assumptive phrase removed, nor can premise 2. Moreover, Dawkins's remarks suggest that he intends the premises to be formulated in terms of assumptions.

The second path that Dawkins may be taking is to move from assumed possibility in the premises to hard reality in the conclusion. This approach is indefensible as well. First of all, it is clear at this juncture that one cannot leap from *probability* to a number of *actual occurrences*, and such is true even when the probability is known. The chance that flipping a fair coin once will result in heads is 0.5000000000; therefore, from a numerical perspective, the expected outcome of tossing the coin a hundred times is fifty heads. What might have happened, though, when Jack tried it, is that his trial of a hundred tosses resulted in forty-seven heads or fifty-three or sixty-two. Second, and of greater import, one surely cannot leap from *imaginary probability*—a make-believe chance of one in a billion—to a number of *actual occurrences*. Even if the assumptions that the anthropic argument puts forth in the first two premises were right, Part I still would fail because its conclusion cannot be submitted as a firm statement about real conditions. Dawkins, if he follows this second path, proceeds illegitimately from suppositions to unsupported claims regarding physical reality. It seems that Dawkins must do so nonetheless, for Part II of the argument relies on establishing that random lifelessness-to-life events are genuine happenings, ones that actually have taken place in the cosmos. Without this reading of the conclusion of Part I, Part II is doomed from the start.

The final problem with Part I is that the Dawkinsian large-numbers sword displays another edge. Grant the one-in-a-billion chance for the sake of analysis. What evidence could one have that the molecule that supposedly began everything met the challenge of survival with success—stated better perhaps, remained intact—bringing about the life-filled earth? Does one say in the anthropic vein that it must have made it, given that people are around to talk about it? To do so would be to embrace a groundless conception. Dawkins's assumed chance is linked to the presumption that what one sees today is the consequence of a rare occurrence on the planet, possibly unique, in which the foundational molecule was formed, but there are many things that could have worked against the molecule's generational role. Broadly speaking, DNA has dual functions, which are executed through its inherent instruction-set: It reproduces itself, and it directs the building of both RNA and, to a greater extent, the proteins that are necessary for cells and their operations. For either of these functions to be carried out, however, it is not enough for there to be merely DNA. Replication is an exacting and complex process that involves much more than the compound itself, and the building of the proteins that form cells is more intricate still. Without the presence of various enzymes to perform critical duties, DNA replication is not even possible. Without other enzymes, and the amino acids of which proteins are made, there is no way to manufacture a cell to house the molecule, rendering it, for all its replicative power, useless as a biological progenitor. What is the likelihood that all these additional life-ingredients were available at the right time and in the same location as the patriarchal molecule? Even if all the necessary components were available, how is it that they would have coalesced to produce a working prototype, along with the full complement of auxiliary products that life requires?

A DOWN-TO-EARTH LAUNCH

There is a theory that chemical evolution gave rise to biological evolution in the earth's ancient history. Perhaps setting the stage for the notion, just after the turn of the twentieth century, Walther Löb began conducting electrochemical experiments whereby he was able to produce organic compounds from certain gases. The theory that living things arose by means of chemical reactions, however, is traced to the 1920s, when Alexander (Aleksandr) Ivanovich Oparin, a Russian biochemist, and subsequently J. B. S. Haldane, a British geneticist, postulated that the complex molecules that are necessary for life, including DNA and proteins, emerged from simpler ones. According to the theory, certain substances, principally inorganic, in the early atmosphere of the earth were subjected to infusions of energy, which brought about important changes, resulting in new compounds. These compounds accumulated in the ocean as rain washed them down to the planet's surface. Methane, ammonia, and hydrogen were key ingredients in the process. In the current version, the narrative turns to several sources of energy as candidates for driving the transformations: the intense radiation of the sun, severe heat of volcanoes, extreme electrical activity of lightning, and so forth. With the Oparin-Haldane idea as a backdrop, Stanley L. Miller, in cooperation with Harold C. Urey, performed an experiment in 1953 in which Miller boiled water to create vapor, mixing it with the (organic) substance methane, along with ammonia and hydrogen, in a closed apparatus. His intent was to simulate the supposed prelife atmospheric environment of the early earth. Next, he introduced electrical sparks to the gaseous mixture. After a period of time, Miller analyzed the resultant gummy liquid and discovered some simple organic molecules, including amino acids.

Drawing on these results, contemporary theorists typically proceed to suggest that elementary chemical units, or monomers, of nucleotides—the basic constituents of bioreplicating compounds, each one made of a sugar, a phosphate group, and a nitrogenous base—joined to form complex chains, or polymers, of the nucleic acid RNA, and possibly DNA. These molecules serve as the foundation that underlies living entities. From there, the theorists propose, a lipid mass that is referred to as a protocell developed, providing a rudimentary membrane that could supply the enclosure that is needed for a replicating compound. This protocell, they hold, became the precursor of the modern cell. Although the Miller-Urey experiment produced no nucleotides and, a fortiori, no nucleic acids, a number of scientists have taken the results to be an indication that life arose in this way, and they have been encouraged by the fact that subsequent trials by other researchers using different materials have produced a range of amino acids. The alleged arising of life from nonliving matter is called abiogenesis.

It is difficult to assign a value to the trials of Miller and others. They show that certain chemical compounds that are vital for life can be produced from other compounds, some of which are not vital, but this fact is to be expected. For instance, living things need not take in hydrogen peroxide (H_2O_2)—indeed, in concentration, it is generally toxic to cells. Yet, it produces water, which all cells of organisms require to sustain metabolism, and oxygen, which nearly all eukaryotic organisms need for normal, aerobic cellular respiration. Basic chemistry proves that many substances form new ones through reactions, as any chemistry set teaches youngsters. The key conjecture for the evolutionists is that, if the ingredients in the experimental mix mimic the early earth environment, then chance might have produced the right compounds for the progression to biological forms.

Both the experimental approach and the concepts that are behind it raise concerns. Regarding the former matter, I will mention briefly a few problems. As the primary energy source in the prebiotic world and therefore the principal one for any reputed amino-acid production, the sun is a key factor in the theoretical generative process. Like other energy factors, however, the sun plays a dual part in the activity, both building molecules and, with commensurate ability, dismantling them. This fact challenges the integrity of the conjectured Oparin-Haldane prebiotic mixture. The utility of methane would have been compromised by the solar fusing of simple molecules of the chemical—probably nearly all of it—to create complex hydrocarbons, thereby preventing participation in the requisite interaction.[15] The sun would have destroyed ammonia in

---

[15] See Charles B. Thaxton, Walter L. Bradley, and Roger L. Olsen, *The Mystery of Life's Origin: Reassessing Current Theories* (New York: Philosophical Library,

short order by breaking that substance into its nitrogen-hydrogen constituents, "reducing its atmospheric concentration to so small a value that it could have played *no* important role in chemical evolution."[16] According to one physicist and author on geophysical topics, it is unlikely that the Oparin-Haldane atmosphere was a feature of the primitive earth.

> If the methane-ammonia hypothesis were correct, there should be geochemical evidence supporting it. What is the evidence for a primitive methane-ammonia atmosphere on earth? The answer is that there is *no* evidence for it, but much against it. The methane-ammonia hypothesis is in major trouble with respect to the ammonia component, for ammonia on the primitive earth would have quickly disappeared. . . .
> If large amounts of methane had ever been present in the earth's atmosphere, geologic evidence for it should also be available. . . . The earliest rocks should contain an unusually large proportion of carbon or organic chemicals. This is not the case.[17]

There is yet another impeding issue: Had amino acids been produced, the sun and other contributors of energy would have acted destructively on them as well: "[M]ost amino acids are especially susceptible to decomposition by irreversible decarboxylation caused by heat."[18] The Miller-Urey apparatus, like others that followed it, shielded the products of amino-acid synthesis from damage by isolating them in a reservoir away from the interposed energy—in the case at hand, an electrical discharge. No such contrived isolation

---

1984), 43. The authors refer to the research that Phillip H. Abelson and P. E. Cloud present on this point.

[16] Ibid. The authors cite Phillip H. Abelson et al. with regard to the reduction of the concentration of ammonia.

[17] Phillip H. Abelson, "Chemical Events on the Primitive Earth," *Proceedings of the National Academy of Sciences of the United States of America* 55, no. 6 (1966): 1365. Abelson was director, and subsequently president, of the Geophysical Laboratory at the Carnegie Institution of Washington from the 1950s to 1970s.

[18] Rene Evard and David Schrodetzki, "Chemical Evolution," *Origins* 3, no. 1 (1976): 14. The authors cite S. L. Miller and L. E. Orgel in connection with this information.

would have existed at the beginning to defend the products of synthesis against the detrimental effects of energy. Without protection, "the destructive forces of electrical discharges or ultraviolet radiation would destroy the prebiotic precursors of life that they had produced."[19]

Regarding the chemical mix, there has been a fair amount of speculation in that respect, evidenced by the fact that the initial concoctions in the various trials since the original experiment vary widely. The most favored substance of recent times for the formation of amino acids and other compounds appears to be hydrogen cyanide (HCN). For the sugar that is needed for a nucleic acid—ribose, for RNA—formaldehyde (CH_2O) is the choice. Unless highly concentrated, however, hydrogen cyanide is hydrolyzed to yield formamide and then formic acid: something that certain organisms, including bees and red ants, use as a weapon. As hydrogen cyanide in the atmosphere descended into the ocean, given that the ocean is nearly all water, hydrolysis would have been assured without some way of protecting the substance from degradation prior to the synthesis of organic materials, thus nullifying any value as a progenitor. There are places on the earth where concentration of inorganic chemicals has occurred—Yellowstone National Park, for example—which may seem to help the case of the theorists, but no like place of concentration of organic chemicals ever has been identified, and no evidence that an oceanic organic soup once existed ever has come to light.[20]

As for formaldehyde, it degenerates rapidly, creating carbon monoxide and hydrogen. The decomposition presents a difficulty for the proposed abiotic origin.

> In the natural situation any formaldehyde would tend to be destroyed. CH_2O is unstable and it decomposes to $CO + H_2$. . . . Formaldehyde if produced at the

---

[19] Ibid., 18.

[20] The hydrolysis of hydrogen cyanide in an oceanic environment and the lack of evidence that organic compounds in concentration existed, or an oceanic soup of them did so, are points appearing in Thaxton, Bradley, and Olsen, *Mystery of Life's Origin*, 48–49, 64–65. Regarding the lack of support for organic pools, see K. Dose, "Peptides and Amino Acids in the Primordial Hydrosphere," in *The Origin of Life and Evolutionary Biochemistry*, ed. K. Dose et al. (New York: Plenum Press, 1974), 75. The aforesaid authors in this note refer to the article by Dose.

top of the atmosphere would not survive the temperatures or radiation there.

Any surviving formaldehyde which reached the alkaline ocean would be subject to further attenuation. Formaldehyde undergoes disproportionation to methyl alcohol plus formic acid.[21]

There are other problems with formaldehyde. It interferes with hydrogen cyanide chemistry. Formaldehyde reacts spontaneously with it to produce cyanohydrin, "a well-known reaction that has vexed workers in the field of prebiotic chemistry relying on an unencumbered availability of HCN in high concentration."[22] The two substances must be separated to prevent interaction, even though, so goes the thinking, both are required—one for the nitrogenous bases that make up a nucleic acid, the other for the sugar component of the nucleic acid's backbone. How these two parts could come to be linked in a prebiotic environment has continued to be an unanswered question.[23]

The polymerization of formaldehyde—the formose reaction—is the sole process that scientists have cited for the synthesis of prebiotic ribose. Yet, the nitrogenous substances that are needed for the building of the bases that compose nucleic acids actually interfere with the crucial process, and any sugar products that might result are destroyed quickly under the applicable conditions.[24] Other scientists also find the reaction to be problematic. It is not "a plausible model for the prebiotic accumulation of sugars," they state, noting that it

---

[21] Abelson, "Chemical Events," 1369.

[22] Stephen J. Mojzsis, Ramanarayanan Krishnamurthy, and Gustaf Arrhenius, "Before RNA and After: Geophysical and Geochemical Constraints on Molecular Evolution," in *The RNA World*, ed. Raymond F. Gesteland, Thomas R. Cech, and John F. Atkins, 2nd ed. (Cold Springs Harbor, NY: Cold Springs Harbor Laboratory Press, 1999), 20. Also refer to p. 17 there. The authors conjecture that cyanohydrin may provide a way out of the formaldehyde trap by leading to nitrogenous bases itself, given certain conditions, but the satisfaction of those conditions is notably speculative. Without substantiation, the supposition is of little value in offering a way to circumvent the inevitable interference quandary.

[23] See, for example, ibid., 24.

[24] This point is expressed in Robert Shapiro, "Prebiotic Ribose Synthesis: A Critical Analysis," *Origins of Life and Evolution of the Biosphere* 18, nos. 1–2 (1988): 71.

requires concentrated solutions, and sugar products that are formed decompose rapidly.[25] Indeed, there is little to suggest that the needed sugar component ever was on hand for a prelife assembly.

> The evidence that is currently available does not support the availability of ribose on the prebiotic earth, except perhaps for brief periods of time, in low concentration, as part of a complex mixture, under circumstances that are unsuitable for nucleotide synthesis.[26]

Finally, with ammonia present, formaldehyde combines with hydrogen cyanide to form glycine; it does not yield any sugars.[27] Relying on the ready accessibility of a sugar is a dubious approach.

Of course, without phosphorous within reach, there would be nowhere to go, even if ribose were on hand, because a critical nucleic acid never would result. Compounding the problem is the fact that phosphorous cannot be extracted easily from minerals that are on the earth, as these minerals are not prone to dissolve. Given the aquatic environment of life's purported origination, it appears that an essential ingredient was not obtainable. Scientists therefore have turned to the heavens as a source: They postulate that certain meteors must have delivered the necessary phosphorous in a more useable form to the terrestrial construction site.[28] Such a conjecture, however, introduces yet another speculative step in the abiogenesis scenario.

A further, more serious problem for the experimental method is that all testing has been based on the supposition that the atmosphere of the earth's ancient past contained no molecular oxygen or oxidizing compounds, unlike the planet's current atmosphere. In the presence of oxygen, such experiments simply collapse. Oxygen thus has been eliminated from the blend of materials in the trials. The sun, however, can break the molecules of a substance—in the case at hand, water in the form of vapor—into constituent elements. This photodissociation of water yields hydrogen and oxygen. Even in

---

[25] C. Reid and L. E. Orgel, "Synthesis of Sugars in Potentially Prebiotic Conditions," *Nature* 216, no. 5114 (1967): 455.

[26] Shapiro, "Prebiotic Ribose Synthesis," 84.

[27] Stated in Evard and Schrodetzki, "Chemical Evolution," 28.

[28] See Alonso Ricardo and Jack W. Szostak, "Origin of Life on Earth," *Scientific American* 301, no. 3 (2009): 57.

small amounts, oxygen would have served to prevent the formation of the critical compounds and would have destroyed, through chemical joining, any that did form. Further, it is probable that just a trifling amount of it would have produced an ozone layer that screened short-wavelength ultraviolet radiation and deprived the presumed prebiotic amalgam of a major source of energy for any relevant surficial synthesis.

> The present calculations indicate that there is an effective ozone shield even for atmospheres containing only 10^{-3} PAL [$^1/_{1000}$ the present atmospheric level] of oxygen. If this O_2 level was reached in very early atmospheres by the purely abiotic photodissociation of atmospheric water vapor it seems unlikely that solar UV radiation was the energy source for the prebiotic synthesis of organic molecules at the earth's surface.[29]

Clearly, a central issue in assessing the theory of chemical evolution is not so much what admixture of toxic chemicals was present in the early atmosphere as what *sort* of atmosphere existed at the time. For chemical evolution to work, the gaseous environment at the outset had to have been *reducing*—that is to say, one in which molecular oxygen and oxidizing agents were effectively absent, thereby precluding oxidation. The Oparin-Haldane model proposes such an atmosphere. The chemist and evolutionist L. E. Orgel puts the point in the following way:

> So far it has proved impossible to obtain amino acids from an atmosphere which contains free oxygen or from a mixture of carbon dioxide, nitrogen, and water. This is a very important negative result, for it argues strongly in favor of the Oparin-Haldane hypothesis that the primitive atmosphere was reducing. *Life could not*

---

[29] A. J. Blake and J. H. Carver, "The Evolutionary Role of Atmospheric Ozone," *Journal of the Atmospheric Sciences* 34, no. 5 (1977): 727. For an additional resource, see Thaxton, Bradley, and Olsen, *Mystery of Life's Origin*, 44, which refers to the article by Blake and Carver. Also see Percival Davis and Dean H. Kenyon, *Of Pandas and People: The Central Question of Biological Origins*, ed. Charles B. Thaxton (Dallas: Haughton Publishing Co., 1989), 48.

have got started in an atmosphere of the type that exists today.[30]

Orgel sets forth an interesting bit of reasoning. His implicit argument follows the pattern that is shown below; I number the steps for reference:

1. Evidence strongly suggests that life could have arisen through chemical evolution only in a reducing-atmosphere environment.
2. Life did arise by means of chemical evolution.
3. Therefore, evidence strongly suggests that the atmosphere of the early earth environment was reducing.

The problem is that premise 2 is an assumption, allowing Orgel to draw the conclusion, but the truth of that premise is the crucial question.

What was the atmospheric makeup of the earth in its primal phase—were free oxygen molecules (O_2) or oxidizing substances there? Geological data suggesting that oxygen was present early in the planet's history have been available for a number of years. Perhaps the decisive discovery in the matter, however, occurred in a NASA-sponsored study in 2011. In this investigation, using the world's oldest minerals, scientists at the New York Center for Astrobiology found that the atmosphere of the Hadean eon—the earth's most ancient past, which lasted from the inception of the planet to four billion years ago, so say the geologists—was *not* the long-assumed *reducing* atmosphere. Quite the opposite, the environmental envelope was marked by an oxygen-rich composition, similar to conditions on the earth at present. The findings, as one report states, "turned these [previous] atmospheric assumptions on their heads."[31] According to the study,

---

[30] L. E. Orgel, *The Origins of Life: Molecules and Natural Selection* (New York: John Wiley and Sons, 1973), 129. The emphasis is mine.
[31] "Early Earth's 'Alien Atmosphere' Theories Nixed—'Dominated by Oxygen-Rich Compounds,'" *Daily Galaxy*, November 4, 2013, accessed April 16, 2015, www.dailygalaxy.com/my_weblog/2013/11/early-earths-alien-atmosphere-theories-nixed-dominated-by-oxygen-rich-compounds-todays-most-popular.html.

> We find that the [magmatic] melts have average oxygen fugacities that are consistent with an oxidation state defined by the fayalite-magnetite-quartz buffer, similar to present-day conditions. Moreover, selected Hadean [eon] zircons (having chemical characteristics consistent with crystallization specifically from mantle-derived melts) suggest oxygen fugacities similar to those of Archaean and present-day mantle-derived lavas as early as ~4,350 Myr [million years] before present. These results suggest that outgassing of Earth's interior later than ~200 Myr into the history of Solar System formation *would not have resulted in a reducing atmosphere.*[32]

The authors of the study did not abandon their acceptance of an evolutionary chronicle for the planet, but the results plainly present a serious impediment to those who endeavor to find life's origin in a prebiotic soup. The standard position of evolutionary biology is that "life first arose from nonliving matter around 3.7 billion years ago."[33] It is too late—conditions that would have prevented the supposed chemical-synthesis launch had existed for more than half a billion years before that time, by the scientists' account. In view of that detail, one may want to recast Orgel's argument to yield the following reasoning:

1. Evidence strongly suggests that life could have arisen through chemical evolution only in a reducing-atmosphere environment.
2. The atmosphere of the early earth environment was not reducing.
3. Therefore, evidence strongly suggests that life did not arise by means of chemical evolution.

The conclusion is worth pondering. Indeed, several years later, after continuing his work in the area and investigating the problems

---

[32] Dustin Trail, E. Bruce Watson, and Nicholas D. Tailby, "The Oxidation State of Hadean Magmas and Implications for Early Earth's Atmosphere," *Nature* 480, no. 7375 (2011): 79. The emphasis is mine.

[33] Ricardo and Szostak, "Origin of Life," 54.

with synthesizing nucleic acids, Orgel coauthors a paper in which he expresses his pessimism about the chance abiogenetic assembly of these foundational molecules. The authors assert that "the de novo appearance of oligonucleotides [short nucleic acid chains] on the primitive earth would have been a near miracle."[34] They are not alone in this conviction. One chemist and molecular biologist lists nearly a score of reasons why the thesis that life arose through the synthesis of nucleic acids is implausible.[35] These scientists do not discard the theory of abiogenesis but postulate that some other course must be the one that the select raw materials followed on their way to life. Others in the field take a stronger stance, noting that one must step back and reconsider the relevant information rather than surrender to dogmatism. The following commentary summarizes the thoughts of two researchers after a thorough review of relevant studies:

> This is what we have attempted to accomplish in this study. We have tried to carefully examine the scientific data presented in the literature dealing with chemical evolution and critically evaluate the results to determine if the conclusions of the investigators are sound. Such a study reveals that chemical evolution does not provide a satisfying solution to the question of the origin of life.[36]

In the face of all these difficulties, the idea of a fortuitous chemical beginning—one without intelligent intervention—continues to have supporters. Apart from experimental issues, though, there are problems with concepts that underlie the theory. In cells, enzymes are required to link monomers to form polymers, but enzymes are proteins, which are polymers, and there are no proteins until amino-acid monomers are linked to form them. How then could they have arisen? Moreover, "DNA and RNA are needed to make protein, protein and RNA are needed to make more DNA, and DNA and

---

[34] Gerald F. Joyce and Leslie E. Orgel, "Prospects for Understanding the Origin of the RNA World," in *RNA World*, 68.

[35] A. G. Cairns-Smith, *Genetic Takeover* (Cambridge: Cambridge University Press, 1982), 56–58.

[36] Evard and Schrodetzki, "Chemical Evolution," 29.

protein are needed to make RNA."[37] The chemical egg-chicken-egg scenario represents a conundrum unto itself.

Some hypothesize that protein was the first to arise, but, of course, protein per se can produce neither DNA nor RNA. Although protein is not sufficient for construction, enzymatic activity, which is characteristic of protein, is indispensable: Without the presence of enzymes to function as catalysts, the formation of lengthy RNA polymers is not forthcoming.

Others think that RNA and protein might have arisen together. The probability of such a double appearance by chance, however, is remote, too much so to be feasible. The proposal is as unsupportable from a mathematical perspective as the supposed arising of DNA in combination with the enzymes that are required for its replication.

The prevailing thought among evolutionists in contemporary times seems to be that RNA, in spite of the need for enzymes to assemble it, was the original fibril of life in the earth's early environment. Evolutionists conceive of this environment as RNA world. The discovery in the late twentieth century that RNA could serve as both a template for replication and a catalyst bolstered the idea. Appropriately, such molecules are referred to as ribozymes. Researchers in this area have employed existing strands of RNA to extend other strands. In one trial, a pair of scientists assembled a "cross-catalytic system involving two RNA enzymes that catalyze each other's synthesis from a total of four component [oligo-nucleotide] substrates."[38] The results, however, are limited in their implication. As one critic notes, the trial did not demonstrate replication but ligation: the joining of two short strands of RNA, using more RNA to accomplish it. The experiment assumes the existence of nucleotides with well-matched bases, which, on the premise that the conditions of the experiment mimic the planet's early state, had to have arisen simply by chance—an extremely unlikely occurrence.[39] Here again then, RNA needs more RNA to

---

[37] Jeffrey P. Tomkins, *The Design and Complexity of the Cell* (Dallas: Institute for Creation Research, 2012), 14.

[38] Tracey A. Lincoln and Gerald F. Joyce, "Self-Sustained Replication of an RNA Enzyme," *Science* 323, no. 5918 (2009): 1229.

[39] Jonathan Sarfati, "Is RNA Self-Replication Evidence for Evolution?" Creation Ministries International, accessed July 10, 2015, creation.com/rna-self-replication.

extend RNA. The fundamental problem of the arising of RNA in the first place remains.

Some viruses have RNA for their genetic material instead of DNA, which may seem to support the belief that RNA came first. No such virus, however, is capable of reproducing itself; all require host cells, which they hijack and force to produce the viral copies from the hosts' DNA. For this reason, they are said to be obligate intracellular parasites. Further, the process of genetic data-transfer in cells is a fixed path that does not originate with RNA. The path is universal—*all* RNA that cells contain comes from DNA.

> The flow of genetic information in cells is . . . from DNA to RNA to protein. . . . All cells, from bacteria to humans, express their genetic information in this way—a principle so fundamental that it is termed the *central dogma* of molecular biology.[40]

If RNA were the first to arise as a molecule that reproduced itself, then its appearance would run counter to the ubiquitous phenomenon that underlies the science that seeks to explain the arising.

In the end, relying on the catalytic properties of RNA does not help one to escape the which-came-first problem. The circularity that is inherent in a supposed initial self-replicating event is a challenging hurdle for the evolutionists—from more than one standpoint. Consider these comments:

> Without evolution it appears unlikely that a self-replicating ribozyme could arise, but without some form of self-replication there is no way to conduct an evolutionary search for the first, primitive self-replicating ribozyme.[41]

Two refinements to the RNA-first conjecture have been proposed. One revision envisages a chemical predecessor as the initial droplet in the life-stream. This ancestral compound would be an

---

[40] Bruce Alberts et al., *Molecular Biology of the Cell*, 4th ed. (New York: Garland Science, 2002), 301.

[41] Joyce and Orgel, "Understanding the Origin," 62.

analogue of RNA that, like its counterpart, could serve as a template to transfer genetic information, and, at some point, it could have transferred it to a molecule of the standard nucleic acid—assuming, of course, that the nucleic acid existed at the time. One of the presumed forerunners is, in fact, more stable than RNA. The revision, however, is also problematic. It introduces an additional barrier to cross on the path to life: There must be a transition from the early molecule to RNA. How did it happen? Indeed, why would it have occurred? What would have caused nature to uproot a successful replicator and replace it with another, potentially less stable one, a change that required not only a shift in chemical makeup but a shift in structure as well? The very notion seems to stand against the underlying premise of evolutionary theory, with its focus on survival. Moreover, although a compound of this sort can be produced under laboratory conditions, no remnants of any such chemical ever have been discovered in either existing cells or fossils.[42]

The second suggested refinement is described best as genetic overthrow.[43] The notion is that a self-replicating system arose generating the seeds of its own demise by producing, through an evolutionary process, another genetic system that took over the replication machinery. There is no transfer of information in this case but an entirely new chemical mechanism. The first problem with this hypothesis is obvious: As an attempt to explain the arrival of RNA on the earth, it offers no advantage over the premise that RNA surfaced spontaneously in the absence of any preexistent genetic or pseudogenetic platform. The initial nucleic acid still must come forth from scratch, so to speak, just as the RNA-first conjecture maintains. The second problem is one that is also apparent in the first proposed refinement: Nature, which is incapable of anticipating improvement, would have discarded a working system to start over, as it were. A suitable justification for the idea is not in the offing.

---

[42] For a discussion of the hypothetical predecessor RNA, see Alberts et al., *Molecular Biology*, 366–67. Also see Joyce and Orgel, "Understanding the Origin," 68–70.

[43] Joyce and Orgel mention this idea in "Understanding the Origin," 70. In the work *Genetic Takeover*, cited above, Cairns-Smith argues that inorganic crystals in clays constituted the initial system on the planet, which nucleic acids eventually replaced.

To make matters worse, harsh conditions on the earth during the supposed primeval period could have destroyed the fragile life-perpetuating fragment, whatever its chemical composition might have been, wiping out any possibility of the continuance of that series. RNA is particularly susceptible to destruction, as it is less resistant to physical damage than DNA because of its configuration. Such early hazards are attributable to a variety of phenomena. Temperature extremes or sudden thermal shifts could undermine nature's budding effort: too hot for continued structural integrity, too cold for generative activity before organizational degradation occurs, or perhaps a change in temperature that is too abrupt for the fragment to handle. An unfriendly chemical environment could be devastating: Volcanoes, for example, emit hydrogen chloride gas, a substance that combines with moisture to create hydrochloric acid. The potential for destructive effects on a would-be replicator is evident. Radiation from the sun, violent ejections of magma, boiling underwater vents, electrical discharges from thunderstorms, physical crushing, and other natural occurrences could take their toll on the delicate molecule. It is ironic that the very conditions that biologists propose as prehistorical energy sources to generate, from a principally inorganic broth, the organic compounds that are necessary to form a self-replicating molecule are the same conditions that could contribute easily to its hasty downfall.

The prolongation of a life seed therefore, even if one grants its arrival in the face of the odds that Dawkins surmises, sits atop a high-risk endeavor of its own. Perhaps all the necessary compounds, including enzymes and a ready supply of nitrogenous bases, were not present when needed, rendering the seed impotent; and all essential amino acids were yet to appear, stopping short any hope of assembling proteins with which to construct a cell. Maybe an imperfect replicator, the initial molecule produced only deformed copies, which could not replicate themselves, or did so without fidelity. Severe atmospheric and geological conditions could have thwarted any creative potential that it might have possessed. Whatever the cause of the nonstarter status might have been, a life-initiating incident would have had to have happened again. Just how many iterations would have been required before the process, at last, was off and running, no one can say.

Suppose that it took half a dozen so-called attempts for a replicator, accompanied by the necessary auxiliary compounds, finally to persist as a functioning unit in the threatening primal backwaters. Although Dawkins notes that the originating event might not have been unique, he does not take up an investigation of repetitious arisings. Under such conditions as I have suggested, would it be the first *viable* occurrence of a spontaneously generated DNA-like structure that carries Dawkins's one-in-a-billion chance, or would *each* occurrence, regardless of whether its product lasts long enough to replicate, face such a severe unlikelihood? If the former alternative prevails, then the probability of a spontaneous assembly is $(^1/_{1,000,000,000})^{1/6}$, or about one in thirty-two. Evolution cannot handle that number, as it destroys the single-branching tree-of-living-things concept and replaces it with that of an orchard. Life may be off to a shaky start, but, in the end, it would matter little: With a probability this high, the self-replicating molecule would be surfacing steadily, with commensurate opportunities for viable instances to establish parallel series. Given that such an event never has been observed— nor could it be observed, so the scientists say, in the earth's present oxygen-rich atmospheric environment—there is no evidence to bear out the supposition. If, on the other hand, each occurrence, workable or otherwise, carries a chance of one in a billion, then the picture is much more bleak. The probability of the replicator compound's arising and continuing is $(^1/_{1,000,000,000})^6$, or one in a septendecillion: 0.000000000000000000000000000000000000000000000000000001 in decimal format—a decidedly unrealistic prospect. Ostensibly, Dawkins intends his stated chance to apply to an active, operational replicator. Both aforesaid cases count against his proposed odds.

The point, of course, is not that six attempts are required for initial success—or one, three, twelve, or any other value. To give a particular number is to make an assumption that is as unfounded as that of Dawkins. The point is that one could not know. Even if one were to believe that the sudden, undirected appearance of life is physically possible, the probability that Dawkins sets forth would be unsupportable in yet another respect: It could be off by multiple orders of magnitude. Given the problems that I noted above with the prebiotic generation of nucleic acids, Dawkins's offhand assignment of probability just bears no weight at all.

ANTHROPIC INEFFECTIVENESS

I would like to return at this juncture to Dawkins's anthropic argument and focus on the second part. After attempting to establish that there are a billion planets where life arose from lifelessness—based on a purported promise of such a happening—Dawkins moves next to assert in Part II of the argument that the earth is one of those planets because conscious beings live on it. Were there, in fact, a billion planets where life sprang into being from lifelessness—as the conclusion of Part I would have it—it would not follow by the rules of logic that the earth would be one of them. Although a minor concern, step 4 assumes that there is a single type of cause of all life in the universe: the random jump to molecular self-replication.

Consider an illustration. Ted believes that a hundred mailboxes in his neighborhood have been damaged by vandalism and that students from the nearby school committed the acts. Ted discovers that his own mailbox is damaged. He concludes that the cause of the damage to his property is the same as the cause of the damage to the property of the other residents in his subdivision. Ted may be right about the mailboxes of his neighbors but wrong about his own. The dents in Ted's mailbox could have been caused by hail, a car that veered off the road, a meteor shower, a bull that escaped from a farm in the area, someone who was angry at Ted for posting a political sign in his yard, vandals from another school, or any number of other things. Similarly, life on the earth could have been brought about by design, even if chance underlay its emergence elsewhere. This logical possibility, although clearly quite unlikely to be the case, is sufficient to counter the premise that is presented in step 4 nevertheless, thereby undermining Dawkins's deduction.

A more serious flaw is found in this part of Dawkins's line of reasoning. The aforesaid step posits as an assumed fact the very issue that is being challenged—that the origin of rational organic existence lies in a fortuitous episode in which life sprang into being mindlessly from chemical substances. Dawkins sees an essential link between the two—between the presence of conscious humans and the irregular incident that started life. The postulated link can hold only if a chance abiogenetic event is a necessary condition of, and evolution is the process that is responsible for, the appearance of intelligence.

The argument does not prove that the ultimate source of what people observe in the biological world around them, and in the mirror, is abiogenesis; instead, it assumes it in the premises. Thus, as before, it is guilty of the fallacy of begging the question; but the fallacy now is not cloaked but obvious. This part of the construction in itself fails.

One may think that Part II of the argument could be salvaged by restructuring step 4 so that the antecedent and the consequent of the conditional statement are reversed. This sentence captures the change:

> 4′. If x happened on a planet, then that planet is populated by y.

The revision, however, would not allow one to reach the conclusion, step 6, for the revision would introduce the logical fallacy of affirming the consequent, rendering the argument invalid. One will recall from chapter 1 that a conditional statement takes the form 'If p, then q' in the propositional calculus. If the conditional is true, then one can be sure of two things: (1) If p is true, then q is true; (2) if q is false, then p is false. It does not follow from the truth of the conditional, however, that, if q is true, then p is true. For example, consider the following three-step reasoning:

> 1. If Billy ate peanuts yesterday, then he has developed a rash.
> 2. Billy has developed a rash.
> 3. Therefore, Billy ate peanuts yesterday.

Billy is allergic to peanuts. Whenever he consumes them, a rash appears on his face and arms. There is no escape. Further, at the present time, red, itching bumps cover his face and arms. Both premises are therefore true. The conclusion, however, is false: Billy's rash was caused by poison ivy, which he encountered while playing hide-and-seek in the wooded lot that is behind his house. In a like manner, the supposed revision of Dawkins's argument would fail.

If one sets aside the thought that the universe was tailor-made for humankind, then with what exactly is one left as an anthropic narrative? There is just something unsettling about the notion that the cosmos that people observe must be the way that it is, or else they would not be there to observe it. In the general form of the anthropic tenet, it says no more than that humans can exist only in a universe in which humans can exist. One could say with no less sensibleness that the people in the stands can see Judy beat her opponent in the tennis match only if she can win. That which is actual can be actual only if it is possible. An anthropic statement, such as the aforementioned general one about humans, is true, but it is inconsequential and uninformative. It offers nothing in the way of enlightenment.

If one adopts a form of the principle based on probability, as Dawkins appears to do, then it must be the notion that something in particular has beaten the odds, and the fact that one perceives it is sufficient to demonstrate that it has done so. The probability of the occurrence of some type of event in any one case is low, but the probability of the occurrence of that type of event across a great many cases is somewhat higher because of the substantial number of opportunities for it to happen. Where one observes a token of the type, that specific incident is one that has taken place against the unlikelihood of its own occurrence. It is the large number of potential occasions for some phenomenon to happen that somehow explains it.

Does such a form of the anthropic principle offer any increased utility? How is it that the principle is supposed to explain the phenomenon? Again, it says no more than that which is actual must be possible. Many instances may increase the potential for its occurrence *somewhere*, but it fails to explain why it occurred *here*. Jack dealt Zach a royal straight flush in spades on the first hand of the Friday-night poker game.[44] The fact that many poker hands have come and gone since the creation of poker increases the probability that someone somewhere will receive a royal straight flush in spades, but it does not increase *Zach's* chance of holding the necessary cards on any given hand, nor does it *explain* his doing so. If it did explain it, then one could use the anthropic principle to account for every hand that Zach holds that night because, no matter *what* cards Jack deals to him, the unlikelihood is, *ceteris paribus*, exactly the same. Suppose that his first hand consists of the following set:

---

[44] The probability that five cards will be dealt consecutively from a shuffled, standard deck, with no other factors involved, resulting in a royal straight flush in spades is $1/2{,}598{,}960$, expressed as a common fraction.

ten of diamonds
queen of hearts
three of clubs
six of clubs
nine of spades

The probability of Zach's being dealt this hand is identical to the probability of his being dealt the royal straight flush in spades, as each card is unique, and no single card is more likely to be dealt than another, assuming consistent conditions. To explain why some particular phenomenon occurred against the odds by drawing on (1) the fact that the chance for it to happen at some time and in some place is promising because of the large number of opportunities for it to happen and (2) the fact that one observes the phenomenon in the present case is to dilute the explanatory force of the principle to the point of impotency. The principle's universal applicability in this respect is also its undoing. If it can account for *everything* that one observes—it applies to every poker hand that anyone ever deals—then it actually can account for *nothing*. The anthropic principle does not help Dawkins; it does not support his thinking regarding the presence of humans on the earth. Would one say of pieces of driftwood, which are lying on a sandy shore and which spell the names of each of the kings of England in proper chronological order, that those little chunks of timber exist; therefore, they must be somewhere—so, why not here, in this exact pattern? If it were otherwise, then it would not be possible to observe the driftwood here, in this exact pattern. Such a declaration would not explain the material's special arrangement on the beach in any way whatsoever. One simply cannot point to the facts and say that the facts explain the facts in a sort of bootstrapping, "Why should it be otherwise than what it is?" In the words of a contemporary philosopher and mathematician, using the anthropic principle in an attempt to account for the arising of humankind through natural selection "confuses a necessary condition (i.e., our being selected) with an explanation (why us)."[45] I will leave the anthropic principle now and proceed to the next leg of Dawkins's

---

[45] William A. Dembski, *Intelligent Design: The Bridge between Science and Theology* (Downers Grove, IL: IVP Academic, 1999), 267.

story. As will be evident soon enough, the improbabilities that I have been discussing pale in comparison with what is coming.

STUMBLING TOWARD COMPLEXITY: A DIM PATH

Once the theoretical self-replicating, life-propagating molecule takes root, Dawkins sees a process of ongoing improvement, driven by two factors: (1) variations in the sets of characteristics of organisms, owing to random genetic alterations, and (2) the honing of those sets of characteristics as nature selects the organisms with superior features for survival and subsequent reproduction.[46] It is not the activity of intelligent agency but a blind process in which whatever biological entities are produced from the previous generation are challenged to live and to reproduce in the world in which they come to be; and the entities that are in a better position to do so will be the ones that take part in the next generational cycle. What Dawkins supports is not merely a theory of biological change but one that also purports to explain the sum of life on the planet. It is a theory that has its basis in the ideas of Charles Darwin and Alfred Russel Wallace.

These men were not the first to advance the view that life evolves. Certain Presocratic philosophers suggested an evolutionary thesis of sorts more than two millennia earlier—refer to chapter 1 for a general discussion of the lives and metaphysical thought of these philosophers of old. Anaximander, for example, hypothesizes that

---

[46] Changes in the characteristics of the members of a given species in a locale can occur because of other dynamics: The random shuffling of dominant and recessive forms of genes is a prime case. In small groups, the effect of such shuffling is statistically somewhat likely to be marked; the possibility of the total loss of a form as a result of chance events underscores the effect. Those events have little impact on large populations, where, *ceteris paribus*, the ratio of expression tends to remain constant. This factor is not central to Dawkins's theory of biological progression; I will not pursue the matter, except in one instance where doing so is helpful. In his theory, variations that genetic mutations cause account for the appearance of novel features, which nature then assesses, as it were, in terms of their heritable potential.

embryos of humans developed originally inside fish or fish-like creatures, which ruptured in due course, releasing adult men and women on the earth. Although not Darwinian per se, Anaximander's tale does incorporate other species in recounting the arrival of people on the planet.

The theory that Empedocles puts forth, however, is particularly noteworthy because of its emphasis—in a rudimentary way, at least—on survival and its link to physical traits, suggestive of the modern version. Like Darwin and Wallace, Empedocles proposes that the beings that populate the earth that humans know are the result of a course of change, but, for the ancient philosopher, it unfolds in a bizarre way. His account identifies four phases. They seem to compose two separate processes comprising two stages each rather than a single process of successive stages. In any case, the first stage is one in which parts of organisms arise by themselves, detached from other parts. These remarks appear in the fragments:

> On it (*Earth*) many foreheads without necks sprang forth, and arms wandered unattached, bereft of shoulders, and eyes strayed about alone, needing brows.
>
> Limbs wandered alone.[47]

As if such occurrences were not strange enough, the next stage is characterized by the combining of the pieces to produce creatures with a variety of configurations.

> Many creatures were created with a face and breast on both sides; offspring of cattle with the fronts of men, and again there arose offspring of men with heads of cattle; and (*creatures made of elements*) mixed in part from men, in part of female sex, furnished with hairy limbs.[48]

The survival aspect comes into play here: The results of various chance assemblages of pieces narrow to the viable ones. Those living

---

[47] Empedocles, frags. 57, 58, in *Ancilla to the Pre-Socratic Philosophers*, trans. Kathleen Freeman (1948; repr., Cambridge: Harvard University Press, 1996), 58.
[48] Ibid., frag. 61, 58–59.

creatures that are equipped well continue to exist, while their lesser-equipped counterparts fade from the scene. As the ill-constructed cease to be, what remains are men, women, and animals resembling those that are observable in the current age.

In the final two phases, living things arise in the world as masses of the ingredients earth, fire, and water—three of the primary substances in ancient Greek thought. These bodies are structurally basic; they are devoid of limbs and organs, and they are without gender. Subsequently, differentiation takes place, producing male and female sexes, and introducing the major divisions between types of creatures: fish that live in the water, birds that populate the air, and the other beasts that roam the land. Empedocles's theory is quite imaginative, hardly the story of evolution as it is told today, but there is an interesting parallel nevertheless: Both chance and suitability for survival play central roles in each of them.[49]

Before the discussion continues, it is important to distinguish between microevolution and macroevolution. Some scientists make no distinction, claiming that there is only evolution *simpliciter*, but the general stance is that there is a line between the two that is scribed according to the extent of inherent differences. One contemporary textbook states, "Microevolution pertains to evolutionary changes within a population, which is all the members of a single species occupying a particular area."[50] Microevolution is a phenomenon whereby organisms of a given species exhibit features, sometimes owing to mutations, that differ from those of the predecessor members, features that may prove to be valuable. Few would argue that nature fails to make provisions for such changes. They offer a flexibility that allows living entities to meet environmental and other conditions in a way that aids continuance of the kind. Those organisms that reproduce are ones that have survived to reach a state of maturity, and it is the genes—the units of hereditary information—of the ones that propagate that shape the characteristics of future generations. If mutations occur, then some of them may

---

[49] For further discussion regarding Empedocles's developmental theory of life, see the summary in W. K. C. Guthrie, *A History of Greek Philosophy*, vol. 2, *The Presocratic Tradition from Parmenides to Democritus* (1965; repr., Cambridge: Cambridge University Press, 1969), 200–211.

[50] Sylvia S. Mader, *Biology*, 9th ed. (New York: McGraw-Hill, 2007), 302.

effect an advantage in survival; so, the chance that helpful changes will be passed to offspring increases. Albeit it does not show that life is the result of intention, a built-in avenue for adaptation—whether for individuals during a lifetime through responses to external and internal conditions, or for species in the course of many lifetimes through heredity—aligns well with a teleological perspective.[51]

The concept of macroevolution, on the other hand, is more inclusive. It is set forth in this way: "In evolutionary biology today the term macroevolution is used to refer to any evolutionary change at or above the level of species."[52] Macroevolution suggests that species themselves are developmental products: The organisms that belong to an individual species stemmed from organisms that did not belong to it. Biological history is compared to a branching tree: Creatures that exist in the present age owe their existence to common ancestors that lie farther down the limbs. Ultimately—and here is the crucial facet of the thesis—all life, in all taxonomic categories, comes from a single point at the base of the trunk: the DNA or RNA replicator-molecule. For macroevolutionists, such as Dawkins, that molecule is the result of a random occurrence. Dawkins puts forward his theory with the intent of eliminating any reliance, no matter how remote, on intelligent design.

Climbing the mountain of life is possible, claims Dawkins, because a jump up the precipice to the pinnacle of complexity is not necessary; there is an alternative path of gradual progression. Inch by inch, the mutation-selection process takes biological forms up the mountain's mild incline opposite the cliff. It ends in the same place on the top—the extreme sophistication of a conscious human, or a functioning eye or wing—but without the extreme improbability that would accompany the sudden appearance of these complex things. Dawkins relies on the accumulation of minor improvements in his gentle-slope analogy. Small changes that are positive—that is to say, ones that provide a benefit for the bearer in surviving and repro-ducing—can be summed, he says, to create a substantial effect.

---

[51] The formation of calluses on the fingertips of guitarists, the increased endurance of cross-country skiers with continued practice, and the muscular hypertrophy of weight lifters are examples of individual adaptation in response to the conditions under which the body is placed, coupled with genetic propensities.

[52] Mader, *Biology*, 310.

What is it that makes natural selection succeed as a solution to the problem of improbability, where chance and design both fail at the starting gate? The answer is that natural selection is a cumulative process, which breaks the problem of improbability up into small pieces. Each of the small pieces is slightly improbable, but not prohibitively so. When large numbers of these slightly improbable events are stacked up in series, the end product of the accumulation is very very improbable indeed, improbable enough to be far beyond the reach of chance. . . . The creationist completely misses the point, because he (women should for once not mind being excluded by the pronoun) insists on treating the genesis of statistical improbability as a single, one-off event. He doesn't understand the power of *accumulation*.

In *Climbing Mount Improbable*, I expressed the point in a parable. One side of the mountain is a sheer cliff, impossible to climb, but on the other side is a gentle slope to the summit. On the summit sits a complex device such as an eye or a bacterial flagellar motor. The absurd notion that such complexity could spontaneously self-assemble is symbolized by leaping from the foot of the cliff to the top in one bound. Evolution, by contrast, goes around the back of the mountain and creeps up the gentle slope to the summit: easy![53]

Easy, is it? I want to see whether it is so.

THE CHASM CHALLENGE

Dawkins admits that improvements are rare, but natural selection identifies and captures them nevertheless as it pushes its way up the mountain. He also says—and I find this point to be of particular interest—that one needs luck to reach the top. Luck, however, is simply something that is introduced to account for a happening,

---

[53] Dawkins, *God Delusion*, 121–22.

which a rational being typically deems to be positive or desirable, in the face of improbability. Dawkins explains,

> The predilection to mutate is always bad, even though individual mutations occasionally turn out to be good. It is best, if more than a little paradoxical, to think of natural selection as favoring a mutation rate of zero. Fortunately for us, and for the continuance of evolution, this genetic nirvana is never quite attained. Natural selection, the second stage in the Darwinian process, is a non-random force, pushing towards improvement. Mutation, the first stage in the process, is random in the sense of not pushing towards improvement. All improvement is therefore, in the first place, lucky.[54]

In an early work, he states,

> It is as though, in our theory of how we came to exist, we are allowed to postulate a certain ration of luck. . . . Given our ration of luck, we can then 'spend' it as a limited commodity over the course of our explanation of our own existence. If we use up almost all our ration of luck in our theory of how life gets started on a planet in the first place, then we are allowed to postulate very little more luck in subsequent parts of our theory, in, say, the cumulative evolution of brains and intelligence. If we don't use up all our ration of luck in our theory of the origin of life, we have some left over to spend on our theories of subsequent evolution, after cumulative selection has got going.[55]

For a theory of science, Dawkins's overt reliance on luck in his exposition of evolution seems to be out of place. One has to wonder just how much luck is needed. According to Dawkins in a later publication, perhaps a considerable amount of it. In speaking of the

---

[54] Richard Dawkins, *Climbing Mount Improbable* (1996; repr., New York: W. W. Norton and Co., 1997), 85–86.
[55] Richard Dawkins, *The Blind Watchmaker: Why the Evidence of Evolution Reveals a Universe without Design* (1986; repr., New York: W. W. Norton and Co., 2006), 207.

arising of life on the earth and its subsequent advancement on the way to biological complexity, he offers these comments:

> It needs some luck to get started, and the 'billions of planets' anthropic principle grants it that luck. Maybe a few later gaps in the evolutionary story also need major infusions of luck, with anthropic justification.[56]

His remark using the phrase 'major infusions of luck' is a pronounced understatement. Indeed, a sudden spring to complexity may be highly improbable, but the creeping-climb approach fares no better. There are some primary steps in the theoretical evolutionary process that must take place—and in the right sequence—to produce conscious humans; and getting there requires quite the favorable chain of fortuitous events. Here are a few of them:

1—One needs luck at the outset to launch the process through the chance assembly of the replicator-molecule, as Dawkins asserts in the previous extract. Again, he says, "[I]t may be that the origin of life is not the only major gap in the evolutionary story that is bridged by sheer luck."[57]

2—One needs luck for a primitive, prokaryotic cell (one that, as is the case with a bacterium, lacks a nucleus, a mitochondrion, and other advanced features) to come about from the originating molecule. Avers Dawkins, "The original replication machines . . . must have been a lot simpler than bacteria."[58]

---

[56] Dawkins, *God Delusion*, 141.

[57] Ibid., 140.

[58] Dawkins, *Mount Improbable*, 286. Some propose the arising of bacteria following the emergence of a protocell, a structure that I mentioned above. If one supposes that such a thing did exist in the earth's early history and supposes further that it served as a stepping stone to the prokaryotic cell, then one may wish to break step 2 into a pair of steps—or perhaps more than a pair. It is unclear whether doing so exacerbates the problem of luck. On the one hand, it poses an intermediary, which may be easier to reach than the end result, but, on the other hand, it adds yet another chasm to the sequence. I will not pursue the issue but leave step 2 as a single gap; using his own probabilities, Dawkins has enough trouble with the milestones that he mentions. In any case, Dawkins assigns a chance of one in a billion to life's origination, apparently without regard to the number of steps that it

3—One needs luck to explain the arising of the type of cell that makes up human bodies—a cell that contains a nucleus and other special components, distinguishing it from the prokaryotic cell that lacks them. Dawkins states that his colleague Mark Ridley "has suggested that the origin of the eucaryotic [or eukaryotic] cell (our kind of cell . . .) was an even more momentous, difficult and statistically improbable step than the origin of life."[59]

4—One needs luck to move from asexual reproduction to sexual reproduction: "There are many theories of why sex exists, and none of them is knock-down convincing." He continues: "But the whole question of sex and why it is there . . . is another story and a difficult one to tell. Maybe one day I'll summon up the courage to tackle it in full."[60]

5—One needs luck to achieve consciousness: "The origin of consciousness might be another major gap whose bridging was of the same order of improbability [as that of the origin of the eukaryotic cell]."[61]

In each instance, the object in question falls on one side or the other of a divide. By a logical law, it is necessarily true that either a self-replicating molecule exists, or it does not exist; a cell is eukaryotic, or it is not eukaryotic; an entity possesses consciousness, or it does not possess it. Dawkins's idea of breaking improbability into small pieces is inapplicable. The aforesaid chasms must be crossed in succession, and the assigned probabilities are multiplicative. The chance of completing the series is the product of the respective probabilities of achieving each of the stages, where the probability that is associated with each stage past the first one depends on the occurrence of the preceding ones. Dawkins sees the problem—in part, at least—

---

might have taken to reach that point. By specifying the probability of the arrival of the end unit that is tied to the spanning of that initial gap—the self-replicator—Dawkins asserts, in effect, that how many incremental changes were needed for it to materialize is not germane. This notion can be extended to the other steps.

[59] Dawkins, *God Delusion*, 140. Note again that the American spelling of the two types of cells differs slightly from that of the British, but the references are identical.

[60] Dawkins, *Mount Improbable*, 85.

[61] Dawkins, *God Delusion*, 140.

mentioning two of the gaps in the musings that appear in the following passage:

> Now suppose that the origin of life, *and* the origin of intelligence given that life is there, are *both* highly improbable events. Then the probability of any one planet, such as Earth, enjoying both strokes of luck is the *product* of the two low probabilities, and this is a far smaller probability.[62]

If no other factors are in play, then his probability claim is correct.

For crossing the gap that is identified in step 1, Dawkins uses a chance of one in a billion. It is plain, I think, that he intends to apply that chance to the reputed period of time that the earth has existed, which, according to current scientific theory, is about four and one-half billion years, as I noted earlier. Compressing the time would serve only to exacerbate the problem of origination. From comments in his later work about great infusions of luck, it is evident that he embraces an improbability of bridging the gaps in steps 3 and 5 that is at least as extreme. Dawkins does not offer a numerical value for the probability of clearing the hurdle in step 2, but there is nothing to support a supposition that the step presents an advancement that is less challenging than the others. Similarly, he does not speculate about step 4. The molecular process that results in the generation of DNA is very different from the sexual behavior of animals that results in the generation of offspring; step 4 embodies an unlikelihood of success that may be more severe than that of its forerunners.

I will use Dawkins's own value of one in a billion thus for the chance of spanning any one of the five gaps; it is consistent, it seems, with his remarks. Given that the process is sequential, such that each step past the first is conditional, in that it can occur only if every previous one in the sequence occurs, the overall probability is the product of the probabilities of the individual increments in the series, taking into account the successor dependencies. Each increment must take place on the *same* planet—*the* planet that is home to humans—and in the right order. The reliance on an anthropic principle does not help Dawkins here. To reach man's kind, evolution must cross each

---

[62] Dawkins, *Blind Watchmaker*, 206.

major chasm, one after the other, and it must cross the entire set of them within the allotted time: the history of the earth.

Suppose then that one permits Dawkins's postulation regarding the probability of the spontaneous emergence of life to stand and that, despite the austerity of the prospect, it happened on the planet that humans occupy at present. Given that the other four major breaks in the flow of life carry potentialities that are, at best, similarly diminutive, the would-be completion of the progression collides with the mathematics of it. Once the protobiotic, self-replicating molecule surfaces on the earth against the odds—granting Dawkins the first milestone for the sake of analysis—the expectation of traversing the four remaining rifts can be calculated in the way that is shown below, yielding one chance in an undecillion:

$$\left(^1/_{1,000,000,000}\right)^4 = {}^1/_{10^{36}}$$

To put this figure in perspective, suppose that Jerry hands a comprehensive dictionary of the English language—a six-inch-thick one—to Jenny, asking her to pick a word at random and to give no clue about what entry she selected. He then asks her to close the book and hand it back to him. Afterward, Jerry thumbs through the pages and attempts to guess correctly what word Jenny chose. He gets only one guess. No one would wager much on such poor odds, but it would take far more than one of these dictionaries to yield an unlikelihood of one in an undecillion. Assuming a traditional word-count value, Jenny would need one and two-thirds nonillion of the massive books. Stacked atop each other, they would create a column that is nearly *twenty-seven trillion light-years* in height. This distance is equivalent to almost three hundred times the diameter of the entire observable universe. Jerry would get a single guess to select not only the *right word* but the right word in the *right dictionary* as well.

Evolutionists would say that a few billion years of planetary history, with a commensurate number of opportunities for life to build on its own past, can improve the picture; yet, that temporal expanse is merely the blink of an eye. A quadrillion attempts every second to cross the gaps would not come even close in ten trillion years. One in an undecillion represents a staggeringly remote probability—too remote to overcome in such a short period of time. The theory of the development of humans from a random prebiotic event seems to be quite fantastic. Even on the supposition that the original self-replicator appeared on the earth, in spite of its near-assured failure to materialize, completing the series using probabilities that align with Dawkins's postulations borders on mathematical absurdity. Dawkins charges intelligent-design supporters with dismissing unexplained phenomena by relying on what he refers to in a rather demeaning manner as "'God of the Gaps' reasoning."[63] Ironically, he brushes past the yawning crevasses in his own theory. Faced with such gaps in the evolutionary model, perhaps Dawkins's account, despite the hope of mitigating improbabilities through incremental change, has run out of luck.

FIRST STEPS IN A NEW DIRECTION

That random mutations occur in the process of heredity is an established finding. According to the theory of evolution, some of these mutations—a small percentage—result in certain organisms' gaining an advantage in the quest to survive and reproduce; other organisms face a drawback from mutations with harmful effects—a much higher percentage. Such benefits and impediments, of course, cannot be traced invariably to genetics, including genetic dispositions that may be switched on by environmental factors. Genes are not the sole cause of the characteristics that appear in progeny.

THE LEARNING-IMITATION COMPONENT

In her autobiography, *It's Always Something*, the comedienne Gilda Radner tells a true story from her childhood about a dog that belonged to the cousin of the family's live-in nurse. The dog became pregnant, and, about a week before she was to give birth to her puppies, the animal came into contact with an operating lawnmower.

---

[63] Dawkins, *God Delusion*, 128. Other naysayers also have made use of this label.

Both hindlegs were severed in the affair. The people rushed the dog to a veterinarian, who said that he could suture the torn tissue in her mangled posterior, or, if they wanted, he could euthanize her. He assured them that, if they chose the former option, then she would be able to bear the puppies. They decided to let the dog live, and the veterinarian stitched the back end of her in place. In the course of the following week, the dog learned to walk by taking two steps with her front legs and then flipping up her limbless rear, executing this procedure repeatedly to make her way around her environment. Eventually, the dog gave birth to six puppies. They were normal in every respect. Something strange happened, however. As the puppies grew older and learned to walk, they all walked on their front legs, flipping up their rears behind them. Their method of locomotion was not the product of genetics but of learning. Their behavior was acquired through observation and imitation. They might have passed this characteristic to their offspring as well, maintaining an attribute that was totally independent of genetics qua genetics, one that might have put each member of the litter at risk. Their peculiar behavior inhibited their ability to run, even though genetically they might have been superior runners. That ability would have surfaced had they had a more normal puppyhood. Genetics alone cannot guarantee the continuance, in a species, of inherited qualities, even when those qualities may outclass those of the competition.

In the wild too, experience and learning play important roles in prolonging an organism's existence. For example, a lioness cub may have a chance encounter with a venomous snake, an incident in which the serpent's fangs barely break the skin on her paw. Stunned and sickened by the event, she will practice caution whenever she approaches the tall grass at the water's edge in the future. Her sister, although genetically exceptional as a consequence of some mutation, did not live to reproduce: A similar encounter a month later had a fatal outcome. She did not have the opportunity to learn to be wary in the high grass before her inexperience killed her. In this case, natural selection did not take hold of the right cub—the improved one—for preserving what was beneficial. Again, it would be too simplistic to think that evolution is so careful a guardian of the genetically superior creatures that it is they that govern with an iron hand the propagation of the species.

Dawkins recognizes the power of imitation among living organisms. In fact, he argues that the tendency to imitate would be favored by natural selection, as it can provide a fast track to acquired skills.[64] At this point, however, he diverges from standard evolutionary theory to build a parallel course, where a new sort of evolution takes hold. It is not biological but cultural, and it is driven by an altogether different sort of replicator, for which Dawkins coins the term 'meme'. As genes impose their instructions on physical bodies, memes, so he asserts, impose their instructions on brains, commandeering them to reproduce themselves in a population. If it merely expressed an analogy, then the proposal would be innocuous enough, perhaps even interesting. Dawkins, however, carries the notion to the extreme, building an entire system around these supposed self-copying societal units. What is disturbing in particular is that he elevates them to the level of being actual, existent entities. Says Dawkins,

> The gene, the DNA molecule, happens to be the replicating entity which prevails on our own planet. There may be others. If there are, provided certain other conditions are met, they will almost inevitably tend to become the basis for an evolutionary process.
>
> . . . I think that a new kind of replicator has recently emerged on this very planet. . . . It is still in its infancy, still drifting clumsily about in its primeval soup, but already it is achieving evolutionary change at a rate which leaves the old gene panting far behind.
>
> The new soup is the soup of human culture. We need a name for the new replicator, a noun which conveys the idea of a unit of cultural transmission, or a unit of *imitation*. 'Mimeme' comes from a suitable Greek root, but I want a monosyllable that sounds a bit like 'gene'. I hope my classicist friends will forgive me if I abbreviate mimeme to *meme*.
>
> Examples of memes are tunes, ideas, catchphrases, clothes fashions, ways of making pots or of building arches. Just as genes propagate themselves in

---

[64] See Richard Dawkins, *Unweaving the Rainbow: Science, Delusion, and the Appetite for Wonder* (Boston: Houghton Mifflin Co., 1998), 305.

> the gene pool by leaping from body to body via sperms
> or eggs, so memes propagate themselves in the meme
> pool by leaping from brain to brain via a process which,
> in the broad sense, can be called imitation. . . . As my
> colleague N. K. Humphrey neatly summed up an earlier
> draft of this chapter: '. . . memes should be regarded as
> living structures, not just metaphorically but techni-
> cally. . . .'[65]

What could a unit of cultural transmission be, and what evidence is there to support the existence of a meme pool? How could anyone classify these fanciful curiosities as living, other than metaphorically, and expect to be taken seriously? In setting forth his meme hypothesis, Dawkins is inventing a gene-like device because of the replicative efficacy of DNA, but his invention has no basis in science. It is obvious that imitation is a process that occurs in the world, but to surmise that it is traceable to an actual pool of elementary, duplicating, brain units is patently untenable. He is multiplying entities beyond necessity in an arrant violation of the law of parsimony. One of his several critics, who himself is an evolutionist and paleobiologist, makes the following claim:

> Perhaps that irritating little tune that continues to bounce
> around your head is a meme? . . . But memes are trivial,
> to be banished by simple mental exercises. In any wider
> context they are hopelessly, if not hilariously, simplistic.
> To conjure up memes . . . reveals a strange imprecision
> of thought.[66]

According to another critic, if the meme conjecture were correct, then one would be deprived of rational thinking, which is surely not the case. He states,

> Just as in Dawkins's scheme of things, biological
> organisms are prisoners of their genes, so our minds
> become prisoners of the memes which colonize them.

---

[65] Richard Dawkins, *The Selfish Gene* (New York: Oxford University Press, 1976), 206–7.

[66] Simon Conway Morris, *Life's Solution: Inevitable Humans in a Lonely Universe* (Cambridge: Cambridge University Press, 2003), 324.

> But, whatever might be said about organisms and genes, minds precisely are not prisoners of memes. . . . We can reject or modify ideas we find rationally wanting, and many of us do. And if we accept an idea after examining it and finding it plausible, our case is precisely not that of our mind having been colonized by a phrase one 'cannot get out of one's head'.[67]

Dawkins's creation of memes is directed ultimately at explaining the spread of religious beliefs: "We are finally equipped to turn to the memetic theory of religion."[68] Continuing, he contends, "Some religious ideas survive because they are compatible with other memes that are already numerous in the meme pool—as part of a memeplex."[69] So, there are not just the imaginary units themselves but also a complex of them. Dawkins is mixing evolution with ideology. The meme hypothesis is not science; it is pseudoscience. Further, it is pseudoscience with an unscientific aim.

A Diversity of Factors

A principal focus of evolution is the genetic alterations, arising through fluctuations in DNA replication, that are passed to offspring, and certain environmental factors that may shape the expression of them. Without these mutations, nature cannot produce novel features. It is important to note, however, that a theorist cannot afford to disengage the workings of other elements that may influence the continued existence of the members of a species. As suggested, learning is one of these elements. It may help organisms to live to the point of reproduction, but it may stand just as well in their way, as the puppies in Radner's story show. Survival and procreation depend on more than the material makeup of a creature as the product of the activity of genes. Hereditary traits cannot be viewed in isolation. An

---

[67] Anthony O'Hear, *Beyond Evolution: Human Nature and the Limits of Evolutionary Explanation* (Oxford: Clarendon Press, 1997), 156.
[68] Dawkins, *God Delusion*, 199.
[69] Ibid.

animal's exploiting what it has inherited, for instance, is as important as the condition of its possessing the hereditary traits themselves. If a faster runner does not run fast when a predator approaches but turns and trots away, then its ability to forward its superior swiftness to the next generation will come swiftly to an end.

There are many other factors that come into play. Unexpected incidents are one, for they can cut short the path of the superior. The randomness on which the theory of evolution relies to improve future generations can work as easily against them. Accidents happen, and any general upsurge in the frequency of them increases the likelihood that an enhanced mutant will be a victim. A better-equipped beast may slip and break a leg, becoming a target for predators; it may fall into a tar pit and perish; or it might be caught in a rock slide from which there is no escape. Opportunity may be the factor that presents the sudden block to nature's favored course. A bird that would have exhibited exceptional eyesight and superior mate-attracting color as an adult may be consumed by a snake that happened upon the chick's nest. In reality, a positive change may be offset by other changes that are negative. An impala that, because of some anatomical variation, might have been able to jump higher than normal for its species may carry a different, concomitant variation that brings visual impairment or perhaps seizures, making it easy prey. Worst of all, it may bring impotence. Indeed, a change, which is otherwise positive, may have detrimental consequences. Lengthened femurs may position an animal to run faster and thereby evade a pursuing predator more effectively; however, those same femurs may make it more likely to lose its footing and be caught by a pursuing predator. It is not difficult to see that a change that may provide some usefulness could be canceled by the very thing that made it useful. There is no assurance, of course, that some one-off, inherited property will be lost in the genetic stream, but neither is there a guarantee that it will be retained simply because of an advantage that it offers.

The thrust of these examples is not that evolution never could work as a result of such opposing forces. It is rather that things other than random genetic mutation and natural selection play an important part in what is taking place in the ongoing, highly intricate parade of life and, more to the point, in the alleged march toward complexity. One cannot discount the multifaceted character of such a dynamic enterprise. Accidents and other events do rise to influence the natural order. They can cause the incidence of expressed properties, owing to dominant and recessive forms of genes, to drift within a population, as noted earlier; and, among small groups, they even can eliminate one form of a given gene from the pool. What is central to the discussion here, though, is that mishaps can terminate potentially beneficial paths that stem from mutations. They can decrease the probability of the perpetuation of alterations that surface in trait-sets, shifts that might further the abilities of the bearers, but this aspect of their occurrence is glazed over by Dawkins's focus on the retention and propagation of positive genetically induced changes. Ironically, Dawkins proposes accidents as a way to explain the progressive development of a particular feature. His explanation, however, as one will see, is implausible.

From these few illustrations, it is evident that the story of life's sustention is not to be single-threaded by those who tell it, for it is an affair with numerous, interleaved forces that affect the outcome. There is value in continuing the investigation of Dawkins's reliance on natural selection as the path to enhancement to see whether it is adequately far-reaching in explanatory power. A paradigm case will help to elucidate the facts.

UPGRADES BY GRADATION: THE CASE FOR EYES ...

To grasp adequately what Dawkins says is occurring in evolution, one needs to understand a bit more fully the mechanism by which natural selection targets variations and capitalizes on them because it is this process, Dawkins avers, that produces advanced physical attributes that appear in descendants. The process rests on an overall principle and consists of three fundamental, interrelated components. As for the principle, evolutionary changes are undirected. As for the components, the changes come in small steps; nature fastens on those that are improvements; and nature retains the improvements and builds on them. Stated succinctly, the entire operation is *purposeless*; and its unfolding is *gradual, selective,* and *cumulative*. If evolution fails in any of these respects, then it fails totally, and there is nothing left open to the theory as a natural way to account for the sophistication that one finds in the biological world.

In support of the concept of gradual change as the sole path to organic complexity, Dawkins attempts to show how reasonable it is for a human eye to develop in a little-by-little manner from no eye at all. Albeit such an intricate thing as an eye, he acknowledges, could not have arisen in a single step from no eye—the odds against such an event's happening are too great—its arising in a single step from something slightly different from itself is conceivable. If one thinks otherwise, then one has selected something that is too different, and one needs to imagine a smaller difference. At some point, the variance will be small enough, according to Dawkins, that one will be comfortable picturing the sophisticated thing's arising in this fashion. The imaginer can consider now that the thing that is slightly different from the eye and which served as its immediate predecessor could have stemmed, in turn, from something that is slightly different from itself, and so forth. Dawkins then asks, "Is there a continuous series of Xs [incremental changes] connecting the modern human eye to a state with no eye at all?"[70] He proceeds to answer the question:

> It seems to me clear that the answer has to be yes, provided only that we allow ourselves a *sufficiently large* series of Xs. You might feel that 1,000 Xs is ample, but if you need more steps to make the total transition plausible in your mind, simply allow yourself to assume 10,000 Xs. And if 10,000 is not enough for you, allow yourself 100,000, and so on. Obviously the available time imposes an upper ceiling on this game, for there can be only one X per generation. . . . What we do know is that geological time is awfully long. . . . Given, say, a *hundred million* Xs, we should be able to construct a plausible series of tiny gradations linking a human eye to just about anything![71]

In quite a stretch of thought, Dawkins is endeavoring to move from imagination to an acceptable depiction of things as they are in

---

[70] Dawkins, *Blind Watchmaker*, 109.
[71] Ibid. The second emphasis is mine. As for Dawkins's claim that geological time is lengthy, one will see in a moment just how fleeting it is.

reality. He is attempting to put forth as plausible a description of how actual complex objects could come to exist through a sequence of minimal adjustments, using invented changes as the foundation for the portrayal. Dawkins says that one can envision the development of an eye from almost any no-eye thing. The fact that one can imagine a succession of small changes that ends in something different from the initial object or the initial state is innocuous enough, but it is of no value. Dawkins has drifted from science into fantasy. An individual can imagine that a turnip turns into a turtle in a series of tiny steps or that a beet becomes a barnacle. For that matter, one can visualize the gradual transmogrification of a rotund reindeer into Santa Claus. Simply being able to think of something does not make it real, regardless of the number of steps in the would-be conversion. Dawkins intends, however, to move the series from the realm of fanciful thought to hard reality in an effort to support a theory that small changes are exactly how complex biological entities emerge on the planet. There is an impediment to this leap from the conceptual to the material. The small steps are random, and randomness takes things in all conceivable directions, so to speak. How is it possible therefore to get through a lengthy series of alterations—Dawkins tosses a nine-figure number on the table—in the real world, not merely in the mind, each of which arises as a result of a coincidence in the real world, not merely in the mind? Further, how is it possible to keep from losing any of them before completing this protracted sequence in the real world, not merely in the mind?

Dawkins believes that he has the answer, in that nature latches onto any change that results in a benefit in survival and reproduction. Continuing with his reasoning, Dawkins holds that it is plausible that *every* element of the series of changes leading to a complex biological feature was produced through random mutation and that—and this point is critical to his theory—*each one* yielded an advantage.

> Considering each member of the series of Xs connecting the human eye to no eye at all, is it plausible that *every one of them* worked sufficiently well that it assisted the survival and reproduction of the animals concerned? . . . [I]s the answer yes? . . . I think that it is.[72]

---

[72] Ibid., 118–19. The emphasis is mine.

Nature thus sees all the steps in a sequence that ends in complexity—millions of steps perhaps, so Dawkins contends—as worthy of retention because they are improvements. That assertion is decidedly ambitious. If Dawkins cannot make it stick, then his theory faces a serious setback.

So, the question to ask initially is this one: What precisely constitutes an improvement? This question brings with it unforeseen issues that will come to light. For the moment, though, note that the answer for an evolutionist, it seems, is simply that an improvement, as it pertains to natural selection, is identified with organismal variance, traced to genetic mutation, that increases the chance of survival and procreative success in a specific locale; and here a troubling matter arises for Dawkins. He attempts to align future features with prior ones in a chain of hereditary paces, whereby each step toward that future represents an enhancement. If possessing the property Φ is more advantageous than not possessing it, in that having Φ increases the probability that an organism will continue to live and eventually will reproduce effectively, then a change in the physical makeup of the immediate offspring of parent organisms, relative to the parents themselves, where that change increases the similarity between those offspring and any future descendants that possess the property Φ must be an improvement too, even if Φ is not realized in the present progeny. That statement is a bit cumbersome; an illustration, which I provide below, will help to clarify the point:

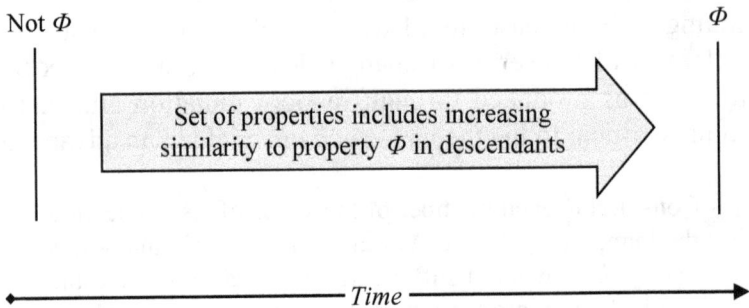

Not Φ Φ

Set of properties includes increasing similarity to property Φ in descendants

— *Time* —

Figure 8.1

If the property Φ signifies, for instance, having eyes that see or wings that are used for flight, then any incremental step along the way toward having such eyes or wings must be an improvement. Such a tenet is necessary because, without it, the theory of evolution falters, as there is no incentive, as it were, for nature to preserve the modification and build on it. Evolution is ignorant of the future; natural selection can act only on what it has at the time. Unless each change that increases the similarity to something that is advantageous is an advantageous change *itself*, it is not possible to explain the future enhancement in terms of a progression that is based on present features.

I recall the many trips that our family took when I was a boy. There were unusual and interesting things to experience on these childhood journeys, and I was fascinated by all of them. During a particular excursion, we stopped at a roadside establishment and came upon an opportunity to see something that none of us ever had seen before: a cow with five legs and six feet. No inquisitive youngster could pass up such a thing. We proceeded to the exhibit—I, at least, with great excitement. The cow appeared to be unbothered by the shortened extra limb, with its pair of feet, as it protruded from the animal's torso, dangling, useless in every sense. Obviously the product of some unfortunate deviation in genetic activity, the creature had been turned into a spectacle. What we saw was a freak, but what would natural selection see? Might a fifth leg be useful? Once it expanded through subsequent generations of mutation-cum-selection until it finally reached the ground, and the neuromuscular structure developed sufficiently, perhaps it could provide a marginal boost in speed across the pasture. An extra pair of feet might increase stability in the muddy fields after a downpour. No one would entertain such a ludicrous idea, of course. The variation was not an improvement then, nor was it a step toward becoming one in the future, even though the potential for it—in a stretched sense—existed. My example here is not intended to be insensitive but to underscore the fact that natural selection can see incremental changes only for what they are in the present. It is blind to what they could become in the future. The cow's extra limb was only what it was: an inoperative deformity.

Dawkins argues nevertheless that even a trifling change along a continuum on the way to some complex, useful feature can be, all by itself, an improvement. Is it so? One of the major criticisms of evolution is that intricate biological devices are of no value unless they are complete, with crucial components in place—the concept of irreducible complexity—as the devices cannot operate unless they are intact. If they cannot operate, then they are useless. If they are useless, then there is no reason for nature to retain them. Dawkins presents his case against the irreducible complexity of the eye:

> 'What is the use of half an eye?' and 'What is the use of half a wing?' are both instances of the argument from 'irreducible complexity'. A functioning unit is said to be irreducibly complex if the *removal of one of its parts* causes the whole to cease functioning. This has been assumed to be self-evident for both eyes and wings.
> ... [I]t is easy to imagine situations in which half an eye would save the life of an animal where 49 per cent of an eye would not. ... A flatworm has an eye that, by any sensible measure, is less than half a human eye. *Nautilus* . . . has an eye that is intermediate in *quality* between flatworm and human.[73]

There is a major problem here with Dawkins's contention. Partway down a course that ends in possessing the property Φ is not the same as possessing the property Φ in part, or to a degree, all along the course. A key distinction exists between, on the one hand, half an eye in the sense of an eye with half the parts that are essential to its function missing and, on the other hand, half an eye in the sense of an eye with a complete, operational structure but with half the acuity of another. The first one cannot see at all; the second one cannot see well. Dawkins blurs this difference, no pun intended, speaking in the quoted passage initially of parts detachment and then of quality. The patent shift in meaning introduces a logical flaw in his argument. The criticism of evolution that is based on irreducible complexity is directed toward the cessation of a device's primary function on the supposition of the subtraction of one or more categories of components that are necessary for the operation of the

---

[73] Dawkins, *God Delusion*, 123–24. The emphases are mine; *Nautilus* is a genus, and hence its name is italicized in the original wording. One has observed that I use only the respective genus names in this work when referring to some creatures.

device. It is *not* based on the extent to which a device with all its components intact and all of them operating is good at what it does. Note that it is not the removal of a part, such as a single photoreceptor, that counts but the removal of a type of part: in this instance, the photoreceptor cells as a group. Without them, the eye does not work.

Thus, Dawkins's version of what it is to be partially eyed is not relevant to his case. In the examples that he gives, his numerical scale is not tied to the *critical completeness* of the structure of the particular organism's eye—flatworm, mollusk, or human—but rather to its *relative capacity*; that is to say, it does not pertain to whether the visual function is realized, in an operational way, in a certain complement of different types of parts but rather to how well the visual feature of the animal performs the function. It does not matter that some organisms' eyes have more types of parts and, as a result, may offer greater capabilities—such as color vision or accommodation for distance—than other organisms' eyes. The point is that the failure to work at all owing to the removal of necessary components is not the same as the failure to work well owing to reduced capacity, *even if* that reduced capacity is associated with a structure that has fewer types of functional parts.

Bob owns a large sedan. It is luxurious, laden with features, and packed with sophisticated electronics to handle various tasks automatically. Driven by a high-capacity, turbocharged engine with eight cylinders, it has a maximum speed capability, on level ground, of 158 miles per hour. Tim owns a compact, economy model. It is neither luxurious nor rich in features. Most operations are manual rather than automatic. Tim's vehicle can reach only 101 miles per hour after extended acceleration. Remove the fuel pump from Bob's car, however, and it will not run at all. Its maximum speed, on level ground, will be zero miles per hour. Tim's vehicle is also subject to this limitation. Remove the photosensitive cells from a flatworm's eye (eyespot), and it will not be able to detect light. The keenness of a normal flatworm eye is effectively immaterial. Dawkins's response to the irreducible complexity charge, with regard to eyes, misses the mark. In an effort to address degrees of completeness of components, Dawkins employs degrees of acuity. It is true that one functioning eye need not be as complex as another functioning eye, even though both are complete. Yet, there are parts that are essential to the operation of *any* eye, regardless of its complexity.

It is not just that there must be photoreceptors, however, for the eye to yield vision. It is also necessary that this special group of cells arises in conjunction with other required parts. Consider Bob's car again; it serves to illustrate this condition of functionality. Aside from the fuel pump, one could remove, for example, the camshaft or the timing belt and thereby prevent the car's performing its essential role of transportation. The same concept applies to vision. Aside from the photoreceptors, one could remove the neural transmission link or the optical processing center and thereby prevent the eye's performing its essential role of sight or light-detection. Whatever components are required for there to be locomotion have to exist in the automobile at once. Likewise, whatever components are required for there to be sight must exist in the organism at once.

Evolution relies on gradual change to construct the complex from the simple. For complex things to come to exist, every retained, incremental step toward realized intricacy must provide a benefit, or the theory fails, for natural selection will take a firm grip only on what produces *immediate* gains. The problem is that numerous components are necessary for the core role of the feature to be expressed: Without all of them in place, the biological device does not work. The development of any one of the components offers no advantage whatsoever unless they all are there—and performing, at minimum, to some extent. Regardless of the other parts of an eye— cornea, lens, vitreous humor, no matter what they may be—there is no advantage to their development if there are no photoreceptors, and no advantage to the development of photoreceptors if there is no way to transmit the impulses, and no advantage to the development of a network to transmit the impulses if there is nothing to receive and process those signals. Evolution not only must account for the progression of functionally rich components through multiple series of random events, followed by the retention of beneficial changes; it must account as well for the simultaneous progression of those components when their contribution to the essential activity of the unit is codependent. It is the function of the whole that explains the parts, and some of the parts are interrelated through an unbreakable bond. What is needed is a type of convergence, but how can evolution accomplish it when it is blind to the future? In the diagram that I provide below, each of the parts p_1, p_2, and p_3 is necessary for the whole, w, to perform its basic function. If p_1 and p_2 are present in w, but p_3 is missing, then this truncated w will not operate. If p_2 and p_3 are present in w, but p_1 is missing, then this truncated w will not work either, and so forth.

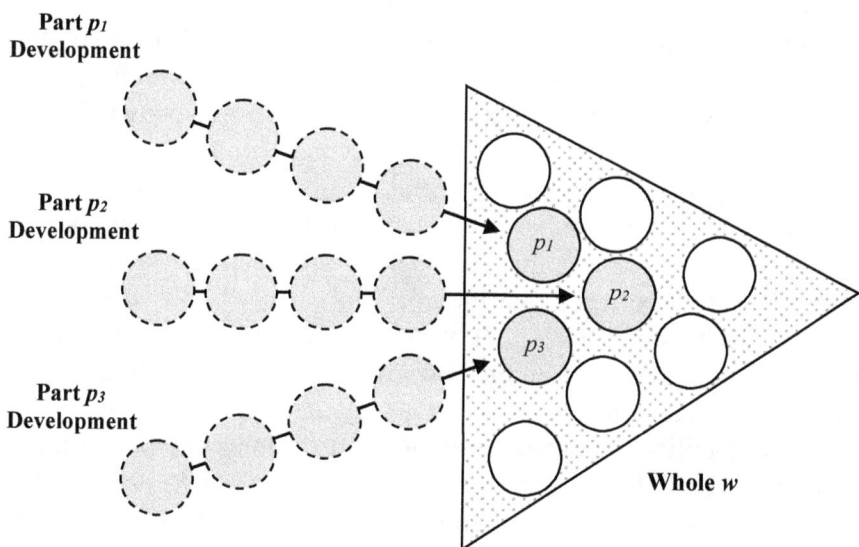

where

    represents a part that is required for the function of the unit and is under development

    represents a part that is required for the function of the unit and is developed to the point of operation

    represents a part that is not required for the function of the unit

Figure 8.2

Each required part, p_1–p_3, must progress toward a whole that is operational only if all the required pieces are there and carrying out their respective duties, however well or poorly they may be doing so. The theory of evolution seeks to explain the development of each constituent in terms of immediate advantage, but there is no advantage to the development of *any* of the indispensable components without the development of *all* the indispensable components. No step along the way toward a full-blown p_1 could offer any future value, let alone present value, unless p_2 and p_3 are positioned for functional status. To be functional, however, they must evolve to maturity, yet they could not have evolved previously, for the theory of evolution requires that there be a benefit to each step. No step along p_2's path could offer any value, prospective or, without doubt, current, unless p_1 and p_3 are positioned for functional status. Again, any value that p_3's development eventually may bring depends on the evolution of p_1 and p_2 to maturity, and it offers no value before then. For each respective member of the set consisting of the components that are required for a feature to operate, a crucial interdependence holds separately between that member and a subset consisting of all the other such components. It is a relation for which Dawkins's theory of gradual advancement toward a whole, itself riding on the back of a stream of immediately advantageous steps, cannot account. The improbability of success in building a complex biological thing shifts exponentially with every part that is required to activate the feature because, without contemporaneous development, the thing will not work; and every step in the development of every one of the parts is the result of a random event. It is an insurmountable obstacle.

In chapter 4, I illustrated how the coordinated-attack problem, a conundrum without a solution, arises. Independent agents must possess the same information at the same point in time to launch a synchronized attack in which all the partakers are simultaneously knowledgeable of the relevant facts. Given their independence, however, communication among the agents is necessary, so that all of them possess the latest requisite information just prior to the assault. The messaging structure itself, however, prohibits the critical convergence because no message can be dispatched by means of a courier without some delay in, and potential failure of, its delivery. If, before undertaking a synchronized, joint action, each agent must await confirmation, from another agent, of the delivery of a dispatched message, where the confirmation itself is a message that requires delivery and confirmation, then an infinite regress results. The vital convergence is not possible; the attack never will occur.

In an analogous way, a coordination problem is at work in evolution. The circularity is not the part-part reliance of each participant in an attack as that participant awaits some confirmatory action of another. Rather, the circularity is a part-whole reliance, where each essential part—and in the face of the need for parallel progression—must await the assembly of the whole to rationalize the development of that part, for it has no utility otherwise; but there is no assembled whole until all the essential parts are developed and in place. It seems that an irreparable defect underlies the theory that biological complexity is the product of evolution.

AND THE CASE FOR WINGS

Aside from eyes, wings are an interesting organismal formation from a slightly different perspective. Once more, Dawkins attempts to explain how it is that incremental changes along the path to a future, complex feature can be classified as improvements themselves. I will take a look at some factors surrounding flight and begin by delving into the way in which gradual change may be at work here. Dawkins alleges,

> Half a wing could save your life by easing your fall from a tree of a certain height. And 51 per cent of a wing could save you if you fall from a slightly taller tree. *Whatever fraction of a wing you have, there is a fall from which it will save your life where a slightly smaller winglet would not.* The thought experiment of trees of different height, from which one might fall, is just one way to see, in theory, that there *must be a smooth gradient of advantage all the way from 1 per cent of a wing to 100 per cent.*[74]

In an earlier work, Dawkins writes,

---

[74] Ibid., 123. The emphases are mine.

[I]f prototype wingflaps worked to break the animal's fall, you cannot say 'Below a certain size the flaps would have been of no use at all'. Once again, it doesn't matter *how* small and un-winglike the first wingflaps were. There must be some height, call it *h*, such that an animal would just break its neck if it fell from that height, but would just survive if it fell from a slightly lower height. In this critical zone, any improvement in the body surface's ability to catch the air and break the fall, however slight that improvement, can make the difference between life and death. Natural selection will then favour slight, prototype wingflaps.[75]

Dawkins is putting forth this accident scenario as a workable account, but his claims are patently unwarranted. Whatever fraction, he says—so, expressing it in the common, numeral format, would the fraction $1/100,000$ make a difference; would $1/1,000,000$ or $1/100,000,000$ have an effect?[76] Any supposition along these lines is exceedingly frail. Even limiting the change to something more substantial, it is not sensible to align every increase in winglet size with an increase in survivability. There are many factors at work in an actual fall—too many to isolate one that controls the outcome and steers the course of evolution. For example, the mass of the animal at the time of the fall is an important component of the event. It is not winglet size per se, or even surface area per se, that contributes to the speed of descent; rather, it is, *ceteris paribus*, the ratio of the mass of the creature to

---

[75] Dawkins, *Blind Watchmaker*, 126.

[76] In light of his example of a series of a hundred million steps to the human eye, quoted earlier, Dawkins must think so. In his book *Mount Improbable*, Dawkins refers to a computer model by biologists Dan Nilsson and Susanne Pelger that depicts the development of a fish eye lens in change increments of 1 percent. See this work by Dawkins, p. 160 ff. Dawkins says that there is nothing special about the number; it could have been 0.005 percent just as well. Although he directs this remark specifically toward the model, it appears that he sets no lower limit on the amount of change that is required to make a difference. His assertion here using the phrase 'whatever fraction' indicates that he, in fact, does not believe that there is a lower limit, within the bounds of biological structure, at least. Assuming that one cell is the smallest possible winglet, the fractional increments vis-à-vis a full wing must be correspondingly infinitesimal, and to think that each increase of a cell can make a difference is just not a plausible stance.

the surface area that is presented to the air beneath it by the entire body, including the winglets, during a fall. A flapping creature that climbs a tree after a huge meal risks a dive to the death no less than its hungry companion with smaller winglets. Replace the miniature airman on a child's toy parachute with a brick, and it will drop like a technology stock showing poor quarterly earnings.

There are countless other conditions that shape the consequences of a tumble from the forest canopy. Stating the obvious, I will list a few. A change in the orientation of the animal's parts during the fall, altering the time that a given degree of air resistance is in effect; barometric pressure and air temperature, affecting density; wind speed and direction; whether the fall occurs in a hail storm; moisture content of the ground; slope of the terrain; type and amount of leaf material atop the soil beneath the tree; whether the forest floor is blanketed with snow; the contour of the partially formed wing and whether its top surface is curved; and the rapidity with which the beast flaps its winglets—all have a bearing on the descending creature's fate. Further, the position of the body as it strikes the ground is as decisive as the height from which the animal drops. Beasts that land on their heads are more likely to break their necks than those that land on their feet, regardless of winglet size. Beasts that prefer to climb only those trees that are surrounded by thick underbrush have an advantage in a fall because they shed speed for a greater period of time—albeit still a short one—as they pass through the undergrowth. Ones that roll like paratroopers when they land have a better chance of survival because, as is the case with their brush-seeking counterparts, they distribute the force of impact temporally.

A better ability to grip, better balance and agility, and stronger legs to help a creature to maneuver about a tree would be of greater benefit to an animal in the canopy, in all probability, than a truncated protuberance that is incapable of allowing the animal to take to the air. Focusing simply on an accidental falling incident discounts the importance of possessing a solid ability to hang onto a tree in the first place and to find food, both of which are important in sustaining life overall. A barely functioning air bag profits little in a vehicular collision, but avoiding a crash altogether by practicing careful and defensive driving is of considerable value in saving a driver's life.

The animal that is good at avoiding a fall is the one that is set to succeed in life, not the clumsy one flapping a nub as it smashes into the ground.

One simply cannot state unequivocally that more winglet is better, hoping to justify a gradual-progression schema; and it will not do to hold that, if all other variables are equal, then the larger wing has the advantage. The question is whether something can survive a plunge in the real world, and an entire range of conditions come into play in a life-and-death episode. One could say just as well that, if all other variables are equal, then the animal that eats little, particularly before ascending a tree, is the one that is more likely than others of its kind to survive. It will weigh less than similar animals that stuff themselves; therefore, less wing is required to slow the descent by resisting the onrush of air as gravity goes to work. The thoughts of one evolutionary biologist, active in the twentieth century, seem to be apropos here. He writes,

> You can drop a mouse down a thousand-yard mine shaft; and, on arriving at the bottom, it gets a slight shock and walks away, so long as the ground is fairly soft. A rat is killed, a man is broken, a horse splashes.[77]

Maybe it is the finicky eaters that make it through falling ordeals, not those with the trivially expanded winglets. According to Dawkins's mishap hypothesis then, falling ought to lead to a gradual decrease in the mass of tree-dwelling animals rather than the development of wings.

What this admittedly tongue-in-cheek listing of potential issues shows, I think, is that Dawkins's sole-aspect approach is a gross oversimplification, and his corresponding explanation with regard to the development of wings is weak, suggesting that his hypothesis concerning the advent of flight based on the accidental plummeting from the tops of trees is misguided. It is not the product of investigation but imagination. To account for the appearance of flight in bird-like creatures, even as a thought experiment, (1) in terms of a single factor and (2) based on the supposition that all microscopic increases

---

[77]J. B. S. Haldane, "On Being the Right Size," in *Possible Worlds and Other Essays* (1927; London: Chatto and Windus, 1928), 19.

in winglet size improve the chance of continued existence is just too simplistic and speculative to be credible.

A critical issue here for Dawkins is that his turning to a sudden-slip scenario in an attempt to explain the development of wings leads to a dilemma. Do these prebird organisms fall out of trees with considerable regularity, or are their plummeting episodes few-and-far-between events? To contend that natural selection values a continuum for the expansion of winglets with the passage of time, on the basis that winglets of increasing size serve as accident buffers of increasing effectiveness, is to contend that accidents are a significant factor in evolution. They can be a significant factor, though, only if they are commonplace occurrences; not limited to the missteps of a prebird species, they include as well random events that take place in a wider context. The upshot is that the survival of the rising stars is called into question, altering the face of natural selection in an important way. Accidents are blind. On the condition that they are prevalent, hereditary supremacy gives way to, to use Dawkins's conceptual prop, luck. The weaker, slower, less agile therefore stand a better chance than evolution has it that they do stand. The lucky ones become, to a degree that is not supported by the premise of natural selection, the ones that nature targets to pass their genes to the next generation. It is not the strong, swift, nimble zebra that lives to breed but the inferior one that happened to cross the river three yards farther downstream as the limb fell. As is true of the drifting of gene-form ratios, alluded to earlier, chance can take hold to control which members of a population survive to reproduce; but here (1) it is improvement arising from mutation that is affected, and (2) chance becomes an overplayed, governing dynamic. Insofar as Dawkins wishes to underscore the impact of accidents on the evolutionary process by building a case for flight, resting on the plummeting from trees, he is arguing against the general provisions of his own theory.

As for the progression to complexity in particular, frequent accidents that occur because of a creature's mistakes, such as tragic slips among the boughs, increase the likelihood that a beast with a just-realized, first step forward will be swept away before nature can build on the step in subsequent generations. Nature will have to wait for another, similar change to surface before it can start again in that direction. The prevention of an accident clearly trumps the use of an ineffective, underdeveloped feature during the occurrence of one. If calamities are common, then those organisms with superior avoidance abilities are in a better position to stay alive than those with anatomical changes that are too immature in their construction to provide any meaningful defense against those calamities. So, as one has seen, the nub-bearers are most likely the losers in a world filled with catastrophes—exactly the opposite of what Dawkins maintains in endeavoring to explain the development of biological complexity.

On the other hand, if the plunges to the ground are the rare exception, then what possible advantage could the winglets afford a member of the species that may possess them? Without an advantage, natural selection will not target the mutant for retention of the characteristic. Without retention, however, there can be no accumulation and ultimately no completely built structure.

There is thus a contrary relationship at work in the attempt to give an account of the emergence of flight in birds by referring to falling incidents. Either the role of natural selection's alleged broad-based targeting of attributes diminishes because accidents in nature are frequent, or whatever explanatory value Dawkins's tumble-from-the-heights mishap story might have had diminishes because they are infrequent. One cannot have it both ways. In any event, from the standpoint of science, the mishap story is of little elucidatory merit.

I believe that there is sufficient reason at this point to discount Dawkins's claim that accidents can account for the purported gradual development of wings for an entire category of organisms. As a result, his supposition that a gradient of advantage must underlie complexity is left unsupported. Dawkins's proposed incremental changes may be devoid of any impact at all, and, in the final analysis, they may be distinct impediments. In reality, a pair of wing-like protrusions on a beast probably would decrease its maneuverability in a tree. Neither half a wing nor 51 percent of a wing would allow the creature to fly. Any farm boy who has clipped the tips of the feathers on the wings of chickens to prevent their flying out of the barnyard knows that not much material has to be removed to ground the fowls. For an animal that cannot fly, a smaller nub may be a better nub; no nub may be even better. A pair of forelimbs having claws with which to grip when in the heights, one has to think, will outperform a pair of paddles with which to thrash.

Natural selection may offer a basis for explaining the utility of genetically spawned variations that provide immediate benefits in survival and breeding, but it lacks the force that is needed to explain the supposed utility of incremental variations that are, so to speak, purely strategic. If a change is not an enhancement, then there is no reason for nature to strive to keep it; and, if a change is actually a hindrance, in spite of future potential, then, according to the theory, it will be purged. One author claims that undeveloped features, in fact, would be such changes and therefore targeted for removal.

> Natural selection would actually cull out animals with partially developed structures because such features tend to hinder survival in the wild. This rules out any type of slow and gradual evolution of wings and support structures.[78]

If incremental changes are not preserved, for whatever reason, then Dawkins's theory is exposed to the problem that he is trying to avoid: the sudden bound up the cliff of his imaginary mountain to the complexity at the peak. I would argue that the probability, though slight, of the sudden arising of a single wing from some mutational fluke, like a fifth leg on a cow, is, given the mathematics of the matter, assuredly greater than that corresponding to the plodding development of a pair of them through a series of mutational flukes and the lack of any advantage in survival that nubs would provide over legs. To support a notion of gradual progress toward winged flight, Dawkins needs a far better account of why evolution would protect precursor protuberances, especially where they are tiny fractions of what a fully developed wing would be—so tiny that, by any reasonable standards, they would be essentially useless, contrary to what Dawkins alleges. Without that account, his theory generates the seeds of its own destruction. Changes that are labeled as improvements, not because they in themselves represent any enhanced ability but because they are footsteps along the path that would end in something that does represent enhanced ability if those changes were

---

[78] Jeffrey P. Tomkins, "Tail-Gliding Bugs Are Not Evidence for Flight Evolution," Institute for Creation Research, accessed July 1, 2013, www.icr.org/article/tail-gliding-bugs-are-not-evidence.

to progress, are misnomers within the structure of the theory of natural selection. It may be that the upward trail on Dawkins's Mount Improbable is just an illusory byproduct of the theory itself rather than a rationale for its veracity. The cart seems to be pulling the horse.[79]

---

[79] The falling scenario represents the bulk of Dawkins's attempt to explain how wings could have come about little by little. He does consider an alternative view, although I will not pursue it in detail. Birds might have stemmed, he postulates, from small, ground-bound dinosaurs rather than from animals that were living in the canopy. Chasing insects, they developed wings from enlarged surfaces on their front legs that aided in making sudden directional changes in pursuit of meals, and, from there, flapping arose. Whether it is the tree to the ground or the ground to the tree, if one goes back far enough, taking the path of the evolutionists' theory, then one reaches a point where the predecessor is on the forest floor. With regard to the idea that winglets would assist in making midair changes because of increased air resistance, it must be noted that the same increase in air resistance would make those limbs harder to wield in fending off deft enemies and less effective than sleek legs in running away from them. A flap-legged creature hardly would be an exemplar of agility. By hypothesis, the animal could not fly, so it could not fly away from a predator as it set out across land. Evasion is the factor in survival here, and anything that reduces the ability to evade capture increases the risk of termination. The flaps might help in making directional changes because of air resistance, but they would come at the cost of speed for the same reason, making the creature easier prey than it would have been without them. Nature very likely would eliminate the flap-bearing organism then, according to evolutionary theory, in favor of organisms without flaps. The ground-to-tree scenario hence offers another example of how a potentially positive change can be offset by detrimental consequences. So, even if winglets could increase the ability of a mutant member of a species to obtain food, the likelihood that winglets would decrease the ability of the animal to stay alive when fleeing from a predator cannot be ignored. The upshot is that the species may fail to achieve enough wing to sail into the trees— ever. I am not suggesting that either Dawkins's ground-bound hypothesis or my criticism of it is an accurate depiction of reality. The grim outcome as I have portrayed it is a plausible prediction, however, if one embraces the hypothesis. The explanation of flight as an evolutionary product of insect-pursuing dinosaurs thus seems to be no better than Dawkins's primary explanation. There is simply too much guessing. Survival is not just a matter of securing things to eat; it is also a matter of avoiding being eaten. As with the tree-tumbling pseudoflyers, the supposition that incrementally longer winglets provide an advantage for the land-dwelling insect chasers is overly imaginative, and it cannot be accepted at face value as the story of the advent of flight in birds. Moreover, both hypotheses are confronted with the same lack of evidence.

THE TRANSITORY AND THE TRANSITIONAL

There is a further problem to note. Improvements are context sensitive. As environmental conditions shift, the value of a change that mutation brings about may change as well. Consider the following case of a pesticide and its effect on insects:

> For example, when a population of insects is sprayed with a deadly chemical like DDT, the most susceptible insects die but the individuals most resistant to the poison survive to breed and leave offspring, which inherit the genes that provide resistance. After many generations of insects have been sprayed, the entire surviving population may be comprised of the DDT-resistant variety, and some new form of insect control will have to be applied. Such changes are not permanent, however, because the resistant mosquitoes are more fit than the others only for as long as the insecticide is applied. When the environment becomes free of the toxic chemical, the insect population tends to revert to what it was before.[80]

What may be an advantage at one point in time may not be so at another. Although natural selection may target the best of breed for the moment, the development of sophisticated features through an evolutionary process would require a certain long-term consistency in general environmental conditions, long enough for the surmised thousands or millions or tens of millions of steps to occur, each building on the retention of past variance. Dawkins assumes that all advantages will be kept because they *are* advantages; however, as noted, that assumption, as an overarching principle, is false.

Indeed, one must take into consideration what is observed in the natural world and ask whether observations support, rather than contradict, the premise that complexity is the product of gradual progression. In the case of wings, for example, if improvement were linked invariably to size, then one would expect to see organisms

---

[80] Phillip E. Johnson, "Evolution: Fact or Fantasy?" in *The Apologetics Study Bible*, ed. Ted Cabal et al. (Nashville: Holman Bible Publishers, 2007), 7.

with at least *some* of the mutation-driven partial-wing advantages exhibited in the organism pool. One does not see them. What accounts for this state of affairs?

Turning to the author of the modern theory of evolution himself, one finds Charles Darwin's recognition of the problem and his attempt to explain this apparent hole in his theory. The absence of current transitional forms, he says, is explainable by the process of natural selection, which, in the course of time, replaces earlier forms with those that are more advanced.

> When we see any structure highly perfected for any particular habit, as the wings of a bird for flight, we should bear in mind that animals displaying early transitional grades of the structure will seldom continue to exist to the present day, for they will have been supplanted by the very process of perfection through natural selection.[81]

This approach is hardly helpful. After all, if 1-percent winglets—or 0.001-percent winglets or whatever number one wishes to use—can produce a survival benefit, as Dawkins argues, then the possessor of 1-percent winglets is more likely than others without them to live long enough to reproduce. One would expect that the offspring pool of the animal would include bearers of 1-percent winglets too; otherwise, the theory's accumulation requirement is plainly bogus. Those beasts, in turn, will survive to produce offspring with such winglets until, at last, another random mutation produces a creature that bears 2-percent winglets, perhaps hundreds of millennia later. The beasts with the smaller winglets do not suddenly cease to reproduce, nor do they suddenly disappear from the face of the earth. There could be millions of them, even billions, all continuing to generate progeny, along with the new model, well into the future. In fact, the 2-percent-winglet protobirds that supersede them, and the 3-percent-winglet protobirds that come next, should be quite prevalent at some point as

---

[81] Charles Darwin, *On the Origin of Species by Means of Natural Selection*, ed. Joseph Carroll (Peterborough, Ontario, Canada: Broadview Press, 2003), 209. The first edition of Darwin's work was published in 1859 under the title *On the Origin of Species by Means of Natural Selection, or the Preservation of Favoured Races in the Struggle for Life.*

well. The key issue is that, if each Dawkinsian whatever-fraction increase in the size of the wing is truly advantageous, and, given that nature's chance of reaching the next rung on the wing-expansion ladder, after making it to those preceding it, is slight, then one ought to come upon creatures displaying percentages of corresponding development across a broad range—if not in the present, then, as a minimum, in the remains from the past. Their absence is obvious.

Unlike his evolution-theory predecessor, however, Dawkins contends that the transitional wing forms *do* exist currently.

> Creationists who attempt to deploy the argument from improbability in their favour always assume that biological adaptation is a question of the jackpot or nothing. Another name for the 'jackpot or nothing' fallacy is 'irreducible complexity' (IC). Either the eye sees or it doesn't. Either the wing flies or it doesn't. There are assumed to be no useful intermediates. But this is simply wrong. Such intermediates abound in practice—which is exactly what we should expect in theory.[82]

If the intermediates abound, as he says, then they ought to be easy to locate. Where are they? Where is the evidence for his hypothesis? Dawkins says, "The forests are replete with gliding or parachuting animals illustrating, in practice, every step of the way up that particular slope of Mount Improbable."[83] His contention is incorrect.

I showed earlier how Dawkins's conflation of completeness and quality in his argument for partial eyes causes the argument to fail. Here, one finds a similar blending of distinct properties. What does the fact that there are gliding and parachuting animals have to do with the development of wings? There are a number of species of gliders, to be sure, but the notion that gliders are intermediates, by virtue of being gliders, runs counter to core evolutionary principles. Flying squirrels, for example, are gliding animals, which have tissue that stretches between their limbs on each side from wrist to ankle. Notably, the feature does not resemble an avian structure at all. It ties

---

[82] Dawkins, *God Delusion*, 122.
[83] Ibid., 123–24.

a forelimb and the corresponding hindlimb together, whereas birds' wings are not attached to their legs. Certain possums (not opossums, in this case) and other gliding animals are similar to squirrels. The use of air resistance as a method of limited travel does not establish biological progression; indeed, in view of these organisms, it contradicts Dawkins's hypothesis. Flying squirrels are rodents, of the order Rodentia. Sugar gliders (possums) are marsupials, of the order Diprotodontia. Evolution has it that birds existed millions of years before either of these particular orders of mammals on the biological time scale. So, Dawkins is challenged to explain how the gliding apparatuses of these creatures represent transitional forms—steps toward the metaphorical summit where the wings of birds allegedly are found. If one deems rodents and marsupials that sail through the trees to be works in progress, then what one sees here is devolution, not evolution, as life runs headlong downhill on Mount Improbable.

One could slice off these gliding mammals to protect the transitional-wing hypothesis and maintain, with regard to the development of wings, that only species of gliders that predate birds on the evolutionary time scale can count as evidence and that such gliders as squirrels and possums must have come about in some other fashion. Of course, in taking this approach, one will have introduced a fatal flaw in the reasoning. The point of Dawkins's mentioning gliders in the first place was to count them as instances of partial development. No hypothesis can be strengthened by eliminating all evidence to the contrary simply because it is evidence to the contrary; it only can be weakened by such an approach and ultimately becomes a candidate for abandonment. Even biologists would take exception to Dawkins's argument, I believe, claiming that the late gliders are examples of convergent evolution. In such a reputed phenomenon, a given feature arises independently in different species and does not indicate a developmental link.

Maple seeds descend to the ground like tiny helicopters, and dandelion seeds ride the air currents like payloads aboard miniature aircraft, but what do these facts show? The wind-resistant parts of the seed units of these plants cannot be classified as emerging wings just because they travel using the medium of air. Reasoning that parts of animals that allow them to glide or parachute are in-between wings merely on the basis that these parts offer resistance to the wind is unsound. Biological entities exist within a framework of physical and chemical laws. It is virtually inevitable that some entities will share features as a consequence, for their structures and functions must operate within that framework. Dogs swim using their legs, pushing against the water to propel themselves forward and to change direction. Would one hold that the existence of a spaniel's limbs is clear evidence of unfinished fin-fabrication? The woods are filled with mammals that swim. Beavers, with their webbed hindfeet, are even better at it than dogs. Does it follow then that beavers possess fractional fins—finlets, one supposes—that represent a higher percentage of completion than that of dogs? At the culmination of this path of improvement lie the fully developed fins of fish. Evolution has it, though, that fish arrived well ahead of mammals on the timeline of life.

This discussion is hardly serious, of course, but here is the crux of this matter: Whether air or water, it is not the fact that things in nature make use of these media in various ways for survival and reproduction that Dawkins needs for his theory. What he needs is *incremental advancement*. The example of gliders-parachuters that Dawkins puts forth as organisms with intermediate wing structures is not germane to his argument. It would be no less constructive to declare that large feet are more effective at slowing a descent from a tree than small feet because they offer greater wind resistance; so, the fact that some organisms possess comparatively large feet demonstrates that big feet are midway steps in the development of wings. The thinking in both instances is faulty: Irrelevance prevails.

What Dawkins must demonstrate is that there are creatures with winglets of gradually increasing size—1 percent of a wholly developed, functional wing, 2 percent, 3 percent, and so forth—not other structures that are complete and that make use of air resistance. If Dawkins's conjecture concerning gradation were correct, then what one would expect to see is a *continuum* of birds or protobirds with ever-increasing winglet sizes, compared with what a typical fully extended wing would be, measured, so one surmises, by the standards of the organisms of today. That continuum, however, is not what one finds at all—either in the forests or, more important, in the fossil record. On the supposition that bit-by-bit feature-progression within an evolutionary model accurately depicts reality, such a continuum ought to be in one of the two. Either the development of the wings of birds is ongoing, in which case there should be at least some partial-formation representatives alive at present; or it was completed years ago, in which case there should be at least some partial-formation representatives among the relics.[84] Paleontologists have uncovered an extraordinary number of fossils. Some indication, even a slight one, of the truth of Dawkins's postulation, were it indeed factual, would be destined to surface somewhere: an incomplete wing of any fraction at all. It is not there. Evidence in support of gradation is striking by its absence. Even evolution's favored foundational flyer, *Archaeopteryx*, heralded as a transitional organism, had full-length wings, as the fossils reveal, complete with a set of feathers.

Charles Darwin continues his defense against the lack of transitional forms. In addition to his endeavoring to account for their current absence, he attempts to account for their historical deficiency. One reason that he cites is the poor state of the fossil record.

> [T]he number of intermediate varieties, which have formerly existed on the earth, [must] be truly enormous. Why then is not every geological formation and every stratum full of such intermediate links? Geology assuredly does not reveal any such finely graduated organic chain; and this, perhaps, is the most obvious and gravest objection which can be urged against my theory. The explanation lies, as I believe, in the extreme imperfection of the geological record.[85]

Darwin maintains that the record is wanting because of the paucity of remains that have been protected from environmental degradation, and such protective conditions are rare. States the evolutionist,

---

[84] During a discussion about evolution, a family member pointed to the fact that partially winged birds do not exist in nature today. This state of affairs suggests that such gradation is not at work currently in the creatures. Nonfunctional wings that appear on large flightless birds are not partial wings; they are whole structures but are incapable of enabling the birds to take to the air. In the case of the ostrich, for example, the relative mass of the animal is a major inhibiting factor.

[85] Darwin, *Origin of Species*, 269.

> But, as by this theory innumerable transitional forms must have existed, why do we not find them embedded in countless numbers in the crust of the earth? . . . I believe the answer mainly lies in the record being incomparably less perfect than is generally supposed; the imperfection of the record being chiefly due to organic beings not inhabiting profound depths of the sea, and to their remains being embedded and preserved to a future age only in masses of sediment sufficiently thick and extensive to withstand an enormous amount of future degradation; and such fossiliferous masses can be accumulated only where much sediment is deposited on the shallow bed of the sea, whilst it slowly subsides. These contingencies will occur only rarely, and after enormously long intervals.[86]

He is saying that one does not find historical evidence of transitional features, because the conditions that preserve organismal structures, including those bearing these features, seldom arise; therefore, one should not expect to find such evidence. In general, the remains of intermediates were lost over the ages as they wore away from the effects of nature.

Is this explanation acceptable? Paleontologists do uncover fossils, after all—millions of them—and even discover soft tissue in some, as I remarked previously. Realistically, one ought to come upon a 1-percent-winged or 2-percent-winged or 3-percent-winged protobird on occasion, or maybe a 30-percent-winged one. Scientists do not see them, however.

Suppose that one argues, paralleling Dawkins's anthropic-basis reasoning, that living beings exist on other planets: There are many planets out there; some of them must have the conditions that are necessary for life and be populated by biological entities, even intelligent ones. The fact that astronomers have not detected them—with any measure of assurance—after years of looking is attributable to the great distances. A person should not expect to locate extraterrestrial life easily, but it is surely present in the cosmos. In taking that stance, one is reversing the role of scientific evidence, claiming that the failure to observe what one seeks is not because it is nonexistent.

---

[86] Ibid., 203.

Certainly, one may keep looking, but it may be that it is simply not there, and any theory that places an emphasis on evidence must hold that such a possibility is a genuine alternative. A plausible explanation for why researchers do not find part-winged early birds in the paleontological search is because there are no such creatures.

The other reason that Darwin gives for the inadequate fossil record is that transitional forms were few in number. He asks one to suppose that winged birds evolved from fish that sail above the water with fins extended. Their counts would not have increased until nature reached a critical point in the development of wings. Darwin writes,

> Thus, to return to our imaginary illustration of the flying-fish, it does not seem probable that fishes capable of true flight would have been developed under many subordinate forms, for taking prey of many kinds in many ways, on the land and in the water, *until their organs of flight had come to a high stage of perfection, so as to have given them a decided advantage over other animals in the battle for life.* Hence, the chance of discovering species with transitional grades of structure in a fossil condition will always be less, from their having existed in lesser numbers, than in the case of species with fully developed structures.[87]

What Darwin is claiming in this passage is that one does not find underdeveloped winglets among the fossils because wings as an evolutionary feature did not take off, so to speak, until they had reached an advanced stage. Only after that point would they be found in large numbers because only after that point were they decidedly advantageous. According to Dawkins, however, each fractional increase in winglet size provides an advantage, as it is the only way to bolster the prospect that natural selection will retain the expansion among the offspring in the ambling toward perfection. Even *the tiniest bit of augmentation* must provide heightened value in the struggle for survival to account for the continued development of the structure.

---

[87] Ibid., 209. The emphasis is mine.

One thus reaches an inconsistency. If an evolutionist holds that Darwin's argument concerning the lack of gradation in fossils is cogent, then explaining the nonappearance of underdeveloped winglets forces a theorist to conclude that they do not yield a benefit in the struggle for life after all. If they do not offer that benefit, then Dawkins's postulation regarding incremental improvement—that it is the road that nature follows, selecting the finest specimens on the way to complex characteristics—is false. The result is that such evolutionary explanations, in attempting to defend the absence of partial wings, press toward self-effacement.

It might be said that one has to look at the big picture when speaking of natural selection, that one should view the process as a whole and over the long haul. Some of the mutants with helpful changes will survive, one may contend. Natural selection will go to work on the ones that make it, pushing toward complexity. It is not the loss of individuals that matters, or the loss of individual paths toward functionally rich features. It is the overall gains of the biological world, taken in its entirety. One does not know what nature will produce in the course of time, only, from a broad perspective, that it will produce organisms that are more complex than their ancestors.

Dawkins's theory is put forth for a purpose. That purpose is to explain—and to explain not just the arising of complexity in general but also the arising of complex things in particular. He must do so because he is attempting to counter the notion that certain biological structures—such as eyes, wings, and bacterial flagellar motors—are irreducibly complex. Irreducible complexity is totally destructive to evolutionary theory. If it can be demonstrated that a given compound structure could not have arisen by a gradual process across multiple generations, then the theory of evolution, by everyone's account, including that of Dawkins, fails. Incremental improvement is the only option open to a Dawkinsian evolutionary story. Without it, the extreme improbability of the chance assemblage of the parts that are necessary to make a sophisticated organic device operate points to intelligent agency. Explaining the staged development of complete complex features is thus critical to Dawkins's thesis, yet his account is unsatisfying. It is not the notion of change among life forms that is unsettling in the theory of evolution, for the variation is real. It is the notable lack of credible support for the conjecture that all complexity in the biological world has come about through this tiny-steps-of-enhancement process, undirected and lumbering as it is.

At this juncture, one comes to the first crucial point as it pertains to the question about improvement. It is a dual point: (1) It is not reasonable to characterize small changes in themselves as enhancements, under a blanket coverage, simply because they could move an organism toward some complex feature that would be useful if it were developed more fully, when the changes in themselves do not produce a biological advantage; and (2) there is a lack of empirical evidence—not to mention logical demonstration—that incremental changes do provide enhancements with the regularity that is required to develop complexity. That lack of evidence in itself is problematic, but, more central to the issue, it counts as evidence to the contrary. One does not see the supposed progression in either the present or the past. The upshot is that the complexity that living organisms exhibit is not explained adequately by drawing on a sequence of gradual beneficial changes, and looking elsewhere to account for complexity is the sensible course.

BETTER AT THE BOTTOM

Dawkins claims, "Natural selection works because it is a cumulative one-way street to improvement."[88] Nature may suffer a misstep on occasion, but, in the final analysis, Dawkins believes, it heads uphill, and only uphill, on his imaginary mountain: "From a given starting point, a path which goes ever upward, never downward, is the path that natural selection would follow."[89] That uphill trail takes life to the top, which represents perfected, intricate systems, as exemplified by eyes and other advanced biological formations.

It is important to note that the path of improvement toward the apex of Dawkins's symbolic high ground is rooted in survival and procreation, not in mounting complexity.

---

[88] Dawkins, *God Delusion*, 141.
[89] Dawkins, *Mount Improbable*, 162.

> There is no long-distance target, no final perfection to serve as a criterion for selection. . . . In real life, the criterion for selection is always short-term, either simple survival or, more generally, reproductive success.[90]

Yet, complexity is where it leads. Picking up part of a passage from Dawkins's writings, quoted in the last chapter, one reads:

> The height of Mount Improbable stands for the combination of perfection and improbability that is epitomized in eyes and enzyme molecules (and gods capable of designing them). To say that an object like an eye or a protein molecule is improbable means something rather precise. The object is made of a large number of parts arranged in a very special way.[91]

How does Dawkins get from the notion of *improvement* to the notion of *complexity*? They are not the same. In his mountain analogy, he blends the two erroneously. Here then is the second crucial point as it comes to light in investigating improvement: Increased biological viability—that is to say, improved chance of survival and procreation—is distinct from increased complexity; a step toward the former property is clearly independent of a step toward the latter one, and conversely. Some species of insects can take far more radiation than *Homo sapiens* before death occurs, handle the total absence of moisture considerably better, and live much longer submerged in water. Insects are notably less complex than humans nonetheless. Tortoises can outlive humans by more than a century and produce hundreds, even thousands, of offspring; yet, they are biologically simple compared with people. The conifer *Pinus longaeva* (the bristlecone pine of North America) can survive five thousand years and release seeds beyond counting; but no tree, no plant, is nearly as complex as the human entity. If organic continuance were linked to complexity, then one would expect these two things to align. Creature-survival relies on satisfactory sensory awareness. It is aided by adaptability, efficiency, resilience, hardiness, strength, swiftness,

---

[90] Dawkins, *Blind Watchmaker*, 72.
[91] Dawkins, *Mount Improbable*, 77–78.

and agility; aside from a superficial connection, complexity is not associated with any of these qualities.

Moreover, a large assemblage of parts, where each part plays a role in the functioning of a system as a whole, increases the probability relative to a simple, basic assemblage, *ceteris paribus*, that something will go wrong. There are more parts to malfunction or to jam, to break or to desynchronize. If the continuance of life is the whole point of biological goings-on, then the simple—in general, it seems—would be better at it. The underlying issue that requires explaining here is why a natural process that is supposed to increase the chance of survival would move toward greater complexity in its products when, as a rule, complexity, where it is something beyond the mere addition of redundant parts, brings with it a heightened risk of failure. There may be no improvement to be gained in advancing toward the sophistication at the summit; doing so may be more likely to worsen the odds of survival than to better them. Once again, one might need to rely on luck. On the premise that humans are the product of natural selection, with its emphasis on preservation and reproduction, one needs a better description of how the complexity of this organism arises out of a process that is independent of it, indifferent to it, and, in actuality, may be in conflict with it.

Finally, given that Dawkins's upward path is the relentless drive toward intricacy, natural selection does not proceed as he suggests, according to other, dissenting scientists. The observations of one evolutionary biologist, whom I quote below, are pertinent:

> Some evolutionary trajectories point to increasing complexity, but simplification can be just as prevalent. Thus, there are a number of excellent examples from among the animals of what appears to our eyes as regressive evolution. These include the flatworms, whose relative simplicity was until recently thought to represent a rather primitive arrangement from which more advance phyla emerged. More extreme reduction is seen in the curious dicyemids . . . and what is effectively a regression to a protistan state has occurred in the myxozoans.[92]

---

[92] Morris, *Life's Solution*, 302–3.

If the entire focus of natural selection is on singling out advantageous variations, then perhaps the downward path to simplicity is more prevalent than Dawkins admits. I believe that he should give it more consideration, as it adds a measure of complexity itself to his proffered explanation of how complex features are built.

MODELING INCREMENTAL IMPROVEMENT

I would like to proceed at this time to examine a challenge for Dawkins's theory that arises from the mathematics of the alleged gradual enhancement that constructs intricate biological systems. In brief, beneficial hereditary outcomes carry decreasing levels of probability as the requirements for the specificity of change increase.

The first phase of the theoretical complexity-building enterprise is random mutation: an aberrant event that resequences the genetic material. In a species that reproduces sexually, the modification must happen in the germ line—the cellular track leading to the production of gametes (the sperm and ova)—if it is to affect organisms through descent. For evolution to work as the means of improvement, some of these modifications must produce, in the progeny, characteristics that provide a benefit in the procession of life, as I remarked above.

There are numerous characteristics that life forms possess, and there are countless possible directions that genetic aberrations can take as parents procreate. As a consequence, many properties of the offspring are subject to change. Underlying the multifarious traits of an organism, regardless of the way in which they may be expressed in the given individual, is an elaborate set of chemical instructions that are embedded in the DNA that makes up the creature's genetic footprint. In short order, I will discuss how the structure of DNA can change and how that event can shape a biological entity's attributes.

For now, I want to spotlight a central problem with Dawkins's approach, which can be exposed in a straightforward manner using a series of three diagrams. The illustrations provide a basic portrayal of alterations in traits—as traits are displayed in the respective corpuses of bearers among the offspring—prompted by the irregular activity of genes. A single organism serves as the progenitor in each of the diagrams. In sexual reproduction, of course, heritable qualities are tied to a parental pair, but the configuration that I have chosen simplifies the illustrations and is sufficient for the current analysis.

The initial drawing shows the dispersion of potential, random change across a broad spectrum of properties. Each line represents a possible variance, and the elliptical figures represent traits, where variations that would offer an advantage to an individual possessor appear in grey. I am not concerned at this point with the likelihood that a specific property will be altered, only with a favorable outcome, regardless of the trait on which the mutation has an influence. The design depicts the improbability as a whole that a haphazard shift in genetic material will produce a *beneficial* trait-change—with respect to *any trait*—in the progeny. There is no predetermined direction here; any mutation that betters the odds that offspring will survive in a given environment and, in turn, reproduce with success will count as effecting an improvement. For clarity reasons, I will limit the discussion to observable physical characteristics.

Dawkins's idea of the development of advanced formations rests, in the main, on the generation of novel features that are adjusted in a stair-step manner to reach some useful state. For evolution to achieve the complexity that Dawkins envisions, it must move from general improvement to focused enhancement. That enhancement consists of independent strings of changes in which multiple elements progress along their respective tracks, driving toward a particular future condition in a bit-by-bit fashion. In a Dawkinsian context then, a complex trait can be viewed as one that has two key facets. (1) It is multidimensional, in that it encompasses two or more developmental elements, each of which must reach a certain stage of completion to assemble a workable end product. In reality thus, a complex trait is a biological composite. Given that the odds of the abrupt appearance of such a thing are prohibitive, (2) it must be built in pieces. As the following series of diagrams will show, however, the piecemeal approach that Dawkins embraces only exacerbates the mathematical difficulty that he faces.

Consider the overall prospect of positive variation, reflected in Figure 8.3. Constraints narrow the course: Figures 8.4 and 8.5. My labels for traits may suggest their general character, coupled with the individuality (indicated by lowercase Greek letters) of distinct ones.

CHANCE OF POSITIVE CHANGE

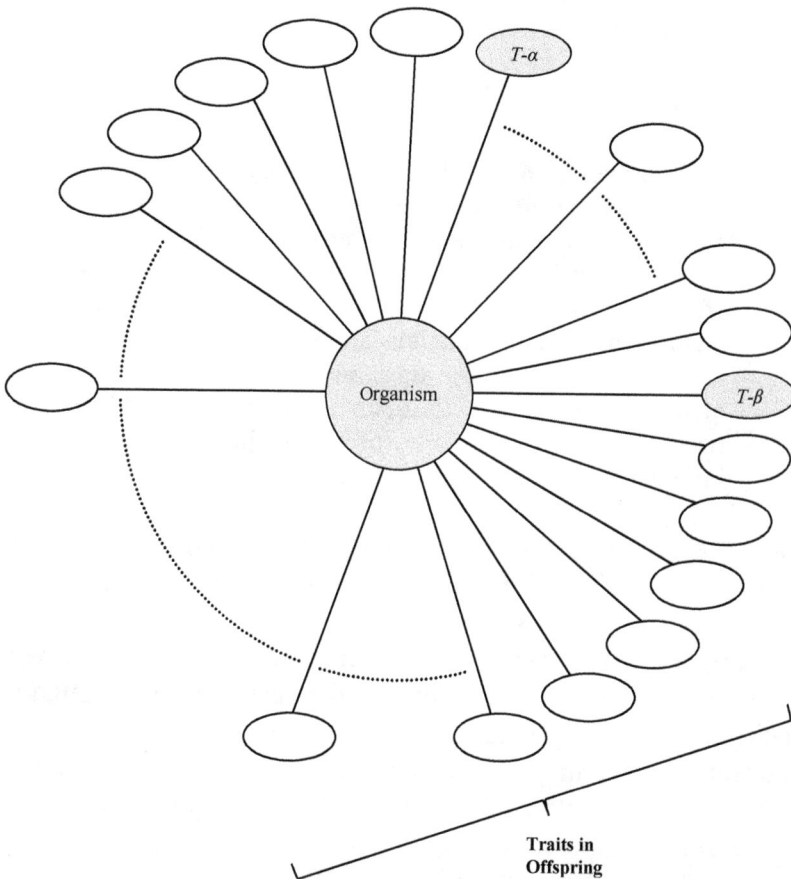

Figure 8.3

What is the chance that a mutation, if it occurs, would prove to have a positive impact, increasing the biological fitness of the individual creature that exhibits the genetic-induced attribute upgrade? Dawkins admits that mutations seldom result in anything that is advantageous. Other biologists agree with that assessment. In an article on hereditary traits and DNA, for example, one author writes,

> Only a tiny fraction of these changes [spontaneous DNA sequence variants] are likely to improve, rather than degrade, the original hereditary information and the trait that derives from it.[93]

Another says,

> "Fitness," as used in evolutionary biology, is a technical term for this idea: it is the probability of surviving or reproducing in a given environment.
> . . . Most important, we know something about the effects of mutations on fitness. The overwhelming majority of random mutations are harmful—that is, they reduce fitness; only a tiny minority are beneficial, increasing fitness. . . . [I]n finely tuned systems, random tweaks are far more likely to disrupt function than to improve it.[94]

What value does one assign to the tiny fraction and the tiny minority that these authors mention—is it, expressed in the common-fraction mode, $^1/_{100,000}$, $^1/_{1,000,000}$, or $^1/_{100,000,000}$? No number can be stated with assurance, but it is clear that these scientists, and Dawkins, believe the figure to be very small. Given that the vast majority of mutations, when they do occur, generate negative effects, nature must overcome this obstacle in inching toward some useful advanced structure. This remote chance constitutes the initial narrowing of probability.

A single isolated change in some physical property of an organism, by the very nature of the sort of change that it is, cannot provide a basis on which to erect a complex biological feature. Even if nature selects it as beneficial, it is a dead end, viewed in light of the potential to play any role in the development of complexity. Such changes are apparent in nature. They can offer a way for species to adapt to their world, positioning them to be successful.

A favored example to which evolutionists point as a case of natural selection at work is a lone incident of color change that

---

[93] David M. Kingsley, "From Atoms to Traits," *Scientific American* 300, no. 1 (2009): 59.

[94] H. Allen Orr, "Testing Natural Selection," *Scientific American* 300, no. 1 (2009): 46.

increases the survivability of an organism by making it more difficult to see in its habitat, whether the organism is predator or prey.[95] A one-off change that is immediately advantageous, though, says effectively nothing about a series of independent changes leading to a novel, compound feature that is advantageous. Other than the fact that, according to the theory, all changes, whether singular or serial, must produce some gain for nature to recognize them, so to speak, as worthy of keeping, the example of camouflage that evolutionists cite has no connection to the development of sophisticated biological elements. Those elements require parallel successions of multifarious alterations that are unrelated except for their contribution to the operation of the end product. The two scenarios are very different.

Dawkins argues against the sudden arising of an assemblage of parts that function together as a unified system because he is aware of the extreme improbability of such a coming to be. Thus, as noted earlier, a complex feature, he avers, must be put together little by little as mutation and selection push toward greater intricacy. For this gradual-development approach to work, some of the positive changes

---

[95] Although its import has been challenged, a case that scientists note in support of evolution is that of peppered moths. The colors of the moths are the physical expression of dominant and recessive forms of genes that are present in the pool. The percentage of living moths possessing light or dark wings has varied with the conditions of the environment. Natural selection purportedly favors one color or the other (additional shades, however, have been reported): The moths that blend better with their surroundings are the ones that are less likely to be spotted by birds and eaten. Prior to the industrial revolution, the light moths were nearly ubiquitous in England. As industry took hold, the dark moths became more common because soot from burning coal covered the countryside and produced a concealing backdrop. It also killed the lichens, exposing the dark bark on trees. Subsequent to efforts to effect cleaner conditions, the light-colored moths again prevailed. Such environmental variations can encourage population shifts toward the more camouflaged creatures, but, of course, no development of new features occurs and no augmentation of existing ones. There are only light and dark moths, of the same species, in differing proportions. Even if a mutation generated a change in the past from the normal light-winged creature to a dark-winged offspring, with a trait that became widespread, the value of the case in arguing for evolution—microevolution here—based on genetic alteration is limited. The shift back to lighter moths was not the result of mutation, only, at best, selection on the basis of current displayed attributes. For opposing commentary, see Dawkins, *Mount Improbable*, 87–88; and Gary Parker, *Creation: Facts of Life—How Real Science Reveals the Hand of God*, rev. ed. (2006; Green Forest, AR: Master Books, 2010), 77–84, 93–94.

that result from mutations must be more than isolated adjustments: They must be the first footfalls down what are to become multiple-step paths. They signal course changes in the properties of progeny.

It is helpful to conceive of a series of these supposed iterative variations as constituting what I will label a 'genetic vector'—not to be confused with terminology in microbiology that applies to DNA cloning. Analogous to its mathematical counterpart, this hereditary construct represents, from a conceptual standpoint, both magnitude and direction. Each positive step in a sequence of changes increases the degree of completeness of some prospective feature—1 percent of a finished formation, 2 percent of that formation, 3 percent of it, and so forth—and the serial pattern as a whole points to the specific yet-to-materialize system that is under development by the evolutionary process.[96] Nothing hinges on the expression that I adopt. The important point is that incremental change must take place along a channel if the proposed accumulation that is needed to build a future structural element is to occur. An evolutionist may object that there is no actual direction, given that evolution is unguided. Nevertheless, the doctrine to which Dawkins subscribes entails the notion that biological advancement, regardless of how it is achieved, is movement *toward* a complex arrangement, even if it is only in retrospect that it becomes recognizable that it was such.

Extending Figure 8.3 can clarify this concept. In the following diagram, the grey figures represent, as before, traits with positive variations—ones that would further the fitness of the possessor in the offspring pool. Among such possible changes is one that corresponds to trait T-β, which, unlike a change that corresponds to trait T-α, would initiate a series that theoretically ends in some intricate and useful structure. Here, evolution takes the first step down a corridor

---

[96] One could represent the value of the changes numerically, although it would be difficult to assign relative worth with any meaningful accuracy. Additional molars, longer claws, and higher mate-attracting skull ridges—all may be positive, but assessing the comparative contribution of each in survival and breeding scarcely could be something in which one could put much confidence. Perhaps a heritable step in the right direction—toward having a useful attribute—could be rendered as +1. This approach could use −1 for harmful mutational outcomes and zero for ones that are neutral in impact. In any event, one can distinguish beneficial changes from nonbeneficial changes in keeping with the theory of evolution; accordingly, it is the beneficial ones that allegedly increase the degree of the system's completion.

that will lead to an expressed complex trait—*any complex trait*—assuming continued progress, in a collaborative context.

CHANCE OF POSITIVE VECTORIAL CHANGE

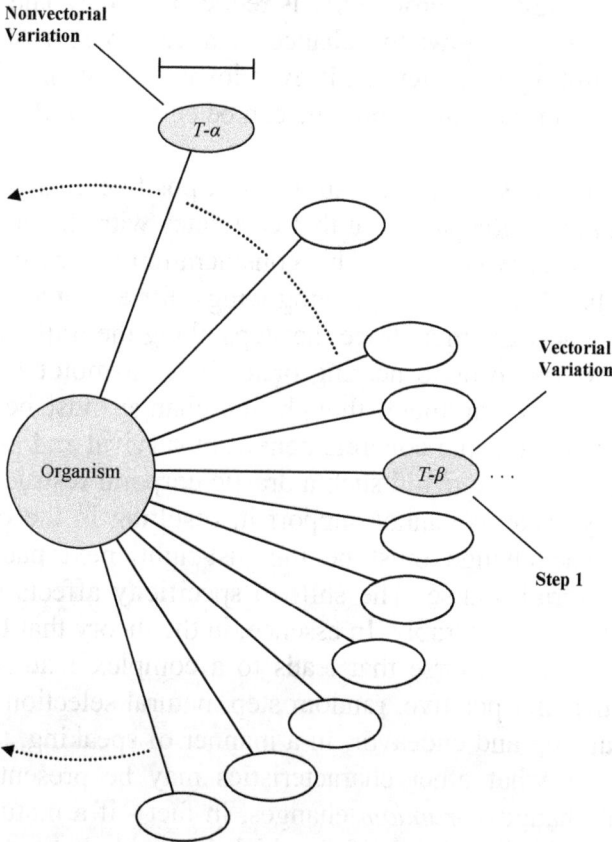

Figure 8.4

The set of traits that belong to genetic vectors is a proper subset of the set of all traits that an organism possesses. Any characteristic can change at random, as a rule, because of mutation. If the odds are against a change's being beneficial, then one must apply those odds across the set of all traits, such that the chance that a beneficial change falls on a vector is reduced accordingly. Stated differently, a benefit is highly unlikely to appear as a consequence of mutation, regardless of circumstances. That low probability applies to all traits as a set. Where select traits—namely, those that have a vectorial basis—are in view, the probability is reduced further: The chance of any improvement is low; the chance of a certain sort of improvement, constituting a smaller set, is even lower. One cannot be certain of precise numerical values, but one can be certain that the likelihood narrows.[97]

Consider now the improbability of a positive change's turning up along a *particular* path, one that correlates with the development of a *particular complex trait*. This consideration is clearly important because, when faced with explaining wings, for example, Dawkins's evolutionary account must trace the steps along the trail that leads to flight, not to vision or to hearing or to flagellar-motor locomotion. More than that requirement, though, the change must be extensive enough to provide some concrete benefit in survival and propagation but limited enough to avoid such a drastic corporal restructuring that the auxiliary systems cannot support it, resulting in the organism's perishing. The change must be the just-right, next pace down a specific vectorial course. The shift in specificity affects the probability numbers considerably. In essence, in the theory that Dawkins is promoting, once a course that leads to a complex feature is established by the first positive, random step, natural selection must take hold of that step and endeavor, in a manner of speaking, to build on *it*—no matter what other characteristics may be present—through subsequent changes—*random* changes, in fact—if a mature product is ever to materialize. Figure 8.5, which I provide below, represents what one finds. Note that many generations may pass between positive steps along the given genetic passageway.

---

[97] Certain types of changes are more likely to occur than others. In reality, the chance of positive change is not spread quite evenly across all traits. This fact does not matter for the analysis in this chapter, however. The concern is not so much with specific improbabilities as with the general concept that they are problematic for evolutionary theory.

CHANCE OF SUBSEQUENT POSITIVE CHANGE THAT IS ASSOCIATED WITH A PARTICULAR VECTOR

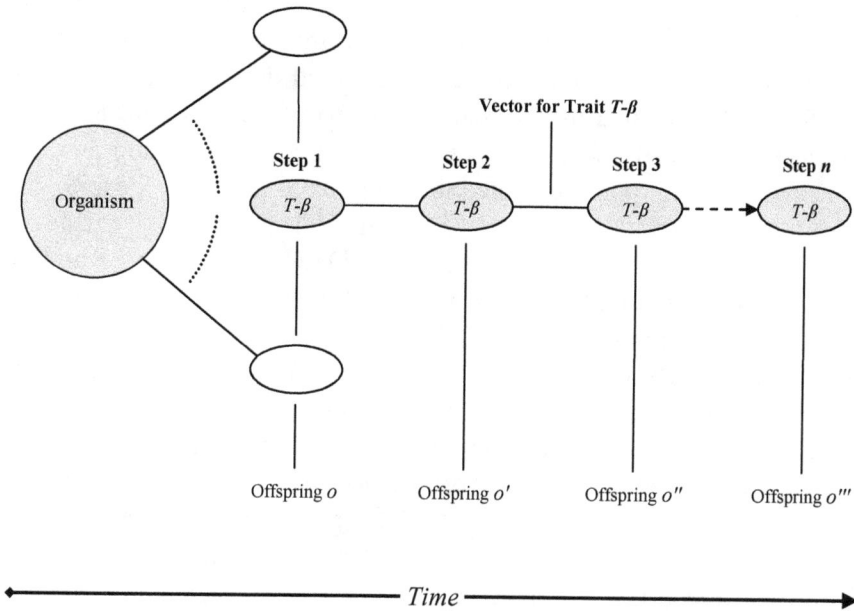

Figure 8.5

The third crucial point about improvement surfaces here. The probability of hitting upon a positive change as a result of mutation, *any* positive change, is very low. The probability of the positive change's launching a genetic vector, *any* genetic vector, is even less. The probability of the positive change's stumbling upon the next incremental pace down a given vectorial corridor, which is the *same* corridor as one down which prior, *related* movement occurred, is remote—mathematically, an anomaly. Such sequential advancement, though, is exactly what is required if evolution is to construct a complex thing through a series of gradual, and gradually improving, random alterations. Even if nature keeps the first mutative step as it begins its supposed accumulation, getting to the second and further steps is still the product of happenstance, for, according to the theory, the changes are haphazard. On the assumption that natural selection will cause all positive changes to be retained, one still is faced with accounting for numerous, indiscriminate differences that must fall on a particular vector on which previous indiscriminate differences fell. Those alterations must be beneficial in the survival-reproduction phenomenon as well to explain the continued development and ultimate completion of a useful feature that nature has begun. Random variation is exactly what it is: *random*. It is an unsystematic process. It has no actual predetermined bearing as it unfolds, despite the notion that advancement toward a finished product by virtue of aggregation is an inherent element of Dawkins's thesis. Random change does not look ahead to see what may be there. Whether it provides an advantage in life, or it does not do so, a mutation-based change in a creature's characteristics is never recognized by nature as something on which it must build. Every deviation in the DNA code, lying behind such a change, is an aberrant event. The aberration is one of the core postulates of evolutionary theory. Without it, natural selection is rendered effectively sterile, for it has no raw material.

The heart of the issue at hand begins to take shape now in the form of a question: The inherited traits that an organism possesses, and their overt expressions, are derived from the creature's DNA, but how are these traits tied to that foundational substance? Answering the question is essential. If all things are equal, and change is entirely random, then the probability of irregular, yet pseudochanneled and cumulative, variation leading to complexity—vectorial variation—stemming from reproductive errors, rests on the probability of the occurrence of specific shifts in the chemical makeup of genes.

To explore the matter, one must turn to the structure of DNA. In eukaryotes, DNA appears in nuclear chromosomes; a very small amount is also present in the mitochondria. This amazing molecule is a polymer consisting of two strands that are linked by a large number of chemical base pairings and twisted into a double-helix configuration. Each strand of this special molecule is a chain that is made of repeating units—nucleotides; and each nucleotide consists of a sugar, a phosphate group, and a chemical base, as I mentioned earlier. A given base is one of four substances: adenine, guanine, thymine, or cytosine, usually referred to by the abbreviated forms A, G, T, and C respectively. Every base connects to its counterpart base in the other strand by means of hydrogen bonds, which keep the structure intact. Purines link to pyrimidines: Adenine pairs consistently with thymine in DNA, and guanine pairs with cytosine. For the reason that the linkings of the four compounds are fixed—adenine to thymine and guanine to cytosine—a copy of the original double helix can be reconstructed from either half, which is exactly what happens. The accuracy of the DNA-replication process is astonishing; even more astonishing, built-in machinery exists to correct things that go awry.

How then *do* mutations occur, and how is it that they generate physical aberrations in offspring? In higher, sexually reproducing life forms, genetic mutations arise during the production of the gametes and issue from the reconfiguration of the sequence of base pairs in the DNA. In turn, this shifting in the base-pair sequence alters the genetic instruction-sets that organisms pass to their progeny. These deviations can affect the construction of proteins from which the body of a given immediate descendant is made, thereby causing a change in its physical properties. One will recall that DNA functions not only to replicate itself but also to govern the building of both RNA and proteins.

MODIFYING THE DNA SEQUENCE

Dawkins makes much of the idea of complexity in his writings, focusing on the macrophysical features of more advanced organisms. One need not look too high in the conjectural evolutionary tree, however, to find complex things. Eukaryotic cells in themselves are wondrous, miniature factories that spawn the production of proteins by means of the information that is embedded in the DNA areas that constitute genes. Genes of eukaryotic organisms are fragmented, in that the protein-coding sections, which are exons, are interspersed with noncoding sections, or introns. The construction method is quite elaborate and requires many chemical compounds to make it work. What follows is a highly simplified overview of how eukaryotic cells utilize the code in genes—more precisely, in their exons—to assemble proteins. The discussion will concentrate on the core production; the mirroring, mitochondrial activity is effectively noncontributing.

851

AN AMBITIOUS BUILDING PLAN

The first phase of protein synthesis is transcription. During this phase, the dual strands of DNA, where they coincide with a gene—a distinctive segment of a DNA molecule, which (excluding the mitochondria) is situated within the nucleus of a cell—separate as the hydrogen bonds between the base pairs uncouple through enzymatic activity. One strand of the segment contains a sequence of nucleotides that serves as a template for constructing a specific protein.[98] This sequence is encoded one nucleotide at a time into complementary nucleotides in RNA, continuing in this fashion until the DNA strand directs the process to terminate by means of an embedded signal. At this stage of the procedure, the RNA compound is precursor messenger RNA, or precursor mRNA (referred to as primary mRNA in some texts); it awaits further processing. During transcription, each base in the DNA template corresponding to the gene is joined by its counterpart in the precursor mRNA molecule; uracil (U) takes the place of thymine here. The other three bases—A, G, and C—are identical to those in DNA. Thus, the DNA single-strand series ACC is matched by the precursor mRNA counterpart series UGG. As the transcription process proceeds, the double helix of the DNA molecule reseals in its wake. The initial end of the emerging RNA string is capped shortly after transcription commences; the other end will be processed as the operation draws to a close.

RNA splicing ensues. The introns, which complement the introns in the DNA template, are removed from the precursor mRNA transcript, and the coding sections—exons that correlate with those in DNA—are joined. Splicing generally begins before transcription concludes. The process is analogous to the editing of a tape for a video program, excising the portions of the tape that will not be shown and then connecting the appropriate pieces of footage to compose a continuous segment. Spliceosomes are the units that conduct this activity, readying the precursor mRNA for the succeeding stage. More than fifty proteins are involved in this complex procedure

---

[98] In certain species, under conditions that can occur later in the production, more than one specific protein may be created in a single construction incident, but such a case is atypical. There is a mechanism, however, that permits different proteins to be assembled on different occasions from the same gene: alternative RNA splicing.

alone. Once the processing is complete, the mature mRNA strip that results exits the nucleus of the cell through one of several tiny pores. These nuclear pores act not only as gateways but also as selective gatekeepers, allowing only properly prepared mature mRNA to pass. The mRNA enters the cytoplasm, bearing sequences of nucleotides in triplets. A succession of three nucleotides—a codon—carries in its bases the code for an amino acid. With four chemical bases, there are 4^3, or sixty-four, possible configurations of nucleotide triplets. As a rule, twenty amino acids form the proteins that make up organisms' cells; each amino acid corresponds to one or more of these codons.

At the next phase of synthesis, through the procedure of translation, which is conducted by ribosomes, polypeptide chains—that is to say, proteins—are assembled using another type of RNA: transfer RNA, or tRNA. Ribosomes themselves are, in fact, the products of cellular construction, produced in the nucleoli of cells. Each ribosome consists of two subunits, which join temporarily when it is time for protein synthesis to occur. A tRNA molecule holds an amino acid at one end of its bent structure, and it has a special set of three nucleotides at the opposite end. The trio of nucleotides forms, in this instance, an anticodon: The bases are the counterparts to the triplet bases in mRNA. The mRNA codon UGG, for example, associates with tRNA bearing the anticodon ACC, which brings with it the amino acid tryptophan. Each series of three nucleotides constituting a codon specifies a particular amino acid or, in the case of three of these triplets, specifies a particular directive instead—namely, to stop the amino-acid chain assembly, marking the end of that individual run.[99] A fourth triplet has a dual function, both providing the code for a specific amino acid and, by virtue of that amino acid, indicating the beginning of a protein-building sequence. A ribosome, working in conjunction with others in a manner that maximizes efficiency, ties amino acids together in the prescribed order, translating the train of triplets in the mRNA and releasing each tRNA molecule after the delivery of its matching amino-acid payload to the construction site. The ribosome continues the linking procedure until the preset stop

---

[99] In some eukaryotic species and in special circumstances, the code that is embedded in two of the stop codons, in addition to the normal, instructional role, can serve as the basis for handling nonstandard amino acids, where each of these codons specifies a given nonstandard amino acid uniquely.

codon in the mRNA informs it that the chain is complete. At that point, the ribosome releases the amino-acid chain, then the mRNA filament, and separates into its dual subunits. Even before synthesis ends, the polypeptide string begins folding into a structured protein, often with the aid of molecular chaperones. This folding activity (sometimes taking place in the endoplasmic reticulum) is necessary to produce a useable biological building block. The activity finishes once the ribosome frees the protein. Support processes involving many compounds enhance this entire operation, and the substance adenosine triphosphate provides an important supply of energy for the synthesis. Intrinsic quality-control routines secure the integrity of the production. In the end, if improperly formed proteins are created, then the cell classifies those proteins as faulty and destroys them.

As an aside, perhaps even more fascinating than the manufacturing activity of cells, with the built-in quality control, is the DNA-repair system that is inherent in cells. When damage to DNA occurs, a consequence of exposure to certain environmental materials, or to radiation or thermal variation—as before, phenomena that scientists draw on in endeavoring to explain the arising of the self-replicating molecule can be the very things that harm it—cellular restoration machinery sets about to return the molecule to a proper configuration. The repair is accomplished by excising a malformed base or, if needed, an entire nucleotide sequence. A cadre of specific enzymes does the work. The cell waits, as it were, for the repair to be completed before it continues with its normal cycle of division, thereby averting the propagation of a problem. Combined with the complexity that cells exhibit in their protein-manufacturing program, this additional procedure heightens the sense that the entire system is a feat of microengineering using chemicals to achieve the end result.

Although I will not pursue further the matter of the complexity of cells with their information-driven protein synthesis and error-correction routines, not to mention their DNA-repair machinery, the same concerns about convergence and gradual progression apply as much to them as they do to eyes and wings, and perhaps more so. Indeed, it takes a stretch of thought to envision how the building process could commence because cells, which produce proteins, would have to exist prior to the manufacture of the proteins of which the cells themselves are made and on which they rely for making more proteins. A troubling circularity surfaces once again. Even evolutionists believe that the cellular factory is an enigma, as this extract reveals:

> It is especially difficult to imagine how protein synthesis evolved because it is now performed by a complex interlocking system of protein and RNA molecules; obviously the proteins could not have existed until an early version of the translation apparatus was already in place.[100]

Their search for answers in purely mechanistic terms continues nevertheless.

A Very Great Array

How many base pairs there are in the DNA of an organism varies with the species, and there is no hard correlation between the complexity of an organism and the number of base pairs in its genetic profile. Humans have two sets of twenty-three chromosomes, including a pair of sex chromosomes—forty-six total—in the nuclei of their somatic cells, which are the cells that make up the general tissues of the body. As I noted previously, the term 'diploid' is applied to cells that possess dual sets of chromosomes. Each sperm and ovum, as a mature germ cell, contains a single set, which joins the corresponding set from the opposite-sex parent in fertilization. As also noted, the term 'haploid' is applied to gametes; only one set of chromosomes is present in each. The human genome—genome sizes are specified using haploid values—contains slightly more than three billion nucleotide pairs. In other species, the number can run from hundreds of millions to hundreds of billions. The genome of a certain species of single-cell, amoeboid creatures contains in excess of half a trillion pairs. The genetic constitution of an animal or plant is thus such that the DNA from which its physical characteristics are derived may contain billions of adenine-thymine, guanine-cytosine bondings.

---

[100] Alberts et al., *Molecular Biology*, 372.

Even in light of the precision with which the entire genetic process proceeds, the great number of base pairs in an organism's genome sets the stage for a mutation to happen. By altering the configuration of bases, a mutation can change the commands in a gene, causing a shift in the way in which a ribosome assembles amino acids to form a protein, or stopping a chain prematurely. There are several ways in which such shifts can take place. In a single chromosome, a substitution of one chemical base for another in a particular location within the structure is possible, altering the pairing accordingly. So, for example, A-T can replace G-C, or conversely. An exchange for a pair's mirror image can occur, where, say, A-T is switched to T-A. Alterations that affect only one site are point mutations; they appear in a sole place along the polymer. There are mutations that affect numerous bases. Existing nucleotides can be relocated to other areas in the structure. Whole blocks of bases can be inverted, reversing the order of their relative positions within the molecule. There can be insertions or deletions of strings of nucleotides. Duplication or even repeated replication of zones can come about, extending the molecular chain as a result.

In addition to these intrachromosomal changes, mutations that involve more than a single chromosome can arise. A segment of a given chromosome can be removed and inserted into a different one, collapsing the source and expanding the target. Segments of two chromosomes can be exchanged, in which case a sequence of base pairs from the first moves to the second, and a sequence from the second moves to the first.

The set of physical traits that an organism displays—its phenotype—is linked to the serial arrangements of chemical base pairs that make up the genetic material. A change in the way in which a DNA molecule's component compounds are arrayed can bring about a change in one or more of these traits. Some changes derive from a single altered base pair, whereas others are traced to a lengthy chain in which an entire sector of DNA—containing perhaps thousands, or even tens of thousands, of chemical bases—is duplicated.

The difference between black and yellow color in Labrador retrievers stems, for instance, from a single base change that inactivates a signal receptor in the pigment cells of yellow dogs. . . . In contrast, the special dorsal stripe of hair in Rhodesian ridgeback dogs comes from the duplication of a 133,000-base-pair region containing three genes that encode a growth factor for fibroblast cells, which amps up production of the growth factor.[101]

Although mutations do take place, the chance of one's affecting any given nucleotide during any given replication of DNA for any given organism is remote. It is approximately one in a billion.

In all cells, DNA sequences are maintained and replicated with high fidelity. The mutation rate, approximately 1 nucleotide change per 10^9 nucleotides each time the DNA is replicated, is roughly the same for organisms as different as bacteria and humans.[102]

Applying the rate in particular to a generational cycle, a scientist offers the following remarks in a technical journal:

We know, for instance, that genetic types originate in mutations of DNA—random changes in the sequence of nucleotides (or string made up of the letters A, G, C and T) that constitutes the "language" of the genome. We also know a good deal about the rate at which a common kind of mutation—the change of one letter of DNA to another—appears: each nucleotide in each gamete in each generation has about one chance in a billion of mutating to another nucleotide.[103]

It is evident that the specificity of change that is needed by Dawkins's theory, with its inbuilt principle of gradation, does present an obstacle. Not just any variant will do in building a particular complex feature; only a certain configuration (or certain configurations) of DNA bases will produce a right result: an acceptable successor

---

[101] Kingsley, "Atoms to Traits," 57.
[102] Alberts et al., *Molecular Biology*, 238.
[103] Orr, "Testing Natural Selection," 46.

increment in the development of that given attribute. If the probability of a given nucleotide change in a reproductive cycle is so low,
and only a very small fraction of changes generate beneficial effects,
then what modification or modifications of the genetic sequence
would it take for a proper next step, complete with accompanying
advantage, to appear in the lineage?

It is already clear that not all the chemical bases in an animal's
genomic makeup are tied to heritable traits. The prevailing belief is
that the percentage of DNA that bears protein-building code in *Homo
sapiens* is fairly low at about 1.5 percent or perhaps slightly higher.
Of the remainder, some is responsible for the structural integrity of
the molecular unit and for activity that is related to the assembly of
amino-acid chains from the DNA blueprints. In contrast to humans,
the percentage of DNA that forms coding sections is notably higher
in many other organisms. Traditionally, much of the noncoding DNA
has been deemed to be nonfunctional and thus branded 'junk DNA'.
It is a lamentable designation, and it is inaccurate. Biologists are
discovering only now the important role that it plays in cellular
construction. The presence of introns provides a pathway for
synthesizing different proteins from a single gene by connecting
exons in diverse sequences to create distinct mRNAs; introns also
may contribute to the regulation of gene expression.[104] Although it
encountered resistance, a late study challenged the traditional stance.

> As part of the Encyclopedia of DNA Elements
> (ENCODE) project, 35 research teams have analyzed 44
> regions of the human genome covering 30 million bases
> and figured out how each base contributes to overall
> genome function. The results . . . provide a litany of new
> insights and drive home how complex our genetic code
> really is. For example, protein-coding DNA makes up
> barely 2% of the overall genome, yet 80% of the bases
> studied showed signs of being expressed, says Ewan
> Birney of the European Molecular Biology Laboratory's
> European Bioinformatics Institute in Hinxton, U.K., who
> led the ENCODE analysis.[105]

---

[104] See Alberts et al., *Molecular Biology*, 318, 436; and Mader, *Biology*, 243.
[105] Elizabeth Pennisi, "DNA Study Forces Rethink of What It Means to Be a
Gene," *Science* 316, no. 5831 (2007): 1556.

Biologists recognize nevertheless that an organism's DNA contains noncoding sections. There are four chemical bases and hence four configurations of linked bases: A-T, T-A, G-C, and C-G. Strictly in view of the mathematics, the number of possible arrangements of paired bases within an organism's protein-coding exons, assuming standard conditions, is determinable by a specific formula:

$$4^{bp}$$

where

b = the number of base pairs in organism's genomic layout
p = the percentage of base pairs in organism's genomic layout that fall in exons and can carry code for proteins

In recent years, scientists investigating the genetic makeup of the common chicken discovered that there are approximately a billion base pairs in its genome.[106] The hypothetical protobird that I have been discussing in this chapter would have a DNA complement of about this size, one would think. Its set of base pairs that constitute protein-coding sections might be on the low end of the scale at, say, 1.5 percent, as is the case with humans; this percentage would be a conservative estimate for the conjectural animal, at least. So, if one uses the stated size, then the number of possible arrangements of corresponding base pairs, lying in exons, is captured by this expression:

$$4^{(1,000,000,000 \times 0.015)}$$

That numerical value is equivalent to the following one, rounded, in scientific notation:

$$7.41173 \times 10^{9,030,899}$$

It is an extraordinary number.[107] It is so large that it would require several books the size of this book just to write it in the conventional,

---

[106] See International Chicken Genome Sequencing Consortium, "Sequence and Comparative Analysis of the Chicken Genome Provide Unique Perspectives on Vertebrate Evolution," *Nature* 432, no. 7018 (2004): 695–716.
[107] I calculated this numerical value using the computational knowledge engine at Wolfram Alpha, accessed July 15, 2013, www.wolframalpha.com.

decimal format. Obviously, counting on a particular chance configuration of the DNA of either parent, or even one of several possible chance configurations, to bring about the next vectorial increment in some advanced-feature-building run is outside the limits of reason. This number, of course, does not include additions that mutational base-pair insertions may occasion.

With a fixed quantity of base pairs, there are factors that reduce the number of changes that can affect the traits of the offspring. For example, the genetic code determines that certain nucleotide triplets produce the same amino acid. One will remember that there are twenty standard amino acids but sixty-four codons, of which three specify stop instructions. Arginine is produced from six different triplets, as are leucine and serine. On the other hand, methionine and tryptophan are produced from only one triplet respectively. Mutations that result in altered codons where the amino acids that those codons prescribe stay the same are referred to as synonymous mutations.

Another factor has a bearing on the number: Changes in amino acids can occur in areas that have no influence on the phenotype. Additionally, some amino acids have biochemical properties that are similar to other amino acids. A mutation that leads to an exchange of one of these protein constituents for its sister may have no significant impact on the physical characteristics of the organism.[108]

These limitations, however, are totally ineffectual in making a difference, given the staggering number of possible configurations. They cannot put a dent in the exponent of the aforesaid figure. Even if the quantity of potential sequences were reduced dramatically, eliminating trillions of trillions of trillions of trillions of trillions of trillions of arrays, the exponent would remain unchanged, and one still would need a set of books to write the value.

The link between specific chemical arrangements and the various physical attributes that organisms exhibit is unquestionably complex, with many factors that can come into play, and research in this field is ongoing. A mutation that involves a large number of bases could trigger a rather pronounced change in an organism's

---

[108] I am indebted to James Bradley, a cell biologist, for his guidance on these two issues. Bradley is a professor emeritus at Auburn University and former director of the Human Odyssey program there.

phenotype, a minor change, or no change at all. One cannot draw a hard correlation between the number of nucleotides that are reformed and some physical characteristic that may materialize as a result, as one sees from the two examples of dogs that Kingsley mentions. There are too many variables in mutations to pin down probabilities of particular outcomes in the progeny; and, beyond what is known about the size of genomes and the percentage of DNA that corresponds to coding sections, the numbers do not establish facts that can be used in extensive predictions. Still, what this exercise reveals is that, strictly from a mathematical standpoint, the set of nucleotides holding the code for proteins in an organism, even though the set may represent a relatively small percentage of the total DNA, yields an astonishingly great number of possible formations. Given so many possibilities, the probability that a random deviation would generate the next positive incremental pace along a genetic vector—perhaps the sole deviation that could generate it—is far too low to think that such a thing could happen even a single time, let alone repeatedly.

One cannot foresee whether a supposed step toward the building of a complex feature derives from a mutation that affects a few base pairs or thousands of them, nor can one foresee what type of mutation would produce it. It may be the result of simple substitutions, or it may be the product of more elaborate modifications. In any case, it is clear that a step that is part of a vectorial progression cannot stem from a mere reversal of a previous mutation that is related to that vector. If a chance alteration in the germ line of a creature causes, say, each of a number of base linkings to flip from A-T to G-C, and, in the reproductive stage of any affected immediate descendant, an offsetting incident causes a full reversion to A-T, then whatever change the original mutation might have wrought will be lost. Evolution must bring about new assemblages of base pairs in DNA without retrogression. The patterning process could not be that of cyclical reversion limited to the same group of nucleotides, for, in that event, a presumed nascent enhancement would be thwarted.

To complicate matters, mutations, as noted earlier, can involve more than the substitution of a few bases in place or the inversion of a block of them. They can include, for example, additions or subtractions of nucleotide chains of varying, indefinite lengths: a possibility that exacerbates the probability problem. Aside from shifts in the positions of existing base pairs in a DNA molecule, the potential for expansion and contraction of chromosomal sequences means that the number of possible changes in heredity is essentially incalculable. All that can be said for certain is that the possibilities are nearly inexhaustible, within the physical constraints of cellular structure. Reason thus dictates that the improbability of a mutation's being the precise one that is needed for the extension of a genetic vector to the next level is so extreme that no theory of gradual, ground-up development that ignores it could be a sensible candidate for acceptance.

The story does not end there, needless to say. Nature must repeat the process as many times as there are footfalls on the road to eyes or wings or other things. Dawkins suggests that the footfalls could number in the scores of millions.[109] Building biological systems through measured progression, all rooted in the random shuffling of DNA nucleotides—with or without nature's selective retention of the best results—stares squarely in the face of the hard fact of mathematical exponentiation.

ANOTHER GREAT ARRAY

One may argue that the odds can be improved by looking not at the number of base pairs in the entire genome in analyzing possible protein-coding configurations but the number of pairs in a single gene, which controls a distinct, heritable organismal characteristic. There are three problems with this approach, however. First, the randomness of change is not restricted to particular genes but affects the full set of chemical bases in the genome. A complex feature, by its very character, requires multiple morphological adjustments, bringing the activity of different genes into play. A random alteration in one gene could undercut the budding feature as easily as a random alteration in another could extend it. Simply paring down the base-pair set to a given gene will not work; the offspring organism is the physical expression of the whole collection.

---

[109] See Dawkins's remarks, quoted earlier in this chapter, regarding the number of steps that could lead to a human eye.

A second, allied problem is that, because convergence underlies complexity, development must proceed along several tracks, as explained earlier. Sight, for instance, requires more than photoreceptors and a proper structure to hold them in place. Neural pathways and the means to interpret the signals must be part of the package. The stereoscopic vision of advanced organisms entails two eyes, signals that cross in the optic chiasma, and the merging of the impulses in the visual cortex to form a single image with a three-dimensional representation. Accommodation (retaining focus with variations in distance) is possible because of a flexible lens in the eye and a ciliary muscle to control its shape. As for flight in birds, it is not enabled merely by the possession of wings. Asymmetric feathers rotate to decrease wind resistance on the upstroke and increase it on the downstroke to give thrust during ascent. Hollow bones reduce weight, allowing birds to soar, and a feathered tail provides stability. In both foregoing examples, an extended arterial network has to emerge to supply burgeoning tissues with oxygen and nutrients.

Each separate series of these associated changes constitutes, in effect, a genetic subvector within the overall development of the particular capability. Accordingly, the vector that matches trait $T\text{-}\beta$ in Figure 8.5 is replaced with multiple channels of concurrent, independent progression that ultimately must link to provide useful functionality. The chance that an operational faculty will surface thus shifts markedly lower as the improbability of the maturation of each component of the multidimensional trait comes into play, and what already carried an extreme level of unlikelihood recedes further. One cannot look at a feature in isolation, just as one cannot carve out a lone gene in determining potential configurations.

There is a final matter. Even if one limits the base-pair set to a single average-size gene, holding the instructions for synthesizing an average-size protein, the number of possible arrangements of these chemically joined units, spanning just the exons in that individual gene, exceeds the estimated quantity of elementary particles in the entire perceptible cosmos by hundreds of orders of magnitude.

Perhaps, though, one can look at probabilities in a slightly different way in hopes of putting the mutation-selection cycle in a more favorable light. It is the proteins that cells construct from amino acids that serve as the bricks and mortar of tissues. These tissues form the body of the organism, providing its phenotypic features and carrying out the various operations that are necessary to sustain life. With only twenty amino acids, does the set of proteins that genetic mutations can generate from them represent a more manageable array of possible outcomes from a mathematical perspective? If so, then it may be that one can focus on the realization of complex features on the basis of different proteins that arise through random mutation rather than on the basis of the different configurations of nucleotides that underlie those proteins. The breadth of possibilities, however, remains extreme.

> Since each of the 20 amino acids is chemically distinct and each can, in principle, occur at any position in a protein chain, there are . . . 20^n different possible polypeptide chains n amino acids long. For a typical protein length of about 300 amino acids, more than 10^{390} (20^{300}) different polypeptide chains could theoretically be made. This is such an enormous number that to produce just one molecule of each kind would require many more atoms than exist in the universe.[110]

Polypeptide chains fold to create structures in three-dimensional space. According to the authors of the passage that appears above, the great majority of the possible serial configurations of polypeptide chains are such that they can assume numerous distinct arrangements when folded. All these conformations are roughly equivalent in stability, and each exhibits properties that differ from those of the other shapes that the particular amino-acid string could take. This variability would prove to be pernicious to any cells that incorporate the structures. How is it possible then to arrive at a collection of proteins that assume unique, stable conformations that can be utilized in cellular construction? Virtually all cellular proteins exhibit this characteristic of a singular, unvarying geometry. The authors assert that, through time and testing, evolution whittled down the immense number of potential outcomes to a workable set. Consider their comments in the excerpt that follows:

---

[110] Alberts et al., *Molecular Biology*, 141.

> The answer lies in natural selection. A protein with an unpredictable variable structure and biochemical activity is unlikely to help the survival of a cell that contains it. Such proteins would therefore have been eliminated by natural selection through the *enormously long trial-and-error process* that underlies biological evolution.[111]

Presumably, nature employs this useable set, which came about through myriad random changes, to build complex features by means of encoded instructions that came about as well through myriad random changes. It is for the development of useful proteins as it is for the development of the advanced eye and feathered wing: Just keep trying . . . and trying . . . and trying. . . . Given enough protein-built animals that are reproducing and enough time, such biological systems for sight and flight are sure to turn up in the evolutionary tree eventually—maybe after a few billion years.

To put this trial-and-error process, alleged to be lengthy, in perspective, I submit the following portrayal. It is elaborate, but see pages 1027–28 (appendix) for an illustration. Imagine that a googol (10^{100}) cells—the number of atoms in the observable universe is only about 10^{80}—sprang into being on the earth with the planet's reputed formation: an event that, say the scientists, took place four billion six hundred million years ago. Imagine further that every one of those cells immediately began producing its own series of average-length polypeptide chains, and has continued to do so since the beginning, without interruption, at the rate of a googol chains every attosecond (one-quintillionth second). Finally, imagine that this production, not limited to the earth, has been occurring on a billion billion planets in the universe for four billion six hundred million years; and not on planets just in the universe that humans know but on a billion billion planets, for that same period of time, in each of a trillion trillion trillion total universes. Even if no two of the polypeptide chains were ever the same anywhere, the number of amino-acid strings that this process would have constructed would be less than one-googolth ($^1/_{googol}$) the number of different chains that it must assemble to deliver just one of each possible average-length sequence. It is far from over, however, because a polypeptide chain that is composed of

---

[111] Ibid. The emphasis is mine.

a few hundred amino acids is merely a run-of-the-mill product. The chains can contain thousands of amino acids; they usually are formed as conjoined subunits of individually folded chains. The resultant increase in the number of possible configurations is inestimable.

Ponder the mathematics. Why would one think that nature had not run out of time in such a mammoth trial-and-error undertaking? Even if nature had not been constrained to test every possibility, the astounding number of them would have overridden all attempts at progress. To erect a biological world atop a blind process where the possibilities are so vast is ambitious beyond reason. How remarkably efficacious natural selection must be, evolutionists are forced to hold, in finding stable building blocks of life with "chemical properties finely tuned to enable the protein to perform a particular catalytic or structural function in the cell."[112] Indeed, the exactitude is striking—

> Proteins are so precisely built that the change of even a few atoms in one amino acid can sometimes disrupt the structure of the whole molecule so severely that all function is lost.[113]

Not even Dawkins's luck can account for precision of this order among potentialities of such radical order.

The insurmountable hurdle that Dawkins faces is not mutation; it is advantageous gradation, issuing from mutation. That genetic profiles will change is likely, offering a measure of flexibility to life as a whole. That a complex feature will have come about by inching aimlessly down a specific course on its way to completion is not a workable premise. Flipping base pairs never will take Dawkins where he wants to go. It already has been established that most mutations are harmful in their effects. The probability of a change's yielding a benefit starts out low and, with the need for specificity, descends rapidly. Dawkins's theory must account for each successive step along a particular genetic vectorial pathway, once it is initiated; but, by any standards, the chance of reaching one of those steps is stunningly remote. Put forth as part of his naturalistic thesis, that treading is a probabilistic implausibility.

---

[112] Ibid., 141–42.
[113] Ibid., 142.

CHANGING THE PHENOTYPE IN A DIFFERENT WAY

Incremental progression toward complex features, such as eyes and wings, is not supported by observation of current phenomena; it is not supported by the fossil record; it is not supported by logical analysis. If evolution is to build complex things, then it appears that it must do so by way of sweeping morphological paces. Perhaps the most likely candidate for bringing about movement of that sort is gene regulation: a type of process control that provides for the expression or suppression of targeted genes—turning on or off particular ones. A primary method of exerting that control rests with a cell's employment of genetic switches. These switches consist of gene regulatory proteins and specific stretches of DNA with which the proteins interact. Epigenetics, a field of study within biology, investigates links between organisms' genes and the physical characteristics of organisms where those links lie outside the strict DNA sequences. Gene regulation is one such connection.

Regulation can take place in multiple places along a cell's protein-construction highway, although transcription is a common point in the DNA-to-RNA-to-polypeptide route. Therefore, not only is the cellular factory packaged with instructions and routines for assembling the microconstituents of tissues; it is programmed as well to exercise control over which genes are expressed, and when they are expressed, through the manipulation of these genetic devices. Often, this modifying activity occurs in response to conditions that are outside the cell in which the devices are set to perform. It is a multifaceted operation that brings with it its own group of wonders as the miniature machinery steers its own production. Regulation, in fact, opens the door to a new level of functional intricacy, with a corresponding level of improbability that chance explains it.

Even if random changes on the molecular plane, however, were to produce major variations in the features of offspring instead of, or in addition to, the diminutive alterations that Dawkins surmises, an evolutionist would have to take note of the contrary side of that two-edged blade. Giant steps bring with them a significant problem. As Dawkins states, creatures are unlikely to survive substantial hereditary changes in their physical structures.

> Organisms are extremely complicated and sensitively adjusted pieces of machinery. If you take a complicated piece of machinery, even one which is not working all that well, and make a very large, random alteration to its insides, the chance that you will improve it is very low indeed. . . . [A] very large random change has the effect of sampling the gigantic set of all possible arrangements. And the vast majority of all possible arrangements are wrong. . . .
>
>   . . . If you think of all possible ways of arranging the bits of an animal, almost all of them would turn out to be dead; more accurately they'd mostly never be born. Each species of animal and plant is an island of workability set in a vast sea of conceivable arrangements most of which would, if they ever came into existence, die.[114]

Scientists, such as Dawkins, must deal with a serious quandary. If an evolutionary model attributes the reputed emergence of biological complexity to a large-scale succession of gradual improvements, then, besides embracing what runs counter to paleontological discoveries, it faces crippling odds in the building of that complexity. If the model does not attribute the reputed arising of complexity to this phased development, then it has to accept the hypothesis that the advanced features of organisms appear all at once, more or less. Yet, too great a change is likely to kill the offspring of any organism, irrespective of species. If a change somehow happens to be the just-right, comprehensive phenotypic restructuring in which a fully functional sophisticated feature materializes in the progeny, then, in all probability, it would not destroy the creature that exhibits the feature; but the sudden coming to be of a complete and usable sophisticated apparatus faces odds that are as insuperable as those of incremental progression. It is a bound up the precipice to the crest of Mount Improbable—exactly what Dawkins was trying to avoid—and one is left wanting a believable naturalistic picture of what the biological world displays.

---

[114] Dawkins, *Mount Improbable*, 98–99.

A GAP IN KIND

Evolutionary theory maintains that the trial-and-error approach that nature adopts is quite effectual in finding ways to ensure the continuance of its products. The core issue to address in assessing the explicatory strength of the theory, however, is not the means but the end. It is not how life persists that is key here but the impetus to make it happen. If to explain, in a satisfactory manner, why evolution is in force is to turn to its twin foundational elements of survival and procreative success, then the perpetuation of life is the cornerstone of the doctrine—the factor that must account for the entire proceedings. It is that toward which the operation drives. Pointing to the workings of the pistons, valves, transmission, and so forth may convey how a car moves, but it does not capture why it moves. To communicate that aspect of its motion, one must introduce the idea of transportation. Although describing the biochemical workings of the cells, tissues, and organs may tell how a creature continues to live, it does not capture why the creature does so; and including adaptation in the biological chronicle of the earth may tell how life meets the challenges of survival, but it does not capture why it occurs. If a process can be explained adequately only in terms of the end toward which it presses, then, even though it may be achieved by means of the mechanistic activity of physical things, the process is, in fact, teleological—and fundamentally so.

Thus, a final problem with Dawkins's view surfaces, and it is an especially perplexing one. Evolution never speaks to the basic question: Why would any living thing attempt to survive, and why would nature be so compelled, as it were, to keep life going on the planet as a whole? The entire theory spins around a world of animate entities that are clinging to their existence as though some hidden, supreme directive were infused into them en masse. Exceptions are rare. Evolution, however, is totally impotent where a quest to preserve oneself is missing. The theory assumes as an axiom that there is an all-encompassing urge to live. Without that urge, the enterprise grinds rather discordantly to a halt; and, as if individual preservation were not sufficiently problematic, the concept of natural selection is not even sensible apart from nature's dogged fixation on this curious mission to sustain life overall through the honing of progeny. Where there is no continuance, there can be no evolution. It is the linchpin of the operation; yet, although it is built into the model as a necessary dynamic, it is not anchored to anything at all. The theory's central tenet is a central stumbling block.

One may protest that science is not concerned with such matters, only with discovering the physical happenings that underlie biological perpetuation. If, however, a naturalist is going to give a full description of life, one that excludes God, then he or she is obliged to make clear why this ubiquitous phenomenon is present. Reminiscent of Dawkins's reliance on the anthropic principle, one might say that life never would have persevered without that drive. Given that humans populate the earth, it must have been in place from the beginning, implanted in each new organism and each new species that arrived on the scene. Such an answer, of course, would be hopelessly inadequate. It explains nothing. *Why* is it there? A theorist has to get from a mindless chemical mass, propelled by pure physical forces, to a being's guarding its own existence—a guarding that is apparent in people, in fish, in bacteria, and even in plants. Try cornering a common American cockroach in a garage and watch its behavior. Instinctively, it will do whatever it takes to escape with its life: run, hide, scurry under a protective barrier, or, when all else fails, fly. One questions how chemicals can give rise to the autonomy of a living organism and then to the unremitting, pull-out-all-the-stops activity that allows it to stay alive, while its internal parts are striding together toward that same end. To cross the gap between an elementary molecule and behavior that aligns with self-preservation, and eventually propagation, in an entity in which such a molecule is embedded, even where that entity has no rational grasp—indeed, underscored by that lack—is to cross the gap between *strict mechanism* and *purpose*. It is the greatest rift of all in the evolutionists' story, for it is not one in probability but in kind, and it is reflected in the deep chasm between two opposing sets of beliefs about reality.

A convincing report of the advent of end-directed behavior is not forthcoming from the Darwinian-Dawkinsian camp. In whatever way hydrogen, oxygen, nitrogen, carbon, and phosphorous might combine to form a nucleotide chain, a material universe cannot bring about the chain's taking all necessary steps to ensure its own persistence or that of the cell-built house in which it resides. Why would nature care, so to speak, whether any living thing at all exists or continues to exist, and why would it be concerned whether anything at all reproduces and perpetuates life on the planet? Why would evolution's alleged trial-and-error routine, showcased as the path to prolongation, even be happening at all? In a world of unthinking biomachinery, what fuels the engine—the cause *in esse* of the whole enterprise, from proteins to progeny? A DNA string is just a mass of chemicals, yet it keeps trying . . . and trying . . . and trying. . . .

CHANCE ENCOUNTERED

Although I have taken liberties with the quotation, the title of this chapter evokes the memory of Neil Armstrong's famous remark as he made history with his momentous step onto the surface of the moon. It was indeed a giant leap for mankind, but the leap to living organisms on a barren planet, and ultimately to *Homo sapiens*, presents a greater challenge for those proffering an evolutionary narrative. Dawkins turns to probability to account for the beginning of life in the universe, drawing on the large number of planets in an attempt to show how it came to be on the earth. Probability is not kind to him, however. His use of the anthropic principle does not explain why life arose; and, in the end, his large-numbers argument turns against him in a mirror-image version at the other end of the scale, where the probabilities that emerge to confront Dawkins are striking in comparison. The genomes of living entities contain vast, ordered collections of nucleotides. The chance of success as evolution waits, as it were, for just the right mutation to produce just the right next pace in some protracted progressive series is too slight to support Dawkins's thesis. The supposed accumulation on which Dawkins relies—his easy trail up the back of the mountain—is very far from the reality that the mathematics reveals. Nature would have to overcome inconceivable odds to construct complex things in the piecemeal fashion that his theory requires. It is an obstacle that the theory cannot surmount. There can be no organic buildup, for biological forms never will make it to the next step in a conjectured

871

progression, not to mention numerous subsequent steps, all while retrograde mutation threatens to undo nature's promising handiwork. The complement of nitrogenous bases in the genes of organisms is so extreme, the random alterations in the respective configurations of their DNA so varied, that the possibilities challenge the mind.

Mutation is inevitable in the course of procreation cycles, but a methodical advancement toward complexity, rooted in mutation, which is what Dawkins's evolutionary rendering requires, is beyond the reach of reason. Every stride in that notional systematic advancement—past the initial one, at least—comes at too high a price to be logically palatable; and nature must overcome the corresponding radical odds not once but again and again, regardless of whether it keeps any improvement. The purported amassing of changes may offer what amounts to a pseudodirection. In actuality, however, the randomness of the process is much more likely to take the offspring down countless side paths than it is to foster the continued development of a characteristic that is the result of indiscriminate genetic shifting, despite the reputed seizing of it for future generations in light of its supposed benefit. Mutations are random, and random is random. Chance reconfiguring is totally insensitive to whatever the consequences of that reconfiguring may be, whether enhancement or degradation. Chance tends to *scatter* its effects; it does not tend to *focus* them, and one cannot count on natural selection to undertake the impossible task of focusing what chance scatters with such forcefulness. With these facts in view, it is difficult to accept the proposal that gradual buildup works as a way of explaining complexity. The giant leap to the summit fares better. At least, one does see a few leaps: the sudden appearance of a cow with an extra leg, for instance, useless as it was. What one does *not* see is a steady stream of tiny trait-shifts on the way to a better beast—as a case in point, incrementally extended winglets on a hypothetical protobird.

To provide an account of complexity, evolution needs to accrue changes that, when looked at from an end-to-end perspective, are steps in the right direction, even though those changes, when looked at individually, may be devoid of any merit. The theory needs to latch onto every bit of variation that comes down the pike, where such variation increases the resemblance to a complete prospective feature. Although indistinct movement toward enhancement may continue to surface from time to time, natural selection must concentrate on alterations that produce immediate rewards. It is not a process that is driven by an understanding of the future. It is blind, short-term, mechanistic, and agnostic. Its philosophy is carpe diem. One cannot count on a species to keep a minuscule change that happens to appear in a member organism, even if it increases the similarity to something that would be an aid in survival, were it to exist in a finished state. Indeed, such a formation may be a detriment to the organism in the immediate term rather than a benefit. In that event, according to the theory of evolution, it will be bred out of existence. If nature fails to retain changes, regardless of the reason, then one is faced with the staggering implausibility of the chance arising of biological sophistication, and intelligent design becomes the reasonable alternative. The premise of natural selection, in spite of Dawkins's assertion to the contrary, is hamstrung by a serious probability problem. The cumulative process on which Dawkins depends in the hope of mitigating the destructive effects of chance falls itself to the destructive effects of chance. The improbability that he is trying to avoid by means of the gentle slope of his metaphorical mountain looms like an avalanche waiting to sweep away the improvements that natural selection supposedly has secured.

In the face of the wondrous, molecular operations of the cellular protein-building factories, pointing with transparency to the embodiment of goal-directed procedures, many biologists—but not all of them, to be sure—have embraced the aimlessness of macroevolutionary theory. It is the correct picture of the history of life on the earth, so they believe, running the course from prebiotic chemicals to humans. If one removes God from the scene, then one removes the overarching rationale for life; and all that one has left as a way to account for its complexity is evolution, for no scientist wants to trust chance alone to handle it. From inside the bubble, so to speak, with only biological systems in view, evolution seems to make sense as a way of describing how what one sees in the natural world came to be. Certainly, there are many likenesses among the members of different species, from their DNA to their morphology, and resemblance is a key piece of evidence that biologists introduce to support an evolutionary position. Specific anatomically similar formations that appear in organisms suggest, in the judgment of many, common descent. They are said to be homologous structures—they are unlike analogous structures, which have parallel functions but unrelated development. A typical instance of homology, say the evolutionists, is the vertebrate forelimb. In every specimen, it contains the same two bones: the radius and the ulna. Those bones vary appreciably in size and play different roles in different vertebrate creatures, yet they are present in all of them; and a credible explanation for this fact, according to the interpretation, is a shared ancestry.

When one attempts to expand the similarity-explanation to cover elements that lie farther down the forelimbs of vertebrates, however, it begins to falter. The number of digits and the number of phalanges (individual bones in the digits) differ widely. Some examples are in order. Human hands, with few exceptions, contain five digits: four fingers and a thumb. There are three phalanges in each finger and two in the thumb. Various other vertebrates exhibit like digit counts for the anterior limbs, albeit the posterior limbs may be dissimilar. Certain species of whales, in contrast, have only four digits in the manus but as many as eight phalanges in a single digit. In a long-finned pilot whale (an oceanic dolphin), the phalanges in one digit can number a dozen or more. Birds have three digits in the anterior extensions. Horses have only one. If a theorist turns to the equal number of bones in the forelimbs as a case of homology, then the theorist must give a reason for digit-phalanx divergence among those same beasts, for it suggests otherwise. There are attempts to do so.[115] As is often true, though, biological evidence can serve to reinforce polarized viewpoints. In the effort to ground evolutionary explanations in the evidence, the import of the equal number of forelimb bones in vertebrates ought not to overshadow the import of the unequal number of bones that are positioned distally.

Furthermore, just raising the matter of homologous structures to bolster the argument for evolution creates problems; indeed, it may bring in evidence that stands against the theory.

> Worse yet for evolution, structures that appear
> homologous often develop under the control of genes

---

[115] See, for instance, Lisa Noelle Cooper et al., "Evolution of Hyperphalangy and Digit Reduction in the Cetacean Manus," *Anatomical Record* 290, no. 6 (2007): 654–72.

that are *not* homologous. In such cases, the thesis that similar structures developed from genes modified during evolutionary descent is precisely falsified.

In frogs, for example, the five digits on each limb grow out from buds on the embryonic paddle; in human embryos, the digits form as the tissue between them is resorbed. Here quite *different* gene-enzyme mechanisms produce *similar* (homologous) patterns. Structures in adult lobsters and crayfish are so similar (homologous) that the same lab instructions can be used for dissecting either, yet the crayfish egg develops directly into the adult form while the lobster egg reaches the homologous pattern through a free-swimming larval stage.[116]

Perhaps the lesson here is that structural likeness per se is not a reliable guarantor of a common source, of some mutual ancestor lying closer to the base of the biological tree. No one would say of the Virginia creeper (*Parthenocissus quinquefolia*) that it is related to humans by virtue of having fivefold palmately compound leaves—its five leaflets extend from the petiole like the digits from the palm of a hand. Resemblance in itself is insufficient to ensure a developmental link. Resemblance can be an *indication* of a shared starting place, but, on this basis, the creative action of an intelligent entity is no less rational an explanation of origination than evolution. When one steps outside the bubble to look at the numbers with which the theory of evolution must deal and the intricacy of the processes that underlie the mechanics of life, the breakdown becomes apparent. Given the extraordinary number of possible arrangements that nature faces as it tries haphazardly to find even suitable proteins to construct the cells of beasts, let alone their complex features, it is clear that geological time is not, as Dawkins claims, "awfully long."[117] On the contrary, it is decidedly short. By concentrating on the biology of evolutionary theory in an effort to explain the development of advanced features of organisms, Dawkins has run roughshod over the logic and the mathematics of it. His thesis no more avoids the ravages of improbability than the all-out spring to the crown of his make-believe mountain; and, in light of the major gaps that evolution must

---

[116] Parker, *Creation: Facts of Life*, 45–46.
[117] Dawkins, *Blind Watchmaker*, 109.

bridge, it is difficult to accept his position as anything worthy of adoption. Dawkins himself declares, "It is grindingly, creakingly, crashingly obvious that, if Darwinism were really a theory of chance, it couldn't work."[118] Yes, I agree—it could not work . . . and, when one delves into the central postulates that evolution sets forth, it becomes apparent that, as a way to account for biological complexity, a theory of chance is exactly what it is.

---

[118] Dawkins, *Mount Improbable*, 77.

PART III

THE TRIFOLD WAY OF THINGS

CHAPTER 9

FUTILITY AND EVIDENCE

[T]hey are zealous for God,
but their zeal is not based on knowledge.

—Rom. 10:2 NIV

The naiveté of children is portrayed in the wonderful ways in which they think. That innocence brings with it an unpretentiousness that is both delightful and on occasion surprising. Children take things at face value; to adults, their behavior can be amusing. When my eldest granddaughter was about five years old, my wife and I took her for a visit to my sister's home. The child and I were playing outdoors, but I wanted to go into the house for a moment. I instructed her to stay put and not to move until I returned. For her safety, it was important, I thought, for her to remain in the general area and not to wander farther into the yard unaccompanied. She agreed. Upon returning shortly afterward, I found that she was completely immobile, feet planted, body fixed to the same spot and in the same pose as when I left her. As though she were one of Rodin's sculptures, her limbs were frozen in position. She had followed my instructions precisely as she had understood them. In an adorable fashion, she literally had not moved.

It is regrettable that some children, for various reasons, are robbed of the joys and privileges of childhood, for it is a precious time of discovery and development, a time when character and values are being shaped. Consider the wisdom of Solomon, as his words in Proverbs reflect: "Train a child in the way he should go, and when he is old he will not turn from it."[1] For many, childhood is that carefree stage of life, enduring until the responsibilities that come with age weigh heavily on the bearer. Perhaps it is because of this fact that, in retrospect, it seems to be a season of blithe wonder, a

---

[1] Prov. 22:6 NIV.

period when the difficulties that are encountered are as fleeting as the butterflies that the little ones chase across the fields. It is not unexpected that many of the fondest memories are from that chapter of life. If one looks carefully, however, then one may see that the incidents of those days, unfolding in such a lighthearted way, sometimes mirror matters of a deeper sort, matters that a more mature mind sees in a different light. Reminiscent of a Lewis Carroll story, there are two levels of understanding awaiting those who engage in the pursuit. In Carroll's *Alice's Adventures in Wonderland*, for example, one discovers, as a child, an exciting tale about a little girl's journey to a strange place. As an adult, one finds the puzzles of the mathematician-author. Here is a playful passage from Carroll's writings:

> "Take some more tea," the March Hare said to Alice, very earnestly.
> "I've had nothing yet," Alice replied in an offended tone: "so I ca'n't take more."
> "You mean you ca'n't take *less*," said the Hatter: "it's very easy to take *more* than nothing."[2]

As I reflect on my own past, a particularly interesting occasion comes to mind. It was a family fishing trip. An avid fisherman, my father so enjoyed the sport that, during the early days of his career, he carried tackle in the trunk of his vehicle while traveling on business. Often, as he came upon farms in the countryside where there were ponds on the property, he stopped to ask permission to try his hand at a few casts. Typically, that permission was granted. I believe that the biggest bass that he ever landed came from a pond so small that he could cast a lure completely across it from the bank. A fishing expedition was bound to be fun for the whole family but especially so for my father.

The day of the outing arrived. Equipped with the appropriate gear, including cane poles for the children, the family set out on the mission, traveling to a group of ponds at a large dairy several miles

---

[2] Lewis Carroll, *Alice's Adventures in Wonderland* in *The Complete Works of Lewis Carroll* (New York: Vintage Books, 1976), 81. Carroll's *Through the Looking Glass* provides another example of a child's story with adult puzzles.

from our house. The excitement mounted as we unloaded the car and hiked across the pasture. At last, we reached the water, where the objects of the quest lay waiting beneath the surface. My father helped us to prepare, and we settled down for the afternoon. Although I do not remember with certainty, it must have been the first such trip for my sister, as her inexperience was soon to be revealed. With anxious expectancy, she focused her gaze on the drifting cork, the piece of the rig that would signal success. Suddenly, the cork submerged, and she knew that a fish had taken the bait. She snatched the unsuspecting creature from its home and held it over dry land. There the fish hung from the end of her line, suspended in midair, just out of her reach. Her gaze as fixed as the angle of the pole, my sister took a step toward it, but it moved ahead, for, when she moved, so did the pole. She took another step, but the fish advanced again. She took another, and then another. Each time, the fish eluded her. As if some bygone Zenonian paradox itself had stepped forward to capture the event, she kept reaching the point where the fish was but never the point where the fish came to be. Eventually, my sister was running at full speed across the meadow, hand outstretched toward the animal, as though the quickened pace somehow could bring it within her grasp. It was too late for any dignity-preserving explanation; my father latched onto the episode for the many reruns that it was destined to have at his whim, and her expense.

There is another element here, however, that underlies the innocence of this story. What it shows in a comical way is that activity is not productivity. Unless one's actions are based on principles that are sound, one's efforts are generally futile. Great effort is no guarantor of success, and acts that are not rooted in what is the case in reality are prone to miss the mark. Like my sister's pursuit of the fish, intellectual pursuits may be performed with zeal, but zeal that is not undergirded by truth is without merit. With this childhood account in mind, I turn now to the matter at hand.

LINK TO REALITY

This work began with an examination of the centuries-old quest to find enlightenment through reasoning. The Western philosophical enterprise arose in the region of Greece as a search for *archē* or *physis*, developing not long afterward into a consideration of deeper and more ponderous concerns. Queries surfaced regarding the nature of change and the conditions of identity, and philosophers began to wonder how knowledge could obtain in an uncertain world. Comprehending how one can know is valuable in its own right, but there is a practical side to knowing too. What people do is dependent on their beliefs, but the overall efficacy of what they do is dependent on beliefs that are grounded suitably. The greater the scope of the issue is and the greater the impact of a choice, the more important it is that one know. God, origin, mind, identity, morality, self, eternity, and purpose—questions about such things inspired diverse accounts in a variety of fields through the centuries in hopes of presenting satisfactory answers. Many who sought understanding, however, were still unsure after the accounts had come to light, and they were continuing to look. Without a portrayal of base reality that is firm enough to support the weight that the hard questions place on it, those questions remain unanswered. Ontology is the instrument that a philosopher employs in an effort to assemble a duly solid picture of existence. It is surely important that there be one, whichever road leads there, for what *is* determines much.

GRAMMAR, LOGIC, AND TRUTH

One will recall the comparison in chapter 1 between grammar and logic. As noted there, the basic units of linguistic communication are sentences. Composed of words and punctuation marks, sentences are carriers. They convey meaning. They express complete thoughts. To make sense—to be comprehensible—what a user of the language constructs must follow the rules of proper formation. Suppose, for example, that one writes the string of letters and figures that appear below:

Hrs /\] ps–ûr .. 5-0/\1 ⌐ apegol ♣ tqz wstl tn‡ ☼ p◊ nk ⌐ b ↔

This string of characters does not constitute a well-formed message in English. Its syntax violates the rules of sentence construction. Letters of the alphabet must be conjoined properly to generate words, and grammar specifies how words and permissible punctuation marks may be concatenated to create legitimate phrases, clauses, and sentences in the language. When the rules are violated, particularly if those violations are severe, no thought whatever may be expressed. What is produced is without meaning. As an instance of communication, the string that is shown above has failed entirely.

Suppose, however, that someone writes this string:

> There is a bright pink horse, which is more than five
> thousand feet in height, eating turquoise apples in the
> pasture and whistling a tune between bites.

This sentence exhibits a proper formation; it expresses a complete thought. One understands the notion that the sequence of characters conveys. It is just that what the sentence asserts is surely false. Indeed, upon reading it or hearing it spoken, one would think that the author of the assertion either has a strange sense of humor or is delusional. The sentence is meaningful, but it does not report the facts as they are. The value of grammar lies in its presentation of the structure whereby it is possible to communicate as one expresses one's thoughts through linguistic formations that are in accordance with syntactical rules. Grammar establishes the framework within which authors assemble the elements of language to transport ideas—through sentences, paragraphs, and ultimately works. Grammar, however, is not concerned with the truth of sentences that one builds in the language; rather, it is concerned with the form that those sentences take. Stating the truth is left to the writer or speaker who is using the rules of language. Two books may be written equally well, but one may be a factual, historical account, whereas the other may be a work of fiction.

Consider how literary compositions are paralleled by philosophical constructs. As grammar gives structure to language, so logic gives structure to arguments. Logic is the discipline that brings the necessary order to philosophical inquiry.[3] It tells one what counts as acceptable articulations of concepts, and it institutes the rules that govern engagement. The utility of logic lies in its presentation of the principles of proper inferential procedures and the formations that accompany them. It defines the ways in which expressed chains of rational thought can proceed legitimately and the ways in which they can go astray. Logic establishes the framework within which those who offer supposed truth assemble the elements of reasoning to set forth ideas—through assertions, arguments, and ultimately systems.

The letters and figures that represent statements in systems of formal, deductive logic work precisely because it is the configuration of deductive arguments that determines their validity. These statements may be any declarations whatever, and they may be true or false. Analogous to the case of grammar, formal, deductive logic, as its name implies, is not concerned directly with the truth of the assertions that make up the premises and conclusions of arguments; rather, it is concerned with the form that those arguments take. An example of deductive reasoning follows. A fully symbolized version, utilizing standard propositional logic elements, accompanies it, showing the form of the argument more clearly. One may wish to review the discussion of truth-functional operators in chapter 1.

Argument—Letters Are Variables Representing Sentences	*Fully Symbolized Version*
If not p, then q.	$-p \supset q$
If q, then not r.	$q \supset -r$
Not s if, and only if, r.	$-s \equiv r$
Not s, or both p and not p.	$-s \vee (p \cdot -p)$
Therefore, p.	$\therefore p$

If one gives p in the first premise of the argument the meaning 'It is a nice day', then p, both in the other premise in which p appears and in

---

[3] To be exact, I must note that logic orders philosophical inquiry in the analytic tradition. Certain nonanalytic movements have forgone the traditional rules of logic to their discredit. A few instances of this rule abandonment will come to light in the current chapter as well as in the next one.

the conclusion, must mean the same thing; but p could stand for any simple proposition that one cares to select, such as 'Lauren is a third-grade student' or 'Osmium is a metal' or 'This horse is pink'. Logic declares that this argument is valid—its structure ensures that it is so—regardless of what sentences are substituted for the variables. Once a variable is instantiated, however, the instantiation must be consistent throughout the argument. To use a different sentence requires using a different variable.[4]

The validity of a deductive argument is based on the condition that, *if* the premises are true, then the conclusion *must* be true. Where that condition holds, the argument is valid; its form makes it so. Informally, or materially, of course, logic does concern itself with the meaning of sentences apart from the structure of the reasoning that those sentences embody. For instance, as chapter 1 explained, the strength of an inductive argument is not established solely by virtue of its form; the content of the assertions that it presents matters. A logician must take into account what the premises state to determine how well they support the conclusion, which is set forth with varying levels of force or probability, not incontrovertible certainty.

In any event, expressing truth in the premises is the job of those who would use arguments to support a chosen position. As with the paragraphs of a book, the key arguments on which one builds a philosophical system may be formed well; but more is needed. The premises must be true. Philosophical constructs can be notably complex, employing numerous arguments that exhibit a range of configurations. Whether deductive or inductive, no argument that relies on false premises is acceptable, regardless of what the conclusion purports. So, not only must arguments exhibit a proper organization; they must put forward true claims as well. Otherwise,

---

[4] Changing the instantiation of a variable that represents a proposition within an argument undercuts the argument's legitimacy. Considered strictly in view of its form, the symbolized argument may exhibit a valid structure, but the change in meaning with instantiation creates an error. The concept is much the same with the meanings of terms in sentences. Richard Dawkins's case against the existence of God, for example, rests on changing the meaning of a word in midstream, as it were, resulting in the material fallacy of equivocation. Arguments must use terms to represent the same things throughout the chain of reasoning, or they are materially fallacious.

in the end, the system that the builder will have erected using them may be nothing more than a chimera. It is not a depiction of what is the case.

ONTOLOGY: A TELLING PARADIGM

With the comparison drawn between grammar and logic, one can see a parallel taking shape in the quest to understand the scope of reality. A novelist may write a clever and imaginative story. The author may develop believable characters, describe a plausible setting, and create an exciting plot that unfolds in a natural way. If the author has done the hard work of preparation and practices care in crafting the storyline, then the book will be internally consistent. No part of it will contradict another part. The entire narrative will cohere in such a way that there is nothing in the writing that precludes the possibility of its being an actual account; nevertheless, the book as a whole bears no resemblance to anything in reality, for it is a work of fiction. It is credible and engaging, and convincing in its presentation: a well-conceived effort. It is, however, simply not truthful. Like a jigsaw puzzle, the pieces fit together neatly to form a complete, interlaced whole, but the picture that is formed when the last puzzle piece is placed is that of a fairytale castle. Although the image appears to be a photograph of an actual palace, complete with moat and drawbridge, perched on a cliff, overlooking a placid sea, it is not a picture of anything at all. There is nothing in existence to which the picture corresponds.

SYSTEMS AND CONSISTENCY

Imagine that there are three boxes, each containing a number of marbles, which may be of as many as three different sizes, with the largest size equal to an inch in diameter. Inside each box is also a card, and on the card is written a pair of principles governing the box and the objects therein. Here are the imaginary boxes:

Box *A*—Items and Principles

Contents: One large, blue marble
         Two medium, yellow marbles
         Two small, red marbles

Principle 1: Red marbles are smaller than yellow ones.
Principle 2: There are always an equal number of yellow
  marbles and red ones.

Box *B*—Items and Principles

Contents: Three large, red marbles
         One medium, blue marble
         One small, yellow marble

Principle 1: Yellow marbles are smaller than red ones.
Principle 2: Red marbles always outnumber yellow ones.

Box *C*—Items and Principles

Contents: Eight large, yellow marbles
         Two large, red marbles

Principle 1: Each marble is either yellow or red.
Principle 2: Yellow marbles always outnumber red ones by
  a ratio of four to one.

Note that the following conditions apply to the set of boxes as it is detailed above:

    1. The contents of each box differ from the contents of each
       of the other boxes.
    2. The contents of each box are in accordance with both the
       principles that govern that box; that is to say, the
       principles are true, insofar as they apply to the contents
       of that box.
    3. No principle is true when it is applied to any box except
       its own.

Suppose now that there is a real box, not an imaginary one, and in it are marbles all of which are an inch in diameter. The contents of this box and the matching principles are shown below:

<u>Box *R*—Items and Principles</u>

Contents: Ten large, nonblue marbles.

Principle 1: All marbles are large.
Principle 2: There are no blue marbles.

In the case of each box, taken individually, the principles that apply to that box are not contradictory, nor are the contents of it out of compliance with the principles. In this sense, each is internally consistent; and there is no evidence that the principles are false, insofar as they apply to their respective boxes. Only one of the imaginary boxes, however, is compatible with what is real.

Like great literary works, theories offering depictions of reality may tell comprehensive and believable stories that follow suitable chains of reasoning. Supported by their logical analyses, purveyors of theories argue that things must be a certain way, but, given the inevitable disparities, the challenge is to know which story—if any—among conflicting ones is correct. What one can know is that at least some of them must be incorrect because, although they may not contradict themselves, they contradict each other. A theorist who erects a system atop false beliefs and false assumptions creates a construct that misses the mark, despite the fact that the theorist may follow accepted inferential rules in building it. The system may be internally consistent, demonstrably so, but fail to reflect the truth.

Some common ground is necessary, of course; otherwise, discourse is not possible. A group of athletes cannot play a game of football if one team's rule book has it that four attempts to progress ten yards are permitted before possession of the ball is lost, and the other team's rules state that three attempts to gain fifteen yards are allowed before the ball is surrendered. Axiomatic truths and rules of logic are the litmus paper of rational thought. They serve as tests of rightness. To dismiss them is to undermine the ability of persons to reason together in dialogue, and human discourse is reduced to sophistry. If one moves away from analytic systems to nonanalytic ones, then even basic and seemingly irrefutable axioms—ones to which no well-versed analytic philosopher would object—sometimes are cast aside. Little effort is needed to find instances of logic-disregard in the literature. Consider first this obviously true assertion:

Every thing is what it is, and not another thing.[5]

Now, contrast it with the following one:

[B]eing is what it is not, and is not what it is.[6]

Again, weigh it against this next proposition:

Everyone is the other, and no one is himself.[7]

Many of the assumptions in the arguments of complex meta-physical systems, however, are not self-evident; therefore, even if the rules are followed, or seem to be followed, there is no guarantee that the developments as a whole reflect what is actually the case. It is not enough that the scaffolding in which postulations are generated within a theory is solid; what those postulations set forth must not be in error. Rules of proper formation can ensure that the *structure* of a system is right, in that its arguments are assembled well, but ensuring that the *content* of the system is right requires demonstrating that the premises of those arguments are true. Logic can point to the chinks in a system's armor with effectiveness, but underwriting the system's veracity is not always easy, as, although logic readily can determine the *consistency* of a theoretical construct, determining its *truth* demands compelling reasoning. Showing that a given system is laden with logical error lends weight nonetheless to a contrary proposal. It

---

[5] Joseph Butler, "Fifteen Sermons Preached at the Rolls Chapel," in *British Moralists, 1650–1800*, ed. D. D. Raphael, vol. 1, *Hobbes–Gay* (Oxford: Oxford University Press, 1969), 335. Butler's work appeared first in 1726; the quotation here is from the 4th ed., dated 1749.

[6] Jean-Paul Sartre, *Being and Nothingness*, trans. Hazel E. Barnes (New York: Philosophical Library, 1956), 68.

[7] Martin Heidegger, *Being and Time*, trans. John Macquarrie and Edward Robinson, 7th ed. (New York: Harper and Row, Publishers, 1962), 165. Heidegger's work was published initially in German in 1927.

is an important point: In philosophy, a formidable offensive against an opposing model is often an effectual initial defense of one's own.

When one turns to theories about what makes up reality—what things exist—three overarching, competing systems step forward to claim representation of the facts. They are

> System I—material, and only material, things exist.
> System II—immaterial, and only immaterial, things exist.
> System III—both material and immaterial things exist.

What distinguishes each of these theoretical models from the others is its ontological classification of substance. A nonstrict materialist may grant references to nonphysical properties but invariably holds that they have no reality apart from the physical things that exhibit them. A strict materialist or physicalist denies such existents. Both subscribe to a materialistic view of one form or the other, which maintains that all substantive entities fall completely within the sphere of corporeality. There is no immaterial substance. There are only physical things as they are expressed in various ways. If the first abovementioned system is upheld, then nothing that is incorporeal and substantive exists anywhere.[8]

By the laws of logic, it is true of necessity that (1) material and immaterial (that is to say, not material) exhaust the possibilities for existent things, and (2) none of the aforesaid systems is consistent with either of the other two. Given that something does exist, which is clearly the case, it follows that one, and only one, of the models is correct. Exactly *one* corresponds to reality as a general account.

An illustration may be beneficial. Note the similarities between Figure 9.1, appearing below, and Figure 4.1 in chapter 4, where I depicted competing geometries.

---

[8] One will recall P. F. Strawson's allowance of a postperson consciousness, but his view is that of materialism nevertheless. The individual entity—the particular—is the person, and the person is material. Anything else is just a fragment, broken off the original entity, and talk of it as though it were something on its own, never linked to any physical entity, is nonsensical in his view.

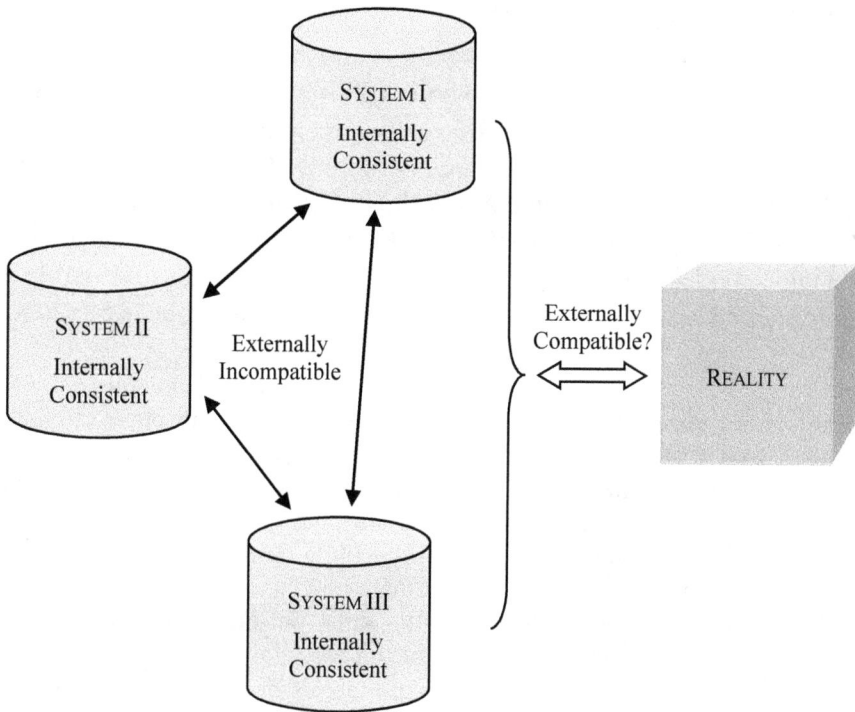

Figure 9.1

In this drawing, each of the three systems is built in such a way that it comprises a coherent set of propositions, some of which are assumed axioms, some of which are submitted premises, and some of which are conclusions of arguments that are based on chains of satisfactory reasoning. Although each system may be internally consistent because of adherence to logical laws, each one is incompatible with the others. It is critical that the postulations of a theory of ontology correspond to reality. If an ontological construct falls short of describing things as they are in actuality, then it fails in its essential purpose. Despite the zeal and toil of the one who built it, however great those things may be, it is the product of utter futility.

891

AN ABERRANT ASYMMETRY

Two authors take a surprisingly different approach to the matter of what is real, asking, "[D]o we really have reason to believe that an objective reality exists?"[9] Physicists Stephen Hawking and Leonard Mlodinow argue that people are not justified in doing so, challenging the exclusivity of an external existence and accordingly that there is a single model that depicts it. They adopt the position that reality is not independent of how humans perceive it. Consider these remarks:

> [W]e shall adopt an approach that we call model-dependent realism. It is based on the idea that our brains interpret the input from our sensory organs by making a model of the world. When such a model is successful at explaining events, we tend to attribute to it, and to the elements and concepts that constitute it, the quality of reality or absolute truth. But there may be different ways in which one could model the same physical situation, with each employing different fundamental elements and concepts. If two such physical theories or models accurately depict the same events, *one cannot be said to be more real than the other*; rather, we are free to use whichever model is most convenient.[10]

> [A] well-constructed model *creates a reality* of its own.[11]

Albeit the authors say that one model is no more real than the other, they apparently mean, by their statement, that what one model posits as real is no more correct than what the other model posits. At any rate, two distinct issues are evident. They are, in order of the authors' focus, (1) how humans think that things are and (2) how things are. Hawking and Mlodinow seem to be embracing the notion that these two issues are actually one and the same: The line between the *doxastic-epistemic* implications of a given workable representation

---

[9] Stephen Hawking and Leonard Mlodinow, *The Grand Design* (New York: Bantam Books, 2010), 34.

[10] Ibid., 7. The emphasis is mine.

[11] Ibid., 172. The emphasis is mine.

and the *ontic* implications of it fades to yield an amorphous whole. I will call this view the strong view of model-dependence—the notion that reality is not fixed but, on the contrary, is determined by the practicality of observations and predictions within a given conceptual framework. If a model's postulations are consonant with what people perceive, and its forecasts align with what takes place in the future, as revealed by the senses, then, so goes the thinking, the model is right. If the model is lacking in these respects, then it is not right. Its being right in this strong sense, however, is its *generating* reality, not its *reflecting* it: What humans accept determines what is real; what is real does not determine what they accept. It is an aberrant reversal of the logical, asymmetric relation that obtains between what exists and how a system portrays it. If one follows the chain of thought, then ultimately observation is not a method of discovery at all. There is nothing in objective reality that is locked down, nothing that is awaiting unearthing other than people's own perceptions.

In such a case then, two obviously conflicting descriptions are both correct, even though they are inconsistent, provided that each explains adequately what people experience by means of their senses. The world is both flat and not flat, as long as no one sails either over the edge or around the globe. When the Apostle Paul and Barnabas put out to sea at Attalia to return to Antioch at the close of Paul's initial missionary journey during the first century, both portrayals could account for their arriving at their destination. Let t_1–t_2 represent the time of the voyage. Model-dependent realism has it that, during the time period, at minimum, of t_1 to t_2, one model of the shape of the earth is, or was, as accurate in describing reality as the other. If one comes to adopt the view, based on subsequent observations, that the world is round, then one discards the flat-world theory; but it ostensibly told the individual what reality was like all along, despite the fact that it made claims that were in direct opposition to the counterpart theory. Given these two propositions:

p_1. The world is flat (core tenet of theory 1).
p_2. The world is not flat (core tenet of theory 2).

it seems that one of the following claims is true, where the symbol '>' means 'is later than':

q_1. Both propositions p_1 and p_2 are true during time t_1–t_2.

q_2. Proposition p_1 is uniquely true during time t_1–t_2 but becomes false at time t_3, where $t_3 > t_2$.

Assertion q_1 defies fundamental logical rules and cannot be accepted as true in any system. It is a contradiction and is to be rejected outright because it is not possible for a proposition and its negation to be true simultaneously. What does one say about q_2? If it is true, then what changes, so that p_1 becomes false at t_3: the human conception of the world or the world itself? If it is the conception of the world that changes, then the door is opened to a form of relativism that is too extreme to allow. As people's notions of existent things shift, the essence of what is real changes. It is not just that people see things differently because things are actually different; rather, things are actually different because people see them differently. There was thus no galaxy-replete cosmos until the twentieth century when Edwin Hubble first saw Andromeda for what it was; it suddenly sprang into being as the idea of the universe changed—billions of stars in a flash. What one is after is the truth. If reality is dependent strictly on how it is perceived or, more to the point, that it is perceived at all, then one rides dangerously close to Protagoras's doctrine that man is the measure of all things. If such is the case, then one ought to stop the search for truth because it is no more than what one thinks that it is, and no more than what one thinks that it is at that particular moment. If, on the other hand, it is the world itself that changes, so that p_1 becomes false at t_3, then the supposition that reality is dependent on a model fails because reality is independent of a depiction of it.

Moving the conceptual into the realm of contingent physicality is an illicit ontological step—one that is found in Richard Dawkins's attempt to explain the advent of life. The thesis that is under review compels one to hold the position that q_1, although self-contradictory, is true nonetheless, as observations at time t_1–t_2 can support either planetary shape; and, with Protagorean dogma in play, all opinions, even if inconsistent, are true. It is not a rational stance. Indeed, the incongruousness of the Hawking-Mlodinow theory is amplified as the theory turns against itself. If a certain model aligns with what is observed and predicted, and the model presents the view that there is an independent reality and that it *alone* accounts for observations and substantiated predictions, then, in light of the alignment, the model is correct: What it maintains agrees with perceptual experience. If it is correct, however, then it is not true that reality depends on how it is portrayed, for, in accordance with the model, reality is independent, which contradicts the position that it is model-dependent. Thus, if what the theory of model-dependence declares is true, then what the theory declares is false. Logic has been hurled into the trash bin.

It appears that the authors' conjecture arises out of quantum physics. In the world of quanta, things behave like both material bits and waves, a duality that produces strange consequences. Probability reigns here, and it is not possible to identify the exact condition of a microphysical particle until it is observed. Measurement somehow seems to select a single state from among the possible ones. A generally recognized description of this phenomenon, albeit not one that is universally recognized, is that the particle exists simultaneously in more than one of its allowed states in what is referred to as superposition. When observation takes place, this cloud of possibilities suddenly gives way to a single definite actuality as a result of the interaction of the microphysical particle with the macrophysical world of the observer and the measuring device. Precisely what happens to effect the change is not understood in depth—assuming that the superposition postulate accurately characterizes the affair—introducing perhaps a contemporary version of the ancient Grecian puzzle: How can one come out of many? There are different attempts to explain it. According to a common rendering of the Copenhagen interpretation (a reference to the work of Niels Bohr and his associates in Denmark in the early twentieth century), there is a collapse of the wave function: a mathematical representation of the amplitude of the wave corresponding to a specific particle; the square of the value correlates proportionally with the probability, per volumetric unit, of finding the object in a given space. Measurement brings the collapse, but whether the change is traced to the awareness of the observer who performs the delimiting act or the physical delimiting itself remains an open issue for those who deem the depiction to be viable. In an extreme rendering of the Copenhagen interpretation, suggested by Werner Heisenberg, the author of the uncertainty principle, it is not meaningful to ask about the details of objects in the subatomic realm prior to measurement, indicating a sort of conditional being. Perhaps this thinking underlies the Hawking-Mlodinow theory.

To show the counterintuitiveness of the putative collapse of the wave function and its fixing the state of an object, the physicist Erwin Schrödinger proposed a famous thought experiment. A live cat is placed in a steel box along with a small amount of radioactive material. A device that detects the decay of even a single atom of the substance is housed in the box. Connected to the device is a relay that engages if the detector senses radioactivity, causing a small hammer to shatter a flask of poison and kill the cat. There is a 50 percent chance that an atom of the substance will undergo nuclear degeneration within an hour. Given the hypothesis of superposition, the cat is both alive and dead until someone opens the box and looks inside, at which point the two possibilities dissolve into one actuality. Reason, of course, dictates that the cat cannot be in both states at once, and peering inside the container only permits one to know in which state the cat is in actuality. The experiment illustrates the fact that one cannot relegate reality, at least in the macrophysical world, to such nebulosity. The question remains whether doing so in the mircophysical world is right. The science at hand suggests that there is a firm distinction between the two worlds, which seems to be arbitrary; and one may wonder why everyday physical objects would not be governed by the same principles that govern the physical bits that compose them. Some believe that they are so governed.

Despite its oddities, the Copenhagen construal continues to enjoy a popular standing among particle physicists. Some scientists, however, have offered opposing interpretations. In the 1950s, Hugh Everett III proposed perhaps the most noted of the divergent views, claiming that there is no collapse at all of the wave function. What happens is that the many possible states of an object continue as actual states in other, parallel universes, each entirely detached from the one of presently shared human experience. In a manner of speaking, the cosmos splits as the measurement occurs, carrying the observer along with it down the single path in which the value of the measurement is realized. At every point where two or more states are possible for any object, the universe branches when observation latches onto a single value from among the possibilities. One of the branches corresponds to the observed state of the object.

Others embrace this many-worlds view, as it is called, believing that it accurately portrays how things are. Max Tegmark, a physicist and cosmologist, maintains that the universe of physical reality as humans know it is a mathematical structure, and only one of many. He supports the concept of an ultimate ensemble theory,

> where not only worlds corresponding to say different sets of initial data or different physical constants are considered equally real, but also worlds ruled by altogether different equations. The only postulate in this theory is that *all structures that exist mathematically exist also physically.*[12]

If it can be described by mathematics, then it exists, so goes the thinking. This approach brings to mind the Pythagoreans, who take numbers to be the ultimate reality, such that, in their metaphysical account, all physical things truly are made of them. In an effort to turn the possible into the actual, Tegmark is turning the abstract into the concrete—what one sees in those philosophers of old. The significance of mathematics lies in depicting reality, not creating it. To assert that an existing, physical universe is erected atop a mere description of it, mathematical or otherwise, seems to be exceedingly ambitious. Other scientists believe nonetheless that a plethora of universes have been spawned, with different laws and fundamental constants; and these units either continued as structures in parallel with the one cosmos that humans know or, what is more likely, collapsed before taking root.

The stance is not limited to science. The philosopher David Lewis argues that every possible world is an actual world. If one can specify conditions through a logically consistent set of propositions, then one can describe a state of affairs that obtains in reality.

> Are there other worlds that are other ways? I say there are. I advocate a thesis of plurality of worlds, or *modal realism*, which holds that our world is but one among many.

---

[12] Max Tegmark, "Is 'the Theory of Everything' Merely the Ultimate Ensemble Theory?" *Annals of Physics*, 270, no. 1 (1998): 1. The emphasis is mine.

> The worlds are many and varied. . . . There are so
> many other worlds, in fact, that absolutely *every* way
> that a world could possibly be is a way that some world
> is.[13]

Logic is the basis for determining allowable states of affairs, not, as Lewis seems to think, the progenitor of their realization. Logic tells one what *can* be the case among contingencies, not that all of them *are* the case. What is possible cannot be made to equal what is.

Apart from these difficulties, as an interpretation of quantum phenomena, the cost of the many-worlds theory is high. This theory generates actual universes without number from potential ones in violation of the law of parsimony. It establishes worlds merely by observing things in the process of measuring them. Perhaps most disturbing of all, it replicates the observer, such that a discrete version of the person who determines the outcome through measurement in a perceptual event arises in parallel universes, and that version splits again with a subsequent perception. A person ceases to be a single entity and is transformed into a multitude of different entities who come to exist in separate worlds. The nonsensicality of this scenario undermines personhood and the uniqueness of the individual; moreover, it defies logical rules. The incident-generated beings cannot be numerically the same as the original, even though they are offshoots of the original, or else nonidentical entities—these generated ones with different histories—would be identical, given that two things that are identical to the same thing must be identical to each other; and that state of affairs—the identity of nonidentical things—is a patent impossibility. They had to have been one and the same person at some juncture nevertheless because they share a set of perspective-specific experiences prior to the initial split, and persons who have such authentic experiences in common must be the same person.

Embracing the strong view of a model-dependent reality may be a natural outcome of (1) understanding the role that observation plays in particle physics and (2) recognizing the uncertainty that is inherent in a subatomic system. One must take care, though, in extending the probability distributions and the position-momentum

---

[13] David Lewis, *On the Plurality of Worlds* (Oxford: Basil Blackwell, 1986), 2.

hinge—key factors that characterize the quantum realm—to models of reality en bloc, where one interprets the conditional lack of fixedness as a sort of fuzzy existence. Albeit surely bizarre, there is no contradiction in saying, as a common interpretation of quantum theory does say, that a particle is in multiple states simultaneously until observed. There *is* a contradiction, however, in saying that a particle both is, and is not, in multiple states simultaneously, or even in a given state simultaneously, just as there *is* a contradiction in saying that reality both is, and is not, in accordance with a particular model's depiction of it, whether that model is one of quantum mechanics or some other field. If two competing conceptions are inconsistent, then both cannot be right. A person cannot move from declaring what is supposedly true *within a model* to declaring that such truth holds *across models* that express contradictory principles. Reality at the base level may be marked by probability and uncertainty in keeping with particle physics, but, if reality is that way, then reality is *that* way; and its being that way is independent of anyone's conception of it. It is just the way that it is, and any theory that denies that axiom would be incorrect. Hawking and Mlodinow, it seems, think that model-dependence solves—or perhaps avoids— the question of existence, and its application is not limited to the microphysical realm. If one leaves the room, they say, then the table may continue to exist while one is away, or it may cease to exist, reappearing in the same place when one returns. One cannot know. Both options account for the observation of the table in the given location, although the former alternative is in a better position to explain a change in the table in the interim, if it occurs, because it is a simpler version. According to the authors, it is all that one can ask.

Assuredly, it is not all that one can ask. It may be that the table appears in front of a subject on each account of reality, the former one reminiscent of John Locke, the latter one of David Hume. It cannot be true, however, that the table, in whatever way one chooses to define it, both does, and does not, exist when one leaves the room. Either Locke is right in his theory of material reality, or he is not right. Either the table continues to be in the room, or it ceases to be there. There is no place for both hypotheses to be in force. Although both may be in agreement with what is observed, only one can correspond to what actually occurs. An account fits the facts of

899

existence, or it does not fit them. Let p_1 represent 'The table remained in the room when no one was looking' and p_2 represent p_1's negation. Suppose that each statement can be subsumed under a different model that may explain observed events. Given that an outright contradiction cannot stand in any circumstances, one of the two propositions—either p_1 or p_2—is false; and, in this case, one of the models is a false proposal. Thus, the theory of model-dependence cannot stand. What people may not know limits *them*; it does not limit *reality* or the *truth of statements about it*. Knowing what reality is like and what reality is like are two different things. A person cannot leap from epistemic restrictions to ontic ones, and such a leap seems to be precisely what these two physicists are attempting to do.

Turning to the notion of origin, one sees an incongruity surface once more. Hawking and Mlodinow maintain, as chapter 6 noted, that the universe exists because of its own spontaneous creation, but that view is just one portrayal of reality. Another view is that God created it. Hawking and Mlodinow cannot declare that the universe created itself without going against their own theory of model-dependent realism. The best that they can do is to say that a conceptual model in which the universe is self-created is not in conflict with what an observer perceives in the universe—but, of course, neither is the competing model of intelligent design. It is not possible that the universe both is, and is not, the product of an act of creation by God. By the law of excluded middle in logic, a proposition asserting that one or the other of the two conditions holds must be true, but, by the law of noncontradiction in logic, a proposition asserting that both of them hold cannot be true. It appears that the two physicists are dismissing not only the need for God in their account but the existence of God too, yet it is impossible both that God exists and that God does not exist. If two models are divided on this point, then it is logically necessary that one of them is a false account. No theory should be so loose with reality, let alone with logic.

Finally, if one endorses the view of Hawking and Mlodinow, then one must accept the unfortunate consequence that no matter what theory of physical reality one presents, solipsism trumps it.[14]

---

[14] See the discussion of Descartes's epistemology in chap. 2 for an explanation of solipsism.

Under a model-dependent view of existence, solipsism is the ultimate stance. If one alleges that things are in actuality just as a conceptualization determines them to be, then, up against any competing account, solipsism always wins. There is no unearthing, no thought, no experience, and no deduction that can prove it to be a false description of reality. Why look for indications of the truth out there? All that one will encounter is oneself. A person and states of that person constitute the sum of what the individual ever can know and ultimately, according to the strict view of solipsism, the sum of what exists. Reality is how one thinks that it is because it cannot be otherwise. One reaches the stagnant dead end of scientific and philosophical inquiry. It is a terrible place to be. Model-dependent realism, at least in the strong sense, is a specious, self-defeating view. Of all the theories about reality, it epitomizes the futile.

A more reasonable position, although it is not one that the two physicists take, is to allow a different view of modeling. With this approach, one would say that there is a reality that is independent of people's notions of it, and people discover the accuracy of their notions as they continue to investigate and learn. Humans may not *know* invariably how things are in the external world, but that world is the way that it is, and its being that way does not require the presence of humans. Physical reality—not in the sense here of objects as aggregate singularities, which is an altogether different issue, but in the sense of the matter and energy that make up the universe and the configurations thereof in space-time—is not the outgrowth of their conceptions, which, in turn, are based on their perceptions. If one assumes otherwise, then it cannot be the case that four ounces of meteoroid material traveling at thousands of feet per second struck and killed Larry on his hiking adventure to a remote wilderness: He did not see it coming, and his body, which tumbled into a ravine, was covered by a rockslide—never to be found. One may not know whether statements (or systems of statements) about the makeup of the physical world and how it is arranged are true or false, but whether the statements *are* true or false is not up to people.

Discovery has genuine merit. One forms beliefs, hypotheses, and theories on the foundation of observation. A person has confidence in what his or her senses reveal, or seem to reveal, and adopts a belief in a relationship between perceptions and the matter in space-time that accounts for them, between awareness of things and a physical reality of which those things are part. Humans build conceptual models of how they judge the universe to operate. They may find at some juncture that certain earlier beliefs were wrong, but they *can* find that they were wrong, at least. Something out there *makes* them wrong. Statements about the basis of the cosmos are true if, and only if, they report what is the case, and it is the senses that tell one when it is so, even if the senses mislead on occasion. Truth is given in the correspondence of what is declared to what does obtain.

It is not possible for reality to be at odds with itself. Any pair of properly formed propositions about actual conditions cannot be contradictory if both propositions are true, for they reflect the facts of an objective existence. An ontological theory, like other theories, has to be internally consistent if it is to be acceptable, but that property is not enough to guarantee that the theory is correct, as Figure 9.1 illustrates. If it is correct, however, then it *must* be consistent in its declarations about reality—it must be coherent in this respect—not because the theory's author avoided contradictions in its creation but because, in describing reality, it is describing how things are. Unlike many theories, consistency in an ontological construct is essentially derivative. An ontological theory that conveys the truth thus sees two cascading requirements, underscored by the discussion to this point:

1. Any proposition that is formulated within the theory and that purports to report what is real must be such that what it reports *corresponds* to what is the case in reality.
2. Any proposition that is formulated within the theory and is such that what it reports corresponds to what is the case in reality must be *consistent* with any other proposition that is formulated within the theory and that purports to report what is real.

Of necessity, what is actual must be possible, and it is not possible for incompatible conditions to hold simultaneously in reality. Hence, if a pair of statements alleges to describe actual conditions, where the individual conditions that the statements describe are in conflict, then it is not possible for both statements to be true. In an ontological system, consistency is a *consequence* of correspondence because reality fixes the truth of propositions about it. In the final analysis, *the laws of logic hold sway over the laws of physics*, even in the strange world of quanta, and one cannot set aside rational principles in any rendition of how physical reality must be.

REALMS OF BEING

Reflecting on the history of human inquiry brings to light two spheres that the curious have sought to explore. It is probably evident from the discourse in this work thus far that an interleaving of matters pertaining to each of them respectively suggests an insep- arability in a thoroughgoing investigation of knowledge. As the topics in the various sections in each chapter determined the tenor, elements of one sphere or the other became primary in order and in focus. It is a pattern that, to a degree, will reappear in coming pages.

The first realm—the ground level, as it were—is that of the physical, where matter and energy form the framework in which exploration takes place, and the senses are the means by which people conduct it. Human comprehension of the material universe has expanded dramatically through the centuries, and a broad body of information concerning physical phenomena has become avail- able. Scientists have come to understand much about the very large as well as the very small—about galactic structures that populate the cosmos and about the diminutive bits of material that make up the things that people see. Science has revealed that the sun is one of two hundred billion or more stars in the Milky Way and that this galaxy spins among countless others in a cosmos of astounding proportions. As fascinating as the enormity of the universe is, the minuteness within that same universe is no less wondrous. Miniature systems of tiny particles buzzing about other tiny particles form the atomic lattice, and some researchers believe now that things that are con- siderably tinier than these microbits may underlie it all.

Science is a mature discipline, incorporating a proven set of practices that, taken together, constitute a structured methodology for acquiring knowledge about physical things. Science depends on examination and experimentation to make advances, and the senses are the collective basis on which the discipline operates: People come to hold beliefs about the world by perceiving it. Although the senses sometimes do deceive, a matter that I have discussed at length, reliance on them is still the standard of the day. People must rely on them; the practicality that allows routine life to carry on demands as much. No one would dive into a bed at night if he or she were unsure that what appears to be a bed is really a bed—or even exists at all. A person would perish from starvation if that person were continually suspicious of the visual and olfactory information that he or she receives and hence refuses to eat. If one did not have confidence that the senses convey trustworthy data, at least most of the time, then, reminiscent of my granddaughter's stance in the yard, one would be as immobile as a Rodinian statue, frozen in a perpetual state of uncertainty, paralyzed by radical doubt.

Such is just not the case. Humans reach out to a material world that they take to be real, and they learn things about it through perception. *In the realm of the physical, perception is the mode of discovery, and it is perception that grounds true beliefs, so that knowledge is possible.* Sometimes, a single glance is sufficient both to engender a belief and to warrant its truth. Sometimes, substantiation through additional inspection is required as other perceptual events converge on it to ensure the integrity of the sensory data. In perceiving, one seldom is mistaken. The chance of error is generally quite low and, in some cases, so low that being wrong is a probabilistic implausibility: The chance is outside the range of rational acknowledgment. In the end, there is a bedrock of verifiability undergirding beliefs about the existence of a material universe and about facts that pertain to it, all resting on the ability to look and see. Ongoing discoveries confirm the truth. Recognition of the fact that matter exists and that it is possible to know about it is universal, or nearly so, discounting the philosophy of George Berkeley; and it is difficult to imagine that any serious person would think that Berkeley is correct: There is an abundance of evidence to the contrary. Samuel Johnson's refutation of immaterialism does have a rather right ring to it.[15] If it is reasonable to eliminate total immateriality—System II

---

[15] Johnson's terse, albeit not incontrovertibly compelling, denial is in chap. 2.

above—as an accurate representation of existence, then the challenge that remains is to determine how extensive is the material. Is it all that there is, or is there something more? Science can point to the matter that everyone—in Western culture, at least—takes to be real, Berkeley aside, but showing that matter is all that *is* real is a wholly different affair. For a discovery of that sort, one must look elsewhere.

None of this discussion is to imply, of course, that reason does not play a crucial part in empirical investigation. On the contrary, it is what binds sensory input to produce a meaningfully interwoven, convincing picture of how the universe is arrayed. It is what lets one predict future occurrences of phenomena, employing laws that are discovered inductively. Beliefs about physical reality arise in perception as the cognitive faculty molds the raw data of sense. Beliefs can be represented as the acceptance of propositions that report ostensible facts, as I covered in chapter 4. There, I discussed the mental grid that becomes for each individual a backdrop against which new information is displayed, compared or contrasted, and judged. Where that information dovetails with an individual's set of previously permitted propositions, it is incorporated. Where it fails to do so, it is rejected. Where it does so in part or, at minimum, does not conflict with the set, it is held in suspension until further information is available. Reason thus works in conjunction with the web of beliefs to screen appearances, helping to shape what people receive as true based on what they sense. That which appears to a subject, and so appears to the subject to reflect what is the case, is superimposed on a background of prior beliefs. Using reason, a subject balances what he or she sees, hears, and touches against what those established beliefs report. It is because of this fact that one is not deceived by the circus act in which an entertainer seems to saw a woman in half, or taken in by the appearance of water some distance down the road on a particularly hot day, realizing that it is merely an illusion that is caused by schlieren. Logical judgment orders the set of beliefs that one holds, including those about material being, and one takes his or her perceptions to be accurate reflections of reality when reason tells the perceiver that there are adequate grounds to do so. To understand the world, an individual relies on what the senses provide, confirmed at times by sensory corroboration. Reason therefore serves to frame a believable picture of the physical cosmos from the perceptual data, but perception is what provides the ultimate link that positions one to know an external existence.

Unlike scientific endeavors, however, nonphysical pursuits—those in the second of the two spheres of exploration—depend little, if at all, on the input of the senses. Often, they take the form of metaphysical inquiries. Relying on thought, they arrive at what must be the case based on conclusions that a theorist draws from proposed premises. Metaphysical findings, like those of other philosophical disciplines, are essentially mental discoveries; they are not the products of perception but of inference. Observation is not an activity that one can bring into play here. No experiment will demonstrate that *archē* is the Boundless or that Platonic forms are real. *In the realm of the mental, logical inference is the mode of discovery, and it is logical inference that grounds true beliefs, so that knowledge is possible.* This state of affairs does increase the challenge of determining the authenticity of metaphysical advances. If one is to uncover anything in the philosophical enterprise, then one must reason his or her way to it; one must use logic. Two persons who disagree about the contents of an opaque box can lift the lid and peer inside to see what it contains. Two persons who disagree about the existence of incorporeal things cannot settle the matter simply by taking a peek. In contrast to scientific hypotheses, which ultimately rest on publicly observable phenomena for their proof or disproof, metaphysical theses are not founded—not more than nominally, at least—on things that one can detect with the senses. Where the premises of supporting arguments are established axioms or rule-based derivations therefrom, there is probably no contestation; but with divergence from the self-evident comes opportunity for dissent. The complexity of metaphysical systems and their nontestable conceptions create avenues for objections to be raised, and the assertions of those systems remain untethered to anything that can anchor their purported truth except the cogency of the reasoning with which they are presented. It is the weight of the inferential constructions that prevents their being set adrift. Truth must correlate with reality, to be sure, but, where observation is precluded, reason rules the court.[16]

---

[16] As a faculty that operates in the cognitive realm, reason, of course, is not limited to scientific and philosophical inquiry. Systems of mathematics, for example, set forth proofs of theorems based on permissible axioms and adopted rules. One can

The diagram that I give below illustrates how an individual perceives material reality and how the rational faculty of the perceiving subject operates in concert with the subject's grid of beliefs to confirm the authenticity of the perceptions. One generally must infer what, if anything, lies beyond that reality, however— whether there are immaterial things and, if so, then whether the mind of the subject is among them. It is the business of ontology to determine the scope of what exists. Metaphysical systems cannot bring one in perceptual contact with what they hold out as incorporeal existents: substantive, nonphysical elements that are constituents of the real. Unlike sensation, in which the sensory link connects persons to the world that they sense, ontology offers no link other than reason itself. Perhaps it is because of this apparent limitation that the scientists Hawking and Mlodinow claim that "philosophy is dead."[17] They believe that physics has supplanted it as the means by which truth is uncovered.

---

expand his or her understanding within the framework of a given system using these demonstrations, as high-school geometry students learn early in their courses of study. What one comes to hold as true is found along a path of inference. Unlike metaphysics, however, geometry is not concerned with the ontological status of mathematical elements. A geometrician does not seek to prove that lines and planes are existent objects in some world of incorporeal things or that angles themselves are real. A scholar of metaphysics, on the other hand, focuses on matters of this sort. In attempting to use logic to prove or disprove the *existence* of such things, however, the philosopher introduces a rift that is not easy to bridge. One can prove unequivocally in Euclidean geometry that the sum of the interior angles of a triangle equals precisely half the sum of the interior angles of a square, but it is another matter to prove unequivocally that there are actual immaterial triangles corresponding to the drawings on one's paper or that the Platonic form Triangularity is real.

[17] Hawking and Mlodinow, *Grand Design*, 5.

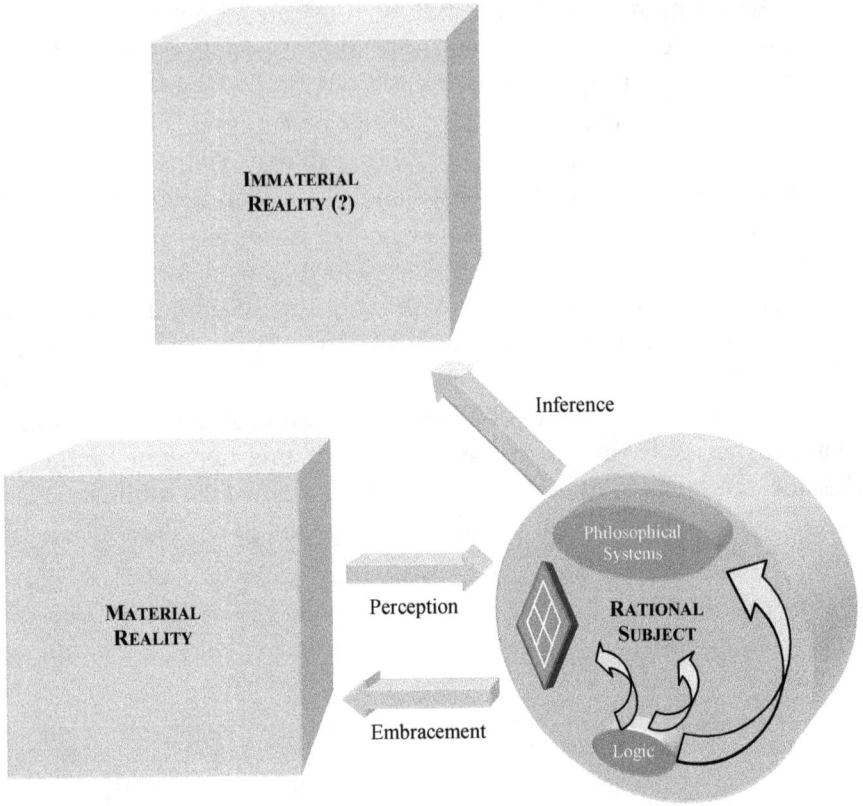

Figure 9.2

Accordingly, one way to navigate around the problem is to collapse reality into the material, an approach that took center stage in the discussion of physical-basis theories in previous chapters. Doing so would mean that science is all that one would need in the pursuit of knowledge because the material is the domain of scientific inquiry. Consider this statement by Hawking:

> We are used to the idea that events are caused by earlier events, which in turn are caused by still earlier events. There is a chain of causality stretching back into the past. But suppose this chain has a beginning.

Suppose there was a first event. What caused it? This was not a question that many scientists wanted to address. They tried to avoid it, either by claiming . . . that the universe didn't have a beginning or by maintaining that the origin of the universe did not lie within the realm of science but belonged to metaphysics or religion. In my opinion, this is not a position any true scientist should take. . . . *We must try to understand the beginning of the universe on the basis of science. It may be a task beyond our powers, but we should at least make the attempt.*[18]

Science is not inherently at odds with either metaphysics or religion. Indeed, all ought to perform complementary roles in a singular, cohesive reality. Must one limit all things at all costs to the physical—a practice that Hawking appears to endorse—and, if so, then why? Is such an approach acceptable in any authentic search for ontological truth?

Take a moment to contemplate a short puzzle that I created. It illustrates an issue that lies at the heart of this discussion.

SQUARES

A square is a figure with exactly four sides
Of equal lines: Their lengths must coincide.
To change one line is to change three more,
Lest there be no square as there was before.
And all interior angles must be ninety degrees;
They can be no less, nor can they be increased.
But suppose that the lines number a dozen instead,
Each the same length and to others connected—
The length of a line determined by juncture:
A point in common with another.
How many squares would it be possible to make,
Adhering to Euclidean geometry's constraints?

---

[18] Stephen Hawking, *The Universe in a Nutshell* (New York: Bantam Books, 2001), 79.

Give it some thought. Turn the page for a clue, if needed.

. . .

What is the puzzle asking? It begins with certain conditions that are required for there to be a square, which is a two-dimensional figure of four lines of equal length forming angles that are also equal. The puzzle proceeds next to increase the number of lines from four to a dozen and specifies how the length of a line is set: It terminates where it intersects another line. Thus,

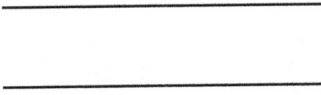

are two lines, but

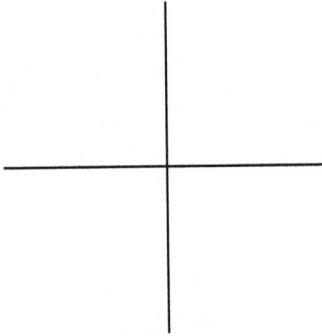

are four because a line ends where it joins another. If there are twelve lines of equal length, then how many squares can one construct? Try it now before continuing.

. . .

One who made five squares—a large figure and four smaller ones—did well. See Figure 9.3.

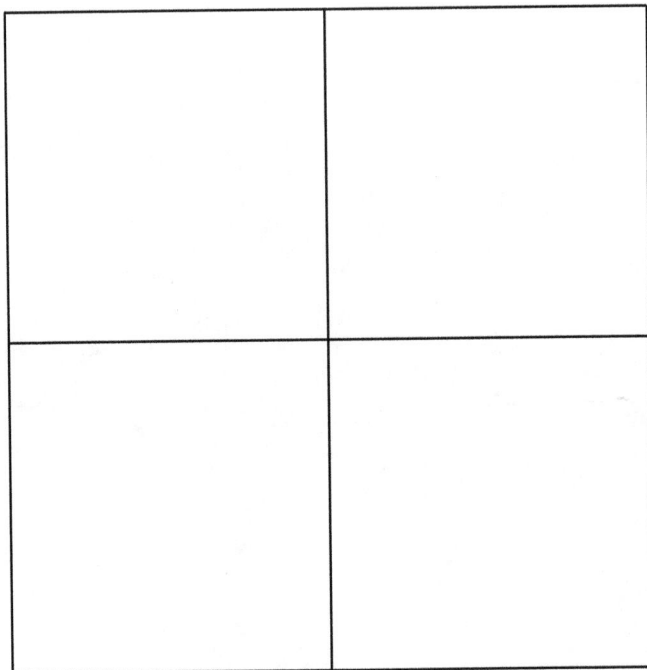

Figure 9.3

On the other hand, there is a better way to solve the puzzle. Ponder it before turning to the end of this chapter for the solution.

. . .

Limiting the scope of the exercise to a single plane produces a solution that falls short of the mark. It is only when one removes the dimensional boundary that the right answer becomes manifest. It is only when one steps back to take an unhindered perspective that the last square comes into view.

Strict science is a discipline that is confined to the exploration of physical phenomena. It is what science is. It cannot venture beyond the scope of its operations to see what may be out there. It never can embrace immateriality. By the very nature of the enterprise, science does not accept the existence of nonphysical things and therefore cannot accept anything as evidence that they are real. It does not understand even what incorporeal existents might be, let alone how to go forth in search of them. The incorporeal is preeliminated without qualification. All answers to all questions must be framed in physical terms. Even if some phenomenon cannot be explained by referring to physical laws, science assumes that there is such an explanation.

I recall a conversation that I had recently with a learned man—a terminal degree in his field. When I noted that there are questions that science cannot answer, his response was, "Yet." What he did not see is that it is not a matter of *time*; it is a matter of *kind*. Some questions are simply not amenable to the kind of answers that scientific endeavors can provide. Science limits by design the objects of its discovery.

The astronomer Carl Sagan once said with apparent confidence, "The Cosmos is all that is or ever was or ever will be."[19] On what basis could he establish his claim? Given that scientific inquiry draws a box around matter and energy in space-time and directs one to look no further, if one finds that the stock answers to his or her questions about reality are suspect and wishes to explore a bit more deeply, then all that one receives from science is a blank stare. In the hands of a number of its practitioners, the discipline is restrained from acknowledging its own limitations. It cannot pursue the incorporeal; as a consequence, science either ignores the question of its existence or denies its existence, supposing that all things are of the physical sort. Ignoring incorporeality is one thing; denying it is quite another. The former approach need not be at odds with scientific methodology, though it may be shortsighted in some cases; the latter

---

[19] Carl Sagan, *Cosmos* (New York: Random House, 1980), 4.

approach, however, is *not scientific at all* but *philosophical*. If an individual maintains that the laws that govern the natural world are universally applicable and yet confined to that world, then the individual cannot stand on those laws to make existential assertions about things that are not part of the natural realm. One author states appropriately,

> No doubt natural science assumes certain preconditions, some of which appear to be essential to its practice. But none of them is derived *from* science; they are philosophical presuppositions that make science possible.[20]

Contrary to the claim by Hawking and Mlodinow, philosophy is not dead; it is alive and well. It is just that philosophy can offer only an intellectual peek at the extent of reality. The irony is that science occupies the weaker position in the quest. It is boxed in by its own modus operandi. Thus, it is not surprising that some of its disciples take on a philosophical role. When science turns to philosophy, however, and brings with it an assemblage of preconceived notions, it surely can go awry. Should one be so bound to physicality when searching for what is real? It is the truth here, after all, that is important. Why then, in the quest for it, would everything not be on the table?

One looks to metaphysics for convincing answers about reality because the self-imposed limits of the scientific enterprise effectively preclude them, but the lack of compatibility among philosophical systems introduces its own set of challenges. In chapter 5, I argued that immateriality is not to be rejected out of hand; the deficiencies of a materialistic view of existence cannot be ignored. Maybe there is something that can bolster the thesis that reality is more than material. Sensory corroboration adds weight to the truth of what one comes to believe in perception; but what besides the indissoluble rules of logic can substantiate assertions that a system puts forward in support of a broad-based reality?

---

[20] Francis J. Beckwith, *Law, Darwinism, and Public Education* (Lanham, MD: Rowman and Littlefield Publishers, 2003), 94.

ON ACCOUNT OF THE EVIDENCE

Probably more than any other thing in life, people want to know the truth about spiritual matters. Does the creative God exist, or are humans merely the result of a godless fluke that ends in the capacity to wonder whether the creative God exists? Is Jesus who He claims to be, and did He perform the many miracles that the Gospels ascribe to Him? Is there an eternal existence awaiting people who depart, or is the end in sight?

Finding God is not the result of a natural perceptual event. An immaterial being cannot be discerned by means of the senses in the normal way that the things in the physical universe can be discerned. Visual discernment of God is possible through the incarnation—the embodiment of God in Jesus Christ—but one cannot perceive the incorporeal Deity in exactly the same manner as he or she sees the rocks and rivers that populate a material world. Reports of sensory encounters with the resurrected Christ do occur, from the Apostle Paul on the Damascus Road in the first century to persons in current times.[21] Few people, though, come to a realization of spiritual things in that way, it seems; observation is not the path that leads there.

> Once, having been asked by the Pharisees when the kingdom of God would come, Jesus replied, "The kingdom of God does not come with your careful observation, nor will people say, 'Here it is,' or 'There it is,' because the kingdom of God is within you."[22]

Nevertheless, people consistently turn to their sensory faculties to tell them what is real. It is characteristic of who humans are. The Scriptures report that even a disciple of Jesus would not believe in Jesus's resurrection without the confirmation that his eyes and his hands yielded. Having walked with his Lord and having seen the miracles that He performed, Thomas still looked for proof from his senses that Jesus was alive.

---

[21] A powerful example of such an experience appears in Richard E. Eby, *Jesus Told Me to . . . Tell Them I Am Coming* (Old Tappan, NJ: Fleming H. Revell Co., 1980). Several, unlike Paul, encountered the resurrected Lord before He ascended.
[22] Luke 17:20–21 NIV.

> But he [Thomas] said to them, *"Unless I see* the
> nail marks in his hands *and put my finger* where the nails
> were, *and put my hand* into his side, *I will not believe
> it."*
>
> A week later his disciples were in the house again,
> and Thomas was with them. Though the doors were
> locked, Jesus came and stood among them and said,
> "Peace be with you!" Then he said to Thomas, "Put your
> finger here; see my hands. Reach out your hand and put
> it into my side. Stop doubting and believe."
>
> Thomas said to him, "My Lord and my God!"
>
> Then Jesus told him, "Because you have *seen* me,
> you have believed."[23]

Thomas would not believe until he observed Jesus firsthand, reaching for perception to tell him the truth about reality. Without the physical evidence, he could not accept the account of the other disciples that they had seen Jesus alive after his death and burial. One may reject the Scriptures, but a key point that the passage makes is enlightening nonetheless.

Finding God is not a matter of mere inference either, however. Logic has the power to assess arguments, and it can persuade theorists who elect to take hold of it of the strength of cases for the existence of God or cases against it; but other arguments and counterarguments are wont to emerge from the wings to cross the stage. If one expects the way to God to be forged solely by deduction, then disappointment most likely awaits one. For this reason, I believe that those who have built their lives on the study of philosophy struggle perhaps most of all with the acceptance of spiritual things.

> But the natural man does not receive the things of the
> Spirit of God, for they are foolishness to him; nor can he
> know *them*, because they are spiritually discerned.[24]

What the rational mind has not uncovered by sight it labors to uncover by reason. The Bible makes it clear that God is a spiritual being, and spiritual entities are not bound by physicality. Is finding

---

[23] John 20:25–29 NIV. The emphases are mine.
[24] 1 Cor. 2:14 NKJV.

God then a matter of accepting as real that which one has not seen or heard oneself, yet trusting the accounts of individuals who report what they have seen and heard? Does one turn to evidence—whether it comes by means of eyewitness testimony or in some other way—to undergird the truth of propositions where direct observation is not available and where logic by itself leaves room for doubt? No living person beheld the arrival of the Mayflower off the coast of Massachusetts in 1620, but no one disbelieves that it happened. It is an accepted fact because it is part of the historical record that is grounded in such beholding. Among the passengers on the ship was William Bradford, a leader within the group who was the principal governor of the fledgling Plymouth Colony. Although he was not the first governor, Bradford served in that role for an overall period of about thirty years. His manuscript testifies to the authenticity of the voyage, the arrival, and the eventual landing. Here is an excerpt from his journal concerning the Pilgrims' entrance into the harbor:

> But to omit other things (that I may be brief) after long beating at sea they fell with that land which is called Cape Cod; the which being made and certainly known to be it, they were not a little joyful. . . .
>
> Being thus arrived in good harbor, and brought safe to land, they fell upon their knees and blessed the God of Heaven who had brought them over the vast and furious ocean, and delivered them from all the perils and miseries thereof, again to set their feet on the firm and stable earth, their proper element.[25]

Bradford gives the date of November 11 for their coming to rest in what presently is known as Provincetown Harbor. He proceeds to record in his manuscript the text of the Mayflower Compact, the signing of which took place aboard the ship, giving the date again at the close of the brief document.

> In witness whereof we have hereunder subscribed our names at Cape Cod, the 11th of November, in the year of

---

[25] William Bradford, *Of Plymouth Plantation: 1620–1647*, a new edition by Samuel Eliot Morison (New York: Alfred A. Knopf, 1979), 59–61.

the reign of our Sovereign Lord King James, of England,
France and Ireland the eighteenth, and of Scotland the
fifty-fourth. Anno Domini 1620.[26]

One has come to see that knowledge is justified true belief.
Proper evidence is one way to provide justificatory support. If there
is an immaterial, spiritual realm, then what is the role that evidence
plays in taking one to its truths? An examination of evidence, and
how it can point to that which one cannot see, is in order.

EVIDENTIAL STRUCTURE

What exactly *is* evidence? An appropriate way to think of it,
aligning with the analysis in chapter 4, is as information in the form
of propositions that support the truth of other propositions. Everyone
believes, for instance, that dinosaurs once roamed the planet: Paleontologists uncover fossilized skeletons of certain configurations, and a
reasonable explanation for the existence of the skeletons is that they
belonged to creatures of the past. The evidence for the proposition

Triceratops existed.

is thus the proposition

Skeletons of configuration type *C* exist.

In turn, people believe that the skeletons exist because what they see
and touch they believe to be real, and further what they see and
touch, in this instance, they believe to be the bones of bygone beasts.
No other explanation for those perceptions seems to fit. Given what
the senses relate and what reason informs observers is the case,
people postulate that living organisms, to which the skeletons correspond, must have existed years ago. No one who is on the earth in

---

[26] Ibid., 76. The date by a modern, Gregorian calendar is November 21, 1620. The
general landing of the Pilgrims at what traditionally is known as Plymouth Rock
occurred in December of that year.

the present age has seen a living example of *Triceratops*, but people hold that these animals walked the planet at some prior time. In this sense then, evidence becomes a set of one or more premises of an argument—premises here that are grounded in observation—such that the set supports the argument's conclusion.

In a trial, a defense attorney may declare that the defendant could not have been at the crime scene: A witness in another city saw him entering a pharmacy minutes before the time of the incident, and he could not have traveled the sixty miles to arrive at the burglarized store in so short a time. The prosecution, on the other hand, argues that the detectives found a business card there, one belonging to the defendant. Tire prints matching his vehicle were in the dirt at the side of the parking lot adjoining the building where the shop is located. His fingerprints were on the recovered stolen property. Moreover, the supposed eyewitness could not have identified the defendant, as it was a dark night and raining, and the witness who claims to have seen the defendant was peering through a cracked windshield in his vehicle more than a hundred feet away. As evidence, there are propositions that each side offers in support of its position; the case for the defense, at this point, may be built on those that yield this argument:

> The defendant, Robert, was in another, distant city at the time of the store burglary, as the eyewitness testified.
> If a person is in one city at a given time, then that person cannot be in another, distant city at approximately the same time.
> Therefore, the defendant was not at the scene of the crime when the burglary took place.
> No person can commit a (hands-on) burglary unless that person is at the scene of the crime at the time that the crime occurs.
> Therefore, the defendant could not have committed the burglary.

The accused either was, or was not, in a distant city at the time of the crime, indicated by the store alarm. There is no other possibility. The attorney presents, as evidence that his client is innocent, the premise that the man was elsewhere when the crime occurred. The argument exhibits a well-constructed form, taking liberties with its representation, but whether it is sound, of course, depends on the truth of the premises, and the first premise of the argument is key. Some of the jurors may be convinced of its truth; others may reject it as false because of the contrary evidence that the prosecution presents; still others may be unsure. There are then two aspects of evidence: an *objective* component that is presented to an individual and the *subjective* perspective of the individual himself or herself—the person's grid of beliefs—on which the former is superimposed. René Descartes's empty-apple-basket approach to the quest for knowledge is inapplicable; a person starts with a set of propositions that he or she has assimilated, and the evidence that the person accepts is that which dovetails with it.

When a person turns to questions the answers to which form the foundation underlying his or her thinking about reality, the individual translates the ostensible facts, arising from various sources, in terms of beliefs that he or she already possesses, just as the person does in other instances, such as the abovementioned one. The belief-set that comes into play, however, is all-encompassing in its scope. It is not about the spatiotemporal particulars of certain events that may pertain to a given trial. It is a totally inclusive view of what things— and what kinds of things—are real. The belief-set marks out, for the individual, a worldview. In spite of what Hawking and Mlodinow may assert, reality is what it is. A worldview represents an accurate interpretation of reality or an inaccurate one, depending on whether the pertinent beliefs that frame it align with what is actually the case; and the order of the aligning is not reversible.

Whenever people examine the evidence for some position, it is therefore important for them to realize that they have perspectives that shape what they think of its reputed veracity. Rational minds can come to diverse opinions in evaluating the same new propositions because sets of other propositions that individuals accept may offer support or present a refutation. In the case of Richard Dawkins, one finds a scientist who, not unexpectedly, adopts a strict view that the only reality is a material one. He rejects the existence of anything that lies outside the physical, alleging that his position is based on an assessment of the evidence; and there is no evidence, he surmises, for a contrary view. If a person does not agree with him, so he thinks, then it is because that person has embraced a position as axiomatic based on faith, with no reasoning to uphold it. His attack on theism rests, in part, on his charge that those who believe in God, accepting intelligent design, refuse to search out the truth when things cannot be explained. They encourage others to end the pursuit: "[J]ust give up and say God did it."[27] They do not base their belief-sets on appropriate grounds: that of evidence and inference. Consider his remarks:

> Fundamentalists know they are right because they have read the truth in a holy book and they know, in advance, that nothing will budge them from their belief. The truth of the holy book is an axiom, not the end product of a process of reasoning. The book is true, and if the evidence seems to contradict it, it is the evidence that must be thrown out, not the book. By contrast, what *I, as a scientist, believe* (for example, evolution) I believe not because of reading a holy book but *because I have studied the evidence*. It really is a very different matter. Books about evolution are believed not because they are holy. They are believed because they present overwhelming quantities of mutually buttressed evidence. In principle, any reader can go and check that evidence. When a science book is wrong, somebody eventually discovers the mistake and it is corrected in subsequent books. That conspicuously doesn't happen with holy books.[28]

With a rather broad-brushed, superficial pronouncement, Dawkins writes as though evidence and what he calls a "holy book" are incompatible. Blanket dismissals, needless to say, seldom represent proper examination or adherence to statistical rules. He continues,

> But my belief in evolution is not fundamentalism, and it is not faith, because I know what it would take to change my mind, and I would gladly do so if the necessary evidence were forthcoming.[29]

---

[27] Richard Dawkins, *The God Delusion* (Boston: Houghton Mifflin Co., 2006), 132.
[28] Ibid., 282. The emphases are mine.
[29] Ibid., 283.

What exactly would count as mind-changing substantiation of a contrary position? Dawkins claims to have studied the evidence, but what were the objects of the inquiry? Has he limited his inspection prematurely? One has seen that the boundaries of science lie in the physical universe, to which the laws of science apply. As it pertains to the point at hand, it seems that Dawkins's stating that he is a scientist is tantamount to his asserting that his investigation is, or was, restricted to the corporeal, and his stating that he, a scientist, has studied the evidence is tantamount to his asserting that the evidence is, or was, restricted to corporeal things. To preclude the nonphysical is to block a priori all biblical reports that point to incorporeal things, along with any other information that may support those reports. Consequently, what Dawkins claims to believe, as is the case with some others in the trade, is not a matter of *science* but *philosophy*. Drawing a hard line around the search cuts short the exploration, and ironically that approach is simply to accept *as axiomatic* the all-inclusiveness of corporeality. At one time, the following proposition was accepted as fact by the general European population: All swans are white. The people knew of no swans anywhere of a different color. Subsequently, black swans were discovered in Australia. The geographically contained examination led to a false belief. Preexclusion without substantial grounds is an injudicious path to travel.

On rare occasion, the weight of one's discoveries may overturn his or her Cartesian apple basket. Things that the person had come to accept as true come to be challenged. One is forced to reevaluate entrenched beliefs in light of a bundle of reputed facts that are convincingly coherent but which stand in opposition to the grid of beliefs that he or she possesses. Return to the aforesaid incident of the burglary. Suppose that three other witnesses come forward to say that the suspect was with them at a birthday party for a friend that evening, far from the city where the theft took place. "We know that Robert was there," they state, and then proceed to explain on what basis they know. They saw him and the uniquely shaped scar on his left cheek; spoke with him, hearing him talk in his familiar, raspy voice; and shook his hand, with its missing index finger. Each attests to knowing Robert and working with him for more than ten years. In the course of the evening, Robert described in considerable detail the project that he was undertaking in his garage: rebuilding a treasured

1963 Chevrolet Corvette split-window coupe. The witnesses had been to his house a few times and had seen the vehicle, they report. Undeniably, it was Robert at the party that night.

Could the witnesses in Robert's defense be wrong? It is highly improbable; the evidence that he was in a location other than that of the crime on the night that it was committed is too weighty to dismiss. As I argued at length in chapter 4, corroboration of perceptions diminishes the probability of error to the point of practically eliminating the possibility of it. With regard to the support for the defense, there are multiple witnesses, testifying to the same fact, and multiple sensory faculties of each witness that confirm it. That someone can be deceived on some particular occasion in no way bars one's knowing, and, when the accounts and the perceptions converge as they do here, one certainly does know. Reports of events, offered by reliable eyewitnesses who observe the events from a suitable position, outweigh circumstantial evidence. As a rule, what a person sees, hears, and touches takes precedence as evidence over what a person conjectures based on circumstances, where the two are in conflict.

As it turns out, Robert, on the day prior to the criminal intrusion, was fleeing from a dog that chased him across the parking lot near the place where the break-in occurred. He had stopped his car at the edge of the lot, leaving tire prints in some soft dirt that had washed there from a recent storm. After Robert exited his vehicle, the dog advanced, and Robert ran into the closest business to escape the aggressive animal. His intention, though, was to go next door to the hardware store to purchase a set of socket wrenches for work on his Corvette. While he was in the first establishment, waiting for the threatening beast to leave, he handled a valuable item, considering it as a gift for his wife—their anniversary was approaching. The contact left his fingerprints. Robert decided to buy the object and removed his wallet from his pocket to get a credit card, but he changed his mind, as he thought that he might find something that she would like better. It was then that his business card fell from his wallet. Finally, on the night of the burglary, Robert stopped at a pharmacy, just before arriving at the party, to purchase aspirin for a headache; there, the first eyewitness spotted him.

CANONICAL CONSIDERATIONS

The Bible describes numerous historical events and presents narratives about numerous individuals. It documents wonders throughout and many prophecies that have been fulfilled. Miraculous occurrences are almost too abundant to list. From the Old Testament to the New, the record is there to see, if one chooses to examine it. Eyewitnesses set forth accounts in detail. As noted above, eyewitness reports carry considerable weight, even more so where there is convergence of reports by multiple witnesses and convergence of multiple perceptions of a given witness—especially if those perceptions come by means of different sensory faculties. In the following passage, the Apostle John gives his testimony concerning what his, and others', ears, eyes, and hands have told them:

> That which was from the beginning, which we have heard, which we have seen with our eyes, which we have looked at and our hands have touched—this we proclaim concerning the Word of life. The life appeared; we have seen it and testify to it, and we proclaim to you the eternal life, which was with the Father and has appeared to us. We proclaim to you what we have seen and heard, so that you also may have fellowship with us. And our fellowship is with the Father and with his Son, Jesus Christ.[30]

It is the Apostle John who records in chapter 9 of the biblical book that bears his name the remarkable healing of a man who was born blind: one of many such events in the life of Jesus as told in the Gospels and foretold by Old Testament prophets. The narrative ends with a profound message for the religious leaders of the day about blindness of a different sort.

As for prophecies, Daniel declares with specificity the four major world empires that dominate the history of humankind prior to the establishing of the kingdom of God on the earth. The first, Babylonia, reached its peak under the ruler Nebuchadnezzar II, who reigned from c. 605 to c. 562 B.C. That empire fell, under successor

---

[30] 1 John 1:1–3 NIV.

leadership, in 539 B.C., when Babylon was captured, marking the beginning of Medo-Persian dominance. The other two—the Grecian and Roman empires—have risen and fallen since then, but the Scriptures have it that the fourth, the roots of which persist, will reemerge in a different form in the future. Wisdom would dictate that one watch the horizon for signs of its imminent appearing as world events continue to unfold. Even a description in the book of Daniel regarding the breakup of the third empire into four pieces after the death of Alexander the Great is exact; and the explicit, detailed account of the Seleucids and Ptolemies—dynasties that developed from two of Alexander's successor generals—as they battled for control in the years that followed is equally precise. It is a matter of historical record. The accuracy of the narratives centuries before the corresponding events took place is astounding, as is the angelic announcement, in Daniel's prophetic text, of the specific number of years from the issuing of the decree (by King Artaxerxes I) to rebuild postexilic Jerusalem to a time in the ministry of Jesus Christ.

The general charge of the atheists is that the biblical record is not true—that the incidents never happened or that they did not happen in the way that they are given. It is, to echo the physicist whom I mentioned at the outset of this work, a collection of fables, so they aver. With such a stance, would one intend to exclude all the recorded occurrences, or just the ones that point to the supernatural, such as miracles, prophecies that came to be fulfilled, and activity in the spiritual realm? There is convergence of canonical references to particular incidents and individuals, offered by different authors on different occasions, but important evidence that substantiates the authenticity of biblical accounts also comes in extracanonical forms. What is one to do then with ancient writings and artifacts that provide confirmation of the biblical testimony?

This topic is rich in extent. I will focus on a pair of examples, discussing briefly one from each testament, where a range of evidence lends support to the truth of the canonical record. First, from the Old Testament, there are the events, near the close of the eighth century B.C., surrounding the military campaign of the Assyrian king Sennacherib against Judah and its ruler Hezekiah, and the subsequent fall of both Assyria's king and its capital city of Nineveh. In the New Testament, one reads of the execution of Jesus

Christ following the combined actions of the ruling political authority—the Roman governor, Pontius Pilate—and the ruling religious authority—the Sanhedrin, headed by the high priest Joseph Caiaphas. There are other cases in point, of course, and one is encouraged to pursue the matter further by examining the historical information that is available through a number of sources.

An Old Testament Case[31]

In the book of the prophet Nahum and in that of Zephaniah, one reads of the coming, utter destruction of the great city of Nineveh, representative of—and later, under Sennacherib, the capital of—a notoriously wicked, cruel society that displayed brutality beyond imagination: the Assyrians. Mutilation, impalement, and torture were typical treatments for vanquished foes of the nation. Assyrian troops skinned their enemies alive and even eviscerated captured children. Their gruesome acts were elements of psychological warfare, which they practiced in an attempt to intimidate and demoralize their opponents. "The Assyrian king Shalmaneser III boasted of erecting a pyramid of chopped-off heads in front of an enemy's city. Other Assyrian kings stacked corpses like cordwood by the gates of defeated cities."[32] Through the prophet Jonah, God warned the people of Nineveh what they were facing: judgment. It was a message that was delivered by a very reluctant prophet, as Jonah was

---

[31] In this section, I will be quoting passages from several ancient documents. In some of the passages, the translators insert comments or terms for clarification. Additionally, they complete missing portions of text, or lacunae, with language that they deem to match the original phraseology. The former extensions usually appear in parentheses, the latter ones in brackets. Artifacts that contain the writings and that are in poor condition require editing to be comprehensible. Note that the remainder of this chapter will introduce numerous historical figures. In many cases, exact dates for their lives are not known. Where the estimates that authors provide differ by more than a few years, I will mention the variance. Some of these individuals possess multiple names; I do not plan to list all the names.

[32] Kenneth L. Barker et al., eds., *Zondervan NIV Study Bible* (1985; repr., Grand Rapids, MI: Zondervan, 2008), 1402, n. to Nah. 3:3. Shalmaneser III reigned from c. 859 to 824 B.C.

interested more in the annihilation of the society than he was in its penitence. The Assyrians did repent for a season—even their king humbled himself and declared a national fast—but that change of attitude did not last, and judgment eventually fell upon them. The prophet Zephaniah foretold God's impending action: "He will stretch out his hand . . . and destroy Assyria, leaving Nineveh utterly desolate and dry as the desert."[33] The devastation of wicked Nineveh was so complete that some believed the city to be merely a myth, denying that it ever even existed—until archaeologists discovered it in 1845, buried under sand for centuries.

Extraordinary discoveries awaited the archaeologists who excavated Nineveh. To appreciate the impact of the findings on the study of ancient history and its relation to narratives in the Bible, one must turn to a series of events that the Old Testament describes, events surrounding the Sennacherib-Hezekiah conflict. It is this conflict that is the subject of the analysis here as I investigate evidence that pertains to its authenticity. A detailed biblical record of the affair appears in three books: 2 Kings 18–19; 2 Chronicles 32; and Isaiah 36–37.

Consider the history that led to the clash. After serving in the capacity of coregent with his father, Hezekiah became the sole head of Judah in c. 715 B.C.[34] He was under the yoke of the Assyrian king Sargon II, paying tribute to the foreign ruler who had conquered the northern kingdom of Israel. When Sargon died in 705 B.C., Hezekiah capitalized on the new leadership and rebelled along with other vassals who were also under the control of Assyria. The successor to the Assyrian throne, Sennacherib, intended to maintain dominance in the region and set out to quell the rebellion. The Bible describes the ensuing events. Sennacherib besieged Judah with force, determined to take its cities for himself. Many communities fell. Even the highly fortified city Lachish was no match for Sennacherib's army, which overran it in 701 B.C. King Hezekiah capitulated, paying a heavy

---

[33] Zeph. 2:13 NIV.

[34] Of archaeological interest, in 1998, a clay impression of a royal stamp seal surfaced, which reads, "Belonging to Hezekiah (son of) Ahaz king of Judah." See Barker et al., *Zondervan Study Bible*, 561, n. to 2 Kings 18:1. Some writers place the beginning of Hezekiah's reign, as well as his death, a decade or so earlier, but the dates that I give for each in this segment are the standard ones.

tribute, but, despite Hezekiah's relinquishment of large sums of gold and silver, the Assyrian king's formidable forces prepared for an assault on Jerusalem.[35] It is not clear whether (1) Sennacherib deemed the tribute, albeit sizeable, to be insufficient, (2) Sennacherib believed that Hezekiah's rebellion required punishment, or (3) some other thinking drove the king's action.[36] Whatever the impetus, Sennacherib's attention turned to the Davidic city. Sennacherib sent his supreme commander and other officers with a large company of soldiers to Jerusalem. They carried a communiqué to Hezekiah, demanding surrender. Defying Hezekiah's God, the Assyrian king declared that the Hebrew God could no more deliver His people from Sennacherib's hand than the gods of the other nations that Sennacherib had conquered had delivered them.

It did not end as the prideful, Assyrian king had expected. The Scriptures report that Hezekiah appealed to God for help against such

---

[35] As the book of 2 Chron., chap. 32, records, when Sennacherib invaded Judah, and Hezekiah realized that the king planned to wage war against Jerusalem, Hezekiah took steps to prepare for an attack. He blocked springs in outlying areas to deprive the enemy of water; repaired the broken sections of the wall around the city; erected towers; built another, outer wall; reinforced the terraces; and produced a large supply of weapons. He encouraged the people, assuring them that God was with them and that God would fight their battles. It is significant that an underground aqueduct that Hezekiah constructed to bring water into the city from the Gihon spring is still observable in Jerusalem and is even operational. Hezekiah's tunnel, as it is called, was quite an engineering feat for this ancient people.

[36] Whether the threatened attack was imminent or occurred later is, to some extent, an open question among historians. A defensible view—the correct one, I would argue—is that the Assyrians set out to come against Jerusalem following their taking of Lachish, even though Hezekiah paid the tribute. Indeed, the Bible reports in 2 Kings 18:14 that Hezekiah sent a message to Sennacherib at Lachish, offering to meet a demand for payment in exchange for withdrawal. An alternative view, although it appears to be a minority position, is that there were two campaigns in Judah: The Judahite king paid the tribute initially, forestalling an attack, but refused to do so several years later, prompting the Assyrians to march against Jerusalem at that time. I believe that the dual-campaign theory is difficult to support, however, as there is no indication of an interruption in Sennacherib's military action: "The king of Assyria sent his supreme commander, his chief officer and his field commander with a large army, from Lachish to King Hezekiah at Jerusalem" (2 Kings 18:17 NIV). In either case, the end result for the Assyrians was the same.

a powerful enemy. Following the Judahite king's prayer, Isaiah the prophet sent a message from God to Hezekiah. God assured Hezekiah of the withdrawal of the Assyrian king.

> "He will not enter this city
> or shoot an arrow here.
> He will not come before it with shield
> or build a siege ramp against it.
> By the way that he came he will return;
> he will not enter this city,"
> declares the LORD.[37]

Further, according to the Scriptures, not only was God going to end the army's plans to attack Jerusalem, but He was going to end Sennacherib's life as well and do so in his home territory. Through Isaiah, God said, "I am going to put such a spirit in him that when he hears a certain report, he will return to his own country, and there I will have him cut down with the sword."[38] The encamped Assyrian forces were decimated in a single night, ostensibly by a potent disease, and one hundred eighty-five thousand Assyrian soldiers died. Sennacherib was forced to return to Nineveh in disgrace, where he eventually was assassinated by two of his sons: Adrammelech and Sharezer. He was killed with the sword as he was worshipping in the temple of his god. Another son—Esarhaddon—succeeded him.

There is intrabiblical corroboration of these events, but is there any corroboration from documents that are outside the Bible? A description of Sennacherib's expedition against Hezekiah also appears in the writings of the Jewish historian Flavius Josephus. Born in A.D. 37 or 38, Josephus died around the turn of the second century. His foremost works are *The Jewish War*, *Jewish Antiquities*, and *Against Apion*. In his work *Antiquities*, Josephus writes of the Assyrian king's advance, Hezekiah's prayer, Isaiah's prophecy, the devastation of the invading army, and Sennacherib's retreat and

---

[37] Isa. 37:33–34 NIV. The passage in 2 Kings 19:32–33 NIV is nearly identical.

[38] 2 Kings 19:7 NIV. This passage also appears, with very minor wording differences, in Isa. 37:7. Although not certain, the reference may be to the report that Sennacherib received about Tirhakah of Cush, the upper Nile region—namely, that Tirhakah was marching out to engage him in battle. See 2 Kings 19:9. 'Tirhakah' is spelled 'Tarhaqa' in some texts.

subsequent death at the hands of his sons. Josephus provides confirming evidence of the incident—the catastrophic plague that struck the Assyrians, Sennacherib's flight to Nineveh, and the king's assassination—from yet another source that is neither Jewish nor Christian: the pagan Chaldean Berosus. Living during the fourth and third centuries B.C., Berosus wrote about Babylonian history. Josephus quotes him in the following passage:

> When the people, as well as the ambassadors, heard what the Assyrian commander said, they related it to Hezekiah, who thereupon put off his royal apparel, and clothed himself with sackcloth, and took the habit of a mourner, and, after the manner of his country, he fell upon his face and begged God, and entreated him to assist them, now they had no other hope of relief. He also sent some of his friends, and some of the priests, to the prophet Isaiah, and desired that he would pray to God, and offer sacrifices for their common deliverance, and so put up supplications to him, that he would have indignation at the expectations of their enemies, and have mercy upon his people. And when the prophet had done accordingly, an oracle came from God to him, and encouraged the king and his friends that were about him; and foretold that their enemies should be beaten without fighting, and should go away in an ignominious manner, and not with that insolence which they now show, for that God would take care that they should be destroyed. He also foretold that Sennacherib, the king of Assyria, should fail of his purpose against Egypt, and that when he came home he should perish by the sword.
>
> . . . Berosus, who wrote of the affairs of Chaldea, makes mention of this King Sennacherib, and that he ruled over the Assyrians, and that he made an expedition against all Asia and Egypt; and says thus:
>
> . . . "Now when Sennacherib was returning from his Egyptian war to Jerusalem, he found his army under Rabshakeh his general in danger [by a plague], for God had sent a pestilential sickness upon his army; and on the very first night of the siege, a hundred fourscore and five thousand, with their captains and generals, were destroyed. So the king was in a great dread and in a

terrible agony at this calamity; and being in great fear for his whole army, he fled with the rest of his forces to his own kingdom, and to his city Nineveh; and when he had abode there a little while, he was treacherously assaulted, and died by the hands of his elder sons, Adrammelech and Sharezer, and was killed in his own temple, which was called Araske [Nisroch]."[39]

When archaeologists unearthed Nineveh, they discovered artifacts having major historical importance. Excavated were items documenting the Assyrian invasion of Judah and, of particular value, ones relating to the biblical narrative concerning Sennacherib and Hezekiah. Archaeologists found Sennacherib's palace and, with it, sculpted stone reliefs displaying vivid scenes of the king's military victory over the town of Lachish. The reliefs depict soldiers with spears and shields, protecting archers and warriors with slingshot weapons. It shows men who are ascending a siege ramp to the city; battering rams; and impaled, Judahite casualties. The researchers also obtained Sennacherib's archives. These official records, which are inscribed in cuneiform on various objects, provide reports of the king's exploits. One such object, the Rassam Cylinder, confirms Hezekiah's payment of a tribute to Sennacherib, noting what the Assyrian king collected.[40] Perhaps the most significant finds for the

---

[39] Flavius Josephus, *Jewish Antiquities* 10.1.3–5, in *The New Complete Works of Josephus*, trans. William Whiston (Grand Rapids, MI: Kregel Publications, 1999), 334–35. Whiston's original translation of Josephus's works appeared in 1737. The quotation from Berosus (or Berossus) puts the number of Assyrian troops who died from the plague—the bracketed expressions are in the Whiston text itself—at one hundred eighty-five thousand: the same number that is in the Bible. On the plague, cf. Isa. 10:12, 16. Flavius Josephus generally is known as simply Josephus.

[40] The amount of gold that the cylinder reports—thirty talents—is identical to that which is noted in the Bible. The silver differs; the Assyrian artifact gives a greater amount. The Assyrians viewed silver as an inferior metal—in comparison with gold—and probably combined it with other materials in calculating the weight or the estimated value of a collection. This fact may account for the difference. For this explanation, see Walter Mayer, "Sennacherib's Campaign of 701 BCE: The Assyrian View," in *'Like a Bird in a Cage': The Invasion of Sennacherib in 701 BCE*, ed. Lester L. Grabbe (London: Sheffield Academic Press, 2003), 183. There is also a clear reference in the Scriptures to the devaluing of sliver relative to gold: "All King Solomon's goblets were gold, and all the household articles in the Palace of the Forest of Lebanon were pure gold. Nothing was made of silver,

study of ancient history are three clay articles in the shape of hex-agonal solids that give Sennacherib's own account of the Assyrian operation in Judah, even mentioning Hezekiah and Jerusalem by name. These artifacts are the Taylor, Chicago, and Jerusalem Prisms.[41]

Collectively, these numerous extracanonical materials confirm the conflict in Judah. There is a considerable degree of alignment between the biblical and the Assyrian accounts of the war. A few of the specifics differ, however, and scholars have turned to them in an effort to understand the unfolding of events. Some authors take these differences to constitute a reason to call into question the authenticity of the biblical account. The primary factors concerning the campaign to seize Judah that have raised doubts are (1) the presence of a phrase in the Assyrian annals that, certain writers surmise, entails an attack on Jerusalem, with all the associated military tactics, including the erecting of a siege ramp, and (2) the lack of any mention in the annals of the plague that destroyed Sennacherib's army when it was preparing to assault that key city. A brief look at each is in order.

THE PRISMS

This report from the Chicago Prism provides a reference to the Assyrian activities in the region; it is essentially the same as that inscribed on the Taylor Prism:

> As to Hezekiah, the Judaean, who did not submit
> to my yoke, I laid siege to 46 of his strong cities,
> fortresses and countless small villages in their vicinity
> (and) conquered (them) by means of building siege
> ramps, drawing battering-rams up close, hand-to-hand
> combat of infantry, mines, breaches and assault ladders.

---

because silver was considered to be of little value in Solomon's days" (1 Kings 10:21 NIV).

[41] The Taylor Prism, named after the person who is believed to be its discoverer, is in the British Museum. The Chicago Prism, or Oriental Institute Prism, belongs to the Oriental Institute in Chicago. The Jerusalem Prism is located in the Israel Museum in Jerusalem.

Himself I enclosed in Jerusalem, his royal city,
like a bird in a cage. I laid out forts against him in order
to repel him from going out of the gate of his city.[42]

The Bible substantiates the fact that the Assyrian king's territory-grab was extensive, although it is silent on the number of Judahite cities that fell. It is the phrase 'like a bird in a cage' that gives scholars pause. Some have argued, contrary to the biblical account, that Sennacherib did storm the walls of Jerusalem. The caged-bird simile, so they think, seems to confirm it.

Such an interpretation, however, cannot be right. The first consideration that counts against the construal is that the expression is actually a very old cliché that refers to one's being cornered or confined. It surfaces in documents that predate Sennacherib's annals by many years and that make its meaning clear. In the fourteenth century B.C., Rib-Hadda, the king of Gubla, a Phoenician city on the coast of the Mediterranean, composed a lengthy series of letters that he directed to Akhenaton, the reigning pharaoh of Egypt at the time. In these communications, which are part of an ancient collection—the Amarna Letters—Rib-Hadda pleads as one of the pharaoh's vassals for military aid, obviously feeling threatened. A number of his letters contain this simile: "Like a bird in a trap: *ki-lu-bi* (cage), so am I in Gubla."[43]

Again, the expression appears in inscriptions, from the eighth century B.C., of the Assyrian king Tiglath-pileser III. Records that were unearthed in the 1800s—the Kalḫu Annals—contain a report, written on a stone slab, of the flight of Rezin, the king of Aram, from Tiglath-pileser's forces. In some texts or portions thereof, Rezin is referred to as Raḫiānu. The following passage is one that uses the alternate identifier:

---

[42] Sennacherib, as translated by Mayer, "Sennacherib's Campaign," 189.

[43] Rib-Hadda, letter EA 74, in *The Amarna Letters*, trans. William L. Moran (Baltimore: Johns Hopkins University Press, 1992), 143. Other letters that employ the bird-in-a-cage simile include EA 78, 79, 81, 90, 105, and 116. Moran published his work initially in 1987 in French. The name 'Rib-Hadda' is spelled 'Rib-Addi' in some material. There are also different spellings of 'Akhenaton' and various other ancient names. The city Gubla is the same as Byblos, the location of which is present-day Lebanon.

> In order to save his life, he (Raḫiānu) fled alone and entered the gate of his city [like] a mongoose. I [im]paled his foremost men alive while making (the people of) his land watch. For forty-five days I set up my camp [aro]und his city and confined him (there) like a bird in a cage.[44]

As in the case of Rib-Hadda, the phraseology indicates captivity or restricted movement, not besiegement. In the end, the Assyrian king did conquer that city, Damascus, and Rezin was killed. This account is found in the Bible in 2 Kings 16. There is also a report of a fragment of the Kalḫu Annals that contains a notice of the death of Rezin, but it has been lost.[45]

The most reasonable position on the use of the caged-bird simile by Sennacherib is therefore evident: Its employment follows that of the earlier writers.

> The true sense of these passages is that of a total blockade, and the hyperbole is employed as a face-saving device to cover for a failure to take the enemy's capital and punish the rebellious king. In the case of Rezin, this was accomplished in the following year (732); in the case of Hezekiah, Sennacherib was forced to make do with heavy tribute delivered to Nineveh after his retreat.[46]

---

[44] Tiglath-pileser III, Kalḫu Annals, inscription on stone slab no. 20, 8′b–12′, in *The Royal Inscriptions of Tiglath-pileser III (744–727 BC) and Shalmaneser V (726–722 BC), Kings of Assyria*, trans. Hayim Tadmor and Shigeo Yamada, ed. Jamie Novotny (Winona Lake, IN: Eisenbrauns, 2011), 59. This text represents Annals Series C, Unit 9. Other passages in *Royal Inscriptions* (and other translations of this passage) use the name 'Rezin'; refer to the inscription on stone slab no. 20, 13′–14′a, 59. One also may wish to turn to K. Lawson Younger Jr., "The Calah Annals (2.117A)," in *The Context of Scripture*, ed. William W. Hallo and K. Lawson Younger Jr., vol. 2, *Monumental Inscriptions from the Biblical World* (Leiden, Netherlands: Brill, 2000), 286. Note that 'Calaḫ' is an alternate spelling of 'Kalḫu'. The brackets in the extract are those of the translators.

[45] See the editorial commentary on p. 57 of the work *Royal Inscriptions*, cited in the previous footnote.

[46] Hayim Tadmor, trans., *The Inscriptions of Tiglath-pileser III, King of Assyria: Critical Edition, with Introductions, Translations, and Commentary* (Jerusalem: The Israel Academy of Sciences and Humanities, 1994), 79, n. to Ann. 23, 11′.

Another consideration for denying an all-out offensive at Jerusalem is that Sennacherib's annals contain an elaborate listing of the elements of siege warfare when describing his attack on the other fortified cities of Judah—siege ramps, battering rams, hand-to-hand combat, mines, breaches, and assault ladders—all of which, rather conspicuously, are missing in his description of the Assyrian operations at Jerusalem.[47] Given that Jerusalem was the seat of power and the most fortified city of Hezekiah's kingdom, such an omission by the arrogant Assyrian ruler is in conflict with the idea that he besieged Judah's capital.[48] If Sennacherib had overrun Jerusalem, then he surely would have removed the defiant Judahite vassal from power, but he failed to do so: Hezekiah remained on the throne until his death in c. 686 B.C.

Although not everyone is convinced, the notion that Sennacherib laid siege to Jerusalem in the Lachishian manner, rather than merely set up barricades, simply lacks support. One scholar summarizes the opinions of several authors on the topic when he writes the following assessment:

> The action that shut up Hezekiah 'like a bird in a cage' was a blockading of the roads and supply routes (Mayer). There was no besieging army at Jerusalem's gate nor any siege mound cast up around Jerusalem. A parallel example is Ashurbanipal's siege of Tyre which was actually a blockade (NN).[49]

Ann. 23, as designated in the work, corresponds to stone slab no. 20, presented in the abovesaid, later publication *Royal Inscriptions*. The phrase 'these passages' in the quotation refers to the appearance of the simile in writings of Tiglath-pileser and Sennacherib.

[47] Paul S. Evans makes this point in *The Invasion of Sennacherib in the Book of Kings: A Source-Critical and Rhetorical Study of 2 Kings 18–19* (Leiden, Netherlands: Brill, 2009), 17–18.

[48] It is noteworthy that the siege ramp at Lachish is still clearly visible nearly three millennia after the Assyrians constructed it. Archaeologists have uncovered more than a thousand iron arrowheads in the ramp and a chain associated with the use of a battering ram. On this latter point, see BiblePlaces.com, "Lachish," accessed May 31, 2016, www.bibleplaces.com/lachish.

[49] Lester L. Grabbe, "Reflections on the Discussion," in *'Like a Bird in a Cage': Invasion of Sennacherib*, 309. The name 'Mayer' refers to Walter Mayer; 'NN' refers to Nadav Na'aman.

In the final analysis, the archaeological discoveries at Nineveh uphold the account in 2 Kings, 2 Chronicles, and Isaiah. Not only is there an independent record in the Assyrian documents themselves of the Sennacherib-Hezekiah incident as it is reported in the Scriptures, but the Assyrian annals offer support as well, according to the view of a number of Assyriologists, for the absence of any battle by the Judahites at Jerusalem. It is reasonable to conclude, in keeping with the biblical narrative, that the intended siege of Jerusalem never took place. It was thwarted before an actual engagement was launched— on the first night of the encampment of the Assyrian troops. Exactly how close they were geographically to Jerusalem at that point remains an open question.

THE PLAGUE

The second issue that arises in a review of the events surrounding the Assyrian operations is the lack of any mention of a plague in Sennacherib's annals. On this basis, some historians have questioned the report in the Scriptures. What is interesting is that the Greek historian Herodotus (c. 484–c. 425 B.C.), in a completely independent account, also describes the destruction of Sennacherib's forces; but he attributes the cause of it, based apparently on a story from the Egyptians, to the activity of mice. Here is the passage:

> Sennacharib [Sennacherib] king of the Arabians and Assyrians led a large army against Egypt. . . . But after the enemy had arrived and night had fallen, an army of field mice swarmed through their camp and chewed up their quivers, bowstrings, and even the handles of their shields, so that on the next day, the enemy found themselves deprived of their weapons and defenseless; many fell as they tried to flee.[50]

---

[50] Herodotus, *The Histories*, 2.141, *The Landmark Herodotus: The Histories*, trans. Andrea L. Purvis, ed. Robert B. Strassler (New York: Pantheon Books, 2007), 182, 184. I provide the more common spelling of the name of the Assyrian king in the quotation.

It is hard to conceive that such a commotion could go unnoticed by a large contingent of trained and experienced military men, failing to safeguard their weapons—the very tools of their trade—particularly given that there almost certainly would have been sentinels who were stationed among the troops to stand watch at night. The essence of what the narrative depicts, though, is the destruction of Sennacherib's forces; the mice may be put forth as a natural cause of an extraordinary event. Indeed, they may be symbolic of an epidemic in the Assyrian camp. Not everyone agrees: Although the ancients connected rodents and disease, they did not blur the distinction between them. There is support for the metaphorical reading nevertheless. Consider these recent comments on the incident by a contributor to the discussion:

> This is Herodotus' version of the Jewish story of the pestilence which destroyed the Assyrian army before Jerusalem. Mice are a Greek symbol of pestilence; it is Apollo Smintheus (the mouse god) who sends and then ends the plague in Homer, *Iliad* I.[51]

Regardless of how Herodotus came to portray the happening in terms of an attack by vermin, the value of the story is that it tells of the mass ruin of Sennacherib's forces. Something happened to cause their downfall. In this respect, Herodotus's portrayal cannot be ignored in looking at extracanonical evidence that lends weight to the biblical description of the episode. The omission from the Assyrian annals of the enormous loss is not surprising, for it is a patent admission of defeat. Had Sennacherib conquered Jerusalem—the most important city in Judah—there unquestionably would have been note of it in his records. One author believes that the Egyptians played some part in the Assyrian rout, in light of Tirhakah's march and Herodotus's remarks. Although I do not agree with his reliance on the Egyptian element as a key part of the explanation for the huge troop loss—insofar, at least, as it may be thought to supplant the nocturnal decimation by a plague—I do agree with him that the story in Herodotus points to an unusual occurrence. I also agree that Sennacherib retreated. The author writes,

---

[51] Strassler, editorial comment, *Landmark Herodotus*, 184, n. 2.141.5a.

The Assyrians do not mention a defeat by the Egyptians, but they are not likely to have done so. What is clear is that Sennacherib returned to Nineveh without defeating Hezekiah, and his listing of the destruction wrought on Judah and the resultant tribute by Hezekiah only confirms the peculiarity in Hezekiah's being allowed to remain on the throne and the strange silence about the taking of Jerusalem.[52]

THE PROPHECY

With the excavation of Nineveh, archaeologists discovered, in addition to the other artifacts, the library of Sennacherib's grandson: the Assyrian ruler Ashurbanipal. The library held a huge number of tablets—approximately a hundred thousand—providing valuable insight into the times. It was under subsequent leadership that Nineveh fell in 612 B.C. to an assault by a coalition of Babylonians, Medes, and Scythians. The fall was recorded in another ancient work, one that is neither Jewish nor Christian: the Babylonian Chronicles. The relevant section of this ancient manuscript contains lacunae, but the record is transpicuous nevertheless. I provide the text, translated with manifest attention to detail by A. Kirk Grayson.

> [The fourteenth year]: The king of Akkad mustered his army [and marched to . . .] The king of the Umman-manda [*marched*] towards the king of Akkad [. . .] . . . they met one another. [The k]ing of Akkad . . . [. . . Cy]axares . . . brought across and they marched along the bank of the Tigris. [. . . they encamp]ed against Nineveh. From the month Sivan until the month Ab—for three [months—. . .] . . . they subjected the city to a heavy siege. [On the Nth day] of the month Ab [. . .] they inflicted a major [defeat upon a g]reat [*people*]. At that time Sin-sharra-ishkun, king of Assyria, [*died*] . . .

---

[52] Lester L. Grabbe, "Of Mice and Dead Men: Herodotus 2.141 and Sennacherib's Campaign in 701 BCE," in *'Like a Bird in a Cage': Invasion of Sennacherib*, 138–39.

[. . .] . . . They carried off the vast booty of the city and
the temple (and) [turned] the city into a ruin heap [. . .][53]

Thus, the prophecy concerning Nineveh, delivered both by Nahum
and by Zephaniah, was fulfilled. The evidence—here, from a pagan
source—is there for those who wish to look.

A New Testament Case

Turning to the New Testament, one finds that there are many
prophecies in the Old Testament that point to events pertaining to
Christ. It is not uncommon for a biblical passage to describe then-
current circumstances or occurrences, even as the weight of the
passage rests with the future. Psalm 22 was written by King David a
millennium before the death of Jesus. This description in the Psalter
of the piercing of the hands and the feet, the mocking and gloating,
the dividing of the garments, and the casting of lots for the clothing
is an unambiguous reference to the crucifixion of Christ as it is
described in the Gospels. The book of Isaiah was written more than
seven hundred years before the death of Jesus; yet, the closing verses
of chapter 52 through chapter 53 of this prophetic author's text give a
forceful depiction of the passion of Christ and declare the purpose
for his crucifixion. In Zechariah, which was written about five
hundred years before the time of Christ, there is this passage by the
prophet:

So they paid me thirty pieces of silver.
     And the LORD said to me, "Throw it to the
potter"—the handsome price at which they priced me!
So I took the thirty pieces of silver and threw them into
the house of the LORD to the potter.[54]

---

[53] Babylonian Chronicle 3, 38–45, in *Assyrian and Babylonian Chronicles*, trans.
A. Kirk Grayson (1975; repr., Winona Lake, IN: Eisenbrauns, 2000), 94. The fourteenth year to which the text refers corresponds to 612–611 B.C., using modern date
standards. The bracketed parts of the quotation appear in the translation.
[54] Zech. 11:12–13 NIV.

The Bible states that Judas Iscariot betrayed Christ for thirty pieces of silver. The amount is recorded in the Gospel of Matthew. Overcome with remorse afterward, Judas returned the money to the religious leaders—they had paid him for the deed—but they had no interest in his sense of guilt. Judas threw the money into the temple. The chief priests there retrieved the coins and used them to buy the potter's field. The parallel is unequivocal.

Just as some denied even the historical existence of Nineveh prior to its eventual unearthing, however, some deny even the historical existence of Jesus Christ. In an essay by the philosopher Bertrand Russell in the early twentieth century, the agnostic and practicing atheist expresses his skepticism: "Historically, it is quite doubtful whether Christ ever existed at all."[55] One should consider the evidence that determines whether Russell's position is defensible.

Beginning with the canon itself, documentation corresponding to the New Testament is substantial and exceeds by a wide margin that of many other ancient works that scholars deem to be reliable. There are approximately four thousand extant Greek manuscripts of the New Testament, either complete or partial, the best examples of which date from around A.D. 350. There are portions of documents, produced one to two centuries earlier, that cover most of this biblical volume. The earliest extant papyrus fragment containing material from the New Testament dates from about A.D. 130; another papyrus document was created near A.D. 200. Together, they present the majority of the Gospel of John. Contrast these details with those pertaining to various other early works, of which merely a few survive, taken from writings that are hundreds of years more recent. Of the several existing manuscripts of Caesar's *Gallic War*, which was composed in the first century B.C., ten or fewer are quality items, and the oldest one is from a period that is almost a millennium after the time of Caesar. Of the 142 books of the Roman history of Titus Livius, or Livy (c. 59 B.C.–c. A.D. 17), fewer than three dozen survive in not more than twenty manuscripts of importance; only one of that number comprises elements that are as old as the fourth century.

---

[55] Bertrand Russell, "Why I Am Not a Christian," in *Why I Am Not a Christian and Other Essays on Religion and Related Subjects*, ed. Paul Edwards (New York: Simon and Schuster, 1957), 16. First given as a lecture, the essay was published in 1927. Russell refers to himself as an agnostic or an atheist, depending on context.

Aside from a few scraps of papyrus dating from around the first century, the accounts that the Greek historians Herodotus and Thucydides (c. 460–c. 400 B.C.) scribed exist in a mere handful of records; and the earliest records that are of use were written more than thirteen hundred years after these men lived.[56] Certainly, no contemporary scholar would doubt the genuineness of these documents, however.[57]

There are references to Christ or His followers in ancient sources besides the canon. In Christian authorship, the first three centuries alone yield an extensive list of writings of the church fathers. From the first through the second century, some who include explicitly 'Jesus', 'Christ', 'the Son of God', or a combination of these identifying designations in their works are Clement of Rome, Ignatius of Antioch, Polycarp of Smyrna, Papias of Hierapolis, Aristides of Athens, Justin Martyr, Apollinaris of Hierapolis, Melito of Sardis, Hegesippus, Athenagoras of Athens, Irenaeus of Lyons— although many place his death slightly after the turn of the following century—and Polycrates of Ephesus. Counting those whose lives extend to the third century brings Clement of Alexandria, Tertullian, Serapion of Antioch, Apollonius of Ephesus, Caius, Hippolytus of Rome, and Origen of Alexandria. Additional documents supplement the writings of these authors. Other writers refer to Christians, the Crucified One, or the Savior, using the corresponding terms in their manuscripts.

What of sources that are not Christian, however—are there any documents apart from those of Christian authorship that substantiate the life of Jesus Christ? Indeed, there are a number of them, and the corroborating support that they provide cannot be overlooked. Various passages that appear in these writings mention not only Jesus Christ but also John the Baptist, who announced the Lord's coming; James and Jude—two other sons of Mary, the mother of Jesus; and the Christians as a group. A prominent segment is found in the writings of Josephus. Besides his references to Old Testament

---

[56] Some sources suggest that the death of Thucydides probably occurred a few years later.

[57] I take the points in this paragraph from F. F. Bruce, *The New Testament Documents: Are They Reliable?* 5th rev. ed. (1960; repr., Grand Rapids, MI: William B. Eerdmans Publishing Co., 1963), 16–18.

persons, Josephus mentions Christ in two places in his *Antiquities*, which he penned in the A.D. 90s, only a few decades after the events surrounding Christ's crucifixion as they are reported in the Gospels. One citation is given here, translated from the Greek text. It has come to be known as the *Testimonium Flavianum*.

> Now there was about this time Jesus, a wise man, if it be lawful to call him a man; for he was a doer of wonderful works, a teacher of such men as receive the truth with pleasure. He drew over to him both many of the Jews and many of the Gentiles. He was [the] Christ. And when Pilate, at the suggestion of the principal men among us, had condemned him to the cross, those that loved him at the first did not forsake him; for he appeared to them alive again the third day, as the divine prophets had foretold these and ten thousand other wonderful things concerning him. And the tribe of Christians, so named from him, are not extinct at this day.[58]

Some scholars hold that this quotation, although accurate in its core historical content, reflects certain editing, given that Josephus was not a convert to Christianity, according to the church father Origen (c. A.D. 185–c. 254).[59] The same passage, however, is presented by another Christian author of the early period; Eusebius Pamphilus (c. A.D. 263–c. 339) preserves the quotation in his historical account of the church, where Josephus's wording remains intact.[60] The tenth-century Christian historian Agapius also cites this passage in an Arabic work titled *Universal History*, but here the

---

[58] Josephus, *Antiquities*, 18:3.3, 590. The bracketed word is in the translation.

[59] See Origen, *Origen Against Celsus*, 1.47, in *The Ante-Nicene Fathers: Translations of the Writings of the Fathers down to A.D. 325*, vol. 4, *Fathers of the Third Century: Tertullian, Part Fourth; Minucius Felix; Commodian; Origen, Parts First and Second*, ed. Alexander Roberts and James Donaldson (1885; repr., New York: Charles Scribner's Sons, 1925), 416.

[60] The quotation appears in Eusebius's *Ecclesiastical History*, 1.11, *The Ecclesiastical History of Eusebius Pamphilus, Bishop of Caesarea in Palestine*, trans. C. F. Crusé; *A Historical View of the Council of Nice*, trans. Isaac Boyle (New York: T. Mason and G. Lane, 1839), 42. Eusebius Pamphilus is known as Eusebius of Caesarea as well. Frequently, he is referred to as simply Eusebius.

phraseology is somewhat different. It speaks of Jesus, and of Pilate's condemning Him to death by crucifixion, but without the personal commitment to Jesus's resurrection and Messiahship. The text reads,

> At this time there was a wise man who was called Jesus. And his conduct was good, and [he] was known to be virtuous. And many people from among the Jews and the other nations became his disciples. Pilate condemned him to be crucified and to die. And those who had become his disciples did not abandon his discipleship. They reported that he had appeared to them three days after his crucifixion and that he was alive; accordingly, he was perhaps the Messiah concerning whom the prophets have recounted wonders.[61]

Despite the differences between this rendering of Josephus's manuscript and the verbiage that appears in *Antiquities*, what the two documents record of certain key historical events is consistent. Josephus's other reference to "Jesus, who was called Christ" is broadly held to be authentic as it is written.[62] Whatever Josephus's view is concerning the resurrected Christ, it is evident from his writings that he does not doubt the fact of Jesus's existence or his crucifixion at the order of Pilate.

Furthermore, there are citations in works with neither Jewish nor Christian authorship. One important source is the noted Roman historian Publius (or Gaius) Cornelius Tacitus, who is referred to as simply Tacitus (c. A.D. 56–c. 120). His two major compilations are *Annals* and *Histories*, comprising together, scholars believe, about thirty books, of which only some survive. Appearing in Tacitus's

---

[61] The extract from the Agapius document is given in Shlomo Pines, *An Arabic Version of the Testimonium Flavianum and Its Implications* (Jerusalem: The Israel Academy of Sciences and Humanities, 1971), 16. Pines cites the full, lengthy Arabic title of Agapius's work; the brief, English title is sufficient for the current purposes. In Pine's quotation, he italicizes the differences between the two renderings, leaving the remainder in Roman type. Doing so is beneficial in a comparative analysis, but I omit the italics here, which facilitates the reading. The bracketed insertion is that of Pines.

[62] Josephus, *Antiquities*, 20.9.1, 656. In that same passage, Josephus also mentions James; and elsewhere he speaks of "John, that was called the Baptist," noting that "Herod killed him." See *Antiquities*, 18.5.2, 595.

writings is a reference to Christ; there are at least two to Christians. The following passage describes Nero's blaming of the great fire of Rome on the Christians, a fire that, it is widely held, Nero himself started. The passage also contains references to the Roman official who sentenced Jesus to death and to the reigning emperor at the time.

> But all human efforts, all the lavish gifts of the emperor, and the propitiations of the gods, did not banish the sinister belief that the conflagration was the result of an order. Consequently, to get rid of the report, Nero fastened the guilt and inflicted the most exquisite tortures on a class hated for their abominations, called Christians by the populace. Christus, from whom the name had its origin, suffered the extreme penalty during the reign of Tiberius at the hands of one of our procurators, Pontius Pilatus.[63]

Tacitus proceeds to elaborate on the horrid treatment by Nero of Christ's followers, including their being covered with animal skins and ripped apart by dogs, nailed to crosses, and turned into human torches to provide light in the evening hours for Nero's parties. Such cruelty hardly was matched even by the Assyrians. Known as simply Nero, this notorious ruler was born Lucius Domitius Ahenobarbus.

There is another reference to the death of Jesus in the ancient documents. A reputed official report by Pontius Pilate regarding the crucifixion appears in a work by Justin Martyr (c. A.D. 110–c. 165).[64] The report is one that Pilate sent, as part of a regular series, to Emperor Tiberius Claudius Nero, or merely Tiberius, as he is generally known. Albeit the documents—Justin refers to them as the Acts of Pontius Pilate—did not survive the centuries, this early Christian theologian mentions them, as they corroborate the facts pertaining to Christ's crucifixion. Note the quotation in the first sentence, which comes from Psalm 22, as does the allusion to the casting of lots for

---

[63] Publius Cornelius Tacitus, *Annals*, 15.44, in *The Complete Works of Tacitus*, trans. Alfred John Church and William Jackson Brodribb, ed. Moses Hadas (New York: Modern Library, 1942), 380. The Latin names 'Christus' and 'Pontius Pilatus' refer respectively to Christ and Pontius Pilate.

[64] Certain writers believe the date of Justin's birth to be approximately a decade earlier.

His clothing, appearing in verses 16 and 18 respectively of that Psalm.

> And the expression, "They pierced my hands and my feet," was used in reference to the nails of the cross which were fixed in His hands and feet. And after he was crucified they cast lots upon His vesture, and they that crucified Him parted it among them. And that these things did happen, you can ascertain from the Acts of Pontius Pilate.[65]

In addition, this sequence of reports that Pilate issued is mentioned elsewhere by Justin. The theologian speaks of Christ's miracles—His healing people and His raising the dead to life— stating, "And that He did those things, you can learn from the Acts of Pontius Pilate."[66] Here then is a reference to an attestation by a pagan official that extends beyond the existence of Christ to deeds that Christ performed, which have to be characterized as supernatural. Justin writes merely a century or so after the events to which he refers. Regrettably, Pilate's original letters have been lost. It is important to know whether there are similar references among pagan manuscripts that point to miraculous occurrences surrounding the life of Jesus.

Looking at another set of evidence is enlightening, this one citing independent accounts by two pagan historians: Thallus, living in the first century, and Phlegon of Tralles, living in the first and second centuries. Their separate recordings of the celestial and terrestrial incidents that took place during the crucifixion of Christ have a principal bearing on the discussion. Just fragments of the three-volume chronicle of Thallus, who wrote only about twenty years after the date of Jesus's death, remain; effectively nothing of Phlegon's original wording has survived. Some of their commentary, however, is preserved in other manuscripts, such as those that the Christian author Sextus Julius Africanus (c. A.D. 160–c. 240) penned,

---

[65] Justin Martyr, *The First Apology*, 35, in *The Ante-Nicene Fathers: Translations of the Writings of the Fathers down to A.D. 325*, vol. 1, *The Apostolic Fathers: Justin Martyr, Irenaeus*, ed. Alexander Roberts and James Donaldson (1885; repr., New York: Charles Scribner's Sons, 1925), 174–75.

[66] Ibid., 48, 179.

947

portions of which are extant.[67] Note that three of the Gospels report that darkness fell over the land from the sixth to the ninth hour (noon to 3:00 p.m.) during the crucifixion of Jesus Christ, and one of the three Gospels, that of Matthew, also reports that a shaking of the earth occurred upon Jesus's death about the ninth hour. Explicit in Julius's writings is the view of the two aforementioned historians that the period of darkness is attributable to a solar eclipse; however, as Julius makes clear, an eclipse *cannot* be the cause.

> On the whole world there pressed a most fearful darkness; and the rocks were rent by an earthquake, and many places in Judea and other districts were thrown down. This darkness Thallus, in the third book of his *History*, calls, as appears to me without reason, an eclipse of the sun. For the Hebrews celebrate the passover on the 14th day according to the moon, and the passion of our Saviour falls on the day before the passover; but an eclipse of the sun takes place only when the moon comes under the sun. And it cannot happen at any other time but in the interval between the first day of the new moon and the last of the old, that is, at their junction: how then should an eclipse be supposed to happen when the moon is almost diametrically opposite the sun? . . . Phlegon records that, in the time of Tiberius Caesar, at full moon, there was a full eclipse of the sun from the sixth hour to the ninth—manifestly that one of which we speak. . . . But it was a darkness induced by God, because the Lord happened then to suffer.[68]

---

[67] The dates that historians give for the life of Julius vary by as much as two decades.

[68] Sextus Julius Africanus, "The Extant Fragments of the Five Books of the Chronography of Julius Africanus," 18.1, in *The Ante-Nicene Fathers: Translations of the Writings of the Fathers down to A.D. 325*, vol. 6, *Fathers of the Third Century: Gregory Thaumaturgus, Dionysius the Great, Julius Africanus, Anatolius and Minor Writers, Methodius, Arnobius*, ed. Alexander Roberts and James Donaldson (1886; repr., New York: Charles Scribner's Sons, 1925), 136–37. George Syncellus (the name is spelled 'Synkellos' as well), writing just after the turn of the ninth century, preserves the Julian quotation in his *Chronography*, providing yet another source. See his citation in *The Chronography of George Synkellos: A Byzantine Chronicle of Universal History from the Creation*, trans. William Adler and Paul Tuffin (Oxford: Oxford University Press, 2002), 466–67.

Although some dispute the reference to the events in nature as ones that occurred at the time of Christ's death, the objection seems to be without merit. Julius's use of the expression 'this darkness' in mentioning Thallus's assertion, followed by a description of the day of the crucifixion in relation to the Jewish calendar, identifies, rather obviously, the darkness as one that befell the earth during Jesus's execution. Julius is astute—and correct—in concluding that there could be no solar eclipse in a lunar period of full moon, which is when the Passover occurred, because the sun and moon are on opposite sides of the earth at that time. An eclipse of the sun at this juncture is nomologically impossible. Further, the actual interval of darkness in an eclipse is never more than a few minutes, whereas the account of Phlegon, like those that appear in the first three Gospels, records a darkness at the crucifixion that lasted three hours: from noon until three o'clock in the afternoon. It would be silly to suggest that the two pagan historians recorded a society's being led by a covering cloud to think that a total eclipse of the sun had occurred.

Julius's report is not alone in citing ancient Greek writings that refer to the events that occurred at the crucifixion of Christ. There are other references to Phlegon's remarks. Eusebius states,

> Jesus Christ, the son of God, our Lord, as the prophecies about Him foretold, went to His Passion in the nineteenth year of the reign of Tiberius. At which time, as we found recorded in other Greek memoranda also word for word as follows, "The sun was eclipsed; there was an earthquake in Bithynia; the greater part of Nicaea was destroyed," and this tallies with the events which accompanied the Passion of our Saviour. And Phlegon also, who compiled the Olympiads, writes about the same events in his 13th book in these very words: "In the fourth year of the 202nd Olympiad an eclipse of the sun took place greater than any hitherto known, and night came on at twelve o'clock [noon], so that even the stars appeared in the sky; and a great earthquake took place in Bithynia, which levelled the greater part of Nicaea."[69]

---

[69] This passage is from the second book of Eusebius's *Chronicle*. The original work, in effect, did not survive, although subsequent chronographers captured it.

Origen also notes, in two places in one of his works, the comments by Phlegon. They are included in the church father's defense against the attacks on Christianity by Celsus. Both citations are given below:

> [A]lthough we are able to show the striking and miraculous character of the events which befell Him [Jesus], yet from what other source can we furnish an answer than from the Gospel narratives, which state that "there was an earthquake, and that the rocks were split asunder, and the tombs opened, and the veil of the temple rent in twain from top to bottom, and that darkness prevailed in the day-time, the sun failing to give light?" But if Celsus believe the Gospel accounts when he thinks that he can find in them matter of charge against the Christians, and refuse to believe them when they establish the divinity of Jesus, our answer to him is: "Sir, either disbelieve all the Gospel narratives, and then no longer imagine that you can found charges upon them; or, in yielding your belief to their statements, look in admiration on the Logos of God. . . . And with regard to the eclipse in the time of Tiberius Caesar, in whose reign Jesus appears to have been crucified, and the great earthquakes which then took place· Phlegon too, I think, has written in the thirteenth or fourteenth book of his Chronicles."[70]

> He [Celsus] imagines also that both the earth-quake and the darkness were an invention; but regarding

---

George Syncellus cites Eusebius in his *Chronography*. I quote from the translation of Syncellus in C. R. Haines, *Heathen Contact with Christianity during Its First Century and a Half, Being All References to Christianity Recorded in Pagan Writings during That Period* (Cambridge: Deighton, Bell and Co., 1923), 57. Also see the parallel translation of the passage as it appears in the previously mentioned *Chronography of George Synkellos*, 471–72. In the fourth century, Jerome translated the second book of Eusebius's *Chronicle* into Latin, manuscripts of which have been preserved. An English rendering of Jerome's work, which includes the quotation from Eusebius that I give here, is available. Consult Roger Pearse et al., "Early Church Fathers – Additional Texts: The Chronicle of St. Jerome," The Tertullian Project, accessed May 9, 2014, www.tertullian.org/fathers/jerome_chronicle_03_part2.htm.

[70] Origen, *Origen Against Celsus*, 2.33, 444–45.

these, we have in the preceding pages made our defence, according to our ability, adducing the testimony of Phlegon, who relates that these events took place at the time when our Saviour suffered.[71]

The Julian analysis, together with the corresponding remarks by the other two authors, does more than document the existence of Christ; it also suggests that the miraculous is associated with Him. There are other allusions, among the Greeks, to miraculous events in Jesus's life. The renowned physician Claudius (or Aelius) Galenus—known as Galen of Pergamum (c. A.D. 130–c. 210)—is cited in a medieval work by Gregory Bar Hebraeus, in which Galen is recorded speaking of Christ or Christians.[72] Galen notes the moral principles in accordance with which the followers of Christ conduct themselves and their acceptance of the Lord's miracles. What is interesting is that Galen appears to accept these supernatural occurrences as well.

> Now this Galen came from the city of Pergamus [Pergamum], and he wrote many books on the craft of the physician, and of these about one hundred works are extant. He revived the Hippocratic system of medicine which had fallen into disuse (or, become antiquated). And when he was told about the mighty deeds and healings which Christ, our Lord, used to do, he said, 'I have no doubt whatsoever that He doeth these things by means of the Divine Power.'[73]

There are several other examples of ancient writings—principally, Greco-Roman—that contain pertinent references. Collectively, they represent a corpus of information that provides important insights. I summarize below some cases that document historical facts and that mention Christ or Christians explicitly by name, except where noted as identifying descriptions:

---

[71] Ibid., 2.59, 455.

[72] Estimates of Galen's death vary by more than a decade.

[73] Gregory Bar Hebraeus, *Chronography*, 1.8, *The Chronography of Gregory Abû'l Faraj, the Son of Aaron, the Hebrew Physician Commonly Known as Bar Hebraeus, Being the First Part of His Political History of the World,* trans. Ernest A. Wallis Budge, vol. 1 (London: Oxford University Press, 1932), 54.

Gaius Plinius Caecilius Secundus (Pliny the Younger), governor of Bithynia in Asia Minor, lived from c. A.D. 61 to c. 113. A substantial amount of Pliny's writings survive in the form of correspondence: ten books of letters that he composed or received. In one such communiqué, delivered to Emperor Trajan (Book 10, Letter 96), Pliny mentions Christ several times. Explaining his dealings with Christians, he seeks the emperor's counsel. Pliny states that he has been conducting trials in which he attempts to force those who are suspected of being Christians to deny their faith, under the threat of punishment, then worship a statue of Trajan and curse Christ, thereby securing their release. Pliny remarks that it is said of those who are devoted followers of Christ that they cannot be made to perform such acts. Persons who continued to express their allegiance to Jesus after being interrogated were executed on the governor's orders or, if they were Roman citizens, sent to Rome for trial. In the letter, Pliny states that individuals who claim to be believers acknowledge gathering, singing hymns to Christ, and binding themselves by oath to moral behavior, such things constituting the whole of their questionable activities.

Marcus Ulpius Traianus (Trajan), Roman emperor, lived from A.D. 53 to 117. In reply to Pliny, Trajan writes a letter telling the governor that he is right to punish those who prove to be Christians but that those who deny their faith and who demonstrate it by supplicating the gods should gain pardon. Trajan directs Pliny, however, not to search actively for Christians and not to accept any anonymous report that accuses someone of being a Christian. Trajan's response is maintained in the collected correspondence of Pliny (Book 10, Letter 97).

Gaius Suetonius Tranquillus (Suetonius), a Roman historian and lawyer, lived from c. A.D. 70 to c. 150, although some place his death a number of years earlier. In his work *The Lives of the Twelve Caesars*, Suetonius refers in *Claudius* (Book 5), 25, to one who is named 'Chrestus'. It is not certain whether the name is an alternate rendering of 'Christus'—the Latin spelling of 'Christ'—or refers to someone else, and scholars are divided on this issue. There is in the same work, however, a clear reference in *Nero* (Book 6), 16, to the severe treatment of Christians.

Publius Aelius Hadrianus (Hadrian), Roman emperor, lived from A.D. 76 to 138. Hadrian composed a letter to Minucius Fundanus, proconsul of Asia, in response to a letter by the predecessor proconsul, Serenius Granianus, regarding the treatment of Christians. In his letter, Hadrian emphasizes due process in dealing with them, taking punitive measures only on proof of wrongdoing. Persons accusing Christians calumniously, having no basis for an allegation other than prejudice, are to be punished severely. The letter is preserved by the second-century church father Justin Martyr in his *First Apology*, 69, and its content is recounted by the third-to-fourth century church father Eusebius in his *Ecclesiastical History*, 4.9. A second letter, which was written to the statesman Servianus, mentions both Christ and Christians, but there is disagreement regarding the letter's authenticity because of its style and content. One scholar believes, however, that it was taken from Phlegon's biography of Hadrian.[74]

Lucian of Samosata, a Greek satirist, lived from c. A.D. 120 to c. 190. Critical of believers, he mentions Christians in several places in his works *Alexander* and *The Death of Peregrinus*. An implicit, but unambiguous, reference to Christ appears in *Peregrinus*, 11: "The Christians, as it is, still worship that great man, who was crucified in Palestine."[75] A second reference to Christ, similar to the first, appears in *Peregrinus*, 13.

Celsus, a subscriber to Neoplatonism, lived around the end of the second century. He wrote a scathing attack on Jesus and Christianity titled *True Doctrine*. In it, he derides and mocks the faith in a broad fashion. The work perished, but much of it is preserved in Origen's notable and lengthy rebuttal *Origen Against Celsus*. Passages in Origen that are attributed to the words of Celsus include direct references to Jesus, albeit in a blasphemous way.

Marcus Annius Verus (Marcus Aurelius Antoninus), Roman emperor and philosopher, lived from A.D. 121 to 180. He sent a letter to the Assembly of Asia concerning the persecution of Christians. The message is one of rebuke, commanding the recipients not to harass

---

[74] See Haines, *Heathen Contact*, 18.
[75] Lucian of Samosata, *Peregrinus*, 11, quoted in Haines, *Heathen Contact*, 81.

believers. In the document, the emperor confirms that he will uphold the previously established policy, which decrees that there will be no disturbance of Christians, except for attempted actions against the Roman government. Those who accuse Christians wrongly, simply on the basis of their faith, are to be held guilty. The letter is preserved in Eusebius's *Ecclesiastical History*, 4.13. The letter also appears in Justin Martyr's *First Apology*, 70, where it is attributed to Titus Antoninus Augustus Pius (Antoninus Pius). It is unclear whether the rescript was dispatched by Marcus Aurelius, Antoninus Pius, or both. It may be that it was composed by Antoninus Pius before his death and issued subsequently by Marcus Aurelius.[76]

Mara Bar Serapion, a Syrian and possibly a Stoic philosopher, probably lived between the late first century and the third century. In a letter to his son, he mentions the Jews' "executing their wise King."[77] The reference, if it is to Jesus, is implicit; nevertheless, history offers no obvious alternative.

Other references exist. According to Eusebius, one by the name of 'Bruttius', writing perhaps around A.D. 150, states that numerous Christians suffered martyrdom under the Roman emperor Titus Flavius Domitianus (Domitian), who lived from A.D. 51 to 96. As for this ruler, Eusebius notes in *Ecclesiastical History*, 3.19–20, that Domitian, according to the church father Hegesippus, issued orders for the slaying of the descendants of David. Learning that there were living grandchildren of Judas—that is to say, Jude, a son of Mary— "called the brother of our Lord, according to the flesh," the emperor sent for them, as they were reputed to be in David's lineage.[78] He inquired about their ancestry, and they confirmed that David was their forefather. The emperor questioned them concerning their tangible assets, then asked them about Christ and His kingdom. After they responded, he dismissed them, treating them derisively as simpletons, but he ordered the persecution to cease.

Passages with oblique references to Jesus or to Christians, varying in transparency, are found in several early pagan writings,

---

[76] This reasonable suggestion is put forth in Haines, *Heathen Contact*, 22.

[77] Mara Bar Serapion, quoted in Bruce, *New Testament Documents*, 114.

[78] Eusebius, *Ecclesiastical History*, 3.20, 102.

including those of the Stoic author Epictetus (c. A.D. 45–c. 120), the Latin orator Marcus Cornelius Fronto (c. A.D. 95–c. 167), and a Greek rhetorician, Publius Aelius Aristides Theodorus (c. A.D. 120–c. 189).[79] The philosopher Numenius of Apamea, who was active around A.D. 170, presents a narrative about Jesus, without actually naming Him, in his dissertation *The Good*, according to Origen in his manuscript *Origen Against Celsus*, 4.51.

There is also nontextual evidence that relates to the crucifixion of Jesus. Although it is not as extensive or conclusive as what was unearthed in Nineveh, each element opens a window on the biblical narrative. In 1968, workers discovered an ancient burial site in Israel. The discovery yielded an ossuary—a stone box into which human bones are placed—holding the skeletal remains of a man. The inscription identified him as Yohanan Ben Ha'galgol. The man's frame revealed that he had been crucified, possibly around A.D. 70 as a result of the uprising against Rome. A nail had penetrated both his heel bones and was still in place, embedded along with fragments of the wooden beam to which he had been attached. An examination of the other bones showed the position of the nails in the forearms.[80] The remains are tangential, but they demonstrate that crucifixion was practiced in early times as a form of execution, and they provide an indication of the method of affixing a victim to the wooden structure.

Other archaeological findings allude to two persons in authority who were associated directly with the condemnation of Jesus: the political figure who sentenced Jesus to death on the cross and the principal religious figure who was behind the advocacy of it. In 1961, an inscribed, stone step in the Roman amphitheater in the ancient city of Caesarea was uncovered. That city was the official residence of Pontius Pilate, governor of Judea from A.D. 26 to 36, during the reign of Emperor Tiberius, who ruled from A.D. 14 to 37. The step contains a phrase in Latin; these words are included: "Pontius Pilate, Prefect [the governor] of Judea."[81] Such a discovery

---

[79] Estimates of the respective dates of the lives of these individuals span a number of years.

[80] A more complete description is available in Gary R. Habermas, *The Historical Jesus: Ancient Evidence for the Life of Christ* (Joplin, MO: College Press Publishing Co., 1996), 173–75.

[81] See Barker et al., *Zondervan Study Bible*, 1568–69, n. to Luke 3:1.

clearly substantiates the life of the ruler who executed Jesus. Among relevant findings are also coins from the period of Pilate's reign.

As for the chief religious leader in Jesus's day, Zvi Greenhut reports that excavations in 1990 of a burial site in the Jerusalem Peace Forest yielded a number of ossuaries.[82] One of them, ossuary number 3, bears a name that is translated as 'Caiaphas'. Another, ossuary number 6, displays two inscriptions that are nearly identical; both may be translated as 'Joseph son of Caiaphas'. The Gospels refer to Caiaphas, without the given name, as the high priest who oversaw the questioning of Jesus as He faced the Sanhedrin just prior to His trial before Pilate. Caiaphas held that position, in the generally accepted view, from A.D. 18 to 36. There is reason to believe that the ossuary is that of the man who denounced Jesus in front of the Jewish council, although the issue of the identity of the individual whose bones were discovered is not settled.[83] Josephus mentions Caiaphas twice in his *Antiquities*, providing both his given name and surname. Note the elucidation of the name, particularly in the second passage, as well as the reference to Pontius Pilate in the first.

> Tiberius Nero . . . was now the third emperor; and he sent Valerius Gratus to be procurator of Judea. . . . This man deprived Ananus of the high priesthood, and appointed Ismael, the son of Phabi, to be high priest. He

---

[82] See Zvi Greenhut, "The 'Caiaphas' Tomb in North Talpiyot, Jerusalem," *Atiqot* 21, no. 21 (1992): 63–71.

[83] Greenhut, along with other archaeologists and scholars, is convinced that the ossuary is that of the high priest Caiaphas. Some have expressed doubts, however, because of the level of the ornamentation on the box, the questionable identification of one of the letters in the inscription, and the inclusion of 'son' in the reference. See Craig A. Evans, *Jesus and the Ossuaries* (Waco: Baylor University Press, 2003), 104–12. Contrary to Evans's assessment, the ossuary appears to be rather ornate, with an etched border, and an elaborate pattern of rosettes and other figures that are carved into the front. Says Greenhut, "This richly decorated ossuary is the finest in the tomb." Consult Greenhut, " 'Caiaphas' Tomb," 65. The slight difference between the two inscriptions on ossuary number 6 is possibly of more significance in attempting to ascertain identity. The inclusion of 'son' in the wording, on the other hand, may be inconsequential, given that 'Caiaphas' is the family name. Some writings, in fact, include the term when referring to him. Despite the open question, the archaeological finding is important enough to be considered in any analysis of historical evidence.

also deprived him in a little time, and ordained Eleazar, the son of Ananus, who had been high priest before, to be high priest; which office, when he had held for a year, Gratus deprived him of it, and gave the high priesthood to Simon, the son of Camithus; and when he had possessed that dignity no longer than a year, Joseph Caiaphas was made his successor. When Gratus had done those things, he went back to Rome, after he had waited in Judea eleven years, when Pontius Pilate came as his successor.[84]

Besides which, he [Vitellius] also deprived Joseph, who was also called Caiaphas, of the high priesthood, and appointed Jonathan, the son of Ananus, the former high priest, to succeed him.[85]

A further discovery of importance awaited. A paper that two authors published in 2011 provides details of the finding and subsequent analysis of an ornate ossuary, said to be from a burial cave in the area of the 'Elah Valley.[86] It displays an inscription, the English translation of which is "Miriam daughter of Yeshua son of Caiaphas, priests of Maʻaziah from Beth 'Imri." Archaeologists give a date range for the artifact of A.D. 70–135, a period the accuracy of which is supported by a pair of oil lamps, also said to be from the cave. The authors bear witness to the authenticity of this valuable artifact.

Since the ossuary in question was not found in a controlled excavation and due to its importance, it was subjected to scientific analyses in order to address the question of authenticity. The examinations focused on the patina coating the stone surface, with emphasis on the inscribed area. The patination of the stone, in and around the inscription, indicates a complex process that

---

[84] Josephus, *Antiquities*, 18.2.2, 588. Ananus was a son of Annas, the high priest from A.D. 6–15. Joseph Caiaphas was Annas's son-in-law.

[85] Ibid., 18.4.3, 593.

[86] Boaz Zissu and Yuval Goren, "The Ossuary of 'Miriam Daughter of Yeshua Son of Caiaphas, Priests [of] Maʻaziah from Beth 'Imri,' " *Israel Exploration Journal* 61, no. 1 (2011): 74–95.

occurred over a prolonged sequence of time, which is
extremely difficult, if not impossible, to replicate in
laboratory conditions. It may be concluded, therefore,
that the patina and the inscription should be considered
authentic beyond any reasonable doubt.[87]

The key significance of the discovery is the documenting of the
priestly family of Caiaphas.

Apart from discoveries that pertain to the crucifixion of Christ,
there is archaeological evidence that points to James, a member of
Jesus's immediate family, as described in the New Testament. An
ossuary surfaced in 2002 with a deeply etched inscription that, when
translated, reads, "James, son of Joseph, brother of Jesus." There is
little or no dissention with respect to the antiquity of the stone box
itself among scholars who have studied the artifact. The inscription,
however, leaves them divided: Some hold that it is genuine; others
disagree. One scholar who writes on the subject states,

> If the James ossuary is indeed the ossuary of
> James, the brother of Jesus, we are in possession of a
> truly significant artifact that confirms and clarifies
> several important aspects of the life and impact of
> James, an important leader in the early Christian
> movement.[88]

Regardless of the lack of consensus, the ossuary is an object
with historical implications that demand attention in any serious
discussion of archaeological support for the life of Christ. Like the
other findings, it is one more piece of information that contributes to
the overall extracanonical picture of ancient history and is to be
counted as deserving of scrutiny.

In the final analysis, the skeptical remarks by Russell concerning the existence of Christ reflect, even prior to the recent discoveries
of relevant archaeological evidence, an uncommon superficiality.
That Christ lived is supported too well by data from a diversity of
sources. As one contemporary author puts it,

---

[87] Ibid., 74.
[88] Evans, *Jesus and the Ossuaries*, 122. See pp. 112–22 of the Evans work for
more detail concerning this artifact.

Some writers may toy with the fancy of a 'Christ-myth', but they do not do so on the ground of historical evidence. The historicity of Christ is as axiomatic for an unbiased historian as the historicity of Julius Caesar. It is not historians who propagate the 'Christ-myth' theories.[89]

THE UPSHOT

So, must one reject the biblical record and *all* these ancient corroborating materials along with it—not after a careful examination of them but simply en masse—as though such things do not count as, to use Dawkins's phrase, mutually buttressed evidence? Dawkins is correct in holding that substantiation of facts leads to assurance of truth. If, however, one ignores information that does not align with a preconceived view solely because it does not align with it, where the preconceptions on which the view is based are adopted without solid grounds, then one surely may miss the truth. Dawkins claims to have studied the evidence, but one must be doubtful of the scope of that review. If it excludes pertinent data, then it is deficient. Even the accounts of the miraculous deserve a fair look, at minimum, and the events surrounding the life and death of Christ—reported both in the Bible and in other early documents—are a sensible place to start. Reality is not determined by how one models it. Facts are independent of one's inclination or disinclination to accept them. Clinging to disinclinations would have brought quantum mechanics to a sudden end years ago, as its proclamations are just too bizarre to be readily believable; and it would have resulted in denying the existence of the extra dimensions of the universe, for no one has experienced even five dimensions, let alone the eleven of M-theory.

In summary, the internal support for the biblical record, both the Old Testament and the New, is there, but the external support adds another facet to the investigation. A careful reading of the ancient texts—Jewish, Christian, and pagan—furnishes a researcher with an array of valuable information, and the evidence that is

---

[89] Bruce, *New Testament Documents*, 119.

generated by an active archaeological enterprise continues to grow. Some of the findings are definitive; others provide implied support. Collectively, the material is certainly sufficient to warrant judicious thought and rigorous, extended study—not wholesale dismissal. Both Dawkins's sweeping rejection of "anything and everything super-natural" and Russell's sweeping rejection of the historicity of Jesus point to investigations that are characterized by a singular incompleteness.[90] It is they, rather than the contender, that exemplify the inadequately considered review of evidence. To look at evidence and then to disallow it following a careful evaluation is one thing; not to look at all is quite another. The latter approach cannot be justified, even if it points to occurrences that defy explanation in terms of physical law.

NONCOMPLIANCE

David Hume maintains in his *Enquiry* that it is not sensible to believe in miracles. The laws of nature bear the greatest degree of probability in accounting for actual events, he says; miracles are violations of these laws. It is therefore more probable, he proceeds to argue, that a report of the occurrence of a miracle is false than it is that a genuine breach of a physical law has occurred. Hume does acknowledge, however, that it is not logically impossible for such a breach to take place.

Like Hume, Dawkins centers on probability but goes to some lengths to explain how events that seem to be miraculous give that impression merely because of the very low likelihood of their happening. Says Dawkins, "So, what do we mean by a miracle? A miracle is something that happens but which is exceedingly surprising."[91] He asks one to suppose that a sculpture of the Virgin Mary waves its hand. It may seem to observers to be miraculous, but physics can offer a reason for the event.

---

[90] Dawkins, *God Delusion*, 36.
[91] Richard Dawkins, *The Blind Watchmaker: Why the Evidence of Evolution Reveals a Universe without Design* (1986; repr., New York: W. W. Norton and Co., 2006), 226.

> In the case of the marble statue, molecules in solid marble are continuously jostling against one another in random directions. The jostlings of the different molecules cancel one another out, so the whole hand of the statue stays still. But if, by sheer coincidence, all the molecules just happened to move in the same direction at the same moment, the hand would move. If they then all reversed direction at the same moment the hand would move back. In this way it is *possible* for a marble statue to wave at us. It could happen. The odds against such a coincidence are unimaginably great but they are not incalculably great. A physicist colleague has kindly calculated them for me. . . . It is theoretically possible for a cow to jump over the moon with something like the same improbability.[92]

There is an inconsistency here. Physics may describe, in theory, how a piece of stone could shift, though the molecules would have to move concurrently in the same direction over a substantial distance, from the molecular perspective, for the shift to be observable. There would be no strict violation of a law of nature in this case, despite the extreme improbability. A cow's jumping over the moon, however, would be a breach of such a law. It is a nomological impossibility. Dawkins's latter example is surely not serious, but the thinking that it reflects is serious. It points to an obscuring of the distinction between the extraordinary and the miraculous. Miracles cannot be *identified* with improbable happenings or surprising incidents, albeit miracles may be both unlikely and unexpected. It is not by virtue of the level of probability or expectation that they are set apart. Dawkins's view, in fact, leads to a trilemma, according to which (1) events that are not nomologically possible, such as a cow's jumping over the moon, carry a probability of occurrence in nature that is greater than zero and are therefore nomologically possible, which is a contradiction; or (2) events that violate the laws of nature are not miracles; yet, by the very meaning of the term 'miracle', such events are indeed miracles, and to declare otherwise would be to exclude them through mere redefinition; or (3) there are no violations of the laws of nature—even moon-jumping-cow events—and therefore no miracles, but this

---

[92] Ibid., 227–28.

assumption eliminates miracles simply by decreeing that no such incidents ever occur. It is the position that some adopt: "[T]here are no miracles, or exceptions to the laws of nature."[93] Likewise, I believe that Dawkins takes this last path. Consider how he does so.

It is important to distinguish between two related concepts of events. A preternatural event—as I will employ the concept of it—is one in which supernatural agency brings about a state of affairs but not by diverging from physical laws. A supernatural event is one in which supernatural agency brings about a state of affairs by moving or operating outside physical laws, in whole or in part. Miraculous occurrences—and it is supernatural agency that sets them apart— may be of either sort, but those of the latter sort provide the more striking evidence that transcendent intelligence exists. I will focus on them going forward. Given his stance regarding the supernatural and his remark that he is a scientist, it seems that Dawkins would accept nothing in support of the premise that reality could be more inclusive than the physical. All contrary indications thus would be inadmissible. What appears to be miraculous is preexcluded as being such, which is tantamount to embracing this argument; I number the steps:

The No-Miracle Argument

1. There is no reality other than physical reality.
2. Everything that happens in physical reality does so wholly in accordance with physical laws.
3. Therefore, everything that happens does so wholly in accordance with physical laws.
4. A miracle is an event that does not happen in accordance with physical laws.
5. If a supposed event does not happen in accordance with physical laws, then it cannot be real.
6. Reality is that which is.
7. Therefore, there are no miracles.

If one accepts the first premise, then one may continue through the argument and accept the conclusion. The argument, though, begs the

---

[93] Hawking and Mlodinow, *Grand Design*, 34.

question, for the issue is whether reality is limited in extent to the physical. The first premise rules out the supernatural, and thereby miracles, by mere declaration. A billion events that follow the laws of nature will not show that no events contravene them. Miracles, if they occur, are evidence to the contrary, not simply unexplained physical phenomena. One cannot preclude them by assumption without tripping on the fallacy. Preelimination without an objective assessment of evidence is a flawed approach. Rejecting the immaterial based on a presupposition that it does not exist will not do.

There is a sister argument with a different, but related, conclusion. It appears below, also with numbered assertions:

The No-God Argument

1. There is no reality other than physical reality.
2. The Judaeo-Christian God, if He is real, is supernatural and hence transcends the physical.
3. Reality is that which is.
4. Therefore, there is no Judaeo-Christian God.

Again, in stating that reality is just physical, the argument eliminates the supernatural, and thereby God, as a premise; it begs the question.

Contrary to Dawkins's claim about the axiomatic adoption of faith-based beliefs, one's acceptance of the things of God, as revealed in the Bible, is not the turning of a deaf ear to evidence. In fact, that same Bible says, "Taste and see that the LORD is good."[94] People are encouraged to go and explore—to learn. That exploration takes one beyond the purview of scientific inquiries while perhaps leaving a foot planted there. It is a search for things that are not part of the corporeal world, but it does not entail dismissing perceptual experience. Indeed, even Jesus, as the Scriptures report, points to publically observable incidents when telling one of His disciples to accept what he says as true: "Believe me when I say that I am in the Father and the Father is in me; or at least believe on the *evidence* of the miracles themselves."[95] One *can* see the physical evidence that

---

[94] Ps. 34:8 NIV.
[95] John 14:11 NIV. The emphasis is mine.

nonphysical things, which one *cannot* see, do exist. The miraculous, if it occurs, *is* evidence that the claims that Jesus advances are right. Consider then an argument that presents a conclusion that differs from the argument that denies miracles. Again, miracles of the supernatural sort are under discussion here. As before, I number the steps.

The Miracle-Reality Argument

1. Physical laws are universal in physical reality: Wherever there is strict physical reality, those laws apply without variance.
2. If there are any events that happen but do not happen in accordance with physical laws, then reality extends beyond the strictly physical.
3. A miracle is an event that does not happen in accordance with physical laws.
4. Therefore, if there are any miracles, then reality extends beyond the strictly physical.

If one allows the physicalists' assumption about the universality of the laws of nature to stand, then the argument is indisputable, though the conclusion is conditional. If, however, there is just one genuine miracle, then the antecedent of the conditional in the conclusion of the argument is satisfied, and it follows that reality does not lie solely within the borders of physicality. It transcends them. In that case, the entire atheistic system of explanation, which denies immateriality on the basis of preimposed boundaries, collapses.

Why would Jesus have pointed to miracles as evidence unless He believed that they supported the truth of His message? One could deny that the incidents occurred, but one could not deny that, if they occurred, then they stood as stark proof of a reality beyond the realm of corporeality. If miracles happen, then Dawkins's assertion that nothing supernatural is real is a false assertion. The question is whether that postulate is true. Publically observable events that can be explained adequately only by incorporating the miraculous into the explanation would be hard evidence.

It is noteworthy that, as the Bible conveys, the religious leaders of Jesus's day *accepted the miracles of Jesus* as factual, but they *rejected Him.* Recorded in the Gospel of John is the account of the raising of Lazarus from the dead. The chief priests and Pharisees were disturbed by the event because it evidenced Jesus's divinity; and, as a result, people were putting their faith in Jesus rather than looking to the Jewish authorities. The motivation for their rejection of Jesus as the Messiah is plain.

> Therefore many of the Jews who had come to visit Mary, and had seen what Jesus did [in raising Lazarus from the dead], put their faith in him. But some of them went to the Pharisees and told them what Jesus had done. Then the chief priests and the Pharisees called a meeting of the Sanhedrin.
>
> "What are we accomplishing?" they asked. "Here is this man performing many miraculous signs. If we let him go on like this, everyone will believe in him, and then the Romans will come and take away both our place and our nation."[96]

What this narrative relates is amazing. The chief priests and Pharisees believed the authenticity of the miracle that Jesus performed in raising Lazarus—that it actually did occur—and the supernatural import of what it signified—that it could not have occurred purely by natural means—but did not receive the one who performed the miracle as the Messiah. They valued the status quo too much to allow anything to jeopardize it. Their solution was to eliminate Jesus: "So from that day on they plotted to take his [Jesus's] life."[97]

What is more amazing is that the chief priests wanted to get rid of not only Jesus but the *evidence* of the miracle too.

> Meanwhile a large crowd of Jews found out that Jesus was there and came, not only because of him but also to see Lazarus, whom he had raised from the dead. So the chief priests made plans to kill Lazarus as well, for on account of him many of the Jews were going over to Jesus and putting their faith in him.[98]

---

[96] Ibid., 11:45–48 NIV.
[97] Ibid., 11:53 NIV.
[98] Ibid., 12:9–11 NIV.

That Jesus was performing supernatural deeds, these men accepted as a fact. It is just that these astounding incidents were of less importance to them than their cultural structure. This point is significant. The actions of the men reflected an intellectual assent, acknowledging the manifestation of the miraculous—publically observed events clearly bore witness to it—yet that acknowledgment was not enough to change their course. As I detailed in chapter 4, what underlies end-state actions is the conjunction of value-factors and beliefs. The problem for the Jewish leaders lay in what they valued, not in what they believed, for they deemed the miracles to be real. Their acts stemmed from what they cherished in light of what they believed.

One could dismiss the entire account, of course, taking the miracle with it, but on what basis? Would it not be because of the assumption that there are no miracles? To eliminate them would require striking much of the Old Testament and the New Testament. I can attest to occurrences in my life that are surely miracles—no other explanation is plausible—and to the comments by puzzled, even stunned, individuals who saw the results; perhaps a future work on the topic would be fitting. Contemporary Christian literature is filled with examples of miraculous events in current times that even a cursory review reveals. All these accounts would need to be excised as well without investigation. The theme here ought to be familiar by now. Dismissal of all evidence—tentative or otherwise—prior to examination of that evidence, particularly where it is in conflict with a favored position, is illogical. Furthermore, it stands in violation of the very principles of proper inquiry to which practitioners in the field of science strive to adhere.

Dawkins's appeal to truth, so he asserts, is based on evidence. He thinks that one must examine it if one is to embrace a system of beliefs. It is thus ironic that Dawkins is willing, based on what science has discovered in biological cells, to accept, of all things, intelligent design, but design that, so he claims, points to, of all things, that for which there is a conspicuous *absence of evidence*: the seeding of the planet earth by extraterrestrial beings. On the other hand, intelligent design for which there is a conspicuous *wealth of evidence*, including what science has discovered in biological cells, design that points with reasonableness to God, he dismisses adamantly. Consider his postulations:

966

It could be that, at some earlier time, somewhere in the universe, a civilization evolved by probably some kind of Darwinian means to a very high level of technology and *designed* a form of life that they seeded onto perhaps this planet. Now, we know the sort of event that must have happened for the origin of life. It was the origin of the first self-replicating molecule. That is a possibility and an intriguing possibility, and I suppose it's possible you might find *evidence of that* if you look at the details of our chemistry and molecular biology—you might find a *signature of some sort of designer*. And that designer could well be a higher intelligence from elsewhere in the universe; but that higher intelligence would itself have had to have come about by some explicable or ultimately explicable process. It couldn't have just jumped into existence spontaneously. That's the point.[99]

Dawkins acknowledges the possibility that life on the earth is designed—the handiwork of intelligent agency. It is difficult to see how he can claim that his position is based on evidence and yet accept a supposition for which there is none at all: the exporting of life by extraterrestrials. Moreover, in admitting that biological forms on the earth may be the product of intelligent design, he has no basis other than fiat for declaring that the intelligent designers are the product of some other process. Could the chemistry and molecular biology of these would-be creatures not also bear the signature of design? Dawkins just opened the door to his own who-designed-the-designer regress. All his fervent arguing against design and in favor of the arising of living things on the earth by a random event in a primeval environment, somehow spun into reality by the anthropic principle, seems to be remarkably diminished. One might wish to ponder this pair of comments by a contemporary of Dawkins:

> No one has been more eloquent than Richard Dawkins in describing how complexity arises from simplicity in biology, so it is ludicrous to suggest he supports the ID [intelligent design] view [of life].

---

[99] Richard Dawkins, in *Expelled: No Intelligence Allowed*, dir. Nathan Frankowski, 95 min. (n.p.: Premise Media, 2008), DVD. The emphases are mine.

> I have personally checked with Dawkins and he agrees with my interpretation of his words.[100]

Such incongruousness is surprising.

A NARROW PATH

Science is a grand enterprise. It has brought much to humanity. Its breakthroughs have improved the lives of people considerably and helped them to achieve marvelous things across history. Scientific discoveries have revealed many wonders, from a world of material building blocks that are almost unimaginably tiny to a cosmos of almost unimaginably colossal proportions. Science and the scientific method operate with great effectiveness within the physical domain. There they stop, though, unable to venture outside that domain to see whether there is anything more. Philosophy, on the other hand, does peer beyond physicality's edge. With its complex theories and nontestable principles in hand, it dares to delve into matters where other fields of study never go. In the final analysis, however, it too proves to be inadequate, as it has no independent means of verification. In the philosophical enterprise, there is only the weight of the machinery of logic to secure the truth. In the mission to understand the scope of reality—whether immaterial things exist—*what science lacks* is the extended reach of metaphysics, and *what metaphysics lacks* is the observability of science.

Evidence is an important indicator of truth; it points to facts that validate beliefs. If one seeks such support for the spiritual, then one can find it; it is there for the taking. Turning to physical evidence that substantiates the existence of the unseen Judaeo-Christian God, or to the various proofs that He is real—if one or more of these proofs is ultimately persuasive—may lead a person to believe in

---

[100] Victor J. Stenger, "Everything Came from Nothing," *Huffington Post*, September 12, 2011, accessed August 30, 2015, huffingtonpost.com/victor-stenger/everything-came-from-noth_b_896992.html.

God. Each of these avenues can constitute a step forward in the search, but, in the end, both of them fall short of having the efficacy that is required to bring a person into a relationship with Him. Knowing that God exists is not the same as knowing God. The first is *propositional*; the second is *experiential*. It is a distinction that surfaced earlier in this work. With knowledge only of the former sort, one's travels will remain unfinished.

Perhaps there is a way to unlock the mysteries of an unseen realm—a path to understanding that leads beyond both observation and logic, abandoning neither but recognizing the limitations of each. Maybe finding God does not depend so much on the eyes or the mind as on something that is deeper within an individual. In His rebuke of Thomas for a lack of faith, as reported in the Gospel of John, Jesus told the disciple that, because he had seen, he believed. It was the evidence that Thomas's senses provided that convinced him of his Lord's resurrection. Jesus then said to Thomas, "[B]lessed are those who have not seen and yet have believed."[101] The path that Jesus wanted Thomas to take was the narrow one of reliance on what Jesus had spoken to him, not on what Thomas's senses or his reasoning conveyed. Jesus wanted the disciple's trust in the revelation that Jesus had given. The Scriptures, in fact, declare, "[W]ithout faith it is impossible to please God."[102]

Evidence serves to confirm one's beliefs in any pursuit of knowledge, but the weight of it in spiritual matters may fall where one would not have expected it to fall. The Bible states, "Now faith is the *substance* of things hoped for, the *evidence* of things not seen."[103] How can faith be substantive? How can it be evidential? Given that knowledge is justified true belief—a key tenet for which I have argued—is it possible for faith to ground beliefs, so that knowing is realizable where incorporeal, spiritual things are concerned? One wonders whether an undetected square of a different order lies at the end of this extradimensional corridor. It is an issue to explore.

An acquaintance asked Bertrand Russell, at a gathering to celebrate his ninetieth birthday, what he would do if he learned after

---

[101] John 20:29 NIV.

[102] Heb. 11:6 NIV.

[103] Ibid., 11:1 KJV. The emphases are mine. The Amplified Bible has the phrase 'proof of things' in place of 'evidence of things' in the translation of this verse.

his departure that, contrary to Russell's belief, God does exist. Here is an account of that dialogue:

> A London lady . . . sat next to him at his party, and over the soup she suggested to him that he was not only the world's most famous atheist but, by this time, very probably the world's oldest atheist. "What will you do, Bertie, if it turns out you've been wrong?" she asked. "I mean, what if—uh—when the time comes, you should *meet* Him? What will you say?" Russell . . . was delighted with the question. His bright, birdlike eyes grew brighter as he contemplated this possible future dialogue, and then he pointed a finger upward and cried, "Why, I should say, 'God, you gave us insufficient evidence!'"[104]

Support for the existence of God is not insufficient. Whether there is evidence of a sort that one does not anticipate encountering in the quest to know, there is certainly evidence of the mainstream sort. A review of both the ancient literature and modern archaeological discoveries reveals an abundance of information, from a range of sources, that substantiates the authenticity of biblical narratives. The corroboration is neither out of sight nor out of reach. It is right before one's nose. One only has to look—and see whether experience will bear out the facts.

Russell died a few years later. Evidence was no longer a factor at that point in anchoring his belief about God, whether because of annihilation or epiphany: Either there was no Russell to know the truth, or he understood it in a profound way.

---

[104] "The Talk of the Town," *New Yorker* 46, no. 1 (1970): 29.

SOLUTION TO THE PUZZLE, SQUARES

By not limiting the thinking to two dimensions—which admittedly the formation of the puzzle leads one to do—a different result is possible, increasing the number of squares to six. Figure 9.4 shows the configuration.

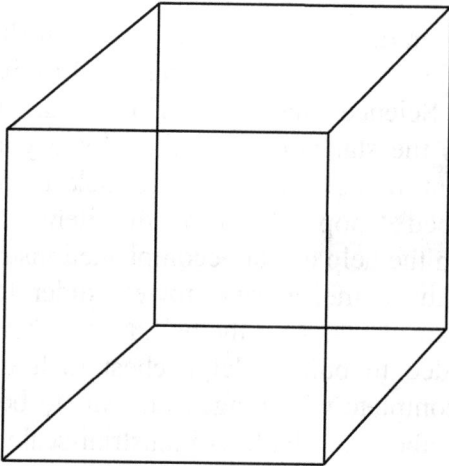

Figure 9.4

CHAPTER 10

THE LONGING FOR BELONGING

A cord of three strands is not quickly broken.

—Eccles. 4:12 NIV

The eighth grade was an unusual period of time for me. Aside from physical education, my classes in school to that point had been academic ones. Science, mathematics, English, history, and other subjects—it was the standard curriculum for a young person. That year was different, though. Boys my age took a woodworking class, which we dubbed 'shop'. Most of the items that the students constructed, with the help of our accomplished instructor, were small accessories for the home: a paper-towel holder for the kitchen or perhaps a knickknack stand for the hall. Not content with the typical projects, I decided to build a large chest to house firewood. My firewood box, complete with hinged lid, was to be functional and a thing of beauty; above all, with its industrial-scale legs, it was to be sturdy. While the other children were handling little pieces of wood, a lumber store delivered a full-size sheet of thick plywood, which my father had helped me to acquire, to the classroom. The piece of lumber was, no doubt, the source of disapproving comments by the surprised students. Even the instructor seemed to be displeased when that unwieldy board arrived and demanded its space on the shop floor. It was to become my prized creation, however, and a gift to my parents. I was excited. I do not remember exactly how my family and I managed to get the huge box in the car for the trip home when the project was finally complete, but perhaps one's memory becomes selective with maturity to shield one from the indignities of the past.

One thing that I do remember about the shop class, though, is something that the instructor shared one day. He was teaching us about the bonding properties of adhesives. Take two pieces of wood, treat them properly with the appropriate glue, and clamp them together securely until the bonding agent has dried overnight. Then, with mechanical aid, try to pull the boards apart. One never will be able to separate those two sections of lumber where they are joined, the instructor said. Instead of a clean break at the seam, the wood itself will splinter and tear as the force of separation rips it apart, leaving a rough, jagged surface. The bond is stronger than the wood. As a result, the joint remains, but the material shatters. It was a lesson that I was to see reappear in a different way many years later.

That cold, predawn hour in January, I was awakened by the stirring of someone who was staying in the room with me as we maintained a supportive presence. Sleep was intermittent for us during those nights in the facility. A member of my family—a person who was extremely close to me—had been in a hospice for no more than a few days, but her precious life on the earth was drawing to a close. She had fought the battle with the determination of a warrior and with an inner strength that stemmed from her spiritual beliefs. In the last weeks, I had begged her not to leave me. What rational person would ask such a thing? How could she promise not to die? What she did in response was to subject herself to whatever was necessary to try to stay alive. Following an aborted procedure, she said to me, "I did it for you." It was because I had pleaded with her not to go away. Her words were piercing. No one who has escaped such an experience can imagine the effect that hearing a loved one speak those words can have. She took her last breath in peace early that morning. Minutes passed, and then a wave of unspeakable, penetratingly deep sorrow swept over me. I grieved in a way that I never had known. The intensity of the emotion stunned me. I thought that I was prepared for it. I was wrong. It was at that moment that what actually had happened engulfed me, although I did not recognize it until later. We had been ripped apart by death. The bond that united us remained intact, but what was left behind was a jagged and severely torn spirit. The bond was stronger than the man.

Relationships take root, develop, and mature in a part of humans that is central to their personhood. They join one person to another at the core of who they are. Although people are different— with diverse gifts, abilities, interests, feelings, thoughts, ambitions, and perspectives—their makeup is not different. All people are put together in the same way. What, though, is that structure, and what is the core part of these beings? What sort of entities are persons?

THE TEACHER

For it is written:

"I will destroy the wisdom of the wise;
    the intelligence of the intelligent I will frustrate."

Where is the wise man? Where is the scholar?
Where is the philosopher of this age? Has not God made
foolish the wisdom of the world?[1]

Sitting in a philosophy class a number of years ago as a young college student, I listened attentively as the professor spoke to the group about his mental capabilities, describing himself as a very intelligent man. He said that, if he did not grasp the point of an argument, then it was because there was no point to be taken. He was referring, as I remember, to an existentialist or phenomenologist who had made certain illogical claims in a work that we were discussing. Philosophical movements in the nonanalytic vein do have their fair share of such claims, to be sure. Here is a sample:

To believe is to know that one believes, and to know that
one believes is no longer to believe. Thus to believe is
not to believe any longer because that is only to believe.[2]

Though hardly a well-articulated postulation, this passage is merely self-contradictory, but some writings of nonanalytic philosophers are sheer nonsense, as this paragraph from a work by Martin Heidegger demonstrates so well:

What testifies to the constant and widespread
though distorted revelation of the nothing in our existence more compellingly than negation? But negation
does not conjure the "not" out of itself as a means for
making distinctions and oppositions in whatever is
given, inserting itself, as it were, in between what is

---

[1] 1 Cor. 1:19–20 NIV.
[2] Jean-Paul Sartre, *Being and Nothingness*, trans. Hazel E. Barnes (New York: Philosophical Library, 1956), 69.

974

given. How could negation produce the not from itself when it can make denials only when something deniable is already granted to it? But how could the deniable and what is to be denied be viewed as something susceptible to the not unless all thinking as such has caught sight of the not already? But the not can become manifest only when its origin, the nihilation of the nothing in general, and therewith the nothing itself, is disengaged from concealment. The not does not originate through negation; rather, negation is grounded in the not that springs from the nihilation of the nothing. But negation is also only one way of nihilating, that is, only one sort of behavior that has been grounded beforehand in the nihilation of the nothing.[3]

The failure to find some meaningful point in the remarks by any given philosopher was to be attributed, the professor declared, to the irrationality of the writing, not to the lack of acumen on the professor's part. He was correct in his assessment of the illogic of some texts, without doubt, but what captured my interest was his assessment of his own intelligence. I believe that he was correct there too. Having enrolled in several of his courses and watched him tackle the arguments of other scholars, I found him to be accomplished and quite bright—erudite, logical, philosophically incisive, and forceful in his criticisms. Completing a terminal degree on an accelerated schedule at a prestigious university, the teacher was a well-versed representative of the analytic tradition. In spite of his brilliance and his self-assuredness, though, on matters of crucial importance in the lives of people, he could offer little help. Probably feeling invincible when young, as most people feel, he experienced an injury in midlife that brought with it an increased awareness of his vulnerability. The lingering effects of that injury seemed to underscore for him the limitations of his being, and, judging from his comments and demeanor, I think that he had begun to face his own mortality seriously.

The word 'philosophy' signifies the love of wisdom. If philosophy were to live up to its name, then it would point the way to

[3] Martin Heidegger, "What Is Metaphysics," in *Martin Heidegger: Basic Writings*, trans. HarperCollins Publishers, ed. David Farrell Krell (London: Harper Perennial, 2008), 104–5. Heidegger's work was published initially in German in 1929.

foundational truths and how to apply them to the issues that confront humankind. Surely then, mortality would not be so troublesome a matter for the field's most accomplished disciples, and they would not struggle to apprehend its universal role in human existence. A teacher of philosophy would be a teacher of the ways of wisdom. I make this statement not to speak against the considerable value of learning, even learning philosophy, and certainly not to belittle a brilliant man. I do it to emphasize the fact that intelligence is not the same as wisdom, and wielding the sword of logic is not the same as guiding others to essential truths. Logic lays bare the ways in which reasoning can go awry—and it does so with decisiveness—but it is not a discipline that offers answers, incontrovertible or otherwise, to the profoundly important questions that everyone comes to face. Philosophy cannot broker an agreement among its followers even on what intelligence is, let alone the mind that exhibits it. How much more elusive is wisdom? A sobering incompleteness is evident here.

Every person wants to understand why the universe exists, why living things exist, and why rational beings exist. Central to the human quest for answers is to know whether reality consists of just a blind, mechanical unfolding of colossal proportions, or it is imbued with purpose. In the end, each individual wants to know the truth about his or her own existence, whether all that there is in the short span of an individual's life is all that there is. States the Psalmist,

> As for man, his days are like grass,
>   he flourishes like a flower of the field;
> the wind blows over it and it is gone,
>   and its place remembers it no more.[4]

It seems to me that there is a common yearning in people—in many people, at least, so my experience suggests—to be a part of something that is greater than they, something that defines in some way who they are. It is a longing for a sense of purpose, I believe—a need to know, driving one on a life-quest to find answers. Deep-seated, it surfaces in moments of quiet reflection.

The Scriptures teach that King David, when he was nearing the end of his life, declared that his son Solomon was to assume the

---

[4] Ps. 103:15–16 NIV.

throne after him. David instructed the priest Zadok and the prophet Nathan to anoint Solomon king over Israel. Solomon's reign began in 970 B.C., centuries before the ancient Greeks initiated their search for *archē*. It is important to consider the account of this man that the Scriptures record.

In a dream, God told the new king to ask for whatever he would have God give to him. Solomon recognized his inexperience in administrative matters and the awesome responsibility of overseeing the nation. He asked God for an understanding heart that he might govern the people and distinguish between right and wrong. That request pleased God.

> So God said to him, "Since you have asked for this and not for long life or wealth for yourself, nor have asked for the death of your enemies but for discernment in administering justice, I will do what you have asked. I will give you a wise and discerning heart, so that there will never have been anyone like you, nor will there ever be. Moreover, I will give you what you have not asked for—both riches and honor—so that in your lifetime you will have no equal among kings. And if you walk in my ways and obey my statutes and commands as David your father did, I will give you a long life."[5]

Solomon became a man of penetrating insight and amazing creativity, and his extended reign was marked by extraordinary peace and wealth. He came to be a teacher with a depth of comprehension that exceeded all others. Word of his abilities spread, so that people traveled from foreign lands to hear him speak. The following passage reflects the extent of the gift:

> God gave Solomon wisdom and very great insight, and a breadth of understanding as measureless as the sand on the seashore. Solomon's wisdom was greater than the wisdom of all the men of the East, and greater than all the wisdom of Egypt. He was wiser than any other man. . . . And his fame spread to all the surrounding nations. . . . Men of all nations came to listen to

---

[5] 1 Kings 3:11–14 NIV.

> Solomon's wisdom, sent by all the kings of the world, who had heard of his wisdom.[6]

Indeed,

> King Solomon was greater in riches and wisdom than all the other kings of the earth. The whole world sought audience with Solomon to hear the wisdom God had put in his heart.[7]

The report of Solomon's exceptional capacity for understanding reached the queen of Sheba, and she traveled to Jerusalem from her home in southwest Arabia, a journey of many miles, to test the gifted ruler with difficult questions. She witnessed firsthand his acumen and his prosperity. The Bible states that "she was overwhelmed."[8] Before her visit concluded, the queen shared her thoughts with him.

> She said to the king, "The report I heard in my own country about your achievements and your wisdom is true. But I did not believe these things until I came and saw with my own eyes. Indeed, not even half was told me; in wisdom and wealth you have far exceeded the report I heard."[9]

During his lifetime, Solomon uttered three thousand proverbs, and his songs numbered more than a thousand. Active in scholastic matters, he described plant life and taught about animals of the region. Late in life, Solomon began an extensive inquiry to learn whether existence on the earth independent of God could hold any significance—any meaning. If sense could be made of it, then this wise leader, who refers to himself as the Teacher, was determined to illuminate it. It is in the book of Ecclesiastes that the king penned his discoveries.[10]

---

[6] Ibid., 4:29–34 NIV.

[7] Ibid., 10:23–24 NIV.

[8] Ibid., 10:5 NIV.

[9] Ibid., 10:6–7 NIV.

[10] The book of Ecclesiastes details the author's quest to understand the human condition and discover whether life holds purpose. That Solomon wrote it is the

Solomon looked at nature and found monotony in the cycles of things. The sun rises and sets, only to repeat the sequence on the following day. The wind blows to the south and turns to the north, going in circular paths, always returning on its course. Streams of water flow to the sea, but the sea is never full, and the waters reemerge at the origins of the streams. There is only repetition and emptiness to be found in these things, nothing in nature itself that brings understanding to life.

The king investigated learning, devoting himself to study. He discovered only meaninglessness there. He turned next to pleasure and mirth in his quest. Again, he could find nothing of lasting value and purpose. He looked at work and power, but these things too were merely "a chasing after the wind."[11] Solomon examined riches but learned that they were like the rest: all for nothing. He came to declare that everything under the sun is marked by barrenness. It is all vanity. Existence on the earth, considered in itself, is absolutely senseless. The words of this insightful king give one pause.

> "Meaningless! Meaningless!"
> says the Teacher.
> "Utterly meaningless!
> Everything is meaningless."[12]

PURVEYORS OF GLOOM

Advancing to the twentieth century, one encounters a remarkable parallel. Perhaps taking a cue from the French atheist and existentialist Jean-Paul Sartre, a man who sees no genuine purpose

---

opinion that I and others have, although the author is not known with certainty. Nevertheless, he describes himself as a son of David, a king in Jerusalem, and greater and wiser than those who ruled over Jerusalem before him. Coupled with the references in 1 Kings, these facts provide solid support for the position that Solomon penned the book.

[11] Eccles. 2:11 NIV. This phrase appears in several places in the book.
[12] Ibid., 1:2 NIV.

underlying human existence, the philosopher Albert Camus holds that efforts to uncover meaning in life fail because it is not there. Camus gives the label 'the Absurd' to the interplay that arises out of the conflict between humans' search for a rationale that grounds their existing and their inability to find it. There is no God to impart meaning, he thinks, and life is utterly devoid of it. It is pointless and irrational. One might represent the general thinking in terms of a deductive line of reasoning, as presented below:

> If God does not exist, then human existence is without any underlying purpose.
> God does not exist.
> Therefore, human existence is without any underlying purpose.

The argument is valid by virtue of its form. Is it sound?

Camus's view of God—and its predictable consequence—is one that has taken root in the mainstream thought of contemporary science and philosophy. Recalling the atomists of old, many in current times believe that there is nothing more than matter, interacting with itself in energy fields in the pseudovoid of space, moving about in a universe of happenstance. Reality is physical, the product of indifferent, natural forces. Nothing immaterial exists, they say, only the physical cosmos. There is no God. There is no design, no planning, no intelligence to account for the existence of people or their world. Life is the result of a chemical quirk. Humankind is the result of random mutations and selection of the best equipped, erected atop that quirk. All that has come to be came from nothing at all, and all is headed into a dismal future as the universe winds down in accordance with the second law of thermodynamics.

Some who take this stand might reject the first premise of the aforestated argument, claiming that purpose in life is possible without God. To think so, however, is to misconstrue the matter. Such purpose would be merely an aim du jour, not an encompassing reason for it all. Those same individuals cannot lay claim to a foundational raison d'être, lest they forfeit the very physicalistic view to which they subscribe. For them, as for Camus, there can be no real point to existence as a whole.

Notably, Solomon agrees with Camus—in a way. Both find meaninglessness in a Godless world. Even so, their views differ markedly. Unlike the twentieth-century philosopher, the ancient king believes that there is a God and that He has "set eternity in the hearts of men."[13] What Solomon's years taught him is that, *if* God is removed from one's global view, *then* life on the earth is senseless and hollow. An acceptable representation of the thinking here is an argument that embraces the first premise of the previous one but varies from that case of reasoning in important respects. Consider then the following logical construction:

> If God does not exist, then human existence is without any underlying purpose; but, if God does exist, then human existence is fundamentally purposive.
> God exists.
> Therefore, human existence is fundamentally purposive.

As for the emptiness of a Godless, mechanized universe, an atheist might state that it is disappointing that the universe is this way, but things are as they are, and one simply must deal with them. Such an assertion is correct to a point. Wishful thinking will not change the facts, and, if nothing other than material bits and the physical forces that drive them exists, then it is indeed disappointing. That issue, however, is the one at hand. Turning to the declarations of another author who finds no grounds for a belief in God, one sees that his too is a world of blind mechanism. The tone of despondency that overlays the writings of Bertrand Russell is unmistakable.

> [E]ven more purposeless, more void of meaning, is the world which Science presents for our belief. Amid such a world, if anywhere, our ideals must henceforth find a home. That Man is the product of causes which had no prevision of the end they were achieving; that his origin, his growth, his hopes and fears, his loves and his beliefs, are but the outcome of accidental collocations of atoms;

---

[13] Ibid., 3:11 NIV. David Jeremiah points out that Solomon sees that the hope of eternity eclipses life's apparent futility, as the quoted passage portrays. Jeremiah's comments aired in a sermon on the broadcast *Turning Point* on February 4, 2007.

that no fire, no heroism, no intensity of thought and feeling, can preserve an individual life beyond the grave; that all the labours of the ages, all the devotion, all the inspiration, all the noonday brightness of human genius, are destined to extinction in the vast death of the solar system, and that the whole temple of Man's achievement must inevitably be buried beneath the débris of a universe in ruins. . . . Only within the scaffolding of these truths, only on *the firm foundation of unyielding despair*, can the soul's habitation henceforth be safely built.[14]

As is the case with Russell, central to the philosophical perspectives of Sartre and Camus is the notion that no agency is behind the presence of humans; no God is around to provide a reason for it. Humans possess the ability to ponder their temporally limited lives as earthly beings. They have but a few years. If there is nothing more—no intelligent Designer of the world; no plan for an individual, conceived by the omniscient and loving Deity; no value placed on one's personhood by the Creator who fashioned it; no continuance past the grave—then what collective purpose could be found in their brief moments on the stage? It is not the purpose of caring for one's children or of advancing the quality of the human condition through medical research that is in view here but the grand aim, the deep-rooted explanation for the sum of reality, a reality that includes sentient, intelligent beings. Without purpose, not only is *meaning* lost, but *value* is lost as well.[15] If humankind is a fluke, drifting in a cosmic sea of mindless mechanism, then, in the final analysis, what truly matters? There is no genuine inherent worth to be found anywhere; and whatever a person does, whatever occurs, it all will be over for that person very soon. It is no wonder that Sartre maintains that any objective meaning in life vanishes when one comes to realize that eternity is just a fantasy. Sartre tries to take the path that one must contrive and assign meaning to existence oneself

---

[14] Bertrand Russell, "A Free Man's Worship," in *Mysticism and Logic* (1917; repr., New York: W. W. Norton and Co., 1929), 47–48. The emphasis is mine. The essay was published initially in *Independent Review* in 1903.

[15] William Lane Craig makes this point in *Reasonable Faith: Christian Truth and Apologetics*, 3rd ed. (Wheaton, IL: Crossway Books, 2008), 74–75.

and, with it, any value that it has, given that neither of these things is there intrinsically. This position, though, only underscores their stark absence, like that of a child's imaginary playmates. Pretending does not make them real. It offers only a make-believe picture of relief from the void. Remarks the atheist,

> [I]f I have eliminated God the Father, there has to be someone to invent values. . . . [T]o say that we invent values means no more or less than this: life has no meaning *a priori*.[16]

Toward the end of his fairly extended years, Sartre seemed to reverse his stance on the existence of God, to the disconcertedness of his long-time companion, Simone de Beauvoir.[17] Camus did not live long. He died in an automobile accident at the age of forty-six.

Both Solomon and Camus—one who believes in God and one who does not believe—see the emptiness of reality without the Supreme Being to convey purpose. It is simply a reality that is, and is for no reason. Such an existence is founded on *coincidence*, not on *rationality*. Reflecting Russell's pointless-world mindset, an undercurrent of hopelessness characterizes the outlook of Sartre and Camus in their writings, despite the fact that Sartre claims something more positive for existentialism as a humanistic philosophy. The question that must be asked, however, is whether what these purveyors of gloom posit is true. If so, then, in a twist, the ultimate futility rests not with the development of an ontological construct that goes wide of the mark, as I discussed in the previous chapter, but with one that lands on dead center.

---

[16] Jean-Paul Sartre, *Existentialism Is a Humanism*, trans. Carol Macomber, ed. John Kulka (New Haven: Yale University Press, 2007), 51. Sartre's book was published originally in French in 1946.

[17] As a youngster, Sartre had blamed God for the pangs of conscience that he had experienced following an incident of misconduct, and he had cursed God repeatedly. Sartre's action would have been irrational if he had not believed in God at the time. Although it appears that he might have come full circle, cognitively assenting to the existence of God is not the same as accepting Him. It is not certain where Sartre stood in his belief about God—or where he stood with the God whom he had spent a lifetime denying—as his days drew to a close.

A Way to View the World

In this work, one has come to see in operation a pair of disparate philosophical pictures of reality. Their differences can be traced to a nascent form of dissent in the metaphysical musings of the ancient Greeks, where a search for *archē* or *physis* yielded contrasting responses to a pair of essential questions. Restated here from the first chapter, those questions are

1. What underlies the generation of things?
2. What underlies the conservation of things?

The ancients wanted to understand how their world and the things that were in it came to be and how those things could continue to exist through change. The investigations that ensued in attempts to answer the aforesaid questions led to other uncertainties, such as those about identity and knowledge, but the questions themselves continued to be central to the pursuit of the truth. Taken globally, the queries bring to the forefront the primary dissimilarities between two comprehensive, but disharmonious, worldviews that have emerged to compete for acceptance in Western thought. Many of the basic ideas that separate them remain intact nearly three millennia after the Greeks pondered these matters, but they have coalesced into two systems of fundamental—and fundamentally different—conceptualizations. One model accepts as real only natural, physical phenomena and processes; the other embraces a broader reality. One model is wholly mechanistic and atheistic; the other is not wholly mechanistic, and it is theistic. There are variations within these two models of being, but the line of demarcation between them is distinct, etched sharply by explanations of origins.[18] Therefore, it comes as no surprise that the question of the existence of the immaterial Judaeo-Christian God lies at the heart of the division.

---

[18] As for variations, one example is the theory that God, having created life, used evolution to bring about the biological forms that appear on the earth today. With regard to this position, intelligent design is behind the presence of life, and God is the source of it nevertheless—the theory is teleological and theistic. It diverges from a literal interpretation, and widely held view, of the Scriptures, however, and, of course, from the naturalism that is central to classic evolutionary theory.

It is worthwhile to consider a set of ideas that has become entrenched in certain circles of modern thought. I outline it below and give it an appropriately descriptive title:

MODEL I

Ontic Naturalism—the Atheistic Worldview

Reality is entirely physical.

The operations of reality are limited to physiochemical mechanism.

Nothing in existence corresponds to the Judaeo-Christian God.

Jesus, if He existed, was merely a man.

The universe came from nothing.

Life came from lifelessness.

The human being is the product of an initial chance event and subsequent evolution.

The rational, human mind came from matter, and it is material.

There is no overall purpose to existence; what exists is the product of blind coincidence, not design.

Naturalism and mechanistic physicalism—or physiochemicalism—are not equivalent doctrines, strictly speaking, although they are aligned. The doctrines merge straightforwardly, however, to form a comprehensive position concerning reality: Nothing apart from matter and physical forces in space-time exists, and all events take place in accordance with the fixed laws of nature; wherefore, proper explanations of all phenomena must be in terms of the physical workings of the cosmos. It is this thinking that characterizes the prevalent framework of modern atheism, and it is this position, under the identifier that I use for the model, that I will consider in the analysis as the chapter proceeds.

Opposing this system of related notions is one that is based on principles that diverge widely from those of its rival. Encompassing both the natural and the supernatural, it bears a fitting designation as well. Contrast the two models, where the tenets in the following set are in direct conflict with the corresponding tenets in the other:

MODEL II

Ontic Metanaturalism—the Theo-Christian Worldview

Reality is not entirely physical but includes the nonphysical.
The operations of reality are not limited to physiochemical
    mechanism.
The Judaeo-Christian God exists.
Jesus exists; He is the Christ, the Son of God.
God created the universe.
God created life.
God created the human being.
God created the rational, human mind, and it is not material.
There is an overall purpose to existence; what exists is the
    product of design, not blind coincidence.

As a general system, each of these models comprises a set of
propositions that cohere, in that no contradictions are expressed;
therefore, each is internally consistent. The two systems are exter-
nally incompatible, though. A configuration that is reminiscent of
those in previous chapters surfaces again here:

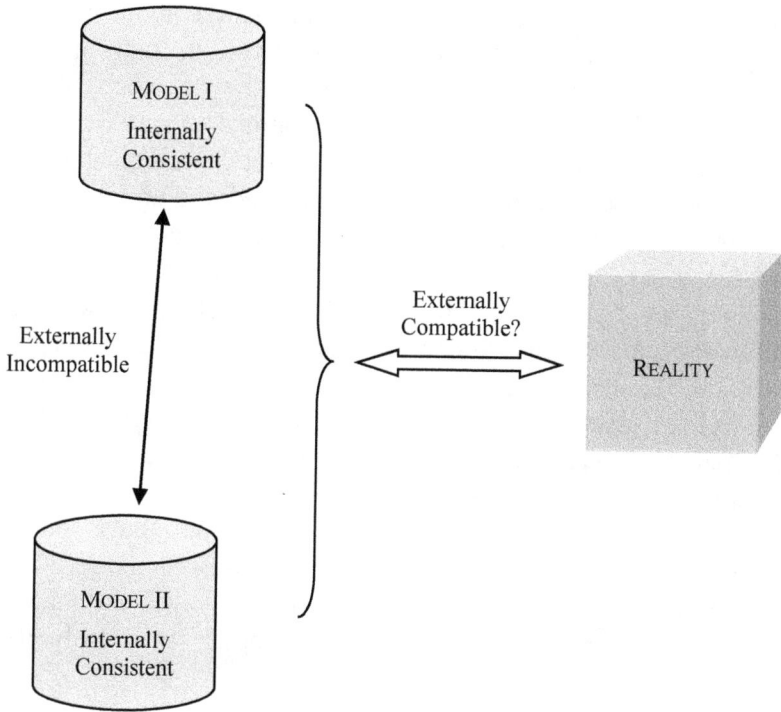

Figure 10.1

The respective originations that the models present predate humanity; therefore, the associated claims of truth cannot be verified by direct observation of the corresponding events. No person witnessed the launch of the universe. Humans could not have observed whether mock-nothingness in the guise of a quantum fluctuation spun it into existence, or a creative act did so—if such an act could be detected. Likewise, no one watched the start of life on the earth. Humans could not have seen whether a chance, molecular episode initiated it, or a divine decree brought it into being—if such a decree could be discerned. Were it possible for people to have been present and somehow to have beheld the beginnings, they probably would not disagree, insofar, at least, as what their perceptions, extended perhaps with the use of tools, could report. When two individuals raise the lid of a box to peer inside, their beliefs about what they see very likely align. In the absence of observation, many evolutionists who look at the evidence believe that the presence of both the universe and living things is to be explained in purely mechanistic terms, and they reject the existence of God. Creationists who look at the evidence believe that the presence of both the universe and living things is to be explained in teleological terms, and they embrace the existence of God. Contrary to the theory of model-dependent realism, the truth cannot be spread equally across the pair. Each camp presents its case in the court of judgment, and every person must take his or her turn on the bench.

Given that the beholding of originations is not possible in the drive to understand the whole of reality, does reason possess the wherewithal to afford that understanding? A succinct statement of the general position of naturalism, with its emphasis on material process, a statement that probably expresses its underlying tenor best, is found here: "[T]he most reasonable belief is that we came from nothing, by nothing and for nothing."[19] Is it truly the most reasonable? Why would one think so?

Many are hesitant to turn to a consideration of an immaterial side of existence because they have dismissed the acceptance of incorporeality as an irrational point of view, and, of course, no intelligent person wants to land in that place. Reflect then on a strident irony: The very rationality that those who put their trust in naturalism value so highly points rather conspicuously outside the sphere of the matter-energy complex. The pillars of the naturalistic-mechanistic model introduce obstacles that are not surmounted readily. If, one by one, reasoning takes its toll on the foundational tenets of a given system, then the attractiveness of a competing proposal increases as the other loses its footing—a point that one will recall from the previous chapter. Issues concerning what is real have surfaced along the way in this work. They intersect here to strain the underpinning for atheism as a spectrum of findings throws a shroud of doubt over its alleged truth.

---

[19] Quentin Smith, "The Uncaused Beginning of the Universe," in *Theism, Atheism, and Big Bang Cosmology*, ed. William Lane Craig and Quentin Smith (Oxford: Clarendon Press, 1993), 135.

Reality

➤ Science, the enterprise that investigates physical reality, is incapable of showing that all reality is physical.

Origin—the Universe

➤ The assertion that the universe arose from nothing at all as a result of instability is nonsensical because it is not possible for that which does not exist to possess any properties. A proposition that purports to ascribe a property—in this case, instability—to the nonexistent is meaningless.

➤ The claim that the universe created itself is self-contradictory because it is not possible for something to exist, to be the generative cause, before it exists, to be the effect of that cause.

➤ On the often-mentioned premise of a cosmogonic big bang, the exactness of the rate at which the particle-space had to have expanded immediately after the event, for the universe to exist at all, determines that the universe is not the product of chance.

Origin—Life and Biological Complexity

➤ Chemical evolution—the materialists' favored path to life from lifeless matter—could not have taken place in a nonreducing atmosphere, yet the atmosphere of the earliest period of the earth was nonreducing, preceding the supposed arising of life by more than half a billion years by the scientists' own time line.

➤ The Dawkinsian explanation of the arising of life by chance from a prebiotic mass of chemical compounds rests on proposed probabilities that are completely speculative, lacking both empirical and logical support; and employing these probabilities in attending to evolution's need to bridge major gaps results in mathematical proscription.

➤ The DNA-RNA-protein-construction scenario introduces a vicious circularity that defies the authenticity of the surmised initial replication incident; and the predominant RNA-first hypothesis, despite the enzymatic property of this nucleic acid—the arrival of which itself falls subject to the charge of circularity—stands conspicuously in opposition to the chemistry on which the hypothesis relies.

➤ Mathematical analysis of the mutation-selection process of developing suitable proteins with which to assemble and operate cells reveals probabilities that lie far outside the domain of reason.

➤ It is illogical to hold that an organismal feature having two or more essential components—those parts that are required for the feature to operate—could arise through incremental improvement. A part offers no advantage without the whole; but there can be no whole until that part is developed, along with the others, which will not happen, according to evolutionary theory, without the part's offering a biological advantage, as it will fail to be targeted by natural selection. This aspect of the theory thus mirrors the coordinated-attack problem, which has no solution.

➤ The construction of complex features of organisms by means of a process of genetic vectorial progression runs counter to the geological record, but, even more problematic, it flies in the face of the radical mathematical exponentiation that lies beneath the biomechanics of such a conjecture.

➤ Evolutionary theory rests on the premise that nature drives toward sustaining life on the earth. It claims to explain how nature purportedly does so: upholding survival and capitalizing on positive hereditary changes. Yet, it is incapable of explaining why insensible nature would be engaged in such an enterprise, whether with regard to individual organisms or to the sum of biological existence. Without the premise, the theory is a nonstarter.

Organismal Identity

➤ There is nothing about matter or material process or material structure that can provide the basis for an adequate explanation of how it is that living organisms continue through time as distinct individuals.

Mind and Agency

➤ Materialism does not offer a satisfactory rendering of the experience of consciousness.

➤ The attributing of agency to a material mind violates the principles of the deterministic universe that materialism embraces.

Evil

➤ The assertion in defense of atheism that evil exists in the world is vacuous without the absolute moral standards of divine law that are necessary to impart meaning to the term 'evil' that the very declaration employs; and attempts to account for it in an alternative manner lead to irrational consequences.

Evidence—the Historical Record

➤ Aside from internal evidence, there is substantial external evidence that supports the biblical narrative, including documentation from Jewish, Christian, and pagan sources, and from archaeological findings; and to dismiss the evidence on the basis that it conflicts with naturalism is to adopt naturalism axiomatically without examination.

When one steps back to look at the dubious character of what the naturalistic stance proffers collectively as an inclusive account of existence, it becomes obvious that believing reasonableness to be its defining attribute requires quite a mental stretch. It is thus difficult to see why one would eliminate from consideration, particularly right out of the gate, a position that acknowledges a broad-based reality.

The metanaturalistic model gazes beyond particles and forces. It posits a single point of origin in its simple explanation of being. It gives a plausible portrayal of the identity of living things. It offers a credible picture of agency and its role in effecting change in the universe. It sets forth an authoritative foundation for distinguishing between good and evil. It recognizes evidence from multiple sources, confirming events that are reported in the biblical canon, even events for which descriptions in terms of physical law are inadequate. It addresses the pair of core questions with which the ancient Greeks wrestled—questions about generation and conservation—by proposing a sole answer to both.

> In the past God spoke to our forefathers through the prophets at many times and in various ways, but in these last days he has spoken to us by his Son, whom he appointed heir of all things, and *through whom he made the universe*. The Son is the radiance of God's glory and the exact representation of his being, *sustaining all things* by his powerful word.[20]

One may choose to reject the theo-Christian view, and some certainly do so, but it cannot be because rationality singles out its major opposing position. The from-by-and-for-nothing story leaves one hard-pressed to accept unhesitatingly its explanation of how things came to be the way that they are. One ought to consider the contrasting view. Like its counterpart, it finds expression in a succinct statement: "For from him [God] and through him and to him are all things."[21]

Reason has its place in building a worldview. It shapes beliefs; it works to counter deception; it uncovers errors in inferential constructions. Reason weaves the tapestry of thought that becomes for each person a mindset, acting as the litmus test of acceptance for new propositions that circumstances occasion. People are not constrained by logic to embrace an atheistic perspective—the cases against the existence of God that I reviewed, needless to say, are not convincing—even as those who brandish arguments for atheism are attempting to dismiss ones to the contrary. Where the weight of reason begins to bow the beams that undergird a given position, however, the appropriate question to ask is whether the scaffolding is sufficiently sound—enough so that a person is willing to place unwavering trust in its assumed veracity, listing though the whole edifice may be. The naturalistic-mechanistic stance regarding reality manifests instability of this sort.

Plato once remarked,

---

[20] Heb. 1:1–3 NIV. The emphases are mine.
[21] Rom. 11:36 NIV.

> The giants among them, of the true earthborn breed,
> would not stick at any point; they would hold out to the
> end, that whatever they cannot squeeze between their
> hands is just nothing at all.[22]

One should not be too hasty in declaring, as do those to whom Plato refers, that reality is solely physical, that nothing nonphysical exists. Sometimes, the only way to see things as they are is to take the view from the top. If one could observe a triangle from the plane in which it lies—making allowances for the visibility of two-dimensional figures—then all that one could detect would be a line. It is not until one exits that plane that the three-sided geometric shape comes to light. Again, it is only after stepping back into the additional dimension of M-theory that physicists can see the several opposing, ten-dimensional string theories as different snapshots of one and the same set of phenomena. Analogously, it may be that one must take a step back from the machinery of the material world to grasp in a comprehensive way the grand context in which it operates.

PERSONAL IDENTITY—ANOTHER LOOK

When one turns to the issue of personhood, the division between the two opposed worldviews that I outlined is brought into sharp focus from a different angle. Theories about the essence of people are rooted in ideas about the mind-body relationship, as chapter 5 discussed. Rejecting the Cartesian notion of an immaterial mental substance, many philosophers believe that there is no mind existing apart from the tangible human frame with which it is correlated in some way. Ontologically speaking, only the physical exists. Given this monistic, materialistic stance, if there is to be a persistent and personal self, then it ultimately must be tied to an individual's physical being: One must rely on the corpus as the

---

[22] Plato, *Sophist*, 247c, trans. F. M. Cornford, in *The Collected Dialogues of Plato, Including the Letters*, trans. Lane Cooper et al., ed. Edith Hamilton and Huntington Cairns (1961; Princeton: Princeton University Press, 1971), 992.

instrument of personhood because, at base, the corpus *is* what a person is. Although contemporary materialists develop different systems, those systems are similar, in that each incorporates the idea that mental talk and physical talk actually point to the same thing— body. Materiality lies at the base of humanity, and one's identity must be grounded in it. The following figure illustrates the concept:

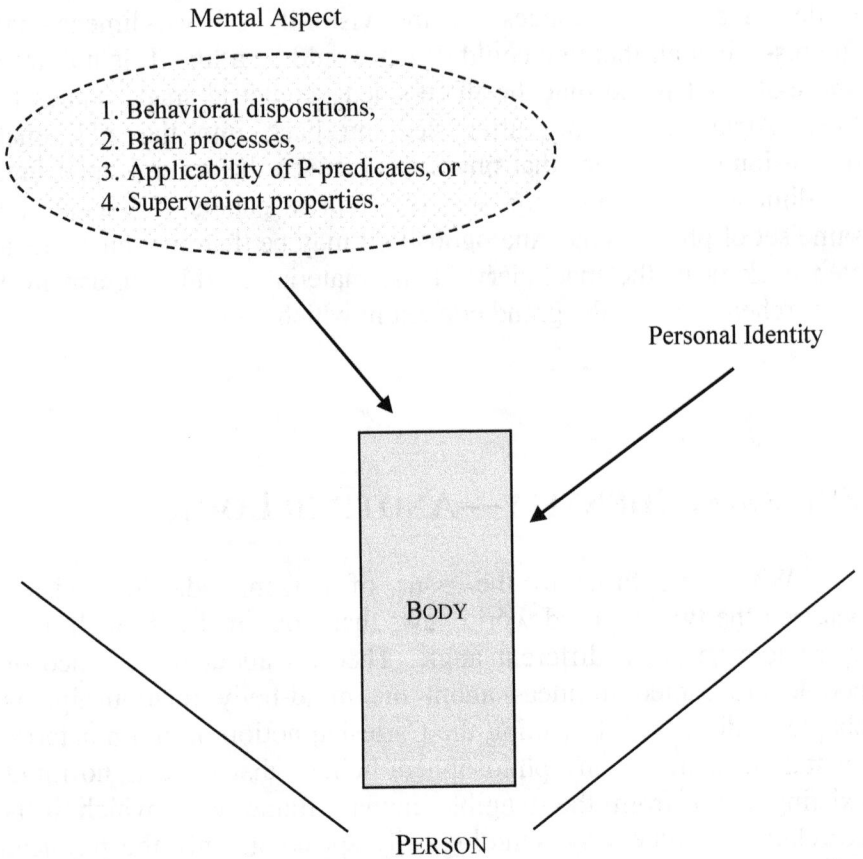

Mental Aspect

1. Behavioral dispositions,
2. Brain processes,
3. Applicability of P-predicates, or
4. Supervenient properties.

Personal Identity

BODY

PERSON

Figure 10.2

I have argued that the failure of materialistic theories to provide satisfactory explanations extends across a broad area. Identity is one stumbling block. Identity subsists in singularity, but the singularity of a material aggregate does not issue from its physical composition. Whether an artifact or an organism, matter is neither (1) what distinguishes a thing from all others things, so that it is unique, nor (2) what achieves continuity for it through successive moments in time. When one looks at persons, matter fares no better. If materialism were to present an accurate picture of reality, then there would not be any immaterial substantive elements at all, and thus there would not be any elements of that sort in people. It would have to be true, in that case, that the bodies of human beings ultimately would be what satisfies the two crucial conditions of the numerical identity of persons: (1) individuation and (2) persistence. From the standpoint of ontology, there would be nothing other than the material mass on which to base those conditions, and herein lies a set of problems.

CORPORAL BEING

Take a look at what zany situations arise from employing matter in an attempt to validate personal identity. One may think that spatiotemporal location of the corpus is adequate for delineation. The body of a man with three severed limbs, however, occupies four positions in space-time. Which location does one say is *his* location? The body of a lady who visited a salon to have her hair trimmed and nails filed occupies hundreds of positions following her appointment. It is irrational to think that the lady herself is both in her car, headed for the sports club, and spread about the salon floor. Worse still is it to think that the existence of the person herself somehow diminished through the activity of the beautician.

As parts are removed from a body during an operation, why does the person remain a whole human entity and not become fractured, at least for the period that a central protoplasmic piece on the table stays alive? Consider conjoined twins. There is one body; there even may be a single heart; but there are two human beings— by definition, one would be prone to claim—because there are twins:

distinct entities. Both beings suffer pain when a common part is injured. Depending on the location of their joining, two voices may cry out in distress when a passerby steps on a foot. The single body occupies one unbroken region in space; how then is a materialist to individuate the beings? Pointing to states of consciousness will not work, for states of consciousness, according to the materialists, *are* states of the body, and there is only one of those things.

One could say that it is not the entire body that makes the person, just the head. The abovementioned twins, however, could be joined at the head. Perhaps one says instead that the decisive component is the brain. Suppose then that there is a loss of a bit of material that composes the brain—maybe a neuron or even an atom belonging to the neuronal cell. If matter is the determinant of personal identity, then identity is lost because

> For any two sets of material particles S_1 and S_2, if $S_1 =$ person p_1, and $S_2 =$ person p_2, then, for any material particle x, if $x \in S_1$, and $x \notin S_2$, then $p_1 \neq p_2$, because $S_1 \neq S_2$.

One is compelled to embrace either Peter Unger's illogical idea of partially existing persons or the absurd notion that a person who is delivering a lecture and who, during the event, loses an atomic brain constituent—a single sodium ion, for instance—suddenly ceases to exist, even though there is no cognitive degradation, and the speaking carries on in a coherent manner without interruption. Neither a partial person nor a nonexistent person can equal a person. *People* do not fade from existence as their brain material diminishes by a particle or two any more than they fade from existence as their muscles atrophy from lack of use, and they do not blink suddenly out of existence either. If the body is the person, then, based on the aforesaid principle, the person cannot survive an atomic or subatomic reduction, which is untenable. Therefore, the body is not the person.

Suppose that one says, on the other hand, that a person does continue to exist with the loss of a material bit. Shedding a microphysical encephalic particle, or even an entire neuron among the hundred billion or so brain cells that a human possesses, is not sufficient to bring about the end of the entity. Accordingly, the principle that appears below applies:

> For any two sets of material particles S_1 and S_2, if $S_1 =$ person p_1, and $S_2 =$ person p_2, then, for any material particle x, if $x \in S_1$, and $x \notin S_2$, then it does not follow that $p_1 \neq p_2$, even though $S_1 \neq S_2$.

With this condition in force, however, matter cannot be that which identifies persons: The diminishing of a piece of it is irrelevant; it has no effect on one's personhood. Therefore, the body is not the person.

Perhaps, one may assert, it is the relative amount of material that matters, not a bit here or there. Imagine then that some brain tissue must be cut asunder as the aforementioned conjoined twins are separated, or part of the brain tissue is removed surgically in an effort to spare the life of at least one of the twins. Is the corpus with the larger amount of the remaining cerebral cortex a person, and, if so, then which person is it? If, to give a response to this question, one must wait to see what memories return to consciousness in any part that is left, then John Locke's memory criterion, unworkable as it is, resurfaces as the decisive standard. If amnesia takes hold, then all identity is lost anyway, regardless of what physical tissue may continue to be viable.

A number of years ago, an acquaintance of mine participated in a golf tournament. On one of his drives, something extraordinary happened: The ball split into multiple pieces. It was such an unusual event that no one knew what to do. An examination of the rule book prompted an official decision and its conveyance: The man was to play the largest piece to the green, after which he could replace the chunk with another, complete ball. No doubt, the choice of club at that point was challenging. The announcement of the ruling brought with it the implicit declaration that a golf ball in play on the fairway is to be identified with the whole or the largest intact piece of the fused group of material bits that a club fired from the tee. Chapter 3 showed that the identity of aggregate, inanimate objects is a product of decree, not discovery, and the case here certainly fits that fact. If one tries to extend the criterion to persons, however, then absurdities result. Not to be gruesome, but suppose that an accident at a factory cuts a human in two, and tissue in each piece remains in a living state for a brief period. To say that the larger piece (assume that it is the lower 55 percent volumetrically) *is* the person is totally unfounded.

If the tissue of the greater part expires before that of the lesser one, then does the person suddenly jump twelve feet across the factory floor to the still-living, smaller portion? If the two segments are of equal size, then what does one say about the person? In contradistinction to golf balls, the identity of people is not a matter of fiat.

To cling to physicality as a criterion, suppose that one goes to the other end of the scale, claiming that the DNA of a person fixes the identity of the individual, making the person unique. That genetic material is essentially the same throughout the body, *ceteris paribus*, with a few exceptions (such as mature erythrocytes, or red blood cells, which lack DNA). So, the person is to be identified with his or her genetic profile. Thus, if a body is severed, then the crucial individuality is maintained by virtue of the peculiarity of the DNA of the cells that compose the pieces.

This approach produces even more ludicrous results. First, with the criterion, it would be *possible* for identical twins—or identical triplets—to be one and the same person (the DNA of identical siblings usually begins to vary slightly in the womb). Then, as identical things must have all qualities and states in common at a given time, one twin could not be asleep if the other is playing croquet; one could not be happy when the other is depressed; and one triplet could not pass without the death of the other two—all spurious limitations.

A second problem arises with the approach: diverse reincorporation. In contrast to the factory-employee case, DNA-bearing parts may be returned to operational status by spreading them among other individuals. Imagine that Larry is killed in a car wreck. Spotting the organ-donor symbol on his license, the ambulance personnel alert the appropriate medical teams, who prepare for transplants. Potential recipients are notified following early testing. Larry's liver is placed in Leonard; his lungs go to Lawrence. The rest of Larry's body is cremated. After surgery, the first recipient moves to a distant country and the second to another. The DNA that allegedly preserves Larry's identity resides in discrete biological systems in discrete locations, and there is no longer a human Larry in existence to which the DNA is tied. DNA alone cannot be the carrier of distinctness for a person.

I realize that all these examples are at the edge of sensibility, but they underscore the fact that a criterion of identity for persons that is based purely on physicality introduces acutely counterintuitive consequences. Matter no more can serve as the determinant of identity for persons than it can serve as the determinant of identity for other things. Using the positions of material in space as the dividing line between individuals generates illogicalities; identifying people strictly with their physical makeup raises Unger's nonsensical notion of partially existing beings who fade from the scene, or else terminates their existence prematurely and irrationally; and linking people to their genetic footprints produces a self-conflicting situation as well as the bizarre loss of personal identity through dissolution.

The body fails the individuation criterion. Given that matter cannot impart unity to itself and must rely on something apart from a cluster of it to bring oneness through time, it also fails the persistence criterion. Materialism struggles with personal identity because matter lacks the efficacy to deliver the required sort of differentiation and the required sort of temporal coherence; both lie beyond its reach. In turning to the physical to bestow distinctiveness and endurance, the materialists' stance falls short in its portrayal of personhood, and one more pillar of support beneath the naturalistic platform shows itself to be of questionable structural integrity.

Personal Identity

➤ Materialism does not provide a satisfactory account of either the individuality of persons or their persistence as individuals.

COGNITIVE BEING

If the identity of people demands more than a strict material-based rendering can provide, then the breadth of personhood must be extended to the immaterial. Such an extension directs the attention initially to the rational mind—an incorporeal existent, so I have argued. Can it bear the weight of personal identity? To do so, it must satisfy the two conditions that are necessary for numerical sameness: (1) distinguish a person from all other people and (2) ensure the person's temporal continuity. The rational mind seems to meet the first condition—that of uniqueness—because thoughts belong only to a single human mind. Jim's thoughts are his thoughts; they can exist in no other person's mind. When Jim acts, the intention that is the defining element of his action resides nowhere else. Consider the second condition: persistence. If the essence of a personal self *is exactly* the thinking part of an individual, as René Descartes believes, then would one not blink out of existence when unconscious? Surely, unawareness in itself, occasioned by dreamless sleep, does not terminate the rational mind of a subject and thereby, on the premise that the mind is the crucial part, terminate the person—recall Jim's adventure to Yellowstone National Park—any more than sleep apnea brings a person's breathing body to an end and thereby ends the person. To claim that sleep terminates the mind introduces an absurdity. Look at why it is so. Nothing can cease to exist, only to come into being again as the same thing, a principle that I have stated frequently. If the mind ceases to be during the evening hours, then no mind that exists the next day can be the same mind as the prior one. There would be no way to explain, in that case, how the memory-thought of a subject's particular previous perception—say, seeing Old Faithful erupt—could arise, along with the memory-thought of the act that it inspired—say, entering a restricted area for a better view—following a nighttime state of slumber. Such a passive-active recollection would have to belong solely to the one who experienced it. No other individual could be the subject of the mental incident that corresponds to the phenomenon from that perceiver-agent's perspective, and that one who experienced it no longer exists, on the supposition at hand, having ceased to be when the mind ceased to be. Descartes holds that the mind does persist in these instances because it continues to think, given that thinking is its essential attribute, even though one cannot remember the thoughts during those times. That conjecture is a product of his dualism, however, and not supported easily by independent reasoning. Perhaps there is a better way to conserve the thinking part of humans.

In reflecting on ways in which the mind might stay intact through dormancy of thought and, in so doing, given the supposition that the mind is the person, underwrite the latter's preservation, three theses, I believe, rise to offer explanations. The first is that the mind persists because the brain of the organism preserves it. I showed in the previous section that linking personhood directly to the physical body, or to a part of it—specifically, the brain—fails as a way to account for personhood. Suppose that, although the mind performs the actual work of maintaining identity, the brain is what conserves the mind, enabling it to perform that work. There are two relevant possibilities for such encephalic preserving. One is that the mind *is* the brain. In chapter 5, I demonstrated that a mental condition can maintain uniformity under varying encephalic conditions, and hence a mental state cannot be strictly identical to a state of the brain. Thus, the mind is not the brain. I submit the following principle as a truism:

> For any two things x and y and any two distinct times t_1 and t_2, if s_1 is the state of x at t_1, and s_2 is the state of x at t_2, and s_1 is qualitatively identical to s_2, and s_3 is the state of y at t_1, and s_4 is the state of y at t_2, and s_3 is not qualitatively identical to s_4, then x is not numerically identical to y.

A thing that is in indistinguishable states at discrete times cannot be numerically identical to a thing that is in diverse states at those same respective times. The mind and the brain are separate existents.

Is it possible, as a second path, for the crucial sustaining to occur through a different relationship, one that is physical and contingent rather than logical, avoiding the absolute equivalence of Smart's identity theory? Emergence, against which I argued earlier as a general theory of mind, is not the answer in this specific case either. If a thing emerges, then it comes to be. Nothing can terminate and resurface as the numerically identical thing. Even if a mind were to emerge with the onset of consciousness following sleep, complete with properties resembling those of a prior mind, it would not be, and could not be, the same one that existed beforehand.

A more likely prospect for the physical relationship is systemic preservation. An organism continues as a single creature for as long as it is alive. Some animals possess states of consciousness—their behavior convincingly supports that view. Whatever awareness an animal may possess is tied to the organismal system, and whatever constancy an organism may experience is given in the life that marks out that entity as a whole. Can these facts be extended to humans, such that the organismal system *Homo sapiens* is capable of the mental conservation that is needed for personal identity, grounded in the workings of the human brain? Attempting to do so introduces an obstacle that is difficult to surmount. There is a hard line between mere sentience and intellection. Beasts lack the mentality that is intrinsic to humans; their conduct is not governed by the pervasive rationality that characterizes people and their acts. The cognizance of Jim qua organism is not the same as the cognizance of Jim qua agent. His seeing the geyser erupt at Yellowstone is a mental happening that is fundamentally dissimilar to his deciding to disobey the rules there and climb over the barrier. His memory of the former event is of something that he sensed; his memory of the latter one is of something that he did.

One dark night, a fox jumped over the fence around the barnyard on Doug's farm and carried away a chicken. An hour later, a man did likewise. The fox was hungry; it was responding to a biological drive. The man was not hungry; he was seeking revenge for Doug's running over his pet iguana after it escaped from its cage and darted into the road. The fox is not—indeed, *could not* be—guilty of a crime. The man, on the other hand, is a vindictive thief. Propositions that ascribe blame, vindication, or praise to behavior are meaningless when applied to organisms as such because organisms cannot perform in the capacity of agents. Agency requires rational thought, but rationality is not part of the organismal system.[23]

Now, it must be possible for the same agent to exist at different times. Otherwise, the man who is charged today with stealing a chicken last week could not be guilty, for he could not have done the deed: The one who perpetrated the crime no longer would exist. Without constancy of agency, morality would be senseless and the basic notions of humanity derailed. No punishment for homicide would be deserved if one delays the investigation; no commendation for a genuinely supererogatory deed would be justified the next day. Such consequences are not defensible. For an entity to continue uninterruptedly as an agent—the same agent—the rational mind of

---

[23] Note that even individuals who lack the normal rationality of mature members of the population are not merely organisms; they are persons too, which the forthcoming analysis will confirm, but they can operate as agents only in a limited way: A central part of agency is truncated. Hence, a civilized society does not hold them accountable for what they do, and societal laws protect them from the penalty to which a fully capable person would be subject upon committing a wrongful deed.

that entity must continue uninterruptedly, even through periods of unconsciousness, because it is the rational mind that makes that entity an agent in the first place. No other mind could be exchanged to fill a temporal gap in the agent's existence, lest the door be opened for the mind of one agent to experience the acts of another. Rationality lies outside the organismal system, however, and the brain is part of that system. Even if Jim's mind as mentality qua organism could be conserved by the brain, Jim's mind as mentality qua agent could not be so conserved. Beasts are not agents. It appears that organismal-encephalic persistence is insufficient to preserve the human mind.

The second thesis, which is a stronger position on systemic preservation, is to hold that the human agential system is what conserves the mind. Rational thought is a necessary part of the expression of the will when an agent acts. The ability to think rationally remains through periods in which it is not exercised because, although acts occur as separate, discontinuous events, agency itself—the potential to perform acts—endures as part of the human agential system. It is inherent in this composite entity. The rational mind thus continues through states of unconsciousness by virtue of this capacity for thought—although, contrary to Descartes, the thinking itself ceases for a time. It continues because the system does so, even though one may not be acting, and therefore thinking, at the moment.

The capacity can persist, however, only if the mind persists because it is a capacity *of* the mind, just as the capacity to bench-press four hundred pounds and to perspire under conditions of muscular exertion are capacities *of* the body and require a body to be exhibited, although a person might have skipped the gym that afternoon and relaxed in a hammock. One must be careful not to conflate capacities, whether mental or physical, and the things that possess them. It would be a mistake to hold that the ability to think rationally *is* the mind, just as it would be a mistake to think that the ability to carry out certain physical feats and operations *is* the body or that the capacity to accelerate from zero to sixty miles per hour in six seconds *is* the car. As noted in chapter 5, capabilities and the things that possess them are distinct. There can be no capacity—no facility from which anything at all can issue—unless there is an ontically substantive existent to possess it. A rational mind is not something that can be pulled into being by the bootstraps of its own capabilities.

It is evident that the capacity for rational thought continues because the mind continues, not the converse. Given that this ability to think is not identical to the mind, however, how is it that one and the same rational mind can carry on unaware? What is the explanation for its temporal cohesion? The body cannot do the work, for the corporal is metaphysically powerless to bring about—and, a fortiori, to sustain—such unity. The systems that compose the human creature fall short of meeting the requirement. Perhaps a plausible candidate remains: thought itself. Thoughts are mental elements, those of thinking. Can recurrent thoughts be the same thoughts and thereby glue a mind together? Although the mind is independent of its elements, if those elements can be identical at discrete times, then perhaps they can deliver identity to the mind through their own identity, yielding mental persistence.

The notion is that Henry can think on more than one occasion of the five-and-one-half-meter-tall giraffe, Cecil, in the nearby zoo, and, because Henry can do so, the very same thought recurs. Thinking is a psychological operation that is represented by a relationship holding among three things: (1) a mental subject (a mind)—that which is doing the thinking, (2) an object—that of which the subject is thinking, and (3) a time—a string of one or more moments at which the mental subject is thinking of the object. As a provisional hypothesis, one might adopt a principle that two thoughts at different times are the same if, and only if, the other two relata of the relationship—the subject and object—are the same. If the same thought arises at different times, then the mind that thinks them must be the same mind. The tentative principle can be stated in this way:

> For any two thoughts x_1 and x_2, and any two distinct times t_1 and t_2, where x_1 is the thought by subject s_1 of object ω_1 at t_1, and x_2 is the thought by subject s_2 of object ω_2 at t_2, $x_1 = x_2$ if, and only if, $s_1 = s_2$, and $\omega_1 = \omega_2$.

The approach, however, is flawed, as it is circular. One cannot use the principle to prove the identity of mental subjects based on the identity of thoughts, as the principle relies on the identity of subjects, as well as objects, to demonstrate that thoughts are identical.

Suppose instead that one proposes that the identical objects of thought alone are sufficient to secure the identity of the minds that think them. The relationship still obtains; thinking requires a thinker, but thoughts are the same where their objects are the same, and the same thoughts entail the same thinker. Consequently, all that is required for the persistence of the subject is the occurrence of identical thought-objects at different times.

There is a problem with this approach too. If the locution 'object of thought' here refers literally to an entity in space-time, then the proposal fails as a way to equate two subjects. Both Henry and Harold can think of Cecil on separate occasions respectively, so that the objects of their thoughts are the same thing, but it does not follow that there is a single mind that is experiencing the thoughts. Moreover, a mind can think of things that have no spatiotemporal existence, such as a purple giraffe that is two hundred meters tall.

Perhaps 'object of thought' refers instead to a mental item: the *idea* of something. Cecil can cease to be one day, following an accident at the restraining wall, yet Henry still can think of him a month later. The object of Henry's thought is the mental element that signifies the physical organism in space-time, not the physical organism itself—somewhat reminiscent of Descartes's key division between the formal reality of ideas and their objective reality. One does not think of *things* exactly but thinks *thoughts of things*. Two people can think of the same giraffe, but the objects of their thoughts—their ideas of the giraffe—differ because the minds that are thinking the thoughts are distinct.

Given this interpretation, though, thoughts that are interrupted either by a period of quiescence or by another thought cannot be identical in the numerical sense, only in the qualitative sense, because the objects of the thoughts can be identical only in this latter sense. Once the idea of something ceases, the object of thought ceases. Whatever idea-object emerges afterward must be numerically different from it, as it cannot persist in a state of nonexistence and return to being—a fact that applies to all things. The qualitative identity of objects of thought at separate times is not strong enough in itself to guarantee the numerical identity of the subjects of those thoughts, however.[24] Although an idea-object, in the present usage of the concept, is unique—it is restricted to the single mind that experiences it—if, to avoid circularity, one sets aside the subject and relies on the idea-objects to effect sameness, then one sets aside the very thing that brings distinctiveness. The former meaning of 'object of thought' then comes into play, but the problem arises when the idea-objects pertain to the nonperceptual. What distinguishes between two equal-duration thoughts of a mathematical value? Henry thinks of the cube root of −8 at noon; Harold thinks of it at 1:00 p.m.—without the temporal reference, persistence would not apply. Henry's idea-object could have all not-perspective-specific properties in common with Harold's if the hour is not a factor; so, the two could be just alike, yet the subjects are distinct. Stringing qualitatively identical idea-objects at discrete times together cannot ensure the numerical identity of the minds that entertain them without presupposing it. A mind is not the patchwork product of its contents, fused to form a monadic entity.

What therefore remains for this hypothesis is the same quandary as before: Where the thoughts of a rational mind cease, the mind ceases, and whatever terminates cannot return to being. If the rational mind of a human agent is to persist, then clearly something else is required—something that is ontically substantial—because the organism cannot serve to anchor the singularity of an agent's mind through the void of unconsciousness; and neither the capacity to think nor a pieced-together collection of thoughts fares any better. If that something else is indeed the bedrock on which personal identity

---

[24] Returning to physical safekeeping for a moment, one may surmise that, if a memory of some incident can be preserved in neurons in the brain, so that it is possible for the same memory to reappear at different times, then perhaps the mind to which the memory occurs can be the same mind as well. One may wish to review the comments in chap. 5 on the link between memory and specific neurons. Memories at different times of the same incident, however, are *not* the same memories. Memories include the condition of consciousness that makes them what they are. Qualitatively identical memories that are related to discrete firings of numerically identical neurons do not demonstrate that there are numerically identical memories. A memory that has ceased to be part of the consciousness of a mind cannot reemerge as the numerically same memory. Like all things, it cannot exist after it ceases, even if that memory, like a previous one, is of the very same event and includes indistinguishable details. A numerically identical mind therefore cannot be built on recurrent memories.

rests, such that *its* persistence is what imparts unity to the individual, then the rational mind is the *beneficiary* of the coherence of people, *not its source*. Given that the physical cannot generate metaphysical cohesion and thus cannot provide identity, this substantive component must be immaterial. What then is it?

COMPLETE BEING

People are beings with physical constitutions. They are also beings with rational faculties. People execute acts in a material world based on reason and, in so doing, manifest the dual character of the human agential system. Acting with understanding, however, is not coextensive with acting with a sense of what is right and wrong. One may open the refrigerator door to get the lemonade because of a desire to quench one's thirst and the belief that a pitcher of it sits on a shelf in there, choosing the lemonade over the tea on the counter. When an agent acts toward an end because of ethical principles, however, taking into account the leadings of conscience, the agent has crossed over from mere *rationality* to *morality*. Rationality can explain agency as a general dynamic. It can account for the deliberation that is behind common election. In itself, though, it is not sufficient to explain the sense of right and wrong that underlies moral choice and that accompanies actions bearing moral qualities. Human beings are capable of deciding what to do when facing standards of righteousness and ethical conduct, and they possess the ability to perform in accordance with them. They have an awareness of what is good and what is evil. They can distinguish fairness and equity from unfairness and inequity. They are satisfied when justice prevails and disturbed when injustice seems to gain the upper hand. Among living creatures, humans are alone in this comprehension. Beasts are not capable of moral discernment. They do not deliberate about taking the high road. They can do nothing from the dictates of conscience, nor can they experience the pangs of guilt. They have no knowledge of right and wrong. They cannot grasp fairness or unfairness, equity or inequity. They do not recognize either justice or its contrary. All these characteristics are peculiar to persons.

I believe that there is a way to describe personal identity that is more forceful than what heretofore has surfaced. Rationality, like risibility, is unique to persons, to be sure, but it is not what truly separates them from other life forms. It is not their defining attribute. The isolating factor is something that is seated more deeply. This work, at its heart, is not one of theology if considering the discipline in an inclusive sense. It is one of apologetics, however, and one that investigates the truth concerning what is real and how knowledge of it is possible. If one turns to the theo-Christian position, then a picture of personhood comes into view that offers meaningful and consistent answers to the basic questions about what persons are and how they can continue through time as unique entities. It is a matter that merits pursuing. In the rest of this chapter, I will undertake the analysis in light of the teaching of the Scriptures. What that teaching reveals is eminently sensible, I maintain, and it contrasts sharply with the deficiencies of materialism as I have identified them in this work.

THE TRINITY OF PERSONHOOD

In the biblical account, God created man in His image, and God is a spiritual being. The Gospel of John records these words of Jesus Christ: "God is spirit."[25] In harmony with the theo-Christian model is the concept that humanity is founded on the spiritual. No one denies the existence of bodies, George Berkeley aside, nor does anyone deny the existence of minds, although different theories portray mentality differently. From the triune God come creatures that are trifold in structure; the Scriptures identify the spirit as the third component: "May your whole spirit, soul and body be kept blameless at the coming of our Lord Jesus Christ."[26] The respective New Testament Greek words for the three facets in this passage are *pneuma*, *psyche*, and *soma*. The spirit—the *pneuma*—mirrors the Creator. It is immaterial, and it is individual. It comes into existence but is future-eternal. It persists. Its persistence does not depend on either the body

---

[25] John 4:24 NIV.
[26] 1 Thess. 5:23 NIV. Cf. 1 Cor. 14:14; and Heb. 4:12.

or the mind; rather, it is conserved by the essential nature that the Creator gives it, one that reflects His own nature. A rational mind cannot subsist on its own, but the mind of a person is preserved through periods of unconsciousness by the immaterial quintessence of the human creature. The spirit provides constancy of personhood beyond both the organismal system and the human agential system.

It follows that this spirit-facet is what makes persons *what* they are because, at the fundamental level, humans are spiritual beings. In a sense, spirituality is the substrate of personhood and bears the weight of it, constituting the core nature—the *physis*, as it were—of humankind, setting it apart from all other kinds of entities in the natural world. Yet, it is also what determines *who* persons are because it fixes personal uniqueness, distinguishing one human being from another. The spirit is the *self*. It is the carrier of personal identity, satisfying the two critical requirements for numerical sameness that I noted earlier: (1) individuation and (2) persistence.

If this view is correct, then part of a person, taken broadly, is not physical, but part is not mental either. Figure 10.3 captures this structure, reflecting a triplex of both corporeal and incorporeal components—elements that make up the personal entity.

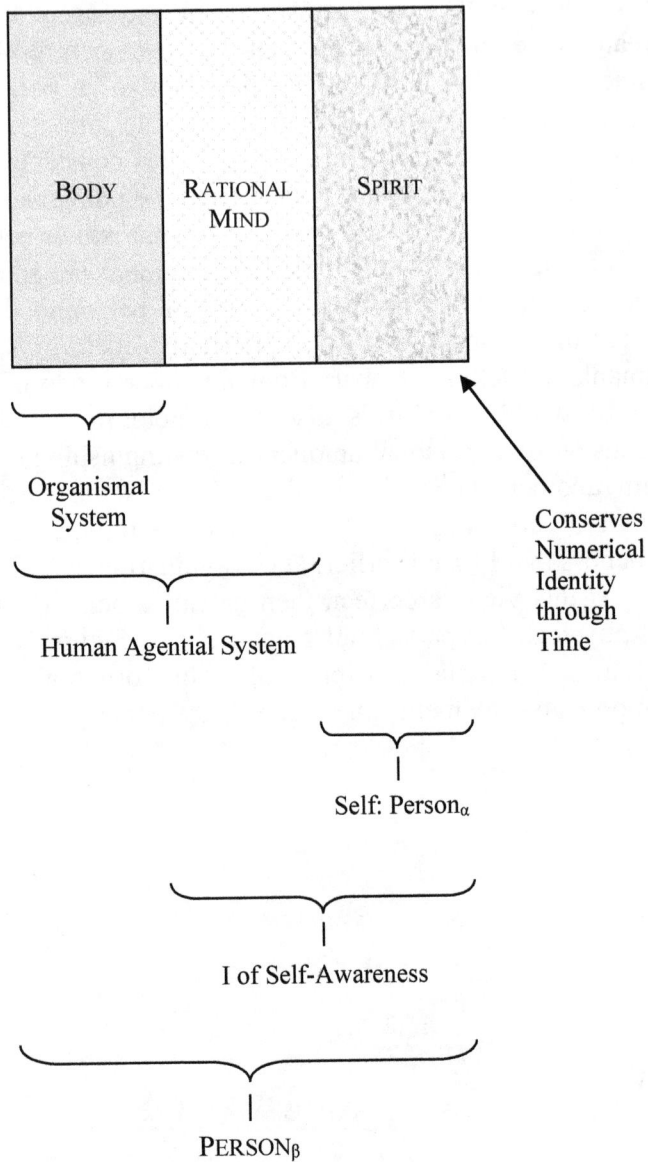

Figure 10.3

I use the term 'person$_\beta$' here, rather than simply 'person', when depicting the personal entity as a whole because, although there is a legitimate sense in which the latter term refers to the trifold being in its entirety, in the more accurate sense, it does not do so. It is the sense that has surfaced just now in the analysis. The person is the nucleus—the essence—of the personal entity. It is the spiritual self, what I label 'person$_\alpha$'. The extended terminology is not important; the concepts that it reflects, however, are central to the discussion.

Those who reject the reality of immaterial minds surely would not admit the reality of immaterial spirits, but existence in that form does explain phenomena that are not explained easily otherwise. Opponents may object that such a representation of persons violates the law of parsimony by multiplying elements—in this case, the ontic components of the human entity. The specific applications of this philosophical principle vary, but, in any application, it is concerned not with the number of elements of a theory but with the proliferation of them beyond what is needed to account for the facts. Of two competing models that offer plausible explanations of a given phenomenon or set of phenomena, the simpler is to be preferred—and will remain so, unless it proves, at some point, to be inadequate. If physicists could describe everything in physical reality effectively without reference to yet another particle, then why look for the Higgs boson and risk being corpuscle-extravagant? They found the elusive particle after decades of searching. Reality is what it is. Given that a suitable account of the numerical identity of persons cannot rest on the body or the mind or the merger of the two, the thesis on the table regarding personhood is reasonable and perhaps even unavoidable.

Ironically, the objection turns against one who raises it, and any materialist who would take this path must examine his or her own theory. The law of parsimony pertains to a range of things, not just entities. It covers causes, dependencies, events, types of phenomena, assumptions, and other factors that play a part in models no less than compositional elements. As a portrayal of the coming into existence of what humans observe, a single-source model is simpler than one incorporating a series of unrelated, happenstance incidents that stem from a spectrum of causes. Strictly from the standpoint of parsimony, the hypothesis of a sole God, acting as a creative agent, is preferable to the contrary hypothesis of purely mechanistic beginnings. Setting aside the illogical universe-from-nothing conception, one is left with this string of random happenings: A fortuitous fluctuation of energy generated the universe, after which a succession of haphazard chemical events generated a self-replicating, nucleotide-constructed molecule, and this occurrence was followed by a plethora of other chance chemical events that generated humans through a process of honing the products of that plethora of chance chemical events. The latter hypothesis is multiplying factors beyond what is needed to give an account of the observable facts.

Suppose that, one day, Bart's trash can and another one in the neighborhood are overturned near the curb where they awaited emptying. Refuse is strewn about the yards at both houses. A lawn down the hill also contains refuse, but the receptacle in that location is upright. Bart believes that one animal is responsible: a large dog that was spotted roaming the neighborhood a few days earlier carrying part of a discarded pizza box in its mouth. The animal rummaged through the trash bins on the three sites, knocking two of them over in the process.

Bill, who lives next door to Bart, advances a different hypothesis. He thinks that a gust blew Bart's receptacle over, given that the last two days have been slightly breezy, and it rolled down the hill to topple the container there, spreading debris at both homes. A municipal employee, who was reading the meters, saw those cans that morning and set them upright, returning Bart's can to his home using the number that the city imprinted on it to identify the address. The worker left the clean-up job to the homeowners. The wind turned Bart's receptacle over a second time, but it was not strong enough to cause the article to take another trip down the street. A raccoon, with its typically nocturnal feeding pattern, upset the third container at some point during the preceding evening, turning it on its side and scattering the contents. That homeowner is the only one of the three to place the trash by the curb at night. The municipal worker spilled coffee on his shirt as he made his rounds in the area— Bill knows him to be an avid coffee-drinker—and he left to go home to change his clothes. Given that he was delayed by the incident, he did not set any containers upright when he returned. Those that were overturned remained in that position.

Both hypotheses may be incorrect, but both cannot be correct. Bart's hypothesis is the simpler of the two. It posits a single cause of the observable state of affairs rather than multiple ones. It lacks the assumption of the targeting event, where Bart's can is hurled down the exact path that is necessary to strike a neighbor's can. It does not presume the corrective action of the municipal employee. It has no repeat wind-toppling episode that leaves Bart's bin in the final position. It does not introduce an unseen animal and its nighttime feeding activity, nor does it rely on a coffee spill that sends the municipal worker home, delaying his routine. Importantly, unlike Bill's hypothesis, it does not include a probabilistic dependency in which one random event—the can down the street topples—can occur only if another random event—Bart's can overturns—occurs first, where both events are strictly the products of chance rather than behavior or agency.

The philosophical tenet of parsimony extends to generational factors. The assumptions that one must set forth to explain origins brings into focus another logical concern for materialistic theories. Taken in isolation, this point against materialism is not decisive, although, of course, it is not a tu quoque, but I believe that it raises questions about the strength of a final support beneath the naturalistic platform.

Parsimony

➤ On the basis of the law of parsimony, what the theory of materialism puts forward to explain the current state of the earth gives ground to that of the theory of a single source.

There is good reason to be leery of adopting a position in which a dozen and a half shortcomings are evident.

When one thinks of Jane, one thinks of her physical presence, her voice, and her mannerisms. One thinks of her personality, her fondness for tennis, and her sense of humor. Are these manifestations of her being sufficient to say that therein is the *essence* of the individual? I do not believe that it is so. In the final analysis, whether Jane cuts her hair or gains a pound from eating the second slice of cheesecake; whether she is filled with excitement as she envisions her vacation to the mountain resort next week, has forgotten all about it, or is unconscious; whether she searched the store before buying just the right gift for a friend's wedding or has lost the ability to move or even to solve simple problems in algebra, Jane is Jane—by virtue of a spiritual core. *She herself is distinct* from all other people. *She herself continues*—through physical change, through mental change, and, if the analysis that I put forth in this section is suitably insightful, then even through the loss of her natural life.

IDENTITY BEYOND THE SELF

The inherent identity of a person, however, does not report the entire account of the self. When Jane was adopted as a child, she became part of a family, with all the responsibilities and privileges that come with daughtership. The adoption effected a legal identity as a member of a familial set, such that her identity from that time forward included not only that of her intrinsic personhood but also that of the relationship into which she entered under the law.

As I noted earlier, experience has demonstrated to me that there is commonly in people a desire to be part of something that they deem to be, in one way or another, greater than they, something with which they can identify. There is an impression of belonging that accompanies it. "I am an *X*," one thinks implicitly, or "I am one of them." The inclusion classifies the individual as a member of a group; from that membership can come a derivative sense of identity for the person through affiliation. The extreme fervor that characterizes loyalty to a college sports team, even among those who never attended the institution, is an example. I know of such people, in fact. More than simply disappointed, they feel personally damaged by the loss of an important game, as though they themselves suffered the defeat. One can become immersed in a job to the point that one's feeling of personal worth is shaken when his or her performance is criticized, even constructively, or the job is no longer there, for whatever reason. I have seen it happen. A certain man whom I know spoke of himself as a "nobody" following unemployment. His identity had come to be bound to his role. When a person is invited to join a fraternity or sorority, an academic or athletic organization, a club or guild, or even a gang, the acceptance unites one with a community of others through a shared connection. The impression of being a part of the whole is likely to be immediate. One's identity is fixed from within, but it is shaped from without by the relationships into which one enters.

If one gives the biblical account of God and the threefold structure of persons due consideration—and I am arguing that such consideration is vital—then one has a basis for understanding that the spirit of an individual is what glues the individual to the existent God. It makes fellowship with Him possible, for, as already stated, God is a spiritual being. Persons possess the special component that allows the connection. Besides its role as the carrier of identity, the spirit serves as the harborer of divinely implanted precepts, which the mind senses in instances of moral reflection and discernment. As adults, people have the privileged ability to comprehend good and evil, to recognize the difference in various contexts, and to choose the good and act in accordance with it. Responsibility accompanies privilege; great responsibility accompanies great privilege. The human capacity to understand moral rightness—to grasp virtue—is a wondrous thing; and, because people possess that capacity, they are accountable for what they do. Like various physical and mental attributes, moral discernment comes with maturity. It is not operational at the beginning, but the predisposition is embedded in the individual; it is innate, and the latent turns active later in life.

Awareness of what is right comes at a price; the failure to do what is right comes with consequences. Faced with divergent courses of action, people must choose. If they choose to do what contravenes God's standards of conduct, then they have missed the mark. No one is free of failure in this regard, for "all have sinned and fall short of the glory of God."[27] Transgression severs the tie to the righteous Creator. Wrongdoing separates people from the holy God. When death takes a loved one, there is a deep-down splintering of a person's being. So too, when an individual is pulled apart from God by an action that violates His principles, there is a jagged tear where the bond with the Creator had been. The conscience testifies to the

---

[27] Rom. 3:23 NIV.

spiritual break. The only way to reestablish the fellowship is by payment of the debt that the transgression generates, but the great privilege of knowing good and evil brings with it a debt upon failure that is also great, too great for one to pay. A lifetime of good works cannot erase sin. "God is love," but He is also "a God of justice."[28] As nature abhors a physical vacuum, so the common adage proclaims, justice abhors a moral vacuum. It *will* be filled, and the scales *will* be balanced.

The Scriptures reveal an offer of substitutionary atonement, and it is through faith, not works. Even though all have chosen iniquity on many occasions, God sent His Son to cover the resultant debt, shielding people from the divine judgment that their wrongdoings surely deserve. It is the perfect, standing in for the imperfect. Here, love and justice intersect. Through acceptance of Jesus Christ as Lord and Savior, the fellowship with God is restored: "[I]f anyone is in Christ, he is a new creation; the old has gone, the new has come!"[29] This regeneration of the personal self, the quiddity of the human entity, forms the spirit anew—every failing is covered— because personal identity lies exactly there. Individuality is given intrinsically in a human's spirit, but, in a profound way, this extrinsic factor also comes into play. It establishes who one is before God. It determines whether the person is in a relationship with the Creator through grace as a member of the familial set. The spiritual pullings-apart that one experiences in life are sealed in Christ, and the tear in the relationship is repaired. Without Christ, the separation remains.

It is not surprising that the angst that one finds in the writings of Sartre and Camus takes center stage in their philosophies, nor is it surprising that Russell's belief in a blind, purposeless universe leads him to hold that truth is founded on despair. In rejecting the actuality of God, these men encounter the inevitable consequence. The inherent meaning and inherent value of life elude their grip. The masked tragedy of such a mindset is that identity is truncated because the relationship with the God who is greater than the individual is what yields not only a sense of purpose for existence but a comprehensive sense of the self as well. It is the sense of a self who belongs.

---

[28] 1 John 4:16 NIV; and Isa. 30:18 NIV—respectively.
[29] 2 Cor. 5:17 NIV.

BELIEVING IS SEEING

The stock articulation of the current atheistic account of reality places much weight on nothing: Humankind came from nothing, by nothing, and for nothing. The theistic account sets forth a dramatically different explanation: Humankind came from God, by God, and for God—people are created to fellowship with their Creator and to honor Him through praise and service. Can anyone prove conclusively that God exists; can anyone show that reality encompasses the immaterial and that it is purposive at its core? A universally accepted logical demonstration of such is not likely to be on the horizon. Science focuses on physical discoveries, and philosophy focuses on metaphysical ones, but neither is a capable mentor where a spiritual pursuit is concerned. That pursuit differs from the others in the objects of discovery, but what counts as knowledge remains fixed, regardless of the realm of inquiry.

I have asserted that knowledge is belief that is true and is grounded suitably, and I have maintained that knowledge is possible. Humans trust their senses to tell them what lies in their surroundings. It is through the experience of perceiving the world that a person comes to hold beliefs about it. Those beliefs take the form of implicit propositions that set forth ostensible facts. Often, those propositions are true—the beliefs align with what is the case in reality—because the senses are trustworthy faculties. A single visual inspection in the right circumstances may be all that is required in many cases to anchor a propositional conviction. Where there is doubt, it can be expelled through corroborative observation: Diverse or recurrent perceptions underwrite the authenticity of what an individual experiences. As the evidence that sensory input provides mounts, the chance that one is wrong in perception descends to the point that being wrong becomes a probabilistic implausibility, confirmed by the rationality of the perceiver. This trio of factors—trust, experience, and evidence—furnishes a reliable base of reasonableness as true beliefs are transformed into knowledge through justification.

When Jeff opens the kitchen door and sees the car in the garage from six feet away, the belief that he forms about its presence is nearly instantaneous. The possibility for error is so low that his being mistaken is not feasible; no further substantiation is necessary, and knowledge accompanies the belief. Such occurrences are those of type *A* in Figure 10.4, where a single visual event yields sufficient evidence, which is represented by the ellipse, to ground the true, propositional belief, which is represented by the diagonal line.

When Jeff sees the left rear quarter of his car from the end of his driveway as he returns to his house from visiting a neighbor, his belief in its presence is all but certain. He continues to gaze, then hears the familiar clicking of the valves after his wife starts the engine to prepare for a trip to the store. A moment later, he smells the exhaust, then sees the tag number when his wife backs the car up the driveway. The convergence of these perceptions substantiates his belief that what his senses report is true. This event is illustrated by type *B* in Figure 10.4, where the instances of perceptual evidence arrive in a compressed period of time. The original sighting carries considerable weight as the belief is formed; the remaining sensory experiences validate the truth of it.

KNOWLEDGE

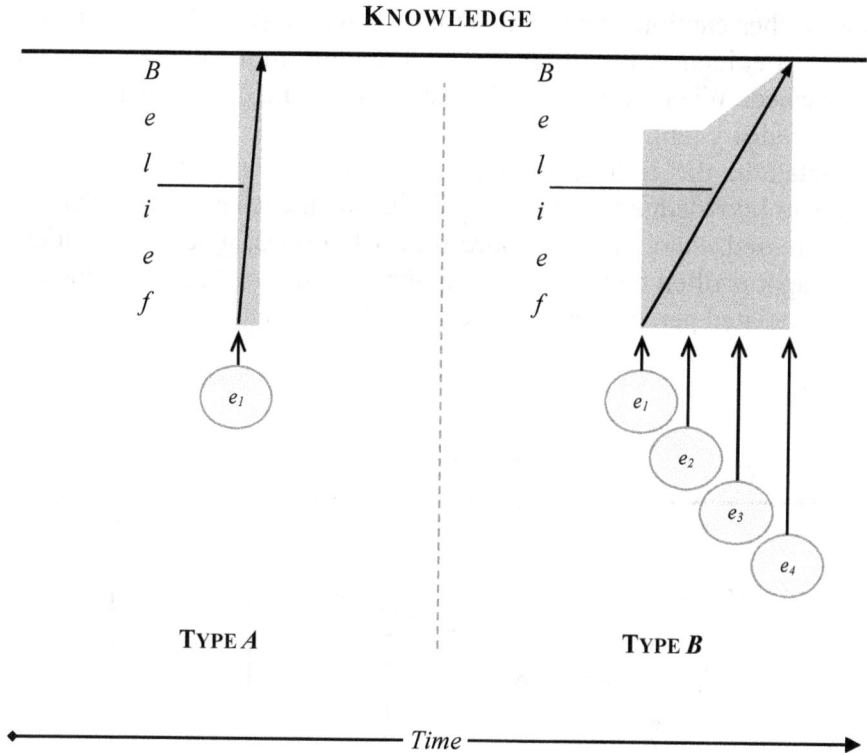

Figure 10.4

In some cases, further investigation is required. One spring morning, Jeff hears rustling in a pile of leaves that he left in his yard during the winter. He believes that a baby bird fell from its nest and fluttered a bit as it sank into the sizeable mound; there are several nests in the trees near the front of his house. He wants to be sure that the sound that he hears is not caused by a copperhead; a neighbor sighted two of them in the vicinity recently. If Jeff is to know, then more perceptual input is required. He moves closer and listens carefully when the wind subsides. He tosses a pebble near the edge of the pile and watches for any movement that indicates a pattern. Distracted by his son's request, Jeff heads for the sidewalk to help the lad, who fell while roller-skating, then returns to his monitoring. He moves around to the other side of the pile and observes. He approaches cautiously and prods the area with a stick. With each new piece of evidence, his belief gains force until, in the end, knowledge is reached: When he brushes the leaves aside, he discovers that there is indeed a young songbird on the ground. This coming to know is depicted in the following diagram as type C. Besides perceptual paths to knowledge that are virtually instantaneous and those that are compressed, there are also more protracted ones, where the evidential support often comes in packets that are interrupted by periods of no associated perceptions. Figure 10.5 illustrates this case.

KNOWLEDGE

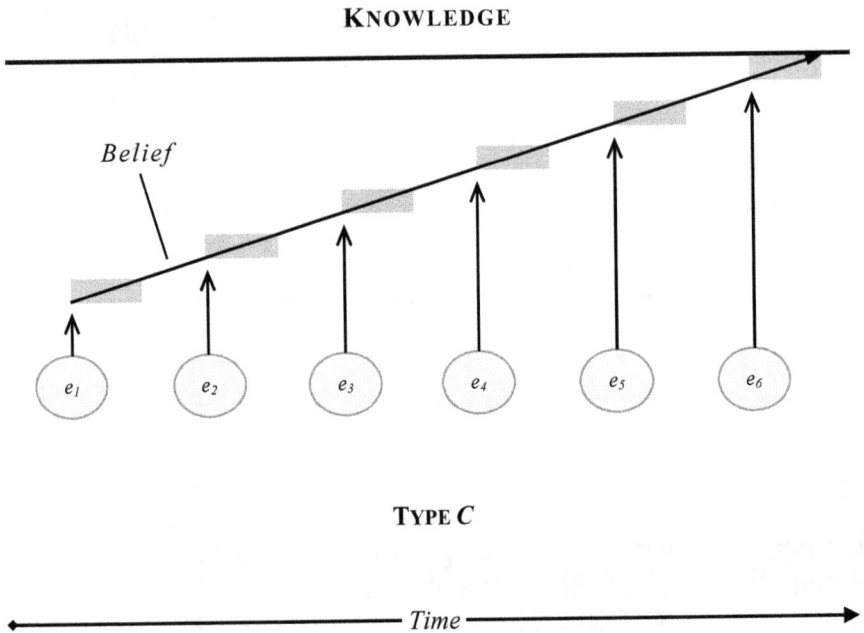

TYPE C

Time

Figure 10.5

Must knowing be limited a priori to the physical, and must evidence point only to physical things? Clearly, there is no logical compulsion for such constraints. The previous chapter, in fact, presented evidence that certain events transcend the world of the material. Many physicists postulate the existence of seven extra dimensions of physical reality that one cannot experience—not to mention the incalculable number of unseen, parallel universes that a few propose. It is not beyond reason to accept the existence of an immaterial dimension of reality that one can experience, though not, on the whole, through perception. If the door to incorporeality is open, then perhaps so is the possibility of acknowledging the truth of propositions pertaining to spiritual matters, founded on the same abovesaid trio of factors—trust, experience, and evidence—albeit in a different way. As is the case with visual inspection under proper conditions, a single incident may be all that is needed both to generate a propositional belief and to ground its truth. Indeed, some report such type-A experiences.[30] They are epiphanies.

In the absence of them in a person's life, however, does one possess enough open-mindedness to step forward in search of the extensiveness of reality, despite the fact that it may include that which a person cannot see? The Bible declares that one is to "think soberly, according as God has dealt to every man the measure of faith."[31] Is it true then that each person has enough inborn trust to set out from the citadel of skepticism on a mission of discovery? I hold that it is so. The stair-step way is the norm for the spiritual journey, but one quite likely does not come to the ground state of believing on this journey by means of visual input, though observing the amazing world may influence some. It is not usually seeing that generates the belief, nor is it even logic, but faith—based on hearing about God. One will recall that "faith is . . . the evidence of things not seen."[32] In Figure 10.5, e_1 represents this initial thrust. Where the experiences that follow serve to support the tentative belief, faith rises again to maintain the course and drive the progression; and, where subsequent encounters converge to ground that belief, knowledge, I submit, is acquired. It is not a jaunt for the day, however. It is an enduring quest, one of determination, one of commitment to learning the truth.

---

[30] Changed lives are the result. The radical transformation that took place in Mac Gober following an encounter with Jesus Christ is a case in point. This man, who was locked in a brutal, biker lifestyle, experienced the miraculous. See his book *Unchained* (Dallas: Word Publishing, 1993).

[31] Rom. 12:3 NKJV.

[32] Heb. 11:1 KJV.

If one's knowledge of God is to be more than an intellectual appreciation, though, then it must be more than *propositional*. It must encompass—indeed, seize upon—the purpose for human existence. Knowing God in this way is not a matter of tangible evidence or logical rules. It is a matter of *relationship*. It is *experiential*, not in the sense of having perceptions that give rise to propositional knowledge of physical reality but in the sense of intimate acquaintance, engendered by revelation; and such knowing is of a different order. God presents a depiction of reality to humankind in His word; trust is the means by which it is possible to take hold of it. The decision to look in earnest rests with the individual, and it is the earnest search that is rewarded: "'You will seek me and find me when you seek me with all your heart. I will be found by you,' declares the LORD."[33] Those who do go forward, God will reach out to meet, for the Scriptures declare that He will draw close to those who draw close to Him.[34] It is what one would expect in a relationship.

The traveler who forges ahead must understand that the path to knowledge here leads through an uncommon wood, where a distinct reversal of the way of the world lies. The human familiarity with the natural domain conditions one to think in a certain way, and familiarity is a forceful guide, but a reality that extends beyond the natural sphere need not be limited to an identical set of operating principles. A Riemannian surface does not conform to Euclidean rules, yet it is no less authentic. Fundamental ontic differences ought to bring different workings into play. In the physical realm, one walks in trust because one has come to rely on the senses, and so one trusts what one sees. In the spiritual realm, one sees because one has come to walk in trust, and so one sees more. The first move there is one of faith, but, unless one is willing to make it, the next stepping stone will lie forever unlit. It is manifest that God wants each person to go after Him, but one must possess the resolve to do so and act accordingly. Faith in contemplation generates the propositional belief about the existence of God. Faith in action generates the paces that, in time, bring confirmation. What awaits one who continues down this path goes beyond knowledge that *God is*; it leads to knowledge of *God*. In

---

[33] Jer. 29:13–14 NIV.
[34] See James 4:8.

accepting the thesis that I have set forth in these pages, the notion that a spiritual realm is part of the makeup of reality comes into focus. *In this realm, faith is the mode of discovery, and ultimately it is faith that grounds true beliefs, so that knowledge is possible.*

DIVERGENT DRIFT

Several years after my encounter with the blind man whom I introduced at the beginning of this work, I was back at the same intersection where we had met. I noticed that the city had installed electronic devices with voice commands to inform pedestrians when it was safe to cross and audible beacons that helped to guide them to the proper place on the opposite side of the street. Provided that pedestrians responded appropriately to what they heard, safe passage effectively was assured. Undoubtedly, those who could not see the road found the apparatuses to be useful. When one cannot determine the correct route by means of direct, visual observation, one is compelled to depend on other means to keep from drifting off course. Even hearing the sonic signals would be of no use, however, if one did not place a measure of confidence in the authenticity of those signals and hence did not set out across the street. Getting to where one wants to go—the valued end—requires one to hold a true belief concerning one's bearing. It is not enough simply to believe, however; without action, the belief is sterile. The corroboration that substantiates what a traveler holds to be true may not emerge with the initial footfall, but, as the evidence that one is proceeding in the right direction continues to mount, little by little, there will come a point at which the belief is grounded with force. Without the first pace forward, there can be no progression toward a goal. If a person, whether sighted or sightless, never puts a foot on the street at the crossroads, trusting in the information that the senses provide—visual or auditory—then that person never will reach the desired destination.

Knowledge is not found in passivity, in the mere idle waiting for beliefs to press themselves upon an unguarded mind. Knowledge is found in the active pursuit of truth. The atheistic worldview and the theo-Christian worldview represent composite interpretations of reality that are not compatible. I have made a case for the latter view in this work in the hope, in part, that one will consider it to be a rational stance and seek to learn more. The election is restricted; it belongs solely to the individual. Each person has to assess the information that is conveyed to him or her about God and His Son through the Scriptures and decide what to do with that information: embrace it, place it aside for the moment, ignore it altogether, or reject it. So says God in the biblical canon: "This day I call heaven and earth as witnesses against you that I have set before you life and death, blessings and curses. Now choose life."[35] Persons are beings with free will. They can choose. They must choose. They must act on their choices. In this most weighty of all decisions, it is imperative that a person act with wisdom, and do so even this day. The implications of the course that one determines are major, and the end state, I would argue, is everlasting.

---

[35] Deut. 30:19 NIV.

EPILOGUE

ERASING THE PAST

"For I will forgive their wickedness
and will remember their sins no more."

—Jer. 31:34 NIV

One of the particularly disturbing experiences of my childhood occurred early during my first school year. Children were issued pencils as part of a program to develop writing skills. Those pencils had no erasers. If a pupil made a mistake, then the developmental exercise ended in disaster; there was just no good way to correct the error. Children make mistakes. The impact—on me, at least—was a long-lasting one. It created an underlying expectation that things that go wrong cannot be fixed. Life seemed to bear out the expectancy. As many can attest, injuries may leave one without the capabilities that existed prior to the incident and even prone to suffer from collateral maladies. In the case of some injuries, such as detached menisciuses or damage to the central nervous system, strictly natural tissue restoration is not forthcoming. A word that is spoken in haste or in anger cannot be retracted. It may remain in the memory of the hearer, and the speaker as well, indefinitely. Unanticipated consequences of a poorly considered choice may bring regrets that linger for decades. One cannot go back to a prior hour to take another path. Several school grades passed before I came to realize that those first pencils were not returning—all the ones in subsequent years were equipped with erasers—but the impression already had been set. The minds of the young are molded easily by what they encounter.

Some choices that people make have a moral aspect. If one selects the wrong course in such cases, then the results can be far more injurious than a misstep on the stairs or an insensitive remark to a friend. They can harm one's very self. The conscience bears witness to that fact. How can the action be reversed? The deed has been executed; the damage has been done. The answer is that forgiveness is available through God's Son and, with that forgiveness, liberation. The misdeeds covered, it is as though they never happened. The Scriptures state, "Therefore, there is now no condemnation for those who are in Christ Jesus."[1]

All the science and all the philosophy are powerless to tell one how to rectify the moral mistakes that come about in life. If, however, one will invest the implanted measure of faith—divinely allotted to every person—and step forward to take hold of the extended, sacrificial hand, then one will have escaped what justice surely requires; one will have "crossed over from death to life."[2] It is not spending years pursuing the mind-bending hypotheses about the quantum world or the abstruse, enigma-laden theories of metaphysics that leads to the answers to humankind's most profound questions. The answers do not lie in complexity but in simplicity. They lie in God's grand, but exclusive, offer to erase one's past and recast one's future.

Take seriously the thought of entering into a relationship with the eternal God in the only way that one can do so: through "Christ, in whom are hidden all the treasures of wisdom and knowledge."[3] The act of entering is more than simply an exercise, performed in faith, leading to a grasp of immaterial reality. It is also an act of wisdom; indeed, it is the wisest act of a lifetime. With each pace ahead comes a fuller understanding of what this mysterious quest is driving all, with such force, to discover. It is to find the way out of the arid wilderness of an incomplete identity. It is "to know the love of Christ that surpasses knowledge."[4] In the end, the experiential transcends the propositional. In the end, what humans search for at the deepest part of their personhood, I believe, is to know the unconditional love of the God who brought them into being.

---

[1] Rom. 8:1 NIV.

[2] John 5:24 NIV.

[3] Col. 2:2–3 NIV.

[4] Eph. 3:19 ESV.

APPENDIX: MATHEMATICS OF UNIQUE PROTEIN SYNTHESIS
FIRST PART—SINGLE PLANET

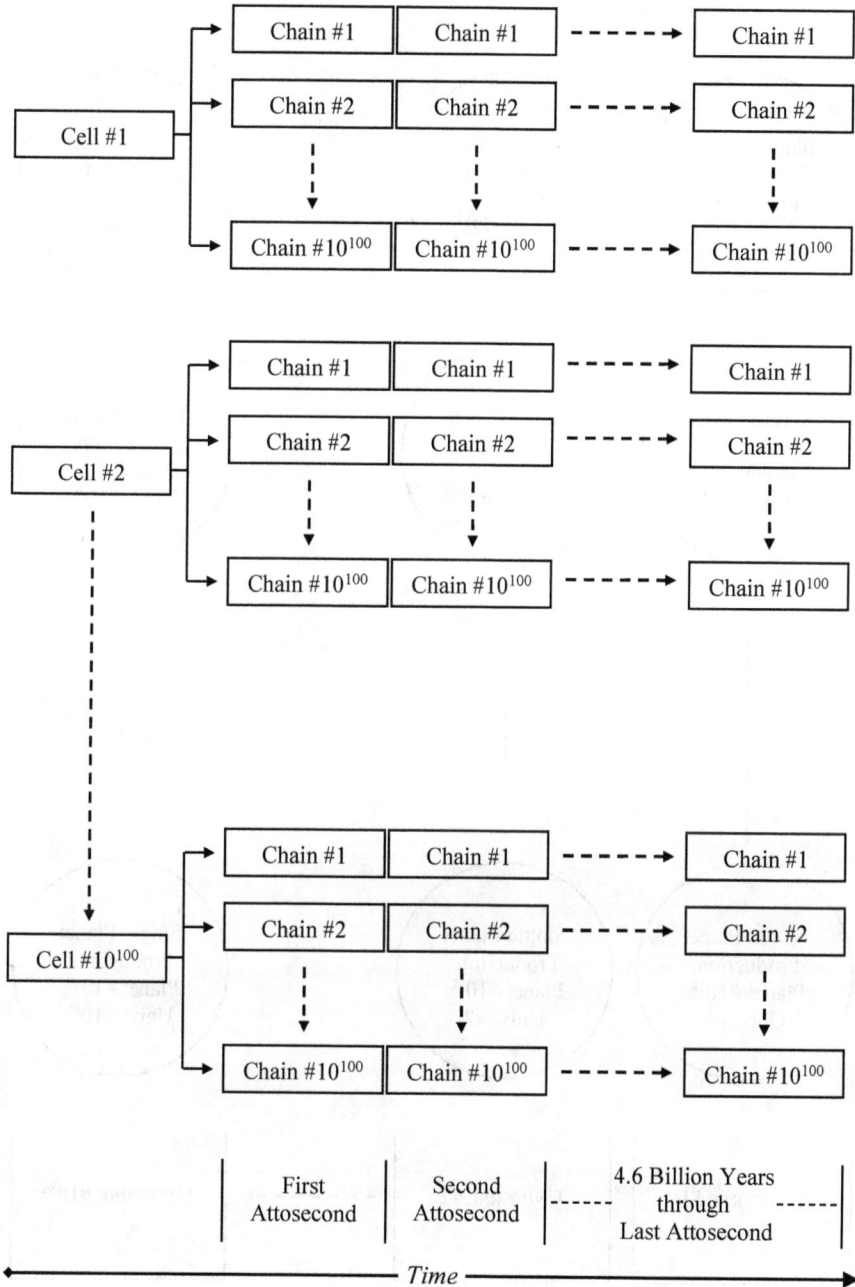

	First Attosecond	Second Attosecond	4.6 Billion Years through Last Attosecond

Time

APPENDIX: MATHEMATICS OF UNIQUE PROTEIN SYNTHESIS (CONT.)
SECOND PART—MULTIPLE PLANETS, MULTIPLE UNIVERSES
OVERALL RESULT: $< {}^1/_{\text{GOOGOL}}$ NUMBER OF POSSIBLE CHAINS

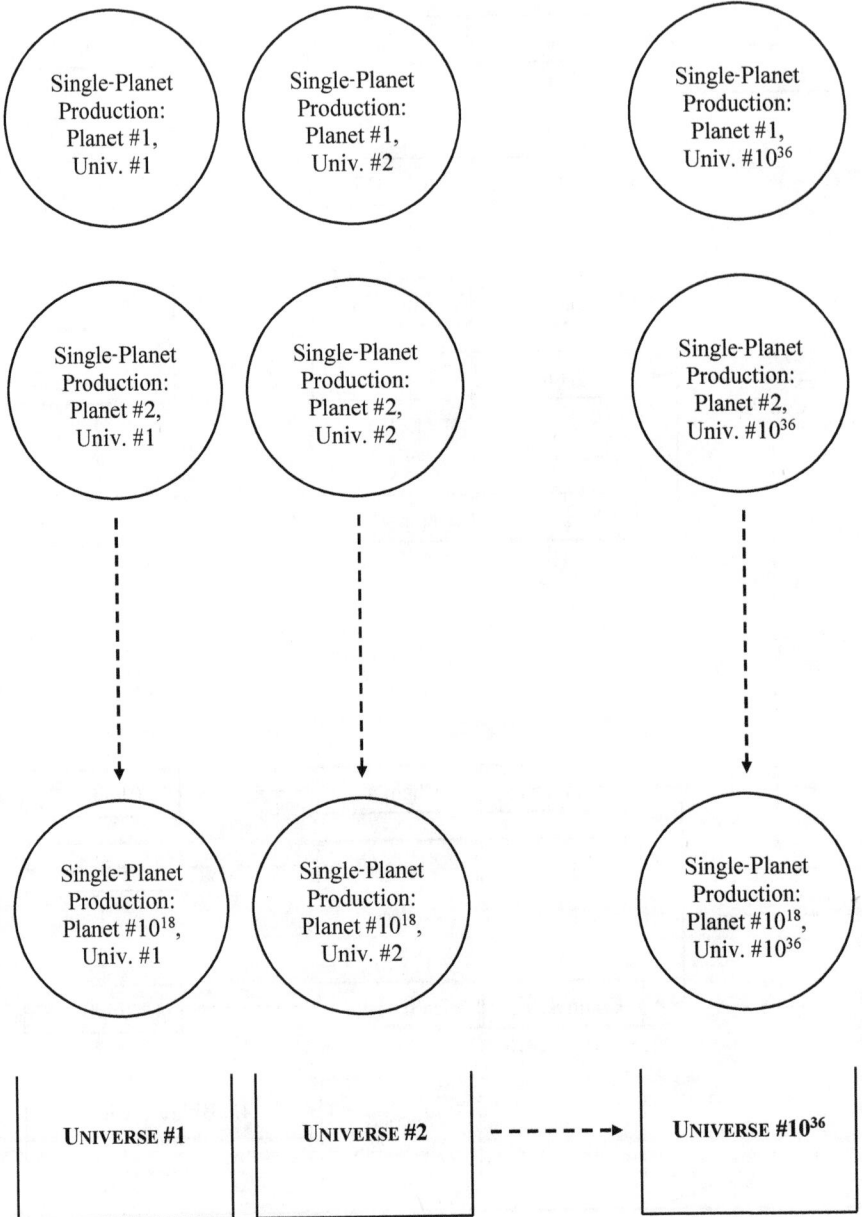

Single-Planet Production: Planet #1, Univ. #1

Single-Planet Production: Planet #1, Univ. #2

Single-Planet Production: Planet #1, Univ. #10^{36}

Single-Planet Production: Planet #2, Univ. #1

Single-Planet Production: Planet #2, Univ. #2

Single-Planet Production: Planet #2, Univ. #10^{36}

Single-Planet Production: Planet #10^{18}, Univ. #1

Single-Planet Production: Planet #10^{18}, Univ. #2

Single-Planet Production: Planet #10^{18}, Univ. #10^{36}

UNIVERSE #1

UNIVERSE #2

UNIVERSE #10^{36}

BIBLIOGRAPHY

Abell, George. *Exploration of the Universe*. 2nd ed. New York: Holt, Rinehart and Winston, 1969.

Abelson, Phillip H. "Chemical Events on the Primitive Earth." *Proceedings of the National Academy of Sciences of the United States of America* 55, no. 6 (1966): 1365–72.

Akkoyunlu, E. A., K. Ekanadham, and R. V. Huber. "Some Constraints and Tradeoffs in the Design of Network Communications." *Association for Computing Machinery SIGOPS Operating System Review Newsletter* 9, no. 5 (1975): 67–74.

Alakkalkunnel, Francis, and Christian Kanzian. "Strawson's Concept of Person—A Critical Discussion." In *Papers of the 25th International Wittgenstein Symposia 11–17 August 2002*; from the Austrian Ludwig Wittgenstein Society archives: A selection of papers from the International Wittgenstein Symposia in Kirchberg am Wechsel, ed. Chr. Kanzian, J. Quitterer, and E. Runggaldier. Accessed October 21, 2014. wab.uib.no/agora-alws.

Albert, David. "On the Origin of Everything." *New York Times Book Review*, March 25, 2012, 20–21.

Alberts, Bruce, et al. *Molecular Biology of the Cell*. 4th ed. New York: Garland Science, 2002.

Alexander of Aphrodisias. *Alexander of Aphrodisias on Aristotle's Metaphysics 1*. Trans. W. E. Dooley. Ithaca: Cornell University Press, 1989.

Allen, R. E. *Plato's* Parmenides: *Translation and Analysis*. Minneapolis: University of Minnesota Press, 1983.

Alston, William P. "Epistemic Circularity." *Philosophy and Phenomenological Research* 47, no. 1 (1986): 1–30.

Anscombe, G. E. M. *Intention*. 2nd ed. 1963. Repr., Ithaca: Cornell University Press, 1974.

———. " 'Whatever Has a Beginning of Existence Must Have a Cause': Hume's Argument Exposed." *Analysis* 34, no. 5 (1974): 145–51.

Aquinas, Saint Thomas. *Summa theologiæ*. Trans. Timothy McDermott. Vol. 2, *Existence and Nature of God*. Cambridge: Blackfriars, 1964.

Aristotle. *Aristotle: Nicomachean Ethics*. Trans. Terence Irwin. 2nd ed. Indianapolis: Hackett Publishing Co., 1999.

———. *Aristotle's Metaphysics*. Trans. Hippocrates G. Apostle. Bloomington: Indiana University Press, 1966.

———. *Aristotle's Physics*. Trans. W. D. Ross. 1936. Repr., Oxford: Clarendon Press, 1966.

————. *The Basic Works of Aristotle*. Trans. E. M. Edghill et al. Ed. Richard McKeon. New York: Random House, 1941.

Armitage, Mark Hollis, and Kevin Lee Anderson. "Soft Sheets of Fibrillar Bone from a Fossil of the Supraorbital Horn of the Dinosaur *Triceratops horridus*." *Acta Histochemica* 115, no. 6 (2013): 603–8. Accessed November 2, 2016. www.sciencedirect.com/science/article/pii/S0065128113000020.

Armstrong, D. M. *Belief, Truth, and Knowledge*. Cambridge: Cambridge University Press, 1973.

Asara, John M., et al. "Protein Sequences from Mastodon and *Tyrannosaurus* [*r*]*ex* Revealed by Mass Spectrometry." *Science* 316, no. 5822 (2007): 280–85.

Associated Press. "Fetus Can't Feel Pain before 24 Weeks, Study Says." Reported by NBC News, June 25, 2010. Accessed November 19, 2013. www.nbcnews.com/id/37920310/ns/health-health_care/t/fetus-cant-feel-pain-weeks-study-says.

Austin, J. L. "Other Minds." In *Philosophical Papers*, ed. J. O. Urmson and G. J. Warnock. 3rd ed. Oxford: Oxford University Press, 1979.

————. *Sense and Sensibilia*. 1962. Repr., London: Oxford University Press, 1970.

Ayer, Alfred J. *The Foundations of Empirical Knowledge*. 1940. Repr., London: Macmillan and Co., 1958.

————. *The Problem of Knowledge*. London: Macmillan and Co., 1956.

Baker, Lynne Rudder. "Metaphysics and Mental Causation." In *Mental Causation*, ed. John Heil and Alfred Mele. Oxford: Clarendon Press, 1993.

Banich, Marie T. *Cognitive Neuroscience and Neuropsychology*. 2nd ed. Boston: Houghton Mifflin Co., 2004.

Bar Hebraeus, Gregory. *The Chronography of Gregory Abû'l Faraj, the Son of Aaron, the Hebrew Physician Commonly Known as Bar Hebraeus, Being the First Part of His Political History of the World*. Trans. Ernest A. Wallis Budge. Vol. 1. London: Oxford University Press, 1932.

Barker, Kenneth L., et al., eds. *Zondervan NIV Study Bible*. 1985. Repr., Grand Rapids, MI: Zondervan, 2008.

Barker, Stephen F. *The Elements of Logic*. 2nd ed. New York: McGraw-Hill Book Co., 1974.

Barnes, Jonathan. *The Presocratic Philosophers*. Vol. 1, *Thales to Zeno*. London: Routledge and Kegan Paul, 1979.

————. *The Presocratic Philosophers*. Vol. 2, *Empedocles to Democritus*. London: Routledge and Kegan Paul, 1979.

Baskin-Robbins. "Our History." Accessed July 24, 2013. www.baskinrobbins.com.

Beckwith, Francis J. *Law, Darwinism, and Public Education.* Lanham, MD: Rowman and Littlefield Publishers, 2003.

Berkeley, George. *George Berkeley: Principles, Dialogues, and Philosophical Correspondence.* Ed. Colin Murray Turbayne. Indianapolis: Bobbs-Merrill Co., 1965.

Bertazzo, Sergio, et al. "Fibres and Cellular Structures Preserved in 75-Million-Year-Old Dinosaur Specimens." *Nature Communications* 6, article no. 7352 (2015): 1–8. Accessed July 17, 2015. www.nature.com/ncomms/2015/150609/ncomms8352/full/ncomms8352.html.

Bible Architecture. "Lachish." Accessed October 28, 2014. www.bible-architecture.info/Lachish.htm.

Bible Hub. Accessed July 25, 2015. www.biblehub.com.

BiblePlaces.com. "Lachish." Accessed May 31, 2016. www.bibleplaces.com/lachish.

Black, Max. "The Identity of Indiscernibles." *Mind* 61, no. 242 (1952): 153–64.

Blake, A. J., and J. H. Carver, "The Evolutionary Role of Atmospheric Ozone." *Journal of the Atmospheric Sciences* 34, no. 5 (1977): 720–28.

Bradford, William. *Of Plymouth Plantation: 1620–1647.* A new edition by Samuel Eliot Morison. New York: Alfred A. Knopf, 1979.

Bruce, F. F. *The New Testament Documents: Are They Reliable?* 5th rev. ed. 1960. Repr., Grand Rapids, MI: William B. Eerdmans Publishing Co., 1963.

Burnet, John. *Early Greek Philosophy.* 4th ed. 1930. Repr., London: Adam and Charles Black, 1971.

———. *Greek Philosophy: Thales to Plato.* 1914. Repr., London: Macmillan and Co., 1932.

Butler, Joseph. *The Analogy of Religion, to the Constitution and Course of Nature. To Which Are Added Two Brief Dissertations: I. On Personal Identity.—II. On the Nature of Virtue.* 23rd ed. Philadelphia: J. B. Lippincott and Co., 1902.

———. "Fifteen Sermons Preached at the Rolls Chapel." In *British Moralists, 1650–1800,* ed. D. D. Raphael. Vol. 1, *Hobbes–Gay.* Oxford: Oxford University Press, 1969.

Cairns-Smith, A. G. *Genetic Takeover.* Cambridge: Cambridge University Press, 1982.

Calladine, C. R., and Horace R. Drew. *Understanding DNA: The Molecule and How It Works.* 2nd ed. San Diego: Academic Press, 1997.

Cantor, Georg. *Contributions to the Founding of the Theory of Transfinite Numbers*. Trans. Philip E. B. Jourdain. New York: Dover Publications, 1915.

Carroll, Lewis. *The Complete Works of Lewis Carroll*. New York: Vintage Books, 1976.

Cartland, Joseph L. "Counting Actions: A Philosophical Inquiry." Ph.D. diss., University of Virginia, 1980.

Celce-Murcia, Marianne, and Diane Larsen-Freeman, with Howard Williams. *The Grammar Book: An ESL/EFL Teacher's Course.* 2nd ed. Boston: Heinle and Heinle Publishers, 1999.

Center for Online Judaic Studies. "Hezekiah's Defeat: The Annals of Sennacherib on the Taylor, Jerusalem, and Oriental Institute Prisms, 700 BCE." Accessed June 16, 2014. www.cojs.org/cojswiki/index.php/Hezekiah%E2%80%99s_Defeat:_The_Annals_of_Sennacherib_on_the_Taylor,_Jerusalem,_and_Oriental_Institute_Prisms,_700_BCE.

Chappell, V. C., ed. *The Philosophy of Mind*. Englewood Cliffs, NJ: Prentice-Hall, 1962.

Cherniss, Harold. *Aristotle's Criticism of Presocratic Philosophy*. 1935. Repr., New York: Octagon Books, 1964.

Chisholm, Roderick M. *Perceiving: A Philosophical Study*. 1957. Ithaca: Cornell University Press, 1969.

Christianson, Gale E. *Edwin Hubble: Mariner of the Nebulae*. New York: Farrar, Straus and Giroux, 1995.

Clegg, James S. "Cryptobiosis—A Peculiar State of Biological Organization." *Comparative Biochemistry and Physiology – Part B: Biochemistry and Molecular Biology* 128, no. 4 (2001): 613–24.

Cleve, Felix M. *The Philosophy of Anaxagoras: An Attempt at Reconstruction*. New York: King's Crown Press, 1949.

Cogan, Mordechai. "Sennacherib: The Capture and Destruction of Babylon (2.119E)." In *The Context of Scripture*, ed. William W. Hallo and K. Lawson Younger. Vol. 2, *Monumental Inscriptions from the Biblical World*. Leiden, Netherlands: Brill, 2000.

———. "Sennacherib's Siege of Jerusalem (2.119B)." In *The Context of Scripture*, ed. William W. Hallo and K. Lawson Younger. Vol. 2, *Monumental Inscriptions from the Biblical World*. Leiden, Netherlands: Brill, 2000.

Cogan, Mordechai, and Hayim Tadmor. "*Excursus:* The Biblical and Assyrian Accounts of Sennacherib's Campaign Compared." In *The Anchor Bible*. Vol. 11, *II Kings: A New Translation with Introduction and Commentary*, trans. Mordechai Cogan and Hayim Tadmor. New York: Doubleday and Co., 1988.

Cooper, Lisa Noelle, et al. "Evolution of Hyperphalangy and Digit Reduction in the Cetacean Manus." *Anatomical Record* 290, no. 6 (2007): 654–72.

Copi, Irving M. *Introduction to Logic*. 3rd ed. 1968. London: Macmillan Co., 1969.

Copleston, Frederick. *Aquinas*. Harmondsworth, England: Penguin Books, 1955.

———. *A History of Philosophy*. Vol. 1, *Greece and Rome*. London: Search Press, 1946.

———. *A History of Philosophy*. Vol. 2, *Augustine to Scotus*. London: Search Press, 1950.

———. *A History of Philosophy*. Vol. 4, *Descartes to Leibniz*. London: Search Press, 1958.

———. *A History of Philosophy*. Vol. 5, *Hobbes to Hume*. London: Search Press, 1959.

Cornford, Francis Macdonald. *Before and After Socrates*. 1932. Repr., Cambridge: Cambridge University Press, 1958.

———. *From Religion to Philosophy: A Study in the Origins of Western Speculation*. New York: Harper and Brothers Publishers, 1957.

———. *Plato and Parmenides: Parmenides'* Way of Truth *and Plato's* Parmenides *Translated with an Introduction and a Running Commentary*. 1939. London: Routledge and Kegan Paul, 1950.

———. *Plato's Cosmology: The* Timaeus *of Plato Translated with a Running Commentary*. 1937. Repr., London: Routledge and Kegan Paul, 1977.

———. *Plato's Theory of Knowledge: The* Theaetetus *and the* Sophist *of Plato Translated with a Running Commentary*. 1935. London: Routledge and Kegan Paul, 1949.

Coursey, J. S., et al. "Atomic Weights and Isotopic Compositions." Physical Measurement Laboratory, National Institute of Standards and Technology. Accessed October 20, 2014. nist.gov/pml/data/comp.cfm.

Craig, William Lane. *The Cosmological Argument from Plato to Leibniz*. New York: Barnes and Noble Books, 1980.

———. *The Kalām Cosmological Argument*. London: Macmillan Press, 1979.

———. *Reasonable Faith: Christian Truth and Apologetics*. 3rd ed. Wheaton, IL: Crossway Books, 2008.

Cross, R. C., and A. D. Woozley. *Plato's* Republic: *A Philosophical Commentary*. London: Macmillan and Co., 1964.

Curley, E. M. *Descartes against the Skeptics*. Cambridge: Harvard University Press, 1978.

Dardis, Anthony. *Mental Causation: The Mind-Body Problem*. New York: Columbia University Press, 2008.

Darrow, Clarence. *The Story of My Life*. New York: Charles Scribner's Sons, 1932.

Darwin, Charles. *On the Origin of Species by Means of Natural Selection*. Ed. Joseph Carroll. Peterborough, Ontario, Canada: Broadview Press, 2003.

Davidson, Donald. "Actions, Reasons, and Causes." *Journal of Philosophy* 60, no. 23 (1963): 685–700.

———. "Agency." In *Agent, Action, and Reason*, ed. Robert Binkley, Richard Bronaugh, and Ausonio Marras. Toronto: University of Toronto Press, 1971.

———. *Essays on Actions and Events*. Oxford: Clarendon Press, 1980.

———. "Thinking Causes." In *Mental Causation*, ed. John Heil and Alfred Mele. Oxford: Clarendon Press, 1993.

Davis, Percival, and Dean H. Kenyon. *Of Pandas and People: The Central Question of Biological Origins*. Ed. Charles B. Thaxton. Dallas: Haughton Publishing Co., 1989.

Dawkins, Richard. *The Blind Watchmaker: Why the Evidence of Evolution Reveals a Universe without Design*. 1986. Repr., New York: W. W. Norton and Co., 2006.

———. *Climbing Mount Improbable*. 1996. Repr., New York: W. W. Norton and Co., 1997.

———. *The God Delusion*. Boston: Houghton Mifflin Co., 2006.

———. *The Greatest Show on Earth: The Evidence for Evolution*. New York: Free Press, 2009.

———. "Ignorance Is No Crime." *Free Inquiry* 21, no. 3 (2001): 7–8.

———. "Put Your Money on Evolution." *New York Times Book Review*, April 9, 1989, 34–35.

———. *River Out of Eden: A Darwinian View of Life*. New York: BasicBooks, 1995.

———. *The Selfish Gene*. New York: Oxford University Press, 1976.

———. *Unweaving the Rainbow: Science, Delusion, and the Appetite for Wonder*. Boston: Houghton Mifflin Co., 1998.

DeLong, Howard. *A Profile of Mathematical Logic*. Reading, MA: Addison-Wesley Publishing Co., 1970.

Dembski, William A. *Intelligent Design: The Bridge between Science and Theology*. Downers Grove, IL: IVP Academic, 1999.

———. "What Every Theologian Should Know about Creation, Evolution, and Design." In *Unapologetic Apologetics: Meeting the Challenges of Theological Studies*, ed. William A. Dembski and Jay Wesley Richards. Downers Grove, IL: InterVarsity Press, 2001.

Descartes, René. *The Philosophical Works of Descartes*. Trans. Elizabeth S. Haldane and G. R. T. Ross. 2 vols. 1911. Repr., Cambridge: Cambridge University Press, 1967.

————. *The Philosophical Writings of Descartes*. Trans. John Cottingham et al. 3 vols. 1984–1991. Cambridge: Cambridge University Press, 1997–2009. Vol. 3 is a reprint.

De Vogel, C. J. *Greek Philosophy: A Collection of Texts*. 3rd ed. Vol. 1, *Thales to Plato*. Leiden, Netherlands: E. J. Brill, 1963.

Dicker, Georges. *Descartes: An Analytical and Historical Introduction*. New York: Oxford University Press, 1993.

Diels, Hermann, trans. *Die Fragmente der Vorsokratiker*. Ed. Walther Kranz. 6th rev. ed. 3 vols. 1951–1952. Repr., Dublin: Weidmann, 1972–1973.

Diogenes Laërtius. *Lives of Eminent Philosophers*. Trans. R. D. Hicks. 2 vols. London: William Heinemann, 1925.

Dolezal, Hubert. *Living in a World Transformed: Perceptual and Performatory Adaptation to Visual Distortion*. New York: Academic Press, 1982.

Dose, K. "Peptides and Amino Acids in the Primordial Hydrosphere." In *The Origin of Life and Evolutionary Biochemistry*, ed. K. Dose et al. New York: Plenum Press, 1974.

Douglas, J. D., and Merrill C. Tenney, eds. *Zondervan Bible Dictionary*. Grand Rapids, MI: Zondervan, 2008.

Duhem, Pierre. *To Save the Phenomena: An Essay on the Idea of Physical Theory from Plato to Galileo*. Trans. Edmund Doland and Chaninah Maschler. Chicago: University of Chicago Press, 1969.

Dull, Charles E., H. Clark Metcalfe, and John E. Williams. *Modern Chemistry*. 1958. New York: Holt, Rinehart and Winston, 1962.

"Early Earth's 'Alien Atmosphere' Theories Nixed—'Dominated by Oxygen-Rich Compounds.' " *Daily Galaxy*, November 04, 2013. Accessed April 16, 2015. www.dailygalaxy.com/my_weblog/2013/11/early-earths-alien-atmosphere-theories-nixed-dominated-by-oxygen rich-compounds-todays-most-popular.html.

Eby, Richard E. *Jesus Told Me to . . . Tell Them I Am Coming*. Old Tappan, NJ: Fleming H. Revell Co., 1980.

Educational Broadcasting Corporation. *Stephen Hawking's Universe*. Vol. 6, *An Answer to Everything*. 60 min. Boston: PBS Video, 1997. Videocassette.

Edwards, Paul, gen. ed. *The Encyclopedia of Philosophy*. 8 vols. 1967. Repr., New York: Macmillan Publishing Co., 1972.

Edwards, Paul, and Arthur Pap, eds. *A Modern Introduction to Philosophy*. Rev. ed. New York: Free Press, 1965.

Elegant Universe, The. Dir. Joseph McMaster and Julia Cort. Disk 1, *Einstein's Dream*, dir. Joseph McMaster. 60 min. Boston: WGBH Boston Video, 2003. DVD.

Epstein, Richard L. *The Semantic Foundations of Logic: Predicate Logic.* New York: Oxford University Press, 1994.

Evans, Craig A. *Jesus and the Ossuaries.* Waco: Baylor University Press, 2003.

———. "Jesus in Non-Christian Sources." In *Studying the Historical Jesus: Evaluations of the State of the Current Research*, ed. Bruce Chilton and Craig A. Evans. Leiden, Netherlands: Brill, 1998.

Evans, Paul S. *The Invasion of Sennacherib in the Book of Kings: A Source-Critical and Rhetorical Study of 2 Kings 18–19.* Leiden, Netherlands: Brill, 2009.

Evard, Rene, and David Schrodetzki. "Chemical Evolution." *Origins* 3, no. 1 (1976): 9–34.

Expelled: No Intelligence Allowed. Dir. Nathan Frankowski. 95 min. N.p.: Premise Media, 2008. DVD.

Fairbairn, Malcolm, and Robert Hogan. "Electroweak Vacuum Stability in Light of BICEP2." *American Physical Society Physical Review Letters* 112, no. 20 (2014): 201801-1–201801-5. Accessed July 20, 2015. journals.aps.org/prl/pdf/10.1103/PhysRevLett.112.201801.

Feynman, Richard P. *The Character of Physical Law.* Cambridge: MIT Press, 1965.

———. *QED: The Strange Theory of Light and Matter.* Princeton: Princeton University Press, 1985.

Fischer, John Michael. "Carbon-14-Dated Dinosaur Bones Are Less Than 40,000 Years Old." Accessed November 5, 2016. www.newgeology.us/presentation48.html.

Fixed Point Foundation. *The God Delusion Debate.* 112 min. Birmingham, AL: Fixed Point Foundation, 2007. DVD.

Flew, Anthony. *A Dictionary of Philosophy.* 1979. Repr., New York: St. Martin's Press, 1982.

Floridi, L. "On the Logical Unsolvability of the Gettier Problem." *Synthese* 142, no. 1 (2004): 61–79.

Fogelin, Robert J. *Berkeley and the Principles of Human Knowledge.* London: Routledge, 2001.

Freeman, Kathleen, trans. *Ancilla to the Pre-Socratic Philosophers.* 1948. Repr., Cambridge: Harvard University Press, 1996.

———. *The Pre-Socratic Philosophers: A Companion to Diels, Fragmente der Vorsokratiker.* 2nd ed. 1949. Repr., Oxford: Basil Blackwell, 1966.

Fuller, B. A. G. *History of Greek Philosophy*. Vol. 1, *Thales to Democritus*. 1923. Repr., New York: Greenwood Press, Publishers, 1968.

Gettier, Edmund L. "Is Justified True Belief Knowledge?" *Analysis* 23, no. 6 (1963): 121–23.

Gibson, A. Boyce. *The Philosophy of Descartes*. 1932. Repr., New York: Russell and Russell, 1967.

Gober, Mac. *Unchained*. Dallas: Word Publishing, 1993.

Goldman, Alvin. *A Theory of Human Action*. Englewood Cliffs, NJ: Prentice-Hall, 1970.

Goodrick, Edward W., and John R. Kohlenberger III. *The NIV Concordance*. Grand Rapids, MI: Zondervan, 1984.

Grabbe, Lester L. "Of Mice and Dead Men: Herodotus 2.141 and Sennacherib's Campaign in 701 BCE." In *'Like a Bird in a Cage': The Invasion of Sennacherib in 701 BCE*, ed. Lester L. Grabbe. Journal for the Study of the Old Testament Supplement Series 363, ser. eds. Andrew Mein, David J. A. Clines, and Philip R. Davies; European Seminar in Historical Methodology 4, ed. Lester L. Grabbe. London: Sheffield Academic Press, 2003.

———. "Reflections on the Discussion." In *'Like a Bird in a Cage': The Invasion of Sennacherib in 701 BCE*, ed. Lester L. Grabbe. Journal for the Study of the Old Testament Supplement Series 363, ser. eds. Andrew Mein, David J. A. Clines, and Philip R. Davies; European Seminar in Historical Methodology 4, ed. Lester L. Grabbe. London: Sheffield Academic Press, 2003.

Graham, Daniel W. "Heraclitus." In *Internet Encyclopedia of Philosophy*, ed. James Fieser et al. Accessed January 10, 2017. www.iep.utm.edu/heraclit/#H3.

Grayson, A. Kirk, trans. *Assyrian and Babylonian Chronicles*. 1975. Repr., Winona Lake, IN: Eisenbrauns, 2000.

Greene, Brian. *The Elegant Universe*. New York: W. W. Norton and Co., 1999.

Greenhut, Zvi. "The 'Caiaphas' Tomb in North Talpiyot, Jerusalem." *Atiqot* 21, no. 21 (1992): 63–71.

Grube, G. M. A. *Plato's Thought*. 1935. Repr., Boston: Beacon Press, 1968.

Guthrie, W. K. C. *A History of Greek Philosophy*. Vol. 1, *The Earlier Presocratics and the Pythagoreans*. 1962. Repr., Cambridge: Cambridge University Press, 1967.

———. *A History of Greek Philosophy*. Vol. 2, *The Presocratic Tradition from Parmenides to Democritus*. 1965. Repr., Cambridge: Cambridge University Press, 1969.

———. *A History of Greek Philosophy*. Vol. 4, *Plato, the Man and His Dialogues: Earlier Period*. Cambridge: Cambridge University Press, 1975.

———. *A History of Greek Philosophy*. Vol. 5, *The Later Plato and the Academy*. Cambridge: Cambridge University Press, 1978.

Habermas, Gary R. *The Historical Jesus: Ancient Evidence for the Life of Christ*. Joplin, MO: College Press Publishing Co., 1996.

Haines, C. R. *Heathen Contact with Christianity during Its First Century and a Half, Being All References to Christianity Recorded in Pagan Writings during That Period*. Cambridge: Deighton, Bell and Co., 1923.

Hajék, Alan. "Waging War on Pascal's Wager." *Philosophical Review* 112, no. 1 (2003): 27–56.

Haldane, J. B. S. "On Being the Right Size." In *Possible Worlds and Other Essays*. 1927. London: Chatto and Windus, 1928.

Hales, Stephen D., and Timothy A. Johnson. "Endurantism, Perdurantism, and Special Relativity." *Philosophical Quarterly* 53, no. 213 (2003): 524–39.

Hallgrímsson, Benedikt, and Brian K. Hall, eds. *Epigenetics: Linking Genotype and Phenotype in Development and Evolution*. Berkeley: University of California Press, 2011.

Hasker, William. *The Emergent Self*. Ithaca: Cornell University Press, 1999.

Hawking, Stephen. *The Universe in a Nutshell*. New York: Bantam Books, 2001.

Hawking, Stephen, and Leonard Mlodinow. *The Grand Design*. New York: Bantam Books, 2010.

Hawley, Katherine. *How Things Persist*. Oxford: Clarendon Press, 2001.

Heidegger, Martin. *Being and Time*. Trans. John Macquarrie and Edward Robinson. 7th ed. New York: Harper and Row, Publishers, 1962.

———. "What is Metaphysics." In *Martin Heidegger: Basic Writings*, trans. HarperCollins Publishers, ed. David Farrell Krell. London: Harper Perennial, 2008.

Heller, Mark. *The Ontology of Physical Objects: Four-Dimensional Hunks of Matter*. New York: Cambridge University Press, 1990.

Hempel, Karl G., and Paul Oppenheim. "Studies in the Logic of Explanation." *Philosophy of Science* 15, no. 2 (1948): 135–75.

Herodotus. *The Landmark Herodotus: The Histories*. Trans. Andrea L. Purvis. Ed. Robert B. Strassler. New York: Pantheon Books, 2007.

Hick, John. *Philosophy of Religion*. Englewood Cliffs, NJ: Prentice-Hall, 1963.

Hill, Christopher S. *Sensations: A Defense of Type Materialism.* Cambridge: Cambridge University Press, 1991.

Holzschuh, Josef, Jean de Pontcharra, and Hugh Miller. "Recent C-14 Dating of Fossils Including Dinosaur Bone Collagen." Accessed November 5, 2016. www.sciencevsevolution.org/Holzschuh.htm.

Honderich, Ted. "The Argument for Anomalous Monism." *Analysis* 42, no. 1 (1982): 59–64.

Hovis, Jeffery K. "Review of Dichoptic Color Mixing." *Optometry and Vision Science* 66, no. 3 (1989): 181–90.

Hughes, G. E., and Morton L. Schagrin. "Formal Logic: Higher-Order Predicate Calculi." In *Encyclopedia Britannica Online*, ed. Mansur G. Abdullah et al. Accessed July 25, 2013. www.britannica.com/EBchecked/topic/213716/formal-logic/65850/Definite-descriptions.

Hume, David. *David Hume: The Philosophical Works.* Ed. Thomas Hill Green and Thomas Hodge Grose. 4 vols. 1882, 1886. Repr., Frankfurt am Main, Germany: Scientia Verlag Aalen, 1964.

Ikeda, Mitsuo, and Ken Sagawa. "Binocular Color Fusion Limit." *Journal of the Optical Society of America* 69, no. 2 (1979): 316–21.

International Chicken Genome Sequencing Consortium. "Sequence and Comparative Analysis of the Chicken Genome Provide Unique Perspectives on Vertebrate Evolution." *Nature* 432, no. 7018 (2004): 695–716.

Jeffrey, Richard C. *Formal Logic: Its Scope and Limits.* New York: McGraw-Hill Book Co., 1967.

Jeremiah, David. Sermon that aired on *Turning Point*, February 4, 2007.

Johnson, Phillip E. "Evolution: Fact or Fantasy?" In *The Apologetics Study Bible*, ed. Ted Cabal et al. Nashville: Holman Bible Publishers, 2007.

Johnston, Mark. "Is There a Problem about Persistence?" *Proceedings of the Aristotelian Society Supplementary Volumes* 61, no. 1 (1987): 107–35.

———. "Particulars and Persistence." Ph.D. diss., Princeton University, 1984.

Josephus, Flavius. *The New Complete Works of Josephus.* Trans. William Whiston. Grand Rapids, MI: Kregel Publications, 1999.

Joyce, George Hayward. *Principles of Natural Theology.* 2nd ed. London: Longmans, Green and Co., 1924.

Joyce, Gerald F. "RNA Evolution and the Origins of Life." *Nature* 338, no. 6212 (1989): 217–24.

Joyce, Gerald F., and Leslie E. Orgel. "Prospects for Understanding the Origin of the RNA World." In *The RNA World*, ed. Raymond F. Gesteland, Thomas R. Cech, and John F. Atkins. 2nd ed. Cold Springs Harbor, NY: Cold Springs Harbor Laboratory Press, 1999.

Judaeus, Philo. *The Works of Philo: New Updated Edition*. Trans. C. D. Yonge. Peabody, MA: Hendrickson Publishers, 1993.

Judd, Deane B., and Gunter Wyszecki. *Color in Business, Science, and Industry*. 3rd ed. New York: John Wiley and Sons, 1975.

Jullo, Eric, et al. "Cosmological Constraints from Strong Gravitational Lensing in Clusters of Galaxies." *Science* 329, no. 5994 (2010): 924–27.

Kahn, Charles H. *The Art and Thought of Heraclitus: An Edition of the Fragments with Translation and Commentary*. Cambridge: Cambridge University Press, 1979.

Kaiser, Walter C., and Duane Garrett, eds. *NIV Archaeological Study Bible*. Grand Rapids, MI: Zondervan, 2005.

Kant, Immanuel. *Immanuel Kant's Critique of Pure Reason*. Trans. Norman Kemp Smith. 1929. Repr., New York: St. Martin's Press, 1965.

———. *Universal Natural History and Theory of the Heavens*. Trans. W. Hastie. Ann Arbor: University of Michigan Press, 1969.

Kenny, Anthony. *Action, Emotion, and Will*. 1963. Atlantic Highlands, NJ: Humanities Press, 1976.

———. *Descartes: A Study of His Philosophy*. New York: Random House, 1968.

Kim, Jaegwon. "The Mind-Body Problem after Fifty Years." In *Current Issues in Philosophy of Mind*, ed. Anthony O'Hear. Royal Institute of Philosophy Supplement 43. Cambridge: Cambridge University Press, 1998.

———. "The Myth of Nonreductive Materialism." *Proceedings and Addresses of the American Philosophical Association* 63, no. 3 (1989): 31–47.

———. *Physicalism, or Something Near Enough*. Princeton: Princeton University Press, 2005.

———. "Supervenience as a Philosophical Concept." *Metaphilosophy* 21, nos. 1–2 (1990): 1–27.

Kingsley, David M. "From Atoms to Traits." *Scientific American* 300, no. 1 (2009): 52–59.

Kirk, G. S. *Heraclitus: The Cosmic Fragments*. 1954. Repr., Cambridge: Cambridge University Press, 2010.

Kirk, G. S., J. E. Raven, and M. Schofield. *The Presocratic Philosophers: A Critical History with a Selection of Texts*. 2nd ed. 1983. Cambridge: Cambridge University Press, 2011.

Krauss, Lawrence M. *A Universe from Nothing: Why There Is Something Rather Than Nothing*. New York: Free Press, 2012.

Kripke, Saul. "Identity and Necessity." In *Identity and Individuation*, ed. Milton K. Munitz. New York: New York University Press, 1971.

————. *Naming and Necessity*. Cambridge: Harvard University Press, 1980.

Lambrecht, Astrid. "Observing Mechanical Dissipation in the Quantum Vacuum: An Experimental Challenge." In *Laser Physics at the Limit*, ed. Hartmut Figger, Dieter Meschede, and Claus Zimmermann. Berlin: Springer-Verlag, 2002.

Leblanc, Hugues, and William A. Wisdom. *Deductive Logic*. 1972. Boston: Allyn and Bacon, 1974.

Lemaître, Georges. *The Primeval Atom: An Essay on Cosmogony*. Trans. Betty H. Korff and Serge A. Korff. Toronto: D. Van Nostrand Co., 1950.

Levin, Janet. "Functionalism." In *Stanford Encyclopedia of Philosophy*, ed. Edward N. Zalta et al. Accessed October 5, 2013. plato.stanford.edu/archives/fall2013/entries/functionalism.

Lewis, David. *On the Plurality of Worlds*. Oxford: Basil Blackwell, 1986.

Liddell, Henry George, and Robert Scott. *A Greek English Lexicon*. 9th ed., rev. and aug. by Henry Stuart Jones with the assistance of Roderick McKenzie. 2 vols. 1940. Repr., Oxford: Clarendon Press, 1951.

Lincoln, Tracey A., and Gerald F. Joyce. "Self-Sustained Replication of an RNA Enzyme." *Science* 323, no. 5918 (2009): 1229–32.

Lindgren, Johan, et al. "Microspectroscopic Evidence of Cretaceous Bone Proteins." *PLOS ONE* 6, no. 4 (2011): e1–e11. Accessed November 2, 2016. journals.plos.org/plosone/article?id=10.1371/journal.pone.0019445.

Locke, John. *An Essay concerning Human Understanding*. Ed. Peter H. Nidditch. 1975. Repr., Oxford: Oxford University Press, 1985.

Luckenbill, Daniel David, trans. *The Annals of Sennacherib*. Oriental Institute Publications. Vol. 2. Chicago: University of Chicago Press, 1924.

Luminet, Jean-Pierre. "Editorial Note to: Georges Lemaître, a Homogeneous Universe of Constant Mass and Increasing Radius Accounting for the Radial Velocity of Extra-Galactic Nebulae." *General Relativity and Gravitation* 45, no. 8 (2013): 1619–33.

Mader, Sylvia S. *Biology*. 9th ed. New York: McGraw-Hill, 2007.

Malcolm, Norman. "The Conceivability of Mechanism." *Philosophical Review* 77, no. 1 (1968): 45–72.

Mallot, Hanspeter A. *Computational Vision: Information Processing in Perception and Visual Behavior*. Trans. John S. Allen. Cambridge: MIT Press, 2000.

Mastin, Luke. "Important Scientists: Georges Lemaître (1894–1966)." The Physics of the Universe. Accessed August 22, 2016. physicsoftheuniverse.com/scientists_lemaitre.html.

Mates, Benson. *Elementary Logic.* 2nd ed. 1972. New York: Oxford University Press, 1975.

Matson, Wallace I. *A History of Philosophy.* New York: American Book Co., 1968.

Mayer, Walter. "Sennacherib's Campaign of 701 BCE: The Assyrian View." In *'Like a Bird in a Cage': The Invasion of Sennacherib in 701 BCE*, ed. Lester L. Grabbe. Journal for the Study of the Old Testament Supplement Series 363, ser. eds. Andrew Mein, David J. A. Clines, and Philip R. Davies; European Seminar in Historical Methodology 4, ed. Lester L. Grabbe. London: Sheffield Academic Press, 2003.

McDowell, Josh. *Evidence for Christianity.* Nashville: Thomas Nelson, 2006.

———. *The New Evidence That Demands a Verdict.* Nashville: Thomas Nelson, 1999.

Melden, A. I. *Free Action.* 1961. London: Routledge and Kegan Paul, 1967.

Merricks, Trenton. *Objects and Persons.* Oxford: Clarendon Press, 2001.

Meyers, Robert G., and Kenneth Stern. "Knowledge without Paradox." *Journal of Philosophy* 70, no. 6 (1973): 147–60.

Michalos, Alex C. *Principles of Logic.* Englewood Cliffs, NJ: Prentice-Hall, 1969.

Mill, John Stuart. *Autobiography of John Stuart Mill.* New York: Columbia University Press, 1924.

Moczydłowska, Małgorzata, Frances Westall, and Frédéric Foucher. "Microstructure and Biogeochemistry of the Organically Preserved Ediacaran Metazoan *Sabellidites.*" *Journal of Paleontology* 88, no. 2 (2014): 224–39.

Mojzsis, Stephen J., Ramanarayanan Krishnamurthy, and Gustaf Arrhenius, "Before RNA and After: Geophysical and Geochemical Constraints on Molecular Evolution." In *The RNA World*, ed. Raymond F. Gesteland, Thomas R. Cech, and John F. Atkins. 2nd ed. Cold Springs Harbor, NY: Cold Springs Harbor Laboratory Press, 1999.

Moon, Truman J., James H. Otto, and Albert Towie. *Modern Biology.* New York: Holt, Rinehart and Winston, 1963.

Moran, William L., trans. *The Amarna Letters.* Baltimore: Johns Hopkins University Press, 1992.

Morris, Simon Conway. *Life's Solution: Inevitable Humans in a Lonely Universe.* Cambridge: Cambridge University Press, 2003.

O'Hear, Anthony. *Beyond Evolution: Human Nature and the Limits of Evolutionary Explanation.* Oxford: Clarendon Press, 1997.

Orgel, L. E. *The Origins of Life: Molecules and Natural Selection.* New York: John Wiley and Sons, 1973.

Orr, H. Allen. "Testing Natural Selection." *Scientific American* 300, no. 1 (2009): 44–50.

Orzel, Chad. *How to Teach Physics to Your Dog.* New York: Scribner, 2009.

Osborne, Catherine. "Heraclitus." In *Routledge History of Philosophy*, ed. G. H. R. Parkinson and S. G. Shanker. Vol. 1, *From the Beginning to Plato*, ed. C. C. W. Taylor. London: Routledge, 1997.

Paley, William. *Natural Theology: or, Evidences of the Existence and Attributes of the Deity, Collected from the Appearances of Nature.* 1802. Repr., Boston: Lincoln and Edmands, 1829.

Pamphilus, Eusebius. *The Ecclesiastical History of Eusebius Pamphilus, Bishop of Caesarea in Palestine.* Trans. C. F. Crusé. *A Historical View of the Council of Nice.* Trans. Isaac Boyle. New York: T. Mason and G. Lane, 1839.

Panek, Richard. *The 4 Percent Universe: Dark Matter, Dark Energy, and the Race to Discover the Rest of Reality.* Boston: Houghton Mifflin Harcourt, 2011.

Parker, Gary. *Creation: Facts of Life—How Real Science Reveals the Hand of God.* Rev. ed. 2006. Green Forest, AR: Master Books, 2010.

Parmenides. *Parmenides of Elea: Fragments.* Trans. David Gallop. Toronto: University of Toronto Press, 1984.

Pasachoff, Jay M., and Alex Filippenko. *The Cosmos: Astronomy in the New Millennium.* Fort Worth: Harcourt College Publishers, 2001.

Pascal, Blaise. *Pensées.* Trans. W. F. Trotter. *The Provincial Letters.* Trans. Thomas M'Crie. New York: Modern Library, 1941.

Pawlicki, Roman, and Maria Nowogrodzka-Zagórska. "Blood Vessels and Red Blood Cells Preserved in Dinosaur Bones." *Annals of Anatomy* 180, no. 1 (1998): 73–77.

Pearse, Roger, et al. "Early Church Fathers – Additional Texts: The Chronicle of St. Jerome." The Tertullian Project. Accessed May 9, 2014. www.tertullian.org/fathers/jerome_chronicle_03_part2.htm.

Pennisi, Elizabeth. "DNA Study Forces Rethink of What It Means to Be a Gene." *Science* 316, no. 5831 (2007): 1556–57.

Pfeiffer, Charles F., Howard F. Vos, and John Rea, eds. *Wycliffe Bible Dictionary.* Peabody, MA: Hendrickson Publishers, 2008.

Pickford, R. W. "Binocular Colour Combinations." *Nature* 159, no. 4034 (1947): 268–69.

Pines, Shlomo. *An Arabic Version of the Testimonium Flavianum and Its Implications*. Jerusalem: Israel Academy of Sciences and Humanities, 1971.

Plantinga, Alvin. *God, Freedom, and Evil*. 1974. London: George Allen and Unwin, 1975.

Plato. *The Collected Dialogues of Plato, Including the Letters*. Trans. Lane Cooper et al. Ed. Edith Hamilton and Huntington Cairns. 1961. Princeton: Princeton University Press, 1971.

———. *The Dialogues of Plato*. Trans. Benjamin Jowett. 2 vols. 1892. Repr., New York: Random House, 1937.

Pliny the Younger. *Pliny, Letters*. Trans. William Melmoth. Rev. W. M. L. Hutchinson. 2 vols. London: William Heinemann, 1915.

Polger, Thomas W. "Are Sensations Still Brain Processes?" *Philosophical Psychology* 24, no. 1 (2011): 1–21.

———. "Functionalism." In *Internet Encyclopedia of Philosophy*, ed. James Fieser et al. Accessed October 5, 2013. www.iep.utm.edu/functism.

Prentice, W. C. H. "New Observations of 'Binocular Yellow.'" *Journal of Experimental Psychology* 38, no. 3 (1948): 284–88.

Putnam, Hilary. "The Nature of Mental States." In *Philosophical Papers*. Vol. 2, *Mind, Language, and Reality*. Cambridge: Cambridge University Press, 1975.

Radner, Gilda. *It's Always Something*. New York: Simon and Schuster, 1989.

Rafelski, J., and B. Müller. *The Structured Vacuum: Thinking about Nothing*. Frankfurt am Main, Germany: Verlag Harri Deutsch, 1985.

Ray, Christopher. *Time, Space, and Philosophy*. London: Routledge, 1991.

Redondo, Jordi. "The Greek Literary Language of the Hebrew Historian Josephus." *Hermes* 128, no. 4 (2000): 420–34.

Reid, C., and L. E. Orgel. "Synthesis of Sugars in Potentially Prebiotic Conditions." *Nature* 216, no. 5114 (1967): 455.

Reid, Thomas. *Essays on the Intellectual Powers of Man*. Cambridge: MIT Press, 1969.

Reijmers, Leon G., et al. "Localization of a Stable Neural Correlate of Associative Memory." *Science* 317, no. 5842 (2007): 1230–33.

Reisz, Robert R., et al. "Embryology of Early Jurassic Dinosaur from China with Evidence of Preserved Organic Remains." *Nature* 496, no. 7444 (2013): 210–14.

Ricardo, Alonso, and Jack W. Szostak. "Origin of Life on Earth." *Scientific American* 301, no. 3 (2009): 54–61.

Ritchie, Mark A. *God in the Pits*. Nashville: Thomas Nelson, 1990.

Roberts, Alexander, and James Donaldson, eds. *The Ante-Nicene Fathers: Translations of the Writings of the Fathers down to A.D. 325.* Vol. 1, *The Apostolic Fathers: Justin Martyr, Irenaeus.* 1885. Repr., New York: Charles Scribner's Sons, 1925.

———. *The Ante-Nicene Fathers: Translations of the Writings of the Fathers down to A.D. 325.* Vol. 3, *Latin Christianity: Its Founder, Tertullian.* 1885. Repr., New York: Charles Scribner's Sons, 1918.

———. *The Ante-Nicene Fathers: Translations of the Writings of the Fathers down to A.D. 325.* Vol. 4, *Fathers of the Third Century: Tertullian, Part Fourth; Minucius Felix; Commodian; Origen, Parts First and Second.* 1885. Repr., New York: Charles Scribner's Sons, 1925.

———. *The Ante-Nicene Fathers: Translations of the Writings of the Fathers down to A.D. 325.* Vol. 6, *Fathers of the Third Century: Gregory Thaumaturgus, Dionysius The Great, Julius Africanus, Anatolius and Minor Writers, Methodius, Arnobius.* 1886. Repr., New York: Charles Scribner's Sons, 1925.

Royal Astronomical Society. "The Flat Universe." Accessed April 24, 2013. www.ras.org.uk/publications/other-publications/2035-cosmology-flat-universe.

Runes, Dagobert D., ed. *Treasury of Philosophy.* New York: Philosophical Library, 1955.

Russell, Bertrand. *Bertrand Russell on God and Religion.* Ed. Al Seckel. Buffalo: Prometheus Books, 1986.

———. "A Free Man's Worship." In *Mysticism and Logic.* 1917. Repr., New York: W. W. Norton and Co., 1929.

———. *A History of Western Philosophy.* New York: Simon and Schuster, 1945.

———. "Why I Am Not a Christian." In *Why I Am Not a Christian and Other Essays on Religion and Related Subjects,* ed. Paul Edwards. New York: Simon and Schuster, 1957.

Ryle, Gilbert. *The Concept of Mind.* New York: Barnes and Noble Books, 1949.

———. *Dilemmas.* 1954. Repr., Cambridge: Cambridge University Press, 1975.

Sagan, Carl, ed. *Communication with Extraterrestrial Intelligence (CETI).* Cambridge: MIT Press, 1973.

———. *Cosmos.* New York: Random House, 1980.

Sakharov, Alex. "Strict Order." MathWorld—a Wolfram web resource, created by Eric W. Weisstein. Accessed April 24, 2013. www.mathworld.wolfram.com/StrictOrder.html.

Sarfati, Jonathan. "Is RNA Self-Replication Evidence for Evolution?" Creation Ministries International. Accessed July 10, 2015. creation.com/rna-self-replication.

Sartre, Jean-Paul. *Being and Nothingness*. Trans. Hazel E. Barnes. New York: Philosophical Library, 1956.

———. *Existentialism Is a Humanism*. Trans. Carol Macomber. Ed. John Kulka. New Haven: Yale University Press, 2007.

Sayers, Sean. *Plato's* Republic: *An Introduction*. Edinburgh: Edinburgh University Press, 1999.

Schweitzer, Mary Higby, Jennifer L. Wittmeyer, and John R. Horner. "Soft Tissue and Cellular Preservation in Vertebrate Skeletal Elements from the Cretaceous to the Present." *Proceedings of the Royal Society B* 274, no. 1607 (2007): 183–97; cor. 274, no. 1629 (2007): 3183.

Schweitzer, Mary Higby, et al. "Analyses of Soft Tissue from *Tyrannosaurus rex* Suggest the Presence of Protein." *Science* 316, no. 5822 (2007): 277–80.

———. "Biomolecular Characterization and Protein Sequences of the Campanian Hadrosaur *B. canadensis*." *Science* 324, no. 5927 (2009): 626–31.

———. "Molecular Analyses of Dinosaur Osteocytes Support the Presence of Endogenous Molecules." *Bone* 52, no. 1 (2013): 414–23.

Searle, John. "Minds, Brains, and Programs." *Behavioral and Brain Sciences* 3, no. 3 (1980): 417–24.

Serway, Raymond A., and John W. Jewett Jr. *Physics for Scientists and Engineers*. 7th ed. Vol. 2. Belmont, CA: Thomson Brooks/Cole, 2008.

Shapiro, Fred. R., ed. *The Yale Book of Quotations*. New Haven: Yale University Press, 2006.

Shapiro, Robert. "The Improbability of Prebiotic Nucleic Acid Synthesis." *Origins of Life* 14, nos. 1–4 (1984): 565–70.

———. "Prebiotic Ribose Synthesis: A Critical Analysis." *Origins of Life and Evolution of the Biosphere* 18, nos. 1–2 (1988): 71–85.

Sider, Theodore. *Four-Dimensionalism: An Ontology of Persistence and Time*. 2001. Oxford: Clarendon Press, 2003.

Simons, Peter. *Parts: A Study in Ontology*. Oxford: Clarendon Press, 1987.

Simplicius. *Simplicius: On Aristotle Physics 1.3–4*. Trans. Pamela Huby and C. C. W. Taylor. London: Bristol Classical Press, 2011.

Singer, Maxine, and Paul Berg. *Genes and Genomes: A Changing Perspective*. Mill Valley, CA: University Science Books, 1991.

Smart, J. J. C. "Sensations and Brain Processes." *Philosophical Review* 68, no. 2 (1959): 141–56.

Smith, Quentin. "The Uncaused Beginning of the Universe." In *Theism, Atheism, and Big Bang Cosmology*, ed. William Lane Craig and Quentin Smith. Oxford: Clarendon Press, 1993.

Sporcle. "Baskin-Robbins 31 Flavors." Accessed July 31, 2013. www.sporcle.com/games/g/baskinrobbins.

Sproul, R. C. "The Mystery of Iniquity: Right Now Counts Forever." *Tabletalk* 32, no. 12 (2008): 4–7.

Star Trek IV: The Voyage Home. Dir. Leonard Nimoy. 119 min. Hollywood, CA: Paramount Pictures, 1986. Videocassette.

Stenger, Victor J. *The Comprehensible Cosmos: Where Do the Laws of Physics Come From?* Buffalo: Prometheus Books, 2006.

———. "Everything Came from Nothing." *Huffington Post*, September 12, 2011. Accessed August 30, 2015. huffingtonpost.com/victor-stenger/ everything-came-from-noth_b_896992.html.

———. *God: The Failed Hypothesis—How Science Shows That God Does Not Exist.* Buffalo: Prometheus Books, 2007.

———. "The Other Side of Time." Secular Web. Accessed October 21, 2014. infidels.org/library/modern/vic_stenger/otherside.html.

Stokes, Michael C. *One and Many in Presocratic Philosophy.* Washington, DC: Center for Hellenic Studies, 1971.

Stratton, George M. "Some Preliminary Experiments on Vision without Inversion of the Retinal Image." *Psychological Review* 3, no. 6 (1896): 611–17.

———. "Upright Vision and the Retinal Image." *Psychological Review* 4, no. 2 (1897): 182–87.

———. "Vision without Inversion of the Retinal Image." *Psychological Review* 4, no. 4 (1897): 341–60.

———. "Vision without Inversion of the Retinal Image." *Psychological Review* 4, no. 5 (1897): 463–81.

Strawson, P. F. *Individuals: An Essay in Descriptive Metaphysics.* 1959. Repr., London: University Paperbacks, 1974.

Strong, Augustus Hopkins. *Systematic Theology.* 3 vols. 1907. Valley Forge, PA: Judson Press, 1972.

Suetonius. *Suetonius: The Lives of the Twelve Caesars.* Trans. Philemon Holland. New York: Heritage Press, 1965.

Sugita, Yoichi. "Global Plasticity in Adult Visual Cortex Following Reversal of Visual Input." *Nature* 380, no. 6574 (1996): 523–26.

Syncellus (Synkellos), George. *The Chronography of George Synkellos: A Byzantine Chronicle of Universal History from the Creation.* Trans. William Adler and Paul Tuffin. Oxford: Oxford University Press, 2002.

Tacitus, Publius Cornelius. *The Complete Works of Tacitus*. Trans. Alfred John Church and William Jackson Brodribb. Ed. Moses Hadas. New York: Modern Library, 1942.

Tadmor, Hayim, trans. *The Inscriptions of Tiglath-pileser III, King of Assyria: Critical Edition, with Introductions, Translations, and Commentary*. Jerusalem: Israel Academy of Sciences and Humanities, 1994.

Tadmor, Hayim, and Shigeo Yamada, trans. Ed. Jamie Novotny. *The Royal Inscriptions of Tiglath-pileser III (744–727 BC) and Shalmaneser V (726–722 BC), Kings of Assyria*. Winona Lake, IN: Eisenbrauns, 2011.

"Talk of the Town, The." *New Yorker* 46, no. 1 (1970): 29.

Taylor, A. E. *A Commentary on Plato's* Timaeus. 1928. Repr., Oxford: Clarendon Press, 1972.

Taylor, Richard. *Ethics, Faith, and Reason*. Englewood Cliffs, NJ: Prentice-Hall, 1985.

Taylor, Richard, and William Lane Craig. "Is the Basis of Morality Natural or Supernatural?" A debate between Richard Taylor and William Lane Craig at Union College, Schenectady, New York, October 8, 1993. Accessed November 4, 2015. www.leaderu.com/offices/billcraig/docs/craig-taylor1.html.

Tegmark, Max. "Is 'the Theory of Everything' Merely the Ultimate Ensemble Theory?" *Annals of Physics* 270, no. 1 (1998): 1–51.

Tenney, Merrill C., Steven Barabas, and Peter deVisser, eds. *Pictorial Bible Dictionary*. 1963. Repr., Nashville: The Southwestern Co., 1974.

Thaxton, Charles B., Walter L. Bradley, and Roger L. Olsen. *The Mystery of Life's Origin: Reassessing Current Theories*. New York: Philosophical Library, 1984.

Thiselton, Anthony C. *A Concise Encyclopedia of the Philosophy of Religion*. Oxford: Oneworld Publications, 2002.

Thomson, Judith Jarvis. "Parthood and Identity across Time." *Journal of Philosophy* 80, no. 4 (1983): 201–20.

Tomkins, Jeffrey P. *The Design and Complexity of the Cell*. Dallas: Institute for Creation Research, 2012.

———. "Tail-Gliding Bugs Are Not Evidence for Flight Evolution." Institute for Creation Research. Accessed July 1, 2013. www.icr.org/article/tail-gliding-bugs-are-not-evidence.

Trail, Dustin, E. Bruce Watson, and Nicholas D. Tailby. "The Oxidation State of Hadean Magmas and Implications for Early Earth's Atmosphere." *Nature* 480, no. 7375 (2011): 79–83.

Tryon, Edward P. "Is the Universe a Vacuum Fluctuation?" *Nature* 246, no. 5433 (1973): 396–97.

Turnbull, Robert G. *The* Parmenides *and Plato's Late Philosophy*. Toronto: University of Toronto Press, 1998.

Tyson, Neil deGrasse, and Donald Goldsmith. *Origins: Fourteen Billion Years of Cosmic Evolution*. New York: W. W. Norton and Co., 2004.

Unger, Peter. *Identity, Consciousness, and Value*. New York: Oxford University Press, 1990.

———. "I Do Not Exist." In *Perception and Identity: Essays Presented to A. J. Ayer, with His Replies*, ed. G. F. Macdonald. Ithaca: Cornell University Press, 1979.

———. "Why There Are No People." *Midwest Studies in Philosophy* 4, no. 1 (1979): 177–222.

Van Impe, Jack and Rexella. *Daniel—Final End Time Mysteries Unsealed, Part 3*. 119 min. Troy, MI: Jack Van Impe Ministries, 1993. Videocassette.

Van Inwagen, Peter. *Material Beings*. Ithaca: Cornell University Press, 1990.

Vannatta, Glen D., A. Wilson Goodwin, and Harold P. Fawcett. *Algebra Two: A Modern Course*. Columbus, OH: Charles E. Merrill Books, 1962.

Van Voorst, Robert E. *Jesus Outside the New Testament: An Introduction to the Ancient Evidence*. Grand Rapids, MI: William B. Eerdmans Publishing Co., 2000.

Vermazen, Bruce, and Merrill B. Hintikka, eds. *Essays on Davidson: Actions and Events*. Oxford: Clarendon Press, 1985.

Vlastos, Gregory. "Zeno's Race Course." In *Studies in Greek Philosophy: Gregory Vlastos*, ed. Daniel W. Graham. Vol. 1, *The Presocratics*. Princeton: Princeton University Press, 1995.

Wahlberg, Tobias Hansson. "Can Persistence Be a Matter of Convention?" *Axiomathes* 21, no. 4 (2011): 507–29.

Walls, Gordon Lynn. *The Vertebrate Eye and Its Adaptive Radiation*. Bloomfield Hills, MI: Cranbrook Institute of Science, 1942.

Watson, James D., and Andrew Berry. *DNA: The Secret of Life*. New York: Alfred A. Knopf, 2003.

Wilczek, Frank. "The Cosmic Asymmetry between Matter and Antimatter." *Scientific American* 243, no. 6 (1980): 82–90.

Wilson, Timothy D. *Strangers to Ourselves: Discovering the Adaptive Unconscious*. Cambridge: Harvard University Press, Belknap Press, 2002.

Winchester, A. M. *Biology and Its Relation to Humankind*. 4th ed. New York: Van Nostrand Reinhold Co., 1969.

WMAP Science Team. "Will the Universe Expand Forever?" National Aeronautics and Space Administration. Accessed August 18, 2019. map.gsfc.nasa.gov/universe/uni_shape.html.

———. "WMAP Produces New Results." Reported as of April 8, 2013. National Aeronautics and Space Administration. Accessed May 20, 2013. map.gsfc.nasa.gov/news.

Wolfram Alpha. "Computational Knowledge Engine." Accessed July 15, 2013. www.wolframalpha.com.

Wright, M. R. "Empedocles." In *Routledge History of Philosophy*, ed. G. H. R. Parkinson and S. G. Shanker. Vol. 1, *From the Beginning to Plato*, ed. C. C. W. Taylor. London: Routledge, 1997.

———. *Empedocles: The Extant Fragments*. New Haven: Yale University Press, 1981.

Yeoman, R. S. *A Guidebook of United States Coins*. 32nd rev. ed. Racine, WI: Western Publishing Co., 1979.

Younger, K. Lawson, Jr. "The Calah Annals (2.117A)." In *The Context of Scripture*, ed. William W. Hallo and K. Lawson Younger. Vol. 2, *Monumental Inscriptions from the Biblical World*. Leiden, Netherlands: Brill, 2000.

Zaimov, Stoyan. "Richard Dawkins Claims Unborn Children Are 'Less Human' Than Pigs; Stirs Firestorm." *Christian Post*, March 14, 2013. Accessed November 19, 2013. www.christianpost.com/news/richard-dawkins-claims-unborn-children-are-less-human-than-pigs-stirs-fire storm-91911/#.

Zissu, Boaz, and Yuval Goren. "The Ossuary of 'Miriam Daughter of Yeshua Son of Caiaphas, Priests [of] Ma'aziah from Beth 'Imri.'" *Israel Exploration Journal* 61, no. 1 (2011): 74–95.

INDEX

This index gives page numbers for direct references and, where appropriate, closely associated indirect ones, which pertain to entries without mentioning them. Topical listings are provided for select items; if page numbers extend beyond those for topics, full listings also are provided. Both the main text and footnotes are included. No identifiers beyond pages are employed for notes, producing a manageable search tool.